Lecture Notes in Computer Science

Lecture Notes in Artificial Intelligence **15943**

Founding Editor

Jörg Siekmann

The series Lecture Notes in Artificial Intelligence (LNAI) was established in 1988 as a topical subseries of LNCS devoted to artificial intelligence.

The series publishes state-of-the-art research results at a high level. As with the LNCS mother series, the mission of the series is to serve the international R & D community by providing an invaluable service, mainly focused on the publication of conference and workshop proceedings and postproceedings.

Clark Barrett · Uwe Waldmann
Editors

Automated Deduction – CADE 30

30th International Conference on Automated Deduction
Stuttgart, Germany, July 28–31, 2025
Proceedings

Springer

Editors
Clark Barrett
Stanford University
Stanford, CA, USA

Uwe Waldmann
Max-Planck-Institute for Informatics
Saarbrücken, Germany

ISSN 0302-9743 ISSN 1611-3349 (electronic)
Lecture Notes in Artificial Intelligence
ISBN 978-3-031-99983-3 ISBN 978-3-031-99984-0 (eBook)
https://doi.org/10.1007/978-3-031-99984-0

LNCS Sublibrary: SL7 – Artificial Intelligence

This Springer imprint is published by the registered company Springer Nature Switzerland AG
The registered company address is: Gewerbestrasse 11, 6330 Cham, Switzerland

Preface

This volume contains the proceedings of the 30th International Conference on Automated Deduction (CADE-30). CADE is the major forum for the presentation of research in all aspects of automated deduction, including foundations, applications, implementations, and practical experience. CADE-30 was held on 28–31 July 2025, hosted at Baden-Württemberg Cooperative State University in Stuttgart, Germany (Duale Hochschule Baden-Württemberg, or DHBW).

CADE-30 emphasized the breadth of topics that are of interest, including applications in and beyond computer science and mathematics, and the use/contribution of automated deduction in AI.

The Program Committee (PC) reviewed 87 submissions this year, of which 37 were accepted (33 full papers and 4 short papers or system descriptions). Reviewing was single-blind, and each submission was reviewed by at least three PC members or their external reviewers. The criteria for evaluation were originality and significance, technical quality, comparison with related work, quality of presentation, and reproducibility of experiments.

The program of the conference included three invited talks:

- "A Decade of Lean: Advancing Proof Automation for Mathematics and Software Verification" by *Leonardo de Moura*, Amazon Web Services, USA
- "Taming Infinity for Verification in First-Order Logic" by *Sharon Shoham*, Tel Aviv University, Israel
- "Choose Your Proofs: Commutativity and Symmetry for Smarter Reasoning" by *Azadeh Farzan*, University of Toronto, Canada

The conference hosted one competition and several workshops:

- CASC-30: The CADE-30 ATP System Competition (July 30)
- ADG 2025: Automated Deduction in Geometry (August 1–2)
- DT 2025: Deduktionstreffen (August 1)
- Weidenbach60: First-Order Reasoning, Below and Beyond: Workshop in Honor of Christoph Weidenbach's 60th Birthday (August 1)
- SC2: 10th International Workshop on Satisfiability Checking and Symbolic Computation (August 2)
- ThEdu 2025, Theorem Proving Components for Educational Software (August 2)
- TPTPTP: The TPTP Tea Party (August 2)

Two best paper awards and three CADE awards were presented at the conference:

- The CADE-30 Best Paper Award, for "More is Less: Adding Polynomials for Faster Explanations in NLSAT" by *Valentin Promies, Jasper Nalbach, Erika Ábrahám, and Paul Wagner*

- The Larry Wos Best Student Paper Award, for "Being Polite is Not Enough (and Other Limits of Theory Combination)" by *Guilherme Toledo, Benjamin Przybocki, and Yoni Zohar*
- The 2025 Herbrand Award for Distinguished Contributions to Automated Reasoning, awarded to Aart Middeldorp, University of Innsbruck, Austria, in recognition of his deep foundational and influential practical contributions to the field of term rewriting, as well as his sustained services to the automated reasoning community.
- The Thoralf Skolem Award for CADE papers that have passed the test of time by being the most influential papers in the field, awarded to each of the following papers:
  - "Associative-Commutative Unification" by *François Fages*, CADE-7 (1984)
  - "Building Decision Procedures for Modal Logics from Propositional Decision Procedures" by *Fausto Giunchiglia and Roberto Sebastiani*, CADE-13 (1996)
  - "Automating the Dependency Pair Method" by *Nao Hirokawa and Aart Middeldorp*, CADE-19 (2003)
  - "The Lean Theorem Prover (System Description)" by *Leonardo de Moura, Soonho Kong, Jeremy Avigad, Floris van Doorn, and Jakob von Raumer*, CADE-25 (2015)
- The Bill McCune PhD Award for a PhD thesis' substantive contributions to the field of Automated Reasoning, awarded to Jannik Vierling, Vienna University of Technology, Austria

Sincere thanks go to the many people who contributed to the success of CADE-30—the authors, the participants, the invited speakers, the members of the PC, the external subreviewers, the general chair, the workshop chair, the publicity chair, the staff at Springer, and the EasyChair team. We'd also like to thank Inna Avrutina, Jan Hladik, Daniela Jung, and the team at DHBW Stuttgart for their help with local organization. CADE-30 gratefully acknowledges the support of the CADE trustees, the board of the Association for Automated Reasoning, ACM SIGLOG, and the sponsors Amazon Web Services and Springer.

July 2025

Clark Barrett
Uwe Waldmann

The original version of the book has been revised. A correction to this book can be found at https://doi.org/10.1007/978-3-031-99984-0_39

Organization

Conference Chair

Stephan Schulz	DHBW Stuttgart, Germany

Program Committee Chairs

Clark Barrett	Stanford University, USA
Uwe Waldmann	MPI for Informatics, Germany

Workshop Chair

Sophie Tourret	Inria Nancy, France

Publicity Chair

Geoff Sutcliffe	University of Miami, USA

Program Committee

Erika Ábrahám	RWTH Aachen University, Germany
Haniel Barbosa	Universidade Federal de Minas Gerais, Brazil
Clark Barrett	Stanford University, USA
Jasmin Blanchette	Ludwig-Maximilians-Universität München, Germany
Maria Paola Bonacina	Università degli Studi di Verona, Italy
Liron Cohen	Ben-Gurion University of the Negev, Israel
Stéphane Demri	LMF, CNRS & ENS Paris-Saclay, France
Huimin Dong	TU Wien, Austria
Katalin Fazekas	TU Wien, Austria
Mathias Fleury	University of Freiburg, Germany
Pascal Fontaine	Université de Liège, Belgium
Carsten Fuhs	Birkbeck, University of London, UK
Silvio Ghilardi	Università degli Studi di Milano, Italy

Alessandro Gianola	INESC-ID and Universidade de Lisboa, Portugal
Iris van der Giessen	University of Amsterdam, The Netherlands
Alberto Griggio	Fondazione Bruno Kessler, Italy
Nao Hirokawa	JAIST, Japan
Mikoláš Janota	Czech Technical University in Prague, Czech Republic
Moa Johansson	Chalmers University of Technology, Sweden
Martin Jonáš	Masaryk University, Czech Republic
Cezary Kaliszyk	University of Melbourne, Australia
Konstantin Korovin	The University of Manchester, UK
Katherine Kosaian	University of Iowa, USA
Laura Kovács	TU Wien, Austria
Peter Lammich	University of Twente, The Netherlands
Kuldeep S. Meel	University of Toronto, Canada
Stephan Merz	Inria Nancy, France
Cláudia Nalon	University of Brasília, Brazil
Jakob Nordström	University of Copenhagen, Denmark and Lund University, Sweden
Nicola Olivetti	LIS, Aix-Marseille University, France
Elaine Pimentel	University College London, UK
André Platzer	Karlsruhe Institute of Technology, Germany
Florian Rabe	FAU Erlangen-Nürnberg, Germany
Andrew Reynolds	University of Iowa, USA
Philipp Rümmer	University of Regensburg, Germany
Tanja Schindler	University of Basel, Switzerland
Renate A. Schmidt	The University of Manchester, UK
Carsten Schürmann	IT University of Copenhagen, Denmark
Mihaela Sighireanu	ENS Paris-Saclay, France
Alexandra Silva	Cornell University, USA
Viorica Sofronie-Stokkermans	University of Koblenz, Germany
Martin Suda	Czech Technical University in Prague, Czech Republic
Yong Kiam Tan	Institute for Infocomm Research and NTU, Singapore
Guilherme Toledo	State University of Campinas, Brazil
Sophie Tourret	Inria Nancy, France
Ali Kemal Uncu	University of Bath, UK
Uwe Waldmann	MPI for Informatics, Germany
Christoph Weidenbach	MPI for Informatics, Germany
Bohua Zhan	Huawei Technologies Co., Ltd., China
Yoni Zohar	Bar-Ilan University, Israel

Additional Reviewers

Alex Aiken
Takahito Aoto
Martin Avanzini
Guy Axelrod
Matthias Baaz
Sage Binder
Benjamin Bogø
Paolo Bottoni
Marvin Brieger
Chad Brown
Paul Brunet
Julia Butte
Julie Cailler
David Cerna
Karel Chvalovský
Robin Coutelier
Martin Desharnais
Sólrún Halla Einarsdóttir
Clemens Eisenhofer
Matthew England
Mauro Ferrari
Tiago Ferreira
Camillo Fiorentini
Yannick Forster
Han Gao
Malvin Gattinger
Thibault Gauthier
Nicola Gigante
Stefano Guerrini
Roland Herrmann
Andreas Herzig
Petra Hozzová
Ullrich Hustadt
Vincent Jackson
Jan Jakubův
Jacques-Henri Jourdan
Aditi Kabra
Jan-Christoph Kassing
Wietze Koops
Daniil Kozhemiachenko
Stéphane Le Roux
Luca Maio
Andrew Marmaduke
Mark Moeller
Sibylle Möhle-Rotondi
Johannes Niederhauser
Andy Oertel
Vincent van Oostrom
Eugenio Orlandelli
Edi Pavlović
Nicolas Peltier
Long Qian
Pedro Quaresma
Daniel Ranalter
João Rasga
Rodrigo Raya
Masahiko Sakai
Teppei Saito
Jan Frederik Schaefer
Michael Schaper
Johannes Schoisswohl
Marcel Schütz
Nicholas Smallbone
Mallku Soldevila
Lara Stoltenow
Melanie Taprogge
René Thiemann
Balazs Toth
Jan Van den Bussche
Conrad Watt
Christoph Wernhard
Hui Yang
Emily Yu
Cheng Zhang
Zhiguang Zhao

Board of Trustees of CADE Inc.

Board of the Association for Automated Reasoning

Invited Talks

A Decade of Lean: Advancing Proof Automation for Mathematics and Software Verification

Leonardo de Moura

Automated Reasoning Group, AWS, USA
leo@lean-fro.org

Abstract. Ten years on from its CADE debut, Lean has evolved from a research prototype into a full-featured formal reasoning platform. Today, it is used to formalize mathematical theories, support AI-driven reasoning, and verify industrial software and hardware. This talk presents the proof automation we have recently integrated into Lean, together with ongoing development efforts:

- "bv_decide" integrates bit-vector reasoning into Lean's tactic framework, dispatching bit-precise verification goals at scale.
- "grind" merges congruence closure, model-based decision procedures, heuristic quantifier instantiation, and Gröbner-basis algebraic reasoning.
- Efficient symbolic evaluation enables scalable software and hardware verification.

We will also survey key Lean success stories in mathematics, AI, and verification; explain the engineering choices that reuse and extend classic CADE techniques; and outline the research opportunities these new tools unlock.

Taming Infinity for Verification in First-Order Logic

Sharon Shoham

Tel Aviv University, Tel Aviv, Israel
sharon.shoham@cs.tau.ac.il

Abstract. First-order logic (FOL) has proven itself useful for modeling and verifying systems with unbounded domains, such as heap-manipulating programs and distributed protocols. FOL strikes a good balance between automation and expressiveness, with uninterpreted functions and relations used to encode the state of a system and quantifiers used to reason about unbounded domains of nodes, processes, messages, etc. However, standard FOL semantics may introduce spurious behaviors that do not exist under the intended semantics of the modeled system, resulting in a semantic gap which may hinder verification efforts. Namely, properties that are true under the intended semantics may have counterexamples under FOL semantics. In this talk we focus on a semantic gap stemming from the presence of unintended infinite first-order structures in the standard FOL semantics. We first present an approach for representing and finding (unintended) infinite counter-models to verification conditions. Even if spurious under the intended semantics, such counter-models are important for debugging verification failures. Naturally, the approach is not complete in general, but we identify a new fragment of FOL for which it is complete, leading to decidability of validity in this fragment. We then discuss several techniques for incorporating the intended semantics, e.g., finite-domain semantics, into the verification process. Importantly, verification is still carried out using standard FOL, despite the undefinability of the intended semantics in FOL.

S. Shoham—The research leading to these results has received funding from the European Research Council under the European Union's Horizon 2020 research and innovation programme (grant agreement No [759102-SVIS]) and from the Israel Science Foundation (grant number 2117/23).

Contents

Rewriting

Formalizations in Isabelle/HOL

Calculi

Non-classical Logics

SAT

Invited Talks

Choose Your Proofs: Commutativity and Symmetry for Smarter Reasoning

Azadeh Farzan(✉)

Department of Computer Science, University of Toronto, Toronto, Canada
azadeh@cs.toronto.edu

Abstract. This paper is a very short overview of a few advancements in automated verification of concurrent programs over the years, with a focus on the role of commutativity and symmetry in proofs. The aim of this line of work is to use commutativity and symmetry to lower the burden of logical reasoning for the backend theorem provers used in automated verification. The paper is not written to list formal results but rather to provide a high-level intuition about how certain contributions fit together in unexpected ways to advance program verification techniques. An interested reader is encouraged to dig deeper into the formal results in the cited papers.

The presented ideas go beyond concurrent programs, but a little bit of focus is helpful in telling a coherent story. Techniques discussed here in part have been used in many other interesting program verification problems including hypersafety verification [2,17], verification of probabilistic programs [29], counting proofs for the verification of parameterized programs [10], verification of recursive programs [2,19], verification of sequential programs [18], termination proofs of sequential [20], concurrent [16], and parameterized programs [20], and general LTL properties [4].

We start with an informal overview of an *operational* style of reasoning about programs that is uniquely suitable for incorporating and exploiting these ideas. Then, we discuss how symmetry and commutativity reasoning fit within the framework.

1 Operational Reasoning for Concurrent Programs

The most common approach to reasoning about program correctness, among *programmers*, is based on operational reasoning. Intuitively, the programmer does an informal analysis of the program in terms of its executions, by categorizing them into a finite set of *cases* or *scenarios*, arguing that the program satisfies a desired property in each case. The classic approach to program correctness, among the *experts in this field*, is based on axiomatic reasoning. Such a proof is constructed in a syntax-directed manner by recursion on the structure of the program. The key feature of the formal path is *modularity*: proofs are constructed by composing proofs of program parts.

When it comes to concurrent and distributed programs, the extension of the axiomatic framework (due to Owicki-Gries [28] and Jones [21] and many

The author has been funded by an NSERC Discovery Grant.

C. Barrett and U. Waldmann (Eds.): CADE 2025, LNAI 15943, pp. 3–14, 2025.
https://doi.org/10.1007/978-3-031-99984-0_1

others) construct a proof of correctness for the whole program out of proofs for individual components (threads or processes) and a modicum of glue that connects them. The guiding principle is based on the notion of *non-interference*: other threads/processes do not interfere with the functionality of the current one, and therefore do not have much impact on its proof of correctness. Certain concurrent programs, for example, cooperative concurrency in which processes work together to achieve some common goal, are not designed based on the principle of non-interference. Axiomatic proof systems have clever workarounds (e.g., ghost state [24]) for these cases, but cleverness is an obstacle to automation: humans are clever, but automated verifiers are not.

In contrast, informal operational arguments accommodate arbitrary global facts into proofs more naturally because they are not bound by the axiomatic view. We embarked on a path to make operational arguments rigorous and algorithmically useful in the style of classical axiomatic proofs [9–12]. All of this early work has been thoroughly and beautifully discussed in Zachary Kincaid's (award-winning) thesis [22].

In this line of work, we argue that operational reasoning can be formalized using axiomatic proofs of a program's behaviours, which are sequences of instructions that are executed in order (without conditional branching, looping, etc). Similar to axiomatic proofs, the smallest (atomic) unit in proofs remains a Hoare triple $\{P\}\,\rho\,\{Q\}$, which consists of two assertions P and Q (called the pre-condition and post-condition of the triple, respectively), and a program behaviour ρ. An operational proof for a program is a mechanism that facilitates the derivation of a Hoare triple $\{\text{Pre}\}\ \rho\ \{\text{Post}\}$ for any program behaviour ρ that satisfies it. We call such Hoare triples *valid*.

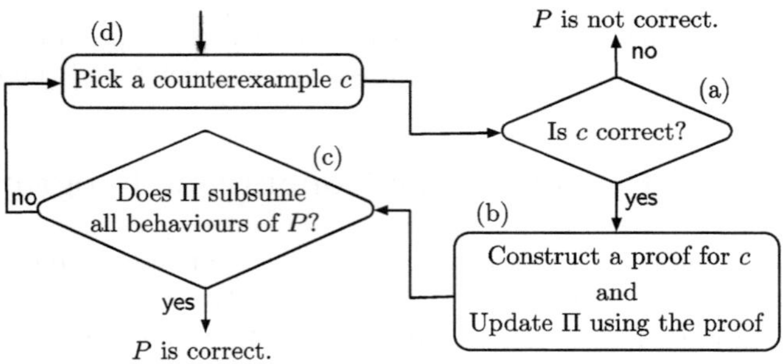

Fig. 1. A Refinement loop For operational-style reasoning. P is a program, and the loop can start in box (c) with an empty proof Π.

To formalize an operational proof, then, we need:

- a mechanism for deriving valid Hoare triples for program behaviours and representing the resulting argument as a coherent formal proof, and
- a way of checking if every program behaviour has been included.

In the context of algorithmic verification, this operational view can be implemented by a refinement loop illustrated in Figure 1. Roughly speaking, boxes (a) and (b) correspond to the first item, and boxes (c) and (d) correspond to the second item listed above.

One can take the view that program behaviours are words over an alphabet of statements Σ. This would make the set of behaviours of P a *language* over that alphabet. In effect, a notion like a control flow graph for the program is a representation for this set of *syntactic* behaviours of the program.

One can also consider Π, the set of behaviours for which the refinement loop has so far produced a formal correctness argument, as another language over the same alphabet. Then, box (c) is a simple language inclusion check. If this check is decidable for the given class of languages, then one has an algorithm for box (c). A counterexample, that is, a witness to the violation of the inclusion check, is then a program behaviour that still needs a proof. Therefore, Π may start from being the empty language in this refinement loop, and then iteratively grow larger based on counterexamples until the program is subsumed.

2 Formalizing Operational Proofs

The counterexample c can be viewed as a *simple* program; for example, in the context of safety, it is a finite run which can be viewed as a sequential program without any branching or looping structure [18]. In the context of liveness [12, 20], it is a simple loop with some initialization and without branching (i.e. a *lasso*). One can use one of the many existing verification techniques (e.g., Craig interpolation or ranking function computation) to verify it, and if it is correct, produce a Hoare/Floyd style proof for it.

The key to this operational framework is how this proof is used to update the existing proof conjecture Π. There are several different proposals for this in the literature. Here, we outline the one from [9] which deals with the verification of concurrent programs with a fixed number of threads[1].

Given a Hoare/Floyd proof of c, one can extract a set of *basic* valid Hoare triples from this proof. They can simply be the set of Hoare triples that appear in the proof. Any such set of Hoare triples H can be associated with an infinite set of Hoare triples $S(H)$, which consists of the Hoare triples that can be obtained from H using the following rules of inference:

- **Sequencing Rule**: if $\{P_1\}\,\tau_1\,\{P_2\}$ and $\{P_2\}\,\tau_2\,\{P_3\}$ are valid triples, then so is $\{P_1\}\,\tau_1;\tau_2\,\{P_3\}$.
- **Conjunction Rule**: if $\{P_1\}\,\tau\,\{Q_1\}$ and $\{P_2\}\,\tau\,\{Q_2\}$ are valid, then so is $\{P_1 \wedge P_2\}\,\tau\,\{Q_1 \wedge Q_2\}$.

We call the set of Hoare triples $PS(H)$ a *proof space*, and call H a *basis* for $PS(H)$. We say that a proof space proves that a set of behaviours $\mathcal{T}$ is correct

[1] We are rewriting the history. In [9], we introduced inductive dataflow graphs. Proof spaces were introduced in [11]. But, in hindsight, one can view inductive dataflow graphs as a limitation of proof spaces.

with respect to a specification *Pre*/*Post* if for each ρ in $\mathcal{T}$, the Hoare triple $\{Pre\}\,\rho\,\{Post\}$ belongs to the proof space $S(H)$ generated by H; that is, there is a derivation of $\{Pre\}\rho\{Post\}$ using the sequencing and conjunction rules, using the Hoare triples in H as axioms.

In [9], we argue how the size of H is polynomial in the number of data dependencies. Importantly, this does not grow exponentially in the number of threads unless the data dependencies do. In other words, the size of the proof is polynomial in the size of a *localized proof*, which can be viewed as a particular presentation of the Floyd/Hoare proof that labels each location ℓ with the conjunction of the global assertion and all local assertions for location ℓ.

The approach shifts the burden of the exponential explosion of dealing with concurrent programs towards checking whether all program behaviours are represented, i.e., to a combinatorial problem. This is in contrast to classic program proofs that end up querying a solver or theorem prover exponentially many times to check a proof.

3 Proof Checking

A proof space is a proof for the program if and only if for every program behaviour, there exists a valid Hoare triple proving its correctness in the proof space. If the proof space is represented by a finite basis, then this means that the Hoare triple for the behaviour must be derived by the repeated application of one of the two rules (sequencing and conjunction).

The existence of such a derivation is reminiscent of the acceptance notion in automata theory, and indeed, there is a formal connection which we exploit. A word (i.e., a sequence of letters) is accepted by an automaton if there exists a run (i.e., a sequence of transitions of the automaton) that leads from an initial state to a final state. The sequencing rule corresponds to the sequencing of transitions of an automaton when we do the following: We associate each statement S of the program with a letter of the alphabet of the automaton, each assertion P to a state of the automaton, and each Hoare triple $\{P\}s\{Q\}$ with a transition from state P to state Q under the letter s. A run ρ is now a word over the alphabet of the automaton. The proof space contains the Hoare triple $\{P\}\rho\{Q\}$ for the run ρ if and only if there exists a sequence of transitions that leads from state P to state Q along the word ρ.

The sequencing rule suffices if we are interested in proof spaces for sequential program proofs. One can use the notion of alternating automata to accommodate the conjunction rule; this allows us to account for concurrent programs with a fixed number of threads. Alternating finite automata offer the most *compact* description of a proof with the potential to be double-exponentially more concise than deterministic finite automata. However, as argued in [9], the price will eventually have to be paid during the subsumption check, but the combinatorial problem remains in PSPACE.

4 Exploiting Symmetry

There is a history of exploiting symmetry in analyzing concurrent systems with the view that systems comprising many identical or isomorphic components may be large, but expressing the structure through the actions of a group of automorphisms of the structure. A shared concurrent program composed of n identical threads is an example of such a structure, where automorphisms can help collapse the $n!$ many permutations of processes.

Let Σ be the set of distinct program statements in a single thread. To represent statements of all threads, we can use the set $\Sigma \times \mathbb{N}$, as a sort of *indexed alphabet*. Note that the Σ component here is tied to code and therefore remains finite, but the $\mathbb{N}$ component is infinite. Then, behaviours of such a program are words over $(\Sigma \times \mathbb{N})^*$.

Let S be the set of all bijections on $\mathbb{N}$ that act on $\Sigma \times \mathbb{N}$ by changing thread identifiers. These form a symmetry group that induces an equivalence relation $\equiv_S$ on program behaviours. Two behaviours are symmetry equivalent if there is a bijection that can rename the thread identifiers of one consistently to those of the other.

In the classic model checking literature [6], exploiting *symmetry* is often done through using the *quotient* up to $\equiv_S$ of the transition graph of the system. The gist is that the quotient is a smaller system that can be soundly verified in place of the original model, saving time and memory in the model checking process.

In [11], our goal was to target the verification of *parameterized* concurrent programs. These are concurrent programs where unboundedly many threads can be spawned from boundedly many thread templates. We use *symmetry* to tackle this newly introduced infinite dimension. Note that even syntactic program runs are not guaranteed to be finitely representable. *Proof Spaces* can be extended with an additional rule [11] to deal with this:

- **Symmetry Rule**: if $\{P\}\,\tau\,\{Q\}$ is a valid, then any triple $\{P'\}\,\tau'\,\{Q'\}$ that can be obtained by consistently renaming thread identifiers in all three components of the Hoare triple is also valid.

For every behaviour ρ in Π, include all other behaviours $\sigma' \equiv_S \sigma$ also in Π. This can be alternatively viewed as computing the symmetry closure of Π (constructed from sequencing and conjunction rules or some other way) up to S and proposes the following proof rule for verification:

$$\frac{\Pi \models \varphi \quad P \subseteq [\Pi]^S}{P \models \varphi} \qquad \text{(SYMMETRY CLOSURE)}$$

Note the contrast between *closing the proof* here and *reducing the program* (i.e. the symmetry quotient) in model checking. For finite-state programs, this translates to a smaller basis for a (finite) proof space that subsumes the program. For parameterized programs, this is vital to yield a *finite* basis for the proof space. One invents and checks the validity of a Hoare triple once, and then it can be used for any other set of thread identifiers up to all automorphisms.

In [11], we show that proof spaces are *complete* wrt Ashcroft invariants, which are universally quantified, over thread identifiers, global invariants that prove the safety of a parameterized program. In [8], we prove that they are *complete* for the verification of Boolean programs. When used in the refinement loop of Figure 1, proof spaces propose an algorithmic path for verification of parameterized programs that is refutation-complete; the refinement loop provides the opportunity for the algorithm to keep refining the abstraction until a true counterexample is found.

5 Predicate Automata

Continuing the argument from Section 3, the sequencing and conjunction rules are accommodated by notions in finite state automata. But, the symmetry rule requires a shift to *data automata* that operate on the *indexed* alphabets. In [11], we introduced the notion of *predicate automata*, as a type of data automata that fits well in the context of modelling parameterized programs and their proofs.

In a predicate automaton, states are predicates applied to thread identifiers. For example, we may use the binary predicate $P(1, 2)$ associated with the assertion $m_1 < m_2$ over the local variables of the two threads with the identifiers 1 and 2. Transitions of predicate automata are specified using first-order logic formulas with free variables, say i and j, in correspondence with the fact that a Hoare triple for an action of, say, Thread 1 can be transformed to a Hoare triple for the *same* action of, say, Thread 2. The language of behaviours proven correct by a proof space is recognized by a predicate automaton that we can construct from the basis of the proof space. Similarly, the set of behaviours of a program is recognized by a predicate automaton that can be constructed from the description of the thread templates. Then, proof checking is reduced to the inclusion problem between languages of predicate automata. In its full generality, the inclusion problem is undecidable, but there exist interesting decidable cases [11]. In [8], we argued that predicate automata have the same expressive power as alternating register automata.

6 Exploiting Commutativity

Atomic program steps a and b *commute* if and only if $a; b$ and $b; a$ have the same semantics (i.e. input-output relation). This leads to a simple observation that if a program run $\rho ab\rho'$ satisfies some specification (e.g. pre/post-condition) and a and b commute, then $\rho ba\rho'$ also satisfies the same specification. It is then convenient to call these and only these program runs *equivalent* under a commutativity relation I that includes the pair (a, b). The equivalence relation $\equiv_I$ induced by I is the reflexive and transitive closure of the relation $\sim_I$ defined as:

$$\sigma \sim_I \sigma' \iff \sigma = \rho ab\rho' \land \sigma' = \rho ba\rho' \land (a, b) \in I.$$

In the refinement loop of Figure 1, this suggests a straightforward way of exploiting commutativity: for every behaviour σ in Π, include all other behaviours $\sigma' \equiv_I \sigma$ also in Π. This amounts to computing the commutativity closure of Π up to I and proposes the following proof rule for verification:

$$\frac{\Pi \models \varphi \quad P \subseteq [\Pi]^I}{P \models \varphi} \qquad \text{(COMMUTATIVITY CLOSURE)}$$

In a sense, we get more mileage out of our efforts to construct proofs by using the commutativity closure of our proof candidate. This proof rule is practically useless. However, since checking the premise $P \subset [\Pi]^I$ is undecidable [3] even for regular languages, which are the simplest class of languages that can be used in our operational reasoning scheme. Therefore, we need a compromise. Consider the following rule:

$$\frac{\Pi \models \varphi \quad \exists \widehat{P} \in \mathit{Red}(P).\ \widehat{P} \subseteq \Pi}{P \models \varphi} \qquad \text{(REDUCTION)}$$

where $\mathit{Red}(P)$ is a set of programs that satisfy the following

$$\widehat{P} \in \mathit{Red}(P) \iff \forall \rho \in P\ \exists \rho' \in \widehat{P}\ \ \rho \equiv_I \rho'$$

The minimal (up to the subset relation) members of $\mathit{Red}(P)$ are quotients of P up to $\equiv_I$. We call these quotient programs *reductions*.

Note that if we let $\mathit{Red}(P)$ be the largest set of programs that are all subsets of behaviours of P and satisfy the above condition, then Rules COMMUTATIVITY CLOSURE and REDUCTION are equivalent, since for this $\mathit{Red}(P)$, we have:

$$(\exists \widehat{P} \in \mathit{Red}(P).\ \widehat{P} \subseteq \Pi) \iff P \subseteq [\Pi]^I$$

and therefore, this new premise is as undecidable as the old one. However, it presents us with a new opportunity: settle for a subset of the reductions in $\mathit{Red}(P)$ so that the premise becomes algorithmically checkable.

The easiest way to achieve this is to let $\mathit{Red}(P)$ include *one* (or finitely many) finitely representable reductions. This is the setup that is used in [13–15]. In [7], we survey some contributions that all stem from exploiting commutativity for program verification in the general form of verifying reductions of programs. We do not repeat that content here. The core concept of how one can enumerate or select reductions, however, is related to the remainder of this paper and is therefore briefly recalled below.

6.1 Contextual Lexicographical Reductions

The more (theoretically) interesting setup is when $\mathit{Red}(P)$ can include infinitely many reductions and yet the entire set remains finitely representable. In [17], we introduce one such expressive set of reductions. The intuitive idea is to let the *lexicographical least element* (LEX) of an equivalence class be the representative of the class, where the lexicographical order is defined based on an order on the alphabet of actions. Each different base order on the alphabet of actions yields a different order on program runs, which yields a different selector from equivalence classes.

Let Σ be an alphabet of program atomic actions. We define a new context-sensitive alphabet order $\prec: \Sigma^* \rightarrow lin(\Sigma)$ where $lin(\Sigma)$ is the set of all possible total orders on Σ. Intuitively, $\prec$ defines an ordering of actions sensitive to the context in which the letters appear in a program run.

Fix a choice of $\prec$ and define a reduction $\widehat{P}_{\prec}$ parametric on this choice as one satisfying the following condition for all $\rho \in P$:

$$\neg(\rho = \sigma_1 b \sigma_2 a \sigma_3 \wedge a \prec_{\sigma_1} b \wedge (a, b\sigma_2) \in I) \implies \rho \in \widehat{P}_{\prec}$$

The left-hand side of the implication determines that the run ρ is the lexicographically least member of its equivalence class up to $\prec$. Therefore, it belongs to the reduction $\widehat{P}$, which only collects these normal forms. Let Red_{lex} be the set of all such reductions for all possible choices of $\prec$. Note that despite there being only finitely many total orders on Σ, there are infinitely many choices for $\prec$, and therefore, infinitely many reductions can be enumerated as long as the program has infinitely many runs. Moreover, each such reduction is *optimal* in the sense that it includes precisely one member of each equivalence class of program behaviours. Therefore, the proof does not need to cover any redundant program behaviours.

The technical breakthrough in [17] is that it puts forward a methodology in which the verification algorithm can simultaneously search in the set of reductions in Red_{lex} *and* for a proof of correctness of such a reduction without introducing any new divergence possibilities beyond the existing ones in software model checking.

The literature surveyed in [7] relies on a program model with boundedly many threads. The problem of how to account for commutativity in *parameterized* programs was mostly in 2023, with the exception of the use of Lipton's movers [25], a limited form of commutativity reasoning, in the tool CIVL [5,23]. Since dealing with symmetry reasoning is vital in dealing with parameterized programs to break down an element of infinity for algorithmic solutions, the question of how to exploit commutativity reasoning in this context also becomes a question of how to accommodate symmetry and commutativity reasoning in a harmonious way in the same framework.

7 Commutativity and Symmetry: Sneak Peek

In [15], we argue why commutativity reasoning can have a huge impact on the verification of parameterized programs. The advantages in simplification of proofs from concurrent programs with a fixed number of threads persist, in that a reduction may have a proof in a simpler assertion language. Parameterization, however, adds an extra layer of complication that has to do with the incompleteness of proofs without ghost variables. For concurrent programs with a fixed number of threads, *program counters* are canonical ghost variables that bring completeness to a Hoare-style proof axiomatic scheme [24]. For parameterized concurrent programs, only access to a full history guarantees the same level of completeness [27]. Proof spaces, for instance, are not complete precisely in scenarios where such ghost variables are needed. In [10], we give one methodology for automatically generating such ghost counters when they are the only ghost state required for the proof.

It is demonstrated through examples in [15] that while verifying the program may require sophisticated ghost variables, like *counters*, a reduction can be verified without any ghost variables, which would put the verification of the reduction within the realm of automated tools that otherwise cannot divine the required ghost state out of thin air.

Let us systematically discuss the problem of adding commutativity reasoning for parameterized programs. Conceptually, we want to take advantage of a proof rule of the following form:

$$\frac{\Pi \models \varphi \quad P \subseteq [[\Pi]^I]^S}{P \models \varphi} \qquad (\textsc{Symmetry \& Commutativity Closure})$$

which remains computationally impossible since $[\Pi]^I$ does not necessarily admit a representation in the same class of language recognizers as Π [1], which are predicate automata [11]. The proof rule as phrased implicitly relies on the identity $[[\Pi]^I]^S = [[\Pi]^S]^I$ to hold, which is only true if S and I are coherent in the sense that when two letters commute, their images under automorphisms of S also commute [1].

The fact that the Symmetry & Commutativity Closure rule cannot be algorithmically implemented suggests that one may have to resort to the same solution that is offered by the Reduction rule. In [15], an approximate solution for this is proposed that, informally put, relies on the verification of a sort of both commutativity and symmetry reduced version of the program, with the caveat that the commutativity reductions are far less expressive than the full set of *contextual lexicographical reduction*. To overcome this, we need a rule like this:

$$\frac{\Pi \models \varphi \quad \exists \widehat{P} \in Red_I(P).\ \widehat{P} \subseteq [\Pi]^S}{P \models \varphi} \qquad (\textsc{Reduction \& Symmetry})$$

The technical challenge present in algorithmically implementing this rule is whether, similar to the rule Reduction reduction, one can put forward an expressive class of reductions, perhaps precisely the class of contextual lexicographical reductions, that can also be represented using predicate automata. Sadly, this is not true for a rather obvious reason. Languages recognized by predicate automata are closed under symmetry [8]. However, contextual lexicographical reductions, by definition *favour* an element of an equivalence class over the rest and *break* symmetry in the process. Hence, $[\Pi]^S$ can be captured by a predicate automaton as before, but a desirable member of $Red_I(P)$ cannot.

Remarkably, it turns out that the flaw is in the definition of *symmetry*, in the sense that it is too limiting. The bijections on natural numbers are sufficient to deal with parameterized programs over shared memory, which are defined through a finite number of thread templates. They, however, cannot capture other types of symmetry existing in other parameterized programs, for instance, the type of symmetry that is present in a parameterized program from the set $Red_I(P)$. If we draw our thread identifiers from a different structure, in particular the set of *ordered rational numbers*, then we recover the ability to distinguish or prefer one thread over another by comparing their identifiers, which is essential in selecting representatives from commutativity equivalence classes [1].

Ordered rational numbers and order-preserving automorphisms also define a symmetry. The good news is that predicate automata can be generalized so that they are parametric on an appropriate notion of symmetry that is suitable for modelling the parameterized program under consideration, and the essential results from [11] can be recovered under this generalization. Hence, the REDUCTION & SYMMETRY rule can be implemented.

8 Summary

Operational proofs offer a clean framework in which symmetry and commutativity can be seamlessly incorporated to lessen the burden of logical reasoning required for automated verification. On the commutativity side, work has been ongoing for quite a few years, and a big remaining challenge is how to algorithmically take advantage of *abstract commutativity*. On the symmetry side, some very recent progress [1] suggests that this area has not received as much attention as needed since the early days of model checking and much more work is required to explore appropriate notions of symmetry in dealing with parameterized programs beyond shared concurrent program, for instance to account of the topological structure in distributed programming [6] or exploit local symmetries [26] in both concurrent and distributed programs.

Disclosure of Interests. The author has no competing interests to declare that are relevant to the content of this article.

References

1. Cheng, R., Farzan, A.: Commutativity and Symmetry in Verification of Parameterized Concurrent Programs. Technical report, University of Toronto, 07 2025
2. Cheng, R., Farzan, A.: Products of recursive programs for hypersafety verification. CoRR, abs/2504.10800 (2025)
3. Diekert, V., Rozenberg, G.: The book of traces. World scientific (1995)
4. Dietsch, D., Heizmann, M., Langenfeld, V., Podelski, A.: Fairness modulo theory: a new approach to ltl software model checking. In: Kroening, D., Păsăreanu, C.S. (eds.) Computer Aided Verification, pp. 49–66. Springer, Cham (2015)

5. Elmas, T., Qadeer, S., Tasiran, S.: A calculus of atomic actions. In: Shao, Z., Pierce, B.C. (eds.) Proceedings of the 36th ACM SIGPLAN-SIGACT Symposium on Principles of Programming Languages, POPL 2009, Savannah, GA, USA, January 21-23, 2009, pp. 2–15. ACM (2009)
6. Allen Emerson, E., Havlicek, J.W., Trefler, R.J.: Virtual symmetry reduction. In: Proceedings of the 15th Annual IEEE Symposium on Logic in Computer Science, LICS '00, p. 121. IEEE Computer Society, USA (2000)
7. Farzan, A.: Commutativity in automated verification. In: 38th Annual ACM/IEEE Symposium on Logic in Computer Science, LICS 2023, Boston, MA, USA, June 26-29, 2023, pp. 1–7. IEEE (2023)
8. Farzan, A., Kincaid, Z.: The beauty of predicate automata. In: On the pursuit of insight and elegance: essays on the occasion of Andreas Podelski's 65th birthday, vol. 14765. LNCS (2025)
9. Farzan, A., Kincaid, Z., Podelski, A.: Inductive data flow graphs. SIGPLAN Not. **48**(1), 129–142 (2013)
10. Farzan, A., Kincaid, Z., Podelski, A.: Proofs that count. SIGPLAN Not. **49**(1), 151–164 (2014)
11. Farzan, A., Kincaid, Z., Podelski, A.: Proof spaces for unbounded parallelism. In: Rajamani, S.K., Walker, D. (eds.) Proceedings of the 42nd Annual ACM SIGPLAN-SIGACT Symposium on Principles of Programming Languages, POPL 2015, Mumbai, India, January 15-17, 2015, pp. 407–420. ACM (2015)
12. Farzan, A., Kincaid, Z., Podelski, A.: Proving liveness of parameterized programs. In: Proceedings of the 31st Annual ACM/IEEE Symposium on Logic in Computer Science, LICS '16, pp. 185–196. Association for Computing Machinery, New York (2016)
13. Farzan, A., Klumpp, D., Podelski, A.: Sound sequentialization for concurrent program verification. In: Proceedings of the 43rd ACM SIGPLAN International Conference on Programming Language Design and Implementation, pp. 506–521 (2022)
14. Farzan, A., Klumpp, D., Podelski, A.: Stratified commutativity in verification algorithms for concurrent programs. In: Proceedings of the ACM on Programming Languages, 7(POPL), 1426–1453 (2023)
15. Azadeh Farzan, Dominik Klumpp, and Andreas Podelski. Commutativity simplifies proofs of parameterized programs. *Proc. ACM Program. Lang.*, 8(POPL):2485–2513, 2024
16. Farzan, A., Lette, D.: Commutativity for concurrent program termination proofs. In: Enea, C., Lal, A. (eds.) Computer Aided Verification - 35th International Conference, CAV 2023, Paris, France, July 17-22, 2023, Proceedings, Part I. LNCS, vol. 13964, pp. 109–131. Springer (2023)
17. Farzan, A., Vandikas, A.: Automated Hypersafety Verification. In: Dillig, I., Tasiran, S. (eds.) CAV 2019. LNCS, vol. 11561, pp. 200–218. Springer, Cham (2019). https://doi.org/10.1007/978-3-030-25540-4_11
18. Heizmann, M., Hoenicke, J., Podelski, A.: Refinement of trace abstraction. In: Palsberg, J., Su, Z. (eds.) Static Analysis, pp. 69–85. Springer, Heidelberg (2009)
19. Heizmann, M., Hoenicke, J., Podelski, A.: Nested interpolants. In: Proceedings of the 37th Annual ACM SIGPLAN-SIGACT Symposium on Principles of Programming Languages, POPL '10, pp. 471–482. Association for Computing Machinery, New York (2010)
20. Heizmann, M., Hoenicke, J., Podelski, A.: Termination analysis by learning terminating programs. In: Biere, A., Bloem, R., (eds.) Computer Aided Verification, pp. 797–813. Springer, Cham (2014)

21. Jones, C.B.: The early search for tractable ways of reasoning about programs. IEEE Ann. Hist. Comput. **25**(2), 26–49 (2003)
22. Kincaid, Z.: Parallel Proofs for Parallel Programs. Ph.D. thesis, University of Toronto (2016)
23. Kragl, B., Qadeer, S.: Layered Concurrent Programs. In: Chockler, H., Weissenbacher, G. (eds.) CAV 2018. LNCS, vol. 10981, pp. 79–102. Springer, Cham (2018). https://doi.org/10.1007/978-3-319-96145-3_5
24. Lamport, L.: Control predicates are better than dummy variables for reasoning about program control. ACM Trans. Program. Lang. Syst. **10**(2), 267–281 (1988)
25. Lipton, R.J.: Reduction: A method of proving properties of parallel programs. Commun. ACM **18**(12), 717–721 (1975)
26. Namjoshi, K.S., Trefler, R.J.: Local symmetry and compositional verification. In: Kuncak, V., Rybalchenko, A. (eds.) VMCAI 2012. LNCS, vol. 7148, pp. 348–362. Springer, Heidelberg (2012). https://doi.org/10.1007/978-3-642-27940-9_23
27. Nieto, L.P.: Completeness of the owicki-gries system for parameterized parallel programs. In: Proceedings of the 15th International Parallel & Distributed Processing Symposium, IPDPS '01, p. 150, USA. IEEE Computer Society (2001)
28. Owicki, S.S., Gries, D.: Verifying properties of parallel programs: an axiomatic approach. Commun. ACM **19**(5), 279–285 (1976)
29. Smith, C., Hsu, J., Albarghouthi, A.: Trace abstraction modulo probability. 3(POPL), January 2019

SMT

Being Polite Is Not Enough (and Other Limits of Theory Combination)

Guilherme V. Toledo[1(✉)], Benjamin Przybocki[2], and Yoni Zohar[1]

[1] Bar-Ilan University, Ramat Gan, Israel
guivtoledo@gmail.com
[2] University of Cambridge, Cambridge, UK

Abstract. In the Nelson–Oppen combination method for satisfiability modulo theories, the combined theories must be stably infinite; in gentle combination, one theory has to be gentle, and the other has to satisfy a similar yet weaker property; in shiny combination, only one has to be shiny (smooth, with a computable minimal model function and the finite model property); and for polite combination, only one has to be strongly polite (smooth and strongly finitely witnessable). For each combination method, we prove that if any of its assumptions are removed, then there is no general method to combine an arbitrary pair of theories satisfying the remaining assumptions. We also prove new theory combination results that weaken the assumptions of gentle and shiny combination.

1 Introduction

Let us start at the middle. Polite theory combination [15] was not the first method to combine two theories (see, e.g., [13,20]). It was also not the last (see, e.g., [5,8,12]). However, it is one of the most influential approaches to theory combination. In fact, it has found its way to the implementation of the state-of-the-art SMT-solver cvc5 [1] (and also CVC4 [3] and CVC3 [2]).

The history of polite combination is illustrated in Fig. 1, that focuses on decidable theories (marked by the large rectangle). The left circle corresponds to decidable theories that can be combined with any other decidable theory over a disjoint signature. We call such theories *combinable*. In [15], it was argued that a sufficient condition for combinability is *politeness*, a technical notion that concerns cardinalities of models. In other words, [15] claimed that the red-hatched region of Fig. 1 is empty. Then, the paper [9] discovered a bug in the proof from [15], and offered to replace politeness by a seemingly stronger notion, *strong politeness* (the name is due to [6]). It was proved in [9] that strongly polite theories are combinable, which positions the small circle that represents strongly polite theories completely within the circle representing combinable theories.

While [9] found a bug in the *proof* of [15], it left two questions open: (i) does politeness imply combinability, as [15] claimed, only with a different proof? and (ii) do polite theories that are not strongly polite exist? In terms of Fig. 1: (i) is the red-hatched region empty? and (ii) is the entire hatched region empty?

C. Barrett and U. Waldmann (Eds.): CADE 2025, LNAI 15943, pp. 17–34, 2025.
https://doi.org/10.1007/978-3-031-99984-0_2

Question (*ii*) was recently resolved in [18,22]: a theory named $\mathcal{T}_f$ was found wandering around the hatched region. However, question (*i*) remained unanswered, as it was unclear whether $\mathcal{T}_f$ resided in the red hatched region or the blue one.

In this paper we solve question (*i*), by placing $\mathcal{T}_f$ in the red-hatched region: it is polite but uncombinable. To show this, we introduce a new decidable theory, named $\mathcal{T}_=$, over a disjoint signature, and prove that its combination with $\mathcal{T}_f$ is *undecidable.*

$\mathcal{T}_f$ and $\mathcal{T}_=$ are not merely mustard watches [16]. They show that being polite is not enough (for theory combination), finally closing the question of politeness vs. combinability, that remained open since [9]. Foundationally, they show that the fix of [9] was indeed necessary. And practically, they justify the implementation overhead of adopting the more complicated definition of strong politeness.

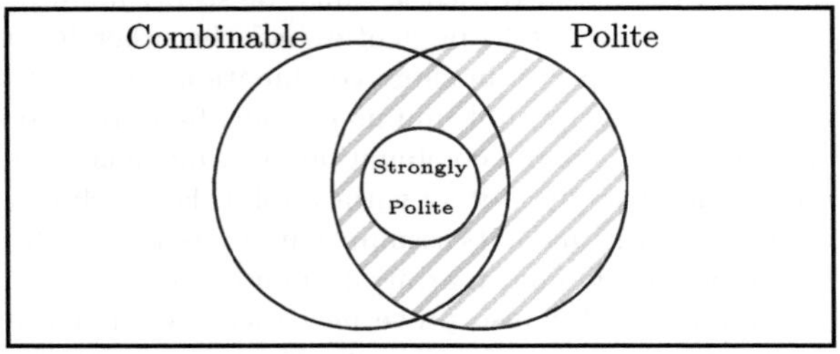

Fig. 1. An illustration of the contributions of [9,15,22] and the current paper.

The existence of $\mathcal{T}_f$ and $\mathcal{T}_=$ can be seen as a *limitation theorem*: they show that the polite combination method cannot be applied if strong politeness is weakened to politeness. We present similar limitation theorems for other combination methods. For the Nelson–Oppen method [13], we show that if only one of the theories is assumed to be stably infinite, then the combination method fails; this was previously proven in [4], but that study did not broach any combination methods other than Nelson–Oppen. We provide a similar treatment for gentle combination [8]. Finally, for a theory to be shiny [19], it has to satisfy three requirements. For each one, we show its necessity as well. Surprisingly, we can reuse $\mathcal{T}_f$ and $\mathcal{T}_=$ for almost all limitation theorems, except for one. Therefore, we use two more theories. The first, $\mathcal{T}_\infty$, is also taken from [22]. The second, $\mathcal{T}_\leq$, is new, and can be seen as a generalization of the theory from [4] that was used for the Nelson-Oppen limitation theorem. For all theories (old and new), we prove that they satisfy the required properties for each limitation theorem.

Additionally, we prove two new combination theorems, based on the gentle and shiny combination methods. These theorems relax some of the requirements for theory combination, while ensuring the decidability of the combined theories. In a sense, the new theorems remedy the limitation theorems that we prove.

This paper is organized as follows. Section 2 surveys notions regarding theory combination. Section 3 proves our main theorems, exhibiting limits of common

$\neq(x_1,\ldots,x_n)=\bigwedge_{i=1}^{n-1}\bigwedge_{j=i+1}^{n}\neg(x_i=x_j)$	$\psi_{\leq n}=\exists\,x_1,\ldots,x_n.\,\forall\,y.\,\bigvee_{i=1}^{n}y=x_i$
$\psi_{\geq n}=\exists\,x_1\ldots x_n.\,\neq(x_1,\ldots,x_n)$	$\psi_{=n}=\psi_{\geq n}\wedge\psi_{\leq n}$

Fig. 2. Cardinality formulas.

combination methods. Section 4 improves the proofs of Sect. 3 by only using theories over finite signatures. Section 5 proves new combination theorems. Section 6 concludes and provides directions for future research.

2 Preliminaries

We use $\mathbb{N}$ to denote the set of naturals including 0, and $\mathbb{N}^*$ to denote $\mathbb{N}\setminus\{0\}$. If X is a set, $|X|$ is its cardinality, and $|\mathbb{N}|=\aleph_0$.

2.1 First-Order Logic

A *signature* is a pair $\Sigma=(\mathcal{F}_\Sigma,\mathcal{P}_\Sigma)$ where: $\mathcal{F}_\Sigma$ is a set of function symbols, each with arity $n\in\mathbb{N}$; and $\mathcal{P}_\Sigma$ is a set of predicate symbols, each with arity $m\in\mathbb{N}$, containing at least the equality $=$, of arity 2. Σ is said to be *empty* if it has no function and predicate symbols other than $=$. Two signatures are said to be *disjoint* if the only symbol they share is $=$. We define *terms*, *literals*, *clauses* (i.e., disjunctions of literals), *cubes* (i.e., conjunctions of literals), *formulas* and *sentences* in the usual way. If t is a unary function symbol and x a variable, we define by induction the terms $t^0(x):=x$ and $t^{n+1}(x):=t(t^n(x))$. The set of variables in a formula φ is denoted by $vars(\varphi)$.

Σ *-interpretations* $\mathcal{A}$ are defined as usual: $dom(\mathcal{A})$ is the *domain* of $\mathcal{A}$; for a function symbol f of arity n, $f^{\mathcal{A}}:dom(\mathcal{A})^n\rightarrow dom(\mathcal{A})$; for a predicate symbol P of arity m, $P^{\mathcal{A}}\subseteq dom(\mathcal{A})^m$; for a variable x, $x^{\mathcal{A}}\in dom(\mathcal{A})$. For a term α, $\alpha^{\mathcal{A}}$ is its value in $\mathcal{A}$, and for a set Γ of terms, $\Gamma^{\mathcal{A}}=\{\alpha^{\mathcal{A}}:\alpha\in\Gamma\}$. If $\mathcal{A}$ satisfies φ, we write $\mathcal{A}\vDash\varphi$. Formulas from Fig. 2 are satisfied by $\mathcal{A}$ when $|dom(\mathcal{A})|$ is: at least n (for $\neq(x_1,\ldots,x_n)$ and $\psi_{\geq n}$); at most n (for $\psi_{\leq n}$); exactly n (for $\psi_{=n}$).

A *theory* $\mathcal{T}$ is a class of all interpretations that satisfy a (finite or infinite) set of sentences $Ax(\mathcal{T})$ called the *axiomatization* of $\mathcal{T}$; φ is said to be $\mathcal{T}$ *-satisfiable* when there is a $\mathcal{T}$-interpretation satisfying φ; it is $\mathcal{T}$ *-valid* when every $\mathcal{T}$-interpretation satisfies φ. Two formulas φ and ψ are $\mathcal{T}$ *-equivalent* when a $\mathcal{T}$-interpretation satisfies φ if and only if it satisfies ψ. $\mathcal{T}$ is *decidable* if the set of $\mathcal{T}$-satisfiable quantifier-free formulas is decidable.

2.2 Theory Combination Theorems

In what follows, Σ, Σ_1,Σ_2 are signatures, and $\mathcal{T}$, $\mathcal{T}_1$, $\mathcal{T}_2$ are Σ, Σ_1,Σ_2-theories, respectively. We assume Σ_1 and Σ_2 are disjoint, and $\mathcal{T}_1$ and $\mathcal{T}_2$ are decidable.

$\Sigma_1 \cup \Sigma_2$ is the signature obtained by collecting all function and predicates symbols from Σ_1 and Σ_2. $\mathcal{T}_1 \oplus \mathcal{T}_2$ is the $\Sigma_1 \cup \Sigma_2$-theory axiomatized by $Ax(\mathcal{T}_1) \cup Ax(\mathcal{T}_2)$.

We start with Nelson–Oppen. $\mathcal{T}$ is *stably infinite* if for every quantifier-free $\mathcal{T}$-satisfiable formula φ there is an infinite $\mathcal{T}$-interpretation $\mathcal{A}$ with $\mathcal{A} \models \varphi$.

Theorem 1 **([13]).** *$\mathcal{T}_1 \oplus \mathcal{T}_2$ is decidable, if both $\mathcal{T}_1$ and $\mathcal{T}_2$ are stably infinite.*

Next, we define politeness. $\mathcal{T}$ is *smooth* if for every quantifier-free $\mathcal{T}$-satisfiable formula φ, $\mathcal{T}$-interpretation $\mathcal{A}$ that satisfies φ, and cardinal $\kappa > |dom(\mathcal{A})|$, there is a $\mathcal{T}$-interpretation $\mathcal{B}$ that satisfies φ with $|dom(\mathcal{A})| = \kappa$ (notice smoothness implies stable infiniteness, as we can choose an infinite κ). $\mathcal{T}$ is *finitely witnessable* if there exists a function *wit* (called a witness) from the quantifier-free formulas of Σ into themselves such that, for every quantifier-free formula φ, one has that: (I) φ and $\exists\, \overrightarrow{x}\, .\, wit(\varphi)$ are $\mathcal{T}$-equivalent, where $\overrightarrow{x} = vars(wit(\varphi)) \setminus vars(\varphi)$; (II) if $wit(\varphi)$ is $\mathcal{T}$-satisfiable there exists a $\mathcal{T}$-interpretation $\mathcal{A}$ that satisfies $wit(\varphi)$ with $dom(\mathcal{A}) = vars(wit(\varphi))^{\mathcal{A}}$. $\mathcal{T}$ is *polite* if it is both smooth and finitely witnessable. The following was stated as a theorem in [15], but its proof was later refuted in [9]. It therefore remained a conjecture, which essentially states that politeness is enough for theory combination.

Conjecture 1 ([15]). $\mathcal{T}_1 \oplus \mathcal{T}_2$ is decidable, provided that $\mathcal{T}_2$ is polite.

Next: strong politeness. Given a finite set of variables V and an equivalence relation E on V, the *arrangement* induced by E on V, denoted by δ_V^E or δ_V if E is clear, is the conjunction, for $x, y \in V$, of all formulas $x = y$, if xEy, or $\neg(x = y)$ otherwise. $\mathcal{T}$ is *strongly finitely witnessable* if it is finitely witnessable, with witness *wit*, which in addition satisfies: (II') for every quantifier-free formula φ, finite set of variables V, and arrangement δ_V on V, if $wit(\varphi) \wedge \delta_V$ is $\mathcal{T}$-satisfiable then there exists a $\mathcal{T}$-interpretation $\mathcal{A}$ that satisfies $wit(\varphi) \wedge \delta_V$ with $dom(\mathcal{A}) = vars(wit(\varphi) \wedge \delta_V)^{\mathcal{A}}$. In that case *wit* is called a strong witness. $\mathcal{T}$ is *strongly polite* if it is smooth and strongly finitely witnessable (it was shown in [14, Theorem 2] that in this definition, smoothness can be replaced by stable infiniteness).

Theorem 2 **([9]).** *$\mathcal{T}_1 \oplus \mathcal{T}_2$ is decidable, provided that $\mathcal{T}_2$ is strongly polite.*

We continue to shiny combination. $\mathcal{T}$ has the *finite model property* if, for every quantifier-free $\mathcal{T}$-satisfiable formula φ[1] and $\mathcal{T}$-interpretation $\mathcal{A}$ that satisfies φ, there exists a $\mathcal{T}$-interpretation $\mathcal{B}$ that satisfies φ with $|dom(\mathcal{B})| < \aleph_0$. Let $\mathbb{N}_\omega = \mathbb{N} \cup \{\aleph_0\}$. The *minimal model function* **minmod** of $\mathcal{T}$ is a function from the quantifier-free formulas of Σ to $\mathbb{N}_\omega$ such that for every quantifier-free $\mathcal{T}$-satisfiable formula φ: (I) there exists a $\mathcal{T}$-interpretation $\mathcal{A}$ that satisfies φ with $|dom(\mathcal{A})| = \mathbf{minmod}(\varphi)$; (II) if $\mathcal{B}$ is a $\mathcal{T}$-interpretation that satisfies φ, $\mathbf{minmod}(\varphi) \leq |dom(\mathcal{B})|$.[2] $\mathcal{T}$ is *shiny* if it is smooth, and it has both the finite model property and a computable minimal model function. Note that [6,7]

[1] This notion is often not restricted to a quantifier-free φ, but in SMT it usually is.

[2] The function **minmod** is only guaranteed to exist if $\mathcal{F}_\Sigma \cup \mathcal{P}_\Sigma$ is countable.

showed that shininess is equivalent to strong politeness for decidable theories. In our context, however, we disassemble these notions to their more rudimentary ingredients, and when doing so, the equivalence does not necessarily hold.

Theorem 3 ([20]). *$\mathcal{T}_1 \oplus \mathcal{T}_2$ is decidable, provided that $\mathcal{T}_2$ is shiny.*

The *spectrum* $Spec(\mathcal{T}, \varphi)$ of $\mathcal{T}$ w.r.t. a quantifier-free formula φ is the set of countable cardinalities of $\mathcal{T}$-interpretations that satisfy φ. Roughly, $\mathcal{T}$ is gentle if, given a conjunction φ of literals, $Spec(\mathcal{T}, \varphi)$ can be computed, and is either a finite set of finite cardinalities or a co-finiteset of cardinalities. Formally, $\mathcal{T}$ is *gentle* if there is an algorithm that, for every conjunction φ of literals, outputs a pair (b, S), with b a boolean and $S \subset \mathbb{N}^*$ is finite, such that (i) if b is true, then $Spec(\mathcal{T}, \varphi) = S$ and (ii) if b is false, then $Spec(\mathcal{T}, \varphi) = \mathbb{N}_\omega \setminus S$. Note that a gentle theory is decidable, because φ is $\mathcal{T}$-satisfiable if and only if $Spec(\mathcal{T}, \varphi) \neq \emptyset$.

Theorem 4 ([8, Theorem 3]). *$\mathcal{T}_1 \oplus \mathcal{T}_2$ is decidable, when $\mathcal{T}_1$ is gentle, and $\mathcal{T}_2$ is either: (i) gentle, (ii) finitely axiomatizable, or (iii) there is an algorithm that, for a conjunction φ of Σ_2-literals, outputs a finite $S \subset \mathbb{N}_\omega$ with $Spec(\mathcal{T}, \varphi) = S$.*

3 Limitations of Theory Combination Methods

In this section, we examine what is the outcome of dropping each assumption on the theories from Theorems 1 to 4. We show that each of these theorems break if we drop any of the assumptions it makes regarding the combined theories.

All of these theorems have the following form: if $\mathcal{T}_1$ and $\mathcal{T}_2$ are over disjoint signatures and are decidable, and in addition, $\mathcal{T}_1$ admits some properties, and $\mathcal{T}_2$ admits some properties, then $\mathcal{T}_1 \oplus \mathcal{T}_2$ is also decidable. Thus, our limitation proofs always consist of examples for theories $\mathcal{T}_1$ and $\mathcal{T}_2$ that admit all but one of the properties, such that $\mathcal{T}_1 \oplus \mathcal{T}_2$ is undecidable.

In Sect. 3.2 we show that the Nelson–Oppen combination method fails if we drop the requirement of stable infiniteness from one of the theories. We show a similar result for gentle combination. In Sect. 3.3, dedicated to polite combination, we show that it fails if we drop any of the requirements for polite combination from $\mathcal{T}_2$. This includes dropping strong finite witnessability in exchange for finite witnessability, namely, replacing strong politeness by politeness. We also show that dropping smoothness from the polite combination method results in failure. In Sect. 3.4, a similar investigation is carried out for shiny theories. For each of the three components of shininess, we show that it is critical for the possibility of combination.

But first, we introduce the theories that will be used to demonstrate the limits of the various combination theorems in Sect. 3.1.

Table 1. Signatures. Predicate symbols are 0-ary. The function symbol is unary.

Name	Function Symbols	Predicate Symbols
Σ_1	$\emptyset$	$\emptyset$
Σ_s	$\{s\}$	$\emptyset$
Σ_P^n	$\emptyset$	$\{P_n \mid n \in \mathbb{N}^*\}$

3.1 The Theories that We Use

Since the Nelson–Oppen and gentle methods require one property each (stable infiniteness and gentleness, respectively), the polite method requires 2 properties (smoothness and strong finite witnessability), and the shiny method requires 3 properties (smoothness, the finite model property, and the computability of the minimal model function), we have $1 + 1 + 2 + 3 = 7$ variants to consider, each removing exactly one property as an assumption from a combination theorem. For each such variant, we need to provide 2 theories, $\mathcal{T}_1$ and $\mathcal{T}_2$ for which the variant fails. So, in total, we need to produce $7 \cdot 2 = 14$ theories as examples.

Remarkably, we are able to cover all the aforementioned variants using only 4 theories, that are defined over 3 signatures. Out of these 4 theories, only 2 are used for all but one of the variants. From these 4 theories, we create 3 ordered pairs of theories ($\mathcal{T}_1$ and $\mathcal{T}_2$). Two pairs are used to show the limits of 3 combination approaches each, and the third pair is used for one limit. Clearly, even if we were only concerned with shininess, 3 distinct ordered pairs would have been necessary, as there are three properties to exclude. Thus, the number of pairs of theories that we present is optimal.

The signatures for the theories are described in Table 1. Σ_1 is simply the empty signature. Atomic formulas are therefore only equalities between variables. Σ_s has a unary function symbol s. And Σ_P^n has infinitely many 0-ary predicate symbols $P_1, P_2, \ldots$.

The 4 theories are described in Table 2. The first two are taken from [22], which introduced and studied a wide collection of theories. $\mathcal{T}_\infty$ is the theory over the empty signature whose models have infinitely many elements.

$\mathcal{T}_f$ is more involved. Its axiomatization as a Σ_s-theory assumes the existence of a non-computable function $f : \mathbb{N}^* \to \{0, 1\}$, such that $f(1) = 1$, and for every $k \geq 1$, f maps half of the numbers between 1 and 2^k to 1, and the other half to 0. Such a function was proven to exist in [22, Lemma 6]. The axiomatization utilizes two derived functions: $f_0(k)$ returns the number of numbers between 1 and k that f maps to 0, while $f_1(k)$ returns the number of numbers between 1 and k that f maps to 1. Obviously, when k is a power of 2, then $f_0(k) = f_1(k)$. Now, f itself is not a part of the signature Σ_s of $\mathcal{T}_f$. Instead, the axiomatization relies on the formulas from Fig. 3, that involve counting elements for which the function symbol s acts as the identity. Intuitively, a finite $\mathcal{T}_f$-interpretation $\mathcal{A}$ with n elements has $f_0(n)$ of them satisfying $s^{\mathcal{A}}(e) \neq e$, and $f_1(n)$ satisfying $s^{\mathcal{A}}(e) = e$; an infinite such interpretation has infinitely many elements of each kind.

$$\psi^{=}_{\geq n} = \exists\, \overrightarrow{x}.[\neq (x_1,\ldots,x_n) \wedge \bigwedge_{i=1}^{n} p(x_i)], \qquad \psi^{\neq}_{\geq n} = \exists\, \overrightarrow{x}.[\neq (x_1,\ldots,x_n) \wedge \bigwedge_{i=1}^{n} \neg p(x_i)],$$

$$\psi^{=}_{=n} = \exists\, \overrightarrow{x}.\ [\neq (x_1,\ldots,x_n) \wedge \bigwedge_{i=1}^{n} p(x_i) \wedge \forall x.\ [p(x) \rightarrow \bigvee_{i=1}^{n} x = x_i]],$$

$$\psi^{\neq}_{=n} = \exists\, \overrightarrow{x}.\ [\neq (x_1,\ldots,x_n) \wedge \bigwedge_{i=1}^{n} \neg p(x_i) \wedge \forall x.\ [\neg p(x) \rightarrow \bigvee_{i=1}^{n} x = x_i]].$$

Fig. 3. Formulas for the axiomatization of $\mathcal{T}_f$. $\overrightarrow{x}$ stands for $x_1, \ldots, x_n$, and $p(x)$ for $s(x) = x$.

The definition of $\mathcal{T}_{\leq}$ assumes an arbitrary non-computable function $F : \mathbb{N}^* \rightarrow \mathbb{N}^* \cup \{\aleph_0\}$ such that the set $\{(m,n) \in \mathbb{N}^* \times \mathbb{N}^* \mid F(m) \geq n\}$ is decidable. Such a function F exists: for example, suppose F maps every $n \in \mathbb{N}^*$ to the number of steps the nth Turing machine (under some encoding) takes to halt, returning $\aleph_0$ if it does not halt. This function is clearly not computable. But, given m and n, we can decide whether $F(m) \geq n$ by executing the mth Turing machine for n steps. If a $\mathcal{T}_{\leq}$-interpretation $\mathcal{A}$ satisfies P_n, then it has at most $F(n)$ elements.[3]

Finally, $\mathcal{T}_{=}$ consists of all Σ^n_P-interpretations $\mathcal{A}$ in which for all $n \in \mathbb{N}^*$, either P_n is interpreted as false, or $|\mathcal{A}| = n$. It therefore allows quantifier-free formulas to enforce finite sizes of models, as P_n being true implies the model has n elements.

Table 2. Theories. $f : \mathbb{N}^* \rightarrow \{0,1\}$ is assumed to be a non-computable function, such that $f(1) = 1$ and, for every $k \geq 0$, f maps half of the numbers between 1 and 2^k to 1, and the other half to 0. $f_i(k)$ is the number of numbers between 1 and k that are mapped by f to i. $F : \mathbb{N}^* \rightarrow \mathbb{N}^* \cup \{\aleph_0\}$ is non-computable, but the set $\{(m,n) \mid F(m) \geq n\}$ is decidable. Formulas from Fig. 3 are used.

Name	Signature	Axiomatization	Source
$\mathcal{T}_\infty$	Σ_1	$\{\psi_{\geq n} : n \in \mathbb{N}^*\}$	[22]
$\mathcal{T}_f$	Σ_s	$\{[\psi^{=}_{\geq f_1(k)} \wedge \psi^{\neq}_{\geq f_0(k)}] \vee \bigvee_{i=1}^{k} [\psi^{=}_{=f_1(i)} \wedge \psi^{\neq}_{=f_0(i)}] : k \in \mathbb{N}^*\}$	[22]
$\mathcal{T}_{\leq}$	Σ^n_P	$\{P_n \rightarrow \psi_{\leq F(n)} : n \in \mathbb{N}^*,\ F(n) \in \mathbb{N}^*\}$	new
$\mathcal{T}_{=}$	Σ^n_P	$\{P_n \rightarrow \psi_{=n} : n \in \mathbb{N}^*\}$	new

3.2 Nelson–Oppen and Gentle Combination

We begin by proving the sharpness of Theorem 1 in the following sense: although two theories can be combined if both are stably-infinite, this is no longer the

[3] $\mathcal{T}_{\leq}$ generalizes the theory TM_∞ from [4].

case if only one has that property. This result was previously proven in [4, Theorem 4.1], but with a different proof.

Theorem 5. *There are decidable theories $\mathcal{T}_1$ and $\mathcal{T}_2$ over disjoint signatures such that $\mathcal{T}_1$ is stably infinite but $\mathcal{T}_1 \oplus \mathcal{T}_2$ is undecidable.*

Proof (sketch).[4] Take $\mathcal{T}_1$ and $\mathcal{T}_2$ to be $\mathcal{T}_f$ and $\mathcal{T}_=$, respectively. Clearly, their signatures (namely Σ_s and Σ_P^n) are disjoint. Further, $\mathcal{T}_f$ is shown in [25, Lemma 54] to be stably infinite; it was also proven to have the same set of quantifier-free satisfiable formulas as the theory of an uninterpreted unary function, which makes it decidable. Finally, although both $\mathcal{T}_f$ and $\mathcal{T}_=$ are decidable, $\mathcal{T}_f \oplus \mathcal{T}_=$ is not. Indeed, the formulas $P_{n+1} \wedge \varphi^=_{\geq f_1(n)+1}$, where

$$\varphi^=_{\geq n} := \bigwedge_{1 \leq i < j \leq n} \neg(x_i = x_j) \wedge \bigwedge_{i=1}^{n} s(x_i) = x_i,$$

are $\mathcal{T}_= \oplus \mathcal{T}_f$-satisfiable if and only if $f(n+1) = 1$, whereas f is a non-computable function.

Clearly, Theorem 1 and the proof of Theorem 5 imply that $\mathcal{T}_=$ is not stably infinite. And indeed, for every n, the formula P_n is $\mathcal{T}_=$-satisfiable, but only by a finite model.

As it turns out, the same theories can be used to show a similar result for gentleness.

Theorem 6. *There are decidable theories $\mathcal{T}_1$ and $\mathcal{T}_2$ over disjoint signatures such that $\mathcal{T}_1$ is gentle, but $\mathcal{T}_1 \oplus \mathcal{T}_2$ is undecidable.*

Proof (sketch). We reuse the proof of Theorem 5, but flip the roles of the theories. Now, we set $\mathcal{T}_1$ to be $\mathcal{T}_=$ and $\mathcal{T}_2$ to be $\mathcal{T}_f$. $\mathcal{T}_f$ and $\mathcal{T}_=$ are both decidable, are over disjoint signatures, but $\mathcal{T}_= \oplus \mathcal{T}_f$ is undecidable. The only thing left to show is that $\mathcal{T}_=$ is gentle, which indeed can be shown.

Theorem 4 and the proof of Theorem 6 tell us that $\mathcal{T}_f$ is not gentle. And indeed, were $\mathcal{T}_f$ gentle, one would be able to calculate f. Similarly, $\mathcal{T}_f$ does not satisfy any of the other two requirements from Theorem 4.

3.3 Polite Combination

Theorem 2 demands two properties from $\mathcal{T}_2$ in order for it to be combinable with any decidable theory $\mathcal{T}_1$ over a disjoint signature: strong finite witnessability and smoothness. We start by showing that if smoothness is removed from the requirements, the theorem fails.

Theorem 7. *There are decidable theories $\mathcal{T}_1$ and $\mathcal{T}_2$ over disjoint signatures such that $\mathcal{T}_2$ is strongly finitely witnessable but $\mathcal{T}_1 \oplus \mathcal{T}_2$ is undecidable.*

[4] Due to lack of space, some proofs are omitted, and can be found in [21].

Proof (sketch). Take $\mathcal{T}_1$ to be $\mathcal{T}_f$ and $\mathcal{T}_2$ to be $\mathcal{T}_=$, as was done in the proof of Theorem 5, where both theories were shown to be decidable while their combination was shown to be undecidable. The only thing that is left to be shown, and indeed can be shown by providing an appropriate strong witness, is that $\mathcal{T}_=$ is strongly finitely witnessable.

As before, Theorem 2 and the proof of Theorem 7 imply that $\mathcal{T}_=$ is not smooth. And indeed, it is not, as it is not even stably infinite.

Next, we show that dropping the strong finite witnessability requirement also leads to a failure in the polite combination method.

Theorem 8. *There are decidable theories $\mathcal{T}_1$ and $\mathcal{T}_2$ over disjoint signatures such that $\mathcal{T}_2$ is smooth but $\mathcal{T}_1 \oplus \mathcal{T}_2$ is undecidable.*

Proof. Take $\mathcal{T}_1$ to be $\mathcal{T}_=$ and $\mathcal{T}_2$ to be $\mathcal{T}_f$, again as in the proof of Theorem 6, only now we rely on the fact that, proven in [25, Lemma 54], that $\mathcal{T}_f$ is smooth, and as we already know, $\mathcal{T}_= \oplus \mathcal{T}_f$ is not decidable.

Clearly, Theorem 2 and the proof of Corollary 1 imply that $\mathcal{T}_f$ is not strongly finitely witnessable. This was also proven in [25, Lemma 56].

Now, $\mathcal{T}_f$ was proven in [25, Lemmas 55] to not be smooth, but it is also finitely witnessable (without being strongly finitely witnessable), which makes it polite. Thus, the proof of Theorem 8 also gives us the following corollary, by again taking $\mathcal{T}_1$ to be $\mathcal{T}_=$ and $\mathcal{T}_2$ to be $\mathcal{T}_f$.

Corollary 1. *There are decidable theories $\mathcal{T}_1$ and $\mathcal{T}_2$ over disjoint signatures such that $\mathcal{T}_2$ is polite but $\mathcal{T}_1 \oplus \mathcal{T}_2$ is undecidable.*

Recall that [15] claimed that politeness is enough for theory combination, but a problem in the proof was later discovered and corrected in [9] by strengthening the politeness assumption to strong politeness. But was the problem of [15] in the proof or in the statement itself? In other words: does Conjecture 1 hold? What we immediately get from Corollary 1 is that it does not.

Corollary 2. *Conjecture 1 does not hold.*

Hence, politeness is not enough for theory combination, which justifies the title of this paper.

3.4 Shiny Combination

In this section we consider the three requirements Theorem 3 makes on one of the combined theories, namely: computability of the minimal model function, the finite model property, and smoothness.

We start with the computability of the minimal model function.

Theorem 9. *There are decidable theories $\mathcal{T}_1$ and $\mathcal{T}_2$ over disjoint signatures such that $\mathcal{T}_2$ is smooth and has the finite model property, but $\mathcal{T}_1 \oplus \mathcal{T}_2$ is undecidable.*

Proof. By taking $\mathcal{T}_1$ to be $\mathcal{T}_=$ and $\mathcal{T}_2$ to be $\mathcal{T}_f$, we can use proofs of previous theorems in order to show most properties that are needed. Further, it was proven in [23, Theorem 2] that $\mathcal{T}_f$ admits the finite model property.

From Theorem 3 and the proof of Theorem 9, $\mathcal{T}_f$ does not have a computable minimal model function, which was also proven in [24, Lemma 126].

For the next sharpness theorem we need the following lemma, according to which for decidable theories, strong finite witnessability implies computability of the minimal model function. This was essentially proven in [6], but was never explicitly stated there; indeed, as they were focused on strong politeness and shininess, they have assumed smoothness, even if that assumption was never actually used in the part of the proof that concerned the computability of the minimal model function.

Lemma 1. *If $\mathcal{T}$ is decidable and strongly finitely witnessable, then it has a computable minimal model function.*

Remark 1. Notice that the reciprocal of Lemma 1 is not true: decidability and computability of the minimal model function do not entail strong finite witnessability. For example, $\mathcal{T}^{\infty}_{even}$, defined in [18] by the axiomatization $\{\neg\psi_{=2\cdot n+1} \mid n \in \mathbb{N}\}$, is proven in [24, Lemma 126] to have a computable minimal model function; furthermore it is decidable, as it satisfies all and only the quantifier-free formulas that are satisfiable in first-order logic, but it is not strongly finitely witnessable (as proven in [18]).

Now, using Lemma 1, we show that shiny combination (Theorem 3) fails without the smoothness requirement. We once again essentially reuse Theorem 5 to obtain the following:

Theorem 10. *There are decidable theories $\mathcal{T}_1$ and $\mathcal{T}_2$ over disjoint signatures such that $\mathcal{T}_2$ has the finite model property and a computable minimal model function, but $\mathcal{T}_1 \oplus \mathcal{T}_2$ is undecidable.*

Proof. Take $\mathcal{T}_1$ and $\mathcal{T}_2$ to be $\mathcal{T}_f$ and $\mathcal{T}_=$, respectively: we have already shown that they are both decidable even though $\mathcal{T}_f \oplus \mathcal{T}_=$ is not. From Lemma 1 and the fact that $\mathcal{T}_=$ is strongly finitely witnessable (which was established in the proof of Theorem 7), we get $\mathcal{T}_=$ has a computable minimal model function. Using then [23, Theorem 2], according to which finite witnessability implies the finite model property, $\mathcal{T}_=$ has the finite model property.

Next, we show that the requirement of the finite model property cannot be removed. Unlike the previous results, we are unable to reuse $\mathcal{T}_=$ and $\mathcal{T}_f$. Therefore, we use the theory $\mathcal{T}_\infty$ from [22] and the theory $\mathcal{T}_\leq$.

Theorem 11. *There are decidable theories $\mathcal{T}_1$ and $\mathcal{T}_2$ over disjoint signatures such that $\mathcal{T}_2$ is smooth and has a computable minimal model function, but $\mathcal{T}_1 \oplus \mathcal{T}_2$ is undecidable.*

Table 3. A finite signature.

Name	0-ary Functions	1-ary Functions	Predicates
Σ_t^a	$\{a\}$	$\{t\}$	$\emptyset$

$$\psi^{orb}_{\geq n}(x) = \bigwedge_{0\leq i<j\leq n-1} \neg(t^i(x) = t^j(x)) \text{ for } n \in \mathbb{N}^* \setminus \{1\}$$

$$\psi^{orb}_{=1}(x) = t(x) = x$$

$$\psi^{orb}_{=n}(x) = \psi^{orb}_{\geq n}(x) \wedge \neg\psi^{orb}_{\geq n+1}(x) \text{ for } n \geq 2$$

Fig. 4. Formulas in Σ_t^a.

Proof. (sketch). Take $\mathcal{T}_1$ to be $\mathcal{T}_{\leq}$ and $\mathcal{T}_2$ to be $\mathcal{T}_{\infty}$, axiomatized in Table 2. Clearly, they are defined over disjoint signatures. $\mathcal{T}_{\infty}$ is smooth and has a computable minimal model function. The proofs for these facts are simple, and are given in [25, Lemma 22] and [24, Lemma 130]. It is also decidable, as it satisfies all quantifier-free formulas in its signature that are satisfiable in first-order logic (and only them). Perhaps surprisingly, it is possible to show that $\mathcal{T}_{\leq}$ is decidable. However, it can also be shown that $\mathcal{T}_{\leq} \oplus \mathcal{T}_{\infty}$ is not.

4 Finite Signatures

Every proof in Sect. 3 uses a pair of theories, one of them always over the infinite signature Σ_P^n (in all cases the used theory is $\mathcal{T}_=$, except for in Theorem 11, where the Σ_P^n-theory $\mathcal{T}_{\leq}$ is used instead). And indeed, both $\mathcal{T}_=$ and $\mathcal{T}_{\leq}$ are theories that are relatively easy to understand. This is, among other things, thanks to the availability of infinitely many predicates.

In this section, we aim to provide finitistic proofs of the limitation theorems from Sect. 3, in the sense that all theories that are used are over finite signatures. Doing so provides a more succinct set of examples, over more minimal signatures. The cost, however, is that the theories that we use in this section are more complex.

4.1 New Theories over Finite Signatures

The two theories over the infinite signature Σ_P^n from Sect. 3 are $\mathcal{T}_=$ and $\mathcal{T}_{\leq}$. They will be replaced by theories over the finite signature Σ_t^a: this signature has a unary function t, a constant a, and no predicates, as described in Table 3.

In order to introduce the new theories, we define the formulas $\psi^{orb}_{\geq n}(x)$ and $\psi^{orb}_{=n}(x)$ in Fig. 4.

The *orbit* (see e.g., [10,17]) of an element e in a Σ_t^a-interpretation $\mathcal{A}$ is the set $\{(t^{\mathcal{A}})^n(e) \mid n \in \mathbb{N}\}$. Since e itself is always an element of this set, the orbit is always non-empty. We sometimes view this set as the following sequence indexed by n: $e, t^{\mathcal{A}}(e), (t^{\mathcal{A}})^2(e), \ldots$ In this context, in an interpretation $\mathcal{A}$ that satisfies $\psi^{orb}_{\geq n}(x)$, we have that there are at least n elements that can be obtained by recursively applying $t^{\mathcal{A}}$ to $x^{\mathcal{A}}$, meaning its orbit has at least n elements; similarly $\mathcal{A}$ satisfies $\psi^{orb}_{=n}(x)$, the orbit of $x^{\mathcal{A}}$ has precisely n elements.

With these formulas, we can now define the new theories over Σ_t^a. These are specified in Table 4. In the finite $\mathcal{T}^2_{orb}$-interpretations, the orbit of the interpretation of the constant symbol a consists of at least half of the elements of the interpretation; meanwhile in the infinite $\mathcal{T}^2_{orb}$-interpretations this orbit is infinite. $\mathcal{T}^{orb}_{\leq}$ is very similar to $\mathcal{T}_{\leq}$, replacing P_n by the assumption that the orbit has size n, and also concluding that the number of elements in the domain is at most $F(n)+n$ (and not $F(n)$ as in $\mathcal{T}_{\leq}$).

Table 4. Theories over the finite signature Σ_t^a. In the definition of $\mathcal{T}^{orb}_{\leq}$, the function F admits the same assumptions as in Fig. 2. The axiomatizations utilize formulas that are defined in Fig. 4.

Name	Signature	Axiomatization	Source
$\mathcal{T}^2_{orb}$	Σ_t^a	$\{\psi^{orb}_{=n}(a) \rightarrow \psi_{\leq 2n} : n \in \mathbb{N}^*\}$	new
$\mathcal{T}^{orb}_{\leq}$	Σ_t^a	$\{\psi^{orb}_{=n}(a) \rightarrow \psi_{\leq F(n)+n} : n \in \mathbb{N}^*,\ F(n) \in \mathbb{N}^*\}$	new

With these new theories, we can now turn to making the proofs of the theorems from Sect. 3 rely solely on finite signatures.

4.2 Finitizing the Proofs of Theorems 5 to 10 and Corollary 1

The proof of Theorem 5 sets $\mathcal{T}_1$ to be $\mathcal{T}_f$ and $\mathcal{T}_2$ to be $\mathcal{T}_{=}$. In order to only use finite signatures, we set $\mathcal{T}_2$ to be $\mathcal{T}^2_{orb}$ instead.[5]

As for $\mathcal{T}_1$, we can still use $\mathcal{T}_f$, but we need to restrict the possible functions f it relies on. To make it clear that the functions f are now required to satisfy some extra properties we denote them by g, so that $\mathcal{T}_f$ becomes $\mathcal{T}_g$. We then require $g : \mathbb{N}^* \rightarrow \{0, 1\}$ to be any non-computable function such that: $g(1) = 1$ and g is zero as often as it is 1 in each interval from 1 to 2^k (as required for f in the definition of $\mathcal{T}_f$); and in addition to the requirements in $\mathcal{T}_f$, we now also require that $g(2n+1) = g(2n+2)$ for all $n \geq 2$. Such functions exist: for an example, take the function $f : \mathbb{N}^* \rightarrow \{0, 1\}$ defined in [22], make $g(1) = g(3) = 1$, $g(2) = g(4) = 0$, and $g(2n+1) = g(2n+2) = f(n+1)$ for $n \geq 2$. Since $\mathcal{T}_f$ is decidable and stably infinite regardless of the specific f, we have $\mathcal{T}_g$ is decidable and stably infinite.

Although it can be shown that $\mathcal{T}^2_{orb}$ is decidable, $\mathcal{T}_g \oplus \mathcal{T}^2_{orb}$ is undecidable. Indeed, were it decidable, one would be able to calculate the function g by

[5] Notice that [4] has also produced a finitary proof of Theorem 5, using a theory named $TM_{\forall\omega}$ over a finite signature.

using the fact that $\psi^{orb}_{=n+1}(a) \wedge \varphi^{=}_{\geq g_1(2n)+2}$ is $\mathcal{T}_g \oplus \mathcal{T}^2_{orb}$-satisfiable if and only if $g(2n+1) = g(2n+2) = 1$ for $n \geq 2$: if we know g up to $2n$ we can calculate $g_1(2n)$, obtain the formula $\psi^{orb}_{=n+1}(a) \wedge \varphi^{=}_{\geq g_1(2n)+2}$, and by testing whether it is $\mathcal{T}_g \oplus \mathcal{T}^2_{orb}$-satisfiable we find the value for $g(2n+1) = g(2n+2)$. We know $g(1) = g(3) = 1$ and $g(2) = g(4) = 0$, and then we proceed from there on forward inductively.

We can mimic the same process for other results from Sect. 3, by replacing $\mathcal{T}_=$ by $\mathcal{T}^2_{orb}$, and instantiating $\mathcal{T}_f$ by $\mathcal{T}_g$ with f satisfying the aforementioned condition. In particular, we can do so in: Theorem 6, by proving that $\mathcal{T}^2_{orb}$ is also gentle; Theorem 7, by proving that $\mathcal{T}^2_{orb}$ is strongly finitely witnessable; Theorem 8, and Corollary 1, by remembering $\mathcal{T}_g$ is both smooth and polite; Theorem 9, as $\mathcal{T}_g$ has the finite model property; and Theorem 10, by proving that $\mathcal{T}^2_{orb}$ has a computable minimal model function, and the finite model property.

4.3 Finitizing the Proof of Theorem 11

Finally, notice that the proof of Theorem 11 sets $\mathcal{T}_1$ to be $\mathcal{T}_{\leq}$, which is defined over an infinite signature, and $\mathcal{T}_2$ to be $\mathcal{T}_\infty$. While we can leave $\mathcal{T}_2$ as $\mathcal{T}_\infty$, we replace $\mathcal{T}_{\leq}$ by its Σ^a_t-variant $\mathcal{T}^{orb}_{\leq}$, in order to get two theories over a finite signature.

The proof that $\mathcal{T}^{orb}_{\leq}$ is decidable follows the proof that $\mathcal{T}^2_{orb}$ is decidable. Yet the combination $\mathcal{T}^{orb}_{\leq} \oplus \mathcal{T}_\infty$ is not decidable, $\psi^{orb}_{=n}(a)$ being satisfiable in it if, and only if, $F(n) = \aleph_0$.

5 New Combination Theorems

In this section we prove new combination theorems, that strengthen Sect. 4 and 3. In Sect. 5.1, we show that the conditions from Sect. 4 can be weakened. In Sect. 5.2, we show that the finite model property *can* be dismissed from shiny combination, as long as we compensate it by requiring another property from the second theory being combined. This does not contradict Theorem 11, as the example there does not meet the additional criterion.

In what follows, we assume that Σ_1 and Σ_2 are disjoint signatures, and that $\mathcal{T}_1$ is a Σ_1-theory, and $\mathcal{T}_2$ a Σ_2-theory.

5.1 Recovering Gentle Combination

Assuming $\mathcal{T}_1$ is gentle, Theorem 4 provided three conditions on $\mathcal{T}_2$, any one of which suffices for theory combination. We prove a strengthening of Theorem 4.

Definition 1. *We say that a theory* $\mathcal{T}$ *has* computable finite spectra *if there is an algorithm that, given a quantifier-free formula* φ *and* $k \in \mathbb{N}^*$, *decides whether* $k \in Spec(\mathcal{T}, \varphi)$.

Intuitively, having computable finite spectra means that we can query the set $Spec(\mathcal{T}, \varphi)$ to check whether it contains a given *finite* cardinality. In contrast to gentleness, it does not imply that we can compute any concrete set S, nor does it require the ability to check whether $\aleph_0$ is in the spectra.

Theorem 12. *Suppose that $\mathcal{T}_1$ is gentle and $\mathcal{T}_2$ has computable finite spectra. Then, $\mathcal{T}_1 \oplus \mathcal{T}_2$ is decidable.*

Each of the three properties in Theorem 4 imply that $\mathcal{T}_2$ has computable finite spectra, so Theorem 12 is indeed a strengthening. We now present two theories that can be combined by Theorem 12 but not by any other combination method discussed in this paper.

Example 1. Fix any $n \in \mathbb{N}^*$ and let $\mathcal{T}_1 = \mathcal{T}_{\leq n}$ be the Σ_1-theory axiomatized by $\{\psi_{\leq n}\}$. Now, let $\mathcal{T}_2$ be $\mathcal{T}_{\leq}$ from Table 2. Then, $\mathcal{T}_{\leq n}$ and $\mathcal{T}_{\leq}$ are decidable, $\mathcal{T}_{\leq n}$ is gentle, and $\mathcal{T}_{\leq}$ has computable finite spectra. By Theorem 12, $\mathcal{T}_{\leq n} \oplus \mathcal{T}_{\leq}$ is decidable. On the other hand, $\mathcal{T}_{\leq}$ does not satisfy any of the three properties in Theorem 4. Furthermore, neither theory is strongly polite, shiny, or stably infinite, and so none of the other combination theorems can be used to decide this combination of theories.

5.2 Recovering Shiny Combination Without Finite Models

In Theorem 11 we have seen that the shiny combination theorem fails if the finite model property is dropped from the definition of shininess. However, we now show that we can do without the finite model property if we impose another condition on the other theory being combined.

Definition 2. *We say that a theory $\mathcal{T}$ is* infinitely decidable *if it is decidable whether a quantifier-free formula is satisfied by an infinite $\mathcal{T}$-interpretation.*

A similar notion to infinite decidability, but also requiring decidability, was defined in [4] and called $\exists_\infty$-decidability, but not considered along gentleness.

Theorem 13. *Let $\mathcal{T}_1$ and $\mathcal{T}_2$ be decidable theories over disjoint signatures. Suppose that $\mathcal{T}_1$ is smooth and has a computable minimal model function and that $\mathcal{T}_2$ is infinitely decidable. Then, $\mathcal{T}_1 \oplus \mathcal{T}_2$ is decidable.*

In the next example, we present 2 theories that can be combined using Theorem 13, but not with any other combination theorem studied in this paper.

Example 2. Let $\mathcal{T}^h_\infty$ be the Σ^n_P-theory axiomatized by

$$\{P_1 \rightarrow \psi_{=1}\} \cup \{P_1 \rightarrow \neg P_n : n \geq 2\} \cup \{P_n \rightarrow \psi_{\geq m} : m, n \geq 2, h(n) = 1\},$$

for $h : \mathbb{N}^* \rightarrow \{0, 1\}$ a non-computable function. Also, consider the theory $\mathcal{T}_\infty$ from Table 2. Both theories are decidable. It can be shown that $\mathcal{T}^h_\infty$ is neither stably infinite nor has computable finite spectra, and so it cannot be combined

Table 5. Summary of the main results. Only 3 tuples of theories were used, and these are assigned different colors in the table.

Approach	Property	Theorem	Infinite		Finite	
			$\mathcal{T}_1$	$\mathcal{T}_2$	$\mathcal{T}_1$	$\mathcal{T}_2$
Nelson–Oppen (Thm. 1)	Stable Infiniteness	Thm. 5	$\mathcal{T}_f$	$\mathcal{T}_=$	$\mathcal{T}_g$	$\mathcal{T}_{orb}^2$
Gentle (Thm. 4)	Gentleness*	Thm. 6	$\mathcal{T}_=$	$\mathcal{T}_f$	$\mathcal{T}_{orb}^2$	$\mathcal{T}_g$
Polite (Thm. 2)	Smoothness	Thm. 7	$\mathcal{T}_f$	$\mathcal{T}_=$	$\mathcal{T}_g$	$\mathcal{T}_{orb}^2$
	Strong Finite Witnessability**	Thm. 8	$\mathcal{T}_=$	$\mathcal{T}_f$	$\mathcal{T}_{orb}^2$	$\mathcal{T}_g$
Shiny (Thm. 3)	Comp. Min. Mod.	Thm. 9	$\mathcal{T}_=$	$\mathcal{T}_f$	$\mathcal{T}_{orb}^2$	$\mathcal{T}_g$
	Smoothness	Thm. 10	$\mathcal{T}_f$	$\mathcal{T}_=$	$\mathcal{T}_g$	$\mathcal{T}_{orb}^2$
	Finite Model Property*	Thm. 11	$\mathcal{T}_{\leq}$	$\mathcal{T}_\infty$	$\mathcal{T}_{\leq}^{orb}$	$\mathcal{T}_\infty$

* Theorems 13 and 12, in a sense, remedy Theorems 11 and 6.
** In particular, Corollary 1 is a consequence of the proof of Theorem 8.

with $\mathcal{T}_\infty$ using the Nelson–Oppen method, the gentle method, or the new method we propose in Theorem 12. It can also be shown that neither theory is strongly polite or shiny, and so they cannot be combined using the polite or shiny methods. But, $\mathcal{T}_\infty$ has a computable minimal model function and is smooth. Further, $\mathcal{T}_\infty^h$ is infinitely decidable. By Theorem 13, $\mathcal{T}_\infty \oplus \mathcal{T}_\infty^h$ is decidable. Thus, Theorem 13 is able to combine two theories that none of the other methods can.[6]

6 Conclusion

For each combination method and each of its associated properties, we have proven in Sect. 3 that the corresponding combination theorem fails if the property is not assumed. The proofs always involve producing two theories that are decidable while their combination is not. The proofs of these results were improved in Sect. 4, where only finite signatures were used.

Table 5 lists the theories used in Sects. 3 and 4. It also lists the original combination theorem whose limits are identified. Notice that for each theorem we produced 2 pairs of theories: one pair for its original proof, and another pair for its improved proof. In total, we were able to prove all theorems, with finite and infinite signatures, using only three quadruples of theories, built from only six theories, by reusing the introduced theories as much as possible.

We have also proven that politeness is not enough for theory combination. Further, we have introduced two new combination theorems, based on shiny and gentle combinations (Theorems 13 and 12).

[6] We use $\mathcal{T}_\infty$ in the example to keep things simple, reusing the theories that are already defined in the paper. However, any decidable theory $\mathcal{T}$ on a countable signature (disjoint from Σ_P^n) with only infinite models could replace $\mathcal{T}_\infty$, such as the theory of dense linear orders without endpoints [11].

The main direction for further work is to find more theorems like Theorems 13 and 12, with the purpose of varying the set of requirements for theory combination. We hope that such theorems will make it to introduce algorithms for new combination of theories. In addition, we are working on stronger limitation theorems: while the classical combination methods provide *sufficient* conditions for combinability, we plan to study *necessary* conditions.

Acknowledgments. We thank Christophe Ringeissen, Pascal Fontaine, and Cesare Tinelli for fruitful discussions that led to and helped writing this paper. Toledo and Zohar were funded by the NSF-BSF grant 2020704, the ISF grant 619/21, and the Colman-Soref fellowship. Przybocki was supported by the NSF Graduate Research Fellowship Program under Grant No. DGE-2140739.

Disclosure of Interests. Yoni Zohar has received research grants from Amazon Web Services.

References

1. Barbosa, H., et al.: cvc5: A Versatile and Industrial-Strength SMT Solver. Presented at the (2022). https://doi.org/10.1007/978-3-030-99524-9_24
2. Barrett, C., Tinelli, C.: CVC3. In: Damm, W., Hermanns, H. (eds.) CAV 2007. LNCS, vol. 4590, pp. 298–302. Springer, Heidelberg (2007).https://doi.org/10.1007/978-3-540-73368-3_34
3. Barrett, C.W., et al.: CVC4. In: Gopalakrishnan, G., Qadeer, S. (eds.) Computer Aided Verification - 23rd International Conference, CAV 2011, Snowbird, UT, USA, July 14-20, 2011. Proceedings. LNCS, vol. 6806, pp. 171–177. Springer (2011).https://doi.org/10.1007/978-3-642-22110-1_14
4. Bonacina, M.P., Ghilardi, S., Nicolini, E., Ranise, S., Zucchelli, D.: Decidability and undecidability results for nelson-oppen and rewrite-based decision procedures. In: Furbach, U., Shankar, N. (eds.) Automated Reasoning, pp. 513–527. Springer, Heidelberg (2006). ISBN 978-3-540-37188-5
5. Bonacina, M.P., Fontaine, P., Ringeissen, C., Tinelli, C.: Theory combination: beyond equality sharing. In: Lutz, C., Sattler, U., Tinelli, C., Turhan, A.-Y., Wolter, F. (eds.) Description Logic, Theory Combination, and All That - Essays Dedicated to Franz Baader on the Occasion of His 60th Birthday. LNCS, vol. 11560, pp. 57–89. Springer (2019). https://doi.org/10.1007/978-3-030-22102-7_3
6. Casal, F., Rasga, J.: Many-sorted equivalence of shiny and strongly polite theories. J. Autom. Reason. **60**(2), 221–236 (2017). https://doi.org/10.1007/s10817-017-9411-y
7. Casal, F., Rasga, J.: Revisiting the equivalence of shininess and politeness. In: McMillan, K., Middeldorp, A., Voronkov, A. (eds.) LPAR 2013. LNCS, vol. 8312, pp. 198–212. Springer, Heidelberg (2013). https://doi.org/10.1007/978-3-642-45221-5_15
8. Fontaine, P.: Combinations of theories for decidable fragments of first-order logic. In: Ghilardi, S., Sebastiani, R., (eds.) Frontiers of Combining Systems, pp. 263–278. Springer, Heidelberg (2009). ISBN 978-3-642-04222-5
9. Jovanović, D., Barrett, C.: Polite theories revisited. In: Fermüller, C.G., Voronkov, A. (eds.) LPAR 2010. LNCS, vol. 6397, pp. 402–416. Springer, Heidelberg (2010).https://doi.org/10.1007/978-3-642-16242-8_29

10. Kilp, M., Knauer, U., Mikhalev, A.V.: Monoids, Acts and Categories: With Applications to Wreath Products and Graphs. A Handbook for Students and Researchers. DE GRUYTER, December 2000. ISBN 9783110152487.https://doi.org/10.1515/9783110812909
11. Kozen, D.: Theory of Computation, 2006th edn. Texts in Computer Science. Springer, London, England (2006)
12. Krstić, S., Goel, A., Grundy, J., Tinelli, C.: Combined satisfiability modulo parametric theories. In: Grumberg, O., Huth, M. (eds.) TACAS 2007. LNCS, vol. 4424, pp. 602–617. Springer, Heidelberg (2007). https://doi.org/10.1007/978-3-540-71209-1_47
13. Nelson, G., Oppen, D.C.: Simplification by cooperating decision procedures. ACM Trans. Program. Lang. Syst. **1**(2), 245–257, October 1979. ISSN 0164-0925. https://doi.org/10.1145/357073.357079
14. Przybocki, B., de Toledo, G.V., Zohar, Y., Barrett, C.W.: The nonexistence of unicorns and many-sorted löwenheim-skolem theorems. In: Platzer, A., Yvonne Rozier, K., Pradella, M., Rossi, M. (eds.) Formal Methods - 26th International Symposium, FM 2024. LNCS, Milan, Italy, September 9-13, 2024, Proceedings, Part I, vol. 4933, pp. 658–675. Springer (2024). https://doi.org/10.1007/978-3-031-71162-6_34
15. Ranise, S., Ringeissen, C., Zarba, C.G.: Combining data structures with nonstably infinite theories using many-sorted logic. In: Gramlich, B. (ed.) 5th International Workshop on Frontiers of Combining Systems - FroCoS'05, vol. 3717. Lecture Notes in Artificial Intelligence, pp. 48–64, Vienna, September 2005, pp. Springer. https://doi.org/10.1007/11559306. https://hal.inria.fr/inria-00000570
16. Ringard, Y.-J.: Mustard watches: an integrated approach to time and food. Equipe de logicue mathématique, prépublications (1990). https://girard.perso.math.cnrs.fr/mustard/article.html
17. Joseph, J.: Rotman. An Introduction to the Theory of Groups. Springer, New York (1995)
18. Sheng, Y., Zohar, Y., Ringeissen, C., Reynolds, A., Barrett, C., Tinelli, C.: Politeness and stable infiniteness: stronger together. In: Platzer, A., Sutcliffe, G. (eds.) CADE 2021. LNCS (LNAI), vol. 12699, pp. 148–165. Springer, Cham (2021). https://doi.org/10.1007/978-3-030-79876-5_9
19. Tinelli, C., Zarba, C.: Combining decision procedures for theories in sorted logics. Technical Report 04-01, Department of Computer Science, The University of Iowa, February 2004. ftp://ftp.cs.uiowa.edu/pub/tinelli/papers/TinZar-RR-04.pdf
20. Tinelli, C., Zarba, C.G.: Combining nonstably infinite theories. J. Autom. Reason. **34**(3), 209–238 (2005)
21. Toledo, G.V., Przybocki, B., Zohar, Y.: Being polite is not enough (and other limits of theory combination) (2025). https://arxiv.org/abs/2505.04870
22. Toledo, G.V., Zohar, Y., Barrett, C.: Combining combination properties: an analysis of stable infiniteness, convexity, and politeness. In: Pientka, B., Tinelli, C. (eds.) Automated Deduction - CADE 29, pp. 522–541. Springer, Cham (2023)
23. Toledo, G.V., Zohar, Y., Barrett, C.: Combining finite combination properties: finite models and busy beavers. In: Sattler, U., Suda, M. (eds.) Frontiers of Combining Systems, pp. 159–175, 2023. Springer, Cham
24. de Toledo, G.V., Zohar, Y.: Combining combination properties: Minimal models (2024)
25. de Toledo, G.V., Zohar, Y., Barrett, C.: An analysis of stable infiniteness, convexity, and politeness, Combining combination properties (2023)

On Symbol Elimination and Uniform Interpolation in Theory Extensions

Viorica Sofronie-Stokkermans(✉)

University of Koblenz, Koblenz, Germany
sofronie@uni-koblenz.de

Abstract. We define a notion of general uniform interpolant, generalizing the notions of cover and of uniform interpolant and identify situations in which symbol elimination can be used for computing general uniform interpolants. We investigate the limitations of the method we propose, and identify theory extensions for which the computation of general uniform interpolants can be reduced to symbol elimination followed by the computation of uniform quantifier-free interpolants in extensions with uninterpreted function symbols of theories allowing uniform quantifier-free interpolation.

1 Introduction

In this paper we study the links between symbol elimination in local theory extensions and the computation of general uniform interpolants in such theories.

We studied possibilities of symbol elimination in local theory extensions in [23,28,29], in relationship with the verification of safety properties in parametric systems: symbol elimination was used to infer (possibly universally quantified) constraints on parameters under which it was guaranteed that certain properties are met, or for invariant strengthening. In [30,32] we continued this study and analyzed possible applications to interpolation in local theory extensions.

Interpolation is widely used in program verification (cf. [14,15,20–22] to mention some of the early papers). Intuitively, interpolants can be used for describing separations between the sets of "good" and "bad" states; they can help to discover relevant predicates in predicate abstraction with refinement and for over-approximation in model checking. It often is desirable to obtain ground interpolants of ground formulae. When defining ground interpolation, sometimes a difference is made between interpreted and uninterpreted function symbols or constants. In [1], a notion of *general ground interpolation* was defined. A theory $\mathcal{T}$ with signature Σ is said to have the *general ground interpolation property* if for every signature Σ' disjoint from Σ and every pair of ground $\Sigma \cup \Sigma'$-formulae A and B, if $A \wedge B \models_{\mathcal{T} \cup \mathsf{UIF}_{\Sigma'}} \perp$ then there exists a ground formula I such that: (i) all constants and all predicate and function symbols from Σ' occurring in I are symbols shared by A and B (no restriction is imposed on the symbols in Σ), and (ii) $A \models_{\mathcal{T} \cup \mathsf{UIF}_{\Sigma'}} I$ and $B \wedge I \models_{\mathcal{T} \cup \mathsf{UIF}_{\Sigma'}} \perp$. The symbols in Σ are regarded as interpreted, those in Σ' as uninterpreted. In [24,26,27,30,32] we

C. Barrett and U. Waldmann (Eds.): CADE 2025, LNAI 15943, pp. 35–55, 2025.
https://doi.org/10.1007/978-3-031-99984-0_3

studied theory extensions $\mathcal{T}_0 \subseteq \mathcal{T}_0 \cup \mathcal{K}$ for which the notion of sharing had to be extended, because of uninterpreted function symbols occurring together in clauses in $\mathcal{K}$. We solved this by introducing closure operators Θ on signatures and imposing that the interpolant contains terms in $\Theta(\Sigma_s \cup C_s)$, where $\Sigma_s \cup C_s$ are the uninterpreted function and predicate symbols, and constants shared by A and B.

Sometimes one needs to find the *strongest* interpolant of two formulae w.r.t. a theory $\mathcal{T}$, or a *(general) uniform interpolant* for a ground formula A w.r.t. a given subset Σ_s of function symbols and a subset C_s of the constants occurring in A for a theory $\mathcal{T}$. This is a formula I containing arbitrary interpreted symbols and only uninterpreted symbols in $\Sigma_s \cup C_s$ (or a suitably defined closure $\Theta(\Sigma_s \cup C_s)$ depending on the theory $\mathcal{T}$), such that $A \models_\mathcal{T} I$ and for all ground formulae B sharing with A only interpreted symbols and symbols in $\Sigma_s \cup C_s$ (resp. $\Theta(\Sigma_s \cup C_s)$) with $A \models_\mathcal{T} B$, we have $I \models_\mathcal{T} B$. Uniform interpolants were studied in the context of non-classical logics and description logics and in verification. In description logics they are studied in relationship with "forgetting" (projecting to a subsignature) (cf. e.g. [16–18]). In verification, uniform interpolants offer an optimal approximation of states in a subsignature; in fact, a strongly related notion – that of cover – was proposed by Gulwani and Musuvathi in [6]. The computation of uniform interpolants allows a more precise approximation or even a precise computation of the reachable states. The problem of uniform interpolation for the theory of uninterpreted function symbols was studied in [2, 5], where several methods were proposed: a method using a version of constraint superposition [2], DAG-methods and tableau methods [5]. In [3] possibilities of uniform interpolation in combinations of theories are investigated.

However, the results in [2,3,5,6] are devised for the case in which all function symbols are seen as interpreted and only constants need to be eliminated: The computed interpolant can contain arbitrary function symbols, but only constants in a specified set C_s. In this paper we extend these results and investigate the possibility of generating general uniform interpolants which contain uninterpreted symbols in specified subsets $\Sigma_s \cup C_s$ (resp. in $\Theta(\Sigma_s \cup C_s)$ for a suitable closure operator), identify classes of theory extensions where *general uniform interpolation* is possible and also investigate the limitations of the method we propose. The main contributions of the paper can be summarized as follows:

- We define a notion of general uniform interpolant generalizing the notions of cover [6] and of uniform interpolant [2] and prove a semantical characterization of general uniform interpolants, extending the one in [2].
- We propose a method for eliminating function symbols with arity ≥ 1 based on an adaptation of a method for symbol elimination we proposed in [32].
- We prove that certain extensions of theories with uninterpreted function symbols have general uniform interpolation, and identify theory extensions for which the computation of *general uniform interpolants* can be reduced to the computation of *uniform interpolants* with methods from [2,3,5].
- We propose a method for computing explicit definitions for functions implicitly definable w.r.t. the signature of the base theory + uninterpreted function

symbols in local theory extensions, and analyze possibilities of computing general uniform interpolants in such extensions.

The paper is structured as follows: In Sect. 2 the main definitions and results on logical theories and local theory extensions which are used in the paper are introduced. In Sect. 3 we recall existing results on $\mathcal{T}$-uniform quantifier-free interpolation. In Sect. 4 we define a notion of general uniform interpolant w.r.t. a theory $\mathcal{T}$. In Sect. 5 we present a method for symbol elimination and investigate conditions under which it can be used for computing general uniform interpolants. In Sect. 6 we analyze extensions with implicitly definable functions. Section 7 contains the conclusions and some plans of future work.
The details of the proofs and additional examples can be found in [34].

2 Preliminaries

We assume known standard definitions from first-order logic such as Π-structures, models, homomorphisms, logical entailment, satisfiability, unsatisfiability. We here introduce the main notions needed in the paper: logical theories and properties of logical theories and local theory extensions.

Notation: In what follows we will denote with (indexed version of) $\overline{x}$ (resp. $\overline{c}$) sequences of variables $x_1, \dots, x_n$ (resp. sequences of constants $c_1, \dots, c_n$).

Logical Theories. We consider signatures of the form $\Pi = (S, \Sigma, \mathsf{Pred})$, where S is a set of sorts, Σ is a family of function symbols and Pred a family of predicate symbols such that for every $f \in \Sigma$ and $P \in \mathsf{Pred}$ their arities $a(f) = s_1 \dots s_n \rightarrow s$ resp. $a(P) = s_1, ..., s_n$ (where $s_1, \dots, s_n, s \in S$) are specified. If we do not want to emphasize the set of sorts, we write $\Pi = (\Sigma, \mathsf{Pred})$. We denote "falsum" with $\perp$. In this paper, a theory $\mathcal{T}$ is described by a set of closed formulae (the axioms of the theory). If F and G are formulae we write $F \models G$ (resp. $F \models_{\mathcal{T}} G$) to express the fact that every model of F (resp. every model of F which is also a model of $\mathcal{T}$) is a model of G. The definitions can be extended in a natural way to the case when F is a set of formulae; in this case, $F \models_{\mathcal{T}} G$ if and only if $\mathcal{T} \cup F \models G$. $F \models \perp$ means that F is unsatisfiable; $F \models_{\mathcal{T}} \perp$ means that there is no model of $\mathcal{T}$ which is also a model of F. If there is a model of $\mathcal{T}$ which is also a model of F we say that F is $\mathcal{T}$-consistent. If C is a fixed countable set of fresh constants, we denote by Π^C the extension of Π with constants in C.

Let $\mathcal{A} = (A, \{f_{\mathcal{A}}\}_{f \in \Sigma}, \{P_{\mathcal{A}}\}_{P \in \mathsf{Pred}})$ be a Π-structure. We denote the universe A of $\mathcal{A}$ with $|\mathcal{A}|$. If $\Pi_1 \subseteq \Pi$, we denote by $\mathcal{A}_{|\Pi_1}$ the reduct of $\mathcal{A}$ to Π_1, and if C is an additional set of constants $\mathcal{A}^C$ is the extension of $\mathcal{A}$ with constants in C (a Π^C-structure with $\mathcal{A}^C_{|\Pi} = \mathcal{A}$ and with interpretations for the constants in C).

For Π-structures $\mathcal{A}$ and $\mathcal{B}$, $\varphi : \mathcal{A} \rightarrow \mathcal{B}$ is an embedding if and only if it is an injective homomorphism and has the property that for every $P \in \mathsf{Pred}$ with arity n and all $(a_1, \dots, a_n) \in |\mathcal{A}|^n$, $(a_1, \dots, a_n) \in P_{\mathcal{A}}$ iff $(\varphi(a_1), \dots, \varphi(a_n)) \in P_{\mathcal{B}}$. In particular, an embedding preserves the truth of all literals. An elementary embedding between two Π-structures is an embedding that preserves the truth of all first-order formulae over Π. Two Π-structures are elementarily equivalent if they satisfy the same first-order formulae over Π.

Let $\mathcal{A}^A$ be the extension of $\mathcal{A}$ where we have an additional constant for each element of A (which we here denote with the same symbol) with the natural expanded interpretation mapping the constant a to the element a of $|\mathcal{A}|$. The *diagram* $\Delta(\mathcal{A})$ of $\mathcal{A}$ is the set of all literals true in $\mathcal{A}^A$ (a set of sentences over the signature Π^A obtained by expanding Π with a new constant a for every element a of $|\mathcal{A}|$). If $\mathcal{A}$ is a Π-structure and $\mathcal{T}$ a theory and $\Delta(\mathcal{A})$ is $\mathcal{T}$-consistent then there exists a Π-structure $\mathcal{B}$ which is a model of $\mathcal{T}$ and into which $\mathcal{A}$ embeds.

Quantifier Elimination, Model Completeness, Model Completion. A theory $\mathcal{T}$ over signature Π *allows quantifier elimination* (QE) if for every formula ϕ over Π there exists a quantifier-free formula ϕ^* over Π which is equivalent to ϕ modulo $\mathcal{T}$. A *model complete* theory has the property that all embeddings between its models are elementary. Every theory which allows quantifier elimination is model complete (cf. [8], Theorem 7.3.1). Thus, since linear rational arithmetic and linear real arithmetic $LI(\mathbb{Q})$, $LI(\mathbb{R})$, and the theory $\mathbb{R}$ of real closed fields, as well as the theory of algebraically closed fields allow quantifier elimination, they are model complete. A theory $\mathcal{T}^*$ is called a *model companion* of $\mathcal{T}$ if (i) $\mathcal{T}$ and $\mathcal{T}^*$ are co-theories (i.e. every model of $\mathcal{T}$ can be extended to a model of $\mathcal{T}^*$ and vice versa), (ii) $\mathcal{T}^*$ is model complete. $\mathcal{T}^*$ is a *model completion* of $\mathcal{T}$ if it is a model companion of $\mathcal{T}$ with the additional property (iii) for every model $\mathcal{A}$ of $\mathcal{T}$, $\mathcal{T}^* \cup \Delta(\mathcal{A})$ is a complete theory ($\Delta(\mathcal{A})$ is the diagram of $\mathcal{A}$).

Stable Infinity, Convexity, Equality Interpolation. A theory $\mathcal{T}$ is stably infinite iff for every ground formula ϕ, if ϕ is $\mathcal{T}$-consistent then there exists also an infinite model $\mathcal{B}$ of $\mathcal{T}$ with $\mathcal{B} \models \phi$. A theory $\mathcal{T}$ with signature $\Pi = (\Sigma, \mathsf{Pred})$ is *convex* if for all conjunctions Γ of ground Π^C-atoms (with additional constants in a set C), and Π^C-terms s_i, t_i, $i \in \{1, \dots, n\}$, if $\Gamma \models_{\mathcal{T}} \bigvee_{i=1}^m s_i \approx t_i$ there exists $i_0 \in \{1, \dots, m\}$ such that $\Gamma \models_{\mathcal{T}} s_{i_0} \approx t_{i_0}$. We say that a convex theory $\mathcal{T}$ has the equality interpolation property if for every conjunction of ground Π^C-literals $A(\overline{c}, \overline{a_1}, a)$ and $B(\overline{c}, \overline{b_1}, b)$, if $A \wedge B \models_{\mathcal{T}} a \approx b$ then there exists a term $t(\overline{c})$ containing only the shared constants $\overline{c}$ such that $A \wedge B \models_{\mathcal{T}} a \approx t(\overline{c}) \ \wedge \ t(\overline{c}) \approx b$. A theory allowing quantifier elimination is equality interpolating [1].

Local Theory Extensions. Let $\Pi_0 = (\Sigma_0, \mathsf{Pred})$ be a signature, and $\mathcal{T}_0$ be a "base" theory with signature Π_0. We consider extensions $\mathcal{T} := \mathcal{T}_0 \cup \mathcal{K}$ of $\mathcal{T}_0$ with new function symbols Σ_1 (*extension functions*) whose properties are axiomatized using a set $\mathcal{K}$ of (universally closed) clauses in the extended signature $\Pi = (\Sigma_0 \cup \Sigma_1, \mathsf{Pred})$, which contain function symbols in Σ_1. If G is a finite set of ground Π^C-clauses, where C is an additional set of constants, and $\mathcal{K}$ a set of Π-clauses, we will denote by $\mathsf{st}(\mathcal{K}, G)$ (resp. $\mathsf{est}(\mathcal{K}, G)$) the set of all ground terms (resp. extension ground terms, i.e. terms starting with a function in Σ_1) which occur in G or $\mathcal{K}$. In this paper we regard every finite set G of ground clauses as the ground formula $\bigwedge_{C \in G} C$. If T is a set of ground Π^C-terms, we denote by $\mathcal{K}[T]$ the set of all instances of $\mathcal{K}$ in which the terms starting with a function symbol in Σ_1 are in T. Let Ψ be a map associating with every finite set T of ground terms a finite set $\Psi(T)$ of ground terms containing T. For any set G of ground Π^C-clauses we write $\mathcal{K}[\Psi_\mathcal{K}(G)]$ for $\mathcal{K}[\Psi(\mathsf{est}(\mathcal{K}, G))]$. We define:

(Loc_f^Ψ) For every finite set G of ground clauses in Π^C it holds that $\mathcal{T}_0 \cup \mathcal{K} \cup G \models \perp$ if and only if $\mathcal{T}_0 \cup \mathcal{K}[\Psi_\mathcal{K}(G)] \cup G$ is unsatisfiable.

Extensions satisfying condition (Loc_f^Ψ) are called *Ψ-local.* If Ψ is the identity we obtain the notion of *local theory extensions* [25]; if in addition $\mathcal{T}_0$ is the theory of pure equality we obtain the notion of *local theories* [4,19].

Hierarchical Reasoning in Local Theory Extensions. Consider a Ψ-local theory extension $\mathcal{T}_0 \subseteq \mathcal{T}_0 \cup \mathcal{K}$. Condition ($\mathsf{Loc}_f^\Psi$) requires that for every finite set G of ground Π^C-clauses, $\mathcal{T}_0 \cup \mathcal{K} \cup G \models \perp$ iff $\mathcal{T}_0 \cup \mathcal{K}[\Psi_\mathcal{K}(G)] \cup G \models \perp$. In all clauses in $\mathcal{K}[\Psi_\mathcal{K}(G)] \cup G$ the function symbols in Σ_1 only have ground terms as arguments, so $\mathcal{K}[\Psi_\mathcal{K}(G)] \cup G$ can be flattened and purified by introducing, in a bottom-up manner, new constants $c_t \in C$ for subterms $t = f(c_1, \dots, c_n)$ where $f \in \Sigma_1$ and c_i are constants, together with definitions $c_t \approx f(c_1, \dots, c_n)$. We obtain a set of clauses $\mathcal{K}_0 \cup G_0 \cup \mathsf{Def}$, where $\mathcal{K}_0$ and G_0 do not contain Σ_1-function symbols and Def contains clauses of the form $c = f(c_1, \dots, c_n)$, where $f \in \Sigma_1$, $c, c_1, \dots, c_n \in C$.

Theorem 1 ([12,13,25]). *Let $\mathcal{K}$ be a set of clauses. Assume that $\mathcal{T}_0 \subseteq \mathcal{T}_0 \cup \mathcal{K}$ is a Ψ-local theory extension. For any finite set G of flat ground clauses (with no nestings of extension functions), let $\mathcal{K}_0 \cup G_0 \cup \mathsf{Def}$ be obtained from $\mathcal{K}[\Psi_\mathcal{K}(G)] \cup G$ by flattening and purification, as explained above. Then the following are equivalent to $\mathcal{T}_0 \cup \mathcal{K} \cup G \models \perp$:*

(i) $\mathcal{T}_0 \cup \mathcal{K}[\Psi_\mathcal{K}(G)] \cup G \models \perp$.

(ii) $\mathcal{T}_0 \cup \mathcal{K}_0 \cup G_0 \cup \mathsf{Con}_0 \models \perp$, *where* $\mathsf{Con}_0 = \{\bigwedge_{i=1}^n c_i \approx d_i \rightarrow c \approx d \mid f(c_1, \dots, c_n) \approx c, f(d_1, \dots, d_n) \approx d \in \mathsf{Def}\}$.

Locality and Embeddability. When establishing links between locality and embeddability we require that the clauses in $\mathcal{K}$ are *flat* and *linear* w.r.t. Σ_1-functions. When defining these notions we distinguish between ground and non-ground clauses: An *extension clause D is flat* when all symbols below a Σ_1-function symbol in D are variables. D is *linear* if whenever a variable occurs in two terms of D starting with Σ_1-functions, the terms are equal, and no term contains two occurrences of a variable. A *ground clause D is flat* if all symbols below a Σ_1-function in D are constants. A *ground clause D is linear* if whenever a constant occurs in two terms in D whose root symbol is in Σ_1, the two terms are identical, and if no term which starts with a Σ_1-function contains two occurrences of the same constant.

In [13] we showed that for extensions with sets of flat and linear clauses Ψ-locality can be proved by proving a weak embeddability condition of partial into total models. The proof in [13] can be extended to situations in which the clauses in $\mathcal{K}$ are not linear if a suitable closure operator is used, cf. [24,31].

Examples of Local Theory Extensions. Using the characterization of locality in terms of weak embeddability of partial models into total models, in [25,27,35,36] we gave several examples of local theory extensions:

(1) Extensions $\mathcal{T}_0 \cup \mathsf{UIF}_\Sigma$ of a theory $\mathcal{T}_0$ with uninterpreted functions in a set Σ;
(2) Extensions of partially ordered theories with a function f satisfying:
$(\mathsf{Mon}_f)\, x_1 \leq y_1 \wedge \dots \wedge x_n \leq y_n \rightarrow f(x_1, \dots, x_n) \leq f(y_1, \dots, y_n)$.
(3) Extensions of any theory $\mathcal{T}_0$ containing a reflexive predicate symbol $\leq$ with functions satisfying conditions $(\mathsf{Bound}^t(f))$ or $(\mathsf{GBound}^t(f))$:
$(\mathsf{Bound}^t(f)) \quad \forall x_1, \dots, x_n (f(x_1, \dots, x_n) \leq t(x_1, \dots, x_n))$
$(\mathsf{GBound}^t(f)) \quad \forall x_1, \dots, x_n (\phi(x_1, \dots, x_n) \rightarrow f(x_1, \dots, x_n) \leq t(x_1, \dots, x_n))$,
where $t(x_1, \dots, x_n)$ is a term in the base signature Π_0 and $\phi(x_1, \dots, x_n)$ a conjunction of literals in the signature Π_0, whose variables are in $\{x_1, \dots, x_n\}$.
(4) Extensions of the theory TOrd of totally ordered sets, $LI(\mathbb{R})$ or the theory of real numbers with functions satisfying $\mathsf{SGc}(f, g_1, \dots, g_n) \wedge \mathsf{Mon}(f, g_1, \dots, g_n)$.
$(\mathsf{SGc}(f, g_1, \dots, g_n)) \quad \forall x_1, \dots, x_n, x (\bigwedge_{i=1}^n x_i \leq g_i(x) \rightarrow f(x_1, \dots, x_n) \leq x)$

Chains of Theory Extensions. In many cases $\mathcal{K} = \mathcal{K}_1 \cup \dots \cup \mathcal{K}_n$ and we have a chain of local theory extensions $\mathcal{T}_0 \subseteq \mathcal{T}_0 \cup \mathcal{K}_1 \subseteq \dots \subseteq \mathcal{T}_0 \cup \mathcal{K}_1 \cup \dots \cup \mathcal{K}_n$, with the property that for every extension all variables occur also below extension functions. In this case checking the satisfiability of a set of ground clauses G can be reduced in n steps to a satisfiability test w.r.t. $\mathcal{T}_0$. Also in this case the number of instances can be expressed using a closure operator Ψ.

Locality Transfer Results. In [13] we analyzed the way locality results can be transferred to combinations of theories.

Theorem 2 ([13]). *Let $\mathcal{T}_0$ be a $\forall\exists$ theory in the signature Π_0, and let Σ_1 and Σ_2 be two disjoint sets of fresh function symbols. Let $\mathcal{K}_i$ be a set of universally closed flat and linear clauses $\Pi_0 \cup \Sigma_i$-clauses for $i = 1, 2$, in which all variables occur below extension functions. If the extensions $\mathcal{T}_0 \subseteq \mathcal{T}_0 \cup \mathcal{K}_i$ are local for $i = 1, 2$ then the extension $\mathcal{T}_0 \subseteq \mathcal{T}_0 \cup \mathcal{K}_1 \cup \mathcal{K}_2$ is local.*

3 Uniform Interpolation

In [2] a notion of quantifier-free uniform interpolation w.r.t. a theory related also to a notion of covers introduced in [6] was defined. We summarize the results on uniform quantifier-free interpolation from [2,3,5] relevant for this paper.

Definition 1 (Uniform interpolation [2]). *Let $\mathcal{T}$ be a theory and $\exists \overline{e} \phi(\overline{e}, \overline{y})$ an existential formula with free variables $\overline{y}$. A quantifier-free formula $\psi(\overline{y})$ is a* $\mathcal{T}$-cover *(or a $\mathcal{T}$-uniform interpolant) of $\exists \overline{e} \phi(\overline{e}, \overline{y})$ iff*

(1) $\mathcal{T} \models \phi(\overline{e}, \overline{y}) \rightarrow \psi(\overline{y})$, and
(2) for every quantifier-free formula $\theta(\overline{y}, \overline{z})$ with $\mathcal{T} \models \phi(\overline{e}, \overline{y}) \rightarrow \theta(\overline{y}, \overline{z})$ we have: $\mathcal{T} \models \psi(\overline{y}) \rightarrow \theta(\overline{y}, \overline{z})$.

A theory $\mathcal{T}$ is said to have uniform quantifier-free interpolation iff every existential formula $\exists \overline{e} \phi(\overline{e}, \overline{y})$ has a $\mathcal{T}$-cover.

Theorem 3 ([2]). *A quantifier-free formula $\psi(\overline{y})$ is a $\mathcal{T}$-cover of $\exists \overline{e} \phi(\overline{e}, \overline{y})$ iff condition (1) in Definition 1 and condition (2') below hold:*

(2') for every model $\mathcal{A}$ of $\mathcal{T}$ and every tuple of elements in the universe of $\mathcal{A}$, $\overline{a}$, such that $\mathcal{A} \models \psi(\overline{a})$ there exists another model $\mathcal{B}$ of $\mathcal{T}$ such that $\mathcal{A}$ embeds into $\mathcal{B}$ and $\mathcal{B} \models \exists \overline{e} \phi(\overline{e}, \overline{a})$.

Remark 1 *We can equivalently formulate the definition of a $\mathcal{T}$-uniform interpolant by considering Π^C-formulae $\phi(\overline{e}, c_1, \dots, c_n)$. A $\mathcal{T}$-uniform interpolant of ϕ w.r.t. $C_s = \{c_1, \dots, c_n\}$ is a Π^C-formula $\psi(c_1, \dots, c_n)$ which contains only constants in $\{c_1, \dots, c_n\}$, and such that (1) $\phi \models_{\mathcal{T}} \psi$, and (2) for every formula θ having only constants in $\{c_1, \dots, c_n\}$ in common with ϕ, if $\phi \models_{\mathcal{T}} \theta$ then $\psi \models_{\mathcal{T}} \theta$.*

In [2] it was proved that the theory UIF_Σ of uninterpreted function symbols in a set Σ allows uniform quantifier-free interpolation; a hierarchical superposition calculus [2] and DAG-methods and tableau methods [5] can be used for the computation of uniform interpolants. The uniform interpolant for a formula ϕ computed with these methods only contains functions in Σ which occur in ϕ.
In [3] it was shown that a universal theory $\mathcal{T}$ has a model completion $\mathcal{T}^*$ iff $\mathcal{T}$ has uniform quantifier-free interpolation and, moreover, situations were identified in which the combination of two theories with uniform quantifier-free interpolation has again uniform quantifier-free interpolation.

Theorem 4 ([3]). *Let $\mathcal{T}_1, \mathcal{T}_2$ be two convex, stably infinite, equality interpolating, universal theories over disjoint signatures admitting uniform quantifier-free interpolation. Then $\mathcal{T}_1 \cup \mathcal{T}_2$ admits uniform quantifier-free interpolation.*

Example 1 *The theory UIF_Σ is universal, convex, stably infinite and equality interpolating [1] and admits uniform quantifier-free interpolation [2]. Therefore for every theory $\mathcal{T}$ with signature disjoint from Σ which is convex, stably infinite, equality interpolating, and universal, if $\mathcal{T}$ admits uniform quantifier-free interpolation then $\mathcal{T} \cup \mathsf{UIF}_\Sigma$ admits uniform quantifier-free interpolation, and for every formula ϕ we can compute a $\mathcal{T} \cup \mathsf{UIF}_\Sigma$-uniform interpolant containing only symbols in the signature of $\mathcal{T}$ and extension symbols occurring in ϕ using the convex combined cover algorithm proposed in [3]. This holds in particular when $\mathcal{T} = LI(\mathbb{R})$. $LI(\mathbb{R})$ has a universal axiomatization, is convex, stably infinite, allows quantifier elimination, hence (i) has also the equality interpolation property [1] and (ii) allows uniform quantifier-free interpolation.*

4 General Uniform Interpolation

We define the notion of general uniform quantifier-free interpolation, and show that the semantic characterization in Theorem 3 (proved in [2]) can be extended to the case of general uniform quantifier-free interpolation.

Let $\Pi = (\Sigma, \mathsf{Pred})$ be a signature where $\Sigma = \Sigma_0 \cup \Sigma_1$, where $\Pi_0 = (\Sigma_0, \mathsf{Pred})$ is a set of interpreted function and predicate symbols and Σ_1 a set of uninterpreted function symbols. Let ϕ be a Π^C-formula and let $\Sigma_s \subseteq \Sigma_1$, $C_s \subseteq C$ be sets of uninterpreted symbols and constants occurring in ϕ. We denote by Π_s the signature $(\Sigma_0 \cup \Sigma_s, \mathsf{Pred})$. We denote by Σ_e the set of uninterpreted function symbols in ϕ which are not in Σ_s and by C_e the set of additional constants in C occurring in ϕ which are not in C_s (the symbols which are eliminated). Let $\Pi_r = (\Sigma_0 \cup (\Sigma_1 \backslash \Sigma_e), \mathsf{Pred})$ and $C_r = C \backslash C_e$ (the set of function and predicate symbols and constants in Π^C which are not eliminated).

Definition 2 (General uniform interpolation). *Let $\mathcal{T}$ be a theory over a signature $\Pi = (\Sigma, \mathsf{Pred})$, where $\Sigma = \Sigma_0 \cup \Sigma_1$, where $\Pi_0 = (\Sigma_0, \mathsf{Pred})$ is a set of interpreted function symbols and Σ_1 a set of uninterpreted function symbols. We say that $\mathcal{T}$ has the* general uniform interpolation property *if for every quantifier-free Π^C-formula ϕ (where C is a set of new constants) and all subsets $\Sigma_s \subseteq \Sigma_1$, $C_s \subseteq C$ of uninterpreted symbols and constants occurring in ϕ there exists a quantifier-free $\Pi_s^{C_s}$-formula ψ such that:*

(1) $\phi \models_{\mathcal{T}} \psi$, and
(2) For every ground formula θ having in common with ϕ only interpreted symbols in Π_0, uninterpreted symbols in Π_s, and constants in C_s if $\phi \models_{\mathcal{T}} \theta$ then $\psi \models_{\mathcal{T}} \theta$.

A formula ψ with the properties (1) and (2) is called a $\mathcal{T}$-general uniform interpolant of ϕ w.r.t. $\Sigma_s \cup C_s$.

Remark 2 *Definition 1 is a special case of Definition 2, in which all function and predicate symbols in the signature of $\mathcal{T}$ are* interpreted, *i.e. can be contained in the uniform interpolant of a formula. We will later also consider the possibility of regarding symbols in Σ_1 as "semi-interpreted": If two function symbols $f, g \in \Sigma_1$ occur together in an axiom of $\mathcal{T}$, and $f \in \Sigma_s$ then the general uniform interpolant is allowed to also contain g. We will model this using a closure operator Θ, and require that the general uniform interpolant of a formula ϕ can contain any Π_0-symbols and only uninterpreted symbols in $\Theta(\Sigma_s \cup C_s)$.*

Theorem 5 *Let $\mathcal{T}$ be a theory with signature $\Pi = (\Sigma_0 \cup \Sigma_1, \mathsf{Pred})$, and let ϕ be a ground Π^C-formula. Let $\Sigma_s \subseteq \Sigma_1$ be a subset of the uninterpreted function symbols occurring in ϕ, and $C_s \subseteq C$ a subset of the constants occurring in ϕ. We use the notation introduced in the paragraph preceding Definition 2. A ground $\Pi_s^{C_s}$-formula ψ is a $\mathcal{T}$-general uniform interpolant of ϕ w.r.t. $\Sigma_s \cup C_s$ iff*

(1) $\mathcal{T} \models \phi \rightarrow \psi$, and
(2') for every Π^C-structure $\mathcal{A}$ such that $\mathcal{A}$ is a model of $\mathcal{T}$ and $\mathcal{A} \models \psi$ there exists another model $\mathcal{B}$ of $\mathcal{T}$ such that $\mathcal{A}_{|\Pi_r^{C_r}}$ embeds into $\mathcal{B}_{|\Pi_r^{C_r}}$ and $\mathcal{B} \models \phi$.

Proof: The proof is similar to the proof given for the case of uniform interpolation in [2]. The details are presented in [34]. □

5 General Uniform Interpolation in Theory Extensions

We present a method for eliminating function symbols based on an adaptation of a method for symbol elimination in theory extensions we proposed in [32]. In [32] we considered theory extensions $\mathcal{T}_0 \cup \mathcal{K}$ with extension symbols Σ, and assumed that the function symbols in a subset $\Sigma_s \subseteq \Sigma$ were underspecified, i.e. considered to be parameters. Given a set G of ground clauses such that $\mathcal{T}_0 \cup \mathcal{K} \cup G$ is satisfiable, we used a form of symbol elimination for deriving a (weakest) universally quantified condition Γ on the parameters in Σ_s such that G becomes unsatisfiable w.r.t. $\mathcal{T} \cup (\mathcal{K} \cup \Gamma)$. This was used in verification, for deriving additional conditions under which certain properties are guaranteed to be inductive invariants [33] and for invariant strengthening [23]. We show that this method can be used for reducing the problem of computing a general uniform interpolant in local theory extensions to the problem of computing uniform interpolants.

Let $\Pi_0 = (\Sigma_0, \mathsf{Pred})$. Let $\mathcal{T}_0$ be a theory with signature Π_0. We consider theory extensions $\mathcal{T}_0 \subseteq \mathcal{T} = \mathcal{T}_0 \cup \mathcal{K}$ with signature $\Pi = \Pi_0 \cup \Sigma$ and sets of ground clauses G over Π^C. We identify sets $\Sigma_s \subseteq \Sigma$ (resp. $C_s \subseteq C$) of function symbols (resp. constants) occurring in G which are considered to be shared and must be kept, and the set $\Sigma_1 = \Sigma \backslash \Sigma_s$. We proceed as follows:

(I) We first eliminate the function symbols in Σ_1 with arity ≥ 1 and the constants which do not occur below functions in Σ_s.
(II) We then use (if possible) methods similar to those developed in [3] to eliminate the remaining constants which are not in $\Sigma_s \cup C_s$.

5.1 (I) Eliminating Function Symbols in Local Theory Extensions

We identify situations in which we can generate, for every set of flat ground clauses G, a ground formula Γ containing only uninterpreted symbols in Σ_s, such that Γ is a general uniform interpolant of G w.r.t. $\Sigma_s \cup \overline{C}_s$, for a subset $\overline{C}_s$ of C containing the constants C_s occurring in G. We will use a method which eliminates symbols in a hierarchical way, by reducing the problem to quantifier elimination in the theory $\mathcal{T}_0$, which is described in Algorithm 1.

We first consider a special type of extensions, in which $\mathcal{K}$ is the disjoint union of a set of $\Pi_0 \cup \Sigma_s$-clauses $\mathcal{K}_s$, a set of $\Pi_0 \cup \Sigma_1$-clauses $\mathcal{K}_1$, and a set of clauses $\mathcal{K}_i$ containing only symbols in Π_0 and symbols in Σ not occurring in G.

Theorem 6 *Assume that $\mathcal{T}_0$ allows quantifier elimination. Let $\mathcal{T}_0 \subseteq \mathcal{T}_0 \cup \mathcal{K}$ be an extension of the theory $\mathcal{T}_0$ with additional function symbols in a set Σ which is the disjoint union of Σ_s, Σ_1 and Σ_i, satisfying a finite set $\mathcal{K}$ of flat and linear clauses such that for every clause in $\mathcal{K}$, every variable occurs below an extension symbol. Let G be a finite set of flat and linear ground $(\Pi_0 \cup \Sigma_s \cup \Sigma_1)^C$-clauses and T a set of flat $(\Pi_0 \cup \Sigma_s \cup \Sigma_1)^C$-terms satisfying the conditions in Algorithm 1, and let Γ_T be the ground formula obtained by applying Algorithm 1.*

Algorithm 1. Algorithm for Function Elimination

Input: Theory extension $\mathcal{T}_0 \subseteq \mathcal{T}_0 \cup \mathcal{K}$ with signature $\Pi = \Pi_0 \cup (\Sigma_s \cup \Sigma_1)$
where $\mathcal{K}$ is a finite set of flat and linear Π-clauses;
G, a finite set of flat and linear ground clauses in the signature Π^C;
T, a finite set of flat ground Π^C-terms s.t. $\mathsf{est}(\mathcal{K}, G) \subseteq T$ and $\mathcal{K}[T]$ is ground.
Output: Ground Π_s^C-formula Γ.

Step 1 Compute the set of Π_0^C-clauses $\mathcal{K}_0 \cup G_0 \cup \mathsf{Con}_0$ from $\mathcal{K}[T] \cup G$ using purification (cf. Thm. 1, extension symbols $\Sigma = \Sigma_s \cup \Sigma_1$).
Step 2 $G_1 := \mathcal{K}_0 \cup G_0 \cup \mathsf{Con}_0$. Among the constants in G_1, identify
(i) the constants $\overline{c}_f$, $f \in \Sigma_s$, where $c_f = f \in \Sigma_s$ is a constant parameter or c_f is introduced by a definition $c_f := f(c_1, \dots, c_k)$ in the hierarchical reasoning method,
(ii) all constants $\overline{c}_p$ occurring as arguments of functions in Σ_s in such definitions.
Let $\overline{c}$ be the remaining constants.
Replace the constants in $\overline{c}$ with existentially quantified variables $\overline{x}$ in G_1, i.e. replace $G_1(\overline{c}_p, \overline{c}_f, \overline{c})$ with $G_1(\overline{c}_p, \overline{c}_f, \overline{x})$, and consider the formula $\exists \overline{x} G_1(\overline{c}_p, \overline{c}_f, \overline{x})$.
Step 3 Compute a quantifier-free formula $\Gamma_1(\overline{c}_p, \overline{c}_f)$ equivalent to $\exists \overline{x} G_1(\overline{c}_p, \overline{c}_f, \overline{x})$ w.r.t. $\mathcal{T}_0$ using a method for quantifier elimination in $\mathcal{T}_0$.
Step 4 Let $\Gamma(\overline{c}_p)$ be the formula obtained by replacing back in $\Gamma_1(\overline{c}_p, \overline{c}_f)$ the constants c_f introduced by definitions $c_f := f(c_1, \dots, c_k)$ with the terms $f(c_1, \dots, c_k)$.

(1) $G \models_{\mathcal{T}_0 \cup \mathcal{K}} \Gamma_T$.
(2) Assume that $\mathcal{T}_0 \subseteq \mathcal{T}_0 \cup \mathcal{K}$ *is a local theory extension, and that* $\mathcal{K} = \mathcal{K}_s \cup \mathcal{K}_1 \cup \mathcal{K}_i$, *where* $\mathcal{K}_s$ *is a set of* $\Pi_0 \cup \Sigma_s$*-clauses,* $\mathcal{K}_1$ *is a set of* $\Pi_0 \cup \Sigma_1$*-clauses, and* $\mathcal{K}_i$ *is a set of* $\Pi_0 \cup \Sigma_i$*-clauses. Let* $\overline{C}_s$ *consist of* C_s *together with all constants in* C *which occur as arguments of functions in* Σ_s *in* G*. Then the formula* Γ *obtained by applying Algorithm 1*[1] *to* $\mathcal{T}_0 \cup \mathcal{K}_s \cup \mathcal{K}_1$, G *and* $T := \mathsf{est}(\mathcal{K}, G)$ *is a* $\mathcal{T}_0 \cup \mathcal{K}$*-general uniform interpolant of* G *w.r.t.* $\Sigma_s \cup \overline{C}_s$.

Proof: The proof can be found in [34]. □

Remark 3 *Theorem 6(2) can be slightly reformulated, by allowing the clauses in* $\mathcal{K}_1$ *to contain symbols in* Σ_s *under the assumption that the extension is* Ψ*-local, for a suitable closure operator* Ψ*, and in Algorithm 1* $\mathcal{K}[\Psi(G)]$ *is used instead of* $\mathcal{K}[G]$ *and* $T = \Psi(\mathsf{est}(\mathcal{K}, G))$*. (cf. [34] for details).*

Proposition 7 *Let* G *be a finite set of flat and linear ground* Π^C*-clauses, and let* Σ_s, Σ_1 *be the extension function symbols occurring in* G *and* $C_s \subseteq C$ *a set of constants occurring in* G*. Let* $\mathcal{T} := \mathcal{T}_0 \cup \mathcal{K}_s \cup \mathcal{K}_1 \cup \mathcal{K}_i$ *be a* Π*-theory, such that all the conditions in Theorem 6(2) hold. Let* Γ *be the* $\mathcal{T}$*-general uniform interpolant for* G *w.r.t.* $\overline{C_s}$ *(with* $C_s \subseteq \overline{C}_s$*) obtained by applying Algorithm 1. If* ψ *is a* $\Pi_s^{C_s}$*-ground formula which is a* $\mathcal{T}_0 \cup \mathcal{K}_s$*-uniform interpolant of* Γ *w.r.t.* C_s *then* ψ *is a* $\mathcal{T}$*-general uniform interpolant of* G *w.r.t.* C_s*.*

[1] Since G does not contain the symbols in Σ_i, the instances computed in Step 1 of Algorithm 1 do not contain instances of $\mathcal{K}_i$, so $\mathcal{K}_i$ can be ignored.

Proof: The proof can be found in [34]. □

Example 2 *Consider the extension of $LI(\mathbb{R})$ with uninterpreted function symbols in $\Sigma = \{f, g\}$. Let $G = (a \leq f(e)) \wedge (e \leq g(b)) \wedge (g(b) \leq a) \wedge (f(e) \leq g(b))$. We want to compute the uniform interpolant of G w.r.t. $\{g, a, e\}$ ($\Sigma_s = \{g\}, C_s = \{a, e\}$). For this, we need to eliminate $\{f, b\}$. To eliminate f we use Alg. 1.*

Step 1: *With the definitions* $\mathsf{Def} := \{e_f \approx f(e), b_g \approx g(b)\}$ *we obtain, after instantiation, purification and simplification:*

$(a \leq e_f) \wedge (e \leq b_g) \wedge (b_g \leq a) \wedge (e_f \leq b_g)$

Step 2: *The constants corresponding to elements in Σ_s are $\{g_e, e, a\}$; b is an argument of g. The remaining constants are: $\{e_f\}$.*

Step 3: *We use quantifier elimination in $\mathcal{T}_0$ to eliminate e_f:*

$\exists e_f((a \leq e_f) \wedge (e \leq b_g) \wedge (b_g \leq a) \wedge (e_f \leq b_g)) \equiv (a \leq b_g) \wedge (e \leq b_g) \wedge (b_g \leq a)$

Step 4: *We obtain $\Gamma = (a \approx g(b) \wedge e \leq g(b))$.*

To eliminate b the $LI(\mathbb{R}) \cup \mathsf{UIF}_{\{g\}}$-uniform interpolant ψ w.r.t. $C_s = \{e, a\}$ can be computed with methods proposed in [2, 3, 5].

5.2 (II) Eliminating Constants Occurring Below Function Symbols

Until now we showed that Algorithm 1 can be used to eliminate extension functions with arity ≥ 1 and constants which do not occur below functions in Σ_s. In a second step, the remaining constants in C_e need to be eliminated. However, this is not always possible, as shown in the next example.

Example 3 *Consider the extension of the theory $LI([0, 1])$ with a function symbol f satisfying axioms $\mathcal{K} = \{\mathsf{Mon}_f, \forall x(f(x) \leq 1)\}$. Let $G = (a \leq b) \wedge (b \leq f(b))$.*

If we try to compute a $\mathcal{T}$-general uniform interpolant of G w.r.t. $\Sigma_s \cup C_s$, where $\Sigma_s = \{f\}$, $C_s = \{a\}$, and $\mathcal{T} = LI([0, 1]) \cup \mathcal{K}$ (or a $\mathcal{T}$-uniform interpolant of G w.r.t. C_s) we notice that no finite formula containing only symbols in Π_0 and a and f has the properties of a $\mathcal{T}$-uniform interpolant w.r.t. C_s. Indeed, the family of all consequences θ of G containing arbitrary Π_0-symbols, but sharing with G the uninterpreted symbols $\{a, f\}$ contains the infinite set $\{a \leq f^n(1) \mid n \in \mathbb{N}\}$. A $\mathcal{T}$-uniform interpolant ψ for G w.r.t. C_s would only contain a finite set of terms, so there would exist $k \in \mathbb{N}$ such that $f^1(1), \ldots, f^k(1)$ occur in ψ, but $f^{k+1}(1)$ does not. Note that $G \not\models_{\mathcal{T}} a \approx 0$ and there exist models of $\mathcal{T}$ and G (hence also of ψ) in which $0 < f^n_{\mathcal{A}}(1) < f^{n-1}_{\mathcal{A}}(1) < 1$ for all $n \geq 1$. Let $\mathcal{A}$ be a model for $\mathcal{T}$ and G (hence also of ψ) in which $a_{\mathcal{A}} > 0$ and $0 < f^k_{\mathcal{A}}(1) < \cdots < f_{\mathcal{A}}(1) < 1$. We can change $\mathcal{A}$ to a model $\mathcal{B}$ in which the values of the terms occurring in ψ have the same value, but the interpretation of f is changed such that if $x < f^{k-1}_{\mathcal{B}}(1)$ we have $f_{\mathcal{B}}(x) = 0$. Since $f^k_{\mathcal{B}}(1) < f^{k-1}_{\mathcal{B}}(1)$, $f^{k+1}_{\mathcal{B}}(1) = 0$. $\mathcal{B}$ is still a model of ψ and of $\mathcal{T}$, but $a > f^{k+1}_{\mathcal{B}}(1)$, so $\psi \not\models_{\mathcal{T}} a \leq f^{k+1}(1)$.

In what follows, we identify situations in which constants can be eliminated.

Extensions with Uninterpreted Function Symbols. We first identify consition under which the union of a theory allowing quantifier elimination with uninterpreted function symbols in a set Σ allows general uniform interpolation.

Theorem 8 *If $\mathcal{T}_0$ is a convex, stably infinite, equality interpolating, universal theory allowing quantifier elimination and $\mathcal{T} = \mathcal{T}_0 \cup \mathsf{UIF}_\Sigma$ is the extension of $\mathcal{T}_0$ with uninterpreted function symbols Σ, then $\mathcal{T}$ has general uniform interpolation.*

Proof: Let Π be the signature of $\mathcal{T}$, C a set of additional constants, and let G be a set of flat and linear ground Π^C-clauses. Let $\Sigma_s \subseteq \Sigma$ and $C_s \subseteq C$ occurring in G, and let $\Sigma_e \cup C_e$ be the symbols in G which are not in Σ_s or C_s, i.e. which we want to eliminate. We can compute a $\mathcal{T}$-general uniform interpolant for G w.r.t. $\Sigma_s \cup C_s$ as follows: We use Algorithm 1 (with $\mathcal{K} = \emptyset$) for eliminating the function symbols in Σ_e with arity ≥ 1 and all constants in C_e which do not occur as arguments of function symbols in Σ_s and obtain a formula Γ, containing symbols in $\Sigma_s \cup C_s \cup C'$, where C' are the constants in C_e occurring below function symbols in Σ_s. We can then use the method proposed in [3] for computing the uniform interpolant ψ of Γ w.r.t. C_s for $\mathcal{T}_0 \cup \mathsf{UIF}_{\Sigma_s}$. We prove that the resulting formula is indeed a $\mathcal{T}$-general uniform interpolant w.r.t. $\Sigma_s \cup C_s$. The details of the proof are presented in [34]. □

We present a situation in which constants can be eliminated using a reduction to uniform interpolation in extensions with free function symbols.

Uniform Interpolation with Θ -Sharing. For local theory extensions $\mathcal{T}_0 \subseteq \mathcal{T}_0 \cup \mathcal{K}$ in which some of the clauses in $\mathcal{K}$ contain both symbols in $\mathcal{K}_s$ and in $\mathcal{K}_1$, or for Ψ-local theory extensions, where Ψ is a closure operator with the property that the set of instances $\mathcal{K}[\Psi(G)]$ might contain function symbols not occurring in G, the conditions in Theorem 6(2) are not met. A solution to this problem is to define an equivalence relation $\simeq$ on the uninterpreted function symbols in Σ_1, such that if $f \simeq g$ and f is shared then g must be considered to be shared as well. We mention two ways of defining such equivalence relations:

(1) Define $f \sim g$ iff there exist c, d such that if $g(d) \in T$ then $f(c) \in \Psi(T)$ or vice versa, and consider the induced equivalence relation $\simeq$.
(2) Define $f \sim g$ iff there exists a clause in $\mathcal{K}$ in which both f and g occur, and consider the induced equivalence relation $\simeq$.

We can then define $\Theta(\Sigma_s) = \{f \mid \exists g \in \Sigma_s \text{ with } f \simeq g\}$, and apply Algorithm 1 with $\Theta(\Sigma_s)$ instead of Σ_s and $T = \mathsf{est}[\Psi(G)]$.

Example 4 *Consider the extension $\mathcal{T} := LI(\mathbb{R}) \cup \mathcal{K}$ of $LI(\mathbb{R})$ with monotone functions f, g satisfying the axioms $\mathcal{K} = \{x{\leq}g(y) \rightarrow f(x){\leq}g(y)\} \cup \mathsf{Mon}_f \cup \mathsf{Mon}_g$. In [27], cf. also [24] we proved that this is a local theory extension.*
Let $G = (a \leq f(e)) \wedge (e \leq g(b)) \wedge (g(b) \leq a)$. We want to compute a $\mathcal{T}$-general uniform interpolant of G w.r.t. $\{g, a, e\}$. Since f and g occur together in an axiom in $\mathcal{K}$ we have $f \sim g$ and we can define, using possibility (2) above, a closure operator Θ with $\Theta(\{g\}) = \{f, g\}$. In this case $\Sigma_e = \{b\}$, so Algorithm 1 does not need to be used for eliminating the function symbols with arity ≥ 1. We have to compute $\exists b((a \leq f(e)) \wedge (e \leq g(b)) \wedge (g(b) \leq a))$ w.r.t. $\mathcal{T}$. However, Example 3 shows that monotonicity axioms can in general be problematic.

We identify situations in which such problems can be avoided. We focus on definitions of closure operators defined according to possibility (2) above.[2]

Definition 3 *Let $\Pi_0 = (\Sigma_0, \mathsf{Pred})$, let $\Pi = (\Sigma_0 \cup \Sigma, \mathsf{Pred})$, where Σ is a set of additional function symbols. Let $\mathcal{K}$ be a set of flat and linear Π-clauses. For $f, g \in \Sigma$ we define $f \sim g$ if and only if there exists a clause in $\mathcal{K}$ in which both f and g occur. Let $\simeq$ be the equivalence relation induced by $\sim$. We define a closure operator $\Theta_{\mathcal{K}}$ by: $\Theta_{\mathcal{K}}(\Sigma_s) := \{f \mid \exists g \in \Sigma_s \text{ with } f \simeq g\}$, for every set $\Sigma_s \subseteq \Sigma$.*

With the notation in Definition 3, let G be a set of ground Π^C-clauses, Σ_s and C_s sets of function symbols and constants occurring in G, Σ_e and C_e the remaining extension symbols resp. constants in G, $\Sigma'_s = \Theta_{\mathcal{K}}(\Sigma_s)$ and $\Sigma_1 = \Theta_{\mathcal{K}}(\Sigma_e)$. Then $\mathcal{K}$ can be written as the disjoint union of three sets of clauses: a set of $\Pi_0 \cup \Sigma'_s$-clauses $\mathcal{K}_s$, a set of $\Pi_0 \cup \Sigma_1$-clauses $\mathcal{K}_1$, and a set of $\Pi_0 \cup \Sigma_i$-clauses $\mathcal{K}_i$, where $\Sigma_i = \Sigma \backslash (\Sigma'_s \cup \Sigma_1)$. Considerations similar to those in Proposition 7 allow us to ignore (w.l.o.g.) the symbols in Σ_i and the clauses in $\mathcal{K}_i$.

We identify a situation in which only constants can be used as arguments of functions in Σ'_s, and computing a $\mathcal{T}$-general uniform interpolant for G w.r.t. $\Sigma'_s \cup C_s$ can be reduced to computing a $\mathcal{T}_0 \cup \mathsf{UIF}_{\Sigma'_s \cup \Sigma_1}$-uniform quantifier-free interpolant.

Lemma 9 *Let $\mathcal{T}_0 \subseteq \mathcal{T}_0 \cup \mathcal{K}_s \cup \mathcal{K}_1$ be a local extension with flat clauses, with signature $\Pi = \Pi_0 \cup \Sigma'_s \cup \Sigma_1$, in which the symbols Σ'_s occurring in $\mathcal{K}_s$ and Σ_1 occurring in $\mathcal{K}_1$ are disjoint, and for every clause in $\mathcal{K}_s \cup \mathcal{K}_1$, every variable occurs below an extension symbol. Let T_0 be a set of Π^C-terms, and $T = \{f(t_1, \dots, t_n) \mid f \in \Sigma'_s, t_i \in T_0\}$. Then for every ground Π^C-formula θ whose terms starting with function symbols in Σ'_s are in T, $\mathcal{T}_0 \cup \mathcal{K}_s \cup \mathcal{K}_1 \cup \theta \models \perp$ if and only if $\mathcal{T}_0 \cup \mathcal{K}_s[T] \cup \mathcal{K}_1 \cup \theta \models \perp$.*

Proof: The direct implication is clear. For the converse, we show that every model $\mathcal{A}$ of $\mathcal{T}_0 \cup \mathcal{K}_s[T] \cup \mathcal{K}_1 \cup \theta$ can be suitably changed to a model $\mathcal{B}$ of $\mathcal{T}_0 \cup \mathcal{K}_s \cup \mathcal{K}_1 \cup \theta$. For this, we use the locality of the extension. For a full proof cf. [34]. □

For the equivalence in Lemma 9 to hold for all ground Π^C-formulae θ, T_0 has to be the set of all Π^C-terms, so $\mathcal{K}_s[T]$ can be infinite. We identify a case in which the set T of terms starting with a function symbol in Σ'_s, and $\mathcal{K}_s[T]$ are finite.

We consider $\mathcal{T}$-general uniform interpolation problems for sets G of ground clauses w.r.t. extension functions Σ_s and constants $C_s \subseteq C$, where C is the set of additional constants occurring in G, and consider $\Sigma'_s = \Theta_{\mathcal{K}}(\Sigma_s)$, where $\mathcal{T} = \mathcal{T}_0 \cup \mathcal{K}$ is a theory extension over a signature with the following properties:

(A1) $\mathcal{T} = \mathcal{T}_0 \cup \mathcal{K}$ is a theory over a signature $\Pi = (S, \Sigma_0 \cup \Sigma'_s \cup \Sigma_1, \mathsf{Pred})$ with set of sorts $S = S_1 \cup S_2$, where $S_1 \cap S_2 = \emptyset$ (an extension of a theory $\mathcal{T}_0$ with signature Π_0 with a finite set of function symbols $\Sigma = \Sigma'_s \cup \Sigma_1$).

[2] In many cases the closure operators on terms used for possibility (1) reflect the condition in possibility (2).

(A2) $\mathcal{K}$ is a finite set of flat and linear Π-clauses, $\mathcal{K} = \mathcal{K}_s \cup \mathcal{K}_1$, where $\mathcal{K}_s$ is a set of $\Pi_0 \cup \Sigma'_s$-clauses, $\mathcal{K}_1$ a set of $\Pi_0 \cup \Sigma_1$-clauses, for every clause in $\mathcal{K}_s \cup \mathcal{K}_1$, every variable occurs below an extension symbol, and the following hold:
(a) For every f in $\Sigma_0 \cup \Sigma'_s \cup \Sigma_1$ with arity ≥ 1, the output sort of f is in S_2.
(b) For every $f \in \Sigma'_s$ with arity $a(f) = s_1, \ldots, s_n \rightarrow s$ we have $s_1, \ldots, s_n \in S_1$.
(c) The constants of sort in S_1 are in $\Sigma'_s \cup C$.

Proposition 10 *Let Π be a many-sorted signature, G be a finite set of flat and linear ground Π^C-clauses, $C_s \subseteq C$ a set of constants occurring in G, and $\mathcal{T}_0 \subseteq \mathcal{T} := \mathcal{T}_0 \cup \mathcal{K}_s \cup \mathcal{K}_1$ be a local theory extension with signature $\Pi = \Pi_0 \cup \Sigma'_s \cup \Sigma_1$, which satisfies conditions* (**A1**) *and* (**A2**). *Let*

$$T := \{f(c_1, \ldots, c_n) \mid f \in \Sigma'_s, a(f) = s_1 \ldots s_n \rightarrow s, \text{ s.t. for } 1 \leq i \leq n \; c_i \text{ is a constant of sort } s_i \text{ in } \Sigma'_s \cup C\}.$$

Let ψ be a ground $(\Pi_0 \cup \Sigma'_s)^{C_s}$-formula. If ψ is a $\mathcal{T}_0 \cup \mathsf{UIF}_{\Sigma'_s} \cup \mathcal{K}_1$-general uniform interpolant of $G \wedge \mathcal{K}_s[T]$ w.r.t. $\Sigma'_s \cup C_s$, then ψ is a $\mathcal{T}_0 \cup \mathcal{K}_s \cup \mathcal{K}_1$-general uniform interpolant of G w.r.t. $\Sigma'_s \cup C_s$.

Proof: The proof is given in [34] □

Theorem 11 *Let $\mathcal{T}_0$ be a convex, stably infinite, equality interpolating, universal many-sorted theory with signature $\Pi_0 = (S, \Sigma_0, \mathsf{Pred})$ allowing quantifier elimination. Let $\Pi = (S, \Sigma_0 \cup \Sigma, \mathsf{Pred})$, G be a set of flat and linear ground Π-clauses with additional constants C, $\Sigma_s \subseteq \Sigma$, $C_s \subseteq C$ be extension functions resp. constants occurring in G and $\Sigma'_s = \Theta_{\mathcal{K}}(\Sigma_s)$ Assume that $\mathcal{T}_0 \subseteq \mathcal{T} := \mathcal{T}_0 \cup \mathcal{K}$ is a local theory extension with signature Π satisfying conditions* (**A1**) *and* (**A2**).

Then a $\mathcal{T}$-general uniform interpolant of G w.r.t. $\Sigma'_s \cup C_s$ can be computed by computing a $\mathcal{T}_0 \cup \mathsf{UIF}_{\Sigma'_s} \cup \mathcal{K}_1$-general uniform interpolant of $G \wedge \mathcal{K}_s[T]$ w.r.t. $\Sigma'_s \cup C_s$, where $T = \{f(c_1, \ldots, c_n) \mid f \in \Sigma'_s, a(f) = s_1 \ldots s_n \rightarrow s$, s.t. for $1 \leq i \leq n, c_i$ is a constant of sort s_i in $\Sigma'_s \cup C\}$. This can be achieved by (i) applying Algorithm 1 to $G \wedge \mathcal{K}_s[T]$, theory $\mathcal{T}_0 \cup \mathsf{UIF}_{\Sigma'_s} \cup \mathcal{K}_1$, and C_s, with set of terms for the instantiation $\mathsf{est}(G \wedge \mathcal{K}_s[T])$, which yields a $\Pi_s^{\overline{C_s}}$-formula Γ, where $C_s \subseteq \overline{C_s}$, and (ii) computing a $\mathcal{T}_0 \cup \mathsf{UIF}_{\Sigma'_s \cup \Sigma_1}$-uniform interpolant of Γ w.r.t. C_s.

Proof: Let $\Pi_s = (S, \Pi_0 \cup \Sigma'_s, \mathsf{Pred})$ and Γ be the $\Pi_s^{\overline{C}_s}$-formula obtained using Algorithm 1 from $G \wedge \mathcal{K}_s[T]$, and the theory $\mathcal{T}_0 \cup \mathsf{UIF}_{\Sigma'_s} \cup \mathcal{K}_1$ and C_s, with set of terms for the instantiation $\mathsf{est}(G \wedge \mathcal{K}_s[T])$. Then, by Theorem 6(2), Γ is a $\mathcal{T}_0 \cup \mathsf{UIF}_{\Sigma'_s} \cup \mathcal{K}_1$-general uniform interpolant of $G \wedge \mathcal{K}_s[T]$ w.r.t. $\Sigma'_s \cup \overline{C}_s$. Let ψ be a $\mathcal{T}_0 \cup \mathsf{UIF}_{\Sigma'_s \cup \Sigma_1}$-uniform interpolant for Γ w.r.t. C_s. Then, by Proposition 7, ψ is a $\mathcal{T}_0 \cup \mathsf{UIF}_{\Sigma'_s} \cup \mathcal{K}_1$-general uniform interpolant for $G \wedge \mathcal{K}_s[T]$ w.r.t. $\Sigma'_s \cup C_s$, i.e., by Proposition 10, a $\mathcal{T}$-general uniform interpolant of G w.r.t. $\Sigma'_s \cup C_s$. □

Example 5 *Let $\mathcal{T}_0$ be the 2-sorted disjoint combination of $LI(\mathbb{R})$ (sort n) and the (model completion of the) pure theory of equality (sort p). Let $\Sigma = \{f, g, h\}$, where $a(f) = \mathsf{n} \rightarrow \mathsf{n}$ and $a(g) = a(h) = \mathsf{p} \rightarrow \mathsf{n}$.*
Let $\mathcal{T}_0 \subseteq \mathcal{T}_0 \cup \mathcal{K}_s \cup \mathcal{K}_1$, where $\mathcal{K}_s = \forall x(g(x) \leq h(x))$ and $\mathcal{K}_1 = \mathsf{Mon}_f$,
$G = (c \leq g(p)) \wedge (h(p) \leq b) \wedge (p \approx q) \wedge (b \leq g(r)) \wedge (r \approx q) \wedge (f(b) \leq c) \wedge (f(b) \approx b),$

and $\Sigma_s = \{g, h\}$, $C_s = \{q, b\}$, *where* $a(q) = \mathsf{p}$ *and* $a(b) = \mathsf{n}$.

$T = \{g(p), g(q), g(r), h(p), h(q), h(r)\}$. *We apply Algorithm 1 to* $\mathcal{T}_0 \cup \mathsf{UIF}_{g,h} \cup \mathcal{K}_1$, $G \wedge \mathcal{K}_s[T]$ *and* $\mathsf{est}(G \wedge \mathcal{K}_s[T])$. *We need to eliminate* f *and* $\{p, r, c\}$.

Step 1: *After instantiation and introducing definitions* $\mathsf{Def} = \{p_g \approx g(p), q_g \approx g(q), r_g \approx g(r), p_h \approx h(p), q_h \approx h(q), r_h \approx h(r), b_f \approx f(b)\}$ *we obtain:*

$(c \leq p_g) \wedge (p_h \leq b) \wedge (p \approx q) \wedge (b \leq r_g) \wedge (r \approx q) \wedge (b_f \leq c) \wedge (b_f \approx b) \wedge$
$(p_g \leq p_h) \wedge (q_g \leq q_h) \wedge (r_g \leq r_h) \wedge (p_g \approx q_g) \wedge (p_h \approx q_h) \wedge (r_g \approx q_g) \wedge (r_h \approx q_h)$.

Step 2: *We classify the constants. The constants introduced for the parameters and their arguments are* $\{p_g, q_g, r_g, p_h, q_h, r_h, p, q, r\}$.

Step 3: *We eliminate* $\{b_f, c\}$ *and obtain:*

$(b \leq p_g) \wedge (p_h \leq b) \wedge (p \approx q) \wedge (b \leq r_g) \wedge (r \approx q) \wedge$
$(p_g \leq p_h) \wedge (q_g \leq q_h) \wedge (r_g \leq r_h) \wedge (p_g \approx q_g) \wedge (p_h \approx q_h) \wedge (r_g \approx q_g) \wedge (r_h \approx q_h)$.

Step 4: *We replace the new constants with the terms they denote and ignore formulae already implied by* $\mathcal{T}_0 \cup \mathcal{K}_s$ *and obtain:*

$(b \leq g(p)) \wedge (h(p) \leq b) \wedge (p \approx q) \wedge (b \leq g(r)) \wedge (r \approx q)$.

We can compute $\exists p, r (b \leq g(p) \wedge h(p) \leq b \wedge p \approx q \wedge b \leq g(r) \wedge r \approx q)$.
It can be seen that it is equivalent to $(b \leq g(q)) \wedge (h(q) \leq b) \wedge (b \leq g(q))$.

6 Definable Functions

If we want to use Proposition 7 for computing a general uniform interpolant, if $\mathcal{K}_s \neq \emptyset$ it might be problematic to compute a $\mathcal{T}_0 \cup \mathcal{K}_s$-uniform interpolant after applying Alg. 1. We show that if $\Sigma_s = \Sigma_f \cup \Sigma_s^d$, $\mathcal{K}_s = \mathsf{UIF}_{\Sigma_f} \cup \mathcal{K}_s^d$, and all symbols in Σ_s^d are definable w.r.t. $\mathcal{T}_0 \cup \mathcal{K}_s$ over the signature $\Pi_0 \cup \Sigma_f$, computing $\mathcal{T}_0 \cup \mathcal{K}_s$-uniform interpolants can be reduced to computing $\mathcal{T}_0 \cup \mathsf{UIF}_{\Sigma_f}$-interpolants.

Definition 4 *Let* $\mathcal{T}$ *be a theory with signature* $\Pi = (\Sigma, \mathsf{Pred})$, *and* $f \in \Sigma$ *with arity* n. *We say that* f *is* explicitly definable *w.r.t.* $\mathcal{T}$ *over the signature* $\Pi_1 \subseteq \Pi$ *iff there exists a* Π_1*-formula* F_f *with free variables* $x_1, \dots, x_n, y$ *such that*

$$\mathcal{T} \models \forall x_1, \dots, x_n, y((f(x_1, \dots, x_n) \approx y) \leftrightarrow F_f(x_1, \dots, x_n, y)).$$

We say that f *is* implicitly definable *w.r.t.* $\mathcal{T}$ *over the signature* Π_1 *if whenever* $\mathcal{T}'$ *is the set of formulae obtained from* $\mathcal{T}$ *by renaming the function and predicate symbols which are not in* Π_1 *(including* f*) to primed versions,*

$$\mathcal{T} \cup \mathcal{T}' \models \forall x_1, \dots, x_n(f(x_1, \dots, x_n) \approx f'(x_1, \dots, x_n)).$$

Proposition 12 *Let* T_0 *be a* $\forall\exists$ *theory with signature* Π_0, *in which ground satisfiability is decidable. Let* Σ *be a set of extension functions and let* $\Sigma_1 \subseteq \Sigma$. *Let* $\mathcal{T}_0 \subseteq \mathcal{T}_0 \cup \mathsf{UIF}_{\Sigma_1} \subseteq \mathcal{T} = \mathcal{T}_0 \cup \mathsf{UIF}_{\Sigma_1} \cup \mathcal{K}$ *be a chain of local theory extensions, where* $\mathcal{K}$ *is a set of flat and linear clauses, such that in every clause every variable occurs below an extension function in* $\Sigma \backslash \Sigma_1$. *Then testing whether a function* $f \in \Sigma \backslash \Sigma_1$ *is implicitly definable w.r.t.* $\mathcal{T}$ *over* $\Pi_1 = \Pi_0 \cup \Sigma_1$ *is decidable.*

Proof: Let $\mathcal{K}'$ be obtained by replacing every function $f \in (\Sigma \backslash \Sigma_1)$ by a primed version. If $\mathcal{T}_0 \cup \mathsf{UIF}_{\Sigma_1} \subseteq \mathcal{T}_0 \cup \mathsf{UIF}_{\Sigma_1} \cup \mathcal{K}$ is local then also $\mathcal{T}_0 \cup \mathsf{UIF}_{\Sigma_1} \subseteq \mathcal{T}_0 \cup \mathsf{UIF}_{\Sigma_1} \cup \mathcal{K}'$ is local, so by Theorem 2 (cf. [13]) $\mathcal{T}_0 \cup \mathsf{UIF}_{\Sigma_1} \subseteq \mathcal{T}_0 \cup \mathsf{UIF}_{\Sigma_1} \cup \mathcal{K} \cup \mathcal{K}'$ is local. f is implicitly definable in Π_1 iff $\mathcal{T}_0 \cup \mathsf{UIF}_{\Sigma_1} \cup \mathcal{K} \cup \mathcal{K}' \models \forall \overline{x}(f(\overline{x}) \approx f'(\overline{x}))$ iff $\mathcal{T}_0 \cup \mathcal{K} \cup \mathcal{K}' \cup f'(\overline{a}) \not\approx f(\overline{a}) \models \perp$, where $\overline{a} = a_1, \dots, a_n$ are new Skolem constants, which can be checked by hierarchical reasoning in local theory extensions. □

Theorem 13 *Let $\mathcal{T}_0 \subseteq \mathcal{T}_0 \cup \mathsf{UIF}_{\Sigma_f} \subseteq \mathcal{T} := \mathcal{T}_0 \cup \mathsf{UIF}_{\Sigma_f} \cup \mathcal{K}$ be a chain of local theory extensions, such that the signature of $\mathcal{T}_0$ is Π_0, the signature of $\mathcal{T}$ is $\Pi = \Pi_0 \cup \Sigma$, where $\Sigma = \Sigma_f \cup \Sigma_d$, and $\mathcal{K}$ is a set of Π-clauses such that for every clause in $\mathcal{K}$, every variable occurs below a Σ_d-symbol. If $f \in \Sigma_d$ is implicitly definable w.r.t. $\mathcal{T}$ over $\Pi_0 \cup \Sigma_f$ then we can use Algorithm 1 to eliminate the function symbols in Σ_d, followed by uniform interpolant computation w.r.t. $\mathcal{T}_0 \cup \mathsf{UIF}_{\Sigma_f}$ to find a $\Pi_0 \cup \Sigma_f$-formula F_f such that $\mathcal{T} \models \forall \overline{x}, y((f(\overline{x}) \approx y) \leftrightarrow F_f(\overline{x}, y))$.*

Proof: We apply Algorithm 1 to $\mathcal{T}_0 \cup \mathsf{UIF}_{\Sigma_f} \cup \mathcal{K}$, $G = f(a_1, \dots, a_n) \approx b$, $\Sigma_s := \Sigma_f$, $C_s := \{a_1, \dots, a_n, b\}$, and $T = \mathsf{est}(\Psi(G))$, for a suitable closure operator Ψ. This yields a $(\Pi_0 \cup \Sigma_f)^C$-formula $\Gamma(\overline{a}, b, \overline{c})$. We prove that if f is implicitly definable, the $\mathcal{T}_0 \cup \mathsf{UIF}_{\Sigma_f}$-uniform interpolant for Γ w.r.t. $\{a_1, \dots, a_n, b\}$, $F_f(\overline{a}, b)$, is the required explicit definition of f. The proof can be found in [34]. □

Theorem 14 *Let $\mathcal{T}_0 \subseteq \mathcal{T}_0 \cup \mathsf{UIF}_{\Sigma_1} \subseteq \mathcal{T} := \mathcal{T}_0 \cup \mathsf{UIF}_{\Sigma_f} \cup \mathcal{K}_s \subseteq \mathcal{T}_0 \cup \mathsf{UIF}_{\Sigma_f} \cup \mathcal{K}_s \cup \mathcal{K}_1$ be a chain of local theory extensions with extension functions in a set $\Sigma = \Sigma_s \cup \Sigma_1$, with $\Sigma_s = \Sigma_f \cup \Sigma_s^d$, where $\mathcal{K}_s, \mathcal{K}_1$ are flat and linear, $\mathcal{K}_s$ is a set of $\Pi_0 \cup \Sigma_s$-clauses in which every variable occurs below a function symbol in Σ_s^d, $\mathcal{K}_1$ a set of $\Pi \cup \Sigma_1$-clauses in which every variable occurs below an extension symbol in Σ_1. Let G be a set of flat and linear ground Π^C-clauses, containing the symbols in Σ_s; C_s a set of constants in G, and Γ be the $\Pi_s^{\overline{C}_s}$-formula obtained after applying Algorithm 1 to $\mathcal{T}$ and G, where $C_s \subseteq \overline{C}_s$. If all function symbols in Σ_s^d are explicitly definable w.r.t. $\mathcal{T}$ over $\Pi_0 \cup \Sigma_f$, then we can compute the $\mathcal{T}$-general uniform interpolant for G w.r.t. $\Sigma_s \cup C_s$ using a reduction to computations of uniform interpolants in $\mathcal{T}_0 \cup \mathsf{UIF}_{\Sigma_f}$.*

Proof: Let Γ be the Π_s^C-formula obtained by applying Algorithm 1. Let Γ_0 be obtained from Γ by replacing every term of the form $f(c)$, where $f \in \Sigma_s$ and $c \in C$ with a new constant $c_{f(c)}$, $\Gamma' = \Gamma_0 \wedge \bigwedge c_{f(c)} = f(c)$, and $\Gamma'' = \Gamma_0 \wedge \bigwedge F_f(c, c_{f(c)})$, where F_f is the explicit definition of f. Then $\mathcal{T}_0 \cup \mathsf{UIF}_{\Sigma_1} \cup \mathcal{K} \models (\Gamma' \leftrightarrow \Gamma'')$. We can prove that the $\mathcal{T}_0 \cup \mathsf{UIF}_{\Sigma_f}$-uniform interpolant of Γ'' w.r.t. C_s is a $\mathcal{T}$-general uniform interpolant of G w.r.t. $\Sigma_s \cup C_s$. For details cf. [34]. □

Example 6 *Consider the following chain of theory extensions of $\mathcal{T}_0 = LI(\mathbb{R})$: $\mathcal{T}_0 \subseteq \mathcal{T}_0 \cup \mathsf{UIF}_h \subseteq \mathcal{T}_0 \cup \mathsf{UIF}_h \cup \mathcal{K}$, where:*

$$\mathcal{K} = \{\forall x(x \leq 3 \rightarrow g(x) \leq f(x) \leq 3x), \forall x(x > 3 \rightarrow f(x) \approx h(x)), \forall x(3x \approx g(x))\}.$$

Let $\Sigma_s = \{f, g, h\}$, $C_s = \{u\}$. We compute $\exists c(c \leq g(u) \wedge c \approx f(c))$ as follows: We show that f is definable w.r.t. $\Pi_0 \cup \{h\}$: Let $\mathcal{K}' = \{\forall x(x \leq 3 \rightarrow g'(x) \leq f'(x))$, $\forall x(x \leq 3 \rightarrow f'(x) \leq 3x), \forall x(x > 3 \rightarrow f(x) \approx h(x)), \forall x(3x \approx g'(x))\}$. We have the chain of theory extensions: $\mathcal{T}_0 \subseteq \mathcal{T}_0 \cup \mathsf{UIF}_h \subseteq \mathcal{T}_0 \cup \mathsf{UIF}_f \cup \mathcal{K} \cup \mathcal{K}'$. This can be *used for checking that* $\mathcal{T}_0 \cup \mathcal{K} \cup \mathcal{K}' \models \forall x(f(x) \approx f'(x))$. *We can prove that* g *is definable w.r.t.* $\Pi_0 \cup \{h\}$; $F_g(a,b) := 3a \approx b$.

We construct a explicit definition for f *by applying Algorithm 1 as follows: The extension* $\mathcal{T}_0 \subseteq \mathcal{T}_0 \cup \mathcal{K}$ *is* Ψ*-local if we choose a closure operator for computing instances as explained in the proof of Theorem 13 (cf. [34]). We instantiate and purify* $\mathcal{K} \cup (f(a) \approx b)$ *using* $\Psi(\mathsf{est}(f(a) \approx b)) = \Psi(\{f(a)\}) = \{f(a), g(a), h(a)\}$. *Then* $\mathcal{K}[\Psi(\mathsf{est}(f(a) \approx b))]$ *is:*
$\{(a \leq 3 \rightarrow g(a) \leq f(a) \leq 3a), (a > 3 \rightarrow f(a) \approx h(a)), (3a \approx g(a)) \wedge f(a) \approx b\}$.
With the definition $\mathsf{Def} := \{a_f \approx f(a), a_g \approx g(a), a_h \approx h(a)\}$ *we obtain:*

$$(a \leq 3 \rightarrow a_g \leq a_f \leq 3a) \wedge (a > 3 \rightarrow a_f \approx a_h) \wedge (3a \approx a_g) \wedge (a_f \approx b).$$

We eliminate a_f, a_g, *then replace* a_h *back with* $h(a)$ *and obtain:*

$$F_f(a,b) := (a \leq 3 \rightarrow b \approx 3a) \wedge (a > 3 \rightarrow b \approx h(a)).$$

We compute $\exists c(c \leq g(u) \wedge c \approx f(c))$ **as Follows:** *We replace* $f(c)$ *with* d_1, $g(u)$ *with* d_2 *and obtain:* $\exists d_1 \exists d_2 \exists c(c \leq d_2 \wedge g(u) \approx d_2 \wedge c \approx d_1 \wedge f(c) \approx d_1)$. *We then replace the atoms* $f(c) \approx d_1$ *and* $g(u) \approx d_2$ *with the definitions and obtain:*

$$\exists d_1 \exists d_2 \exists c(c \leq d_2 \wedge 3u \approx d_2 \wedge c \approx d_1 \wedge (c \leq 3 \rightarrow d_1 \approx 3c) \wedge (c > 3 \rightarrow d_1 \approx h(c)))$$
$$\equiv 0 \leq 3u \vee \exists d_1(d_1 \leq 3u \wedge d_1 > 3 \wedge d_1 \approx h(d_1)).$$

To eliminate d_1 *we can use a method for uniform interpolation in* $\mathcal{T}_0 \cup \mathsf{UIF}_{\{h\}}$.

7 Conclusions

We generalized the notion of cover [6] and uniform interpolant [2] to a notion of general uniform interpolant, and proved a semantical characterization of uniform interpolants generalizing a result in [2]. We then proposed a method for symbol elimination in local theory extensions and analyzed possibilities of using it to compute general uniform interpolants for ground formulae w.r.t. such theories. We showed that general uniform interpolants can be computed in extensions with uninterpreted function symbols, then studied general uniform unification for "semi-interpreted" extension symbols and identified conditions (somewhat similar to the conditions on combinations of tame theories in [3], or the acyclicity conditions in [2]) under which the computation of uniform interpolants can be reduced to the computation of uniform interpolants for extensions with uninterpreted function symbols. Finally, we proposed a method for computing explicit definitions (w.r.t. local theory extensions) for functions implicitly definable in terms of the base signature and uninterpreted function symbols, and showed that we can use these definitions to reduce the task of computing general uniform interpolants to uniform interpolation in extensions with uninterpreted function symbols. Example 3 shows that in some cases we cannot construct general uniform interpolants, but that some infinite sets of formulae might have the properties of general uniform interpolants. Such phenomena were studied in description logics, where it was shown that uniform interpolants do not always exist, but can often be expressed using fixpoint operators. In [2] a constraint superposition calculus was used to compute uniform interpolants in the theory of uninterpreted function symbols, and was proved to terminate. However, such calculi might not terminate in the presence of additional axioms. It is not clear whether forms of symbol elimination based on resolution and/or superposition used for interpolant generation [7] can be used to obtain uniform interpolants. We hope that calculi such as the melting calculus [11] we studied in relationship with local theory extensions in [9,10], could be used for obtaining finite representations of infinite sets of clauses.

Acknowledgment. We thank the reviewers for their helpful comments. The research reported here was funded by the Deutsche Forschungsgemeinschaft (DFG, German Research Foundation) – grant 465447331.

Disclosure of Interests. The author has no competing interests to declare that are relevant to the content of this article.

References

1. Bruttomesso, R., Ghilardi, S., Ranise, S.: Quantifier-free interpolation in combinations of equality interpolating theories. ACM Trans. Comput. Log. 15(1), 5:1–5:34 (2014)
2. Calvanese, D., Ghilardi, S., Gianola, A., Montali, M., Rivkin, A.: Model completeness, uniform interpolants and superposition calculus. J. Autom. Reason. **65**(7), 941–969 (2021)
3. Calvanese, D., Ghilardi, S., Gianola, A., Montali, M., Rivkin, A.: Combination of uniform interpolants via Beth definability. J. Autom. Reason. **66**(3), 409–435 (2022)
4. Ganzinger, H.: Relating semantic and proof-theoretic concepts for polynominal time decidability of uniform word problems. In: 16th Annual IEEE Symposium on Logic in Computer Science, Boston, Massachusetts, USA, June 16-19, 2001, Proceedings, pp. 81–90. IEEE Computer Society (2001)
5. Ghilardi, S., Gianola, A., Kapur, D.: Uniform interpolants in EUF: Algorithms using DAG-representations. Log. Methods Comput. Sci., 18(2) (2022)
6. Gulwani, S., Musuvathi, M.: Cover algorithms and their combination. In: Drossopoulou, S. (ed.) ESOP 2008. LNCS, vol. 4960, pp. 193–207. Springer, Heidelberg (2008). https://doi.org/10.1007/978-3-540-78739-6_16
7. Hoder, K., Kovács, L., Voronkov, A.: Interpolation and symbol elimination in Vampire. In: Giesl, J., Hähnle, R. (eds.) IJCAR 2010. LNCS (LNAI), vol. 6173, pp. 188–195. Springer, Heidelberg (2010). https://doi.org/10.1007/978-3-642-14203-1_16
8. Hodges, W.: Model theory, vol. 42. Cambridge University Press, Encyclopedia of mathematics and its applications (1993)
9. Horbach, M., Sofronie-Stokkermans, V.: Obtaining finite local theory axiomatizations via saturation. In: Fontaine, P., Ringeissen, C., Schmidt, R.A. (eds.) FroCoS 2013. LNCS (LNAI), vol. 8152, pp. 198–213. Springer, Heidelberg (2013). https://doi.org/10.1007/978-3-642-40885-4_14
10. Horbach, M., Sofronie-Stokkermans, V.: Locality transfer: From constrained axiomatizations to reachability predicates. In: Demri, S., Kapur, D., Weidenbach, C. (eds.) IJCAR 2014. LNCS (LNAI), vol. 8562, pp. 192–207. Springer, Cham (2014). https://doi.org/10.1007/978-3-319-08587-6_14

11. Horbach, M., Weidenbach, C.: Deciding the inductive validity of FOR ALL THERE EXISTS * queries. In E. Grädel and R. Kahle, editors, *Computer Science Logic, 23rd international Workshop, CSL 2009, 18th Annual Conference of the EACSL, Proceedings*. LNCS (LNAI), vol. 5771, pp. 332–347. Springer (2009)
12. Ihlemann, C., Jacobs, S., Sofronie-Stokkermans, V.: On local reasoning in verification. In: Ramakrishnan, C.R., Rehof, J. (eds.) Tools and Algorithms for the Construction and Analysis of Systems, 14th International Conference, TACAS 2008, Held as Part of the Joint European Conferences on Theory and Practice of Software, ETAPS 2008, Proceedings, LNCS (LNAI), vol. 4963, pp. 265–281. Springer (2008)
13. Ihlemann, C., Sofronie-Stokkermans, V.: On hierarchical reasoning in combinations of theories. In: Giesl, J., Hähnle, R. (eds.) IJCAR 2010. LNCS (LNAI), vol. 6173, pp. 30–45. Springer, Heidelberg (2010). https://doi.org/10.1007/978-3-642-14203-1_4
14. Jhala, R., McMillan, K.L.: Interpolant-based transition relation approximation. In: Etessami, K., Rajamani, S.K. (eds.) CAV 2005. LNCS, vol. 3576, pp. 39–51. Springer, Heidelberg (2005). https://doi.org/10.1007/11513988_6
15. Kapur, D., Majumdar, R., Zarba, C.G.: Interpolation for data structures. In: Young, M., Devanbu, P.T. (eds.) Proceedings of the 14th ACM SIGSOFT International Symposium on Foundations of Software Engineering, FSE 2006, pp. 105–116. ACM (2006)
16. Konev, B., Walther, D., Wolter, F.: Forgetting and uniform interpolation in extensions of the description logic $\mathcal{EL}$. In: Grau, B.C., Horrocks, I., Motik, B., Sattler, U. (eds.) *Proceedings of the 22nd International Workshop on Description Logics (DL 2009)*, vol. 477. CEUR Workshop Proceedings. CEUR-WS.org (2009)
17. Konev, B., Walther, D., Wolter, F.: Forgetting and uniform interpolation in large-scale description logic terminologies. In: Boutilier, C. (ed.) IJCAI 2009, Proceedings of the 21st International Joint Conference on Artificial Intelligence, pp. 830–835 (2009)
18. Lutz, C., Wolter, F.: Foundations for uniform interpolation and forgetting in expressive description logics. In: Walsh, T. (ed.) IJCAI 2011, Proceedings of the 22nd International Joint Conference on Artificial Intelligence, pp. 989–995. IJCAI/AAAI (2011)
19. McAllester, D.A.: Automatic recognition of tractability in inference relations. J. ACM **40**(2), 284–303 (1993)
20. McMillan, K.L.: Interpolation and SAT-based model checking. In: Hunt, W.A., Somenzi, F. (eds.) CAV 2003. LNCS, vol. 2725, pp. 1–13. Springer, Heidelberg (2003). https://doi.org/10.1007/978-3-540-45069-6_1
21. McMillan, K.L.: An interpolating theorem prover. In: Jensen, K., Podelski, A. (eds.) Tools and Algorithms for the Construction and Analysis of Systems, 10th International Conference, TACAS 2004, Held as Part of the Joint European Conferences on Theory and Practice of Software, ETAPS 2004, Proceedings, LNCS (LNAI), vol. 2988, pp. 16–30. Springer (2004)
22. McMillan, K.L.: Applications of Craig interpolants in model checking. In: Halbwachs, N., Zuck, L.D. (eds.) Tools and Algorithms for the Construction and Analysis of Systems, 11th International Conference, TACAS 2005, Held as Part of the Joint European Conferences on Theory and Practice of Software, ETAPS 2005, Proceedings, LNCS (LNAI), vol. 3440, pp. 1–12. Springer (2005)
23. Peuter, D., Sofronie-Stokkermans, V.: On invariant synthesis for parametric systems. In: Fontaine, P. (ed.) CADE 2019. LNCS (LNAI), vol. 11716, pp. 385–405. Springer, Cham (2019). https://doi.org/10.1007/978-3-030-29436-6_23

24. Peuter, D., Sofronie-Stokkermans, V., Thunert, S.: On P-interpolation in local theory extensions and applications to the study of interpolation in the description logics $\mathcal{EL}$, $\mathcal{EL}^+$. In: Pientka, B., Tinelli, C. (eds.) Automated Deduction - CADE 29 - 29th International Conference on Automated Deduction, Proceedings, LNCS (LNAI), 14132, pp. 419–437. Springer (2023)
25. Sofronie-Stokkermans, V.: Hierarchic reasoning in local theory extensions. In: Nieuwenhuis, R. (ed.) CADE 2005. LNCS (LNAI), vol. 3632, pp. 219–234. Springer, Heidelberg (2005). https://doi.org/10.1007/11532231_16
26. Sofronie-Stokkermans, V.: Interpolation in local theory extensions. In: Furbach, U., Shankar, N. (eds.) IJCAR 2006. LNCS (LNAI), vol. 4130, pp. 235–250. Springer, Heidelberg (2006). https://doi.org/10.1007/11814771_21
27. Sofronie-Stokkermans, V.: Interpolation in local theory extensions. Logical Methods Comput. Sci. **4**(4) (2008)
28. Sofronie-Stokkermans, V.: Hierarchical reasoning for the verification of parametric systems. In: Giesl, J., Hähnle, R. (eds.) IJCAR 2010. LNCS (LNAI), vol. 6173, pp. 171–187. Springer, Heidelberg (2010). https://doi.org/10.1007/978-3-642-14203-1_15
29. Sofronie-Stokkermans, V.: Hierarchical reasoning and model generation for the verification of parametric hybrid systems. In: Bonacina, M.P. (ed.) CADE 2013. LNCS (LNAI), vol. 7898, pp. 360–376. Springer, Heidelberg (2013). https://doi.org/10.1007/978-3-642-38574-2_25
30. Sofronie-Stokkermans, V.: On interpolation and symbol elimination in theory extensions. In: Olivetti, N., Tiwari, A. (eds.) IJCAR 2016. LNCS (LNAI), vol. 9706, pp. 273–289. Springer, Cham (2016). https://doi.org/10.1007/978-3-319-40229-1_19
31. Sofronie-Stokkermans, V.: Representation theorems and locality for subsumption testing and interpolation in the description logics $\mathcal{EL}$, $\mathcal{EL}^+$ and their extensions with n-ary roles and numerical domains. Fund. Inform. **156**(3–4), 361–411 (2017)
32. Sofronie-Stokkermans, V.: On interpolation and symbol elimination in theory extensions. Log. Methods Comput. Sci., 14(3) (2018)
33. Sofronie-Stokkermans, V.: Parametric systems: Verification and synthesis. Fund. Inform. **173**(2–3), 91–138 (2020)
34. Sofronie-Stokkermans, V.: On symbol elimination and uniform interpolation in theory extensions. (Extended Version) Arxiv:2506.01664 [cs.LO], https://doi.org/10.48550/arXiv.2506.01664 (2025)
35. Sofronie-Stokkermans, V., Ihlemann, C.: Automated reasoning in some local extensions of ordered structures. In: 37th International Symposium on Multiple-Valued Logic, ISMVL 2007. IEEE Computer Society (2007)
36. Sofronie-Stokkermans, V., Ihlemann, C.: Automated reasoning in some local extensions of ordered structures. Multiple-Valued Logic Soft Comput. **13**(4–6), 397–414 (2007)

What's Decidable About Arrays With Sums?

Roland Herrmann[1(✉)] and Philipp Rümmer[1,2]

[1] University of Regensburg, Regensburg, Germany
{roland.herrmann,philipp.ruemmer}@ur.de
[2] Uppsala University, Uppsala, Sweden

Abstract. The theory of arrays, supported by virtually all SMT solvers, is one of the most important theories in program verification. The standard theory of arrays, which provides *read* and *write* operations, has been extended in various different ways in past research, among others, by adding extensionality, constant arrays, function mapping (resulting in combinatorial array logic), counting, and projections. This paper studies array theories extended with *sum constraints,* which capture properties of the sum of all elements of an integer array. The paper shows that the theory of extensional arrays extended with constant arrays and sum constraints can be decided in non-deterministic polynomial time. The decision procedure works both for finite and infinite index sorts, as long as the cardinality is fixed a priori. In contrast, adding sum constraints to combinatorial array logic gives rise to an undecidable theory. The paper concludes by studying several fragments in between standard arrays with sums and combinatorial arrays with sums, aiming at providing a complete characterization of decidable and undecidable fragments.

1 Introduction

Arrays are fundamental in Computer Science because they provide a structured way to store and manage multiple values of the same type efficiently. They allow fast access to elements through indexing, enabling optimization of algorithms in terms of both time and space complexity. Reasoning about arrays is therefore a crucial part of verification of programs, and the theory of arrays is one of the most important theories supported by SMT solvers. The standard theory of arrays, proposed by McCarthy [10], has been extended over the years in various directions; among others, by adding extensionality, constant arrays and function mapping (resulting in combinatorial array logic CAL [11]), counting [5], or projections [3], aiming at a theory in which programs and specifications can be concisely encoded and efficiently analyzed.

In this paper, we consider array theories extended with *sum constraints,* which capture properties of the sum of elements in an integer array. Sum constraints are frequently used in specifications and are made available in specification languages like JML [7] and ACSL [2] in the form of *extended quantifiers,* yet are currently not supported by any SMT solver. In verification tools,

C. Barrett and U. Waldmann (Eds.): CADE 2025, LNAI 15943, pp. 56–74, 2025.
https://doi.org/10.1007/978-3-031-99984-0_4

sum constraints are therefore handled through quantified axioms [8] or intricate encodings [1] that are passed to the SMT solver. Exploring the possibility to support sum constraints directly in an SMT solver, we survey known decidability results for arrays extended with sums. We provide a simplified proof that Combinatorial Array Logic extended with sum constraints is undecidable. We then propose a new decision procedure for extensional arrays extended with sum constraints, that operates for both finite and infinite index sets uniformly, as long as their cardinality is fixed a priori. We overcome the interaction between the residual sums and the default values arising from constant arrays uniformly. The decision procedure is presented in a sequential manner, grouped into a preparation phase, simple rule applications, and rewriting of the sum constraints. This structure makes the procedure particularly comprehensible and easy to reason about.

Contributions of the Paper: (1) We formalize our view of sum constraints and prove that the extension of CAL by sum constraints is undecidable in Sect. 4. (2) We survey results from the literature about arrays with sums in Sect. 5. (3) Our main contribution is a decision procedure for the satisfiability problem of quantifier-free formulae of extensional arrays with constant arrays and sums in Sect. 6, which runs in non-deterministic polynomial time. (4) We examine further extensions of our fragment on decidability in Sect. 7. Overall, this results in an overview of decidability and undecidability results and the problems that arise when we add sum constraints, serving both as a reference and starting point for ongoing research.

2 Related Work

A basic theory of arrays was introduced by McCarthy [10]. The satisfiability problem of quantifier-free formulae in an (extensional or non-extensional) array theory is NP-complete [15]. Our work uses the results and the framework of Combinatory Array Logic (CAL) [11] as a starting point, which extends extensional array theory by adding a constant array operator and element-wise function applications. An extension to CAL is Cartesian Array Logic (CaAL) [3], which supports n-ary arrays and adds a projection operator that corresponds to partial function application; adding projections to the theory comes at the cost of NEXPTIME-complexity of the corresponding satisfiability problem. All these theories have in common that the operators used in the constraints are designed to extract single elements of the array or act on an array uniformly. In contrast, an extension to statements specific to arrays as a whole is provided by the Array Folds Logic (AFL) [5], which enables counting elements in an array. However, AFL can not reason about the sum of all elements in an array. The projection operator in CaAL can only model finite sums (see Example 1). The work of Rodrigo Raya [13] is, to the best of our knowledge, the only decision procedure supporting summation of elements for infinite arrays. However, the results from the summation process are solely used to reason about cardinality constraints on index sets, and can neither be stored in another array nor compared to other array elements. The details are discussed in Sect. 5.

3 Preliminaries

We give some preliminaries and recollect the notions of the array theories that we refer to later. For foundations on logic we refer to [6]. First, we formally define the notion of a theory.

Definition 1 (Signature). *Let Σ^S be a set of sorts, Σ^F a set of function symbols and Σ^P a set of predicate symbols, where each $f \in \Sigma^F$, respectively $p \in \Sigma^P$ is endowed with a corresponding arity and sorts from Σ^S. Then we call the triple $\Sigma = (\Sigma^S, \Sigma^F, \Sigma^P)$ a signature.*

Definition 2 (Theory). *Let $\Sigma = (\Sigma^S, \Sigma^F, \Sigma^P)$ be a signature. A first-order formula over Σ is called Σ-sentence if it has no free variables. A Σ-theory is a signature Σ together with a collection of Σ-sentences closed under entailment.*

Axioms of particular interest are those that make a statement about the cardinality of our theory.

Definition 3 (cardinality axioms). *Let $n \in \mathbb{N}$. We define the following axioms (independent of the underlying signature) for theories with equality:*

$$\exists x_1, \ldots, x_n. \bigwedge_{(i,j)\in\{1,\ldots,n\}^2, i\neq j} x_i \neq x_j \qquad (\geq n) \qquad (1)$$

$$\forall x_1, \ldots, x_n. \bigvee_{(i,j)\in\{1,\ldots,n\}^2, i\neq j} x_i = x_j \qquad (< n) \qquad (2)$$

We say a theory

- *has cardinality at least n if it includes the axiom $(\geq n)$.*
- *has cardinality less than n if it includes the axiom $(< n)$.*
- *has cardinality n if it includes $(\geq n)$ and $(< n+1)$.*
- *is bounded if there exists an $n \in \mathbb{N}$ such that it includes $(< n)$.*
- *is unbounded if it includes the axioms $(\geq n)$ for all $n \in \mathbb{N}$.*
- *has fixed cardinality if it is either infinite or there exists an $n \in \mathbb{N}$ such that it has cardinality n.*

We describe array theories as conservative extensions of some base theory.

Definition 4 (conservative extension). *Let T_i be a theory with signature Σ_i and axioms A_i for $i \in \{1, 2\}$. Then T_2 is called a conservative extension of T_1 if (1) $\Sigma_1 \subseteq \Sigma_2$, and (2) formulae ϕ definable in T_1 are entailed by A_1 iff they are entailed by A_2, i.e., $A_1 \models \phi$ iff $A_2 \models \phi$.*

We assume a base theory with satisfiability problem of quantifier-free formulae in NP. For our purposes, arrays are introduced by adding a new sort denoted by $I \Rightarrow E$, for two sorts I and E, where we call I the index sort and E the element sort. Nested array sorts are allowed. The function symbols, predicate symbols, and axioms depend on the array theory we want to consider. In any case, they are conservative extensions of our base theory. The most basic array theory, also known as McCarthy arrays, can be defined as follows.

Definition 5. *Let T be our base theory with signature $(\Sigma^S, \Sigma^F, \Sigma^P)$ and corresponding axioms. Then the associated array theory is the following extension.*

- *Σ^S is extended to Σ^S_A, which is the least set such that $\Sigma^S \subseteq \Sigma^S_A$ and for all $I, E \in \Sigma^S_A$ we have $(I \Rightarrow E) \in \Sigma^S_A$.*
- *for all sorts $I, E \in \Sigma^S_A$, the set Σ^F is extended by an operator $read(\cdot,\cdot) : ((I \Rightarrow E), I) \rightarrow E$, sometimes also called select, and an operator $write(\cdot,\cdot,\cdot) : ((I \Rightarrow E), I, E) \rightarrow (I \Rightarrow E)$, sometimes called store. We abbreviate $read(a, i)$ by $a[i]$.*

The following axioms, representing the semantics of read and write, are added to extend our base theory to the theory of McCarthy arrays:

$$\forall a : (I \Rightarrow E), i : I, v : E. \qquad write(a, i, v)[i] = v \tag{3}$$

$$\forall a : (I \Rightarrow E), i : I, j : I, v : E. \qquad i = j \vee write(a, i, v)[j] = a[j]. \tag{4}$$

The above extension is indeed conservative. As a next extension, we consider extensionality of arrays, that is, we can reason about equality of arrays as a whole. Therefore, we add the following axioms:

$$\forall a : (I \Rightarrow E), b : (I \Rightarrow E). \exists i : I. \qquad a = b \vee a[i] \neq b[i]. \tag{5}$$

We call the resulting theory the extensional array theory. If the satisfiability problem of the base theory is in NP, then the satisfiability problem of a formula in the corresponding extensional array theory is in NP, too [15, Theorem 3]. To show NP membership, we can abstract away the array symbols and end up with an equi-satisfiable formula in the base theory.

For the rest of the paper, we assume that the quantifier-free theory of integers without multiplication, called Linear Integer Arithmetic (LIA) (we omit the prefix "quantifier-free" in the following), is included in the base theory, and we assume a "core solver" that decides satisfiability of quantifier-free formulae in the base theory in non-deterministic polynomial time. Note that LIA can be reduced in polynomial time to Presburger Arithmetic (PA), that is, the theory of natural numbers without multiplication, which is NP-complete.

Closely related to summation is the star operator introduced in [12].

Remark 1 (LIA).* For later use, we introduce the notion of a star operator on sets of integer vectors. Let $S \subseteq \mathbb{Z}^n$ be a set of integer vectors, then we define

$$S^* := \left\{ \sum_{i=1}^{n} \boldsymbol{x}_i \mid n \in \mathbb{N} \text{ and } \boldsymbol{x}_1, \ldots, \boldsymbol{x}_n \in S \right\}. \tag{6}$$

Then LIA* is the theory of Linear Integer Arithmetic extended by constraints of the form $\boldsymbol{x} \in \{\boldsymbol{z} \mid F(\boldsymbol{z})\}^*$, where $\boldsymbol{x}$ is a vector of integer terms and $\boldsymbol{z}$ a vector of integer variables, both of size $n \in \mathbb{N}$, and F is a LIA formula in which the variables $\boldsymbol{z}$ can occur. In [12] it is shown that the satisfiability problem of LIA* formulae is NP-complete.

Another important extension of extensional arrays is Combinatorial Array Logic (CAL), which adds constant array constructors $K(\cdot) : E \to (I \Rightarrow E)$ and point-wise function applications $map_f : (I \Rightarrow E)^n \to (I \Rightarrow E)$ as new function symbols to the signature, where $f : E^n \to E$ is a function in the base theory. The semantics of the new functions are defined by the following axioms:

$$\forall v : E, i : I. \qquad K(v)[i] = v. \tag{7}$$

$$\forall a_1, \ldots, a_n : (I \Rightarrow E), i : I. \quad map_f(a_1, \ldots, a_n)[i] = f(a_1[i], \ldots, a_n[i]) \tag{8}$$

The satisfiability problem of quantifier-free CAL formulae is NP-complete as well. The decision procedure provided in [11] follows the same idea as those for the theory of extensional arrays: one carries reads through map_f terms and adds one additional read for every array, representing all values that are not constrained, to detect contradictions arising from the constant array operator.

4 Sum Constraints

We formalize what we mean by a sum constraint, which is a constraint on an array that refers to the sum of all array elements. The difficulty with sums is that we make a statement about all elements in the array, of which there may be infinitely many. There are two aspects we need to take into account: whether the sum exists, and, if it does, what its value is. Finite sums always exist, while the sum of infinite arrays only exists if almost all array elements have value zero. To address this undefinedness, we introduce a new relation symbol $sum : ((I \Rightarrow \mathbb{Z}), \mathbb{Z})$, which intuitively holds for an array a and an integer k if the sum of the elements of a exists and is equal to k.

The semantics of sum is defined by two axiom schemata. Evidently the axiom only applies to arrays with $\mathbb{Z}$ as element sort. If an array has only finitely many non-zero elements, the sum exists, which is expressed by the following axiom schema, where $distinct(i_1, \ldots, i_n)$ evaluates to true if and only if $i_1, \ldots, i_n$ are pairwise distinct:

$$\forall i_1, \ldots i_n : I, v_1, \ldots, v_n, w : \mathbb{Z}.\ distinct(i_1, \ldots, i_n) \to \left(sum(write(\ldots(write(K(0), i_1, v_1) \ldots i_n, v_n), w) \leftrightarrow w = \sum_{i=1}^{n} v_i \right) \tag{9}$$

We used the fact that an array which is zero almost everywhere arises from a finite number of write operators from $K(0)$. However, the number of non-zero elements is not known in general, which results in infinitely many axioms, one for each $n \in \mathbb{N}$.

As finiteness cannot be expressed in first-order logic, as a consequence of the compactness Theorem [6, Theorem 4.6], we use an axiom schema in second-order logic to describe the cases in which a sum is not defined. We write *injective*(f) for the formula expressing injectivity of f:

$$\forall a : (I \Rightarrow \mathbb{Z}), v : \mathbb{Z}.\\ \Big(\exists f : \mathbb{Z} \rightarrow I.\big(\mathit{injective}(f) \land \forall n : \mathbb{Z}.\ a[f(n)] \neq 0\big)\Big) \rightarrow \neg \mathit{sum}(a, v) \tag{10}$$

Definition 6. *Let T be a base theory including LIA, where all sorts have fixed cardinality. Then we define Summation Array Logic (SAL) as the extensional array theory extended by the constant array operator and the sum predicate and their corresponding axioms.*

With our description of sums, we obtain the following undecidability result. The result is related to the one given in [13], which however holds for a richer array theory including Boolean algebra expressions over index sets (see Sect. 5.2).

Theorem 1. *Consider CAL extended by sum constraints and $\mathbb{Z}$ with Linear Integer Arithmetic as index and element sort. Then satisfiability of quantifier-free formulae in the resulting theory is undecidable.*

Proof. We prove this by reduction from Hilbert's tenth problem [9], which states that the problem whether diophantine equations have a solution is undecidable. To this end, it suffices to show that we can express equations of the form $z = x \cdot y$ for integer variables $x, y, z \in \mathbb{Z}$. The function $f : \mathbb{Z} \rightarrow \mathbb{Z}$, which evaluates to 1 if its argument is greater or equal to zero, and to zero otherwise, can be defined in LIA by the formula $(x_1 < 0 \land x_2 = 0) \lor (x_1 \geq 0 \land x_2 = 1)$. Furthermore, the function $g : \mathbb{Z}^2 \rightarrow \mathbb{Z}$ with $g(x_1, x_2) = x_2$ if $x_1 = 1$ and $g(x_1, x_2) = 0$ otherwise, can be defined in LIA by the formula $(x_3 = x_2 \land x_1 = 1) \lor (x_3 = 0 \land x_1 \neq 1)$. Hence, we can define the following formula in CAL.

$$b = \mathit{map}_f(a) \land \mathit{sum}(b, x) \land c = \mathit{map}_g(b, K(y)) \land \mathit{sum}(c, z). \tag{11}$$

The first constraint requires b to have values 0 or 1, since f has those as its image. Together with the second constraint on the sum of b, b necessarily has x entries with 1 and the rest with 0 in order to be satisfiable. Finally, the application of g to b and $K(y)$ sets all non-zero values of b to y and the rest to 0, which enforces b to have exactly x entries with the value y, i.e. $\mathit{sum}(c, z) \Leftrightarrow z = \sum_{i=1}^{x} y = x \cdot y$.

5 Arrays With Sums in the Literature

5.1 Cardinality of the Index Sort

Consider any array theory with finite (bounded) index sorts. If we add sum constraints, we obviously maintain decidability: we may simply impose reads on all array indices. Then we can replace the sum operator by the actual formula computing the sum, as in axiom 9. This transforms any formula with sum constraints to an ordinary formula in the theory without sum constraints. However, this will lead to a $\mathcal{O}(|I|)$ blowup of the formula for the imposed reads, where I is the index sort.

Lemma 1. *Let T be an array theory whose satisfiability problem is decidable and whose index sorts are bounded. Then the theory extended by sum constraints is decidable as well.*

Another procedure that is built on CAL is the Cartesian Array Logic (CaAL) [3]. It is introduced to represent quantum states as multi-dimensional arrays of the form $\{0,1\}^n \Rightarrow \mathbb{C}$, where $\mathbb{C}$ denotes the complex numbers. In this logic, a projection operator is available, which (as a special case) can model sum constraints, as shown by the following example.

Example 1. Let $proj_k(a, i)$ denote the projection operator from CaAL to the array $a : \{0,1\}^n \Rightarrow \mathbb{C}$, which is the projection of the k-th index variable to the value i, defined as follows using notation for multidimensional arrays:

$$proj_k(a,i)[i_0,\ldots,i_{n-1}] = a[i_0,\ldots,\underbrace{i}_{k\text{-th position}},\ldots,i_{n-1}]. \tag{12}$$

Now consider $a : \{0,1\}^n \Rightarrow \mathbb{C}$. Then the sum s of a can be calculated by the following formula, where map_+ denotes element-wise addition of arrays:

$$a_0 = a \wedge s = a_n[\,] \wedge \bigwedge_{i=1}^{n} a_i = map_+(proj_0(a_{i-1}, 0), proj_0(a_{i-1}, 1)) \tag{13}$$

Although the size of this formula is only linear in n, solving the formula boils down to constructing a number of read operations that is exponential in n; in the end, a decision procedure has to construct reads for all locations of the array a. This is an explanation for why the decision procedure in [3] runs in non-deterministic exponential time in general. The construction of the sum using the projection operator is not possible for infinite index sorts in CaAL. Hence, the proof of Theorem 1 does not carry over to the case of CaAL.

In order to handle arrays with infinite index sort, it is necessary that we have information about all elements in the array, even if they do not explicitly occur in a constraint. In the decision procedure for CAL [11], a fresh index variable is introduced to represent the default value. However, this is only possible because the index sort has infinite cardinality. Some changes in the decision procedure for CAL are necessary to support finite index sorts [11].

5.2 Other Sum Constraints

A different definition of a sum constraint is used by Rodrigo Raya in [13]. In [14], Raya et al. describe a satisfiability preserving translation from CAL to quantifier-free Boolean algebra formulae with Presburger Arithmetic and interpreted index sets (QFBAPAI). A formula in QFBAPAI has the following form [14, Def. 5]

$$F(S_1,\ldots,S_k) \wedge \bigwedge_{i=1}^{k} S_i = \{r \in I \mid \varphi_i(x_1[r],\ldots,x_n[r],c_1,\ldots,c_m)\}, \tag{14}$$

where F is a Boolean algebra formula with Linear Integer Arithmetic constraints on the cardinality of the set variables $S_1, \ldots, S_k$, φ_i are formulae in the existential fragment of the element theory, I is the index sort of the arrays, $x_1, \ldots, x_n$ are array variables and $c_1, \ldots, c_m$ are variables of the element sort. Without going into further detail, the idea behind the transformation is to abstract away the constraints in the element theory to constraints on index sets, for example a read constraint $v = \mathit{read}(a, i)$ can be equivalently described by $\{i\} \subseteq \{l \mid a[l] = v\}$ as part of the formula F. In [13], sum constraints are added to this logic which results in formulae of the following form

$$F(S_1, \ldots, S_k, \boldsymbol{\sigma}) \wedge \bigwedge_{i=1}^{k} S_i = \{n \in I \mid \varphi_i(\boldsymbol{c}[n])\} \wedge \boldsymbol{\sigma} = \sum (\!|\boldsymbol{c}[n] \mid \varphi_0(\boldsymbol{c}[n])|\!), \quad (15)$$

where $\boldsymbol{c}$ is a tuple of arrays and $(\!|\cdot|\!)$ denotes multi-sets. First note that this does not allow variables in the element sort, which would result in undecidability similar to Theorem 1 and is stated in [13, Corollary 6]. The summation process has the same intended semantics as ours in Sect. 4.

Example 2. A minimal example of a sum in QFBAPAI with sums is the following formula

$$|S| < \sigma \wedge S = \{n \in I \mid \varphi(c[n])\} \wedge \sigma = \sum (\!|c[n] \mid \varphi_0(c[n])|\!). \quad (16)$$

The formula φ specifies the set of indices included in S, depending on the value of the array c at the index. Formula φ could for example select those indices where the value at this index is even: $\varphi(x) \equiv \exists y.\ 2 \cdot y = x$. Formula φ_0 restricts the values of the array that add to the sum. To obtain the sum over the whole array we simply choose $\varphi_0 \equiv \mathit{true}$. Then the original formula translates to "the number of indices where an even value is stored is smaller than the sum over all values of the array". This is satisfiable for the array $K(0)$. No matter how we choose φ and φ_0, the resulting formula will always make a statement on the cardinality of an index set in relation to the (partial) sum of an array.

In comparison, formulas in our theory of arrays with sums can take the form $\mathit{sum}(a, v) \wedge v = \mathit{read}(b, i)$. The sum is used to constrain elements of the b. In particular, we can store the sum of one array in another array.

6 Array Theory With Constant Arrays and Sums

In this section, we provide a decision procedure which runs in non-deterministic polynomial time for the array theory with sums defined in definition 6. Note that we allow finite and infinite index sorts as long as they have fixed cardinality. Nested arrays are also allowed.

Remark 2 (flattened form). We assume that our formulae are in flattened form, meaning that the left-hand side of every equality is a variable. For readability, however, we will initially write literals in non-flattened form and immediately transform them afterwards. Any formula can be converted into flattened form in linear time by adding at most two fresh variables per atom, splitting the atom into three atoms, for instance $x+1 = y-2$ can be transformed to $a = x+1 \wedge b = y-2 \wedge a = b$ with fresh variables a, b.

We end up with the following set of constraints we want to reason about.

Definition 7 (Arr_{cs}). *Let Arr_{cs} be the set of all sets which consist of constraints of the following form.*

$$\begin{array}{ll} v = \mathit{read}(a,i) & (\mathit{read}) \\ a = \mathit{write}(b,i,v) & (\mathit{write}) \\ a = b, a \neq b & ((\mathit{in})\mathit{equality\ of\ arrays}) \\ x = y, x \neq y & ((\mathit{in})\mathit{equality\ of\ variables}) \\ a = K(v) & (\mathit{const}) \\ \mathit{sum}(a,v) & (\mathit{sum\ predicate}) \\ p(v_1,\ldots,v_n) & (\mathit{base\ theory\ predicate}) \end{array}$$

where p is a predicate in the base theory, not involving array variables. We say that an element $\varphi \in \mathsf{Arr}_{cs}$ is satisfiable if and only if $\bigwedge_{c\in\varphi} c$ is satisfiable.

For the time being, we do not allow constraints of the form $\neg \mathit{sum}(a,v)$ in the input formula. There are two possibilities: the sum does not exist, or the sum does not have the desired value. The latter case can be expressed by $\mathit{sum}(a,w) \wedge v \neq w$.

The decision procedure to determine satisfiability of an element $\varphi \in \mathsf{Arr}_{cs}$ is presented as a sequence $\varphi = F_{-3}, F_{-2}, F_{-1}, F_0, \ldots, F_n$ in Arr_{cs} such that F_{-3} is satisfiable if and only if F_n is. The steps to derive F_{i+1} from F_i are described in the following. We start by an example to illustrate the procedure.

Example 3. Consider the following satisfiable set of constraints, where $i, j, x, v, w : \mathbb{Z}$ and $a, b : \mathbb{Z} \Rightarrow \mathbb{Z}$ in Arr_{cs}:

$$\varphi = \begin{Bmatrix} a = \mathit{write}(b,i,v), b = \mathit{write}(c,j,w), c = K(x), \\ \mathit{sum}(a,w), \mathit{sum}(b,12) \end{Bmatrix} \tag{17}$$

First, we non-deterministically guess an *arrangement,* defining which variables have equal and which have distinct values. One possible guess could be to assume that all occurring index variables are pairwise distinct, i.e. $\mathit{distinct}(i,j)$, and $a = b \neq c$ holds. It will turn out that this is indeed an arrangement that yields satisfiability of the formula. In order to treat the sum constraints later, we impose reads on all occurring index and array variables, plus one additional read on a fresh index i_a on a, representing the "residual" of the sum, i.e., the sum of array elements at indices distinct from i and j. If we abbreviate $r_d^k := (v_{d,k} = \mathit{read}(d,k))$, φ is equi-satisfiable to

$$\varphi \cup \{r_d^k \mid k \in \{i,j,i_a\}, d \in \{a,b,c\}\} \cup \{\mathit{distinct}(i,j,i_a), a = b, b \neq c\} \tag{18}$$

since adding additional variables and reads does not change satisfiability. Next, we can infer additional constraints that we add to our set of constraints by a set of inference rules derived from the axioms of our theory. The inference rule derived from the axiom for the constant array operator implies $v_{c,i} = v_{c,j} = v_{c,i_a} = x$. The inference rules derived from the axioms on read and write infer $v_{b,i} = v_{b,i_a} = x, v_{b,j} = w, v_{a,i_a} = x, v_{a,j} = w, v_{a,i} = v$, which can be illustrated as follows.

$$\begin{array}{r|c|c|c|c|c|c|c|} a = & \cdots & i : v & \cdots & j : w & \cdots & i_a : x & \quad\text{x}\quad \\ b = & \cdots & i : x & \cdots & j : w & \cdots & i_a : x & \quad\text{x}\quad \end{array} \tag{19}$$

Since a and b have an infinite index sort, in order to satisfy $sum(a, w)$, respectively $sum(b, v)$, a and b need to be zero almost everywhere. Since they arise from $K(x)$ they have the value x almost everywhere, in particular we can deduce $x = 0$. Note that this implies that the array has value zero everywhere except at i and j, and that the residual sum is zero. Finally, we can rewrite the sum constraints to $v+w+x = w$ and $x+w+x = 12$, since we assume that the residual of the sums is "compressed" at i_a. We can solve these equations algebraically and obtain $x = v = 0, w = 12$. A model of the arrays as functions $\mathbb{Z} \to \mathbb{Z}$ can be constructed by setting c to 0 everywhere, and setting $a = b$ to the function that returns 12 for input 0 and zero elsewhere.

The first steps from F_{-3} to F_0 summarize the introduction of all necessary fresh variables and reads. In the above example, the (simplified) set F_0 is (18).

Definition 8 (Indices for extensionality). *Let $\varphi \in \mathsf{Arr}_{cs}$. For each pair of array variables of the same sort $a, b : I \Rightarrow E$, let $k_{a,b}$ be a fresh index variable, $v^a_{a,b}, v^b_{a,b}$ fresh element variables, and define $F_{-2} := F_{-3} \cup \{v^a_{a,b} = read(a, k_{a,b}) \mid a, b : I \Rightarrow E$ occur in $F_{-3}\}$ as the formula with indices for extensionality.*

The variable $k_{a,b}$ serves as an index variable to verify the extensionality axiom in the case of inequality, which may eventually be identified with an already existing variable.

Definition 9 (Arrangement). *Let K be a set of variables of the same sort. An arrangement of K is a partition of K into equivalence classes, that is sets $K_1, \ldots, K_n \subseteq K$ such that $\dot{\bigcup} K_i = K$. Let $\{K_1, \ldots, K_n\}$ be an arrangement of K, then we define*

$$arr(\{K_1, \ldots, K_n\}) = \bigcup_{i=1}^{n} \bigcup_{a,b \in K_i} \{a = b\} \cup \bigcup_{i=1}^{n} \bigcup_{j=1}^{i-1} \bigcup_{a \in K_i, b \in K_j} \{a \neq b\}. \tag{20}$$

Definition 10 (Chosen arrangements). *Let F_{-2} be a formula with indices for extensionality. For all variables of each sort σ in F_2 including array sorts non-deterministically choose an arrangement $\mathcal{K}_\sigma$. Let $\delta_a : E$ be a fresh variable for each array $a : I \Rightarrow E$ in F_{-2} which we will call the default value. Then choose an arrangement $\mathcal{K}_{\sigma,\delta}$ for all default values of each sort σ in F_2 as well. For each sort σ in F_2, either include $\bot$ into one equivalence class of $\mathcal{K}_{\sigma,\delta}$ or add a new equivalence to $\mathcal{K}_{\sigma,\delta}$ which consists only of $\bot$. We define $F_{-1} := F_{-2} \cup \bigcup_\sigma arr(\mathcal{K}_\sigma) \cup arr(\mathcal{K}_{\sigma,\delta})$ as the formula with chosen arrangements.*

The default values serve as auxiliary variables that indicate the value of an array at an index that is not explicitly mentioned in the formula through a read. For instance, the elements of a constant array $K(x)$ necessarily need to be x, hence the default value should be x. The equivalence class with $\perp$ indicates that the arrays within this class (which may also be none) do not necessarily have a default value. This allows us to choose the values at indices that are not explicitly mentioned in the formula as illustrated by the following example.

Example 4. Consider the following satisfiable set of constraints, where $i : \mathbb{Z}$ and $a, b : \mathbb{Z} \Rightarrow \mathbb{Z}$ in Arr_{cs}

$$\varphi = \{a = \mathit{write}(b, i, v), \mathit{read}(b, i) = 8, \mathit{sum}(a, 10), \mathit{sum}(b, 12)\}. \quad (21)$$

We first choose an arrangement; as we will see, in this example, the arrangement $a \neq b$ gives rise to a solution. In contrast to Example 3, there is no constant array involved. Hence, we may choose $\delta_a = \delta_b = \perp$ as arrangement for default values. For comparison: in Example 3, the only satisfying arrangement for default values is $\delta_a = \delta_b = \delta_c \neq \perp$. Clearly a and b need to be zero almost everywhere to satisfy the sum constraints. However, this does not imply that their respective default values need to be zero, which would cause all elements except at i to be zero. Here the role of $\perp$ comes into play: we are free to choose infinitely many elements as zero but there might exist finitely many non-zero elements at indices other than i. We assume that those, adding up to the residual sum of the arrays, are compressed at a fresh index i_a. Since a and b are equal at all indices other than i the residual sums coincide as well, which is ensured by inference rules instantiating the read and write axioms. Hence, it suffices to add the constraints $\mathit{read}(a, i) = v, \mathit{read}(a, i_a) = s, \mathit{read}(b, i_a) = s, i \neq i_a$ to φ, which can be illustrated as follows.

$a =$	0	$i : v$	0	$i_a : s$	0
$b =$	0	$i : 8$	0	$i_a : s$	0

(22)

Note that the element at index i is not included in the residual sum of a and therefore explicitly added to the formula since otherwise the respective residual sums of a and b do not coincide. The sum constraints can then be rewritten as $v + s = 10$ and $8 + s = 12$ which can be solved algebraically and yields the solution $s = 4, v = 6$. Clearly, many other solutions exist, for instance by constructing arrays that store at four distinct indices the element 1; but to find just one solution, we can assume that the only non-zero entries are at i and i_a.

Lemma 2. *Let $\varphi \in \mathit{Arr}_{cs}$. Then φ is satisfiable if and only if there exist arrangements $\mathcal{K}_{\sigma_1}, \ldots, \mathcal{K}_{\sigma_n}$ for all occurring variables and sorts $\sigma_1, \ldots, \sigma_n$ in φ such that $\varphi \cup \bigcup_{i=1}^{n} \mathit{arr}(\mathcal{K}_{\sigma_i})$ is satisfiable.*

Remark 3. Intuitively, the default value of an array should be preserved through write operators, for instance $a = \mathit{store}(K(x), i, v)$ should have the value x everywhere except at i, i.e. $\delta_a = x = \delta_{K(x)}$. However, this is only true for infinite index sorts. Consider arrays $a, b : \{0\} \Rightarrow \mathbb{Z}$ and the following formula:

$$a = K(0) \wedge b = \mathit{write}(a, 0, 1) \wedge c = K(1) \wedge b = c \quad (23)$$

Any array that is constant should have a corresponding default value. Then $a = K(0)$ and $b = c = K(1)$ would imply $\delta_a = 0$ and $\delta_b = \delta_c = 1$. If we allow to propagate default values through write operators we obtain $0 = \delta_a = \delta_b = \delta_c = 1$, which is a contradiction. However, the formula is satisfiable with $a = K(0)$ and $b = c = K(1)$ which is due to the fact that all elements of the index sort are already explicitly mentioned in the formula. Therefore, we need to compare the number of constrained indices with the cardinality of the index sort.

Definition 11 (Index equivalence classes). *Let $a : (I \Rightarrow E)$ be an array variable occurring in a formula $\varphi \in \mathsf{Arr}_{cs}$. We write $[i]$ for the equivalence class of variable i according to an arrangement. Then $ct(a)$ is the least set of equivalence classes (according to an arrangement) of index variables that satisfies:*

- *for all constraints $v = read(a, i)$, we have $[i] \in ct(a)$;*
- *for all constraints $a = write(b, i, v)$, we have $ct(b) \subseteq ct(a)$ and $[i] \in ct(a)$;*
- *for all constraints $a = b$ we have $ct(b) = ct(a)$.*

Definition 12 (Weak equivalence [4]**).** *Let $\varphi \in \mathsf{Arr}_{cs}$. Two array variables a, b are called weakly equivalent if there exists a sequence of array variables $a = a_1, \ldots, a_n = b$ such that for all $i \in \{1, \ldots, n-1\}$ either $a_i = write(a_{i+1}, j, v) \in \varphi$, $a_{i+1} = write(a_i, j, v) \in \varphi$ for some j, v or $a_i = a_{i+1} \in \varphi$. We define $WE(a) := \{b \mid b$ is weakly equivalent to $a\}$.*

Definition 13 (Indices for residual sums). *Let F_{-1} be a formula with chosen arrangements. Let S' be the set of all array variables $a : I \Rightarrow \mathbb{Z}$ with $sum(a, v) \in F_{-1}$ for some v and $|ct(a)| < |I|$. Let $S \subseteq S'$ be a subset that contains exactly one array variable for each weak equivalence class in S'. For $a \in S$ define $ct(WE(a)) := \bigcup_{c \in WE(a)} ct(c)$. Then we define the formula with all necessary reads and indices for residual sums as*

$$F_0 := F_{-1} \cup \bigcup_{a \in S} \left(\begin{array}{l} \{v = read(b, i) \mid b \in WE(a), [i] \in ct(WE(a))\} \\ \cup \{\varepsilon_a = read(a, i_a) \mid |ct(WE(a))| < |I|\} \\ \cup \{i \neq i_a \mid [i] \in ct(WE(a)), |ct(WE(a))| < |I|\} \end{array} \right) \quad (24)$$

Note that only one ε_a for each weak equivalence class suffices to represent the residual of the sum on the indices which are not constrained in the formula.

Deriving F_0 from F_{-3}, only a polynomial number of constraints and fresh variables have been added. The next steps can be described by a set of inference rules, similar to those in the decision procedure for CAL in [11]. The rules are depicted in Fig. 1. They can be read top-down, i.e., the premise is the set of constraints above the line and the consequence is the set of constraints below the line. Premises $a' = a$ between array variables express that a rule is applicable if a', a coincide, or if those arrays are assumed to be equal in the arrangement. If $\phi \subseteq F_i$ and we have an inference rule with ϕ as the premise, then the consequence ψ can be added to F_i, i.e., $F_{i+1} = F_i \cup \psi$. The inference rules $idx, \Downarrow, \Uparrow, ext, K \Downarrow$ are adjusted versions of those in [11] for CAL and model the axioms. Rules δ_a-*const*, δ_a-*write* and δ_a-*equality* are introduced to handle the default values. We restrict the usage of δ_a-*write* and δ_a-*equality* to the case where $|ct(b)| < |I|$, as discussed in Remark 3. Rule *cong* ensures functional consistency for any function symbol f. We assume that the core solver returns unsatisfiable if $\bot$ occurs.

$$\frac{a = write(b,i,v)}{a[i] = v}\ idx \qquad \frac{a = write(b,i,v) \quad w = a'[j] \quad a' = a \quad i \neq j}{w = b[j]}\ \Downarrow$$

$$\frac{a = K(v) \quad w = a'[j] \quad a' = a}{a[j] = v}\ K\Downarrow \qquad \frac{a = write(b,i,v) \quad w = b'[j] \quad b' = b \quad i \neq j}{w = a[j]}\ \Uparrow$$

$$\frac{a : (I \to E) \quad b : (I \to E) \quad a \neq b}{a[k_{a,b}] \neq b[k_{a,b}]}\ ext \qquad \frac{a = K(v)}{\delta_a = v}\ \delta_a\text{-}const$$

$$\frac{b = write(a,i,v) \quad \delta_a \neq \delta_b}{\bot}\ \delta_a\text{-}write \qquad \frac{a = b \quad \delta_a \neq \delta_b}{\bot}\ \delta_a\text{-}equality$$

$$\frac{x = y \quad f(x) \neq f(y)}{\bot}\ cong$$

Fig. 1. Inference rules

Lemma 3. *The inference rules δ_a-const, δ_a-write and δ_a-equality are sound in the following sense: if a formula $\varphi \in \mathsf{Arr}_{cs}$ is satisfiable then there exists an arrangement of the default values such that whenever F_i is satisfiable, then the set F_{i+1} obtained by applying one of the rules is satisfiable as well.*

Proof. Rule δ_a-*const* is sound since there are no axioms referring to the default values that could be violated after the rule application and it is already ensured by the axiom for the constant array constructor that if $a = K(v)$ and $a = K(w)$ then $v = w$, hence $\delta_a = v$ is well-defined. Assume for a contradiction that for all arrangements of the default values, there is an application of δ_a-*write*, respectively δ_a-*equality*, possible. The only way to obtain such a situation according to our rules is that both arrays a, b arise from a constant array along a sequence of write and equality constraints, otherwise we would be able to change the default values to make a rule application impossible. Therefore there exists $k \in I \setminus \bigcup ct(b) \neq \emptyset$ such that $read(a,k) = \delta_a \neq \delta_b = read(b,k)$, which is a contradiction to the axiom for read and write, respectively extensionality.

We apply the inference rules until we reach a fixed point F_k for some $k \in \mathbb{N}$. In order to handle the sum constraints, we use a set of rewrite rules.

$$sum(a,v) \rightsquigarrow_\infty \sum_{[i] \in ct(a)} read(a,i) = v \wedge \delta_a = 0 \tag{25}$$

$$sum(a,v) \rightsquigarrow_n \sum_{[i] \in ct(a)} read(a,i) = v \tag{26}$$

$$sum(a,v) \rightsquigarrow_n^{\delta_a} \sum_{[i] \in ct(a)} read(a,i) + (|I| - |ct(a)|) \cdot \delta_a = v \tag{27}$$

A rewrite rule $\phi \rightsquigarrow \psi$ applied to F_i results in $F_{i+1} = (F_i \setminus \phi) \cup \psi$. The first rewrite rule is restricted to $|I| = \infty$, the second one to $|I| < \infty$ and $\delta_a = \bot$ and the third one is restricted to $|I| < \infty$ and $\delta_a \neq \bot$.

Lemma 4. *Let $F_i \in \mathsf{Arr}_{cs}$ be the current set of constraints such that the application of inference rules has reached a fixed point. Then the rewrite rules on sum constraints preserve satisfiability of F_i.*

Proof. For $i_1, \ldots, i_{n+m}$ such that $distinct(i_1, \ldots, i_{n+m})$ holds, we have

$$\begin{aligned} & sum(write(\ldots(write(K(0), i_1, v_1) \ldots i_{n+m}, v_{n+m}), \sum_{i=1}^{n+m} v_i) \\ \Leftrightarrow \quad & sum(write(\ldots(write(K(0), i_1, v_1) \ldots i_{n+1}, \sum_{i=n+1}^{n+m} v_i), \sum_{i=1}^{n+m} v_i). \end{aligned} \tag{28}$$

Therefore, if a sum constraint satisfies the axioms, then there exists a representation of the sum as rewritten that satisfies the formula. The residual of the sum is compressed at the fresh indices that may have been introduced previously before applying the inference rules. The soundness of $\rightsquigarrow_n^{\delta_a}$ follows from the fact that additional reads evaluate to the default value as in the proof of Lemma 3.

Theorem 2. *The following procedure is sound and complete for determining satisfiability of quantifier-free formulae in Arr_{cs}, i.e. there exists an arrangement such that the procedure returns satisfiable iff the original formula is satisfiable.*

1. *Step by step add the additional variables, reads and arrangements to subsequently obtain the sequence $F_{-3}, F_{-2}, F_{-1}, F_0$, as defined in Definitions 8, 10 and 13.*
2. *Apply the inference rules until a fixed point F_k is reached.*
3. *Apply the rewrite rules to all sum constraints to obtain F_{k+n}.*
4. *Let a core solver decide satisfiability of F_{k+n}.*

Proof. Soundness: Adding additional variables and reads does not change satisfiability. Adding arrangements is sound by Lemma 2. The inference rules are sound since they are direct instantiations of the axioms and by Lemma 3. The rewrite rules on sums are sound by Lemma 4. The last step is sound by assumption on our core solver.

Completeness: It suffices to show that any satisfiable model of the core solver in the last step gives rise to a model that satisfies the original formula.
Let M be a model provided by the core solver. We extend M to a model M^λ for our original formula as in [11]. Array variables are interpreted as functions. The read, write and constant array operator have their expected interpretations, see [11] for details. We choose for every sort E a default value $\delta_E \in M^\lambda(E)$ and $\delta_{\mathbb{Z}} = 0$. Then we define the interpretation of an array variable $a : I \Rightarrow E$ as

$$M^\lambda(a)(\iota) = \begin{cases} M^\lambda(v) & \text{if } v = read(a, i) \text{ exists and } M^\lambda(i) = \iota \\ M^\lambda(\delta_a) & \text{else if } \delta_a \neq \bot \\ \delta_E & \text{else if } \delta_a = \bot \end{cases} \tag{29}$$

This interpretation is well-defined: Assume we have $v = read(a, i) \wedge w = read(a, j)$ with $i = j$. Then by the inference rule for congruence for the function symbol *read*, we obtain $M(v) = M(read(a, i)) = M(read(a, j))) = M(w)$, in particular $M^\lambda(a)(M^\lambda(i))$ is well-defined. We show that all axioms are satisfied.

- Write-axioms and Extensionality-axiom: We only show that the write axioms hold, the extensionality axiom works analogously. Assume we have $a = write(b, i, v)$. Then $M^\lambda(a)(M^\lambda(i)) = M^\lambda(v)$ is fulfilled by the inference rule idx. For all $\iota \in M^\lambda(\bigcup ct(b)) \setminus \{M^\lambda(i)\}$, we have $M^\lambda(a)(\iota) = M^\lambda(b)(\iota)$ by definition of the interpretation of arrays on $M^\lambda(\bigcup ct(b))$ and the inference rules $\Downarrow$ and $\Uparrow$. For all $\iota \in M^\lambda(I) \setminus M^\lambda(\bigcup ct(a))$ we have $M^\lambda(a)(\iota) = M^\lambda(\delta_a) = M^\lambda(\delta_b) = M^\lambda(b)(\iota)$, since the rule $\delta_a - write$ is not applicable.
- Constant array axiom: Assume we have $a = K(v)$. Then we have $M^\lambda(a)(\iota) = M^\lambda(v)$ for all $\iota \in M^\lambda(I)$, either because of $K \Downarrow$ for $\iota \in M^\lambda(\bigcup ct(a))$ or because of δ_a-$const$.
- sum-axioms: The choice $\delta_\mathbb{Z} = 0$ immediately shows that the axioms on infinite sums trivially hold. Then the rewrite rules are direct instantiations of the sum axioms for finite sums, according to our interpretation of arrays.

Theorem 3. *The above decision procedure runs in non-deterministic polynomial time.*

7 Overview of Decidability Results

We have shown that CAL with sums is undecidable, but that by removing the element-wise function applications, e.g., the map_f operators, we can retain decidability. We consider the following extensions of Arr_{cs} to examine the frontier of decidability:

- Adding another specific aggregation function. As an example we examine the minimum, respectively maximum of an array, i.e., $min(a) = x$.
- Pointwise function applications of functions with arity one, e.g. $b = map_f(a)$.

Lemma 5. *Minimum* $\min(a)$ *and maximum* $\max(a)$ *of an array can be defined in CAL.*

Proof. We consider the maximum operator. As an auxiliary function, the minimum $z = \min(x, y)$ of two integers x, y is defined by the following LIA formula:

$$z = \min(x, y) \;\Leftrightarrow\; (z = x \wedge x \leq y) \vee (z = y \wedge y \leq x \wedge x \neq y). \qquad (30)$$

Then $max(a) = x$ if and only if $a = map_{min(\cdot,\cdot)}(a, K(x)) \wedge \exists i.\ read(a, i) = x$.

Theorem 4. *The satisfiability problem of formulas in* Arr_{cs}*, extended by constraints of the form* $max(a) = c$ *and* $min(a) = c$*, for constants* $c \in \mathbb{Z}$*, is decidable.*

Proof. Since minimum and maximum operator are subsumed by CAL, we can propagate reads through the corresponding *map* operators as in the decision procedure in [11]. If an array is not weakly equivalent to both an array involved in a sum constraint and an array in a minimum, respectively maximum operator the respective decision procedures from Sect. 6 and [11] apply. Therefore, without loss of generality let a be an array variable with infinite index sort, occurring in constraints $max(a) = c$ and $sum(a, v)$, where $c \in \mathbb{Z}$ is an integer constant. Then $sum(a, v)$ can be rewritten as

$$\Big(v - \sum_{[i] \in ct(a)} read(a, i)\Big) \in \{x \mid x \leq c\}^*. \tag{31}$$

Since c is an integer constant, the above is a LIA^* formula and can be decided in non-deterministic polynomial time.

Remark 4. If we allow minimum/maximum constraints comparing an array with a variable, like in $\max(a) = x$, the resulting formula of the rewrite process in the proof of Theorem 4 is not a LIA^* formula, since the characteristic function of the set for the star operator contains additional variables. It is still open whether the satisfiability problem of this extension is decidable or not.

We adapt the definition of weak equivalence in the presence of map_f by also allowing $a_i = map_f(a_{i+1})$ in Definition 12. Furthermore, if $a = map_f(b)$ occurs, then $ct(a)$ also satisfies $ct(b) = ct(a)$.

Theorem 5. *The satisfiability problem of formulas in Arr_{cs}, extended by point-wise function applications of functions of arity one, i.e., constraints of the form $a = map_f(b)$ where f is a LIA function of arity one, restricted to at most one sum constraint per weak equivalence class of array variables, is decidable.*

Proof. Let a be an array variable occuring in a sum constraint $sum(a, v)$ in the formula. Due to Lemma 1 we can assume that a has infinite index sort. We make a case distinction depending on whether a is weakly equivalent to a constant array. (1) If a is weakly equivalent to a constant array, then $\delta_a \neq \bot$. Hence, we have $\delta_a = 0$ in order to satisfy the sum constraint. In this case, the sum constraint can be rewritten as in (25) and the decision procedure for CAL applies. (2) If a is not weakly equivalent to a constant array, we can freely choose all remaining values. For each function application map_f in the formula we can compute the range of f, which is a semilinear set. Since $map_f(map_g(b)) = map_{f \circ g}(b)$ we can assume that all map operators are of the form $a = map_{f_i}(a_i)$ for $i \in \{1, \ldots, n\}$. Let F_i be the respective formula that describes the image of f_i as a semilinear set, then define $F := \wedge_{i=1}^{n} F_i$. Then a sum constraint $sum(a, v)$ can be rewritten as

$$\Big(v - \sum_{[i] \in ct(a)} read(a, i)\Big) \in \{x \mid F(x)\}^*. \tag{32}$$

The above constraint asks whether the values that are not explicitly mentioned in the formula can form a sum that coincides with the difference between v and the sum of all explicitly mentioned values of a, which is decidable as a LIA^* formula.

Remark 5. The minimum and maximum operator without variables can be modeled by functions of arity one: $max(a) = c \Leftrightarrow a = map_{min(\cdot,c)}(a) \wedge read(a,i) = x$. For variables to be meaningfully included in an element-wise function application to an array, a function of arity greater than one is needed. For instance, $a = map_{min}(a, K(x))$ states $max(a) \leq x$, whereas $a = map_{min(\cdot,c)}(a)$ states $max(a) \leq c$ and c can not be a variable since otherwise $min(\cdot, c)$ is not a LIA function. Note that the undecidability proof in Theorem 1 only needs function applications of arity two.

8 Conclusion and Future Work

We provided a sound and complete decision procedure for an extensional array theory with constant arrays and sum constraints. The implementation of the procedure is ongoing work. We furthermore discussed the difficulties of defining sums over arrays and the borders of decidability that arise. Our decision procedure proves that decidability can be preserved for adding sums, however gets lost if we add pointwise function applications as in CAL. We examined additional decidability results for further extensions of our fragment.

Sum constraints can be seen as one of the most used and desired operators of the form $(I \Rightarrow E) \rightarrow E$. A direct generalization of our decision procedure would be to consider the element sort of the array to be an arbitrary Abelian semigroup $(E, *)$. Furthermore, one could look for other interesting operators for array theories to add to the decision procedure, such as minimum and maximum in the general case (discussed in Sect. 7). The question whether adding specific function applications, such as minimum and maximum operators with variables, preserves decidability remains open if we allow variables. A further goal is to explore the space between the theories CAL and CaAL to find array theories that can succinctly model quantum circuits (which is the main purpose of CaAL), have lower complexity than NEXPTIME, but also include summation to reason about probabilities.

Acknowledgement. This work was supported by the Swedish Research Council through grant 2021-06327, and by the Knut and Alice Wallenberg Foundation through project UPDATE. The authors thank the CADE reviewers for insightful comments!

Disclosure of Interests. The authors have no competing interests to declare that are relevant to the content of this article.

References

1. Amilon, J., Esen, Z., Gurov, D., Lidström, C., Rümmer, P.: Automatic program instrumentation for automatic verification. In: Enea, C., Lal, A. (eds.) Computer Aided Verification - 35th International Conference, CAV 2023, Paris, France, July 17-22, 2023, Proceedings, Part III. Lecture Notes in Computer Science, vol. 13966, pp. 281–304. Springer (2023). https://doi.org/10.1007/978-3-031-37709-9_14, https://doi.org/10.1007/978-3-031-37709-9_14

2. Baudin, P., Filliâtre, J.C., Marché, C., Monate, B., Moy, Y., Prevosto, V.: ACSL: ANSI/ISO C Specification Language. http://frama-c.com/acsl.html
3. Chen, Y.F., Rümmer, P., Tsai, W.L.: A Theory of Cartesian Arrays (with Applications in Quantum Circuit Verification). In: Pientka, B., Tinelli, C. (eds.) Automated Deduction – CADE 29, pp. 170–189. Springer Nature Switzerland, Cham (2023). https://doi.org/10.1007/978-3-031-38499-8_10
4. Christ, J., Hoenicke, J.: Weakly Equivalent Arrays. In: Lutz, C., Ranise, S. (eds.) Frontiers of Combining Systems, pp. 119–134. Springer International Publishing, Cham (2015). https://doi.org/10.1007/978-3-319-24246-0_8
5. Daca, P., Henzinger, T.A., Kupriyanov, A.: Array folds logic. In: Chaudhuri, S., Farzan, A. (eds.) Computer Aided Verification, pp. 230–248. Springer International Publishing, Cham (2016). https://doi.org/10.1007/978-3-319-41540-6_13
6. Harrison, J.: Handbook of Practical Logic and Automated Reasoning. Cambridge University Press, Cambridge (2009). https://doi.org/10.1017/CBO9780511576430, https://www.cambridge.org/core/books/handbook-of-practical-logic-and-automated-reasoning/EB6396296813CB562987E8C37AC4520D
7. Leavens, G.T., Baker, A.L., Ruby, C.: JML: A notation for detailed design. In: Kilov, H., Rumpe, B., Simmonds, I. (eds.) Behavioral Specifications of Businesses and Systems, The Kluwer International Series in Engineering and Computer Science, vol. 523, pp. 175–188. Springer (1999). https://doi.org/10.1007/978-1-4615-5229-1_12
8. Leino, K.R.M., Monahan, R.: Reasoning about comprehensions with first-order SMT solvers. In: Shin, S.Y., Ossowski, S. (eds.) Proceedings of the 2009 ACM Symposium on Applied Computing (SAC), Honolulu, Hawaii, USA, March 9-12, 2009, pp. 615–622. ACM (2009). https://doi.org/10.1145/1529282.1529411, https://doi.org/10.1145/1529282.1529411
9. Matiyasevich, Y.V.: Hilbert's Tenth Problem. MIT Press, Cambridge (1993)
10. McCarthy, J.: Towards a Mathematical Science of Computation. In: Fetzer, J.H., Colburn, T.R., Fetzer, J.H., Rankin, T.L. (eds.) Program Verification, vol. 14, pp. 35–56. Springer Netherlands, Dordrecht (1993). https://doi.org/10.1007/978-94-011-1793-7_2, http://link.springer.com/10.1007/978-94-011-1793-7_2, series Title: Studies in Cognitive Systems
11. Moura, L.d., Bjørner, N.: Generalized, Efficient Array Decision Procedures, September 2009, https://www.microsoft.com/en-us/research/publication/generalized-efficient-array-decision-procedures/
12. Piskac, R., Kuncak, V.: Linear Arithmetic with Stars. In: Gupta, A., Malik, S. (eds.) Computer Aided Verification, pp. 268–280. Springer, Berlin, Heidelberg (2008). https://doi.org/10.1007/978-3-540-70545-1_25
13. Raya, R.: Combinatory Array Logic with Sums, May 2024. https://doi.org/10.48550/arXiv.2311.06582, http://arxiv.org/abs/2311.06582, arXiv:2311.06582 [cs] version: 2
14. Raya, R., Kunčak, V.: NP Satisfiability for Arrays as Powers. In: Finkbeiner, B., Wies, T. (eds.) Verification, Model Checking, and Abstract Interpretation, pp. 301–318. Springer International Publishing, Cham (2022). https://doi.org/10.1007/978-3-030-94583-1_15
15. Stump, A., Barrett, C., Dill, D., Levitt, J.: A decision procedure for an extensional theory of arrays. In: Proceedings 16th Annual IEEE Symposium on Logic in Computer Science, pp. 29–37. IEEE Comput. Soc, Boston, MA, USA (2001). https://doi.org/10.1109/LICS.2001.932480, http://ieeexplore.ieee.org/document/932480/

Cazamariposas: Automated Instability Debugging in SMT-based Program Verification

Yi Zhou(✉), Amar Shah, Zhengyao Lin, and Marijn J. H. Heule, and Bryan Parno

Carnegie Mellon University, Pittsburgh, PA, USA
{yizhou5,amarshah,zhengyal,mheule,bparno}@cs.cmu.edu

Abstract. Program verification languages such as Dafny and F* often rely heavily on Satisfiability Modulo Theories (SMT) solvers for proof automation. However, SMT-based verification suffers from instability, where semantically irrelevant changes in the source program can cause spurious proof failures. While existing mitigation techniques emphasize preemptive measures, we propose a complementary approach that focuses on diagnosing and repairing specific instances of instability-induced failures. Our key technique is a novel differential analysis to pinpoint problematic quantified formulas in an unstable query. We implement this technique in Cazamariposas, a tool that automatically identifies such quantified formulas and suggests fixes. We evaluate Cazamariposas on multiple large-scale systems verification projects written in three different program verification languages. Our results demonstrate Cazamariposas' effectiveness as an instability debugger. In the majority of cases, Cazamariposas successfully isolates the issue to a single problematic quantifier, while providing a stabilizing fix.

Keywords: SMT · Program Verification · Proof Instability.

1 Introduction

Satisfiability Modulo Theories (SMT) solvers play a prominent role in automated program verification. In verifiers such as Dafny [22], F* [30], or Verus [20], SMT solvers can often discharge complex verification conditions automatically, despite the generally undecidable program properties. In this way, SMT solvers significantly reduce the need for manual proof steps, facilitating the verification of large-scale software systems [15,19,26].

However, the solvers must resort to incomplete heuristics to reason about undecidable program properties. Consequently, SMT-based program verifiers suffer from a persistent problem of *proof instability* [16,34], where trivial, non-semantic changes to the source program result in spurious proof failures. For instance, an SMT solver may fail to verify (i.e., return an inconclusive result on) a previously-proven verification condition after a simple variable renaming, even though the program's semantics remain unchanged.

Instability is a major impediment to the industrial deployment of automated verification [12]. In particular, instability disrupts the usual development work

C. Barrett and U. Waldmann (Eds.): CADE 2025, LNAI 15943, pp. 75–94, 2025.
https://doi.org/10.1007/978-3-031-99984-0_5

flow, incurring time and resource costs to debug spurious failures. Worse yet, the solver provides little insight as to why it rejects the modified query. As a result, the developer has limited recourse beyond blindly modifying their source code in the hopes of nudging the solver into an accepting state [31].

While prior work [1,21,33] has tried to preemptively mitigate instability (with partial success—see Sec. 2), we propose a complementary approach to debug and repair unstable SMT queries. In more detail, we automatically provide the developer with query-specific *repair strategies*, targeting the quantified formulas causing instability. In fact, for 61% the queries in our study, there is only a *single* quantified formula to blame! In other words, we can repair most of the unstable proofs by limiting the impact of just one ill-behaved quantified formula.

We introduce a *differential analysis* to identify such problematic formulas. We leverage the fact that by definition [34], semantically equivalent variants of an unstable query create a mix of verification successes and failures. We thus compare the quantifier-instantiation profiles between succeeding and failing variants, highlighting the formulas that are over/under-instantiated in the failing variants. We further refine the analysis using novel proof and trace mining techniques, exploiting the causal relation between the instantiations.

We implement our analysis in Cazamariposas, an SMT-level instability debugging tool. Cazamariposas takes as input an unstable SMT query Φ and provides a repair strategy as output. For example, suppose our analysis points to an over-instantiated formula ϕ within Φ. Cazamariposas confirms that removing ϕ from Φ stabilizes the query, and then it encourages the developer to remove the source-level construct that introduced ϕ to Φ. Crucially, we ensure that the repair strategy is sound with respect to program-verification semantics (Sec. 4).

We evaluate Cazamariposas on a diverse set of benchmarks, with 615 unstable SMT queries collected from 12 system verification projects written in Dafny [22], F* [30], or Verus [20]. We find that Cazamariposas successfully repairs 70% of the unstable queries, of which 87% involve a single quantified formula (Sec. 5).

2 Notation and Related Work

2.1 Notation

We use a conjunctive formula $\Phi = \bigwedge_{i=0}^{n} \psi_i$ to represent an SMT query, where each ψ_i is an assertion. We slightly abuse the notation here by treating Φ as a set of assertions. For example, we use $\Phi \setminus \{\psi\}$ and $\Phi \cup \{\psi\}$ to denote a new query with an assertion ψ removed or added, respectively.

We assume the *goal-axioms* structure in program verification queries [33]. In particular, $\psi_0 = \neg\theta$ is the negation of the properties of the procedure under verification. Meanwhile, $\Lambda = \bigwedge_{i=1}^{n} \psi_i$ is a conjunction of *axioms* encoding the semantics of: **(1)** the verification language's constructs, and **(2)** other developer-written procedures that have already been verified. By checking that $\Phi = \Lambda \wedge \neg\theta$ is unsatisfiable, the SMT solver confirms that θ is a logical consequence of Λ.

The use of quantifiers is common in program verification. For ease of exposition, we use single-variable quantified formulas (e.g., $\phi = \forall x.\varphi$) as examples as long as it is clear how the method under discussion generalizes to quantification over multiple variables. We use Ω to represent the set of quantified formulas (including all the nested ones) in Φ.

For a universally quantified formula $\phi = \forall x.\varphi$, we use $\varphi[x \mapsto t]$ to denote the result of capture-free substitution of some ground term t for all free occurrences of x in φ. We refer to $\varphi[x \mapsto t]$ as an *instantiation* of ϕ, and t as the *instantiating term*. We use the calligraphic $\mathcal{I}^{\phi}$ to denote a set of instantiations of ϕ. For convenience, we define $\mathcal{I}^{\phi} = \{\}$ if ϕ is existentially quantified.

We analyze the quantifier reasoning process based on solver-generated logs. Concretely, for a given query Φ, we leverage the Z3 [11] solver to produce a pair of proof and trace $(\mathfrak{p}, \mathfrak{t})$ logs where $\mathfrak{p}$ is a proof tree of unsatisfiability [6], and $\mathfrak{t}$ records the all the solver-discovered instantiations. We use $\mathcal{I}^{\phi}_{\mathfrak{p}}$ and $\mathcal{I}^{\phi}_{\mathfrak{t}}$ to denote the set of instantiations of ϕ in $\mathfrak{p}$ and $\mathfrak{t}$, respectively.

SMT-based verification languages rely heavily on pattern-based quantifier instantiation [23,24]. Each universally quantified formula $\forall x.\varphi$ is associated with (at least) one syntactic *pattern* π, where π would be a ground term expect for the free variable x in it. The body φ remains hidden until a ground term $\pi[x \mapsto t]$ enters the solver's context, at which point the solver creates the instantiation $\varphi[x \mapsto t]$. We refer to $\pi[x \mapsto t]$ as the *triggering term*.

2.2 Related Work

Proof instability is an obstacle to wide-scale industrial adoption of SMT-based verification. Galois highlights the "fragility of proofs" which can be "highly sensitive to minor changes in logical terms" [12]. Similarly, Amazon complains about the serious challenge of "lack of monotonicity and stability in runtimes" [28]. Numerous other large-scale verification projects cite SMT instability as a key pain point [2,9,10,13,16,19,27].

In prior work, researchers applied source-program-level analysis to choose better syntactic patterns for user-introduced quantified formulas, hoping to produce more stable SMT queries [21]. More recently, Bordis and Leino propose using *free facts* [7], where quantified axioms are replaced by specific instantiations before the query is dispatched to the solver. Both techniques have shown some improvement, although they rely on ad hoc measures of instability.

In our Mariposa work [34], we presented a statistically rigorous approach to characterizing proof instability. At a high level, the Mariposa tool takes in an SMT query-solver pair (Φ, s), and outputs whether the query Φ is stable, unstable, or unsolvable when run with solver s. Intuitively, Mariposa generates semantically-equivalent *mutants* of Φ and if the solver's performance varies significantly across the mutants, Φ is unstable on s.

Mariposa creates the mutants by (1) reordering assertions, (2) α-renaming variables, or (3) changing the random seed. Therefore, for two mutants Φ_1 and Φ_2 of Φ, there is a one-to-one correspondence in terms of the function symbols and the formulas between Φ_1 and Φ_2. It is thus possible to compare how the "same" quantified formula ϕ is instantiated in Φ_1 and Φ_2, even though ϕ may appear in different forms.

As part of the Mariposa project, we also curated a collection of program verification queries. In particular, we included several large-scale systems-verification projects written in Dafny [22] and F* [30] as a part of the Mariposa benchmark suite, where we found non-trivial amounts of instability.

In our follow-up work, we demonstrate that proof stability is strongly connected to the relevance of axioms [33]. In general, given a verification goal θ, if Λ is populated with unnecessary or irrelevant axioms, then the query is more likely to experience instability. We then introduce SHAKE, a context-pruning technique that reduces the number of irrelevant axioms in program verification queries, mitigating the instability on the Mariposa benchmark suite by 29% on Z3 and 41% on cvc5.

Amrollahi et al. preprocess an SMT query to put it into a canonical form [1] so as to normalize away semantically irrelevant source-level changes. They demonstrate mixed results, reducing instability on one Mariposa benchmark by 20%, while increasing it on another by 76%. Cumulatively, their approach increased instability by 4%.

In contrast to these approaches based on preemptive preprocessing, in this work, we propose to diagnose and repair specific instances of unstable proofs. Our approach draws inspiration from the field of automated theorem proving [18,29]. In particular, our query-specific diagnosis draws a parallel to the axiom selection problem [17], where the goal is to select a small subset of axioms from a large set of axioms to prove a theorem. Oftentimes, axiom selection is done using techniques from machine learning [5].

3 Motivating Examples

When a programmer encounters instability, fixing it often requires considerable effort. When a proof in an automated verification language fails, conventional wisdom suggests various manual debugging techniques [25,31,32], including:

1. Adding source-level assertions to help guide the solver towards deriving important intermediate facts, and to trigger important quantifiers.
2. Adding source-level annotations to hide function definitions that are unnecessary for the proof. These annotations cause the verifier to encode the function such that the SMT solver treats it as uninterpreted.

We observe that these techniques target different problems at the SMT level. When the solver quickly returns `unknown` because of insufficient information, this may be addressed at the source level by adding source-level assertions. If the solver "times out" because it has spent too much time exploring extraneous parts of the proof space, this may be addressed at the source level by hiding unnecessary functions definitions.

In Sec. 4.3, we describe how Cazamariposas is able to automatically differentiate between the two cases above and suggest the appropriate fixes. In contrast, developers often struggle to find such fixes. To illustrate this, below we present two examples [1] from the Verus benchmarks (Sec. 5.2) where Cazamariposas identifies a fix that the original programmers missed.

3.1 Diagnosing and Repairing Unnecessary Instantiations

Our first example, a lemma `lemma_from_after` written in Verus, has an unstable proof. In the original source code, the developer added a Verus annotation asking the solver to spin off a separate SMT query just for this lemma (normally Verus proves many goals incrementally in the same SMT context). Verus developers often use this annotation to try to improve stability, but Cazamariposas' measurements indicate it is still unstable.

To fix this proof's instability, the developer can try to hide various functions definitions using Verus's `hide` keyword. However, from the developer's perspective, it is not obvious which function might be to blame for the instability. The file containing `lemma_from_after` has 6 function definitions, and it imports 27 other Rust crates, each of which contributes many more functions that might be causing the instability. A priori, it is not even clear that hiding a function definition is the correct fix. The developer might instead guess that adding assertions to the body of `lemma_from_after` will improve stability.

In contrast, Cazamariposas explains that `make_stateful_set` is the cause, an unrelated function imported from a completely different crate. Cazamariposas suggests that the developer hide `make_stateful_set`, which produces a stable SMT query.

3.2 Diagnosing and Repairing Missing Instantiations

In the Verus code below, the function `entry_alive_wraps` on line 7 proves that every index `i` from `low` to `high` is alive if and only if `BUFFER_SIZE + i` is alive. Liveness is defined via `entry_alive`, which among other operations, performs a division. At the SMT level, Verus represents division with the function `Euc_Div`, which is guarded to prevent division by 0. The original SMT query for `entry_alive_wraps` is unstable because the solver gets stuck going from `Euc_Div` to SMT-LIB's built-in division operator. As a developer, diagnosing such is quite difficult, let alone finding a fix.

```
1  const BUFFER_SIZE = ...
2
3  fn entry_alive(i: int) -> bool {
4   (i / BUFFER_SIZE) % 2 == 0
5  }
6
7  fn entry_alive_wraps(low: nat, high: nat)
8   ensures forall|i: nat|low <= i < high ==>
9     entry_alive(i, BUFFER_SIZE) == entry_alive(i + BUFFER_SIZE, BUFFER_SIZE)
10 {}
```

In contrast, Cazamariposas automatically diagnoses the problem at the SMT level and suggests a fix. At the SMT level, the ensures clause on

[1] We have simplified the examples here and placed the full versions in our technical report [35].

`entry_alive_wraps` is negated, turning the universal quantifier on line 8 into an existential. Cazamariposas experiments with Skolemizing the quantified variable (i.e., turning it into a constant) and then searches for universal quantifiers in the query that might benefit from instantiation with the new Skolem constant. In this case, it identifies an instantiation of a quantifier about `Euc_Div` that stabilizes the proof. It suggests this fix to the developer, who can then use appropriate Verus-level syntax to apply the fix.

4 The Cazamariposas Methodology

Cazamariposas produces SMT-level *query edits* as repair strategies for proof instability. For example, given an unstable query Φ, Cazamariposas may pinpoint a quantified axiom ϕ_i (for $i \neq 0$) such that $\Phi^* = \Phi \setminus \{\phi_i\}$ is stable. (We note that removing ϕ_i is sound since Φ^* maintains the original verification goal.) The developer can then apply an analogue of this SMT-level edit as a source-level change (e.g., hiding the procedure axiomatized by ϕ_i in this case), stabilizing the proof.

Cazamariposas follows an "edit-and-test" scheme to identify stabilizing repair strategies. Conceptually, for each quantified axiom $\phi_i \in (\Lambda \cap \Omega)$, Cazamariposas goes through the following:

- Hypothesize that quantifier reasoning over ϕ_i is the cause of instability.
- Select a *query edit* on Φ to reduce the reasoning obligations over ϕ_i.
- Apply the query edit to create a *candidate query* Φ^*.
- Test the stability of Φ^* using Mariposa.
- If Φ^* is not stable, dismiss the hypothesis for now.
- If Φ^* is stable, report ϕ_i as a cause of instability.

In Sec. 4.1, we discuss how we ensure that a query edit **(1)** weakens a particular target axiom, and **(2)** preserves the rest of the query context. With this design, if Φ^* is stable, the edit is also a sound repair strategy.

While the "edit-and-test" scheme is conceptually simple, the vast number of quantified axioms makes it impractical to exhaustively test the stability impact of each ϕ_i individually. Therefore, as illustrated in Figure 1 and described in Sec. 4.2-4.4, Cazamariposas must efficiently prioritize the likely suspects. In particular, we leverage the fact that an unstable query Φ has at least one passing mutant Φ_s and one failing mutant Φ_f. This allows us to compare the instantiations of ϕ_i between Φ_f and Φ_s, as we explained in Sec. 2.

More concretely, we obtain from the solver a trace log $\mathfrak{t}$ for Φ_f, and a proof log $\mathfrak{p}$ for Φ_s. In theory, our method generalizes to multiple traces and proofs. In practice, collecting even one pair of $(\mathfrak{t}, \mathfrak{p})$ can entail difficulties (Sec. 5). Hence, we focus our discussion on one such pair. We use $\mathcal{I}_{\mathfrak{t}}^{\phi_i}$ and $\mathcal{I}_{\mathfrak{p}}^{\phi_i}$ to denote the instantiation set of ϕ_i in $\mathfrak{t}$ and $\mathfrak{p}$, respectively.

We first triage (Sec. 4.2) which kind of instability-induced failure we face: either a *quick unknown* (QU) or a *slow timeout* (TO). We then compute key metrics to distinguish the potentially problematic quantified axioms (Sec. 4.3). Next, using the metrics and the failure mode, we select the query edits most

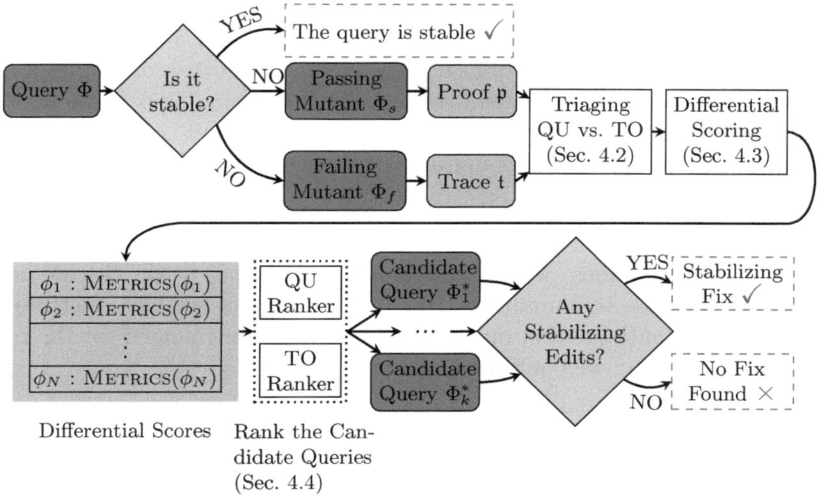

Fig. 1: The Design of Cazamariposas. We have colored the SMT queries, data, and Mariposa calls. We use METRICS(ϕ_i) to represent the metrics in Sec. 4.3. For simplicity, we have omitted doubleton edits.

likely to stabilize the query (Sec. 4.4). Finally, we use Mariposa to evaluate the edits, and if any succeed in stabilizing the query, we report success and suggest the corresponding edit as a repair.

4.1 Testing the Axioms for Stability

We start with our methodology to evaluate the stability impact of an individual axiom using query edits leveraging the proof log $\mathfrak{p}$. More formally, we define a *singleton edit* as a pair (ϕ_i, a_i), where $\phi_i \in (\Lambda \cap \Omega)$, and a_i is an *action* among the following:

- **del**: delete ϕ_i from the query.
- **inst**: augment ϕ_i with its proof instantiations (i.e., $\mathcal{I}_{\mathfrak{p}}^{\phi_i}$) as new axioms.
- **inst-del**: replace ϕ_i with $\mathcal{I}_{\mathfrak{p}}^{\phi_i}$ in the query.
- **sk**: Skolemize an existentially quantified assertion, ϕ_i.

We formally define the edits in Table 1. We use $f_{\phi_{ix}}$ to denote a Skolem constant from some existential assertion $\phi_i = \exists x.\varphi$.

Action a_i	Applicability ϕ_i	Edited Candidate Φ^*
del	$\phi_i \in (\Lambda \cap \Omega)$	$\Phi \setminus \{\phi_i\}$
inst	$\phi_i \in \Lambda, \phi_i = \forall x.\varphi$	$\Phi \cup \mathcal{I}_{\mathfrak{p}}^{\phi_i}$
inst-del		$(\Phi \cup \mathcal{I}_{\mathfrak{p}}^{\phi_i}) \setminus \{\phi_i\}$
sk	$\phi_i \in \Phi, \phi_i = \exists x.\varphi$	$(\Phi \cup \{\varphi[x \mapsto f_{\phi_{ix}}]\}) \setminus \{\phi_i\}$

Table 1: **Cazamariposas Query Edits**

Intuitively, the edits are meant to reduce or eliminate a solver's reasoning over ϕ_i, so a stabilized candidate also points to ϕ_i as a cause of instability. We now discuss some basic properties of the edit actions, including soundness, which ensures that a stabilizing edit is also a valid repair strategy.

Soundness. We define the soundness of the candidate Φ^* as:

$$\Phi^* \vdash \bot \implies \Phi \vdash \bot$$

We demonstrate soundness with a case analysis. When $a_i = \mathbf{sk}$, the queries Φ^* and Φ are equivalent, so soundness trivially holds. Since we have restricted **sk** to be the only potential action on the goal, θ remains unchanged for the rest of the actions. Therefore, we could instead show that:

$$\Lambda^* \vdash \theta \implies \Lambda \vdash \theta$$

which holds as long as Λ^* is no stronger than Λ. When $a_i = \mathbf{inst}$, because the elements of $\mathcal{I}_{\mathrm{p}}^{\phi_i}$ are tautological consequences of ϕ_i, Λ^* is as strong as Λ. When $a_i \in \{\mathbf{del}, \mathbf{inst\text{-}del}\}$, Λ^* might be weaker than Λ.

Completeness. We define completeness of the axiom set as follow:

$$\Lambda \vdash \theta \implies \Lambda^* \vdash \theta$$

The proof instantiation set $\mathcal{I}_{\mathrm{p}}^{\phi_i}$ is sufficient to establish θ by definition, so we maintain completeness. However, since the edits may weaken the axioms, we do sacrifice a broader sense of completeness. Specifically, **del** and **inst-del** may remove a quantified axiom ϕ_i, while the $\mathcal{I}_{\mathrm{p}}^{\phi_i}$ is only a finite subset of all possible instantiations of ϕ_i. Therefore do not guarantee that $\Lambda^* \vdash \phi_i$.

Composability. We note that if we perform a series of singleton edits $\Delta = \langle ..., (\phi_i, a_i), ... \rangle$, we also maintain soundness and completeness. Intuitively, when instability arises from the interaction of multiple quantified axioms, singleton edits (i.e., $\|\Delta\| = 1$) might fail to capture the cause, and thus we need to consider $\|\Delta\| \geq 2$. In the case where $\|\Delta\| = 2$, we call Δ a *doubleton edit.*

Practicality. In Cazamariposas, we focus on the SMT level to ensure applicability to multiple languages. Eventually, we would like to apply the edit actions to the source code, which we leave as future work. The query edits do generally correspond to source-level features in Dafny, F*, and Verus:

- **del** corresponds to source-level visibility control mechanisms. For example, Dafny's `opaque` keyword hides the definition of a function.
- **inst** corresponds to quantifier instantiations as source-level annotations.
- **sk** corresponds to Hilbert's choice as a language construct. For example, Dafny's `var x :| P(x)` assigns `x` an arbitrary value such that `P(x)` holds.

However, the translation might not always be straightforward. As we discussed in Sec. 2, the axioms may also encode the semantics of language constructs. For example, **del** on an axiom for higher-order functions has no direct source-level equivalent. More specific to **inst**, if the repair adds a large number of instantiations to the source code, it is arguably impractical due to maintenance and readability concerns. Nevertheless, we have some empirical evidence that the repairs are often practical, which would make it interesting to explore automatic translation in the future.

Complexity. Another more pressing concern is the complexity of the search space. Consider a query Φ with n applicable singleton edits. The total number of potential candidates is roughly:

$$\sum_{i=1}^{\|\Delta\|} \binom{n}{i} = \binom{n}{1} + \binom{n}{2} + \dots + \binom{n}{\|\Delta\|}$$

The combinatorial explosion makes it infeasible to test all candidates. Meanwhile, if a stabilizing edit involves too many axioms, it also become less realistic to reenact the repair at the source level.

Given these considerations, we limit our experiments to two classes: *singleton* and *doubleton* edits, i.e., $\|\Delta\| \leq 2$. Nevertheless, a massive search space remains for each class, with typically thousands of quantified axioms in a query. We thus further introduce a parameter k to limit the number of candidates we test for full stability. Specifically, we first test k singleton edits, and then k doubleton edits if the former fails to stabilize the query.

4.2 Triaging the Failure Mode

Given our methodology to test the stability of individual axioms, we now discuss how to select the most promising candidates. We begin by triaging the high-level cause of the underlying instability. Specifically, we observe two distinct modes of an instability-induced failure, which we name *quick unknown* (QU) and *slow timeout* (TO). In a QU, the solver quickly terminates (e.g., in < 1 second) with an `unknown` result, despite being given a generous timeout and resource limit. Meanwhile, for a TO, the solver runs on the query until it runs out of its time budget.

As we discuss in depth in Sec. 5.3, the two failure modes correspond to different instantiation profiles, signifying different underlying causes of instability. In a QU, the solver only explores a small number of instantiations before giving up. We therefore hypothesize that the solver is failing because it is missing key instantiations to prove the goal θ. In contrast, a TO is associated with orders of magnitude more instantiations, suggesting that the solver is spending significant time and resources on quantifier reasoning irrelevant to θ.

4.3 Calculating the Differential Metrics

We now introduce measures to quantify the degree of insufficient or excessive instantiation. We define the metrics for quantified formula $\phi_i \in \Omega$, levering the proof instantiation set $\mathcal{I}_{\mathfrak{p}}^{\phi_i}$ and the trace instantiation set $\mathcal{I}_{\mathfrak{t}}^{\phi_i}$. (In Sec. 4.4, we discuss how to aggregate the metrics to rank potential edits over the quantified axioms.) Specifically, we compute the following metrics here:

- DEFICIT($\phi_i, \mathfrak{p}, \mathfrak{t}$) $= \|\mathcal{I}^{\phi_i}_{\mathfrak{p}\text{-}\mathfrak{t}}\|$, where $\mathcal{I}^{\phi_i}_{\mathfrak{p}\text{-}\mathfrak{t}} = \mathcal{I}^{\phi_i}_{\mathfrak{p}} \setminus \mathcal{I}^{\phi_i}_{\mathfrak{t}}$. Intuitively, $\mathcal{I}^{\phi_i}_{\mathfrak{p}\text{-}\mathfrak{t}}$ is the set of instantiations in the proof but not in the trace. When $\|\mathcal{I}^{\phi_i}_{\mathfrak{p}\text{-}\mathfrak{t}}\|$ is large, the solver may be missing instantiations of ϕ_i that are crucial to reaching `unsat`.
- EXCESS($\phi_i, \mathfrak{p}, \mathfrak{t}$) $= \|\mathcal{I}^{\phi_i}_{\mathfrak{t}\text{-}\mathfrak{p}}\|$, where $\mathcal{I}^{\phi_i}_{\mathfrak{t}\text{-}\mathfrak{p}} = \mathcal{I}^{\phi_i}_{\mathfrak{t}} \setminus \mathcal{I}^{\phi_i}_{\mathfrak{p}}$. Intuitively, $\mathcal{I}^{\phi_i}_{\mathfrak{t}\text{-}\mathfrak{p}}$ is the set of instantiations in the trace but not in the proof. When $\|\mathcal{I}^{\phi_i}_{\mathfrak{t}\text{-}\mathfrak{p}}\|$ is large, the solver may be wasting time and resources instantiating ϕ_i without making progress towards proving the goal.

When ϕ_i is existentially quantified, $\mathcal{I}^{\phi_i}_{\mathfrak{t}}$ and $\mathcal{I}^{\phi_i}_{\mathfrak{p}}$ are both empty, so DEFICIT and EXCESS are trivially 0. In that case, we introduce the following metric based on the instantiations that depend on ϕ_i:

- CONTINGENCY($\phi_i, \mathfrak{p}$) $= \sum_{\phi_j \in \Omega} \|\{I \mid I \in \mathcal{I}^{\phi_j}_{\mathfrak{p}}, f_{\phi_{ix}} \sqsubseteq I\}\|$, where ϕ_i creates the the Skolem constant $f_{\phi_{ix}}$, $\phi_j \in \Omega$ is some (universally) quantified formula, $I \in \mathcal{I}^{\phi_j}_{\mathfrak{p}}$ is some instantiation of ϕ_j containing $f_{\phi_{ix}}$, and $f_{\phi_{ix}} \sqsubseteq I$ denotes that $f_{\phi_{ix}}$ is a sub-term of I. Intuitively, the metric reflects the proof instantiations that depend on $f_{\phi_{ix}}$. When ϕ_i has a high CONTINGENCY score, other quantified formulas cannot be sufficiently instantiated until ϕ_i is Skolemized.

Naively, we could already start prioritizing the quantified axioms based on these scores alone, but this would provide only crude guidance without considering the dependence between the formulas. Thus, we next discuss how we aggregate the scores and choose the most promising edit actions for each axiom.

4.4 Ranking the Candidate Queries

As mentioned in Sec. 4.1, we use a parameter k to limit the number of candidates we test for full stability, where we first consider top-k singleton edits, and then doubleton edits if none of the singleton edits is stabilizing. We describe how to compute the scores for the singleton and doubleton edits in this section. The output of this stage are two partial maps, SSCORE and DSCORE.

1. We score each axiom ϕ_i, and then select an appropriate edit for it. When there are multiple possible actions on ϕ_i, we commit to one that is likely stabilizing. More formally, we create a partial map:

$$\text{SSCORE} = \{(\phi_i, a_i) \mapsto s_i \mid \phi_i \in \Phi\}$$

   where $a_i \in \{\mathbf{del}, \mathbf{inst}, \mathbf{inst\text{-}del}, \mathbf{sk}\}$ is the chosen edit action.
2. We then score ordered pairs of quantified assertions, along with the most promising actions for each assertion. More formally, we create another partial map:

$$\text{DSCORE} = \{\langle(\phi_i, a_i), (\phi_d, a_j)\rangle \mapsto s_{ij} \mid \phi_i, \phi_j \in \Phi\}$$

   where $a_i, a_j \in \{\mathbf{del}, \mathbf{inst}, \mathbf{inst\text{-}del}, \mathbf{sk}\}$ are the chosen edit actions. $\langle(\phi_i, a_i), (\phi_j, a_j)\rangle$ is the doubleton edit we apply (in order). We note that both maps are partial because we may not find an applicable action for certain assertions.

We split the discussion on the ranking of edits based on the hypothesized failure mode (QU or TO), as the two failure modes require different strategies.

Ranking Edits for QU We start with how we handle QU failures, which is more straightforward. At the general triage (Sec. 4.2) stage, we hypothesize that the QU failures are due to the absence of certain instantiations. Intuitively, we are looking for under-instantiated axioms, where **inst** is applicable, i.e.,

$$\text{SScore} = \{(\phi_i, \textbf{inst}) \mapsto s_i \mid \phi_i \in \Phi\}$$

There are various ways to use the differential scores to set s_i. Plausible contenders include:

1. (Deficit, $-\text{Excess}$)
2. ($-\text{Excess}$, Deficit)
3. $\kappa \cdot \text{Deficit} - \text{Excess}$ (for some constant κ)
4. $\text{Deficit}/\text{Excess}$

We experimented with multiple examples of each of these heuristics. Eventually we settled on the first one, using Deficit as the primary metric.

However, the picture becomes complicated when instantiations contain Skolem constants. In that case, we cannot fully materialize all of ϕ_i's proof instantiations $\mathcal{I}_{\mathfrak{p}}^{\phi_i}$, unless all its Skolem dependencies are met. If the actual materializable instantiation count is 0 (indicating that no instantiations can be created without Skolemization), then we drop ϕ_i in the singleton phase.

We address this issue in the doubleton stage. Specifically, we use the Contingency score to select the first axiom ϕ_i for **sk**; i.e., the quantified assertion with the most "contingent" instantiations depending on its Skolem constant. When choosing the second axiom ϕ_j, we only consider ϕ_j candidates that depend on the Skolem constant $f_{\phi_{ix}}$ in their instantiations, and we can apply **inst** to ϕ_j. More formally,

$$\text{DScore} = \{\langle(\phi_i, \textbf{sk}), (\phi_j, \textbf{inst})\rangle \mapsto s_{ij} \mid \phi_i, \phi_j \in \Phi\}$$

where $s_{ij} = (\text{Contingency}(\phi_i, \mathfrak{p}), \text{Deficit}(\phi_j, \mathfrak{p}, \mathfrak{t}))$, and $\exists I \mid I \in \mathcal{I}_{\mathfrak{p}}^{\phi_j}, f_{\phi_{ix}} \sqsubseteq I$.

Ranking Edits for TO In the general triage stage (Sec. 4.2), we hypothesize that in a TO failure, the solver is spending significant time and resources on irrelevant quantified formulas. For this failure mode, we focus on the *quantified axioms* in Λ as targets. Intuitively, we want to suppress the excessive instantiations in order to stabilize the query, under the constraint that we cannot edit the goal itself (since we want to our edits to preserve soundness).

A natural choice would be to use the Excess for SScore, and then apply **del** to the axiom ϕ_i with the highest Excess. However, the situation is more complex than QU in two ways. **(1)** We cannot simply delete an arbitrary ϕ_i with a high Excess. The axiom may be necessary for the proof, and deleting it will render the goal un-provable (i.e., creating incompleteness). **(2)** Even if ϕ_i is indeed unnecessary, other excessively instantiated axioms may also be contributing to the instability.

Problem (1) is easier to address. We use the **inst-del** edit action, replacing the axiom ϕ_i with its instantiations from the successful proof trace $\mathcal{I}_{\mathfrak{p}}^{\phi_i}$. Intuitively, this eliminates the need (and the ability) for the solver to instantiate ϕ_i:

since $\mathcal{I}_{\mathfrak{p}}^{\phi_i}$ is sufficient for the proof, this action works around the incompleteness issue.

Problem (2) is more challenging. Anecdotally, if we focus solely on the EXCESS score, the debugging process turns into a "whack-a-mole" situation, where we delete one axiom, only to find another axiom with high EXCESS taking its place, and we fail to stabilize the query. Hence, to successfully repair the query, we need a mechanism to identify the underlying cause of the excessive instantiations.

Dependency Analysis In order to locate the root cause of TO instability, we further analyze the causal relations between the instantiations. Our notion of causality extends the *instantiation graph* from the SMTSCOPE (formerly the Axiom Profiler) [4], a tool to analyze instantiation loops and other sources of poor performance in pattern-based SMT solvers. Below, we describe Axiom Profiler's approach and then our extension.

The instantiation graph is a directed acyclic graph over the terms (instantiations) in a trace log $\mathfrak{t}$. More formally, we model this as a graph G_0 with the node set:

$$\{(I, \phi_i) \mid I \in \mathcal{I}_{\mathfrak{t}}^{\phi_i}, \phi_i \in \Omega\}$$

where each instantiation is labeled with its quantified formula ϕ_i. Edges in the graph indicate the causal relations, which include the following:

- **Instantiating Dependency**: an instantiation causes another one to materialize due to a matched pattern. Let (I_s, ϕ_s) and (I_d, ϕ_d) be two nodes in G_0, where $\phi_d = \forall x.\varphi_j$ is guarded by the pattern π_j. Suppose a sub-term of I_s matches π_j, i.e., $\pi_j[x \mapsto t] \sqsubseteq I_s$ for some ground term t. This match triggers the creation of $I_d = \varphi_j[x \mapsto t]$, corresponding to an edge $(I_s, \phi_s) \rightarrow (I_d, \phi_d)$ in G_0.
- **Equational Dependency**: an equational rewrite (from one instantiation) contributes to another instantiation. Continuing the example above, I_s may only trigger π_j after additional equality rewrites. Consider a quantified formula $\phi_{eq} = \forall x.p(x) \cong q(x)$ and one of its instantiations $I_{eq} = p(a) \cong q(a)$. The solver might have to rewrite I_s with I_{eq} first, and then the rewrite result, $I_s[p(a) \mapsto q(a)]$, triggers the creation of I_d. In that case, there is also an edge $(I_{eq}, \phi_{eq}) \rightarrow (I_d, \phi_d)$ in G_0.

We further extend this graph G_0 from prior work into a graph G_1 to capture two additional types of dependencies.

- **Skolemizing Dependency**: a Skolem constant is a sub-term of an instantiation. Consider the existentially quantified $\phi_i = \exists x.\varphi_i$ with Skolem constant $f_{\phi_{ix}}$. There might be some node (I_d, ϕ_d) in G_1 such that $f_{\phi_{ix}} \sqsubseteq I_d$. In that case, we add the node $(f_{\phi_{ix}}, \phi_s)$, and the edge $(f_{\phi_{ix}}, \phi_s) \rightarrow (I_d, \phi_d)$ to G_1. This form of dependency follows the same intuition as in our definition of CONTINGENCY, except we apply it to the trace log here.
- **Nesting Dependency**: an instantiation is a (previously-nested) quantified formula, which creates further instantiations. For example, consider (I_s, ϕ_s), where $\phi_s = \forall x.(f(x) \wedge \forall y.g(x, y))$, and $I_s = f(t) \wedge \forall y.g(t, y)$ for some ground term t. Let $\phi_d = \forall y.g(t, y)$ be the nested quantified formula. Intuitively, I_s is

the reason why ϕ_d exists at all. We thus add an edge from (I_s, ϕ_s) to every (I_d, ϕ_d), where $I_d \in \mathcal{I}_{\mathfrak{t}}^{\phi_d}$.

The graph G_1 captures the four types of dependencies we discussed above, which offers a rather low-level view of the instantiation reasoning in the trace. We further process G_1 so that it reflects the relation between the quantified formulas.

1. We collapse G_1 into a multi-edge graph G_2. We initialize G_2 with Ω as its nodes. For each edge $(I_s, \phi_s) \rightarrow (I_d, \phi_d)$ in G_1, we create an edge $\phi_s \rightarrow \phi_d$.
2. We reduce G_2 into a weighted simple graph G_3. For each pair of neighboring nodes ϕ_s and ϕ_d with $m_{s,d}$ parallel edges in G_2, we keep one edge $\phi_s \rightarrow \phi_d$ in G_3 with the weight $m_{s,d}$.
3. We normalize the edge weights in G_3, where we set the weight for $\phi_s \rightarrow \phi_d$ in G_3 to:
$$w_{s,d} = \frac{m_{s,d}}{\sum_{\phi_i \rightarrow \phi_d} m_{i,d}}$$
Intuitively, $w_{s,d}$ reflects the normalized "impact" of ϕ_s on ϕ_d over all the in-coming edges (via other ϕ_i) to ϕ_d.

Hence the output of our dependency analysis is a directed simple graph G_3 over Ω, where each edge weight $w_{s,d}$ captures (or rather, approximates) the normalized impact of ϕ_s over ϕ_d. For example, $w_{s,d} = 0.5$ signifies that ϕ_s has an *immediate impact* on 50% of the instantiations of ϕ_d.

We then compute the transitive impact through fixed-point iterations. Concretely, for $\phi_i \in \Lambda$, we consider the reachable subgraph G_{ϕ_i} in G_3. We initialize a ratio $r_d = 0$ for each ϕ_d in G_{ϕ_i}, except for ϕ_i, where we set $r_i = 1$. We then update each ratio $r_d = \sum_s r_s \cdot w_{s,d}$. After the fixed-point computation terminates, we use the weighted sum of Excess as the final score for ϕ_i:

$$\text{SScore} = \{(\phi_i, a_i) \mapsto \sum_{\phi_j \in \Omega} \text{Excess}(\phi_j, \mathfrak{t}, \mathfrak{p}) \cdot r_j \mid \phi_i \in \Lambda\}$$

The fixed-point computation is non-decreasing by transitivity. However, there is no theoretical guarantee that it will converge. In particular, when G_{ϕ_i} contains a cycle, a node's ratio may approach a limit at an exponentially decaying rate. Nevertheless, this is not a threat to practical usage. In particular, since floating point numbers represent the ratios, the convergence criteria must be threshold-based. For our implementation, we consider a ratio to have converged if its increment from the previous iteration is $\leq 10^{-4}$.

Now that we have the scores for each axiom, we proceed to choose the singleton edit action. We do so with a simple heuristic: if we can delete an axiom without causing incompleteness, we choose **del**. Otherwise, we instantiate the axiom with its proof instantiations, using **inst-del**. However, if there is Skolemization dependency preventing us from fully materializing the proof instantiations, we choose **inst** instead. Finally, if we have no other choice beyond Skolemization (**sk**), we select it.

Given this setup, ranking the doubleton edits is simple. We use the fixed-point computation to estimate the impact of each pair of axioms; i.e., we initialize

$r_i = 1, r_j = 1$ for the pair (ϕ_i, ϕ_j), and then iterate over the nodes in G_3 to update the ratios. We then use the same weighted sum of Excess to calculate the final score for each pair. We also use the same heuristic to choose the edit actions for each pair.

5 Evaluation

In this section we perform an evaluation of Cazamariposas. We start with a brief overview of the implementation in Sec. 5.1, followed by a discussion of the benchmarks used in our evaluation Sec. 5.2. We then present the results of our evaluation, structured around two research questions: (1) Does the experimental data support our hypothesis about the different failure modes? and (2) How effective is Cazamariposas at identifying stabilizing edits?

5.1 Implementation

Our implementation of Cazamariposas is in 4,730 lines of Python, publicly available on GitHub [8], as a part of the Mariposa tool-chain. Here we also discuss our use of other tools and the configuration settings.

Mariposa We use Mariposa twice in our workflow, first to test whether the initial query Φ is stable and finally to test whether our various fixes are stable. We run Mariposa with its standard configuration, creating 180 total mutants for each query for full stability test. We use the default timeout of 60 seconds for the Mariposa benchmarks, but for the Verus benchmarks, we align the timeout limit with the project artifacts, which use 10 seconds.

Z3 We use a recent version of the Z3 solver (4.13.0). We evaluate Cazamariposas with Z3, as Dafny, $F^\star$, and Verus are designed with Z3 in mind. Past work [34] has shown that other solvers such as cvc5 [3] and Vampire [18] are not optimized for these verification languages, resulting in large numbers of unsolvable queries.

Z3 provides proof-production functionality, which can be complicated to use in practice. Enabling proof production often causes Z3 to take a different path, completely failing on an otherwise solvable query. To work around this, we have employed the following strategies: (1) use Z3 to find an unsatisfiable core first and then produce a proof from the core, (2) use 4 different versions of Z3 solver, (3) use an extended timeout of 1 hour, and (4) use up to 256 mutants. We note that these configuration are for finding proofs, not for testing stability. Despite all of these strategies, we were unable to get proofs for 4 Mariposa queries and 3 Verus queries. In our evaluation, we count these cases as if Cazamariposas *fails to find a fix*. Ideally the proof-production failures can be addressed within the SMT solver.

SmtScope We created a fork of SmtScope [14] to parse the Z3 trace logs, and then we enhance their instantiation graph as described in Sec. 4.4.

5.2 Verus Benchmark Set

In addition to the Mariposa benchmark with 545 unstable queries (from five systems projects written in Dafny and F*), we curate a new benchmark set comprised of SMT queries from ten Verus verification projects. Between these Verus projects, there are a total of 7,584 queries of which 7,514 (~99%) are stable and 70 (~1%) are unstable. We refer the readers to a detailed breakdown of projects in our technical report [35].

We conduct all of our stability tests, for benchmark creation and evaluation, all on the same set of machines with an Intel Core i9-9900K (max 5.00 GHz) CPU, 128 GB of RAM, and Ubuntu 20.04.3.

In summary, we evaluate Cazamariposas on 70 unstable Verus queries and 545 unstable Mariposa queries, for a total of unstable 615 queries.

5.3 Failure Mode Distinction

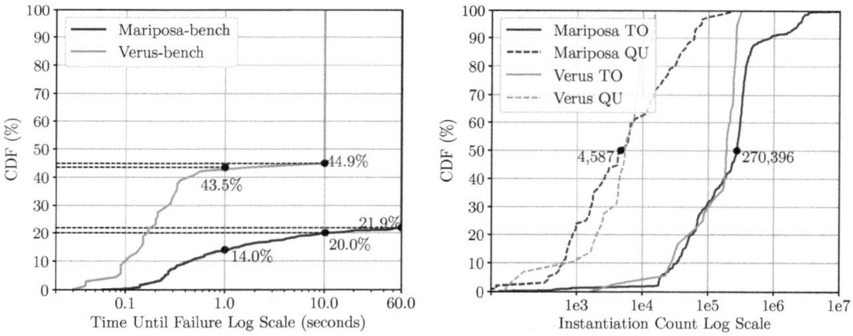

(a) Bimodal Mutant Failure Time (b) Instantiation Count Distributions

Fig. 2: **Failure Mode Distinction**. In (a) we plot the runtime of the failed mutants Φ_f, **before** the triage. In (b), we plot the instantiation count for the failed mutants Φ_f based on the failure modes triage.

Cazamariposas's first step is to triage a query's failure mode into either quick unknown (QU) or slow timeout (TO). Here we present empirical evidence for the distinction. In Figure 2a, for each original query Φ in the benchmarks, we report the runtime of its failed mutant Φ_f. The plot is in log scale, and we observe that the distribution for each benchmark is bimodal. For Verus-bench, ~43% of the failures occur within 1 second, barely any occur between 1 and 10 seconds, and the rest fail at 10 seconds. For Mariposa-bench, the distribution is more spread out, but the separation is still clear, where ~19% queries fail within 10 seconds, and ~78% time out after 60 seconds. There is almost no middle ground between the two modes. The x-axis of Figure 3 shows how many queries from each benchmark Cazamariposas ultimately classifies as QU versus TO.

In Figure 2b, we examine our hypothesis that QU failures are due to insufficient instantiation, and TO failures are due to excessive instantiation. We perform our triage, and then plot the instantiation counts based on the failure modes. Note the log-scale on x-axis, which highlights that the TO failures have orders of magnitude more instantiations than the QU failures. For example, in Mariposa TO, the median instantiation count is 270, 396 while in Mariposa QU, the median is 4, 587. The separation is also clear within Verus benchmark.

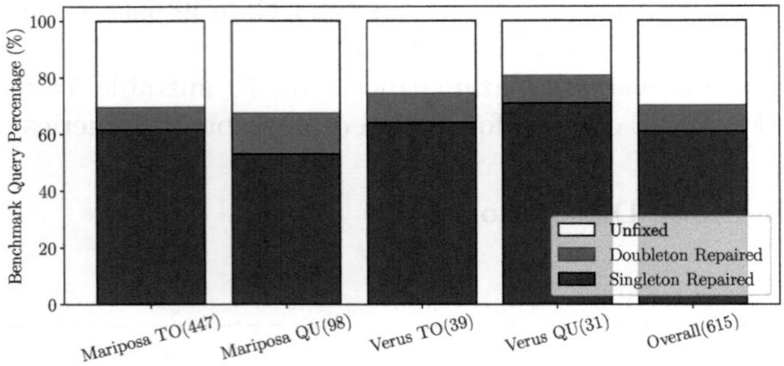

Fig. 3: Percentage of Benchmark Queries Repaired.

5.4 Stabilizing Edits Found

Next, we evaluate Cazamariposas' ability to automatically identify stabilizing edits. Recall that Cazamariposas first tries $k = 10$ singleton edits, and if none works, it tries 10 doubleton edits. Overall, Cazamariposas repairs 431/615 ($\approx$ 70%) of the benchmark queries. Figure 3 provides more details, reporting Cazamariposas' performance on the two benchmarks, subdivided by the underlying failure type (TO vs. QU). We note that Mariposa TO accounts for the largest absolute number of queries. Cazamariposas appears to be more effective on Verus queries in either failure type. Nevertheless, Cazamariposas repairs approximately 69% of the Mariposa queries and 77% of the Verus queries. This compares favorably to the best results from prior work (Sec. 2), which stabilized 29% of the Mariposa benchmark. We also observe that 375/615 ($\approx$ 61%) queries can be stabilized with a single edit. Doubleton edits subsequently provide a small but noticeable boost.

We also evaluate how well Cazamariposas ranks the stabilizing edits. First, in Figure 4a, we show the distribution of the number of quantified formulas in the original queries. For example, in Mariposa TO, the median count is 5, 965, which is a large search space for possible edits. The median count is lower in Verus QU, making it potentially more tractable to fully explore.

Now that we have sense of the search space, we evaluate how well Cazamariposas identifies the useful edits. In Figure 4b, we report the minimal rank of

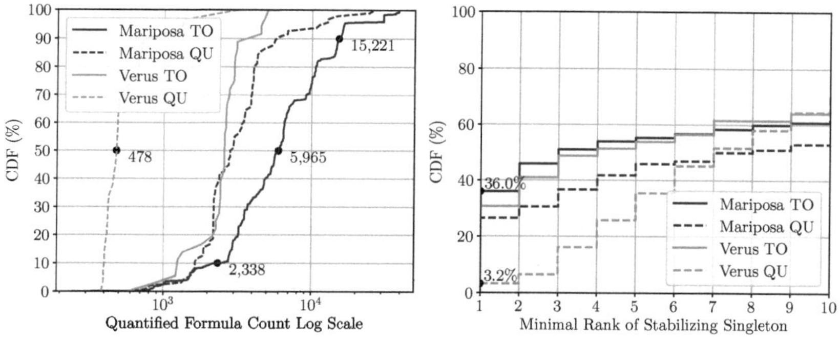

(a) Quantified Formula Count. (b) Rank of Stabilizing Edits.

Fig. 4: Finding Repairs Among Large Number of Quantified Formulas.

the stabilizing singleton edits. Specifically in singletons, given a query, Cazamariposas produces a ranked list of 10 edits, and we report the rank of the first stabilizing edit within this list. We note the endpoints of the CDFs on the y-axis. It is the probability that Cazamariposas finds a stabilizing edit within the first 10 singleton edits, which corresponds to Figure 3. We note the start points of the CDFs on the y-axis. This is the probability that the first edit Cazamariposas tries would directly work. For a Mariposa TO query, Cazamariposas has a 36% chance of finding a stabilizing edit with one shot.

6 Conclusions

Proof instability is a major impediment to industrial use of automated program verification tools. Hence, we propose a new approach that targets specific instances of instability. Using a novel differential analysis, we automatically classify the type of instability a query is experiencing, rank the problematic quantifiers in the query, and then efficiently identify targeted query edits that stabilize the query. We implement this approach in Cazamariposas and evaluate it on SMT queries from numerous verification projects written in three automated verification languages. Cazamariposas successfully repairs 70% of the unstable queries.

Acknowledgments

We thank Jay Bosamiya and the anonymous reviewers for their valuable feedback on the paper. We thank Jonáš Fiala for his help with using and modifying SMTSCOPE.

This work was supported in part by the National Science Foundation (NSF) under grant 2224279, funding from AFRL and DARPA under Agreement FA8750-24-9-1000, and the Future Enterprise Security initiative at Carnegie Mellon CyLab (FutureEnterprise@CyLab).

Disclosure of Interests: The authors have no competing interests to declare that are relevant to the content of this article.

References

1. Amrollahi, D., Preiner, M., Niemetz, A., Reynolds, A., Charikar, M., Tinelli, C., Barrett, C.: Using normalization to improve SMT solver stability (2024), https://arxiv.org/abs/2410.22419
2. Backes, J., Bolignano, P., Cook, B., Dodge, C., Gacek, A., Luckow, K., Rungta, N., Tkachuk, O., Varming, C.: Semantic-based automated reasoning for AWS access policies using SMT. In: Formal Methods in Computer Aided Design (FMCAD) (2018). https://doi.org/10.23919/FMCAD.2018.8602994
3. Barbosa, H., Barrett, C., Brain, M., Kremer, G., Lachnitt, H., Mann, M., Mohamed, A., Mohamed, M., Niemetz, A., Nötzli, A., et al.: cvc5: A Versatile and Industrial-Strength SMT Solver. In: Tools and Algorithms for the Construction and Analysis of Systems (TACAS) (2022). https://doi.org/10.1007/978-3-030-99524-9_24
4. Becker, N., Müller, P., Summers, A.J.: The axiom profiler: Understanding and debugging SMT quantifier instantiations. In: Tools and Algorithms for the Construction and Analysis of Systems (TACAS) (2019)
5. Blanchette, J.C., Kühlwein, D., Geschke, S., Loewe, B., Schlicht, P.: A survey of axiom selection as a machine learning problem. In: Infinity, Computability, and Metamathematics: Festschrift Celebrating the 60th Birthdays of Peter Koepke and Philip Welch. Tributes, College Publications (2014)
6. Böhme, S.: Proof reconstruction for Z3 in Isabelle/HOL. In: International Workshop on Satisfiability Modulo Theories (2009)
7. Bordis, T., Leino, K.R.M.: Free facts: An alternative to inefficient axioms in Dafny. In: Formal Methods: 26th International Symposium (FM) (2024). https://doi.org/10.1007/978-3-031-71162-6_8
8. Cazamariposas. https://github.com/secure-foundations/mariposa, accessed Feb. 2025
9. Chakarov, A., Geldenhuys, J., Heck, M., Hicks, M., Huang, S., Jaloyan, G.A., Joshi, A., Leino, R., Mayer, M., McLaughlin, S., Mritunjai, A., Claudel, C.P., Porncharoenwase, S., Rabe, F., Rapoport, M., Reger, G., Roux, C., Rungta, N., Salkeld, R., Schlaipfer, M., Schoepe, D., Schwartzentruber, J., Tasiran, S., Tomb, A., Torlak, E., Tristan, J., Wagner, L., Whalen, M., Willems, R., Xiang, J., Byun, T.J., Cohen, J., Wang, R., Jang, J., Rath, J., Syeda, H.T., Wagner, D., Yuan, Y.: Formally verified cloud-scale authorization. In: International Conference on Software Engineering (ICSE) (2025), https://www.amazon.science/publications/formally-verified-cloud-scale-authorization
10. Cutler, J.W., Disselkoen, C., Eline, A., He, S., Headley, K., Hicks, M., Hietala, K., Ioannidis, E., Kastner, J., Mamat, A., McAdams, D., McCutchen, M., Rungta, N., Torlak, E., Wells, A.M.: Cedar: A new language for expressive, fast, safe, and analyzable authorization. In: Proceedings of the ACM Conference on Object-Oriented Programming Systems, Languages, and Applications (OOPSLA) (Apr 2024). https://doi.org/10.1145/3649835
11. De Moura, L., Bjørner, N.: Z3: An efficient SMT solver. In: Tools and Algorithms for the Construction and Analysis of Systems (TACAS) (2008). https://doi.org/10.1007/978-3-540-78800-3_24

12. Dodds, M.: Formally Verifying Industry Cryptography. IEEE Security and Privacy Magazine (2022). https://doi.org/10.1109/MSEC.2022.3153035
13. Ferraiuolo, A., Baumann, A., Hawblitzel, C., Parno, B.: Komodo: Using Verification to Disentangle Secure-Enclave Hardware from Software. In: Proceedings of the ACM Symposium on Operating Systems Principles (SOSP) (2017). https://doi.org/10.1145/3132747.3132782
14. Fiala, J.: SmtScope (2025), https://github.com/viperproject/smt-scope, accessed Feb. 2025
15. Hawblitzel, C., Howell, J., Kapritsos, M., Lorch, J.R., Parno, B., Roberts, M.L., Setty, S., Zill, B.: IronFleet: Proving practical distributed systems correct. In: Proceedings of the ACM Symposium on Operating Systems Principles (SOSP) (2015)
16. Hawblitzel, C., Howell, J., Lorch, J.R., Narayan, A., Parno, B., Zhang, D., Zill, B.: Ironclad Apps: End-to-end security via automated full-system verification. In: Proceedings of the USENIX Symposium on Operating Systems Design and Implementation (OSDI) (October 2014)
17. Hoder, K., Voronkov, A.: Sine qua non for large theory reasoning. In: International Conference on Automated Deduction. pp. 299–314. Springer (2011)
18. Kovács, L., Voronkov, A.: First-order theorem proving and Vampire. In: Computer Aided Verification (CAV) (2013)
19. Lattuada, A., Hance, T., Bosamiya, J., Brun, M., Cho, C., LeBlanc, H., Srinivasan, P., Achermann, R., Chajed, T., Hawblitzel, C., Howell, J., Lorch, J., Padon, O., Parno, B.: Verus: A practical foundation for systems verification. In: Proceedings of the ACM Symposium on Operating Systems Principles (SOSP) (November 2024)
20. Lattuada, A., Hance, T., Cho, C., Brun, M., Subasinghe, I., Zhou, Y., Howell, J., Parno, B., Hawblitzel, C.: Verus: Verifying Rust programs using linear ghost types. In: Proceedings of the ACM Conference on Object-Oriented Programming Systems, Languages, and Applications (OOPSLA) (December 2023)
21. Leino, K.R.M., Pit-Claudel, C.: Trigger selection strategies to stabilize program verifiers. In: Chaudhuri, S., Farzan, A. (eds.) Proceedings of the International Conference on Computer Aided Verification (CAV) (2016)
22. Leino, K.R.M.: Dafny: An automatic program verifier for functional correctness. In: Logic for Programming, Artificial Intelligence, and Reasoning (LPAR) (2010)
23. Moskal, M.: Programming with triggers. In: Proceedings of the Workshop on Satisfiability Modulo Theories (2009)
24. de Moura, L., Bjørner, N.: Efficient e-matching for SMT solvers. In: Conference on Automated Deduction (CADE) (2007)
25. Profiling Z3 and solving proof performance issues. https://fstar-lang.org/tutorial/book/under_the_hood/uth_smt.html#profiling-z3-and-solving-proof-performance-issues
26. Protzenko, J., Parno, B., Fromherz, A., Hawblitzel, C., Polubelova, M., Bhargavan, K., Beurdouche, B., Choi, J., Delignat-Lavaud, A., Fournet, C., Kulatova, N., Ramananandro, T., Rastogi, A., Swamy, N., Wintersteiger, C., Zanella-Beguelin, S.: EverCrypt: A Fast, Verified, Cross-Platform Cryptographic Provider. In: Proceedings of the IEEE Symposium on Security and Privacy (May 2020)
27. Reitz, A., Fromherz, A., Protzenko, J.: StarMalloc: Verifying a modern, hardened memory allocator. Proc. ACM Program. Lang. (Oct 2024). https://doi.org/10.1145/3689773
28. Rungta, N.: A billion SMT queries a day (invited paper). In: Shoham, S., Vizel, Y. (eds.) Proceedings of the International Conference on Computer Aided Verification (CAV) (2022)

29. Schulz, S., Cruanes, S., Vukmirović, P.: Faster, higher, stronger: E 2.3. In: Fontaine, P. (ed.) Proc. of the 27th CADE, Natal, Brasil. pp. 495–507. No. 11716 in LNAI, Springer (2019)
30. Swamy, N., Hriţcu, C., Keller, C., Rastogi, A., Delignat-Lavaud, A., Forest, S., Bhargavan, K., Fournet, C., Strub, P.Y., Kohlweiss, M., Zinzindohoue, J.K., Zanella-Béguelin, S.: Dependent Types and Multi-Monadic Effects in F*. In: Proceedings of the ACM Symposium on Principles of Programming Languages (POPL) (2016)
31. Tomb, A., Tristan, J.B.: Avoiding verification brittleness in Dafny. https://dafny.org/blog/2023/12/01/avoiding-verification-brittleness/ (2023)
32. Verification debugging when verification fails. https://dafny.org/dafny/DafnyRef/DafnyRef#sec-brittle-verification
33. Zhou, Y., Bosamiya, J., Li, J., Heule, M., Parno, B.: Context pruning for more robust SMT-based program verification. In: Proceedings of the Formal Methods in Computer-Aided Design (FMCAD) Conference (October 2024)
34. Zhou, Y., Bosamiya, J., Takashima, Y., Li, J., Heule, M., Parno, B.: Mariposa: Measuring SMT instability in automated program verification. In: Proceedings of the Formal Methods in Computer-Aided Design (FMCAD) (October 2023)
35. Zhou, Y., Shah, A., , Lin, Z., Heule, M., Parno, B.: Cazamariposas: Automated Instability Debugging in SMT-based Program Verification (Technical Report). Tech. rep., Carnegie Mellon University (June 2025), doi.org/10.1184/R1/29207189

Boosting MCSat Modulo Nonlinear Integer Arithmetic via Local Search

Enrico Lipparini[1,2](✉), Thomas Hader[3], Ahmed Irfan[4], and Stéphane Graham-Lengrand[4]

[1] University of Cagliari, Cagliari, Italy
enrico.lipparini@unica.it
[2] University of Genoa, Genoa, Italy
[3] TU Wien, Vienna, Austria
thomas.hader@tuwien.ac.at
[4] SRI International, Menlo Park, CA, USA
{ahmed.irfan,stephane.graham-lengrand}@sri.com

Abstract. The Model Constructing Satisfiability (MCSat) approach to the SMT problem extends the ideas of CDCL from the SAT level to the theory level. Like SAT, its search is driven by incrementally constructing a model by assigning concrete values to theory variables and performing theory-level reasoning to learn lemmas when conflicts arise. Therefore, the selection of values can significantly impact the search process and the solver's performance. In this work, we propose guiding the MCSat search by utilizing assignment values discovered through local search. First, we present a theory-agnostic framework to seamlessly integrate local search techniques within the MCSat framework. Then, we highlight how to use the framework to design a search procedure for (quantifier-free) Nonlinear Integer Arithmetic ($\mathcal{NIA}$), utilizing accelerated hill-climbing and a new operation called *feasible-sets jumping*. We implement the proposed approach in the MCSat engine of the Yices2 solver, and empirically evaluate its performance over the $\mathcal{NIA}$ benchmarks of SMT-LIB.

1 Introduction

Satisfiability Modulo Theory (SMT) is the problem of deciding the satisfiability of a first-order formula with respect to defined background theories. SMT solvers are the core backbone of a vast range of verification and synthesis tools that require reasoning about expressive logical theories such as real/integer arithmetic [3,16]. One of the major state-of-the-art approaches to SMT is the Model Constructing Satisfiability calculus (MCSat) [15,29], which generalizes the ideas of Conflict-Driven Clause Learning (CDCL) to the theory level, and which has been shown to perform particularly well on complex theories such as nonlinear arithmetic. In the MCSat approach, the solver progressively constructs a *theory model*, similarly to how SAT solvers construct Boolean models. Theory reasoning is used to assess the consistency of partial models, provide explanations of infeasibility, decide theory variables, and propagate theory constraints.

C. Barrett and U. Waldmann (Eds.): CADE 2025, LNAI 15943, pp. 95–115, 2025.
https://doi.org/10.1007/978-3-031-99984-0_6

When extending the partial model with a new assignment to a theory variable, picking a good value is critical for the overall performance of the solver. Heuristics used by state-of-the-art solvers pick values on the basis of compatibility with the current search state and of computational cheapness. This has a major drawback: these heuristics only consider knowledge of the current search state, neglecting information on how likely a particular assignment is to lead to a satisfying model eventually.

In this work, we address the problem of choosing good values for variable decisions by augmenting the current search state knowledge with insights provided by local search techniques. Following the logic-to-optimization approach [19,37], we associate to the logical formula a cost function that represents the *distance from a model*, and use local search to find assignments that have a small cost. These assignments are then used to guide future MCSat decisions.

Although local search has already been used in the context of SMT, either as a standalone solver [6,35,46] or as a CDCL(T) theory solver [48], our work is the first to propose a tight integration of local search within the MCSat framework, creating a powerful synergy between the reasoning capabilities of MCSat and the intuition provided by local search which boosts performance for both satisfiable and unsatisfiable instances. Our novel approach is flexible enough to allow calls to local search at any point during the MCSat search, seamlessly fitting with the current state. As MCSat progresses through decisions, propagations, and conflicts, the local search problem is instantiated accordingly: (i) the cost function is built upon the simplification of the original formula under current state assumptions, (ii) initial local search assignments are based on the current search state as well as cached values, and (iii) local search moves are enhanced by information on intervals of feasible assignments to theory variables as tracked by the MCSat engine.

While our approach can be applied to any theory supported by MCSat, in this work we showcase its application to the theory of nonlinear integer arithmetic ($\mathcal{NIA}$). In particular, we design a procedure based on a new operation called *feasible-sets jumping*, which allows to move between feasible intervals, and on accelerated hill-climbing [26], to move inside feasible intervals.

Contributions. In this work we: (i) design a theory-agnostic framework to tightly integrate local search techniques within the MCSat approach in order to guide variable decisions, (i) use the framework to define a local search procedure for the theory of nonlinear integer arithmetic, that makes use of feasible-sets jumping and accelerated hill-climbing, and (i) show the practical applicability of our method using our implementation in the MCSat engine of Yices2 [17] on the quantifier-free $\mathcal{NIA}$ benchmark set of SMT-LIB [2].

Structure. In Sect. 2, we provide the necessary background. Section 3 describes a deep integration of local search techniques within the MCSat framework from a general point of view, which is applied in Sect. 4 to define a local search approach for non-linear integer arithmetic. In Sect. 5, we show and discuss the results of our experiments before presenting related work in Sect. 6 and concluding in Sect. 7.

2 Preliminaries

We assume basic knowledge on the standard first-order quantifier-free logical setting and standard notions of theory, satisfiability, and logical consequence. We write logical *variables* with $x, y, \ldots$, and concrete *values* with $\alpha, \beta, \ldots$ (the domain of concrete values is theory specific, e.g. $\mathbb{Z}$ for integer arithmetic, $\mathbb{R}$ for real arithmetic). An *assignment* μ is a map from variables to values of matching type. If ϕ is a formula, we denote with $Vars(\phi)$ the set of its (free) variables. We use C to denote clauses, and L to denote literals. Nonlinear Integer Arithmetic ($\mathcal{NIA}$) is the theory consisting of arbitrary Boolean combinations of Boolean variables and arithmetic atoms of the form of polynomial equalities and polynomial inequalities over integer variables. The theory is undecidable by Matiyasevich's theorem [40].

2.1 SMT and MCSat

SMT [3] is the problem of deciding the satisfiability of a first-order formula with respect to some theory or combination of theories. Two of the major approaches for SMT solving are the Conflict-Driven Clause Learning with theory support (CDCL(T)) [3,42] and the MCSat approach. In the former, theory solvers augment a propositional SAT engine with theory reasoning procedures which are capable of deciding a conjunction of literals (i.e. atomic formulas and their negations) in a particular theory. A propositional model (of the Boolean abstraction of the formula) found by the SAT solver is then checked by all theory engines for theory consistency.

The latter, MCSat, applies CDCL-like mechanisms to perform theory reasoning directly. It can be used either as a theory solver for a specific theory (e.g. in Z3 [14] for non-linear arithmetic over the reals and the integers [4]), or as a fully-fledged stand-alone engine able to handle multiple theories (e.g. in Yices2 for non-linear arithmetic over the reals [30] and over the integers [28], bit-vectors [21], arrays [27], and finite fields [24,25]; as well as in SMT-RAT [13] for non-linear real arithmetic [33]). The MCSat architecture consists of a core solver, an assignment trail, and plugins for theory reasoning. Figure 1 illustrates the high level flow of the MCSat framework.

The core solver incrementally constructs a partial model consisting of Boolean and theory assignments (stored in a *trail*), maintaining the invariant that none of the constraints evaluate to false under the partial model. The trail contains three kinds of elements: *propagated literals* (literals implied to be true by the current state), *decided literals* (literals that we assume to be true), and *model assignments* (assignments of first-order variables to concrete values). Propagations, conflict analysis, lemmas generation, and variable decisions are all handled by theory plugins (including a Boolean plugin that is responsible for propositional reasoning). In general, plugins also keep a *feasibility set* for each variable of their competence, containing the values that are consistent with the current trail and are, thus, candidates to be picked for deciding the variable.

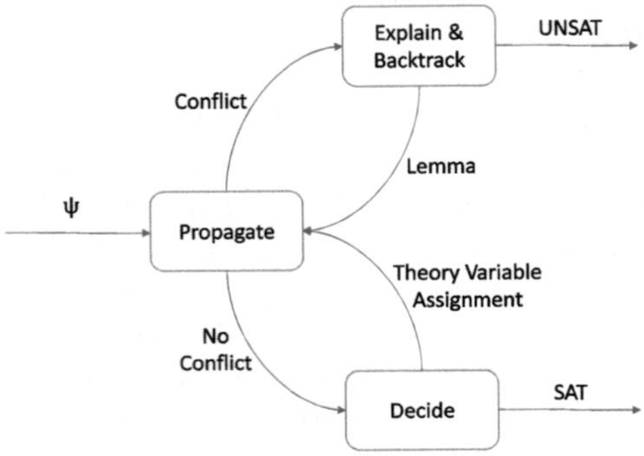

Fig. 1. The MCSat framework consists of the following steps: 1) Propagate the trail. 2) If a conflict is found during propagation, check if there is any decision to backtrack over. If not, return UNSAT. Otherwise, explain the conflict using a lemma, backtrack the trail, and repeat step 1. 3) If no conflict is found during propagation, decide on a variable that is not on the trail. If there is nothing left to decide, return SAT. Otherwise, add the decided variable to the trail and repeat step 1.

When the core solver selects a variable for decision, the choice of the value to assign to the variable is handled by the theory plugin responsible for its type. Some solvers (e.g. Yices2) implement a heuristic called *value cache* (a generalization of SAT phase saving [43]), that keeps track of the last value assigned to a variable when the assignment is undone. Then, when a decision has to be made for the variable, the cached value will be used, provided that it is still in the feasibility set; otherwise, it will simply be ignored, and other heuristics will be used (e.g. picking a default value such as 0).

In the following, we will denote with M the trail, with $v[M](x)$ the value of the variable x in the trail (which may be equal to `undef` if the variable is not assigned in the trail), and with $v[M](L)$ the value of the literal L under the assignment in M which may be true ($\top$) or false ($\bot$) if L can be fully evaluated under such assignment, or `undef` otherwise. We denote with $feasible_M(x)$ the feasibility set of x in M, i.e. all values that can be chosen for x in the current search state given by M. For arithmetical theories, we have that $feasible_M(x) \subseteq \mathbb{R}$, and, in particular, that $feasible_M(x)$ is the union of a finite set of *feasible intervals*, i.e. $feasible_M(x) = \bigcup_{i \in [0:m]} I_i$. We assume that theory plugins provide a function $pick\_value(S)$ that returns a value from a set S.

Example 1. Assume a search problem in $\mathbb{Z}$ with variables x, y, and z given by the input formula ϕ.

$$\phi = (\neg(x \geq 1) \vee (xy = 1)) \wedge (\neg(xy = 1) \vee (x + 2yz > 0)) \wedge (z^2 > 1)$$

A possible trail at some point during the search is

$$M = [(z^2 > 1) \mapsto \top, x \mapsto 1, (x \geq 1) \mapsto \top, (xy = 1) \mapsto \top]$$

On M elements are either decided or propagated. The feasibility sets are given by $\mathit{feasible}_M(z) = (-\infty, -1) \cup (1, \infty)$ and $\mathit{feasible}_M(y) = \{1\} = \mathit{feasible}_M(x)$. Since $\mathit{feasible}_M(y)$ is a singleton, we can propagate the assignment $y \mapsto 1$ on M. We further have that $v[M]((x + 2yz > 0)) = \mathtt{undef}$ and $v[M](x) = 1$.

2.2 Local Search

We define a local search problem as a triple $(\mu_0, f_c, \mathit{moves})$, where:

- μ_0 is an initial assignment for a set of variables *Vars*,
- f_c is a cost function from the set of assignments to $\mathbb{R}_{\geq 0}$,
- *moves* is a neighbor relation between assignments.

A local search algorithm starts from the initial assignment μ_0 and iteratively explores neighboring assignments according to the *moves* relation. We say that μ' is a *move from* μif $(\mu, \mu') \in \mathit{moves}$. A move μ' is *accepted* if $f_c(\mu') < f_c(\mu)$. When a move is accepted, the new assignment becomes the current assignment and the search continues until either: a zero-cost assignment is found, there are no more possible moves (meaning that the current assignment represents a *local minimum*), or a given stopping criterion is reached (e.g. number of moves).

The problem of finding a solution for an SMT formula ϕ can be encoded as a local search problem, e.g., by following the logic-to-optimization approach [19, 37, 38], in which a formula ϕ is mapped to a term $\mathcal{L}2\mathcal{O}(\phi)$ that represents the *distance from a solution.*

In principle, the $\mathcal{L}2\mathcal{O}$ operator can be defined for any theory for which the concept of distance between terms makes sense. Here, we limit ourselves to arithmetic theories. We introduce an arithmetic function symbol d of arity 2 and we assume a fixed interpretation d that satisfies the properties of metric distance, i.e. symmetry, positivity, reflexivity, and triangle inequality. We also assume the existence of a fixed constant term ϵ, such that $\epsilon > 0$. The specific choice of d and ϵ is theory-dependent.

We recursively define $\mathcal{L}2\mathcal{O}$ as follows:

$$
\begin{aligned}
&\mathcal{L}2\mathcal{O}(b) &&\stackrel{\text{def}}{=} ITE(b, 0, 1)\\
&\mathcal{L}2\mathcal{O}(\neg b) &&\stackrel{\text{def}}{=} ITE(b, 1, 0)\\
&\mathcal{L}2\mathcal{O}(t_1 = t_2) &&\stackrel{\text{def}}{=} d(t_1, t_2)\\
&\mathcal{L}2\mathcal{O}(t_1 \leq t_2) &&\stackrel{\text{def}}{=} ITE(t_1 \leq t_2,\ 0,\ d(t_1, t_2))\\
&\mathcal{L}2\mathcal{O}(t_1 < t_2) &&\stackrel{\text{def}}{=} ITE(t_1 < t_2,\ 0,\ d(t_1, t_2) + \epsilon)\\
&\mathcal{L}2\mathcal{O}(t_1 \neq t_2) &&\stackrel{\text{def}}{=} ITE(t_1 \neq t_2,\ 0,\ 1)\\
&\mathcal{L}2\mathcal{O}(\phi_1 \wedge \phi_2) &&\stackrel{\text{def}}{=} \mathcal{L}2\mathcal{O}(\phi_1) + \mathcal{L}2\mathcal{O}(\phi_2)\\
&\mathcal{L}2\mathcal{O}(\phi_1 \vee \phi_2) &&\stackrel{\text{def}}{=} \mathcal{L}2\mathcal{O}(\phi_1) \cdot \mathcal{L}2\mathcal{O}(\phi_2)\\
&\mathcal{L}2\mathcal{O}(ITE(\phi_c, \phi_1, \phi_2) &&\stackrel{\text{def}}{=} ITE(\phi_c,\ \mathcal{L}2\mathcal{O}(\phi_1),\ \mathcal{L}2\mathcal{O}(\phi_2))\\
&\mathcal{L}2\mathcal{O}(\neg ITE(\phi_c, \phi_1, \phi_2)) &&\stackrel{\text{def}}{=} ITE(\phi_c,\ \mathcal{L}2\mathcal{O}(\neg\phi_1),\ \mathcal{L}2\mathcal{O}(\neg\phi_2))
\end{aligned}
$$

It is easy to check that a complete assignment μ satisfies ϕ if and only if $\mathcal{L}2\mathcal{O}(\phi)$ evaluates to 0 under μ.

In the following, with a slight abuse of notation, we denote with $\mathcal{L}2\mathcal{O}(\phi)$ also the corresponding arithmetic function determined by the interpretation d and the constant ϵ, and we define the *cost function* associated to ϕ as $f_c \stackrel{\text{def}}{=} \mathcal{L}2\mathcal{O}(\phi)$.

Example 2. Let $\phi \stackrel{\text{def}}{=} b \wedge x = y^2$, and $\mathrm{d}(t_1, t_2) \stackrel{\text{def}}{=} |t_1 - t_2|$. Then, the cost function associated to ϕ is

$$f_c \stackrel{\text{def}}{=} \mathcal{L}2\mathcal{O}(\phi) = ITE(b, 0, 1) + |x - y^2|$$

Now, let $\mu_0 \stackrel{\text{def}}{=} \{b \mapsto \bot \ ; \ x \mapsto 4 \ ; \ y \mapsto 1\}$ be a starting assignment. We have that $f_c(\mu_0) = ITE(\bot, 0, 1) + |4 - 1^2| = 1 + 3 = 4$. If we consider the move $\mu_1 \stackrel{\text{def}}{=} \{b \mapsto \top \ ; \ x \mapsto 4 \ ; \ y \mapsto 1\}$ that flips b, then $f_c(\mu_1) = ITE(\top, 0, 1) + |4 - 1^2| = 0 + 3 = 3$, hence the move is improving and is accepted. Then, if we consider the move $\mu_2 \stackrel{\text{def}}{=} \{b \mapsto \top \ ; \ x \mapsto 4 \ ; \ y \mapsto 2\}$ that increases the value of y by 1, we have $f_c(\mu_1) = ITE(\top, 0, 1) + |4 - 2^2| = 0 + 0 = 0$. Hence we have found a zero for f_c, i.e. a satisfying assignment for ϕ.

In general, local search is not guaranteed to find a solution of ϕ, if there is any. Nevertheless, it returns a *local minimum/best-effort value* of the cost function in the neighborhood of the initial assignment.

3 Deep Combination of Local Search and MCSat

We propose a deep combination of MCSat and local search where: (i) the current state of MCSat is used to instantiate a local search problem and (ii) the results of the local search help guiding future MCSat decisions. Assuming we have a local search procedure LS, we discuss how to instantiate LS (Sect. 3.1), as well as how to use the result of LS within MCSat (Sect. 3.2).

3.1 Instantiating the Local Search Problem

For the instantiation of LS, we determine the initial assignment and the formula upon which the cost function is constructed. Both choices are of fundamental importance. A good initial assignment is essential to find a good local minimum of the cost function. A *good local minimum* is a local minimum that meets two conditions: (i) it has a smaller cost compared to the cost of the initial assignment and (i) its assignment values are likely to be accepted by MCSat, i.e., they are consistent with the current trail. Passing a simplified formula that takes the truth value of propagated and decided literals into account is also essential to tailor the search to the current MCSat state and to avoid unnecessary computations.

Initial Assignment. For every model assignment $x \mapsto \alpha$ in M, the assigned variable is treated as a constant that takes its respective assigned value (i.e., x is treated as the constant α) and is not allowed to be changed in LS. This reduces the dimension of the LS search space, and avoids moves inconsistent with the

Algorithm 1. Initial assignment for LS

Input: a set $Vars(\phi)$, a trail M, a value cache $cache$, a feasibility map $feasible_M$
Output: an initial assignment μ_0. a set of fixed variables $VarsFixed \subseteq Vars(\phi)$

```
VarsFixed ← ∅
for x ∈ Vars(φ) do
    if v[M](x) ≠ undef then                              ▷ check if x has a value in the trail
        μ0(x) ← v[M](x)                                  ▷ assign trail value
        VarsFixed.add(x)
    else if cache(x) ≠ undef and cache(x) ∈ feasible_M(x) then
        μ0(x) ← cache(x)                                 ▷ assign feasible cached value
    else
        μ0(x) ← pick_value(feasible_M(x))                ▷ assign any feasible value
```

current trail. For initial assignment of variables that are unassigned in M, a reasonable choice is to use cached values of previous search states, if present in the value cache. However, cached values are not guaranteed to be in the feasibility set, as they might be the result of a previous decision that eventually led to a conflict. Hence, we first check if the cached value is feasible. If it is not, or there is no cached value, we pick any value from the feasibility set by asking the appropriate theory plugin. The procedure for choosing the initial assignment is shown in Algorithm 1. Note that, for all the variables, the feasibility set cannot be empty. An empty feasibility set indicates an inconsistent trail which is resolved using conflict resolution before starting LS. MCSat maintains the invariant that, for a consistent trail, the feasibility set of all variables is non-empty.

Formula for LS. Every Boolean assignment $L \mapsto \{\top, \bot\}$ in M represents the truth value of the literal L that is assumed to hold at the current search state

Algorithm 2. Formula for LS

Input: a formula ϕ, a trail M
Output: a subformula ϕ_{LS} of ϕ

```
φ_LS ← ⊤                                                 ▷ formula to be passed to LS
for C ∈ φ do
    C_LS ← ⊥
    for L ∈ C do
        if v[M](L) = ⊤ then                              ▷ if literal is assigned to true in trail
            C_LS ← ⊤                                     ▷ substitute the clause with true
            φ_LS ← φ_LS ∧ L                              ▷ store literal
            break
        else if v[M](L) = ⊥ then                         ▷ if literal is assigned to false in trail
            φ_LS ← φ_LS ∧ ¬L                             ▷ store literal (with correct polarity)
            continue                                     ▷ ignore literal in the clause
        else
            C_LS ← C_LS ∨ L                              ▷ keep literal in the clause
    φ_LS ← φ_LS ∧ C_LS                                   ▷ store simplified clause
```

(either because of a propagation or a decision). We can use this information to simplify the original formula before passing it to LS. For a given clause $C \stackrel{\text{def}}{=} L \vee L_1 \vee \ldots$, if $v[M](L) = \top$, then, for LS, it suffices to find an assignment that satisfies L, since such an assignment would satisfy C as well. Hence, in this case, we shall pass to LS just L instead of C. On the other hand, if $v[M](L) = \bot$, then there is no incentive for LS to try to find an assignment that makes L true, as any such assignment would be inconsistent with the trail and will be discarded by MCSat immediately. Thus, L is removed from the clause that is passed to LS. Note that, by just removing L from the clause, we still may end up with an assignment that evaluates L to $\top$. Therefore, for literals that are assigned to $\bot$ in the trail, we add, just once, $\neg L$ to the formula that we pass to LS. This procedure is shown in Algorithm 2.

3.2 Guiding MCSat Decisions

During the search, we periodically call LS to suggest values for MCSat to choose in subsequent decisions. As a heuristic to decide when to call LS, we are utilizing a polynomially increasing conflict threshold. Initially, this limit is set to 50, and then it is increased according to the polynomial $50 \cdot \text{ls\_calls} \cdot \log_{10}(\text{ls\_calls} + 9)^3$, where ls_calls represents the number of times LS has been called. A similar heuristic is used by SAT solvers to decide when to perform certain cache clearing operations [8]. Once the threshold is reached, we wait until the last conflict has been resolved and all consequences of that conflict are propagated. Then we start LS to guide any further decisions.

The return of LS consists of a complete assignment that contains *suggested values* for future variable decisions. These suggested values are put in the MCSat value cache – recall that the values in the cache are picked first during variable decisions, provided that they are feasible. Note that, during the choice of the initial assignment to pass to LS, we had relied on (feasible) cached values as well. If a cached value was feasible and LS changed its value, it means that such change led to a smaller cost, hence got us closer to a solution. Therefore, replacing the old cached value with the newly found suggestion improves the cache quality. On the other hand, if the cached value was not feasible, then any change to a feasible value improves the cache quality.

Furthermore, LS keeps track of the activity of each variable during its execution. The most active variables have contributed most to the decrease of the cost during LS. We suggest those variables to MCSat as good choices for subsequent decisions. This way, variables that were more active during the local search phase will have a higher impact on the MCSat search.

4 Local Search for Nonlinear Integer Arithmetic

As explained in Sect. 3.1, LS receives an initial assignment μ_0 and a formula ϕ from MCSat. The formula ϕ is used to construct the cost function f_c using the logic-to-optimization approach (Sect. 2.2), i.e. $f_c \stackrel{\text{def}}{=} \mathcal{L}2\mathcal{O}(\phi)$. To apply that, we must first define the distance function d and the strict inequality constant ϵ for integers. For d, we choose a consistent and computationally cheap definition $\mathrm{d}(t_1, t_2) \stackrel{\text{def}}{=} |t_1 - t_2|$. For ϵ, our choice is $\epsilon \stackrel{\text{def}}{=} 1$, since $t < 0$ is interchangeable with $t + 1 \leq 0$ for integers.

The building blocks of local search are *moves*. We contemplate three types of moves (or *modes*): one for Boolean variables, and two for integer variables. Given an assignment μ, we have the following types of moves:

- *Boolean flips*: For a Boolean variable b, the assignment $\mu_{\neg b} \stackrel{\text{def}}{=} \mu[b \mapsto \neg\mu(b)]$ obtained by changing the value of b to the negation of its value assigned by μ is a *flip move* from μ.
- *Hill-climbing moves*: In the basic version of hill-climbing, for an integer variable x, the assignments $\mu_{x+1} \stackrel{\text{def}}{=} \mu[x \mapsto \mu(x) + 1]$ and $\mu_{x-1} \stackrel{\text{def}}{=} \mu[x \mapsto \mu(x) - 1]$ obtained by mapping x to the successor and predecessor of its value assigned by μ are moves from μ.
- *Feasible-set-jumps*: For an integer variable x, with feasibility set $\mathit{feasible}(x) = \bigcup_{i \in [0:m]} I_i$, and $x \in I_j$ (for a given $j \in [0 : m]$), the assignments $\mu_{\text{left}} \stackrel{\text{def}}{=} \mu[x \mapsto \mathit{pick\_value}(I_{j-1})]$, and $\mu_{\text{right}} \stackrel{\text{def}}{=} \mu[x \mapsto \mathit{pick\_value}(I_{j+1})]$ obtained by picking a value from the left and right feasible intervals of I_j (provided they exist, i.e., respectively, that $j-1 \in [0 : m]$, and $j+1 \in [0 : m]$) are moves from μ.

Our specific strategy of the local search algorithm is outlined in Algorithm 3. The algorithm starts with a list of variables *vars* (and an associated *feasible*

Algorithm 3. LS main algorithm

Input: a list *vars*, a feasibility map *feasible*, an initial assign. μ_0, a cost function f_c
Output: a final assignment μ^* with $f_c(\mu^*) \leq f_c(\mu_0)$

$\mu^* \leftarrow \mu_0$ ▷ best assignment
$\mathit{cost}^* \leftarrow f_c(\mu_0)$ ▷ best cost
for $\mathit{mode} \in$ {bool-flips, fs-jumps, hill-climb} **do**
  $\mathit{n\_vars} \leftarrow 0$ ▷ no. of vars visited since last improvement
  while $\mathit{n\_vars} < \mathrm{len}(\mathit{vars})$ **and** $\mathit{cost}^* \neq 0$ **do**
    $x \leftarrow \mathit{vars}[\mathit{n\_vars}]$ ▷ pick next variable
    $\alpha \leftarrow \mu^*(x)$ ▷ value assigned to x
    while $\alpha_{new} \leftarrow$ MOVE.choose($x, \alpha, \mathit{feasible}, \mathit{mode}$) **do**
      $\mu_{new} \leftarrow \mu^*[x \mapsto \alpha_{new}]$ ▷ create new assignment
      $\mathit{cost}_{new} \leftarrow f_c(\mu_{new})$
      $\mathit{success} \leftarrow \mathit{cost}_{new} < \mathit{cost}^*$ ▷ check if the move has improved
      if *success* **then**
        $\mu^* \leftarrow \mu_{new}$ ▷ update best assignment
        $\mathit{cost}^* \leftarrow \mathit{cost}_{new}$ ▷ update best cost
        $\mathit{n\_vars} \leftarrow 0$ ▷ reset no. of vars visited
        vars.to_front(x) ▷ move x to the front of the list
      MOVE.notify($x, \alpha, \alpha_{new}, \mathit{feasible}, \mathit{mode}, \mathit{success}$)
    $\mathit{n\_vars} \leftarrow \mathit{n\_vars} + 1$ ▷ increas no. of vars visited

map), an initial assignment μ_0, and a cost function f_c. The goal of the procedure is to return an assignment μ^* that improves over the initial assignment μ_0 w.r.t. the cost function, i.e. $f_c(\mu^*) < f_c(\mu_0)$.

At the beginning, the best assignment coincides with the initial assignment (Line 1). First, we cycle over modes (Line 3). Then, we enter in a loop over the variables (Line 5). The loop breaks only in two cases: if all the variables have already been visited since the last improvement (in which case, it means we have reached a local minimum w.r.t. the current mode moves), or if the current cost is equal to 0 (in which case it means we have found a solution). At each loop iteration, we pick the next variable (Line 6). Here, for simplicity, we assume that there are no fixed variables (in practice, these variables are just ignored and treated as constants). Then, for the current variable x, we enter in a second loop (Line 8), in which we select new values for x. These values are determined by a move selection module, which we discuss below. The loop breaks only when there are no more moves available. For each value, a new assignment is built by re-assigning x to the new value (Line 9), and the cost of the new assignment is computed (Line 10). We then check whether the current cost is lower than the previous cost (Line 11). If so, then the new assignment becomes the best assignment (Line 13), and x is moved to the front of the list (Line 16). If not, then we try other moves for x, if there are any. In both cases, we notify the move selection module whether the suggested move has led to a success or not (Line 17). The move selection module works as following.

Boolean Flips Mode. Here, the logic is rather straightforward, as there is only one move possible per variable. Regardless of whether the move has success or not, the cycle over moves terminates, and the algorithm proceeds with the cycles over variables or over modes.

Accelerated Hill-Climbing Mode. The simple hill-climbing moves presented earlier, in which we add or subtract 1 to the current value, can be quite slow in converging toward a local minimum when the search space is huge. For this reason, we *accelerate* hill-climbing by keeping, for each variable, an adaptive *step_size*, which is incremented or decremented according to a fixed acceleration parameter *acc* (in our setting $acc = 1.2$) and on the base of the success of previous moves. At the beginning, *step_size* is set to 1 (i.e., we start with simple hill-climbing moves). At each iteration, we try four moves, corresponding to adding to the current value the product between *step_size* and one of the following: acc, $\frac{1}{acc}$, $\frac{-1}{acc}$, $-acc$. Since we are working with integers, every step value is rounded to the nearest integer. If one of the moves has success, then we set *step_size* to be equal to the best successful step (thus keeping the best velocity). If none of the moves has success, then we stop the moves cycle, and we set *step_size* to $\frac{step\_size}{acc}$ (thus decelerating over this variable for future moves).

Feasible-Set-Jumping Mode. There are two possible versions of fs-jumping: *global* and *local.* In global fs-jumping, given a fixed variable, we try *all* possible jumps over the feasibility set, i.e. we try one jump per feasible interval. While this may give a wide-ranging view over the feasibility set, it can also be very costly, hence we limit global fs-jumping to one time per variable (per LS call). Local fs-jumping, on the contrary, only explores the left and the right feasible intervals w.r.t. to the interval that contains the current value. If one fs-jump is successful, e.g. the one to the left interval, then we continue on that direction and explore the interval further left. As soon as we find that both left and right fs-jumps do not improve, then we stop, hence avoiding to span over all feasible intervals like in the global fs-jumping.

5 Experiments

Implementation. We have implemented our method in the MCSat engine of the YICES2 SMT solver, adding a module for the interaction with LS. We will denote the version of YICES2 that makes use of LS as YICES2$_{LS}$ and the baseline version (without any local search) as YICES2$_{base}$.

Setup. We have run our experiments on a cluster equipped with AMD EPYC 7502 CPUs running at 2.5 GHz, using a timeout of 300 s, and a memory limit of 8GB. We have compared the base version of YICES2 with the LS-boosted version YICES2$_{LS}$ as well as with the state-of-the-art SMT solvers CVC5 [1] (version 1.2.0), MATHSAT5 [11] (version 5.6.11), and Z3 [14] (version 4.13.3). We have also included in the comparison HYBRIDSMT [48], which runs a portfolio composed by the LS solver LocalSMT [6] (used as a standalone tool) and a LocalSMT-boosted version of Z3's CDCL(T) – see also related work (Sect. 6).

Benchmarks. We have considered all the SMT-LIB [2] (Version 2024 [44]) benchmarks from the QF_NIA category. This is a class of 25443 benchmarks, among which 14990 and 5183 come with a known status of "sat" and "unsat", respectively, and another 5270 have an "unknown" satisfiability status.

Results. In the presentation of the results, we consider both a short time limit and a long time limit. We set the short time limit to 24s, as in the respective SMT-COMP track [47], and the long time limit to 300s, due to resource constraints. The results are shown in Table 1 and Table 2, respectively. In the columns, we separate per benchmark family; on the rows, for each solver, we report the amount of overall benchmarks solved, and, in parenthesis, the amount of benchmarks solved restricted to sat and unsat instances, respectively. We also include two portfolios between Z3 (resp., HYBRIDSMT) and YICES2$_{LS}$, that work as follows: we run Z3 (resp., HYBRIDSMT) for half of the time limit (i.e., 12s/150s), then, if it has not terminated, we run YICES2$_{LS}$ for the remaining time.

Discussion. First, we observe that, with both time limits, Yices2$_{LS}$ solves a significant number of benchmarks more than Yices2$_{base}$. In particular, on both satisfiable and unsatisfiable instances, it improves (or matches) Yices2$_{base}$ results over all families, except one. Improving on unsatisfiable benchmarks is noteworthy: indeed, while, in general, local search is geared toward proving satisfiability, integrating it within MCSat enables to generate better lemmas. This is witnessed

Table 1. Summary of results for $\mathcal{NIA}$ benchmarks with a timeout of 24 s.

	cvc5	HybridSMT	MathSAT5	Yices2$_{base}$	Yices2$_{LS}$	Z3	Portfolio (Z3 + Yices2$_{LS}$)	Portfolio (HybridSMT + Yices2$_{LS}$)
VeryMax	7799 (5465) (2334)	13555 (10427) (3128)	11233 (7615) (3618)	13695 (9461) (4234)	**14269** (10019) (4250)	13975 (9599) (4376)	14848 (10271) (4577)	15428 (11105) (4323)
calypto	171 (79) (92)	174 (78) (96)	168 (79) (89)	174 (79) (95)	174 (79) (95)	**176** (80) (96)	176 (80) (96)	176 (80) (96)
ezsmt	**8** (8) (0)	**8** (8) (0)	**8** (8) (0)	**8** (8) (0)	**8** (8) (0)	**8** (8) (0)	8 (8) (0)	8 (8) (0)
LassoRank	97 (4) (93)	**105** (4) (101)	**105** (4) (101)	91 (4) (87)	96 (4) (92)	104 (4) (100)	102 (4) (98)	104 (4) (100)
Dartagnan	320 (11) (309)	**354** (10) (344)	327 (12) (315)	142 (1) (141)	87 (0) (87)	352 (9) (343)	344 (9) (335)	347 (9) (338)
LCTES	**1** (0) (1)	**1** (0) (1)	**1** (0) (1)	0 (0) (0)	0 (0) (0)	**1** (0) (1)	1 (0) (1)	1 (0) (1)
MathProbl	107 (100) (7)	93 (86) (7)	141 (134) (7)	122 (115) (7)	**303** (296) (7)	118 (111) (7)	300 (293) (7)	305 (298) (7)
leipgiz	72 (70) (2)	**151** (150) (1)	114 (112) (2)	102 (101) (1)	111 (110) (1)	120 (119) (1)	119 (118) (1)	148 (147) (1)
UltAut23	16 (8) (8)	10 (7) (3)	17 (7) (10)	7 (7) (0)	7 (7) (0)	**21** (8) (13)	20 (8) (12)	9 (7) (2)
mcm	9 (9) (0)	**56** (56) (0)	3 (3) (0)	6 (6) (0)	6 (6) (0)	5 (5) (0)	5 (5) (0)	46 (46) (0)
sqrtmodinv	2 (0) (2)	7 (0) (7)	0 (0) (0)	0 (0) (0)	0 (0) (0)	**17** (0) (17)	17 (0) (17)	6 (0) (6)
UltAut	**7** (0) (7)	**7** (0) (7)	**7** (0) (7)	**7** (0) (7)	**7** (0) (7)	**7** (0) (7)	7 (0) (7)	7 (0) (7)
AProVE	1816 (1251) (565)	2212 (1572) (640)	2085 (1556) (529)	2328 (1615) (713)	**2356** (1642) (714)	2289 (1612) (677)	2380 (1657) (723)	2371 (1649) (722)
UltLasso	**32** (6) (26)	31 (6) (25)	**32** (6) (26)	**32** (6) (26)	**32** (6) (26)	**32** (6) (26)	32 (6) (26)	32 (6) (26)
Total	10457 (7011) (3446)	16764 (12404) (4360)	14241 (9536) (4705)	16714 (11403) (5311)	**17456** (12177) (5279)	17225 (11561) (5664)	18359 (12459) (5900)	18988 (13359) (5629)

not only by the higher amount of benchmarks solved overall, but also by the lower amount of conflicts and theory variables assignments occurred. On unsatisfiable benchmarks solved by both tools, on average (resp. median), Yices2_{LS} encountered 225 (resp. 4) fewer conflicts and 27826 (resp. 36) fewer theory variables assignments than Yices2_{base}. Note that, on average (resp. median), Yices2_{base} encountered 1669 (resp. 458) conflicts and 79842 (resp. 10537) theory variable

Table 2. Summary of results for $\mathcal{NIA}$ benchmarks with a timeout of 300 s.

	cvc5	HybridSMT	MathSAT5	Yices2_{base}	Yices2_{LS}	Z3	Portfolio (Z3 + Yices2_{LS})	Portfolio (HybridSMT + Yices2_{LS})
VeryMax	10489 (7122) (3367)	**17060** (12093) (4967)	13651 (9509) (4142)	14549 (10164) (4385)	15160 (10719) (4441)	16304 (11044) (5260)	16698 (11366) (5332)	17303 (12156) (5147)
calypto	173 (79) (94)	175 (78) (97)	169 (79) (90)	174 (79) (95)	175 (79) (96)	**177** (80) (97)	177 (80) (97)	177 (80) (97)
ezsmt	**8** (8) (0)	**8** (8) (0)	**8** (8) (0)	**8** (8) (0)	**8** (8) (0)	**8** (8) (0)	8 (8) (0)	8 (8) (0)
LassoRank	98 (4) (94)	**106** (4) (102)	105 (4) (101)	93 (4) (89)	97 (4) (93)	**106** (4) (102)	104 (4) (100)	105 (4) (101)
Dartagnan	350 (17) (333)	**369** (14) (355)	347 (18) (329)	311 (7) (304)	288 (3) (285)	368 (14) (354)	363 (13) (350)	367 (13) (354)
LCTES	1 (0) (1)	**2** (0) (2)	1 (0) (1)	0 (0) (0)	0 (0) (0)	**2** (0) (2)	1 (0) (1)	1 (0) (1)
MathProbl	177 (170) (7)	107 (100) (7)	183 (176) (7)	124 (117) (7)	**311** (304) (7)	118 (111) (7)	314 (307) (7)	327 (320) (7)
leipgiz	89 (87) (2)	**156** (155) (1)	126 (124) (2)	104 (103) (1)	111 (110) (1)	135 (134) (1)	134 (133) (1)	154 (153) (1)
UltAut23	16 (8) (0)	10 (7) (3)	17 (7) (10)	7 (7) (0)	7 (7) (0)	**21** (8) (13)	21 (8) (13)	10 (7) (3)
mcm	17 (17) (0)	**69** (69) (0)	10 (10) (0)	9 (9) (0)	9 (9) (0)	10 (10) (0)	11 (11) (0)	64 (64) (0)
sqrtmodinv	2 (0) (2)	10 (0) (10)	0 (0) (0)	0 (0) (0)	0 (0) (0)	**17** (0) (17)	17 (0) (17)	8 (0) (8)
UltAut	**7** (0) (7)	**7** (0) (7)	**7** (0) (7)	**7** (0) (7)	**7** (0) (7)	**7** (0) (7)	7 (0) (7)	7 (0) (7)
AProVE	1939 (1330) (609)	2352 (1640) (685)	2180 (1622) (558)	2337 (1621) (716)	**2367** (1647) (720)	2339 (1640) (699)	2394 (1661) (733)	2387 (1656) (731)
UltLasso	**32** (6) (26)	31 (6) (25)	**32** (6) (26)	**32** (6) (26)	**32** (6) (26)	**32** (6) (26)	32 (6) (26)	32 (6) (26)
Total	13398 (8848) (4550)	**20435** (14174) (6261)	16836 (11563) (5273)	17755 (12125) (5630)	18572 (12896) (5676)	19644 (13059) (6585)	20281 (13597) (6684)	20950 (14467) (6483)

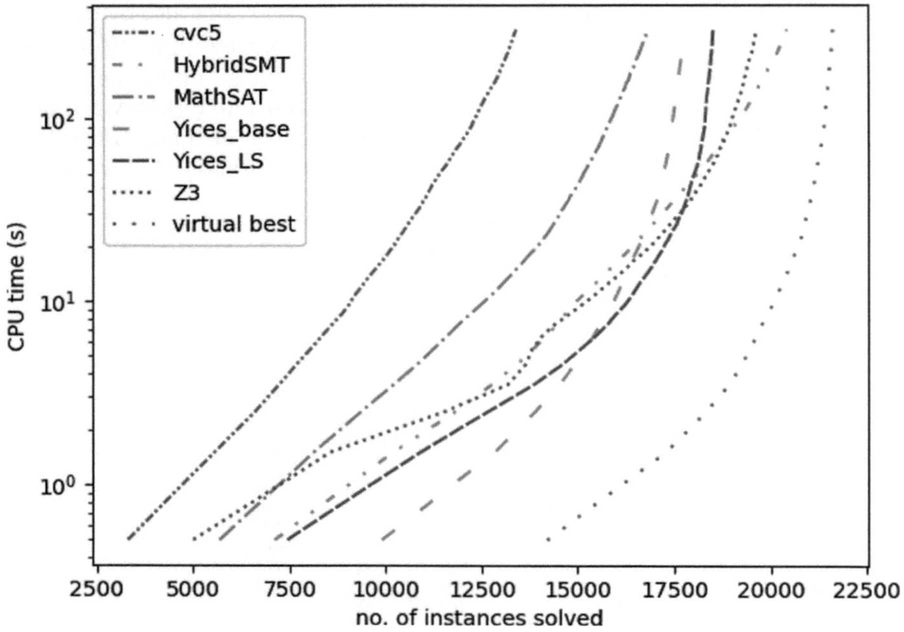

Fig. 2. Plots showing the number of instances solved (x axis) within given time in seconds (y axis) in log scale.

assignments. These numbers show that there is a considerable amount of benchmarks for which the number of conflicts and theory variable assignments is significantly lower (note that such a lower median w.r.t. average implies a pronounced right-skewness).

Overall, we see that, in the 24s track, YICES2$_{LS}$ solves more benchmarks than any other solver, while, in the 300s track, it comes third, after HYBRIDSMT and Z3. The complementarity of YICES2$_{LS}$ w.r.t. both tools can be witnessed by the scatter plots in Fig. 3, and by the results of the portfolios in Tables 1 and 2. Note that Z3 internally utilizes portfolio tactics that combine multiple solving techniques sequentially (clearly observable in Figs. 2 and 3). HYBRIDSMT runs a higher-level portfolio that combines the LS-based LocalSMT and Z3. The results of the portfolios that include YICES2$_{LS}$ show that our approach brings significant diversity to the strategies already used in state-of-the-art portfolio approaches.

Since HYBRIDSMT is the only other solver that – to the best of our knowledge – leverages local search techniques for $\mathcal{NIA}$, it is interesting to compare the improvements it brings to Z3 with the improvements that YICES2$_{LS}$ brings over YICES2$_{base}$. We can see that, with a 300s time limit, the improvements are comparable, as both tools solve around 800 benchmarks more than their base solvers. With a 24s time limit, however, we see that YICES2$_{LS}$ is able to solve around 700 benchmarks more than YICES2$_{base}$, while, on the contrary,

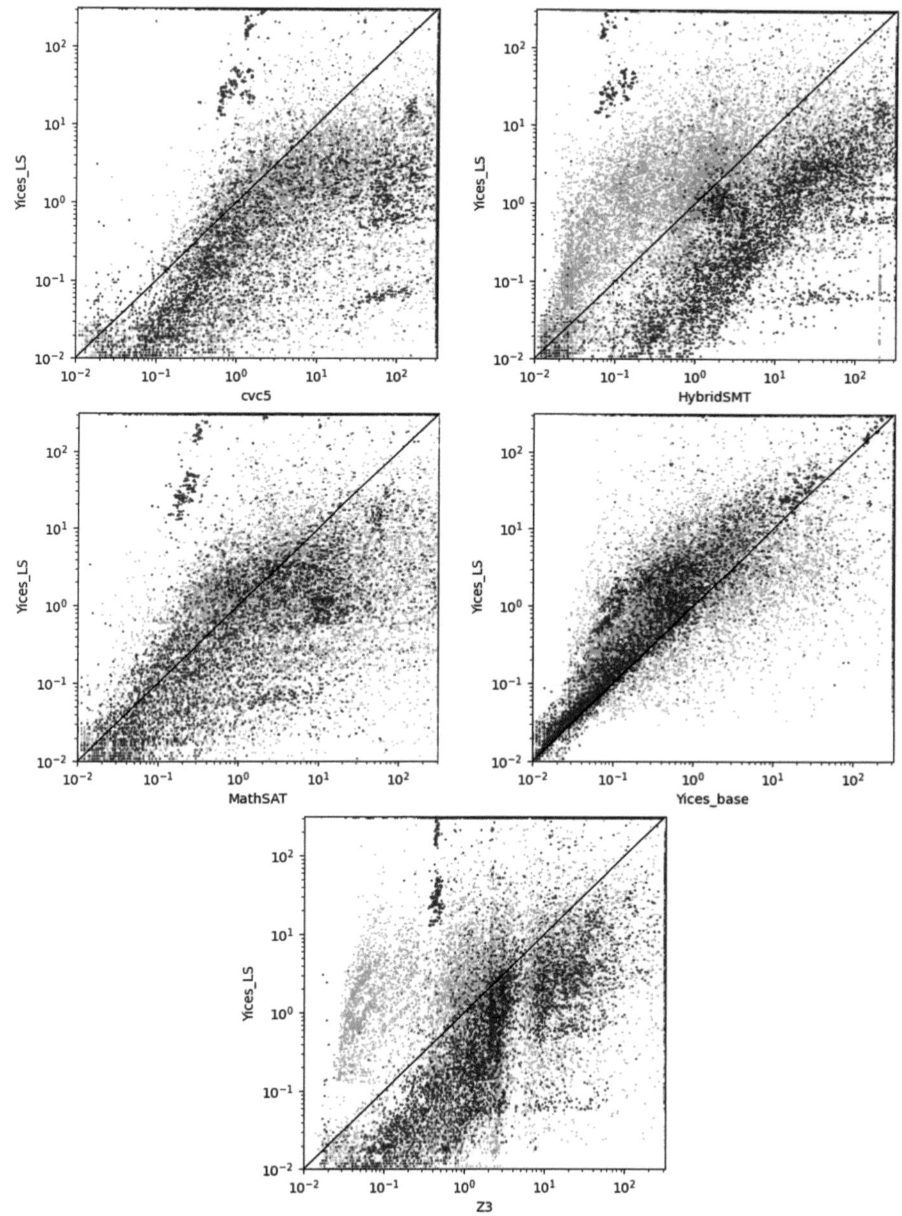

Fig. 3. Scatter plots comparing YICES2$_{LS}$ to CVC5, HYBRIDSMT, MATHSAT5, YICES2$_{base}$, and Z3, respectively; on sat. (orange) and unsat. (blue) instances. (Color figure online)

HYBRIDSMT loses around 450 benchmarks compared to Z3. Figure 2 shows that the point at which using local search pays off is much earlier for YICES2$_{LS}$ (<10 s) than for HYBRIDSMT (just below 100 s).

6 Related Work

In propositional SAT solving, local search techniques have been successfully used to solve difficult satisfiable problems [31] as well as unsatisfiable instances [45]. Recently, their tight integration in the propositional CDCL framework has been shown to improve performance [7,8] and are now considered a key component of state-of-the-art SAT solvers. In the context of SMT, on the other hand, the adoption of LS is a lot less widespread.

In [22], the LS-based SAT solver WalkSAT has been used in combination with a theory solver as an alternative to the classic CDCL(T) approach; however, the use of local search remained limited to the Boolean level. For the theory of bit-vectors, the idea of Boolean flips in SAT solving has been transposed to the bit level by introducing *bit-flips* [18], possibly augmented with propagations [41].

The adoption of LS for arithmetic theories is more recent. For the theories of Linear Integer Arithmetic ($\mathcal{LIA}$) [5] and Multi-linear Real Arithmetic [34] a *critical move* operation is used to change the value of a variable that appears in a literal violated by the current assignment in order to make the literal satisfied. To deal with the nonlinear arithmetic constraints, the *cell-jumping* technique is used, which first isolates the roots of a falsified polynomial w.r.t. to a variable (by fixing the value of the other variables), thus decomposing the real space into finitely many intervals (*cells*, in the CAD [12] terminology), and then tries to satisfy the polynomial by changing the value of the variable by jumping around these cells. This technique has been implemented in LocalSMT for $\mathcal{NIA}$ [6], and as a tool in Maple [35] and on top of Z3 [46] for $\mathcal{NRA}$.

Local search has also been used as a sub-routine for *global search* techniques, as in the case of floating points [19], and of $\mathcal{NRA}$ possibly augmented with transcendental functions ($\mathcal{NTA}$) [36,37,39]. In these works, numerical optimization algorithms, e.g. the gradient-descent, are used to find local minima, while stochastic jumping is used to move away from a local minimum in order to explore other regions in search for a global minimum.

All the methods discussed so far for arithmetic theories are only able to prove satisfiability; if they fail, then all the knowledge that has been acquired by the search is lost. HybridSMT [48] addresses this issue, for the case of $\mathcal{NIA}$, by integrating LocalSMT within Z3's CDCL(T). In particular, LocalSMT takes as input a subformula corresponding to a Boolean skeleton solution, and, if it does not find an integer solution for the subformula, it returns the best assignment found and the conflict frequency for atoms. This information is used to improve phase selection (i.e. Boolean assignments) and variable ordering. Although both HybridSMT and our method share the idea of integrating LS within a reasoning calculus (CDCL(T) and MCSat, respectively), there are some substantial difference. First, in HybridSMT, LS takes into account complete Boolean variable assignments. In our framework, LS can take as input both Boolean and theory variable assignments, either partial or complete. Additionally, while in HybridSMT LS can only suggest assignments for (and ordering of) Boolean literals, we extend that to theory variables as well. Moreover, there is a theory-specific difference in our approach. LocalSMT relies on cell-jumps, which require to perform potentially very expensive root isolation sub-routines at every step. In contrast, our method uses fs-jumps that rely on feasibility intervals already maintained by the theory plugin in the MCSat framework. This eliminates the need for additional computation and can be viewed as a lazy version of cells, progressively refined on-demand. Furthermore, we pair fs-jumps with hill-climbing to move inside feasible intervals.

Most state-of-the-art solvers do not use local search for $\mathcal{NIA}$ problems. Bit-blasting [20] aims at proving satisfiability by iteratively imposing bounds on the variables and then encoding the obtained sub-formula into an equi-satisfiable Boolean formula, which is then handled by a SAT solver. In the branch-and-bound approach [28,32] the integer domain is relaxed by allowing variables to range over real numbers. Incremental Linearization [9,10] leverages decision procedures for $\mathcal{LIA}$ by abstracting non-linear multiplications with uninterpreted functions and then incrementally axiomatize them.

7 Conclusion

In this work, we have introduced a theory-independent framework for integrating local search into the MCSat calculus. By combining local search intuition with MCSat reasoning capabilities, our approach leverages logic-to-optimization formalization to provide guidance to the core MCSat solver. Specifically, we addressed the theory of nonlinear integer arithmetic by proposing a local search procedure based on feasibility-set jumping and hill-climbing.

We implemented our approach in the YICES2 SMT solver, and empirically demonstrated its improvements for both satisfiable and unsatisfiable instances. Our results show that the new YICES2 solver with local search compares favorably and often outperforms other SMT solvers; in particular, it manages to solve a significant amount of benchmarks not solved by other state-of-the-art tools. Moreover, our results show that the new YICES2 is able to reach solutions or proofs more efficiently, compared to the baseline YICES2, in terms of the number of decisions and conflicts. Our findings indicate that this new approach complements existing techniques used by other solvers, as evident in the experimental results (see virtual best and portfolio solvers in the plots and tables).

In the future, we aim to extend our approach to other theories such as finite fields and bit-vectors, and conduct more comprehensive experimental evaluations. Additionally, we plan to integrate this approach with different caching schemes, including value and target caches, along with periodic recaching in MCSat [23].

Acknowledgments. This material is based upon work supported in part by NSF grant 2016597. Any opinions, findings and conclusions or recommendations expressed in this material are those of the author(s) and do not necessarily reflect the views of the US Government or NSF.

The work of Enrico Lipparini was partially supported by project PRIN 2022 DeLiCE (F53D23009130001) under the MUR National Recovery and Resilience Plan funded by the European Union – NextGenerationEU.

Disclosure of Interests. The authors have no competing interests to declare that are relevant to the content of this article.

References

1. Barbosa, H., et al.: cvc5: a versatile and industrial-strength SMT solver. In: Fisman, D., Rosu, G. (eds.) Tools and Algorithms for the Construction and Analysis of Systems - 28th International Conference, TACAS 2022, Held as Part of the European Joint Conferences on Theory and Practice of Software, ETAPS 2022, Munich, Germany, April 2-7, 2022, Proceedings, Part I, Lecture Notes in Computer Science, vol. 13243, pp. 415–442. Springer (2022)
2. Barrett, C., Fontaine, P., Tinelli, C.: The Satisfiability Modulo Theories Library (SMT-LIB) (2016). www.SMT-LIB.org
3. Barrett, C.W., Sebastiani, R., Seshia, S.A., Tinelli, C.: Satisfiability modulo theories. In: Biere, A., Heule, M., van Maaren, H., Walsh, T. (eds.) Handbook of Satisfiability. Frontiers in Artificial Intelligence and Applications, 2nd edn., vol. 336, pp. 1267–1329. IOS Press (2021)
4. Bjørner, N., Nachmanson, L.: Arithmetic solving in z3. In: Gurfinkel, A., Ganesh, V. (eds.) Computer Aided Verification, pp. 26–41. Springer, Cham (2024)
5. Cai, S., Li, B., Zhang, X.: Local search for SMT on linear integer arithmetic. In: Shoham, S., Vizel, Y. (eds.) Computer Aided Verification, pp. 227–248. Springer, Cham (2022)
6. Cai, S., Li, B., Zhang, X.: Local search for satisfiability modulo integer arithmetic theories. ACM Trans. Comput. Logic **24**(4) (2023)
7. Cai, S., Zhang, X.: Deep cooperation of CDCL and local search for SAT. In: Li, C.-M., Manyà, F. (eds.) SAT 2021. LNCS, vol. 12831, pp. 64–81. Springer, Cham (2021). https://doi.org/10.1007/978-3-030-80223-3_6
8. Cai, S., Zhang, X., Fleury, M., Biere, A.: Better decision heuristics in CDCL through local search and target phases. J. Artif. Int. Res., 74 (2022)
9. Cimatti, A., Griggio, A., Irfan, A., Roveri, M., Sebastiani, R.: Experimenting on solving nonlinear integer arithmetic with incremental linearization. In: Beyersdorff, O., Wintersteiger, C.M. (eds.) SAT 2018. LNCS, vol. 10929, pp. 383–398. Springer, Cham (2018). https://doi.org/10.1007/978-3-319-94144-8_23
10. Cimatti, A., Griggio, A., Irfan, A., Roveri, M., Sebastiani, R.: Incremental linearization for satisfiability and verification modulo nonlinear arithmetic and transcendental functions. ACM Trans. Comput. Logic **19**(3) (2018)
11. Cimatti, A., Griggio, A., Schaafsma, B.J., Sebastiani, R.: The MathSAT5 SMT solver. In: Piterman, N., Smolka, S.A. (eds.) TACAS 2013. LNCS, vol. 7795, pp. 93–107. Springer, Heidelberg (2013). https://doi.org/10.1007/978-3-642-36742-7_7
12. Collins, G.E.: Quantifier elimination for real closed fields by cylindrical algebraic decompostion. In: Brakhage, H. (ed.) Automata Theory and Formal Languages, pp. 134–183. Springer, Heidelberg (1975)

13. Corzilius, F., Kremer, G., Junges, S., Schupp, S., Ábrahám, E.: SMT-RAT: an open source C++ toolbox for strategic and parallel SMT solving. In: SAT (2015)
14. De Moura, L., Bjørner, N.: Z3: an efficient SMT solver. In: Proceedings of the Theory and Practice of Software, 14th International Conference on Tools and Algorithms for the Construction and Analysis of Systems, TACAS'08/ETAPS'08, pp. 337–340. Springer, Heidelberg (2008)
15. de Moura, L., Jovanović, D.: A model-constructing satisfiability calculus. In: Giacobazzi, R., Berdine, J., Mastroeni, I. (eds.) VMCAI 2013. LNCS, vol. 7737, pp. 1–12. Springer, Heidelberg (2013). https://doi.org/10.1007/978-3-642-35873-9_1
16. de Moura, L.M., Bjørner, N.S.: Satisfiability modulo theories: introduction and applications. Commun. ACM **54**(9), 69–77 (2011)
17. Dutertre, B.: Yices 2.2. In: Biere, A., Bloem, R. (eds.) Computer-Aided Verification (CAV'2014). Lecture Notes in Computer Science, vol. 8559, pp. 737–744. Springer (2014)
18. Fröhlich, A., Biere, A., Wintersteiger, C., Hamadi, Y.: Stochastic local search for Satisfiability Modulo Theories. In: Proceedings of the AAAI Conference on Artificial Intelligence, vol. 29, no. 1 (2015)
19. Fu, Z., Su, Z.: XSat: a fast floating-point satisfiability solver. In: Chaudhuri, S., Farzan, A. (eds.) CAV 2016. LNCS, vol. 9780, pp. 187–209. Springer, Cham (2016). https://doi.org/10.1007/978-3-319-41540-6_11
20. Fuhs, C., Giesl, J., Middeldorp, A., Schneider-Kamp, P., Thiemann, R., Zankl, H.: SAT solving for termination analysis with polynomial interpretations. In: Marques-Silva, J., Sakallah, K.A. (eds.) SAT 2007. LNCS, vol. 4501, pp. 340–354. Springer, Heidelberg (2007). https://doi.org/10.1007/978-3-540-72788-0_33
21. Graham-Lengrand, S., Jovanović, D., Dutertre, B.: Solving Bitvectors with MCSAT: explanations from bits and pieces. In: Peltier, N., Sofronie-Stokkermans, V. (eds.) IJCAR 2020. LNCS (LNAI), vol. 12166, pp. 103–121. Springer, Cham (2020). https://doi.org/10.1007/978-3-030-51074-9_7
22. Griggio, A., Phan, Q.-S., Sebastiani, R., Tomasi, S.: Stochastic local search for SMT: combining theory solvers with WalkSAT. In: Tinelli, C., Sofronie-Stokkermans, V. (eds.) Frontiers of Combining Systems, pp. 163–178. Springer, Heidelberg (2011)
23. Hader, T., Irfan, A., Graham-Lengrand, S.: Decision heuristics in MCSat. In: Computer Aided Verification (2025, to appear)
24. Hader, T., Kaufmann, D., Irfan, A., Graham-Lengrand, S., Kovács, L.: MCSat-based finite field reasoning in the Yices2 SMT solver (short paper). In: IJCAR (1). Lecture Notes in Computer Science, vol. 14739, pp. 386–395. Springer (2024)
25. Hader, T., Kaufmann, D., Kovács, L.: SMT solving over finite field arithmetic. In: LPAR. EPiC Series in Computing, vol. 94, pp. 238–256. EasyChair (2023)
26. Hernando, L., Mendiburu, A., Lozano, J.: Hill-climbing algorithm: let's go for a walk before finding the optimum. pp. 1–7 (2018)
27. Irfan, A., Graham-Lengrand, S.: Arrays reasoning in MCSat. In: SMT@CAV. CEUR Workshop Proceedings, vol. 3725, pp. 24–35. CEUR-WS.org (2024)
28. Jovanović, D.: Solving nonlinear integer arithmetic with MCSAT. In: Bouajjani, A., Monniaux, D. (eds.) Verification, Model Checking, and Abstract Interpretation, pp. 330–346. Springer, Cham (2017)
29. Jovanovic, D., Barrett, C., de Moura, L.: The design and implementation of the model constructing satisfiability calculus. In: International Conference on Formal Methods in Computer-Aided Design (FMCAD), pp. 173–180. IEEE (2013)
30. Jovanović, D., de Moura, L.: Solving non-linear arithmetic. ACM Commun. Comput. Algebra **46**(3/4), 104–105 (2013)

31. Kautz, H.A., Sabharwal, A., Selman, B.: Incomplete algorithms. In: Biere, A., Heule, M., van Maaren, H., Walsh, T. (eds.) Handbook of Satisfiability. Frontiers in Artificial Intelligence and Applications, 2nd edn., vol. 336, pp. 213–232. IOS Press (2021)
32. Kremer, G., Corzilius, F., Ábrahám, E.: A generalised branch-and-bound approach and its application in SAT modulo nonlinear integer arithmetic. In: Gerdt, V.P., Koepf, W., Seiler, W.M., Vorozhtsov, E.V. (eds.) CASC 2016. LNCS, vol. 9890, pp. 315–335. Springer, Cham (2016). https://doi.org/10.1007/978-3-319-45641-6_21
33. Kremer, G., Ábrahám, E.: Modular strategic SMT solving with SMT-RAT. Acta Universitatis Sapientiae, Informatica **10**(1), 5–25 (2018)
34. Li, B., Cai, S.: Local search for SMT on linear and multi-linear real arithmetic. In: 2023 Formal Methods in Computer-Aided Design (FMCAD), pp. 1–10 (2023)
35. Li, H., Xia, B., Zhao, T.: Local search for solving satisfiability of polynomial formulas. In: Enea, C., Lal, A. (eds.) Computer Aided Verification, pp. 87–109. Springer, Cham (2023)
36. Lipparini, E.: Satisfiability modulo Nonlinear Arithmetic and Transcendental Functions via Numerical and Topological methods. Ph.D. thesis (2024)
37. Lipparini, E., Cimatti, A., Griggio, A., Sebastiani, R.: Handling polynomial and transcendental functions in SMT via unconstrained optimisation and topological degree test. In: Bouajjani, A., Holík, L., Wu, Z. (eds.) Automated Technology for Verification and Analysis, pp. 137–153. Springer, Cham (2022)International Publishing
38. Lipparini, E., Ratschan, S.: Satisfiability of non-linear transcendental arithmetic as a certificate search problem. In: Rozier, K.Y., Chaudhuri, S. (eds.) NASA Formal Methods, pp. 472–488. Springer, Cham (2023)
39. Lipparini, E., Ratschan, S.: Satisfiability of non-linear transcendental arithmetic as a certificate search problem. J. Autom. Reason. **69**(1) (2025)
40. Matiyasevich, Y.V.: Hilbert's Tenth Problem. MIT Press, Cambridge (1993)
41. Niemetz, A., Preiner, M., Biere, A.: Propagation based local search for bit-precise reasoning. Formal Methods Syst. Des. **51**(3), 608–636 (2017)
42. Nieuwenhuis, R., Oliveras, A., Tinelli, C.: Solving SAT and SAT modulo theories: from an abstract Davis-Putnam-Logemann-Loveland procedure to DPLL(T). J. ACM **53**(6), 937–977 (2006)
43. Pipatsrisawat, K., Darwiche, A.: A lightweight component caching scheme for satisfiability solvers. In: Marques-Silva, J., Sakallah, K.A. (eds.) SAT 2007. LNCS, vol. 4501, pp. 294–299. Springer, Heidelberg (2007). https://doi.org/10.1007/978-3-540-72788-0_28
44. Preiner, M., Schurr, H.-J., Barrett, C., Fontaine, P., Niemetz, A., Tinelli, C.: SMT-LIB release 2024 (non-incremental benchmarks) (2024)
45. Prestwich, S., Lynce, I.: Local search for unsatisfiability. In: Biere, A., Gomes, C.P. (eds.) SAT 2006. LNCS, vol. 4121, pp. 283–296. Springer, Heidelberg (2006). https://doi.org/10.1007/11814948_28
46. Wang, Z., Zhan, B., Li, B., Cai, S.: Efficient local search for nonlinear real arithmetic. In: Dimitrova, R., Lahav, O., Wolff, S. (eds.) Verification, Model Checking, and Abstract Interpretation, pp. 326–349. Springer, Cham (2024)

47. Weber, T., Conchon, S., Déharbe, D., Heizmann, M., Niemetz, A., Reger, G.: The SMT competition 2015–2018. J. Satisf. Boolean Model. Comput. **11**(1), 221–259 (2019)
48. Zhang, X., Li, B., Cai, S.: Deep combination of CDCL(T) and local search for satisfiability modulo non-linear integer arithmetic theory. In: Proceedings of the IEEE/ACM 46th International Conference on Software Engineering, ICSE '24, New York, NY, USA. Association for Computing Machinery (2024)

More is Less: Adding Polynomials for Faster Explanations in NLSAT

Valentin Promies(✉), Jasper Nalbach, Erika Ábrahám, and Paul Wagner

RWTH Aachen University, Aachen, Germany
{promies,nalbach,abraham}@cs.rwth-aachen.de

Abstract. To check the satisfiability of (non-linear) real arithmetic formulas, modern satisfiability modulo theories (SMT) solving algorithms like NLSAT depend heavily on *single cell construction*, the task of generalizing a sample point to a connected subset (cell) of $\mathbb{R}^n$, that contains the sample and over which a given set of polynomials is sign-invariant.

In this paper, we propose to speed up the computation and simplify the representation of the resulting cell by dynamically extending the considered set of polynomials with further linear polynomials. While this increases the total number of (smaller) cells generated throughout the algorithm, our experiments show that it can pay off when using suitable heuristics due to the interaction with Boolean reasoning.

Keywords: Single Cell Construction · Cylindrical Algebraic Decomposition · Real Algebra · SMT Solving

1 Introduction

Satisfiability checking deals with the problem of deciding whether a first-order logic formula admits a solution. *Satisfiability modulo theories (SMT)* solvers use specialized algorithms to tackle this problem for different theories. While the targeted problems are generally hard (NP-complete for propositional logic, and even undecidable for integer arithmetic), modern SMT solvers are highly efficient and widely used as integrated engines, e.g. for automated deduction [5,17].

In this paper, we focus on the *quantifier-free* fragment of *non-linear real arithmetic (NRA)*, denoted as *QF-NRA*, whose formulas are Boolean combinations of polynomial constraints with rational coefficients and real-valued variables. The *cylindrical algebraic decomposition (CAD)* method [11], which is in general a quantifier elimination procedure for NRA, was the first tractable technique for solving the satisfiability problem for QF-NRA. A CAD partitions the search space of the variables into a finite number of *cells*, such that all polynomials in the input formula are sign-invariant - and thus the input formula is truth-invariant - within each CAD cell. Consequently, we can decide the satisfiability problem by checking one point from each cell. Despite major improvements by, e.g., McCallum [23,24], Lazard [21], and Brown [8], CAD still scales poorly, often due to expensive *resultant* computations.

C. Barrett and U. Waldmann (Eds.): CADE 2025, LNAI 15943, pp. 116–135, 2025.
https://doi.org/10.1007/978-3-031-99984-0_7

Inspired by CAD, one of the most successful SMT-solving techniques for QF-NRA is *NLSAT* [19], an instance of the *model constructing satisfiability calculus (MCSAT)* [25] by Jovanic and de Moura. NLSAT extends DPLL+CDCL-style propositional reasoning with a dual approach for the theory. The propositional part consists of deciding truth values for constraints, Boolean propagation, and Boolean conflict resolution. Dually, the theory part decides real values for theory variables, accompanied by theory propagation to assure that theory assignments evaluate constraints *consistently* with the Boolean assignment, and theory conflict resolution. Steps from both parts are interleaved, maintaining consistent partial assignments to guide each other towards a solution.

If all possible values for an unassigned theory variable would contradict the Boolean assignment of some constraint, then the current theory assignment cannot be extended consistently. This situation is resolved using an *explanation* backend, which generalizes the conflict's reason to a lemma (called explanation) that not only excludes the current conflicting assignment but also further similar situations from the future search. For example, given the formula $(x_1^2 + x_2^2 - 1 < 0 \ \vee \ x_2 > 0)$, NLSAT could decide the first constraint to be true, and then assign $x_1 = 2$. Now, no value of x_2 would satisfy $x_1^2 + x_2^2 - 1 < 0$, as it simplifies to $x_2^2 < -3$ under $x_1 = 2$. However, if $x_1^2 + x_2^2 - 1 < 0$ holds, then any value $x_1 > 1$ would require x_2^2 to be negative. Thus we can generalize the value $x_1 = 2$ to $x_1 > 1$ by learning the lemma $(\neg(x_1^2 + x_2^2 - 1 < 0) \ \vee \ x_1 \leq 1)$.

Explanations should be efficiently computable and generalize as strongly as possible. Note that the learnt clause may contain literals not present in the input formula (like $x_1 < 1$ above), thus the generalization technique is crucial for completeness. NLSAT uses CAD techniques to generalize a sample point to a single cell around it. However, NLSAT computes cells *locally* w.r.t. a sample and a subset of the constraints, which offers potential for simpler computations and larger cells. While improvements of Brown and Košta [9], Li and Xia [22], and Nalbach et al. [28] use this potential and avoid certain resultant computations, single cell construction remains a major factor for the running time.

Contributions. The cost of computing a resultant of two polynomials depends on their degree. If one of the polynomials is linear, the resultant is generally cheap to compute. In this paper, we dynamically insert linear polynomials during the cell construction from [28], effectively under-approximating the bounds on the cell. This reduces the effort of the construction by replacing expensive resultant computations with simpler ones. It also affects the quality of the cell for NLSAT: The representation is simpler, but the cell covers less of the search space. This paper follows up on the extended abstract [29], in which we briefly introduced this idea. In particular, our contributions include the following:

- We generalize the ideas from [29] and provide a clear algorithmic formulation.
- We elaborate on the reasons for potential non-termination of NLSAT using the modified single cell construction by providing an example, and adapt the method to guarantee termination.
- We explore several variants of our method, including different ways of constructing additional polynomials and criteria for when to insert them.

– We provide an extensive experimental evaluation of these variants, using our implementation in the SMT solver SMT-RAT [12,30].

Structure. In Sect. 2 we recall some background, including the levelwise single cell construction from [28], which we adapt for under-approximation in Sect. 3. We explore variants of our approach in Sect. 4 and discuss experiments in Sect. 5. In Sect. 6 we conclude with an outlook on future work.

Related Work. Some incomplete but fast explanation backends for NLSAT are not based on CAD, but on Fourier-Motzkin variable elimination [18], virtual substitution [2], or interval constraint propagation [20].

The general idea of using linear approximations or abstractions for QF-NRA has been explored before. For example, the `ksmt` calculus [6] transforms each formula into a set of linear arithmetic clauses and a set of non-linear constraints and then incrementally constructs a model, mainly performing linear reasoning. Partial assignments which falsify a non-linear constraint are generalized to conjunctions of linear constraints, using local linear approximations of the non-linear functions. Incremental linearization [10] computes a linear abstraction of the input formula by replacing all multiplications with uninterpreted functions, possibly allowing to derive unsatisfiability by purely linear reasoning. The abstraction is refined incrementally by adding linear arithmetic axioms for the individual multiplications. Neither of these methods is complete, though `ksmt` was shown to be δ-complete.

2 Preliminaries

We assume that the reader has some basic knowledge about multivariate polynomials, logic and SMT solving. For an introduction, we refer to, e.g., [4,13].

Let $\mathbb{N}$, $\mathbb{Q}$, and $\mathbb{R}$ be the sets of natural (incl. 0), rational, respectively real numbers. For $k \in \mathbb{N}$, let $[k] := \{1, \ldots, k\}$; for $r \in \mathbb{R}^k$ and $i \in [k]$ let r_i be the ith entry in r, $r_{[i]} := (r_1, \ldots, r_i)$, and $r_{[0]} = ()$. For the extent of this paper, we fix some $n \in \mathbb{N} \setminus \{0\}$ and ordered real-valued variables $x_1 \prec \ldots \prec x_n$.

Polynomials. For $i \in [n]$, let $\mathbb{Q}[x_1, \ldots, x_i]$ be the set of all polynomials in $x_1, \ldots, x_i$ with rational coefficients (for $i = 0$, this is $\mathbb{Q}$). We can write any $p \in \mathbb{Q}[x_1, \ldots, x_i]$ as a univariate polynomial $p = c_d x_i^d + c_{d-1} x_i^{d-1} + \ldots + c_1 x_i + c_0$ in x_i with either $d = 0$ or $c_d \neq 0$, with *degree* $\deg_{x_i}[p] := d$, *coefficients* $\text{coeff}_{x_i}[p] := \{c_0, \ldots, c_d\} \subset \mathbb{Q}[x_1, \ldots, x_{i-1}]$, and *leading coefficient* $\text{ldcf}_{x_i}[p] := c_d$. Given $r \in \mathbb{R}^i$, we write $p(r)$ for the evaluation $p(r_1, \ldots, r_i) \in \mathbb{R}$. Given $r \in \mathbb{R}^{i-1}$ and $r' \in \mathbb{R}$, let $p(r, x_i) \in \mathbb{R}[x_i]$ result from p by substituting $r_1, \ldots, r_{j-1}$ for $x_1, \ldots, x_{j-1}$, and we write $p(r, r')$ for $p(r_1, \ldots, r_{j-1}, r')$.

Real Roots. Let $p \in \mathbb{Q}[x_1, \ldots, x_i]$. A *(real) root* of p is a point $r \in \mathbb{R}^i$ so that $p(r) = 0$; the *variety* of p is the set of its roots. The roots of univariate polynomials build the set of *(real) algebraic numbers* $\bar{\mathbb{Q}} := \{r \in \mathbb{R} \mid \exists q \in \mathbb{Q}[x].q(r) = 0\}$.

Given $r \in \bar{\mathbb{Q}}^{i-1}$, one can compute $\text{realRoots}(p, r) := \{r_j \in \mathbb{R} \mid p(r, r_j) = 0\}$, i.e. the *roots of* p *over* r. If $\text{realRoots}(p, r) = \mathbb{R}$, then we say that p is *nullified over* r. Otherwise, $\text{realRoots}(p, r)$ is a finite set of algebraic numbers.

Let $j \in \mathbb{N}$. An *indexed root expression* $\text{root}_{x_i}[p, j] : \mathbb{R}^{i-1} \to \mathbb{R} \cup \{\bot\}$ maps each $r \in \mathbb{R}^{i-1}$ to the j-th root of p over r if it exists, and to $\bot$ otherwise:

$$\text{root}_{x_i}[p, j](r) := \begin{cases} \bot & \text{if } \text{realRoots}(p, r) = \mathbb{R} \text{ or } j > |\text{realRoots}(p, r)|, \text{ and else} \\ z_j & \text{where } \text{realRoots}(p, r) = \{z_1, \dots, z_k\}, z_1 < \dots < z_k. \end{cases}$$

We refer to the polynomial p of an indexed root expression $\xi = \text{root}_{x_i}[p, j]$ by $\xi.p$, and we say that the level of ξ is i. The set of indexed root expressions of level i is $\text{IRE}(i)$. Given $P \subseteq \mathbb{Q}[x_1, \dots, x_i]$ and $r \in \bar{\mathbb{Q}}^{i-1}$, one can compute the *indexed root expressions defined over* r: $\text{irExp}(P, r) := \{\xi \in \text{IRE}(i) \mid \xi.p \in P \text{ and } \xi(r) \neq \bot\}$.

The *resultant* of two polynomials $p, q \in \mathbb{Q}[x_1, \dots, x_i]$ w.r.t. x_i is a polynomial $\text{res}_{x_i}[p, q] \in \mathbb{Q}[x_1, \dots, x_{i-1}]$, such that for all $r \in \mathbb{R}^{i-1}$ it holds: if there is $r' \in \mathbb{R}$ with $p(r, r') = 0 = q(r, r')$, then $\text{res}_{x_i}[p, q](r) = 0$. The *discriminant* of p is $\text{disc}_{x_i}[p] := \text{res}_{x_i}[p, p']$, where p' is the derivative of p w.r.t x_i.

Formulas. A formula of the quantifier-free fragment of (non-linear) real arithmetic (QF-NRA) is a Boolean combination of (polynomial) *constraints* of the form $p \sim 0$, with $p \in \mathbb{Q}[x_1, \dots, x_n]$ and $\sim \in \{<, >, =, \leq, \geq, \neq\}$. An *extended constraint* has the form $x_i \sim \xi$, where $\xi \in \text{IRE}(i)$ is an indexed root expression.

Cells. A *cell* is a non-empty connected set $S \subseteq \mathbb{R}^i$ for some $i \in [n]$. We call S (semi-)*algebraic* if it is the solution set of a conjunction of constraints and extended constraints. We call p *sign-invariant* over S, if the sign of $p(r)$ is the same for all points $r \in S$ (i.e. $\forall r \in S.\ p(r) \sim 0$ for a fixed $\sim \in \{<, =, >\}$). We call S sign-invariant for $P \subset \mathbb{Q}[x_1, \dots, x_i]$, if all $p \in P$ are sign-invariant over S.

2.1 Levelwise Single Cell Construction

Given a constraint set C and an assignment $s \in \mathbb{R}^i$, if all extensions of s evaluate some constraints from C to false, then we say that s is *inconsistent* with C. In NLSAT, if the theory assignment is inconsistent with the constraints C defined to be true by the Boolean assignment, then we generalize s to a cell $S \subseteq \mathbb{R}^i$, whose points are all inconsistent with C. To do so, we derive a set $P \subset \mathbb{Q}[x_1, \dots, x_i]$ of projection polynomials, such that $s \in S$ and the sign-invariance of P over S assures that all points in S are inconsistent with C. The learned explanation is then $(\neg C \vee \neg \varphi_S)$, where φ_S is a conjunction of extended constraints defining S.

Definition 1. *Given* $i \in [n]$, $P \subset \mathbb{Q}[x_1, \dots, x_i]$ *and* $s \in \mathbb{R}^i$, *the problem of* single cell construction *(SCC) is to compute a description of an algebraic cell* $S \subseteq \mathbb{R}^i$ *so that* $s \in S$ *and all* $p \in P$ *are sign-invariant over* S.

We now recall the *levelwise* SCC approach [28] by Nalbach et al., which is summarized in Algorithm 1, and which we will modify in Sect. 3.

Algorithm 1: `levelwise-scc`(P, s)

Input : A finite $P \subseteq \mathbb{Q}[x_1, \ldots, x_i]$, and $s \in \mathbb{R}^i$ (with $i \in [n]$).
Output: A description $(I_1 \wedge \ldots \wedge I_i)$ of a sign-invariant cell for P containing s

1 **for** $j = i, \ldots, 1$ **do**
2     $P_j := P \cap (\mathbb{Q}[x_1, \ldots, x_j] \setminus \mathbb{Q}[x_1, \ldots, x_{j-1}])$
3   **if** realRoots$(p, s_{[j-1]}) = \mathbb{R}$ for some $p \in P_j$ **then return** *FAIL*
4     $\{\xi_1, \ldots, \xi_k\} :=$ irExp$(P_j, s_{[j-1]})$ s.t. $\xi_1(s_{[j-1]}) \leq \ldots \leq \xi_k(s_{[j-1]})$
5   **if** $k = 0$ **then** $I_j := (true)$
6   **else if** $s_j = \xi_\ell(s_{[j-1]})$ for some ℓ **then** $I_j := (x_j = \xi_\ell)$
7   **else if** $s_j > \xi_k(s_{[j-1]})$ **then** $I_j := (\xi_k < x_j)$
8   **else if** $s_j < \xi_1(s_{[j-1]})$ **then** $I_j := (x_j < \xi_1)$
9   **else** $I_j := (\xi_\ell < x_j \wedge x_j < \xi_{\ell+1})$ for the ℓ with $\xi_\ell(s_{[j-1]}) < s_j < \xi_{\ell+1}(s_{[j-1]})$
10   **add** to P discriminants and coefficients ensuring delineability
11   **add** to P resultants ensuring sign-invariance
12 **return** $(I_1 \wedge \ldots \wedge I_i)$

Let $i \in [n]$, $s \in \mathbb{R}^i$, $P \subset \mathbb{Q}[x_1, \ldots, x_i]$, and for $j \in [i]$ let P_j be the polynomials from P with largest variable x_j (i.e. those containing x_j, but not $x_{j+1}, \ldots, x_i$). For each dimension $j = i, \ldots, 1$, the algorithm determines a *symbolic interval* I_j of the form $(x_j = \xi)$, $(x_j < \xi)$, $(x_j > \xi)$, or $(\xi < x_j \wedge x_j < \xi')$ for some $\xi, \xi' \in \text{IRE}(j)$, bounding the value of x_j w.r.t. the lower variables $x_1, \ldots, x_{j-1}$. For all $r \in \mathbb{R}^{j-1}$ with $\xi(r) \neq \bot \neq \xi'(r)$, I_j defines a *concrete interval* $I_j(r) \subseteq \mathbb{R}$ which is $\{\xi(r)\}$, $(-\infty, \xi(r))$, $(\xi(r), \infty)$, or $(\xi(r), \xi'(r))$, respectively.

The final cell described by $I_1 \wedge \ldots \wedge I_i$ is *locally cylindrical*, i.e., I_1 defines a concrete interval $S_1 \subseteq \mathbb{R}$, and for $j = 2, \ldots, i$, the root expressions in I_j are defined everywhere over S_{j-1}, and they specify the cell

$$S_j = \{(r, r') \in \mathbb{R}^j \mid r \in S_{j-1} \wedge r' \in I_j(r)\}.$$

To determine I_j, we assign $x_1, \ldots, x_{j-1}$ to the underlying sample $s_{[j-1]}$, and compute realRoots$(p, s_{[j-1]})$ for all $p \in P_j$. These roots witness the indexed root expressions in Line 4. The greatest root below (or equal to) s_j and the smallest root above (or equal to) s_j provide the interval boundaries (if they do not exist, $-\infty$ and ∞ are used). Thus, the polynomials in P_j are sign-invariant over $\{s_{[j-1]}\} \times I_j(s_{[j-1]})$.

The idea is now that the to-be-constructed underlying cell $S_{j-1} \subseteq \mathbb{R}^{j-1}$ will be a neighbourhood around $s_{[j-1]}$ over which the root expressions in I_j define total continuous functions such that S_j is a sign-invariant cell for P_j containing $s_{[j]}$. To obtain an underlying cell with the desired properties, the concepts of delineability and order-invariance (a strengthening of sign-invariance) are used:

Definition 2 (Delineability [11]**).** *Let* $j \in [n-1]$ *and* $S \subseteq \mathbb{R}^j$ *be a cell. A non-zero polynomial* $p \in \mathbb{Q}[x_1, \ldots, x_{j+1}]$ *is* delineable *over* S *if there exist* $k \geq 0$ *continuous functions* $\theta_1, \ldots, \theta_k : S \to \mathbb{R}$ *and constants* $m_1, \ldots m_k \in \mathbb{N}$ *such that for all* $r \in S$ *holds* $\theta_1(r) < \ldots < \theta_k(r)$, realRoots$(p, r) = \{\theta_1(r), \ldots, \theta_k(r)\}$, *and for all* $\ell = 1, \ldots, k$ *the multiplicity of the root* $\theta_\ell(r)$ *in* $p(r, x_{j+1})$ *is* m_ℓ.

Definition 3 (Order-invariance [23]). *The* order of $p \in \mathbb{Q}[x_1, \ldots, x_j]$ at $r \in \mathbb{R}^j$*, denoted* $ord(p, r)$*, is the minimum* k *so that some partial derivative of* p *of total order* k *does not evaluate to* 0 *at* r *(or* ∞*, if all evaluate to* 0*). We call* p order-invariant *on* $R \subseteq \mathbb{R}^j$ *if* $ord(p, r) = ord(p, r')$ *for all* $r, r' \in R$.

The indexed root expressions of p determined in Line 4 witness the θ functions. That these are well-defined continuous functions is assured by the delineability of p. The method uses the fact that p is delineable over the underlying cell S_{j-1} if $\text{disc}_{x_j}[p]$ is order-invariant on S_{j-1} and $\text{ldcf}_{x_j}[p]$ is sign-invariant over S_{j-1}; thus it adds these polynomials to P and ensures their properties on the next level, thereby restricting I_{j-1} and the levels below.

The method still has to ensure that no root function crosses the cell boundaries (the root expressions in I_j) over S_{j-1}, because this would imply a sign change of some polynomial within S_j. For this purpose, we use that for any two $\xi, \xi' \in \text{irExp}(P_j, s_{[j-1]})$ and $\sim \in \{<, =\}$ with $\xi(s_{[j-1]}) \sim \xi'(s_{[j-1]})$, it holds: If $\text{res}_{x_j}[\xi.p, \xi'.p]$ is order-invariant on S_{j-1}, then $\xi(r) \sim \xi'(r)$ for all $r \in S_{j-1}$.

Since only intersections of roots with the cell boundaries are relevant, it suffices to maintain a *partial* ordering of the root functions, ensured by certain resultants (Line 11). For example, if $\xi_1, \ldots, \xi_k$ are as in Algorithm 1 and $I_j = (\xi_\ell < x_j \wedge x_j < \xi_{\ell+1})$, then we could add $\{\text{res}_{x_j}[\xi_{\ell'}.p, \xi_\ell.p] \mid \ell' < \ell\} \cup \{\text{res}_{x_j}[\xi_{\ell+1}.p, \xi_{\ell'}.p] \mid \ell + 1 < \ell'\}$, ensuring that $\xi_1, \ldots, \xi_{\ell-1}$ stay below (or equal to) ξ_ℓ and $\xi_{\ell+2}, \ldots, \xi_k$ stay above (or equal to) $\xi_{\ell+1}$. By exploiting transitivity, other partial orderings and thus other sets of resultants are also viable; this is a heuristic decision. However, the resultant $\text{res}_{x_i}[\xi_\ell.p, \xi_{\ell+1}.p]$ of the bounds is always added to ensure connectedness of S_j.

Note that this method fails if any of the encountered polynomials is nullified on the underlying sample, because then delineability cannot be ensured in the same way. The method can detect this and return "FAIL", and a different, complete approach is used instead. To further ensure that no polynomial $p \in P_j$ is nullified over any other point in S_{j-1}, some $c \in \text{coeff}_{x_j}[p]$ with $c(s_{[j-1]}) \neq 0$ is also added to P in Line 10. After adding all required polynomials to P, if $j > 1$, then the method proceeds with the construction of I_{j-1} in the same way.

Example 1. Figure 1 illustrates an example with a given sample $s \in \mathbb{R}^2$ and polynomials $P = \{p_1, p_2, p_3\} \subset \mathbb{Q}[x_1, x_2]$. The line labelled with p_1 indicates the variety of p_1 i.e. those points $r \in \mathbb{R}^2$ with $p_1(r) = 0$, and similarly for p_2, p_3.

We start at level 2, where $P_2 = P$. At $x_1 = s_1$, there is one root of p_2 below s_2 and one root of each polynomial above s_2. The roots closest to s_2 define the symbolic interval $I_2 := (\xi_1 < x_2 \wedge x_2 < \xi_2)$ (Fig. 1a). To ensure correctness of this interval for all values of x_1 in the underlying cell (to be computed at level 1), the discriminants and leading coefficients of p_1, p_2, p_3 are added to P (dash-dotted lines in Fig. 1b). Moreover, adding $\text{res}_{x_2}[p_3, p_1]$ and $\text{res}_{x_2}[p_3, p_2]$ (dashed lines in Fig. 1b) ensures that none of the root functions cross the upper interval bound defined by p_1 over I_1. Note that the crossing of ξ_3 and ξ_4 is irrelevant, and the corresponding resultant of p_1 and p_2 is thus avoided. On level 1, we isolate the roots of these polynomials and use the closest to s_1 as interval boundaries, resulting in the shaded cell (Fig. 1c).

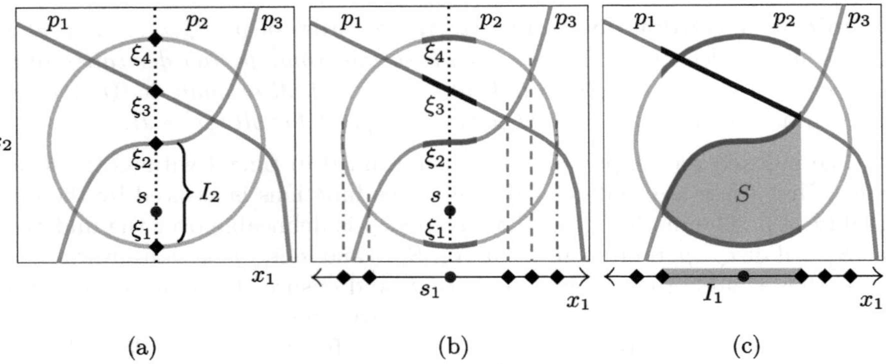

Fig. 1. Illustration of the levelwise construction described in Example 1.

3 Adding Polynomials to Avoid Expensive Resultants

The running time of SCC is dominated by discriminant and resultant computations. Given $p, q \in \mathbb{Q}[x_1, \ldots, x_n]$ with $d_j = \deg_{x_j}[p]$, $e_j = \deg_{x_j}[q]$ for all $j \in [n]$, the resultant of p and q requires $\mathcal{O}(d_n e_n)$ polynomial multiplications and, in the worst case, its degree w.r.t. any x_j is $d_n e_j + d_j e_n$. Given $P \subset \mathbb{Q}[x_1, \ldots, x_n]$ with maximal degree d in any variable, the degree and time complexity of resultants during SCC grows doubly exponential in worst-case (d^{2^n}), as resultants of resultants are computed iteratively. The levelwise method already mitigates the effort for computing resultants, e.g. it avoids involving polynomials of high degree. However, some cannot be avoided, e.g. polynomials defining the bounds of an interval are always included in some resultant computations.

Our approach is as follows: If a high-degree polynomial p would define a bound of a symbolic interval I_j, then we add a new *linear* polynomial $p_* = (x_j - c)$ to P, whose root $c \in \mathbb{Q}$ lies *strictly* between that bound and the sample s_j. Using this as a new, under-approximating bound for I_j allows replacing expensive resultants of p and some $q \in P$ by resultants of p_* with q, which are simply computed by substituting c for x_j in q, and their degree is bounded by the one of q. The choice of c ensures that (1) the resulting cell still contains the sample, (2) all other roots remain outside the cell, and (3) the underlying levels still generalize to some larger cell. Towards the latter, c should not be equal to any polynomial's root, as the cell then would only generalize to a section $I_{j-1} = (x_{j-1} = \xi)$ on the level below as the resultant of that polynomial with p_* would have a root at $s_{[j-1]}$.

Example 2. In Example 1 (depicted in Fig. 2a), the levelwise method cannot avoid the resultants $\text{res}_{x_2}[p_2, p_3]$ and $\text{res}_{x_2}[p_3, p_1]$, which are expensive if p_1, p_2 and p_2 have high degree. Adding a linear polynomial p_* with a root ξ_* between s and ξ_2, lets us use ξ_* as upper bound of I_2, and it suffices to compute only the cheap resultants of p_* with p_1, p_2, p_3 (like shown in Fig. 2b). Figure 2c shows

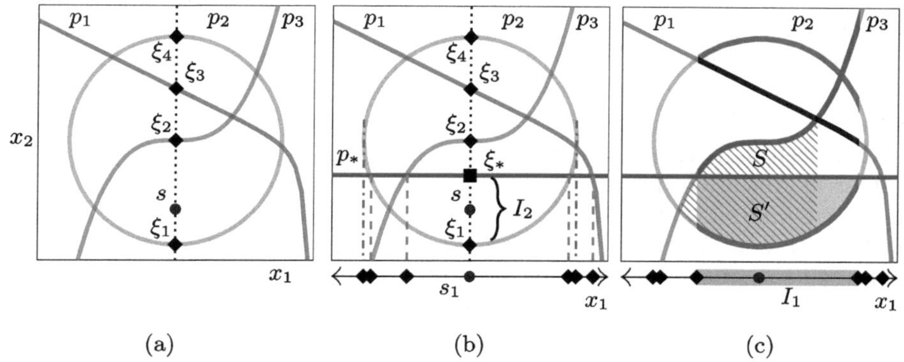

Fig. 2. Approximated cell using a new linear polynomial

the resulting cell S' (pink, shaded) and the original cell S (hatched). Importantly, p_1, p_2 and p_3 are sign-invariant over S'. Note that we might also under-approximate the lower bound of I_2, or the bounds of I_1, leading to an even smaller cell, but also reducing computations.

We generalize this approach and modify `levelwise-scc`, so that on each level, it can dynamically extend the working set P with arbitrary polynomials, resulting in our new method `apx-scc` shown in Algorithm 2, which adds Line 4. The method `apx-criteria` decides whether adding new polynomials is beneficial, by checking e.g. whether the symbolic interval I_j would be defined by a polynomial with high degree. If the criteria are fulfilled, `apx-polys` computes a set of new polynomials (called *auxiliary* polynomials) that are added to P. The auxiliary polynomials have roots at favourable positions, admitting an easier set of resultants to be computed. We discuss the different approaches for implementing `apx-criteria` and `apx-polys` in Sect. 4.

Adding auxiliary polynomials makes the maximal possible sign-invariant cell around the given sample point smaller, hence we compute some kind of *under-*

Algorithm 2: `apx-scc`(P, s)

Input : A finite $P \subseteq \mathbb{Q}[x_1, \ldots, x_i]$ and $s \in \mathbb{R}^i$ (with $i \in [n]$).
Output: A description $(I_1, \ldots, I_i)$ of a sign-invariant cell for P containing s

1 **for** $j = i, \ldots, 1$ **do**
2     $P_j := P \cap (\mathbb{Q}[x_1, \ldots, x_j] \setminus \mathbb{Q}[x_1, \ldots, x_{j-1}])$
3   **if** realRoots$(p, s_{[j-1]}) = \mathbb{R}$ for some $p \in P_j$ **then return** *FAIL*
4   **if** `apx-criteria`$(P_j, s_{[j]})$ **then** $P := P \cup$ `apx-polys`$(P_j, s_{[j]})$
5   **compute** I_j as before (Lines 2-9 in Algorithm 1)
6   **add** to P polynomials ensuring delineability and sign-invariance (Lines 10-11 in Algorithm 1)
7 **return** $(I_1, \ldots, I_i)$

---

approximation. However, as shown in Fig. 2c, the cell computed by `apx-scc` is not necessarily a subset of the cell computed by `levelwise-scc`, as strengthening the bounds of I_j might allow weakening some bound of I_{j-1}. In any case, both the original and the approximated cell (S and S') are subsets of the maximal sign-invariant cell S_{max} for P. While $S = S_{max}$ may hold, it always holds $S' \subsetneq S_{max}$.

Our modification has two main benefits for the usage in NLSAT: (1) Avoiding expensive resultant computations means that explanations can be computed much faster; and (2) during later computations, NLSAT needs to isolate the roots of the cell boundaries over further sample points, for checking whether a given sample lies in the excluded cell - the effort for these computations may be drastically reduced by polynomials of lower degree (or even degree 1). On the other hand, the under-approximated cells may lead to more cells generated throughout the search, and even lead to non-termination, as we will see in Sect. 3.1.

It is important to note that our modification does not eliminate the strong degree growth entirely, because the discriminants needed for delineability are also resultants. Moreover, for sections $I_j = (x_j = \xi)$ we cannot compute meaningful approximations, forcing us to fall back to the default method.

Theorem 1 (Correctness). *Let $P \subset \mathbb{Q}[x_1, \ldots, x_i]$ be finite and $s \in \mathbb{R}^i$. If* `apx-scc`*(P, s) yields the cell $S \subseteq \mathbb{R}^i$, then $s \in S$ and P is sign-invariant over S.*

Proof. The idea is that the original method could produce the same cell, when given an appropriately modified input. For each $j \in [i]$, let $Q_j \subset \mathbb{Q}[x_1, \ldots, x_j]$ be the set of polynomials added by `apx-scc` on level j, and let $Q := Q_1 \cup \ldots \cup Q_i$. Consider the cell $S' \subseteq \mathbb{R}^i$ computed by `levelwise-scc`$(P \cup Q, s)$. As that method is correct, $s \in S'$ and $P \cup Q$ is sign-invariant over S'. By definition of sign-invariance, this implies that P is sign-invariant over S'.

We show $S = S'$ to complete the proof: The polynomials in Q_j do not impact the computations of the levels $j + 1, \ldots, i$, because $Q_j \cap P_k = \emptyset$ for each $k \neq j$. Thus, both `levelwise-scc` and `apx-scc` compute each level j only based on $P \cup \bigcup_{k=j}^{i} Q_k$. As their computations do not differ (apart from adding Q_j), they compute exactly the same intervals and projections. □

3.1 Incompleteness

Like `levelwise-scc`, our approach fails in the case of nullification and is thus incomplete as a stand-alone procedure. However, one can detect nullification and resort to a complete construction for that cell. More critically, the termination of NLSAT is no longer guaranteed when using `apx-scc` for explanations.

Example 3 (Non-Termination). We continue Example 2. After excluding the approximated cell from the search, NLSAT chooses a new value for y. This value can lie between the auxiliary cell boundary and the root of p_3, leading to the sample s' as shown in Fig. 3a. Since s' and s are in the same maximal sign-invariant cell for p_1, p_2, p_3, it leads to a conflict with the same constraints, and thus `apx-scc` is called with the same polynomials. When computing the new explanation, another auxiliary boundary is introduced between s' and p_3, and

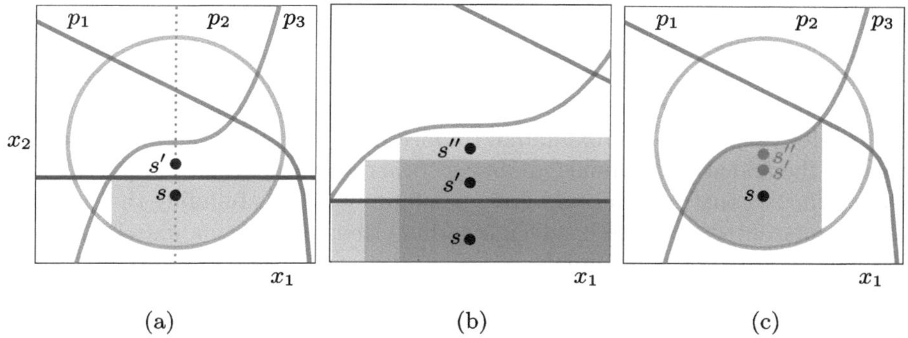

Fig. 3. Non-termination of NLSAT with under-approximating cells, as described in Example 3. Figure (b) zooms in on the area between p_3 and the approximation.

this behaviour repeats, leading to a sample s'' as in Fig. 3b. This can repeat indefinitely, and NLSAT will run into the same conflict over and over, without ever covering the entire search space. This behaviour cannot occur with the original construction, as is illustrated in Fig. 3c.

Note that NLSAT does not always run into this situation. It might also choose samples that are further away, thus escaping the conflict. Thanks to the Boolean structure of the formula, the remaining search space might still be covered by approximated cells for other conflicts, which involve different sets of polynomials.

We can also express this with formal terms from [19]: the termination of NLSAT relies on the fact that a *finite basis* explanation function is used. That is, for every input formula φ, there is a *finite* set $B(\varphi) \subset \mathbb{Q}[x_1, \ldots, x_n]$ such that in all possible runs of NLSAT, all explanations use only polynomials from B. Since there are runs of NLSAT for which our explanation produces *infinitely* many different literals, `apx-scc` does not yield a *finite basis* explanation function.

Retaining Completeness. If we ensure that in every run of NLSAT, we add only finitely many auxiliary polynomials, then termination is guaranteed again. The reasoning is that there will be a point after which the output of `apx-scc` is always equal to the original levelwise construction `levelwise-scc`. Since this is a finite-basis explanation function, termination will be guaranteed.

Lemma 1 (Termination). *A run of NLSAT using* `apx-scc` *terminates iff* `apx-criteria`*($P_j, s_{[j]}$) returns* `true` *only finitely many times during that run.*

To make use of this lemma, we provide additional information to `apx-criteria`, like the number n_{cells} of so far approximated cells. Then, `apx-criteria` could return `false` whenever n_{cells} exceeds some fixed threshold, fulfilling the condition from Lemma 1 and thus implying termination.

However, the optimal threshold will vary depending on the input formula. A more flexible approach is to gradually strengthen the criteria as the number of approximated cells increases. For example, we only add a polynomial if a cell boundary is defined by some $p \in P$ with $\deg_{x_p}[j] \geq c \cdot n_{cells} + d$, where $c, d \in \mathbb{Q}_{\geq 0}$.

This avoids the behaviour from Example 3, since $c \cdot n_{cells} + d$ eventually exceeds the degree of the involved polynomials, but other cells with more expensive resultants are still approximated. Importantly, this only ensures termination because the added polynomials are linear; otherwise, the degrees of polynomials derived in the construction could grow indefinitely, always fulfilling the criterion.

The guarantee may also be given by other criteria, e.g. using individual counters for the involved polynomials.

4 Variants

We now present several instantiations for `apx-polys` and `apx-criteria`. The first three methods approximate a cell boundary: Given the sample $s_{[j]}$ and some $p \in P$, whose root ξ would be a bound of I_j, we construct some p_* with a root $c \in \mathbb{Q}$ between s_j and $b := \xi(s_{[j-1]})$.

Simple Approach. At the beginning of Sect. 3, we already introduced the idea of adding polynomials $x_j - c$ defining a constant bound c on x_j. We now elaborate on the choice of c. Although choosing c close to b restricts I_j less, it may shrink the underlying cell depending on the shape of p's variety. This can be observed in Fig. 3: the closer the approximate bound is to the actual bound, the smaller becomes I_1 (the interval for x_1). It is thus not immediately clear what to choose. More importantly, this approach can produce numbers $c = {}^{num}/_{den}$ with large bit size $log(num) + log(den)$, causing significant overhead in operations like substituting c into high-degree polynomials. Therefore, we choose c with a minimal bit size using a method based on the *Stern-Brocot tree* [7,31].

The following two approaches try to provide better approximations of the cell boundary, hoping to increase the cell's quality for NLSAT.

Taylor. We want to construct p_* so that its gradient at its root $(s_{[j-1]}, c)$ is equal to the gradient of p at its root $r := (s_{[j-1]}, b)$:

$$p_* \quad = \quad \frac{\partial p}{\partial x_j}(r) \cdot (x_j - c) + \sum\nolimits_{k \in [j-1]} \left(\frac{\partial p}{\partial x_k}(r) \cdot (x_k - s_k) \right)$$

This is a slight modification of the *first-order Taylor expansion* of p at r, the difference being that the constant term $p(r)$ is left out as it is always zero, and that $(x_j - c)$ is used instead of $(x_j - r_j)$ in the first term. This ensures that p_* has its root at $(s_{[j-1]}, c)$ instead of r. Now, clearly

$$p_*(s_{[j-1]}, c) = 0 \text{ and } \frac{\partial p_*}{\partial x_k}(s_{[j-1]}, c) = \frac{\partial p}{\partial x_k}(r) \text{ for all } k \in [j].$$

The idea is that the root functions of p and p_* will behave similarly around $s_{[j-1]}$, as illustrated in Fig. 4a. The dashed line is the root of the tangent to p_3 at (s_{j-1}, b), which is then shifted to pass through c.

Unfortunately, if some sample coordinate s_k is *irrational*, then (1) we cannot use the term $(x_k - s_k)$, since we require *rational* coefficients, and (2) the gradients $\partial p/\partial x_k(r)$ are harder to compute and might also be irrational. We tackle (1) by omitting the summand corresponding to x_k for the k where s_k is irrational, and (2) by finding rational approximations of the gradients: Each (irrational) algebraic number can be isolated using an open interval containing a single root of its defining polynomial; this interval can be refined arbitrarily by bisection. For $k \in [j]$, let $g_k \approx \partial p/\partial x_k(r)$ be a rational approximation, then we get

$$p_* \quad = \quad g_j \cdot (x_j - c) + \sum_{k \in [j-1] \text{ s.t. } s_k \in \mathbb{Q}} \Big(g_k \cdot (x_k - s_k) \Big)$$

Both mitigations harm the quality of the approximation, as some gradients are only approximately equal, or not counted in at all.

Piecewise Linear. Instead of approximating the boundary at a single point, we can use piecewise linear interpolation. For this purpose, we determine an interval $D \subseteq \mathbb{R}$ around s_{j-1} so that p is delineable over

$$\{s_{[j-2]}\} \times D = \{(s_{[j-2]}, s') \in \mathbb{R}^{j-1} \mid s' \in D\} \subseteq \mathbb{R}^{j-1},$$

i.e. $\text{disc}_{x_j}[p]$ and certain coefficients of p are sign-invariant over that set. We now know that ξ is a total continuous function over $\{s_{[j-2]}\} \times D$, which is needed for deriving a meaningful interpolation.

We then choose $k \in \mathbb{N}$ support points $d_1 < \ldots < d_k$ from D such that $s_{j-1} \in \{d_1, \ldots, d_k\}$, and for each $\ell \in [k]$ we compute the value $\xi((s_{[j-2]}, d_\ell))$ of the root function at that support point (in practice, we only isolate it in a rational interval). Each of those values is under-approximated by choosing a value $d'_\ell \in \mathbb{Q}$ "close" to the boundary $\xi((s_{[j-2]}, d_\ell))$ such that $(s_{[j-2]}, d_\ell, d'_\ell) \in \mathbb{R}^j$ is inside the cell. We require that one support point d_ℓ is equal to s_{j-1}, because this guarantees that $(s_{[j-2]}, d_\ell, d'_\ell)$ (for this particular ℓ) is between the bound and the sample point.

The approximate bound then consists of $k-1$ pieces, which connect the points $\{(s_{[j-2]}, d_\ell, d'_\ell) \in \mathbb{R}^j \mid \ell \in [k]\}$ and which are defined by the roots of

$$p_*^{(\ell)} := (d_{\ell+1} - d_\ell)(x_j - d'_\ell) - (d'_{\ell+1} - d'_\ell)(x_{j-1} - d_\ell), \quad \ell \in [k-1].$$

That is, p_* is a piecewise function so that for $r \in \mathbb{R}^j$ holds $p_*(r) = p_*^{(\ell)}(r)$ if $d_\ell \leq r \leq d_{\ell+1}$ (or $\ell = k$ if $d_k \leq r$). We can encode this function by a minimum over maximum of linear functions as described in [32,33], and thus derive an QF-NRA formula. Further, we can adapt the subsequent cell construction to handle such compound interval bounds by using the techniques described in [26]: We compute the resultant of each $p_*^{(\ell)}$ with the polynomials below or above the interval and filter out roots of the resultants witnessing spurious intersections. This approach is illustrated in Fig. 4b where the intersections with the dashed lines are filtered out.

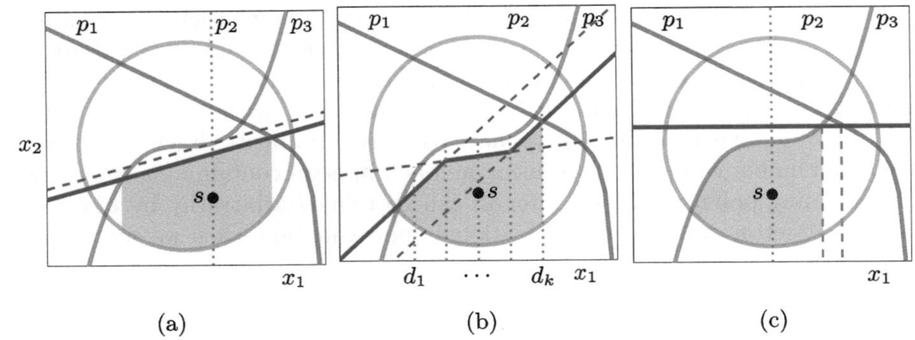

Fig. 4. Variants of the modified construction: (a) using Taylor expansion, (b) using piecewise linear bounds, and (c) adding roots outside the cell.

There are two cases where we cannot apply this approach (and thus need to apply e.g. the simple approach): (1) Like the Taylor approach, if s_{j-1} is irrational, we cannot construct p_*, because $s_{j-1} = d_\ell$ for some $\ell \in [k]$, and thus we cannot use the term $x_{j-1} - d_\ell$. (2) If $D = \{s_{j-1}\}$, i.e. D contains only one point, we cannot choose more than one support point. However, at least two points are needed to construct one piece of the approximate boundary. This case happens e.g. when the discriminant of p (the original boundary-defining polynomial) has a root ξ_{disc} at $s_{[j-1]}$, which means that the next level will collapse to a section $I_{j-1} = (x_{j-1} = \xi_{disc})$ anyway and the behaviour of p_* around the sample does not matter as much.

Roots Outside the Cell. We could also introduce polynomials p_* with a root function ξ_* between the cell boundary ξ and some other root ξ' outside the cell. Instead of $\text{res}_{x_j}[\xi.p, \xi'.p]$, we compute $\text{res}_{x_j}[\xi.p, p_*]$ and $\text{res}_{x_j}[p_*, \xi'.p]$ and then use transitivity, which may simplify the projection. While this has the advantage of leaving the top level I_i unchanged, the underlying cell may still be restricted by the new resultants. This is illustrated in Fig. 4c.

Approximation Criteria. In addition to varying the way *how* auxiliary polynomials are computed, we can also adapt *when* they are computed, by using different instantiations of `apx-criteria`.

As our goal is to avoid expensive resultant computations, we are interested in quantities which influence the resultant complexity on the current level. A simple (yet effective in practice) criterion depends on the degree of the boundary-defining polynomial $p \in \mathbb{Q}[x_1, \ldots, x_i]$: the bound is approximated if $\deg_{x_i}[p]$ exceeds a fixed threshold. This has some limitations: (1) It can happen that `levelwise-scc` would not compute any (expensive) resultants with p, but this criterion would still advise inserting auxiliary polynomials. While this defeats the purpose of avoiding expensive resultants, it is not completely useless as it still simplifies the cell description. (2) Different thresholds will be optimal for different kinds of input problems, and it is not easy to guess a good one a priori.

Addressing the first issue, one can additionally check whether a resultant of p with another nonlinear polynomial would be computed. However, this did not improve the performance in our preliminary experiments. The second issue is (partially) addressed with the dynamic termination criterion from Sect. 3.1, where the threshold for the degree grows with the number of approximated cells.

Instead of the degree $\deg_{x_i}[p]$, we might also consider similar measures, e.g. the *sum-of-total-degrees* of p's monomials, which has been used for CAD projection orderings [15].

Transfer to CAlC. Similar to NLSAT, the *cylindrical algebraic covering (CAlC)* method [1,27] tries to extend a partial assignment $s \in \mathbb{R}^i$ to a full model. It uses the same theoretical framework as the levelwise construction to derive symbolic intervals to be excluded from the search. In particular, it also ensures that certain root functions ξ, ξ' do not intersect by making $\text{res}_{x_{i+1}}[\xi.p, \xi'.p]$ order-invariant. We can apply our technique and dynamically introduce a polynomial with a root between ξ, ξ', replacing an expensive resultant by two simpler ones, but shrinking the underlying cell. This will introduce similar issues regarding termination, which can be solved in similar ways as presented above for SCC.

5 Experiments

We implemented several variants of our approach in the SMT-RAT solver [12,30], allowing us to use its existing implementations of the levelwise SCC and NLSAT. SMT-RAT also uses explanation backends based on the Fourier-Motzkin variable elimination (FM) [18], interval constraint propagation (ICP) [20], and virtual substitution (VS) [2], which are fast, but may fail to provide an explanation, especially for polynomials of degree 3 or higher. The backends are called sequentially (FM, ICP, VS, SCC), so that the single cell construction is only needed when all other backends fail. We compare the following variants for SCC:

`Baseline`: The original levelwise SCC.

`Simple-j`: For `j` $\in \{3, 4, 5, 6\}$, cell bounds defined by polynomials of degree `j` or higher are approximated by simple polynomials of the form $x_j - c$. Termination is ensured by limiting the number of approximated cells to 50.

`Simple-*`: a virtual best portfolio of the `Simple-j` variants.

`Dynamic`: Uses the dynamic termination criterion from Sect. 3.1. A cell bound is approximated by a simple polynomial of the form $x_j - c$, if the defining polynomial has degree higher than or equal to $1/5 \cdot n_{cells} + 3$, where n_{cells} is the number of so far approximated cells.

`Taylor`: Like `Dynamic`, but using Taylor approximations as in Sect. 4.

`PWL-j`: For `j` $\in \{2, 4, 6\}$, like `Dynamic`, but using piecewise linear approximations with `j` pieces, as presented in Sect. 4.

`PWL-*`: a virtual best portfolio of the `PWL-j` variants.

`Outside`: If the lower (resp. upper) cell bound and another root function below (resp. above) that bound are defined by two non-linear polynomials, one of which fulfils the dynamic criterion, then we add a polynomial (of the form $x_j - c$) whose root lies outside the cell, between the bound and the other root, as explained in Sect. 4.

Moreover, we also compare to the state-of-the-art `cvc5` [14] solver (version 1.2.1), which uses incremental linearization and cylindrical algebraic coverings.

We used the QF-NRA benchmark set from SMT-LIB [3], but only consider the 1684 instances where SMT-RAT calls SCC at least once, since there is no difference between the variants on the other instances. The tests were conducted on identical Intel®Xeon®8468 Sapphire CPUs with 2.1 GHz per core, with a time limit of 1 min and memory limit of 4GB per instance.

The results are summarized in Fig. 5. While `cvc5` usually solves more instances than SMT-RAT on the entire QF-NRA set, already the `Baseline` solver outperforms `cvc5` on our restricted benchmark set.

Simple Approximations. Already the `Simple-j` variants solve around 45 instances more than `Baseline`. However, these variants excel (partly) on different instances: the virtual portfolio `Simple-*` solves at least 18 instances more than each `Simple-j` variant.

`Dynamic` almost matches this performance, solving 58 instances more than `Baseline`, and it is in fact the best (non-portfolio) variant in our tests. Interestingly, the differences in solved satisfiable instances and unsatisfiable instances are almost equal (30 more satisfiable, 28 more unsatisfiable). This suggests that our explanations can not only help NLSAT find a model more quickly, but the Boolean structure of the unsatisfiable problems often still allows to cover the search space with the under-approximated cells.

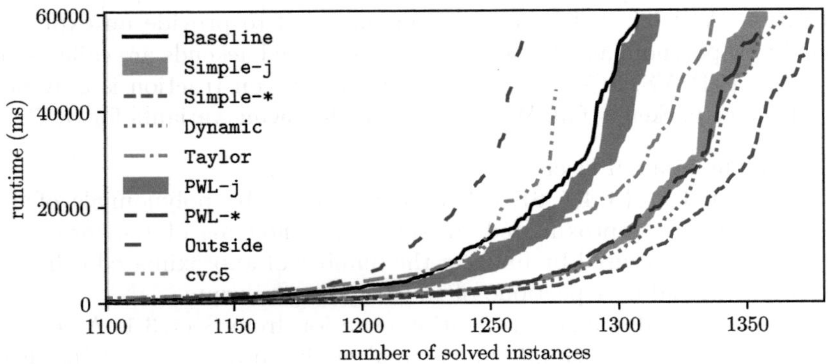

Fig. 5. Performance profile. The purple area covers all `PWL-j` variants, the green area covers all `Simple-j` variants.

Figure 6 shows a more detailed comparison between `Dynamic` and `Baseline`. Looking at the running times, `Dynamic` can solve many instances within one

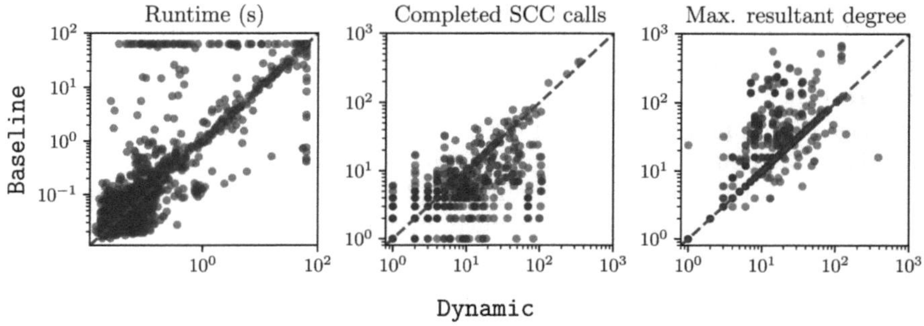

Fig. 6. Scatter plots comparing `Dynamic` with `Baseline`

second, for which `Baseline` needs multiple seconds or even times out. On the other hand, there are very few instances on which `Dynamic` is significantly slower, even though the number of SCC calls is usually much higher. This is expected: the approximated cells can be computed faster, but they cover less of the search space. Moreover, our approach often significantly reduces the maximum degree of any computed resultant. However, we did not find a clear reduction of degrees of discriminants and coefficients.

Other Variants. The `Taylor` and `PWL-j` variants performed slightly better than `Baseline`, but worse than the simple approximations. It seems that the induced overhead outweighs potential benefits of better approximations. In particular, our investigations often showed large bit sizes of the rational coefficients in the auxiliary polynomials and their resultants. Another reason could be that the cell representation is less convenient, which is supported by the underwhelming performance of `Outside`, which solves fewer instances than `Baseline`. While it does avoid some resultants like the other variants, it does not simplify the cell representation. Accordingly, this seems to be a significant factor.

Transfer to the CAlC Method. We also tested our modification in the context of the *cylindrical algebraic covering (CAlC)* method [27], which is implemented in SMT-RAT as well. Now considering all 12154 instances of the QF_NRA benchmark set, there is no significant difference between the baseline CAlC implementation (solving 9964 instances) and our modification (solving 9975 instances). Once again, this might indicate that NLSAT especially benefits from simpler cell descriptions (which are not used in CAlC) and from compensating smaller cells by Boolean reasoning.

A Note on Non-termination. In Sect. 3.1, we showed that our approach can lead to non-termination with some sort of "looping" behaviour and presented ways to combat this. Naturally, it would be interesting to know how often this occurs in practice. As it is quite hard to reliably detect this behaviour, we have no concrete data. However, when turning off the limit on approximated cells, the `Simple-j` variants time out significantly more often (solving around 40 instances less than with the limit), hinting at the importance of our termination criteria. However, there are other influences in practice: When sampling new values, SMT-RAT prioritizes simple numbers, e.g. integers over rational numbers, and thus even the variants without the hard bound might (temporarily) escape looping when the gap between the actual cell boundary and the approximation becomes small. Then it may still time out in other parts of the computation or get caught in another loop.

6 Conclusions

We modified the levelwise single cell construction for NLSAT and CAlC by dynamically inserting linear polynomials into the projection to avoid expensive high-degree polynomials in resultant computations and description of the resulting cell, at the cost of smaller cells - which are unterstood as "under-approximations". We introduced various variants to introduce such polynomials, as well as criteria to mitigate potential non-termination of NLSAT and CAlC.

In our experiments, our approach could significantly improve the running time of NLSAT. Interesingly, relatively simple under-aproximations performed best, while more complex approximations did not pay off, suggesting that the gains are mainly due to simpler root isolation in NLSAT.

There are several directions for further research: Firstly, we conjecture that more intricate variants of `apx-criteria` may further improve efficiency. This is not an easy task: In experiments not presented here, various other approaches based e.g. on the sum-of-total-degrees of the polynomials or involving the degrees of all polynomials on a level did not yield better results. Secondly, our approach can only reduce computational effort for resultants, but not yet for discriminants, which have an even greater impact. Thirdly, the basic modification of the CAlC method had little impact, which might be improved. Finally, we guarantee termination of NLSAT by resorting to the original levelwise construction at some point. Alternatively, we may consider δ-completeness instead, as done e.g. in [6,16], and cover cells up to some precision δ.

Acknowledgments. J. Nalbach and V. Promies were supported by the DFG project SMT-ART (AB 461/9-1), and J. Nalbach and P. Wagner by the DFG RTG 2236 UnRAVeL. Computing resources were granted under the RWTH project rwth1560.

Data Availability Statement. Our implementation, experimental results, and tools for reproducing them are available at https://doi.org/10.5281/zenodo.14916587

Disclosure of Interests. The authors have no competing interests to declare that are relevant to the content of this article.

References

1. Ábrahám, E., Davenport, J.H., England, M., Kremer, G.: Deciding the consistency of non-linear real arithmetic constraints with a conflict driven search using cylindrical algebraic coverings. J. Log. Algebraic Methods Program. **119**, 100633 (2021). https://doi.org/10.1016/J.JLAMP.2020.100633
2. Ábrahám, E., Nalbach, J., Kremer, G.: Embedding the virtual substitution method in the model constructing satisfiability calculus framework. In: England, M., Ganesh, V. (eds.) Proc. of SC^2'17. CEUR Workshop Proceedings, vol. 1974. CEUR-WS.org (2017). https://ceur-ws.org/Vol-1974/EAb.pdf
3. Barrett, C., Stump, A., Tinelli, C.: The SMT-LIB standard – version 2.0. In: Proceedings of SMT '10 (2010). http://theory.stanford.edu/~barrett/pubs/BST10.pdf
4. Barrett, C., Tinelli, C.: Satisfiability Modulo Theories, pp. 305–343. Springer (2018). https://doi.org/10.1007/978-3-319-10575-8_11
5. Blanchette, J.C., Böhme, S., Paulson, L.C.: Extending sledgehammer with SMT solvers. In: Bjørner, N.S., Sofronie-Stokkermans, V. (eds.) Proc. of CADE'11. LNCS, vol. 6803, pp. 116–130. Springer (2011). https://doi.org/10.1007/978-3-642-22438-6_11
6. Brauße, F., Korovin, K., Korovina, M., Müller, N.: A CDCL-style calculus for solving non-linear constraints. In: Herzig, A., Popescu, A. (eds.) Frontiers of Combining Systems, pp. 131–148. Springer (2019)
7. Brocot, A.: Calcul des rouages par approximation: Nouvelle méthode. Revue chronométrique. Journal des horlogers, scientifique et pratique **3**, 186–194 (1861). https://gallica.bnf.fr/ark:/12148/bpt6k1661912
8. Brown, C.W.: Improved projection for cylindrical algebraic decomposition. J. Symb. Comput. **32**(5), 447–465 (2001). https://doi.org/10.1006/JSCO.2001.0463
9. Brown, C.W., Košta, M.: Constructing a single cell in cylindrical algebraic decomposition. J. Symb. Comput. **70**, 14–48 (2015). https://doi.org/10.1016/J.JSC.2014.09.024
10. Cimatti, A., Griggio, A., Irfan, A., Roveri, M., Sebastiani, R.: Incremental linearization for satisfiability and verification modulo nonlinear arithmetic and transcendental functions. ACM Trans. Comput. Log. **19**(3), 19:1–19:52 (2018). https://doi.org/10.1145/3230639
11. Collins, G.E.: Quantifier elimination for real closed fields by cylindrical algebraic decomposition. In: Barkhage, H. (ed.) Automata Theory and Formal Languages, 2nd GI Conference, Kaiserslautern, May 20-23, 1975. LNCS, vol. 33, pp. 134–183. Springer (1975). https://doi.org/10.1007/3-540-07407-4_17
12. Corzilius, F., Kremer, G., Junges, S., Schupp, S., Ábrahám, E.: SMT-RAT: an open source C++ toolbox for strategic and parallel SMT solving. In: Proc. of SAT'15. LNCS, vol. 9340, pp. 360–368. Springer (2015). https://doi.org/10.1007/978-3-319-24318-4_26
13. Cox, D.A., Little, J., O'Shea, D.: Ideals, varieties, and algorithms - an introduction to computational algebraic geometry and commutative algebra (2. ed.). Undergraduate Texts in Mathematics, Springer (1997). https://doi.org/10.1007/978-3-662-41154-4
14. cvc5: An efficient open-source automatic theorem prover for satisfiability modulo theories (SMT) problems. https://cvc5.github.io/
15. Dolzmann, A., Seidl, A., Sturm, T.: Efficient projection orders for CAD. In: Gutierrez, J. (ed.) Proc. of ISSAC'04, pp. 111–118. ACM (2004). https://doi.org/10.1145/1005285.1005303

16. Gao, S., Kong, S., Clarke, E.M.: dreal: An SMT solver for nonlinear theories over the reals. In: Bonacina, M.P. (ed.) Proc. of CADE'13. LNCS, vol. 7898, pp. 208–214. Springer (2013). https://doi.org/10.1007/978-3-642-38574-2_14
17. Giesl, J., et al.: Analyzing program termination and complexity automatically with aprove. J. Autom. Reason. **58**(1), 3–31 (2017). https://doi.org/10.1007/S10817-016-9388-Y
18. Jovanovic, D., Barrett, C., de Moura, L.: The design and implementation of the model constructing satisfiability calculus. In: Proceedings of FMCAD'13, pp. 173–180 (2013). https://doi.org/10.1109/FMCAD.2013.7027033
19. Jovanovic, D., de Moura, L.M.: Solving non-linear arithmetic. In: Proceedings of IJCAR'12. LNCS, vol. 7364, pp. 339–354. Springer (2012). https://doi.org/10.1007/978-3-642-31365-3_27
20. Kremer, G.: Cylindrical algebraic decomposition for nonlinear arithmetic problems. Ph.D. thesis, RWTH Aachen University, Germany (2020). https://publications.rwth-aachen.de/record/792185
21. Lazard, D.: An Improved Projection for Cylindrical Algebraic Decomposition, pp. 467–476. Springer (1994). https://doi.org/10.1007/978-1-4612-2628-4_29
22. Li, H., Xia, B.: Solving satisfiability of polynomial formulas by sample-cell projection. CoRR abs/2003.00409 (2020). https://arxiv.org/abs/2003.00409
23. McCallum, S.: An improved projection operation for cylindrical algebraic decomposition. In: Caviness, B.F. (ed.) Proceedings of EUROCAL'85. LNCS, vol. 204, pp. 277–278. Springer (1985). https://doi.org/10.1007/3-540-15984-3_277
24. McCallum, S.: On projection in cad-based quantifier elimination with equational constraint. In: Geddes, K.O., Salvy, B., Dooley, S.S. (eds.) Proc. of ISSAC '99, pp. 145–149. ACM (1999). https://doi.org/10.1145/309831.309892
25. de Moura, L.M., Jovanovic, D.: A model-constructing satisfiability calculus. In: Giacobazzi, R., Berdine, J., Mastroeni, I. (eds.) Proc of VMCAI'13. LNCS, vol. 7737, pp. 1–12. Springer (2013). https://doi.org/10.1007/978-3-642-35873-9_1
26. Nalbach, J., Ábrahám, E.: Merging adjacent cells during single cell construction. In: Boulier, F., Mou, C., Sadykov, T.M., Vorozhtsov, E.V. (eds.) Proc. of CASC'24. LNCS, vol. 14938, pp. 252–272. Springer (2024). https://doi.org/10.1007/978-3-031-69070-9_15
27. Nalbach, J., Kremer, G.: Extensions of the cylindrical algebraic covering method for quantifiers. CoRR abs/2411.03070 (2024). https://doi.org/10.48550/ARXIV.2411.03070
28. Nalbach, J., Ábrahám, E., Specht, P., Brown, C.W., Davenport, J.H., England, M.: Levelwise construction of a single cylindrical algebraic cell. J. Symb. Comput. **123**, 102288 (2024). https://doi.org/10.1016/j.jsc.2023.102288
29. Promies, V., Nalbach, J., Ábrahám, E.: Under-approximation of a single algebraic cell (extended abstract). In: Brown, C.W., Kaufmann, D., Nalon, C., Steen, A., Suda, M. (eds.) Proc. of IJCAR'24. CEUR Workshop Proceedings, vol. 3717, pp. 132–136. CEUR-WS.org (2024). https://ceur-ws.org/Vol-3717/short3.pdf
30. SMT-RAT, a toolbox for strategic and parallel satisfiability modulo theories solving. https://github.com/ths-rwth/smtrat
31. Stern, M.: Ueber eine zahlentheoretische Funktion. Journal für die reine und angewandte Mathematik (Crelles Journal) **1858**(55), 193–220 (1858). https://doi.org/10.1515/crll.1858.55.193

32. Xu, J., Van Den Boom, T., De Schutter, B., Luo, X.L.: Minimal conjunctive normal expression of continuous piecewise affine functions. IEEE Trans. Autom. Control **61**(5), 1340–1345 (2016). https://doi.org/10.1109/TAC.2015.2465212
33. Xu, J., van den Boom, T.J., De Schutter, B.: Irredundant lattice piecewise affine representations and their applications in explicit model predictive control. In: Decision and Control (CDC 2014), pp. 4416–4421. IEEE (2014). https://doi.org/10.1109/CDC.2014.7040078

Ground Truth: Checking VAMPIRE Proofs via Satisfiability Modulo Theories

Michael Rawson[3](✉), Andrei Voronkov[1,2], Johannes Schoisswohl[4], and Anja Petković Komel[4]

[1] EasyChair
[2] University of Manchester, United Kingdom
[3] University of Southampton, United Kingdom, michael@rawsons.uk
[4] TU Wien, Austria

Abstract. The VAMPIRE automated theorem prover is extended to output proofs in such a way that each inference is represented by a quantifier-free SMT instance. If every instance is unsatisfiable, the proof can be considered verified by an external SMT solver. This pragmatic form of proof checking places only a very light burden on the SMT solver, and can easily handle inferences that other systems may find difficult, such as theory inferences or extensive ground reasoning. The method is considerably easier to implement than proof formats based on small kernels and covers a greater variety of modern-day inferences.

Keywords: automated theorem proving · SMT · verified proofs

VAMPIRE [27] is an advanced automated theorem prover (ATP) for first-order logic, extended to reason in a polymorphic logic with *theories* such as real arithmetic and datatypes. For various reasons, not least VAMPIRE's complexity, users are sometimes unwilling to take VAMPIRE's proofs on trust, and so they *check* them to increase their confidence in the proof. User attitudes and requirements vary, and so too their methods of checking proofs. In particular, some users require that the proof be reconstructed in another format, such as the internal language and logic of an interactive theorem prover.

One way of checking proofs [42] is to use an external ATP[5] to replay proofs inference-by-inference, invoking the external ATP to re-prove each step in the proof. The external ATP could be an "old faithful" theorem prover like Otter [29], assumed free of bugs due to long service, a system so small that it is hard to doubt its correctness, like leanCoP [34], or an ATP that itself produces checkable proofs, like Metis [22]. The underlying assumption here is that each step in the proof is small enough that it can be easily re-proved by the external ATP, but in practice this is not always the case. This is exacerbated with modern inference systems that may involve many premises and implicit deductions [45, 46] or

[5] Or even the ATP itself: VAMPIRE developers sometimes use VAMPIRE to check VAMPIRE proof steps. The resulting ouroboros nevertheless catches bugs.

C. Barrett and U. Waldmann (Eds.): CADE 2025, LNAI 15943, pp. 136–149, 2025.
https://doi.org/10.1007/978-3-031-99984-0_8

reasoning modulo theory [25, 37]. For reconstructing proofs the inference-by-inference method works but is labour-intensive in practice [18, 21].

Instead, a degenerate form of this approach is popular for proof automation in interactive theorem proving. Here, there are usually many more axioms than necessary to prove a given conjecture. A strong ATP like VAMPIRE is used to find a proof in the presence of superfluous axioms. The proof is then discarded, recording only which axioms were necessary to find the proof. A proof is then found *again* using only these axioms and the interactive theorem prover's internal proof search. Isabelle's *Sledgehammer* [30] uses this to great effect. Here it is even more likely that the reconstructing ATP is unable to find a proof.

Finally, it is possible to modify ATPs to output proofs directly in the format desired for checking. This could be an interactive theorem prover's logic, an intermediate language designed for inter-operation [4], or a language specifically designed only for proof checking [6]. In principle this approach means that proof checking is straightforward and guaranteed to work. Unfortunately, doing this in practice is also labour-intensive. Typically, formats designed for checking proofs require spelling out simple inferences in great detail, do not accept ATP shorthands (e.g. treating the equality predicate as symmetric), and cannot reason modulo theory. This last limitation is particularly vexing as VAMPIRE grows more capability for reasoning with theories, while small proof checking systems are unlikely to offer built-in theory reasoning. In some cases VAMPIRE relies on the Z3 SMT solver [32] to perform inferences such as theory instantiation [38], so VAMPIRE does not even "know" what theory reasoning was done.

We propose a new technique for proof checking (Section 1) that:

- is simple to implement
- is simple to check, using only an incremental SMT solver
- is fast, not requiring excess time in practice
- is relatively human-readable
- provides counter-examples for debugging proof steps

We also discuss its implementation in VAMPIRE (Section 2), carry out experiments on a large subset of TPTP [43] and several SMT-LIB [36] logics (Section 3) and propose a way to completely reconstruct VAMPIRE proofs in other systems using the technique (Section 5.1).

Preliminaries. We assume familiarity with automated and interactive theorem proving, the resolution calculus [5], and satisfiability modulo theories (SMT) [10]. Some exposure to the SMT-LIB input language may help [9]. Notation is standard, but we occasionally use a bar over variables $\bar{x}$ or terms $\bar{t}$ to indicate possibly-many variables or terms in that context.

1 Universal Inferences as Ground SMT Instances

Saturation theorem proving [5] is the gold standard for reasoning in first-order logic. Proofs are performed by contradiction. First, the input set of formulas is preprocessed and brought into clausal normal form, then inference rules are applied deriving new clauses until at some point the empty clause, witnessing contradiction, is derived. Completeness of state-of-the-art saturation theorem provers builds on *Herbrand's Theorem*, which might be stated as "a set of clauses is unsatisfiable iff there are ground instances which are ground unsatisfiable". This means that in order to find a proof we can first compute all ground instances of a clause, and then use a complete ground inference system on them.

Example 1. Consider the clauses $\forall x, y.P(y) \vee Q(x,a)$, $\forall z.\neg Q(b,z)$, and $\forall w.\neg P(w)$. We first compute the grounding

$$\begin{array}{cc} P(a) \vee Q(a,a) & \neg Q(b,a) \\ P(b) \vee Q(a,a) & \neg Q(b,b) \\ P(a) \vee Q(b,a) & \neg P(a) \\ P(b) \vee Q(b,a) & \neg P(b) \end{array}$$

then apply ground *binary resolution* twice to derive a contradiction:

$$\dfrac{\dfrac{P(b) \vee Q(b,a) \qquad \neg Q(b,a)}{P(b)} \qquad \neg P(b)}{\square}$$

The grounding of a set of clauses is typically very large, and becomes infinite in the presence of function symbols. This makes directly enumerating ground instances and searching for applicable inferences in the ground set impractical. Modern first-order theorem provers instead bypass grounding by working with universally-quantified clauses and using *unification* [5] to compute the most general instance of two clauses that makes an inference rule applicable.

Example 2. Consider the clauses from example 1. We apply non-ground binary resolution twice to derive a contradiction, without first computing a grounding.

$$\dfrac{\dfrac{\forall x, y.P(y) \vee Q(x,a) \qquad \forall z.\neg Q(b,z)}{\forall y.P(y)} \qquad \forall w.\neg P(w)}{\square}$$

The idea of using unification instead of explicit grounding is called *lifting* [5] and can be seen as compressing a (potentially infinite) set of inferences into a single inference. Lifting is a core principle of modern first-order theorem provers that sets them apart from Nelson-Oppen style SMT solvers.

1.1 Proposed Technique

Proof-checking such *lifted* inferences between quantified formulae poses a challenge for SMT solvers and automated theorem provers alike, especially when mixing theory reasoning with uninterpreted functions. This is where our method ties in. Suppose we wish to check that a particular inference occurring in a proof is sound. This means that we will need to show the conclusion $\forall \bar{x}.\ C[\bar{x}]$ follows from the premises $\forall \bar{y}.P_i[\bar{y}]$. We can show this by refutation. For that, we first negate and Skolemise the conclusion to obtain $\neg C[\bar{\sigma}]$. If there are instances of the premises $P_i[\bar{t_i}]$ that, taken together, refute $\neg C[\bar{\sigma}]$, we can conclude that the inference is valid. As our calculus uses lifting by unification such terms $\bar{t_i}$ can be directly found by using the unifying substitution θ computed in the rule application: first we instantiate the premises with θ, and then we replace all variables $\bar{x}$ that occured in the conclusion $C[\bar{x}]$ with the respective Skolem constants $\bar{\sigma}$.

Example 3. Take the first inference from example 2. The rule uses binary resolution unifying $Q(x, a)$ and $Q(b, z)$ computing the unifier $\theta = \{x \mapsto b, z \mapsto a\}$. In order to prove that the rule is sound we can instantiate the premises with the unifier, and instantiate the remaining free variable y with the Skolem constant σ in order to get the instantiated premises $P(\sigma) \vee Q(b, a)$ and $\neg Q(b, a)$. Negating the conjecture produces $\neg P(\sigma)$. This set of clauses is unsatisfiable iff the inference is sound.

As the resulting set of clauses is ground, it is most easily refuted by an SMT solver implementing a ground decision procedure.

Inhabited Sorts An edge case occurs when two variables are being unified. In this case the unifier will contain variables that are not present in the conclusion, thus $P_i[\bar{t_i}]\theta$ cannot be grounded by using the conclusion's Skolem constants. In such a case these variables can be instantiated with any ground term. If there are no constant symbols in the signature we can introduce a new Skolem symbol as sorts in first-order logic are assumed to be inhabited.

Example 4. Consider the last inference from example 2. Binary resolution is used to unify $P(y)$ and $P(w)$ computing the unifier $\theta = \{w \mapsto y\}$. If we apply θ to the premises we obtain the two non-ground clauses $P(y)$, $\neg P(y)$. In order to ground them we can choose any arbitrary ground term for y, say b, to obtain the ground premises $P(b)$, $\neg P(b)$.

1.2 Abilities and Limitations

As explained at the beginning of this section, most of VAMPIRE's inferences *lift* ground inferences, which means that they can be covered by our method. This includes the core superposition calculus, simplification rules such as subsumption resolution, and most rules of the ALASCA calculus [25] for arithmetic reasoning. Further we support simple preprocessing rules like definition unfolding, AVATAR [45] inferences except definition introduction (including the dreaded `avatar sat refutation`), and axiomiatised theories; these rules do not instantiate variables in premises and can be implemented systematically. Our implementation in VAMPIRE uses the same code for 58 such rules.

The key benefit of our approach is that the queries posed to the SMT solver are ground and relatively small compared to the size of the whole proof, which means that they are easily checked by state-of-the-art decision procedures. In contrast to checking every proof step without transforming it into the relevant ground instances, with our method the SMT solver can not only check the correctness of a rule application, but also give a counter-example if some proof-step is not correct. This can give insight into why a given inference is not sound.

However, there are some limitations to our new approach. Notably most preprocessing steps cannot be handled, as they are not sound inferences but transform the entire problem into an equisatisfiable form [20], relying on global properties of the whole problem (like freshness of introduced symbols) instead of performing a valid clause-to-clause inference. Proof steps in this category are usually found in the conversion to normal form, such as Skolemisation or definition introduction. We note that these steps also cause other proof checking systems trouble [19, 42]. This does also occasionally occur *during* proof search, such as when introducing definitions for AVATAR or clausifying higher-order terms on the fly [33].

Further unsupported inferences are those that cannot be grounded. Quantifier elimination rules used by the ALASCA [25,40] calculus, for example deriving $a \leq b$ from $\forall x : \mathbb{Q}.\ a \leq x \vee x \leq b$, where an instance for x cannot be found by unification. Still further limitations occurs with VAMPIRE's support for induction [26]. SMT solvers can check theory tautologies such as axiomatisations of arithmetic, but do not by design detect that a particular induction scheme is valid. Nascent support for induction [39] may later prove useful here.

2 Implementation

To demonstrate the method, we have a proof-of-concept implementation in VAMPIRE[6]. When activated with the flag `-p smtcheck`, VAMPIRE does not produce its usual proof format but instead an SMT-LIB script [9] suitable for processing by an incremental SMT solver such as Z3 [32] or `cvc5` [8]. If the SMT solver produces only `unsat` outputs, the proof can be considered verified by the SMT solver. Messages beginning "sorry" indicate that a step cannot yet be checked and should be further inspected or processed. Errors or `sat` responses (which cause an error) indicate a bug in VAMPIRE or the SMT solver.

2.1 Script Format

The script first declares symbols from the input problem (including sorts, if necessary) and provides a constant for each sort (Section 1.1). Then, for each inference in VAMPIRE's proof, the script:

1. Uses an SMT-LIB `(push)` command to isolate the context for this inference.
2. Declares new Skolem constants from the negated conjecture.
3. Asserts the instances of the premises required.
4. Asserts the negated conjecture.
5. Checks satisfiability, `(check-sat)`. The construct `(set-info :status unsat)` is used to produce an error and halt if any steps fail checking.

[6] https://github.com/vprover/vampire

6. Clears the assertions and declared Skolems with (pop).

For inferences that are not yet or cannot be implemented, the (echo ...) command is used to inform the user that the inference must be taken on trust. No satisfiability check occurs in this case. Figure 1 shows a single inference.

```
; signature declared once at the start of the script
(declare-sort iota 0) ; the built-in default sort
(declare-fun |_identity| () iota) ; user-provided symbols
(declare-fun |_multiply| (iota iota) iota)

(push) ; inference starts here
(declare-const v0 iota) ; Skolem constant
(declare-const v1 iota) ; Skolem constant
(assert (or (=
  (|_multiply| (|_multiply| v0 v0) v1)
  (|_multiply| v0 (|_multiply| v0 v1))))) ; premise
(assert (or (= |_identity| (|_multiply| v0 v0)))) ; premise
(assert (not (=
  (|_multiply| v0 (|_multiply| v0 v1))
  (|_multiply| |_identity| v1)))) ; conclusion
(set-info :status unsat)
(check-sat)
(pop) ; inference finishes here
```

Fig. 1. A self-contained extract from a group theory proof, deriving $x \cdot (x \cdot y) = e \cdot y$ from $x \cdot (y \cdot z) = (x \cdot y) \cdot z$ and $x \cdot x = e$. Note the instantiation of both axioms with appropriate Skolem constants from the conclusion. User provided symbols are |_quoted|.

The user must presently trust that VAMPIRE soundly instantiates and correctly transcribes clauses present in the script. This situation could be improved with greater support for definitions in SMT-LIB: (define-fun ...) would allow us to define a clause in terms of its variables and later instantiate it soundly by using the definition. However, our understanding is that this construct may be treated as a universally-quantified formula rather than a macro by the SMT solver, so we were unwilling to use it for this reason. A version of (define-fun ...) that *must* be treated as a macro would be very useful for us. An anonymous reviewer kindly suggested that using SMT solvers' support for annotations/*triggers* [31] would be another way to guide quantifier instantiation. We carried out a short experiment and can confirm that trigger-based instantiation works for this use-case. Like define-fun, however, triggers also rely on a well-behaved quantifier instantiation routine.

VAMPIRE supports both SMT-LIB and TPTP input problems. As some of the features of TPTP are not supported in SMT-LIB, proofs of these TPTP problems cannot be checked in a straightforward manner. Proofs which make use of polymorphism [11] cannot be checked, although the recent SMT-LIB 2.7 standard and the upcoming SMT-LIB 3 should make this possible. If this were not the case, *monomorphisation* would be an option, creating one function for each instantiation of a polymorphic function. Arithmetic functions in TPTP [44] that are not supported by SMT-LIB (e.g. the floor function $\lfloor\cdot\rfloor : \mathbb{R} \to \mathbb{R}$) also cause trouble: some of these we "polyfill" by injecting a suitable translation, others simply cannot be proof checked currently.

2.2 Computing Instances

When printing a proof, we now need to compute the instances of the premises required for proof checking. It may at first appear that a substitution must be kept for each inference during proof search, but in fact this is overkill. Instead, we record only enough information to recover the substitution we need. Taking binary resolution as a representative example, we record which literals from the parent clauses were resolved upon. At proof-printing time, we then re-unify the literals to produce the required premise substitution. The overhead of this implementation technique is non-zero, but small. Vampire loses only 5 proofs out of 7,839 in a single-strategy configuration over TPTP when the `--proof_extra full` flag is set.

3 Experiments

The proof-of-concept implementation covers all Vampire's core search inferences, AVATAR, theory axioms, and the more common ALASCA inferences. Other inferences are skipped, reporting a warning but allowing proof checking to continue. To test this implementation, we ran Vampire:

1. In its default mode for 10 seconds over TPTP 9.0.0 problem set, covering the CNF, FOF, and TF0 languages with arithmetic but excluding known-satisfiable instances. `ARI502_1` was excluded as it uses TPTP rational arithmetic features that cannot be easily translated to SMT-LIB.
2. Using a fixed ALASCA configuration[7] for 10 seconds over the non-incremental SMT-LIB 2024 [36] problem set restricted to the `LRA`, `NRA`, and `UFLRA` logics.

In total this generated 13,159 SMT-LIB proof scripts. Generally these are short, but there are some outliers. The largest script came from the TPTP problem `SWV545-1.010`, weighing in at 331MB. The proof with the greatest number of checked inferences is TPTP's `NUM378+1.010.015` with 378,298.

We ran the Z3 [32] and cvc5 [8] SMT solvers on the scripts. No unsoundness was found in Vampire's proofs, although a known ALASCA bug was rediscovered. After pulling the fix from upstream, all proofs checked successfully. Z3 is more permissive with identifiers than cvc5, which rejected a handful of TPTP proof scripts, but suitably escaping identifiers fixed the problem. Z3 could check

[7] `-alasca on -to qkbo -uwa alasca_main`

all instances, but cvc5 times out on the final AVATAR refutation (an unsatisfiable SAT instance) for the TPTP problems `ALG034+1`, `ALG035+1`, and `ALG101+1`. Switching cvc5's SAT solver [17] resolved this.

3.1 Quantified Proof Scripts

We have gone to some effort in order to produce *ground* SMT proof scripts. However, SMT solvers have good support for handling quantifiers [7], so this may not be needed in practice. In order to check this, we produced quantified scripts that simply include the universally-quantified premises and the negated conjecture for each step. We found that although the SMT solvers dispatched many proof steps quickly, unsurprisingly there are some VAMPIRE steps for which both Z3 and cvc5 run out of time. Out of 4,194 quantified scripts produced from the SMT-LIB set of problems above, 85 exceeded a 10-second timeout when checked with Z3, and a further 19 required in excess of 1 second to check. For comparison, all ground scripts were checked in less than 0.2 seconds. After these extreme cases, the difference between the two falls rapidly, and the majority can be checked in less than 0.05 seconds.

4 Comparison with Other Methods

There are several approaches to proof-checking the output of ATPs. Verifying all proof steps with a small kernel of an interactive theorem prover (ITP), especially when an ITP has been around long enough to be tried and tested (like Coq [16], Agda [1] or Isabelle [23]), is currently deemed most trusted. Ideally the amount of proof search during the verification phase is reduced to a minimum, and outputting proofs directly in an ITP-checkable format can be done for the core calculus [12, 14, 15, 24, 35]. Some features of VAMPIRE that our approach struggles with are directly expressible in this manner, like polymorphism, induction and introducing definitions. Additionally, exporting proofs directly to ITPs contributes to interoperability [4]. However, in the presence of theories extending the core calculus, this becomes less feasible in practice. ITPs have some limited support to reason with theories — the tactic *omega* in Coq is the canonical example — but they tend to be inefficient compared to SMT solvers. It would also require carrying around superfluous (to VAMPIRE) information and produce proofs of unreasonable size in some cases.

A similar approach to ours is treating every (quantified, not ground) inference in a proof as a separate conjecture and re-deriving each individual step from the premises it refers to, using an external ATP. As we are dealing with non-ground problems, no decision procedures exist, which means ATPs and SMT solvers alike may time out on at least some valid proof steps, which we confirm occurs in practice in Section 3.1. In contrast, with our approach we are guaranteed that SMT solvers can prove sound proof steps, and can even obtain witnesses for unsoundness (i.e. counter-models) if an unsound proof step is detected. An example for this is the tool *ekstrakto* [19], which re-derives required steps from a

TSTP proof using external ATPs that produces proof in the $\lambda\Pi$-modulo calculus [12, 14, 15, 24]. An advantage of such an approach is that it can in principle work on most first-order provers without modification, but in practice success is limited, as it fails to handle advanced proof search features like AVATAR inferences or theories.

Proofs can also be checked by a separate verifier designed for a specific proof format. *Theory-Extensible Sequent Calculus (TESC)* [6] is a proof format for first-order ATPs. The calculus subsumes a large fraction of first-order formulas handled by VAMPIRE, including reasoning with AVATAR. Not all problems solved by VAMPIRE can be translated from the TSTP trace to TESC automatically, and the support for reasoning with theories is limited. There are three verifiers for TESC currently available, one of which is formalized in ITP Agda [1], enhancing the trustworthiness of the verifier. One can also verify the proof steps semantically as in GDV [42]: here not only are proof steps checked as in Section 3.1 with a trusted ATP, but additionally some of the proof structure is checked, for example that the parents of inferences exist and that a refutation ends in falsum.

Similar techniques are applied to SMT solvers. Proofs emitted in the recently proposed format Alethe [41] (currently cvc5 [8] and veriT [13] support this format), can be verified either by a separate verifier Carcara [2] (not formally checked); imported to Isabelle via the `smt` tactic [28], checking each step of the proof with Isabelle's internal kernel; or imported to Coq using the SMTCoq plugin [3].

5 Conclusion

We introduced a method for efficiently checking proofs produced from state-of-the-art saturation theorem provers. Any valid inference that lifts a ground inference is supported in principle. Checking each individual quantified proof step is reduced to a ground satisfiability check which can be performed efficiently by the decision procedures present in SMT solvers. We therefore support, out of the box, proofs that involve theory reasoning (like arithmetic), which pose a severe challenge to other ATP proof checking systems. In practice, even very lengthy, difficult VAMPIRE proofs are efficiently verified by third-party SMT solvers.

5.1 Fully Reconstructed Proofs

Users who wish to fully reconstruct proofs in their system of choice may object that we have not addressed this, only moved trust from VAMPIRE to the SMT solver. However, SMT proof technology is improving rapidly with several recent proposals, and it seems likely that in the near future this will be possible. Using our method, a proof could be fully reconstructed by gluing together the SMT unsatisfiability proof for each VAMPIRE inference together into one long continuous proof. The host system would still need to check that premise instances are instances of known clauses (Section 2.1), that the input has been reproduced faithfully, and deal with inferences that are not yet possible (Section 1.2), but the hard part of reconstructing VAMPIRE proofs is done.

Acknowledgments. We acknowledge funding from the ERC Consolidator Grant ARTIST 101002685, the COST Action CA20111 EuroProofNet, the TU Wien SecInt Doctoral College, the FWF SFB project SpyCoDe F8504, the WWTF ICT22-007 grant ForSmart, and the Amazon Research Award 2023 QuAT. We thank the anonymous reviewers for their suggestions.

Disclosure of Interests. The authors have no competing interests to declare that are relevant to the content of this article.

References

1. The Agda proof assistant. https://wiki.portal.chalmers.se/agda/ (2021)
2. Andreotti, B., Lachnitt, H., Barbosa, H.: Carcara: An efficient proof checker and elaborator for SMT proofs in the alethe format. In: Sankaranarayanan, S., Sharygina, N. (eds.) Tools and Algorithms for the Construction and Analysis of Systems - 29th International Conference, TACAS 2023, Held as Part of the European Joint Conferences on Theory and Practice of Software, ETAPS 2022, Paris, France, April 22-27, 2023, Proceedings, Part I. Lecture Notes in Computer Science, vol. 13993, pp. 367–386. Springer (2023). https://doi.org/10.1007/978-3-031-30823-9_19, https://doi.org/10.1007/978-3-031-30823-9_19
3. Armand, M., Faure, G., Grégoire, B., Keller, C., Théry, L., Werner, B.: A modular integration of sat/smt solvers to coq through proof witnesses. In: Jouannaud, J.P., Shao, Z. (eds.) Certified Programs and Proofs. pp. 135–150. Springer Berlin Heidelberg, Berlin, Heidelberg (2011)
4. Assaf, A., Burel, G., Cauderlier, R., Delahaye, D., Dowek, G., Dubois, C., Gilbert, F., Halmagrand, P., Hermant, O., Saillard, R.: Dedukti: a logical framework based on the $\lambda\Pi$-calculus modulo theory. CoRR **abs/2311.07185** (2023). https://doi.org/10.48550/ARXIV.2311.07185, https://doi.org/10.48550/arXiv.2311.07185
5. Bachmair, L., Ganzinger, H.: Resolution theorem proving. In: Robinson, J.A., Voronkov, A. (eds.) Handbook of Automated Reasoning (in 2 volumes), pp. 19–99. Elsevier and MIT Press (2001). https://doi.org/10.1016/B978-044450813-3/50004-7, https://doi.org/10.1016/b978-044450813-3/50004-7
6. Baek, S.: A formally verified checker for first-order proofs. In: Cohen, L., Kaliszyk, C. (eds.) 12th International Conference on Interactive Theorem Proving, ITP 2021, June 29 to July 1, 2021, Rome, Italy (Virtual Conference). LIPIcs, vol. 193, pp. 6:1–6:13. Schloss Dagstuhl - Leibniz-Zentrum für Informatik (2021). https://doi.org/10.4230/LIPICS.ITP.2021.6, https://doi.org/10.4230/LIPIcs.ITP.2021.6
7. Barbosa, H.: New techniques for instantiation and proof production in SMT solving. Ph.D. thesis, Université de Lorraine (2017)
8. Barbosa, H., Barrett, C.W., Brain, M., Kremer, G., Lachnitt, H., Mann, M., Mohamed, A., Mohamed, M., Niemetz, A., Nötzli, A., Ozdemir, A., Preiner, M., Reynolds, A., Sheng, Y., Tinelli, C., Zohar, Y.: cvc5: A versatile and industrial-strength SMT solver. In: Fisman, D., Rosu, G. (eds.) Tools and Algorithms for the Construction and Analysis of Systems - 28th International Conference, TACAS 2022, Held as Part of the European Joint Conferences on Theory and Practice of Software, ETAPS 2022, Munich, Germany, April 2-7, 2022, Proceedings, Part I. Lecture Notes in Computer Science, vol. 13243, pp. 415–442. Springer (2022). https://doi.org/10.1007/978-3-030-99524-9_24, https://doi.org/10.1007/978-3-030-99524-9_24

9. Barrett, C., Stump, A., Tinelli, C., et al.: The SMT-LIB standard: Version 2.0. In: Proceedings of the 8th international workshop on Satisfiability Modulo Theories (Edinburgh, UK). vol. 13, p. 14 (2010)
10. Barrett, C.W., Tinelli, C.: Satisfiability modulo theories. In: Clarke, E.M., Henzinger, T.A., Veith, H., Bloem, R. (eds.) Handbook of Model Checking, pp. 305–343. Springer (2018). https://doi.org/10.1007/978-3-319-10575-8_11, https://doi.org/10.1007/978-3-319-10575-8_11
11. Blanchette, J.C., Paskevich, A.: TFF1: the TPTP typed first-order form with rank-1 polymorphism. In: Bonacina, M.P. (ed.) Automated Deduction - CADE-24 - 24th International Conference on Automated Deduction, Lake Placid, NY, USA, June 9-14, 2013. Proceedings. Lecture Notes in Computer Science, vol. 7898, pp. 414–420. Springer (2013). https://doi.org/10.1007/978-3-642-38574-2_29, https://doi.org/10.1007/978-3-642-38574-2_29
12. Bonichon, R., Delahaye, D., Doligez, D.: Zenon: An extensible automated theorem prover producing checkable proofs. In: Dershowitz, N., Voronkov, A. (eds.) Logic for Programming, Artificial Intelligence, and Reasoning. pp. 151–165. Springer Berlin Heidelberg, Berlin, Heidelberg (2007)
13. Bouton, T., Oliveira, D.C.B.D., Déharbe, D., Fontaine, P.: verit: An open, trustable and efficient smt-solver. In: Schmidt, R.A. (ed.) Automated Deduction - CADE-22, 22nd International Conference on Automated Deduction, Montreal, Canada, August 2-7, 2009. Proceedings. Lecture Notes in Computer Science, vol. 5663, pp. 151–156. Springer (2009). https://doi.org/10.1007/978-3-642-02959-2_12, https://doi.org/10.1007/978-3-642-02959-2_12
14. Burel, G., Bury, G., Cauderlier, R., Delahaye, D., Halmagrand, P., Hermant, O.: First-order automated reasoning with theories: When deduction modulo theory meets practice. Journal of Automated Reasoning **64**(6), 1001–1050 (2020). https://doi.org/10.1007/s10817-019-09533-z
15. Bury, G.: Integrating rewriting, tableau and superposition into SMT. Theses, Université Sorbonne Paris Cité (Jan 2019), https://theses.hal.science/tel-02612985
16. The Coq proof assistant, version 2021.02.2. https://coq.inria.fr/ (2021)
17. Fazekas, K., Niemetz, A., Preiner, M., Kirchweger, M., Szeider, S., Biere, A.: IPASIR-UP: user propagators for CDCL. In: Mahajan, M., Slivovsky, F. (eds.) 26th International Conference on Theory and Applications of Satisfiability Testing, SAT 2023, July 4-8, 2023, Alghero, Italy. LIPIcs, vol. 271, pp. 8:1–8:13. Schloss Dagstuhl - Leibniz-Zentrum für Informatik (2023). https://doi.org/10.4230/LIPICS.SAT.2023.8, https://doi.org/10.4230/LIPIcs.SAT.2023.8
18. Fleury, M., Blanchette, J.: Translation of proofs provided by external provers. Tech. rep., Tech. rep. Techniche Universität München (2014)
19. Haddad, M.Y.E.: Integrating Automated Theorem Provers in Proof Assistants. (Utiliser des démonstrateurs automatiques dans un assistant à la preuve). Ph.D. thesis, University of Paris-Saclay, France (2021), https://tel.archives-ouvertes.fr/tel-03387912
20. Heule, M., Kiesl, B.: The potential of interference-based proof systems. In: Reger, G., Traytel, D. (eds.) ARCADE 2017, 1st International Workshop on Automated Reasoning: Challenges, Applications, Directions, Exemplary Achievements, Gothenburg, Sweden, 6th August 2017. EPiC Series in Computing, vol. 51, pp. 51–54. EasyChair (2017). https://doi.org/10.29007/VR7N, https://doi.org/10.29007/vr7n
21. Hurd, J.: Integrating gandalf and HOL. In: Bertot, Y., Dowek, G., Hirschowitz, A., Paulin-Mohring, C., Théry, L. (eds.) Theorem Proving in Higher Order

Logics, 12th International Conference, TPHOLs'99, Nice, France, September, 1999, Proceedings. Lecture Notes in Computer Science, vol. 1690, pp. 311–322. Springer (1999). https://doi.org/10.1007/3-540-48256-3_21, https://doi.org/10.1007/3-540-48256-3_21

22. Hurd, J.: First-order proof tactics in higher-order logic theorem provers. Design and Application of Strategies/Tactics in Higher Order Logics, number NASA/CP-2003-212448 in NASA Technical Reports pp. 56–68 (2003)
23. Isabelle. https://isabelle.in.tum.de/ (2016)
24. Korovin, K.: iprover – an instantiation-based theorem prover for first-order logic (system description). In: Armando, A., Baumgartner, P., Dowek, G. (eds.) Automated Reasoning. pp. 292–298. Springer Berlin Heidelberg, Berlin, Heidelberg (2008)
25. Korovin, K., Kovács, L., Reger, G., Schoisswohl, J., Voronkov, A.: ALASCA: reasoning in quantified linear arithmetic. In: Sankaranarayanan, S., Sharygina, N. (eds.) Tools and Algorithms for the Construction and Analysis of Systems - 29th International Conference, TACAS 2023, Held as Part of the European Joint Conferences on Theory and Practice of Software, ETAPS 2022, Paris, France, April 22-27, 2023, Proceedings, Part I. Lecture Notes in Computer Science, vol. 13993, pp. 647–665. Springer (2023). https://doi.org/10.1007/978-3-031-30823-9_33, https://doi.org/10.1007/978-3-031-30823-9_33
26. Kovács, L., Hozzová, P., Hajdú, M., Voronkov, A.: Induction in saturation. In: Benzmüller, C., Heule, M.J.H., Schmidt, R.A. (eds.) Automated Reasoning - 12th International Joint Conference, IJCAR 2024, Nancy, France, July 3-6, 2024, Proceedings, Part I. Lecture Notes in Computer Science, vol. 14739, pp. 21–29. Springer (2024). https://doi.org/10.1007/978-3-031-63498-7_2, https://doi.org/10.1007/978-3-031-63498-7_2
27. Kovács, L., Voronkov, A.: First-order theorem proving and VAMPIRE. In: Sharygina, N., Veith, H. (eds.) Computer Aided Verification - 25th International Conference, CAV 2013, Saint Petersburg, Russia, July 13-19, 2013. Proceedings. Lecture Notes in Computer Science, vol. 8044, pp. 1–35. Springer (2013). https://doi.org/10.1007/978-3-642-39799-8_1, https://doi.org/10.1007/978-3-642-39799-8_1
28. Lachnitt, H., Fleury, M., Aniva, L., Reynolds, A., Barbosa, H., Nötzli, A., Barrett, C., Tinelli, C.: Isarare: Automatic verification of smt rewrites in isabelle/hol. In: Finkbeiner, B., Kovács, L. (eds.) Tools and Algorithms for the Construction and Analysis of Systems. pp. 311–330. Springer Nature Switzerland, Cham (2024)
29. McCune, W.: OTTER 3.3 reference manual. CoRR **cs.SC/0310056** (2003), http://arxiv.org/abs/cs/0310056
30. Meng, J., Paulson, L.C.: Translating higher-order clauses to first-order clauses. J. Autom. Reason. **40**(1), 35–60 (2008). https://doi.org/10.1007/S10817-007-9085-Y, https://doi.org/10.1007/s10817-007-9085-y
31. Moskal, M.: Programming with triggers. In: Proceedings of the 7th International Workshop on Satisfiability Modulo Theories. pp. 20–29 (2009)
32. de Moura, L.M., Bjørner, N.S.: Z3: an efficient SMT solver. In: Ramakrishnan, C.R., Rehof, J. (eds.) Tools and Algorithms for the Construction and Analysis of Systems, 14th International Conference, TACAS 2008, Held as Part of the Joint European Conferences on Theory and Practice of Software, ETAPS 2008, Budapest, Hungary, March 29-April 6, 2008. Proceedings. Lecture Notes in Computer Science, vol. 4963, pp. 337–340. Springer (2008). https://doi.org/10.1007/978-3-540-78800-3_24, https://doi.org/10.1007/978-3-540-78800-3_24

33. Nummelin, V., Bentkamp, A., Tourret, S., Vukmirovic, P.: Superposition with first-class booleans and inprocessing clausification. In: Platzer, A., Sutcliffe, G. (eds.) Automated Deduction - CADE 28 - 28th International Conference on Automated Deduction, Virtual Event, July 12-15, 2021, Proceedings. Lecture Notes in Computer Science, vol. 12699, pp. 378–395. Springer (2021). https://doi.org/10.1007/978-3-030-79876-5_22, https://doi.org/10.1007/978-3-030-79876-5_22
34. Otten, J., Bibel, W.: leancop: lean connection-based theorem proving. J. Symb. Comput. **36**(1-2), 139–161 (2003). https://doi.org/10.1016/S0747-7171(03)00037-3, https://doi.org/10.1016/S0747-7171(03)00037-3
35. Petković Komel, A., Rawson, M., Suda, M.: Case study: Verified VAMPIRE proofs in the $\lambda\Pi$-calculus modulo. CoRR **abs/2503.15541** (2025). https://doi.org/10.48550/ARXIV.2503.15541, https://doi.org/10.48550/arXiv.2503.15541
36. Preiner, M., Schurr, H., Barrett, C.W., Fontaine, P., Niemetz, A., Tinelli, C.: SMT-LIB release 2024 (non-incremental benchmarks) (version 2024.04.23). https://doi.org/10.5281/zenodo.11061097 (Apr 2024). https://doi.org/10.5281/ZENODO.11061097, https://doi.org/10.5281/zenodo.11061097, accessed on YYYY-MM-DD.
37. Reger, G., Bjørner, N.S., Suda, M., Voronkov, A.: AVATAR modulo theories. In: Benzmüller, C., Sutcliffe, G., Rojas, R. (eds.) GCAI 2016. 2nd Global Conference on Artificial Intelligence, September 19 - October 2, 2016, Berlin, Germany. EPiC Series in Computing, vol. 41, pp. 39–52. EasyChair (2016). https://doi.org/10.29007/K6TP, https://doi.org/10.29007/k6tp
38. Reger, G., Suda, M., Voronkov, A.: Unification with abstraction and theory instantiation in saturation-based reasoning. In: Beyer, D., Huisman, M. (eds.) Tools and Algorithms for the Construction and Analysis of Systems - 24th International Conference, TACAS 2018, Held as Part of the European Joint Conferences on Theory and Practice of Software, ETAPS 2018, Thessaloniki, Greece, April 14-20, 2018, Proceedings, Part I. Lecture Notes in Computer Science, vol. 10805, pp. 3–22. Springer (2018). https://doi.org/10.1007/978-3-319-89960-2_1, https://doi.org/10.1007/978-3-319-89960-2_1
39. Reynolds, A., Kuncak, V.: Induction for SMT solvers. In: D'Souza, D., Lal, A., Larsen, K.G. (eds.) Verification, Model Checking, and Abstract Interpretation - 16th International Conference, VMCAI 2015, Mumbai, India, January 12-14, 2015. Proceedings. Lecture Notes in Computer Science, vol. 8931, pp. 80–98. Springer (2015). https://doi.org/10.1007/978-3-662-46081-8_5, https://doi.org/10.1007/978-3-662-46081-8_5
40. Schoisswohl, J., Kovács, L., Korovin, K.: VIRAS: conflict-driven quantifier elimination for integer-real arithmetic. In: Bjørner, N.S., Heule, M., Voronkov, A. (eds.) LPAR 2024: Proceedings of 25th Conference on Logic for Programming, Artificial Intelligence and Reasoning, Port Louis, Mauritius, May 26-31, 2024. EPiC Series in Computing, vol. 100, pp. 147–164. EasyChair (2024). https://doi.org/10.29007/KG4V, https://doi.org/10.29007/kg4v
41. Schurr, H., Fleury, M., Barbosa, H., Fontaine, P.: Alethe: Towards a generic SMT proof format (extended abstract). In: Keller, C., Fleury, M. (eds.) Proceedings Seventh Workshop on Proof eXchange for Theorem Proving, PxTP 2021, Pittsburg, PA, USA, July 11, 2021. EPTCS, vol. 336, pp. 49–54 (2021). https://doi.org/10.4204/EPTCS.336.6, https://doi.org/10.4204/EPTCS.336.6
42. Sutcliffe, G.: Semantic derivation verification: Techniques and implementation. Int. J. Artif. Intell. Tools **15**(6), 1053–1070 (2006). https://doi.org/10.1142/S0218213006003119, https://doi.org/10.1142/S0218213006003119

43. Sutcliffe, G.: The TPTP problem library and associated infrastructure - from CNF to th0, TPTP v6.4.0. J. Autom. Reason. **59**(4), 483–502 (2017). https://doi.org/10.1007/S10817-017-9407-7, https://doi.org/10.1007/s10817-017-9407-7
44. Sutcliffe, G., Schulz, S., Claessen, K., Baumgartner, P.: The TPTP typed first-order form with arithmetic. In: Bjørner, N.S., Voronkov, A. (eds.) Logic for Programming, Artificial Intelligence, and Reasoning - 18th International Conference, LPAR-18, Mérida, Venezuela, March 11-15, 2012. Proceedings. Lecture Notes in Computer Science, vol. 7180, pp. 406–419. Springer (2012). https://doi.org/10.1007/978-3-642-28717-6_32, https://doi.org/10.1007/978-3-642-28717-6_32
45. Voronkov, A.: AVATAR: the architecture for first-order theorem provers. In: Biere, A., Bloem, R. (eds.) Computer Aided Verification - 26th International Conference, CAV 2014, Held as Part of the Vienna Summer of Logic, VSL 2014, Vienna, Austria, July 18-22, 2014. Proceedings. Lecture Notes in Computer Science, vol. 8559, pp. 696–710. Springer (2014). https://doi.org/10.1007/978-3-319-08867-9_46, https://doi.org/10.1007/978-3-319-08867-9_46
46. Xu, Y., Liu, J., Chen, S., Zhong, X., He, X.: Contradiction separation based dynamic multi-clause synergized automated deduction. Inf. Sci. **462**, 93–113 (2018). https://doi.org/10.1016/J.INS.2018.04.086, https://doi.org/10.1016/j.ins.2018.04.086

SMT and Functional Equation Solving over the Reals: Challenges from the IMO

Chad E. Brown[1], Karel Chvalovský[1], Mikoláš Janota[1(✉)], Mirek Olšák[3], and Stefan Ratschan[2]

[1] Czech Technical University in Prague, CIIRC, Prague, Czechia
mikolas.janota@cvut.cz
[2] Czech Academy of Sciences, Institute of Computer Science, Prague, Czech Republic
[3] University of Cambridge, Cambridge, UK

Abstract. We use SMT technology to address a class of problems involving uninterpreted functions and nonlinear real arithmetic. In particular, we focus on problems commonly found in mathematical competitions, such as the International Mathematical Olympiad (IMO), where the task is to determine all solutions to constraints on an uninterpreted function. Although these problems require only high-school-level mathematics, state-of-the-art SMT solvers often struggle with them. We propose several techniques to improve SMT performance in this setting.

Keywords: SMT · Quantifier elimination · IMO · lemmas · real arithmetic · instantiations

1 Introduction

The *AIMO Challenge*[1] has garnered significant interest from researchers, particularly within the machine learning community, by focusing on mathematical olympiad problems [14,29]. However, this challenge is also highly relevant to the field of automated reasoning. In a previous study [8], the authors formally addressed the problem of functional equations, which involves determining all functions that satisfy a given set of equations. The problem is best illustrated by a simple example where one is to find all $f : \mathbb{R} \to \mathbb{R}$, s.t.

$$\forall xy. f(x + y) = xf(y) + yf(x). \tag{1}$$

Setting y to 0, yields $\forall x. f(x) = f(0)x$, revealing that f must be linear and is entirely determined by the value of $f(0)$. Furthermore, substituting $x = 0$ reveals that f must be identically zero, meaning the unique solution is $f(x) = 0$ (formally, $f = \lambda x. 0$). A solution should provide a clear description of *all* possible functions f, potentially parameterized by constants.

[1] https://aimoprize.com/.

C. Barrett and U. Waldmann (Eds.): CADE 2025, LNAI 15943, pp. 150–163, 2025.
https://doi.org/10.1007/978-3-031-99984-0_9

The initial approach of the authors [8] fixes a template (a polynomial with parameters as coefficients) for the function f and then determines how this template should be parameterized to solve the given problem. The values of the parameters are obtained by real quantifier elimination. Then, it is required to prove that all possible solutions must fit within the template. To illustrate, consider the "linear" template $f(x) = ax + b$ in Eq. (1) where applying quantifier elimination on $\forall x$ gives all the possible values of a and b, which is simply $a = b = 0$. In the second phase, it needs to be proven that all possible f must be linear, which can be stated as follows.

$$(\forall xy.f(x+y) = xf(y) + yf(x)) \Rightarrow (\exists a, b \forall x.f(x) = ax + b) \tag{2}$$

It turns out that proving such an implication is the bottleneck of the approach. That is, even if it is easy to find every f within the template that solves the equality, proving that the template is sufficient to cover all the solutions, is hard for state-of-the-art solvers for Satisfiability Modulo Theories (SMT).

The problem under investigation presents a dual challenge: function synthesis and comprehensive coverage verification ("there are no more f's"). Function synthesis alone represents a significant computational challenge with numerous methodological approaches [2,7,16,18,19,30], which we address through a template-based methodology [36] coupled with quantifier elimination [13,37,39]. The principal contribution of this paper, however, lies in establishing the comprehensive coverage verification. We introduce novel inference techniques that enhance solvers' performance by generating auxiliary lemmas and strategic quantifier instantiations prior to invoking SMT solvers. These techniques generalize to other challenging problems in real arithmetic that, despite their compact representation, present considerable difficulty in solving.

The key contributions of this paper are as follows:

- Development of an exploratory procedure that discovers novel lemmas to facilitate proof construction.
- Formulation of specialized instantiation-based techniques designed for computationally intensive quantified problems.
- Implementation of these advances in a unified framework that leverages state-of-the-art SMT solvers.
- Introduction of a benchmark suite to evaluate these techniques, demonstrating meaningful performance improvements over the existing method.

2 Preliminaries

Throughout the paper, a basic understanding of first-order logic is expected [35]. We use SMT solvers [5] mainly in a black-box fashion, where the primary target is the combination of the theories of nonlinear real arithmetic and uninterpreted functions (`UFNRA`).

By a *substitution* in a formula ϕ we mean a mapping from all free variables of ϕ to terms and its application is denoted as $\phi[x_1 \mapsto t_1, \ldots, x_n \mapsto t_n]$ where all x_i are replaced by the corresponding term t_i simultaneously. For a vector of variables $\boldsymbol{x}$, a quantified formula $\forall \boldsymbol{x}.\, \phi$, and a substitution s, an *instantiation* is the formula $\forall \boldsymbol{x}'.\, \phi[s]$, where $\boldsymbol{x}'$ are the free variables introduced by s.

SMT solvers attempt to solve quantified problems by adding quantifier instantiations.[2] These instantiations only introduce ground terms so that they can be sent to the ground subsolver. There is a large body of research on quantifier instantiation in SMT, with syntactic-driven approaches (*e-matching* [15] or syntax-guided instantiation [28]), semantic-driven (*model-based* [16,33]), *conflict-based* [34], and *enumerative instantiation* [21,32]. Our experiments also use the automated theorem prover VAMPIRE [22] as an SMT solver. VAMPIRE does not explicitly instantiate but relies on superposition [35].

Quantifier Elimination (QE). We need to be able to handle nonlinear arithmetic over the real numbers. The corresponding logical theory—the theory of real closed fields—allows QE [37]. This means, that there is an algorithm that takes any formula with the signature $\{0, 1, +, \times, =, \leq\}$ (in practice, further symbols that can be expressed in terms of these) and computes a quantifier-free formula that is equivalent w.r.t. the axioms of the theory of real closed fields. QE in the theory of real-closed fields is highly costly, both in theory [13,39] and in practice. Hence it is usually beneficial, and often indispensable, to exploit the specific structure of the quantifier elimination problems at hand. For QE we use QEPCAD [9,12] via the tool Tarski [38]. Additional techniques are discussed in Sect. 3.1.

3 Problem Statement and Templates Revisited

In many cases, the problem is given as an equation, just as in example (1), but more complicated problem descriptions may appear. For instance, apart from the equation there might also exist the requirement that the function f must be monotone, injective, etc. Similarly, the solution to a problem might be a single function but also more complicated classes of functions often appear, e.g. identity with a positive shift, which can be described as $\exists c.\, c > 0 \wedge \forall x.\, f(x) = x + c$. We formalize this in the following.

The *input* to a problem is a *specification* of a function $f : \mathbb{R} \to \mathbb{R}$, which is a sentence Φ_{spec} in the language of first-order real arithmetic augmented with a unary function symbol f.[3]

A *solution* to a problem is a specification Φ_{sol} that is logically equivalent to the specification Φ_{spec} but in *solved form*, defined as follows. A sentence of the form $\exists \boldsymbol{a}.\Gamma \wedge \forall x.f(x) = t$ is in *solved form* iff f occurs in neither Γ nor

---

[2] If formulas are not prenex, new instantiations are added in the form of the implication $(\forall \boldsymbol{x}.\, \phi) \to \phi[s]$, but through this paper we assume prenex form.

[3] Competitions may contain problems with multiple functions and with different domains, e.g. $\mathbb{Q}$. These we currently do not support. We do support certain restrictions on the reals, e.g. $\mathbb{R}^+$ but we avoid discussing this here for the purpose of conciseness.

t. We consider $\exists \boldsymbol{a}.\forall x.f(x) = t$ to be the same as the special case where Γ is $\top$. Note that the solution might also be the empty class of functions, in which case $\Gamma = \bot$. A disjunction $\Psi_1 \vee \Psi_2$ is in *solved form* if each disjunct is.

In Example (1), the given specification Φ_{spec} is $\forall xy.f(x+y) = xf(y)+yf(x)$. The corresponding solved form Φ_{sol} is $\forall x.f(x) = 0$.

Finding a solution to a specification Φ_{spec} is done in two phases: First construct a candidate solution Φ_{sol}, and then attempt to prove $\Phi_{\text{spec}} \Leftrightarrow \Phi_{\text{sol}}$. If this fails, potentially look for another candidate solution.

When proving $\Phi_{\text{spec}} \Leftrightarrow \Phi_{\text{sol}}$, we focus on the implication $\Phi_{\text{spec}} \Rightarrow \Phi_{\text{sol}}$, i.e. that the class of functions described by the solution Φ_{sol} covers all functions specified by Φ_{spec}. Typically, this implications is significantly harder to prove and the converse follows by the construction of Φ_{sol}.

In the context of an SMT problem, proving $\Phi_{\text{spec}} \Rightarrow \Phi_{\text{sol}}$ corresponds to assuming $\Phi_{\text{spec}} \wedge \neg\Phi_{\text{sol}}$ and proving unsatisfiability. We typically start with a skolemized version of $\neg\Phi_{\text{sol}}$, introducing new constants.

Following the initial work [8], we look for solutions in the quadratic polynomial template $ax^2 + bx + c$. To obtain all possible solutions within the template, we first plug the template into the specification formula and then eliminate all quantified variables using QE. This results in a formula containing only a, b, c, from which the solved form is obtained heuristically, see [8, Sec.3.3].

Note that the coefficients appear a, b, c appear quantified existentially in the solution as per solved form. However, since we are dealing with a polynomial template, they can be eliminated by setting $c = f(0)$, $a = (f(1) + f(-1))/2 - c$, $b = f(1) - a - c$, see [8, Sec. 3.1] and *Lagrange interpolation* [10]. For example, $\exists c.\, c > 0 \wedge \forall x.\, f(x) = x + c$ is simplified to $f(0) > 0 \wedge \forall x.\, f(x) = x + f(0)$.

To reduce the computational cost of QE, we also use variations of the quadratic template by setting some of the coefficients to 0 (linear $bx+c$, quadratic monomial ax^2, constant c), see [8, Sec. 3.1]. An alternative, specialized technique that improves QE for equations is described in Sect. 3.1.

At this stage, all solutions of the specification are within the template. But there may exist other solutions, *outside* of the template. The earlier approach [8] tried to prove that any f satisfying the specification must follow the template. We have, however, observed that it is more efficient to first find the solution within the template and then prove that there are no other solutions.

Coming back to the introductory example (1), rather than proving that the solution must be linear, we first identify the solution $f(x) = 0$, and then prove that this is the only solution possible, leading to the following SMT problem.

$$\forall xy.f(x+y) = xf(y) + yf(x) \quad (3) \qquad\qquad \neg(\forall x.f(x) = 0) \quad (4)$$

We surmise that the reason why these proofs are easier for the SMT solver is that there are constants from the proposed solution. As noted above, the formula (4) is skolemized as $f(c) \neq 0$, with c being a fresh constant. While we could rely on the SMT solver to perform the skolemization, we explicitly perform it in our implementation, since the skolem constant is useful for our techniques.

3.1 Quantifier Elimination on Equalities

The high cost of quantifier elimination in the theory of real-closed fields warrants the exploitation of the specific structure of the problems we target. In our case, we have problems that are the result of substituting a template for the function symbols in the given specification formula. In many problems, the specification formula is a functional equation [23]. Applying the template to it yields a formula of the form $\forall \boldsymbol{x}.\ P(\boldsymbol{a}, \boldsymbol{x}) = 0 \land F$, where P is a polynomial, $\boldsymbol{a}$ stands for the parameters of the template, and $\boldsymbol{x}$ stands for the universally quantified variables of the original functional equation. The part F may come from additional requirements on the function, e.g. f is non-decreasing.

Now observe that the only polynomial that is zero everywhere is the zero polynomial. Hence, denoting $P(\boldsymbol{a}, \boldsymbol{x})$ as a polynomial in $\boldsymbol{x}$ with parametric coefficients $p_1(\boldsymbol{a}), \ldots, p_k(\boldsymbol{a})$, we can rewrite the problem to the form

$$p_1(\boldsymbol{a}) = 0 \land \cdots \land p_k(\boldsymbol{a}) = 0 \land \forall \boldsymbol{x}.F,$$

which is usually considerably easier to solve. Moreover, in the special case where F is not present, this already describes the result of quantifier elimination. For example, substituting the template $ax^2 + bx + c$ into Eq. (1), one arrives at a polynomial equation in the variables a, b, c, x, y that contains (among others) the monomials $ax^2, (b - c)x, c$, resulting in a system of equations that contains (again among others) the equations $a = 0, b - c = 0, c = 0$, from which one can immediately read off the solution $a = 0, b = 0, c = 0$.

In our computations, we use the SymPy package [25] to obtain the concrete values of the coefficients.

4 Quantifier Instantiation

Our initial experiments indicate, that the reason why problems are not being solved, is the difficulty of finding the right quantifier instantiations. In general, the ground part could potentially also be difficult because it requires the theory of nonlinear real arithmetic, but by manually testing with the appropriate quantifier instantiations, we have observed that the SMT solvers are typically successful. SMT instantiation techniques are tailored to work fast within the DPLL(T) framework, which explains why they have less success on problems that are small but highly challenging. In this section we introduce instantiation techniques targeting such problems.

Our experiments also use the automated theorem prover Vampire, which does not explicitly instantiate during proving but also benefits from our techniques because we explicitly add instantiations into the input formula.

4.1 Partial Instantiations with Simple Terms

As seen in our introductory example (1), valuable information can be obtained by substituting concrete values, such as 0 and 1, which will likely simplify the problem. Even though cvc5 has the enumerative mode [21], it only relies on the ground terms in the formula—and 0,1 might not be in it—and furthermore, it always grounds *all* variables under a quantifier. However, partial instantiations, where some variables are left as the original variables, provide powerful facts (recall that substituting 0 for x in (1) immediately shows that f must be linear). It may also be helpful to instantiate with other small ground terms, e.g., skolem constants. We illustrate this on the problem **U10** from [27]:

$$f(x^2 + y) + f(f(x) - y) = 2f^2(x) + 2y^2. \tag{5}$$

For our purposes, here we assume the solution $f(x) = x^2$ has been found and it only remains to prove there are no more solutions. As an SMT problem, this means we assume the identity (5) and assume $f(c) \neq c^2$ for a constant c. The resulting problem is unsatisfiable, although CVC5 and VAMPIRE are unable to determine unsatisfiability with a 10 min time limit.

It is enough to instantiate (x, y) in (5) with six relatively small instantiations: $(0, 0)$, $(0, f(0))$, $(0, -c^2)$, $(c, 0)$, $(c, f(c))$ and $(c, -c^2)$. Let us briefly consider why these instantiations are enough. The instantiations $(0, 0)$ and $(0, f(0))$ easily yield $f(0) = 0$. The instantiation $(c, f(c))$ yields $f(c^2 + f(c)) = 2f^2(c) + 2(f(c))^2$ while $(c, -c^2)$ yields $f(f(c) + c^2) = 2f^2(c) + 2c^4$, which together give $(f(c))^2 = c^4$. Since we know $f(c) \neq c^2$, we must have $f(c) = -c^2$. Combining this with $f(f(c) + c^2) = 2f^2(c) + 2c^4$ we have $f^2(c) = -c^4$. The instantiation $(c, 0)$ yields $f(c^2) = f^2(c)$, hence $f(c^2) = -c^4$ and $f(c^2) = f(f(c)) = f(-c^2)$. The instantiation $(0, -c^2)$ yields $f(-c^2) + f(c^2) = 2c^4$ and so $-2c^4 = 2c^4$ giving $c = 0$. However, $c = 0$ contradicts $f(0) = 0$ and $f(c) \neq c^2$.

If we add these six instantiations manually, both CVC5 and VAMPIRE refute the problem within 1 s. The largest term used in the instantiations above is $-c^2$ (or, more properly, $-(c \cdot c)$). An early partially successful experiment was to enumerate all terms up to the size of $-c^2$ and try selected pairs of instantiations using these terms. However, it proved more successful to use *partial* instantiations. Note that in each of the 6 pairs above the instantiation for x is simply 0 or c. This led us to try instantiating each variable with a very small term (e.g., 0 and c) and leave the other variable free. This yields four partially instantiated versions of (5). We also have the option of including the original equation (5) with both variables free. If we include only the four partially instantiated equations, VAMPIRE (using a portfolio) refutes the resulting problem in less than 3 s. The specific strategy in the portfolio that solves the problem takes 0.2 s. An inspection of the proof generated by VAMPIRE demonstrates that it is using instantiations beyond the six pairs described above. In particular, VAMPIRE effectively uses the pair $(c, -f(-c))$ for (x, y) at one point of the proof, which is not one of the six pairs with which we started.

Our implementation considers a slightly larger set of small terms for partial instantiations, with the minimal set being 0, 1 and all skolems in the problem (e.g., c in **U10**) and the maximum set additionally including other ground terms occurring in the equation (e.g., 2 in **U10**). When using 0, 1 and c for the partial instantiations, VAMPIRE (using the strategy that solves the problem with 0 and c) can still find a refutation, but in 0.44 s. When using 0, 1, 2 and c for the partial instantiations, VAMPIRE (with the same strategy) solves the problem in 2.3 s.

4.2 Theory-Unification by Equation Solving

E-matching is an SMT technique for finding instantiations that results in terms that already appear in the formula modulo equality [15]. For our purposes, equality alone is insufficient as we also need *theory reasoning*. In particular, we would like matching to be aware of real arithmetic. This is illustrated by the following example (Úloha 6 by Musil [27]). Consider the following specification for f.

$$\forall xy.\ f(x+y) - f(x-y) = xy \tag{6}$$

The quadratic template gives the candidate solution $f(x) = x^2/4 + f(0)$, which is negated and skolemized, resulting in the following.

$$f(c) \neq c^2/4 + f(0). \tag{7}$$

To prove that all possible f are covered, unsatisfiability of (6)∧(7) needs to be shown. This is done by substituting both x and y with $c/2$ in (6):

$$f\,(c/2 + c/2) - f\,(c/2 - c/2) = c^2/4 \tag{8}$$

$$f(c) = c^2/4 + f(0) \tag{9}$$

Traditional E-matching cannot discover this substitution because $c/2$ does not occur in the existing formula. One could try to factor the term $c^2/4$, but we take a different approach. We observe it is often useful to derive instantiations where f is simply applied to x. Ideally, we obtain a definition-like equality, i.e. $f(x) = t$, where t does not contain f, or f is only applied on ground terms.

We look for such instantiations by the following heuristic. Collect all the arguments A to f in a quantified subexpression—consider only top-level arguments in the form of a polynomial. Non-deterministically partition A into A_z and A_0. Find a substitution that makes all the arguments in A_z equal to a fresh variable z and sets all arguments in A_0 to 0. Add all instantiations by the obtained substitutions. The Python package SymPy [25] is used to solve the equations.

In example (6), considering all possible subsets of $\{x+y, x-y\}$ yields the following equations and their corresponding solutions

$$\begin{array}{lcr} x+y=z, x-y=0 & \cdots & x \mapsto z/2, y \mapsto z/2 \\ x+y=0, x-y=z & \cdots & x \mapsto z/2, y \mapsto -z/2 \\ x+y=z, x-y=z & \cdots & x \mapsto z, y \mapsto 0 \\ x+y=0, x-y=0 & \cdots & x \mapsto 0, y \mapsto 0 \end{array}$$

The first substitution yields, after simplification, $\forall z.\, f(z) - f(0) = z^2/4$. Then the underlying SMT solver just needs to substitute c for z to obtain a contradiction as in (9).

Note that setting arguments in A_0 to 0 is a somewhat arbitrary choice, but in our benchmarks, 0 typically leads to further simplification in the formula. An alternative would be to substitute a fresh constant k and solve for it as well.

5 Lemma Generation

Coming up with lemmas that improve the solvers' performance is a notoriously challenging task, but we propose to look for useful conjectures by generating relevant ground instances of simple equations. For example, in (1), it holds that $f(0) = 0$, $f(1) = 0$, $f(0) = f(1)$, etc. We generate such simple statements (essentially by brute-force) and test whether they hold in the given formula to be solved. If they do, we add them to the problem, as an additional axiom.

The equations are generated systematically from terms of small depths. We start with a small set of initial terms 0, 1, skolem constants, and possible other numbers occurring in the problem. These are subsequently combined using addition, subtraction, multiplication, and the application of the function f.

Since this systematic process quickly explodes, we try to limit the conjectures being generated by making substitution into the candidate solution. For example, to show that $f(x) = x \vee f(x) = -x$ (two solutions), we substitute a skolem c, an initial term, for x, and obtain $f(c) = c \vee f(c) = -c$ as a conjecture. This makes it possible to express more general conjectures for problems with multiple solutions. Moreover, we also add the individual equations as conjectures, e.g. $f(c) = c$ and $f(c) = -c$ to obtain them sooner.

We use the previous techniques to iteratively generate conjectures. Conjectures that are proven are then added to our original SMT problem as lemmas and we attempt to solve the SMT problem again. If we fail, we restart the conjecture-generating process from scratch. This has various advantages. First, as we use a portfolio of solvers, they can exchange these proven lemmas. Second, the derived lemmas influence quantifier instantiations. Moreover, we prune conjectures for redundancies by quickly checking whether they follow from the previously derived lemmas alone. Note that these quick checks involve only ground formulas.

6 Experiments

The implementation and data is available at [20]. For QE we use Tarski [38] due its capability to read SMT. Alternatively, one could also use Z3's QE functionality but we had a better experience with Tarski overall. For SMT queries several solvers and their configurations are used, run in parallel and stopping all, once one finishes. We use Z3 [26][4], VAMPIRE [22][5], and CVC5 [4][6] in several configurations: {`enum-inst`}, {`no-e-matching, enum-inst`}, {`simplification=none, enum-inst`}, {`mbqi`}, {`no-e-matching, no-cbqi, enum-inst`}. The experiments were performed on machines with two AMD EPYC 7513 32-Core processors and with 514 GiB RAM with 10 problem instances run in parallel. Each problem instance has the CPU time limit3600 sand calls up to 8 SMT solvers in parallel. Each SMT solver has the time limit 120s (5s for lemmas).

As in [8], we use a problem collection by Musil [27] comprising 79 problem instances from several sources. We collected more problems from competitions. We scraped the problems from Art Of Problem Solving (AoPS) [1] for International, Regional, and National contests. Then we heuristically filtered problems resembling functional equations, obtaining 754 problems as text. Then we translated these problems to our custom language for functional equations, which we converted into SMT. This procedure successfully produced 343 problems.

To evaluate the techniques we have performed an ablation study of the proposed approaches. A summary of the results can be found in Table 1. The default approach is to first run SMT queries with additional instances obtained by Theory-Unification (TU), see Sect. 4.2. This part corresponds to −PI−L in Table 1. If this fails, we produce more instances using partial instantiations (PI), see Sect. 4.1, and query SMT solvers again. The problems solved by these two steps correspond to −L in Table 1. If this also fails, we run the lemma generation loop (L) interleaved with SMT queries when new lemmas are proven, see Sect. 5, until the time limit. We also consider the *virtual best solver (VBS)*, which considers the shortest solving time for each instance across all configurations of our tool. The results show that all the techniques contribute to the default mode. Lemmas and partial generation have the greatest impact—turning them off causes a loss of half of the instances.

Table 1. The number of solved problems. The default (Def.) uses EQ, PI, TU and L. In −EQ the original equation is removed during PI. +FI means partial instantiations of equation by simple terms and terms obtained by one application of $+,-,\times$, or f from them into up to three variables. −PI means no partial instantiations (Sect. 4.1) by simple terms into one variable. −TU means no Theory-Unification (Sect. 4.2). −L means no lemmas (Sect. 5). Base is −PI−TU−L. VBS is the virtual best solver.

		Def.	−EQ	−EQ+FI	−PI	−TU	−PI−TU	−L	−PI−L	−TU−L	Base	VBS
Musil	total	21	21	20	18	17	13	19	17	14	13	22
	unique	0	0	1	0	0	0	0	0	0	0	
AoPS	total	77	75	64	60	76	47	64	39	58	33	87
	unique	2	1	5	2	1	0	0	0	0	0	

[4] version 4.12.1, with default options and `-memory:32768`.

[5] version 4.8 linked with Z3 4.9.1.0 and options `-input_syntax smtlib2 -mode portfolio -schedule smtcomp_2018 -cores 1`.

[6] version 1.1.3-dev.72.2b4ca00c2.

6.1 Example Solved Problem

To demonstrate the current capabilities, we show an example of a problem that the system could solve, contrary to its predecessor. We also show the standard human solution to give a sense of difficulty. It is problem 19 of the 2005 Postal Coaching contest in India. In our benchmark, it can be found under the AoPS code `c1068820h2554984p21862259`.

Find all functions $f : \mathbb{R} \mapsto \mathbb{R}$ such that $f(xy + f(x)) = xf(y) + f(x)$ for all $x, y \in \mathbb{R}$. Let (a, b) denote plugging $x = a$ and $y = b$ into the original equation. To solve the problem, we start with two substitutions.

$$\begin{aligned} (0, x): \quad & f(f(0)) = f(0), \\ (f(0), 0): \quad & f(f(f(0))) = f(0)^2 + f(0). \end{aligned}$$

By combining these two equations, we obtain $f(0)^2 = 0$, therefore $f(0) = 0$. Now, we plug $(x, 0)$ into the original equation and obtain $f(f(x)) = f(x)$. We continue with two symmetric substitutions

$$\begin{aligned} (x, f(x)): \quad & f(xf(x) + f(x)) = xf(x) + f(x), \\ (f(x), x): \quad & f(f(x)x + f(x)) = f(x)^2 + f(x). \end{aligned}$$

Notice that the left hand sides are equal, and equating the right hand sides simplifies to $f(x)^2 = xf(x)$, equivalently $f(x) = 0$, or $f(x) = x$.

In theory, for any real number x, there could be an independent choice of whether $f(x) = x$ or $f(x) = 0$. Now, we will prove that in fact, across all the values of x, the choice must be the same.

For contradiction, assume that there are two nonzero numbers a, b such that $f(a) = a$ and $f(b) = 0$. Let us plug (a, b) into the equation: $f(ab + a) = a$. Because $a \neq 0$, our characterization of possible values for $f(x)$ forces $a = ab + a$. However, this equation simplifies to $ab = 0$, and cannot be satisfied by nonzero values. Therefore, the only two solutions are $f(x) = 0$ for all $x \in \mathbb{R}$, and $f(x) = x$ for all $x \in \mathbb{R}$. We easily check that these two functions satisfy the given equation.

Our solver automatically solves the same problem as follows. First, using the template and quantifier elimination it is easy to obtain the two solutions, and as usual it remains to prove there are no other solutions. That is, the solver needs to prove unsatisfiability of the identity $f(xy + f(x)) = xf(y) + f(x)$ along with the two skolemized disequations $f(c_1) \neq c_1$ and $f(c_2) \neq 0$. Using the techniques described in this paper, the solver additionally adds partial instantiations of $f(xy + f(x)) = xf(y) + f(x)$. The solver then generates and proves lemmas. First, it derives lemmas $f(0) = 0$ and $f(1) = 1 \vee f(1) = 0$. Second, it derives $f(c_1) = 0$, $f(c_2) = c_2$ and $f(1) = 1$ using the previously derived lemmas. Each lemma was proven using VAMPIRE. Using all these lemmas, the unsatisfiability of the whole set can be shown instantly by all solvers in our portfolio but one.[7] Note that our informal proof above shows that if $f(a) = a$ and $f(b) = 0$, then either a or b must be 0. By the same argument, the automatically derived lemmas $f(c_1) = 0$ and $f(c_2) = c_2$ imply either c_1 or c_2 must be 0, contradicting $f(0) = 0$.

[7] The one is CVC5 called with enumeration and no simplification.

7 Conclusions and Future Work

We develop a pipeline that solves for all real functions satisfying a specification Φ_{spec}. We first use quantifier elimination in order to solve for all quadratic solutions to the specification, giving a candidate solution Φ_{sol} satisfying $\Phi_{\text{sol}} \Rightarrow \Phi_{\text{spec}}$. We then try to prove $\Phi_{\text{spec}} \Rightarrow \Phi_{\text{sol}}$ in order to conclude Φ_{sol} exhausts the class of all solutions. Such implications are challenging for SMT solvers and we have combined several novel techniques (and several SMT solvers) to automatically justify the implication.

One of the techniques is to instantiate some quantifiers before calling the SMT solver. We look for instantiations by solving equations (over the theory of the reals) and sometimes simply use small instantiations. Apart from instantiations, we also generate and prove potential lemmas and add them to the problem. This approach enables synergy between SMT solvers since one solver may prove a lemma and another solver uses the lemma in the final proof.

The introduced techniques significantly contribute to the number of problems solved, which suggests that such techniques may be useful in a more general SMT setting. Proving that there are no more solutions is also of interest in automated synthesis, since more (unknown) solutions indicate ambiguity in the specification—ambiguity has been studied by Kunčak et al. [24] in the context of synthesis but only for specifications that admit deskolemizing f (meaning that f is always applied to the same arguments).

We found some helpful instantiations by solving equations. A more general version of this technique would be to use *rigid E-unification* to solve equations in the theory of the reals along with the assumed equations for the unary function f [3]. Some limited support for linear arithmetic in E-matching has been developed by Hoenicke and Schindler [17]. We leave this for future work. Unification with abstraction [31] can help Vampire obtain useful instantiations for clauses with theory and nontheory parts (e.g., some parts purely involving reals and other parts involving the uninterpreted function symbol f). Updating to use more recent work on unification with abstraction [6] may be a fruitful avenue of future work. Another topic for future work is to improve the synthesis of potential lemmas in order to produce lemmas beyond disjunctions of ground equations.

Another interesting topic for future research is how to handle richer templates. For example, we could consider the quotient of two polynomials (of bounded degree). Having a polynomial in the denominator introduces issues with how division by zero is handled (or avoided).

Acknowledgments. The research was supported by the Ministry of Education, Youth and Sports within the dedicated program ERC CZ under the project POSTMAN no. LL1902, by the Czech Science Foundation grant no. 25-17929X, and by the European Union under the project ROBOPROX (reg. no. CZ.02.01.01/00/22_008/0004590). This article is part of the RICAIP project that has received funding from the European Union's Horizon 2020 research and innovation programme under grant agreement No 857306. Stefan Ratschan's work was supported by the research programme of the

Strategy AV21 AI: Artificial Intelligence for Science and Society and institutional support RVO:67985807.

Disclosure of Interests. The authors have no competing interests to declare that are relevant to the content of this article.

References

1. Art of problem solving. https://artofproblemsolving.com/community/c13_contest_collections
2. Alur, R., et al.: Syntax-guided synthesis. In: 2013 Formal Methods in Computer-Aided Design, pp. 1–8 (2013). https://doi.org/10.1109/FMCAD.2013.6679385
3. Backeman, P., Rümmer, P.: Free variables and theories: revisiting rigid E-unification. In: Lutz, C., Ranise, S. (eds.) FroCoS 2015. LNCS (LNAI), vol. 9322, pp. 3–13. Springer, Cham (2015). https://doi.org/10.1007/978-3-319-24246-0_1
4. Barbosa, H., et al.: cvc5: A versatile and industrial-strength SMT solver. In: Tools and Algorithms for the Construction and Analysis of Systems, TACAS. LNCS, vol. 13243, pp. 415–442. Springer (2022). https://doi.org/10.1007/978-3-030-99524-9_24
5. Barrett, C., Tinelli, C.: Satisfiability modulo theories. In: Handbook of Model Checking, pp. 305–343. Springer, Cham (2018). https://doi.org/10.1007/978-3-319-10575-8_11
6. Bhayat, A., Korovin, K., Kovács, L., Schoisswohl, J.: Refining unification with abstraction. In: Piskac, R., Voronkov, A. (eds.) LPAR 2023: Proceedings of 24th International Conference on Logic for Programming, Artificial Intelligence and Reasoning, Manizales, Colombia, 4–9 June 2023. EPiC Series in Computing, vol. 94, pp. 36–47. EasyChair (2023). https://doi.org/10.29007/H65J
7. Bradley, A.R., Manna, Z., Sipma, H.B.: What's decidable about arrays? In: Emerson, E.A., Namjoshi, K.S. (eds.) VMCAI 2006. LNCS, vol. 3855, pp. 427–442. Springer, Heidelberg (2005). https://doi.org/10.1007/11609773_28
8. Brown, C.E., Janota, M., Olšák, M.: Symbolic computation for all the fun. In: Brown, C.W., Kaufmann, D., Nalon, C., Steen, A., Suda, M. (eds.) Joint Proceedings of the 9th Workshop on Practical Aspects of Automated Reasoning (PAAR) and the 9th Satisfiability Checking and Symbolic Computation Workshop (SC-Square), 2024 co-located with the 12th International Joint Conference on Automated Reasoning (IJCAR 2024). CEUR Workshop Proceedings, vol. 3717, pp. 111–121. CEUR-WS.org (2024). https://ceur-ws.org/Vol-3717/paper6.pdf
9. Brown, C.W.: QEPCAD B: a system for computing with semi-algebraic sets via cylindrical algebraic decomposition. SIGSAM Bull. **38**(1), 23–24 (2004). https://doi.org/10.1145/980175.980185
10. Burden, R.L., Faires, J., Douglas, A.: Numerical Analysis, 10th edn. Cengage Learning, Boston (2015)
11. Caviness, B.F., Johnson, J.R. (eds.): Quantifier Elimination and Cylindrical Algebraic Decomposition. Springer, Wien (1998). https://doi.org/10.1007/978-3-7091-9459-1
12. Collins, G.E., Hong, H.: Partial cylindrical algebraic decomposition for quantifier elimination. J. Symb. Comput. **12**(3), 299–328 (1991). https://doi.org/10.1016/S0747-7171(08)80152-6

13. Davenport, J.H., Heintz, J.: Real quantifier elimination is doubly exponential. J. Symb. Comput. **5**, 29–35 (1988). https://doi.org/10.1016/S0747-7171(88)80004-X
14. Dekoninck, J., Balunović, M., Jovanović, N., Petrov, I., Vechev, M.: MathConstruct: challenging LLM reasoning with constructive proofs. In: ICLR 2025 Workshop: VerifAI: AI Verification in the Wild (2025). https://openreview.net/forum?id=nHW2tiGMrb
15. Detlefs, D., Nelson, G., Saxe, J.B.: Simplify: a theorem prover for program checking. J. ACM **52**(3), 365–473 (2005). https://doi.org/10.1145/1066100.1066102
16. Ge, Y., de Moura, L.: Complete instantiation for quantified formulas in satisfiabiliby modulo theories. In: Bouajjani, A., Maler, O. (eds.) CAV 2009. LNCS, vol. 5643, pp. 306–320. Springer, Heidelberg (2009). https://doi.org/10.1007/978-3-642-02658-4_25
17. Hoenicke, J., Schindler, T.: Incremental search for conflict and unit instances of quantified formulas with e-matching. In: Henglein, F., Shoham, S., Vizel, Y. (eds.) VMCAI 2021. LNCS, vol. 12597, pp. 534–555. Springer, Cham (2021). https://doi.org/10.1007/978-3-030-67067-2_24
18. Hozzová, P., Kovács, L., Norman, C., Voronkov, A.: Program synthesis in saturation. In: Pientka, B., Tinelli, C. (eds.) Automated Deduction - CADE 29 - 29th International Conference on Automated Deduction. LNCS, vol. 14132, pp. 307–324. Springer, Cham (2023). https://doi.org/10.1007/978-3-031-38499-8_18
19. Hozzová, P., Amrollahi, D., Hajdu, M., Kovács, L., Voronkov, A., Wagner, E.M.: Synthesis of recursive programs in saturation. In: International Joint Conference on Automated Reasoning IJCAR (2024). https://doi.org/10.1007/978-3-031-63498-7_10
20. Janota, M.: Allfun (2025). https://doi.org/10.5281/zenodo.15554870
21. Janota, M., Barbosa, H., Fontaine, P., Reynolds, A.: Fair and adventurous enumeration of quantifier instantiations. In: Formal Methods in Computer-Aided Design, pp. 256–260. IEEE (2021). https://doi.org/10.34727/2021/ISBN.978-3-85448-046-4_35
22. Kovács, L., Voronkov, A.: First-order theorem proving and VAMPIRE. In: Sharygina, N., Veith, H. (eds.) CAV 2013. LNCS, vol. 8044, pp. 1–35. Springer, Heidelberg (2013). https://doi.org/10.1007/978-3-642-39799-8_1
23. Kuczma, M.: An introduction to the theory of functional equations and inequalities. Birkhäuser Basel (2009). https://doi.org/10.1007/978-3-7643-8749-5
24. Kuncak, V., Mayer, M., Piskac, R., Suter, P.: Complete functional synthesis. In: PLDI, pp. 316–329. ACM (2010). https://doi.org/10.1145/1806596.1806632
25. Meurer, A., et al.: SymPy: symbolic computing in Python. PeerJ Comput. Sci. **3**, e103 (2017). https://www.sympy.org
26. de Moura, L., Bjørner, N.: Z3: an efficient SMT solver. In: Ramakrishnan, C.R., Rehof, J. (eds.) TACAS 2008. LNCS, vol. 4963, pp. 337–340. Springer, Heidelberg (2008). https://doi.org/10.1007/978-3-540-78800-3_24
27. Musil, V.: Funkcionální rovnice (2024). https://prase.cz/library/FunkcionalniRovniceVM/FunkcionalniRovniceVM.pdf, online library of the Matematický korespondenční seminář PraSe (PRAžský SEminář), Downloaded 8 March 2024
28. Niemetz, A., Preiner, M., Reynolds, A., Barrett, C., Tinelli, C.: Syntax-guided quantifier instantiation. In: TACAS 2021. LNCS, vol. 12652, pp. 145–163. Springer, Cham (2021). https://doi.org/10.1007/978-3-030-72013-1_8
29. Petrov, I., et al.: Proof or bluff? Evaluating LLMs on 2025 USA math Olympiad (2025). https://arxiv.org/abs/2503.21934

30. Ratschan, S.: Deciding predicate logical theories of real-valued functions. In: Leroux, J., Lombardy, S., Peleg, D. (eds.) 48th International Symposium on Mathematical Foundations of Computer Science (MFCS 2023), LIPIcs, vol. 272, pp. 76:1–76:15. Schloss Dagstuhl – Leibniz-Zentrum für Informatik, Dagstuhl, Germany (2023). https://doi.org/10.4230/LIPIcs.MFCS.2023.76
31. Reger, G., Suda, M., Voronkov, A.: Unification with abstraction and theory instantiation in saturation-based reasoning. In: Beyer, D., Huisman, M. (eds.) TACAS 2018. LNCS, vol. 10805, pp. 3–22. Springer, Cham (2018). https://doi.org/10.1007/978-3-319-89960-2_1
32. Reynolds, A., Barbosa, H., Fontaine, P.: Revisiting enumerative instantiation. In: Beyer, D., Huisman, M. (eds.) TACAS 2018. LNCS, vol. 10806, pp. 112–131. Springer, Cham (2018). https://doi.org/10.1007/978-3-319-89963-3_7
33. Reynolds, A., Tinelli, C., Goel, A., Krstić, S., Deters, M., Barrett, C.: Quantifier instantiation techniques for finite model finding in SMT. In: Bonacina, M.P. (ed.) CADE 2013. LNCS (LNAI), vol. 7898, pp. 377–391. Springer, Heidelberg (2013). https://doi.org/10.1007/978-3-642-38574-2_26
34. Reynolds, A., Tinelli, C., de Moura, L.M.: Finding conflicting instances of quantified formulas in SMT. In: Formal Methods in Computer-Aided Design, FMCAD, pp. 195–202. IEEE (2014). https://doi.org/10.1109/FMCAD.2014.6987613
35. Robinson, J.A., Voronkov, A. (eds.): Handbook of Automated Reasoning (in 2 volumes). Elsevier and MIT Press (2001). https://www.sciencedirect.com/book/9780444508133/handbook-of-automated-reasoning
36. Srivastava, S., Gulwani, S., Foster, J.S.: Template-based program verification and program synthesis. Int. J. Softw. Tools Technol. Transf. **15**(5–6), 497–518 (2013). https://doi.org/10.1007/S10009-012-0223-4
37. Tarski, A.: A Decision Method for Elementary Algebra and Geometry. University of California Press, Berkeley (1951). https://doi.org/10.2307/jj.8501420, also in [11]
38. Vale-Enriquez, F., Brown, C.W.: Polynomial constraints and unsat cores in Tarski. In: Davenport, J.H., Kauers, M., Labahn, G., Urban, J. (eds.) ICMS 2018. LNCS, vol. 10931, pp. 466–474. Springer, Cham (2018). https://doi.org/10.1007/978-3-319-96418-8_55, https://www.usna.edu/Users/cs/wcbrown/tarski/index.html, code obtained from https://github.com/chriswestbrown/tarski
39. Weispfenning, V.: The complexity of linear problems in fields. J. Symb. Comput. **5**(1–2), 3–27 (1988). https://doi.org/10.1016/S0747-7171(88)80003-8

Rewriting

Lexicographic Combination of Reduction Pairs

Teppei Saito(✉) and Nao Hirokawa(✉)

JAIST, Nomi, Japan
{saito,hirokawa}@jaist.ac.jp

Abstract. We present a simple criterion for combining reduction pairs lexicographically. The criterion is applicable to arbitrary classes of reduction pairs, such as the polynomial interpretation, the matrix interpretation, and the Knuth–Bendix order. In addition, we investigate a variant of the matrix interpretation where the lexicographic order is employed instead of the usual component-wise order. Effectiveness is demonstrated by experiments and examples, including Touzet's Hydra Battle.

Keywords: Term rewriting · Termination · Dependency pairs

1 Introduction

Lexicographic combination is a powerful method to combine termination measures into a more complex one. To illustrate it, consider the term rewrite system:

$$1: \quad \mathsf{f}(\mathsf{f}(x)) \to \mathsf{g}(\mathsf{g}(\mathsf{f}(x))) \qquad\qquad 2: \quad \mathsf{g}(\mathsf{g}(x)) \to x$$

For example, it has the following rewrite sequence:

$$\mathsf{f}(\mathsf{f}(\mathsf{f}(x))) \xrightarrow{1} \mathsf{f}(\mathsf{g}(\mathsf{g}(\mathsf{f}(x)))) \xrightarrow{2} \mathsf{f}(\mathsf{f}(x)) \xrightarrow{1} \mathsf{g}(\mathsf{g}(\mathsf{f}(x))) \xrightarrow{2} \mathsf{f}(x)$$

If the numbers of occurrences of f and g are measured, the sequence turns into the descending sequence with respect to the lexicographic order $>^{\mathsf{lex}}$:

$$(3,0) >^{\mathsf{lex}} (2,2) >^{\mathsf{lex}} (2,0) >^{\mathsf{lex}} (1,2) >^{\mathsf{lex}} (1,0)$$

In this manner, lexicographic combination can be used for showing termination of the rewrite system. More formally speaking, the measure can be expressed as the lexicographic combination of two linear polynomial interpretations [21], namely $\mathcal{A}$ and $\mathcal{B}$ defined by $\mathsf{f}_{\mathcal{A}}(x) = x + 1$, $\mathsf{g}_{\mathcal{A}}(x) = x$, $\mathsf{f}_{\mathcal{B}}(x) = x$, and $\mathsf{g}_{\mathcal{B}}(x) = x + 1$. Here $\mathcal{A}$ counts the number of occurrences of f, while $\mathcal{B}$ counts that of g.

There has been a long line of research concerning termination analysis of term rewrite systems. Among others, the dependency pair framework [1,10,12–14] is a powerful method for automated termination analysis. Decreasing measures for the method are typically given in the form of *reduction pairs* consisting of preorders and well-founded orders on terms. Unfortunately, in general, lexicographic

C. Barrett and U. Waldmann (Eds.): CADE 2025, LNAI 15943, pp. 167–186, 2025.
https://doi.org/10.1007/978-3-031-99984-0_10

combinations of reduction pairs are not reduction pairs. To overcome this, we give a simple criterion for a combination to be a reduction pair.

Actually, the previous example implicitly uses the folklore that lexicographic combinations of *monotone* reduction pairs are (monotone) reduction pairs, see [3,9,27]. Our main result can be conceived as an extension of it. For example, let us consider the following term rewrite system

$$\mathsf{s}(x) + y \to \mathsf{p}(\mathsf{s}(x)) + \mathsf{s}(y) \qquad\qquad \mathsf{p}(\mathsf{s}(x)) \to x$$

which encodes addition in a tricky way, using the successor symbol s and the predecessor symbol p. The dependency pair framework tells us that the termination is established if one can find a reduction pair $(\geqslant, >)$ that fulfills the following set of constraints.

$$\mathsf{s}(x) + y \geqslant \mathsf{p}(\mathsf{s}(x)) + \mathsf{s}(y) \qquad\qquad \mathsf{p}(\mathsf{s}(x)) \geqslant x$$
$$\mathsf{s}(x) +^\sharp y > \mathsf{p}(\mathsf{s}(x)) +^\sharp \mathsf{s}(y) \qquad\qquad \mathsf{s}(x) +^\sharp y > \mathsf{p}^\sharp(\mathsf{s}(x))$$

Here, $+^\sharp$ and $\mathsf{p}^\sharp$ are fresh symbols introduced by the method. To do this, one can use the lexicographic combination of the following linear polynomial interpretations $\mathcal{A}$ and $\mathcal{B}$:

$$\mathsf{s}_\mathcal{A}(x) = x + 1 \quad \mathsf{p}_\mathcal{A}(x) = x \quad \mathsf{p}^\sharp_\mathcal{A}(x) = 0 \quad x +_\mathcal{A} y = x \quad x +^\sharp_\mathcal{A} y = x$$
$$\mathsf{s}_\mathcal{B}(x) = x + 1 \quad \mathsf{p}_\mathcal{B}(x) = 0 \quad \mathsf{p}^\sharp_\mathcal{B}(x) = 0 \quad x +_\mathcal{B} y = x \quad x +^\sharp_\mathcal{B} y = x$$

The resulting lexicographic combination satisfies the constraints: Thanks to lexicographic comparison, the constraint $\mathsf{p}(\mathsf{s}(x)) \geqslant x$ is not subject to comparison by the second interpretation $\mathcal{B}$, as it is interpreted to $x + 1 > x$ in the first interpretation $\mathcal{A}$. This allows us to use $\mathsf{p}_\mathcal{B}(x) = 0$, which helps to satisfy the remaining constraints. A problem here is that, in contrast to the previous example, the algebras $\mathcal{A}$ and $\mathcal{B}$ are not monotone, as $\mathsf{p}_\mathcal{B}(x) = 0$ disregards the argument x. Although the folklore does not apply, our result can justify that the resulting combination is indeed a reduction pair, which facilitates a successful termination proof.

The polynomial interpretation [21], the matrix interpretation [8], and the Knuth–Bendix order [19] are typical methods for constructing reduction pairs. We also show how to use these methods with lexicographic combination, demonstrating it with the term rewrite system of the Battle of Hercules and Hydra [18] due to Touzet [28]. As a by-product, we obtain a variant of the matrix interpretation with the lexicographic order instead of the standard component-wise order. As remarked in [8,23], this has been an open question.

In the context of the dependency pair framework, repetitive application of reduction pair processors [12,13] and the rule removal method [27] can be regarded as alternative methods for combining reduction pairs in a lexicographic manner. Examples and experimental data show that our method is complementary to those methods and particularly useful for relative termination.

The structure of the paper. After recalling some preliminaries in Sect. 2, a criterion for lexicographic combination and termination proofs with it are presented in Sect. 3. The termination proof of the Hydra Battle is discussed in Sect. 4. Then, as a generalization of lexicographic combination of the linear polynomial interpretation, Sect. 5 studies a variant of the matrix interpretation with the lexicographic order. Experimental data and related work are discussed in Sect. 6 and Sect. 7.

2 Preliminaries

Throughout the paper, we assume familiarity with term rewriting [2,25]. In this section, we briefly recall notions and notations for term rewriting and termination analysis based on the dependency pair framework.

Let $\mathcal{F}$ be a signature and $\mathcal{V}$ an infinite set of variables. The set of terms built from $\mathcal{F}$ and $\mathcal{V}$ is denoted by $\mathcal{T}(\mathcal{F}, \mathcal{V})$, or simply by $\mathcal{T}$. The root symbol $\mathrm{root}(t)$ of a non-variable term $t = f(t_1, \ldots, t_n)$ is f. A mapping $\sigma : \mathcal{V} \to \mathcal{T}$ is called a *substitution* if $\sigma(x) \neq x$ for only finitely many variables x. Given a term t, the term obtained by replacing each variable occurrence x in t with $\sigma(x)$ is denoted by $t\sigma$. Let $\Box$ be a fresh constant symbol. A *context* is a term with exactly one occurrence of $\Box$. The term obtained by replacing $\Box$ in a context C with a term t is denoted by $C[t]$. We write $s \trianglerighteq t$ if $s = C[t]$ for some context C, and moreover we write $s \triangleright t$ if $s \trianglerighteq t$ and $s \neq t$. Let $\hookrightarrow$ be a relation on terms. The relation $\hookrightarrow$ is said to be *closed under substitutions* if $s\sigma \hookrightarrow t\sigma$ whenever $s \hookrightarrow t$ and σ is a substitution. Similarly, $\hookrightarrow$ is said to be *closed under contexts* if $C[s] \hookrightarrow C[t]$ whenever $t \hookrightarrow u$ and C is a context.

A *rewrite rule* $\ell \to r$ is a pair (ℓ, r) of terms such that ℓ is not a variable and every variable occurring in r also occurs in ℓ. A set of rewrite rules is called a *term rewrite system* (TRS). The *rewrite step* $\to_\mathcal{R}$ of a TRS $\mathcal{R}$ is defined as follows: $s \to_\mathcal{R} t$ if $s = C[\ell\sigma]$ and $t = C[r\sigma]$ for some rewrite rule $\ell \to r \in \mathcal{R}$, context C, and substitution σ. When $C = \Box$, it is written as $s \xrightarrow{\epsilon}_\mathcal{R} t$. Given a term t and a variable x, we write $|t|_x$ for the number of occurrences of x in t. A term rewrite system $\mathcal{R}$ is *non-duplicating* if $|\ell|_x \geqslant |r|_x$ for all $\ell \to r \in \mathcal{R}$ and variables x. A term t is *terminating* with respect to a relation $\hookrightarrow$ on terms if there is no infinite sequence $t \hookrightarrow t_1 \hookrightarrow t_2 \hookrightarrow \cdots$ starting from t. *Termination* of the relation $\hookrightarrow$ is defined as absence of non-terminating terms. A TRS $\mathcal{R}$ is *terminating* if $\to_\mathcal{R}$ is. Let $\hookrightarrow^*$ denote the reflexive and transitive closure of a relation $\hookrightarrow$. Given TRSs $\mathcal{R}$ and $\mathcal{S}$, the relation $\to_{\mathcal{R}/\mathcal{S}}$ is defined on terms as follows: $s \to_{\mathcal{R}/\mathcal{S}} t$ if $s \to_\mathcal{S}^* u \to_\mathcal{R} v \to_\mathcal{S}^* t$ for some terms u and v. We say that $\mathcal{R}$ is *relatively terminating* with respect to $\mathcal{S}$, or $\mathcal{R}/\mathcal{S}$ is terminating, if $\to_{\mathcal{R}/\mathcal{S}}$ is terminating.

We recall the dependency pair framework [1,12–14]. Let $\mathcal{R}$ be a TRS. We define $\mathcal{D}_\mathcal{R}$ as $\{f \mid f(\ell_1, \ldots, \ell_n) \to r \in \mathcal{R}\}$. Elements in $\mathcal{D}_\mathcal{R}$ are called *defined symbols*. Given a term t of the form $f(t_1, \ldots, t_n)$ with $f \in \mathcal{D}_\mathcal{R}$, we write $t^\sharp$ for $f^\sharp(t_1, \ldots, t_n)$. Here $f^\sharp$ is a fresh n-ary function symbol corresponding to f. The set of such terms $t^\sharp$ is denoted by $\mathcal{T}^\sharp$. The TRS $\mathsf{DP}(\mathcal{R})$ is defined as follows:

$$\mathsf{DP}(\mathcal{R}) = \{\ell^\sharp \to t^\sharp \mid \ell \to r \in \mathcal{R}, r \trianglerighteq t, \mathrm{root}(t) \in \mathcal{D}_\mathcal{R},\ \text{and } \ell \not\triangleright t\}$$

Rules in $\mathsf{DP}(\mathcal{R})$ are called *dependency pairs*. *Dependency pair problems* are pairs $(\mathcal{P}, \mathcal{R})$ of TRSs with $\mathcal{P} \subseteq \mathcal{T}^\sharp \times \mathcal{T}^\sharp$ and $\mathcal{R} \subseteq \mathcal{T} \times \mathcal{T}$. A dependency pair problem $(\mathcal{P}, \mathcal{R})$ is *finite* if there exists no infinite sequence of the form $s_1 \to_{\mathcal{R}}^* t_1 \xrightarrow{\epsilon}_{\mathcal{P}} s_2 \to_{\mathcal{R}}^* t_2 \xrightarrow{\epsilon}_{\mathcal{P}} \cdots$, where each s_i is terminating with respect to $\mathcal{R}$.

Theorem 1. *A TRS $\mathcal{R}$ is terminating if and only if $(\mathsf{DP}(\mathcal{R}), \mathcal{R})$ is finite.*

A pair of a preorder $\geqslant$ and a strict order $>$ on the same set is an *order pair* if $a > d$ whenever $a \geqslant b > c \geqslant d$. An order pair is *well-founded* if $>$ is well-founded. An order pair $(\geqslant, >)$ on terms is *stable* if $\geqslant$ and $>$ are closed under substitutions. A well-founded stable order pair is a *reduction pair* if $\geqslant$ is closed under contexts. If in addition $>$ is closed under contexts, $(\geqslant, >)$ is called a *monotone* reduction pair. The next theorem is known as the reduction pair processor.

Theorem 2. *Let $(\geqslant, >)$ be a reduction pair. A dependency pair problem $(\mathcal{P}, \mathcal{R})$ with $\mathcal{P} \cup \mathcal{R} \subseteq \geqslant$ is finite if and only if $(\mathcal{P} \setminus >, \mathcal{R})$ is finite.*

Thus, a TRS $\mathcal{R}$ is terminating if $\mathsf{DP}(\mathcal{R}) \subseteq >$ and $\mathcal{R} \subseteq \geqslant$ for some reduction pair $(\geqslant, >)$. This simple criterion can also be used for showing relative termination. We say that a TRS $\mathcal{R}$ *dominates* a TRS $\mathcal{S}$ if r has no defined symbols of $\mathcal{R}$ for all rules $\ell \to r \in \mathcal{S}$.

Theorem 3. ([15]). *Let $\mathcal{R}$ and $\mathcal{S}$ be TRSs such that $\mathcal{R}$ dominates $\mathcal{S}$ and $\mathcal{S}$ is non-duplicating. If there exists a reduction pair $(\geqslant, >)$ with $\mathsf{DP}(\mathcal{R}) \subseteq >$ and $\mathcal{R} \cup \mathcal{S} \subseteq \geqslant$ then $\mathcal{R}/\mathcal{S}$ is terminating.*

Let $\mathcal{F}$ be a signature. An *$\mathcal{F}$-algebra* $\mathcal{A}$ is a pair $(A, \{f_\mathcal{A}\}_{f \in \mathcal{F}})$ where A is a non-empty set, called the *carrier* of $\mathcal{A}$, and each $f_\mathcal{A}$ is an n-ary function on A, called the interpretation of an n-ary function symbol f. Let $\mathcal{A}$ be an $\mathcal{F}$-algebra. A function α from $\mathcal{V}$ to A is called an *assignment* for $\mathcal{A}$. It is extended to the homomorphism $[\alpha]_\mathcal{A} : \mathcal{T}(\mathcal{F}, \mathcal{V}) \to A$ as follows:

$$[\alpha]_\mathcal{A}(x) = \begin{cases} \alpha(x) & \text{if } x \text{ is a variable} \\ f_\mathcal{A}([\alpha]_\mathcal{A}(t_1), \ldots, [\alpha]_\mathcal{A}(t_n)) & \text{if } t = f(t_1, \ldots, t_n) \end{cases}$$

Assume that $\mathcal{A}$ is equipped with an order pair $(\geqslant, >)$ on A. The algebra $\mathcal{A}$ is *well-founded* if $>$ is well-founded, and *weakly monotone* if $f_\mathcal{A}(a_1, \ldots, a_i, \ldots, a_n) \geqslant f_\mathcal{A}(a_1, \ldots, b, \ldots, a_n)$ whenever $f \in \mathcal{F}$ and $a_i \geqslant b$. We write $s \geqslant_\mathcal{A} t$ and $s >_\mathcal{A} t$ if $[\alpha]_\mathcal{A}(s) \geqslant [\alpha]_\mathcal{A}(t)$ and $[\alpha]_\mathcal{A}(s) > [\alpha]_\mathcal{A}(t)$ hold for all assignments α, respectively. It is known that $(\geqslant_\mathcal{A}, >_\mathcal{A})$ is a reduction pair if $\mathcal{A}$ is weakly monotone and well-founded.

The *matrix interpretation* [8] provides a semantic method to construct reduction pairs. The carrier of a matrix interpretation $\mathcal{A}$ is the set of vectors $\boldsymbol{x}$ of natural numbers of a fixed dimension $d > 0$. Vectors are ordered by the componentwise order pair $(\geqslant, >)$ defined as follows: $(x_1, \ldots, x_d)^T \geqslant (y_1, \ldots, y_d)^T$ if $x_i \geqslant y_i$ for all $i \in \{1, \ldots, d\}$; if in addition $x_1 > y_1$ then $(x_1, \ldots, x_d)^T > (y_1, \ldots, y_d)^T$.

We write $(A)_{i,j}$ or simply $A_{i,j}$ for the entry at the i-th row and the j-th column. Moreover, $\boldsymbol{e}_i$ stands for the unit vector $(0,\ldots,1,\ldots,0)^T$ having 1 only at the i-th coordinate, and O (resp. $\mathbf{0}$) for the zero matrix (resp. vector) with 0 in all entries. The interpretation $f_{\mathcal{A}}$ of each n-ary function symbol f is of the form

$$f_{\mathcal{A}}(\boldsymbol{x}_1,\ldots,\boldsymbol{x}_n) = A_1\boldsymbol{x}_1 + \ldots + A_n\boldsymbol{x}_n + \boldsymbol{a}$$

where $A_1,\ldots,A_n$ are $d \times d$ matrices of natural numbers and $\boldsymbol{a} \in \mathbb{N}^d$. The pair $(\geqslant_{\mathcal{A}}, >_{\mathcal{A}})$ is a reduction pair. The special class of the matrix interpretation with $d = 1$ is called the *linear polynomial interpretation.*

The *Knuth–Bendix order* (KBO) [19] is another way to construct reduction pairs. A *weight function* is a pair of a positive integer w_0 and a function w from function symbols to natural numbers with $w(c) \geqslant w_0$ for all constants c. The *weight* $w(t)$ of a term t is defined inductively: $w(x) = w_0$ for variables x, and $w(t) = w(f) + \sum_i w(t_i)$ for $t = f(t_1,\ldots,t_n)$. We write $f^n(t)$ for the n-times application of a unary function symbol f to a term t. Let (w_0, w) be a weight function and $\succ$ a precedence, that is, a strict order on function symbols. The Knuth–Bendix order $>_{\mathsf{kbo}}$ is inductively defined as follows: $s >_{\mathsf{kbo}} t$ if $|s|_x \geqslant |t|_x$ for all variables x, and

1. $w(s) > w(t)$, or
2. $w(s) = w(t)$ and one of the following conditions holds.
   a. $s = f^n(t)$ for some $n > 0$ and t is a variable.
   b. $s = f(s_1,\ldots,s_m)$, $t = g(t_1,\ldots,t_n)$, and either
      i. $f \succ g$ or
      ii. $f = g$ and there is an i such that $s_i >_{\mathsf{kbo}} t_i$ and $s_j = t_j$ for all $j < i$.

The weight function (w_0, w) is *admissible* for $\succ$, if $f \succ g$ for other function symbols g whenever f is a unary function symbol with $w(f) = 0$. If $\succ$ is well-founded and (w_0, w) is admissible for $\succ$, then $(\geqslant_{\mathsf{kbo}}, >_{\mathsf{kbo}})$ is a monotone reduction pair, where $\geqslant_{\mathsf{kbo}}$ stands for the reflexive closure of $>_{\mathsf{kbo}}$. (We note that in that case $>_{\mathsf{kbo}}$ is a so-called reduction order.)

Argument filtering [1] is a popular transformation for building reduction pairs with the Knuth–Bendix order. As the name suggests, this transformation filters out arguments from a given term. Formally, an *argument filter* π is a mapping that associates each n-ary function symbol f to an integer i or a list $[i_1,\ldots,i_m]$ of integers over $\{1,\ldots,n\}$. The *argument filtering* $\hat{\pi}$ is defined as follows:

$$\hat{\pi}(t) = \begin{cases} t & \text{if } t \text{ is a variable} \\ \hat{\pi}(t_i) & \text{if } t = f(t_1,\ldots,t_n) \text{ and } \pi(f) = i \\ f(\hat{\pi}(t_{i_1}),\ldots,\hat{\pi}(t_{i_m})) & \text{if } t = f(t_1,\ldots,t_n) \text{ and } \pi(f) = [i_1,\ldots,i_m] \end{cases}$$

Note that arities of function symbols may change by applying $\hat{\pi}$. Given a binary relation R on terms, we write $s \mathrel{R^\pi} t$ if $\hat{\pi}(s) \mathrel{R} \hat{\pi}(t)$.

Proposition 4. *Let* $(\geqslant, >)$ *be a reduction pair. Then* $(\geqslant^\pi, >^\pi)$ *is a reduction pair for every argument filter* π.

3 Combinability Criterion

Lexicographic combination is a well-known method to turn two order pairs into a single order pair which is capable of capturing a more complicated termination measure.

Definition 5. *Let* $(\geqslant_1, >_1)$ *and* $(\geqslant_2, >_2)$ *be order pairs on a set* X. *The* lexicographic combination $(\geqslant_{12}, >_{12})$ *is the pair of relations on* X *defined as follows:*

- $x \geqslant_{12} y$ *if* $x >_1 y$, *or both* $x \geqslant_1 y$ *and* $x \geqslant_2 y$.
- $x >_{12} y$ *if* $x >_1 y$, *or both* $x \geqslant_1 y$ *and* $x >_2 y$.

Lexicographic combinations of reduction pairs satisfy all conditions to be reduction pairs, except for closure under contexts of preorders.

Example 6. Consider the reduction pairs $(\geqslant_{\mathcal{A}}, >_{\mathcal{A}})$ and $(\geqslant_{\mathcal{B}}, >_{\mathcal{B}})$ induced by the following linear polynomial interpretations $\mathcal{A}$ and $\mathcal{B}$:

$$\mathsf{f}_{\mathcal{A}}(x) = 0 \qquad \mathsf{a}_{\mathcal{A}} = 1 \qquad \mathsf{b}_{\mathcal{A}} = 0$$
$$\mathsf{f}_{\mathcal{B}}(x) = x \qquad \mathsf{a}_{\mathcal{B}} = 0 \qquad \mathsf{b}_{\mathcal{B}} = 1$$

Although $\mathsf{a} \geqslant_{\mathcal{AB}} \mathsf{b}$ follows from $\mathsf{a} >_{\mathcal{A}} \mathsf{b}$, the desired inequality $\mathsf{f}(\mathsf{a}) \geqslant_{\mathcal{AB}} \mathsf{f}(\mathsf{b})$ for closure under contexts does not hold. Even worse, the flipped inequality $\mathsf{f}(\mathsf{b}) >_{\mathcal{AB}} \mathsf{f}(\mathsf{a})$ follows from $\mathsf{f}(\mathsf{b}) \geqslant_{\mathcal{A}} \mathsf{f}(\mathsf{a})$ and $\mathsf{f}(\mathsf{b}) >_{\mathcal{B}} \mathsf{f}(\mathsf{a})$.

As noted in [32], the problem in Example 6 is that, in the first component $\mathsf{f}_{\mathcal{A}}(x) = 0$ is not monotone with respect to the argument x, while $\mathsf{f}_{\mathcal{B}}(x) = x$ is dependent on x in the second component. This observation suggests the following definitions.

Definition 7. *Let* $(\geqslant, >)$ *be an order pair on terms. Let* f *be an* n*-ary function symbol. The* i*-th argument position of* f *is* $>$-monotone *(or monotone with respect to* $>$*) if*

$$t_i > u \implies f(t_1, \ldots, t_i, \ldots, t_n) > f(t_1, \ldots, u, \ldots, t_n)$$

for all terms $t_1, \ldots, t_n, u$. *Similarly, the position is* $\geqslant$-invariant *if*

$$f(t_1, \ldots, t_i, \ldots, t_n) \geqslant f(t_1, \ldots, u, \ldots, t_n)$$

for all terms $t_1, \ldots, t_n, u$. *An order pair* $(\geqslant, >)$ *is said to be* normal *if* $> \subseteq \geqslant$ *holds. We say that an order pair* $(\geqslant_1, >_1)$ *on terms is* combinable *with another order pair* $(\geqslant_2, >_2)$ *on terms if* $(\geqslant_1, >_1)$ *is normal and every argument position of any function symbol is* $>_1$*-monotone or* $\geqslant_2$*-invariant. If the order of combination can be inferred from the context, we may simply call them combinable.*

If we consider the equivalence relation $\sim$ induced by $\geqslant$, invariance is equivalent to $f(t_1, \ldots, t_i, \ldots, t_n) \sim f(t_1, \ldots, u, \ldots, t_n)$ for all $t_1, \ldots, t_n, u$. This justifies its name.

Recall the form of linear polynomial interpretations $\mathcal{A}$:

$$f_{\mathcal{A}}(x_1, \ldots, x_n) = a_0 + a_1 x_1 + \cdots + a_n x_n$$

Trivially, the i-th argument position of f is monotone with respect to $>_{\mathcal{A}}$ if $a_i > 0$, and invariant with respect to $\geqslant_{\mathcal{A}}$ otherwise. Moreover, $(\geqslant_{\mathcal{A}}, >_{\mathcal{A}})$ is normal.

Example 8 (continued from Example 6). The first argument position of f is neither monotone with respect to $>_{\mathcal{A}}$ nor invariant with respect to $\geqslant_{\mathcal{B}}$. Thus, $(\geqslant_{\mathcal{A}}, >_{\mathcal{A}})$ is *not* combinable with $(\geqslant_{\mathcal{B}}, >_{\mathcal{B}})$.

We have similar facts for matrix interpretations $\mathcal{A}$: let the interpretation of an n-ary function symbol f be $f_{\mathcal{A}}(\boldsymbol{x}_1, \ldots, \boldsymbol{x}_n) = A_1\boldsymbol{x}_1 + \cdots + A_n\boldsymbol{x}_n + \boldsymbol{a}$. The i-th argument position of f is monotone if $(A_i)_{1,1} > 0$, and invariant if $A_i = O$, see [8]. Again, $(\geqslant_{\mathcal{A}}, >_{\mathcal{A}})$ is normal.

Lemma 9. *Let $(\geqslant_1, >_1)$ be a reduction pair combinable with another reduction pair $(\geqslant_2, >_2)$. Then $\geqslant_{12}$ is closed under contexts.*

Proof. It is sufficient to show the monotonicity of $\geqslant_{12}$, meaning that if $t_i \geqslant_{12} u$ then $C[t_i] \geqslant_{12} C[u]$ for an arbitrary context C of the form $f(t_1, \ldots, \Box, \ldots, t_n)$. Suppose $t_i \geqslant_{12} u$. If it follows from $t_i \geqslant_1 u$ and $t_i \geqslant_2 u$, then $C[t_i] \geqslant_{12} C[u]$ follows from the assumptions that $\geqslant_1$ and $\geqslant_2$ are closed under contexts. Otherwise, $t_i \geqslant_{12} u$ follows from $t_i >_1 u$. According to the combinability, the i-th argument position of f is monotone in $>_1$ or invariant in $\geqslant_2$. In the former case $C[t_i] >_1 C[u]$ follows from $t_i >_1 u$. In the latter case, $t_i \geqslant_1 u$ from the normality, and therefore $C[t_i] \geqslant_1 C[u]$ from the closure under contexts. The invariance yields $C[t_i] \geqslant_2 C[u]$. Hence, in either case $C[t_i] \geqslant_{12} C[u]$ is concluded. □

Theorem 10. *Lexicographic combinations of combinable reduction pairs are reduction pairs.*

Remark 11. The normality requirement cannot be dropped from the combinability criterion (Theorem 10), see [24]. However, normality is a mild requirement, in the sense that typical reduction pairs like the Knuth–Bendix order [19], the recursive path order [6,16], the matrix interpretation [8], and the polynomial interpretation [21] are all normal reduction pairs. Furthermore, lexicographic combinations of normal reduction pairs are normal.

We demonstrate a termination proof based on lexicographic combination.

Example 12. Recall the TRS $\mathcal{R}$ in the introduction:

$$1\colon\ \mathsf{s}(x) + y \to \mathsf{p}(\mathsf{s}(x)) + \mathsf{s}(y) \qquad\qquad 2\colon\ \mathsf{p}(\mathsf{s}(x)) \to x$$

The set $\mathsf{DP}(\mathcal{R})$ consists of the two dependency pairs:

$$3\colon\ \mathsf{s}(x) +^\sharp y \to \mathsf{p}(\mathsf{s}(x)) +^\sharp \mathsf{s}(y) \qquad\qquad 4\colon\ \mathsf{s}(x) +^\sharp y \to \mathsf{p}^\sharp(\mathsf{s}(x))$$

Let $\mathcal{A}$ and $\mathcal{B}$ be the linear interpretations given by:

$$\begin{array}{lllll} \mathsf{s}_{\mathcal{A}}(\underline{x}) = x + 1 & \mathsf{p}_{\mathcal{A}}(\underline{x}) = x & \mathsf{p}^{\sharp}_{\mathcal{A}}(x) = 0 & \underline{x} +_{\mathcal{A}} y = x & \underline{x} +^{\sharp}_{\mathcal{A}} y = x \\ \mathsf{s}_{\mathcal{B}}(x) = x + 1 & \mathsf{p}_{\mathcal{B}}(\overline{x}) = 0 & \mathsf{p}^{\sharp}_{\mathcal{B}}(\overline{x}) = 0 & x +_{\mathcal{B}} \overline{y} = x & x +^{\sharp}_{\mathcal{B}} \overline{y} = x \end{array}$$

Here monotone positions in $\mathcal{A}$ and invariant positions in $\mathcal{B}$ are indicated by underlining and overlining, respectively. The induced reduction pairs are combinable, so let $(\geqslant_{\mathcal{AB}}, >_{\mathcal{AB}})$ be their lexicographic combination. Then $\geqslant_{\mathcal{AB}}$ orients the rules in $\mathcal{R}$ while $>_{\mathcal{AB}}$ orients those in $\mathsf{DP}(\mathcal{R})$:

$$\begin{array}{llll} 1\colon\ x+1 \geqslant_{\mathcal{A}} x+1 & 2\colon\ x+1 >_{\mathcal{A}} x & 3\colon\ x+1 \geqslant_{\mathcal{A}} x+1 & 4\colon\ x+1 >_{\mathcal{A}} 0 \\ 1\colon\ x+1 \geqslant_{\mathcal{B}} 0 & & 3\colon\ x+1 >_{\mathcal{B}} 0 & \end{array}$$

Hence, the termination of $\mathcal{R}$ is concluded by Theorems 1 and 2.

Remark 13. The following fact gives an alternative method for combining reduction pairs lexicographically: Given reduction pairs $(\geqslant_1, >_1)$ and $(\geqslant_2, >_2)$, the pair $(\geqslant_1 \cap \geqslant_2, >_{12})$ forms a reduction pair, where $>_{12}$ is defined as in Definition 5. Theorem 2 with such a reduction pair is equivalent to successive application of the same theorem. However, this approach cannot handle Example 12 with the reduction pairs used there, as it imposes the additional constraint $\mathsf{p}(\mathsf{s}(x)) \geqslant_{\mathcal{B}} x$. This prevents a successful termination proof, as mentioned in the introduction. It is worth noting that the use of the usable rule criterion [14,27] for Theorem 2 is not helpful here as $\mathsf{p}(\mathsf{s}(x)) \to x$ is a usable rule.

If monotone and invariant positions of combined reduction pairs are identified, one can combine multiple reduction pairs by successively applying Theorem 10. Let $(\geqslant_{12}, >_{12})$ be the lexicographic combination of combinable reduction pairs $(\geqslant_1, >_1)$ and $(\geqslant_2, >_2)$.

Lemma 14. *If the i-th argument position of a function symbol is $>_2$-monotone and $>_2$ is non-empty then the position is $>_1$-monotone. Similarly, if the i-th argument position of a function symbol is $\geqslant_1$-invariant and $>_1$ is non-empty then the position is $\geqslant_2$-invariant.*

Proof. We only show the first claim because the second is shown in a similar way. Due to the non-emptiness of $>_2$, there are terms t and u with $t >_2 u$. By monotonicity $f(t, \ldots, t, \ldots, t) >_2 f(t, \ldots, u, \ldots, t)$ is obtained. If the i-th argument position of f were $\geqslant_2$-invariant, we would also have $f(t, \ldots, u, \ldots, t) \geqslant_2 f(t, \ldots, t, \ldots, t)$, which leads to a contradiction. So the i-th argument position of f is not $\geqslant_2$-invariant, and therefore the claim follows from the combinability. □

Theorem 15. *If the i-th argument of a function symbol is $>_2$-monotone and $>_2$ is non-empty, then it is $>_{12}$-monotone too. Similarly, if the i-th argument of a function symbol is $\geqslant_1$-invariant and $>_1$ is non-empty, then it is $\geqslant_{12}$-invariant too.*

Proof. Again, we only show the first claim. Let $t = f(t_1, \ldots, t_i, \ldots, t_n)$, $u = f(t_1, \ldots, u', \ldots, t_n)$, and $t_i >_{12} u'$. If $t_i >_{12} u'$ is due to $t_i >_1 u'$ then Lemma 14 yields $t >_1 u$, from which $t >_{12} u$ follows. Otherwise, $t_i \geqslant_1 u'$ and $t_i >_2 u'$. As $\geqslant_1$ is closed under contexts and the i-th position is $>_2$-monotone, the inequalities $t \geqslant_1 u$ and $t >_2 u$ follow. Hence, $t >_{12} u$ is concluded. □

The non-emptiness condition in Theorem 15 cannot be dropped, see [24]. In practice, this is not a problem, because a usual reduction pair (including those mentioned in Remark 11) can be extended to another one $(\geqslant, >)$ so that satisfies $\mathsf{c}_1 > \mathsf{c}_2$ for fresh constant symbols c_1 and c_2.

Example 16 (continued from Example 12). We show the termination of the extended system $\mathcal{R}' = \mathcal{R} \cup \{0 + y \to y\}$. The set $\mathsf{DP}(\mathcal{R}')$ coincides with $\mathsf{DP}(\mathcal{R})$. The linear interpretation $\mathcal{C}$ with

$$0_{\mathcal{C}} = 1 \quad \mathsf{s}_{\mathcal{C}}(\underline{x}) = x \quad \mathsf{p}_{\mathcal{C}}(\underline{x}) = x \quad \mathsf{p}^{\sharp}_{\mathcal{C}}(x) = 0 \quad \underline{x} +_{\mathcal{C}} \underline{y} = x + y \quad \underline{x} +^{\sharp}_{\mathcal{C}} y = x$$

satisfies $0 + y >_{\mathcal{C}} y$ and $\mathcal{R}' \cup \mathsf{DP}(\mathcal{R}) \subseteq \geqslant_{\mathcal{C}}$. Therefore, $\mathcal{R} \subseteq \geqslant_{\mathcal{CAB}}$ and $\mathsf{DP}(\mathcal{R}) \subseteq >_{\mathcal{CAB}}$ are obtained if we extend $\mathcal{A}$ and $\mathcal{B}$ with $0_{\mathcal{A}} = 0$ and $0_{\mathcal{B}} = 0$. The combinability can be verified by Theorem 15. Hence, $\mathcal{R}$ is terminating.

As a side note, order of combination does not matter to combinability: Let $(\geqslant_1, >_1)$, $(\geqslant_2, >_2)$, and $(\geqslant_3, >_3)$ be reduction pairs such that $>_1$, $>_2$, and $>_3$ are non-empty. If $(\geqslant_1, >_1)$ is combinable with $(\geqslant_2, >_2)$ and also $(\geqslant_2, >_2)$ with $(\geqslant_3, >_3)$, then, by Theorem 15, $(\geqslant_{12}, >_{12})$ is combinable with $(\geqslant_3, >_3)$ and $(\geqslant_1, >_1)$ with $(\geqslant_{23}, >_{23})$.

4 Termination of the Battle of Hercules and Hydra

In this short section, we demonstrate a termination proof based on heterogeneous combination of reduction pairs. Among others, we pick up Touzet's TRS encoding of the Battle of Hercules and Hydra [28]; see also [7] for its backgrounds. Touzet's rewrite system $\mathcal{H}$ consists of the following eleven rules:

$$\begin{array}{rlrr}
1: & \mathbin{[\!]} \circ x \to \circ \mathbin{[\!]} x & 6: & \mathsf{H}(0, x) \to \circ\, x \\
2: & \bullet \mathbin{[\!]} x \to \mathbin{[\!]} \bullet \bullet\, x & 7: & \bullet\, \mathsf{H}(\mathsf{H}(0, y), z) \to \mathsf{c}^1(y, z) \\
3: & \circ\, x \to \bullet \mathbin{[\!]} x & 8: & \bullet\, \mathsf{H}(\mathsf{H}(\mathsf{H}(0, x), y), z) \to \mathsf{c}^2(x, y, z) \\
4: & \bullet\, x \to x & 9: & \bullet\, \mathsf{c}^1(x, y) \to \mathsf{c}^1(x, \mathsf{H}(x, y)) \\
5: & \mathsf{c}^1(y, z) \to \circ\, z & 10: & \bullet\, \mathsf{c}^2(x, y, z) \to \mathsf{c}^2(x, \mathsf{H}(x, y), z) \\
 & & 11: & \mathsf{c}^2(x, y, z) \to \circ\, \mathsf{H}(y, z)
\end{array}$$

Symbols $\mathbin{[\!]}$, $\circ$, and $\bullet$ are unary function symbols and their parentheses are omitted here.

While the original termination proof of $\mathcal{H}$ uses a sophisticated algebra on $\mathbb{O} \times \mathbb{N} \times \mathbb{N}$, our proof employs the combination of an ordinal interpretation on $\mathbb{O}$ and a

Knuth–Bendix order. Here $\mathbb{O}$ is the set of all ordinal numbers below ε_0. In order to ease the proof, we introduce an easy corollary of Theorems 1 and 2. Below, we write $\mathcal{E}\mathsf{mb}$ for the TRS consisting of the *embedding rule* $f(x_1, \ldots, x_n) \to x_i$ for all n-ary function symbols f and $1 \leqslant i \leqslant n$.

Corollary 17. *A TRS $\mathcal{R}$ is terminating if $\mathcal{R} \subseteq >$ and $\mathcal{E}\mathsf{mb} \subseteq \geqslant$ for some reduction pair $(\geqslant, >)$.*

Proof. Define $s \geqslant^\natural t$ and $s >^\natural t$ as $s^\natural \geqslant t^\natural$ and $s^\natural > t^\natural$, respectively. Here $t^\natural$ replaces all marked symbols $f^\sharp$ in t by the corresponding unmarked symbols f. Then $(\geqslant^\natural, >^\natural)$ is a reduction pair with $\mathcal{R} \subseteq \geqslant^\natural$. To show termination by Theorems 1 and 2, it remains to show $\mathsf{DP}(\mathcal{R}) \subseteq >^\natural$. Since every dependency pair $\ell^\sharp \to t^\sharp$ admits a rule $\ell \to r \in \mathcal{R}$ with $r \to^*_{\mathcal{E}\mathsf{mb}} t$, we have $\ell > r \geqslant t$ and thus $\ell^\sharp >^\natural t^\sharp$. □

Actually, we use the Knuth–Bendix order together with argument filtering. For verifying combinability, we need to identify monotone and invariant positions. Consider an arbitrary argument filter π. For brevity, we write $i \in \pi(f)$ if $\pi(f) = i$ or $\pi(f) = [\ldots, i, \ldots]$. Let $(\geqslant, >)$ be a monotone reduction pair. Not surprisingly, the i-th argument position of a function symbol f is $>^\pi$-monotone if $i \in \pi(f)$, and $\geqslant^\pi$-invariant otherwise.

We are ready to prove the termination of $\mathcal{H}$. Consider the algebra $\mathcal{O}$ on $\mathbb{O}$ with interpretations:

$$\begin{array}{llll}
\mathsf{0}_{\mathcal{O}} = 0 & \mathsf{c}^1_{\mathcal{O}}(\underline{x}, y) = y + \omega^{x+1} & \circ_{\mathcal{O}}(\underline{x}) = x & [\!]_{\mathcal{O}}(\underline{x}) = x \\
\mathsf{H}_{\mathcal{O}}(\underline{x}, \underline{y}) = \omega^x \oplus y & \mathsf{c}^2_{\mathcal{O}}(\underline{x}, y, \underline{z}) = z \oplus \omega^{y+\omega^{x+1}} & \bullet_{\mathcal{O}}(\underline{x}) = x &
\end{array}$$

Here $\oplus$ stands for natural addition and monotone positions are indicated by underlining. Remark that the second argument positions of c^1 and c^2 are not monotone, since the first argument position of $+$ on ordinals is not monotone (e.g. $1 + \omega = 0 + \omega$). The above interpretation is borrowed from the original proof. According to [28, Lemma 3], we have $\{5, 6, 11\} \cup (\mathcal{E}\mathsf{mb} \setminus \{12\text{–}14\}) \subseteq >_{\mathcal{O}}$ and $\{1\text{–}4, 7\text{–}10, 12\text{–}14\} \subseteq \geqslant_{\mathcal{O}}$, where $12\text{–}14$ denote the rules $\circ\, x \to x$, $\bullet\, x \to x$, and $[\!]\; x \to x$ in $\mathcal{E}\mathsf{mb}$, respectively. By taking the argument filter π with $\pi(\mathsf{0}) = \pi(\mathsf{H}) = \pi(\mathsf{c}^1) = \pi(\mathsf{c}^2) = [\,]$, and $\pi(\circ) = \pi(\bullet) = \pi([\!]) = [1]$ the rules in the latter group are simplified as follows:

$$\begin{array}{llll}
1:\; [\!] \circ x \to \circ [\!]\; x & 4:\; \bullet\, x \to x & 9:\; \bullet\, \mathsf{c}^1 \to \mathsf{c}^1 & 12:\; \circ\, x \to x \\
2:\; \bullet [\!]\; x \to [\!] \bullet \bullet\, x & 7:\; \bullet\, \mathsf{H} \to \mathsf{c}^1 & 10:\; \bullet\, \mathsf{c}^2 \to \mathsf{c}^2 & 13:\; \bullet\, x \to x \\
3:\; \circ\, x \to \bullet [\!]\; x & 8:\; \bullet\, \mathsf{H} \to \mathsf{c}^2 & & 14:\; [\!]\; x \to x
\end{array}$$

Consider the Knuth–Bendix order $>_{\mathsf{kbo}}$ induced from the precedence $\bullet \succ [\!] \succ \circ \succ \mathsf{c}^1 \succ \mathsf{c}^2$ and the admissible weight function (w_0, w) with:

$$w(\circ) = 2 \quad w_0 = w(\mathsf{0}) = w(\mathsf{H}) = w(\mathsf{c}^1) = w(\mathsf{c}^2) = w([\!]) = 1 \quad w(\bullet) = 0$$

It is not difficult to see that the Knuth–Bendix order orients the above simplified rules strictly, and thus, $\{1\text{–}4, 7\text{–}10, 12\text{–}14\} \subseteq >^\pi_{\mathsf{kbo}}$. As non-monotone argument positions with respect to $>_{\mathcal{O}}$ are filtered out by π, the reduction pairs $(\geqslant_{\mathcal{O}}, >_{\mathcal{O}})$ and $(\geqslant^{\pi}_{\mathsf{kbo}}, >^{\pi}_{\mathsf{kbo}})$ are combinable. Hence, the termination is concluded by Corollary 17.

Remark 18. We stress that the use of Theorem 10 is crucial for obtaining a termination proof (see [24]). In particular, the rule removal method [27] is not applicable because the reduction pair induced from Touzet's interpretation $\mathcal{O}$ lacks monotonicity.

5 Echelon-Form Matrix Interpretation

In this section, we investigate another technique to construct reduction pairs based on lexicographic comparison. The underlying observation is that, linear polynomial interpretations combined lexicographically (by the combinability criterion) can be regarded as a variant of the matrix interpretation which uses the lexicographic order pairs $(\geqslant^{\mathsf{lex}}, >^{\mathsf{lex}})$. Here $(x_1, \ldots, x_n)^T >^{\mathsf{lex}} (y_1, \ldots, y_n)^T$ if there exists an index $1 \leqslant i \leqslant n$ such that $x_i > y_i$ and $x_j = y_j$ for all $j < i$. The relation $\geqslant^{\mathsf{lex}}$ is the reflexive closure of $>^{\mathsf{lex}}$.

Example 19 (continued from Example 16). The three linear interpretations $\mathcal{C}$, $\mathcal{A}$, and $\mathcal{B}$ can be combined into the single algebra $\mathcal{M}$ on $\mathbb{N}^3$ with the interpretations:

$$\mathsf{s}_{\mathcal{M}}(\boldsymbol{x}) = \begin{pmatrix} 1&0&0 \\ 0&1&0 \\ 0&0&1 \end{pmatrix} \boldsymbol{x} + \begin{pmatrix} 0 \\ 1 \\ 1 \end{pmatrix} \qquad \mathsf{p}_{\mathcal{M}}(\boldsymbol{x}) = \begin{pmatrix} 1&0&0 \\ 0&1&0 \\ 0&0&0 \end{pmatrix} \boldsymbol{x} \qquad \mathsf{0}_{\mathcal{M}} = \boldsymbol{e}_1$$

$$\boldsymbol{x} +_{\mathcal{M}} \boldsymbol{y} = \begin{pmatrix} 1&0&0 \\ 0&1&0 \\ 0&0&1 \end{pmatrix} \boldsymbol{x} + \begin{pmatrix} 1&0&0 \\ 0&0&0 \\ 0&0&0 \end{pmatrix} \boldsymbol{y} \quad \boldsymbol{x} +^{\sharp}_{\mathcal{M}} \boldsymbol{y} = \begin{pmatrix} 1&0&0 \\ 0&1&0 \\ 0&0&1 \end{pmatrix} \boldsymbol{x} \quad \mathsf{p}^{\sharp}_{\mathcal{M}}(\boldsymbol{x}) = \boldsymbol{0}$$

For instance, $\mathsf{p}_{\mathcal{M}}(\boldsymbol{x}) = (x_1, x_2, 0) = (\mathsf{p}_{\mathcal{C}}(x_1), \mathsf{p}_{\mathcal{A}}(x_2), \mathsf{p}_{\mathcal{B}}(x_3))$ holds for $\boldsymbol{x} = (x_1, x_2, x_3)^T$. If we equip $\mathcal{M}$ with $\geqslant^{\mathsf{lex}}$, the reduction pair $(\geqslant_{\mathcal{M}}, >_{\mathcal{M}})$ coincides with the lexicographic combination employed in Example 16.

Let $\mathcal{M}$ be such a matrix interpretation equipped with the lexicographic order. Although $\mathcal{M}$ is well-founded, it cannot afford weak monotonicity for free (cf. Example 6), which is a relevant property for $(\geqslant_{\mathcal{M}}, >_{\mathcal{M}})$ to be a reduction pair. Below, we show that weak monotonicity is characterized by *(column) echelon-form* matrices.

Let A be an $m \times n$ matrix. The matrix A is in *(column) echelon form* if the following property holds for all $1 \leqslant i \leqslant m$ and $2 \leqslant j \leqslant n$: If $A_{k,j-1} = 0$ for all $k < i$ then $A_{i,j} = 0$. By definition, every echelon-form matrix is a lower-triangular matrix. In particular, $A_{1,j} = 0$ is enforced for every $2 \leqslant j$, as the premise is vacuously satisfied.

Example 20. The 2×2 and 3×3 echelon-form matrices are classified as follows:

$$\begin{pmatrix} 0&0 \\ *&0 \end{pmatrix} \quad \begin{pmatrix} +&0 \\ *&* \end{pmatrix} \quad \begin{pmatrix} 0&0&0 \\ 0&0&0 \\ *&0&0 \end{pmatrix} \quad \begin{pmatrix} 0&0&0 \\ +&0&0 \\ *&*&0 \end{pmatrix} \quad \begin{pmatrix} +&0&0 \\ *&0&0 \\ *&*&0 \end{pmatrix} \quad \begin{pmatrix} +&0&0 \\ *&+&0 \\ *&*&* \end{pmatrix}$$

Here $+$ stands for an arbitrary positive natural number, and $*$ for an arbitrary non-negative integer. The matrices $\left(\begin{smallmatrix}0&0\\0&1\end{smallmatrix}\right)$ and $\left(\begin{smallmatrix}0&0&0\\0&0&0\\0&1&0\end{smallmatrix}\right)$ are not in echelon form, so not all lower-triangular matrices are in echelon form.

Lemma 21. *Let A be an $m \times n$ matrix in echelon form. Then $A\boldsymbol{x} \geqslant^{\mathsf{lex}} A\boldsymbol{y}$ whenever $\boldsymbol{x} \geqslant^{\mathsf{lex}} \boldsymbol{y}$.*

Proof. We proceed by mathematical induction on m. If $n = 1$ then the claim is trivial, so assume $n > 1$ and let $\boldsymbol{x} = \left(\begin{smallmatrix}x_1\\\boldsymbol{x}'\end{smallmatrix}\right)$ and $\boldsymbol{y} = \left(\begin{smallmatrix}y_1\\\boldsymbol{y}'\end{smallmatrix}\right)$. We further analyze the first column of A. If $A_{i,1} = 0$ for all $1 \leqslant i < m$ (which is in particular true when $m = 1$), from the echelon formedness it holds that $A_{i,j} = 0$ except for $i = m$ and $j = 1$, and therefore

$$A\boldsymbol{x} = \begin{pmatrix}\mathbf{0}\\A_{m,1}x_1\end{pmatrix} \geqslant^{\mathsf{lex}} \begin{pmatrix}\mathbf{0}\\A_{m,1}y_1\end{pmatrix} = A\boldsymbol{y}.$$

Otherwise, by calculation, we have:

$$A = \begin{pmatrix}\mathbf{0} & O\\A_{i,1} & \mathbf{0}^T\\\boldsymbol{a} & A'\end{pmatrix} \qquad A\boldsymbol{x} = \begin{pmatrix}\mathbf{0}\\A_{i,1}x_1\\\boldsymbol{a}x_1 + A'\boldsymbol{x}'\end{pmatrix} \qquad A\boldsymbol{y} = \begin{pmatrix}\mathbf{0}\\A_{i,1}y_1\\\boldsymbol{a}y_1 + A'\boldsymbol{y}'\end{pmatrix}$$

Here $A_{i,1}$ is the first positive entry at the i-th row with $1 \leqslant i < m$, $\boldsymbol{a}$ is a vector of length $m - i > 0$, and A' is an $(m-i) \times (n-1)$ echelon-form matrix. If $\boldsymbol{x} \geqslant^{\mathsf{lex}} \boldsymbol{y}$ is due to $x_1 > y_1$ then $A_{i,1}x_1 > A_{i,1}y_1$ and therefore $A\boldsymbol{x} \geqslant^{\mathsf{lex}} A\boldsymbol{y}$. Otherwise, $x_1 = y_1$ and $\boldsymbol{x}' \geqslant^{\mathsf{lex}} \boldsymbol{y}'$. By the induction hypothesis $A'\boldsymbol{x}' \geqslant^{\mathsf{lex}} A'\boldsymbol{y}'$ and therefore $A\boldsymbol{x} \geqslant^{\mathsf{lex}} A\boldsymbol{y}$. □

Lemma 22. *Let A be an $m \times n$ matrix. If $\boldsymbol{x} \geqslant^{\mathsf{lex}} \boldsymbol{y}$ implies $A\boldsymbol{x} \geqslant^{\mathsf{lex}} A\boldsymbol{y}$ for all vectors $\boldsymbol{x}, \boldsymbol{y}$ of natural numbers, then A is in echelon form.*

See [24] for the proof of Lemma 22. Let $\mathcal{M}$ be an algebra whose carrier is the set of vectors of natural numbers ordered lexicographically and interpretations $f_{\mathcal{M}}(\boldsymbol{x}_1, \ldots, \boldsymbol{x}_n) = A_1\boldsymbol{x}_1 + \cdots + A_n\boldsymbol{x}_n + \boldsymbol{a}$ are built from echelon-form matrices $A_1, \ldots, A_n$. We dub such an algebra *echelon-form matrix interpretation.*

Theorem 23. *The pair $(\geqslant_{\mathcal{M}}, >_{\mathcal{M}})$ is a reduction pair for every echelon-form matrix interpretation $\mathcal{M}$.*

As expected, a lexicographic combination of d linear polynomial interpretations (satisfying the combinability criterion) corresponds to a d-dimensional echelon-form matrix interpretation whose non-diagonal entries are all zero.

Theorem 24. *Let $\mathcal{A}_1, \ldots, \mathcal{A}_d$ be linear polynomial interpretations such that $>_{\mathcal{A}_i}$ is non-empty for all $1 \leqslant i \leqslant d$, and $\mathcal{A}_i$ and $\mathcal{A}_{i+1}$ are combinable for all $1 \leqslant i < d$. Let $(\geqslant, >)$ is the lexicographic combination of $\mathcal{A}_1, \ldots, \mathcal{A}_d$. Then there is a d-dimensional echelon-form matrix interpretation $\mathcal{M}$ such that $(\geqslant, >)$ is identical to $(\geqslant_{\mathcal{M}}, >_{\mathcal{M}})$.*

To characterize strict monotonicity for $m \times n$ matrices A (i.e., the property that $\boldsymbol{x} >^{\mathsf{lex}} \boldsymbol{y}$ implies $A\boldsymbol{x} >^{\mathsf{lex}} A\boldsymbol{y}$), it suffices to additionally assume $n \leqslant m$ and $A_{i,i} > 0$ for all $1 \leqslant i \leqslant n$. Such an echelon-form matrix is called *positive.*

Example 25. The echelon-form matrix $A = \begin{pmatrix} 1 & 0 \end{pmatrix}$ is not positive, while A^T is. Indeed, A is not strictly monotone, as witnessed by $A\begin{pmatrix} 0 \\ 1 \end{pmatrix} = \begin{pmatrix} 0 \\ 0 \end{pmatrix} = A\begin{pmatrix} 0 \\ 0 \end{pmatrix}$.

Lemma 26. *Let A be an $m \times n$ positive echelon-form matrix. Then $A\boldsymbol{x} >^{\mathsf{lex}} A\boldsymbol{y}$ whenever $\boldsymbol{x} >^{\mathsf{lex}} \boldsymbol{y}$.*

Proof. We proceed by mathematical induction on n. The case $n = 1$ is trivial. Otherwise, write $\boldsymbol{x}, \boldsymbol{y}$ and A as follows:

$$\boldsymbol{x} = \begin{pmatrix} x_1 \\ \boldsymbol{x}' \end{pmatrix} \qquad \boldsymbol{y} = \begin{pmatrix} y_1 \\ \boldsymbol{y}' \end{pmatrix} \qquad A = \begin{pmatrix} A_{1,1} & \mathbf{0}^T \\ \boldsymbol{a} & A' \end{pmatrix}$$

Here $A_{1,1}$ is the first positive entry, $\boldsymbol{a}$ is a vector of length $m-1$, and A' is an $(m-1) \times (n-1)$ positive echelon-form matrix. A calculation shows that

$$A\boldsymbol{x} = \begin{pmatrix} A_{1,1}x_1 \\ \boldsymbol{a}x_1 + A'\boldsymbol{x}' \end{pmatrix} \qquad A\boldsymbol{y} = \begin{pmatrix} A_{1,1}y_1 \\ \boldsymbol{a}y_1 + A'\boldsymbol{y}' \end{pmatrix}$$

If $\boldsymbol{x} >^{\mathsf{lex}} \boldsymbol{y}$ is by $x_1 > y_1$ then $A_{1,1}x_1 > A_{1,1}y_1$ and therefore $A\boldsymbol{x} >^{\mathsf{lex}} A\boldsymbol{y}$. Otherwise, $x_1 = y_1$ and $\boldsymbol{x}' >^{\mathsf{lex}} \boldsymbol{y}'$. By the induction hypothesis $A'\boldsymbol{x}' >^{\mathsf{lex}} A'\boldsymbol{y}'$ and therefore $A\boldsymbol{x} >^{\mathsf{lex}} A\boldsymbol{y}$. □

Lemma 27. *Let A be an $m \times n$ matrix. If $\boldsymbol{x} >^{\mathsf{lex}} \boldsymbol{y}$ implies $A\boldsymbol{x} >^{\mathsf{lex}} A\boldsymbol{y}$ for all vectors $\boldsymbol{x}, \boldsymbol{y}$ of natural numbers, then A is a positive echelon-form matrix.*

See [24] for the proof of Lemma 27. Now we can characterize monotone and invariant positions of echelon-form matrix interpretations $\mathcal{M}$. Let the interpretation of an n-ary function symbol f be $f_{\mathcal{M}}(\boldsymbol{x}_1, \ldots, \boldsymbol{x}_n) = A_1\boldsymbol{x}_1 + \cdots + A_n\boldsymbol{x}_n + \boldsymbol{a}$. The i-th argument position of f is monotone if A_i is positive, and invariant if $A_i = O$. Besides, $(\geqslant_{\mathcal{M}}, >_{\mathcal{M}})$ is normal.

We again tame the Hydra, using an echelon-form matrix interpretation which has a positive non-diagonal entry and therefore goes beyond a combination of linear polynomial interpretations.

Example 28. Recall the TRS $\mathcal{H}$ in Sect. 4. Instead of the Knuth–Bendix order, we establish the termination by the combination of the ordinal interpretation $\mathcal{O}$ with the next echelon-form matrix interpretation $\mathcal{M}$:

$$\bullet_{\mathcal{M}}(\boldsymbol{x}) = \begin{pmatrix} 1 & 0 \\ 1 & 1 \end{pmatrix}\boldsymbol{x} + \begin{pmatrix} 0 \\ 1 \end{pmatrix} \quad \circ_{\mathcal{M}}(\boldsymbol{x}) = \begin{pmatrix} 2 & 0 \\ 0 & 1 \end{pmatrix}\boldsymbol{x} + \begin{pmatrix} 3 \\ 0 \end{pmatrix} \quad [\!]_{\mathcal{M}}(\boldsymbol{x}) = \begin{pmatrix} 2 & 0 \\ 0 & 1 \end{pmatrix}\boldsymbol{x} + \begin{pmatrix} 2 \\ 0 \end{pmatrix}$$

The other interpretations $\mathsf{0}_{\mathcal{M}}$, $\mathsf{H}_{\mathcal{M}}(\overline{\boldsymbol{x}}, \overline{\boldsymbol{y}})$, $\mathsf{c}^1{}_{\mathcal{M}}(\overline{\boldsymbol{x}}, \overline{\boldsymbol{y}})$, and $\mathsf{c}^2{}_{\mathcal{M}}(\overline{\boldsymbol{x}}, \overline{\boldsymbol{y}}, \overline{\boldsymbol{z}})$ are defined as the constant vector $\mathbf{0}$. One can confirm the combinability, $\mathcal{R} \subseteq >_{\mathcal{OM}}$, and $\mathcal{E}\mathsf{mb} \subseteq \geqslant_{\mathcal{OM}}$. For instance, the orientations $[\!] \circ x >_{\mathcal{M}} \circ [\!]\ x$ and $\bullet\, [\!]\ x >_{\mathcal{M}} [\!] \bullet \bullet\, x$ of the first two rules in $\mathcal{H}$ are verified as follows:

$$1\colon \begin{pmatrix} 4 & 0 \\ 0 & 1 \end{pmatrix}\boldsymbol{x} + \begin{pmatrix} 8 \\ 0 \end{pmatrix} >^{\mathsf{lex}} \begin{pmatrix} 4 & 0 \\ 0 & 1 \end{pmatrix}\boldsymbol{x} + \begin{pmatrix} 7 \\ 0 \end{pmatrix} \quad 2\colon \begin{pmatrix} 2 & 0 \\ 2 & 1 \end{pmatrix}\boldsymbol{x} + \begin{pmatrix} 2 \\ 3 \end{pmatrix} >^{\mathsf{lex}} \begin{pmatrix} 2 & 0 \\ 2 & 1 \end{pmatrix}\boldsymbol{x} + \begin{pmatrix} 2 \\ 2 \end{pmatrix}$$

So, the termination of $\mathcal{H}$ is again concluded.

The standard matrix interpretation with the component-wise order and our echelon-form matrix interpretation are incomparable. For example, the termination of the TRS $\mathcal{R}$

$$\mathsf{f}(x,\mathsf{s}(y),z) \to \mathsf{f}(x,y,\mathsf{s}(\mathsf{s}(z))) \qquad \mathsf{f}(\mathsf{s}(x),y,z) \to \mathsf{f}(x,z,y) \qquad \mathsf{f}(x,y,z) \to y$$

can be shown by the echelon-form matrix interpretation $\mathcal{A}$:

$$\mathsf{f}_{\mathcal{A}}^{(\sharp)}(\boldsymbol{x},\boldsymbol{y},\boldsymbol{z}) = \boldsymbol{x} + \begin{pmatrix}1&0&0\\0&0&0\\0&1&0\end{pmatrix}\boldsymbol{y} + \begin{pmatrix}1&0&0\\0&0&0\\0&0&0\end{pmatrix}\boldsymbol{z} + \boldsymbol{e}_1 \qquad \mathsf{s}_{\mathcal{A}}(\boldsymbol{x}) = \boldsymbol{x} + \boldsymbol{e}_2$$

It is easy to verify $\mathsf{DP}(\mathcal{R}) \subseteq {>_{\mathcal{A}}}$ and $\mathcal{R} \subseteq {\geqslant_{\mathcal{A}}}$. On the other hand, any standard matrix interpretation cannot satisfy them. This is seen by a complexity consideration: Let $[n] = \mathsf{s}^n(x)$ and $t_n = \mathsf{f}^\sharp(\mathsf{f}([n],[1],[0]),[1],[0])$. Then

$$t_n \to_{\mathcal{R}}^* \mathsf{f}^\sharp([2^n],[1],[0]) \to_{\mathsf{DP}(\mathcal{R})}^* \mathsf{f}^\sharp([0],[2^{2^n}],[0]) \to_{\mathsf{DP}(\mathcal{R})}^{2^{2^n}} \mathsf{f}^\sharp([0],[0],[2^{1+2^n}])$$

holds for every $n \in \mathbb{N}$. Observe that the number of rewrite steps by $\mathsf{DP}(\mathcal{R})$ is double exponential. However, the interpretation of t_n cannot bound such a number from above; see the proof of [8, Lemma 7].

For the converse, we consider the TRS $\mathcal{R} = \{\mathsf{f}(\mathsf{a}) \to \mathsf{f}(\mathsf{b}), \mathsf{g}(\mathsf{b}) \to \mathsf{g}(\mathsf{a})\}$. Then $\mathsf{DP}(\mathcal{R}) = \{\mathsf{f}^\sharp(\mathsf{a}) \to \mathsf{f}^\sharp(\mathsf{b}), \mathsf{g}^\sharp(\mathsf{b}) \to \mathsf{g}^\sharp(\mathsf{a})\}$. The next standard matrix interpretation $\mathcal{A}$ satisfies $\mathcal{R} \subseteq {\geqslant_{\mathcal{A}}}$ and $\mathsf{DP}(\mathcal{R}) \subseteq {>_{\mathcal{A}}}$:

$$\mathsf{a}_{\mathcal{A}} = \begin{pmatrix}1\\0\end{pmatrix} \qquad \mathsf{b}_{\mathcal{A}} = \begin{pmatrix}0\\1\end{pmatrix} \qquad \mathsf{f}_{\mathcal{A}}(\boldsymbol{x}) = \begin{pmatrix}1&1\\0&0\end{pmatrix}\boldsymbol{x} \qquad \mathsf{g}_{\mathcal{A}}(\boldsymbol{x}) = \begin{pmatrix}1&1\\1&1\end{pmatrix}\boldsymbol{x}$$

$$\mathsf{f}^\sharp_{\mathcal{A}}(\boldsymbol{x}) = \begin{pmatrix}1&1\\0&1\end{pmatrix}\boldsymbol{x} \qquad \mathsf{g}^\sharp_{\mathcal{A}}(\boldsymbol{x}) = \begin{pmatrix}0&1\\0&0\end{pmatrix}\boldsymbol{x}$$

Here, it is essential that a and b are incomparable with respect to the underlying component-wise order. Indeed, there is no echelon-form matrix interpretation $\mathcal{A}$ with $\mathcal{R} \subseteq {\geqslant_{\mathcal{A}}}$ and $\mathsf{DP}(\mathcal{R}) \subseteq {>_{\mathcal{A}}}$ due to totality of the lexicographic order: Any interpretation $\mathcal{A}$ satisfies $\mathsf{a} \geqslant_{\mathcal{A}} \mathsf{b}$ or $\mathsf{b} \geqslant_{\mathcal{A}} \mathsf{a}$. If $\mathsf{a} \geqslant_{\mathcal{A}} \mathsf{b}$ holds then $\mathsf{g}^\sharp(\mathsf{a}) \geqslant_{\mathcal{A}} \mathsf{g}^\sharp(\mathsf{b})$ by monotonicity. Similarly, if $\mathsf{b} \geqslant_{\mathcal{A}} \mathsf{a}$ then $\mathsf{f}^\sharp(\mathsf{b}) \geqslant_{\mathcal{A}} \mathsf{f}^\sharp(\mathsf{a})$. In either case it contradicts to $\mathsf{DP}(\mathcal{R}) \subseteq {>_{\mathcal{A}}}$.

6 Experiments

In order to evaluate the presented methods, we have implemented a prototype tool for proving termination and relative termination of (finite) TRSs. The tool uses the dependency pair framework (Theorems 1 and 2) together with two standard refinements: an iterative cycle analysis based on strongly connected components in dependency graphs [1,10,13], and the usable rule criterion [14]. For relative termination, the tool uses the relative version of Theorem 1 (a generalization of Theorem 3), which cannot be used with the usable rule criterion due to lack of minimality, see [15]. We compare the three classes of reduction pairs and their lexicographic combinations.

Table 1. Experiments on 1528 termination problems.

	L	LL	LLL	E_1	E_2	E_3	E_4	S_2	S_2S_2	$S_2S_2S_2$	E_1E_1	E_1L	LE_1
proved	372	389	389	464	562	566	564	593	619	617	506	496	406
timeout	*8*	*8*	*8*	*8*	*14*	*28*	*84*	*24*	*39*	*60*	*8*	*8*	*8*

Table 2. Experiments on 57 relative termination problems.

	L	LL	LLL	E_1	E_2	E_3	E_4	S_2	S_2S_2	$S_2S_2S_2$	E_1E_1	E_1L	LE_1
proved	4	20	22	8	43	45	47	10	47	47	41	30	27
timeout	*0*	*0*	*0*	*0*	*0*	*0*	*0*	*0*	*0*	*0*	*0*	*0*	*0*

- L: lexicographic path orders [16] with argument filtering.
- E_d: echelon-form matrix interpretations on $\mathbb{N}^d$ with $0, 1$-matrix coefficients equipped with the lexicographic order (Section 5).
- S_d: matrix interpretations on $\mathbb{N}^d$ with $0, 1$-matrix coefficients equipped with the standard component-wise order [8]. Note that S_1 is the same as E_1.

Suitable precedences, argument filters, and interpretations are searched by the SMT solver Z3 [22]; see [4,31] for the SAT/SMT encoding techniques. The experiments were run on a PC with Intel Core i5-1340P CPU (4.6 GHz) and 8 GB memory with 60 seconds timeout for each (relative) termination problem.[1]

Table 1 summarizes the experimental results on 1528 termination problems in the TRS Standard category of the Termination Problem Database [26]. For instance, the numbers in column E_1L are read as follows: In the aforementioned setting, lexicographic combinations of E_1 (linear interpretations) with L (the lexicographic path order with argument filtering) proved termination of 496 TRSs, while termination analysis on 13 TRSs did not finish within 60 seconds. In general, combination gives us more proofs. For example, while L and E_1 produce 503 proofs in total, the union of L, E_1, LE_1, and E_1L amounts to 533 proofs. The experimental results show that the echelon-form matrix interpretation (E_2) outperforms lexicographic combination of linear polynomials (E_1E_1). The union of all methods amounts to 649 proofs, which include eight proofs missed by the state-of-the-art termination tool NaTT [29] (version 2.3.2).

Table 2 summarizes the experimental results on relative termination. The TRS Relative category in the database contains 57 relative termination problems where Theorem 3 is applicable. Two of these problems are known to be relatively non-terminating. The union of E_4 and LL amounts to 50 proofs. We note that the union includes 5 problems missed by the 2022 version of NaTT, and 11 missed by another powerful termination tool AProVE [11,17]. The following example (`INVY_15/#3.42`) is one of the 11 problems.[2]

[1] The tool and the full experimental data are available at https://www.jaist.ac.jp/project/saigawa/25cade/.

[2] This problem can be solved by NaTT.

Example 29. Consider the relative termination problem of $\mathcal{R}/\mathcal{S}$. Here $\mathcal{R}$ consists of the rules

$$\begin{aligned} \mathsf{half}(\mathsf{0}) &\to \mathsf{0} & \mathsf{lastbit}(\mathsf{0}) &\to \mathsf{0} \\ \mathsf{half}(\mathsf{s}(\mathsf{0})) &\to \mathsf{0} & \mathsf{lastbit}(\mathsf{s}(\mathsf{0})) &\to \mathsf{s}(\mathsf{0}) \\ \mathsf{half}(\mathsf{s}(\mathsf{s}(x))) &\to \mathsf{s}(\mathsf{half}(x)) & \mathsf{lastbit}(\mathsf{s}(\mathsf{s}(x))) &\to \mathsf{lastbit}(x) \\ \mathsf{conv}(\mathsf{0}) &\to \mathsf{cons}(\mathsf{nil}, \mathsf{0}) \\ \mathsf{conv}(\mathsf{s}(x)) &\to \mathsf{cons}(\mathsf{conv}(\mathsf{half}(\mathsf{s}(x))), \mathsf{lastbit}(\mathsf{s}(x))) \end{aligned}$$

and $\mathcal{S} = \{\mathsf{rand}(x) \to x,\ \mathsf{rand}(x) \to \mathsf{rand}(\mathsf{s}(x))\}$. The set $\mathsf{DP}(\mathcal{R})$ consists of

$$\begin{aligned} \mathsf{half}^\sharp(\mathsf{s}(\mathsf{s}(x))) &\to \mathsf{half}^\sharp(x) & \mathsf{conv}^\sharp(\mathsf{s}(x)) &\to \mathsf{conv}^\sharp(\mathsf{half}(\mathsf{s}(x))) \\ \mathsf{lastbit}^\sharp(\mathsf{s}(\mathsf{s}(x))) &\to \mathsf{lastbit}^\sharp(x) & \mathsf{conv}^\sharp(\mathsf{s}(x)) &\to \mathsf{half}^\sharp(\mathsf{s}(x)) \\ & & \mathsf{conv}^\sharp(\mathsf{s}(x)) &\to \mathsf{lastbit}^\sharp(\mathsf{s}(x)) \end{aligned}$$

The following echelon-form matrix interpretation $\mathcal{A}$ on $\mathbb{N}^3$ satisfies $\mathsf{DP}(\mathcal{R}) \subseteq {>_\mathcal{A}}$ and $\mathcal{R} \cup \mathcal{S} \subseteq {\geqslant_\mathcal{A}}$.

$$\begin{aligned} &\mathsf{0}_\mathcal{A} = \mathbf{0} & &\mathsf{nil}_\mathcal{A} = \mathbf{0} & &\mathsf{lastbit}_\mathcal{A}(\boldsymbol{x}) = \boldsymbol{e}_1 & &\mathsf{conv}_\mathcal{A}(\boldsymbol{x}) = \mathbf{0} \\ &\mathsf{s}_\mathcal{A}(\boldsymbol{x}) = \boldsymbol{x} + \boldsymbol{e}_2 & &\mathsf{cons}_\mathcal{A}(\boldsymbol{x}, \boldsymbol{y}) = \mathbf{0} & &\mathsf{lastbit}^\sharp_\mathcal{A}(\boldsymbol{x}) = \boldsymbol{x} & &\mathsf{conv}^\sharp_\mathcal{A}(\boldsymbol{x}) = \boldsymbol{x} + \boldsymbol{e}_1 \end{aligned}$$

$$\mathsf{half}_\mathcal{A}(\boldsymbol{x}) = \begin{pmatrix} 1 & 0 & 0 \\ 0 & 1 & 0 \\ 0 & 0 & 0 \end{pmatrix} \boldsymbol{x} \qquad \mathsf{half}^\sharp_\mathcal{A}(\boldsymbol{x}) = \boldsymbol{x} \qquad \mathsf{rand}_\mathcal{A}(\boldsymbol{x}) = \begin{pmatrix} 1 & 0 & 0 \\ 0 & 0 & 0 \\ 0 & 0 & 0 \end{pmatrix} \boldsymbol{x} + \boldsymbol{e}_1$$

Since $\mathcal{R}$ dominates $\mathcal{S}$ and $\mathcal{S}$ is non-duplicating, the above inclusions together with Theorem 3 entail the termination of $\mathcal{R}/\mathcal{S}$.

Remark 30. The particular usefulness of our lexicographic combination in relative termination can be explained in terms of the usable rule criterion, which gives fewer constraints on the quasi-order $\geqslant$ of a reduction pair $(\geqslant, >)$. However, as mentioned earlier in this section, the technique cannot be applied with Theorem 3 for relative termination, due to absence of minimality of dependency pair problems. In contrast, Theorem 10 can be used with Theorem 3 (as it does not rely on minimality) and allows us to ignore some rules in latter components of lexicographic combination, provided that the combinability condition is met.

Further experimental comparison with the weighted path order [30] and the max/plus interpretation is found in [24].

7 Conclusion

We have presented a simple criterion for combining reduction pairs based on monotone and invariant positions. By examples and experiments, the criterion is shown to be complementary to existing methods of lexicographic combination of reduction pairs. In particular, the experiments show that state-of-the-art tools may benefit from our method. We have also elucidated when the matrix interpretation with the lexicographic order induces a reduction pair. We conclude the paper by stating related work and future work.

Our combinability criterion (Theorem 10) is inspired by Touzet's work [28]. It is easy to confirm the precise correspondence between her original interpretation $\mathcal{A}$ and Example 28. For instance, $\bullet_{\mathcal{A}}((x, m, n)) = (x, m, m + n + 1)$ corresponds to $\bullet_{\mathcal{O}}(x) = x$ and $\bullet_{\mathcal{M}}((\begin{smallmatrix} m \\ n \end{smallmatrix})) = (\begin{smallmatrix} 1 & 0 \\ 1 & 1 \end{smallmatrix})(\begin{smallmatrix} m \\ n \end{smallmatrix}) + (\begin{smallmatrix} 0 \\ 1 \end{smallmatrix})$. We anticipate that the use of lexicographic combination eases termination analysis of challenging rewrite systems such as Goodstein sequences [32].

The ordinal interpretation in a certain form is the echelon-form matrix interpretation and lexicographic combination of the linear polynomial interpretation. To see this, consider linear polynomial interpretations

$$f_{\mathcal{A}}(x_1, \ldots, x_n) = a_0 + \sum_i a_i x_i \qquad f_{\mathcal{B}}(y_1, \ldots, y_n) = b_0 + \sum_i b_i y_i$$

with $a_i, b_i \in \mathbb{N}$ and the interpretation $f_{\mathcal{O}}$ on ordinal numbers below ω^2 given by:

$$f_{\mathcal{O}}(\omega x_1 + y_1, \ldots, \omega x_n + y_1) = \omega(a_0 + a_1 x_1 + \cdots + a_n x_n) + (b_0 + b_1 y_1 + \cdots + b_n y_n)$$

Here x_i and y_i range over $\mathbb{N}$. Then, $(\geqslant_{\mathcal{O}}, >_{\mathcal{O}})$ is order isomorphic to $(\geqslant_{\mathcal{AB}}, >_{\mathcal{AB}})$. In general, an n-times combination of the linear polynomial interpretation corresponds to an ordinal interpretation below ω^n. For instance, the echelon-form matrix interpretation $\mathsf{rand}_{\mathcal{A}}$ of Example 29 corresponds to $\mathsf{rand}_{\mathcal{O}}(\omega^2 x_1 + \omega x_2 + x_3) = \omega^2(x_1 + 1)$ with $x_1, x_2, x_3 \in \mathbb{N}$. Actually, it is equivalent to $\mathsf{rand}_{\mathcal{O}}(x) = x + \omega^2$ for $x < \omega^3$.

Theorem 24 states a correspondence between the echelon-form matrix interpretation and a special class of lexicographic combination with linear polynomials. A possible line of future work is to extend this result to a broader class of lexicographic combination.

Adapting the echelon-form matrix interpretation for AC termination is another direction for future work. As shown in [3,21], lexicographic combination of *non-linear* polynomial interpretations is an effective proof method for AC termination. We believe that the non-linear matrix interpretation [5], using matrices instead of vectors, is a key for the work. Speaking of matrix, theoretical and experimental comparison of existing matrix methods (including [20,23]) to ours is yet to be done. In particular, we anticipate that derivational complexity is useful to distinguish the powers of the matrix-based methods.

Acknowledgments. We are grateful to the anonymous reviewers for the valuable comments and suggestions. This research was supported by JST SPRING Grant Number JPMJSP2102 and JSPS KAKENHI Grant Numbers JP22K11900 and JP25KJ1363.

Disclosure of Interests. The authors have no competing interests to declare that are relevant to the content of this article.

References

1. Arts, T., Giesl, J.: Termination of term rewriting using dependency pairs. Theor. Comput. Sci. **236**, 133–178 (2000). https://doi.org/10.1016/S0304-3975(99)00207-8
2. Baader, F., Nipkow, T.: Term Rewriting and All That. Cambridge University Press (1998). https://doi.org/10.1017/CBO9781139172752
3. Ben Cherifa, A., Lescanne, P.: Termination of rewriting systems by polynomial interpretations and its implementation. Sci. Comput. Program. **9**(2), 137–159 (1987). https://doi.org/10.1016/0167-6423(87)90030-X
4. Codish, M., Giesl, J., Schneider-Kamp, P., Thiemann, R.: SAT solving for termination proofs with recursive path orders and dependency pairs. J. Autom. Reason. **49**, 53–93 (2012). https://doi.org/10.1145/1890028.1890030
5. Courtieu, P., Gbedo, G., Pons, O.: Improved matrix interpretation. In: van Leeuwen, J., Muscholl, A., Peleg, D., Pokorný, J., Rumpe, B. (eds.) SOFSEM 2010. LNCS, vol. 5901, pp. 283–295. Springer, Heidelberg (2010). https://doi.org/10.1007/978-3-642-11266-9_24
6. Dershowitz, N.: Orderings for term-rewriting systems. Theor. Comput. Sci. **17**, 279–301 (1982). https://doi.org/10.1016/0304-3975(82)90026-3
7. Dershowitz, N., Moser, G.: The Hydra battle revisited. In: Rewriting, Computation and Proof, Essays Dedicated to Jean-Pierre Jouannaud on the Occasion of his 60th Birthday. LNCS, vol. 4600, pp. 1–27 (2007). https://doi.org/10.1007/978-3-540-73147-4_1
8. Endrullis, J., Waldmann, J., Zantema, H.: Matrix interpretations for proving termination of term rewriting. J. Autom. Reasoning **40**(2-3), 195–220 (2008). https://doi.org/10.1007/S10817-007-9087-9
9. Geser, A.: Relative Termination. Ph.D. thesis, University of Passau, Germany (1990). http://vts.uni-ulm.de/docs/2012/8146/vts_8146_11884.pdf
10. Giesl, J., Arts, T., Ohlebusch, E.: Modular termination proofs for rewriting using dependency pairs. J. Symbolic Comput. **34**, 21–58 (2002). https://doi.org/10.1006/jsco.2002.0541
11. Giesl, J., et al.: Analyzing program termination and complexity automatically with AProVE. J. Autom. Reasoning **58**, 3–31 (2017). https://doi.org/10.1007/s10817-016-9388-y
12. Giesl, J., Thiemann, R., Schneider-Kamp, P.: The dependency pair framework: combining techniques for automated termination proofs. In: Baader, F., Voronkov, A. (eds.) LPAR 2005. LNCS (LNAI), vol. 3452, pp. 301–331. Springer, Heidelberg (2005). https://doi.org/10.1007/978-3-540-32275-7_21
13. Hirokawa, N., Middeldorp, A.: Automating the dependency pair method. Inf. Comput. **199**(1–2), 172–199 (2005). https://doi.org/10.1016/J.IC.2004.10.004
14. Hirokawa, N., Middeldorp, A.: Tyrolean termination tool: techniques and features. Inf. Comput. **205**(4), 474–511 (2007). https://doi.org/10.1016/J.IC.2006.08.010
15. Iborra, J., Nishida, N., Vidal, G., Yamada, A.: Relative termination via dependency pairs. J. Autom. Reasoning **58**, 391–411 (2017). https://doi.org/10.1007/s10817-016-9373-5
16. Kamin, S., Lévy, J.: Two generalizations of the recursive path ordering. Tech. rep., University of Illinois (1980), unpublished manuscript
17. Kassing, J.C., Vartanyan, G., Giesl, J.: A dependency pair framework for relative termination of term rewriting. In: Proceedings of 12th International Joint Conference on Automated Reasoning. LNCS, vol. 14740, pp. 360–380 (2024). https://doi.org/10.1007/978-3-031-63501-4_19

18. Kirby, L., Paris, J.: Accessible independence results for Peano arithmetic. Bull. London Math. Soc. **14**, 285–325 (1982). https://doi.org/10.1112/blms/14.4.285
19. Knuth, D., Bendix, P.: Simple word problems in universal algebras. In: Leech, J. (ed.) Computational Problems in Abstract Algebra, pp. 263–297. Pergamon Press (1970)
20. Koprowski, A., Waldmann, J.: Arctic termination ...below zero. In: Voronkov, A. (ed.) RTA 2008. LNCS, vol. 5117, pp. 202–216. Springer, Heidelberg (2008). https://doi.org/10.1007/978-3-540-70590-1_14
21. Lankford, D.: On proving term rewriting systems are noetherian. Louisiana Technical University, Tech. rep. (1979)
22. de Moura, L., Bjørner, N.: Z3: an efficient SMT solver. In: Ramakrishnan, C.R., Rehof, J. (eds.) TACAS 2008. LNCS, vol. 4963, pp. 337–340. Springer, Heidelberg (2008). https://doi.org/10.1007/978-3-540-78800-3_24
23. Neurauter, F., Middeldorp, A.: Revisiting matrix interpretations for proving termination of term rewriting. In: Proceedings of 22nd International Conference on Rewriting Techniques and Applications. LIPIcs, vol. 10, pp. 251–266 (2011). https://doi.org/10.4230/LIPICS.RTA.2011.251
24. Saito, T., Hirokawa, N.: Lexicographic combination of reduction pairs (extended version) (2025), under preparation
25. Terese: Term Rewriting Systems. Cambridge University Press (2003)
26. Termination Community: The Termination Problem Database (TPDB). https://github.com/TermCOMP/TPDB. Accessed 05 Dec 2023
27. Thiemann, R., Giesl, J., Schneider-Kamp, P.: Improved modular termination proofs using dependency pairs. In: Basin, D., Rusinowitch, M. (eds.) IJCAR 2004. LNCS (LNAI), vol. 3097, pp. 75–90. Springer, Heidelberg (2004). https://doi.org/10.1007/978-3-540-25984-8_4
28. Touzet, H.: Encoding the Hydra battle as a rewrite system. In: Proceedings of 23rd International Symposium on Mathematical Foundations of Computer Science. LNCS, vol. 1450, pp. 267–276 (1998). https://doi.org/10.1007/BFb0055776
29. Yamada, A., Kusakari, K., Sakabe, T.: Nagoya termination tool. In: Dowek, G. (ed.) RTA 2014. LNCS, vol. 8560, pp. 466–475. Springer, Cham (2014). https://doi.org/10.1007/978-3-319-08918-8_32
30. Yamada, A., Kusakari, K., Sakabe, T.: A unified ordering for termination proving. Sci. Comput. Program. **111**, 110–134 (2015). https://doi.org/10.1016/j.scico.2014.07.009
31. Zankl, H., Hirokawa, N., Middeldorp, A.: KBO orientability. J. Autom. Reason. **43**, 173–201 (2009). https://doi.org/10.1007/s10817-009-9131-z
32. Zankl, H., Winkler, S., Middeldorp, A.: Beyond polynomials and Peano arithmetic - automation of elementary and ordinal interpretations. J. Symbolic Comput. **69**, 129–158 (2015). https://doi.org/10.1016/J.JSC.2014.09.033

Confluence of Almost Parallel-Closed Generalized Term Rewriting Systems

Salvador Lucas(✉)

DSIC & VRAIN, Universitat Politècnica de València, Valencia, Spain
slucas@dsic.upv.es

Abstract. *Generalized Term Rewriting Systems* (GTRSs) extend Conditional Term Rewriting Systems by (i) selecting the arguments of function symbols on which rewritings are allowed and (ii) allowing for more general conditions in rules, namely, atoms defined by a set of Horn clauses. They are useful to model and analyze properties of computations with sophisticated languages like Maude. Toyama proved that left-linear and *almost parallel-closed* Term Rewriting Systems (TRSs) are confluent. In this paper, we generalize and extend his result to GTRSs *without requiring left-linearity*. This improves Toyama's result, as we show with some examples. Also, Toyama's result entails confluence of weakly orthogonal TRSs, thus providing a syntactic criterion for proving confluence *without requiring termination*. We similarly introduce *weakly V-orthogonal* GTRSs, which are confluent. Weak V-orthogonality checking is implemented in the confluence tool CONFident, to improve its ability to deal with context-sensitive and conditional term rewriting systems.

Keywords: Conditional rewriting · Confluence · Program analysis

1 Introduction

A *Generalized Term Rewriting System (GTRS)* is a tuple $\mathcal{R} = (\mathcal{F}, \Pi, \mu, H, R)$, where $\mathcal{F}$ (resp. Π) is a signature of *function (resp. predicate) symbols*, with $\to, \to^* \in \Pi$; μ is a *replacement map* selecting *active* arguments of function symbols that can be rewritten [18]; H is a set of *definite Horn clauses* $A \Leftarrow c$, where the predicate symbol of A is not $\to$ or $\to^*$; and R is a set of *rewrite rules* $\ell \to r \Leftarrow c$ where ℓ is not a variable. [21, Definition 51]. In both cases, c is a sequence of atoms (Fig. 1)[1]. GTRSs aim to provide a sufficiently expressive class of (first-order) rewriting-based systems covering features in use in existing languages

[1] In the following, we mark in red the non-active, or *frozen* subterms in rules. Although only the pdf version of the submission display them, the distinction can still be helpful, avoiding more 'invasive' notations such as underlining or overlining.

Supported by project PID2021-122830OB-C42 funded by MCIN/AEI/10.13039/501100011033 and by "ERDF A way of making Europe" and by the grant CIPROM/2022/6 funded by Generalitat Valenciana.

C. Barrett and U. Waldmann (Eds.): CADE 2025, LNAI 15943, pp. 187–206, 2025.
https://doi.org/10.1007/978-3-031-99984-0_11

$$\mathsf{Neq}(0, \mathsf{s}(n)) \tag{1}$$
$$\mathsf{Neq}(\mathsf{s}(n), 0) \tag{2}$$
$$\mathsf{Neq}(\mathsf{s}(m), \mathsf{s}(n)) \Leftarrow \mathsf{Neq}(m, n) \tag{3}$$
$$\mathsf{from}(n) \to n : \mathsf{from}(\mathsf{s}(n)) \tag{4}$$
$$\mathsf{rm}(x, \mathsf{nil}) \to \mathsf{nil} \tag{5}$$
$$\mathsf{rm}(x, x : xs) \to \mathsf{rm}(x, xs) \tag{6}$$
$$\mathsf{rm}(x, y : xs) \to y : \mathsf{rm}(x, xs) \Leftarrow \mathsf{Neq}(x, y) \tag{7}$$
$$\mathsf{edups}(\mathsf{nil}) \to \mathsf{nil} \tag{8}$$
$$\mathsf{edups}(x : \mathsf{nil}) \to x : \mathsf{nil} \tag{9}$$
$$\mathsf{edups}(x : x : xs) \to \mathsf{edups}(x : xs) \tag{10}$$
$$\mathsf{edups}(x : y : xs) \to x : \mathsf{rm}(x, \mathsf{edups}(y : xs)) \Leftarrow \mathsf{Neq}(x, y) \tag{11}$$

Fig. 1. A GTRS to eliminate duplicates of natural numbers from lists

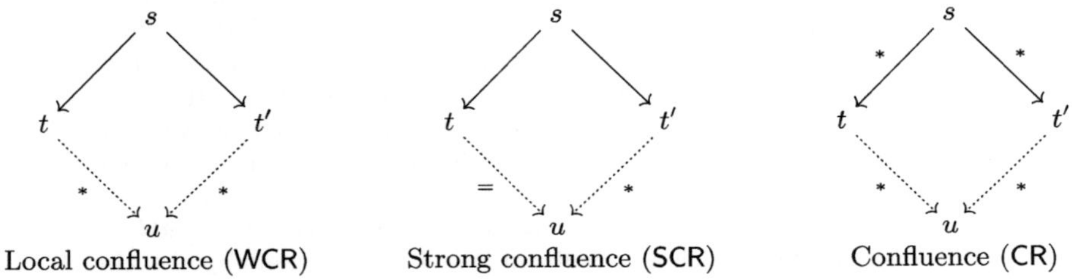

Fig. 2. Different confluence properties

(e.g., Maude [3], cf., [22, Section 8]), so that they can be faithfully modeled and their computational properties can be investigated through GTRSs. The semantic description of a GTRS as a first-order theory, is directly obtained from its specification. This permits the use of logic-based engines (theorem provers, model generators, etc.) for analysis and verification purposes. For instance, the usual classes of CTRSs (*join*, *oriented*, *semi-equational* [26, Definition 7.1.3]) can be investigated as particular cases of GTRSs where the specific evaluation of conditions is made explicit by means of appropriate Horn clauses, see [21, Section 7.3]. Furthermore,"unexplored" classes of CTRSs, where such evaluation schemes can be mixed, even in different conditions of the same rule, can also be easily investigated using GTRSs by applying existing results (also those in this paper).

A binary relation $\to$ on a set A is *(locally, strongly) confluent* if for all s, t, and t' in A, the corresponding diagram in Fig. 2 commutes (where $\to^*$ is the reflexive and transitive closure of $\to$ and $\to^=$ is $\to$ extended with the equality on A: $\to \cup \{=\}$). Strong confluence (SCR) implies confluence (CR), which implies local confluence (WCR), i.e., SCR $\Rightarrow$ CR $\Rightarrow$ WCR. Local confluence characterizes confluence of terminating relations. In contrast to [21], where local confluence of *terminating* GTRSs [22] was characterized, here we investigate confluence of (possibly) *non-terminating* GTRSs using *strong confluence* of *parallel rewriting*. For instance, $\mathcal{R}$ in Fig. 1 is *not* terminating due to rule (4). Confluence of $\mathcal{R}$ cannot be proved using the methods in [21]. Our new results permit a proof of confluence (Example 9).

After some preliminary definitions in Sect. 2, Sect. 3 recalls the basics of GTRSs. Section 4 recalls conditional pairs for analyzing confluence of GTRSs. Section 5 introduces parallel rewriting with GTRSs. Section 6 shows how to prove strong confluence of parallel rewriting with GTRSs and hence its confluence. Section 7 introduces weak V-orthogonality as a syntactic criterion to prove confluence of GTRSs. Section 8 shows the application and improvements of our results when applied to CS-TRSs [18] and CTRSs [13] as particular GTRSs [21, Section 7.3]. Section 9 discusses some implementation issues and the impact of our results in the performance of the tool CONFident [9] which implements some of them. Section 10 discusses related work. Section 11 concludes.

2 Preliminaries

In the following, we often write *iff* instead of *if and only if*. We assume some familiarity with the basic notions of abstract reduction systems and term rewriting [2,26,34] and first-order logic [5,24]. Some notions and notations from [8,18] are also recalled here and used in the remainder of the paper.

Signatures, Terms, Positions. A *signature* is a set of symbols each with a fixed *arity* (the number of arguments it is supposed to have), often given by a mapping *ar*. In this paper, $\mathcal{X}$ denotes a countably infinite set of *variables* and $\mathcal{F}$ denotes a *signature* of *function symbols* $\{f, g, \ldots\}$ with $\mathcal{F} \cap \mathcal{X} = \emptyset$. The set of terms built from $\mathcal{F}$ and $\mathcal{X}$ is $\mathcal{T}(\mathcal{F}, \mathcal{X})$. The set of variables occurring in t is $\mathcal{V}ar(t)$. Terms are viewed as labeled trees in the usual way. *Positions* p are sequences of positive integers used to address subterms $t|_p$ of t. The root position of a term is denoted as Λ. $\mathcal{P}os(t)$ is the set of all positions of t. Positions are ordered by the *prefix ordering* $\leq$ on sequences: we write $p \leq q$ iff p is a prefix of q (we often say that q is *below* p). We write $p < q$ if $p \leq q$ and $p \neq q$. If $p \not\leq q$ and $q \not\leq p$, we say that p and q are *disjoint* (or *parallel*, written $p \parallel q$). The set of positions of a subterm s of t is denoted $\mathcal{P}os_s(t)$. The set of positions of non-variable symbols in t is denoted as $\mathcal{P}os_{\mathcal{F}}(t)$.

Substitutions, Unification. A renaming ρ is a bijection from $\mathcal{X}$ to $\mathcal{X}$. A substitution σ is a mapping $\sigma : \mathcal{X} \to \mathcal{T}(\mathcal{F}, \mathcal{X})$ from variables into terms which is homomorphically extended to a mapping (also denoted σ) $\sigma : \mathcal{T}(\mathcal{F}, \mathcal{X}) \to \mathcal{T}(\mathcal{F}, \mathcal{X})$. In this paper we assume that substitutions σ satisfy $\sigma(x) = x$ except for a *finite* set of variables. Thus, we often write $\sigma = \{x_1 \mapsto t_1, \ldots, x_n \mapsto t_n\}$ to denote a substitution. Terms s and t *unify* if there is a substitution σ (i.e., a *unifier*) such that $\sigma(s) = \sigma(t)$. If s and t unify, then there is a (unique, up to renaming) *most general unifier* (*mgu*) θ of s and t satisfying that, for any other unifier σ of s and t, there is a substitution τ such that, for all $x \in \mathcal{X}$, $\sigma(x) = \tau(\theta(x))$.

Table 1. Generic sentences of the first-order theory of a GTRS

Label	Sentence
$(\mathrm{Rf})^{\bowtie}$	$(\forall x)\ x \bowtie x$
$(\mathrm{Co})^{\bowtie,\bowtie'}$	$(\forall x, y, z)\ x \bowtie y \wedge y \bowtie' z \Rightarrow x \bowtie' z$
$(\mathrm{Pr})^{\bowtie}_{f,i}$	$(\forall x_1, \ldots, x_k, x'_i)\ x_i \bowtie x'_i \Rightarrow f(x_1, \ldots, x_i, \ldots, x_k) \bowtie f(x_1, \ldots, x'_i, \ldots, x_k)$
$(\mathrm{HC})_{A \Leftarrow A_1,\ldots,A_n}$	$(\forall x_1, \ldots, x_p)\ A_1 \wedge \cdots \wedge A_n \Rightarrow A$
	where $x_1, \ldots, x_p$ are the variables occurring in $A_1, \ldots, A_n$ and A

Syntactic Replacement Restrictions. Given a signature $\mathcal{F}$, a *replacement map* is a mapping μ such that, for all $f \in \mathcal{F}$, $\mu(f) \subseteq \{1, \ldots, ar(f)\}$ [18]. In particular, $\mu_\top$ restricts no replacement: $\mu_\top(f) = \{1, \ldots, ar(f)\}$ for all $f \in \mathcal{F}$. The set $\mathcal{P}os^\mu(t)$ of *active positions* of t is $\mathcal{P}os^\mu(t) = \{\Lambda\}$, if $t \in \mathcal{X}$, and $\mathcal{P}os^\mu(t) = \{\Lambda\} \cup \{i.p \mid i \in \mu(f), p \in \mathcal{P}os^\mu(t_i)\}$, if $t = f(t_1, \ldots, t_k)$. Positions of *active* non-variable symbols in t are denoted as $\mathcal{P}os^\mu_\mathcal{F}(t)$. The set of *active* positions of a subterm s of t is denoted $\mathcal{P}os^\mu_s(t)$. Given a term t, $\mathcal{V}ar^\mu(t)$ (resp. $\mathcal{V}ar^{\not\mu}(t)$) is the set of variables occurring at active (resp. frozen) positions in t.

First-Order Logic. We consider signatures Π of *predicate symbols.* Atoms and formulas are built as usual. A first-order theory (FO-theory for short) Th is a set of sentences. In the following, given an FO-theory Th and a formula φ, $\mathsf{Th} \vdash \varphi$ means that φ is *deducible* from (or a *logical consequence* of) Th by using a correct and complete deduction method (e.g., resolution [27]).

Feasibility Sequences. A feasibility condition (or just *f-condition*) γ is an atom [8]. Sequences $\mathsf{F} = (\gamma_i)_{i=1}^n = (\gamma_1, \ldots, \gamma_n)$ of f-conditions are called *f-sequences.* We often drop 'f-' when no confusion arises. Given an FO-theory Th, a condition γ is Th-*feasible* (or just *feasible*) if $\mathsf{Th} \vdash \sigma(\gamma)$ holds for some substitution σ; otherwise, it is *infeasible.* A sequence F is Th-feasible (or just *feasible*) iff there is a substitution σ such that, for all $\gamma \in \mathsf{F}$, γ is Th-feasible.

3 Generalized Term Rewriting Systems

Computations with GTRSs $\mathcal{R} = (\mathcal{F}, \Pi, \mu, H, R)$ are defined by deduction in an associated FO-theory [21, Section 7.3]

$$\overline{\mathcal{R}} = \{(\mathrm{Rf})^{\to^*}, (\mathrm{Co})^{\to,\to^*}\} \cup \{(\mathrm{Pr})^{\to}_{f,i} \mid f \in \mathcal{F}, i \in \mu(f)\} \cup \{(\mathrm{HC})_\alpha \mid \alpha \in H \cup R\},$$

where (see Table 1), $(\mathrm{Rf})^{\to^*}$ expresses *reflexivity* of many-step rewriting; $(\mathrm{Co})^{\to,\to^*}$ expresses *compatibility* of one-step and many-step rewriting; for each k-ary function symbol f and $i \in \mu(f)$, $(\mathrm{Pr})^{\to}_{f,i}$ enables the *propagation* of rewriting steps in the i-th immediate *active* subterm $t|_i$ of a term t with root symbol f; finally, for each Horn clause $\alpha \in H \cup R$, $(\mathrm{HC})_\alpha$ provides the usual *implicative* form. We often use (numeric or symbolic) labels α to refer to clauses and rules $A \Leftarrow c$, written $\alpha : A \Leftarrow c$. For instance (1) is the first clause of $\mathcal{R}$ in Fig. 1.

Example 1. For $\mathcal{R} = (\mathcal{F}, \Pi, \mu, H, R)$ in Fig. 1, $\mathcal{F} = \{\mathsf{0}, \mathsf{s}, \mathsf{:}, \mathsf{from}, \mathsf{nil}, \mathsf{rm}, \mathsf{edups}\}$; $\Pi = \{\to, \to^*, \mathsf{Neq}\}$; $\mu(\mathsf{s}) = \{1\}$, $\mu(\mathsf{:}) = \{2\}$, $\mu(\mathsf{from}) = \emptyset$, $\mu(\mathsf{rm}) = \{2\}$, and $\mu(\mathsf{edups}) = \{1\}$; $H = \{(1), (2), (3)\}$, and $R = \{(4), \ldots, (11)\}$, with:

$$\overline{\mathcal{R}} = \{(\mathrm{Rf})^{\to^*}, (\mathrm{Co})^{\to,\to^*}, (\mathrm{Pr})^{\to}_{\mathsf{s},1}, (\mathrm{Pr})^{\to}_{:,2}, (\mathrm{Pr})^{\to}_{\mathsf{rm},2}(\mathrm{Pr})^{\to}_{\mathsf{edups},1}, (\mathrm{HC})_{(1)}, \ldots, (\mathrm{HC})_{(11)}\}.$$

We write $s \to_{\mathcal{R}} t$ (resp. $s \to^*_{\mathcal{R}} t$) if $\overline{\mathcal{R}} \vdash s \to t$ (resp. $\overline{\mathcal{R}} \vdash s \to^* t$). In the proofs, we also use the following result [21, Proposition 58] which provides a (more familiar) definition based on the replacement of redexes at active positions.

Proposition 1. *Let $\mathcal{R} = (\mathcal{F}, \Pi, \mu, H, R)$ be a GTRS and $s, t \in \mathcal{T}(\mathcal{F}, \mathcal{X})$. Then, $s \to_{\mathcal{R}} t$ iff there is $p \in \mathcal{P}os^{\mu}(s)$ and $\ell \to r \Leftarrow c \in R$ such that (i) $s|_p = \sigma(\ell)$ for some substitution σ, (ii) for all $A \in c$, $\overline{\mathcal{R}} \vdash \sigma(A)$ holds, and (iii) $t = s[\sigma(r)]_p$.*

A GTRS $\mathcal{R}$ is (locally, strongly) confluent (resp. terminating) if $\to_{\mathcal{R}}$ is (locally, strongly) confluent (resp. terminating). A rule $\ell \to r \Leftarrow c$ is ($\overline{\mathcal{R}}$-)feasible if c is. Only feasible rules contribute to $\to_{\mathcal{R}}$-rewriting steps and hence to confluence. As in [25, Definition 6.1], rules $\ell \to r \Leftarrow c$ in GTRSs are classified according to the distribution of variables: type 1, if $\mathcal{V}ar(r) \cup \mathcal{V}ar(c) \subseteq \mathcal{V}ar(\ell)$; type 2, if $\mathcal{V}ar(r) \subseteq \mathcal{V}ar(\ell)$; type 3, if $\mathcal{V}ar(r) \subseteq \mathcal{V}ar(\ell) \cup \mathcal{V}ar(c)$; and type 4, otherwise. A rule of type n is often called an n-rule. A GTRS $\mathcal{R}$ is called an n-GTRS if all its rules are of type n; if $\mathcal{R}$ contains at least one n-rule which is *not* an m-rule for some $m < n$, then we say that $\mathcal{R}$ is a *proper* n-GTRS.

Example 2. The GTRS $\mathcal{R}$ in Fig. 1 is a 1-GTRS.

Replacement maps μ permit a *weaker* notion of linearity which we exploit below.

Definition 1 (μ-Linear Term; μ-Left-linear Rule and GTRS). *A term t is* μ-linear *if no active variable in t occurs twice (active or not): for all $x \in \mathcal{X}$, $\mathcal{P}os^{\mu}_x(t) \neq \emptyset \Rightarrow \mathcal{P}os_x(t) = \{x\}$. A rule $\ell \to r \Leftarrow c$ is* μ-left-linear *if ℓ is μ-linear. A GTRS $\mathcal{R} = (\mathcal{F}, \Pi, \mu, H, R)$ is μ-left-linear if all rules are.*

Definition 2 (μ-compatible rule). *A rule $\ell \to r \Leftarrow c$ is* μ-compatible *if (i) no active variable in ℓ is frozen in r, i.e., $\mathcal{V}ar^{\mu}(\ell) \cap \mathcal{V}ar^{\not\mu}(r) = \emptyset$, and (ii) no active variable in ℓ occurs in c, i.e., $\mathcal{V}ar^{\mu}(\ell) \cap \mathcal{V}ar(c) = \emptyset$.*

Linearity and $\mu_\top$-linearity coincide; and unconditional rules are $\mu_\top$-compatible.

4 Conditional Pairs For Confluence of GTRSs

In the following, we consider *conditional pairs* $\langle s, t\rangle \Leftarrow c$, where s and t are terms and the *conditional part* c is a sequence of atomic conditions [21, Section 5].

Definition 3. [21, Def. 19] *Let $\mathcal{R}$ be a GTRS. A conditional pair $\langle s,t\rangle \Leftarrow c$ is*

- $\overline{\mathcal{R}}$-feasible *(or just* feasible *if no confusion arises) if c is $\overline{\mathcal{R}}$-feasible.*
- $\overline{\mathcal{R}}$-joinable *(or just* joinable*) if for all substitutions σ, whenever $\overline{\mathcal{R}} \vdash \sigma(\gamma)$ holds for all $\gamma \in c$, there is u such that $\sigma(s) \to^*_{\mathcal{R}} u$ and $\sigma(t) \to^*_{\mathcal{R}} u$.*
- Trivial, *if $s = t$.*

Trivial and infeasible conditional pairs are joinable. As joinability of conditional pairs $\langle s,t\rangle \Leftarrow c$ depends on the satisfaction of c by a substitution σ, the notion of *triviality* can also be treated in this way (i.e., modulo a *substitution*).

Definition 4 (s-trivial Conditional Pair). *A conditional pair $\langle s,t\rangle \Leftarrow c$ is* s-trivial *if for all substitutions σ, if $\sigma(c)$ holds, then $\sigma(s) = \sigma(t)$.*

Trivial conditional pairs are s-trivial, but not vice versa (see Example 4 below). In [21, Theorem 62], local confluence of GTRSs is characterized as the joinability of two groups of conditional pairs: (proper and improper) *conditional critical pairs* (CCPs) and *conditional variable pairs* (CVPs) [21, Definition 59].

Definition 5. *Let $\mathcal{R}$ be a GTRS, and $\alpha : \ell \to r \Leftarrow c$, $\alpha' : \ell' \to r' \Leftarrow c'$ be variable disjoint rules of $\mathcal{R}$ (rename if necessary).*

- *Let $p \in \mathcal{P}os^{\mu}_{\mathcal{F}}(\ell)$ be a nonvariable active position of ℓ such that $\ell|_p$ and ℓ' unify with* mgu *θ. Then, $\langle \theta(\ell[r']_p), \theta(r)\rangle \Leftarrow \theta(c), \theta(c')$, labeled $\pi_{\alpha,p,\alpha'}$, is a* conditional critical pair *(CCP) of $\mathcal{R}$ with* critical position *p. If $p = \Lambda$, we say that $\pi_{\alpha,p,\alpha'}$ is a* root *CCP; otherwise, we call it* inner *CCP. Furthermore,*
  - *If $p = \Lambda$ and α and α' are variants of the* same *rule, then $\pi_{\alpha,p,\alpha'}$ is an* improper *CCP (iCCP for short; note that iCCPs are root CCPs);*
  - *otherwise, $\pi_{\alpha,p,\alpha'}$ is a* proper *CCP (pCCP for short).*

  Let $\mathsf{pCCP}(\mathcal{R})$ *be the set of* feasible *pCCPs of $\mathcal{R}$. Let* $\mathsf{iCCP}(\mathcal{R})$ *be the set of* feasible *iCCPs of proper 3- or 4-rules in $\mathcal{R}$.*
- *Let $x \in \mathcal{V}ar^{\mu}(\ell)$ be an active variable of ℓ, $p \in \mathcal{P}os^{\mu}_{x}(\ell)$ be an active position of x in ℓ, and x' be a fresh variable. Then, $\langle \ell[x']_p, r\rangle \Leftarrow x \to x', c$, labeled $\pi_{\alpha,x,p}$, is a* conditional variable pair *(CVP) with* critical variable *x and critical position p. Let* $\mathsf{CVP}(\alpha)$ *be the set of feasible CVPs of a rule α.*

Remark 1 (Variable Peaks and CVPs). As explained in [21, Section 5.2.1], the role of CVPs is handling *variable peaks*, i.e., local peaks $t \xleftarrow{p} \sigma(\ell) \xrightarrow{\Lambda} \sigma(r)$ involving a rule $\ell \to r \Leftarrow c$, an active position p, a substitution σ, and a term t so that the reduction at p occurs "below a variable x of ℓ", i.e., there is $q \in \mathcal{P}os^{\mu}_{x}(\ell)$ such that $q \leq p$. The notion of "variable peak" from [4, Section 2.3], is implicit in the proofs of [16, Section 5, Case 1] and [12, Lemmata 3.1, 3.2, 3.3].

Example 3. As for the 1-GTRS $\mathcal{R}$ in Fig. 1, we have:

- *Proper* conditional *critical* pairs (pCCPs): $\pi_{(6),\Lambda,(7)'}$ and $\pi_{(10),\Lambda,(11)'}$, i.e.,

$$\langle x : \mathsf{rm}(x, xs), \mathsf{rm}(x, xs)\rangle \Leftarrow \mathsf{Neq}(x, x) \quad (12)$$

$$\langle x : \mathsf{rm}(x, \mathsf{edups}(x : xs)), \mathsf{edups}(x : xs)\rangle \Leftarrow \mathsf{Neq}(x, x) \quad (13)$$

Table 2. FO-sentences for parallel rewriting with GTRS

Label	Sentence
$(\mathrm{PPr})^{\bowtie}_{f}$	$(\forall x_1, x'_1, \ldots, x_k, x'_k)\ \bigwedge_{i\in\mu(f)} x_i \bowtie x'_i \Rightarrow f(x_1, \ldots, , x_k) \bowtie f(x'_1, \ldots, x'_k)$
(RPR)	$(\forall x, y)\ x \to y \Rightarrow x \mathrel{+\!\!\!\!\!\!\to} y$

- *Improper* conditional *critical* pairs (iCCPs): $\pi_{(7),\Lambda,(7)'}$ and $\pi_{(11),\Lambda,(11)'}$, i.e.,

$$\langle y : \mathsf{rm}(x, xs), y : \mathsf{rm}(x, xs)\rangle \Leftarrow \mathsf{Neq}(x, y) \tag{14}$$
$$\langle x : \mathsf{rm}(x, \mathsf{edups}(y : xs)), x : \mathsf{rm}(x, \mathsf{edups}(y : xs))\rangle \Leftarrow \mathsf{Neq}(x, y) \tag{15}$$

- Conditional *variable* pairs (CVPs): $\pi_{(6),xs,2.2}$, $\pi_{(7),xs,2.2}$ and $\pi_{(11),xs,1.2.2}$, i.e.,

$$\langle \mathsf{rm}(x, y : xs'), \mathsf{rm}(x, xs)\rangle \Leftarrow xs \to xs' \tag{16}$$
$$\langle \mathsf{rm}(x, y : xs'), y : \mathsf{rm}(x, xs)\rangle \Leftarrow xs \to xs', \mathsf{Neq}(x, y) \tag{17}$$
$$\langle \mathsf{edups}(x : y : xs'), x : \mathsf{rm}(x, \mathsf{edups}(y : xs))\rangle \Leftarrow xs \to xs', \mathsf{Neq}(x, y) \tag{18}$$

The pCCPs (12) and (13) are infeasible: no term t makes $\mathsf{Neq}(t, t)$ provable. Thus, $\mathsf{pCCP}(\mathcal{R}) = \emptyset$. The iCCPs (14) and (15) come from 1-rules, i.e., $\mathsf{iCCP}(\mathcal{R}) = \emptyset$. Finally, $\mathsf{CVP}(\mathcal{R}) = \{(16), (17), (18)\}$.

Note that CVPs $\langle s, t\rangle \Leftarrow c$ *cannot* be trivial: s contains an occurrence of a fresh variable not occuring in t. However, they can be s-trivial.

Example 4. Consider the GTRS

$$\mathsf{a} \to \mathsf{b} \tag{19}$$
$$\mathsf{f}(x) \to \mathsf{f}(\mathsf{b}) \Leftarrow x \to^* \mathsf{b} \tag{20}$$

The CVP $\pi_{(20),x,1}$: $\langle \mathsf{f}(x'), \mathsf{f}(\mathsf{b})\rangle \Leftarrow x \to x', x \to^* \mathsf{b}$ is s-trivial: only $\sigma = \{x \mapsto \mathsf{a}, x' \mapsto \mathsf{b}\}$ satisfies the conditional part; hence, $\sigma(\mathsf{f}(x')) = \sigma(\mathsf{f}(\mathsf{b}))$.

5 Parallel Rewriting with GTRSs

We say that P is a set of *(pairwise) disjoint positions* if for all $p, p' \in P$, $p \neq p'$ implies $p \parallel p'$. Roughly speaking, *parallel reduction* $\mathrel{+\!\!\!\!\!\!\to}$ is the simultaneous contraction in a term s of a set of redexes at *disjoint* (active) positions of s.

Definition 6 (Parallel Reduction with GTRSs). *Given a GTRS $\mathcal{R}$, terms s and t, and a set $P = \{p_1, \ldots, p_n\} \subseteq \mathcal{P}os^{\mu}(s)$ of disjoint (active) positions in s, $s \xrightarrow{P}_{\mathcal{R}} t$ is a* parallel reduction step *from s to t if there are rules $\alpha_i : \ell_i \to r_i \Leftarrow c_i \in \mathcal{R}$ and substitutions σ_i, $1 \leq i \leq n$, such that $s|_{p_i} = \sigma_i(\ell_i)$, $\sigma_i(c_i)$ holds, and $t = s[\sigma_1(r_1)]_{p_1} \cdots [\sigma_n(r_n)]_{p_n}$. We often write $s \xrightarrow{P} t$, $s \mathrel{+\!\!\!\!\!\!\to}_{\mathcal{R}} t$, or even $s \mathrel{+\!\!\!\!\!\!\to} t$.*

Definition 6 is (hopefully) more intuitive for the purpose of this paper. A deductive style can also be used to equivalently define parallel rewriting by using

$$\overline{\mathcal{R}}^{\mathrel{+\!\!\!\!\to}} = \overline{\mathcal{R}} \cup \{(\mathrm{Rf})^{\mathrel{+\!\!\!\!\to}}, (\mathrm{Rf})^{\mathrel{+\!\!\!\!\to}^*}, (\mathrm{Co})^{\mathrel{+\!\!\!\!\to},\mathrel{+\!\!\!\!\to}^*}, (\mathrm{RPR})\} \cup \{(\mathrm{PPr})_f^{\mathrel{+\!\!\!\!\to}} \mid f \in \mathcal{F}\}$$

where $\mathrel{+\!\!\!\!\to}$ and $\mathrel{+\!\!\!\!\to}^*$ are new (binary) predicates, and some new sentences from Table 2 are used together with those in Table 1. Here, $(\mathrm{PPr})_f^{\mathrel{+\!\!\!\!\to}}$ represents the (simultaneous) *propagation of parallel rewriting* on active arguments of function symbols; and (RPR) says that rewriting steps are parallel rewriting steps. Then, $s \mathrel{+\!\!\!\!\to}_{\mathcal{R}} t$ (resp. $s \mathrel{+\!\!\!\!\to}_{\mathcal{R}}^* t$) if $\overline{\mathcal{R}}^{\mathrel{+\!\!\!\!\to}} \vdash s \mathrel{+\!\!\!\!\to} t$ (resp. $\overline{\mathcal{R}}^{\mathrel{+\!\!\!\!\to}} \vdash s \mathrel{+\!\!\!\!\to}^* t$) holds. The notion of $\overline{\mathcal{R}}^{\mathrel{+\!\!\!\!\to}}$-feasible conditional pair is as in Definition 3, but replacing $\overline{\mathcal{R}}$ by $\overline{\mathcal{R}}^{\mathrel{+\!\!\!\!\to}}$.

Remark 2 Since $\overline{\mathcal{R}}^{\mathrel{+\!\!\!\!\to}}$ includes $\overline{\mathcal{R}}$ and *no* deductive power for formulas built with $\mathcal{F}$ and Π is added, $\overline{\mathcal{R}}^{\mathrel{+\!\!\!\!\to}}$-feasibility and $\overline{\mathcal{R}}$-feasibility of CCPs and CVPs coincide.

6 Strong Confluence and Confluence of GTRSs

Strong confluence, as depicted in Fig. 2, middle, is defined as follows.

Definition 7 (Strong Confluence [12, page 801]**).** *A relation* $\to \subseteq A \times A$ *is* strongly confluent *if, for all* $s, t, t' \in A$*, if* $s \to t$ *and* $s \to t'$*, then there is* $u \in A$ *such that* $t \to^{=} u$ *and* $t' \to^* u$*.*

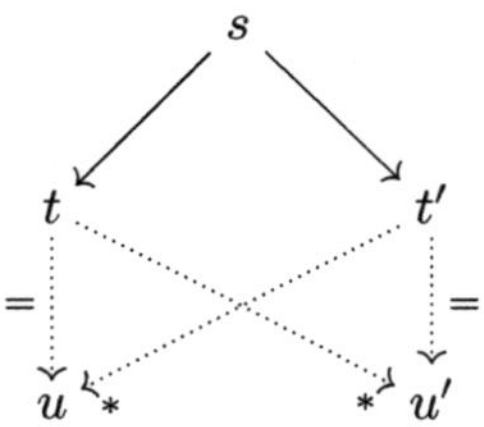

Due to the *asymmetry* in the treatment of t and t' in Definition 7 (see also Fig. 2, middle), strong confluence equivalently corresponds to commutation of the diagram displayed to the right (from [12, Figure 7]). Accordingly, $s, t \in A$ are *strongly* $\to$*-joinable* (or just *strongly joinable* if no confusion arises), if there are $u, u' \in A$ such that $s \to^{=} u \,{}^*\!\!\leftarrow t$ and $s \to^* u' \,{}^{=}\!\!\leftarrow t$ [2, Definition 6.3.2]. For abstract reduction relations $\to$, strong confluence implies confluence [12, Lemma 2.5], often written $\mathsf{SCR}(\to) \Rightarrow \mathsf{CR}(\to)$. For *linear* TRSs $\mathcal{R}$ (i.e., for all rules $\ell \to r$, both ℓ and r are linear), strong $\to_{\mathcal{R}}$-joinability of all its critical pairs implies strong confluence (hence confluence) of $\mathcal{R}$ [12, Lemma 3.2]. In general, linearity *cannot* be weakened into *left-linearity* [12, page 814]. Left-linearity works, though, if *strong confluence of* $\mathrel{+\!\!\!\!\to}_{\mathcal{R}}$ is addressed instead [12, Lemma 3.3]. In general, $\mathsf{SCR}(\mathrel{+\!\!\!\!\to}_{\mathcal{R}})$ does *not* imply $\mathsf{SCR}(\to_{\mathcal{R}})$.

Example 5 For $\mathcal{R} = \{\mathsf{a} \to \mathsf{b}, \mathsf{f}(x) \to \mathsf{c}(x,x)\}$, $\mathrel{+\!\!\!\!\to}_{\mathcal{R}}$ is strongly confuent (by Theorem 2 in Sect. 7) but $\to_{\mathcal{R}}$ is *not* strongly confluent: we have $\mathsf{f}(\mathsf{b}) \,{}_{\mathcal{R}}\!\!\xleftarrow{1} \mathsf{f}(\mathsf{a}) \xrightarrow{\Lambda}_{\mathcal{R}} \mathsf{c}(\mathsf{a},\mathsf{a})$, but $\mathsf{f}(\mathsf{b})$ and $\mathsf{c}(\mathsf{a},\mathsf{a})$ are not strongly $\to_{\mathcal{R}}$-joinable.

Proposition 2 (Confluence of $\to$ as Strong Confluence of $\mathrel{+\!\!\!\!\to}$). *Strong confluence of* $\mathrel{+\!\!\!\!\to}$ *implies confluence of* $\to$*:* $\mathsf{SCR}(\mathrel{+\!\!\!\!\to}) \Rightarrow \mathsf{CR}(\to)$ *[6, page 216].*

We silently use this fact along the paper.

Definition 8 (Strongly $\nrightarrow\!\!\!\!\!\!\;\|$-Joinable Conditional Pair). *A conditional pair* $\langle s,t\rangle \Leftarrow c$ *is* strongly $\mathrel{+\!\!\!\!\!\rightarrow}$-joinable *if for all substitutions* σ *such that* $\sigma(c)$ *holds,* $\sigma(s)$ *and* $\sigma(t)$ *are strongly* $\mathrel{+\!\!\!\!\!\rightarrow}$*-joinable.*

Since $\mathrel{+\!\!\!\!\!\rightarrow}$ is reflexive, $\to^{=} \subseteq \mathrel{+\!\!\!\!\!\rightarrow}$. Also, $\to^*$ and $\mathrel{+\!\!\!\!\!\rightarrow}^*$ coincide. Therefore,

Proposition 3 *If* $\pi : \langle s,t\rangle \Leftarrow c$ *is strongly* $\to$*-joinable, it is strongly* $\mathrel{+\!\!\!\!\!\rightarrow}$*-joinable.*

Furthermore, $\mathrel{+\!\!\!\!\!\rightarrow}$ and $\mathrel{+\!\!\!\!\!\rightarrow}^{=}$ coincide. Thus, *strong* $\mathrel{+\!\!\!\!\!\rightarrow}$*-joinability* of $\langle s,t\rangle \Leftarrow c$ is as follows: for all σ such that $\sigma(c)$ holds, there are terms u and u' such that

$$\sigma(s) \mathrel{+\!\!\!\!\!\rightarrow} u \; {}^*\!\!\mathrel{\leftarrow\!\!\!\!\!+} \sigma(t) \text{ and } \sigma(s) \mathrel{+\!\!\!\!\!\rightarrow}^* u' \mathrel{\leftarrow\!\!\!\!\!+} \sigma(t) \tag{21}$$

We introduce the notion of *parallel* CVP, which is more appropriate for parallel rewriting. Given a term s, $m > 0$, numbers $n_i > 0$ for $1 \leq i \leq m$, pairwise disjoint positions p_{ij} of s and terms t_{ij} for all $1 \leq i \leq m$ and $1 \leq j \leq n_i$, we write $s(([t_{ij}]_{p_{ij}})_{j=1}^{n_i})_{i=1}^{m}$ to denote the simultaneous replacement of $s|_{p_{ij}}$ in s by t_{ij}. Similarly, for variables x_i, $1 \leq i \leq m$ and variables x'_{ij} for all $1 \leq i \leq m$ and $1 \leq j \leq n_i$, we write $((x_i \mathrel{+\!\!\!\!\!\rightarrow} x'_{ij})_{j=1}^{n_i})_{i=1}^{m}$ to denote the sequence of parallel reduction statements $x_i \mathrel{+\!\!\!\!\!\rightarrow} x'_{ij}$ for all $1 \leq i \leq m$ and $1 \leq j \leq n_i$.

Definition 9 (Parallel CVP). *Let* $\alpha : \ell \to r \Leftarrow c$ *be a rule,* $\mathcal{V}ar^{\mu}(\ell) = \{x_1,\ldots,x_m\}$ *and, for all* $1 \leq i \leq m$, $Q_i = \{q_{i1},\ldots,q_{in_i}\} = \mathcal{P}os^{\mu}_{x_i}(\ell)$ *for some* $n_i \geq 1$. *The* Parallel CVP *(PCVP)* $\pi_{\alpha,x_1,\ldots,x_m,Q_1,\ldots,Q_m}$ *of* α *(or* $\pi_{\alpha,\boldsymbol{x},\boldsymbol{Q}}$ *if no confusion arises) is:*

$$\langle \ell(([x'_{ij}]_{q_{ij}})_{j=1}^{n_i})_{i=1}^{m}, r\rangle \Leftarrow ((x_i \mathrel{+\!\!\!\!\!\rightarrow} x'_{ij})_{j=1}^{n_i})_{i=1}^{m}, c \tag{22}$$

where x'_{ij} *are fresh variables for all* $1 \leq i \leq m, 1 \leq j \leq n_i$.

By [21, Proposition 34], CVPs of TRSs are joinable. However, CVPs (or PCVPs) of TRSs do *not* need to be strongly $\to$-joinable (or strongly $\mathrel{+\!\!\!\!\!\rightarrow}$-joinable).

Example 6 The following non-left-linear TRS $\mathcal{R}$ (from [12, page 813])

$$\mathsf{f}(x,x) \to \mathsf{a} \tag{23}$$

$$\mathsf{g}(x) \to \mathsf{f}(x,\mathsf{g}(x)) \tag{24}$$

$$\mathsf{c} \to \mathsf{g}(\mathsf{c}) \tag{25}$$

is a well-known example of a TRS without critical pairs which is however not confluent due to non-left-linearity [15] and [14, Exercise 3.1.2]. The PCVP $\pi_{(23),x,\{1,2\}}$:

$$\langle \mathsf{f}(x',x''),\mathsf{a}\rangle \Leftarrow x \mathrel{+\!\!\!\!\!\rightarrow} x', x \mathrel{+\!\!\!\!\!\rightarrow} x'' \tag{26}$$

is *not* strongly $\mathrel{+\!\!\!\!\!\rightarrow}$-joinable: $\sigma = \{x \mapsto \mathsf{c}, x' \mapsto \mathsf{g}(\mathsf{c}), x'' \mapsto \mathsf{c}\}$ satisfies the conditional part of (26). However, $\mathsf{f}(\mathsf{g}(\mathsf{c}),\mathsf{c})$ and a are not strongly $\mathrel{+\!\!\!\!\!\rightarrow}$-joinable: a is irreducible and $\mathsf{f}(\mathsf{g}(\mathsf{c}),\mathsf{c})$ does *not* reduce to a in a single $\mathrel{+\!\!\!\!\!\rightarrow}$-step, as required. Note that the same substitution shows that the CVP $\pi_{(23),x,1} : \langle \mathsf{f}(x',x),\mathsf{a}\rangle \Leftarrow x \to x'$ is not strongly $\mathrel{+\!\!\!\!\!\rightarrow}$-joinable nor (by Proposition 3) strongly $\to$-joinable.

However, we have the following.

Proposition 4 *PCVPs of μ-left-linear and μ-compatible rules are strongly $\nrightarrow\!\!\!\!\!\!\!\!\;\;\;\;$ $\#\!\!\!\rightarrow$-joinable.*

Remark 3 (Feasibility of PCVPs) PCVPs $\pi_{\alpha,\boldsymbol{x},\boldsymbol{Q}}$ of $\overline{\mathcal{R}}$-feasible rules $\alpha : \ell \to r \Leftarrow c$ are *always* $\overline{\mathcal{R}}^{\#\!\!\!\rightarrow}$-feasible: every substitution σ satisfying c is extended to deal with fresh variables x'_{ij} by $\sigma(x'_{ij}) = \sigma(x_i)$ for all $1 \leq i \leq n$. By reflexivity of $\#\!\!\!\rightarrow$, such extended σ satisfies the conditional part $((x_i \#\!\!\!\rightarrow x'_{ij})_{j=1}^{n_i})_{i=1}^{m}, c$ of $\pi_{\alpha,\boldsymbol{x},\boldsymbol{Q}}$.

However, infeasibility of *all* CVPs for a rule α implies strong $\#\!\!\!\rightarrow$-joinability of the PCVP $\pi_{\alpha,\boldsymbol{x},\boldsymbol{Q}}$.

Proposition 5 *Let $\mathcal{R}$ be a GTRS and α be a rule of $\mathcal{R}$. If* $\mathsf{CVP}(\alpha) = \emptyset$, *then the PCVP $\pi_{\alpha,\boldsymbol{x},\boldsymbol{Q}}$ is strongly $\#\!\!\!\rightarrow$-joinable.*

As for CVPs, PCVPs cannot be trivial, but they can be s-trivial. The following result establishes the essential property of PCVPs in the realm of this paper. For GTRSs, it plays the role of the *Parallel Moves Lemma* (see, e.g., [2, Lemma 6.4.4] for TRSs), but left-linearity is replaced by strong $\#\!\!\!\rightarrow$-joinability of PCVPs.

Proposition 6 *Let $\alpha : \ell \to r \Leftarrow c$ be such that $\pi_{\alpha,\boldsymbol{x},\boldsymbol{Q}}$ is strongly $\#\!\!\!\rightarrow$-joinable, σ be a substitution, and $P \subseteq \mathcal{P}os^{\mu}(\sigma(\ell))$ be such that $P \cap \mathcal{P}os_{\mathcal{F}}(\ell) = \emptyset$. If $t \xleftarrow{P} \sigma(\ell) \xrightarrow{\Lambda} \sigma(r)$, then t and $\sigma(r)$ are strongly $\#\!\!\!\rightarrow$-joinable.*

Definition 10 (Parallel-closed Conditional Pair). $\langle s, t\rangle \Leftarrow c$ *is* parallel-closed *if for all substitutions σ such that $\sigma(c)$ holds, we have $\sigma(s) \#\!\!\!\rightarrow \sigma(t)$.*

Toyama proved that left-linear TRSs such that (i) all root CPs are strongly joinable and (ii) all inner CPs are parallel-closed are confluent [35, Corollary 3.2]. TRSs satisfying (i) and (ii) are often called *almost parallel-closed*, see, e.g., [29, Definition 8], although Toyama did not use such a denomination.

Definition 11 (Almost parallel-closed *GTRS***).** *A GTRS $\mathcal{R}$ is* almost parallel-closed *if (i) $\overline{\mathcal{R}}$-feasible root CCPs are strongly $\#\!\!\!\rightarrow$-joinable and (ii) $\overline{\mathcal{R}}$-feasible inner CCPs are parallel closed.*

Our main result adapts Toyama's result to GTRSs. Here, left-linearity is replaced by strong $\#\!\!\!\rightarrow$-joinability of PCVPs. For TRSs, left-linearity becomes a *sufficient condition* for strong $\#\!\!\!\rightarrow$-joinability of PCVPs (Proposition 4).

Theorem 1 *Let $\mathcal{R}$ be an almost parallel-closed GTRS such that for all $\overline{\mathcal{R}}$-feasible rules $\alpha \in \mathcal{R}$, the PCVP $\pi_{\alpha,\boldsymbol{x},\boldsymbol{Q}}$ is strongly $\#\!\!\!\rightarrow$-joinable. Then, $\#\!\!\!\rightarrow_{\mathcal{R}}$ is strongly confluent. Hence, $\mathcal{R}$ is confluent.*

We adapt the proof of [2, Theorem 6.4.8] to prove Theorem 1. The following result generalizes [2, Lemma 6.4.1]; it immediately follows from CSR's *closedness under active contexts*, see [18, Section 4].

Lemma 1 *Let $P \subseteq \mathcal{P}os^{\mu}(s)$ be a set of active, disjoint, positions. If $s|_p \mathrel{\#\!\!\!\to} t|_p$ for all $p \in P$, then $s[s|_p]_{p\in P} \mathrel{\#\!\!\!\to} s[t|_p]_{p\in P}$.*

Proof (of Theorem 1) Given a term s, consider a local $\mathrel{\#\!\!\!\to}$-peak $t_0 \xleftarrow{P_0} s \xrightarrow{P_1} t_1$ for sets P_0 and P_1 of disjoints active positions in s and terms t_0 and t_1. The *size* of a term t, denoted $|t|$, is the cardinality of $\mathcal{P}os(t)$. The following *complexity measure* of the peak above is used of the proof [2, Definition 6.4.6]:

$$m(s, P_0, P_1) = \sum_{b\in P_0^{\geq P_1}} |(s|_b)| + \sum_{b\in P_1^{\geq P_0}} |(s|_b)|$$

where $P_i^{\geq P_{1-i}}$ is the subset of positions of P_i which are *below* some position of P_{1-i}, and $|t|$ denotes the *size* of t. Now, for $i = 0, 1$, let

$$A_i = \{p \in P_i \mid \nexists q \in P_{1-i} \text{ such that } q < p\} \text{ and } A = A_0 \cup A_1.$$

That is, for $i = 0, 1$, A_i is the set of positions in P_i which are not "covered" by any position q in P_{1-i}. Thus, A is the set of redex positions not strictly below some other redex position.

We prove the existence of u and u' such that $t_0 \mathrel{\#\!\!\!\to} u \mathrel{{}^*\!\!\leftarrow\!\!\!\#} t_1$ and $t_0 \mathrel{\#\!\!\!\to^*} u' \mathrel{\leftarrow\!\!\!\#} t_1$ by induction on $m(s, P_0, P_1)$. First, note that, by [2, Lemma 6.4.3] $t_0 = s[t_0|_p]_{p\in A}$ and $t_1 = s[t_1|_p]_{p\in A}$. Thus, for each $p \in A$, we show that there are terms u_p and u'_p such that $t_0|_p \mathrel{\#\!\!\!\to} u_p \mathrel{{}^*\!\!\leftarrow\!\!\!\#} t_1|_p$ and $t_0|_p \mathrel{\#\!\!\!\to^*} u'_p \mathrel{\leftarrow\!\!\!\#} t_1|_p$; then, Lemma 1 implies $t_0 \mathrel{\#\!\!\!\to} s[u_p]_{p\in A} \mathrel{{}^*\!\!\leftarrow\!\!\!\#} t_1$ and $t_0 \mathrel{\#\!\!\!\to^*} s[u'_p]_{p\in A} \mathrel{\leftarrow\!\!\!\#} t_1$ and we can let u to be $s[u_p]_{p\in A}$ and u' to be $s[u'_p]_{p\in A}$.

Consider $p \in A$; without loss of generality, we assume $p \in P_1$. There are $\alpha : \ell \to r \Leftarrow c \in \mathcal{R}$ and a substitution σ such that $s|_p = \sigma(\ell)$, $t_1|_p = \sigma(r)$, and $\sigma(c)$ holds. Now, let $B_p = \{q \mid p.q \in P_0\}$ be the set of redex positions addressed by P_0 which are below p. Note that $\sigma(\ell) \xrightarrow{B_p} t_0|_p$. We distinguish two cases:

1. There is no critical overlap, i.e.,$B_p \cap \mathcal{P}os^{\mu}_{\mathcal{F}}(\ell) = \emptyset$ and all elements of B_p are below variable positions of ℓ. Since the PCVP $\pi_{\alpha,x,Q}$ is strongly $\mathrel{\#\!\!\!\to}$-joinable, by Proposition 6, $t_1|_p = \sigma(r)$ and $t_0|_p$ are strongly $\mathrel{\#\!\!\!\to}$-joinable, i.e., $t_1|_p \mathrel{\#\!\!\!\to} u_p \mathrel{{}^*\!\!\leftarrow\!\!\!\#} t_0|_p$ and $t_1|_p \mathrel{\#\!\!\!\to^*} u'_p \mathrel{\leftarrow\!\!\!\#} t_0|_p$ for some terms u_p and u'_p.
2. There is a critical overlap, i.e., some $q_0 \in B_p$ and rule $\alpha_0 : \ell_0 \to r_0 \Leftarrow c_0 \in \mathcal{R}$ (sharing no variables with α), such that
   - $q_0 \in \mathcal{P}os^{\mu}_{\mathcal{F}}(\ell)$,
   - $s|_{p.q_0} = \sigma(\ell_0)$ (with σ conveniently extended to variables in α_0), $\sigma(c_0)$ holds, and $t_0|_{p.q_0} = \sigma(r_0)$, and
   - there is a pCCP $\pi_{\alpha,q_0,\alpha_0} : \langle u, v\rangle \Leftarrow \theta(c), \theta(c_0)$, where $u = \theta(\ell)[\theta(r_0)]_{q_0}$ and $v = \theta(r)$ for the mgu θ of $\ell|_{q_0}$ and ℓ_0, and a substitution τ such that $t_1|_p = \tau(v)$;
   - we also define $t = (s|_p)[\sigma(r_0)]_{q_0} = \sigma(\ell)[\sigma(r_0)]_{q_0} = \sigma(\ell)[t_0|_{p.q_0}]_{q_0} = \tau(u)$. Note that $\sigma(\ell) \xrightarrow{q_0} t$ and $t \xrightarrow{Q_0} t_0|_p$, if $Q_0 = B_p - \{q_0\}$.

   We consider two cases:

(a) $\pi_{\alpha,q_0,\alpha_0}$ is a root CCP, i.e., $q_0 = \Lambda$, which, since $q_0 \in B_p$ and by disjointness of positions in B_p, implies $B_p = \{\Lambda\}$. Hence $t_0|_p = \sigma(r)$. Therefore, $u = \theta(r_0)$ and $v = \theta(r)$. Then, by condition (i) in Definition 11, $\pi_{\alpha,q_0,\alpha_0}$ is $\mathrel{\parallel\!\!\!\!\!\rightarrow}$-strongly joinable, i.e., $\sigma(u) = t_0|_p = \sigma(r_0) \mathrel{\parallel\!\!\!\!\!\rightarrow} u_p \mathrel{{}^*\!\!\leftarrow\!\!\!\!\!\parallel} \sigma(r) = t_1|_p = \sigma(v)$ and $\sigma(u) = \sigma(r_0) \mathrel{\parallel\!\!\!\!\!\rightarrow}^* u'_p \mathrel{\leftarrow\!\!\!\!\!\parallel} \sigma(r) = \sigma(v)$ for terms u_p and u'_p.

(b) $\pi_{\alpha,q_0,\alpha_0}$ is an inner CCP, hence a pCCP. Thus, by by condition (ii) in Definition 11, it is parallel closed, i.e., $\varsigma(u) \mathrel{\parallel\!\!\!\!\!\rightarrow} \varsigma(v)$ for all substitutions ς satisfying its conditional part $\theta(c), \theta(c_0)$. In particular, $t = \sigma(\ell)[\sigma(r_0)]_{q_0} = \sigma(u) \xrightarrow{Q_1} \sigma(v) = \sigma(r)$ for some set Q_1 of disjoint positions. Thus, we have a peak $t_1|_p \xleftarrow{Q_1} t \xrightarrow{Q_0} t_0|_p$. As in the last paragraph of the proof of [2, Theorem 6.4.8], we have $m(t, Q_0, Q_1) < m(s, P_0, P_1)$. Thus, by the induction hypothesis, there are terms u_p and u'_p such that $t_1|_p \mathrel{\parallel\!\!\!\!\!\rightarrow} u_p \mathrel{{}^*\!\!\leftarrow\!\!\!\!\!\parallel} t_0|_p$ and $t_1|_p \mathrel{\parallel\!\!\!\!\!\rightarrow}^* u'_p \mathrel{\leftarrow\!\!\!\!\!\parallel} t_0|_p$.

The following diagram summarizes the proof (*P.C.* means *Parallel Closedness*):

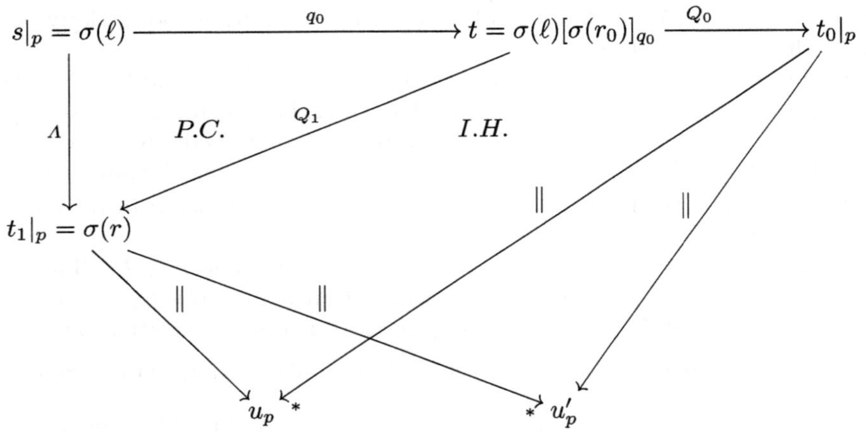

Example 7. The following GTRS $\mathcal{R}$ implements a test of evenness/oddity of numbers in Peano's notation through a "labeling" with symbols even and odd.

$$\mathsf{isEven}(0) \quad (27)$$
$$\mathsf{isEven}(\mathsf{s}(\mathsf{s}(n))) \Leftarrow \mathsf{isEven}(n) \quad (28)$$
$$0 + x \to x \quad (29)$$
$$x + 0 \to x \quad (30)$$
$$x + y \to y + x \quad (31)$$
$$\mathsf{test}(x) \to \mathsf{even}(x) \Leftarrow \mathsf{isEven}(x) \quad (32)$$
$$\mathsf{test}(x) \to \mathsf{odd}(x) \Leftarrow \mathsf{isEven}(\mathsf{s}(x)) \quad (33)$$

We have the following CCPs and PCPVs:

$$\langle 0, 0 \rangle \quad (34)$$
$$\langle x + 0, x \rangle \quad (35)$$
$$\langle 0 + x, x \rangle \quad (36)$$

$$\langle \mathsf{odd}(x), \mathsf{even}(x)\rangle \Leftarrow \mathsf{isEven}(x), \mathsf{isEven}(\mathsf{s}(x)) \tag{37}$$
$$\langle \mathsf{0} + x', x\rangle \Leftarrow x \nrightarrow\!\!\!\!\!\!\!\nrightarrow x' \tag{38}$$
$$\langle x' + \mathsf{0}, x\rangle \Leftarrow x \nrightarrow\!\!\!\!\!\!\!\nrightarrow x' \tag{39}$$
$$\langle x' + y', y + x\rangle \Leftarrow x \nrightarrow\!\!\!\!\!\!\!\nrightarrow x', y \nrightarrow\!\!\!\!\!\!\!\nrightarrow y' \tag{40}$$
$$\langle \mathsf{test}(x'), \mathsf{even}(x)\rangle \Leftarrow x \nrightarrow\!\!\!\!\!\!\!\nrightarrow x', \mathsf{isEven}(x) \tag{41}$$
$$\langle \mathsf{test}(x'), \mathsf{odd}(x)\rangle \Leftarrow x \nrightarrow\!\!\!\!\!\!\!\nrightarrow x', \mathsf{isEven}(\mathsf{s}(x)) \tag{42}$$

The CCPs (34)–(37) are all strongly $\nrightarrow\!\!\!\!\!\!\!\nrightarrow$-joinable (in particular, (37) is $\overline{\mathcal{R}}$-*infeasible* as no substitution σ simultaneously satisfies $\mathsf{isEven}(x)$ and $\mathsf{isEven}(\mathsf{s}(x))$. By Proposition 4, the PCVPs (38)–(40) are strongly $\nrightarrow\!\!\!\!\!\!\!\nrightarrow$-joinable. Also note that the CVP $\pi_{(41),x,1}$: $\langle \mathsf{test}(x'), \mathsf{even}(x)\rangle \Leftarrow x \to x', \mathsf{isEven}(x)$ is $\overline{\mathcal{R}}$-infeasible: if $\sigma(x)$ can be rewritten to $\sigma(x')$, then $\mathsf{isEven}(\sigma(x))$ does not hold. By Proposition 5, (41) is strongly $\nrightarrow\!\!\!\!\!\!\!\nrightarrow$-joinable. Similarly for (42). By Theorem 1, $\mathcal{R}$ is confluent.

Example 8. Let $\mathcal{R}'$ be $\mathcal{R}$ in Example 6 extended with the rule

$$\mathsf{f}(x, y) \to \mathsf{a} \tag{43}$$

By Proposition 4, the PCVPs of the left-linear rules (24), (25), and (43) are strongly $\nrightarrow\!\!\!\!\!\!\!\nrightarrow$-joinable. Also, $\pi_{(23),x,\{1,2\}}$: $\langle \mathsf{f}(x', x''), \mathsf{a}\rangle \Leftarrow x \nrightarrow\!\!\!\!\!\!\!\nrightarrow x', x \nrightarrow\!\!\!\!\!\!\!\nrightarrow x''$ is strongly $\nrightarrow\!\!\!\!\!\!\!\nrightarrow$-joinable: $\mathsf{f}(x', x'') \to_{(43)} \mathsf{a}$ and therefore $\sigma(\mathsf{f}(x', x'')) \to_{(43)} \mathsf{a}$ for every substitution σ satisfying the conditional part of $\pi_{(23),x,\{1,2\}}$. The trivial root CCP $\pi_{((23)),\Lambda,(43)}$: $\langle \mathsf{a}, \mathsf{a}\rangle$ is strongly $\nrightarrow\!\!\!\!\!\!\!\nrightarrow$-joinable. There is no inner CCP. By Theorem 1, $\nrightarrow\!\!\!\!\!\!\!\nrightarrow_{\mathcal{R}'}$ is strongly confluent and $\mathcal{R}'$ confluent.

TRSs $\mathcal{R} = (\mathcal{F}, R)$ are GTRSs $\mathcal{R} = (\mathcal{F}, \Pi, \mu_\top, H, R)$, where $\Pi = \{\to, \to^*\}$ and $H = \emptyset$. Then, $\mu_\top$-left-linearity boils down to left-linearity, and $\mu_\top$-compatibility trivially holds. Thus, Proposition 4 proves left-linearity as a *sufficient condition* for strong $\nrightarrow\!\!\!\!\!\!\!\nrightarrow$-joinability of PCVPs of unconditional rules. However, Example 8 shows left-linearity as *not necessary.* Thus, when applied to TRSs, Theorem 1 strictly subsumes [35, Corollary 3.2].

7 Weak V-Orthogonality

Weak orthogonality tests of TRSs amount at checking *syntactic conditions* [14, Definition 3.1.1] which imply confluence:

- W-ORTH$_1$: *left-linearity* of rules (no variable occurs twice in left-hand sides);
- W-ORTH$_2$: all critical pairs $\langle s, t\rangle$ are *trivial*, i.e., $s = t$.

We generalize this approach to almost parallel-closed GTRSs using Theorem 1. Due to the use of conditions in rules, the (in)feasibility of rules and conditional pairs is considered as a "natural" feature to deal with. Apart from this, we obtain a *syntactic criterion* guaranteeing confluence of GTRSs. The requirement in Theorem 1, is achieved if rules α are μ-left-linear and μ-compatible (Proposition 4) or $\mathsf{CVP}(\alpha) = \emptyset$ (Proposition 5). Trivial CCPs are strongly $\nrightarrow\!\!\!\!\!\!\!\nrightarrow$-joinable and parallel-closed (s-triviality is *not* a syntactic condition as joinability of conditions must be tested). This motivates the following.

Definition 12. (Weakly V-orthogonal *GTRS***).** *A GTRS* $\mathcal{R} = (\mathcal{F}, \Pi, \mu, H, R)$ *is* weakly V-orthogonal *if*

- WV-ORTH$_1$*: for all* $\alpha \in R$*,* $\mathsf{CVP}(\alpha) = \emptyset$ *or* α *is* μ*-left-linear and* μ*-compatible;*
- WV-ORTH$_2$*: all CCPs in* $\mathsf{pCCP}(\mathcal{R}) \cup \mathsf{iCCP}(\mathcal{R})$ *are trivial.*

Remark 4 ('V-' of weak V-orthogonality). Prefix V- stresses the explicit treatment of *variable peaks* using CVPs and PCVPs, see Remark 1.

By WV-ORTH$_2$, weakly V-orthogonal GTRSs are almost parallel-closed (feasible iCCPs of $\mathcal{R}$ which are *not* in $\mathsf{iCCP}(\mathcal{R})$ come from 1- or 2-rules; thus, they are trivial and hence strongly $\twoheadrightarrow\!\!\!\!\!\!\Vert\;_{\mathcal{R}}$-joinable). As a corollary of Theorem 1, we obtain:

Theorem 2. *Let* $\mathcal{R}$ *be a weakly V-orthogonal GTRSs. Then,* $\twoheadrightarrow\!\!\!\!\!\!\Vert\;_{\mathcal{R}}$ *is strongly confluent and* $\mathcal{R}$ *is confluent.*

Example 9. The rules of $\mathcal{R}$ in Fig. 1 are all μ-left-linear and μ-compatible. Thus, WV-ORTH$_1$ holds. And WV-ORTH$_2$ also holds: $\mathsf{pCCP}(\mathcal{R}) = \mathsf{iCCP}(\mathcal{R}) = \emptyset$ (Example 3). Thus, $\mathcal{R}$ is weakly V-orthogonal and confluent.

8 Application to Some Rewriting-Based Systems

In this section we show how the results in this paper improve existing results for some rewriting-based systems which can be seen as particular cases of GTRSs.

Application to TRSs. For TRSs, weak V-orthogonality boils down to weak orthogonality [14, Definition 3.1.1]. However, as a GTRS, $\mathcal{R}'$ in Example 8 uses $\mu_\top$ and it is not ($\mu_\top$-)left-linear. Hence, it is not weakly V-orthogonal, as WV-ORTH$_1$ does not hold. However, Theorem 1 proves $\twoheadrightarrow\!\!\!\!\!\!\Vert\;_{\mathcal{R}'}$ strongly confluent and $\mathcal{R}'$ confluent (Example 8). Note that [35, Corollary 3.2] does *not* apply to $\mathcal{R}'$.

Application to CS-TRSs. A Context-Sensitive Term Rewriting System (CS-TRS) $\mathcal{R} = (\mathcal{F}, \mu, R)$, where R is a set of unconditional rules [18] are GTRSs $\mathcal{R} = (\mathcal{F}, \Pi, \mu, H, R)$, where $\Pi = \{\to, \to^*\}$ and H is empty.

Example 10. Consider the following CS-TRS $\mathcal{R}$ from COPS[1] (1336.trs):

$$\mathsf{f}(x, x) \to \mathsf{plus}(\mathsf{plus}(x, x), x) \qquad\qquad \mathsf{plus}(x, y) \to \mathsf{plus}(y, x)$$

where $\mu(f) = \emptyset$ for all $f \in \mathcal{F}$. Since all variables in the left-hand sides of rules are frozen and $\mathsf{pCCP}(\mathcal{R}) = \mathsf{iCCP}(\mathcal{R}) = \emptyset$, $\mathcal{R}$ is V-orthogonal and confluent.

Left-linear CS-TRSs $\mathcal{R}$ without μ-critical pairs (i.e., unconditional critical pairs π whose critical position is active, i.e., $\pi \in \mathsf{pCCP}(\mathcal{R})$) and such that for all $\ell \to r$ in $\mathcal{R}$ and active variables x in ℓ, (i) x occurs nowhere else in ℓ and (ii) x is not frozen in r are called μ-orthogonal [23, Definition 35]. Weakly V-orthogonal CS-TRSs properly *include* them. For instance, $\mathcal{R}$ in Example 10 is weakly V-orthogonal but not μ-orthogonal.

[1] Confluence Problems database https://cops.uibk.ac.at/.

Application to CTRSs. A CTRS $\mathcal{R} = (\mathcal{F}, R)$, with R a set of rules $\ell \to r \Leftarrow s_1 \approx t_1, \ldots, s_n \approx t_n$ for a predicate symbol $\approx$, is a GTRS $\mathcal{R} = (\mathcal{F}, \Pi, \mu_\top, H, R)$, where $\Pi = \{\to, \to^*, \approx\}$, no replacement restriction is considered (due to $\mu_\top$), and H depends on the (fixed) *evaluation semantics* (*join*, *oriented*, or *semi-equational* [26, Definition 7.1.3]) for the conditions $s \approx t$ in rules, see [21, Figure 2].

Example 11. The following (non-terminating and non-left-linear) oriented 2-CTRS $\mathcal{R}$ (i.e., $\approx$ is interpreted as $\to^*$):

$$\mathsf{a} \to \mathsf{b} \qquad \mathsf{c} \to \mathsf{g}(\mathsf{c}) \qquad \mathsf{f}(x, x) \to x \Leftarrow \mathsf{h}(\mathsf{b}, y) \approx \mathsf{h}(x, \mathsf{g}(y)), y \approx \mathsf{c}$$

is *not* weakly orthogonal [14, Definition 4.0.5]. However, the only CVPs, i.e.,

$$\langle \mathsf{f}(x', x), x\rangle \Leftarrow x \to x', \mathsf{h}(\mathsf{b}, y) \approx \mathsf{h}(x, \mathsf{g}(y)), y \approx \mathsf{c}$$
$$\langle \mathsf{f}(x, x'), x\rangle \Leftarrow x \to x', \mathsf{h}(\mathsf{b}, y) \approx \mathsf{h}(x, \mathsf{g}(y)), y \approx \mathsf{c}$$

are *infeasible*: if σ satisfies the (common) conditional part, then $\sigma(x) \to_{\mathcal{R}} \sigma(x')$ holds. However, $\sigma(\mathsf{h}(\mathsf{b}, y)) = \mathsf{h}(\mathsf{b}, \sigma(y)) \to^*_{\mathcal{R}} \mathsf{h}(\sigma(x), \mathsf{g}(\sigma(y))) = \sigma(\mathsf{h}(x, \mathsf{g}(y)))$ requires $\mathsf{b} = \sigma(x)$, which contradicts reducibility of $\sigma(x)$. Since $\mathsf{CVP}(\mathcal{R}) = \mathsf{pCCP}(\mathcal{R}) = \mathsf{iCCP}(\mathcal{R}) = \emptyset$, $\mathcal{R}$ is weakly V-orthogonal and confluent.

Application to CS-CTRSs. A CS-CTRS [19] $\mathcal{R} = (\mathcal{F}, \mu, R)$, with R a set of conditional rules is a GTRS $\mathcal{R} = (\mathcal{F}, \Pi, \mu, H, R)$ with H as explained for CTRSs. Confluence of *terminating* CS-CTRSs can be proved by using the results in [21].

Example 12. Let $\mathcal{R}'$ be the 1-GTRS $\mathcal{R}$ in Example 4 with $\mu(\mathsf{f}) = \emptyset$. Note that $\mathcal{R}'$ is *not terminating*: $\mathsf{f}(\mathsf{b}) \to_{\mathcal{R}'} \mathsf{f}(\mathsf{b}) \to_{\mathcal{R}'} \cdots$. However, $\mathsf{CVP}(\mathcal{R}') = \mathsf{pCCP}(\mathcal{R}') = \mathsf{iCCP}(\mathcal{R}') = \emptyset$. Thus, $\mathcal{R}'$ is weakly V-orthogonal and hence confluent.

9 Implementation

Kaplan showed one-step conditional rewriting *undecidable* [13]. Thus, for GTRSs $\mathcal{R}$, strong $\nrightarrow\!\!\!\!\to_{\mathcal{R}}$-joinability is undecidable, as one-step rewriting is part of $\nrightarrow\!\!\!\!\to$-joinability. For TRSs, joinability is also *undecidable* in absence of termination, which is a main focus of this paper, as confluence of terminating GTRSs $\mathcal{R}$ is characterized as the joinability of all pairs in $\mathsf{CCP}(\mathcal{R}) \cup \mathsf{CVP}(\mathcal{R})$ [21, Theorem 68]. Even in this case, as a consequence of Kaplan's observation (still valid for terminating CTRSs), confluence of terminating GTRSs is undecidable. However, there are opportunities to mechanize the use of Theorem 1.

Example 13. A mechanized proof of $\mathcal{R}$ in Example 7 is possible as follows:

1. strong $\to$-joinability of CCPs (34)–(36) is easy;
2. the $\overline{\mathcal{R}}$-infeasibility of (37) can be proved with AGES [7]: by [8, Theorem 1], the $\overline{\mathcal{R}}$-feasibility of the conditional part of (37) implies the provability of

$$(\exists x)(\mathsf{isEven}(x) \wedge \mathsf{isEven}(\mathsf{s}(x))) \tag{44}$$

in $\overline{\mathcal{R}}$. A model of $\overline{\mathcal{R}} \cup \{\neg(44)\}$ is obtained with AGES, thus witnessing the infeasibility of (37).

3. Strong $\nrightarrow\!\!\!\!\parallel$-joinability of the PCVPs (38)–(40) follows by Proposition 4. We use AGES again to prove $\overline{\mathcal{R}}$-infeasibility of the CVPs $\pi_{(32),x,1}$ and $\pi_{(33),x,1}$ as above. By Proposition 5 strong $\nrightarrow\!\!\!\!\parallel_{\mathcal{R}}$-joinability of (41) and (42) follows.

Strong $\rightarrow$-joinability tests of unconditional pairs $\langle s,t\rangle$ can be achieved as the $\overline{\mathcal{R}}$-feasibility of the sequence $s^{\downarrow} \rightarrow^{=} x, s^{\downarrow} \rightarrow^{*} x', t^{\downarrow} \rightarrow^{*} x, t^{\downarrow} \rightarrow^{=} x'$, where x and x' are different variables, and given a term u, $u^{\downarrow}$ is the *grounded* version of u obtained by replacing each variable x in u by a constant c_x, see, e.g., [1, page 224]. The tool infChecker [8] is currently able to perform such tests for particular GTRSs (e.g., CS-CTRSs) but not for arbitrary GTRSs. Strong $\nrightarrow\!\!\!\!\parallel$-joinability tests are defined as the $\overline{\mathcal{R}}^{\nrightarrow\!\!\!\!\parallel}$-feasibility of $s^{\downarrow} \nrightarrow\!\!\!\!\parallel x, s^{\downarrow} \nrightarrow\!\!\!\!\parallel^{*} x', t^{\downarrow} \nrightarrow\!\!\!\!\parallel^{*} x, t^{\downarrow} \nrightarrow\!\!\!\!\parallel x'$ (21). However, infChecker is not able (yet) to deal with parallel rewriting predicates $\nrightarrow\!\!\!\!\parallel$ and $\nrightarrow\!\!\!\!\parallel^{*}$. Furthermore, with *conditional pairs* $\langle s,t\rangle \Leftarrow c$ grounding variables in s and t does not work, in general, as only variables whose instantiation satisfies the conditional part should be considered, see [9, Section 5.5].

Theorem 2 was implemented as part of the confluence tool CONFident to prepare its participation in the 2023 edition of the Confluence Competition, CoCo 2023[2]. CONFident and ConfCSR [31] participated in the CSR category of CoCo 2023, where CS-TRSs and CS-CTRSs are mixed (176 CS-TRSs and 287 CS-CTRSs). Since ConfCSR does not handle CS-CTRSs (whose confluence is (dis)proved by CONFident by using the results in this paper together with [9,21]), the following table displays the information for CS-TRSs in [9, Table 10 (left)] for the CoCo 2023 *full run* benchmarks set (full details in [9, Section 8]):

Tool	Yes	No	Maybe	Solved	Total
ConfCSR	28	83	65	111	176
CONFident 2024	49	83	44	132	176

For instance, $\mathcal{R}$ in Example 10 was solved by using the results in this paper.[3]

10 Related Work

In a revised version of [32], Suzuki, Middeldorp, and Ida defined a left-linear CTRS $\mathcal{R}$ as *orthogonal* if there is no proper CCP [33, page 3]. Sternagel and Sternagel only consider *feasible* CCPs in their notion of *orthogonality modulo infeasibility* [30, Definition 2]. However, confluence of such orthogonal CTRSs only follows if *additional* requirements on the structure of the rules are fulfilled. As illustrated by the CTRS in Example 11, there are weakly V-orthogonal CTRSs which are not orthogonal (modulo infeasibility). The following example shows that there are orthogonal CTRSs which are *not* weakly V-orthogonal.

[2] https://project-coco.uibk.ac.at/2023/.

[3] The report produced by CONFident for CoCo 2023 uses the now deprecated term "strong orthogonality" instead of weak V-orthogonality, see http://cops.uibk.ac.at/results/2023/CSR/CONFident/1336.trs/615314450.txt.

Example 14. The following orthogonal oriented 3-CTRS $\mathcal{R}$ [33, Example 4.4]

$$\mathsf{a} \to \mathsf{b} \tag{45}$$

$$\mathsf{b} \to \mathsf{c} \tag{46}$$

$$\mathsf{f}(x) \to y \Leftarrow x \approx y \tag{47}$$

is confluent by [33, Corollary 4.7]. However, $\mathcal{R}$ is *not* weakly V-orthogonal: the iCCP $\pi_{(47),\Lambda,(47)} : \langle y, y' \rangle \Leftarrow x \approx y, x \approx y'$ of the conditional rule is not trivial.

Note, however, that *neither* $\to_{\mathcal{R}}$ nor $\#_{\mathcal{R}}$ for $\mathcal{R}$ in Example 14 are strongly confluent. For instance, $\sigma = \{x \mapsto \mathsf{a}, y \mapsto \mathsf{a}, y' \mapsto \mathsf{c}\}$ satisfies the conditional part of the iCCP $\pi_{(47),\Lambda,(47)}$ in the example, but $\sigma(y) = \mathsf{a} \neq \mathsf{c} = \sigma(y')$ are not strongly $\#_{\mathcal{R}}$-joinable. Thus, the proof of confluence of orthogonal CTRSs in [33] does not follow from proofs of strong confluence of $\#_{\mathcal{R}}$ as done in this paper.

11 Conclusions and Future Work

We have investigated strong confluence of parallel rewriting with almost parallel-closed GTRSs (Theorem 1), strictly extending a previous result for left-linear TRSs [35, Corollary 3.2]. Here, left-linearity is replaced by the strong $\#$-joinability of PCVPs (Definition 9). Left-linearity of TRSs can be seen as a sufficient condition for strong $\#$-joinability of PCVPs (Proposition 4 and Example 8).

We have derived an extended and generalized syntactic criterion, *weak V-orthogonality*, which guarantees strong confluence of parallel rewriting and hence confluence of GTRSs. It is the first orthogonality-like result for GTRSs. Advantages of weak V-orthogonality with respect to previous notions of (weak) orthogonality (for CTRSs, see [20] for an account) are: (i) Left-linearity is relaxed into either (a) μ-left-linearity and μ-compatibility, or (b) infeasibility of CVPs of rules; (ii) It focuses on conditional critical pairs and parallel conditional variable pairs, paying no attention to other structural aspects of rules; (iii) Our Theorem 2 requires no additional syntactic restrictions on rules and (iv) it does *not* depend on any particular evaluation mode of conditions (using reachability, joinability, etc.). Our results are useful to prove confluence of CS-TRSs and CTRSs (Sect. 8). Theorem 2 was implemented as part of the tool CONFident and tested in the 2023 International Competition of Confluence, CoCo 2023.

Future Work. We are working to update CONFident and infChecker to give support to the use of Theorems 1 and 2 with arbitrary GTRSs, as discussed in Sect. 9. From a theoretical point of view, the results in [6,10,11,17,28,29,36] can also be used to improve our results. In particular, Gramlich investigated *parallel critical pairs* of a TRS, where *simultaneous, parallel overlaps* between the left-hand side of a rule and the left-hand sides of other rules of are considered [6, Definition 9], and proved a confluence result for left-linear TRSs [6, Theorem 14] improving on [35, Corollary 3.2]. We believe that Gramlich's idea can be applied to GTRSs.

Acknowledgements. I thank the reviewers for their detailed and useful comments.

Disclosure of Interests. The author has no competing interests to declare that are relevant to the content of this article.

References

1. Avenhaus, J., Loría-Sáenz, C.: On conditional rewrite systems with extra variables and deterministic logic programs. In: Pfenning, F. (ed.) LPAR 1994. LNCS, vol. 822, pp. 215–229. Springer, Heidelberg (1994). https://doi.org/10.1007/3-540-58216-9_40
2. Baader, F., Nipkow, T.: Term Rewriting and All That. Cambridge University Press (1998)
3. Clavel, M., et al.: All About Maude - A High-Performance Logical Framework, How to Specify, Program and Verify Systems in Rewriting Logic, volume 4350 of Lecture Notes in Computer Science. Springer, Cham (2007). https://doi.org/10.1007/978-3-540-71999-1
4. Dershowitz, N., Okada, M., Sivakumar, G.: Confluence of conditional rewrite systems. In: Kaplan, S., Jouannaud, J.-P. editors, Conditional Term Rewriting Systems, 1st International Workshop, Proceedings, volume 308 of Lecture Notes in Computer Science, pp. 31–44. Springer, Berlin, Heidelberg (1987). https://doi.org/10.1007/3-540-19242-5_3
5. Fitting, M.: First-Order Logic and Automated Theorem Proving. Springer, New York, NY (1996). https://doi.org/10.1007/978-1-4612-2360-3
6. Gramlich, B.: Confluence without termination via parallel critical pairs. In: Kirchner, H. (ed.) Trees in Algebra and Programming — CAAP '96, pp. 211–225. Springer, Berlin, Heidelberg (1996). https://doi.org/10.1007/3-540-61064-2_39
7. Gutiérrez, R., Lucas, S.: Automatic generation of logical models with AGES. In: Fontaine, P. (ed.) CADE 2019. LNCS (LNAI), vol. 11716, pp. 287–299. Springer, Cham (2019). https://doi.org/10.1007/978-3-030-29436-6_17
8. Gutiérrez, R., Lucas, S.: Automatically proving and disproving feasibility conditions. In: Peltier, N., Sofronie-Stokkermans, V. (eds.) IJCAR 2020. LNCS (LNAI), vol. 12167, pp. 416–435. Springer, Cham (2020). https://doi.org/10.1007/978-3-030-51054-1_27
9. Gutiérrez, R., Lucas, S., Vítores, M.: Proving Confluence in the Confluence Framework with CONFident. Fundam. Informaticae **192**(2), 167–217 (2024)
10. Hirokawa, N., Kim, D., Shintani, K., Thiemann, R.: Certification of confluence- and commutation-proofs via parallel critical pairs. In: Timany, A., Traytel, D., Pientka, B., Blazy, S., editors, Proceedings of the 13th ACM SIGPLAN International Conference on Certified Programs and Proofs, CPP 2024, London, UK, January 15-16, 2024, pp. 147–161. ACM (2024)
11. Hirokawa, N., Nagele, J., van Oostrom, V., Oyamaguchi, M.: Confluence by critical pair analysis revisited. In: Fontaine, P. (ed.) CADE 2019. LNCS (LNAI), vol. 11716, pp. 319–336. Springer, Cham (2019). https://doi.org/10.1007/978-3-030-29436-6_19
12. Huet, G.P.: Confluent Reductions: abstract properties and applications to term rewriting systems. J. ACM **27**(4), 797–821 (1980)
13. Kaplan, S.: Conditional rewrite rules. Theor. Comput. Sci. **33**, 175–193 (1984)

14. Klop, J.W.: Chapter 1: Term rewriting systems. In: Abramsky, S., Gabbay, D., Maibaurn, T., (eds), Handbook of Logic in Computer Science, pp. 1–116. Oxford University Press (1992)
15. Klop, J.W.: A counterexample to the Church-Rosser property for Lambda calculus with surjective pairing. Technical report, Department of Mathematics, Utrecht University. Preprint No. 102 (1979)
16. Knuth, D.E., Bendix, P.E.: Simple word problems in universal algebra. In: Leech, J., (ed), Computational Problems in Abstract Algebra, pp. 263–297. Pergamon Press (1970)
17. Liu, J., Jouannaud, J.-P., Ogawa, M.: Confluence of layered rewrite systems. In: Kreutzer, S., (ed), 24th EACSL Annual Conference on Computer Science Logic, CSL 2015, September 7-10, 2015, Berlin, Germany, vol. 41 of LIPIcs, pp. 423–440. Schloss Dagstuhl - Leibniz-Zentrum für Informatik (2015)
18. Lucas, S.: Context-sensitive rewriting. ACM Comput. Surv. **53**(4), 78:1–78:36 (2020)
19. Lucas, S.: Applications and extensions of context-sensitive rewriting. J. Logical Algebraic Methods Program. **121**, 100680 (2021)
20. Lucas, S.: A roadmap to orthogonality of conditional term rewriting systems. In: Nishida, N., Chenavier, C., (eds), 13th International Workshop on Confluence, IWC 2024, pp. 28–34 (2024)
21. Lucas, S.:. Local confluence of conditional and generalized term rewriting systems. J. Logical Algebraic Methods Program. **136**, 100926, 1–23 (2024)
22. Lucas, S.: Termination of generalized term rewriting systems. In: Rehof, J. (ed), 9th International Conference on Formal Structures for Computation and Deduction (FSCD 2024), volume 299 of Leibniz International Proceedings in Informatics (LIPIcs), pp. 29:1–29:18, Dagstuhl, Germany. Schloss Dagstuhl – Leibniz-Zentrum für Informatik (2024)
23. Lucas, S., Vítores, M., Gutiérrez, R.: Proving and disproving confluence of context-sensitive rewriting. J. Logical and Algebraic Methods Program. **126**, 100749 (2022)
24. Mendelson, E.: Introduction to mathematical logic (4. ed.). Chapman and Hall (1997)
25. Middeldorp, A., Hamoen, E.: Completeness results for basic narrowing. Appl. Algebra Eng. Commun. Comput. **5**, 213–253 (1994)
26. Ohlebusch, E.: Advanced Topics in Term Rewriting. Springer, New York, NY (2002). https://doi.org/10.1007/978-1-4757-3661-8
27. Robinson, J.A.: A machine-oriented logic based on the resolution principle. J. ACM **12**(1), 23–41 (1965). https://doi.org/10.1145/321250.321253
28. Schöpf, J., Mitterwallner, F., Middeldorp, A.: Confluence of logically constrained rewrite systems revisited. In: Benzmüller, C., Heule, M.J.H., Schmidt, R.A. (eds.) Automated Reasoning: 12th International Joint Conference, IJCAR 2024, Nancy, France, July 3–6, 2024, Proceedings, Part II, pp. 298–316. Springer Nature Switzerland, Cham (2024). https://doi.org/10.1007/978-3-031-63501-4_16
29. Shintani, K., Hirokawa, N.: Compositional confluence criteria. In: Felty, A.P., ed, 7th International Conference on Formal Structures for Computation and Deduction, FSCD 2022, August 2-5, 2022, Haifa, Israel, volume 228 of *Leibniz International Proceedings in Informatics (LIPIcs)*, pp. 28:1–28:19. Schloss Dagstuhl - Leibniz-Zentrum für Informatik (2022)
30. Sternagel, C., Sternagel, T.: Certifying confluence of almost orthogonal CTRSs via exact tree automata completion. In: Kesner, D., Pientka, B., (eds), 1st International Conference on Formal Structures for Computation and Deduction, FSCD 2016

Proceedings in Informatics (LIPIcs), pp. 29:1–29:16. Schloss Dagstuhl - Leibniz-Zentrum für Informatik (2016)
31. Stevanovic, F., Mitterwallner, F.: CoCo 2023 Participant: ConfCSR. In: 12th International Workshop on Confluence, IWC 2023, p. 63 (2023)
32. Suzuki, T., Middeldorp, A., Ida, T.: Level-confluence of conditional rewrite systems with extra variables in right-hand sides. In: Hsiang, J. (ed.) RTA 1995. LNCS, vol. 914, pp. 179–193. Springer, Heidelberg (1995). https://doi.org/10.1007/3-540-59200-8_56
33. Suzuki, T., Middeldorp, A., Ida, T.: Level-Confluence of conditional rewrite systems with extra variables in right-hand sides (1995). revised version of [32], http://cl-informatik.uibk.ac.at/users/ami/research/publications/proceedings/95rta.pdf
34. Terese. Term rewriting systems, volume 55 of Cambridge tracts in theoretical computer science. Cambridge University Press (2003)
35. Toyama, Y.: Commutativity of term rewriting systems. In: Fuchi, K., Kott, L., (eds), Programming of Future Generation Computer, II. Proceedings of the Second Franco-Japanese Symposium on Programming of Future Generation Computers, Cannes, France, 9-11, November, 1987, pp. 393–407. North-Holland (1988)
36. van Oostrom, V.: Developing developments. Theor. Comput. Sci. **175**(1), 159–181 (1997)

The Computability Path Order for Beta-Eta-Normal Higher-Order Rewriting

Johannes Niederhauser(✉) and Aart Middeldorp

Department of Computer Science, University of Innsbruck, Innsbruck, Austria
{johannes.niederhauser,aart.middeldorp}@uibk.ac.at

Abstract. We lift the computability path order and its extensions from plain higher-order rewriting to higher-order rewriting on $\beta\eta$-normal forms where matching modulo $\beta\eta$ is employed. The resulting order NCPO is shown to be useful on practical examples. In particular, it can handle systems where its cousin NHORPO fails even when it is used together with the powerful transformation technique of neutralization. We also argue that automating NCPO efficiently is straightforward using SAT/SMT solvers whereas this cannot be said about the transformation technique of neutralization. Our prototype implementation supports automatic termination proof search for NCPO and is also the first one to automate NHORPO with neutralization.

Keywords: Higher-Order Rewriting · Termination · Lambda Calculus

1 Introduction

Higher-order rewriting is known for its abundance of different formalisms where it is often unclear whether results for a particular notion of higher-order rewriting can be transferred to other kinds of higher-order rewriting [12]. In this paper, we are only concerned with one particular formalism, namely a slightly modified version of the higher-order rewrite systems (HRSs) à la Nipkow [16]. However, as the goal of this paper is to lift a particular termination method from one formalism to another, a short discussion about differences and similarities of the used formalisms is necessary. First and foremost, when we talk about higher-order rewriting in this paper, we mean the particular flavor of higher-order rewriting which considers terms of the simply-typed lambda calculus as objects to be rewritten. Within this class of higher-order rewrite formalisms, we further distinguish between *plain* and *normal* higher-order rewriting: Plain higher-order rewriting uses plain syntactic matching and views lambda calculus' β-reduction as a proper rewrite rule which has to be oriented for termination. On the other hand, normal higher-order rewriting uses matching modulo $\beta\eta$, which means that terms which are $\beta\eta$-equivalent should also be equivalent with respect to the reduction order that is used for establishing termination. Nipkow's HRSs are a premier example of normal higher-order rewriting. HRSs are an interesting formalism for automated reasoning as they can directly represent the terms of

C. Barrett and U. Waldmann (Eds.): CADE 2025, LNAI 15943, pp. 207–225, 2025.
https://doi.org/10.1007/978-3-031-99984-0_12

higher-order logic and as such are part of the meta-theory of interactive theorem provers like Isabelle [21]. Furthermore, they come with a critical pair lemma [16] which is vital for automated equational reasoning with techniques such as completion [7]. In particular, automated confluence analysis of higher-order rewriting typically uses HRSs, as witnessed in the Confluence Competition (2015–2020).[1]

While many termination methods are available for plain higher-order rewriting [2,10,12], the situation for normal higher-order rewriting is different. For a long time, powerful termination methods for HRSs were only based on van de Pol's results [22] which employ the monotone algebra approach [25], i.e., semantic termination arguments which are difficult to automate except for more specialized cases like polynomial interpretations of fixed shape [5]. An early version of the *higher-order recursive path order* (HORPO) which is designed for plain higher-order rewriting was adapted for the important subclass of pattern HRSs in [23], an implementation of this approach is available in the tool CSI^ho [19]. Furthermore, the formalism of *algebraic functional systems with meta-variables* (AFSMs) captures both plain and normal rewriting and therefore makes a larger number of termination methods available for HRSs [12]. An implementation of these methods is available in the tool WANDA [13]. However, WANDA has not been optimized for HRSs and the theory developed around it only establishes termination for systems where all left-hand sides are patterns [17]. A powerful recursive path order specifically designed for HRSs and without the restriction to patterns as left-hand sides of rules was missing until Jouannaud and Rubio lifted their definite version of HORPO [10] from plain to normal higher-order rewriting, resulting in NHORPO [11]. However, the important extension of HORPO by the computability closure [10] is not considered. Instead, a novel transformation technique named *neutralization* is introduced. Its goal is to simplify a given system with respect to the applicability of NHORPO without affecting the system's termination behavior.

The aim of this paper is to develop a syntax-directed reduction order for normal higher-order rewriting which is sufficiently powerful compared to NHORPO with neutralization but easier to automate using SAT/SMT solvers. Our starting point is the *computability path order* (CPO) [2] which is defined for plain higher-order rewriting. CPO is an extension of HORPO which incorporates computability closure [3] in a sophisticated way. We follow the general approach from [11] to lift the extension of core CPO with accessible subterms and small symbols to HRSs, resulting in the *$\beta\eta$-normal computability path order* (NCPO). In particular, we will show that there are HRSs which NCPO can prove terminating but where NHORPO (with or without neutralization) as well as the HORPO implementations in WANDA [13] and CSI^ho [19] fail.

In designing a reduction order for normal higher-order rewriting, one has to deal with the well-known problems that well-founded orders which are compatible with $\beta\eta$ cannot be *monotone* (closed under contexts) and *stable* (closed under substitutions) in general as the following examples show:

---

[1] https://project-coco.uibk.ac.at/.

Example 1. Consider $\mathsf{a} > \mathsf{b}$. If $>$ is closed under contexts, we should also have $(\lambda y.\mathsf{c})\mathsf{a} > (\lambda y.\mathsf{c})\mathsf{b}$. If we also want $>$ to be compatible with $\beta\eta$, we obtain $\mathsf{c} > \mathsf{c}$ which means that $>$ cannot be well-founded. Now consider $Fx > x$. If $>$ is closed under substitutions, we should also have $(\lambda x.x)\mathsf{a} > \mathsf{a}$. If we also want $>$ to be compatible with $\beta\eta$, we obtain $\mathsf{a} > \mathsf{a}$ which again means that $>$ cannot be well-founded.

In [22], van de Pol models substitutions via contexts using β-reduction, thereby eliminating the second problem. For the first problem, two different orders $>_1$ and $>_2$ are introduced and it is shown that $s >_1 t$ implies $C[s] >_2 C[t]$ for all terms s, t and contexts C. Since the relations between $>_1$ and $>_2$ are intrinsically semantic, it is not clear how this approach can be transferred to path orders. In [11], both problems were solved by restricting the order $>$ to $\beta\eta$-normal forms and layering it with its plain version ($\sqsupset$) in a way such that $s > t$ implies $s\sigma\!\downarrow\, \sqsupset^+ t\sigma\!\downarrow$ for all substitutions σ where $s\!\downarrow$ denotes the $\beta\eta$-normal form of a term s. Then, monotonicity and well-foundedness of the plain version can be used in order to show that $(>, \sqsupset)$ is a reduction order. We will utilize this approach in order to define a reduction order $(>, \sqsupset)$ where $>$ is NCPO and $\sqsupset$ is CPO.

The remainder of this paper is structured as follows. Section 2 introduces the basic concepts including the type of higher-order rewriting which we are concerned with in this paper as well as an appropriate notion of $\beta\eta$-normal higher-order reduction orders. Section 3 describes the necessary ingredients of our order regarding types, the important concept of nonversatile terms as well as accessible subterms. Based on this, NCPO is introduced in Sect. 4 and proven to be a correct termination method for HRSs in Sect. 5. Finally, our prototype implementation of NCPO is described and compared to NHORPO with neutralization in Sect. 6 before we conclude in Sect. 7. The full version of this paper which includes all proof details is available on arXiv [20].

2 Preliminaries

In this paper, we consider higher-order rewriting on simply-typed lambda terms [1,4]. Given a set $\mathcal{B}$ of base types, the set of simple types $\mathcal{T}$ is defined inductively: If $a \in \mathcal{B}$ then $a \in \mathcal{T}$, and for $U, V \in \mathcal{T}$ also $U \to V \in \mathcal{T}$. We follow the usual convention that the function space constructor $\to$ is right-associative, i.e., $a \to b \to c$ denotes $a \to (b \to c)$. Throughout this text, lowercase letters $a, b, c, \ldots$ denote base types while upper case letters $T, U, V, \ldots$ denote arbitrary types. For each type $U \in \mathcal{T}$ we consider an infinite set of variables $\mathcal{V}_U$ as well as a set of function symbols $\mathcal{F}_U$ where $\mathcal{V}_U \cap \mathcal{F}_U = \varnothing$ and $\mathcal{V}_U \cap \mathcal{V}_V = \mathcal{F}_U \cap \mathcal{F}_V = \varnothing$ for $V \neq U$. We denote the set of all variables by $\mathcal{V} = \bigcup\{\mathcal{V}_U \mid U \in \mathcal{T}\}$. The set of all function symbols $\mathcal{F} = \bigcup\{\mathcal{F}_U \mid U \in \mathcal{T}\}$ is referred to as the *signature*. We associate with each function symbol f an arity $\mathsf{ar}(f) \in \mathbb{N}$. The set of well-typed lambda terms of a type U (Λ_U) is defined as follows:

- $\mathcal{V}_U \subseteq \Lambda_U$,

- if $f \in \mathcal{F}_{T_1 \to \cdots \to T_{\mathsf{ar}(f)} \to U}$ and $t_i \in \Lambda_{T_i}$ for $1 \leqslant i \leqslant \mathsf{ar}(f)$ then $f(t_1, \ldots, t_n) \in \Lambda_U$,
- if $x \in \mathcal{V}_U$ and $s \in \Lambda_V$ then $\lambda x.s \in \Lambda_{U \to V}$,
- if $s \in \Lambda_{U \to V}$ and $t \in \Lambda_U$ then $st \in \Lambda_V$.

The set $\Lambda = \bigcup\{\Lambda_U \mid U \in \mathcal{T}\}$ contains all well-typed lambda terms. We define the function $\tau\colon \Lambda \to \mathcal{T}$ as $\tau(s) = U$ if $s \in \Lambda_U$. Throughout this paper we only consider well-typed lambda terms. We also follow the convention that application is left-associative, i.e. *stu* denotes $(st)u$. Note that our definition of lambda terms with function symbols of fixed arity neither poses a limitation nor adds expressive power as we can always set $\mathsf{ar}(f) = 0$ for all $f \in \mathcal{F}$ (the "return type" of a function symbol does not have to be a base type) and denote $f(t_1, \ldots, t_n)$ by the corresponding application $ft_1 \cdots t_n$. The addition of function symbols with fixed arity is solely needed for an adequate definition of a recursive path order on lambda terms. We sometimes use the shorthand $f(\bar{t})$ to denote the application of f to the list of arguments $\bar{t}$.

We write $\mathsf{FV}(s)$ for the set of free variables of a term s. The term $s[x/t]$ denotes the term where all free occurrences of x have been replaced by t without capturing the free variables of t (*capture-avoiding substitution*). Due to the fact that infinitely many variables are available for each type, this can always be done by renaming the bound variables accordingly (*α-renaming*). In the remainder, we abstract away from this technicality by viewing lambda terms as equivalence classes modulo α-renaming.

Two fundamental concepts in lambda calculus are the notions of β- and η-reduction which are defined as the rule schemas $(\lambda x.s)t \to_\beta s[x/t]$ and $\lambda x.ux \to_\eta u$ if $x \notin \mathsf{FV}(u)$. Note that both β- and η-reduction preserve types. Every term s has a unique $\beta\eta$-normal form which we denote by $s{\downarrow}$. Rewriting to $\beta\eta$-normal form and the set of $\beta\eta$-normal forms are denoted by $\to^!_{\beta\eta}$ and $\mathsf{NF}(\beta\eta) \subseteq \Lambda$, respectively.

A substitution σ is a mapping from variables to terms of the same type where $\mathcal{D}\mathsf{om}(\sigma) = \{x \mid \sigma(x) \neq x\}$ is finite. We often write σ as a set of variable bindings. Given a substitution $\sigma = \{x_1 \mapsto t_1, \ldots, x_n \mapsto t_n\}$, we define $s\sigma$ as the simultaneous capture-avoiding substitution $s[x_1/t_1, \ldots, x_n/t_n]$. The free variables of a substitution are defined as follows: $\mathsf{FV}(\sigma) = \bigcup\{\mathsf{FV}(\sigma(x)) \mid x \in \mathcal{D}\mathsf{om}(\sigma)\}$. A substitution is said to be *away from* a finite set of variables X if $(\mathcal{D}\mathsf{om}(\sigma) \cup \mathsf{FV}(\sigma)) \cap X = \varnothing$. We follow the convention that the postfix operations of substitution application as well as $\downarrow$ bind stronger than lambda abstractions and applications, i.e., $u\sigma{\downarrow}v\sigma{\downarrow} = (u\sigma{\downarrow})(v\sigma{\downarrow})$ and $\lambda x.t\sigma{\downarrow} = \lambda x.(t\sigma{\downarrow})$. If $\bar{t} = (t_1, \ldots, t_n)$, we allow ourselves to write $\bar{t}\sigma$ ($\bar{t}\sigma{\downarrow}$) as a shorthand for $(t_1\sigma, \ldots, t_n\sigma)$ $((t_1\sigma{\downarrow}, \ldots, t_n\sigma{\downarrow}))$.

Contexts C are lambda terms which contain exactly one occurrence of the special symbol $\square$ which can assume any type. We write $C[s]$ for the lambda term C where $\square$ is replaced by s without employing capture-avoiding substitution. A binary relation $R \subseteq \Lambda \times \Lambda$ is *monotone* if $s \mathrel{R} t$ implies $C[s] \mathrel{R} C[t]$ for every context C. Furthermore, we say that a term t is a *subterm* of s ($s \trianglerighteq t$) if there exists a context C such that $s = C[t]$ and define the proper subterm relation $s \triangleright t$ as $s \trianglerighteq t$ and $s \neq t$. Since we view lambda terms as equivalence classes modulo

α-renaming, the subterm relation is also defined modulo α-renaming. Hence, we have e.g. $\lambda x.t \rhd t[x/z]$ for a fresh variable z. Now, we are able to define the notion of higher-order rewriting we are concerned with in this paper.

Definition 1. *A* rewrite rule *is a tuple* $\ell \to r$ *with* $\ell, r \in \mathsf{NF}(\beta\eta)$ *where* ℓ *is not of the form* $xs_1 \cdots s_n$, $\tau(\ell) = \tau(r)$ *and* $\mathsf{FV}(r) \subseteq \mathsf{FV}(\ell)$. *A* higher-order rewrite system (HRS) *is a set of rewrite rules. Given an* HRS $\mathcal{R}$, *there is a* rewrite step $s \to_{\mathcal{R}} t$ *if there exist a rule* $\ell \to r \in \mathcal{R}$, *a substitution* σ *and a context* C *such that* $s = C[\ell\sigma\downarrow] \in \mathsf{NF}(\beta\eta)$ *and* $t = C[r\sigma\downarrow]\downarrow$.

Note that $\to_{\mathcal{R}} \subseteq \mathsf{NF}(\beta\eta) \times \mathsf{NF}(\beta\eta)$ as $C[\ell\sigma\downarrow], C[r\sigma\downarrow]\downarrow \in \mathsf{NF}(\beta\eta)$ by definition. Hence, both rules and rewrite steps only consider terms in their unique $\beta\eta$-normal form whereas matching is performed modulo $\beta\eta$. In the original definition of HRSs [16], the long $\beta\eta$-normal form based on η-expansion instead of η-reduction is used. Using $\beta\eta$-normal forms instead of long $\beta\eta$-normal forms leads to a different rewrite relation and might change the termination behavior of a given rewrite system (cf. Example 2). The reason of our deviation from the standard definition of Nipkow's HRSs is that higher-order recursive path orders usually have a hard time dealing with lambdas, and we wanted keep Theorem 1 simple by using the same canonical form for rewriting as well as higher-order reduction orders. Furthermore, higher-order rewriting on $\beta\eta$-normal forms is interesting in its own right [8,9]. Note that NHORPO [11] can accommodate any orientation of η by adding an appropriate wrapper around the core order which is only defined on $\beta\eta$-normal forms. We expect that a similar strategy works for NCPO, thus making it applicable to the original formulation of HRSs by Nipkow. Another difference from the usual definition of HRSs is that we allow rules of non-base type. However, this is not new [9]. In all other aspects, our definition is equivalent to the original one given in [16].

Example 2. Let $\mathcal{B} = \{a\}$ and consider the function symbols $\mathsf{c} \in \mathcal{F}_a$, $\mathsf{f} \in \mathcal{F}_{a \to a}$ and $\mathsf{g} \in \mathcal{F}_{a \to a \to a}$ as well as the variable $x \in \mathcal{V}_a$. The $\beta\eta$-normal term f cannot be rewritten using the HRS $\mathcal{R}$ consisting of the single rule $\mathsf{f}x \to \mathsf{g}x\mathsf{c}$. However, for its η-long normal form $\lambda y.\mathsf{f}y$ we have $\lambda y.\mathsf{f}y \to_{\mathcal{R}} \lambda y.\mathsf{g}y\mathsf{c}$ in the standard definition of HRSs.

Next, we recall some important definitions about relations which are used throughout this paper. Given a binary relation R, R^+ and R^* denote its transitive and transitive-reflexive closure, respectively. The composition of a two binary relations R and S is defined as follows: $a\ R \cdot S\ b$ if there exists an element c such that $a\ R\ c$ and $c\ S\ b$. A *preorder* is a reflexive and transitive relation. Given a relation $>$ we denote its inverse by $<$ and its reflexive closure by $\geqslant$. Note that the reflexive closure of a binary relation R defined as $R \subseteq A \times A$ contains all elements of the set A even when the strict part of R assumes additional properties of the elements in A which belong to the relation. A binary relation R on a set A is *well-founded* if there is no infinite sequence $a_1\ R\ a_2\ R \cdots$ where $a_i \in A$ for $i \in \mathbb{N}$. We say that an HRS $\mathcal{R}$ is *terminating* if $\to_{\mathcal{R}}$ is well-founded. We now define the notion of $\beta\eta$-normal higher-order reduction orders.

Definition 2. *A* $\beta\eta$-normal higher-order reduction order *is a pair* $(>, \sqsupset)$ *which satisfies the following conditions:*

- $\sqsupset \subseteq \Lambda \times \Lambda$ *is a well-founded relation,*
- $\sqsupset$ *is monotone,*
- $\rightarrow_\beta, \rightarrow_\eta \subseteq \sqsupset$,
- $s > t$ *implies* $s\sigma\downarrow \sqsupset^+ t\sigma\downarrow$ *for all* $s, t \in \mathsf{NF}(\beta\eta)$ *and substitutions* σ.

We often refer to the last condition as $\beta\eta$-normal stability. *An* HRS $\mathcal{R}$ *is* compatible *with a* $\beta\eta$*-normal higher-order reduction order* $(>, \sqsupset)$ *if* $\ell >^+ r$ *for all* $\ell \rightarrow r \in \mathcal{R}$.

As in [11], the intuition behind this definition is that $>$ will be used to orient the rules of HRSs while relying on the termination proof of its plain variant $\sqsupset$. Despite calling $(>, \sqsupset)$ an order, we do not demand transitivity of any of its components. In the context of higher-order rewriting, this is standard as $\sqsupset$ contains β-reduction which is not transitive. By taking the identity substitution, we can see that $\beta\eta$-normal stability implies $> \subseteq \sqsupset^+$. The following theorem shows that $\beta\eta$-normal higher-order reduction orders can be used to show termination of our flavor of HRSs.

Theorem 1. *If an* HRS $\mathcal{R}$ *is compatible with a* $\beta\eta$*-normal higher-order reduction order* $(>, \sqsupset)$*, then* $\mathcal{R}$ *is terminating.*

Proof. For a proof by contradiction, consider an infinite rewrite sequence $s_1 \rightarrow_\mathcal{R} s_2 \rightarrow_\mathcal{R} \cdots$. By definition, $s_1 = C[\ell\sigma\downarrow]$ and $s_2 = C[r\sigma\downarrow]\downarrow$ for some $\ell \rightarrow r \in \mathcal{R}$ where σ is a substitution and C is a context such that $C[\ell\sigma\downarrow] \in \mathsf{NF}(\beta\eta)$. By assumption, $\ell >^+ r$, so $\ell\sigma\downarrow \sqsupset^+ r\sigma\downarrow$ follows from $\beta\eta$-normal stability and we obtain $C[\ell\sigma\downarrow] \sqsupset^+ C[r\sigma\downarrow]$ by monotonicity of $\sqsupset$. Finally, $C[(\ell\sigma)\downarrow] \sqsupset^+ C[(r\sigma)\downarrow]\downarrow$ since $\sqsupset$ contains $\beta\eta$-reduction. Hence, we can transform the infinite sequence $s_1 \rightarrow_\mathcal{R} s_2 \cdots$ into the infinite descending sequence $s_1 \sqsupset^+ s_2 \cdots$ which contradicts well-foundedness of $\sqsupset$. Thus, $\mathcal{R}$ is terminating. □

3 Ingredients of the Order

We start by recalling the notion of nonversatile terms from [11, Definition 4.1]. Intuitively, a term is nonversatile if the application of any substitution together with the subsequent $\beta\eta$-normalization only affects its proper subterms. As this is needed in the inductive proof of $\beta\eta$-normal stability, an NCPO comparison $s > t$ is only defined for nonversatile s. The sufficient condition for nonversatility given in the subsequent lemma is an improvement over the one given in [11, Lemma 4.2].[2]

Definition 3. *The set* $\Lambda_{\mathsf{nv}} \subseteq \mathsf{NF}(\beta\eta)$ *of* nonversatile *terms is defined as follows:*

[2] In fact, subgoal 3 of Example 4.8 in [11] cannot be handled with the corresponding sufficient condition.

- $\mathcal{V} \cap \Lambda_{\mathsf{nv}} = \varnothing$,
- $f(\bar{t}) \in \Lambda_{\mathsf{nv}}$ *for all* $f \in \mathcal{F}$ *and* $\bar{t} \in \Lambda^{\mathsf{ar}(f)}$,
- $uv \in \Lambda_{\mathsf{nv}}$ *if* $(uv)\sigma\downarrow = u\sigma\downarrow v\sigma\downarrow$ *for all substitutions* σ,
- $\lambda x.u \in \Lambda_{\mathsf{nv}}$ *if* $(\lambda x.u)\sigma\downarrow = \lambda x.u\sigma\downarrow$ *for all substitutions* σ.

Terms which are not nonversatile are said to be versatile.

Example 3. The terms $\mathsf{c}x$ and $\lambda x.\mathsf{f}(yx)$ are nonversatile while the terms yx and $\lambda x.\mathsf{f}(yx)x$ are versatile as can be seen by taking the substitution $\{y \mapsto \lambda z.\mathsf{d}\}$.

Lemma 1. *The following terms are nonversatile if they are $\beta\eta$-normal forms:*

(i) applied function symbols $f(\bar{t})$,
(ii) applications uv *with nonversatile* u,
(iii) abstractions $\lambda x.ux$ *where* $ux \trianglerighteq vw$ *implies that* $vw \in \Lambda_{\mathsf{nv}}$,
(iv) abstractions $\lambda x.u$ *with* $u \neq vx$ *where*
  - $u \in \mathcal{V} \cup \Lambda_{\mathsf{nv}}$,
  - *if* $u = v(w_1w_2)$ *then* $w_1w_2 \in \Lambda_{\mathsf{nv}}$,
  - *if* $u = v(\lambda y.w)$ *then* $\lambda y.w \in \Lambda_{\mathsf{nv}}$.

Besides the usual inference rules on terms, reduction orders derived from HORPO [10] require appropriate orders on types. The next definition recalls the notion of admissible type orders from CPO [2].

Definition 4. *We define the left (right) argument relation on types* $\rhd_l$ ($\rhd_r$) *as follows:* $T \to U \rhd_l T$ ($T \to U \rhd_r U$). *An order* $\succ_{\mathcal{T}}$ *on types is admissible if*

- $\rhd_r \subseteq \succ_{\mathcal{T}}$,
- $\gtrdot = (\succ_{\mathcal{T}} \cup \rhd_l)^+$ *is well-founded,*
- *if* $T \to U \succ_{\mathcal{T}} V$ *then* $U \succeq_{\mathcal{T}} V$ *or* $V = T \to U'$ *with* $U \succ_{\mathcal{T}} U'$.

Given a type T *and* $a \in \mathcal{B}$ *we write* $a \gtrdot_{\mathcal{B}} T$ ($a \geqslant_{\mathcal{B}} T$) *if* $a \gtrdot b$ ($a \geqslant b$) *for every* $b \in \mathcal{B}$ *occurring in* T.

Lemma 2. (Lemma 2.3 from [2]). *Given a well-founded order* $\succ_{\mathcal{B}}$ *on base types, let* $\succ_{\mathcal{T}}$ *be the smallest order on types containing* $\succ_{\mathcal{B}}$ *and* $\rhd_r$ *such that* $V \succ_{\mathcal{T}} V'$ *implies* $U \to V \succ_{\mathcal{T}} U \to V'$ *for all* U, V, V'. *Then,* $>_{\mathcal{T}}$ *is admissible.*

Example 4. Let $\mathcal{B} = \{a, b, c\}$ where $a \succ_{\mathcal{B}} b \succ_{\mathcal{B}} c$ and consider the order $\succ_{\mathcal{T}}$ defined in the previous lemma. We have $a \to b \succ_{\mathcal{T}} a \to c$ because $b \succ_{\mathcal{T}} c$. However, $c \succ_{\mathcal{T}} b \to b$ does not hold because $b \to b \rhd_r b$ and therefore $c \succ_{\mathcal{T}} b \to b \succ_{\mathcal{T}} b$ which contradicts well-foundedness of $\succ_{\mathcal{T}}$ together with $b \succ_{\mathcal{T}} c$.

Unlike their first-order versions, higher-order recursive path orders do not enjoy the subterm property because we cannot have $\mathsf{f}(\mathsf{g}(x)) > x$ in general: If $\mathsf{f} \in \mathcal{F}_{a \to a \to a}$ and $\mathsf{g} \in \mathcal{F}_{(a \to a) \to a}$ for some $a \in \mathcal{B}$ then this is an encoding of the untyped lambda calculus (where f represents application and g represents abstraction) and therefore not terminating. Thus, if we want to recursively define $f(\bar{t}) > v$ by $t_i \geqslant v$ for some i, we usually have to check whether $\tau(t_i) \succeq_{\mathcal{T}} \tau(v)$

holds for the given admissible type order $\succ_{\mathcal{T}}$. In particular, this means that establishing $s > t$ by choosing some $s \rhd s'$ and showing $s' \geqslant t$ is only possible if we check that there is a weak decrease in the admissible type order for all intermediate terms in the recursive definition of $\rhd$. CPO extends HORPO by allowing these checks to be dismissed for the special case of accessible subterms which are determined by type-related properties. To this end, we start by introducing the concepts of (positive and negative) base type positions in a type taken from [2, Definition 7.2].

Definition 5. *The sets* $\mathcal{P}\mathsf{os}^+(T)$, $\mathcal{P}\mathsf{os}^-(T)$ *and* $\mathcal{P}\mathsf{os}_a(T)$ *of* positive base type positions, negative base type positions *and* positions of $a \in \mathcal{B}$ *in a type* $T \in \mathcal{T}$ *are inductively defined as sets of finite strings over* $\{1,2\}$ *(where* ϵ *denotes the empty string) as follows:*

$$\mathcal{P}\mathsf{os}^+(a) = \mathcal{P}\mathsf{os}_a(a) = \{\epsilon\} \qquad \mathcal{P}\mathsf{os}^-(a) = \varnothing \qquad \mathcal{P}\mathsf{os}_a(b) = \varnothing \text{ if } a \neq b$$

$$\mathcal{P}\mathsf{os}_a(U \to V) = \{1p \mid p \in \mathcal{P}\mathsf{os}_a(U)\} \cup \{2p \mid p \in \mathcal{P}\mathsf{os}_a(V)\}$$

$$\mathcal{P}\mathsf{os}^+(U \to V) = \{1p \mid p \in \mathcal{P}\mathsf{os}^-(U)\} \cup \{2p \mid p \in \mathcal{P}\mathsf{os}^+(V)\}$$

$$\mathcal{P}\mathsf{os}^-(U \to V) = \{1p \mid p \in \mathcal{P}\mathsf{os}^+(U)\} \cup \{2p \mid p \in \mathcal{P}\mathsf{os}^-(V)\}$$

Example 5. Let $\mathcal{B} = \{a, b\}$ and consider $T = (a \to b) \to (a \to b)$. We have $\mathcal{P}\mathsf{os}^+(T) = \{11, 22\}$ and $\mathcal{P}\mathsf{os}^-(T) = \{12, 21\}$. Furthermore, $\mathcal{P}\mathsf{os}_a(T) = \{11, 21\}$ and $\mathcal{P}\mathsf{os}_b(T) = \{12, 22\}$.

Next, we define the notions of accessible arguments of function symbols and basic base types as given in [2, Definitions 7.3 & 7.4].

Definition 6. *With every* $f \in \mathcal{F}_{T_1 \to \cdots \to T_n \to a}$ *we associate a set* $\mathsf{Acc}(f)$ *of* accessible *arguments of* f *such that* $i \in \mathsf{Acc}(f)$ *implies* $a \geqslant_{\mathcal{B}} T_i$ *and* $\mathcal{P}\mathsf{os}_a(T_i) \subseteq \mathcal{P}\mathsf{os}^+(T_i)$ *for all* $1 \leqslant i \leqslant n$. *Furthermore, we say that* $a \in \mathcal{B}$ *is* basic *if the following conditions hold:*

- $T \prec_{\mathcal{T}} a$ *implies that* T *is a basic base type,*
- *for all* $f \in \mathcal{F}_{T_1 \to \cdots \to T_n \to a}$ *and* $i \in \mathsf{Acc}(f)$, $T_i = a$ *or* T_i *is a basic base type.*

Note that the condition $T \prec_{\mathcal{T}} a$ is straightforward to check with the admissible type order from Lemma 2 as only base types can be smaller than base types. In general, it is possible to have base types which are bigger than function types while retaining admissibility of the type order [2].

Next, we define the notion of nonversatilely accessible subterms. The definition closely follows the one given in [2, Definition 7.5] but with appropriate restrictions regarding nonversatility.

Definition 7. *We write* $s \rhd_{\mathsf{b}}^{\mathsf{nv}} t$ *if* t *is a subterm of* $s \in \Lambda_{\mathsf{nv}}$ *reachable by nonversatile intermediate terms in the recursive definition of* $\rhd$, t *is of basic base type and* $\mathsf{FV}(t) \subseteq \mathsf{FV}(s)$, *i.e., no bound variables have become free. Furthermore,* $s \rhd_{\mathsf{a}} t$ *if there are* $a \in \mathcal{B}$, $f \in \mathcal{F}_{T_1 \to \cdots \to T_n \to a}$, $s_i \in \Lambda_{T_i}$ *for* $1 \leqslant i \leqslant n$ *and* $j \in \mathsf{Acc}(f)$ *such that* $s = f(s_1, \ldots, s_{\mathsf{ar}(f)})s_{\mathsf{ar}(f)+1} \cdots s_n$ *and* $s_j \unrhd_{\mathsf{a}} t$. *Here,* $\rhd_{\mathsf{b}}^{\mathsf{nv}}, \rhd_{\mathsf{a}} \subseteq \mathsf{NF}(\beta\eta) \times \mathsf{NF}(\beta\eta)$. *A term* t *is* nonversatilely accessible *in a nonversatile term* s *if* $s \rhd_{\mathsf{b}}^{\mathsf{nv}} t$ *or* $s \rhd_{\mathsf{a}} t$.

Finally, we define the notion of structurally smaller terms with respect to a set of variables X. It is an important ingredient of CPO with accessible subterms as it facilitates a way of using the set X with which the order is parameterized in places where it would otherwise lead to non-termination. Once again, we can immediately use the corresponding definition given in [2, Definition 7.8].

Definition 8. *Let X be a finite set of variables. We say that a term t is* structurally smaller *than a term s, written $s \rhd_{@}^{X} t$, if there are $a \in \mathcal{B}$, $x_1, \ldots, x_k \in X$ and $u \in \Lambda$ such that $\tau(s) = \tau(t) = a$, $t = ux_1 \cdots x_k$, $s \rhd_{\mathsf{a}} u$ and $\mathcal{P}\mathsf{os}_a(\tau(x_i)) = \varnothing$ for all $1 \leqslant i \leqslant k$. Here, $\rhd_{@}^{X} \subseteq \mathsf{NF}(\beta\eta) \times \Lambda$.*

Note that if $s \rhd_{@}^{X} t$ then t may not be in $\beta\eta$-normal form. The following important result is required for $\beta\eta$-normal stability and explains why nonversatility is needed in $\rhd_{\mathsf{b}}^{\mathsf{nv}}$ but not in $\rhd_{\mathsf{a}}$ and $\rhd_{@}^{X}$ where it is guaranteed by the original definition.

Lemma 3. *The following statements hold:*

(i) If $s \rhd_{\mathsf{b}}^{\mathsf{nv}} t$ then $s\sigma\downarrow \rhd_{\mathsf{b}}^{\mathsf{nv}} t\sigma\downarrow$ for all substitutions σ.
(ii) If $s \rhd_{\mathsf{a}} t$ then $s\sigma\downarrow \rhd_{\mathsf{a}} t\sigma\downarrow$ for all substitutions σ.
(iii) If $s \rhd_{@}^{X} t$ then $s\sigma\downarrow \rhd_{@}^{X} t'$ for some $t' \to_{\beta\eta}^{!} t\sigma\downarrow$ whenever σ is away from X.
(iv) If $s \rhd_{@}^{X} t$ and $t \in \Lambda_{\mathsf{nv}}$ then $s\sigma\downarrow \rhd_{@}^{X} t\sigma\downarrow$ for all substitutions σ away from X.

4 The Beta-Eta-Normal Computability Path Order

First, we briefly recapitulate the definition of the multiset and lexicographic extension of orders. Given an order $>$, let $(s_1, \ldots, s_n) >_{\mathsf{lex}} (t_1, \ldots, t_m)$ if there exists an $i \leqslant \mathsf{min}(n, m)$ such that $s_i > t_i$ and $s_j = t_j$ for all $j < i$. Given two multisets M and N we write $M >_{\mathsf{mul}} N$ if $N = (M \setminus X) \uplus Y$ where $\varnothing \neq X \subseteq M$ and for all $y \in Y$ there exists an $x \in X$ such that $x > y$. It is well-known that these extensions preserve well-foundedness.

In the following, let $\succ_{\mathcal{T}}$ be an admissible order on types and $\succsim_{\mathcal{F}}$ a preorder on $\mathcal{F}$ called *precedence* with a well-founded strict part $\succ_{\mathcal{F}} = \succsim_{\mathcal{F}} \setminus \precsim_{\mathcal{F}}$ and the equivalence relation $\simeq_{\mathcal{F}} = \succsim_{\mathcal{F}} \cap \precsim_{\mathcal{F}}$. Furthermore, for every $f \in \mathcal{F}$ we fix a status $\mathsf{stat}(f) \in \{\mathsf{mul}, \mathsf{lex}\}$ such that symbols equivalent in $\simeq_{\mathcal{F}}$ have the same status. We also assume that $\mathcal{F}$ is partitioned into sets $\mathcal{F}_{\mathsf{b}}$ and $\mathcal{F}_{\mathsf{s}}$ of *big* and *small* symbols such that the following conditions hold: $\mathcal{F}_{\mathsf{b}} \cap \mathcal{F}_{\mathsf{s}} = \varnothing$, if $f \succsim_{\mathcal{F}} g$ and $g \in \mathcal{F}_{\mathsf{b}}$ then $f \in \mathcal{F}_{\mathsf{b}}$, and whenever $f \in \mathcal{F}_{T_1 \to \cdots T_n \to a} \cap \mathcal{F}_{\mathsf{s}}$ then

- $\mathsf{ar}(f) = n$ implies $a \geqslant_{\mathcal{B}} T_i$ and $\mathsf{S}\mathcal{P}\mathsf{os}_a(T_i) = \varnothing$ for all $1 \leqslant i \leqslant n$ where $\mathsf{S}\mathcal{P}\mathsf{os}_a(\cdot)$ is defined as in [2, Definition 8.9],
- $\mathsf{ar}(f) < n$ implies $\mathsf{Acc}(f) = \varnothing$ as well as $a \geqslant_{\mathcal{B}} T_i$ and $T_{\mathsf{ar}(f)+1} \to \cdots \to T_n \to a \geqslant T_i$ for all $1 \leqslant i \leqslant \mathsf{ar}(f)$.

We are now able to lift CPO with accessible subterms and small symbols [2] to an appropriate component of a $\beta\eta$-normal higher-order reduction order.

$\langle \mathcal{F}_{\mathsf{b}} \rhd \rangle$ $f(\bar{t}) >^X v$ if $f \in \mathcal{F}_{\mathsf{b}}$ and $t_i \trianglerighteq_{\mathsf{b}}^{\mathsf{nv}} \cdot \trianglerighteq_{\mathsf{a}} \cdot \geqslant_\tau v$ for some i

$\langle \mathcal{F}_{\mathsf{b}} = \rangle$ $f(\bar{t}) >^X g(\bar{u})$ if $f \in \mathcal{F}_{\mathsf{b}}$, $f \simeq_{\mathcal{F}} g$, $f(\bar{t}) >^X u_i$ for all i and $\bar{t}\ (>_\tau \cup \rhd_{@}^{X} \cdot \geqslant_\tau)_{\mathsf{stat}(f)}\ \bar{u}$

$\langle \mathcal{F}_{\mathsf{b}} \succ \rangle$ $f(\bar{t}) >^X g(\bar{u})$ if $f \in \mathcal{F}_{\mathsf{b}}$, $f \succ_{\mathcal{F}} g$ and $f(\bar{t}) >^X u_i$ for all i

$\langle \mathcal{F}_{\mathsf{b}} @ \rangle$ $f(\bar{t}) >^X uv$ if $f \in \mathcal{F}_{\mathsf{b}}$, $f(\bar{t}) >^X u$ and $f(\bar{t}) >^X v$

$\langle \mathcal{F}_{\mathsf{b}} \lambda \rangle$ $f(\bar{t}) >^X \lambda y.v$ if $f \in \mathcal{F}_{\mathsf{b}}$, $f(\bar{t}) >^{X \cup \{z\}} v[y/z]$, $\tau(y) = \tau(z)$ and z fresh

$\langle \mathcal{F}_{\mathsf{b}} \mathcal{V} \rangle$ $f(\bar{t}) >^X y$ if $f \in \mathcal{F}_{\mathsf{b}}$ and $y \in X$

$\langle @ \rhd \rangle$ $tu >^X v$ if $t \geqslant^X v$ or $u \geqslant_\tau^X v$

$\langle @ = \rangle$ $tu >^X t'u'$ if $t = t'$ and $u >^X u'$ or $tu >_{@}^{X} t'$ and $tu >_{@}^{X} u'$ where $tu >_{@}^{X} v$ if $t >_\tau^X v$ or $u \geqslant_\tau^X v$ or $tu >_\tau^X v$

$\langle @ \lambda \rangle$ $tu >^X \lambda y.v$ if $tu >^X v[y/z]$, $\tau(y) = \tau(z)$ and z fresh

$\langle @ \mathcal{F}_{\mathsf{s}} \rangle$ $tu >^X f(\bar{v})$ if $f \in \mathcal{F}_{\mathsf{s}}$ and $tu >_\tau^X v_i$ for all i

$\langle @ \mathcal{V} \rangle$ $tu >^X y$ if $y \in X$

$\langle \lambda \rhd \rangle$ $\lambda x.t >^X v$ if $t[x/z] \geqslant_\tau^X v$, $\tau(x) = \tau(z)$ and z fresh

$\langle \lambda \rhd \eta \rangle$ $\lambda x.t >^X v$ if $t[x/z] \geqslant_\tau^X vz$, $\tau(x) = \tau(z)$ and z fresh

$\langle \lambda = \rangle$ $\lambda x.t >^X \lambda y.v$ if $t[x/z] >^X v[y/z]$, $\tau(x) = \tau(y) = \tau(z)$ and z fresh

$\langle \lambda \neq \rangle$ $\lambda x.t >^X \lambda y.v$ if $\lambda x.t >^X v[y/z]$, $\tau(x) \neq \tau(y) = \tau(z)$ and z fresh

$\langle \lambda \mathcal{F}_{\mathsf{s}} \rangle$ $\lambda x.t >^X f(\bar{v})$ if $f \in \mathcal{F}_{\mathsf{s}}$ and $\lambda x.t >_\tau^X v_i$ for all i

$\langle \lambda \mathcal{V} \rangle$ $\lambda x.t >^X y$ if $y \in X$

$\langle \mathcal{F}_{\mathsf{s}} \rhd \rangle$ $f(\bar{t}) >^X v$ if $f \in \mathcal{F}_{\mathsf{s}}$ and $t_i \geqslant_\tau v$ for some i

$\langle \mathcal{F}_{\mathsf{s}} = \rangle$ $f(\bar{t}) >^X g(\bar{u})$ if $f \in \mathcal{F}_{\mathsf{s}}$, $f \simeq_{\mathcal{F}} g$, $f(\bar{t}) >_\tau^X u_i$ for all i and $\bar{t}\ (>_\tau)_{\mathsf{stat}(f)}\ \bar{u}$

$\langle \mathcal{F}_{\mathsf{s}} \succ \rangle$ $f(\bar{t}) >^X g(\bar{u})$ if $f \in \mathcal{F}_{\mathsf{s}}$, $f \succ_{\mathcal{F}} g$ and $f(\bar{t}) >_\tau^X u_i$ for all i

$\langle \mathcal{F}_{\mathsf{s}} @ \rangle$ $f(\bar{t}) >^X uv$ if $f \in \mathcal{F}_{\mathsf{s}}$, $f(\bar{t}) >_\tau^X u$ and $f(\bar{t}) >_\tau^X v$

$\langle \mathcal{F}_{\mathsf{s}} \mathcal{V} \rangle$ $f(\bar{t}) >^X y$ if $f \in \mathcal{F}_{\mathsf{s}}$ and $y \in X$

Fig. 1. Rules of NCPO.

Definition 9. *Given a finite set X of variables, the order $>^X \subseteq \mathsf{NF}(\beta\eta) \times \mathsf{NF}(\beta\eta)$ is inductively defined in Fig. 1 where we implicitly assume $s \in \Lambda_{\mathsf{nv}}$ whenever $s >^X t$. Furthermore, $s >_\tau^X t$ if $s >^X t$ and $\tau(s) \succeq_{\mathcal{T}} \tau(t)$, and $>$ $(>_\tau)$ is a shorthand for $>^{\varnothing}$ $(>_\tau^{\varnothing})$.*

Note that $>^X$ is well-defined by induction on the tuple (s, t) with respect to the well-founded relation $(\rhd, \rhd)_{\mathsf{lex}}$. It is defined like CPO with accessible subterms and small symbols [2] but with the restriction to terms in $\beta\eta$-normal form where we additionally require that the first argument of $>^X$ as well as the first argument and all intermediate terms in the recursive definition of the subterm relation

$\rhd_{\mathsf{b}}^{\mathsf{nv}}$ are nonversatile. Furthermore, the rules $\langle @\beta \rangle$ and $\langle \lambda\eta \rangle$ which orient β- and η-reduction, respectively, have been removed. We also weakened the rule $\langle \mathcal{F}_{\mathsf{s}}= \rangle$ by disallowing $\rhd_{@}^{X} \cdot \geqslant_{\mathcal{T}}$ in the comparison of the arguments as used in $\langle \mathcal{F}_{\mathsf{b}}= \rangle$. Finally, we added the rule $\langle \lambda\rhd\eta \rangle$ which is inspired by rule (11) from NHORPO [11]. We refer to $>_{\mathcal{T}}$ as the $\beta\eta$-normal computability path order (NCPO) and use the symbol $\sqsupset$ with the same decorations as $>$ to denote CPO with accessible subterms and small symbols. We illustrate the definition on a number of examples and emphasize some differences between NCPO and NHORPO together with the transformation technique of neutralization. For our purposes, it is sufficient to know that the definition of NHORPO is similar to the one of NCPO without the extensions of accessible subterms and small symbols but with fewer rules, without a set X of variables and a weak decrease in the admissible type order in each recursive invocation. Furthermore, the transformation technique of neutralization maps terms to terms with the same termination behavior. The goal is to transform terms which are beyond the scope of NHORPO into terms which NHORPO can deal with. In particular, the transformation may apply a function symbol's arguments of nonbase type to special terms and apply β-reduction in order to minimize the number of lambda abstractions. A detailed definition can be found in [11].

Example 6. In this first example, we use the rule $\langle \lambda\rhd\eta \rangle$ which is not part of CPO to prove termination of the symbolic differentiation example from [11]. Let $\mathcal{B} = \{\mathsf{r}\}$ and consider the function symbols $\mathsf{sin}, \mathsf{cos} \in \mathcal{F}_{\mathsf{r} \to \mathsf{r}}$, $\mathsf{diff} \in \mathcal{F}_{(\mathsf{r} \to \mathsf{r}) \to \mathsf{r} \to \mathsf{r}}$ and $+, \times \in \mathcal{F}_{(\mathsf{r} \to \mathsf{r}) \to (\mathsf{r} \to \mathsf{r}) \to \mathsf{r} \to \mathsf{r}}$ as well as the variables $x \in \mathcal{V}_{\mathsf{r}}$ and $F, G \in \mathcal{F}_{\mathsf{r} \to \mathsf{r}}$. Furthermore, $\mathsf{ar}(\mathsf{sin}) = \mathsf{ar}(\mathsf{cos}) = \mathsf{ar}(\mathsf{diff}) = 1$ and $\mathsf{ar}(+) = \mathsf{ar}(\times) = 2$. We will use infix notation for $+$ and $\times$. The HRS $\mathcal{R}$ defining the symbolic differentiation of sin and $\times$ is defined by the following two rules:

$$\mathsf{diff}(\lambda x.\mathsf{sin}(Fx)) \to (\lambda x.\mathsf{cos}(Fx)) \times \mathsf{diff}(F)$$
$$\mathsf{diff}(F \times G) \to (\mathsf{diff}(F) \times G) + (F \times \mathsf{diff}(G))$$

For the termination proof with NCPO, all function symbols can be big with multiset status and we will use the precedence $\mathsf{diff} \succ_{\mathcal{F}} \mathsf{sin}, \mathsf{cos}, +, \times$. Note that all subterms of left-hand sides except for variables and the application Fx are nonversatile. Since $\mathcal{R}$ is an HRS, $\tau(\ell) = \tau(r)$ for all $\ell \to r \in \mathcal{R}$, so we only have to check $\ell > r$ for all $\ell \to r \in \mathcal{R}$. For the first rule, we apply $\langle \mathcal{F}_{\mathsf{b}}\succ \rangle$ to get the two proof obligations $\mathsf{diff}(\lambda x.\mathsf{sin}(Fx)) > \lambda x.\mathsf{cos}(Fx)$ and $\mathsf{diff}(\lambda x.\mathsf{sin}(Fx)) > \mathsf{diff}(F)$. For the former one, we proceed by $\langle \mathcal{F}_{\mathsf{b}}\lambda \rangle$, $\langle \mathcal{F}_{\mathsf{b}}\succ \rangle$ and $\langle \mathcal{F}_{\mathsf{b}}@ \rangle$ to obtain the subgoals $\mathsf{diff}(\lambda x.\mathsf{sin}(Fx)) >^{\{z\}} F$ and $\mathsf{diff}(\lambda x.\mathsf{sin}(Fx)) >^{\{z\}} z$. We can directly resolve the second subgoal with $\langle \mathcal{F}_{\mathsf{b}}\mathcal{V} \rangle$. For the first goal, applying $\langle \mathcal{F}_{\mathsf{b}}\rhd \rangle$ and then $\langle \lambda\rhd\eta \rangle$ yields the goal $\mathsf{sin}(Fy) > Fy$ which can be handled by $\langle \mathcal{F}_{\mathsf{b}}\rhd \rangle$. For the remaining proof obligation $\mathsf{diff}(\lambda x.\mathsf{sin}(Fx)) > \mathsf{diff}(F)$ we apply $\langle \mathcal{F}_{\mathsf{b}}= \rangle$ and $\langle \lambda\rhd\eta \rangle$ to obtain the goal $\mathsf{sin}(Fx) >_{\mathcal{T}} Fx$ which is again handled by $\langle \mathcal{F}_{\mathsf{b}}\rhd \rangle$.[3] Now consider

[3] In [11], the same reasoning is used to handle this subcase but an application of the rule corresponding to $\langle \lambda\rhd\eta \rangle$ is not allowed by their definition as F is a variable. Furthermore, as already mentioned, $\lambda x.\mathsf{sin}(Fx)$ is nonversatile by our sufficient condition but not by the one given in [11].

the second rule. From two applications of $\langle \mathcal{F}_{\mathsf{b}} \succ \rangle$ we obtain the proof obligations $\mathsf{diff}(F \times G) > \mathsf{diff}(F)$, $\mathsf{diff}(F \times G) > G$, $\mathsf{diff}(F \times G) > F$ and $\mathsf{diff}(F \times G) > \mathsf{diff}(G)$ which can be resolved by two applications of $\langle \mathcal{F}_{\mathsf{b}} \rhd \rangle$ or $\langle \mathcal{F}_{\mathsf{b}} = \rangle$ followed by one application of $\langle \mathcal{F}_{\mathsf{b}} \rhd \rangle$, respectively.

Note that the argumentation given for the last rule also works for NHORPO as can be confirmed by both our implementation of NHORPO as well as the prototype implementation linked from [11]. Hence, NHORPO does not need neutralization in order to prove termination of the preceding example even though this is claimed in [11]. However, as already mentioned, the original implementation of NHORPO cannot orient the first rule as the used sufficient condition for nonversatility is too weak. Interestingly, neutralization can make up for that, so the proof checked by the original implementation is correct but for different reasons than the ones given in [11]. The following example shows that NCPO can prove termination of systems where NHORPO succeeds only if neutralization is employed.

Example 7. In this example we use accessible subterms to prove termination of the computation of negation normal forms of formulas in first-order logic in the framework of $\beta\eta$-normal higher-order rewriting using NCPO. We need to distinguish between terms and formulas, so let the set of base types under consideration be $\mathcal{B} = \{t, f\}$. Furthermore, we consider the logical connectives represented by the function symbols $\neg \in \mathcal{F}_{f \to f}$, $\wedge, \vee \in \mathcal{F}_{f \to f \to f}$ and $\forall, \exists \in \mathcal{F}_{(t \to f) \to f}$ which are all considered to be big. We set $\mathsf{ar}(\neg) = \mathsf{ar}(\forall) = \mathsf{ar}(\exists) = 1$ and $\mathsf{ar}(\wedge) = \mathsf{ar}(\vee) = 2$ and allow us to use syntactic sugar in writing as few parentheses as possible by establishing that the unary function symbols bind stronger than the binary function symbols. Furthermore, we use infix notation for $\wedge$ and $\vee$. As variables, we will use $P, Q \in \mathcal{V}_f$ and $R \in \mathcal{V}_{t \to f}$. Hence, the HRS $\mathcal{R}$ for the computation of negational normal forms in first-order logic is given as the following set of rules:

$$\neg\neg P \to P \qquad \neg(P \wedge Q) \to \neg P \vee \neg Q \qquad \neg\forall R \to \exists(\lambda x. \neg(Rx))$$
$$\neg(P \vee Q) \to \neg P \wedge \neg Q \qquad \neg\exists R \to \forall(\lambda x. \neg(Rx))$$

Note that all non-variable subterms of the left-hand sides are nonversatile. We choose $f \succ_{\mathcal{T}} t$ and let all function symbols have multiset status. Furthermore, set $\neg \succ_{\mathcal{F}} \wedge, \vee, \forall, \exists$. We have $\neg\neg P > P$ by applying $\langle \mathcal{F}_{\mathsf{b}} \rhd \rangle$ twice. For $\neg(P \wedge Q) > \neg P \vee \neg Q$, applying $\langle \mathcal{F}_{\mathsf{b}} \succ \rangle$ yields the subgoals $\neg(P \wedge Q) > \neg P$ and $\neg(P \wedge Q) > \neg Q$ which are handled by $\langle \mathcal{F}_{\mathsf{b}} = \rangle$ since $P \wedge Q >_\tau P, Q$ by $\langle \mathcal{F}_{\mathsf{b}} \rhd \rangle$. We obtain $\neg(P \vee Q) > \neg P \wedge \neg Q$ in the same way. This leaves us with establishing $\neg\forall R > \exists(\lambda x. \neg(Rx))$ as the final rule can again be oriented with the same strategy. By applying $\langle \mathcal{F}_{\mathsf{b}} \succ \rangle$, $\langle \mathcal{F}_{\mathsf{b}} \lambda \rangle$ and $\langle \mathcal{F}_{\mathsf{b}} = \rangle$ we obtain $\forall R >_\tau \cup \rhd_{@}^{\{x\}} \cdot \geqslant_\tau Rx$ as proof obligation. Note that $\forall R >_\tau Rx$ is impossible as x does not occur in the left-hand side. However, we can establish $\forall R \rhd_{@}^{\{x\}} Rx$ which is enough to fulfill the proof obligation. Since $f \geqslant_{\mathcal{B}} t \to f$ and $\{2\} = \mathcal{P}\mathsf{os}_f(t \to f) \subseteq \mathcal{P}\mathsf{os}^+(t \to f) = \{2\}$ we can set $1 \in \mathsf{Acc}(\forall)$. Hence, $\forall R \rhd_{\mathsf{a}} R$. Furthermore, $\tau(\forall R) = \tau(Rx) = f$ and $\mathcal{P}\mathsf{os}_f(t) = \varnothing$, so $\forall R \rhd_{@}^{\{x\}} Rx$ as desired.

Example 8. In this example, we demonstrate the usefulness of small function symbols by proving termination of the map function together with a function that increments lists of natural numbers in successor notation. This is a slightly modified subsystem of `AotoYamada_05__014` from the termination problem database.[4] Proving termination of the full system for plain higher-order rewriting needs the transitive closure of CPO as shown in [2, Example 8.20], but this does not help in our setting as the "middle term" is not in $\beta\eta$-normal form.[5] Consider the set of base types $\mathcal{B} = \{\mathsf{a}, \mathsf{b}\}$ as well as the function symbols $\mathsf{0} \in \mathcal{F}_{\mathsf{b}}$, $\mathsf{nil} \in \mathcal{F}_{\mathsf{a}}$, $\mathsf{s} \in \mathcal{F}_{\mathsf{b}\to\mathsf{b}}$, $\mathsf{plus} \in \mathcal{F}_{\mathsf{b}\to\mathsf{b}\to\mathsf{b}}$, $\mathsf{inc} \in \mathcal{F}_{\mathsf{a}\to\mathsf{a}}$, $\mathsf{map} \in \mathcal{F}_{(\mathsf{b}\to\mathsf{b})\to\mathsf{a}\to\mathsf{a}}$ and $\mathsf{cons} \in \mathcal{F}_{\mathsf{b}\to\mathsf{a}\to\mathsf{a}}$. We set $\mathsf{ar}(\mathsf{0}) = \mathsf{ar}(\mathsf{nil}) = 0$, $\mathsf{ar}(\mathsf{s}) = \mathsf{ar}(\mathsf{plus}) = \mathsf{ar}(\mathsf{inc}) = 1$ and $\mathsf{ar}(\mathsf{map}) = \mathsf{ar}(\mathsf{cons}) = 2$. We will use the variables $x, y \in \mathcal{F}_{\mathsf{b}}$, $v \in \mathcal{F}_{\mathsf{a}}$ and $F \in \mathcal{V}_{\mathsf{b}\to\mathsf{b}}$. Consider the HRS $\mathcal{R}$ consisting of the following rules:

$$\mathsf{plus}(\mathsf{0})\,x \to x \qquad \mathsf{plus}(\mathsf{s}(y))\,x \to \mathsf{s}(\mathsf{plus}(y)\,x)$$
$$\mathsf{map}(F, \mathsf{nil}) \to \mathsf{nil} \qquad \mathsf{map}(F, \mathsf{cons}(x, v)) \to \mathsf{cons}(Fx, \mathsf{map}(F, v))$$
$$\mathsf{inc}(v) \to \mathsf{map}(\mathsf{plus}(\mathsf{s}(\mathsf{0})), v)$$

We choose $\mathsf{a} \succ_{\mathcal{T}} \mathsf{b}$, consider all function symbols except for s to be big and let them all have multiset status. The used precedence is $\mathsf{inc} \succ_{\mathcal{F}} \mathsf{map} \succ_{\mathcal{F}} \mathsf{cons}, \mathsf{nil}$ and $\mathsf{plus} \succ_{\mathcal{F}} \mathsf{s}$. Accessible arguments are not needed. Note that all non-variable subterms of the left-hand sides are nonversatile. The first rule follows directly from $\langle @\rhd \rangle$. For the second rule, we apply $\langle @\mathcal{F}_{\mathsf{s}} \rangle$ to obtain the subgoal $\mathsf{plus}(\mathsf{s}(y))\,x >_{\tau} \mathsf{plus}(y)\,x$. We proceed by $\langle @{=} \rangle$ and choose the proof obligations $\mathsf{plus}(\mathsf{s}(y)) >_{\tau} \mathsf{plus}(y)$ as well as $x \geqslant_{\tau} x$. The second one is obviously true while the first rule can be resolved by $\langle \mathcal{F}_{\mathsf{b}}{=} \rangle$ and $\langle \mathcal{F}_{\mathsf{s}}\rhd \rangle$. The third rule follows directly from $\langle \mathcal{F}_{\mathsf{b}}\rhd \rangle$. For the fourth rule, we apply $\langle \mathcal{F}_{\mathsf{b}}\succ \rangle$ to obtain the subgoal $\mathsf{map}(F, \mathsf{cons}(x, v)) > Fx$ which follows from $\langle \mathcal{F}_{\mathsf{b}}@ \rangle$ and three applications of $\langle \mathcal{F}_{\mathsf{b}}\rhd \rangle$ as well as the subgoal $\mathsf{map}(F, \mathsf{cons}(x, v)) > \mathsf{map}(F, v)$ which follows from $\langle \mathcal{F}_{\mathsf{b}}{=} \rangle$ and $\langle \mathcal{F}_{\mathsf{b}}\rhd \rangle$. Finally, the fifth rule can be oriented by applying $\langle \mathcal{F}_{\mathsf{b}}\succ \rangle$ four times as well as $\langle \mathcal{F}_{\mathsf{b}}\rhd \rangle$ once.

The previous example cannot be handled by NHORPO (with or without neutralization) as the rule for the recursive case of plus needs small symbols which are neither part of NHORPO nor added by neutralization.

5 Correctness Proof

We start by a technical result for CPO with accessible subterms which is needed for establishing $\beta\eta$-normal stability of $(>_{\tau}, \sqsupset_{\tau})$. In particular, it states an important connection between $\rhd_{@}^{X}$ and $\sqsupset^{X}$.

Lemma 4. *Let X be a finite set of variables and consider the term $f(t_1, \ldots, t_n)$ with $f \in \mathcal{F}_{\mathsf{b}}$. If $t_i \rhd_{@}^{X} \cdot \sqsupset_{\tau} v$ for some $1 \leqslant i \leqslant n$ then $f(t_1, \ldots, t_n) \sqsupset^{X} v$.*

[4] https://github.com/TermCOMP/TPDB.

[5] Actually, our modification also has to be applied to [2, Example 8.20] because admissible type orders as defined in [2] do not support equivalent base types.

Note that the previous lemma holds for both CPO with accessible subterms and NCPO. Hence, it allows us to do the usual optimizations in the implementation of the rule $\langle \mathcal{F}_\mathsf{b}{=}\rangle$ given in Fig. 2. This can be justified in both cases as follows: If $t_i \geqslant_\tau u_j$ then $f(\bar{t}) >^X u_j$ by $\langle \mathcal{F}_\mathsf{b}\rhd\rangle$ and if $t_i \rhd^X_@ \cdot \geqslant_\tau u_j$ then $f(\bar{t}) >^X u_j$ by Lemma 4. The following lemma is the main result needed for establishing $\beta\eta$-normal stability of the pair $(>_\tau, \sqsupset_\tau)$.

$$\langle \mathcal{F}_\mathsf{b}{=}\mathsf{mul}\rangle \quad f(\bar{t}) >^X g(\bar{u}) \text{ if } f \simeq_\mathcal{F} g,\ \mathsf{stat}(f) = \mathsf{mul} \text{ and } \bar{t}\ (>_\tau \cup \rhd^X_@ \cdot \geqslant_\tau)_\mathsf{mul}\ \bar{u}$$

$$\langle \mathcal{F}_\mathsf{b}{=}\mathsf{lex}\rangle \quad f(\bar{t}) >^X g(\bar{u}) \text{ if } f \simeq_\mathcal{F} g,\ \mathsf{stat}(f) = \mathsf{lex} \text{ and } \exists i.\, t_i >_\tau \cup \rhd^X_@ \cdot \geqslant_\tau u_i \text{ and } \forall j < i.\, t_j = u_j \text{ and } \forall j > i.\, f(\bar{t}) >^X t_j$$

Fig. 2. Optimized Rules for the Implementation of $\langle \mathcal{F}_\mathsf{b}{=}\rangle$.

Lemma 5. *Let $s >^X t$. For every $\beta\eta$-normal substitution σ away from X we have $s\sigma{\downarrow} \sqsupset^X t'$ for some $t\sigma \to^*_{\beta\eta} t' \to^!_{\beta\eta} t\sigma{\downarrow}$. Additionally, if $t = uv$ then $t' = u'v'$ with $u\sigma \to^*_{\beta\eta} u' \to^!_{\beta\eta} u\sigma{\downarrow}$ and $v\sigma \to^*_{\beta\eta} v' \to^!_{\beta\eta} v\sigma{\downarrow}$.*

Theorem 2. *The pair $(>_\tau, \sqsupset_\tau)$ is a $\beta\eta$-normal higher-order reduction order.*

Proof. Since $\sqsupset_\tau$ contains $\beta\eta$-reduction by definition, [2, Lemma 8.2] establishes its monotonicity and [2, Theorem 8.14] its well-foundedness, we are left to prove $\beta\eta$-normal stability. Let $s >_\tau t$ and σ be a substitution. By Lemma 5 we obtain $s\sigma{\downarrow} \sqsupset t'$ for some $t' \to^!_{\beta\eta} t\sigma{\downarrow}$. Since types are preserved under the application of substitutions as well as $\beta\eta$-conversions between well-typed terms, we obtain $s\sigma{\downarrow} \sqsupset_\tau t'$. Finally, we obtain $s\sigma{\downarrow} \sqsupset^+_\tau t\sigma{\downarrow}$ as $\beta\eta$-steps are included in $\sqsupset_\tau$. □

6 Implementation

A prototype implementation of NCPO is available at GitHub.[6] In contrast to the implementations of NHORPO with neutralization as well as CPO linked from [2,11], respectively, our implementation is not a mere termination checker which requires all parameters of the order as input but searches for suitable parameters using SAT/SMT which is standard practice for termination tools such as [6,13]. Implementing the search for parameters also allows one to quickly find mistakes like in [2, Example 8.19] where it is claimed that small symbols are needed whereas this is not true. Running the prototype implementation linked from [2] with the parameters generated from our prototype implementation confirms our findings.

Our prototype is implemented in Haskell and uses the recent Hasmtlib package[7] to encode the termination problems into the SMT-LIB 2 format[8] and communicate with SMT solvers which have to be installed separately. We use the

[6] https://github.com/niedjoh/hrsterm.
[7] https://github.com/bruderj15/Hasmtlib.
[8] https://smt-lib.org/.

well-known TPTP THF format [24] as the input format of our prototype implementation. Our parser supports a suitable fragment of TPTP THF which consists of unit clauses where equality is the only allowed predicate. Variables in rules are handled by universal quantification. In particular, the chosen input format does not support applied function symbols with fixed arities but solely relies on application. We think this is appropriate as in higher-order problems, fixed arities are a superfluous limitation in general and only needed as additional structure for termination techniques based on path orders. Hence, our implementation transforms the input into a representation using applied function symbols with fixed arities for the termination proof. The transformation chooses the maximal possible arity for each function symbol which depends on the minimal number of arguments which it is applied to in the problem. This gives us as much structure as possible without having to write the arities down explicitly.

The SMT encoding of NCPO contains more recursive cases and more global conditions than the one for NHORPO, but except for mild cases like $\rhd^X_@$, terms only need to be decomposed. In particular, we can easily encode the search for precedences and admissible type orders of the class given in Lemma 2 by assigning an integer variable to each function symbol and base type. The remaining parameters regarding the status of each function symbol, which base types are basic, accessible arguments and small symbols can be encoded by boolean variables. Apart from some global conditions, the encoding then just needs to assert orientability of each rule in a given HRS by taking the disjunction of all applicable cases in the definition of NCPO and proceed recursively. Unlike stated in [11], this drastically changes for the transformation technique of normalization. In an efficient encoding, one would have to syntactically analyze $\beta\eta$-normal forms of transformed terms of the original system depending on parameters which are only given symbolically as the goal of the encoding is to search for suitable values for them. This seems to be impossible unless the concrete values of these parameters are hard-coded in a big disjunction which makes the encoding much more verbose than the usual encodings of precedences and the like. In our reimplementation of NHORPO and neutralization, we precomputed the terms resulting from the concrete parameters of neutralization in Haskell and used the SMT solver interactively to try to find a solution for each encoding in turn.

Apart from our reimplementation of NHORPO, we know of two other fully automated implementations of HORPO which are applicable to higher-order rewriting modulo $\beta\eta$, WANDA [13] and CSI^ho [19]. WANDA implements a variation of HORPO for the different rewrite formalism of AFSMs. AFSMs can model our $\beta\eta$-normal flavor of HRSs by replacing the free variables with meta-variables, their applications by meta-applications and employing a $\beta\eta$-first reduction strategy which rewrites a term to $\beta\eta$-normal form before performing a rewrite step. However, a formal proof of such a result is only available for a transformation of the subclass of pattern HRSs in $\beta\eta$-long normal form [12, Transformation 3.4] to AFSMs. Furthermore, WANDA only supports a β-first strategy, so in general the HORPO implementation in WANDA and our implementation of NHORPO/NCPO cannot be directly compared. CSI^ho is a confluence tool which implements a basic variant of HORPO which can be used for pattern HRSs [23] in $\beta\eta$-long normal form. Hence, it is also not possible to directly compare the HORPO implementation of CSI^ho with our prototype. Nevertheless, a comparison with both WANDA and CSI^ho is instructive as the investigated termination problems only differ in the treatment of η.

Table 1. Experimental results.

problem	NCPO	NHORPO	NHORPO+neutralization
Example 6 (extended)	✓ 0.080 s	✓ 0.022 s	✓ 0.410 s
Example 7	✓ 0.043 s	× 0.011 s	✓ 2.286 s
Example 8	✓ 0.020 s	× 0.010 s	× 0.322 s
[2, Example 5.2]	✓ 0.015 s	× 0.009 s	✓ 0.009 s
[2, Example 7.1]	✓ 0.021 s	× 0.011 s	× 33.968 s
[2, Example 8.19]	✓ 0.026 s	× 0.011 s	× 12.408 s
[11, Example 7.1]	✓ 0.032 s	× 0.013 s	✓ 0.498 s
[11, Example 7.2]	× 0.016 s	× 0.010 s	× 0.340 s
[11, Example 7.3]	✓ 0.025 s	× 0.011 s	✓ 0.166 s
`neutr.p`	× 0.012 s	× 0.008 s	✓ 0.025 s
`neutrN.p`	✓ 0.018 s	✓ 0.010 s	✓ 0.030 s

Table 1 compares our implementation of NCPO with our reimplementation of NHORPO with and without neutralization on a small set of problems. In all configurations, termination (✓) or the unsatisfiability of the encoding (×) are checked using the SMT solver Z3 [18]. Here, unsatisfiability of the encoding means that termination cannot be established with the given method, and does not imply nontermination. Furthermore, the table contains the execution time of each invocation on an Intel Core i7-7500U CPU running at a clock rate of 2.7 GHz with 15.5 GiB of main memory. As has already been pointed out in [11], NHORPO on its own is quite weak, so it is intended to be used together with neutralization. For four problems, neutralization on top of NHORPO is not enough: As already discussed, Example 8 needs small symbols and [2, Example 8.19] does not work because (N)HORPO enforces all subgoals to be weakly oriented in the admissible order on types while this is not the case for (N)CPO. Furthermore, [2, Example 7.1] shows that neutralization does not subsume accessible subterms. Finally, note that [11, Example 7.2] is not solvable by any of the three methods. In [11] it is claimed that NHORPO with neutralization is able to prove its termination but the proof given there does not work since it contains comparisons where the left-hand side is versatile. Indeed, our experiments confirm that there does not exist a suitable parameter assignment for neutralization which enables a termination proof with NHORPO. The existence of `neutr.p` shows that NCPO and NHORPO with neutralization have incomparable power. Note that NCPO succeeds in establishing termination of a neutralized version (`neutrN.p`) of this problem. With respect to execution time, it can be seen that a search for suitable parameters of NCPO does not take much more time than the corresponding search for NHORPO parameters. For neutralization, the number of parameters and therefore the execution time of our search method can explode quickly in the presence of function symbols with big arities which have more than one argument of nonbase type. However, there may be a more efficient encoding of the search for the neutralization parameters than the one implemented by us. We also evaluated the HORPO implementations in WANDA and CSI^ho on the problems given in Table 1. The HORPO implementation in WANDA yields termination proofs for `neutr.p` and `neutrN.p` which shows that it is incomparable with NHORPO. The HORPO implementation in CSI^ho performs worse than NHORPO which is to be expected because it is based on a very basic version of HORPO. The examples as well as a script to reproduce our experiments are available on the GitHub repository of our prototype implementation.

7 Conclusion

In this paper, we lifted the computability path order with its extensions for accessible subterms and small symbols [2] from plain to $\beta\eta$-normal higher-order rewriting. In order to achieve that goal, we followed the approach from [11] based on $\beta\eta$-normal stability which allowed us to use monotonicity and well-foundedness of CPO instead of proving the corresponding properties once more for the new order. In addition, we gave an improved sufficient condition for terms to be nonversatile which is an important ingredient of the used approach. The resulting order, dubbed NCPO, can prove termination of systems which are out of reach for all other HORPO implementations targeting normal higher-order rewriting known to us. Moreover, NCPO and NHORPO with neutralization, its strongest competitor, are of incomparable power. Contrary to what is claimed in [11], we find it much more difficult to encode the search for suitable parameters of NHORPO with neutralization than for NCPO. Thus, we think that NCPO is a powerful and lightweight alternative to NHORPO with neutralization.

As far as future work is concerned, transitivity of NCPO is an open question. For NHORPO and CPO, the inclusion of β-reduction in the order justifies that it is not transitive, but this is not the case for NCPO. If $>_\tau$ were not transitive, then merely checking $\ell >_\tau r$ for each rule would not be a complete method for establishing termination with $(>_\tau, \sqsupset_\tau)$ using Theorem 1. Furthermore, the logical next step towards a powerful termination technique for normal higher-order rewriting would be the integration of NCPO into a dependency pair technique for normal higher-order rewriting as defined for example in [15]. Finally, given the complex nature and wide-ranging pitfalls inherent in higher-order termination as well as the mistakes found especially in [11], formalizations of higher-order termination methods are needed. To the best of our knowledge, a formalization of a basic variant of HORPO without computability closure [14] is the only existing work in that direction.

Acknowledgments. We thank the anonymous reviewers for their valuable comments which improved the presentation of the paper.

Disclosure of Interests. The authors have no competing interests to declare that are relevant to the content of this article.

References

1. Barendregt, H.P.: Lambda calculi with types. In: Abramsky, S., Gabbay, D.M., Maibaum, T.S.E. (eds.) Handbook of Logic in Computer Science, vol. 2, pp. 117–309. Oxford University Press (1992). https://doi.org/10.1093/oso/9780198537618.003.0002
2. Blanqui, F., Jouannaud, J.P., Rubio, A.: The computability path ordering. Logical Methods Comput. Sci. **11**(4), 3:1–3:45 (2015). https://doi.org/10.2168/LMCS-11(4:3)2015
3. Blanqui, F., Jouannaud, J.P., Okada, M.: The calculus of algebraic constructions. In: Narendran, P., Rusinowitch, M. (eds.) Proc. 10th International Conference on Rewriting Techniques and Applications. LNCS, vol. 1631, pp. 301–316 (1999). https://doi.org/10.1007/3-540-48685-2_25
4. Church, A.: A formulation of the simple theory of types. J. Symb. Log. **5**(2), 56–68 (1940). https://doi.org/10.2307/2266170
5. Fuhs, C., Kop, C.: Polynomial interpretations for higher-order rewriting. In: Tiwari, A. (ed.) Proc. 23rd International Conference on Rewriting Techniques and Applications. Leibniz Int. Proc. Inform. **15**, 176–192 (2012). https://doi.org/10.4230/LIPIcs.RTA.2012.176
6. Giesl, J., et al.: Analyzing program termination and complexity automatically with AProVE. J. Autom. Reason. **58**(1), 3–31 (2016). https://doi.org/10.1007/s10817-016-9388-y
7. Hirokawa, N., Middeldorp, A., Sternagel, C., Winkler, S.: Abstract completion, formalized. Logical Methods Comput. Sci. **15**(3), 19:1–19:42 (2019). https://doi.org/10.23638/LMCS-15(3:19)2019
8. Jouannaud, J.P.: Higher-order rewriting: Framework, confluence and termination. In: Middeldorp, A., van Oostrom, V., van Raamsdonk, F., de Vrijer, R. (eds.) Processes, Terms and Cycles: Steps on the Road to Infinity: Essays Dedicated to Jan Willem Klop on the Occasion of His 60th Birthday, LNCS, vol. 3838, pp. 224–250. Springer Berlin Heideberg (2005). https://doi.org/10.1007/11601548_14
9. Jouannaud, J.P., Li, J.: Church–Rosser properties of normal rewriting. In: Cégielski, P., Durand, A. (eds.) Proc. 22nd International Conference on Rewriting Techniques and Applications. Leibniz Int. Proc. Inform, vol. 16, pp. 350–365 (2012). https://doi.org/10.4230/LIPIcs.CSL.2012.350
10. Jouannaud, J.P., Rubio, A.: Polymorphic higher-order recursive path orderings. J. ACM **54**(1), 1–48 (2007). https://doi.org/10.1145/1206035.1206037
11. Jouannaud, J.P., Rubio, A.: Normal higher-order termination. ACM Trans. Comput. Logic **16**(2), 13:1–13:38 (2015). https://doi.org/10.1145/2699913
12. Kop, C.: Higher Order Termination. Ph.D. thesis, Vrije Universiteit Amsterdam (2012)
13. Kop, C.: WANDA - a higher order termination tool (system description). In: Ariola, Z.M. (ed.) Proc. 5th International Conference on Formal Structures for Computation and Deduction. Leibniz Int. Proc. Inform, vol. 167, pp. 36:1–36:19 (2020). https://doi.org/10.4230/LIPIcs.FSCD.2020.36

14. Koprowski, A.: Coq formalization of the higher-order recursive path ordering. Appl. Algebra Eng. Commun. Comput. **20**(5), 379–425 (2009). https://doi.org/10.1007/s00200-009-0105-5
15. Kusakari, K., Isogai, Y., Sakai, M., Blanqui, F.: Static dependency pair method based on strong computability for higher-order rewrite systems. IEICE Trans. Inform. Syst. **E92.D**(10), 2007–2015 (2009). https://doi.org/10.1587/transinf.E92.D.2007
16. Mayr, R., Nipkow, T.: Higher-order rewrite systems and their confluence. Theoret. Comput. Sci. **192**(1), 3–29 (1998). https://doi.org/10.1016/S0304-3975(97)00143-6
17. Miller, D.: A logic programming language with lambda-abstraction, function variables, and simple unification. J. Log. Comput. **1**(4), 497–536 (1991). https://doi.org/10.1093/logcom/1.4.497
18. de Moura, L., Bjørner, N.: Z3: An efficient SMT solver. In: Ramakrishnan, C.R., Rehof, J. (eds.) Proc. 14th International Conference on Tools and Algorithms for the Construction and Analysis of Systems. LNCS, vol. 4963, pp. 337–340 (2008). https://doi.org/10.1007/978-3-540-78800-3_24
19. Nagele, J.: Mechanizing Confluence: Automated and Certified Analysis of First- and Higher-Order Rewrite Systems. Ph.D. thesis, University of Innsbruck (2017)
20. Niederhauser, J., Middeldorp, A.: The computability path order for beta-eta-normal higher-order-rewriting (full version). CoRR **abs/2505.20121** (2025). https://doi.org/10.48550/arXiv.2505.20121
21. Nipkow, T., Wenzel, M., Paulson, L.C. (eds.): Isabelle/HOL. LNCS, vol. 2283. Springer, Heidelberg (2002). https://doi.org/10.1007/3-540-45949-9
22. van de Pol, J.: Termination of Higher-Order Rewrite Systems. Ph.D. thesis, Utrecht University (1996)
23. van Raamsdonk, F.: On termination of higher-order rewriting. In: Middeldorp, A. (ed.) Proc. 12th International Conference on Rewriting Techniques and Applications. LNCS, vol. 2051, pp. 261–275 (2001). https://doi.org/10.1007/3-540-45127-7_20
24. Sutcliffe, G.: The TPTP problem library and associated infrastructure. J. Autom. Reason. **59**(4), 483–502 (2017). https://doi.org/10.1007/s10817-017-9407-7
25. Zantema, H.: Termination of term rewriting: interpretation and type elimination. J. Symb. Comput. **17**(1), 23–50 (1994). https://doi.org/10.1006/jsco.1994.1003

Sort-Based Confluence Criteria for Non-Left-Linear Higher-Order Rewriting

Thiago Felicissimo[1](✉) and Jean-Pierre Jouannaud[2]

[1] INRIA, Nantes, France
thiago.felicissimo@inria.fr
[2] Université Paris-Saclay, INRIA, Deducteam, Laboratoire de Méthodes Formelles, Paris, France
jeanpierre.jouannaud@gmail.com

Abstract. Powerful confluence criteria for higher-order rewriting exist for left-linear systems, even in the presence of critical pairs and non-termination. On the other hand, confluence criteria that allow for mixing non-termination and non-left-linearity are either extremely limited or hardly usable in practice. In this paper, we study confluence criteria which explore sort information to make proving higher-order confluence possible, even in the presence of non-termination and non-left-linearity. We give many interesting examples of systems covered by our results, including a (confluent) variant of Klop's counterexample, and a calculus issuing from a dependent type theory with cumulative universes.

Keywords: Higher-Order Rewriting · Left Non-Linear Rules · Confluence

1 Introduction

When proving confluence of higher-order rewrite systems, one generally has to be in one of the following two cases. If the rewrite system being considered is terminating, then by the critical pair criterion it suffices to check that critical pairs are joinable [24]. In most situations this requirement is too restrictive, but if the system is left-linear then many criteria that avoid termination exist, such as orthogonality [20] and development-closedness [26]. If however neither left-linearity nor termination hold, then few criteria allow showing confluence. In such cases, proving confluence can indeed become a subtle problem: as shown by Klop [19], even adding the simple rule $f(\mathsf{X}, \mathsf{X}) \to a$ to the untyped λ-calculus destroys its confluence.

In this paper, we propose criteria that leverage sort information to prove confluence of higher-order systems that are neither left-linear nor terminating. To do this, we define the *confined sorts* of a system $\mathcal{R}$ as those that can appear in instantiations of non-linear metavariables. Then, assuming that the subsystem $\mathcal{R}_c \subseteq \mathcal{R}$ operating in the confined sorts is confluent, we show how confluence of $\mathcal{R}$ can be established by closing the critical pairs of $\mathcal{R}_{nc} := \mathcal{R} \setminus \mathcal{R}_c$ using *decreasing*

C. Barrett and U. Waldmann (Eds.): CADE 2025, LNAI 15943, pp. 226–245, 2025.
https://doi.org/10.1007/978-3-031-99984-0_13

diagrams [27]. More precisely, we provide a criterion that assumes termination of $\mathcal{R}_c$ (Theorem 1) and another which does not (Theorem 2), but requires one to consider the more advanced notion of *cyclic critical pairs* [23]. Finally, we also give a combination criterion (Theorem 3), which allows to prove confluence of a non-left-linear system by splitting it into two, such that the *weakly confined* sorts of one does not interfere with the ones of the other.

Our results prove confluence of many interesting examples not covered by any published criterion (but some of them are covered by our previous non-published work [5,8]). These include for instance a confluent variant of Klop's counterexample, given at Fig. 1. Very minor changes to it can break its confluence (see Remark 3), showing that establishing this property is a non-trivial matter.

The full proofs of our results are given in the appendix of the technical report [9], so as to make the paper more accessible to non-specialists.

$0 : \mathsf{tm}$	$@ : (\mathsf{tm}, \mathsf{tm})\mathsf{tm}$	$\mathrm{Eq}(0, \mathrm{S}(\mathtt{N})) \to \bot$	$\mathrm{Eq}(\mathrm{S}(\mathtt{N}), 0) \to \bot$
$\mathrm{S} : (\mathsf{tm})\mathsf{tm}$	$\lambda : (\{\mathsf{tm}\}\mathsf{tm})\mathsf{tm}$	$\mathrm{Eq}(\mathrm{S}(\mathtt{N}), \mathrm{S}(\mathtt{M})) \to \mathrm{Eq}(\mathtt{N}, \mathtt{M})$	$\mathrm{Eq}(\mathtt{N}, \mathtt{N}) \to \top$
$\top, \bot : \mathsf{prop}$	$\mathrm{Eq} : (\mathsf{tm}, \mathsf{tm})\mathsf{prop}$	$@(\lambda(x.\mathtt{T}\{x\}), \mathtt{U}) \to \mathtt{T}\{\mathtt{U}\}$	

Fig. 1. Higher-order deduction modulo with natural numbers

2 Preliminaries

We work within a formalism of sorted second-order rewriting. This can be seen as Hamana's Second-order Computational Systems [13], simply-typed Combinatory Reduction Systems (CRSs) [20], or Pattern Rewrite Systems (PRSs) [24] with only function symbols of order at most two and variables of order at most one. In particular, this allows us to use criteria developed for any of these formalisms.

Variables, metavariables and function symbols Given a set A, let A^* be the set of lists of elements in A, written $\boldsymbol{a} = a_1, \ldots, a_k$, and let ε be the empty list.

Let $\mathcal{S}$ be a set of *sorts*, written s, as in multi-sorted first-order logic/rewriting (sorts can also be understood as syntactic classes). We assume we are given:

- An infinite set of *variables* $x, y, z, \cdots \in \mathcal{V}$, each equipped with a sort.
- An infinite set of *metavariables* $\mathtt{X}, \mathtt{T}, \mathtt{U}, \cdots \in \mathcal{M}$, each equipped with a *(simple) arity*, that is, an element of $\mathcal{S}^* \times \mathcal{S}$ written as $\{\boldsymbol{s}\}s$. Metavariables are referred to by characters in upper-case `typewriter font`, but we may use the letter e for being a variable or meta-variable, indifferently.
- A *signature* Σ of *function symbols* $f, g, h \in \mathcal{F}$, each equipped with a *binding arity* [11], that is, an element of $(\mathcal{S}^* \times \mathcal{S})^* \times \mathcal{S}$ written as $(\{\boldsymbol{s}_1\}s'_1, \ldots, \{\boldsymbol{s}_k\}s'_k)s$. Function symbols are referred to either by the letters f, g, h or by names in blue serif font, as in the example of Fig. 1.

An arity $\{s_1, \ldots, s_k\}s$ indicates that the metavariable takes k arguments, each of sort s_i, and produces a term of sort s. A binding arity $(\{\boldsymbol{s}_1\}s'_1, \ldots, \{\boldsymbol{s}_k\}s'_k)s$ indicates that the symbol takes k arguments, each of sort s'_i and binding variables of sorts $\boldsymbol{s}_i$, and produces a term of sort s. We write the assignment of a variable (resp. metavariable or symbol) to its sort (resp. arity or binding arity) as $x : s$ (resp. $\mathsf{X} : \{\boldsymbol{s}\}s$ or $f : (\{\boldsymbol{s}_1\}s'_1, \ldots, \{\boldsymbol{s}_k\}s'_k)s$), and often abbreviate $\{\varepsilon\}s$ and $(\varepsilon)s$ as s. We assume infinitely many variables and metavariables for each sort and arity. We however consider Σ to be variable and chosen by the user, and so we do **not** assume that we have a function symbol for each possible binding arity.

Terms The set $\mathcal{T}_s$ of *terms* of sort s is defined by the following rules. Terms are defined simultaneously with *abstractions*: given a list of variables $\boldsymbol{x} : \boldsymbol{s}$ and a term $t \in \mathcal{T}_{s'}$ we have the abstraction $\boldsymbol{x}.t \in \mathcal{T}_{\{\boldsymbol{s}\}s'}$ of arity $\{\boldsymbol{s}\}s'$. As usual, terms and abstractions are considered modulo α-equality. In the following, any definition made for terms is tacitly extended to abstractions $\boldsymbol{x}.t$ by treating the variables $\boldsymbol{x}$ as bound. We can abstract abstractions by taking $\boldsymbol{x}.(\boldsymbol{y}.t) := \boldsymbol{x}\boldsymbol{y}.t$, and an abstraction $\boldsymbol{x}.t$ with $\boldsymbol{x}$ empty is often implicitly coerced to the term t.

$$\frac{x : s}{x \in \mathcal{T}_s} \qquad \frac{\mathsf{X} : \{s_1, \ldots, s_k\}s \quad t_i \in \mathcal{T}_{s_i} \quad (i = 1, \ldots, k)}{\mathsf{X}\{t_1, \ldots, t_k\} \in \mathcal{T}_s} \qquad \frac{f : (\{\boldsymbol{s}_1\}s'_1, \ldots, \{\boldsymbol{s}_k\}s'_k)s \quad \boldsymbol{x}_i.t_i \in \mathcal{T}_{\{\boldsymbol{s}_i\}s'_i} \quad (i = 1, \ldots, k)}{f(\boldsymbol{x}_1.t_1, \ldots, \boldsymbol{x}_k.t_k) \in \mathcal{T}_s}$$

We write $\mathsf{fv}(t)$ for the set of free variables of t, $\mathsf{mv}(t)$ for its set of metavariables, $\mathsf{mv}^l(t)$ for its set of *linear* metavariables (occurring only once), and $\mathsf{mv}^{nl}(t)$ for its *non-linear* metavariables, defined as $\mathsf{mv}^{nl}(t) := \mathsf{mv}(t) \setminus \mathsf{mv}^l(t)$. A term t is said to be *ground* if $\mathsf{fv}(t) = \emptyset$, *meta-free* if $\mathsf{mv}(t) = \emptyset$, and *linear* if $\mathsf{mv}^{nl}(t) = \emptyset$.

Substitutions. A *substitution* σ is a set of pairs either of the form $x \mapsto t$ with $x : s$ and $t \in \mathcal{T}_s$, or $\mathsf{X} \mapsto \boldsymbol{x}.t$ with $\mathsf{X} : \{\boldsymbol{s}\}s'$ and $\boldsymbol{x}.t \in \mathcal{T}_{\{\boldsymbol{s}\}s'}$, such that each variable or metavariable appears to the left of $\mapsto$ at most once. The application of a substitution σ to a term t or an abstraction $\boldsymbol{x}.t$ is written $t[\sigma]$ or $(\boldsymbol{x}.t)[\sigma]$. The main cases of their definitions are $x[\sigma] := t$ if $x \mapsto t \in \sigma$, $\mathsf{X}\{\boldsymbol{t}\}[\sigma] := u[\boldsymbol{x} \mapsto \boldsymbol{t}[\sigma]]$ if $\mathsf{X} \mapsto \boldsymbol{x}.u \in \sigma$ and $(\boldsymbol{x}.t)[\sigma] := \boldsymbol{x}.t[\sigma]$. As usual, we must rename bound variables to avoid capturing. We define the application of σ to another substitution τ, written $\tau[\sigma]$, by applying σ point-wise to all entries of τ. We define $\mathsf{dom}(\sigma)$ by: $x \in \mathsf{dom}(\sigma)$ iff $x \mapsto t \in \sigma$ for some t, and $\mathsf{X} \in \mathsf{dom}(\sigma)$ iff $\mathsf{X} \mapsto \boldsymbol{x}.t \in \sigma$ for some $\boldsymbol{x}.t$.

Positions. We define *positions* $p, q, \ldots$ as words over natural numbers, and write ε for the empty word and $p \cdot q$ for word concatenation. We write $\leq$ for the prefix order and $\leq_{\mathsf{lex}}$ for the lexicographic extension of the order on natural numbers. We say that p, q are *parallel* when they are incomparable with respect to $\leq$.

Given a term t or abstraction $\boldsymbol{x}.t$, we write $\mathcal{P}os(t)$ and $\mathcal{P}os(\boldsymbol{x}.t)$ for their sets of positions. Given a position p of t or $\boldsymbol{x}.t$, the operations $t|_p$ and $(\boldsymbol{x}.t)|_p$ take the *(abstracted) subterm at* p, whose body is often denoted by t^p. These are defined simultaneously by $t|_\varepsilon := t$ and $\mathsf{X}\{\ldots, t_i, \ldots\}|_{ip} := t_i|_p$ and $f(\ldots, \boldsymbol{x}_i.t_i, \ldots)|_{ip} :=$

$(\boldsymbol{x}_i.t_i)|_p$ and $(\boldsymbol{x}.t)|_p := \boldsymbol{x}.t|_p$. A position p is *functional* if $t|_p = \boldsymbol{x}.t^p$ with t^p headed by a function symbol, and *nested* if, for some $q < p$, we have $t|_q = \boldsymbol{x}.t^q$ with t^q headed by a metavariable (otherwise said, the path from ε to p in t passes through a metavariable at some point). A metavariable X of t is said to be *strongly linear* if it is linear and occurs at a non-nested position, and we write $\mathsf{mv}^{sl}(t)$ for the set of such metavariables, and $\mathsf{mv}^{nsl}(t) := \mathsf{mv}(t) \setminus \mathsf{mv}^{sl}(t)$. Finally, given $p \in \mathcal{P}os(t)$ and an abstraction $\boldsymbol{x}.u$ of same arity as $t|_p = \boldsymbol{x}.t^p$, we write $t\{\!|\boldsymbol{x}.u|\!\}_p$ for the result of replacing t^p by u in t.

Patterns. A *pattern* is an abstraction $\boldsymbol{x}.t$ (written just t if $\boldsymbol{x} = \varepsilon$) such that $\mathsf{fv}(t) \subseteq \boldsymbol{x}$ and, for all p, if $t|_p = \boldsymbol{y}.\mathsf{X}\{\boldsymbol{u}\}$ then $\boldsymbol{u} = \boldsymbol{y}$.[1] Two patterns $\boldsymbol{x}.t$, $\boldsymbol{x}.u$ are *disjoint* if $\mathsf{mv}(t) \cap \mathsf{mv}(u) = \emptyset$. A *pattern unification problem* is an equation $\boldsymbol{x}.t \stackrel{?}{=} \boldsymbol{x}.u$ where the left- and right-hand sides are disjoint patterns of same arity. A substitution σ with $\mathsf{dom}(\sigma) = \mathsf{mv}(t) \cup \mathsf{mv}(u)$ for which $(\boldsymbol{x}.t)[\sigma] = (\boldsymbol{x}.u)[\sigma]$ is called a *unifier* of $\boldsymbol{x}.t \stackrel{?}{=} \boldsymbol{x}.u$. A unifier θ is more general than a unifier σ if there exists τ such that $\theta[\tau] = \sigma$. A major property of pattern unification is that it is decidable and, in the positive case, enjoys most-general unifiers (mgus).

Abstract Rewriting. Given a binary relation $\longrightarrow$ over some set $\mathcal{A}$, we write $\longrightarrow^=$ for its reflexive closure, $\longrightarrow\!\!\!\!\!\rightarrow$ for its reflexive-transitive closure and $\twoheadleftarrow\!\!\!\twoheadrightarrow$ for its reflexive-symmetric-transitive closure (also called its associated *conversion*). Given two such relations $\underset{1}{\longrightarrow}, \underset{2}{\longrightarrow}$, we write $\underset{1}{\longrightarrow} \cdot \underset{2}{\longrightarrow}$ for $\{(a, c) \mid \exists b.a \underset{1}{\longrightarrow} b \text{ and } b \underset{2}{\longrightarrow} c\}$. If the relation R under consideration is not denoted by an arrow, we also employ the notation R^* for its reflexive-transitive closure.

A binary relation $\longrightarrow$ is said to be *confluent* when $\twoheadleftarrow \cdot \twoheadrightarrow \subseteq \twoheadrightarrow \cdot \twoheadleftarrow$ and *terminating* when there is no infinite sequence $a \longrightarrow a' \longrightarrow a'' \longrightarrow \dots$.

An important result about abstract rewriting that will be useful in this paper is van Oostrom's *decreasing diagrams criterion* [27]. Suppose some well-founded set of *labels* $\mathcal{L}$ and a family of binary relations $\mathfrak{F} = \{\underset{\alpha}{\longrightarrow}\}_{\alpha \in \mathcal{L}}$, all of them over $\mathcal{A}$. We say that family $\mathfrak{F}$ is *decreasing* if every *divergence* $\underset{\alpha}{\longleftarrow} \cdot \underset{\beta}{\longrightarrow}$ is included in a *decreasing diagram* (DD in short), that is:

$$\underset{\alpha}{\longleftarrow} \cdot \underset{\beta}{\longrightarrow} \subseteq \underset{<\alpha}{\twoheadleftarrow\!\!\!\twoheadrightarrow} \cdot \underset{\beta}{\longrightarrow}^{=} \cdot \underset{<\alpha,\beta}{\twoheadleftarrow\!\!\!\twoheadrightarrow} \cdot {}^{=}\!\underset{\alpha}{\longleftarrow} \cdot \underset{<\beta}{\twoheadleftarrow\!\!\!\twoheadrightarrow}$$

where $\underset{<\alpha}{\longrightarrow}$ denotes $\bigcup_{\gamma<\alpha} \underset{\gamma}{\longrightarrow}$ and $\underset{<\alpha,\beta}{\longrightarrow}$ denotes $\underset{<\alpha}{\longrightarrow} \cup \underset{<\beta}{\longrightarrow}$. Van Oostrom's criterion asserts that, if $\mathfrak{F}$ is decreasing, then the relation $\bigcup_\alpha \underset{\alpha}{\longrightarrow}$ is confluent [17, 27].

Term Rewriting. A *rewrite rule* is a pair $\ell \to r$ whose left-hand side ℓ is a pattern not equal to a metavariable, and whose right-hand side r is a ground term of same sort as ℓ, such that $\mathsf{mv}(r) \subseteq \mathsf{mv}(\ell)$. A *rewrite system* $\mathcal{R}$ is a set

[1] In most works one only asks $\boldsymbol{u}$ to be a subset of $\boldsymbol{y}$ [22]. To simplify technicalities, here we chose to consider *fully extended* patterns, for which $\boldsymbol{u} = \boldsymbol{y}$.

of rewrite rules, and we sometimes name its elements using natural numbers k, writing $k : \ell \to r$.

Given a term t, a rewrite system $\mathcal{R}$ and a position $p \in \mathcal{P}os(t)$, we say that t rewrites to u with $\mathcal{R}$ at p, written $t \xrightarrow[\mathcal{R}]{p} u$ (possibly omitting $\mathcal{R}$ and/or p), if for some σ with $\mathsf{dom}(\sigma) = \mathsf{mv}(\ell)$, we have $t|_p = \boldsymbol{x}.(\ell[\sigma])$ and $u = t\{\!|\boldsymbol{x}.(r[\sigma])|\!\}_p$. We write $\sigma \longrightarrow \sigma'$ if $\mathsf{dom}(\sigma) = \mathsf{dom}(\sigma')$ and for some $e \in \mathsf{dom}(\sigma)$ we have $\sigma(e) \longrightarrow \sigma'(e)$ and that the restrictions of σ, σ' to $\mathsf{dom}(\sigma) \setminus \{e\}$ are equal. The definitions of confluence and termination are lifted from abstract rewriting to rewrite systems $\mathcal{R}$ **by considering the restriction of** $\xrightarrow[\mathcal{R}]{}$ **to meta-free terms** (e.g., $\mathcal{R}$ is confluent if the restriction of $\xrightarrow[\mathcal{R}]{}$ to meta-free terms is confluent).

3 Sort Confinement

In this section, we define the concept of *sort confinement*, a simple powerful idea with roots in [3,5] and which will serve as the basis for our criteria.

Sort Pre-order. We define the *sort pre-order* $\preceq$ in $\mathcal{S}$ by $s \preceq s'$ when there is some meta-free $t \in \mathcal{T}_{s'}$ and $p \in \mathcal{P}os(t)$ such that $t|_p = \boldsymbol{x}.t^p$ with $t^p \in \mathcal{T}_s$.

Note that this definition is only interesting because we ask t to be meta-free, otherwise we could just take the term $\mathsf{X}\{x\}$ with $x : s$ and $\mathsf{X} : \{s\}s'$. For the same reason, this definition would not make sense in higher-order frameworks such as Pattern Rewrite Systems (PRSs) [24], in which one does not make a distinction between variables and metavariables. Note also that $\preceq$ is a property of the user-specified signature Σ alone: it exists independently of any given rewrite system. Finally, it is easy to see that $\preceq$ is indeed reflexive and transitive, but not anti-symmetric, and moreover that it is decidable for finite Σ.

Confined Sorts. Given a rewrite system $\mathcal{R}$, we define its *confined sorts* to be

$$\mathcal{S}_c(\mathcal{R}) := \{s \in \mathcal{S} \mid \exists \ell \to r \in \mathcal{R},\ \mathsf{X} \in \mathsf{mv}^{nl}(\ell) \cup \mathsf{mv}^{nsl}(r),\ \text{st. } \mathsf{X} : \{...\}s' \text{ with } s \preceq s'\}$$

and we define its confined part $\mathcal{R}_c$ to be the rules in $\mathcal{R}$ with sort in $\mathcal{S}_c(\mathcal{R})$, and its non-confined part to be $\mathcal{R}_{nc} := \mathcal{R} \setminus \mathcal{R}_c$. A meta-free term t is then said to be *confined* if it is of a confined sort. In other words, $\mathcal{S}_c(\mathcal{R})$ isolates the sorts that can appear inside (1) meta-free instances of non-linear metavariables of ℓ or (2) meta-free instances of non-strongly linear metavariables of r, and $\mathcal{R}_c$ contains exactly the rules from $\mathcal{R}$ that can act on confined terms. This notion of confinement can be weakened by dropping (2), yielding the *weakly confined sorts*:

$$\mathcal{S}_{wc}(\mathcal{R}) := \{s \in \mathcal{S} \mid \exists \ell \to r \in \mathcal{R},\ \mathsf{X} \in \mathsf{mv}^{nl}(\ell),\ \text{st. } \mathsf{X} : \{\dots\}s' \text{ with } s \preceq s'\}$$

Example 1. Consider the rewrite system $\mathcal{R}$ containing the rules $\Uparrow(\mathsf{N}, \mathsf{N}, \mathsf{X}) \to \mathsf{X}$ and $@(\lambda(x.\mathsf{T}\{x\}), \mathsf{U}) \to \mathsf{T}\{\mathsf{U}\}$, where $@ : (\mathsf{tm}, \mathsf{tm})\mathsf{tm}$, $\lambda : (\{\mathsf{tm}\}\mathsf{tm})\mathsf{tm}$ and $\Uparrow : (\mathsf{nat}, \mathsf{nat}, \mathsf{tm})\mathsf{tm}$. The sort pre-order $\preceq$ is given by $\{(\mathsf{nat}, \mathsf{nat}), (\mathsf{nat}, \mathsf{tm}), (\mathsf{tm}, \mathsf{tm})\}$, therefore we obtain $\mathcal{S}_c(\mathcal{R}) = \{\mathsf{nat}, \mathsf{tm}\}$, $\mathcal{R}_c = \mathcal{R}$ and $\mathcal{S}_{wc}(\mathcal{R}) = \{\mathsf{nat}\}$.

In the next sections, we introduce criteria for proving confluence of a system whose confined part $\mathcal{R}_c$ is confluent (Theorems 1 and 2), or to combine two systems such that one does not interfere with the weakly confined sorts of another (Theorem 3). These can then be combined as building blocks for proving confluence of larger systems (as illustrated in Example 11).

4 A Criterion for When $\mathcal{R}_c$ Is Terminating

We start with our first and more basic criterion, which requires the confined system $\mathcal{R}_c$ to be terminating. This allows us to start gently, by recalling some preliminary notions such as lifting, overlaps and critical pairs, before moving to more advanced variants of these concepts in Sect. 5.

Lifting. Because a subterm at position p depends on the sequence of variables bound on the path from the root to p, one needs to introduce the concept of *lifting* [24]. Given a fixed list of sorts $\boldsymbol{s}$, let $(-)^*$ be a function that picks for each metavariable $\mathsf{X} : \{s_\mathsf{X}\}s_\mathsf{X}$ a unique metavariable $\mathsf{X}^* : \{\boldsymbol{s}, s_\mathsf{X}\}s_\mathsf{X}$—formally, we assume one such function for each choice of $\boldsymbol{s}$. Given $\boldsymbol{x} : \boldsymbol{s}$ and a finite set of metavariables $\mathcal{M}'$, we define the *lifting substitution* $\mathsf{lift}_{\boldsymbol{x}}$ (omitting $\mathcal{M}'$ from the notation) to be the one containing $\mathsf{X} \mapsto \boldsymbol{y}.\mathsf{X}^*\{\boldsymbol{x}, \boldsymbol{y}\}$ for each $\mathsf{X} : \{s_\mathsf{X}\}s_\mathsf{X}$ in $\mathcal{M}'$. In the case where $\boldsymbol{s} = \varepsilon$ we assume $(-)^*$ to be the identity, so that $t[\mathsf{lift}_\varepsilon] = t$ for all t. Given a substitution σ defined over $\mathcal{M}'$, we then write $\boldsymbol{x}.\sigma$ for the *abstraction of $\boldsymbol{x}$ in σ*, which is defined as the substitution containing $\mathsf{X}^* \mapsto \boldsymbol{xy}.t$ for each $\mathsf{X} \mapsto \boldsymbol{y}.t \in \sigma$. Importantly, we have $\mathsf{lift}_{\boldsymbol{x}}[\boldsymbol{x}.\sigma] = \sigma$.

Overlaps and Critical Pairs. Given disjoint patterns t_1 and $\boldsymbol{y}.t_2$, we say that t_1 *overlaps $\boldsymbol{y}.t_2$ at p* when p is a functional position of t_2 and, writing $(\boldsymbol{y}.t_2)|_p = \boldsymbol{x}.t_2^p$, the unification problem $\boldsymbol{x}.t_1[\mathsf{lift}_{\boldsymbol{x}}] \stackrel{?}{=} \boldsymbol{x}.t_2^p$ admits a meta-free unifier. Note that, if $\boldsymbol{x} = \varepsilon$, the problem becomes just $t_1 \stackrel{?}{=} t_2^p$, as lifting with ε is the identity.

Let $\ell_1 \to r_1, \ell_2 \to r_2$ be two rules renamed apart and p a position such that ℓ_1 overlaps ℓ_2 at p and, if $p = \varepsilon$, then the rules are not equal up to renaming. In this case, the rules yield the *critical pair* $\langle \ell_2\{\!|\boldsymbol{x}.r_1[\mathsf{lift}_{\boldsymbol{x}}]|\!\}_p[\theta], r_2[\theta]\rangle$, with θ the mgu of the problem $\boldsymbol{x}.\ell_1[\mathsf{lift}_{\boldsymbol{x}}] \stackrel{?}{=} \boldsymbol{x}.\ell_2^p$ where $\ell_2|_p = \boldsymbol{x}.\ell_2^p$.

Example 2. Consider the rules $g(\mathsf{Y}, \mathsf{Y}) \to \mathsf{Y}$ and $f(x.g(\mathsf{X}\{x\}, x)) \to \mathsf{X}\{a\}$. The first lhs overlaps the second at position 1. Indeed, we have $f(x.g(\mathsf{X}\{x\}, x))|_1 = x.g(\mathsf{X}\{x\}, x)$ and $g(\mathsf{Y}, \mathsf{Y})[\mathsf{lift}_x] = g(\mathsf{Y}^*\{x\}, \mathsf{Y}^*\{x\})$, yielding the unification problem $x.g(\mathsf{Y}^*\{x\}.\mathsf{Y}^*\{x\}) \stackrel{?}{=} x.g(\mathsf{X}\{x\}, x)$, which admits the meta-free unifier $\theta = \{\mathsf{X} \mapsto x.x, \mathsf{Y}^* \mapsto x.x\}$. This is actually an mgu, so we obtain the critical pair $\langle f(x.x), a\rangle$.

Rule Labeling. An important ingredient of our criteria will be the use of *rule labeling* [27,29], a technique for proving confluence of term rewrite systems using decreasing diagrams. However, because in our case we will only need to label non-confined rules, we give an adaptation of the usual definition to our setting.

A *labeled rewrite system* is a system $\mathcal{R}$ equipped with a well-founded set $\mathcal{L}$ of *labels* and an assignment of a label for each rule in $\mathcal{R}_{nc}$. If a rule $\ell \to r \in \mathcal{R}_{nc}$ is labelled by α, we denote this by writing $\ell \to_\alpha r$. Given some $\alpha \in \mathcal{L}$, we define $\mathcal{R}_\alpha := \{\ell \to r \mid \ell \to_\alpha r \in \mathcal{R}_{nc}\}$, $\mathcal{R}_{<\alpha} := \mathcal{R}_c \cup (\bigcup_{\gamma<\alpha} \mathcal{R}_\gamma)$ and $\mathcal{R}_{<\alpha,\beta} := \mathcal{R}_{<\alpha} \cup \mathcal{R}_{<\beta}$. Note that the confined rules are always included in $\mathcal{R}_{<\alpha}$, so one can think of them as being labelled by a new bottom element c adjoined to $\mathcal{L}$.

The Criterion. We are now ready to give our first criterion. In order to simplify notations, we often drop the $\mathcal{R}$ of $\mathcal{R}_{nc}$, $\mathcal{R}_c$, $\mathcal{R}_\alpha$, etc., under an arrow, keeping its subscript, allowing us to write, e.g., $\underset{c}{\longrightarrow}$ for $\underset{\mathcal{R}_c}{\longrightarrow}$ or $\underset{<\alpha}{\longrightarrow}$ for $\underset{\mathcal{R}_{<\alpha}}{\longrightarrow}$. Moreover, recall that a position $q \in \mathcal{P}os(t)$ is non-nested if the path from ε to q in t does not pass through a metavariable—a condition needed in the higher-order setting for the stability of $\longrightarrow$ under substitution [9, Proposition 4].

Theorem 1. *Given some labeled rewrite system $\mathcal{R}$, suppose that:*

(a) *$\mathcal{R}_c$ is confluent and terminating.*
(b) *For all $\ell \to r \in \mathcal{R}_{nc}$ and $\ell_c \to r_c \in \mathcal{R}_c$, ℓ_c does not overlap ℓ.*
(c) *If $\langle u_1, u_2\rangle$ is a critical pair of $\ell_1 \to_{\alpha_1} r_1, \ell_2 \to_{\alpha_2} r_2 \in \mathcal{R}_{nc}$, then*

$$u_1 \underset{<\alpha_1}{\twoheadleftarrow\!\!\twoheadrightarrow} u_1' \xrightarrow[\alpha_2]{q_1}{}^{=} u_1'' \underset{<\alpha_1,\alpha_2}{\twoheadleftarrow\!\!\twoheadrightarrow} u_2'' \;{}^{=}\!\xleftarrow[\alpha_1]{q_2} u_2' \underset{<\alpha_2}{\twoheadleftarrow\!\!\twoheadrightarrow} u_2$$

for some u_1', u_1'', u_2', u_2'' with q_i non-nested in u_i'.

Then $\mathcal{R}$ is confluent.

In **(c)**, recall that $u_i' \xrightarrow{q_i}{}^{=} u_i''$ means either $u_i' = u_i''$ or $u_i' \xrightarrow{q_i} u_i''$, so in the first case we can take q_i to be any position in u_i', and by taking $q_i = \varepsilon$ the non-nesting constraint is trivially verified. Moreover, as can be guessed by its shape, the closing diagram is a DD for some suitable labeling, to be given in Sect. 7.

Remark 1. Note that condition **(c)** behaves the same for symmetric root critical pairs, in the sense that, if ℓ_1 and ℓ_2 each overlap the other one at ε, then the two generated critical pairs $\langle r_1[\theta], r_2[\theta]\rangle$ and $\langle r_2[\theta], r_1[\theta]\rangle$ (where θ is the mgu of $\ell_1 \overset{?}{=} \ell_2$) either both satisfy or do not satisfy **(c)**. Therefore, in such a situation, it suffices to verify the condition for one of the critical pairs.

Let us now see an example of how the criterion can be applied.

Example 3. Consider the following example. The symbol Eq checks equality of two lists for a given prefix length. The elements $x.t$ of such lists denote functions $f : \mathbb{N} \to \mathbb{N}$ defined only in terms of zero, successor and addition. The five rules for $+$ ensure that, if $x.t$ and $x.u$ are ground and meta-free, of arity $\{\mathsf{nat}\}\mathsf{nat}$ and represent the same function, then they are convertible, morally justifying why the check provided by Eq is complete. We can then add symbols for generating infinite lists of functions and compare their prefixes. As an example, we add Λ_1 and Λ_2 which generate the sequences $f, f^2, f^4, f^8, \ldots$ and $f, 2f, 4f, 8f, \ldots$.

$$\begin{array}{lll}
0 : \mathsf{nat} \quad S : (\mathsf{nat})\mathsf{nat} & +(0, \mathsf{M}) \to \mathsf{M} & +(S(\mathsf{N}), \mathsf{M}) \to S(+(\mathsf{N}, \mathsf{M})) \\
+ : (\mathsf{nat}, \mathsf{nat})\mathsf{nat} & +(\mathsf{N}, 0) \to \mathsf{N} & +(\mathsf{N}, S(\mathsf{M})) \to S(+(\mathsf{N}, \mathsf{M})) \\
\Lambda_1, \Lambda_2 : (\{\mathsf{nat}\}\mathsf{nat})\mathsf{tm} & +(\mathsf{N}, +(\mathsf{M}, \mathsf{P})) \to +(+(\mathsf{N}, \mathsf{M}), \mathsf{P}) & \mathrm{Eq}(0, \mathsf{X}, \mathsf{Y}) \to \top \\
\mathrm{cons} : (\{\mathsf{nat}\}\mathsf{nat}, \mathsf{tm})\mathsf{tm} & \multicolumn{2}{l}{\mathrm{Eq}(S(\mathsf{P}), \mathrm{cons}(x.\mathsf{N}\{x\}, \mathsf{X}), \mathrm{cons}(x.\mathsf{N}\{x\}, \mathsf{Y})) \to \mathrm{Eq}(\mathsf{P}, \mathsf{X}, \mathsf{Y})} \\
\mathrm{Eq} : (\mathsf{nat}, \mathsf{tm}, \mathsf{tm})\mathsf{tm} & \multicolumn{2}{l}{\Lambda_1(x.\mathsf{N}\{x\}) \to \mathrm{cons}(x.\mathsf{N}\{x\}, \Lambda_1(x.\mathsf{N}\{\mathsf{N}\{x\}\}))} \\
\top : \mathsf{tm} & \multicolumn{2}{l}{\Lambda_2(x.\mathsf{N}\{x\}) \to \mathrm{cons}(x.\mathsf{N}\{x\}, \Lambda_2(x.+(\mathsf{N}\{x\}, \mathsf{N}\{x\})))}
\end{array}$$

Let us now prove confluence using Theorem 1. The only confined sort is nat, so $\mathcal{R}_c$ contains the five rules defining $+$. Using first-order techniques, it is easy to see that $\mathcal{R}_c$ is terminating and confluent, showing **(a)**. Condition **(b)** is also easily verified and **(c)** is trivial, given that there are no critical pairs in $\mathcal{R}_{nc}$.

The following example, although covered by first-order techniques [3], illustrates how the choice of the labeling can intervene when applying Theorem 1.

Example 4. Considering the following non-terminating system, containing a symmetric equality check for natural numbers.

$$\begin{array}{llll}
0 : \mathsf{tm} & \mathrm{Eq} : (\mathsf{tm}, \mathsf{tm})\mathsf{prop} & 1 : \mathrm{Eq}(0, S(\mathsf{N})) \to \bot & 3 : \mathrm{Eq}(S(\mathsf{N}), 0) \to \bot \\
S : (\mathsf{tm})\mathsf{tm} & \top, \bot : \mathsf{prop} & 2 : \mathrm{Eq}(\mathsf{N}, \mathsf{M}) \to \mathrm{Eq}(\mathsf{M}, \mathsf{N}) & 4 : \mathrm{Eq}(\mathsf{N}, \mathsf{N}) \to \top
\end{array}$$

Let us prove its confluence using Theorem 1. The only confined sort is tm and therefore $\mathcal{R}_c$ is empty, so it suffices to check condition **(c)**. We have the following critical pairs (ignoring symmetric counterparts):

- $\langle \mathrm{Eq}(0, S(\mathsf{X})), \bot \rangle$ with rules 2 and 3, closes as $\mathrm{Eq}(0, S(\mathsf{X})) \xrightarrow{\varepsilon} \bot$ with rule 1.
- $\langle \mathrm{Eq}(S(\mathsf{X}), 0), \bot \rangle$ with rules 2 and 1, closes as $\mathrm{Eq}(S(\mathsf{X}), 0) \xrightarrow{\varepsilon} \bot$ with rule 3.
- $\langle \mathrm{Eq}(\mathsf{X}, \mathsf{X}), \top \rangle$ with rules 2 and 4, closes as $\mathrm{Eq}(\mathsf{X}, \mathsf{X}) \xrightarrow{\varepsilon} \top$ with rule 4.

Therefore, we can conclude confluence by labeling rules 1 and 3 the same.

5 A Criterion for When $\mathcal{R}_c$ Is Potentially Non-Terminating

The termination requirement for $\mathcal{R}_c$ in Theorem 1 is unfortunately violated in many examples of interest, such as the one of Fig. 1. In this section, we show how this restriction can be dropped at the cost of considering more complex notions of unification, overlaps and critical pairs.

Linearization Let us assume for every metavariable X and position p, a fresh metavariable X_p uniquely determined by X and p. Given a term t, we write $\hat{t}$ for the linear term obtained by replacing each occurrence of a non-linear metavariable X at position p by X_p. Given $\mathsf{X} \in \mathsf{mv}(\hat{t})$, define $\check{\mathsf{X}} \in \mathsf{mv}(t)$ by $\check{\mathsf{X}} := \mathsf{X}$ when $\mathsf{X} \in \mathsf{mv}(t)$, otherwise X is of the form Y_p for some $\mathsf{Y} \in \mathsf{mv}(t)$ and p, so define $\check{\mathsf{X}} := \mathsf{Y}$. Given a substitution σ with $\mathsf{dom}(\sigma) = \mathsf{mv}(\hat{t})$, we say that σ is *equalized* if for every $\mathsf{X}, \mathsf{Y} \in \mathsf{mv}(\hat{t})$ with $\check{\mathsf{X}} = \check{\mathsf{Y}}$ we have $\sigma(\mathsf{X}) = \sigma(\mathsf{Y})$. When σ is equalized, we can define the substitution $\check{\sigma} := \{\check{\mathsf{X}} \mapsto \boldsymbol{x}.u \mid \mathsf{X} \mapsto \boldsymbol{x}.u \in \sigma\}$ which satisfies $\hat{t}[\sigma] = t[\check{\sigma}]$. Moreover, given σ with $\mathsf{dom}(\sigma) = \mathsf{mv}(\hat{t})$, we write $\sigma^{\#}$ for the substitution of domain $\mathsf{mv}(t)$ obtained by sending the linear X to $\sigma(\mathsf{X})$ and the non-linear X to $\sigma(\mathsf{X}_p)$ with p being the minimal (for $\leq_{\mathsf{lex}}$) position for X in t—hence, we have $\sigma^{\#} = \check{\sigma}$ when σ is equalized. Intuitively, the $\#$ operator truncates its input substitution so as to obtain a substitution of domain $\mathsf{mv}(t)$. Finally, if σ is defined over $\mathsf{mv}(\hat{t}_1) \cup \mathsf{mv}(\hat{t}_2)$ with $\mathsf{mv}(t_1) \cap \mathsf{mv}(t_2) = \emptyset$, we write $\check{\sigma}$ and $\sigma^{\#}$ for $\check{\sigma}_1 \cup \check{\sigma}_2$ and $\sigma_1^{\#} \cup \sigma_2^{\#}$, where σ_i is the restriction of σ to $\mathsf{mv}(\hat{t}_i)$.

Example 5. The linearization of $t = \mathrm{Eq}(\mathsf{X}, \mathsf{X})$ yields the linear pattern $\hat{t} = \mathrm{Eq}(\mathsf{X}_1, \mathsf{X}_2)$. The substitution $\sigma = \{\mathsf{X}_i \mapsto 0\}$ is equalized for $\hat{t}$, and thus $\check{\sigma}$ is well-defined and satisfies $\hat{t}[\sigma] = t[\check{\sigma}]$ and $\check{\sigma} = \sigma^{\#}$. On the order hand, $\tau = \{\mathsf{X}_1 \mapsto 0, \mathsf{X}_2 \mapsto \mathrm{S}(0)\}$ is not equalized, hence $\tau^{\#} = \{\mathsf{X} \mapsto 0\}$ but $\check{\tau}$ is not well-defined.

Cyclic Unification. Given disjoint patterns $\boldsymbol{x}.t_1, \boldsymbol{x}.t_2$ and a rewrite system $\mathcal{R}$, we consider the $\mathcal{R}$-*cyclic unification problem* $\boldsymbol{x}.t_1 \stackrel{?}{=} \boldsymbol{x}.t_2$, whose $\mathcal{R}$-*cyclic unifiers* are defined as the (syntactic) unifiers σ of the linearized problem $\boldsymbol{x}.\hat{t}_1 \stackrel{?}{=} \boldsymbol{x}.\hat{t}_2$ that satisfy the condition: for all $\mathsf{X}, \mathsf{Y} \in \mathsf{mv}(\hat{t}_1) \cup \mathsf{mv}(\hat{t}_2)$, if $\check{\mathsf{X}} = \check{\mathsf{Y}}$ then $\sigma(\mathsf{X}) \xleftrightarrow[\mathcal{R}]{*} \sigma(\mathsf{Y})$. The following example motivates the terminology of "cyclic": this notion of unification allows for solutions which are morally infinite, but represented in a finite way by the rewrite system $\mathcal{R}$.

Example 6. Consider the $\mathcal{R}$-cyclic unification problem $\mathrm{Eq}(\mathsf{X}, \mathsf{X}) \stackrel{?}{=} \mathrm{Eq}(\mathsf{Y}, \mathrm{S}(\mathsf{Y}))$. Its linearization is $\mathrm{Eq}(\mathsf{X}_1, \mathsf{X}_2) \stackrel{?}{=} \mathrm{Eq}(\mathsf{Y}_1, \mathrm{S}(\mathsf{Y}_{2\cdot 1}))$, which admits the syntactic unifier (actually, mgu) $\theta = \{\mathsf{X}_1 \mapsto \mathsf{Z}_1, \mathsf{X}_2 \mapsto \mathrm{S}(\mathsf{Z}_2), \mathsf{Y}_1 \mapsto \mathsf{Z}_1, \mathsf{Y}_{2\cdot 1} \mapsto \mathsf{Z}_2\}$. Assuming a term ∞ such that $\infty \xrightarrow[\mathcal{R}]{*} \mathrm{S}(\infty)$, we obtain a cyclic unifier with $\sigma := \theta[\mathsf{Z}_i \mapsto \infty]$. Indeed, we then have $\sigma(\mathsf{X}_1) \xleftrightarrow[\mathcal{R}]{*} \sigma(\mathsf{X}_2)$ and $\sigma(\mathsf{Y}_1) = \sigma(\mathsf{Y}_{2\cdot 1})$.

As suggested by the above example, the set of cyclic unifiers of $\boldsymbol{x}.t_1 \stackrel{?}{=} \boldsymbol{x}.t_2$ can be characterized by the mgu of the associated linearized problem $\boldsymbol{x}.\hat{t}_1 \stackrel{?}{=} \boldsymbol{x}.\hat{t}_2$. For this, suppose that $\boldsymbol{x}.\hat{t}_1 \stackrel{?}{=} \boldsymbol{x}.\hat{t}_2$ admits an mgu θ and consider the set $\mathcal{C}_f$ obtained by simplifying the set of equations $\mathcal{C}_0 := \{\theta(\mathsf{X}) \stackrel{?}{=} \theta(\mathsf{Y}) \mid \mathsf{X}, \mathsf{Y} \in \mathsf{dom}(\theta) \text{ with } \check{\mathsf{X}} = \check{\mathsf{Y}}\}$ until no more possible with the following decomposition rule:

$$\{\boldsymbol{x}.f(\boldsymbol{x}_1.t_1, \ldots, \boldsymbol{x}_k.t_k) \approx \boldsymbol{x}.f(\boldsymbol{x}_1.t'_1, \ldots, \boldsymbol{x}_k.t'_k)\} \cup \mathcal{C} \quad \rightsquigarrow \quad \{\boldsymbol{x}\boldsymbol{x}_i.t_i \approx \boldsymbol{x}\boldsymbol{x}_i.t'_i\}_{i=1,\ldots,k} \cup \mathcal{C}$$

We define the *associated congruence* of θ, denoted $\simeq_\theta$ (or just $\simeq$ when θ is obvious), to be the smallest equivalence relation stable under context containing $t_1[\boldsymbol{x} \mapsto \boldsymbol{u}] \simeq t_2[\boldsymbol{x} \mapsto \boldsymbol{u}]$ for each $\boldsymbol{x}.t_1 \approx \boldsymbol{x}.t_2 \in \mathcal{C}_f$ and $\boldsymbol{u}$ of the appropriate arity. The pair $(\theta, \simeq)$ is then called a *description of cyclic unifiers (dcu)* for the cyclic unification problem $t_1 \stackrel{?}{=} t_2$. Because mgus are unique up to renaming and $\simeq$ is uniquely determined for each θ, it follows that dcus are unique up to renaming.

Example 7. Take the cyclic unification problem $\mathrm{Eq}_3(\mathrm{S}(\mathsf{X}), \mathsf{X}, \mathrm{S}(\mathsf{Z})) \stackrel{?}{=} \mathrm{Eq}_3(\mathsf{Y}, \mathsf{Y}, \mathsf{Y})$. Its linearization is $\mathrm{Eq}_3(\mathrm{S}(\mathsf{X}_{1\cdot 1}), \mathsf{X}_2, \mathrm{S}(\mathsf{Z})) \stackrel{?}{=} \mathrm{Eq}_3(\mathsf{Y}_1, \mathsf{Y}_2, \mathsf{Y}_3)$, which admits the mgu $\theta = \{\mathsf{X}_{1\cdot 1} \mapsto \mathsf{W}_1, \mathsf{X}_2 \mapsto \mathsf{W}_2, \mathsf{Z} \mapsto \mathsf{W}_3, \mathsf{Y}_1 \mapsto \mathrm{S}(\mathsf{W}_1), \mathsf{Y}_2 \mapsto \mathsf{W}_2, \mathsf{Y}_3 \mapsto \mathrm{S}(\mathsf{W}_3)\}$. The calculation of $\mathcal{C}_0$ yields $\{\mathsf{W}_1 \approx \mathsf{W}_2, \mathrm{S}(\mathsf{W}_1) \approx \mathsf{W}_2, \mathrm{S}(\mathsf{W}_1) \approx \mathrm{S}(\mathsf{W}_3), \mathsf{W}_2 \approx \mathrm{S}(\mathsf{W}_3)\}$, and by simplifying $\mathrm{S}(\mathsf{W}_1) \approx \mathrm{S}(\mathsf{W}_3)$ into $\mathsf{W}_1 \approx \mathsf{W}_3$ we obtain $\simeq$ as the congruence generated by $\mathcal{C}_f = \{\mathsf{W}_1 \approx \mathsf{W}_2, \mathrm{S}(\mathsf{W}_1) \approx \mathsf{W}_2, \mathsf{W}_1 \approx \mathsf{W}_3, \mathsf{W}_2 \approx \mathrm{S}(\mathsf{W}_3)\}$. So we have the dcu $(\theta, \simeq)$.

Let us say that τ $\mathcal{R}$-realizes $\simeq$ if $u_1 \simeq u_2$ implies $u_1[\tau] \overset{*}{\underset{\mathcal{R}}{\longleftrightarrow}} u_2[\tau]$. The following characterization result justifies the name of "description of solutions".

Proposition 1. (Characterization of cyclic unifiers). *Suppose that $\mathcal{R}$ is confluent and that $\boldsymbol{x}.t_1$, $\boldsymbol{x}.t_2$ are disjoint patterns such that, for all $\ell \to r \in \mathcal{R}$, ℓ does not overlap $\boldsymbol{x}.\hat{t}_i$. If $\boldsymbol{x}.t_1 \stackrel{?}{=} \boldsymbol{x}.t_2$ admits an $\mathcal{R}$-cyclic unifier, then it admits a dcu $(\theta, \simeq)$. Moreover, a meta-free σ with $\mathsf{dom}(\sigma) = \mathsf{mv}(\hat{t}_1, \hat{t}_2)$ is an $\mathcal{R}$-cyclic unifier of $t_1 \stackrel{?}{=} t_2$ iff there is a meta-free τ that $\mathcal{R}$-realizes $\simeq$ and satisfies $\sigma = \theta[\tau]$.*

Cyclic Overlap. The definition of cyclic overlaps is then obtained by directly adapting the standard one. Given patterns t_1 and $\boldsymbol{y}.t_2$ with disjoint sets of metavariables, we say that t_1 *$\mathcal{R}$-cyclicly overlaps $\boldsymbol{y}.t_2$ at p* if p is a functional position of t_2 and, writing $(\boldsymbol{y}.t_2)|_p = \boldsymbol{x}.t_2^p$, the cyclic unification problem $\boldsymbol{x}.t_1[\mathsf{lift}_{\boldsymbol{x}}] \stackrel{?}{=} \boldsymbol{x}.t_2^p$ admits some meta-free $\mathcal{R}$-cyclic unifier.

Remark 2. As a consequence of Proposition 1, if $\boldsymbol{x}.t_1[\mathsf{lift}_{\boldsymbol{x}}] \stackrel{?}{=} \boldsymbol{x}.t_2^p$ admits a dcu $(\theta, \simeq)$ such that no meta-free τ realizes $\simeq$, then t_1 does not cyclicly overlap $\boldsymbol{y}.t_2$ at p, a reasoning which is often useful to rule out the existence of a cyclic overlap.

Let $\ell_1 \to r_1, \ell_2 \to r_2$ be two rules renamed apart and p a position such that ℓ_1 $\mathcal{R}$-cyclicly overlaps ℓ_2 at p and, if $p = \varepsilon$, then the rules are not equal up to renaming. We then have the *$\mathcal{R}$-cyclic critical pair* $\langle \ell_2\{\!|\boldsymbol{x}.r_1[\mathsf{lift}_{\boldsymbol{x}}]|\!\}_p[\theta^{\#}], r_2[\theta^{\#}], \simeq \rangle$ with $(\theta, \simeq)$ a dcu for $\boldsymbol{x}.\ell_1[\mathsf{lift}_{\boldsymbol{x}}] \stackrel{?}{=} \boldsymbol{x}.\ell_2^p$ where $\ell_2|_p = \boldsymbol{x}.\ell_2^p$ (note that a dcu must exist, by Proposition 1). As can be seen, the truncation operator $\#$ is used to get a substitution $\theta^{\#}$ defined over $\mathsf{mv}(\ell_1[\mathsf{lift}_{\boldsymbol{x}}]) \cup \mathsf{mv}(\ell_2^p)$ from θ. One might think that we are loosing information doing this, however this is compensated by the fact that we also store $\simeq$, which will be used for joining critical pairs.

Example 8. Looking at Example 9 and taking $\mathcal{R}$ to contain only rule 4, it is easy to see that the lhs of rule 1 $\mathcal{R}$-cyclicly overlaps the lhs of rule 2 at ε. Their left-hand sides admit the dcu $(\theta, \simeq)$ given in Example 7, which yields $\theta^{\#} = \{\mathsf{X} \mapsto \mathsf{W}_1, \mathsf{Z} \mapsto \mathsf{W}_3, \mathsf{Y} \mapsto \mathrm{S}(\mathsf{W}_1)\}$. Therefore, this overlap yields the cyclic critical pair $\langle \mathrm{Eq}_3(\mathrm{S}(\mathsf{W}_1), \mathsf{W}_1, \mathsf{W}_3), \top, \simeq \rangle$.

The Criterion. We are now finally ready to state our result. In its statement, we write $\underset{\simeq;\mathcal{R}}{\twoheadleftarrow\!\!\twoheadrightarrow}$ for the reflexive-symmetric-transitive closure of $\underset{\mathcal{R}}{\longrightarrow} \cup \simeq$.

Theorem 2. *Given some labeled rewrite system $\mathcal{R}$, suppose that:*

(a) *$\mathcal{R}_c$ is confluent.*
(b) *For all $\ell \to r \in \mathcal{R}_{nc}$ and $\ell_c \to r_c \in \mathcal{R}_c$, ℓ_c does not overlap $\hat{\ell}$.*
(c) *If $\langle u_1, u_2, \simeq\rangle$ is an $\mathcal{R}_c$-cyclic critical pair of $\ell_1 \to_{\alpha_1} r_1, \ell_2 \to_{\alpha_2} r_2 \in \mathcal{R}_{nc}$, then*

$$u_1 \underset{\simeq;<\alpha_1}{\twoheadleftarrow\!\!\twoheadrightarrow} u_1' \overset{q_1}{\underset{\alpha_2}{\longrightarrow}}{}^{=} u_1'' \underset{\simeq;<\alpha_1,\alpha_2}{\twoheadleftarrow\!\!\twoheadrightarrow} u_2'' \;{}^{=}\!\overset{q_1}{\underset{\alpha_1}{\longleftarrow}} u_2' \underset{\simeq;<\alpha_2}{\twoheadleftarrow\!\!\twoheadrightarrow} u_2$$

for some u_1', u_1'', u_2', u_2'' with q_i non-nested in u_i'.

Then $\mathcal{R}$ is confluent.

This criterion looks very similar to Theorem 1, with the crucial difference that we do not require termination of $\mathcal{R}_c$ anymore. In order to compensate this, we now need to consider $\mathcal{R}_c$-cyclic critical pairs in **(c)** and, as explained previously, we can employ the congruence $\simeq$ for closing them. Moreover, we have also strengthened the second assumption, by requiring that left-hand sides in $\mathcal{R}_c$ do not overlap the *linearized* left-hand sides in $\mathcal{R}_{nc}$—see Remark 4 for why this stronger assumption is needed. Finally, note that Remark 1 still holds for this second criterion. Let us now see how the criterion can be applied.

Example 9. Consider the following toy example equipped with any labeling, and let us show its confluence using Theorem 2.

$0, \infty : \mathsf{tm}$	$1 : \mathrm{Eq}_3(\mathrm{S}(\mathsf{X}), \mathsf{X}, \mathrm{S}(\mathsf{Z})) \to \mathrm{Eq}_3(\mathrm{S}(\mathsf{X}), \mathsf{X}, \mathsf{Z})$
$\mathrm{S} : (\mathsf{tm})\mathsf{tm}$	$2 : \mathrm{Eq}_3(\mathsf{Y}, \mathsf{Y}, \mathsf{Y}) \to \top$
$\mathrm{Eq}_3 : (\mathsf{tm}, \mathsf{tm}, \mathsf{tm})\mathsf{prop}$	$3 : \mathrm{Eq}_3(\mathrm{S}(\mathsf{V}), 0, \mathsf{V}) \to \bot$
$\top, \bot : \mathsf{prop}$	$4 : \infty \to \mathrm{S}(\infty)$

The only confined sort is tm, hence $\mathcal{R}_c = \{\infty \to \mathrm{S}(\infty)\}$, which is confluent by orthogonality, showing **(a)**. Condition **(b)** is easily verified. For **(c)** we need to check cyclic critical pairs between 1 and 2, 1 and 3, and 2 and 3. For 1 and 2, we have $\langle \mathrm{Eq}_3(\mathrm{S}(\mathsf{W}_1), \mathsf{W}_1, \mathsf{W}_3), \top, \simeq\rangle$, given in Example 8, and its symmetric counterpart—which, as explained in Remark 1, we do not need to consider. It can be closed with the diagram $\mathrm{Eq}_3(\mathrm{S}(\mathsf{W}_1), \mathsf{W}_1, \mathsf{W}_3) \simeq \mathrm{Eq}_3(\mathsf{W}_1, \mathsf{W}_1, \mathsf{W}_1) \overset{\varepsilon}{\longrightarrow} \top$ and ε is trivially non-nested. Regarding cyclic critical pairs between 1 and 3 and between 2 and 3, their cyclic unification problems each admit a dcu $(\theta, \simeq)$ whose congruence $\simeq$ identifies 0 and $\mathrm{S}(t)$ for some t. Yet, no meta-free τ realizes $\simeq$ given that, by confluence of $\mathcal{R}_c$, $0[\tau] \underset{c}{\twoheadleftarrow\!\!\twoheadrightarrow} \mathrm{S}(t)[\tau]$ is impossible. So, by Remark 2, they do not cyclicly overlap.

This example already shows the strength of our criterion even for the first-order fragment. Indeed, none of the major first-order confluence checkers (CSI [25], ACP [4], etc.) are able to prove its confluence—for this experiment, we used the above system without sorts as, by persistency of first-order confluence [2], it is confluent without sorts iff it is confluent with sorts. More generally, we are not aware of any criterion that is able to show its confluence, apart from ours. For our next example, let us see a confluent variant of Klop's counterexample.

Example 10. Consider the system of Fig. 1 equipped with any labeling, and let us show its confluence using Theorem 2. Once again, the only confined sort is tm, hence $\mathcal{R}_c$ contains only the β-rule, which is confluent by orthogonality, showing **(a)**. Condition **(b)** is again easily verified. For **(c)**, we only have a cyclic critical pair $\langle \mathrm{Eq}(\mathsf{W}_1, \mathsf{W}_2), \top, \simeq\rangle$ (and its symmetric counterpart), with $\simeq$ satisfying $\mathsf{W}_1 \simeq \mathsf{W}_2$, which can be closed with the diagram $\mathrm{Eq}(\mathsf{W}_1, \mathsf{W}_2) \simeq \mathrm{Eq}(\mathsf{W}_1, \mathsf{W}_1) \xrightarrow{\varepsilon} \top$.

Remark 3. Consider the system obtained by adding $\mathrm{Eq}(\mathrm{S}(\mathsf{M}), \mathsf{M}) \to \bot$ to Fig. 1. This extension breaks confluence, as now we can reproduce *Huet's counterexample* [16], by defining ∞ with the fixpoint combinator of the untyped λ-calculus:

$$\top \longleftarrow \mathrm{Eq}(\infty, \infty) \twoheadrightarrow \mathrm{Eq}(\mathrm{S}(\infty), \infty) \longrightarrow \bot$$

Note that the plain critical pairs of $\mathcal{R}_{nc}$ still satisfy condition **(c)** of Theorem 1, so this also shows why considering plain critical pairs instead of cyclic ones in condition **(c)** of Theorem 2 would not be enough.

Confluence can however be restored by removing the β-rule: indeed, without β, $\mathrm{Eq}(\mathsf{N}, \mathsf{N})$ does not cyclicly overlap $\mathrm{Eq}(\mathrm{S}(\mathsf{M}), \mathsf{M})$, given that the congruence $\simeq$ of their dcu satisfies $\mathsf{W}_1 \simeq \mathrm{S}(\mathsf{W}_1)$, which is not realizable anymore.

Finally, changing in Fig. 1 the sorts of Eq, $\top, \bot$ to tm also breaks confluence, as we can then reproduce Klop's counterexample.

Remark 4. Unlike with Theorem 1, for Theorem 2 it is not sufficient to consider in **(b)** only overlaps with non-linearized lhs of $\mathcal{R}_{nc}$. Indeed, consider the rules $\infty \to \mathrm{S}(\infty)$, $\max(\mathsf{X}, \mathsf{X}) \to \mathsf{X}$ and $\mathrm{Eq}(\max(\mathrm{S}(\mathsf{X}), \mathsf{X}), \mathsf{X}) \to \bot$, where $\infty : \mathsf{tm}$, $\max : (\mathsf{tm}, \mathsf{tm})\mathsf{tm}$, $\mathrm{Eq} : (\mathsf{tm}, \mathsf{tm})\mathsf{prop}$ and $\bot : \mathsf{prop}$. The confined part $\mathcal{R}_c$ contains the rules for ∞ and max, and can be shown confluent by [18, Theorem 2] (actually, $\mathcal{R}_c$ is a variant of [18, Example 9]), proving **(a)**. Condition **(c)** is trivially satisfied, as there are no cyclic overlaps in $\mathcal{R}_{nc}$. Finally, neither ∞ nor $\max(\mathsf{X}, \mathsf{X})$ overlaps $\mathrm{Eq}(\max(\mathrm{S}(\mathsf{X}), \mathsf{X}), \mathsf{X})$. Yet, confluence fails, given that

$$\bot \longleftarrow \mathrm{Eq}(\max(\mathrm{S}(\infty), \infty), \infty) \longrightarrow \mathrm{Eq}(\max(\mathrm{S}(\infty), \mathrm{S}(\infty)), \infty) \longrightarrow \mathrm{Eq}(\mathrm{S}(\infty), \infty)$$

and $\mathrm{Eq}(\mathrm{S}(\infty), \infty)$ does not reduce to $\bot$. Of course, if we remove the rule $\infty \to \mathrm{S}(\infty)$ then $\mathcal{R}_c$ becomes terminating, so we obtain confluence using Theorem 1.

6 A Combination Criterion

We have seen how Theorems 1 and 2 can be applied to show the confluence of systems for which no other published criterion was available before. Nevertheless, it is often useful to split the system under consideration in two so as to allow the application of two different criteria, each one fitting the fragment under choice. To this end, we provide the following combination criterion. Here, given a set of sorts $\mathcal{S}' \subseteq \mathcal{S}$, we write $\mathcal{R}|_{\mathcal{S}'}$ for the set of rules of $\mathcal{R}$ whose sort is in $\mathcal{S}'$.

Theorem 3. *Let $\mathcal{R}_1, \mathcal{R}_2$ be (non-necessarily disjoint) rewrite systems such that:*

(1) *$\mathcal{R}_1$ and $\mathcal{R}_2$ are both confluent.*
(2) $\mathcal{R}_2|_{\mathcal{S}_{wc}(\mathcal{R}_1)} = \mathcal{R}_1|_{\mathcal{S}_{wc}(\mathcal{R}_2)} = \emptyset$.
(3) *There are no critical pairs between rules of $\mathcal{R}_1$ and $\mathcal{R}_2$.*

Then $\mathcal{R}_1 \cup \mathcal{R}_2$ is confluent.

So, to split a system $\mathcal{R}$ into $\mathcal{R}_1 \cup \mathcal{R}_2$, we must ensure that **(3)** no critical pairs exist between them, and **(2)** that one cannot operate on the weakly confined sorts of the other. If these conditions are satisfied, then it suffices to show confluence of each system separately. Let us now see how this can be applied.

Example 11. Consider an extension of Example 10 with the following rules (from [24]), adding connectives and rules for computing the negation normal form.

$\neg : (\mathsf{prop})\mathsf{prop}$	$\neg(\neg(\mathsf{X})) \rightarrow \mathsf{X}$	
$\vee, \wedge : (\mathsf{prop}, \mathsf{prop})\mathsf{prop}$	$\neg(\wedge(\mathsf{X}, \mathsf{Y})) \rightarrow \vee(\neg(\mathsf{X}), \neg(\mathsf{Y}))$	$\neg(\forall(x.\mathsf{X}\{x\})) \rightarrow \exists(x.\neg(\mathsf{X}\{x\}))$
$\exists, \forall : (\{\mathsf{tm}\}\mathsf{prop})\mathsf{prop}$	$\neg(\vee(\mathsf{X}, \mathsf{Y})) \rightarrow \wedge(\neg(\mathsf{X}), \neg(\mathsf{Y}))$	$\neg(\exists(x.\mathsf{X}\{x\})) \rightarrow \forall(x.\neg(\mathsf{X}\{x\}))$

If we now try to apply Theorem 2 we realize that no labeling satisfying condition **(c)** can be found. Instead, we can apply Theorem 3 to split the rewrite system into $\mathcal{R}_1 \cup \mathcal{R}_2$, where $\mathcal{R}_1$ is the set of rules of Example 10 and $\mathcal{R}_2$ the set of rules given above. Indeed, it is easy to see that there are no critical pairs between $\mathcal{R}_1$ and $\mathcal{R}_2$, and moreover we have $\mathcal{S}_{wc}(\mathcal{R}_1) = \{\mathsf{tm}\}$ and $\mathcal{S}_{wc}(\mathcal{R}_2) = \emptyset$ and thus $\mathcal{R}_2|_{\mathcal{S}_{wc}(\mathcal{R}_1)} = \mathcal{R}_1|_{\mathcal{S}_{wc}(\mathcal{R}_2)} = \emptyset$. To conclude, it thus suffices to show that $\mathcal{R}_1$ and $\mathcal{R}_2$ are both confluent. In Example 10 we have already shown $\mathcal{R}_1$ to be confluent when considering a smaller signature, and it is easy to see that the added connectives do not change the sort pre-order, hence the argument given in Example 10 is still valid. For the confluence of $\mathcal{R}_2$, we can exploit its termination to conclude confluence by closing the critical pairs—see [24, Example 4.9].

Example 12. The following system (taken from [8]) contains a fragment of the rewrite rules for defining dependent type theory with cumulative Tarski-style universes. Here, we write $\Uparrow_t^u(v)$ for $\Uparrow(t, u, v)$ and $\Pi_t(u, x.v)$ for $\Pi(t, u, x.v)$.

$0 : \mathsf{nat}$	$\max : (\mathsf{nat}, \mathsf{nat})\mathsf{nat}$	$\max(0, \mathsf{Y}) \to \mathsf{Y}$	$\Uparrow^{\mathsf{X}}_{\mathsf{X}}(\mathsf{T}) \to \mathsf{T}$
$\mathrm{S} : (\mathsf{nat})\mathsf{nat}$	$\Uparrow : (\mathsf{nat}, \mathsf{nat}, \mathsf{tm})\mathsf{tm}$	$\max(\mathsf{X}, 0) \to \mathsf{X}$	$\Uparrow^{\mathsf{Z}}_{\mathsf{Y}}(\Uparrow^{\mathsf{Y}}_{\mathsf{X}}(\mathsf{T})) \to \Uparrow^{\mathsf{Z}}_{\mathsf{X}}(\mathsf{T})$
$\Pi : (\mathsf{nat}, \mathsf{tm}, \{\mathsf{tm}\}\mathsf{tm})\mathsf{tm}$		$\max(\mathrm{S}(\mathsf{X}), \mathrm{S}(\mathsf{Y})) \to \mathrm{S}(\max(\mathsf{X}, \mathsf{Y}))$	
$@ : (\mathsf{tm}, \mathsf{tm})\mathsf{tm}$		$\Uparrow^{\mathsf{Y}}_{\mathsf{X}}(\Pi_{\mathsf{X}}(\mathsf{A}, x.\mathsf{B}\{x\})) \to \Pi_{\mathsf{Y}}(\Uparrow^{\mathsf{Y}}_{\mathsf{X}}(\mathsf{A}), x.\Uparrow^{\mathsf{Y}}_{\mathsf{X}}(\mathsf{B}\{x\}))$	
$\lambda : (\{\mathsf{tm}\}\mathsf{tm})\mathsf{tm}$		$@(\lambda(x.\mathsf{T}\{x\}), \mathsf{U}) \to \mathsf{T}\{\mathsf{U}\}$	

Let us show confluence with Theorem 3. For this, take $\mathcal{R}_2$ containing only the β-rule and $\mathcal{R}_1$ containing the other rules. Confluence of $\mathcal{R}_2$ follows by orthogonality, and confluence of $\mathcal{R}_1$ follows because all critical pairs close and the system is terminating. We also have $\mathcal{R}_1|_{\mathcal{S}_{wc}(\mathcal{R}_2)} = \mathcal{R}_1|_{\emptyset} = \emptyset$ and $\mathcal{R}_2|_{\mathcal{S}_{wc}(\mathcal{R}_1)} = \mathcal{R}_2|_{\{\mathsf{nat}\}} = \emptyset$, and we can directly verify that there are no critical pairs between $\mathcal{R}_1$ and $\mathcal{R}_2$. Therefore, we can conclude confluence of $\mathcal{R}_1 \cup \mathcal{R}_2$.

Remark 5. In the above example, note that the metavariable U of sort tm occurs nested in the right-hand side of the β-rule. Therefore, the sort tm, which is not weakly confined, is confined. This shows the benefit of considering weakly confined sorts in Theorem 3, otherwise condition **(2)** would not be satisfied.

Example 13. Consider the following extension of System F with an operator allowing to cast a term of type A to any other type A', along with a rewrite rule for eliminating identity casts. As shown by Girard in his PhD thesis [12], this system is non-normalizing even when considering only well-typed System F terms. Nevertheless, we can prove it to be confluent on all terms using Theorem 3.

$@ : (\mathsf{tm}, \mathsf{tm})\mathsf{tm}$	$\lambda : (\{\mathsf{tm}\}\mathsf{tm})\mathsf{tm}$	$@(\lambda(x.\mathsf{T}\{x\}), \mathsf{U}) \to \mathsf{T}\{\mathsf{U}\}$	
$\mathrm{inst} : (\mathsf{tm}, \mathsf{ty})\mathsf{tm}$	$\Lambda : (\{\mathsf{ty}\}\mathsf{tm})\mathsf{tm}$	$\mathrm{inst}(\Lambda(x.\mathsf{T}\{x\}), \mathsf{A}) \to \mathsf{T}\{\mathsf{A}\}$	
$\to : (\mathsf{ty}, \mathsf{ty})\mathsf{ty}$	$\forall : (\{\mathsf{ty}\}\mathsf{ty})\mathsf{ty}$	$\mathrm{cast} : (\mathsf{ty}, \mathsf{ty}, \mathsf{tm})\mathsf{tm}$	$\mathrm{cast}(\mathsf{A}, \mathsf{A}, \mathsf{T}) \to \mathsf{T}$

Let us take $\mathcal{R}_1$ containing the two β-rules, and $\mathcal{R}_2$ containing the rule for cast. The system $\mathcal{R}_1$ is confluent by orthogonality, and $\mathcal{R}_2$ is confluent by the critical pair criterion, since it is terminating and has no critical pairs. We also have $\mathcal{R}_1|_{\mathcal{S}_{wc}(\mathcal{R}_2)} = \mathcal{R}_1|_{\{\mathsf{ty}\}} = \emptyset$ and $\mathcal{R}_2|_{\mathcal{S}_{wc}(\mathcal{R}_1)} = \mathcal{R}_2|_{\emptyset} = \emptyset$, and there are no critical pairs between $\mathcal{R}_1$ and $\mathcal{R}_2$. We thus conclude confluence of $\mathcal{R}_1 \cup \mathcal{R}_2$.

Proof Idea. We now discuss informally how we prove Theorem 3—the full proof can be found in the technical report [9]. Recall that Hindley-Rosen's lemma states that the union of two relations $\underset{1}{\longrightarrow}, \underset{2}{\longrightarrow}$ is confluent whenever each $\underset{i}{\longrightarrow}$ is confluent and the two commute (that is, when $\underset{1}{\twoheadleftarrow} \cdot \underset{2}{\twoheadrightarrow} \subseteq \underset{2}{\twoheadrightarrow} \cdot \underset{1}{\twoheadleftarrow}$). Because of condition **(1)**, to show confluence of $\mathcal{R}_1 \cup \mathcal{R}_2$ it therefore suffices to prove that $\underset{\mathcal{R}_1}{\longrightarrow}$ and $\underset{\mathcal{R}_2}{\longrightarrow}$ commute on meta-free terms (recall that we only show confluence for meta-free terms). This can be established by adapting the well-known technique of showing that *orthogonal rewriting* $\Longrightarrow$ (also called *simultaneous* or *multi-step rewriting*) satisfies the diamond property, a technique notably found in proofs of confluence by orthogonality [6]. Indeed, because $\xrightarrow[\mathcal{R}_i]{} \subseteq \underset{\mathcal{R}_i}{\Longrightarrow} \subseteq \xrightarrow[\mathcal{R}_i]{}\!\!\!\!\rightarrow$, we have that $\xrightarrow[\mathcal{R}_i]{}\!\!\!\!\rightarrow$ and $\underset{\mathcal{R}_i}{\Longrightarrow}^*$ are equal, so to show that $\mathcal{R}_1$ and $\mathcal{R}_2$ commute we can instead show $\underset{\mathcal{R}_1}{\Longleftarrow} \cdot \underset{\mathcal{R}_2}{\Longrightarrow} \subseteq \underset{\mathcal{R}_2}{\Longrightarrow} \cdot \underset{\mathcal{R}_1}{\Longleftarrow}$ on meta-free terms, a result analogous to the diamond property but when mixing different rewrite systems.

The proof of the above result then relies on the following key property: if $t \underset{\mathcal{R}_1}{\Longrightarrow} t'$ then the $\mathcal{R}_2$ redexes in t are never destroyed (and vice versa for $t \underset{\mathcal{R}_2}{\Longrightarrow} t'$). To ensure this in the left-linear case, it is sufficient to ask for absence of critical pairs (condition **(3)**). However, in the non-left-linear case, a redex can also be destroyed by changing the value of non-linear occurrences of the same metavariable: for instance, if $f(\mathsf{X}, \mathsf{X}) \to \mathsf{X} \in \mathcal{R}_1$ and $a \to b \in \mathcal{R}_2$, then the reduction $f(a, a) \underset{\mathcal{R}_2}{\Longrightarrow} f(a, b)$ destroys the redex $f(\mathsf{X}, \mathsf{X})[\mathsf{X} \mapsto a]$. This problem is ruled out by condition **(2)**, which ensures that a rule from $\mathcal{R}_1$ cannot operate inside meta-free instances of non-left-linear metavariables of $\mathcal{R}_2$, and vice versa. Therefore, conditions **(2)** and **(3)** combined allow us to show $\underset{\mathcal{R}_1}{\Longleftarrow} \cdot \underset{\mathcal{R}_2}{\Longrightarrow} \subseteq \underset{\mathcal{R}_2}{\Longrightarrow} \cdot \underset{\mathcal{R}_1}{\Longleftarrow}$ on meta-free terms, and thus conclude the proof of Theorem 3.

7 Proof Idea for Theorems 1 and 2

We now explain the idea of the proofs for Theorems 1 and 2—the full proofs appear in the technical report [9]. It turns out that their proofs can be factored out by instead proving a unifying theorem (Theorem 4) which is then shown to imply Theorems 1 and 2. To state it, we first recall the notion of $\mathcal{R}$-*critical pairs.*

Given a rewrite system $\mathcal{R}$ and two patterns $\boldsymbol{x}.t$ and $\boldsymbol{x}.u$ of same arity, an $\mathcal{R}$-*unification problem* is a pair $\boldsymbol{x}.t \stackrel{?}{=} \boldsymbol{x}.u$, and an $\mathcal{R}$-*unifier* for it is a substitution σ with $\mathsf{dom}(\sigma) = \mathsf{mv}(t_1) \cup \mathsf{mv}(t_2)$ and $(\boldsymbol{x}.t)[\sigma] \xleftrightarrow[\mathcal{R}]{}\!\!\!\!\rightarrow (\boldsymbol{x}.u)[\sigma]$. Given patterns t_1 and $\boldsymbol{y}.t_2$ with disjoint sets of metavariables, we then say that t_1 $\mathcal{R}$-*overlaps* $\boldsymbol{y}.t_2$ *at* p if p is a functional position of t_2 and, writing $(\boldsymbol{y}.t_2)|_p = \boldsymbol{x}.t_2^p$, the unification problem $\boldsymbol{x}.t_1[\mathsf{lift}_{\boldsymbol{x}}] \stackrel{?}{=} \boldsymbol{x}.t_2^p$ admits some meta-free $\mathcal{R}$-unifier. Finally, given two rules $\ell_1 \to r_1, \ell_2 \to r_2$ renamed apart and a position p such that ℓ_1 $\mathcal{R}$-overlaps ℓ_2 at p, we have the $\mathcal{R}$-*critical pair* $\langle \ell_2\{\!|\boldsymbol{x}.r_1[\mathsf{lift}_{\boldsymbol{x}}]|\!\}_p[\sigma], r_2[\sigma]\rangle$ for each meta-free $\mathcal{R}$-unifier σ of the associated $\mathcal{R}$-unification problem. Note that, compared with the previous notions of overlap, we do not discard the case $p = \varepsilon$ when the rules are the same. Moreover, we do not use mgus or dcus to capture critical pairs in a finite way: for each overlap, we have potentially infinitely many critical pairs, one for every meta-free unifier σ. We can now state the unifying theorem:

Theorem 4. *Given some labeled rewrite system* $\mathcal{R}$*, suppose that:*

(i) $\mathcal{R}_c$ *is confluent.*
(ii) *If* $t \xleftrightarrow[c]{}\!\!\!\!\rightarrow \ell[\sigma]$ *for some* $\ell \to r \in \mathcal{R}_{nc}$ *and* t, σ *both meta-free with* $\mathsf{dom}(\sigma) = \mathsf{mv}(\ell)$*, then* $t \xrightarrow[c]{}\!\!\!\!\rightarrow \ell[\sigma']$ *for some* σ' *with* $\sigma \xrightarrow[c]{}\!\!\!\!\rightarrow \sigma'$*.*

(iii) *If* $\langle u_1, u_2 \rangle$ *is an* $\mathcal{R}_c$*-critical pair of* $\ell_1 \to_{\alpha_1} r_1, \ell_2 \to_{\alpha_2} r_2 \in \mathcal{R}_{nc}$*, then*

$$u_1 \underset{<\alpha_1}{\twoheadleftarrow\!\!\!\twoheadrightarrow} u'_1 \xrightarrow[\alpha_2]{q_1}{}^{=} u''_1 \underset{<\alpha_1,\alpha_2}{\twoheadleftarrow\!\!\!\twoheadrightarrow} u''_2 \;{}^{=}\!\xleftarrow[\alpha_1]{q_2} u'_2 \underset{<\alpha_2}{\twoheadleftarrow\!\!\!\twoheadrightarrow} u_2$$

for some u'_1, u''_1, u'_2, u''_2 *with* q_i *non-nested in* u'_i*.*

Then $\mathcal{R}$ *is confluent.*

Even though the above theorem is stronger than Theorems 1 and 2, it is much harder to use in practice, since condition **(ii)** quantifies over infinitely many σ and t. Similarly, in **(iii)** we have to verify an infinite number of $\mathcal{R}_c$-critical pairs, given that, as explained, we do not use most general unifiers (which may not exist) in the definition of $\mathcal{R}_c$-critical pairs. This is why we chose to present the above result as an auxiliary tool, rather than a main result of this paper.

Proof Idea. To prove Theorem 4, we introduce a relation $\rhd\!\!\xrightarrow[\alpha]{}$ which allows to rewrite with $\mathcal{R}_c$ before matching a rule in $\mathcal{R}_\alpha$: we have $t \rhd\!\!\xrightarrow[\alpha]{p} u$ when $t|_p = \boldsymbol{x}.t^p$ and $t_p \underset{c}{\twoheadrightarrow} \ell[\sigma]$ and $u = t\{\!|\boldsymbol{x}.(r[\sigma])|\!\}_p$ for some $\ell \to r \in \mathcal{R}_\alpha$. Let us write $\underset{<\alpha}{\leftrightsquigarrow}$ for the reflexive-symmetric-transitive closure of $(\bigcup_{\beta<\alpha} \rhd\!\!\xrightarrow[\beta]{}) \cup \underset{c}{\twoheadrightarrow}$. We can then show both that $\underset{c}{\twoheadleftarrow} \cdot \rhd\!\!\xrightarrow[\alpha]{} \subseteq \rhd\!\!\xrightarrow[\alpha]{} \cdot \underset{c}{\twoheadleftarrow}$ and $\xleftarrow[\alpha_1]{}\!\!\lhd \cdot \rhd\!\!\xrightarrow[\alpha_2]{} \subseteq \underset{<\alpha_1}{\leftrightsquigarrow} \cdot \rhd\!\!\xrightarrow[\alpha_2]{}{}^{=} \cdot \underset{<\alpha_1,\alpha_2}{\leftrightsquigarrow} \cdot {}^{=}\!\xleftarrow[\alpha_1]{}\!\!\lhd \cdot \underset{<\alpha_2}{\leftrightsquigarrow}$ on meta-free terms, and moreover we have $\underset{c}{\twoheadleftarrow} \cdot \underset{c}{\twoheadrightarrow} \subseteq \underset{c}{\twoheadrightarrow} \cdot \underset{c}{\twoheadleftarrow}$ on meta-free terms by assumption **(i)**. This proves that $(\bigcup_\alpha \rhd\!\!\xrightarrow[\alpha]{}) \cup \underset{c}{\twoheadrightarrow}$ is decreasing on meta-free terms and thus confluent, by labeling $\rhd\!\!\xrightarrow[\alpha]{}$ with α and $\underset{c}{\twoheadrightarrow}$ with a new bottom element $\bot$ adjoined to $\mathcal{L}$. Because $(\bigcup_\alpha \rhd\!\!\xrightarrow[\alpha]{}) \cup \underset{c}{\twoheadrightarrow}$ and $\xrightarrow[\mathcal{R}]{}$ generate the same transitive closure, we conclude confluence of $\mathcal{R}$.

The proofs of both Theorems 1 and 2 then go by showing that, under the assumptions of these theorems, we can prove condition **(ii)** and moreover reduce $\mathcal{R}$-critical pairs to either plain critical pairs or $\mathcal{R}$-cyclic critical pairs, which can then be closed in an appropriate way by assumption, proving **(iii)**. Therefore, confluence follows by Theorem 4.

8 Towards Automating Our Criteria

Applying critical-pair criteria like Theorems 1 to 3 for checking confluence usually involves a large number of mechanical calculations, whose automation is therefore often helpful. While we leave the automation of our criteria for future work, in this section we take a first step in this direction by sketching how they could be used to decompose a finite rewrite system $\mathcal{R}$ into a set of subsystems $\mathbf{R}$ such that $\mathcal{R}$ is confluent whenever $\mathcal{R}'$ is confluent for all $\mathcal{R}' \in \mathbf{R}$. This strategy could then be used as the basis for a future implementation, by relying on existing tools to verify confluence of the obtained subsystems.

We now define a procedure $\text{D}\textsc{ecomp}(-)$ which, given a finite rewrite system $\mathcal{R}$, returns $\mathbf{R}$ satisfying the property claimed above. We first start by using

Theorem 3 to split $\mathcal{R}$ into as many fragments $\mathcal{R}^1, \ldots, \mathcal{R}^n$ with disjoint signatures as possible, in such a way that they pairwise satisfy condition **(2)**—note that condition **(3)** is automatically ensured by the assumption that the signatures are disjoint. In the next step, we calculate the confined part $\mathcal{R}^i_c$ of $\mathcal{R}^i$ and, if $\mathcal{R}^i_c$ equals $\mathcal{R}^i$, we add $\mathcal{R}^i$ to $\mathbf{R}$, otherwise we attempt to apply Theorem 1 or Theorem 2. To know which result to apply, we try to prove termination of $\mathcal{R}^i_c$ by applying existing techniques—such as the ones implemented by the automated termination prover Wanda [21]. If termination can be proved, we try to verify conditions **(b)** and **(c)** of Theorem 1, otherwise we try to verify conditions **(b)** and **(c)** of Theorem 2. If the conditions are satisfied, we check confluence of $\mathcal{R}^i_c$ by recursively calling $\textsc{Decomp}(\mathcal{R}^i_c)$ and adding the calculated subsystems to $\mathbf{R}$, otherwise we simply add $\mathcal{R}^i$ to $\mathbf{R}$. It is a direct consequence of Theorems 1 to 3 that $\mathcal{R}$ is confluent if $\mathcal{R}'$ is confluent for all $\mathcal{R}' \in \textsc{Decomp}(\mathcal{R})$.

Finally, let us comment on how the conditions of Theorems 1 to 3 can be verified. Conditions **(b)** of Theorem 1, **(b)** of Theorem 2, and **(2)** of Theorem 3 are obviously decidable, the hard work is verifying conditions **(c)** of Theorem 1 and **(c)** of Theorem 2. For these verifications, one could adapt the strategy employed in various previous work, which encode the problem using arithmetic constraints [1,14]. In the specific case of Theorem 2, a further complication is the use of the congruence $\simeq$ for closing cyclic critical pairs. To address this, in the cases where the equations in $\mathcal{C}_f$ are all first-order, one could try to use (ground) completion to calculate a rewrite system for $\simeq$, treating the metavariables as new function symbols. The same strategy may sometimes also work for higher-order equations.

9 Related and Future Work

The core strategy of our work, of using sort information to rule out reductions inside non-linear metavariables of rules, already appears in some forms in the literature. We were directly inspired by the unpublished work of Assaf *et al.* [5], which introduces a confined syntactic class where instances of non-linear metavariables live. This was generalized in unpublished work by Felicissimo [8], by instead considering a framework of sorted rewriting. As we do in Sect. 3, he instead uses the sort pre-order to define confinement *a posteriori* in terms of the sorts of non-linear metavariables. Unbeknownst to him, this idea had already appeared independently in the first-order setting: Aoto *et al.* [3] use the same sort-based strategy to forbid reductions inside non-linear metavariables, and moreover also employ decreasing diagrams for closing critical pairs. Their work however differs significantly from ours by (1) being restricted to the first-order setting, and (2) imposing the confined fragment to be terminating—a restriction we drop in Theorem 2. They moreover leverage persistency of first-order confluence to treat unsorted systems, a strategy we cannot employ given that confluence is not persistent in higher-order rewriting.

A different work stemming from Assaf *et al.* and closely related to ours is the one by Férey and Jouannaud [10], which provides a criterion establishing higher-order non-left-linear confluence in a set of *layered* terms. Unfortunately, the abstract characterization of this set impairs the applicability of their result.

The work by Klein and Hirokawa [18] is also very much related to ours. Their criterion resembles in particular our Theorem 4: both statements use the notion of $\mathcal{R}$-critical pairs and the proofs both employ a rewrite relation applying a directed form of matching modulo. Their result however departs from ours by (1) being restricted to the first-order setting, and (2) requiring a relative termination condition. On the other hand, thanks to this termination hypothesis, they allow for closing critical pairs very liberally, without the need for decreasing diagrams.

The notion of cyclic unification and cyclic critical pairs originates in the work by Liu *et al.* [23], though our definitions are actually considerably different. Their criterion also allows proving confluence of non-left-linear non-terminating systems by closing cyclic critical pairs with decreasing diagrams, but is restricted to the first-order setting. Moreover, their result constrains the use of the congruence $\simeq$ to the bottom of the closing diagram, hence they cannot handle cases like Example 9 which require the application of $\simeq$ before a rewrite step.

Finally, our Theorem 3 is closely related to van Oostrom and van Raamsdonk's weakly orthogonal combination criterion [28]. Their result, which imposes left-linearity, would be a particular case of ours, had they not relaxed **(3)** to allow for trivial critical pairs, which we believe could also be handled in our case.

For future work, Theorems 1 and 2 could be adapted to instead use weak confinement, by employing a form of orthogonal rewriting in their proofs. Indeed, the only reason sorts of non-linear and nested metavariables of right-hand sides are considered confined is to prevent the duplication of non-confined redexes, which ceases to be a problem if one can reduce non-overlapping redexes in a single step. This adaptation should be doable, at the cost of having to consider *nested critical pairs* (also known as *multi-multi* [15]), as in Dowek *et al.* [7].

Acknowledgements. The authors thank Loïc Pujet for suggesting Example 13 and the anonymous reviewers for their helpful comments and remarks.

Disclosure of Interests. The authors have no competing interests to declare that are relevant to the content of this article.

References

1. Aoto, T.: Automated Confluence Proof by Decreasing Diagrams based on Rule-Labelling. In: Lynch, C., editor. Proceedings of the 21st International Conference on Rewriting Techniques and Applications, volume 6 of Leibniz International Proceedings in Informatics (LIPIcs), pp. 7–16, Dagstuhl, Germany, 2010. Schloss Dagstuhl – Leibniz-Zentrum für Informatik
2. Aoto, T., Toyama, Y.: Persistency of confluence. JUCS - J. Univ. Comput. Sci. **3**(11), 1134–1147 (1997)
3. Aoto, T., Toyama, Y., Uchida, K.: Proving confluence of term rewriting systems via persistency and decreasing diagrams. In: Dowek, G., editor, Rewriting and Typed Lambda Calculi, pp. 46–60, Cham (2014). Springer International Publishing

4. Aoto, T., Yoshida, J., Toyama, Y.: Proving confluence of term rewriting systems automatically. In: Treinen, R., editor, Rewriting Techniques and Applications, pp. 93–102, Berlin, Heidelberg (2009). Springer Berlin Heidelberg
5. Assaf, A., Dowek, G., Jouannaud, J.P., Liu, J.: Untyped confluence in dependent type theories. In: Proceedings Higher-Order Rewriting Workshop, Proc. Higher-Order rewriting Workshop, Porto, Portugal, June 2016. Easy-Chair (2016)
6. Bezem, M., Klop, J.W., de Vrijer, R.: Term rewriting systems (2003)
7. Dowek, G., Férey, G., Jouannaud, J.-P., Liu, J.: Confluence of left-linear higher-order rewrite theories by checking their nested critical pairs. Math. Struct. Comput. Sci. **32**(7), 898–933 (2022)
8. Felicissimo. T.: A confluence criterion for non left-linearity in a $\beta\eta$-free reformulation of HRSs. In: 11th International Workshop on Higher-Order Rewriting (HOR 2023) (2023)
9. Felicissimo, T., Jouannaud, J.P.: Sort-based confluence criteria for non-left-linear higher-order rewriting. Technical report https://hal.science/hal-04973508 (2025)
10. Férey, G., Jouannaud, J.-P.: Confluence in non-left-linear untyped higher-order rewrite theories. In: Veltri, N., Benton, N., Ghilezan, S., editors, PPDP 2021: 23rd International Symposium on Principles and Practice of Declarative Programming, Tallinn, Estonia, September 6-8, 2021, pp. 8:1–8:14. ACM (2021)
11. Fiore, M.P., Plotkin, G.D., Turi, D.: Abstract syntax and variable binding. In: 14th Annual IEEE Symposium on Logic in Computer Science, Trento, Italy, July 2-5, 1999, pp. 193–202. IEEE Computer Society (1999)
12. Girard, J.Y.: Interprétation fonctionnelle et élimination des coupures de l'arithmétique d'ordre supérieur. PhD thesis (1972)
13. Hamana, M.: Complete algebraic semantics for second-order rewriting systems based on abstract syntax with variable binding. Math. Struct. Comput. Sci. **32**(4), 542–573 (2022)
14. Hirokawa, N., Middeldorp, A.: Decreasing diagrams and relative termination. J. Autom. Reason. **47**, 481–501 (2011)
15. Hirokawa, N., Nagele, J., Oostrom, V.V., Oyamaguchi, M., et al. Critical peaks redefined-$\phi \sqcup \psi = \top$. In: 6th International Workshop on Confluence (2017)
16. Huet, G.: Confluent reductions: Abstract properties and applications to term rewriting systems: Abstract properties and applications to term rewriting systems. J. ACM (JACM) (1980)
17. Jouannaud, J.-P., van Oostrom, V.: Diagrammatic confluence and completion. In: Albers, S., Marchetti-Spaccamela, A., Matias, Y., Nikoletseas, S., Thomas, W. (eds.) ICALP 2009. LNCS, vol. 5556, pp. 212–222. Springer, Heidelberg (2009). https://doi.org/10.1007/978-3-642-02930-1_18
18. Klein, D., Hirokawa, N.: Confluence of non-left-linear TRSs via relative termination. In: Bjørner, N., Voronkov, A. (eds.) Logic for Programming, Artificial Intelligence, and Reasoning, pp. 258–273. Springer Berlin Heidelberg, Berlin, Heidelberg (2012). https://doi.org/10.1007/978-3-642-28717-6_21
19. Klop, J.W.: Combinatory reduction systems. PhD thesis, Univ. Utrecht (1980)
20. Klop, J.W., van Oostrom, V., van Raamsdonk, F.: Combinatory reduction systems: introduction and survey. Theor. Comput. Sci. **121**(1-2), 279–308 (1993)
21. Kop, C.: WANDA - a Higher Order Termination Tool. In: Zena M. Ariola, editor, 5th International Conference on Formal Structures for Computation and Deduction (FSCD 2020), volume 167 of Leibniz International Proceedings in Informatics (LIPIcs), pp. 36:1–36:19, Dagstuhl, Germany, 2020. Schloss Dagstuhl – Leibniz-Zentrum für Informatik

22. Libal, T., Miller, D.: Functions-as-constructors higher-order unification: extended pattern unification. Ann. Math. Artif. Intell. **90**(5), 455–479 (2022)
23. Liu, J., Jouannaud, J.-P., Ogawa, M.: Confluence of layered rewrite systems. In: Kreutzer, S.,editor, 24th EACSL Annual Conference on Computer Science Logic (CSL 2015), volume 41 of Leibniz International Proceedings in Informatics (LIPIcs), pp. 423–440, Dagstuhl, Germany, 2015. Schloss Dagstuhl – Leibniz-Zentrum für Informatik
24. Mayr, R., Nipkow, T.: Higher-order rewrite systems and their confluence. Theoret. Comput. Sci. **192**(1), 3–29 (1998)
25. Nagele, J., Felgenhauer, B., Middeldorp, A.: CSI: New evidence – a progress report. In: de Moura, L., editor, Automated Deduction – CADE 26, pp. 385–397, Cham, (2017) Springer International Publishing
26. van Oostrom, V.: Developing developments. Theoret. Comput. Sci. **175**(1), 159–181 (1997)
27. van Oostrom, V.: Confluence by decreasing diagrams: converted. In: Voronkov, A., eds., Rewriting Techniques and Applications, pp. 306–320, Berlin, Heidelberg (2008). Springer Berlin Heidelberg
28. Oostrom, V., Raamsdonk, F.: Weak orthogonality implies confluence: the higher-order case. In: Nerode, A., Matiyasevich, Y.V. (eds.) Logical Foundations of Computer Science, pp. 379–392. Springer Berlin Heidelberg, Berlin, Heidelberg (1994). https://doi.org/10.1007/3-540-58140-5_35
29. Zankl, H., Felgenhauer, B., Middeldorp, A.: Labelings for decreasing diagrams. J. Autom. Reason. **54**(2), 101–133 (2015)

Formalizations in Isabelle/HOL

Verified Path Indexing

Mohamed Chaabani[1,2] and Simon Robillard[1(✉)]

[1] LIRMM, Université de Montpellier and CNRS, Montpellier, France
{mohamed.chaabani,simon.robillard}@lirmm.fr
[2] LIMOSE, University of Boumerdès, Boumerdès, Algeria

Abstract. The indexing of syntactic terms is a key component for the efficient implementation of automated theorem provers. This paper presents the first verified implementation of a term indexing data structure, namely a formalization of path indexing in the proof assistant Isabelle/HOL. We define the data structure, maintenance operations, and retrieval operations, including retrieval of unifiable terms, instances, generalizations and variants. We prove that maintenance operations preserve the invariants of the structure, and that retrieval operations are sound and complete.

1 Introduction

In the realm of program verification, automated deduction algorithms hold a special place. They are a cornerstone of automated program verification, and as such, they are also a natural target for verification. Indeed, verified automated deduction programs would be useful not only as trusted implementations, but also as witnesses to the usability of program verification. After all, if the program verification community hopes to convince industrial actors to adopt and use its techniques for software development, it should first be able to do the same.

However, automated deduction algorithms present a particularly difficult challenge for formal verification, as they rely on a rich and complex meta-theory, as well as on optimized implementations and data structures that are crucial for performance. Many efforts have been undertaken to formalize the meta-theory of CDCL SAT solving [1], first-order resolution [10], or saturation theorem proving [13]. These formalizations focus on high-level properties of the calculi used in automated reasoning tools. They are typically expressed in a relational rather than functional style, and thus do not directly yield executable programs. The second step toward formal verification of automated deduction techniques is to formalize and verify the algorithms and data structures used to implement the calculi. State-of-the-art (non-verified) automated deduction tools employ advanced algorithms and data structures. In order to obtain verified executable automated reasoning tools with a decent performance, these implementation-oriented details have to be verified as well. For example, the verified SAT solver IsaSAT [2] relies on a two-watched-literal data structure for unit propagation and conflict detection, similarly to its unverified competitors.

C. Barrett and U. Waldmann (Eds.): CADE 2025, LNAI 15943, pp. 249–260, 2025.
https://doi.org/10.1007/978-3-031-99984-0_14

Automated reasoning tools for first-order logic are significantly more complex than those for propositional logic, and for now, a verified executable prover for first-order logic has yet to be implemented. One key ingredient for performance in automated reasoning in first-order logic is efficient term indexing. Virtually all modern reasoning techniques for first-order logic are based on term unification, and therefore require a way to find unifiable terms among a set of candidates. The term unification problem is quasi-linear in the size of the candidate terms, but since theorem provers can handle millions of candidates, it is not feasible to iterate through pairs of candidates and attempt to unify them. Instead, theorem provers rely on specialized data structures to store terms and retrieve those that are unifiable with a given query term.

This paper presents the formalization[1], in the Isabelle/HOL proof assistant [7,8], of path indexing [9,12], a term indexing technique that relies on a trie to store candidate terms. After an introduction to Isabelle/HOL (Sect. 2) and its notations, and some preliminary notions on terms and term indexing (Sect. 3), this paper presents the formalization of path indexing (Sect. 4). We define the data structure, its invariants, maintenance and retrieval operations, and we sketch the correctness proofs for the different operations. This work represents the first verified implementation of a term indexing technique. Although path indexing has been studied from the perspective of implementation and performance [3,6], this is also, to our knowledge, the first detailed proof of correctness for this technique.

2 Proofs and Programs in Isabelle/HOL

Isabelle/HOL is an interactive proof assistant for higher-order logic. It offers powerful features that simplify and automate the proof process: its rewriting engine allows substituting terms with equivalents, the axiom of substitution allows replacing any subterm of the proof with an equal term, and the rule of extensionality allows proving the equality of two functions by proving that they produce the same result for each argument.

Isabelle allows the definition of inductive datatypes. For example, the type of lists can be defined as follows:

datatype *'a list* =
  Nil ([])
  | *Cons* (*hd*: *'a*) (*tl*: *'a list*) (**infix** # *65*)

This is a polymorphic definition with a type parameter *'a*, that declares *Nil* and *Cons* as the two constructors of the type. In addition, it also defines two partial functions *hd* and *tl* to access the two arguments of lists built from *Cons*, and adds notations [] and # for the constructors, the second being an infix operator. Predicates can likewise be defined inductively, for example list membership can be defined as:

[1] Available at https://seafile.lirmm.fr/f/d76bb08ee2cf4cacb823/.

```
inductive ListMem :: 'a ⇒ 'a list ⇒ bool where
  ListMem x (x # xs)
| ListMem x xs ⟹ ListMem x (y # xs)
```

In this definition, Isabelle's metalogical implication, $\Longrightarrow$, is used to set the condition for the second case. Within statements, the object-logic implication, denoted $\longrightarrow$ must be used instead. The first notation is not to be confused with the notation for function types, $\Rightarrow$.

We can also define functions such as the following

```
fun nth :: 'a list ⇒ nat ⇒ 'a where
  nth [] n = undefined
| nth (x # xs) n = (case n of 0 ⇒ x | Suc m ⇒ nth xs m)
```

that performs pattern matching on a value of *nat*, the type of natural numbers with constructors *0* and *Suc*, in order to return the *nth* element of the list. The Isabelle library use the infix notation *l ! i* for *nth l i*, and we will use this notation in the following. Functions can be partial (non-exhaustive), but their termination must be proven. In simple cases such as the structural recursion above, this obligation is discharged automatically.

Isabelle also features type definitions that identify a new type with a subset of an existing type. For example finite maps are defined as

```
typedef ('a, 'b) fmap = {m. finite {a. m a ≠ None} } :: ('a ⇒ 'b option) set
```

the subset of partial functions (*a ⇒ 'b option*) that are defined for a finite number of values. Such a definition requires a proof that the newly defined type is inhabited. It also introduces coercion functions. The Lifting package allows functions on the supertype to be conveniently adapted to the subtype, provided that the necessary proofs of membership are given. We will use finite maps in this formalization, and in particular we rely on the following notations: *fmempty* stands for the map that associates every value to *None*, *fmdom' m* and *fmran' m* are the domain and range of a map *m*, *m $$ v* is the evaluation of *m* at value *v*, while *m $$! k* is the evaluation of *m* at value *v* provided that *v ∈ fmdom' m* (i.e., $$ is a total function that returns an element of *'b option*, while $$! returns an element of *'b* and may be undefined).

3 Preliminaries

This formalization relies on a pre-existing definition of syntactic terms, available in the Archive of Formal Proofs (AFP), the main repository of Isabelle formalizations. The definition is the following:

```
datatype ('f,'v) term =
  Var 'v
| Fun 'f ('f,'v) term list
```

This definition is parameterized by a type $'f$ of function symbols, and a type $'v$ of variables. Since there are no constraints on the number of arguments that a function symbol is applied to, symbols in terms are uniquely identified by a pair of type $('f \times nat)$, the second element being the arity. For example, the term *Fun s [Fun s []]* is valid but features two distinct symbols $(s,\ 1)$ and $(s,\ 0)$.

A *term index* is a data structure that stores a set S of terms, and that is able, given a query term t, to retrieve all the terms $s \in S$ that satisfy $R(s,t)$, for some R called the retrieval condition. In practice, there are four retrieval conditions that are of particular interest, all related to unification problems ($t \cdot \sigma$ denotes the application of a substitution σ to a term t):

definition *term-unification* :: *('f, 'v) term* ⇒ *('f, 'v) term* ⇒ *bool* **where**
term-unification t1 t2 = (∃σ :: *('f, 'v) subst. t1* · σ = *t2* · σ)

definition *term-instantiation* :: *('f, 'v) term* ⇒ *('f, 'v) term* ⇒ *bool* **where**
term-instantiation t1 t2 = (∃σ :: *('f, 'v) subst. t1* = *t2* · σ)

definition *term-generalization* :: *('f, 'v) term* ⇒ *('f, 'v) term* ⇒ *bool* **where**
term-generalization t1 t2 = *term-instantiation t2 t1*

definition *term-variant* :: *('f, 'v) term* ⇒ *('f, 'v) term* ⇒ *bool* **where**
term-variant t1 t2 = (∃σ :: *('f, 'v) subst.* (∀*t* ∈ *subst-range* σ. *is-Var t*) ∧ *t1* · σ = *t2*)

For example, retrieval of unifiable terms is used to implement resolution rules or to find closing substitutions in analytical tableaux. Resolution theorem provers rely on retrieval of instances to implement forward subsumption and demodulation, and retrieval of generalizations for backward subsumption and demodulation. Aside from automated deduction, other applications that perform computations over terms can benefit from term indexing, including functional programming, logic programming and deductive databases. For an overview of these applications, and what retrieval conditions they use, we refer the reader to the work of Sekar et al. [11].

Like many term indexing techniques, path indexing is a so-called *imperfect filter*, i.e., its retrieval conditions are broader that the aforementioned relations. Consequently, the set that is returned for a given query is a superset of the intended result, and must be filtered using a standard unification algorithm (which is also an opportunity to construct the unifiers, for applications that need that information). More specifically, the retrieval conditions used in path indexing ignores the *non-linearity* of terms, i.e., the fact that a single variable may occur multiple times in the query term and/or indexed terms, and the resulting constraints w.r.t. term unification. Instead, it relies on the following relations as retrieval conditions:

inductive *linear-unification* :: *('f, 'v) term* ⇒ *('f, 'v) term* ⇒ *bool* **where**
linear-unification (Var x) t
| *linear-unification t (Var x)*
| *length args1* = *length args2* ⟹

$(\forall i.\ i < length\ args1 \longrightarrow linear\text{-}unification\ (args1\ !\ i)\ (args2\ !\ i)) \Longrightarrow$
$linear\text{-}unification\ (Fun\ f\ args1)\ (Fun\ f\ args2)$

inductive *linear-instance* :: $('f,\ 'v)\ term \Rightarrow ('f,\ 'v)\ term \Rightarrow bool$ **where**
linear-instance t (Var x)
| $length\ args1 = length\ args2 \Longrightarrow$
$(\forall i.\ i < length\ args1 \longrightarrow linear\text{-}instance\ (args1\ !\ i)\ (args2\ !\ i)) \Longrightarrow$
$linear\text{-}instance\ (Fun\ f\ args1)\ (Fun\ f\ args2)$

definition *linear-generalization t e* = *linear-instance e t*

inductive *linear-variant* :: $('f,\ 'v)\ term \Rightarrow ('f,\ 'v)\ term \Rightarrow bool$ **where**
linear-variant (Var x) (Var y)
| $length\ args1 = length\ args2 \Longrightarrow$
$(\forall i.\ i < length\ args1 \longrightarrow linear\text{-}variant\ (args1\ !\ i)\ (args2\ !\ i)) \Longrightarrow$
$linear\text{-}variant\ (Fun\ f\ args1)\ (Fun\ f\ args2)$

We can check that these relations are necessary conditions for their non-linear counterparts, and the set returned by the index for a given query is in fact a superset of the intended result, e.g.:

lemma *linear-unification-necessary-condition*:
term-unification t1 t2 $\Longrightarrow$ *linear-unification t1 t2*

Since path indexing ignores the specific names of variables, we introduce the following datatype to describe the symbols that it operates on, together with a function that extracts said symbol from a term:

datatype *'f symbol* =
Star
| *F 'f nat*

fun *to-symbol* :: $('f,\ 'v)\ term \Rightarrow 'f\ symbol$ **where**
to-symbol (Var x) = Star
| *to-symbol (Fun f ts) = F f (length ts)*

Path indexing relies on the *path strings* (simply called *paths* in the following) of terms to index them. A path string is a list of symbol-number pairs that corresponds to a path from the root to a node in the tree structure of a term.

type-synonym *'f tpath* = $('f\ symbol \times nat)\ list$

Although this is not specified in the type itself, in a valid path, each symbol s can only be paired with a number i such that $i <$ *symbol-arity* s, except if *symbol-arity* $s = 0$, in which case, i is *0* by convention.

We may use paths to navigate a term, e.g., *subterm-at-path t p t'* holds if and only if t' is the subterm found by following the path p from the root of t:

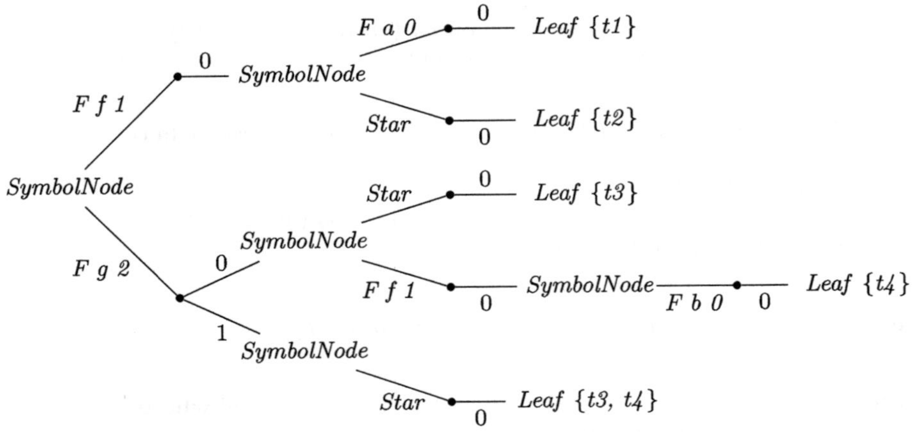

Fig. 1. The path indexing trie that stores the four following terms:
- *t1* ≡ *Fun f* [*Fun a* []],
- *t2* ≡ *Fun f* [*Var x*],
- *t3* ≡ *Fun g* [*Var x*, *Var y*] and
- *t4* ≡ *Fun g* [*Fun f* [*Fun b* []], *Var x*].

inductive *subterm-at-path* :: ('*f*,'*v*) *term* ⇒'*f tpath* ⇒ ('*f*,'*v*) *term* ⇒ *bool* **where**
  subterm-at-path t [] *t*
| $i <$ *length fargs* ⟹ *fargs* ≠ [] ⟹ *subterm-at-path* (*fargs* ! *i*) *p t* ⟹
    subterm-at-path (*Fun f fargs*) ((*F f* (*length fargs*), *i*) # *p*) *t*

In particular, we are interested in the paths to leaves (constant or variables) of a term. A string p is a path to a leaf of a term t if and only if it satisfies *path-of-term t p*, defined as follows:

inductive *path-of-term* :: ('*f*,'*v*) *term* ⇒'*f tpath* ⇒ *bool* **where**
  path-of-term (*Var x*) [(*Star*, *0*)]
| *path-of-term* (*Fun f* []) [(*F f 0*, *0*)]
| *ts* ≠ [] ⟹ $i <$ *length ts* ⟹ *path-of-term* (*ts* ! *i*) *p* ⟹
    path-of-term (*Fun f ts*) ((*F f* (*length ts*), *i*) # *p*)

When we mention the *paths of a term t*, we refer exclusively to those paths p that satisfy *path-of-term t p*. For example, given the variable x and the symbols a, f, and g, the term *Fun f* [*Fun g* [*Var x*], *Fun a*] has two paths, namely [(*F f 2*, *0*), (*F g 1*, *0*), (*Star*, *0*)] and [(*F f 2*, *1*), (*F a 0*, *0*)].

4 Path Indexing

4.1 Structure and Invariants

In path indexing, terms are stored in a *trie*, a tree structure in which edges are decorated with symbol-number pairs. We define this structure as follows:

datatype *(plugins del: size)* *('f,'v) trie* =
  Leaf ('f,'v) term set
| *SymbolNode (children: (('f symbol, (nat, ('f, 'v) trie) fmap) fmap))*

Each node stores its children in nested *fmaps*, with the outer maps indexed by *'f symbols* and the inner maps indexed by *nats*. The terms themselves are stored in the leaves of the trie. Figure 1 gives an example of a path indexing trie.

Because the recursive structure of this datatype is obfuscated by the maps, the *size* function that is automatically generated by Isabelle as a termination measure for the datatype is of no help in this case. Instead, we deactivate this feature and define our own function, based on the depth of the trie, prove its termination and register it as a termination measure. The proof of termination for functions that are defined by structural induction can subsequently be discharged automatically. This is, for example, the case with the following function, that collects all the terms stored in the trie:

fun *to-set* :: *('f,'v) trie* ⇒ *('f,'v) term set* **where**
  to-set (Leaf x) = x
| *to-set (SymbolNode m)* = ⋃ *(to-set* ‘ ⋃ *(fmran'* ‘ *(fmran' m)))*

where the backquote ‘ denotes the application of a function to all the elements of a set.

Just as we use paths to navigate the tree structure of terms, we can use them to navigate tries. In particular, the trie *tr2* is the subtree of the trie *tr1* found by following the path *p* along the edges if and only if *subtrie-at-path tr1 p tr2*, defined as follows:

inductive *subtrie-at-path* :: *('f,'v) trie* ⇒ *'f tpath* ⇒ *('f,'v) trie* ⇒ *bool* **where**
  subtrie-at-path tr [] tr
| *m1 $$ s = Some m2* ⟹ *m2 $$ i = Some tr* ⟹
    subtrie-at-path tr ps tr0 ⟹ *subtrie-at-path (SymbolNode m1) ((s, i) # ps) tr0*

The main invariant of a path indexing trie is that each term is stored in the leaves that are found at the end of paths of that term:

definition *sound-storage* :: *('f, 'v) trie* ⇒ *bool* **where**
  sound-storage tr =
    (∀ *t p*. (∃ *s*. *subtrie-at-path tr p (Leaf (insert t s))*) ⟶ *path-of-term t p*)

where *insert* is the set insertion function. Since a term is stored in multiple leaves (as many as the constants and variables in that term), we must define a second invariant that ensures that any term present in the trie is present in all the relevant leaves of that trie:

definition *complete-storage* :: *('f, 'v) trie* ⇒ *bool* **where**
  complete-storage tr =
(∀ *t*∈*to-set tr*. ∀ *p*. *path-of-term t p* ⟶ (∃ *s*. *subtrie-at-path tr p (Leaf (insert t s))*))

We define a third invariant that ensures that the structure of the trie is consistent with the arity of symbols, and that edges decorated with a symbol of arity 0 lead to a leaf. This property is needed in many proofs to eliminate vacuous cases.

inductive *well-structured* :: $('f,\ 'v)$ *trie* $\Rightarrow$ *bool*
and *well-structured-map-entry* :: *'f symbol* $\Rightarrow$ (*nat*, ($'f$, $'v$) *trie*) *fmap* $\Rightarrow$ *bool*
where
  $(\forall s.\ s \in fmdom'\ m \longrightarrow well\text{-}structured\text{-}map\text{-}entry\ s\ (m\ \$\$!\ s)) \Longrightarrow$
    well-structured (*SymbolNode m*)
| $fmdom'\ m = \{0\} \Longrightarrow (\forall t.\ t \in fmran'\ m \longrightarrow (\exists s.\ t = Leaf\ s)) \Longrightarrow$
    well-structured-map-entry Star m
| $fmdom'\ m = \{0\} \Longrightarrow (\forall t.\ t \in fmran'\ m \longrightarrow (\exists s.\ t = Leaf\ s)) \Longrightarrow$
    well-structured-map-entry (*F f 0*) *m*
| $arity \neq 0 \Longrightarrow fmdom'\ m = \{..< arity\} \Longrightarrow$
    $(\forall t.\ t \in fmran'\ m \longrightarrow well\text{-}structured\ t) \Longrightarrow$
      well-structured-map-entry (*F f arity*) *m*

Lastly, we define a fourth invariant that ensures that the trie contains no empty leaves or childless nodes, except possibly the root itself. While not needed for functional correctness, this is a desirable property that should be preserved by maintenance operations, in particular term removal.

inductive *minimal-storage* :: ($'f$,$'v$) *trie*$\Rightarrow$ *bool* **where**
  $x \neq \{\} \Longrightarrow minimal\text{-}storage\ (Leaf\ x)$
| $(\forall t \in fmran'\ m.\ \forall r \in fmran'\ t.\ minimal\text{-}storage\ r \wedge r \neq SymbolNode\ fmempty) \Longrightarrow$
    minimal-storage (*SymbolNode m*)

Proofs on tries require induction, however, properties *sound-storage* and *complete-storage* hold only for the root of the trie, and not for subtries. To address this, these invariants must be reformulated in a way that accounts for the position (given by a path) of a subtrie within the trie.

definition *sound-storage-from-position* :: ($'f$, $'v$) *trie* $\Rightarrow$ *'f tpath* $\Rightarrow$ *bool* **where**
  sound-storage-from-position tr p =
$(\forall t\ p2\ s.\ subtrie\text{-}at\text{-}path\ tr\ p2\ (Leaf\ (insert\ t\ s)) \longrightarrow path\text{-}of\text{-}term\ t\ (p\ @\ p2))$

definition *complete-storage-from-position* :: ($'f$, $'v$) *trie* $\Rightarrow$ *'f tpath* $\Rightarrow$ *bool* **where**
  complete-storage-from-position tr p =
    $(\forall t \in to\text{-}set\ tr.\ \forall p2.\ path\text{-}of\text{-}term\ t\ (p\ @\ p2) \longrightarrow$
      $(\exists s.\ subtrie\text{-}at\text{-}path\ tr\ p2\ (Leaf\ (insert\ t\ s))))$

where @ is the *append* operator on lists. The properties *sound-storage* and *complete-storage* of the root are simply special cases of the above, from the path/position []. We can easily verify that, given the correct position, these properties hold recursively for subtries, e.g.:

lemma *complete-storage-from-position-subtrie*:
  assumes *complete-storage-from-position* (*SymbolNode m1*) *p*
    and *m1* $\$\$\ f$ = *Some m2* **and** *m2* $\$\$\ i$ = *Some tr*
  shows *complete-storage-from-position tr* (p @ [(f, i)])

With these invariants, we can define a new type for valid tries:

typedef ($'f$, $'v$) *index* = { *tr* :: ($'f$, $'v$) *trie*. *well-structured tr* $\wedge$ *sound-storage tr*
    $\wedge$ *complete-storage tr* $\wedge$ *minimal-storage tr* }

Note that the root of such a trie must be a *SymbolNode*. In particular the empty trie is *SymbolNode fmempty* rather than an empty leaf.

4.2 Maintenance Operations

We have formalized and proved the correctness of a term insertion function and a term deletion function. Both functions traverse the trie from the root node to the leaves, following the paths of the term to insert/delete, updating or creating/deleting nodes along the path as needed.

Let us briefly define some helper functions used in the insertion function. *insert-leaf tr t* is defined only if *tr* is a *Leaf*, in which case it adds the term *t* to the terms contained in that leaf. *update-entry* is a higher-order function that modifies a map in the following way: given a map *m*, a key *k*, a function *f* and a default value *v*, *update-entry m k f v* outputs the map that associates *k* to *Some* (*f* (*m* $$! *k*)) if *k* is defined in *m*, and to *Some* (*f v*) otherwise, and associates other keys *k'* to *m* $$ *k'*. *update-entries* is similar but operates on a list of keys rather than a single key (the update function *f* also take the key as parameter). We can now define the auxiliary recursive function *insert-aux*, such that *insert-aux tr t1 t2* is a trie where the term *t2* is present in all the leaves found on the paths of term *t1*.

fun *insert-aux* :: ('*f*, '*v*) *trie* ⇒ ('*f*, '*v*) *term* ⇒ ('*f*, '*v*) *term* ⇒ ('*f*, '*v*) *trie* **where**
insert-aux (*Leaf s*) *t t0* = *undefined*
| *insert-aux* (*SymbolNode m*) (*Var x*) *t0* =
SymbolNode (*update-entry m Star* (λ*m2*. *update-entry m2 0* (λ*tr*. *insert-leaf tr t0*) (*Leaf* {})) *fmempty*)
| *insert-aux* (*SymbolNode m*) (*Fun f* []) *t0* =
SymbolNode (*update-entry m* (*F f 0*) (λ*m2*. *update-entry m2 0* (λ*tr*. *insert-leaf tr t0*) (*Leaf* {})) *fmempty*)
| *insert-aux* (*SymbolNode m*) (*Fun f fargs*) *t0* =
SymbolNode (*update-entry m* (*F f* (*length fargs*))
(λ*m2*. *update-entries m2* [*0..<length fargs*] (λ*i tr*. *insert-aux tr* (*fargs* ! *i*) *t0*) *empty-trie*) {$$})

This auxiliary function is called by the main insertion function

definition *insert-term* :: ('*f*, '*v*) *trie* ⇒ ('*f*, '*v*) *term* ⇒ ('*f*, '*v*) *trie* **where**
insert-term tr t = *insert-aux tr t t*

which we lift to the type of valid tries

lift-definition *index-insert* :: ('*f*, '*v*) *index* ⇒ ('*f*, '*v*) *term* ⇒ ('*f*, '*v*) *index* **is** *insert-term*

The type of this lifted function indicates the preservation of the four invariants, which we need to prove. The proof of preservation of *well-structured* and *minimal-storage* are direct, but for *sound-storage* and *complete-storage*, we need to generalize, e.g., for completeness, with the following lemma:

lemma *insert-preserves-complete*:
assumes *well-structured tr* **and** *complete-storage-from-position tr p*
and *subterm-at-path t p t'*
shows *complete-storage-from-position* (*insert-aux tr t' t*) *p*

Finally we specify the behavior of *insert-term* w.r.t. the content of the trie, using the function *to-set* and set insertion:

lift-definition *index-to-set* :: *('f, 'v) index* ⇒ *('f, 'v) term set* **is** *to-set*

theorem *index-insert-spec*: *index-to-set* (*index-insert tr t*) = *insert t* (*index-to-set tr*)

Here, for the proof of membership of the newly inserted term, it is enough to focus on a single arbitrary path of that term.

The term removal function, not shown here, works in the same way as insertion, however, it also ensures that leaves and nodes are deleted from the trie if they are emptied by the removal. We prove that it preserves the invariants, and we specify its behavior w.r.t. the content of the trie, as we did for term insertion.

4.3 Retrieval Operations

We have formalized and proved the correctness of four retrieval operations, namely retrieval of unifications, generalizations, instances and variants. We only present here the formalization of the *retrieve-unifications* function, but similar ideas are used for the other functions.

We first define the function *var-terms* that returns all the terms in the leaf under a *Star* edge, if any. We use the partial lookup function $$!, since in a *well-structured* node, the key 0 must be defined for the map *m2*.

```
fun var-terms :: (('f symbol, (nat, ('f, 'v) trie) fmap) fmap) ⇒ ('f, 'v) term set where
  var-terms m = (case m $$ Star of None ⇒ {} | Some m2 ⇒ to-set (m2 $$! 0))
```

Then we can define the main function for the retrieval of terms that are unifiable with a given query term:

```
fun retrieve-unifications :: ('f, 'v) trie ⇒ ('f, 'v) term ⇒ ('f, 'v) term set where
  retrieve-unifications (Leaf ts) t = undefined
| retrieve-unifications (SymbolNode m) (Var x) = to-set (SymbolNode m)
| retrieve-unifications (SymbolNode m) (Fun f fargs) =
    var-terms m ∪
    (case m $$ (F f (length fargs)) of
       None ⇒ {}
     | Some m2 ⇒ if fargs = [] then to-set (m2 $$! 0)
                   else ⋂ i ∈ fmdom' m2. retrieve-unifications (m2 $$! i) (fargs ! i))
```

Finally we can lift the function to the type *index* and prove its specification:

```
lift-definition index-retrieve-unifications ::
          ('f, 'v) index ⇒ ('f, 'v) term ⇒ ('f, 'v) term set is retrieve-unifications
```

```
theorem index-retrieve-unifications-spec:
 index-retrieve-unifications tr t1 = {t2. t2 ∈ index-to-set tr ∧ linear-unification t1 t2}
```

For this, we need to show that the answer set only contains elements from *to-set* that are linear unifications of the query term (soundness), and that all linear unifications in *to-set* are in the answer set (completeness). Once again this is achieved through more general inductive lemmas, e.g., for completeness:

lemma *retrieve-unifications-complete*:
 assumes *well-structured tr* **and** *complete-storage-from-position tr p*
  and *sound-storage-from-position tr p*
  and *linear-unification t t'* **and** $t'' \in$ *to-set tr* **and** *subterm-at-path t'' p t'*
 shows $t'' \in$ *retrieve-unifications tr t*

5 Conclusion

We have presented an Isabelle/HOL formalization of path indexing, the first verified implementation of a term indexing data structure. In future work, we plan to formalize other term indexing techniques, starting with discrimination trees. While Isabelle allows code extraction, to obtain efficient implementations, we will need to verify imperative code with mutable data structures, as opposed to the purely functional implementation presented here. Refinement techniques exist to derive, from functional Isabelle programs, Imperative HOL code [4] or even an LLVM intermediate representation [5].

Disclosure of Interests. The authors have no competing interests to declare that are relevant to the content of this article.

References

1. Blanchette, J.C., Fleury, M., Lammich, P., Weidenbach, C.: A verified SAT solver framework with learn, forget, restart, and incrementality. J. Autom. Reason. **61**, 333–365 (2018)
2. Fleury, M., Blanchette, J.C., Lammich, P.: A verified SAT solver with watched literals using imperative HOL. In: Proceedings of the 7th ACM SIGPLAN International Conference on Certified Programs and Proofs, pp. 158–171 (2018)
3. Graf, P.: Path indexing for term retrieval. Technical report, Max-Planck-Institut für Informatik (1992)
4. Lammich, P.: Automatic data refinement. In: International Conference on Interactive Theorem Proving, pp. 84–99. Springer (2013)
5. Lammich, P.: Generating verified LLVM from Isabelle/HOL. In: 10th International Conference on Interactive Theorem Proving (ITP 2019). Schloss Dagstuhl-Leibniz-Zentrum für Informatik (2019)
6. McCune, W.: Experiments with discrimination-tree indexing and path indexing for term retrieval. J. Autom. Reason. **9**(2), 147–167 (1992)
7. Nipkow, T., Klein, G.: Concrete semantics with Isabelle/HOL. Springer (2014)
8. Nipkow, T., Paulson, L.C., Wenzel, M.: Isabelle/HOL: a proof assistant for higher-order logic. LNCS, vol. 2283. Springer (2002)

9. Ramesh, R., Ramakrishnan, I., Warren, D.S.: Automata-driven indexing of Prolog clauses. In: Proceedings of the 17th ACM SIGPLAN-SIGACT Symposium on Principles of Programming Languages, pp. 281–291 (1989)
10. Schlichtkrull, A., Blanchette, J., Traytel, D., Waldmann, U.: Formalizing Bachmair and Ganzinger's ordered resolution prover. J. Autom. Reason. **64**(7), 1169–1195 (2020)
11. Sekar, R., Ramakrishnan, I., Voronkov, A.: Term indexing. In: Handbook of Automated Reasoning, pp. 1853–1964. Elsevier (2001)
12. Stickel, M.E.: The path-indexing method for indexing terms. SRI International, Artificial Intelligence Center (1989)
13. Waldmann, U., Tourret, S., Robillard, S., Blanchette, J.: A comprehensive framework for saturation theorem proving. J. Autom. Reason., 1–41 (2022)

Simplified and Verified: A Second Look at a Proof-Producing Union-Find Algorithm

Lukas Stevens[1(✉)] and Rebecca Ghidini[1,2,3]

[1] Department of Computer Science, Technical University of Munich, Boltzmannstr. 3, Garching, Germany
lukas.stevens@in.tum.de
[2] École normale supérieure, Département d'informatique de l'ENS, CNRS, PSL University, 75005 Paris, France
rebecca.ghidini@info.ens.psl.eu
[3] Inria, Paris, France

Abstract. Using Isabelle/HOL, we verify a union-find data structure with an explain operation due to Nieuwenhuis and Oliveras. We devise a simpler, more naive version of the explain operation whose soundness and completeness is easy to verify. Then, we prove the original formulation of the explain operation to be equal to our version. Finally, we refine this data structure to Imperative HOL, enabling us to export efficient imperative code. The formalisation provides a stepping stone towards the verification of proof-producing congruence closure algorithms which are a core ingredient of Satisfiability Modulo Theories (SMT) solvers.

Keywords: Equivalence closure · Interactive theorem proving · Satisfiability modulo theories · Proof-producing decision procedure

1 Introduction

The Union-Find (UF) data structure maintains the equivalence closure of a relation, which is given as a sequence of pairs or, in terms of the UF data structure, UNION operations. It is fundamental to efficiently implement well-known graph algorithms such as Kruskal's [14] minimum spanning-tree algorithm. There, it tracks which vertices belong to the same connected component and are, in that sense, equivalent. Beyond graph algorithms, its applicability extends to the domain of theorem proving as it routinely forms the basis of congruence closure algorithms, which are widely used by Satisfiability Modulo Theories (SMT) solvers. To increase their trustworthiness, current SMT solvers such as cvc5 [3], E [26], Vampire [13], veriT [4], and Z3 [18] can output detailed proofs when they determine an input formula to be unsatisfiable. To produce these proofs, it is crucial to have congruence closure algorithms that efficiently explain why they consider two terms to be equal. The first such algorithm was presented

C. Barrett and U. Waldmann (Eds.): CADE 2025, LNAI 15943, pp. 261–279, 2025.
https://doi.org/10.1007/978-3-031-99984-0_15

by Nieuwenhuis and Oliveras [20,21], who extended the UF data structure with an EXPLAIN operation to obtain a Union-Find-Explain (UFE) data structure. Verifying this data structure in Isabelle/HOL is the focus of our paper.

Why, then, should we verify a data structure that already produces proofs? Our answer is three-fold. (1) While the data structure's proofs guarantee soundness, we also prove its completeness. (2) Executing code exported from Isabelle depends on a substantial trusted computing base (TCB), including the target language's compiler and runtime. (3) Whereas SMT solvers typically operate with a large TCB, adding to the TCB of interactive theorem provers is usually discouraged. Proof-producing algorithms—such as those introduced in earlier work by the first author [27]—enable integration without increasing the TCB.

1.1 Contributions

We present, to our knowledge, the first formalisation of the UFE data structure as introduced by Nieuwenhuis and Oliveras [20]. In their work, they present two variants of this data structure. Here, we only formalise the first variant, leaving the other for future work. We devise a simpler, more naive version of the EXPLAIN operation, for which soundness and completeness is easier to prove. Then, we prove the original version of the EXPLAIN operation to be extensionally equal to the simple one. Based on an existing formalisation of the UF data structure by Lammich [15], we develop a more abstract formalisation of the data structure, hiding implementation details. Finally, we refine the UFE data structure to Imperative HOL [5] using Lammich's [15] separation logic framework, enabling generation of efficient imperative code.

The formalisation is available online.[1] Since everything is verified, we omit proofs and focus on outlining the structure of the formalisation.

1.2 Related Work

Efficient implementations of the UF data structure have been known for a long time. In particular, Galler and Fisher [9] represent the data structure as a forest of rooted trees and propose the union-by-size heuristic, which gives $\mathcal{O}(\log n)$ running time for UNION and FIND for a data structure over n elements. Another heuristic, called path compression, was presented by Aho et al. [1]. Analysing the complexity of the data structure when combining both heuristics turned out to be challenging, but Tarjan [28] and Tarjan and van Leeuwen [29] eventually proved an amortised running time of $\mathcal{O}(n + m\,\alpha(m+n, n))$ for a sequence of at most $n-1$ UNION and m FIND operations where α is the inverse Ackermann function. This means that any one operation runs in almost constant time, amortised.

While the paper on the UFE data structure [20] is widely cited, there is limited follow-up literature on this data structure. It does, however, form the basis of proof-producing congruence closure algorithms, which are crucial in the

[1] https://doi.org/10.5281/zenodo.15557955.

field of SMT solving. There, they remain an active area of research; for example, when we are interested in efficiently finding small proofs [8].

The literature of verified algorithms and data structure is vast so we refer to a survey [22] for an overview. Focusing on the UF data structure, there is a formalisation in Coq [7], where the amortised complexity is analysed by Charguéraud and Pottier [6] in a separation logic with time credits. Similarly, in Isabelle, there is a formalisation of the data structure [15] that was later extended with a complexity analysis by Haslbeck and Lammich [11]. More recently, there is formalisation by Guttmann [10] taking a relation-algebraic view.

1.3 Notation

Isabelle/HOL [23] conforms to everyday mathematical notation for the most part. We establish notation and in particular some essential data types together with their primitive operations that are specific to Isabelle/HOL.

We write $t::'a$ to specify that the term t has the type $'a$ and $'a \Rightarrow 'b$ for the space of total functions from type $'a$ to type $'b$.

Sets with elements of type $'a$ have the type $'a\ set$. The cardinality of a set A is denoted by $|A|$.

We use $'a\ list$ to describe the type of lists, which are constructed using the empty list [] or the infix cons constructor (#), and are appended with the infix operator (@). The length of list xs is denote by $|xs|$. The function set converts a list into a set. We write $xs\ !\ i$ to access the i-th element of the list xs.

To represent partial values of type $'a$, we use the type $'a\ option$ with the constructors None and Some. We also define an order on this type by letting None be smaller than Some and lifting the order on the underlying type $'a$, i.e. we have that $(\mathsf{Some}\ x \leq \mathsf{Some}\ y) = (x \leq y)$.

Relations are denoted with the type synonym $'a\ rel$, which expands to $('a \times 'a)\ set$. For a relation r, Field r are those elements that occur as a component of a pair $p \in r$. Furthermore, we use r^{-1} to denote the inverse and r^* to denote the reflexive transitive closure of r.

Throughout our formalisation we employ *locales* [2], which are named contexts of types, constants and assumptions about them.

2 Basic Union-Find

2.1 Background

Given a set of n elements $A = \{a_1, \ldots, a_n\}$, the UF data structure keeps track of a partition of A into disjoint sets $A_1, \ldots, A_k$, i.e. $A = A_1 \uplus \cdots \uplus A_k$. Equivalently, one can view the partition as a partial equivalence relation with the equivalence classes $A_1, \ldots, A_k$. The equivalence relation is partial because $A::'a\ set$ might only be a subset of the type $'a$. We initialise the data structure by partitioning A into singleton sets of elements, so we have that $A = \{a_1\} \uplus \cdots \uplus \{a_n\}$. Those sets are merged by subsequent UNION operations where UNION a_i a_j merges the set containing a_i with the one that contains a_j. Each set in the partition contains one particular element that serves as its representative. We will denote the representative of an element a in the UF data structure uf as rep-of uf a. Accordingly, two elements have the same representative exactly when they belong to the same set in the partition. For any element a_i, the FIND operation returns its representative rep-of uf a_i.

The data structure can be implemented as a forest of rooted trees where each tree encodes an equivalence class. The edges of a tree in the forest are directed towards the root, which is the representative of the corresponding equivalence class. To preserve this invariant, we initialise the forest with n vertices but without any edges and, for every UNION of a_i and a_j, we add a directed edge from rep-of uf a_i to rep-of uf a_j to the forest.

We encode such a forest as a list l of length n, where at each index i of l, we save the index of the parent of the element a_i, denoted by $l\ !\ i$. If a_i is a root, then the list stores i itself at index i, i.e. $l\ !\ i = i$.

2.2 In Isabelle/HOL

The UF algorithm was formalised in Isabelle/HOL by Lammich [15]. The code can be found in an entry [16] of the Archive of Formal Proofs (AFP).[2] Lammich defines a function rep-of, which, as described above, follows the parent pointers until we arrive at the root, where the parent pointer is self-referential.

rep-of :: $nat\ list \Rightarrow nat \Rightarrow nat$

rep-of l i = let $pi = l\ !\ i$ in if $pi = i$ then i else rep-of l pi

Looking closely at this definition, we see that this function is only well-defined for some inputs l and a: for every element $a < |l|$, its parent must be in the list, i.e. we must have $l\ !\ a < |l|$, and the parent pointers must be cycle-free in order for the function to terminate. Functions in Isabelle/HOL must be total, so Isabelle introduces a constant rep-of-dom :: $nat\ list \times nat \Rightarrow bool$ that characterises the inputs for which rep-of terminates. Then, it adds rep-of-dom (l, a) as a premise to the defining equation of rep-of. The intuition above is cast into a predicate ufa-invar that defines such well-formed lists l.

ufa-invar :: $nat\ list \Rightarrow bool$

ufa-invar $l = \forall i{<}|l|.$ rep-of-dom $(l, i) \wedge l\ !\ i < |l|$

Building on the formalisation, we define the abstract data type (ADT) ufa as the set of all l::$nat\ list$ that satisfy ufa-invar l.

typedef $ufa = \{l \mid$ ufa-invar $l\}$.

This introduces a new type without any predefined operations. To equip it with functionality, we lift the operations on the underlying list due to Lammich [15] to the ADT using Isabelle's lifting infrastructure [12], yielding (1) ufa-α :: $ufa \Rightarrow (nat \times nat)\ set$, (2) ufa-rep-of :: $ufa \Rightarrow nat \Rightarrow nat$, (3) ufa-init :: $nat \Rightarrow ufa$, and (4) ufa-union :: $ufa \Rightarrow nat \Rightarrow nat \Rightarrow ufa$. Their meaning is the following:

[2] The code is in the theory file `Examples/Union_Find.thy`.

(1) $\mathsf{ufa}\text{-}\alpha\ uf$ is the partial equivalence relation represented by uf,
(2) $\mathsf{ufa\text{-}rep\text{-}of}\ uf\ x$ is the representative of the equivalence class containing x,
(3) $\mathsf{ufa\text{-}init}\ n$ initialises the data structure with n elements with each element being its own representative, and
(4) $\mathsf{ufa\text{-}union}\ uf\ x\ y$ returns a UF data structure where the equivalence classes of x and y are merged. This is implemented by updating the underlying list at index $\mathsf{rep\text{-}of}\ l\ x$ to $\mathsf{rep\text{-}of}\ l\ y$.

Formally, the above operations fulfil the properties stated below:

- $\mathsf{ufa\text{-}rep\text{-}of}\ uf\ x = \mathsf{ufa\text{-}rep\text{-}of}\ uf\ y \longleftrightarrow (x, y) \in \mathsf{ufa}\text{-}\alpha\ uf$ if $\{x, y\} \subseteq \mathsf{Field}\ (\mathsf{ufa}\text{-}\alpha\ uf)$,
- $\mathsf{ufa}\text{-}\alpha\ (\mathsf{ufa\text{-}init}\ n) = \{(x, x) \mid x < n\}$, and
- $\mathsf{ufa}\text{-}\alpha\ (\mathsf{ufa\text{-}union}\ uf\ x\ y) = \mathsf{per\text{-}union}\ (\mathsf{ufa}\text{-}\alpha\ uf)\ x\ y$

where $\mathsf{per\text{-}union}\ R\ x\ y$ is the equivalence relation that results from merging the respective equivalence classes in the relation R that x and y belong to.

But what happens if x or y is not an element of the partial equivalence relation R? In that case, the equivalence relation is unchanged, which means that $\mathsf{per\text{-}union}\ R\ x\ y = R$. This, however, can be seen as a misuse of the UF data structure, since we initialise it with a fixed set of elements A and expect the user to only work with these elements. Therefore, we introduce the following definitions that characterise valid union(s) with regard to this initial set.

$\mathsf{valid\text{-}union} :: ufa \Rightarrow nat \Rightarrow nat \Rightarrow bool$
$\mathsf{valid\text{-}union}\ uf\ a\ b = a \in \mathsf{Field}\ (\mathsf{ufa}\text{-}\alpha\ uf) \wedge b \in \mathsf{Field}\ (\mathsf{ufa}\text{-}\alpha\ uf)$

$\mathsf{valid\text{-}unions} :: ufa \Rightarrow (nat \times nat)\ list \Rightarrow bool$
$\mathsf{valid\text{-}unions}\ uf\ us = \forall\,(x, y){\in}\mathsf{set}\ us.\ \mathsf{valid\text{-}union}\ uf\ x\ y$

3 Simple Certifying Union-Find Algorithm

Building on the UF ADT, we now develop a simple EXPLAIN operation that, for a given list of equations $us{::}('a \times 'a)\ list$, takes two elements x and y and produces a certificate that $x = y$ modulo us. The certificate is given in terms of a data type *eq-prf* with its corresponding system $\vdash_=$ of inference rules as seen in Fig. 1. As expected, we have inference rules that utilise the reflexivity, symmetry, and transitivity of equality as well as an assumption rule. To improve readability, we use the infix operator $\triangledown$ to denote the proof term for transitivity.

We prove that $\vdash_=$ is sound and complete with respect to the equivalence relation induced by us, i.e. the equivalence closure of us. In Isabelle, we define

$\mathsf{symcl} :: 'a\ rel \Rightarrow 'a\ rel$
$\mathsf{symcl}\ r = r \cup r^{-1}$

$\mathsf{equivcl} :: 'a\ rel \Rightarrow 'a\ rel$
$\mathsf{equivcl}\ r = (\mathsf{symcl}\ r)^*$

and prove the theorem below.

$$\frac{i < |us| \qquad us \; ! \; i = (x,\, y)}{us \vdash_{=} \mathsf{AssmP}\ i : (x,\, y)} \qquad \frac{}{us \vdash_{=} \mathsf{ReflP}\ x : (x,\, x)}$$

$$\frac{us \vdash_{=} p : (x,\, y)}{us \vdash_{=} \mathsf{SymP}\ p : (y,\, x)} \qquad \frac{us \vdash_{=} p_1 : (x,\, y) \qquad us \vdash_{=} p_2 : (y,\, z)}{us \vdash_{=} p_1 \bigtriangledown p_2 : (x,\, z)}$$

Fig. 1. The system of inference rules $\vdash_{=}$ on the data type *eq-prf* of proofs. We write $us \vdash_{=} p : (x,\, y)$ to say that p proves $x = y$ assuming the equalities us.

Theorem 1. (Soundness and Completeness of $\vdash_{=}$). *If* $us \vdash_{=} p : (x,\, y)$ *then* $(x,\, y) \in \mathsf{equivcl}\ (\mathsf{set}\ us)$. *Conversely, If* $(x,\, y) \in \mathsf{equivcl}\ (\mathsf{set}\ us)$ *then* $\exists p.\ us \vdash_{=} p : (x,\, y)$.

Our goal is to implement the EXPLAIN operation using a UF data structure, so we fix an initial UF data structure uf. For a list of equations us or, in terms of the UF data structure, UNION operations, the current state of the UF data structure is then equal to $\mathsf{ufa\text{-}unions}\ uf\ us$ where we define

$\mathsf{ufa\text{-}unions} :: ufa \Rightarrow (nat \times nat)\ list \Rightarrow ufa$
$\mathsf{ufa\text{-}unions} = \mathsf{foldl}\ (\lambda uf\ (x,\, y).\ \mathsf{ufa\text{-}union}\ uf\ x\ y).$

Here, we require the unions us to be valid unions with respect to uf. Moreover, it must hold that $\mathsf{ufa\text{-}}\alpha\ uf \subseteq \mathsf{nat\text{-}rel}$ because the only way to justify an equality from an empty list of equations using $\vdash_{=}$ is by reflexivity. Finally, we also constrain us to be *effective* unions meaning that no union shall be redundant with respect to the unions preceeding it. Note that redundant unions have no effect on the state of the UF data structure anyways so there is no need to record them. We formalise effectiveness with the following definitions.

$\mathsf{eff\text{-}union} :: ufa \Rightarrow nat \Rightarrow nat \Rightarrow bool$
$\mathsf{eff\text{-}union}\ uf\ a\ b = \mathsf{valid\text{-}union}\ uf\ a\ b \wedge \mathsf{ufa\text{-}rep\text{-}of}\ uf\ a \neq \mathsf{ufa\text{-}rep\text{-}of}\ uf\ b$

$\mathsf{eff\text{-}unions} :: ufa \Rightarrow (nat \times nat)\ list \Rightarrow bool$
$\mathsf{eff\text{-}unions}\ uf\ [] = \mathsf{True}$
$\mathsf{eff\text{-}unions}\ uf\ ((a,\, b)\ \#\ us) =$
$\quad \mathsf{eff\text{-}union}\ uf\ a\ b \wedge \mathsf{eff\text{-}unions}\ (\mathsf{ufa\text{-}union}\ uf\ a\ b)\ us$

Similarly to ufa, we encapsulate pairs $(uf,\, us)$ that are well-formed with respect to the constraints above by an ADT ufe. We choose this simple representation of the UFE data structure to ease formal reasoning, while a more efficient implementation is described in Sect. 5.2.

$\mathsf{typedef}\ ufe = \{(uf,\, us) \mid \mathsf{ufa\text{-}}\alpha\ uf \subseteq \mathsf{nat\text{-}rel} \wedge \mathsf{eff\text{-}unions}\ uf\ us\}$

We lift operations on such pairs $(uf,\, us)$ to obtain (1) $\mathsf{unions} :: ufe \Rightarrow (nat \times nat)\ list$, (2) $\mathsf{uf\text{-}ds} :: ufe \Rightarrow ufa$, (3) $\mathsf{ufe\text{-}init} :: nat \Rightarrow ufe$, and (4) both $\mathsf{ufe\text{-}union} :: ufe \Rightarrow nat \Rightarrow nat \Rightarrow ufe$ and its dual (5) $\mathsf{rollback} :: ufe \Rightarrow ufe$. The meaning of these operations is the following: (1) $\mathsf{unions}\ ufe$ is the list of unions us, (2) uf-ds ufe represents the current state of the UUF data structure, i.e. ufa-unions uf us, (3) ufe-init n initialises the data structure with n elements and an empty list of unions, (4) ufe-union ufe a b appends an effective union (a, b) to us, and (5) rollback ufe removes the last union from us. Furthermore, we lift the remaining operations on ufa to ufe via uf-ds, replacing the prefix ufa by ufe. For example, we lift ufa-rep-of by letting ufe-rep-of $ufe \equiv$ ufa-rep-of (uf-ds ufe).

```
explain :: ufe ⇒ nat ⇒ nat ⇒ nat eq-prf
explain ufe x y =
  if unions ufe = [] then ReflP x
  else let ufe0 = rollback ufe; (a, b) = last (unions ufe);
           a-b-P = AssmP |unions ufe0|
       in if ufe-rep-of ufe0 x = ufe-rep-of ufe0 y then explain ufe0 x y
          else if ufe-rep-of ufe0 x = ufe-rep-of ufe0 a
               then explain ufe0 x a ▽ a-b-P ▽ explain ufe0 b y
               else explain ufe0 x b ▽ SymP a-b-P ▽ explain ufe0 a y

explain-partial :: ufe ⇒ nat ⇒ nat ⇒ nat eq-prf option
explain-partial ufe x y =
  if (x, y) ∈ equivcl (set (unions ufe)) then Some (explain ufe x y)
  else None
```

Fig. 2. A simple implementation of the EXPLAIN operation.

At last, we implement the EXPLAIN operation as depicted in Fig. 2. The algorithm assumes that the given elements x and y are equal modulo unions ufe.

If unions $ufe = []$, then x and y must be equal which we certify with ReflP x.

Otherwise, we distinguish between two cases: (1) The elements x and y are already equal modulo unions (rollback ufe), so we proceed recursively with rollback ufe. (2) In the case where the most recent equation $a = b$ is necessary for $x = y$ to hold, we either have $x = a$ and $b = y$ or $x = b$ and $a = y$ modulo unions (rollback ufe). Assuming the former holds—the other case is symmetric—we recursively construct the certificates for $x = a$ and $b = y$. Together with the assumption $a = b$, we obtain $x = y$ by transitivity. The termination of explain is easily proven because the length of unions ufe decreases in each recursive call. Dually, this termination argument gives rise to the following induction principle.

Lemma 1 (Induction on ufe). *In order to prove P ufe for all ufe, we have two inductive cases, both fixing an arbitrary ufe: (1) Assume* ufe-α $ufe \subseteq$ nat-rel *as well as* unions $ufe = []$ *and show P ufe. (2) Assume* eff-union (uf-ds ufe) a b *as well as P ufe and show P* (ufe-union ufe a b).

We condense the intuition above into the completeness theorem below, which we prove using the induction principle from Lemma 1.

Theorem 2 (Completeness of explain**).** *If* $(x, y) \in$ equivcl (set (unions ufe)) *then* unions $ufe \vdash_=$ explain $ufe\ x\ y : (x, y)$.

The explain function is not sound, though. This is because it always returns a certificate, even if x and y are not equal modulo us. To account for this case, we wrap explain into a partial function explain-partial (cf. Fig. 2) that fails if $x = y$ is not provable. Soundness and completeness can then be lifted from the soundness of $\vdash_=$ and the completeness of explain, respectively. Note that membership of equivcl can actually be implemented using UF operations as the following lemma demonstrates. Moreover, it holds that $x \in$ Field (ufa-α uf) $\longleftrightarrow$ $x < n$ where n is the length of the list representing uf.

Lemma 2. *We have* $(x, y) \in$ equivcl (set (unions ufe)) iff $x = y \vee x \in$ Field (ufe-α ufe) $\wedge$ $y \in$ Field (ufe-α ufe) $\wedge$ ufe-rep-of $ufe\ x$ = ufe-rep-of $ufe\ y$.

4 Efficient Certifying Union-Find Algorithm

In the previous section, we developed an EXPLAIN operation that iteratively removes the most recent union from a list of unions, identifying which of them, when viewed as equalities, are necessary to prove the input arguments equal. Iterating through all equalities seems inefficient, though. Intuitively, we aim to return only those on the path between the arguments, viewing the equalities as an undirected graph. To realise this, Nieuwenhuis and Oliveras [20] use a UF data structure represented as forest of rooted trees as described in Sect. 2.1. They modify the data structure such that, for each union between a and b, the newly added edge in the forest gets annotated with (a, b). To understand why this allows for a more efficient implementation of the EXPLAIN operation, suppose that we want to certify that x is equal to y. Clearly, only the edges of the subtree rooted at the lowest common ancestor (LCA) of x and y, as illustrated in Fig. 3, are relevant to explain why x is equal to y. Furthermore, let (a, b) be the most recent union on either of the paths from the LCA to x or y. Here, we assume w.l.o.g. that (a, b) is on the path to x. The corresponding edge separates the tree rooted at the LCA into two subtrees as indicated by the patterns, one containing a and the other one b. Moreover, the paths from the LCA can't overlap, so x and y also belong to different subtrees. Ultimately, to certify the equality of x and y, we recursively prove that x is equal to a and y to b. Then, we put everything together using transitivity and the equality $a = b$. This terminates since (a, b) is the most recent union and we only consider less recent unions in the recursive steps. All in all, this gives a $\mathcal{O}(k \log n)$ EXPLAIN operation on a UF data structure with union-by-size, where k is the number of unions required for an explanation [20]. This is an improvement over the naive algorithm where we iterate over all (up to $n - 1$) unions.

To achieve optimal almost constant running time for UNION and FIND, we need path compression in addition to union-by-size. Path compression, however, is incompatible with the EXPLAIN operation, so Nieuwenhuis and Oliveras [20] propose to maintain two copies of the UF data structure, one with and one without path compression.

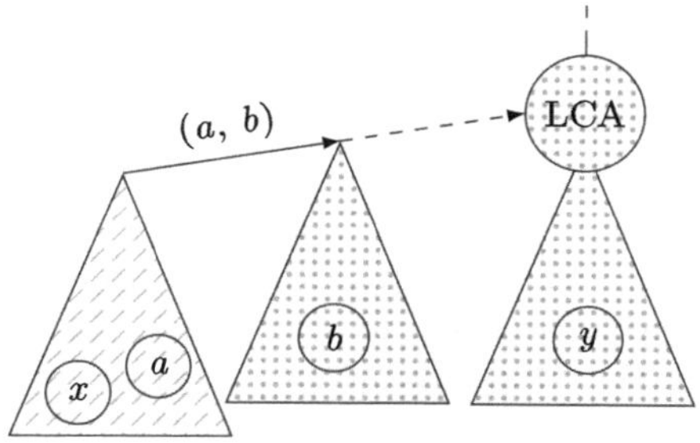

Fig. 3. For arguments x and y, explain′ considers an edge annotated with $(a,\ b)$ that separates the subtree rooted at the LCA of x and y into two subtrees: one containing x and a and the other one containing y and b.

4.1 Implementation

To obtain an efficient EXPLAIN operation, we leverage the structure of the UF data structure, which is a forest of rooted trees. We make this structure accessible by defining a function ufa-parent-of :: $ufa \Rightarrow nat \Rightarrow nat$ via lifting, where ufa-parent-of $uf\ x$ returns the parent of x. This function is related to ufa-rep-of in the obvious way, i.e. we have ufa-parent-of $uf\ x = x$ *iff* ufa-rep-of $uf\ x = x$ for $x \in$ Field (ufa-α uf). With this, we formalise the concept of UFE forests, define the notion of associated unions within this forest, and introduce the two auxiliary functions that are the ingredients to the efficient EXPLAIN operation.

UFE Forests. It is often useful to view the forest of rooted trees underpinning the UF data structure as a graph. For this purpose, we use the graph theory library [25] due to Noschinski, which is available as an entry of the AFP [24]. The library allows us to represent a graph as a record with the fields verts and arcs for its vertices and edges, where edges are pairs of vertices. The forest induced by a UF data structure is then defined as follows.

ufa-forest-of uf =
  let vs = Field (ufa-α uf)
  in ⦇verts = vs,
      arcs = $\{$(ufa-parent-of $uf\ x$, x) $\mid x \in vs \land$ ufa-parent-of $uf\ x \neq x\}$⦈

ufe-forest-of $ufe \equiv$ ufa-forest-of (uf-ds ufe)

Note that we choose (somewhat arbitrarily) to direct the edges away from the root because it aligns more naturally with the notion of a directed rooted tree. Additionally, this choice ensures compatibility with the *directed-forest* locale, which we implemented on top of the graph library. For brevity, we omit the details here and direct the reader to the formalisation, but suffice it to say that typical properties of forests, e.g. the absence of cycles, are proved in this locale. To collect facts that are specific to UF forests, we define a locale *ufa-forest* fixing a UF data structure uf. In the context of this locale, we show that ufa-forest-of uf fulfils the requirements of a *directed-forest*, meaning that the facts in the latter locale transfer over to the former. Similarly, we introduce the locale *ufe-forest* fixing a UFE data structure ufe, where uf-ds ufe is a *ufa-forest.*

Associated Unions. As illustrated by Fig. 3, we annotate each edge of the UFE forest with the union that caused its creation, i.e. for an effective union (a, b), we annotate the newly created edge e between the ufe-rep-of ufe a and ufe-rep-of ufe b with (a, b). We say that (a, b) is the *associated union* of e. Since the underlying UF data structure is expressed in terms of parent pointers, we actually associate the union (a, b) with ufe-rep-of ufe a. Furthermore, we use an index into unions ufe rather than storing the union (a, b) directly. This concept is formalised in the constant au-ds :: $ufe \Rightarrow nat \Rightarrow nat$ *option* whose specific implementation we skip over here; instead, we only state its characteristic properties:

- If unions $ufe = []$ *then* au-ds $ufe = (\lambda x.$ None$)$.
- For an effective union (a, b), i.e. if we have eff-union (uf-ds ufe) a b, it holds that au-ds (ufe-union ufe a b) $=$ (au-ds ufe)(ufe-rep-of ufe $a \mapsto |$unions $ufe|$), where $(f(x \mapsto y))\ z =$ (if $z = x$ then Some y else $f\ z$).

Determining the LCA in a UFE Forest. $\langle proof \rangle \langle proof \rangle$
The first auxiliary functions lists the elements on the path from the representative to some element. Similarly to ufa-rep-of, this function is only well-defined for elements $x \in$ Field (ufa-α uf) of a given UF data structure uf. Now, let px be the path from the representative of x to x and py be the path from y's representative to y. Then, every element of a common prefix of px and py is a common ancestor of x and y and the LCA is exactly the last element of the longest common prefix of px and py.

```
awalk-verts-from-rep :: ufa ⇒ nat ⇒ nat list
awalk-verts-from-rep uf x =
  let px = ufa-parent-of uf x
  in if px = x then [x] else awalk-verts-from-rep uf px @ [x]

ufa-lca :: ufa ⇒ nat ⇒ nat ⇒ nat
ufa-lca uf x y =
  let px = awalk-verts-from-rep uf x; py = awalk-verts-from-rep uf y
  in last (longest-common-prefix px py)
```

Again, we abbreviate ufe-lca $ufe \equiv$ ufa-lca (uf-ds ufe). It holds that ufa-lca is indeed an LCA provided that the arguments share the same representative and thus are in the same tree of the forest. For brevity, we omit the definition of lca here and refer to the formalisation instead.

Lemma 3. *If* $\{x, y\} \subseteq$ Field (ufa-α uf) *and* ufa-rep-of uf x = ufa-rep-of uf y, *then* pre-digraph.lca (ufa-forest-of uf) (ufa-lca uf x y) x y.

We later prove key properties of EXPLAIN using the induction principle from Lemma 1, making it essential to understand how the auxiliary functions behave under effective unions. The lemma below shows that ufa-lca is invariant under a union (a, b) if its arguments share the same representative beforehand. Otherwise, the union introduces an edge from the representative of a to that of b, connecting the trees that x and y belong to at their respective roots. Due to the orientation of this new edge, we know that the LCA of x and y must be the representative of b after performing the union.

Lemma 4. *Assume* eff-union uf a b *and* $\{x, y\} \subseteq$ Field (ufa-α uf). *If* ufa-rep-of (ufa-union uf a b) x = ufa-rep-of (ufa-union uf a b) y *then* ufa-lca (ufa-union uf a b) x y = (if ufa-rep-of uf x = ufa-rep-of uf y then ufa-lca uf x y else ufa-rep-of uf b).

Finding the Most Recent Union on a Path. For the second auxiliary function, we walk the path from the second argument x to the first argument y and return the most recent associated union, i.e. the maximum index with respect to unions ufe on that path. In Isabelle, we define the following function.

find-newest-on-path :: $ufe \Rightarrow nat \Rightarrow nat \Rightarrow nat\ option$
find-newest-on-path ufe y x =
  if $y = x$ then None
  else max (au-ds ufe x) (find-newest-on-path ufe y (ufe-parent-of ufe x))

As explained earlier, we only use this function on an element in conjunction with its LCA relative to another element. Thus, there is a path between the two arguments and the function is well-defined for such inputs. The path, however, can be empty, in which we return None, making the function partial.

As before, we are interested in how the function behaves under effective unions. Since unions only join trees at their roots, existing paths in the tree are unchanged by unions, so, for elements in the same equivalence class, the function is invariant under unions. If, on the other hand, two elements only become part of the same equivalence class as a result of a union (a, b), then (a, b) must be on the path between those elements and, as it is the most recent union, the function returns the index of that union.

Lemma 5. *Assume that* eff-union (uf-ds ufe) a b *and* y *is reachable from* x *in* ufe-forest-of (ufe-union ufe a b), *then it holds that* find-newest-on-path (ufe-union ufe a b) x y = (if ufe-rep-of ufe x = ufe-rep-of ufe y then find-newest-on-path ufe x y else Some |unions ufe|).

Explain. With the auxiliary functions in place, we are set to implement the efficient EXPLAIN operation as shown in Fig. 4.

Given arguments x and y, we first check whether they are equal and, if so, we justify their equality by reflexivity.

Otherwise, we determine the LCA of the two elements and the most recent associated union on both of the paths from the elements to the LCA. Note that, if the LCA is equal to x or to y, the respective path to the LCA is empty; nevertheless, it is impossible that both x and y are equal to the LCA because we are in the case where $x \neq y$. Consider, for the sake of an explanation, the case where the most recent union (ax, bx) is on the path to x. This means, as illustrated in Fig. 3, that x and ax as well as y and bx are in the same subtree, respectively. Thus, we call explain′ recursively and, using transitivity, combine the resulting proofs of $x = ax$ and $bx = y$ with the assumption that $ax = bx$.

The last case, where the most recent union is on the path from y to the LCA, is symmetric, which, accordingly, requires us to apply the symmetry rule after using the assumption rule on the most recent union.

As we will show below, explain′ only terminates for specific inputs. The domain on which the function is well-defined is again characterised by a domain predicate explain′-dom :: $ufe \Rightarrow nat \times nat \Rightarrow bool$.

```
explain' :: ufe ⇒ nat ⇒ nat ⇒ nat eq-prf
explain' ufe x y =
  if x = y then ReflP x
  else let lca = ufe-lca ufe x y;
           newest-x = find-newest-on-path ufe lca x;
           newest-y = find-newest-on-path ufe lca y
       in if newest-y ≤ newest-x
          then let (ax, bx) = unions ufe ! the newest-x
               in explain' ufe x ax ▽ AssmP (the newest-x) ▽
                  explain' ufe bx y
          else let (ay, by) = unions ufe ! the newest-y
               in explain' ufe x by ▽ SymP (AssmP (the newest-y)) ▽
                  explain' ufe ay y
```

Fig. 4. Efficient version of the EXPLAIN operation.

4.2 Correctness

Verifying the functional correctness of explain′ requires proving termination as well as soundness and completeness. We prove termination directly, while we obtain soundness and completeness by showing extensional equality of explain′ and explain. As explain′, like explain, does not validate its input, we assume for the remainder of this section that (1) $\{x, y\} \subseteq$ Field (ufe-α ufe) and (2) ufe-rep-of $ufe\ x =$ ufe-rep-of $ufe\ y$.

To establish termination of explain′, we first prove that termination remains invariant under an effective union using the invariance of find-newest-on-path and ufe-lca under an effective union (see Lemmas 4 and 5). From this, the termination of explain′ follows by induction on ufe.

Lemma 6. *Assume* explain′-dom ufe $(x,\ y)$ *and* eff-union (uf-ds ufe) a b, *then it holds that* explain′-dom (ufe-union ufe a b) $(x,\ y)$.

Theorem 3 (Termination). explain′-dom ufe $(x,\ y)$

By Theorem 3 and the invariance of the auxiliary functions under effective unions, we deduce that explain′ is also invariant under effective unions.

Lemma 7. *If* eff-union (uf-ds ufe) a b *then* explain′ (ufe-union ufe a b) x y = explain′ ufe x y.

Given the definition of explain, we now understand the behaviour of both explain and explain′ under effective unions. Thus we conclude, by induction on ufe, that explain is extensionally equal to explain′.

Theorem 4 (Correctness). explain ufe x y = explain′ ufe x y

5 Refinement to an Efficiently Executable Specification

In the previous section, we described a refined recursion scheme for EXPLAIN that avoids iterating through all input equalities. To turn this into an efficiently executable specification, we refine two aspects of the UFE data structure.

First, we employ the union-by-size heuristic [9], i.e. we always attach the tree with fewer elements to the one with more elements during a UNION. This ensures that all trees in the UF data structure have height at most $\mathcal{O}(\log n)$ where n is the number of elements of the data structure. This yields $\mathcal{O}(\log n)$ running time for UNION and FIND as well as $\mathcal{O}(k \log n)$ for EXPLAIN.

Then, we take this functional UFE data structure and refine it to an imperative specification, thereby giving a concrete implementation. In doing that, we are careful to refine lists by arrays, guaranteeing constant time access to e.g. the parent of an element in the UF data structure. Additionally, we maintain a copy of the UF data structure with path compression as described in Sect. 4, improving the performance of UNION and FIND to almost constant running time.

5.1 Union-by-Size Heuristic

As mentioned in Sect. 2.2, our formalisation of the UF data structure extends a formalisation by Lammich [15,16]. The latter formalisation already introduces the union-by-size heuristic, but it does so during the refinement to Imperative HOL. We raise the union-by-size heuristic to the purely functional level of HOL, which lets us exploit Isabelle's lifting and transfer infrastructure [12]. In addition, we introduce another optimisation: we represent the UF data structure as a single list of integers, eliminating the data structure recording the size information.

As a prerequisite for the union-by-size heuristic, we define a function that determines the equivalence class of an element x in the data structure uf. More specifically, we use the relational image operator (``) on the equivalence relation ufa-α uf to obtain all the elements that are equivalent to x. The associated size of an element is then the cardinality of its equivalence class.

ufa-eq-class :: $ufa \Rightarrow nat \Rightarrow nat\ set$ ufa-size :: $ufa \Rightarrow nat \Rightarrow nat$

ufa-eq-class $uf\ x =$ ufa-α uf `` $\{x\}$ ufa-size $uf\ x = |$ufa-eq-class $uf\ x|$

With this, we perform the UNION operation such that the element with the smaller size is always passed as the first argument. The underlying implementation of the data structure always updates the parent pointer of the representative of the first argument to the representative of the second argument, thus yielding a UNION operation that attaches smaller trees in the UF forest to larger trees.

ufa-union-size :: $ufa \Rightarrow nat \Rightarrow nat \Rightarrow ufa$
ufa-union-size $ufa\ x\ y =$
  let $rep\text{-}x =$ ufa-rep-of $ufa\ x$; $rep\text{-}y =$ ufa-rep-of $ufa\ y$
  in if ufa-size $ufa\ rep\text{-}x <$ ufa-size $ufa\ rep\text{-}y$ then ufa-union $ufa\ x\ y$
    else ufa-union $ufa\ y\ x$

Looking closely at the definition, we see that ufa-size is only ever used on the representative of an element. Moreover, in the representation of ufa as a list of natural numbers, the representatives are exactly those where the parent pointer is self-referential. Ultimately, we integrate both insights and encode the UF data structure as an ADT $ufsi$, which is implemented by a list of integers: we use a negative number to indicate that a parent pointer is self-referential, using the absolute value of the number as the size at the same time. The other parent pointers are encoded as non-negative numbers as before.

5.2 From Functional to Imperative Specification

To obtain an imperative specification, we formulate a refined version of the EXPLAIN operation in the heap monad provided by the Imperative HOL [5] framework. This framework comes with an extension to Isabelle's code generator allowing us to generate imperative code in several target languages including Standard ML. Since Imperative HOL only comes with limited capabilities to analyse programs in its heap monad, we bring in Lammich's [15] separation logic framework for Imperative HOL. The framework lets us reason about the state of the heap using heap assertions, which describe data stored on the heap and their properties. All our data structures are ultimately represented as arrays on the heap, so we ensure with heap assertions that the content of the arrays represents our data structures throughout the operations we perform on them.

With the automation provided by Lammich's framework, it is straightforward to implement the operations and prove their correctness. The process is similar to the refinement of the UF data structure [15]. Thus, we forgo a discussion of how individual functions are refined and refer to the formalisation instead.

The only remaining noteworthy detail is the representation of the UFE data structure in Imperative HOL. Our implementation consists of a UF data structure, a partial function recording the associated union of each parent pointer, and the chronological list of unions. The UF data structure is represented as an array of integers. For the associated unions, we use an array of options to represent the partial function. This works as the domain is actually fixed, i.e. the domain of the partial function is exactly the elements of the UF data structure, which, in our case, are the natural numbers up to some fixed n. Lastly, we represent the list of unions as a dynamic array using the type *array-list*. The type wraps an array together with a natural number indicating how many cells of the array, counting from the first position, are occupied. We can then grow the array dynamically by pushing elements to the end, doubling its size each time it becomes fully occupied. Hence, we achieve amortised constant running time for adding new unions and constant time random access, which are the operations required by the EXPLAIN operation. We assemble these components into a record type $ufe\text{-}imp$. Finally, we extend $ufe\text{-}imp$ with a UF data structure with path compression, thus obtaining the record type $ufe\text{-}c\text{-}imp$.

We define a heap assertion is-ufe :: $ufe \times nat \Rightarrow ufe\text{-}imp \Rightarrow assn$ that relates instances of the ADT ufe with instances of $ufe\text{-}imp$. The assertion just relates the components of $ufe\text{-}imp$ with the corresponding functions on ufe, so we omit it for brevity. The only aspect requiring further explanation is the natural number n in the first argument. Its purpose is to ensure that the elements of the initial UF data structure and the domain of the associated unions are both the numbers up to n. To obtain the assertion is-ufe-c :: $ufe \times nat \Rightarrow ufe\text{-}c\text{-}imp \Rightarrow assn$, we additionally require that the representatives in the UF data structure with path compression corresponds to the representatives in the UFE data structure.

Again, refining the operations on $ufe\text{-}c\text{-}imp$ is routine; so, we only show the final correctness theorem for explain-partial-imp, an imperative version of explain′ that ensures soundness following the approach of explain-partial in Sect. 3.

Theorem 5. *We prove the following Hoare triple, which entails total correctness in the Separation Logic Framework [16]:* $<\mathsf{is\text{-}ufe\text{-}c}\ (ufe,\ n)\ ufe\text{-}c\text{-}imp>$ explain-partial-imp $ufe\text{-}c\text{-}imp\ x\ y$ $<\lambda r.\ \mathsf{is\text{-}ufe\text{-}c}\ (ufe,\ n)\ ufe\text{-}c\text{-}imp * \uparrow (r = \mathsf{explain\text{-}partial}\ ufe\ x\ y)>_t$

6 Benchmarking the Exported Code

In the previous section, we obtained an executable imperative specification of the UFE data structure, from which we can export code to functional target languages while utilising their respective support for imperative programming like destructive array updates in Standard ML (SML). This raises the question whether exporting imperative code to a functional language is a good fit, performance wise. In addition, SMT solvers are usually implemented in imperative language such as C++. Therefore, we compare the exported SML code against a hand-written C++ implementation of the executable specification.

We analyse the performance on two test cases: (1) in the former case, the number of proof steps for an EXPLAIN operation is linear in the number of elements but the depth of the UF forest is constant, (2) while in the latter, the depth of the UF forest as well as the number of proof steps is logarithmic in the number of elements. For both cases, we choose a natural number n, initialise the UFE data structure with 2^n elements, perform UNION operations that results in the desired UF forest, and finally perform a number (i.e. 1000 and 100000, respectively) of EXPLAIN operations with the arguments drawn from the uniform distribution over $0, \ldots, 2^n - 1$. We identify the test cases by functions wide and balanced, which both have type $nat \Rightarrow (nat \times nat)\ list$. Figure 5 illustrates the resulting UF forests or, more specifically, trees.

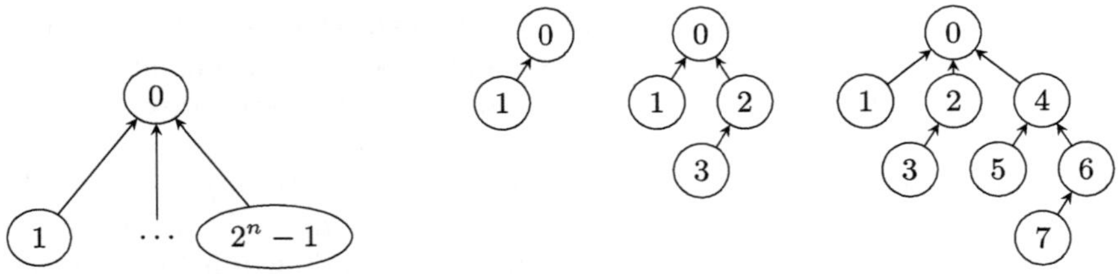

(a) UF tree for wide n. (b) UF trees for balanced n where $n \in \{1, 2, 3\}$.

Fig. 5. The UF trees resulting from performing the UNION operations with the arguments given by wide and balanced.

To perform our measurements, we compiled the exported Standard ML code with MLton[3] version 20210117, and the C++ code with g++[4] version 13.3.0. The results are shown in Table 1. The code export of Isabelle uses arbitrary sized integers to ensure soundness with respect to the executable specification while the C++ uses machine integers, so we also include a version of the exported code, annotated by (Int), that uses machine integers.

The observed running time overhead of using arbitrary sized integers is roughly a factor of 2–2.5, matching that observed by Lammich and Tuerk [17]. The difference between SML with machine integers and C++ is roughly a factor of 2 for the UNION operations and a factor of 1.5 for the EXPLAIN operations throughout both test cases. The second test case exhibits some outliers: notably, between $n = 23$ to $n = 24$ for SML and between $n = 24$ and $n = 25$ for SML (Int). This variance is due to garbage collection becoming a significant factor at large heap sizes, e.g. for $n = 25$ the heap grows to above 5 GB.

Overall, we found that employing a functional language results in a modest performance overhead when working with machine integers. We note that to soundly export such code, it would be necessary to change the element type of the UFE data structure from natural numbers to fixed-width words. This

[3] http://mlton.org.
[4] https://gcc.gnu.org.

Table 1. Wall-clock running times in seconds as measured on an Intel Core i7 4790k. For each n, we recorded the running time for performing the UNION operations and the EXPLAIN operations (separated by a slash).

Impl.	18	19	20	21	22
SML	0.025/18.428	0.075/36.129	0.072/70.696	0.157/140.209	0.393/280.684
SML (Int)	0.011/8.341	0.011/16.249	0.024/29.695	0.051/62.442	0.092/131.532
C++	0.004/3.672	0.007/7.354	0.015/15.113	0.031/31.120	0.062/71.066

(a) Running times for wide n.

Impl.	22	23	24	25	26
SML	0.722/1.879	0.899/2.583	1.552/2.082	4.770/2.396	14.610/3.014
SML (Int)	0.174/0.750	0.227/0.781	0.695/0.900	2.474/0.920	2.785/1.027
C++	0.087/0.369	0.199/0.460	0.350/0.550	0.752/0.620	1.451/0.728

(b) Running times for balanced n.

is plausible future work, as the number of elements is fixed for any instance of the data structure, and the only necessary operations on the elements are comparisons and indexing into arrays—operations that fixed-width words also support.

7 Conclusion and Future Work

We developed a formalisation of the UF data structure with an EXPLAIN operation based on a paper by Nieuwenhuis and Oliveras [20]. The formalisation includes a more naive version of the EXPLAIN operation than the one presented in the paper. We proved their equivalence as well as their soundness, completeness, and termination. Finally, we refined the functional representation of the data structure to an imperative one, allowing us to export efficient code.

In future work, we plan to verify the other variant of the UFE data structure as presented by Nieuwenhuis and Oliveras. This variant also forms the basis of their congruence closure algorithm, which is the logical next step. Ultimately, we want to work towards a verified, proof-producing version of the Nelson-Oppen algorithm [19] for the combination of theories.

Acknowledgements. We thank Tobias Nipkow for reviewing a draft version of this paper and the anonymous referees for their thoughtful feedback.

Disclosure of Interests. The authors have no competing interests to declare that are relevant to the content of this article.

References

1. Aho, A.V., Hopcroft, J.E., Ullman, J.D.: The Design and Analysis of Computer Algorithms. Addison-Wesley (1974). ISBN 0-201-00029-6
2. Ballarin, C.: Locales and locale expressions in Isabelle/Isar. In: Types for Proofs and Programs, pp. 34–50. Springer, Heidelberg (2003). https://doi.org/10.1007/978-3-540-24849-1_3
3. Barbosa, H., et al.: cvc5: A versatile and industrial-strength SMT solver. In: Tools and Algorithms for the Construction and Analysis of Systems. LNCS, vol. 13243, pp. 415–442, Springer (2022). https://doi.org/10.1007/978-3-030-99524-9_24
4. Bouton, T., Caminha B. de Oliveira, D., Déharbe, D., Fontaine, P.: veriT: an open, trustable and efficient SMT-solver. In: Conference on Automated Deduction, pp. 151–156, Springer, Heidelberg (2009). https://doi.org/10.1007/978-3-642-02959-2_12
5. Bulwahn, L., Krauss, A., Haftmann, F., Erkök, L., Matthews, J.: Imperative functional programming with Isabelle/HOL. In: Theorem Proving in Higher Order Logics, pp. 134–149. Springer, Heidelberg (2008). https://doi.org/10.1007/978-3-540-71067-7_14
6. Charguéraud, A., Pottier, F.: Verifying the correctness and amortized complexity of a union-find implementation in separation logic with time credits. J. Autom. Reason. **62**(3), 331–365 (2019). https://doi.org/10.1007/s10817-017-9431-7
7. Conchon, S., Filliâtre, J.C.: A persistent union-find data structure. In: Workshop on ML, pp. 37–46. Association for Computing Machinery, New York (2007). https://doi.org/10.1145/1292535.1292541
8. Flatt, O., Coward, S., Willsey, M., Tatlock, Z., Panchekha, P.: Small proofs from congruence closure. In: Formal Methods in Computer-Aided Design, pp. 75–83. IEEE (2022). https://doi.org/10.34727/2022/ISBN.978-3-85448-053-2_13
9. Galler, B.A., Fisher, M.J.: An improved equivalence algorithm. Commun. ACM **7**(5), 301–303 (1964). https://doi.org/10.1145/364099.364331
10. Guttmann, W.: Verifying the correctness of disjoint-set forests with Kleene relation algebras. In: Relational and Algebraic Methods in Computer Science, pp. 134–151. Springer, Cham (2020). https://doi.org/10.1007/978-3-030-43520-2_9
11. Haslbeck, M.P.L., Lammich, P.: Refinement with time - refining the run-time of algorithms in Isabelle/HOL. In: Interactive Theorem Proving, pp. 20:1–20:18 (2019). https://doi.org/10.4230/LIPIcs.ITP.2019.20
12. Huffman, B., Kunčar, O.: Lifting and transfer: a modular design for quotients in Isabelle/HOL. In: Certified Programs and Proofs. LNCS, pp. 131–146. Springer (2013). https://doi.org/10.1007/978-3-319-03545-1_9
13. Kovács, L., Voronkov, A.: First-order theorem proving and Vampire. In: Computer Aided Verification, pp. 1–35. Springer, Heidelberg (2013). https://doi.org/10.1007/978-3-642-39799-8_1
14. Kruskal, J.B.: On the shortest spanning subtree of a graph and the traveling salesman problem. Proc. Am. Mathe. Soc. **7**(1), 48–50 (1956). https://doi.org/10.2307/2033241
15. Lammich, P.: Refinement to imperative HOL. J. Autom. Reason. **62**(4), 481–503 (2017). https://doi.org/10.1007/s10817-017-9437-1
16. Lammich, P., Meis, R.: A separation logic framework for imperative HOL. Archive of Formal Proofs (2012). ISSN 2150-914x. https://isa-afp.org/entries/Separation_Logic_Imperative_HOL.html. Formal proof development

17. Lammich, P., Tuerk, T.: Applying data refinement for monadic programs to Hopcroft's algorithm. In: Interactive Theorem Proving, pp. 166–182. Springer, Heidelberg (2012). https://doi.org/10.1007/978-3-642-32347-8_12
18. de Moura, L.M., Bjørner, N.S.: Proofs and refutations, and Z3. In: International Workshop on the Implementation of Logics, CEUR Workshop Proceedings, vol. 418. CEUR-WS.org (2008). https://ceur-ws.org/Vol-418/paper10.pdf
19. Nelson, G., Oppen, D.C.: Simplification by cooperating decision procedures. ACM Trans. Program. Lang. Syst. **1**(2), 245–257 (1979). https://doi.org/10.1145/357073.357079
20. Nieuwenhuis, R., Oliveras, A.: Proof-producing congruence closure. In: Term Rewriting and Applications, pp. 453–468. Springer, Heidelberg (2005). https://doi.org/10.1007/978-3-540-32033-3_33
21. Nieuwenhuis, R., Oliveras, A.: Fast congruence closure and extensions. Inf. Comput. **205**(4), 557–580 (2007). https://doi.org/10.1016/j.ic.2006.08.009
22. Nipkow, T., Eberl, M., Haslbeck, M.P.L.: Verified textbook algorithms: a biased survey. In: Automated Technology for Verification and Analysis, pp. 25–53. Springer, Heidelberg (2020). https://doi.org/10.1007/978-3-030-59152-6_2
23. Nipkow, T., Paulson, L.C., Wenzel, M.: Isabelle/HOL — A Proof Assistant for Higher-Order Logic. LNCS, vol. 2283. Springer (2002)
24. Noschinski, L.: Graph theory. Archive of Formal Proofs (2013). ISSN 2150-914x. https://isa-afp.org/entries/Graph_Theory.html. Formal proof development
25. Noschinski, L.: A graph library for Isabelle. Math. Comput. Sci. **9**(1), 23–39 (2015). https://doi.org/10.1007/S11786-014-0183-Z
26. Schulz, S., Cruanes, S., Vukmirović, P.: Faster, higher, stronger: E 2.3. In: Conference on Automated Deduction. LNAI, vol. 11716, pp. 495–507. Springer (2019). https://doi.org/10.1007/978-3-030-29436-6_29
27. Stevens, L., Nipkow, T.: A verified decision procedure for orders in Isabelle/HOL. In: Automated Technology for Verification and Analysis, pp. 127–143. Springer, Cham (2021)
28. Tarjan, R.E.: Efficiency of a good but not linear set union algorithm. J. ACM **22**(2), 215–225 (1975). https://doi.org/10.1145/321879.321884
29. Tarjan, R.E., van Leeuwen, J.: Worst-case analysis of set union algorithms. J. ACM **31**(2), 245–281 (1984). https://doi.org/10.1145/62.2160

Faithful Logic Embeddings in HOL—Deep and Shallow

Christoph Benzmüller[1,2](✉)

[1] Otto-Friedrich-Universität Bamberg, Kapuzinerstraße 16, 96047 Bamberg, Germany
[2] Freie Universität Berlin, Kaiserswerther Str. 16–18, 14195 Berlin, Germany
christoph.benzmueller@uni-bamberg.de, c.benzmueller@fu-berlin.de

Abstract. Deep and shallow embeddings of non-classical logics in classical higher-order logic have been explored, implemented, and used in various reasoning tools in recent years. This paper presents a method for the simultaneous deployment of deep and shallow embeddings of various degrees in classical higher-order logic. This enables flexible, interactive and automated theorem proving and counterexample finding at meta and object level, as well as automated faithfulness proofs between these logic embeddings. The method is beneficial for logic education, research and application and is illustrated here using a simple propositional modal logic. However, this approach is conceptual in nature and not limited to this simple logic context.

Keywords: Logic embeddings · Faithfulness · Automated Reasoning

1 Motivation and Introduction

Deep embeddings of logics, or more generally of domain-specific languages, in a suitable metalogic, such as classical higher-order logic (HOL) [6,28], are typically based on explicitly introduced abstract data types. They essentially axiomatically characterize the structure and the meaning of the new language. Shallow embeddings, on the other hand, identify the embedded languages directly as fragments of the metalogic and they typically require few or no axiom postulates.[1] Deep and shallow embeddings of logics in HOL effectively and elegantly support interactive and automated reasoning with and about such logics within existing HOL theorem proving systems. Consequently, they have received increased attention in recent years. Shallow embeddings, for example, are well suited to automate even quantified modal logics, enabling applications in areas such as

[1] Gibbons and Wu characterize the two notions as follows [35, p.2]: *"[...] a deep embedding consists of a representation of the abstract syntax as an algebraic datatype, together with some functions that assign semantics to that syntax by traversing the algebraic datatype. A shallow embedding eschews the algebraic datatype, and hence the explicit representation of the abstract syntax of the language; instead, the language is defined directly in terms of its semantics."*.

C. Barrett and U. Waldmann (Eds.): CADE 2025, LNAI 15943, pp. 280–301, 2025.
https://doi.org/10.1007/978-3-031-99984-0_16

computational metaphysics [17]. Deep embeddings, on the other hand, are well suited to enable reasoning about the syntactic structure of embedded logics.

The contributions of this paper are manifold: First, a technique for the simultaneous provision of deep and shallow embeddings in metalogic HOL is presented, with the effect that computer-supported faithfulness proofs between the embeddings are not only enabled, but may—at least for simple embedded logics—now even be fully automated in HOL. This is, to the best of the authors' knowledge, a novel result. Second, this paper discusses shallow embedding alternatives differing in the degree of semantic dependencies that are explicitly encoded and maintained. More precisely, heavyweight (maximal) and lightweight (minimal) shallow embeddings are contrasted as extremes, and doing so, the paper hints at the full spectrum that exists between these extremes, which is in fact relevant for practice. For example, while a minimal shallow embedding for a normal modal logic only needs to explicitly encode the crucial semantic dependency on possible worlds [11], the explicit maintenance of an additional dependency, namely on dynamically updated domains of possible worlds, becomes relevant in case the logic is extended by a public announcement operator [13]. Third, the paper hints at opportunities for logic education, and for research, about and with logic embeddings within modern proof assistants and theorem provers for HOL. These range from metalogical studies to object logic applications using interactive proof and disproof, as well as automated theorem proving and counterexample finding, while allowing precise control over the particular level (object- or metalevel) at which reasoning takes place. Fourth, the paper presents some preliminary studies on whether shallow or deep embeddings are better suited for certain reasoning tasks. Fifth, using the Löb axiom of provability logic, the paper briefly sketches how research on the detection of semantic correspondences could possibly be supported by the presented technique in the future.

Since this paper and associated material is intended to be used in logic education, simple propositional modal logic (PML) [19,34,56] has been chosen to illustrate the addressed ideas, and Isabelle/HOL [50] has been chosen as the host proof assistant system for the experiments conducted. Reasons for using Isabelle/HOL include (i) its very good proof automation support with e.g. the `sledgehammer` [20] tool, (ii) the availability of the (counter-)model finder `nitpick` [21], and (iii) its powerful user interface, which allows for user-friendly LaTeX-quality representations. In principle, this paper could have taken advantage of Isabelle/HOL's special support for computer-verifiable paper writing to generate a document directly from the Isabelle/HOL sources, as is the case, for example, with all the articles published in the Archive of Formal Proofs. However, the author has decided against this idea and in favor of screenshots of the source code in order to save space. Furthermore, the visual highlighting and indenting in these screenshots makes them more useful for teaching and illustration purposes by drawing attention to the most important information.

Organization of the paper: Sects. 2 and 3 briefly introduce PML and HOL, before Sects. 4–6 present deep, maximally shallow, and minimally shallow embeddings of PML in HOL. These are connected by automated faithfulness proofs given in Sect. 7. Various experiments with the presented embeddings are presented in Sect. 8, before Sect. 9 discusses related work and Sect. 10 concludes the paper.

2 Propositional Modal Logic (PML)

The *syntax* of PML is defined by the grammar $\varphi, \psi := a \mid \neg\varphi \mid \varphi \supset \psi \mid \Box\varphi$, where $a \in \mathcal{S}$ are propositional symbols declared in a (nonempty) signature $\mathcal{S}$. Further logical connectives can be defined as usual, e.g.: $\varphi \vee \psi := \neg\varphi \supset \psi$, $\varphi \wedge \psi := \neg(\varphi \supset \neg\psi)$, $\Diamond\varphi := \neg\Box\neg\varphi$, $\top := p \supset p$ (for some $p \in \mathcal{S}$), and $\bot := \neg\top$.

A *semantics* for PML, called relational semantics or possible-world semantics, determines the truth of a formula φ relative to a so-called possible world w and a relational model $\mathcal{M}$. A relational model $\mathcal{M}$ is a tuple $\langle \mathcal{W}, \mathcal{R}, \mathcal{V} \rangle$, where $\mathcal{W}$ is a set of possible worlds (the universe), $\mathcal{R}$ is a binary relation on W (called the accessibility relation), $\mathcal{V}$ is a valuation function that assigns a truth value to each symbol $a \in \mathcal{S}$ in each world $w \in \mathcal{W}$, where $\mathcal{S}$ is the signature of propositional symbols. $\langle \mathcal{W}, \mathcal{R} \rangle$ is called a *frame*. Formally, the truth of a formula φ with respect to a given model $\langle \mathcal{W}, \mathcal{R}, \mathcal{V} \rangle$ and a possible world $w \in \mathcal{W}$ is defined as follows:

$$\langle \mathcal{W}, \mathcal{R}, \mathcal{V} \rangle, w \models a \text{ iff } \mathcal{V}(a)(w) \text{ is true}$$
$$\langle \mathcal{W}, \mathcal{R}, \mathcal{V} \rangle, w \models \neg\varphi \text{ iff not } \langle \mathcal{W}, \mathcal{R}, \mathcal{V} \rangle, w \models \varphi$$
$$\langle \mathcal{W}, \mathcal{R}, \mathcal{V} \rangle, w \models \varphi \supset \psi \text{ iff } \langle \mathcal{W}, \mathcal{R}, \mathcal{V} \rangle, w \models \varphi \text{ implies } \langle \mathcal{W}, \mathcal{R}, \mathcal{V} \rangle, w \models \psi$$
$$\langle \mathcal{W}, \mathcal{R}, \mathcal{V} \rangle, w \models \Box\varphi \text{ iff for all } v \text{ with } \mathcal{R}wv \text{ we have } \langle \mathcal{W}, \mathcal{R}, \mathcal{V} \rangle, v \models \varphi$$

Note that in this recursive definition of truth the only parameter altered is the possible world w in the $\Box$-clause, which states that a formula φ is 'necessary' in a world w if and only if (iff) φ is true at all worlds v that are reachable from w via the accessibility relation $\mathcal{R}$. Based on the above definitions a notion of validity can be defined: A formula φ is valid (in so called base modal logic **K**) iff $\langle \mathcal{W}, \mathcal{R}, \mathcal{V} \rangle, w \models \varphi$ for all $\mathcal{W}$, $\mathcal{R}$, $\mathcal{V}$, and $w \in \mathcal{W}$.

Different systems of modal logic beyond base logic **K** can be obtained by requiring (combinations of) so called *frame conditions*. For example, a frame is called (i) reflexive iff Rxx for all $x \in \mathcal{W}$, (ii) symmetric iff Rxy implies Ryx, for all $x, y \in \mathcal{W}$, and (iii) transitive iff Rxy and Ryz implies Rxz, for all $x, y, z \in \mathcal{W}$. Moreover, there are well-known correspondences, known as Sahlqvist correspondences [55], between such semantic conditions and the validity of certain axiom schemata. For example, (i) corresponds to the validity of axiom schema M: $\Box\varphi \supset \varphi$, (ii) to B: $\varphi \supset \Box\Diamond\varphi$ and (iii) to 4: $\Box\varphi \supset \Box\Box\varphi$.

A *proof system* for modal logic **K** is obtained by adding the schematic necessitation rule, stating that 'if φ is a theorem of **K**, then so is $\Box\varphi$' and the distribution axiom schema $\Box(\varphi \supset \psi) \supset (\Box\varphi \supset \Box\psi)$ to the principles of classical propositional logic. The latter can be captured by a simple Hilbert calculus [57,63] consisting of the modes ponens rule, 'if φ and $\varphi \supset \psi$ are theorems (of **K**), then so is ψ', and the three axiom schemata H1: $\varphi \supset (\psi \supset \varphi)$, H2: $(\varphi \supset (\psi \supset \gamma)) \supset ((\varphi \supset \psi) \supset (\varphi \supset \gamma))$ and H3: $(\neg\varphi \supset \neg\psi) \supset (\psi \supset \varphi))$.

Well known modal logics beyond **K** (which works without additional frame conditions) include the logic **S4** with e.g. the frame conditions (i) and (iii) and the logic **S5** with e.g. the frame conditions (i), (ii) and (iii). Thus, by adding the schematic axioms (M)+(4) or (M)+(B)+(4) to the proof system for modal logic **K** above, proof systems for **S4** and **S5** are obtained.

3 Classical Higher-Order Logic (HOL)

The *syntax* of HOL is defined by $s, t := p_\alpha \mid X_\alpha \mid (\lambda X_\alpha s_\beta)_{\alpha\Rightarrow\beta} \mid (s_{\alpha\Rightarrow\beta} t_\alpha)_\beta$, where $\alpha, \beta, o \in \mathcal{T}$ and with $\mathcal{T}$ being a set of *simple types* defined by $\alpha, \beta := o \mid i \mid (\alpha \Rightarrow \beta)$. Type o, called `bool` in Isabelle/HOL, denotes truth values, i individuals, and $\Rightarrow$ is the function type constructor. The p_α in the syntax of HOL are typed constants symbols declared in the sets S_α of a given signature $\mathscr{S} = (S_\alpha)_{\alpha\in\mathcal{T}}$. The X_α are typed variables (distinct from the p_α). Complex HOL terms are constructed from given HOL terms via λ-abstraction $(\lambda X_\alpha s_\beta)_{\alpha\Rightarrow\beta}$ and function application $(s_{\alpha\Rightarrow\beta} t_\alpha)_\beta$. HOL is thus a logic of terms defined on top of the simply typed λ-calculus, and terms of type o are called *formulas*. The type of each term is given as a subscript and may be omitted if obvious in context. It is assumed that signature $\mathscr{S}$ contains the following *primitive logical connectives*: $\neg_{o\Rightarrow o}$, $\vee_{o\Rightarrow o\Rightarrow o}$, $=_{\alpha\Rightarrow\alpha\Rightarrow\alpha}$ (short: $=^\alpha$) and $\Pi_{(\alpha\Rightarrow o)\Rightarrow o}$ (short: Π^α). Further logical connectives or shorthand notations can be introduced as usual; e.g. $\longrightarrow_{o\Rightarrow o\Rightarrow o} := \lambda X_o \lambda Y_o (\neg X \vee Y)$ and $\forall X_\alpha\, \varphi_o := \Pi^\alpha(\lambda X_\alpha\, \varphi)$.

The definition of a *semantics* for HOL starts with the notion of a *frame* $\mathcal{D}$, a collection $\{\mathcal{D}_\alpha\}_{\alpha\in T}$ of nonempty sets $\mathcal{D}_\alpha$, such that $\mathcal{D}_o = \{T, F\}$ (for the truth values true and false). $\mathcal{D}_i$ is chosen freely and $\mathcal{D}_{\alpha\Rightarrow\beta}$ are collections of functions mapping $\mathcal{D}_\alpha$ into $\mathcal{D}_\beta$. A *model* for HOL is a tuple $\mathcal{M} = \langle\mathcal{D}, I\rangle$, where $\mathcal{D}$ is a frame, and I is a family of typed interpretation functions mapping constant symbols $p_\alpha \in C_\alpha$ to appropriate elements of $\mathcal{D}_\alpha$, called the *denotation* of p_α. The logical connectives $\neg, \vee, \Pi$ and $=$ are given their expected standard denotations, for example, $I(\neg)$ is such that $I(\neg)(T) = F$ and $I(\neg)(F) = T$, and $I(\Pi^\alpha)$ is such that for all $s \in \mathcal{D}_{\alpha\Rightarrow o}$ we have $I(\Pi^\alpha)(s) = T$ iff $s(a) = T$ for all $a \in \mathcal{D}_\alpha$.

A *variable assignment* g maps variables X_α to elements in $\mathcal{D}_\alpha$, and $g[d/W]$ denotes the g' identical to g, except for variable W, which is now mapped to d.

The *denotation* $[\![s_\alpha]\!]^{M,g}$ of an HOL term s_α on a model $\mathcal{M} = \langle\mathcal{D}, I\rangle$ under assignment g is an element $d \in \mathcal{D}_\alpha$ defined by $[\![p_\alpha]\!]^{\mathcal{M},g} = I(p_\alpha)$, $[\![X_\alpha]\!]^{\mathcal{M},g} = g(X_\alpha)$, $[\![(s_{\alpha\Rightarrow\beta} t_\alpha)_\beta]\!]^{\mathcal{M},g} = [\![s_{\alpha\Rightarrow\beta}]\!]^{\mathcal{M},g}([\![t_\alpha]\!]^{\mathcal{M},g})$, and $[\![(\lambda X_\alpha s_\beta)_{\alpha\Rightarrow\beta}]\!]^{\mathcal{M},g} =$ the $f : \mathcal{D}_\alpha \longrightarrow \mathcal{D}_\beta$ s.t. $\forall d \in \mathcal{D}_\alpha : f(d) = [\![s_\beta]\!]^{\mathcal{M},g[d/X_\alpha]}$. Note that from the given definitions it e.g. follows $[\![\forall X_\alpha \varphi_o]\!]^{\mathcal{M},g} = T$ iff$[\![\varphi_o]\!]^{\mathcal{M},g[d/X_\alpha]} = T$ for all $d \in \mathcal{D}_\alpha$.

In a *standard model* a domain $\mathcal{D}_{\alpha\Rightarrow\beta}$ is defined as the set of all total functions from $\mathcal{D}_\alpha$ to $\mathcal{D}_\beta$: $\mathcal{D}_{\alpha\Rightarrow\beta} = \{f \mid f : \mathcal{D}_\alpha \Rightarrow \mathcal{D}_\beta\}$. In a *Henkin model* (or general model) [2,39] function spaces are not necessarily required to be the full set of functions: $\mathcal{D}_{\alpha\Rightarrow\beta} \subseteq \{f \mid f : \mathcal{D}_\alpha \Rightarrow \mathcal{D}_\beta\}$. However, it is required that every term still denotes.

s_o is *valid in* $\mathcal{M}$ *under assignment* g, denoted as $\mathcal{M}, g \models^{\mathtt{HOL}} s_o$, iff $[\![s_o]\!]^{\mathcal{M},g} = T$. s_o is *valid in* $\mathcal{M}$, denoted as $\mathcal{M} \models^{\mathtt{HOL}} s_o$, iff $\mathcal{M}, g \models^{\mathtt{HOL}} s_o$ for all assignments g, and s_o is *valid*, denoted as $\models^{\mathtt{HOL}} s_o$, iff s_o is valid in all Henkin models $\mathcal{M}$.

Each standard model is obviously also a Henkin model. Consequently, if $\models^{\mathtt{HOL}} s_o$, then s_o is also valid in all standard models.

Due to Gödel [36], sound and complete mechanizations of HOL with standard semantics cannot be achieved. For HOL with Henkin semantics, however, sound and complete calculi exist; see e.g. [7,9]. Relevant for this paper is that Isabelle/HOL is also sound and complete for HOL, and that HOL as presented is sufficiently well suited as a metalogic for the work presented in this paper.

4 Deep Embedding of PML in HOL

This section presents a deep embedding of PML in HOL. Both the PML language and its semantics are formalized very closely following the definitions given in Sect. 2. This formalization, and all others presented in this paper, are based on some uniformly assumed conventions, resp. preliminaries. These preliminaries are provided in a file `PMLinHOL_preliminaries.thy`, see Fig. 1. Useful comments are provided; they are encapsulated in orange delimiters $-<\ >$.

Relevant at this point is that a type $\mathcal{S}$ is introduced to represent the signature $\mathcal{S}$ of PML, i.e. a (finite or infinite) set of propositional logic symbols; type `w` is the type of possible worlds, $\mathcal{W} := \mathtt{w} \Rightarrow \mathtt{bool}$ is the predicate type of possible worlds (we regard predicates of this type as characteristic functions for the associated sets of possible worlds), $\mathcal{R} := \mathtt{w} \Rightarrow \mathtt{w} \Rightarrow \mathtt{bool}$ is the type of accessibility relations between possible worlds, and $\mathcal{V} := \mathcal{S} \Rightarrow \mathtt{w} \Rightarrow \mathtt{bool}$ is the type of evaluation functions (these definitions are shown in lines 4–9). Well known predicates and functions on relations are introduced (in lines 11–19), and $\forall w{:}W.\, \varphi$ (see lines 21–22) is a W-predicate guarded quantifier that unfolds into $\forall w.\, W\, w \longrightarrow \varphi$, where W is of type $\mathcal{W}$. An important remark concerns the sharing of, e.g., the signature type $\mathcal{S}$ between all embeddings introduced in this paper. This sharing is essential for enabling the faithfulness proofs between the embeddings as presented in Sect. 7.

The deep embedding of PML in HOL is defined in file `PMLinHOL_deep.thy` and presented at top of Fig. 2. After importing `PMLinHOL_preliminaries.thy`, this file starts out with defining an abstract datatype[2] introducing the inductively defined logic language PML, which introduces atomic formulas a^d (for $a \in \mathcal{S}$), negated formulas $\neg^d\varphi$, implication formulas $\varphi \supset^d \psi$, and boxed formulas $\Box^d\varphi$ (see line 4). The superscript ^{d} is used to mark all deeply embedded connectives so that they can be properly distinguished from their counterparts defined in the following sections. In these sections, the alternative superscripts ^{s} (maximal shallow) and ^{m} (minimal shallow) are used accordingly.

In accordance with Sect. 2 the further logical connectives $\vee^d$, $\wedge^d$, $\Diamond^d$, $\top^d$, and $\bot^d$ are introduced as defined terms (lines 6–10).[3] Then the primitive recursive definition of truth in a world w for a given model $\langle W, R, V\rangle$, termed `RelativeTruthD` and noted as $\langle W, R, V\rangle, w \models^d \varphi$, is given (lines 12–16). This definition follows one to one, even in presentation style, the definition introduced in Sect. 2. Based on this, the validity $\models^d \varphi$ of a deeply embedded formula φ is defined as relative truth w.r.t. all sets of worlds W, accessibility relations R, valuation functions V, and worlds $w \in W$ (line 18). Finally, in order to support a convenient, simultaneous unfolding of the introduced definitions, a bag `DefD` is defined (in lines 20–21), which bundles them and adds them also to the simplifier `simp` of Isabelle/HOL.

---

[2] Such a datatype declaration corresponds to, and unfolds into, a rather large set of axioms in HOL that could be postulated instead. Using the Isabelle/HOL command `print_theorems`, this set can be inspected by the user.

[3] Abbreviations could be used instead. They are always unfolded implicitly, while definition unfolding is an explicit operation, leading to more options for control. In

```
theory PMLinHOL_preliminaries  imports Main                    (* Christoph Benzmüller, 2025 *)
begin
—‹Type declarations common for both the deep and shallow embedding›
 typedecl w —‹Type for possible worlds›
 typedecl 𝒮 —‹Type for propositional constant symbols›
 consts p::𝒮 q::𝒮 —‹Some propositional constant symbols›
 type_synonym 𝒲 = "w⇒bool"  —‹Type for sets of possible worlds›
 type_synonym ℛ = "w⇒w⇒bool"  —‹Type for accessibility relations›
 type_synonym 𝒱  = "𝒮⇒w⇒bool"  —‹Type for valuation functions›
—‹Some useful predicates for accessibility relations›
 abbreviation(input) "reflexive      ≡ λR::ℛ. ∀x. R x x"
 abbreviation(input) "symmetric      ≡ λR::ℛ. ∀x y. R x y ⟶ R y x"
 abbreviation(input) "transitive     ≡ λR::ℛ. ∀x y z. (R x y ∧ R y z)  ⟶ R x z"
 abbreviation(input) "equivrel       ≡ λR::ℛ. reflexive R ∧ symmetric R ∧ transitive R"
 abbreviation(input) "irreflexive    ≡ λR::ℛ. ∀x. ¬R x x"
 abbreviation(input) "euclidean      ≡ λR::ℛ. ∀x y z. R x y ∧ R x z ⟶ R y z"
 abbreviation(input) "wellfounded    ≡ λR::ℛ. ∀P::𝒲. (∀x. (∀y. R y x ⟶ P y) ⟶ P x) ⟶  (∀x. P x)"
 abbreviation(input) "converserel    ≡ λR::ℛ. λy. λx. R x y"
 abbreviation(input) "conversewf     ≡ λR::ℛ. wellfounded (converserel R)"
—‹Bounded universal quantifier: ‹∀x:W. φ› stands for ‹∀x. W x ⟶ φ x››
 abbreviation(input) "BAll W φ ≡ ∀x::w. W x ⟶ φ x" syntax "BAll"::"pttrn⇒𝒲⇒bool⇒bool" ("(3∀(_/:_)./_)" [0,0,10]10)
 translations "∀x:W. φ" ⇌ "CONST BAll W (λx. φ)"
—‹Backward implication; useful to have› abbreviation(input) Bimp (infixr "⟵" 50) where "φ ⟵ ψ ≡ ψ ⟶ φ"
—‹Further settings› declare[[syntax_ambiguity_warning=false]] nitpick_params[user_axioms,expect=genuine]
end
```

Fig. 1. Preliminaries.

5 Maximal Shallow Embedding of PML in HOL

The shallow embedding of PML in HOL presented in the middle part of Fig. 2, which is formalized in file `PMLinHOL_shallow.thy`, is a *maximal* (heavyweight) shallow embedding in the following sense: PML formulas φ are associated here with HOL predicate terms φ_σ of type $\sigma := \mathcal{W} \Rightarrow \mathcal{R} \Rightarrow \mathcal{V} \Rightarrow \mathtt{w} \Rightarrow \mathtt{bool}$ (see line 4), thus explicitly encoding the entire semantic dependencies of a PML formula φ_σ on a set of worlds W, an accessibility relation R, a valuation function V and a world w. Remember, that $\mathcal{W}$, $\mathcal{R}$, $\mathcal{V}$, and $\mathtt{w}$ have been uniformly declared for all embeddings presented in this paper in the imported preliminaries file.

Exploiting λ-abstraction and the logical connectives $\neg$ and $\longrightarrow$ from metalogic HOL, the definitions of deeply embedded negation $\neg^s$ and implication $\supset^s$ (in lines 6–8), recursively pass on all the dependencies as mentioned:[4] $\neg^s\varphi := \lambda W R V w. \neg(\varphi W R V w)$ and $\varphi \supset^s \psi := \lambda W R V w. (\varphi W R V w) \longrightarrow (\psi W R V w)$. Atoms a^s, for $a \in \mathcal{S}$, are evaluated (in line 5) using the explicitly maintained valuation function V, that is, $a^s := \lambda W R V w. V a w$. The only case where parts of the recursively passed on dependencies are actually modified is (in line 8) for $\Box^s\varphi$, since here the world in which φ is recursively evaluated may change with the transition, via the accessibility relation R, to world v: $\Box^s\varphi := \lambda W R V w. \forall v.\ R w v \longrightarrow (\varphi W R V v)$. The definition of the other logical connectives $\vee^s$, $\wedge^s$, $\Diamond^s$, $\top^s$ and $\bot^s$ (in lines 10–14) is analogous to the deep embedding and as given in Sect. 3.

---

any case, readers new to Isabelle/HOL can simply focus on the indented definition equations here (and in other figures), at least at first reading.

[4] Dot-notation is used, whereby the scope opened by . is reaching as far to the right as consistent with the formula structure. The term $\lambda W R V w. \neg(\varphi W R V w)$ thus corresponds to $\lambda W \lambda R \lambda V \lambda w(\neg(\varphi W R V w))$.

```
theory PMLinHOL_deep imports PMLinHOL_preliminaries                (* Christoph Benzmüller, 2025 *)
begin
—‹Deep embedding (of propositional modal logic in HOL)›
 datatype PML = AtmD 𝒮 ("_^d") | NotD PML ("¬^d") | ImpD PML PML (infixr "⊃^d" 93) | BoxD PML ("□^d")
—‹Further logical connectives as definitions›
 definition OrD    (infixr "∨^d" 92)  where   "φ∨^dψ ≡ ¬^dφ ⊃^d ψ"
 definition AndD   (infixr "∧^d" 95)  where   "φ∧^dψ ≡ ¬^d(φ ⊃^d ¬^dψ)"
 definition DiaD   ("◇^d_")           where   "◇^dφ ≡ ¬^d(□^d(¬^dφ)) "
 definition TopD   ("⊤^d")            where   "⊤^d ≡ p^d ⊃^d p^d"
 definition BotD   ("⊥^d")            where   "⊥^d ≡ ¬^d ⊤^d"
—‹Definition of truth of a formula relative to a model ‹⟨W,R,V⟩› and a possible world w›
 primrec RelativeTruthD :: "𝒲⇒ℛ⇒𝒱 ⇒w⇒PML⇒bool" ("⟨_,_,_⟩,_ ⊨^d _") where
     "⟨W,R,V⟩, w ⊨^d a^d        = (V a w)"
   | "⟨W,R,V⟩, w ⊨^d ¬^dφ       = (¬ ⟨W,R,V⟩, w ⊨^d φ)"
   | "⟨W,R,V⟩, w ⊨^d φ ⊃^d ψ    = (⟨W,R,V⟩, w ⊨^d φ ⟶ ⟨W,R,V⟩, w ⊨^d ψ)"
   | "⟨W,R,V⟩, w ⊨^d □^dφ       = (∀v:W. R w v ⟶ ⟨W,R,V⟩, v ⊨^d φ)"
—‹Definition of validity›
 definition ValD ("⊨^d _") where "(⊨^d φ) ≡ (∀W R V. ∀w:W. ⟨W,R,V⟩,w ⊨^d φ)"
—‹Collection of definitions in a bag called DefD›
 named_theorems DefD declare OrD_def[DefD,simp] AndD_def[DefD,simp] DiaD_def[DefD,simp]
  TopD_def[DefD,simp] BotD_def[DefD,simp] RelativeTruthD_def[DefD,simp] ValD_def[DefD,simp]
end
```

```
theory PMLinHOL_shallow imports PMLinHOL_preliminaries                (* Christoph Benzmüller, 2025 *)
begin
—‹Shallow embedding (of propositional modal logic in HOL)›
 type_synonym σ = "𝒲⇒ℛ⇒𝒱⇒w⇒bool"
 definition AtmS::"𝒮⇒σ"      ("_^s")              where   "a^s ≡ λW R V w. V a w"
 definition NegS::"σ⇒σ"      ("¬^s")              where   "¬^s φ ≡ λW R V w. ¬(φ W R V w)"
 definition ImpS::"σ⇒σ⇒σ"   (infixr "⊃^s" 93)    where   "φ ⊃^s ψ ≡ λW R V w. (φ W R V w) ⟶ (ψ W R V w)"
 definition BoxS::"σ⇒σ"      ("□^s")              where   "□^s φ ≡ λW R V w. ∀v:W. R w v ⟶ (φ W R V v)"
—‹Further logical connectives as definitions›
 definition OrS     (infixr "∨^s" 92)  where   "φ ∨^s ψ ≡ ¬^sφ ⊃^s ψ"
 definition AndS    (infixr "∧^s" 95)  where   "φ ∧^s ψ ≡ ¬^s(φ ⊃^s ¬^sψ)"
 definition DiaS    ("◇^s")            where   "◇^sφ ≡ ¬^s (□^s (¬^sφ)) "
 definition TopS    ("⊤^s")            where   "⊤^s ≡ p^s ⊃^s p^s"
 definition BotS    ("⊥^s")            where   "⊥^s ≡ ¬^s ⊤^s"
—‹Definition of truth of a formula relative to a model ‹⟨W,R,V⟩› and a possible world w›
 definition RelativeTruthS :: "𝒲⇒ℛ⇒𝒱 ⇒w⇒σ⇒bool" ("⟨_,_,_⟩,_ ⊨^s _") where "⟨W,R,V⟩,w ⊨^s φ ≡ φ W R V w"
—‹Definition of validity›
 definition ValS ("⊨^s _") where "⊨^s φ ≡ ∀W R V. ∀w:W. ⟨W,R,V⟩,w ⊨^s φ"
—‹Collection of definitions in a bag called DefS›
 named_theorems DefS declare AtmS_def[DefS,simp] NegS_def[DefS,simp] ImpS_def[DefS,simp]
  BoxS_def[DefS,simp] OrS_def[DefS,simp] AndS_def[DefS,simp] DiaS_def[DefS,simp] TopS_def[DefS,simp]
  BotS_def[DefS,simp] RelativeTruthS_def[DefS,simp] ValS_def[DefS,simp]
end
```

```
theory PMLinHOL_shallow_minimal imports PMLinHOL_preliminaries                (* Christoph Benzmüller, 2025 *)
begin
—‹The acessibility relation R and the valuation function V are introduced as constants at the meta-level HOL›
 consts R::ℛ V::𝒱
—‹Shallow embedding (of propositional modal logic in HOL)›
 type_synonym σ = "w⇒bool"
 definition AtmM::"𝒮⇒σ"      ("_^m")              where   "a^m ≡ λw. V a w"
 definition NegM::"σ⇒σ"      ("¬^m")              where   "¬^m φ ≡ λw.  ¬φ w"
 definition ImpM::"σ⇒σ⇒σ"   (infixr "⊃^m" 93)    where   "φ ⊃^m ψ ≡ λw. φ w ⟶ ψ w"
 definition BoxM::"σ⇒σ"      ("□^m")              where   "□^m φ ≡ λw. ∀v. R w v ⟶ φ v"
—‹Further logical connectives as definitions›
 definition OrM     (infixr "∨^m" 92)  where   "φ ∨^m ψ ≡ ¬^mφ ⊃^m ψ"
 definition AndM    (infixr "∧^m" 95)  where   "φ ∧^m ψ ≡ ¬^m(φ ⊃^m ¬^mψ)"
 definition DiaM    ("◇^m_")           where   "◇^mφ ≡ ¬^m (□^m (¬^mφ)) "
 definition TopM    ("⊤^m")            where   "⊤^m ≡ p^m ⊃^m p^m"
 definition BotM    ("⊥^m")            where   "⊥^m ≡ ¬^m ⊤^m"
—‹Definition of truth of a formula relative to a model ‹⟨W,R,V⟩› and a possible world w›
 definition RelativeTruthM :: "w⇒σ⇒bool" ("_ ⊨^m _") where "w ⊨^m φ ≡ φ w"
—‹Definition of validity›
 definition ValM ("⊨^m _") where "⊨^m φ  ≡ ∀w::w. w ⊨^m φ"
—‹Collection of definitions in a bag called DefM›
 named_theorems DefM declare AtmM_def[DefM,simp] NegM_def[DefM,simp] ImpM_def[DefM,simp]
  BoxM_def[DefM,simp] OrM_def[DefM,simp] AndM_def[DefM,simp] DiaM_def[DefM,simp] TopM_def[DefM,simp]
  BotM_def[DefM,simp] RelativeTruthM_def[DefM,simp] ValM_def[DefM,simp]
end
```

Fig. 2. PML in HOL: deep (top), maximal shallow (mid), and minimal shallow (bot).

Truth in a world w for a given model $\langle W, R, V\rangle$, called `RelativeTruthS` and noted as $\langle W, R, V\rangle, w \models^s \varphi$, is then defined (see line 16) as the application of φ to W, R, V and w. Analogous to the deep embedding from above, validity $\models^s \varphi$ of an embedded formula φ is defined as relative truth w.r.t. all sets of worlds W, accessibility relations R, valuation functions V, and worlds $w \in W$ (line 18). Also analogous to above, a bag `DefS` is defined (lines 20–22), which conveniently bundles all the definitions given in this file and adds them to the simplifier. Note that not a single axiom is being introduced in this maximal shallow embedding, with the effect, that PML is being characterized here as a proper, albeit quite heavyweight, fragment of the language of HOL.

6 Minimal Shallow Embedding of PML in HOL

The maximal shallow embedding presented in Sect. 5 explicitly maintains more dependencies than seemingly necessary, since the set of worlds W, the accessibility relation R, and the valuation function V are never modified in any of the given definitions, but simply passed on. Therefore, it makes sense to treat these static dependencies as parameters in the metalogic HOL. This is the core idea of the *minimal* (lightweight) shallow embedding of PML in HOL as shown at the bottom of Fig. 2 and formalized in file `PMLinHOL_shallow_minimal.thy`.

To implement this idea, W is now implicitly identified with type `w` of HOL at the metalevel, and the constant symbols `R` and `V` are introduced in metalogic HOL to represent the semantic notions R and V of PML (see line 4). Most importantly, the modified HOL type $\sigma := \mathtt{w} \Rightarrow \mathtt{bool}$ is now taken as the type of the embedded formulas φ_σ, indicating that PML formulas in this minimal embedding now depend only on possible worlds.[5] Hence, instead of maintaining dependencies on W, R, V, and w, the definitions of the logical connectives a^m, $\neg^m$, $\supset^m$, and $\Box^m$ now only explicitly maintain a dependency on worlds w (lines 7–10). Their definitions are thus, where `V` and `R` are the above-mentioned constant symbols in metalogic HOL: $a^s := \lambda w.\, \mathtt{V}\, a\, w$, $\neg^m\varphi := \lambda w.\, \neg(\varphi\, w)$ and $\varphi \supset^m \psi := \lambda w.\, \varphi\, w \longrightarrow \psi\, w$, and $\Box^m\varphi := \lambda w.\, \forall v.\, \mathtt{R}\, w\, v \longrightarrow \varphi\, v$. The definition of the other logical connectives $\vee^m$, $\wedge^m$, $\Diamond^m$, $\top^m$, and $\bot^m$ (in lines 12–16) is analogous to before. Truth in a world w, for a given model $\langle W, R, V\rangle$ maintained at the meta-level HOL, called `RelativeTruthM` and noted as $w \models^m \varphi$, is then defined (see line 18) as the application of the embedded formula φ to w. Consequently, validity $\models^m \varphi$ of an embedded formula φ is defined as relative truth w.r.t. to all worlds w (line 20). The bag `DefM` defined (in lines 22–24) is analogous to `DefD` and `DefS` from before. Again, not a single axiom is introduced. So PML is once again characterized as a proper fragment of HOL, but now more lightweight.

[5] Note that this is also the core idea of the well-known standard translation of PML into first-order logic [19], which, in fact, is implemented here by exploiting λ-conversion and compositionality directly in the metalogical HOL without the need for explicit recursive definitions.

7 Faithfulness Automated

The deep embedding presented in Sect. 4 and the maximal and minimal shallow embeddings presented in Sect. 5 and Sect. 6 have been carefully designed to allow for automated proofs of mutual faithfulness within the metalogic HOL. A relevant aspect is the sharing of the signature $\mathcal{S}$ of propositional symbols between all embeddings. The automated faithfulness proofs are shown in Fig. 3.

```
1  theory PMLinHOL_faithfulness imports PMLinHOL_deep PMLinHOL_shallow PMLinHOL_shallow_minimal (* C.B., 2025 *)
2  begin
3  —‹Mappings: deep to maximal shallow and deep to minimal shallow›
4   primrec DpToShMax ("⦇_⦈") where "⦇aᵈ⦈ = aˢ" | "⦇¬ᵈ φ⦈ = ¬ˢ ⦇φ⦈" | "⦇φ ⊃ᵈ ψ⦈ = ⦇φ⦈ ⊃ˢ ⦇ψ⦈" | "⦇□ᵈ φ⦈ = □ˢ ⦇φ⦈"
5   primrec DpToShMin ("⟦_⟧") where "⟦aᵈ⟧ = aᵐ" | "⟦¬ᵈ φ⟧ = ¬ᵐ ⟦φ⟧" | "⟦φ ⊃ᵈ ψ⟧ = ⟦φ⟧ ⊃ᵐ ⟦ψ⟧" | "⟦□ᵈ φ⟧ = □ᵐ ⟦φ⟧"
6  —‹Proving faithfulness between deep and maximal shallow›
7   theorem Faithful1a:  "∀W R V. ∀w:W. ⟨W,R,V⟩,w ⊨ᵈ φ ⟷ ⟨W,R,V⟩,w ⊨ˢ ⦇φ⦈"   apply induct by auto
8   theorem Faithful1b:  "⊨ᵈ φ ⟷ ⊨ˢ ⦇φ⦈"                                 using Faithful1a by auto
9  —‹Proving faithfulness between deep and minimal shallow›
10  theorem Faithful2:   "∀w. ⟨(λx::w. True),R,V⟩,w ⊨ᵈ φ ⟷ w ⊨ᵐ ⟦φ⟧"        apply induct by auto
11 —‹Proving faithfulness maximal shallow and minimal shallow›
12  theorem Faithful3:   "∀w. ⟨(λx::w. True),R,V⟩,w ⊨ˢ ⦇φ⦈ ⟷ w ⊨ᵐ ⟦φ⟧"       apply induct by auto
13 —‹Additional check for soundness for the minimal shallow embedding›
14  lemma Sound1: "⊨ᵐ ψ ⟷ (∃φ. ψ=⟦φ⟧ ∧ ⊨ᵈ φ)" by (smt Faithful2 DefM DefD RelativeTruthD.simps ext[of ψ "⟦x⊃ᵈx⟧"])
15  lemma Sound2: "⊨ᵐ ψ ⟷ (∃φ. ψ=⟦φ⟧ ∧ ⊨ᵐ ⟦φ⟧)" using Sound1 by blast
16 end
```

Fig. 3. Automated faithfulness proofs between different embeddings of PML in HOL.

The starting points are the mapping functions $\llparenthesis . \rrparenthesis$ and $[\![.]\!]$ (in lines 4–5), which map deeply embedded formulas to maximally and minimally embedded counterparts, respectively. Using these mappings the following faithfulness statements, which are formulated relative to the deeply embedded proof language PML, are proved automatically by induction (see lines 7–12):

$$\forall WRV.\forall w{:}W.\ \langle W,R,V\rangle, w \models^d \varphi \longleftrightarrow \langle W,R,V\rangle, w \models^s \llparenthesis\varphi\rrparenthesis \qquad (\texttt{Faithful1a})$$

$$\models^d \varphi \longleftrightarrow \models^s \llparenthesis\varphi\rrparenthesis \qquad (\texttt{Faithful1b})$$

$$\forall w.\ \langle(\lambda x_w.\top), \mathtt{R}, \mathtt{V}\rangle, w \models^d \varphi \longleftrightarrow w \models^m [\![\varphi]\!] \qquad (\texttt{Faithful2})$$

$$\forall w.\ \langle(\lambda x_w.\top), \mathtt{R}, \mathtt{V}\rangle, w \models^s \llparenthesis\varphi\rrparenthesis \longleftrightarrow w \models^m [\![\varphi]\!] \qquad (\texttt{Faithful3})$$

Theorems `Faithful1a` and `Faithful1b` are rather obvious; they establish the desired faithfulness correspondence between deeply embedded formulas and their maximally shallow counterparts. Theorems `Faithful2` and `Faithful3`, on the other hand, require some explanation. The former states that if W is taken as $\lambda x_{\mathtt{w}}.\top$, i.e. the universe of possible worlds denoted by type `w` in metalogic HOL, and if R and V are replaced by the metalogical constant symbols `R` and `V` in HOL, denoting accessibility between worlds and evaluation of propositional symbols from $\mathcal{S}$ in worlds, then each deeply embedded formula φ faithfully corresponds to its minimally shallow counterpart $[\![\varphi]\!]$. The latter formulates an analogous correspondence between maximal shallow formulas $\llparenthesis\varphi\rrparenthesis$ and minimal shallow formulas $[\![\varphi]\!]$. Together, these theorems show the intended correspondences between all the introduced embeddings, and they provide a valuable foundation for working with them simultaneously and interchangeably in applications. Moreover, the surjection theorems `Sound1` and `Sound2` can be automated by `sledgehammer` for the minimal shallow embedding, but not yet for the maximal one.

8 Experiments

The possibilities that the linked embeddings offer, e.g., for logic education, are illustrated with some experiments. The experiments performed also test the soundness of our embeddings, and assess proof automation and counterexample finding for them with `sledgehammer` and `nitpick`. The embedding that has performed best in this regard is the minimal shallow embedding. This is why file `PMLinHOL_shallow_minimal_tests.thy`, see Fig. 4, is presented here.[6]

```
1  theory PMLinHOL_shallow_minimal_tests imports PMLinHOL_shallow_minimal        (* Christoph Benzmüller, 2025 *)
2  begin
3  —‹Hilbert calculus: proving that the schematic axioms and rules are implied by the embedding›
4   lemma H1: "⊨^m φ ⊃^m (ψ ⊃^m φ)" by auto
5   lemma H2: "⊨^m (φ ⊃^m (ψ ⊃^m γ)) ⊃^m ((φ ⊃^m ψ) ⊃^m (φ ⊃^m γ)) " by auto
6   lemma H3: "⊨^m (¬^mφ ⊃^m ¬^mψ) ⊃^m (ψ ⊃^m φ)" by auto
7   lemma MP: "⊨^m φ ⟹ ⊨^m (φ ⊃^m ψ) ⟹ ⊨^m ψ" by auto
8  —‹Reasoning with the Hilbert calculus: interactive and fully automated›
9   lemma HCderived1: "⊨^m (φ ⊃^m φ)" —‹sledgehammer(H1 H2 H3 MP) returns: by (metis H1 H2 MP)›
10   proof -  have 1: "⊨^m φ ⊃^m ((ψ ⊃^m φ) ⊃^m φ)" using H1 by auto
11            have 2: "⊨^m (φ ⊃^m ((ψ ⊃^m φ) ⊃^m φ)) ⊃^m ((φ ⊃^m (ψ ⊃^m φ)) ⊃^m (φ ⊃^m φ))" using H2 by auto
12            have 3: "⊨^m (φ ⊃^m (ψ ⊃^m φ)) ⊃^m (φ ⊃^m φ)" using 1 2 MP by meson
13            have 4: "⊨^m φ ⊃^m (ψ ⊃^m φ)" using H1 by auto
14            thus ?thesis using 3 4 MP by meson qed
15  lemma HCderived2: "⊨^m φ ⊃^m (¬^mφ ⊃^m ψ) " by (metis H1 H2 H3 MP)
16  lemma HCderived3: "⊨^m (¬^mφ ⊃^m φ) ⊃^m φ" by (metis H1 H2 H3 MP)
17  lemma HCderived4: "⊨^m (φ ⊃^m ψ) ⊃^m (¬^mψ ⊃^m ¬^mφ) " by auto
18 —‹Modal logic: the schematic necessitation rule and distribution axiom are implied›
19  lemma Nec: "⊨^m φ ⟹ ⊨^m □^mφ" by (smt DefM)
20  lemma Dist:  "⊨^m □^m(φ ⊃^m ψ) ⊃^m (□^mφ ⊃^m □^mψ) " by auto
21 —‹Correspondence theory: correct statements›
22  lemma cM:  "reflexive R ⟷ (∀φ. ⊨^m □^mφ ⊃^m φ)" by auto
23  lemma cBa: "symmetric R ⟶ (∀φ. ⊨^m φ ⊃^m □^m◇^mφ)" by auto
24  lemma cBb: "symmetric R ⟵ (∀φ. ⊨^m φ ⊃^m □^m◇^mφ)" by (metis DefM)
25  lemma c4a: "transitive R ⟶ (∀φ. ⊨^m □^mφ ⊃^m □^m(□^mφ))" by (smt DefM)
26  lemma c4b: "transitive R ⟵ (∀φ. ⊨^m □^mφ ⊃^m □^m(□^mφ))" by auto
27 —‹Correspondence theory: incorrect statements›
28  lemma "reflexive R ⟶ (∀φ. ⊨^m □^mφ ⊃^m □^m(□^mφ))" nitpick[card w=3,show_all] oops —‹nitpick: Counterexample›
29 —‹Simple, incorrect validity statements›
30  lemma "⊨^m φ ⊃^m □^mφ" nitpick[card w=2, card 𝒮= 1] oops —‹nitpick: Counterexample: modal collapse not implied›
31  lemma "⊨^m □^m( □^mφ ⊃^m  □^mψ) ∨^m □^m( □^mψ ⊃^m  □^mφ)" nitpick[card w=3] oops —‹nitpick: Counterexample›
32  lemma "⊨^m (◇^m(□^m φ)) ⊃^m  □^m(◇^m φ)" nitpick[card w=2] oops —‹nitpick: Counterexample›
33 —‹Implied axiom schemata in S5›
34  lemma KB: "symmetric R ⟶ (∀φ ψ.  ⊨^m (◇^m(□^mφ)) ⊃^m  □^m(◇^mφ))" by auto
35  lemma K4B: "symmetric R ∧ transitive R ⟶ (∀φ ψ. ⊨^m □^m( □^mφ ⊃^m  □^mψ) ∨^m □^m( □^mψ ⊃^m  □^mφ))" by (smt DefM)
36 end
```

Fig. 4. Experiments: Hilbert system and Sahlqvist correspondences.

Derived Hilbert Calculus. The first experiments (see lines 4–7) confirm that the schematic axioms `H1-H3` and the modus ponens rule `MP` of the propositional

[6] Corresponding files for the deep and the maximal shallow embeddings are shown in the appendix of [5]. The Isabelle/HOL sources are available at http://logikey.org/tree/master/CoursesAndTutorials/2025-CADE-DeepShallow and also in [15].

Hilbert calculus from Sect. 2 are implied by the minimal shallow embedding (local versions of `H1-H3` and `MP` rule are also implied; this is not shown here). The `auto` tactic, and with it, the simplifier `simp` are used, which has access to the definitions in bundle `DefM`. The φ, ψ and γ are schematic variables of type σ in the metalogic HOL. The proofs were originally found by calling `sledgehammer`.

Hilbert Style Proofs Automated and Interactive. The next experiment (in lines 9–14) demonstrates automated and interactive reasoning using the schematic axioms and rules of the Hilbert calculus introduced earlier. It is shown that the formula schema $\varphi \supset^m \varphi$ is derivable in the given Hilbert calculus. By preventing access to the definitions in the bag `DefM`, e.g. with the command `sledgehammer(H1 H2 H3 MP)`, the automated theorem provers orchestrated by `sledgehammer` can be forced to search for proofs in the given Hilbert calculus only, and they succeed here. They find out that only `H1` and `H2` and `MP` are needed to obtain the result. In the given situation, the reconstruction of a proof from `H1` and `H2` and `MP` is then possible with Isabelle's trusted `metis` tool. For educational purposes it is relevant that proofs from the literature can be easily mapped one to one to proofs in our setting. This is illustrated here with an interactive derivation (in lines 10–14) that is following a proof from a Wikipedia entry [63] on Hilbert systems. Further derived axiom schemata are proved automatically at the level of the Hilbert calculus (in lines 15–16). If such attempts fail (as was initially the case in line 17), then either interactive proof is needed or, as is demonstrated here with the call of `auto`, the unfolding of the definitions of the shallow embedding in metalogic HOL (within `auto`) may in fact help to still find a proof automatically. Depending on prior knowledge and teaching objectives, students can be asked to solely provide interactive proofs in such exercises rather than using automation tools. It is also important to note that Isabelle/HOL's proof tactics support, and in particular the Eisbach package, can be used to further enhance the automation of proofs at the level of embedded logic.[7]

Correspondence Theory Automated. Modal logic textbooks typically include exercises on the well known Sahlqvist correspondences [55] (see lines 22–26). Using the definitions in bag `DefM`, such correspondences are here automated in Isabelle/HOL. More exhaustive experiments on such (and similar) correspondences have been reported in prior work [3,8,43,51].

Disproving Correspondences. Even more interesting than automatically proving the Sahlqvist correspondences is disproving falsely assumed correspondences. For example, when `nitpick` is called on the false conjecture, that in PML models with reflexive accessibility relations R the axiom schema $\Box^m\varphi \supset^m \Box^m\Box^m\varphi$ is implied (see line 28), the counterexample shown in Fig. 5 is reported back.

As prior work demonstrates, see e.g. [8,14,51], `nitpick` often provides intuitive and sometimes even surprising counterexamples when used in conjunction with shallow embeddings.[8] This is not only useful for teaching logic, but can

[7] The Eisbach package was e.g. used in [41,42] to define and automate proof methods for a non-trivial shallow embedding of abstract object theory AOT [64] in HOL.

[8] Prior work [8,43] also illustrates how counterexamples reported by `nitpick` can be systematically converted into statements that verifiably disprove the false conjectures; the method presented there could indeed be fully automated.

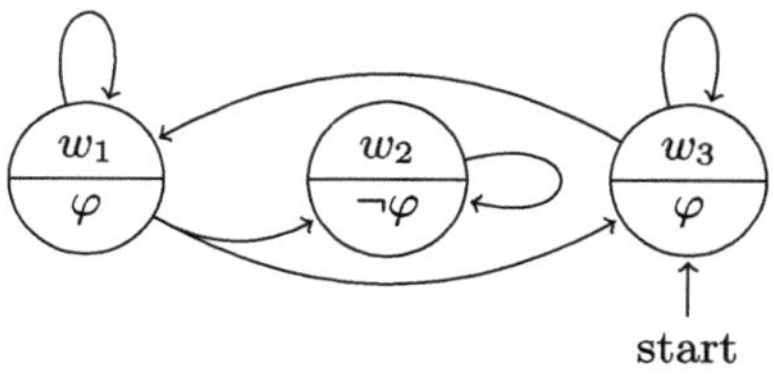


```
Nitpick found a counterexample for card w = 3:
 Skolem constants:
  ??.BoxM.v = w_1
  ??.BoxM.v = w_2
  ??.ValM.w = w_3
  φ = (λx. _)(w_1 := True, w_2 := False, w_3 := True)
 Constant:
  R =
   (λx. _)
   (w_1 := (λx. _)(w_1 := True, w_2 := True, w_3 := True),
    w_2 := (λx. _)(w_1 := False, w_2 := True, w_3 := False),
    w_3 := (λx. _)(w_1 := True, w_2 := False, w_3 := True))
```

Fig. 5. Counterexample reported by `nitpick` in line 28 of Fig. 4

also be useful for research studies, see e.g. [14]. However, some non-classical logics have only infinite models, and then the finite model finder `nitpick` is no longer applicable; this is e.g. the case for Lorini's T-STIT logic [46], which was embedded in HOL by Meder [47]. Developing infinite model finding tools and integrating them into proof assistants such as Isabelle/HOL is thus an important research challenge. So too is the automated, domain-specific provision of intuitive counterexample diagrams like the one on the left in Fig. 5.

For further false conjectures (in lines 30–32 of Fig. 4), including the modal collapse formula $\varphi \supset^m \Box^m \varphi$, intuitive counterexamples are generated by `nitpick`. Finally, examples of simple modal theorems (in lines 34–35), such as the KB theorem $\Diamond^m \Box^m \varphi \supset^m \Box^m \Diamond^m \varphi$, are automated efficiently using `smt` solvers in combination with definition unfolding in metalogic HOL.

Reasoning at Object Level. Figure 6 presents further experiments. After proving the schematic modal principle $K\Diamond$ (in line 4) an object level proof example [56, Ex. 6.10] is studied (in lines 6–14): $\Box^m p^m \supset^m (\Diamond^m q^m \supset^m \Diamond^m (p^m \wedge^m q^m))$, where p and q are propositional symbols from the PML signature $\mathcal{S}$. This statement is again effectively automated via definition unfolding at the metalevel HOL (line 6), while the presented interactive proof (in lines 8–14) uses the propositional Hilbert calculus from before in combination with the modal rule of necessitation, the distribution axiom of base logic **K** and the newly introduced $K\Diamond$-principle.

```
 1 theory PMLinHOL_shallow_minimal_further_tests imports PMLinHOL_shallow_minimal_tests        (* C.B., 2025 *)
 2 begin
 3 —‹Implied modal principle›
 4  lemma K_Dia: "⊨^m (□^m(φ ⊃^m ψ)) ⊃^m ((◇^mφ) ⊃^m ◇^mψ)"    by auto
 5 —‹Example 6.10 of Sider (2009) Logic for Philosophy›
 6  lemma T1a: "⊨^m □^mp^m ⊃^m ((◇^mq^m) ⊃^m ◇^m (p^m ∧^m q^m))" by auto —‹fast automation in meta-logic HOL›
 7  lemma T1b: "⊨^m □^mp^m ⊃^m ((◇^mq^m) ⊃^m ◇^m (p^m ∧^m q^m))"
 8   proof -                                         —‹alternative interactive proof in modal object logic K›
 9    have 1: "⊨^m p^m ⊃^m (q^m ⊃^m (p^m ∧^m q^m))"          unfolding AndM_def using H1 H2 H3 MP by metis
10    have 2: "⊨^m □^m(p^m ⊃^m (q^m ⊃^m (p^m ∧^m q^m)))"                     using 1 Nec        by metis
11    have 3: "⊨^m □^mp^m ⊃^m □^m(q^m ⊃^m (p^m ∧^m q^m))"                    using 2 Dist MP    by metis
12    have 4: "⊨^m (□^m(q^m ⊃^m (p^m ∧^m q^m))) ⊃^m ((◇^mq^m) ⊃^m ◇^m(p^m ∧^m q^m))" using K_Dia   by metis
13    have 5: "⊨^m □^mp^m ⊃^m ((◇^mq^m) ⊃^m ◇^m (p^m ∧^m q^m))"              using 3 4 H1 H2 MP by metis
14    thus ?thesis . qed
15 end
```

Fig. 6. Experiments: Simple proof in modal logic **K**.

Larger object-level proof examples could now be presented, studied and automated using the minimal shallow embedding. Prior studies have shown that this approach is generally competitive, in particular, when it comes to automating quantified modal logics; see e.g. the recent experiments reported in [60]. Recipes for embedding modal quantifiers and extensive application studies for quantified modal logics have been presented in prior works; see e.g. [12,17].

```
1  theory PMLinHOL_shallow_minimal_Loeb_tests imports PMLinHOL_shallow_minimal   (* Christoph Benzmüller, 2025 *)
2  begin
3  —‹Löb axiom: with the minimal shallow embedding automated reasoning tools are still partly responsive›
4    lemma Loeb1:  "∀φ. ⊨ᵐ □ᵐ( □ᵐφ ⊃ᵐφ) ⊃ᵐ □ᵐφ" nitpick[card w=1,card 𝒮=1] oops —‹nitpick: Counterexample.›
5    lemma Loeb2:  "(conversewf R ∧ transitive R) ⟶ (∀φ. ⊨ᵐ □ᵐ(□ᵐφ ⊃ᵐφ) ⊃ᵐ □ᵐφ)" —‹sh: Proof found› oops
6    lemma Loeb3:  "(conversewf R ∧ transitive R) ⟵ (∀φ. ⊨ᵐ □ᵐ(□ᵐφ ⊃ᵐφ) ⊃ᵐ □ᵐφ)" —‹sh: No Proof› oops
7    lemma Loeb3a: "conversewf R ⟵ (∀φ. ⊨ᵐ □ᵐ(□ᵐφ ⊃ᵐφ) ⊃ᵐ □ᵐφ)" unfolding DefM by blast
8    lemma Loeb3b: "transitive R ⟵ (∀φ. ⊨ᵐ □ᵐ(□ᵐφ ⊃ᵐφ) ⊃ᵐ □ᵐφ)" —‹sledgehammer: No Proof› oops
9    lemma Loeb3c: "irreflexive R ⟵ (∀φ. ⊨ᵐ □ᵐ(□ᵐφ ⊃ᵐφ) ⊃ᵐ □ᵐφ)" —‹sledgehammer: Proof found› oops
10 end
```

Fig. 7. Experiments: Studying the Löb-axiom of provability logic.

Experiments with the Löb-Axiom. Figure 7 presents automation experiments with the Löb-axiom of provability logic [24]. A first observation, interesting for education and research, is that via definition unfolding the schematic axioms are automatically converted into corresponding formulas in metalogic HOL. For the Löb-axiom (in line 4) we thus obtain after definition unfolding the HOL formula $\forall \varphi\, w. (\forall v. \mathtt{R}wv \longrightarrow (\forall z. \mathtt{R}vz \longrightarrow \varphi z) \longrightarrow \varphi v) \longrightarrow (\forall v. \mathtt{R}wv \longrightarrow \varphi v)$. When using the maximal shallow embedding instead, the Löb-axiom unfolds into the expected much heavier HOL formula $\forall \varphi\, W R\, V\, x. W\, x \longrightarrow (\forall z. W\, z \longrightarrow Rxz \longrightarrow (\forall x. Wx \longrightarrow Rzx \longrightarrow \varphi WRVx) \longrightarrow \varphi WRVz) \longrightarrow (\forall z. Wz \longrightarrow Rxz \longrightarrow \varphi WRVz)$, which also explains why automated reasoning is generally much harder for maximal shallow embeddings than for minimal shallow embeddings. The utilisation of the features of the presented framework enables students and researchers to explore frame properties for non-trivial properties independently and to subsequently simplify them. Proof automation or interactive proof can then be employed to investigate their equivalence to already known properties, as illustrated in Fig. 7 (in lines 5–9). As shown, such proof automation attempts succeed for the following conjectures: (line 5) the converse well-foundedness of the accessibility relation `R` in combination with the transitivity of `R` implies the Löb axiom, (line 7) the Löb axiom implies converse well-foundedness of `R`, and (line 9) the Löb axiom implies the irreflexivity of `R`. Whenever transitivity is an implicant to be proved, proof automation still fails (see lines 6 and 8). Here interactive proof is still required or, alternatively, improved HOL theorem proving systems, in particular provers that can suitably guess non-trivial instantiations for higher-order variables.[9]

Performance: Examples so Far. The performance of `sledgehammer` and `nitpick` for the different embeddings for the example proof problems as discussed so far

[9] For more on this challenge topic see e.g. the experiments reported in [16].

is briefly discussed:[10] *Minimal shallow embedding:* Proofs for 36 out of 38 valid statements (theorems, lemmas and substatements in interactive proofs) were found by calls to `sledgehammer`. `Nitpick` reported counterexamples for 5 out of 5 invalid statements. Reconstruction of `sledgehammer` proofs with trusted tactics failed in 2 cases. *Maximal shallow embedding:* Proofs for 34 out of 38 valid statements were found by `sledgehammer`. Countermodels for 4 out of 5 invalid statements were found by `nitpick`. Reconstruction of `sledgehammer` proofs with trusted tactics failed in 4 cases. *Deep embedding:* Proofs for 32 out of 38 valid statements were found by `sledgehammer`; in particular, there were no proofs delivered for the Löb examples. Countermodels for 5 out of 5 invalid statements were found by nitpick. Reconstruction of proofs failed in 2 cases.

Performance: Formula Classification. Further experiments were carried out in order to assess the performance of the different embeddings more rigorously. These tests focused on the classification of PML formula examples with respect to the logics in the modal logic cube [34] defined by the schematic axioms $T := \Box\varphi \supset \varphi$, $B := \varphi \supset \Box\Diamond\varphi$ and $4 := \Box\varphi \supset \Box\Box\varphi$, respectively by their semantic counterparts $Ts :=$ `reflexiv` R, $Bs :=$ `symmetric` R and $4s :=$ `transitiv` R (with R being the accessibility relation). The example formulas studied were:

F_1: $\Diamond\Diamond\varphi \supset \Diamond\varphi$
F_2: $\Diamond\Box\varphi \supset \Box\Diamond\varphi$
F_3: $\Diamond\Box\varphi \supset \Box\varphi$
F_4: $\Box\Diamond\Box\Diamond\varphi \supset \Box\Diamond\varphi$
F_5: $\Diamond(\varphi \wedge \Diamond\psi)) \supset (\Diamond\varphi \wedge \Diamond\psi)$
F_6: $((\Box(\varphi \supset \psi)) \wedge \Diamond\Box\neg\psi) \supset \neg\Diamond\psi$
F_7: $\Diamond\varphi \supset \Box(\varphi \vee \Diamond\varphi)$
F_8: $\Diamond(\Box\varphi) \supset (\varphi \vee \Diamond\varphi)$
F_9: $(\Box\Diamond\varphi \wedge \Box\Diamond\neg\varphi) \supset \Diamond\Diamond\varphi$
F_{10}: $(\Box(\varphi \supset \Box\psi) \wedge \Box\Diamond\neg\psi) \supset \neg\Box\psi$

The automatically identified weakest logics in the modal cube in which these formulas are valid are as follows: F_1: **K4**, F_2: **KB**, F_3: **KB4**, F_4: **KB/K4**, F_5: **K4**, F_6: **KB4**, F_7: **KB4**, F_8: **KT/KB**, F_9: **KT**, and F_{10}: **KT**.

Explained in abstract terms, for all $M \subseteq \{T, B, 4\}$, $N \subseteq \{Ts, Bs, 4s\}$ and $F \in \{F_1, \ldots, F_{10}\}$, `sledgehammer` and `nitpick` were called to assess the validity of the following sets of proof problems (each one consisting of $3^2 \times 10 = 80$ entries): $M \models^d F$, $N \models^d F$, $M \models^s F$, $N \models^s F$, $M \models^m F$, $N \models^m F$. `sledgehammer` and `nitpick` were thereby invoked in two modes, with and without prior application of Isabelle/HOL's simplifier `simp` to the proof problem under consideration. Consequently, for each set of problems, a total of 160 calls to each tool were conducted (80 with prior simplification and 80 without).

The results of these experiments, conducted with the same hardware as mentioned in Footnote 10, are presented in Fig. 8. The best results are highlighted. These are the maxima for the informative cases 'counterexample found' and 'no (finite) counterexample found' for `nitpick`, and 'proof found' for `sledgehammer`. For the 'unknown' and 'no proof' cases, which don't provide any useful information, the minima are shown as the best results. A overall score is reported, which was computed by adding the results obtained for the informative cases.

[10] A MacBook Pro 16,1 (6-Core Intel Core i7 processor, 2,6 GHz, 6 Cores, 256 KB L2 Cache per Core, 12 MB L3 Cache, 16 GB Memory) and Isabelle 2025 in standard configuration was used, which sets a 30 s prover timeout for `sledgehammer`.

	nitpick			sledgehammer		
	A	*B*	*C*	*D*	*E*	score
Problems	counterex.	no counterex.	unknown	proof found	no proof	
$M \models^m F$	**84(42/42)**	72(36/36)	4(2/2)	73(**38**/35)	87(**42**/45)	229
$N \models^m F$	**84(42/42)**	**76(38/38)**	**0(0/0)**	**76(38/38)**	**84(42/42)**	**236**
$M \models^s F$	32(16/16)	0(0/0)	128(64/64)	32(24/8)	128(56/72)	64
$N \models^s F$	**84(42/42)**	0(0/0)	76(38/38)	66(**38**/28)	94(**42**/52)	150
$M \models^d F$	16(10/6)	74(0/74)	70(70/**0**)	33(16/17)	127(64/63)	123
$N \models^d F$	32(8/24)	56(0/56)	72(72/**0**)	70(**38**/32)	90(**42**/48)	158

Fig. 8. Performance results of the automated PML formula classification task conducted with `nitpick` and `sledgehammer` (explanation: the first entry 73(**38**/35) in column *D*, e.g., states that 73 proofs were reported in total by `sledgehammer` for the problem set $M \models^m F$, with 38 proofs found with prior application of the simplifier `simp` and 35 without; analogous for the other entries).

The results obtained are briefly discussed. Perfect experimentation results were obtained for the problem set $N \models^m F$, that is, the minimal shallow embedding when used in combination with the semantical frame conditions Ts, Bs and $4s$. In this setting `nitpick` either provided a counterexample for each formula classification task or reported that there was no (finite) counterexample. The latter judgments were then supplemented by proofs from `sledgehammer` that confirmed the validity of these formulas. The second best performance was achieved with the minimal shallow embedding when used in combination with the axiom schemata T, B and 4. The maximal shallow embedding returned some good results for the problem set $N \models^s F$ regarding counterexample finding with `nitpick` and regarding theorem proving with `sledgehammer` when prior simplification was applied. However, in this setting, `nitpick` was unable to identify any formulas with no (finite) countermodels. For the deep embedding the performance results obtained with `nitpick` regarding counterexample finding significantly dropped in comparison to the minimal shallow embedding. The numbers reported for the deep embedding regarding the identification of formulas with no (finite) countermodels are still good though.[11] Interestingly, the maximal number of 38 proofs was still obtained by `sledgehammer` in the deep embedding when prior simplification was applied. Future work should extend the experiments presented to more challenging test formulas F and also include the further axiom schemata (and their corresponding semantic conditions) from the modal logic cube [34]. Additionally, it seems useful to replay, now using all the embeddings as provided in this paper, the metalogical cube verification experiments reported in prior work [3,8].

[11] However, some seemingly self-contradictory answers by `nitpick` in this setting with and without prior simplification for some problems require further consideration.

9 Related Work and Implications for LogiKEy

The notions of deep and shallow embeddings appear to originate from the work of Boulton et al. [25], and the connections between the two have been discussed in numerous related papers, see e.g. [40,53,61,62] and the references therein. However, to the best of the author's knowledge, no previous work has succeeded in integrating deep and (various degrees of) shallow embeddings in the form presented and, in particular, in enabling mutual faithfulness proofs between them.

Deep Embeddings. Exemplary developments and applications of non-trivial deep logic embeddings include self-verifications of the HOL light logic [1,38], a formalization of the Core Why3 logic [29], and a provably sound implementation of a differential dynamic logic [23], to name a few. For examples of deep embeddings of logics and their calculi in the Coq proof assistant [18], see e.g. [58] and the references therein, and Isabelle/HOL examples are presented in [22,31–33]. Further related work on the self-verification or bootstrapping of theorem provers can be found in [26], and more recently in [27] in the context of Lean [48].

Shallow Embeddings. Exemplary work in this category, which Nipkow called the extensional approach [49], includes a mechanization of HOL reasoning in first-order set theory [37], the techniques presented in [40] to overcome some problems of shallow embedding for reasoning over the syntax of embedded languages, a shallow embedding for pure type systems in first-order logic [30], and various other works such as [44,54]; see also the references given in [62]. Note also that the automation support for various quantified non-classical logics as realized in the HOL theorem prover Leo3 [59,60] is based on minimal shallow embeddings.

Implications for LogiKEy. The logic-pluralistic knowledge and reasoning methodology LogiKEy [10], see Fig. 9, leverages higher-order logic (HOL) as a unifying metalogic to enable the modeling of diverse object logics, so far, primarily

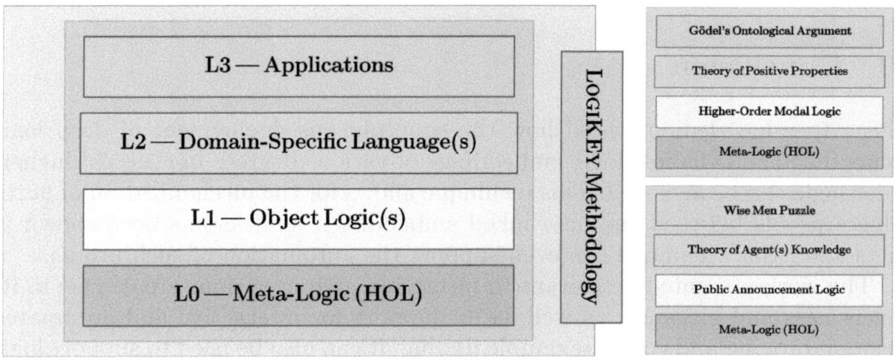

Fig. 9. The logic-pluralistic knowledge representation and reasoning methodology LogiKEy (left) and two concrete applications of it (right): Studies on Gödel's ontological argument [17] (top) and an automation of the wise men puzzle [13] (bottom).

via using shallow semantic embeddings. LogiKEy has been used in a range of application domains and contexts. Very different kinds of object logics have been embedded LogiKEy over the past decade, including, for example, free logic [14], modal higher-order logic [17], public announcement logic [13], conditional logic [4] and dyadic deontic logic with a preference-based semantics [51].

This paper shows how the LogiKEy approach could benefit in the future from providing faithful, deep and shallow embeddings of all object logics under consideration. This would allow the embeddings to be used interchangeably in applications. The technique presented has also the potential to replace or complement pen-and-paper faithfulness proofs in prior works, such as the ones reported in [4,12,13], by computer-verified proofs in Isabelle/HOL. This in turn will be relevant for enabling applications in areas that require highest levels of trust. For this note that a particular application direction of LogiKEy is normative and legal reasoning in the context of AI regulation, see also [10,45].

This paper also illustrates the conceptual modifications applied in prior LogiKEy papers when transitioning from lightweight shallow embeddings of non-classical logics, such as those used to encode higher-order modal logic [12] or conditional logic [4], which consider only dependencies on possible worlds, to more heavyweight shallow embeddings, as, for example, required to embed public announcement logic [13]; in the latter work additional dependencies on evaluation domains had to be encoded. Note on the other hand, that previous work has often avoided the explicit modeling of atoms, signatures, and evaluations, which has been essential for the work presented in this paper. Moreover, the presented technique should eventually help to overcome challenges in application contexts that require the combined use of deep and shallow embeddings. The Fatio protocol for multi-agent argumentation [52] is such an example. Most importantly, the presented technique for linking deep and shallow embeddings will be very fruitful for furthering the use of LogiKEy in university-level logic courses, including the author's courses on universal logical reasoning that have been taught for many years at FU Berlin and now at the University of Bamberg.

10 Conclusion

This paper has demonstrated how the simultaneous deployment of deep logic embeddings and shallow logic embeddings of various degrees in classical higher-order logic can be achieved. This technique allows for the mechanization of faithfulness proofs between the interlinked embeddings, and, as has been shown in this paper, this technique can even support the automation of such proofs.

The work presented is relevant to future research in various areas. Due to its conciseness and elegance, as well as its support for interactive and automated theorem proving and counterexample finding, it can also be used to support logic education effectively. The latter application direction was the main motivation for illustrating this approach using simple propositional modal logic in this paper. This logic is routinely used as introductory material in logic courses worldwide. The Isabelle/HOL sources provided and explained in this paper should be easily reusable to support such courses, and they should also be easily transferable to other higher-order proof assistant systems.

Acknowledgements. I am grateful to the reviewers of this paper for their valuable feedback. I would also like to thank D. Fuenmayor, D. Kirchner, L. Pasetto and E. Zalta for their comments and all those who have contributed to LogiKEy in the past. My thanks also go to Deepl for the fruitful exchange that (hopefully) helped to improve the quality of the wording of this paper.

Disclosure of Interests. The authors have no competing interests to declare that are relevant to the content of this article.

References

1. Abrahamsson, O., Myreen, M.O., Kumar, R., Sewell, T.: Candle: a verified implementation of HOL light. In: Andronick, J., de Moura, L. (eds.) 13th International Conference on Interactive Theorem Proving, ITP 2022, 7–10 August 2022, Haifa, Israel. LIPIcs, vol. 237, pp. 3:1–3:17. Schloss Dagstuhl - Leibniz-Zentrum für Informatik (2022). https://doi.org/10.4230/LIPICS.ITP.2022.3
2. Andrews, P.B.: General models and extensionality. J. Symb. Log. **37**(2), 395–397 (1972). https://doi.org/10.2307/2272982
3. Benzmüller, C.: Verifying the modal logic cube is an easy task (for higher-order automated reasoners). In: Siegler, S., Wasser, N. (eds.) Verification, Induction, Termination Analysis. LNCS (LNAI), vol. 6463, pp. 117–128. Springer, Heidelberg (2010). https://doi.org/10.1007/978-3-642-17172-7_7
4. Benzmüller, C.: Cut-elimination for quantified conditional logic. J. Philos. Log. **46**(3), 333–353 (2016). https://doi.org/10.1007/s10992-016-9403-0
5. Benzmüller, C.: Faithful logic embeddings in HOL — deep and shallow (2025). https://doi.org/10.48550/arXiv.2502.19311
6. Benzmüller, C., Andrews, P.: Church's type theory. In: Zalta, E.N., Nodelman, U. (eds.) The Stanford Encyclopedia of Philosophy, 2024 edn. Metaphysics Research Lab, Stanford University. Spring (2024). https://plato.stanford.edu/archives/spr2024/entries/type-theory-church/
7. Benzmüller, C., Brown, C., Kohlhase, M.: Higher-order semantics and extensionality. J. Symb. Log. **69**(4), 1027–1088 (2004). https://doi.org/10.2178/jsl/1102022211
8. Benzmüller, C., Claus, M., Sultana, N.: Systematic verification of the modal logic cube in Isabelle/HOL. In: Kaliszyk, C., Paskevich, A. (eds.) PxTP 2015, vol. 186, pp. 27–41. EPTCS (2015). https://doi.org/10.4204/EPTCS.186.5
9. Benzmüller, C., Miller, D.: Automation of higher-order logic. In: Gabbay, D.M., Siekmann, J.H., Woods, J. (eds.) Handbook of the History of Logic, Volume 9—Computational Logic, pp. 215–254. Elsevier, North Holland (2014). https://doi.org/10.1016/B978-0-444-51624-4.50005-8
10. Benzmüller, C., Parent, X., van der Torre, L.: Designing normative theories for ethical and legal reasoning: LogiKEy framework, methodology, and tool support. Artif. Intell. **287**, 103348 (2020). https://doi.org/10.1016/j.artint.2020.103348
11. Benzmüller, C., Paulson, L.C.: Multimodal and intuitionistic logics in simple type theory. Log. J. IGPL **18**(6), 881–892 (2010). https://doi.org/10.1093/jigpal/jzp080

12. Benzmüller, C., Paulson, L.C.: Quantified multimodal logics in simple type theory. Log. Univers. **7**(1), 7–20 (2013). https://doi.org/10.1007/s11787-012-0052-y
13. Benzmüller, C., Reiche, S.: Automating public announcement logic with relativized common knowledge as a fragment of HOL in LogiKEy. J. Log. Comput. **33**(6), 1243–1269 (2023). https://doi.org/10.1093/logcom/exac029
14. Benzmüller, C., Scott, D.S.: Automating free logic in HOL, with an experimental application in category theory. J. Autom. Reason. **64**(1), 53–72 (2019). https://doi.org/10.1007/s10817-018-09507-7
15. Benzmüller, C.: Faithful logic embeddings in HOL—deep and shallow (Isabelle/HOL dataset). Arch. Formal Proofs (2025). https://isa-afp.org/entries/FaithfulPMLinHOL.html
16. Benzmüller, C., Fuenmayor, D., Steen, A., Sutcliffe, G.: Who finds the short proof? Log. J. IGPL **32**, 442–464 (2024). https://doi.org/10.1093/jigpal/jzac082
17. Benzmüller, C., Scott, D.S.: Notes on Gödel's and Scott's variants of the ontological argument. Monatshefte für Mathematik (2025). https://doi.org/10.1007/s00605-025-02078-x
18. Bertot, Y., Casteran, P.: Interactive Theorem Proving and Program Development. Springer (2004)
19. Blackburn, P., van Benthem, J.: Modal logic: a semantic perspective. In: Blackburn, P., van Benthem, J.F.A.K., Wolter, F. (eds.) Handbook of Modal Logic, Studies in Logic and Practical Reasoning, North-Holland, vol. 3, pp. 1–84 (2007). https://doi.org/10.1016/S1570-2464(07)80004-8
20. Blanchette, J.C., Böhme, S., Paulson, L.C.: Extending sledgehammer with SMT solvers. In: Bjørner, N., Sofronie-Stokkermans, V. (eds.) CADE 2011. LNCS (LNAI), vol. 6803, pp. 116–130. Springer, Heidelberg (2011). https://doi.org/10.1007/978-3-642-22438-6_11
21. Blanchette, J.C., Nipkow, T.: Nitpick: a counterexample generator for higher-order logic based on a relational model finder. In: Kaufmann, M., Paulson, L.C. (eds.) ITP 2010. LNCS, vol. 6172, pp. 131–146. Springer, Heidelberg (2010). https://doi.org/10.1007/978-3-642-14052-5_11
22. Blanchette, J.C., Popescu, A., Traytel, D.: Soundness and completeness proofs by coinductive methods. J. Autom. Reason. **58**(1), 149–179 (2017). https://doi.org/10.1007/S10817-016-9391-3
23. Bohrer, R., Rahli, V., Vukotic, I., Völp, M., Platzer, A.: Formally verified differential dynamic logic. In: Proceedings of the 6th ACM SIGPLAN Conference on Certified Programs and Proofs, CPP 2017, pp. 208–221. Association for Computing Machinery, New York, NY, USA (2017). https://doi.org/10.1145/3018610.3018616
24. Boolos, G.S.: The Logic of Provability. Cambridge University Press (1994)
25. Boulton, R.J., Gordon, A.D., Gordon, M.J.C., Harrison, J., Herbert, J., Tassel, J.V.: Experience with embedding hardware description languages in HOL. In: Stavridou, V., Melham, T.F., Boute, R.T. (eds.) Theorem Provers in Circuit Design, Proceedings of the IFIP TC10/WG 10.2 International Conference on Theorem Provers in Circuit Design: Theory, Practice and Experience, Nijmegen, The Netherlands, 22–24 June 1992, Proceedings. IFIP Transactions, North-Holland, vol. A-10, pp. 129–156 (1992)
26. Carneiro, M.: Metamath zero: designing a theorem prover prover. In: Benzmüller, C., Miller, B. (eds.) CICM 2020. LNCS (LNAI), vol. 12236, pp. 71–88. Springer, Cham (2020). https://doi.org/10.1007/978-3-030-53518-6_5
27. Carneiro, M.: Lean4Lean: towards a verified typechecker for Lean, in Lean (2024). https://doi.org/10.48550/arXiv.2403.14064

28. Church, A.: A formulation of the simple theory of types. J. Symb. Log. **5**(2), 56–68 (1940). https://doi.org/10.2307/2266170
29. Cohen, J.M., Johnson-Freyd, P.: A formalization of core Why3 in Coq. Proc. ACM Program. Lang. **8**(POPL), 1789–1818 (2024). https://doi.org/10.1145/3632902
30. Czajka, L.: A shallow embedding of pure type systems into first-order logic. In: Ghilezan, S., Geuvers, H., Ivetic, J. (eds.) 22nd International Conference on Types for Proofs and Programs (TYPES 2016). Leibniz International Proceedings in Informatics (LIPIcs), vol. 97, pp. 9:1–9:39. Schloss Dagstuhl – Leibniz-Zentrum für Informatik, Dagstuhl, Germany (2018). https://doi.org/10.4230/LIPIcs.TYPES.2016.9
31. From, A.H., Jacobsen, F.K.: Verifying a sequent calculus prover for first-order logic with functions in Isabelle/HOL. In: Andronick, J., de Moura, L. (eds.) 13th International Conference on Interactive Theorem Proving (ITP 2022). Leibniz International Proceedings in Informatics (LIPIcs), vol. 237, pp. 13:1–13:22. Schloss Dagstuhl – Leibniz-Zentrum für Informatik, Dagstuhl, Germany (2022). https://doi.org/10.4230/LIPIcs.ITP.2022.13
32. From, A.H.: A Naive prover for first-order logic. Arch. Formal Proofs (2022). https://isa-afp.org/entries/FOL_Seq_Calc3.html
33. From, A.H., Villadsen, J.: Soundness and completeness of implicational logic. Arch. Formal Proofs (2022). https://isa-afp.org/entries/Implicational_Logic.html
34. Garson, J.: Modal logic. In: Zalta, E.N., Nodelman, U. (eds.) The Stanford Encyclopedia of Philosophy, 2024 edn. Metaphysics Research Lab, Stanford University. Spring (2024). https://plato.stanford.edu/archives/spr2024/entries/logic-modal/
35. Gibbons, J., Wu, N.: Folding domain-specific languages: deep and shallow embeddings (functional pearl). In: Jeuring, J., Chakravarty, M.M.T. (eds.) Proceedings of the 19th ACM SIGPLAN International Conference on Functional Programming, Gothenburg, Sweden, 1–3 September 2014, pp. 339–347. ACM (2014). https://doi.org/10.1145/2628136.2628138
36. Gödel, K.: Über formal unentscheidbare Sätze der Principia Mathematica und verwandter Systeme I. Monatshefte für Mathematik und Physik **38**(1), 173–198 (1931). https://doi.org/10.1007/BF01700692
37. Guilloud, S., Gambhir, S., Gilot, A., Kuncak, V.: Mechanized HOL reasoning in set theory. In: Bertot, Y., Kutsia, T., Norrish, M. (eds.) 15th International Conference on Interactive Theorem Proving, ITP 2024, 9–14 September 2024, Tbilisi, Georgia. LIPIcs, vol. 309, pp. 18:1–18:18. Schloss Dagstuhl - Leibniz-Zentrum für Informatik (2024). https://doi.org/10.4230/LIPICS.ITP.2024.18
38. Harrison, J.: Towards self-verification of HOL light. In: Furbach, U., Shankar, N. (eds.) IJCAR 2006. LNCS (LNAI), vol. 4130, pp. 177–191. Springer, Heidelberg (2006). https://doi.org/10.1007/11814771_17
39. Henkin, L.: Completeness in the theory of types. J. Symb. Log. **15**(2), 81–91 (1950). https://doi.org/10.2307/2266967
40. Kaposi, A., Kovács, A., Kraus, N.: Shallow embedding of type theory is morally correct. In: Hutton, G. (ed.) MPC 2019. LNCS, vol. 11825, pp. 329–365. Springer, Cham (2019). https://doi.org/10.1007/978-3-030-33636-3_12
41. Kirchner, D.: Computer-verified foundations of metaphysics and an ontology of natural numbers in Isabelle/HOL. Ph.D. thesis, Freie Universität, Berlin (2022). https://doi.org/10.17169/refubium-35141
42. Kirchner, D., Benzmüller, C., Zalta, E.N.: Mechanizing principia Logico-Metaphysica in functional type theory. Rev. Symb. Log. **13**(1), 206–218 (2020). https://doi.org/10.1017/S1755020319000297

43. Lachnitt, H.: Systematic verification of the intuitionistic modal logic cube in Isabelle/HOL. Bachelor thesis, Freie Universität, Berlin (2017)
44. Lammich, P., Meis, R.: A separation logic framework for imperative HOL. Arch. Formal Proofs **2012** (2012). https://www.isa-afp.org/entries/Separation_Logic_Imperative_HOL.shtml
45. Lawniczak, L., Benzmüller, C.: Logical modalities within the European AI act: an analysis. In: Maranhão, J. (ed.) Proceedings of the 20th International Conference on Artificial Intelligence and Law. Association for Computing Machinery, New York, NY, USA (2025, in print)
46. Lorini, E.: Temporal logic and its application to normative reasoning. J. Appl. Non-Class. Log. **23**(4), 372–399 (2013). https://doi.org/10.1080/11663081.2013.841359
47. Meder, P.: Deontic agency and moral luck. Master's thesis, University of Luxembourg (2018). https://hdl.handle.net/10993/39770
48. de Moura, L., Kong, S., Avigad, J., van Doorn, F., von Raumer, J.: The Lean theorem prover (system description). In: Felty, A.P., Middeldorp, A. (eds.) CADE 2015. LNCS (LNAI), vol. 9195, pp. 378–388. Springer, Cham (2015). https://doi.org/10.1007/978-3-319-21401-6_26
49. Nipkow, T.: Hoare logics in Isabelle/HOL. In: Schwichtenberg, H., Steinbrüggen, R. (eds.) Proof and System-Reliability, pp. 341–367. Springer, Netherlands, Dordrecht (2002). https://doi.org/10.1007/978-94-010-0413-8_11
50. Nipkow, T., Wenzel, M., Paulson, L.C. (eds.): Isabelle/HOL. LNCS, vol. 2283. Springer, Heidelberg (2002). https://doi.org/10.1007/3-540-45949-9
51. Parent, X., Benzmüller, C.: Conditional normative reasoning as a fragment of HOL. J. Appl. Non-Class. Log. **34**, 561–592 (2024). https://doi.org/10.1080/11663081.2024.2386917
52. Pasetto, L., Benzmüller, C.: Implementing the Fatio protocol for multi-agent argumentation in LogiKEy. In: Benzmüller, C., Otten, J., Ramanayake, R. (eds.) Proceedings of the 5th International Workshop on Automated Reasoning in Quantified Non-Classical Logics (ARQNL 2024), Nancy, France, 1 July 2024, vol. CEUR-3875, pp. 38–47. CEUR Workshop Proceedings. CEUR-WS.org, Nancy, France (2024). https://ceur-ws.org/Vol-3875/ARQNL2024_paper4.pdf
53. Prinz, J., Kavvos, G.A., Lampropoulos, L.: Deeper shallow embeddings. In: Andronick, J., de Moura, L. (eds.) 13th International Conference on Interactive Theorem Proving, ITP 2022, 7–10 August 2022, Haifa, Israel. LIPIcs, vol. 237, pp. 28:1–28:18. Schloss Dagstuhl - Leibniz-Zentrum für Informatik (2022). https://doi.org/10.4230/LIPICS.ITP.2022.28
54. Rabe, M.N., Lammich, P., Popescu, A.: A shallow embedding of hyperCTL. Arch. Formal Proofs **2014** (2014). https://www.isa-afp.org/entries/HyperCTL.shtml
55. Sahlqvist, H.: Completeness and correspondence in the first and second order semantics for modal logic. Stud. Log. Found. Math. **82**, 110–143 (1975). https://doi.org/10.1016/S0049-237X(08)70728-6
56. Sider, T.: Logic for Philosophy. Oxford University Press, New York (2009)
57. Smullyan, R.: A Beginner's Guide to Mathematical Logic. Dover Books on Mathematics, Dover Publications (2014). https://books.google.ae/books?id=n6S-AwAAQBAJ
58. Sozeau, M., et al.: The MetaCoq project. J. Autom. Reason. **64**(5), 947–999 (2020). https://doi.org/10.1007/S10817-019-09540-0
59. Steen, A., Benzmüller, C.: Extensional higher-order paramodulation in Leo-III. J. Autom. Reason. **65**(6), 775–807 (2021). https://doi.org/10.1007/s10817-021-09588-x

60. Steen, A., Sutcliffe, G., Benzmüller, C.: Solving quantified modal logic problems by translation to classical logics. J. Log. Comput., 1–23 (2025). https://doi.org/10.1093/logcom/exaf006
61. Svenningsson, J., Axelsson, E.: Combining deep and shallow embedding for EDSL. In: Loidl, H.-W., Peña, R. (eds.) TFP 2012. LNCS, vol. 7829, pp. 21–36. Springer, Heidelberg (2013). https://doi.org/10.1007/978-3-642-40447-4_2
62. Wang, Z., Cao, Q., Tao, Y.: Verifying programs with logic and extended proof rules: deep embedding vs. shallow embedding. J. Autom. Reason. **68**(3), 18 (2024). https://doi.org/10.1007/S10817-024-09706-5
63. Wikipedia contributors: Hilbert system — Wikipedia, the free encyclopedia (2024). https://en.wikipedia.org/w/index.php?title=Hilbert_system&oldid=1257978821. Accessed 18 Feb 2025
64. Zalta, E.N.: Principia Logico-Metaphysica (Draft/Excerpt) (2025). https://mally.stanford.edu/principia.pdf. Accessed 27 May 2025

A Stepwise Refinement Proof that SCL(FOL) Simulates Ground Ordered Resolution

Martin Bromberger[1], Martin Desharnais[1,2](✉), and Christoph Weidenbach[1]

[1] Max Planck Institute for Informatics, Saarland Informatics Campus, Saarbrücken, Germany
{mbromber,desharnais,weidenbach}@mpi-inf.mpg.de
[2] Graduate School of Computer Science, Saarland Informatics Campus, Saarbrücken, Germany

Abstract. Recently, it has been demonstrated that SCL(FOL) can simulate ground ordered resolution [6]. We revisit this result and provide a new formal proof in Isabelle/HOL. The existing pen-and-paper proof is monolithic and challenging to comprehend. In order to improve clarity, we develop an alternative proof structured as eleven (bi)simulation steps between the two calculi, transitioning from ordered resolution to SCL(FOL). A key simulation lemma ensures that, under certain conditions, one simulation direction can be automatically lifted to the other. Consequently, for each of the eleven steps, it suffices to establish only one direction of simulation. The complete proof is included in the *Archive of Formal Proofs*.

Keywords: interactive theorem proving · (ground) first-order logic · SCL · non-redundant clause learning · ordered resolution

1 Introduction

The SCL ("Clause Learning from Simple Models" or simply "Simple Clause Learning") family of sound and complete calculi lifts a conflict-driven clause learning (CDCL) approach [2,19] to first-order logic [5,7,8,15,17]. SCL(FOL) is a calculus for first-order logic without equality. Given a clause set, it iteratively builds a ground literal candidate model. If the candidate model conflicts with some clause, SCL(FOL) infers a new non-ground clause from the candidate model and the conflicting clause via resolution. The new clause is added to the clause set, and SCL(FOL) backtracks to a smaller, conflict-free candidate model. Soundness and completeness proofs for SCL(FOL) were first carried out on paper [8] and later in the Isabelle/HOL proof assistant [4].

Ordered resolution (ORD-RES) is a refinement of resolution where a term ordering restricts inferences to literals that are maximal in their respective

C. Barrett and U. Waldmann (Eds.): CADE 2025, LNAI 15943, pp. 302–322, 2025.
https://doi.org/10.1007/978-3-031-99984-0_17

clauses. It can be viewed as superposition [1] restricted to first-order logic without equality. In general, ORD-RES derives also redundant clauses, but if inferences are guided by the model construction contained in its proof of refutational completeness, only non-redundant clauses are generated. The model construction is effective for the ground case but not for the case with variables as there are infinitely many ground instances of clauses with variables. But even with this strategy where ORD-RES generates only non-redundant clauses, it differs significantly from SCL(FOL) as demonstrated by the following example.

Consider the example from [6] of proving that the ground clauses $\mathsf{P(a)} \vee \mathsf{P(a)}$ and $\mathsf{P(a)} \longrightarrow \mathsf{Q(b)}$ entail $\mathsf{Q(b)}$. After negation of the conjecture, we obtain the clause set $N = \{\mathsf{P(a)} \vee \mathsf{P(a)}, \neg\mathsf{P(a)} \vee \mathsf{Q(b)}, \neg\mathsf{Q(b)}\}$. We assume the symbol precedence $\mathsf{a} \prec \mathsf{b} \prec \mathsf{P} \prec \mathsf{Q}$ that we lift [1] to terms, atoms, literals, and clauses with respect to a Knuth–Bendix ordering where all symbols have weight one [16].

Then, following Definition 16, ORD-RES first constructs the candidate model $\{\}$, meaning that no atom is considered true, and finds the minimal false clause $\mathsf{P(a)} \vee \mathsf{P(a)}$; factoring infers the clause $\mathsf{P(a)}$. At this point, the clause set becomes $N \cup \{\mathsf{P(a)}\}$. Then it constructs a new candidate model $\{\mathsf{P(a)}, \mathsf{Q(b)}\}$, meaning that only the atoms $\mathsf{P(a)}$ and $\mathsf{Q(b)}$ are considered true, with minimal false clause $\neg\mathsf{Q(b)}$; ordered resolution on $\neg\mathsf{P(a)} \vee \mathsf{Q(b)}$ and $\neg\mathsf{Q(b)}$ infers $\neg\mathsf{P(a)}$ and the clause set changes to $N \cup \{\mathsf{P(a)}, \neg\mathsf{P(a)}\}$. The final candidate model is $\{\mathsf{P(a)}\}$ with minimal false clause $\neg\mathsf{P(a)}$ resulting in an ORD-RES inference of the empty clause $\bot$.

SCL(FOL) only factorizes clauses in the context of resolution inferences. It does not learn the clauses that ORD-RES inferred through factoring, but it still keeps track of them in our simulation to act as if they had been learned. SCL(FOL) first builds the candidate model $[\mathsf{P(a)}, \mathsf{Q(b)}]$, keeping track that the clause $\mathsf{P(a)}$ can be inferred from $\mathsf{P(a)} \vee \mathsf{P(a)}$, and then detects a conflict with the clause $\neg\mathsf{Q(b)}$; it performs conflict resolution, learns the clause $\neg\mathsf{P(a)}$, and backtracks to the empty candidate model. At this point, the clause set becomes $N \cup \{\neg\mathsf{P(a)}\}$ matching the respective state of the ORD-RES run. Then it builds the candidate model $[\mathsf{P(a)}]$, detects a conflict with $\neg\mathsf{P(a)}$, performs conflict resolution, and infers the empty clause $\bot$.

In this paper, we revisit the simulation proof between ground ORD-RES and SCL(FOL) from [6]. More precisely, SCL(FOL) does not simulate ORD-RES in general, but it simulates the optimal, model driven strategy of ORD-RES. We reuse the existing strategy for ground ORD-RES but provide a new strategy for SCL(FOL) and a new simulation proof. Our contributions are as follows. We specify a new, simpler strategy for regular SCL(FOL) that simulates ground ordered resolution learning non-redundant clauses. The strategy is expressed as a simple transition relation closely following SCL(FOL)'s rules. We provide a strong bisimulation proof between the ORD-RES and SCL(FOL) strategies. Our proof is modular: It consists of eleven refinement steps focusing on different aspects of the two strategies. We provide a general lemma that lifts a simulation between two transition systems meeting some conditions to a bisimulation, Lemma 15, and apply to all refinement steps depicted in Fig. 1. We formalized all the above in Isabelle/HOL. Our formalization consists of approximately 26 000 non-blank lines[1] and is available in the *Archive of Formal Proofs* [11]. Our work is part of the IsaFoL (Isabelle Formalization of Logic) effort [3].

The paper is now organized as follows. Section 2 provides a short overview of the SCL(FOL) calculus. Section 3 contains a bird eyes view of the overall simulation proof explaining every single step. Due to the space limit we focus in Sect. 4 on three aspects of this proof: Sect. 4.1 presents our general lemma lifting a simulation to a bisimulation, Sect. 4.2 presents our deterministic strategy for ground ORD-RES that only learns non-redundant clauses, and Sect. 4.3 presents our deterministic strategy for SCL(FOL). Finally, Sect. 5 provides a discussion of our results and a comparison to related work.

2 Background

We briefly repeat basic notions regarding the SCL(FOL) calculus formalized by Bromberger et al. [4]. We consider an untyped, first-order logic without equality.

The calculus is parametrized by a binary relation $\prec_B$ on ground atoms such that each ground atom has finitely many lesser ground atoms (i.e., $\forall \beta.\ \mathsf{finite}\{A \mid A \prec_B \beta\}$). An example of such an ordering is the Knuth–Bendix ordering [16] without zero-weight symbols. An annotated literal is the pairing of a literal with an optional annotation. We call it a *decision literal* when the annotation is absent, detonated $\dagger$, and a *propagation literal* when the annotation is a grounding closure of the clause the literal originated from. The literal of an annotated literal $\mathcal{K}$ is denoted by $\mathsf{lit}\,\mathcal{K}$. A *trail* is a finite sequence of annotated ground literals; it grows from left to right. Appending an annotated literal $\mathcal{K}$ to a trail Γ is written $\Gamma, \mathcal{K}$. Concatenating two trails Γ_1 and Γ_2 is written Γ_2, Γ_1. A literal L is true under trail Γ if L is in Γ and false under Γ if the complement of L is in Γ. A literal L is defined in a trail Γ if L is true or false under Γ; otherwise, it is undefined. These four properties are lifted from literals to clauses.

The calculus is defined as a transition system operating on states $\langle \Gamma; U; \mathcal{C} \rangle$, where Γ is a trail, U is a finite set of learned clauses, and $\mathcal{C}$ is either $\dagger$ or a clause closure $\langle C; \gamma \rangle$ such that $C\gamma$ is ground and false in Γ. The transition relation $\Rightarrow_{\mathrm{SCL}}^{N,\beta}$ is a binary predicate between states and is parameterized by the finite set N of initial clauses and the bounding ground atom β that restricts the considered atoms. It is defined as the disjunction of the following rules.

Propagate $\langle \Gamma; U; \dagger \rangle \Rightarrow_{\text{Propagate}}^{N,\beta} \langle \Gamma, (L\mu\gamma)^{\langle L\mu; C_0\mu; \gamma \rangle}; U; \dagger \rangle$
Side conditions:

1. $(L \vee C) \in N \cup U$
2. γ is a grounding substitution for $L \vee C$
3. $\forall K \in (L \vee C).\ \mathsf{atom}\,(K\gamma) \preceq_B \beta$
4. $C_0 = \{K \in C \mid K\gamma \neq L\gamma\}$
5. $C_1 = \{K \in C \mid K\gamma = L\gamma\}$

[1] Counted using `grep -Ev '^[[:blank:]]*$'`.

6. $C_0\gamma$ is false under Γ
7. $L\gamma$ is undefined in Γ
8. μ is the idempotent MGU for $\{\mathsf{atom}\ K \mid K \in (L \vee C_1)\}$

Decide $\langle \Gamma; U; \dagger \rangle \Rightarrow^{N,\beta}_{\text{Decide}} \langle \Gamma, (L\gamma)^{\dagger}; U; \dagger \rangle$
Side conditions:

1. γ is a grounding substitution for L
2. $L\gamma$ is undefined in Γ
3. $\mathsf{atom}\ (L\gamma) \preceq_B \beta$

Conflict $\langle \Gamma; U; \dagger \rangle \Rightarrow^{N,\beta}_{\text{Conflict}} \langle \Gamma; U; \langle C; \gamma \rangle \rangle$
Side conditions:

1. $C \in N \cup U$
2. γ is a grounding substitution for C
3. $C\gamma$ is false under Γ

These rules construct a (partial) model via the trail Γ for $N \cup U$ until a conflict (i.e., a clause false under Γ) is found. The above rules always terminate, because there are only finitely many ground atoms A with $A \prec_B \beta$. It might be necessary to successively increase β for full refutational completeness.

Skip $\langle \Gamma, \mathcal{K}; U; \langle C; \gamma \rangle \rangle \Rightarrow^{N,\beta}_{\text{Skip}} \langle \Gamma; U; \langle C; \gamma \rangle \rangle$
Side conditions:

1. $\mathsf{comp}\ (\mathsf{lit}\ \mathcal{K}) \notin C\gamma$

Factorize $\langle \Gamma; U; \langle L' \vee L \vee C; \gamma \rangle \rangle \Rightarrow^{N,\beta}_{\text{Factorize}} \langle \Gamma; U; \langle (L \vee C)\mu; \gamma \rangle \rangle$
Side conditions:

1. $L\gamma = L'\gamma$
2. μ is the idempotent MGU for $\{\mathsf{atom}\ L, \mathsf{atom}\ L'\}$

Resolve $\langle \Gamma; U; \langle L \vee C; \gamma_C \rangle \rangle \Rightarrow^{N,\beta}_{\text{Resolve}} \langle \Gamma; U; \langle (C\rho_C \vee D\rho_D)\mu; \gamma \rangle \rangle$
Side conditions:

1. $\Gamma = \Gamma', (K\gamma_D)^{\langle K; D; \gamma_D \rangle}$
2. $K\gamma_D = \mathsf{comp}\ (L\gamma_C)$
3. ρ_C and ρ_D are renaming substitutions such that the variables of $(L \vee C)\rho_C$ and $(K \vee D)\rho_D$ are disjoint
4. μ is the idempotent MGU for $\{\mathsf{atom}\ L\rho_C, \mathsf{atom}\ K\rho_D\}$
5. γ'_C and γ'_D are adaptations of γ_C and γ_D to the renaming substitutions ρ_C and ρ_D respectively
6. γ is a merged grounding substitution of γ'_C for the variables of $(L \vee C)\rho_C$ and γ'_D for the variables of $(K \vee D)\rho_D$

These rules perform conflict resolution by repeatedly applying factoring or resolution steps and shrinking the trail until the decision literal is found that originally led to the conflict.

Backtrack $\langle \Gamma, \Gamma', K^{\dagger}; U; \langle L \vee C; \gamma \rangle \rangle \Rightarrow^{N,\beta}_{\text{Backtrack}} \langle \Gamma; \{L \vee C\} \cup U; \top \rangle$
Side conditions:

1. $K = \mathsf{comp}\,(L\gamma)$
2. $\nexists \gamma'.\ (L \vee C)\gamma'$ is ground and false under Γ

The clause $L \vee C$ added by the rule Backtrack to U is called a *learned clause.* The empty clause $\bot$ can only be generated by the rule Resolve or be already present in N. Hence, as usual for CDCL-style calculi, the generation of $\bot$, together with the clauses in $N \cup U$, represents a resolution refutation.

A sequence of SCL rule applications is called a *reasonable run* if the rule Decide does not enable an immediate application of rule Conflict. A sequence of SCL rule applications is called a *regular run* if it is a reasonable run and the rule Conflict has precedence over all other rules. Clauses learned in a regular run are always non-redundant.

3 Proof Outline

Figure 1 presents the calculi we formalized and the simulations we proved. At the very top, ORD-RES corresponds to ground ordered resolution. At the very bottom, we arrive at SCL(FOL). In between, ORD-RES-1 is a deterministic strategy for ORD-RES that we successively refine to ORD-RES-11, which is a deterministic strategy for SCL(FOL). All refinement steps follow the same pattern.

1. We define a new calculus as a transition system that changes some aspect of the previous calculus.
2. We prove that this new calculus is well-behaved, sometimes conditionally w.r.t. a safety predicate.
3. We define a matching relation.
4. We prove that the new calculus agrees with the previous one on final states.
5. We prove either a forward or a backward simulation.
6. We lift the simulation to a bisimulation.

ORD-RES-1 is a deterministic and refutationally complete calculus that uses model construction to guide the order of the inference rules. This model construction is the same as the one used in the proof of refutational completeness of the ordered resolution calculus. The idea is to iterate over the clause set, starting from the least clause following the clause ordering, and iteratively build a candidate model. At each iteration, either the candidate model already makes the considered clause true, or the candidate model can be extended to make the clause true, or the least false clause has been found and model construction

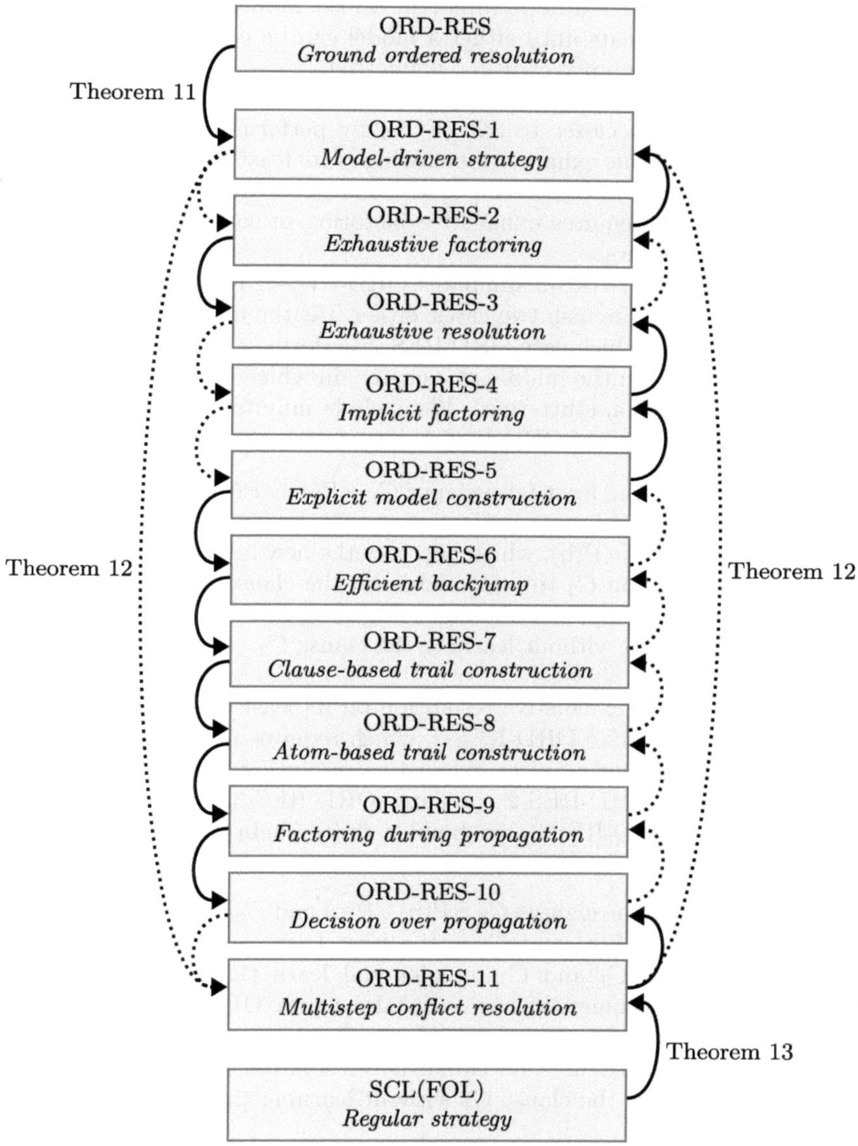

Fig. 1. The calculi and proven simulations. An arrow from a calculus $\mathcal{A}$ to a calculus $\mathcal{B}$ means that $\mathcal{A}$ simulates $\mathcal{B}$ (i.e., if $\mathcal{B}$ makes a transition, then $\mathcal{A}$ eventually also makes some corresponding transitions). A bisimulation consists of both an up- and a down-facing arrow. A solid arrow was proven manually by case analysis. A dotted arrow was proven using either our lifting Lemma 15 or composition of simulations.

stops. If found, the least false clause is then used with either the factoring or the resolution rule to infer a new non-redundant clause. Model construction followed by clause inference repeats until either a model can be constructed that makes all clauses true, or the empty clause $\bot$ is inferred.

ORD-RES-2 brings us closer to SCL(FOL) by performing multiple factoring steps at once. It performs exhaustive factoring of its least false clause in a single step. This is in contrast to ORD-RES-1, which requires multiple steps, but closer to SCL(FOL), which requires exhaustive factoring in some circumstances and allows factoring in others.

We prove that ORD-RES-2 simulates ORD-RES-1. For each factoring step of ORD-RES-1, we distinguish two cases: either it is the ultimate step in a chain of factoring steps—in which case ORD-RES-2 performs a step of its exhaustive-factoring rule, or it is in the middle of a chain—in which case ORD-RES-2 does nothing and waits (a.k.a. stuttering). We exclude infinite stuttering by proving that the least false clause of ORD-RES-1 gets strictly smaller by factoring.

Example 1. Consider the least false clause $C_1 = \mathsf{P}(\mathsf{a}) \vee \mathsf{P}(\mathsf{b}) \vee \mathsf{P}(\mathsf{b}) \vee \mathsf{P}(\mathsf{b})$ where $\mathsf{P}(\mathsf{a}) \prec \mathsf{P}(\mathsf{b})$. ORD-RES-1 uses its factoring rule on C_1 to infer and learn the clause $C_2 = \mathsf{P}(\mathsf{a}) \vee \mathsf{P}(\mathsf{b}) \vee \mathsf{P}(\mathsf{b})$, which becomes the new least false clause. It then uses its factoring rule on C_2 to infer and learn the clause $C_3 = \mathsf{P}(\mathsf{a}) \vee \mathsf{P}(\mathsf{b})$. In contrast, ORD-RES-2 uses its exhaustive-factoring rule on C_1 to directly infer and learn the clause C_3 without learning the clause C_2.

ORD-RES-3 performs exhaustive resolution on its least false clause in a single step. This is in contrast to ORD-RES-2, which requires multiple steps, but like SCL(FOL), which always requires exhaustive resolution during conflict resolution. We prove that ORD-RES-2 simulates ORD-RES-3. For each exhaustive-resolution step of ORD-RES-3, we build a finite chain of resolution steps of ORD-RES-2.

Example 2. Consider the clauses $C_1 = \mathsf{P}(\mathsf{b}) \vee \mathsf{P}(\mathsf{c})$ and $C_2 = \mathsf{P}(\mathsf{a}) \vee \neg\mathsf{P}(\mathsf{c}) \vee \neg\mathsf{P}(\mathsf{c})$ where $\mathsf{P}(\mathsf{a}) \prec \mathsf{P}(\mathsf{b}) \prec \mathsf{P}(\mathsf{c})$ and C_2 is the least false clause. ORD-RES-2 uses its resolution rule on C_1 and C_2 to infer and learn the clause $C_3 = \mathsf{P}(\mathsf{a}) \vee \mathsf{P}(\mathsf{b}) \vee \neg\mathsf{P}(\mathsf{c})$, which becomes the new least false clause. ORD-RES-2 then uses its resolution rule on C_1 and C_3 to infer and learn the clause $C_4 = \mathsf{P}(\mathsf{a}) \vee \mathsf{P}(\mathsf{b}) \vee \mathsf{P}(\mathsf{b})$. In contrast, ORD-RES-2 uses its exhaustive-resolution rule on C_1 and C_2 to directly infer and learn the clause C_4 without learning the clause C_3.

ORD-RES-4 does not learn factorized clauses but instead registers clauses for implicit factoring. This is in contrast to ORD-RES-3, which learns the factorized clauses, but like SCL(FOL), which performs implicit factoring when propagating a literal. ORD-RES-4 keeps track of both a set N of known clauses and a set $\mathcal{F} \subseteq N$ of to-implicitly-factorize clauses. The set of considered clauses consists of the known clauses from N except that the clauses from $\mathcal{F}$ are replaced by their exhaustively factorized version.

We prove that ORD-RES-4 simulates ORD-RES-3. For each exhaustive-factoring step of ORD-RES-3, we prove that ORD-RES-4 can perform an implicit-factoring step. This requires us to prove that model construction of the considered clauses of both calculi agree and reach the same least false clause.

Example 3. Consider the clause set $N = \{C_1 = \mathsf{P(a)} \lor \mathsf{P(a)} \lor \mathsf{P(a)}, C_2 = \mathsf{P(b)} \lor \mathsf{P(b)} \lor \mathsf{P(b)}\}$ where $\mathsf{P(a)} \prec \mathsf{P(b)}$. At first, ORD-RES-4 keeps track of the known clauses N and to-implicitly-factorize clauses $\{\} \subseteq N$. ORD-RES-4 then uses its implicit-factoring rule to register that C_1 should be implicitly factorized. ORD-RES-4 now keeps track of the known clauses N and to-implicitly-factorize clauses $\{C_1\} \subseteq N$; the considered clauses are $\{\mathsf{P(a)}, C_2\}$. ORD-RES-4 then uses its implicit-factoring rule again to register that C_2 should be implicitly factorized. ORD-RES-4 now keeps track of the known clauses N and to-implicitly-factorize clauses $\{C_1, C_2\} \subseteq N$; the considered clauses are $\{\mathsf{P(a)}, \mathsf{P(b)}\}$.

ORD-RES-5 explicitly builds a partial model that closely matches the implicit model construction by iterating over clauses. The partial model is expressed as a partial function from atoms to clauses: The domain represents all atoms considered true and the codomain uniquely identifies the clauses that made each atoms true. The calculus has rules to emulate the implicit model construction from ORD-RES-4.

We prove that ORD-RES-5 simulates ORD-RES-4. For each step of ORD-RES-4, we build a finite chain of model-construction steps of ORD-RES-5 and prove that the models used by both calculi are equivalent.

Example 4. Consider the clauses $C_1 = \mathsf{P(a)}$, $C_2 = \mathsf{P(b)} \lor \mathsf{P(c)}$, and $C_3 = \neg\mathsf{P(c)}$ where $\mathsf{P(a)} \prec \mathsf{P(b)} \prec \mathsf{P(c)}$. ORD-RES-5 starts with the empty model (i.e., encoded by the empty function). The first clause considered is C_1, which is false. To make it true, the model is expanded with the atom $\mathsf{P(a)}$ (i.e., encoded by the function $\{\mathsf{P(a)} \mapsto C_1\}$). The next clause considered is C_2, which is also false. To make it true, the model is expanded with the atom $\mathsf{P(c)}$ (i.e., encoded by the function $\{\mathsf{P(a)} \mapsto C_1, \mathsf{P(c)} \mapsto C_2\}$). The next clause considered is C_3, which is the least false clause. ORD-RES-5 performs a resolution inference and learns the clause $\mathsf{P(b)}$. Then, the candidate model is thrown away and model construction restarts with the empty model.

ORD-RES-6 performs a backjump when learning a new clause. This prevents rebuilding similar partial models from scratch again and again. When ORD-RES-5 performs a factoring or resolution step, it discards its partial model and restarts model construction from scratch. Because model construction is deterministic, the new partial model will be very similar to the previous one. A better strategy is to use a backjump—a special case of backtracking that keeps as much of the model as possible.

We prove that ORD-RES-5 simulates ORD-RES-6. For each step of ORD-RES-6, we build the finite chain of model-construction steps of ORD-RES-5 to build the same model as the one kept by ORD-RES-6.

Example 5. Consider again the clauses $C_1 = \mathsf{P(a)}$, $C_2 = \mathsf{P(b)} \vee \mathsf{P(c)}$, and $C_3 = \neg\mathsf{P(c)}$ from Example 4. ORD-RES-6 starts the same. It constructs the candidate model $\{\mathsf{P(a)} \mapsto C_1, \mathsf{P(c)} \mapsto C_2\}$, identifies C_3 as the least false clause, and learns the clause $\mathsf{P(b)}$ by resolution. But instead of throwing away the candidate model, ORD-RES-6 keep as much of it as possible and backjumps to the model $\{\mathsf{P(a)} \mapsto C_1\}$.

ORD-RES-7 explicitly builds a partial model as a trail of annotated literals. This change of the model encoding gets us closer to SCL(FOL), which also works with a trail of annotated literals. The true atoms encoded in the model of ORD-RES-6 become positive literals in the trail. The atoms that were implicitly false in the model of ORD-RES-6 become negative literals in the trail. The literals are annotated with the clause that produced them.

We prove that ORD-RES-6 simulates ORD-RES-7. For each step of ORD-RES-7, we prove that ORD-RES-6 either performs a corresponding step, or waits for ORD-RES-7 to iteratively build its trail. When matching states, we have to prove that the two model representations are equivalent.

Example 6. Consider again the clauses $C_1 = \mathsf{P(a)}$, $C_2 = \mathsf{P(b)} \vee \mathsf{P(c)}$, and $C_3 = \neg\mathsf{P(c)}$ from Example 5. ORD-RES-7 constructs the candidate model $[\mathsf{P(a)}^{C_1}, \neg\mathsf{P(b)}, \mathsf{P(c)}^{C_2}]$, identifies C_3 as the least false clause, learns the clause $\mathsf{P(b)}$ by resolution, and backjumps to the model $[\mathsf{P(a)}^{C_1}]$.

ORD-RES-8 explicitly builds a partial model as a trail of literals by iterating over atoms. The ORD-RES-7 calculus is made very complex by the fact that it iterates over clauses to construct the model: when considering then next clause, many (negative) literals could need to be added to the trail. The ORD-RES-8 calculus significantly simplifies model construction by iterating over atoms from smallest to largest. When considering an atom, model construction propagates a positive literal if there is a corresponding propagating clause and decides a negative literal otherwise.

We prove that ORD-RES-7 simulates ORD-RES-8. For each step of ORD-RES-8, we prove that ORD-RES-7 either performs a corresponding step, or waits for ORD-RES-7 to iterates over clauses that have no effect on the trail.

Example 7. Consider again the clauses $C_1 = \mathsf{P(a)}$, $C_2 = \mathsf{P(b)} \vee \mathsf{P(c)}$, and $C_3 = \neg\mathsf{P(c)}$ from Example 6. ORD-RES-8 first considers the atom $\mathsf{P(a)}$, notices that it can be propagated by the clause C_1, and extends the trail with a positive literal: $[\mathsf{P(a)}^{C_1}]$. ORD-RES-8 then considers the atom $\mathsf{P(b)}$, notices no propagating clause, and extends the trail with a negative literal: $[\mathsf{P(a)}^{C_1}, \neg\mathsf{P(b)}]$. ORD-RES-8 then considers the atom $\mathsf{P(c)}$, notices that it can be propagated by the clause C_2, and extends the trail with a positive literal: $[\mathsf{P(a)}^{C_1}, \neg\mathsf{P(b)}, \mathsf{P(c)}^{C_2}]$.

ORD-RES-9 learns the necessary implicit factoring during propagation. ORD-RES-8 still has an explicit rule to learn which clauses should be factorized, but SCL(FOL) has no such rule. The solution is to perform this task when propagating a positive literal on the trail.

We prove that ORD-RES-8 simulates ORD-RES-9. One step of ORD-RES-9 that both learns a implicit factoring and propagates corresponds to two steps of ORD-RES-8; all other steps of ORD-RES-9 are the same as in ORD-RES-8.

Example 8. Consider again the clauses $C_1 = \mathsf{P}(\mathsf{a}) \vee \mathsf{P}(\mathsf{a}) \vee \mathsf{P}(\mathsf{a})$ and $C_2 = \mathsf{P}(\mathsf{b}) \vee \mathsf{P}(\mathsf{b}) \vee \mathsf{P}(\mathsf{b})$ from Example 3. ORD-RES-9 first considers the atom $\mathsf{P}(\mathsf{a})$ and finds that it could be propagated if the clause C_1 was factorized. It learns to implicitly factorize C_1 to $\mathsf{P}(\mathsf{a})$ and extends the trail with a positive literal: $[\mathsf{P}(\mathsf{a})^{\mathsf{P}(\mathsf{a})}]$. It then considers the atom $\mathsf{P}(\mathsf{b})$ and finds that it could be propagated if the clause C_2 was factorized. It learns to implicitly factorize C_2 to $\mathsf{P}(\mathsf{b})$ and extends the trail with a positive literal: $[\mathsf{P}(\mathsf{a})^{\mathsf{P}(\mathsf{a})}, \mathsf{P}(\mathsf{b})^{\mathsf{P}(\mathsf{b})}]$.

ORD-RES-10 favors decisions over propagations and propagates if, and only if, a conflict is imminent. This is because SCL(FOL) performs exhaustive resolution w.r.t. all literals propagated after the decision that caused the conflict. This is in contrast to ORD-RES-9, which performs resolution only w.r.t. one literal.

We prove that ORD-RES-9 simulates ORD-RES-10. A positive-decision step of ORD-RES-10 corresponds to a propagation step of ORD-RES-9; all other steps are the same in both calculi.

Example 9. Consider the clauses $C_1 = \mathsf{P}(\mathsf{a})$, $C_2 = \neg\mathsf{P}(\mathsf{a}) \vee \mathsf{P}(\mathsf{b})$, $C_3 = \neg\mathsf{P}(\mathsf{b}) \vee \mathsf{P}(\mathsf{c})$, and $C_4 = \neg\mathsf{P}(\mathsf{b}) \vee \neg\mathsf{P}(\mathsf{c}) \vee \neg\mathsf{P}(\mathsf{c})$ where $\mathsf{P}(\mathsf{a}) \prec \mathsf{P}(\mathsf{b}) \prec \mathsf{P}(\mathsf{c})$. ORD-RES-9 builds the trail $[\mathsf{P}(\mathsf{a})^{C_1}, \mathsf{P}(\mathsf{b})^{C_2}, \mathsf{P}(\mathsf{c})^{C_3}]$. In contrast, ORD-RES-10 builds the trail $[\mathsf{P}(\mathsf{a}), \mathsf{P}(\mathsf{b}), \mathsf{P}(\mathsf{c})^{C_3}]$. The atoms $\mathsf{P}(\mathsf{a})$ and $\mathsf{P}(\mathsf{b})$ were decided (i.e., the positive literals are not annotated) because adding them to the trail did not make any clause false. The atom $\mathsf{P}(\mathsf{c})$ was propagated (i.e., the positive literal is annotated with C_3) because adding it to the trail made the clause C_4 false.

ORD-RES-11 splits the exhaustive resolution step into multiple steps to detect a conflict, perform one resolution step at a time, skip literals from the trail, and backjump. This resolves the last difference with SCL(FOL), which has a multistep conflict resolution mechanism.

We prove that ORD-RES-11 simulates ORD-RES-10. For each step of ORD-RES-10, we build a non-empty sequence of corresponding steps of ORD-RES-11. For each exhaustive-resolution step of ORD-RES-10, we build a finite sequence of conflict step, resolution steps, trail-skipping steps, and backjumping step in ORD-RES-11; all other steps of ORD-RES-10 have a single corresponding step in ORD-RES-11.

Example 10. Consider again the clauses $C_1 = \mathsf{P}(\mathsf{a})$, $C_2 = \neg\mathsf{P}(\mathsf{a}) \vee \mathsf{P}(\mathsf{b})$, $C_3 = \neg\mathsf{P}(\mathsf{b}) \vee \mathsf{P}(\mathsf{c})$, and $C_4 = \neg\mathsf{P}(\mathsf{b}) \vee \neg\mathsf{P}(\mathsf{c}) \vee \neg\mathsf{P}(\mathsf{c})$ from Example 9. ORD-RES-11 first builds the trail $[\mathsf{P}(\mathsf{a}), \mathsf{P}(\mathsf{b}), \mathsf{P}(\mathsf{c})^{C_3}]$ and detects that the clause C_4 is false. ORD-RES-11 then performs a resolution step between C_3 and C_4 to infer the clause $\neg\mathsf{P}(\mathsf{b}) \vee \neg\mathsf{P}(\mathsf{b}) \vee \neg\mathsf{P}(\mathsf{c})$. This is followed by a second resolution step between it and C_3 to infer the clause $\neg\mathsf{P}(\mathsf{b}) \vee \neg\mathsf{P}(\mathsf{b}) \vee \neg\mathsf{P}(\mathsf{b})$. This last inferred clause is then learned and ORD-RES-11 backjumps to the trail $[\mathsf{P}(\mathsf{a})]$.

This concludes our sequence of refinements, and we can now present our three main theorems. The first one states that ORD-RES-1 is a strategy for ORD-RES (i.e., the transitions of ORD-RES-1 are a subset of the transitions of ORD-RES).

Theorem 11 (ORD-RES-1 Strategy for ORD-RES). *Let N and N' be finite sets of ground clauses. If $N \Rightarrow_{\text{ORD-RES-1}} N'$, then $N \Rightarrow_{\text{ORD-RES}} N'$.*

The second theorem composes all bisimulations between ORD-RES-1 and ORD-RES-11. This essentially means that the two calculi behave the same.

Theorem 12 (Bisimulation between ORD-RES-1 and ORD-RES-11). *There exists a bisimulation between ORD-RES-1 and ORD-RES-11.*

The last theorem states that ORD-RES-11 is a strategy for regular SCL(FOL) (i.e., the transitions of ORD-RES-11 can be projected onto a subset of the transitions of regular SCL(FOL)).

Theorem 13 (ORD-RES-11 Strategy for Regular SCL(FOL)). *There exist projection functions $proj_{atm}$, $proj_{clss}$, and $proj_{state}$ such that the following statements hold for any finite set N of ground clauses, for any ground atom β, and for any ORD-RES-11 states S and S'.*

1. *The initial state of ORD-RES-11 can be projected onto the initial state of SCL(FOL) (i.e., $proj_{state}\ \langle N; \{\}; \{\}; \epsilon; \dagger\rangle = \langle \epsilon; \{\}; \dagger\rangle$).*
2. *If*
   - *all atoms in N are less than or equal to β (i.e., $\forall A \in \mathsf{atoms_{clss}}\, N.\ A \preceq \beta$)*
   - *S is reachable from the initial state (i.e., $\langle N; \{\}; \{\}; \epsilon; \dagger\rangle \Rightarrow^{*}_{\text{ORD-RES-11}} S$)*
   - *there is a transition from S to S' (i.e., $S \Rightarrow_{\text{ORD-RES-11}} S'$)*

   then the transition from S to S' can be projected onto a corresponding regular SCL(FOL) transition (i.e., $(proj_{state}\ S) \Rightarrow_{\textit{Reg-SCL}}^{proj_{clss}\, N,\, proj_{atm}\, \beta} (proj_{state}\ S')$).

The symbol † denotes that an optional value is absent (i.e., an optional value can either be a value x or †).

Theorems 11 to 12 can be found in theory Simulation_SCLFOL_ORDRES of the Isabelle/HOL formalization. Theorems 11 corresponds to sublocale declaration backward_simulation_with_measuring_function. Theorems 13 corresponds to theorem ord_res_11_is_strategy_for_regular_scl. Theorems 12 corresponds to theorem bisimulation_ord_res_1_ord_res_11.

4 Details

We now provide a more formal presentation of our lemma to lift a simulation to a bisimulation (Sect. 4.1), of the ORD-RES-1 strategy for ground ordered resolution (Sect. 4.2), and of the ORD-RES-11 strategy for SCL(FOL) (Sect. 4.3). The interested reader can refer to the Isabelle/HOL formalization for more details.

4.1 Lifting a Simulation to a Bisimulation

Two transition systems may be expressed differently but represent similar computations. This relationship is formally expressed by a simulation. Informally, a transition system $\mathcal{A}$ simulates a transition system $\mathcal{B}$ if $\mathcal{A}$ is able to do everything that $\mathcal{B}$ can do. If the similarity goes both way, we say that there is a bisimulation between $\mathcal{A}$ and $\mathcal{B}$.

Definition 14 (Simulation and Bisimulation [9,12,18]**).** *Let $\mathcal{R}$ and $\mathcal{Q}$ be transition relations. Let $\overset{i}{\sim}$ be an annotated matching relation between states of $\mathcal{R}$ and $\mathcal{Q}$ for any annotation i. Let $\sqsubset$ and $\prec$ be two well-founded relations on annotations. We say that $\mathcal{Q}$* simulates *$\mathcal{R}$ w.r.t. $\sim$ and $\sqsubset$ if, following a step of $\mathcal{R}$, $\mathcal{Q}$ either progresses or waits finitely often (i.e., if $\forall i\ a\ b.\ a \overset{i}{\sim} b \longrightarrow \mathcal{R}\ a\ a' \longrightarrow (\exists b'\ i'.\ \mathcal{Q}^+\ b\ b' \wedge a' \overset{i'}{\sim} b') \vee (\exists i'.\ a' \overset{i'}{\sim} b \wedge i' \sqsubset i)$). We say that there is a* bisimulation *between $\mathcal{R}$ and $\mathcal{Q}$ w.r.t. $\sim$, $\prec$, and $\sqsubset$ if both $\mathcal{R}$ simulates $\mathcal{Q}$ w.r.t. $\sim$ and $\prec$, and $\mathcal{Q}$ simulates $\mathcal{R}$ w.r.t. $\sim$ and $\sqsubset$.*

One change we introduced compared to [12] is that a bisimulation may use a different well-founded relation for each simulation direction. What did not change is that a bisimulation requires its two simulations to be w.r.t. the same matching relation. This incurs significant complexity: The definition of the matching relation must contain invariants strong enough for both simulations, and the two simulation proofs must show the preservation of these strong invariants.

Fortunately, a folklore lemma states that it is possible to reverse a simulation between two deterministic transition systems. For example, assuming that $\mathcal{R}$ and $\mathcal{Q}$ are deterministic transition relations and that $\mathcal{R}$ simulates $\mathcal{Q}$ w.r.t. a matching relation $\sim$, the folklore lemma states that there exists another matching relation $\approx$, such that $\mathcal{Q}$ simulates $\mathcal{R}$ w.r.t. $\approx$. This is, however, not enough for a bisimulation between $\mathcal{R}$ and $\mathcal{Q}$, which requires both simulations to be w.r.t. the same matching relation.

We extended the folklore lemma such that, under certain conditions, it lifts a simulation to a bisimulation w.r.t. a new matching relation. This result should not surprise any expert, but we nevertheless could not find it explicitly stated, let alone rigorously proven, in the literature. This lifting lemma not only allows us to simplify our matching relations and prove only half of the simulations, but it also allows us to choose the direction to prove. This is especially useful because one of the directions is usually much easier to prove than the other; which one is simpler varies depending on the exact two transition systems considered.

Lemma 15 (Lifting a Simulation to a Bisimulation). *Let $\mathcal{R}$ and $\mathcal{Q}$ be transition relations. Let $\sim$ be an annotated matching relation between states of $\mathcal{R}$ and $\mathcal{Q}$. Let $<$ be a well-founded relation on annotations. If*

- *$\mathcal{R}$ is right-unique (i.e., $\forall x\ y\ z.\ \mathcal{R}\ x\ y \longrightarrow \mathcal{R}\ x\ z \longrightarrow y = z$)*
- *$\mathcal{Q}$ is right-unique (i.e., $\forall x\ y\ z.\ \mathcal{Q}\ x\ y \longrightarrow \mathcal{Q}\ x\ z \longrightarrow y = z$)*

- *states matching w.r.t.* $\sim$ *agree on whether they are stuck*[2] *or not (i.e.,* $\forall i\ x\ y.\ x \overset{i}{\sim} y \longrightarrow (x \text{ is stuck} \longleftrightarrow y \text{ is stuck})$*)*
- $\mathcal{Q}$ *simulates* $\mathcal{R}$ *w.r.t.* $\sim$ *and* $<$

then there exists a matching relation $\approx$ *and a well-founded relation* $\ll$ *such that the following statements holds:*

- *States matching w.r.t.* $\sim$ *also match w.r.t.* $\approx$ *(i.e.,* $\forall i x y.\ x \overset{i}{\sim} y \longrightarrow (\exists j.\ x \overset{j}{\approx} y)$*).*
- *States matching w.r.t.* $\approx$ *either are both stuck and matching w.r.t.* $\sim$*, or can both progress to states matching w.r.t.* $\sim$ *(i.e.,* $\forall j\ x\ y.\ x \overset{j}{\approx} y \longrightarrow x \text{ is stuck} \wedge y \text{ is stuck} \wedge (\exists i.\ x \overset{i}{\sim} y) \vee (\exists x'\ y'.\ \mathcal{R}^{+}\ x\ x' \wedge \mathcal{Q}^{+}\ y\ y' \wedge (\exists i.\ x' \overset{i}{\sim} y'))$*).*
- *There is a bisimulation between* $\mathcal{R}$ *and* $\mathcal{Q}$ *w.r.t.* $\approx$ *and* $\ll$ *and* $\ll$*.*

Lemma 15 corresponds to lemma lift_strong_simulation_to_bisimulation of theory Lifting_Simulation_To_Bisimulation [9]. Note that Definition 14 defines a bisimulation w.r.t. two arbitrary well-founded relations and that Lemma 15's ultimate conclusion uses the same relation twice.

Lemma 15 still constraints the matching relation: On top of being sufficiently strong to prove a simulation, it must ensure that the two transitions systems finish at the same time (i.e., they agree on stuck states). This means that simulation proofs often have to create a chain of steps to ensure that both transition systems reach a stuck state in tandem. Consider, e.g., the refinement step from ORD-RES-4 to ORD-RES-5 where the implicit and instantaneous model construction is replaced by an explicit and iterative model construction. The matching relation has the following requirements: the two calculi agree on the sets of initial, learned, and to-implicitly-factorize clauses, the invariants of both calculi hold, and the next clause that ORD-RES-5 will consider must be the least false clause implicitly identified by ORD-RES-4.

4.2 ORD-RES-1: A Strategy for Ground Ordered Resolution

The proof of refutational completeness of ground resolution is based on building a model for a saturated clause set. This model takes the form of an Herbrand interpretation (i.e., a set of atoms that are considered true) and is usually built by two mutually recursive functions.

Definition 16 (Model Construction for Ground Ordered Resolution [1]). *The mutually recursive functions* epsilon *and* interp *generate an Herbrand interpretation for a given clause set:*

[2] In the context of a transition relation $\mathcal{R}$, we say that a state x is *stuck* if there is no possible transition starting from it (i.e., if $\nexists y.\ \mathcal{R}\ x\ y$).

$$\forall N\ D.\ \mathsf{epsilon}\ N\ D = \{A \mid D \in N \land A \textit{ is strictly maximal in } D \land \\ \mathsf{interp}\ \{C \in N \mid C \prec D\} \not\models_{\mathsf{cls}} D\}$$

$$\forall N.\ \mathsf{interp}\ N = \bigcup_{D \in N} \mathsf{epsilon}\ N\ D$$

The model construction iterates over the clause set, starting from the least clause following the ordering $\prec$, and collects a set of atoms considered true. At each iteration, epsilon returns a subsingleton set of atoms to add to the interpretation: either the considered clause is already true w.r.t. the interpretation, in which case epsilon returns the empty set, or epsilon returns a single atom that makes the clause true. We say that a clause C is *productive* w.r.t. N if $\mathsf{epsilon}\ N\ C \neq \{\}$. Note that the produced atom is unique (i.e., $\forall N\ C.\ |\mathsf{epsilon}\ N\ C| \leq 1$), because the strictly maximal element in a clause is unique w.r.t. the total ordering $\prec$.

The ORD-RES-1 calculus is a deterministic strategy for ground ordered resolution that uses model construction to guide the inference rules. If model construction succeeds, the clause set is satisfiable and the calculus has nothing more to do. If model construction fails, there exists a (unique) least false clause on which to perform either factoring or resolution.

Definition 17 (Least False Clause). *We say that a ground clause C is the* least false clause *in a clause set N if it is the least clause not made true by model construction (i.e., if it is the least in $\{D \in N \mid \mathsf{interp}\ \{C \in N \mid C \preceq D\} \not\models D\}$).*

The calculus is defined as a transition system $\langle \Rightarrow_{\mathsf{ORD\text{-}RES\text{-}1}}; \mathsf{final}_{\mathsf{ORD\text{-}RES\text{-}1}} \rangle$, where $\Rightarrow_{\mathsf{ORD\text{-}RES\text{-}1}}$ is a transition relation and $\mathsf{final}_{\mathsf{ORD\text{-}RES\text{-}1}}$ is a predicate identifying final states; a state is a finite set of ground clauses.

Definition 18 (ORD-RES-1 Transition Relation). *The transition relation $\Rightarrow_{\mathsf{ORD\text{-}RES\text{-}1}}$ is specified by the following rules.*

Factoring $N \Rightarrow_{\mathsf{ORD\text{-}RES\text{-}1}} (N \cup \{D'\})$
Side conditions:

1. *D is the least false clause in N*
2. *L is a maximal literal in D*
3. *L is a positive literal*
4. *D' is inferred by factoring of D*

Resolution $N \Rightarrow_{\mathsf{ORD\text{-}RES\text{-}1}} (N \cup \{D'\})$
Side conditions:

1. *D is the least false clause in N*
2. *L is a maximal literal in D*
3. *L is a negative literal*

4. $C \in N$
5. C produces the atom of L during model construction for N
6. D' is inferred by resolution on C and D

The rules of $\Rightarrow_{\text{ORD-RES-1}}$ are similar to their counterparts in ground ORD-RES but add several supplementary side conditions to deterministically ascertain which inferences should be performed. More specifically, the first side condition of both rules uniquely selects the main clause on which to operate. The second side condition uniquely selects the literal to inspect. The third condition inspects the selected literal and distinguishes whether a factoring or resolution inference should be performed. In the case of a resolution inference, the fourth and fifth side conditions uniquely select the second clause on which resolution should be performed. The ultimate side condition of both rules is the same as in ground ordered resolution.

Definition 19 (ORD-RES-1 Final States). *A state N is considered final by* $\mathsf{final}_{\text{ORD-RES-1}}$ *either if it contains the empty clause or if the constructed model makes all clauses true (i.e., if $\bot \in N \vee (\forall D \in N.\ \mathsf{interp}\{C \in N \mid C \preceq D\} \models D)$).*

4.3 ORD-RES-11: A Strategy for Regular SCL(FOL)

The ORD-RES-11 calculus is a deterministic strategy for regular SCL(FOL) that constructs the same model and learns essentially the same clauses as ORD-RES-1. It is defined as a transition system $\langle \Rightarrow_{\text{ORD-RES-11}}; \mathsf{final}_{\text{ORD-RES-11}} \rangle$, where $\Rightarrow_{\text{ORD-RES-11}}$ is a transition relation and $\mathsf{final}_{\text{ORD-RES-11}}$ is a predicate identifying final states. A state is a tuple $\langle N; U_r; \mathcal{F}; \Gamma; \mathcal{C} \rangle$ consisting of a finite set N of initial ground clauses, a finite set U_r of ground clauses learned by exhaustive resolution, a finite set $\mathcal{F} \subseteq N \cup U_r$ of clauses to implicitly factorize, a partial model Γ expressed as a trail of annotated literals, and an optional conflicting clause $\mathcal{C}$. Before defining the transition relation and predicate on final states, we first introduce a few intermediate definitions to hide complex and repetitive formulas.

Definition 20 (Implicit Exhaustive Factoring). *The unary function* efac *performs exhaustive factoring of a ground clause through repeated application of the factoring rule (i.e., $\forall C.\ \mathsf{efac}\ C = (\iota C'.\ \mathsf{ground\_factoring}^*\ C\ C' \wedge (\nexists C''.\ \mathsf{ground\_factoring}\, C'\, C''))$).*[3] *The binary function* iefac *performs exhaustive factoring of a ground clause through* efac *if it is a member of the provided clause set (i.e., $\forall \mathcal{F}\ C.\ \mathsf{iefac}\ \mathcal{F}\ C = (\mathsf{if}\ C \in \mathcal{F}\ \mathsf{then}\ \mathsf{efac}\ C\ \mathsf{else}\ C)$).*

Definition 21 (False Clause w.r.t. ORD-RES-11). *We say that a ground clause C is* false *w.r.t. $\langle N; U_r; \mathcal{F}; \Gamma; \mathcal{C} \rangle$ if $C \in \{\mathsf{iefac}\, \mathcal{F}\ C \mid C \in N \cup U_r\}$ and C is false under Γ.*

[3] The syntax $\iota x.\ P\ x$ corresponds to the definite description operator and denotes the unique x for which the predicate P holds.

Definition 22 (Propagating Clause w.r.t. ORD-RES-11). *We say that a ground clause C is* propagating *a ground literal L w.r.t. $\langle N; U_r; \mathcal{F}; \Gamma; \mathcal{C}\rangle$ if $C \in \{\mathsf{iefac}\, \mathcal{F}\; C \mid C \in N \cup U_r\}$, and L is undefined in Γ, and L is a maximal literal in C, and the clause $\{K \in C \mid K \neq L\}$ is false under Γ.*

Definition 23 (Undefined Atom w.r.t. ORD-RES-11). *We say that a ground atom A is* undefined *w.r.t. $\langle N; U_r; \mathcal{F}; \Gamma; \mathcal{C}\rangle$ if $A \in \{A_2 \in \mathsf{atoms_{clss}}\,(N \cup U_r) \mid \forall A_1 \in \mathsf{atoms_{trail}}\; \Gamma.\; A_1 \prec_{\mathsf{t}} A_2\}$[4].*

Using these definitions, we can now proceed to define the ORD-RES-11 calculus. Our transition system is close to the one of SCL(FOL) [8], except it splits the Decide rule into two rules and incorporates the non-redundant clause learning of ORD-RES-1 into the side conditions of the rules.

Definition 24 (ORD-RES-11 Transition Relation). *The transition relation $\Rightarrow_{\mathsf{ORD\text{-}RES\text{-}11}}$ consists of the following rules.*

DecideNeg $\langle N; U_r; \mathcal{F}; \Gamma; \dagger\rangle \Rightarrow_{\mathsf{ORD\text{-}RES\text{-}11}} \langle N; U_r; \mathcal{F}; \Gamma, \neg A^{\dagger}; \dagger\rangle$
Side conditions:

1. *there is no false clause w.r.t. $\langle N; U_r; \mathcal{F}; \Gamma; \dagger\rangle$*
2. *A is the least undefined atom w.r.t. $\langle N; U_r; \mathcal{F}; \Gamma; \dagger\rangle$*
3. *there is no propagating clause for the literal A w.r.t. $\langle N; U_r; \mathcal{F}; \Gamma; \dagger\rangle$*

DecidePos $\langle N; U_r; \mathcal{F}; \Gamma; \dagger\rangle \Rightarrow_{\mathsf{ORD\text{-}RES\text{-}11}} \langle N; U_r; \mathcal{F}'; \Gamma, A^{\dagger}; \dagger\rangle$
Side conditions:

1. *there is no false clause w.r.t. $\langle N; U_r; \mathcal{F}; \Gamma; \dagger\rangle$*
2. *A is the least undefined atom w.r.t. $\langle N; U_r; \mathcal{F}; \Gamma; \dagger\rangle$*
3. *C is the least propagating clause for the literal A w.r.t. $\langle N; U_r; \mathcal{F}; \Gamma; \dagger\rangle$*
4. *$\mathcal{F}' = \mathcal{F} \cup (\mathsf{if}\ (A$ is the greatest literal in $C)\ \mathsf{then}\ \{\}\ \mathsf{else}\ \{C\})$*
5. *there is no false clause w.r.t. $\langle N; U_r; \mathcal{F}'; \Gamma, A^{\dagger}; \dagger\rangle$*

Propagate $\langle N; U_r; \mathcal{F}; \Gamma; \dagger\rangle \Rightarrow_{\mathsf{ORD\text{-}RES\text{-}11}} \langle N; U_r; \mathcal{F}'; \Gamma, A^{\mathsf{efac}\ C}; \dagger\rangle$
Side conditions:

1. *there is no false clause w.r.t. $\langle N; U_r; \mathcal{F}; \Gamma; \dagger\rangle$*
2. *A is the least undefined atom w.r.t. $\langle N; U_r; \mathcal{F}; \Gamma; \dagger\rangle$*
3. *C is the least propagating clause for the literal A w.r.t. $\langle N; U_r; \mathcal{F}; \Gamma; \dagger\rangle$*
4. *$\mathcal{F}' = \mathcal{F} \cup (\mathsf{if}\ (A$ is the greatest literal in $C)\ \mathsf{then}\ \{\}\ \mathsf{else}\ \{C\})$*
5. *there is a false clause w.r.t. $\langle N; U_r; \mathcal{F}'; \Gamma, A^{\dagger}; \dagger\rangle$*

Conflict $\langle N; U_r; \mathcal{F}; \Gamma; \dagger\rangle \Rightarrow_{\mathsf{ORD\text{-}RES\text{-}11}} \langle N; U_r; \mathcal{F}; \Gamma; D\rangle$
Side conditions:

1. *D is the least false clause w.r.t. $\langle N; U_r; \mathcal{F}; \Gamma; \dagger\rangle$*

[4] The unary functions $\mathsf{atoms_{clss}}$ and $\mathsf{atoms_{trail}}$ return the finite sets of all atoms occurring respectively in a clause set and in a trail of annotated literals.

Skip $\langle N; U_r; \mathcal{F}; \Gamma, L^-; D\rangle \Rightarrow_{\mathsf{ORD\text{-}RES\text{-}11}} \langle N; U_r; \mathcal{F}; \Gamma; D\rangle$
Side conditions:

1. $\mathsf{comp}\, L \notin D$

Resolve $\langle N; U_r; \mathcal{F}; \Gamma, L^C; D\rangle \Rightarrow_{\mathsf{ORD\text{-}RES\text{-}11}} \langle N; U_r; \mathcal{F}; \Gamma, L^C; D'\rangle$
Side conditions:

1. $\mathsf{comp}\, L \in D$
2. $D' = (C - \{L\}) \cup (D - \{\mathsf{comp}\, L\})$

Backtrack $\langle N; U_r; \mathcal{F}; \Gamma, L^\dagger; D\rangle \Rightarrow_{\mathsf{ORD\text{-}RES\text{-}11}} \langle N; U_r \cup \{D\}; \mathcal{F}; \Gamma; \dagger\rangle$
Side conditions:

1. $\mathsf{comp}\, L \in D$

The rules DecideNeg, DecidePos, and Propagate iteratively construct a trail that serves as (partial) candidate model for the clauses $\{\mathsf{iefac}\, \mathcal{F}\, C \mid C \in N \cup U_r\}$. The rule Conflict is used as soon as the candidate model is in conflict with at least one clause. The rules Skip and Resolve resolve the found conflict by performing exhaustive resolution between the conflicting clause and the clause found in the trail annotations. At the end of conflict resolution, the Backtrack rule removes the last decision that lead to the conflict and learns a new non-redundant clause.

ORD-RES-11 is purposefully defined similarly to the formalized SCL(FOL) calculus [4, Section 2]. One difference is that the rules of ORD-RES-11 are for ground clauses while the rules of SCL(FOL) are for non-ground clauses; this simplifies the ground rules because they do not need to handle variables through grounding substitutions, renaming substitutions, or most general unifiers. Another difference is that the rules of ORD-RES-11 have several side conditions to deterministically choose which clause and literal to work upon while the rules of SCL(FOL) use a "don't care" non-determinism approach to allow maximal flexibility. A final difference is that the rules of ORD-RES-11 have side conditions to embed the restrictions of a regular SCL(FOL) strategy [4, Definition 3] (i.e., that decisions do not immediately lead to a conflict and that the Conflict rule has precedence over all other). Theorem 13 shows that ORD-RES-11 constitutes a regular strategy of SCL(FOL).

Definition 25 (ORD-RES-11 Final States). *A state $\langle N; U_r; \mathcal{F}; \Gamma; \mathcal{C}\rangle$ is considered final by $\mathsf{final}_{\mathsf{ORD\text{-}RES\text{-}11}}$ either if $\mathcal{C} = \dagger$ and there are neither false clauses nor undefined atom w.r.t. $\langle N; U_r; \mathcal{F}; \Gamma; \mathcal{C}\rangle$ or if $\mathcal{C} = \bot$ and the trail Γ is empty.*

5 Related Work and Discussion

This work was enabled by the growing trend of formalizing the metatheory of logical calculi in proof assistants. Particularly important to us were the availability of formalizations of superposition, ordered resolution, and SCL(FOL). The first candidate was a formalization of a generalization of superposition [20]. However, this formalization represents clauses as sets, which essentially forces factoring to be implicit. We wanted to stay close to the original formulation of clauses as multisets and respective completeness proof with explicit factoring [1] and decided against reusing [20]. The next candidate was a formalization of the superposition calculus [13,14] representing clauses as multisets. However, it only has native support for equations and not for non-equational atoms. This would have required us to encode predicates, which we did not want to deal with. Therefore, we decided to manually extract a formalization for ground ordered resolution out of this formalization. Another possibility would have been to use the formalization of a variant of ground ordered resolution [21,22]. However, this calculus consists of a single resolution rule with built-in factorization, which does not match the use of factorization in SCL(FOL) and ordered resolution with respect to the non-redundant clause learning strategy, ORD-RES-1. Finally, SCL(FOL) was recently formalized [4,10]. This formalization provides a non-ground calculus, but it can be used with relatively little overhead on a ground clause set.

In this paper, we formalize the simulation result of [6] in Isabelle/HOL. They define a strategy for ground ordered resolution, a strategy for SCL(FOL), and prove a simulation between the two. Their pen-and-paper proof is however monolithic and challenging to comprehend. This represents a significant challenge for a formalization in a proof assistant which works better for modular proofs made of small and simple proof steps.

To improve clarity, we developed an alternative proof structure for our Isabelle/HOL formalization. We reused the model-based strategy for ordered resolution specified in [6] and performed ten further refinement steps, proving a bisimulation between the steps. To ease these refinement steps, we proved a lifting lemma to get a bisimulation from a simulation. We then showed that the calculus resulting from the ultimate refinement step is a strategy of regular SCL(FOL). Our SCL(FOL) strategy looks very different to the one from [6], but we claim that they are equivalent in the sense that they learn the same clauses in the same order. In summary, we have one strategy for ordered resolution, one strategy for regular SCL(FOL), and a bisimulation proof that the two strategies are equivalent.

The Isabelle/HOL formalization was invaluable because it forced us to consider corner cases and allowed us to notice small mistakes in the initial specification of some of the calculi. The tooling for proof automation, such as the Sledgehammer command and the order proof method, helped us tremendously by allowing to quickly discharge simple subgoals and focus on the big picture.

Disclosure of Interests. The authors have no competing interests to declare that are relevant to the content of this article.

References

1. Bachmair, L., Ganzinger, H.: Rewrite-based equational theorem proving with selection and simplification. J. Log. Comput. **4**(3), 217–247 (1994). ISSN: 0955-792X. https://doi.org/10.1093/logcom/4.3.217
2. Bayardo, R.J., Schrag, R.: Using CSP look-back techniques to solve exceptionally hard SAT instances. In: Freuder, E.C. (ed.) CP 1996. LNCS, vol. 1118, pp. 46–60. Springer, Heidelberg (1996). https://doi.org/10.1007/3-540-61551-2_65
3. Blanchette, J.C.: Formalizing the metatheory of logical calculi and automatic provers in Isabelle/HOL (invited talk). In: Mahboubi, A., Myreen, M.O. (eds.) Proceedings of the 8th ACM SIGPLAN International Conference on Certified Programs and Proofs. CPP 2019, Cascais, Portugal, 14 January 2019–15 January 2019, pp. 1–13. Association for Computing Machinery, 14 January 2019. ISBN: 978-1-4503-6222-1. https://doi.org/10.1145/3293880.3294087. The IsaFoL (Isabelle Formalization of Logic) repository is hosted at https://github.com/IsaFoL/IsaFoL
4. Bromberger, M., Desharnais, M., Weidenbach, C.: An Isabelle/HOL formalization of the SCL(FOL) calculus. In: Pientka, B., Tinelli, C. (eds.) Automated Deduction – CADE 29. Proceedings of the 29th International Conference on Automated Deduction, CADE 2023. LNCS, Rome, Italy, 1 July 2023–4 July 2023, vol. 14132, pp. 116– 133. Springer, Cham, 2 September 2023. ISBN: 978-3-031-38498-1. https://doi.org/10.1007/978-3-031-38499-8_7
5. Bromberger, M., Fiori, A., Weidenbach, C.: Deciding the Bernays-Schoenfinkel fragment over bounded difference constraints by simple clause learning over theories. In: Henglein, F., Shoham, S., Vizel, Y. (eds.) VMCAI 2021. LNCS, vol. 12597, pp. 511–533. Springer, Cham (2021). https://doi.org/10.1007/978-3-030-67067-2_23
6. Bromberger, M., Jain, C., Weidenbach, C.: SCL(FOL) can simulate non-redundant superposition clause learning. In: Pientka, B., Tinelli, C. (eds.) Automated Deduction – CADE 29. Proceedings of the 29th International Conference on Automated Deduction. CADE 2023. LNCS, Rome, Italy, 1 July 2023–4 July 2023, vol. 14132, pp. 134–152. Springer, Cham, 3 September 2023. ISBN: 978-3-031-38498-1. https://doi.org/10.1007/978-3-031-38499-8_8
7. Bromberger, M., Schwarz, S., Weidenbach, C.: Exploring partial models with SCL. In: Konev, B., Schon, C., Steen, A. (eds.) Proceedings of the Workshop on Practical Aspects of Automated Reasoning Co-Located with the 11th International Joint Conference on Automated Reasoning (FLoC/IJCAR 2022), Haifa, Israel, 11–12 August 2022, vol. 3201. CEUR Workshop Proceedings. CEURWS.org (2022). http://ceur-ws.org/Vol-3201/paper5.pdf
8. Bromberger, M., Schwarz, S., Weidenbach, C.: SCL(FOL) Revisited (2023). https://doi.org/10.48550/arXiv.2302.05954. arXiv: 2302.05954 [cs.LO]
9. Desharnais, M.: A generic framework for verified compilers. Arch. Formal Proofs (2020). https://isa-afp.org/entries/VeriComphtml. Formal proof development. ISSN: 2150-914x
10. Desharnais, M.: A formalization of the SCL(FOL) calculus: simple clause learning for first-order logic. Arch. Formal Proofs (2023). https://isa-afp.org/entries/Simple_Clause_Learning.html. Formal proof development. ISSN: 2150-914x
11. Desharnais, M.: SCL simulates nonredundant ground resolution. Arch. Formal Proofs (2024). https://isa-afp.org/entries/SCL_Simulates_Ground_Resolution.html. Formal proof development. ISSN: 2150-914x

12. Desharnais, M., Brunthaler, S.: A generic framework for verified compilers using Isabelle/HOL's locales. In: Nipkow, T., Paulson, L., Wenzel, M. (eds.) Isabelle Workshop (2020). https://sketis.net/isabelle/isabelle-workshop-2020
13. Desharnais, M., Toth, B.: A modular formalization of superposition. Arch. Formal Proofs (2024). https://isaafp.org/entries/Superposition_Calculus.html. Formal proof development. ISSN: 2150-914x
14. Desharnais, M., Toth, B., Waldmann, U., Blanchette, J., Tourret, S.: A modular formalization of superposition in Isabelle/HOL. In: Bertot, Y., Kutsia, T., Norrish, M. (eds.) 15th International Conference on Interactive Theorem Proving. ITP 2024, Tbilisi, Georgia, 9 September 2024–14 September 2024. Leibniz International Proceedings in Informatics (LIPIcs), vol. 309, pp. 12:1–12:20. Schloss Dagstuhl – Leibniz-Zentrum für Informatik, Dagstuhl, Germany, 2 September 2024. ISBN: 978-3-95977-337-9. https://doi.org/10.4230/LIPIcs.ITP.2024.12
15. Fiori, A., Weidenbach, C.: SCL clause learning from simple models. In: Fontaine, P. (ed.) CADE 2019. LNCS (LNAI), vol. 11716, pp. 233–249. Springer, Cham (2019). https://doi.org/10.1007/978-3-030-29436-6_14
16. Knuth, D.E., Bendix, P.B.: Simple word problems in universal algebras. In: Leech, J. (ed.) Computational Problems in Abstract Algebra, pp. 263–297. Pergamon Press (1970)
17. Leidinger, H., Weidenbach, C.: SCL(EQ): SCL for first- order logic with equality. In: Blanchette, J., Kovács, L., Pattinson, D. (eds.) Automated Reasoning - 11th International Joint Conference, IJCAR 2022. LNCS, Haifa, Israel, 8–10 August 2022, Proceedings, vol. 13385, pp. 228–247. Springer (2022). https://doi.org/10.1007/978-3-031-10769-6_14
18. Leroy, X.: A formally verified compiler back-end. J. Autom. Reason. **43**(4), 363–446 (2009). ISSN: 0168- 7433. https://doi.org/10.1007/s10817-009-9155-4
19. Marques Silva, J.P., Sakallah, K.A.: GRASP-a new search algorithm for satisfiability. In: Proceedings of International Conference on Computer Aided Design, pp. 220–227 (1996). https://doi.org/10.1109/ICCAD.996.569607
20. Peltier, N.: A variant of the superposition calculus. Arch. Formal Proofs (2016). https://www.isa-afp.org/entries/SuperCalc.html
21. Schlichtkrull, A., Blanchette, J., Traytel, D., Waldmann, U.: Formalizing Bachmair and Ganzinger's ordered resolution prover. J. Autom. Reason. **64**(7), 1169–1195 (2020). https://doi.org/10.1007/s10817-020-09561-0
22. Schlichtkrull, A., Blanchette, J.C., Traytel, D., Waldmann, U.: Formalization of Bachmair and Ganzinger's ordered resolution prover. Arch. Formal Proofs (2018). https://isa-afp.org/entries/Ordered_Resolution_Prover.html. Formal proof development. ISSN: 2150-914x

Calculi

Interoperability of Proof Systems with SC-TPTP

Simon Guilloud[1(✉)], Julie Cailler[2], Sankalp Gambhir[1], Auguste Poiroux[1], Yann Herklotz[1], Thomas Bourgeat[1], and Viktor Kunčak[1]

[1] EPFL, Lausanne, Switzerland
{simon.guilloud,sankalp.gambhir,auguste.poiroux,yann.herklotz, thomas.bourgeat,viktor.kuncak}@epfl.ch
[2] University of Lorraine, CNRS, Inria, LORIA, Nancy, France
julie.cailler@loria.fr

Abstract. We introduce SC-TPTP, an extension of the TPTP derivation format that supports sequent formalism, enabling seamless proof exchange between interactive theorem provers and first-order automated theorem provers. We provide a way to represent non-deductive steps—Skolemization, clausification, and Tseitin normal form—as deductive steps within the format. Building upon the existing support in the Lisa proof assistant and the Goéland theorem prover, SC-TPTP ecosystem is further enhanced with proof output interfaces for Egg and Prover9, as well as proof reconstruction support for HOL Light, Lean, and Rocq.

1 Introduction

Interoperability of proof systems, in particular automated and interactive theorem provers (ATPs and ITPs), involves several related but distinct challenges, including translation of statements across different logical foundations, alignment of concepts between mathematical libraries, and transfer of proofs. Focussing on proof transfer, this paper proposes a standardized format for export and import of proofs in an extension of first-order logic, integrating it into a variety of proof-producing and proof-consuming systems. Such standardized proof formats have multiple uses [49,59], of which we highlight three. First, ATPs deploy complex algorithms and heuristics to solve difficult problems, making them vulnerable to bugs. A standardized proof format and corresponding proof checker enable proof assistants with a small trusted kernel to verify the correctness of automated provers. This validation helps to evaluate ATPs in benchmarks and competitions, ultimately enhancing the trustworthiness of theorem provers.

Another key use is the collection of proofs from different tools, similar to the TSTP solution library [55], enabling comparisons of proof objects across various metrics, facilitating analysis and serving as training material for AI tools such as large language models. These proof collections are most valuable when the proofs are expressed in a unified format. One final use of standardized proofs,

C. Barrett and U. Waldmann (Eds.): CADE 2025, LNAI 15943, pp. 325–340, 2025.
https://doi.org/10.1007/978-3-031-99984-0_18

which we illustrate in this paper, is the ability for users of interactive theorem provers (ITPs) to invoke automated theorem provers (ATPs) as tactics. These tactics, known as *hammers*, are available in many ITPs [21,34,46], but do not always ensure the translation and validation of the ATP's proof. Some ITPs treat the ATP as an oracle, bypassing the formal kernel of the ITP and accepting the ATP-proven statement as an axiom, which necessitates trust in both the ATP and the translation process. Other hammers involve running an internal tactic that, while less powerful, is proof-producing, using lemmas discovered by the ATP or filling in intermediate steps in place of the ATP when possible [46]. This approach requires effectively rediscovering the proof, which can fail.

Challenges. As noted in [9], "One of the main difficulties with proof reconstruction is that each prover has its own (often undocumented) proof format and inference rules". For this reason, most existing proof reconstruction implementations focus on one source and one target system and are done most often with SMT solvers, for which there is an ongoing effort to establish proof formats [1,13,14,26,39,53]. A standardized format with well-documented syntax, proof steps, and parameters will help minimize the duplication of work. In general, if n systems each import proofs from m other systems, this requires $n \cdot m$ implementations, including parsing, translation, and proof reconstruction. With one middle ground format, only $n + m$ such implementations are required.

Approach. We propose to use a list of sequents in an extension of first-order logic (FOL) as the foundation for a concrete proof format, SC-TPTP. FOL is widely used by many relevant tools and, as past work on proof transfer and interoperability highlights, the practical challenges are significant even without the added complexity of unifying diverse logical foundations. For our deduction system, we adopt sequent calculus, a well-established formalism with both theoretical and practical benefits. Notably, it can naturally represent proofs from tableaux calculus, resolution calculus, and natural deduction.

We base our proof format on the TPTP derivation format, due to its prevalence in the field, its human-readable syntax, and the number of tools already compatible with it. TPTP (Thousands of Problems for Theorem Provers) [57] is a large collection of problems used to test and evaluate automated theorem provers. It also serves as a specification format [58] for writing these problems and their derivations, where lists of formulas are each deduced from previous ones or from axioms. However, TPTP does not specify which proof steps are allowed, their parameters, or how formulas are derived. To address this, we introduce SC-TPTP, which stands for *Sequent Calculus - TPTP*.

A preliminary proposal for SC-TPTP was presented in [18], introducing its use in interfacing the Lisa proof assistant [29] and the Goéland ATP [19], enabling proof exchange between the two systems. The initial version raised questions about generalizing the format to more proof systems and representing clausification, as many ATPs rely on clausification via Tseitin normal form and Skolemization. Since these two transformations only preserve satisfiability, they differ from sequent calculus rules. In this paper, we present our approach to representing Tseitin normal form and Skolemization within a purely deductive proof, demonstrating proof reconstruction for the resolution-based prover Prover9.

Contributions. Our main contributions are as follows:

- We present a refined version of the SC-TPTP proof format (and extend the underlying TPTP syntax) [18], introducing schematic symbols and structure sharing for terms and formulas.
- We describe how important non-deductive and satisfiability-preserving steps, in particular Tseitin's transform, can be performed in a purely deductive logical system suitable for interactive theorem provers.
- We make available a set of utilities to handle certification of clausification automatically, to ease adoption of the format by more tools.
- We implement SC-TPTP interfaces for additional ITPs including HOL Light, as a representative of the HOL-family of proof assistants, Lean and Rocq (partial support), as representatives of dependently typed proof assistants and extend the support in Lisa, as a representative of systems based on set theory. This provides the users of these proof assistant with the ability to invoke ATPs supporting SC-TPTP as hammers *with proof reconstruction.* Beyond Goéland, we implement SC-TPTP proof production for additional ATPs: Prover9, a resolution-based solver which makes use of our approach to certifying clausification, and egg, a popular e-graph based tool for reasoning with equality.

The above implementations, an independent proof checker, and a library of utilities to parse, manipulate, and transform SC-TPTP proofs are available at

https://github.com/orgs/SC-TPTP/repositories.

The appendices of this publication can be found in the full version [28].

2 The SC-TPTP Format

SC-TPTP is based on the TPTP format, where proofs are represented with *derivations.* A derivation is a list of annotated formulas, each of which is equipped with a name, a role, and, in some cases, an indication of how the formula was deduced. Formulas are essentially part of the FOFX grammar in TPTP.

Example 1. Given the valid formula $\exists x.\ \forall y.\ (d(x) \Rightarrow d(y))$, an automated prover might produce the following SC-TPTP proof for the *drinker's paradox* conjecture:

```
fof(phi, let, ?[X]: ![Y]: (d(X) ⇒ d(Y))).
fof(f1, plain, [d(X), d(Y)] ⟶ [d(Y0), d(Y)],
        inference(hyp, [status(thm), 1], [])).
fof(f2, plain, [d(X)] ⟶ [(d(Y) ⇒ d(Y0)), d(Y)],
        inference(rightImplies, [status(thm)], [f1])).
fof(f3, plain, [d(X)] ⟶ [![Y0] : (d(Y) ⇒ d(Y0)), d(Y)],
        inference(rightForall, [status(thm), 0, 'Y0'], [f2])).
fof(f4, plain, [d(X)] ⟶ [$phi, d(Y)],
        inference(rightExists, [status(thm), 0, $fot(Y)], [f3])).
fof(f5, plain, [] ⟶ [$phi, d(X) ⇒ d(Y)],
        inference(rightImplies, [status(thm), 1], [f4])).
fof(f6, plain, [] ⟶ [$phi, ![Y]: (d(X) ⇒ d(Y))],
        inference(rightForall, [status(thm), 1, 'Y'], [f5])).
fof(f7, plain, [] ⟶ [$phi],
        inference(rightExists, [status(thm), 0, $fot(X)], [f6])).
```

In general, an annotated formula in SC-TPTP follows the pattern `fof(name, role, statement, annotation)`.

- The **name** of a step is an identifier that later proof steps refer to.
- SC-TPTP recognizes five **roles**: `axiom` indicates that the formula is an axiom and can be used as a leaf in the derivation, `conjecture` does not have a logical meaning in the proof and indicates what the proof is supposed to prove, `plain` indicates a valid statement, deduced from previously statements or axioms, `assumption` is used if the step does not have any premises, and `let`, a new role, is used to introduce shorthands, such as `phi` in the first line of the example proof above. Let statements should not be referred to as premises of future steps; instead, they introduce a new defined constant symbol, which can be used in first-order formulas. Any occurrence of `$phi` is a shorthand (without any variable renaming) of the formula it stands for. Let bindings enable structure sharing for proofs, which often need to repeatedly state the same assumptions. Terms can also be bound to identifiers using annotated terms (not present in normal TPTP syntax), e.g. `fot(t, let, f(X, c))`.
- The **statement** is either a formula, or a sequent. A sequent is a pair of sets of formulas of the form $[\phi_1, ...] \longrightarrow [\psi_1, ...]$. A formula is a shortcut for the sequent with an empty left side and one formula on the right side.
- The **annotation** indicates how the formula was derived and is of the form `inference(stepName, [status(thm),` $p_1, \ldots, p_n$`], [`$r_1, \ldots, r_n$`])`. Following the SZS ontologies [56], `status(thm)` indicates the logical status of the formula. In SC-TPTP, all derived statements are `thm`. The p_i are parameters used to efficiently check and transform the proof, and depend on the specific proof step. The r_i's are the premise of the steps. They always correspond to names of previous annotated formulas.

Proof Step Levels. The basic steps of sequent calculus, along with substitution of equal terms or equivalent formulas, and the instantiation of free schematic symbols ([28, Appendix B]), define the logic of SC-TPTP. These steps are low-level and can be efficiently simulated by any proof system that supports first-order logic. However, outputting strict sequent calculus proofs is a stringent requirement for theorem provers. To facilitate the adoption of the format, SC-TPTP proofs allow various proof steps, which are organized into *levels*.

The first level includes exactly the steps from [28, Appendix B], while subsequent levels are flexible and expected to evolve. The second level contains more advanced proof steps for which an algorithm exists to eliminate them, i.e., processing an SC-TPTP proof and unfolding every occurrence of the proof into level 1 steps.

The third level consists of steps that lack such an implementation but are easily deduced and verified by most proof assistants. With moderate effort, a level 3 step can be converted into a level 2 step. The fourth level contains arbitrary sound deductive steps that cannot be reliably unfolded and may be difficult to implement in a proof-producing form.

These levels offer useful stepping stones to make a solver proof-producing, without needing to implement every proof reconstruction detail, such as congruence closure or negation normal form, which can be time-consuming.

Schematic Symbols. We extend the syntax from [18] by introducing support for schematic formulas, predicates, and functions. Semantically, schematic symbols are halfway between constant symbols and variables: they can be instantiated by terms and formulas but cannot be bound. In higher-order systems, there is no true distinction between schematic symbols and higher-order variables. However, in first-order logic, they are essential for expressing theorem and axiom schemas. For example, in the induction schema of Peano arithmetic, $P(0) \wedge (\forall n.\ P(n) \Rightarrow P(n+1)) \Rightarrow \forall n.\ P(n)$, P is a schematic predicate of arity 1 that can be instantiated by any formula with one free variable. Schematic symbols also allow proving generic theorems useful in first-order logic without relying on specific axioms. For instance, the De Morgan law used to compute negation normal form $\neg(\phi \vee \psi) \Leftrightarrow \neg\phi \wedge \neg\psi$ is generic over the formulas ϕ and ψ, which are formally schematic formulas. Schematic symbols are conservative over strict first-order logic and typically supported by first-order proof assistants, such as in Mizar and Lisa. In Metamath [40], schematic variables are referred to as metavariables, while in Isabelle/FOL, higher-order variables in the meta language can play this role. In SC-TPTP, schematic predicates and functions start with capital letters.

Epsilon Terms. An important addition to SC-TPTP is the support for reasoning with Hilbert's epsilon operator ϵ. This operator is a term level quantifier with the following introduction rule:

$$\frac{\Gamma \vdash \Delta, \phi}{\Gamma \vdash \Delta, \phi[x := (\epsilon x.\phi)]}\ \texttt{rightEpsilon}$$

Informally, $\epsilon x.\ \phi$ denotes an arbitrary element satisfying ϕ, if such an element exists. This addition to sequent calculus is conservative [62], a property known as the Epsilon Theorem. Our motivation for introducing epsilon terms is to allow efficient certification of Skolemization. Constructive deskolemization, the problem of computing a proof of a formula ϕ from a proof of a formula ϕ', where ϕ' is the result of applying Skolemization to ϕ, is hard: all known methods have exponential or non-elementary blow-up [3], depending on whether inner or outer Skolemization is used. This happens even when the proof is cut-free [4].

An epsilon-term $\epsilon x.\phi$ can be seen as a Skolem function $f(y_1, ..., y_n)$ where y_is are all the free variables of ϕ except for x. This enables certification of Skolemization in purely deductive proofs with a linear number of substitution steps. The downside is that the target system must support epsilon terms, but this is the case in many proof assistants[1]. SC-TPTP proofs use `#` to denote ϵ.

Logic Options to Classify Proofs. SC-TPTP uses annotations in the TPTP header to indicate logical features used in the proof and advanced SC-TPTP features. Such logical annotations ([28, Appendix A]), are written similarly to the *Specialist Problem Class* (SPC) annotations in TPTP. A declaration:

```
% Logic    : classical_epsilon_schem_let
```

for example, indicates that the proof uses classical logic (`classical`), permitting sequents with multiple formulas on the right-hand side, epsilon choice operator (`epsilon`), schematic predicates or functions (`schem`), and uses defined expressions (`let`) that are defined with the `let` role.

3 Simulating Non-Deductive Proofs

Some common proof strategies used by ATP are not *deductive*, meaning they do not derive a true conclusion from true premises but instead transform the entire problem. Typical examples include *proofs by contradiction*, *Tseitin's transform* and *Skolemization*. Most proof assistants, however, are based on purely deductive logic and cannot accept or prove these steps. When applied correctly, these strategies preserve soundness, and since sequent calculus is complete, any statement proven using non-deductive strategies will also have a proof in strict sequent calculus. However, finding a pure sequent calculus proof can be computationally difficult and time-consuming. Deskolemization, in particular, can blow up the size of the proofs [3, 4]. In any case, for all these classes of steps, it is not possible to simply define them as logical steps in SC-TPTP and unfold them locally. Eliminating them from an ATP proof requires modifying the proof globally.

For the sake of conciseness, we briefly illustrate our approach to certifying Tseitin's transform, which makes use of `let` statements and schematic symbols. A detailed explanation of how these non-deductive steps can be performed in both forward and backward proofs in SC-TPTP is available in [28, Appendix E].

Suppose that we have a formula ϕ given as an axiom, and we aim to deduce $\bot$. The structure of the desired proof from the clausified axioms will be as follows:

[1] It is called `The` in Mizar, `@` in HOL Light and HOL4, ϵ in Lisa, `Some` in Isabelle and `epsilon` in Rocq and Lean (requires non-constructive axioms).

$$\cfrac{\cfrac{\vdash a_1 \vee ... \vee a_n \qquad ... \qquad \vdash z_1 \vee ... \vee z_n}{\vdots}}{\vdash \bot}$$

Where $a_1 \vee ... \vee a_n$, ..., $z_1 \vee ... \vee z_n$ are the clauses resulting from the Tseitin transform of ϕ. But the clauses are not in general consequences of ϕ, as the transformation only preserves satisfiability.

Suppose ϕ contains $a \wedge b$ as a subterm. We simulate the first step of the Tseitin's transform as follows:

$$\cfrac{\cfrac{\cfrac{\cfrac{\cfrac{\vdash \phi(a \wedge b)}{A \Leftrightarrow (a \wedge b) \vdash \phi(A)}\ 1. \quad \cfrac{}{A \Leftrightarrow (a \wedge b) \vdash \neg A \vee a}\ 2. \quad \cfrac{}{A \Leftrightarrow (a \wedge b) \vdash \neg A \vee b}\ 3. \quad \cfrac{}{A \Leftrightarrow (a \wedge b) \vdash A \vee \neg a \vee \neg b}\ 4.}{\vdots}}{A \Leftrightarrow (a \wedge b) \vdash \bot}}{(a \wedge b) \Leftrightarrow (a \wedge b) \vdash \bot}\ 5.\ \texttt{instPred}}{\vdash \bot}\ 6.\ \texttt{elimIffRefl}$$

Step 1 is `rightSubstIff`. Steps 2, 3, and 4 are constant-size tautologies. Then the resolution proof follows normally, independently of the $A \Leftrightarrow (a \wedge b)$ on the left-hand side.

Finally, we eliminate the assumption. Step 5 allows instantiating the schematic formula A with an arbitrary formula. To justify equisatisfiability of the Tseitin transform, we need to ensure that A is fresh. This is enforced here by step 5. If A was not a fresh symbol but already appearing in ψ for example, the initial part of the proof would still work, but step 5 would fail. Step 6 finally eliminates the trivial assumption.

Note that every single step can be unfolded into a constant number of level 1 steps, making the whole proof of Tseitin transformation linear. All steps are deductive and can be locally checked, independently of the rest of the proof. The SC-TPTP utilities (Sect. 4.3) contain tools to automatically perform this transformation on a proof, as well as Skolemization, allowing a prover operating on clauses to assume that the input formula is already clausified Fig. 1.

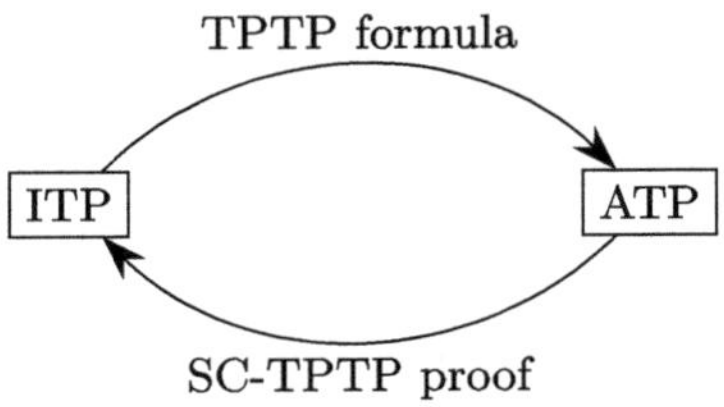

Fig. 1. SC-TPTP for hammers

4 Tools Connected Using SC-TPTP

SC-TPTP was already supported by Lisa and Goéland. We add SC-TPTP interfaces to a selection of systems with a variety of logical foundations and principle to demonstrate a broad potential of the approach.

4.1 Automated Theorem Provers Producing SC-TPTP Proofs

The following ATPs are able to produce proofs in the SC-TPTP format, that can be readily verified by one of the ITP in Sect. 4.2.

Goéland. Goéland [17,19] is an automated theorem prover for first-order logic with equality. It relies on a concurrent tableaux-based proof-search procedure that allows it to conduct a fair branch exploration. The prover can perform deskolemization [50] and produce machine-checkable proofs in Rocq, LambdaPi and SC-TPTP. [28, Appendix F] provides an example of a proof produced by Goéland.

Prover9. Prover9 [38] is an automated theorem prover for first-order logic with equality that implements the resolution and paramodulation calculi, thus relying on clausification. We implement proof producton for Prover9 in two steps. First, we implement it when the input problem is clausal, that is, the conjecture is `$false` and each axiom is a single clause `[a, b, ...]`, naturally represented as the sequent `[]` $\longrightarrow$ `[a, b, ...]`. The steps of a resolution proofs directly correspond to proof steps of SC-TPTP: the resolution step is similar to a `cut` step, and the instantiation is exactly the `instFun` step. Then, we separately implement certification of clausification, which uses Prover9 as a subroutine and modify the output proof, as described in Sect. 3. The resulting procedure takes arbitrary first order formulas as input and outputs verifiable SC-TPTP proofs.

egg. egg [61] (short for E-Graphs Good) is not a traditional ATP but a tool implementing high-performance E-graphs [42] and saturation, often used to optimize programs. It can, however, be seen as solving a fragment of first-order logic with equality, where the equivalence relation is the union of $\Leftrightarrow$ and $=$. egg has already been used for theorem proving in the Coquetier project [15].

egg outputs explanations for pairs of equivalent expressions [25,43]. We add TPTP input for egg, which supports quantified equalities and equivalences as assumptions and conjecture, and transforms egg justifications into SC-TPTP proofs.

egg is also able to find the smallest representative in an equivalence class, motivating using SC-TPTP for more than yes/no answers. We implement the experimental `simplify` role for annotated formulas and terms, exclusive to conjectures, which prompts the solver to find a simplified version of the given term or formula, and prove its equivalence to the original. For example:

```
fof(a1, axiom, (! [Xx]: (Xx = sf(sf(sf(sf(sf(Xx))))))).
fof(a2, axiom, (! [Xx]: (Xx = sf(sf(sf(Xx)))))).
fot(c, simplify, (p(sf(c)))).
...
fof(f15, plain, [] --> [(p(sf(c)) <=> p(c))], inference( ... )).
```

This feature is currently supported only by egg. [28, Appendix F] provides examples of a proof produced by our egg wrapper, with level 1 and level 2 steps.

4.2 Interactive Theorem Provers Validating SC-TPTP Proofs

Lisa. Lisa [29] is a proof assistant based on first order logic and set theory. Its logical system is an extension of sequent calculus, making proof import straightforward, whereas exporting a problem requires a simple form of monomorphization. We developed a dedicated tactic for several provers, illustrated in the examples below. Our proof reconstruction implementation is largely shared across these tactics. The simplicity of the connection of Lisa to automated provers is an argument in favor of using FOL as the foundation for a proof assistant.

```
val divide_mult_shift = Theorem((
      ∀(x, x/t1 === x), ∀(x, ∀(y, x/y === t1/(y/x))),
      ∀(x, ∀(y, (x/y)*y === x))) |- ((t2/t3)*(t3/t2))/t1 === t1):
   have(thesis) by Egg

val drinkers2 = Theorem(∃(x, ∀(y, d(x) ==> d(y)))):
   have(thesis) by Goeland

val thm = Theorem((∀(x, P(x)) ∨ ∀(y, Q(y))) ==> (P(∅) ∨ Q(∅)) ):
   have(thesis) by Prover9
```

HOL Light. HOL Light [30] is an LCF-style interactive theorem prover based on higher-order logic implemented in OCaml. We contribute an extensible way to generically construct interfaces to external provers for use in HOL Light, and a TPTP parser in OCaml using `ocamllex` and `menhir` supporting the FOFX fragment with the SC-TPTP extensions decribed here. Our implementation provides a function `sctptp_tac`, which, given a way to construct invocations to an external solver, can be instantiated in one line as a reusable tactic. Instantiations `EGG`, `GOELAND`, and `PROVER9` for the respective ATPs are included. Each accepts a list of existing theorems to use as axioms, and a sequent to prove, and returns a `thm` object proving the sequent if a proof was found and reconstructed. The following are examples of HOL Light invocations of Goéland and egg:

```
(* syntax: PROVER [premises] [antecedants] conclusion *)
# let drinkers = GOELAND [] [] `?x:ind. !y. d(x) ==> d(y)`;;
val drinkers : thm = |- exists x. forall y. d x ==> d y
# let div_mult_shift = EGG [] [
    `!x. x/t1 = x`; `!x y. x/y = t1/(y/x)`; `!x y. (x/y)*y = x`
    ] `((t2/t3)*(t3/t2))/t1 = t1`;;
val div_mult_shift : thm =
  forall v3 v5. v3/v5 = t1/(v5/v3), forall v3 v5. v3/v5 * v5 = v3,
  forall v3. v3/t1 = v3 |- (t2/ t3 * t3/t2) / t1 = t1
```

To transform the original problem (possibly containing higher-order terms) into a first-order SC-TPTP query, we adapted the monomorphization procedure from the existing implementation of the Meson tactic in HOL Light. All higher-order terms are abstracted into named untyped first-order constants. During proof reconstruction, however, the types for all terms must be recovered. To this end, we implement a type inference and unification procedure similar to that of the simply-typed lambda calculus.

Lean. Lean [23] is an interactive theorem prover based on dependent type theory. In our framework, proof reconstruction is implemented using the standard Lean 4 tactic interface. We developed custom tactics, `egg`, `prover9`, and `goeland`, that automate the entire workflow, including sequent export to TPTP, invocation of the underlying ATP, and subsequent parsing, reification, reconstruction, and checking of the proof within Lean 4, allowing, e.g., the following use.

```
example ( α : Type) [Nonempty α] (d : α → Prop) :
  ∃ y : α, ∀ x : α, (d x → d y) := by goeland
```

Our development uses the monomorphization and reification tools from the Lean Auto project [37,47]. We adapt its mechanism for exporting formulas from the TH0 to the FOF format within the TPTP framework. In the translation of TPTP expressions to Lean expressions, we use type inference to recover information about types of variables. Our proof reconstruction system is implemented using a backward proof strategy within a single global context, allowing us to leverage the Lean 4 tactic proof mode.

Rocq. Similar to the more recent Lean, Rocq is a proof assistant based on a dependently typed calculus. Building upon a proof validating interface between Rocq and egg in the Coquetier project [15], we have developed a prototype that uses SC-TPTP to reconstruct proof statements in the intuitionistic fragment of first-order logic. This interface is currently more limited than one for Lean because it does not make use of monomorphization and supports less level 3 proof steps, but it already provides another path for validating some of the proofs of automated solvers.

4.3 SC-TPTP Utilities and Central Repository

To support the SC-TPTP format, we release a library of tools and utilities to handle SC-TPTP proofs at https://github.com/SC-TPTP/sc-tptp. The library provides a parser and an independent proof checker for SC-TPTP proofs, as well as functions able to unfold level 2 proof steps into level 1 proof, such as a proof-producing implementation of an e-graph able to unfold the `congruence` proof step. It also contains a module able to certify clausification and extend proofs of formulas in CNF provided by ATPs relying on clausification to form a complete proof of the original formula, which is central to SC-TPTP support for Prover9. The library further contains helpers, examples, test cases and documentation. The repository also contains links and forks of tools with SC-TPTP support. The suite of tools is under active development.

5 Related Work

An excellent review of hammers for proof assistants is [9]. In the domain of proof system interoperability but in a very different direction, logical framework such as dedukti [2] and the Lambdapi [24] proof assistant aim at unifying different mathematical foundations to facilitate the sharing of mathematical libraries [10]. SC-TPTP on the other hand is a proof exchange format, that is, a *data* exchange format, and is designed as such. More practically, Dedukti/Lambdapi files are not adequate to represent sequent calculus proof data in such a way that it is easy to export and import. Accessorily, it is not possible to naturally represent sequents in Dedukti with set semantics. It is also worth noting that most proof systems (ATPs and ITPs) already have some support for the TPTP format.

In the SMT community, diverse proof formats have emerged: LFSC [54] was originally used by cvc5 [6] and its predecessors. Z3 [22] has its own format [41]. While there is yet no universally accepted format, efforts have been carried toward this goal [8,32]. The Alethe [52] format is based on SMT-LIB [7], the SMT equivalent of the TPTP World, and supported by cvc5 and veriT [16].

The SAT solving community has developed a series of increasingly more optimized and efficient format for certifying proofs of SAT solvers: the DRAT [48,60] format, LRAT [20] and GRAT [36], VeriPB [11,27] and the corresponding VeriPB-CakePB checker [12] These formats are used in the yearly SAT Competition [31] and produced by state-of-the-art SAT solvers. This long chain of improvements suggests that the current version of SC-TPTP will similarly go through various refinements and improvements over the years.

Closer to our approach, extension of the `TPTP` syntax to the connection calculus [45] was implemented in the leanCoP [44] and Connect++ [33] provers, although intermediate steps do not correspond to logical formulas. Efforts for supporting the connection calculus and Connect++ in SC-TPTP are ongoing.

The TESC format [5] offers a one-sided sequent based proof format with an independent, verified, proof checker supporting ad-hoc extension to support theories. However, this makes verification and reconstruction of proofs theory-specific as well. A tool is provided to compile proofs from TPTP to TESC, then used to check proofs from Vampire [35] and E [51], but the work does not attempt to reconstruct said proofs within a foundational ITP.

6 Conclusion

We have presented SC-TPTP, a proof format for representing proofs in first-order logic with equality, enabling verification of proofs produced by first-order ATPs and transfer of first-order proofs between proof systems. We demonstrated how clausification can be represented in the format and implemented SC-TPTP interfaces in several types of automated and interactive theorem provers.

While in proof assistants with first-order foundations all statements can easily be fed into first-order ATP, systems based on more complex logics, in particular dependent types, typically require monomorphization to maximize usability. This is a largely independent process implemented by hammers in these systems; we hope in the future to more closely integrate SC-TPTP with existing hammers in ITPs.

Acknowledgements. The authors thank reviewers and members of the ATP community who expressed interest and provided feedback. They address particular thanks to Geoff Sutcliffe and Sean Holden. Sankalp Gambhir was supported by the Swiss NSF project number 200021_219474 awarded to Viktor Kunčak.

Disclosure of Interests. The authors have no competing interests.

References

1. Armand, M., Faure, G., Grégoire, B., Keller, C., Théry, L., Werner, B.: A modular integration of SAT/SMT solvers to Coq through proof witnesses. In: Jouannaud, J.-P., Shao, Z. (eds.) CPP 2011. LNCS, vol. 7086, pp. 135–150. Springer, Heidelberg (2011). https://doi.org/10.1007/978-3-642-25379-9_12
2. Assaf, A., et al.: A Logical Framework based on the λΠ-calculus modulo theory. Tech. rep., arXiv (2023)
3. Avigad, J.: Eliminating definitions and Skolem functions in first-order logic. In: Proceedings 16th Annual IEEE Symposium on Logic in Computer Science, pp. 139–146 (2001).https://doi.org/10.1109/LICS.2001.932490
4. Baaz, M., Hetzl, S., Weller, D.: On the complexity of proof Deskolemization. J. Symb. Log. **77**(2), 669–686 (2012)
5. Baek, S.: A formally verified checker for first-order proofs. In: Cohen, L., Kaliszyk, C. (eds.) 12th International Conference on Interactive Theorem Proving (ITP 2021). Leibniz International Proceedings in Informatics (LIPIcs), vol. 193, pp. 6:1–6:13. Schloss Dagstuhl – Leibniz-Zentrum für Informatik, Dagstuhl, Germany (2021). https://doi.org/10.4230/LIPIcs.ITP.2021.6
6. Barbosa, H., et al.: cvc5: A Versatile and Industrial-Strength SMT Solver. In: CPP 2011. LNCS, vol. 7086, pp. 415–442. Springer, Cham (2022). https://doi.org/10.1007/978-3-030-99524-9_24
7. Barrett, C.W., Stump, A., Tinelli, C.: The SMT-LIB Standard Version 2.0. Tech. rep., Stanford University (2010)

8. Besson, F.: A flexible proof format for SMT: A Proposal. In: Fontaine, P., Théry, L. (eds.) PxTP 2011: First International Workshop on Proof eXchange for Theorem Proving (2011)
9. Blanchette, J.C., Kaliszyk, C., Paulson, L.C., Urban, J.: Hammering towards QED. J. Formalized Reason. **9**(1), 101–148 (2016). https://doi.org/10.6092/issn.1972-5787/4593
10. Blanqui, F.: Translating HOL-light proofs to Coq. In: Proceedings of 25th Conference on Logic for Programming, Artificial Intelligence and Reasoning, pp. 1–18 (2024). https://doi.org/10.29007/6k4x
11. Bogaerts, B., Gocht, S., McCreesh, C., Nordström, J.: Certified dominance and symmetry breaking for combinatorial optimisation. J. Artif. Intell. Res. **77**, 1539–1589 (2023). https://doi.org/10.1613/jair.1.14296
12. Bogaerts, B., McCreesh, C., Myreen, M.O., Nordstrom, J., Oertel, A., Tan, Y.K.: Documentation of VeriPB and CakePB for the SAT Competition 2023. Tech. rep. (2023)
13. Böhme, S., Fox, A., Sewell, T., Weber, T.: Reconstruction of Z3's bit-vector proofs in HOL4 and Isabelle/HOL. In: Jouannaud, J.-P., Shao, Z. (eds.) CPP 2011. LNCS, vol. 7086, pp. 183–198. Springer, Heidelberg (2011). https://doi.org/10.1007/978-3-642-25379-9_15
14. Böhme, S., Weber, T.: Fast LCF-style proof reconstruction for Z3. In: Kaufmann, M., Paulson, L.C. (eds.) ITP 2010. LNCS, vol. 6172, pp. 179–194. Springer, Heidelberg (2010). https://doi.org/10.1007/978-3-642-14052-5_14
15. Bourgeat, T.: Specification and Verification of Sequential Machines in Rule-Based Hardware Languages. Thesis, Massachusetts Institute of Technology (Feb (2023)
16. Bouton, T., Caminha B. de Oliveira, D., Déharbe, D., Fontaine, P.: veriT: an open, trustable and efficient SMT-solver. In: Schmidt, R.A. (ed.) CADE 2009. LNCS (LNAI), vol. 5663, pp. 151–156. Springer, Heidelberg (2009). https://doi.org/10.1007/978-3-642-02959-2_12
17. Cailler, J.: Designing an Automated Concurrent Tableau-Based Theorem Prover for First-Order Logic. Ph.D. thesis, Université de Montpellier (2023)
18. Cailler, J., Guilloud, S.: SC-TPTP: an extension of the TPTP derivation format for sequent-based calculus. In: 9th Workshop on Practical Aspects of Automated Reasoning (2024)
19. Cailler, J., Rosain, J., Delahaye, D., Robillard, S., Bouziane, H.L.: Goéland: a concurrent tableau-based theorem prover (System Description). In: Blanchette, J., Kovács, L., Pattinson, D. (eds.) Automated Reasoning, pp. 359–368. Lecture Notes in Computer Science, Springer International Publishing, Cham (2022). https://doi.org/10.1007/978-3-031-10769-6_22
20. Cruz-Filipe, L., Heule, M., Hunt, W.A., Kaufmann, M., Schneider-Kamp, P.: Efficient certified RAT verification. In: de Moura, L. (ed.) CADE 2017. LNCS (LNAI), vol. 10395, pp. 220–236. Springer, Cham (2017). https://doi.org/10.1007/978-3-319-63046-5_14
21. Czajka, Ł, Kaliszyk, C.: Hammer for Coq: automation for dependent type theory. J. Autom. Reason. , 423–453 (2018). https://doi.org/10.1007/s10817-018-9458-4
22. de Moura, L., Bjørner, N.: Z3: an efficient SMT solver. In: Ramakrishnan, C.R., Rehof, J. (eds.) TACAS 2008. LNCS, vol. 4963, pp. 337–340. Springer, Heidelberg (2008). https://doi.org/10.1007/978-3-540-78800-3_24
23. de Moura, L., Kong, S., Avigad, J., van Doorn, F., von Raumer, J.: The lean theorem prover (system description). In: Felty, A.P., Middeldorp, A. (eds.) CADE 2015. LNCS (LNAI), vol. 9195, pp. 378–388. Springer, Cham (2015). https://doi.org/10.1007/978-3-319-21401-6_26

24. Deducteam: Deducteam/lambdapi. Deducteam (2024)
25. Flatt, O., Coward, S., Willsey, M., Tatlock, Z., Panchekha, P.: Small proofs from congruence closure. In: 2022 Formal Methods in Computer-Aided Design (FMCAD), pp. 75–83 (2022).https://doi.org/10.34727/2022/isbn.978-3-85448-053-2_13
26. Fontaine, P., Marion, J.-Y., Merz, S., Nieto, L.P., Tiu, A.: Expressiveness + automation + soundness: towards combining SMT solvers and interactive proof assistants. In: Hermanns, H., Palsberg, J. (eds.) TACAS 2006. LNCS, vol. 3920, pp. 167–181. Springer, Heidelberg (2006). https://doi.org/10.1007/11691372_11
27. Gocht, S., Nordström, J.: Certifying parity reasoning efficiently using pseudo-boolean proofs — supplemental material (2022). https://doi.org/10.5281/zenodo.7083485
28. Guilloud, S., et al.: Interoperability of Proof Systems with SC-TPTP (Full Version). Tech. rep., EPFL (2025). https://infoscience.epfl.ch/handle/20.500.14299/247663
29. Guilloud, S., Gambhir, S., Kuncak, V.: LISA – A modern proof system. In: 14th Conference on Interactive Theorem Proving, pp. 17:1–17:19. Leibniz International Proceedings in Informatics, Daghstuhl, Bialystok (2023)
30. Harrison, J.: HOL light: an overview. In: Berghofer, S., Nipkow, T., Urban, C., Wenzel, M. (eds.) TPHOLs 2009. LNCS, vol. 5674, pp. 60–66. Springer, Heidelberg (2009). https://doi.org/10.1007/978-3-642-03359-9_4
31. Heule, M.J.H., Iser, M., Järvisalo, M., Suda, M.: Proceedings of SAT Ccompetition 2024: Solver, Benchmark and Proof Checker Descriptions. University of Helsinki (2024)
32. Hoenicke, J., Schindler, T.I.: A Simple Proof Format for SMT. In: International Workshop on Satisfiability Modulo Theories (2022)
33. Holden, S.B.: Connect++: a new automated theorem prover based on the connection calculus. In: Otten, J., Bibel, W. (eds.) Proceedings of the 1st International Workshop on Automated Reasoning with Connection Calculi (AReCCa 2023) Affiliated with the 32nd International Conference on Automated Reasoning with Analytic Tableaux and Related Methods (TABLEAUX 2023), Prague, Czech Republic, September 18, 2023. CEUR Workshop Proceedings, vol. 3613, pp. 95–106. CEUR-WS.org (2023)
34. Kaliszyk, C., Urban, J.: Learning-assisted automated reasoning with flyspeck. J. Autom. Reason. **53**(2), 173–213 (2014). https://doi.org/10.1007/s10817-014-9303-3
35. Kovács, L., Voronkov, A.: First-order theorem proving and VAMPIRE. In: Sharygina, N., Veith, H. (eds.) CAV 2013. LNCS, vol. 8044, pp. 1–35. Springer, Heidelberg (2013). https://doi.org/10.1007/978-3-642-39799-8_1
36. Lammich, P.: The GRAT tool chain. In: Gaspers, S., Walsh, T. (eds.) SAT 2017. LNCS, vol. 10491, pp. 457–463. Springer, Cham (2017). https://doi.org/10.1007/978-3-319-66263-3_29
37. Lean Prover Community: Leanprover-community/lean-auto. leanprover-community (2025)
38. McCune, W.: Prover9 and Mace4
39. McLaughlin, S., Barrett, C., Ge, Y.: Cooperating theorem provers: a case study combining HOL-light and CVC lite. Electron. Notes Theor. Comput. Sci. **144**(2), 43–51 (2006). https://doi.org/10.1016/j.entcs.2005.12.005
40. Megill, N., Wheeler, D.A.: Metamath: A Computer Language for Mathematical Proofs. Lulu.com, Morrisville (2019)
41. Moura, L.D., Bjørner, N.S.: Proofs and refutations, and Z3. In: LPAR Workshops (2008)

42. Nelson, G., Oppen, D.C.: Fast decision procedures based on congruence closure. J. ACM **27**(2), 356–364 (1980). https://doi.org/10.1145/322186.322198
43. Nieuwenhuis, R., Oliveras, A.: Proof-producing congruence closure. In: Giesl, J. (ed.) RTA 2005. LNCS, vol. 3467, pp. 453–468. Springer, Heidelberg (2005). https://doi.org/10.1007/978-3-540-32033-3_33
44. Otten, J., Bibel, W.: leanCoP: lean connection-based theorem proving. J. Symb. Comput. **36**(1), 139–161 (2003). https://doi.org/10.1016/S0747-7171(03)00037-3
45. Otten, J., Holden, S.B.: A syntax for connection proofs. In: Otten, J., Bibel, W. (eds.) Proceedings of the 1st International Workshop on Automated Reasoning with Connection Calculi (AReCCa 2023) Affiliated with the 32nd International Conference on Automated Reasoning with Analytic Tableaux and Related Methods (TABLEAUX 2023), Prague, Czech Republic, September 18, 2023. CEUR Workshop Proceedings, vol. 3613, pp. 84–94. CEUR-WS.org (2023)
46. Paulson, L.C., Susanto, K.W.: Source-level proof reconstruction for interactive theorem proving. In: Schneider, K., Brandt, J. (eds.) TPHOLs 2007. LNCS, vol. 4732, pp. 232–245. Springer, Heidelberg (2007). https://doi.org/10.1007/978-3-540-74591-4_18
47. Qian, Y., Clune, J., Barrett, C., Avigad, J.: Lean-auto: an interface between lean 4 and automated theorem provers (2025). https://arxiv.org/abs/2505.14929
48. Rebola-Pardo, A., Cruz-Filipe, L.: Complete and efficient DRAT proof checking. In: 2018 Formal Methods in Computer Aided Design (FMCAD), pp. 1–9 (2018).https://doi.org/10.23919/FMCAD.2018.8602993
49. Reger, G., Suda, M.: Checkable proofs for first-order theorem proving. In: ARCADE 2017. 1st International Workshop on Automated Reasoning: Challenges, Applications, Directions, Exemplary Achievements, pp. 55–63. EasyChair EPiC Series in Computing (2017)
50. Rosain, J., Bonichon, R., Cailler, J., Hermant, O.: A generic Deskolemization strategy. In: Proceedings of 25th Conference on Logic for Programming, Artificial Intelligence and Reasoning, pp. 246–227 (2024). https://doi.org/10.29007/g1tm
51. Schulz, S., Cruanes, S., Vukmirović, P.: Faster, higher, stronger: E 2.3. In: Fontaine, P. (ed.) CADE 2019. LNCS (LNAI), vol. 11716, pp. 495–507. Springer, Cham (2019). https://doi.org/10.1007/978-3-030-29436-6_29
52. Schurr, H.J., Fleury, M., Barbosa, H., Fontaine, P.: Alethe: towards a generic SMT proof format (extended abstract). Electron. Proc. Theor. Comput. Sci. **336**, 49–54 (2021). https://doi.org/10.4204/EPTCS.336.6
53. Schurr, H.-J., Fleury, M., Desharnais, M.: Reliable reconstruction of fine-grained proofs in a proof assistant. In: Platzer, A., Sutcliffe, G. (eds.) CADE 2021. LNCS (LNAI), vol. 12699, pp. 450–467. Springer, Cham (2021). https://doi.org/10.1007/978-3-030-79876-5_26
54. Stump, A., Oe, D.: Towards an SMT proof format. In: Proceedings of the Joint Workshops of the 6th International Workshop on Satisfiability Modulo Theories and 1st International Workshop on Bit-Precise Reasoning, pp. 27–32. SMT '08/BPR '08, Association for Computing Machinery, New York, NY, USA (2008).https://doi.org/10.1145/1512464.1512470
55. Sutcliffe, G.: TPTP, TSTP, CASC, etc. In: Diekert, V., Volkov, M.V., Voronkov, A. (eds.) CSR 2007. LNCS, vol. 4649, pp. 6–22. Springer, Heidelberg (2007). https://doi.org/10.1007/978-3-540-74510-5_4
56. Sutcliffe, G.: The SZS ontologies for automated reasoning software. In: Rudnicki, P., Sutcliffe, G., Konev, B., Schmidt, R.A., Schulz, S. (eds.) Proceedings of the LPAR 2008 Workshops, Knowledge Exchange: Automated Provers and Proof Assistants, and the 7th International Workshop on the Implementation of Logics, Doha,

Qatar, November 22, 2008. CEUR Workshop Proceedings, vol. 418. CEUR-WS.org (2008)
57. Sutcliffe, G.: The TPTP problem library and associated infrastructure. J. Autom. Reason. **59**(4), 483–502 (2017). https://doi.org/10.1007/s10817-017-9407-7
58. Sutcliffe, G.: The logic languages of the TPTP world. Logic J. IGPL **31**(6), 1153–1169 (2023). https://doi.org/10.1093/jigpal/jzac068
59. Weber, T.: Designing proof formats: a user's perspective. In: International Workshop on Proof Exchange for Theorem Proving (2011)
60. Wetzler, N., Heule, M., Hunt, W.A.: DRAT-trim: efficient checking and trimming using expressive clausal proofs. In: Sinz, C., Egly, U. (eds.) SAT 2014. LNCS, vol. 8561, pp. 422–429. Springer, Cham (2014). https://doi.org/10.1007/978-3-319-09284-3_31
61. Willsey, M., Nandi, C., Wang, Y.R., Flatt, O., Tatlock, Z., Panchekha, P.: EGG: fast and extensible equality saturation. Proc. ACM Progr. Lang. **5**(POPL), 23:1–23:29 (2021). https://doi.org/10.1145/3434304
62. Zach, R.: Semantics and proof theory of the epsilon calculus. In: Ghosh, S., Prasad, S. (eds.) ICLA 2017. LNCS, vol. 10119, pp. 27–47. Springer, Heidelberg (2017). https://doi.org/10.1007/978-3-662-54069-5_4

Cut Elimination for Negative Free Logics with Definite Descriptions

Andrzej Indrzejczak(✉)

Department of Logic, University of Lodz, Lodz, Poland
andrzej.indrzejczak@filhist.uni.lodz.pl

Abstract. We present a sequent calculus GNFL for negative free logic with definite descriptions in the classical and intuitionistic versions, with empty and nonempty domains. It is shown constructively that GNFL satisfies the cut elimination theorem and its cut-free version satisfies the subformula property.

Keywords: Definite Descriptions · Negative Free Logic · Sequent Calculus · Cut Elimination Theorem

1 Introduction

The name free logic (FL) applies to wide spectrum of logical systems having different origins and applications. The only common assumption is the admission of non-denoting terms. In the tradition of philosophical logic, the most popular approach is realised by positive free logics (PFL), where some atomic sentences with non-denoting terms may be true. By contrast, in negative free logic (NFL) all predicates are strict, i.e. satisfied only by denoting terms, hence all atomic formulae with non-denoting terms are simply false. Additionally, neutral free logics are considered, where atoms with non-denoting terms are treated as neither true, nor false. In each family, we may also consider universally free systems, where empty domains are admitted in the models. In this paper we focus on NFL in both variants; the latter will be abbreviated as UNFL (universal NFL).

NFL (UNFL), in contrast to PFL, was developed for several applications in constructive mathematics and computer science and more often considered in the intuitionistic version. However, the specific axioms and rules may be used also with the classical basis, as was noted by Feferman [12]. Moreover, the name NFL is not common in this area of applications; many authors prefer different names, and different axiomatisations, so sometimes it is difficult to realise that these names apply to the same logic. Scott [31], as the first, examined the intuitionistic version under the name logic of existence predicate which, in abbreviated form,

Funded by the European Union (ERC, ExtenDD, project number: 101054714). Views and opinions expressed are however those of the author(s) only and do not necessarily reflect those of the European Union or the European Research Council. Neither the European Union nor the granting authority can be held responsible for them.

C. Barrett and U. Waldmann (Eds.): CADE 2025, LNAI 15943, pp. 341–360, 2025.
https://doi.org/10.1007/978-3-031-99984-0_19

was also applied by Feferman (the logic of existence) and by Troelstra and van Dalen [34] (as E-logic). On the other hand, researchers dealing with the classical version, often prefer the name NFL. We will keep the name NFL (UNFL) but consider both the intuitionistic and classical variant, using in many places the schematic name (U)(I)NFL which covers four variants of this logic.

It should be noted that some authors (e.g. Feferman [12], Beeson [4]) prefer the versions of these logics with variables fixed as always denoting terms, assuming that such systems are better for dealing with partial untyped combinatory and lambda calculi (Feferman [12]). These variants of (U)(I)NFL are called usually the logics of partial terms (see Beeson [4], Farmer [11]) or the logics of definedness (Feferman [12]). Troelstra and van Dalen [34], who provide an extensive comparison of both approaches in the context of constructive mathematics, call them E^+-logics to keep a uniform notation. It seems that this sort of logics is in a sense closer to classical logic, since one may adequately characterise them on the basis of pure classical logic, i.e. with quantifier rules restricted to variables, but not requiring existential premisses/conclusions, stated in terms of the existence predicate. This is why such logics are called quasi free logics in [15]. In what follows we focus only on (U)(I)NFL where all terms (including variables) can be non-denoting. The proof theory of the logic of definedness (under the name RDD – Russellian logic of definite descriptions) was already investigated in [17]. The separate treatment of both types of NFL is justified since in the setting of proof theory they have significantly different bases.

We do not restrict the analysis to (U)(I)NFL in languages with simple terms only. One of the most important class of non-denoting terms are *definite descriptions*, expressions of the form 'the so and so', such as 'the author of «On Denoting»'. Definite descriptions (DD) are commonly used in natural languages as well as in mathematics ('the sum of 7 and 5'). A DD is called proper if it denotes a unique object. If it fails to do so, because nothing or more than one thing satisfies it, we call it improper. In artificial languages the iota-operator $\imath$, due to Peano and popularised by Russell, is used to formalise definite descriptions; 'the φ' is represented by $\imath x\varphi$. We follow this route although an alternative solution can be succesfully applied, by means of binary quantifier (see e.g. Neale [24] or Kürbis [21,22]).

Since several rival theories of DD were formulated, the question which approach is the best one, at least for some applications, arises. The basic theory of DD in NFL is the same as in PFL, in the sense that the same axiom, usually called Lambert's axiom, may be used. Due to the specific features of NFL, this theory of DD is in fact as strong as Russell's theory of DD ([30,36]) which plays a central role in this area. It is a standard point of reference of almost all works devoted to the analysis of DD, widely accepted by formal logicians; numerous textbooks count as witnesses for this claim (like influential Quine [29], Copi [10] or Barwise and Etchemendy [3]).

At first sight the examination of DD in the setting of modern proof theory, and in particular, the resuscitation of the Russellian approach to DD in the setting of NFL, may seem to be of small interest for automated deduction, if at all. There are plenty of provers and checkers dealing with several reasoning tasks in reasonably efficient ways. However, introducing term-forming operators like the $\imath$-operator, equipped with well-behaved rules, may offer a more direct way of dealing with the translation of arguments in natural languages and several improvements in the formal proving/disproving process. One may easily check an arbitrary textbook in mathematics and find several short informal proofs using multiple DD. In many cases their shortness, in contrast to formal proofs, follows from the direct application of complex terms. Let us illustrate the point with a simple example:

The (only) daughter of Alice is the wife of Ben. The daughter of Alice is a scientist. So, the wife of Ben is a scientist.

Its formalisation using the $\imath$ operator yields:

$\imath x(Dxa) = \imath x(Wxb), S(\imath x(Dxa)) \vdash S(\imath x(Wxb))$

The conclusion is immediate by Leibniz' law. On the other hand if we apply the standard formalisation we obtain:

$\exists x(Dxa \wedge Wxb \wedge \forall y(Dya \wedge Wyb \rightarrow y = x)), \exists x(Dxa \wedge Sx \wedge \forall y(Dya \rightarrow y = x)) \vdash$
$\exists x(Wxb \wedge Sx \wedge \forall y(Wyb \rightarrow y = x))$

This is much more complex and requires more laborious proof. One might say that in such cases we can avoid troubles by introducing functional terms, which is a standard solution applied in systems of automated deduction. However, applying DD in place of functional terms has many advantages. First of all DD are more expressive than functional terms, since arbitrary functional term $f^n(t_1, \dots, t_n)$ can be represented as a description $\imath x F^{n+1}(x, t_1, \dots, t_n)$. On the other hand, not every DD, even if proper, can be represented as a functional term; consider description like 'the child I saw yesterday'. It is not clear which parts of this expression should be treated as a functor and which as arguments. In the example under consideration we can use a functional term $w(b)$ as representing 'the wife of Ben' (assuming that polygamy is excluded!) but not $d(a)$ as representing 'the daughter of Alice' since the relation 'being a daughter of' is not functional. In general, the main difference is that using the $\imath$-operator we can obtain a term from any formula, whereas we can introduce a function only if this formula expresses a functional relation.

Moreover, the application of functional terms instead of DD, unnecessarily enriches the language with another sort of functors in addition to predicates, which has an impact on the formalisation of arguments and evaluation of their correctness. For example: 'Ann has children' follows from 'Ann is the mother of Ben'. However, proving validity for its formal representation $a = m(b) \vdash \exists x(Cxa)$ requires two enthymematic premisses: $\forall xy(Mxy \vee Fxy \leftrightarrow Cyx)$ and $\forall xy(x = m(y) \leftrightarrow Mxy)$. The latter premiss is a kind of bridge principle allowing us to transfer some information conveyed by predicates to related functions and vice versa. In general, they show how the information encoded by functional terms is represented by predicates and they are necessary in the analysis of obviously valid arguments. Using DD instead of functional terms saves us from the need for bridge principles and has also some advantage for solving sat-problems.

The application of functional terms often easily leads to generating infinite Herbrand models even when finite models are allowed. For example from $\forall x(a = f(x))$ we infer an infinite chain $a = f(a), a = f(f(a)), a = f(f(f(a))), \ldots$. On the other hand, from the corresponding $\forall x(a = \imath y F(y, x))$ we can obtain a single-element model satisfying $a = a, F(a, a)$, where F is a binary predicate corresponding to the unary functional term f.

Summing up, using formal proof systems with the $\imath$-operator we may:

1. provide shorter and more direct formalisations;
2. obtain shorter proofs for valid arguments;
3. avoid infinite countermodels for invalid arguments.

We restricted considerations to extremely simple examples, since the lack of space does not allow us to expand them. However, the usefulness of formal devices like the $\imath$-operator and other term-forming operators has recently been better recognised. Some works may be briefly addressed here as good witnesses for these claims. One of the examples is a differential dynamic logic – a logic used for verification of hybrid systems – where DD were added to enable partial, non-differentiable, and discontinuous terms. Such an extended system was successfully implemented in the theorem prover *KeYamera* X [8]. Another interesting case of implementing a logic with DD is the work by Oppenheimer and Zalta who used NFL with DD to formalise Anselm's ontological argument and verified its validity with the automated reasoning tool *PROVER9* [27]. Scott and Benzmüller implemented FL using *Isabelle/HOL* [6]. The same framework was used by Blumson to encode Oppenheimer and Zalta's formalisation of Anselm's ontological argument [7]. Recently the advantages of introducing DD have also been noticed in the description logics community. In logics which allow the use of nominals, they serve as a means to refer to individual objects. However, nominals are simply proper names and as such bear no characteristics of the named objects. Having access to DD allows a human user to comprehend the kind of object they are dealing with (see e.g. [1,26]).

The number of nonaxiomatic proof systems for (U)(I)NFL is relatively small. There is a natural deduction system of Tennant [33] for NFL with DD and an analytic tableau system of Indrzejczak and Zawidzki [20]. As for the treatment in terms of sequent calculi (SC), Gratzl [13] provided SC for NFL but without DD, where cut is eliminable partially (so called 'inessential cuts', in Takeuti's sense [32], cannot be removed). More recent works which cover also NFL include Pavlović and Gratzl [28] and Indrzejczak [15]; both provide cut-free SC but for logics without DD. The results from [15] were extended to variety of FL with DD in [14]. However, the subformula property does not hold in cut-free systems provided there, so they are not analytic. Eventually, for quasi NFL with DD (called there RDD, after Russell) an improved result was introduced in [17]. A cut-free SC satisfying also the subformula property was obtained by proliferation of rules dealing with different kinds of identities to avoid problems in the constructive proof of cut elimination. The main contribution of this paper is a cut-free and analytic SC for (U)(I)NFL constructed along similar lines. In

Sect. 3 we provide a more detailed comparison of the family of systems presented here with SC for RDD introduced in [17].

2 Preliminaries

We will use a standard first-order language with quantifiers $\forall, \exists$, identity predicate $=$ and iota-operator $\imath$ forming definite descriptions from formulae of the language. The definition of a term and formula is standard. Terms are either complex, i.e. DD of the form $\imath x\varphi$, where φ is a formula, or simple, i.e. individual variables. The latter, for technical convenience, are divided into bound $x, y, z, \ldots$ and free variables (parameters) $a, b, c, \ldots$. In the metalanguage φ, ψ, χ denote any formulae and $\Gamma, \Delta, \Pi, \Sigma$ their multisets. Metavariables $t, s, t_1, \ldots$ denote arbitrary terms, metavariables $d, d', d_1, \ldots$ denote any description if its structure is not essential in the context. $\varphi[t_1/t_2]$ is officially used for the operation of correct substitution of a term t_2 for all occurrences of a term t_1 in φ, and similarly $\Gamma[t_1/t_2]$ for a uniform substitution in all formulae in Γ.

It will be useful to introduce some distinctions concerning atomic formulae. We will keep this name for any formula which consists of a predicate symbol R^n (but not an identity!) followed by a list of n arguments (not necessarily different). Atomic formulae and identities are divided into:

- p-atomic (proper) with all arguments being simple;
- q-atomic (quasi) with at least one argument being DD;
- s-identities (simple) with both arguments being simple;
- m-identities (mixed) with exactly one argument being DD;
- d-identities (descriptive) with both arguments being DD.

$t_1 \approx t_2$ will be used to mean either $t_1 = t_2$ or $t_2 = t_1$. This convention is just for compactness of presentation of the calculus; otherwise we need to display six schemata of rules for the iota-operator, instead of three.

Complexity of formulae and terms is defined in the following way:

$c(t) = 0$, for t being a variable (bound or free)
$c(\imath x\varphi) = c(\neg\varphi) = c(\forall x\varphi) = c(\exists x\varphi) = c(\varphi) + 1$
$c(\varphi * \psi) = c(\varphi) + c(\psi) + 1$, for $* \in \{\wedge, \vee, \rightarrow, \leftrightarrow\}$
$c(R^n t_1 \ldots t_n) = \sum_{i=1}^{n} c(t_i) + 1$
$c(t_1 = t_2) = c(t_1) + c(t_2)$

One may easily observe that all atomic formulae have complexity at least 1 (proper atomic), whereas s-identities have complexity 0. This is an important factor in proving cut elimination.

The notion of a subformula of given formula φ is standard but with the important proviso that if $\imath x\psi$ is a term occurring in φ, then $\psi[x/v]$, where v is a variable (free or bound) is a subformula of φ. Note that instances of ψ with x replaced with some DD are not counted as subformulae of φ. The same applies to quantified formulae, i.e., $\psi[x/a], \psi[x/y]$ are subformulae of $\forall x\psi$ but $\psi[x/\imath y\chi]$ is not. Hence for each proper subformula ψ of φ, $c(\psi) < c(\varphi)$.

(U)(I)NFL can be characterised axiomatically by addition of the following axioms/rules to (intuitionistic) classical propositional logic (see e.g. [5]):

$\exists I$ $\varphi[x/t] \wedge Et \rightarrow \exists x\varphi$
$\exists E$ if $\vdash \varphi[x/a] \wedge Ea \rightarrow \psi$, then $\vdash \exists x\varphi \rightarrow \psi$, where a is not in ψ
$\forall I$ if $\vdash \psi \wedge Ea \rightarrow \varphi[x/a]$, then $\vdash \psi \rightarrow \forall x\varphi$, where a is not in ψ
$\forall E$ $\forall x\varphi \wedge Et \rightarrow \varphi[x/t]$
$SP1$ $R^n t_1 \ldots t_n \rightarrow Et_1 \wedge \ldots \wedge Et_n$
$SP2$ $t_1 = t_2 \rightarrow Et_1 \wedge Et_2$
RR $Et \rightarrow t = t$
LL $t_1 = t_2 \wedge \varphi[x/t_1] \rightarrow \varphi[x/t_2]$.

where R^n denotes arbitrary predicate, while E is a unary predicate of existence defined in FL with identity as $Et := \exists x(x = t)$. $SP1, SP2$ are strictness principles for predicates, RR is (a restricted) reflexivity and LL a Leibniz Law. DD are usually characterised by means of Lambert's axiom:

LA $\forall x(x = \imath y\varphi \leftrightarrow \forall y(\varphi \leftrightarrow y = x))$, where x is not in φ

which provides the basic theory of DD in free logics.

If we want to restrict the logic to nonempty domains (i.e. not universal) we must add one more axiom of existence:

EX $\exists x Ex$.

In what follows we will be not using a predicate of existence, since in NFL Et may be defined as $t = t$ due to RR and $SP2$. So to simplify the calculus (to reduce the number of rules in particular) we will use the latter formula to express existence. However, it is possible to use Et but at the expense of addition suitable rules for dealing with Et in the antecedent and succedent of a sequent.

3 The Sequent Calculus for (U)(I)NFL

Our sequent calculus GNFL is standard in the sense that rules are defined on sequents $\Gamma \Rightarrow \Delta$ which are ordered pairs of finite multisets of formulae called the antecedent and the succedent, respectively, with Δ restricted to at most one formula in the intuitionistic variant. The calculus GNFL on the classical basis consists of the rules from Fig. 1. Let us recall that formulae displayed in the schemata of rules are active, whereas the remaining ones are parametric and together make a context. In particular, all active formulae in the premisses are called side formulae, and the one in the conclusion is the principal formula. Proofs are defined in a standard way as finite trees with nodes labelled by sequents. The height of a proof $\mathcal{D}$ of $\Gamma \Rightarrow \Delta$ is defined as the number of nodes of a branch of maximal lenght in $\mathcal{D}$. $\vdash_k \Gamma \Rightarrow \Delta$ means that $\Gamma \Rightarrow \Delta$ has a proof of the height at most k. For obtaining GU(I)NFL we must cancel ($R2$).

For the intuitionistic variant GINFL we need only to restrict the succedents to at most one formula which means that we can get rid of ($\Rightarrow C$) and need alternative rules for $\vee, \leftrightarrow$:

$$(\Rightarrow\vee 1)\ \frac{\Gamma\Rightarrow\varphi}{\Gamma\Rightarrow\varphi\vee\psi}\qquad(\Rightarrow\vee 2)\ \frac{\Gamma\Rightarrow\psi}{\Gamma\Rightarrow\varphi\vee\psi}$$

$$(\leftrightarrow\Rightarrow 1)\ \frac{\Gamma\Rightarrow\varphi\qquad\psi,\Gamma\Rightarrow\chi}{\varphi\leftrightarrow\psi,\Gamma\Rightarrow\chi}\qquad(\leftrightarrow\Rightarrow 2)\ \frac{\Gamma\Rightarrow\psi\qquad\varphi,\Gamma\Rightarrow\chi}{\varphi\leftrightarrow\psi,\Gamma\Rightarrow\chi}$$

$$(Cut)\ \frac{\Gamma\Rightarrow\Delta,\varphi\qquad\varphi,\Pi\Rightarrow\Sigma}{\Gamma,\Pi\Rightarrow\Delta,\Sigma}\qquad(AX)\ \varphi\Rightarrow\varphi$$

$$(\neg\Rightarrow)\ \frac{\Gamma\Rightarrow\Delta,\varphi}{\neg\varphi,\Gamma\Rightarrow\Delta}\qquad(\Rightarrow\neg)\ \frac{\varphi,\Gamma\Rightarrow\Delta}{\Gamma\Rightarrow\Delta,\neg\varphi}\qquad(W\Rightarrow)\ \frac{\Gamma\Rightarrow\Delta}{\varphi,\Gamma\Rightarrow\Delta}$$

$$(\Rightarrow\wedge)\ \frac{\Gamma\Rightarrow\Delta,\varphi\qquad\Gamma\Rightarrow\Delta,\psi}{\Gamma\Rightarrow\Delta,\varphi\wedge\psi}\qquad(\wedge\Rightarrow)\ \frac{\varphi,\psi,\Gamma\Rightarrow\Delta}{\varphi\wedge\psi,\Gamma\Rightarrow\Delta}\qquad(\Rightarrow W)\ \frac{\Gamma\Rightarrow\Delta}{\Gamma\Rightarrow\Delta,\varphi}$$

$$(\vee\Rightarrow)\ \frac{\varphi,\Gamma\Rightarrow\Delta\qquad\psi,\Gamma\Rightarrow\Delta}{\varphi\vee\psi,\Gamma\Rightarrow\Delta}\qquad(\Rightarrow\vee)\ \frac{\Gamma\Rightarrow\Delta,\varphi,\psi}{\Gamma\Rightarrow\Delta,\varphi\vee\psi}\qquad(C\Rightarrow)\ \frac{\varphi,\varphi,\Gamma\Rightarrow\Delta}{\varphi,\Gamma\Rightarrow\Delta}$$

$$(\rightarrow\Rightarrow)\ \frac{\Gamma\Rightarrow\Delta,\varphi\qquad\psi,\Gamma\Rightarrow\Delta}{\varphi\rightarrow\psi,\Gamma\Rightarrow\Delta}\qquad(\Rightarrow\rightarrow)\ \frac{\varphi,\Gamma\Rightarrow\Delta,\psi}{\Gamma\Rightarrow\Delta,\varphi\rightarrow\psi}\qquad(\Rightarrow C)\ \frac{\Gamma\Rightarrow\Delta,\varphi,\varphi}{\Gamma\Rightarrow\Delta,\varphi}$$

$$(\leftrightarrow\Rightarrow)\ \frac{\Gamma\Rightarrow\Delta,\varphi,\psi\qquad\varphi,\psi,\Gamma\Rightarrow\Delta}{\varphi\leftrightarrow\psi,\Gamma\Rightarrow\Delta}\qquad(\forall\Rightarrow)\ \frac{\varphi[x/b],\Gamma\Rightarrow\Delta}{b=b,\forall x\varphi,\Gamma\Rightarrow\Delta}\qquad(\Rightarrow\exists)\ \frac{\Gamma\Rightarrow\Delta,\varphi[x/b]}{b=b,\Gamma\Rightarrow\Delta,\exists x\varphi}$$

$$(\Rightarrow\leftrightarrow)\ \frac{\varphi,\Gamma\Rightarrow\Delta,\psi\qquad\psi,\Gamma\Rightarrow\Delta,\varphi}{\Gamma\Rightarrow\Delta,\varphi\leftrightarrow\psi}\qquad(\Rightarrow\forall)\ \frac{a=a,\Gamma\Rightarrow\Delta,\varphi[x/a]}{\Gamma\Rightarrow\Delta,\forall x\varphi}\qquad(\exists\Rightarrow)\ \frac{a=a,\varphi[x/a],\Gamma\Rightarrow\Delta}{\exists x\varphi,\Gamma\Rightarrow\Delta}$$

$$(\imath\Rightarrow 1)\ \frac{\Gamma\Rightarrow\Delta,c\approx b\qquad\varphi[x/b],\Gamma\Rightarrow\Delta}{c\approx\imath x\varphi,b=b,\Gamma\Rightarrow\Delta}\qquad(\imath\Rightarrow 2)\ \frac{\Gamma\Rightarrow\Delta,\varphi[x/b]\qquad c\approx b,\Gamma\Rightarrow\Delta}{c\approx\imath x\varphi,b=b,\Gamma\Rightarrow\Delta}$$

$$(\Rightarrow\imath)\ \frac{a=a,\varphi[x/a],\Gamma\Rightarrow\Delta,c\approx a\qquad c\approx a,\Gamma\Rightarrow\Delta,\varphi[x/a]}{c=c,\Gamma\Rightarrow\Delta,c\approx\imath x\varphi}\qquad(E)\ \frac{b=c,\Gamma\Rightarrow\Delta}{a=b,a=c,\Gamma\Rightarrow\Delta}$$

$$(=\Rightarrow)\ \frac{a_1=d_1,a_2=d_2,a_1=a_2,\Gamma\Rightarrow\Delta}{d_1=d_2,\Gamma\Rightarrow\Delta}\qquad(R1)\ \frac{b=b,\Gamma\Rightarrow\Delta}{\varphi[x/b],\Gamma\Rightarrow\Delta}$$

$$(\Rightarrow=)\ \frac{\Gamma\Rightarrow\Delta,b_1=d_1\quad\Gamma\Rightarrow\Delta,b_2=d_2\quad\Gamma\Rightarrow\Delta,b_1=b_2}{\Gamma\Rightarrow\Delta,d_1=d_2}\qquad(R2)\ \frac{a=a,\Gamma\Rightarrow\Delta}{\Gamma\Rightarrow\Delta}$$

$$(Str\Rightarrow)\ \frac{a_1=d_1,\ldots,a_n=d_n,\varphi[x_1/a_1\ldots x_n/a_n],\Gamma\Rightarrow\Delta}{\varphi[x_1/d_1\ldots x_n/d_n],\Gamma\Rightarrow\Delta}\qquad(L)\ \frac{\varphi[x/b],\Gamma\Rightarrow\Delta}{a=b,\varphi[x/a],\Gamma\Rightarrow\Delta}$$

$$(\Rightarrow Str)\ \frac{\Gamma\Rightarrow\Delta,b_1=d_1\qquad\ldots\qquad\Gamma\Rightarrow\Delta,b_n=d_n\qquad\Gamma\Rightarrow\Delta,\varphi[x_1/b_1\ldots x_n/b_n]}{\Gamma\Rightarrow\Delta,\varphi[x_1/d_1\ldots x_n/d_n]}$$

where in rules $(\Rightarrow\forall),(\exists\Rightarrow),(\Rightarrow\imath),(Str\Rightarrow),(=\Rightarrow),(R2)$, $a,a_1,...,a_n$ are fresh parameters (eigenvariable), $b,b_1,...,b_n,c$ are arbitrary parameters, d,d_1,d_2 arbitrary definite descriptions and t arbitrary terms. φ in $(R1)$ is either p-atomic formula, or s- or m-identity with at least one occurrence of parameter b. φ in (L) is p-atomic formula, while φ is $(Str\Rightarrow),(\Rightarrow Str)$ is q-atomic formula with occurrences of n different DD $(n\geq 1)$.

Fig. 1. Calculus GNFL

The propositional part of G(U)(I)NFL is essentially the calculus G1c and G1i of Troelstra and Schwichtenberg [35] but with all rules invertible like in G3. The rules for quantifiers are those of NFL with additional existence premisses ($a = a$) or conclusions ($b = b$) instead of usual Ea, Eb like in [15]. Note that in ($\forall \Rightarrow$), ($\Rightarrow \exists$) we have identities not with arbitrary terms t but with arbitrary variables b. The last ten rules (plus ($R2$) if needed) displayed in Fig. 1 characterise atomic formulae and identities. In particular, ($Str \Rightarrow$) corresponds to the strictness principle for arbitrary predicates and ($=\Rightarrow$) for d-identities. ($\Rightarrow Str$), ($\Rightarrow=$) have nothing to do with strictness but permit proving some instances of LL. Note that in both ($Str \Rightarrow$) and ($\Rightarrow Str$) φ in the premiss is q-atomic. In general, what is important for this rich collection of specific rules dealing with different kinds of identities and atomic formulae, is a division of labour essential for proving cut elimination while keeping the subformula property. By contrast, in [14] only one rule was provided as a counterpart of LL, namely:

$$(=)\ \frac{\Gamma \Rightarrow \Delta, t_1 = t_2 \qquad \Gamma \Rightarrow \Delta, \varphi[x/t_1] \qquad \varphi[x/t_2], \Gamma \Rightarrow \Delta}{\Gamma \Rightarrow \Delta}$$

where φ is an atomic formula or identity.

The variety of calculi for FL with DD with this rule, introduced in [14], were proved cut-free, but it is easy to notice that the subformula property is broken since arbitrary atomic formula (or identity) is allowed in the premisses of the rule. This defect was removed in [17], but only for RDD (quasi NFL), by replacing ($=$) with the set of specialised rules for different kinds of identities and atomic formulae. Basically, the same strategy is applied here to obtain cut-free system satisfying the subformula property. The main difference between the logic RDD from [17], and the logics considered here is connected with the treatment of variables which all denote in RDD. Semantically, we could say that RDD is a special case of the more general situation, considered in the present text, and obtained by limiting the class of models to those where assignment function in models is total. The more general case forces us to introduce syntactic device for signalling existence, and reformulation of quantifier rules accordingly; in [17] they were classical, whereas here they are taken from free logic. Since DD are characterised by means of quantified formulae, and suitable rules for them are obtained by means of decomposition of these formulae, they also differ, and the present rules contain additional existence statements either in the premisses or in the conclusion, where necessary. Moreover, the single rule ($\imath \Rightarrow$) from [17], intuitionistically incorrect, is replaced with two rules which are intuitionistically correct. Also ($R1$) differs from suitable rule in [17], where only $b = b$ in the premiss is present. ($R2$) is an additional rule for excluding emptiness of domains which was not admitted in RDD. It is interesting that rules for d-identities and ($Str \Rightarrow$), ($\Rightarrow Str$) for q-atoms may be left the same as in [17]. They do not require changes, like additional $a = a$ in the premiss, since ($R1$) always allows one to deduce $a = a$ from any $a = d$. Summing up, the changes in rules, comparing to those in [17], seem to be not very big, but the details of proofs of the equivalence with axiomatic systems, and cut elimination, are sometimes significantly more complicated.

Let us note that the following holds for G(U)(I)NFL:

1. If $\vdash \Gamma \Rightarrow \Delta$ has a cut-free proof, then the only terms occurring in it are those already occuring in Γ, Δ or eigenvariables.
2. If $\vdash \Gamma \Rightarrow \Delta$ has a cut-free proof, then it is constructed from subformulae of formulae occurring in Γ, Δ and atomic formulae satisfying the subformula property.

The notion of an atomic formulae satisfying the subformula property needs some explanation since there are cases of atomic formulae that are not subformulae of any formula of Γ, Δ but may be instances of such subformulae. In case of $(Str \Rightarrow), (\Rightarrow Str)$ we have p-atomic instances of q-atomic formulae from the conclusion. In case of $(=\Rightarrow), (\Rightarrow=)$ we have m- and s-identities which are instances of d-identities from the conclusion. In case of $(\imath \Rightarrow 1), (\imath \Rightarrow 2), (\Rightarrow \imath)$ we have s-identities which are instances of m-identities from the conclusion. In all these cases note that the complexity of instances occurring in the premisses is strictly lower than that of the principal formula being instantiated. Additionally we have only introduction of s-identities in some rules, so never the complexity of the union of formulae in each premiss is greater than the complexity of the conclusion.

It remains to show that this calculus is adequate for (U)(I)NFL and that cut can be constructively eliminated from arbitrary proofs. Note that all proofs will be presented in the version which is either intuitionistic or can be easily restored. Also to save space we often omit explicit applications of structural rules.

4 Adequacy

First of all, since theory of identity in (U)(I)NFL is weaker than standard one, it may be not clear that such properties like symmetry or transitivity, which were implicitly used in proofs, can be proved by means of the rules of G(U)(I)NFL. Here are some proofs:

$$\dfrac{\dfrac{b = a \Rightarrow b = a}{a = b, a = a \Rightarrow b = a}\,(E)}{a = b \Rightarrow b = a}\,(C\Rightarrow),(R1)$$

For m-identities symmetry is secured by the formulation of rules in terms of $\approx$. For d-identities it holds obviously by $(Str \Rightarrow), (\Rightarrow Str)$. Transitivity for s-identities:

$$\dfrac{\dfrac{\dfrac{a = c \Rightarrow a = c}{b = a, b = c \Rightarrow a = c}\,(E)}{a = b, a = a, b = c \Rightarrow a = c}\,(E)}{a = b, b = c \Rightarrow a = c}\,(C\Rightarrow),(R1)$$

For other combinations of terms it can be easily obtained either by direct proofs or by using symmetry.

Theorem 1. *If (U)(I)NFL $\vdash \varphi$, then G(U)(I)NFL $\vdash\Rightarrow \varphi$*

Proof. Since (Cut) simulates Modus Ponens it is enough to show that the axioms of (U)(I)NFL are provable and the rules are derivable in the calculus. Et will be represented by $\exists x(x = t)$. The case of RR is simple. If t is a parameter, we have:

$$\dfrac{\dfrac{\dfrac{b = b \Rightarrow b = b}{a = a, a = b \Rightarrow b = b}\,(W \Rightarrow),(R1)}{\exists x(x = b) \Rightarrow b = b}\,(\exists \Rightarrow)}{\Rightarrow \exists x(x = b) \rightarrow b = b}\,(\Rightarrow\rightarrow)$$

For $\exists x x = d \rightarrow d = d$ we have:

$$\dfrac{\dfrac{\dfrac{a = d \Rightarrow a = d \qquad a = d \Rightarrow a = d \qquad a = a \Rightarrow a = a}{a = a, a = d \Rightarrow d = d}\,(\Rightarrow=),(W \Rightarrow)}{\exists x(x = d) \Rightarrow d = d}\,(\exists \Rightarrow)}{\Rightarrow \exists x(x = d) \rightarrow d = d}\,(\Rightarrow\rightarrow)$$

The proofs of sequents corresponding to both denotation principles are similar. Let us take as an example an instance of $SP1$ $Rbd \Rightarrow \exists x(x = b) \wedge \exists x(x = d)$:

$$\dfrac{\dfrac{\dfrac{\dfrac{b = b \Rightarrow b = b}{b = b \Rightarrow \exists x(x = b)}\,(C \Rightarrow),(\Rightarrow \exists)}{Rba \Rightarrow \exists x(x = b)}\,(R1) \qquad \dfrac{\dfrac{a = d \Rightarrow a = d}{a = a, a = d \Rightarrow \exists x(x = d)}\,(\Rightarrow \exists)}{a = d \Rightarrow \exists x(x = d)}\,(C \Rightarrow),(R1)}{a = d, Rba \Rightarrow \exists x(x = b) \wedge \exists x(x = d)}\,(\Rightarrow \wedge),(W \Rightarrow)}{Rbd \Rightarrow \exists x(x = b) \wedge \exists x(x = d)}\,(Str \Rightarrow)$$

both branches show different ways of proving the cases of t_i being a parameter and a DD. Other subcases, as well as the case of $SP2$ are similar.

The proof of LA is slightly more complicated. Let $\mathcal{D}_1$ and $\mathcal{D}_2$ be:

$$\dfrac{\dfrac{\dfrac{\varphi[y/b] \Rightarrow \varphi[y/b] \qquad b = a \Rightarrow b = a}{b = b, a = \imath y\varphi, \varphi[y/b] \Rightarrow b = a}\,(\imath \Rightarrow 2) \qquad \dfrac{b = a \Rightarrow b = a \qquad \varphi[y/b] \Rightarrow \varphi[y/b]}{b = b, a = \imath y\varphi, b = a \Rightarrow \varphi[y/b]}\,(\imath \Rightarrow 1)}{b = b, a = \imath y\varphi \Rightarrow \varphi[y/b] \leftrightarrow b = a}\,(\Rightarrow\leftrightarrow)}{a = a, a = \imath y\varphi \Rightarrow \forall y(\varphi \leftrightarrow y = a)}\,(\Rightarrow \forall),(W \Rightarrow)$$

$$\dfrac{\dfrac{\dfrac{\dfrac{b = a \Rightarrow b = a \qquad \varphi[y/b] \Rightarrow \varphi[y/b]}{\varphi[y/b] \leftrightarrow b = a, b = a \Rightarrow \varphi[y/b]}\,(\leftrightarrow\Rightarrow 2)}{b = b, \forall y(\varphi \leftrightarrow y = a), b = a \Rightarrow \varphi[y/b]}\,(\forall \Rightarrow)}{\forall y(\varphi \leftrightarrow y = a), b = a \Rightarrow \varphi[y/b]}\,(R1) \qquad \dfrac{\dfrac{\varphi[y/b] \Rightarrow \varphi[y/b] \qquad b = a \Rightarrow b = a}{\varphi[y/b] \leftrightarrow b = a, \varphi[y/b] \Rightarrow b = a}\,(\leftrightarrow\Rightarrow 1)}{b = b, \forall y(\varphi \leftrightarrow y = a), \varphi[y/b] \Rightarrow b = a}\,(\forall \Rightarrow)}{a = a, \forall y(\varphi \leftrightarrow y = a) \Rightarrow a = \imath y\varphi}\,(\Rightarrow \imath)$$

then by $(\Rightarrow\leftrightarrow)$ on their roots followed by $(\Rightarrow \forall)$ we obtain $\Rightarrow \forall x(x = \imath y\varphi \leftrightarrow \forall y(\varphi \leftrightarrow y = x))$.

The proof of EX is trivial by $(R2)$ and $(\Rightarrow \exists)$. On the other hand, the proof of LL is considerably complex, due to many cases to consider. It goes by induction on the complexity of φ and we omit the cases where φ is a quantified or boolean formula, since they are proven in a standard way (see, e.g. [25]). However, we must check all cases of φ atomic or identity. The case composed of three s-identities is provable directly by (E) but we still have the following subcases that cover all possible combinations of parameters and descriptions as arguments with φ being an identity or an atomic formula:

1. $b = c, b = d \Rightarrow c = d$
2. $b = d, b = c \Rightarrow d = c$
3. $d = b, d = c \Rightarrow b = c$
4. $d_1 = d_2, d_1 = b \Rightarrow d_2 = b$
5. $d_1 = b, d_1 = d_2 \Rightarrow b = d_2$
6. $b = d_1, b = d_2 \Rightarrow d_1 = d_2$
7. $d_1 = d_2, d_1 = d_3 \Rightarrow d_2 = d_3$
8. $b = c, \varphi[x/b] \Rightarrow \varphi[x/c]$
9. $b = d, \varphi[x/b] \Rightarrow \varphi[x/d]$
10. $d = b, \varphi[x/d] \Rightarrow \varphi[x/b]$
11. $d_1 = d_2, \varphi[x/d_1] \Rightarrow \varphi[x/d_2]$

Ad 1 ($d := \imath x\varphi$):

$$(R1)\ \dfrac{(\Rightarrow \imath)\ \dfrac{(R1)\ \dfrac{(\imath \Rightarrow 1)\ \dfrac{b = c, c = a \Rightarrow b = a \qquad \varphi[x/a] \Rightarrow \varphi[x/a]}{a = a, b = c, b = \imath x\varphi, c = a \Rightarrow \varphi[x/a]}}{b = c, b = \imath x\varphi, c = a \Rightarrow \varphi[x/a]} \qquad \dfrac{\varphi[x/a] \Rightarrow \varphi[x/a] \qquad b = a, b = c \Rightarrow c = a}{a = a, b = c, b = \imath x\varphi, \varphi[x/a] \Rightarrow c = a}}{c = c, b = c, b = \imath x\varphi \Rightarrow c = \imath x\varphi}}{b = c, b = \imath x\varphi \Rightarrow c = \imath x\varphi}$$

Ad. 2: It holds by 1 and symmetry on $c = d$. Ad 3:

$$(R1)\ \dfrac{(\imath \Rightarrow 1)\ \dfrac{(\imath \Rightarrow 2)\ \dfrac{b = b \Rightarrow b = b \qquad \varphi[x/b] \Rightarrow \varphi[x/b]}{b = b, \imath x\varphi = b \Rightarrow \varphi[x/b]} \qquad b = c \Rightarrow b = c}{b = b, \imath x\varphi = b, \imath x\varphi = c \Rightarrow b = c}}{\imath x\varphi = b, \imath x\varphi = c \Rightarrow b = c}$$

Ad 4:

$$\dfrac{\dfrac{a_1 = d_1, d_1 = b \Rightarrow a_1 = b \qquad \dfrac{a_2 = b, a_2 = d_2 \Rightarrow d_2 = b}{a_1 = b, a_2 = d_2, a_1 = a_2 \Rightarrow d_2 = b}\ (E)}{a_1 = d_1, a_2 = d_2, a_1 = a_2, d_1 = b \Rightarrow d_2 = b}\ (Cut)}{d_1 = d_2, d_1 = b \Rightarrow d_2 = b}\ (=\Rightarrow)$$

where both leaves are provable; the left by 3, the right by 2.

Ad 5: by 4 and symmetry on $d_2 = b$. Ad 6:

$$\dfrac{\dfrac{b = d_1 \Rightarrow b = d_1 \qquad b = d_2 \Rightarrow b = d_2 \qquad b = b \Rightarrow b = b}{b = b, b = d_1, b = d_2 \Rightarrow d_1 = d_2}\ (\Rightarrow=)}{b = d_1, b = d_2 \Rightarrow d_1 = d_2}\ (R1)$$

Ad 7:

$$\dfrac{\dfrac{b=d_2\Rightarrow b=d_2 \qquad c=d_3\Rightarrow c=d_3 \qquad \dfrac{a=d_1, b'=d_1\Rightarrow a=b' \qquad \dfrac{\dfrac{b=c\Rightarrow b=c}{b'=b, b'=c\Rightarrow b=c}\,(E)}{a=b', a=b, b'=c\Rightarrow b=c}\,(E)}{a=d_1, a=b, b'=d_1, b'=c\Rightarrow b=c}\,(Cut)}{\dfrac{a=d_1, b=d_2, a=b, b'=d_1, c=d_3, b'=c\Rightarrow d_2=d_3}{a=d_1, b=d_2, a=b, d_1=d_3\Rightarrow d_2=d_3}\,(=\Rightarrow)}\,(\Rightarrow=)}{d_1=d_2, d_1=d_3\Rightarrow d_2=d_3}\,(=\Rightarrow)$$

where the second leaf to the right is provable by 3.

Ad 8. If φ is p-atomic it follows by (L). Otherwise it has some occurrences of DD (say $d_1, ..., d_n$) and requires additional work:

$$\dfrac{\dfrac{S_1\dots S_n \qquad \dfrac{\varphi[x/c, y_1/a_1\dots y_n/a_n]\Rightarrow\varphi[x/c, y_1/a_1\dots y_n/a_n]}{b=c, \varphi[x/b, y_1/a_1\dots y_n/a_n]\Rightarrow\varphi[x/c, y_1/a_1\dots y_n/a_n]}\,(L)}{b=c, a_1=d_1, \dots, a_n=d_n, \varphi[x/b, y_1/a_1\dots y_n/a_n]\Rightarrow\varphi[x/c, y_1/d_1\dots y_n/d_n]}\,(\Rightarrow Str)}{b=c, \varphi[x/b, y_1/d_1\dots y_n/d_n]\Rightarrow\varphi[x/c, y_1/d_1\dots y_n/d_n]}\,(Str\Rightarrow)$$

where $S_1\dots S_n$ is a number of sequents of the form $a_1=d_1\Rightarrow a_1=d_1\ \dots\ a_n=d_n\Rightarrow a_n=d_n$.

Ad 9. It holds immediately by $(\Rightarrow Str)$ if d is the only DD occuring only in $\varphi[x/d]$. Otherwise we have also some other descriptions in $\varphi[x/b]$ and we must first apply $(Str\Rightarrow)$ to change them all into parameters. Then the proof goes like in the case 8.

Ad 10. Assume for simplifying a proof figure (i.e. to diminish the number of inessential branches) that only one other description is present in φ:

$$\dfrac{\dfrac{a'=d'\Rightarrow a'=d' \qquad \dfrac{a=d, d=b\Rightarrow a=b \qquad \dfrac{\varphi[x/b, y/a']\Rightarrow\varphi[x/b, y/a']}{a=b, \varphi[x/a, y/a']\Rightarrow\varphi[x/b, y/a']}\,(L)}{a=d, d=b, \varphi[x/a, y/a']\Rightarrow\varphi[x/b, y/a']}\,(Cut)}{a=d, a'=d', d=b, \varphi[x/a, y/a']\Rightarrow\varphi[x/b, y/d']}\,(\Rightarrow Str)}{d=b, \varphi[x/d, y/d']\Rightarrow\varphi[x/b, y/d']}\,(Str\Rightarrow)$$

where the middle leaf is provable by case 3. In case no other DD are present in φ, the application of $(\Rightarrow Str)$ is not required; in case there is more than one, we simply obtain more axiomatic branches of the form $a_i=d_i\Rightarrow a_i=d_i$.

Ad 11: The proof is similar but with the additional application of $(=\Rightarrow)$ as the first (from the root) inference on $d_1=d_2$, and possibly some applications of $(Str\Rightarrow)$ if additional DD are present in φ.

Having proved that LL holds in full generality for G(U)(I)NFL we can show also that the restriction of $(\forall\Rightarrow), (\Rightarrow\exists)$ to parameters as the only admissible instantiated terms is inessential since the general cases are provable (for derivability of $\exists E, \forall I$, cf. [15]). Let us illustrate it with $\forall E$ applied to some d:

$$\dfrac{\dfrac{\dfrac{\varphi[x/a], a=d\Rightarrow\varphi[x/d]}{\forall x\varphi, a=a, a=d\Rightarrow\varphi[x/d]}\,(\forall\Rightarrow)}{\forall x\varphi, \exists x(x=d)\Rightarrow\varphi[x/d]}\,(\exists\Rightarrow)}{\Rightarrow\forall x\varphi\wedge\exists x(x=d)\rightarrow\varphi[x/d]}\,(\Rightarrow\rightarrow), (\wedge\Rightarrow)$$

where the leaf is an instance of LL. □

Hence G(U)(I)NFL is sufficiently strong; we must show that it is not too strong.

Theorem 2. *If G(U)(I)NFL* $\vdash\Rightarrow \varphi$*, then (U)(I)NFL* $\vdash \varphi$

Proof. It is sufficient to show derivability of specific rules of G(U)(I)NFL in the propositional basis of GNFL enriched with axioms, since quantifier rules of G(U)(I)NFL were shown derivable in [15]. The cases of $(E), (L), (\Rightarrow=), (\Rightarrow Str)$ are rather obvious; all are derivable by cuts with instances of LL. For example, derivability of $(\Rightarrow=)$ requires only cuts (and contractions) on the premisses with $b = d, b' = d', b = b' \Rightarrow d = d'$ which is obviously derivable by cut from two instances of LL: $b = d, b = b' \Rightarrow b' = d'$ and $b' = d, b' = d' \Rightarrow d = d'$.

Similarly for derivability of $(\Rightarrow Str)$ by series of cuts on instances of LL: $b_1 = d_1, \varphi[x_1/b_1, x_2/b_2..., x_n/b_n] \Rightarrow \varphi[x_1/d_1, x_2/b_2..., x_n/b_n]$, ..., $b_n = d_n$, $\varphi[x_1/d_1, x_2/d_2..., x_n/b_n] \Rightarrow \varphi[x_1/d_1, x_2/d_2..., x_n/d_n]$ we get $b_1 = d_1, ..., b_n = d_n, \varphi[x_1/b_1, x_2/b_2..., x_n/b_n] \Rightarrow \varphi[x_1/d_1, x_2/d_2......, x_n/d_n]$ which by cuts with the premisses of $(\Rightarrow Str)$ and contractions yields its conclusion.

In case of $(\Rightarrow \imath)$ from premisses we derive (1) $\Gamma \Rightarrow \Delta, \forall x(\varphi \leftrightarrow x = c)$. From $\Rightarrow \forall y(y = \imath x\varphi \leftrightarrow \forall x(\varphi \leftrightarrow x = y)$ and $\forall y(y = \imath x\varphi \leftrightarrow \forall x(\varphi \leftrightarrow x = y), c = c \Rightarrow c = \imath x\varphi \leftrightarrow \forall x(\varphi \leftrightarrow x = c)$ we obtain $c = c \Rightarrow c = \imath x\varphi \leftrightarrow \forall x(\varphi \leftrightarrow x = c)$, and then $c = c, \forall x(\varphi \leftrightarrow x = c) \Rightarrow c = \imath x\varphi$. This by cut with (1) yields $c = c, \Gamma \Rightarrow \Delta, c = \imath x\varphi$.

For $(\imath \Rightarrow 1)$: From premisses we derive: (1) $b = c \rightarrow \varphi[x/b], \Gamma \Rightarrow \Delta$. By $\Rightarrow \forall y(y = \imath x\varphi \leftrightarrow \forall x(\varphi \leftrightarrow x = y)$ and $\forall y(y = \imath x\varphi \leftrightarrow \forall x(\varphi \leftrightarrow x = y), c = c \Rightarrow c = \imath x\varphi \leftrightarrow \forall x(\varphi \leftrightarrow x = c)$ we obtain $c = c \Rightarrow c = \imath x\varphi \leftrightarrow \forall x(\varphi \leftrightarrow x = c)$, and then $c = c, c = \imath x\varphi \Rightarrow \forall x(\varphi \leftrightarrow x = c)$. This leads by cut with provable $\forall x(\varphi \leftrightarrow x = c), b = b \Rightarrow b = c \rightarrow \varphi[x/b]$ to $c = c, b = b, c = \imath x\varphi \Rightarrow b = c \rightarrow \varphi[x/b]$ and by cut with (1) to $c = c, b = b, c = \imath x\varphi, \Gamma \Rightarrow \Delta$ which by $(R1)$ on $c = c$ yields the conclusion.

For $(R1)$:

$$\dfrac{\varphi[x/b] \Rightarrow \exists x(x = b) \qquad \dfrac{\dfrac{a = a, a = b \Rightarrow b = b \qquad b = b, \Gamma \Rightarrow \Delta}{a = a, a = b, \Gamma \Rightarrow \Delta}\,(Cut)}{\exists x(x = b), \Gamma \Rightarrow \Delta}\,(\exists\Rightarrow)}{\varphi[x/b], \Gamma \Rightarrow \Delta}\,(Cut)$$

Derivability of $(R2)$ (a, b fresh):

$$\dfrac{\Rightarrow \exists xy(x = y) \qquad \dfrac{\dfrac{\dfrac{a = a, \Gamma \Rightarrow \Delta}{a = a, b = b, b = a, \Gamma \Rightarrow \Delta}\,(W\Rightarrow)}{b = b, \exists y(b = y), \Gamma \Rightarrow \Delta}\,(\exists\Rightarrow)}{\exists xy(x = y), \Gamma \Rightarrow \Delta}\,(\exists\Rightarrow)}{\Gamma \Rightarrow \Delta}\,(Cut)$$

Derivability of $(=\Rightarrow)$:

$$
\dfrac{S \qquad \dfrac{\dfrac{\dfrac{\dfrac{a = d, a' = d', d = d' \Rightarrow a = a' \qquad a = a', a = d, a' = d', \Gamma \Rightarrow \Delta}{a = d, a' = d', d = d', \Gamma \Rightarrow \Delta}\,(Cut), (C \Rightarrow)}{a = a, a = d, a' = a', a' = d', d = d', \Gamma \Rightarrow \Delta}\,(W \Rightarrow)}{\exists x(x = d), \exists x(x = d'), d = d', \Gamma \Rightarrow \Delta}\,(\exists \Rightarrow)}{\exists x(x = d) \wedge \exists x(x = d'), d = d', \Gamma \Rightarrow \Delta}\,(\wedge \Rightarrow)}{d = d', \Gamma \Rightarrow \Delta}\,(Cut), (C \Rightarrow)
$$

where the middle leaf is derivable from two instances of LL and S is $d = d' \Rightarrow \exists x(x = d) \wedge \exists x(x = d')$ provable from $SP2$. $(Str \Rightarrow)$ is proven similarly. □

5 Cut Elimination

Let us focus on *regular proofs*, where every parameter, which is fresh by side condition on the respective rule, is fresh in the entire proof, not only on the branch where the application of this rule takes place. Thus no eigenvariable is introduced more than once in the whole regular proof. It holds for G(U)(I)NFL:

Lemma 1. *1. If* $\vdash_k \Gamma \Rightarrow \Delta$*, then* $\vdash_k \Gamma[a/b] \Rightarrow \Delta[a/b]$.
2. If $\vdash \Gamma \Rightarrow \Delta$*, then* $\Gamma \Rightarrow \Delta$ *has a regular proof.*

Proof. The first point is a familiar property of substitution, which is proven in the standard way by induction on the height of the proof (see e.g. [25]). The second point follows from the first by systematic application of substitution. □

In what follows we assume that we deal only with regular proofs as there is no loss of generality. As usual we prove cut elimination by inductive proof showing how to systematically reduce the complexity of cut formulae and transform every (regular) proof into a cut-free proof. The reduction is based on two inductive parameters: the cut-rank, which, for our purposes, is defined in terms of the complexity of the cut-formula φ: $r\varphi = c(\varphi) + 1$, and the height of the proof.

It is sufficient to show that all logical rules are *substitutive* and *reductive*. These notions were introduced by Ciabattoni [9] and applied for general form of cut elimination proof in hypersequent calculi in [23] but can be also used in the present setting. Substitutivity is connected with the fact that multisets of formulae may be safely substituted for a cut formula which is parametric. It secures the induction on the height of a proof in cases when the cut formula is not principal in at least one premiss of cut. Rules with side conditions concerning fresh parameters are not fully substitutive but we can easily overcome the problem applying lemma 1.1. Reductivity (also called coherency in [2]) is responsible for induction on the rank. Let us say that a pair of introduction rules $(\Rightarrow \star)$, $(\star \Rightarrow)$ for a constant $\star$ is reductive if an application of cut on cut formulae introduced by these rules may be replaced by a series of cuts made on less complex formulae, in particular on their subformulae.

One may easily check that all rules (including structural ones) are substitutive (modulo lemma 1.1) and all logical rules are reductive (modulo substitution in the case of rules with eigenvariables). For connectives and free quantifiers it is known (see e.g. [28] or [15] for free quantifiers, with the change of Et for $t = t$).

It remains to check the rules for atomic formulae and identities. It can be easily shown that their role as active formulae in proofs is strictly determined. If φ is p-atomic, it can be a principal formula only in the antecedent, due to (L) or $(R1)$. Similarly, if it is an s-identity, it can be active only in the antecedent, due to (E) or $(R1)$. Hence, if such formulae are cut-formulae in the right premiss of cut, then their occurrences in the left premiss of cut are always parametric w.r.t. the rule immediately applied over cut in the left premiss. Accordingly, we can always apply induction on the height of the left premiss of cut in case of these formulae. In the remaining three cases, if in at least one premiss it is also parametric, again induction on the height is applicable. If in both premisses of cut, respective cut formula is the principal formula of the preceding rules, then it can be introduced on both sides only by the rules which are pairwise reductive, namely:

1. if φ is q-atomic, it can be principal on both sides only via $(Str \Rightarrow), (\Rightarrow Str)$;
2. if it is d-identity, it can be principal on both sides only via $(=\Rightarrow)$ and $(\Rightarrow=)$;
3. if it is m-identity, it can be principal on the left only via $(\Rightarrow \imath)$ and on the right either via $(R1)$ or $(\imath \Rightarrow 1)$ or $(\imath \Rightarrow 2)$.

We will demonstrate the reductivity of the cases 1 and 3. To simplify proof figures let $\varphi := Rd_1d_2$ in case 1.

$$\dfrac{\dfrac{\Gamma \Rightarrow \Delta, b_1 = d_1 \quad \Gamma \Rightarrow \Delta, b_2 = d_2 \quad \Gamma \Rightarrow \Delta, Rb_1b_2}{\Gamma \Rightarrow \Delta, Rd_1d_2} \qquad \dfrac{a_1 = d_1, a_2 = d_2, Ra_1a_2, \Pi \Rightarrow \Sigma}{Rd_1d_2, \Pi \Rightarrow \Sigma}}{\Gamma, \Pi \Rightarrow \Delta, \Sigma}$$

By lemma 1.1 we obtain $b_1 = d_1, b_2 = d_2, Rb_1b_2, \Pi \Rightarrow \Sigma$ to unify parameters with those present in the premisses of the application of $(\Rightarrow Str)$ and proceed by series of cuts as follows:

$$\dfrac{\dfrac{\Gamma \Rightarrow \Delta, b_1 = d_1 \qquad \dfrac{\Gamma \Rightarrow \Delta, b_2 = d_2 \qquad \dfrac{\Gamma \Rightarrow \Delta, Rb_1b_2 \qquad b_1 = d_1, b_2 = d_2, Rb_1b_2, \Pi \Rightarrow \Sigma}{b_1 = d_1, b_2 = d_2, \Gamma, \Pi \Rightarrow \Delta, \Sigma}}{b_1 = d_1, \Gamma, \Gamma, \Pi \Rightarrow \Delta, \Delta, \Sigma}}{\Gamma, \Gamma, \Gamma, \Pi \Rightarrow \Delta, \Delta, \Delta, \Sigma}}{\Gamma, \Pi \Rightarrow \Delta, \Sigma}\;(Contractions)$$

All cuts have strictly lower rank. In particular, recall that in the case of identities their rank is always the sum of complexities of arguments+1, whereas in the case of atomic formulae we add 1 to this number. Note that this is required for the special case of q-atomic cut formula introduced by $(Str \Rightarrow)$ and $(\Rightarrow Str)$, and having just one occurrence of d. Then m-identity $a = d$ in premisses is of rank $n = c(d) + 1$, whereas the principal formula of this rule application is of rank $n + 1$.

Case 3 adresses cuts on m-identities which are principal formulae in both premisses of cut. Hence the left premiss is introduced by $(\Rightarrow \imath)$:

$$\dfrac{a = a, \varphi[x/a], \Gamma \Rightarrow \Delta, c = a \qquad c = a, \Gamma \Rightarrow \Delta, \varphi[x/a]}{c = c, \Gamma \Rightarrow \Delta, c = \imath x\varphi}$$

If in the right premiss of cut $c = \imath\varphi$ was introduced by the application of $(R1)$, then the premiss is $c = c, \Pi \Rightarrow \Sigma$, and the conclusion of cut is directly inferred from it by applications of $(W \Rightarrow), (\Rightarrow W)$. If the right premiss was obtained by means of $(\imath \Rightarrow 1)$ or $(\imath \Rightarrow 2)$ we proceed by induction on the rank. Let it be $(\imath \Rightarrow 1)$ (the case of $(\imath \Rightarrow 2)$ is analogous), so we have:

$$\frac{\Pi \Rightarrow \Sigma, c = b \qquad \varphi[x/b], \Pi \Rightarrow \Sigma}{c = \imath x\varphi, b = b, \Pi \Rightarrow \Sigma}$$

where the conclusion of cut is $b = b, c = c, \Gamma, \Pi \Rightarrow \Delta, \Sigma$. By lemma 1.1 we obtain: $b = b, \varphi[x/b], \Gamma \Rightarrow \Delta, c = b$ and $c = b, \Gamma \Rightarrow \Delta, \varphi[x/b]$ from the premisses of $(\Rightarrow \imath)$ to unify parameters with those present in the premisses of the application of $(\imath \Rightarrow 1)$ and proceed as follows:

$$\dfrac{\dfrac{\Pi \Rightarrow \Sigma, c = b \qquad \dfrac{c = b, \Gamma \Rightarrow \Delta, \varphi[x/b] \qquad \varphi[x/b], \Pi \Rightarrow \Sigma}{c = b, \Gamma, \Pi \Rightarrow \Delta, \Sigma}\,(Cut)}{\Gamma, \Pi, \Pi \Rightarrow \Delta, \Sigma, \Sigma}\,(Cut)}{b = b, c = c, \Gamma, \Pi \Rightarrow \Delta, \Sigma}\,(W \Rightarrow), (C \Rightarrow), (\Rightarrow C)$$

All cuts have lower rank.

These transformations guarantee elimination of cuts. To avoid problems with contractions we follow the elegant strategy originally introduced for hypersequent calculi (see [23]), but applicable also to standard sequent calculi (see e.g. [16]), where the cut elimination theorem follows from two lemmata:

Lemma 2 (Right reduction). *Let $\mathcal{D}_1 \vdash \Gamma \Rightarrow \Delta, \varphi$ and $\mathcal{D}_2 \vdash \varphi^k, \Pi \Rightarrow \Sigma$ with $r\mathcal{D}_1, r\mathcal{D}_2 < r\varphi$, and φ principal in $\Gamma \Rightarrow \Delta, \varphi$, then we can construct a proof $\mathcal{D}$ such that $\mathcal{D} \vdash \Gamma^k, \Pi \Rightarrow \Delta^k, \Sigma$ and $r\mathcal{D} < r\varphi$.*

Lemma 3 (Left reduction). *Let $\mathcal{D}_1 \vdash \Gamma \Rightarrow \Delta, \varphi^k$ and $\mathcal{D}_2 \vdash \varphi, \Pi \Rightarrow \Sigma$ with $r\mathcal{D}_1, r\mathcal{D}_2 < r\varphi$, then we can construct a proof $\mathcal{D}$ such that $\mathcal{D} \vdash \Gamma, \Pi^k \Rightarrow \Delta, \Sigma^k$ and $r\mathcal{D} < r\varphi$.*

where in both lemmata $r\mathcal{D}$ denotes the proof-rank, i.e. the maximal cut-rank in $\mathcal{D}$, φ^k, Γ^k denote $k > 0$ occurrences of φ, Γ, respectively.

Proof. Both lemmata successively make reductions on the height of the right and then on the left premiss of cut. Substitutivity and reductivity of rules secure the satisfaction of both lemmata. More precisely, lemma 2 is proved by induction on the height of $\mathcal{D}_2$. Note that the cases of φ being s-identity or p-atomic do not apply to this lemma since neither of this formulae can be the principal formula in the end-sequent of $\mathcal{D}_1$. Lemma 3 holds by induction on the height of $\mathcal{D}_1$, but with some important differences with the proof of lemma 2. First note that we do not require φ to be principal in $\varphi, \Pi \Rightarrow \Sigma$ so it covers also the cases of φ p-atomic or s-identity. In all these cases we just apply the induction hypothesis. This guarantees that even if p-atomic formula or s-identity is our φ, introduced in the right premiss by one of the rules (E), (L), $(R1)$, the induction on the height is done on the left premiss, and we always obtain the expected result. Now, in cases where one occurrence of φ in $\Gamma \Rightarrow \Delta, \varphi^k$ is principal we first apply the induction hypothesis to eliminate all other $k-1$ occurrences of φ in premisses and then we apply the respective rule. Since the only new occurrence of φ is principal we can make use of the lemma 2 again and obtain the result, possibly after some applications of structural rules. □

Theorem 3 (Cut elimination). *If G(U)(I)NFL $\vdash \Gamma \Rightarrow \Delta$, then it has a cut-free proof.*

Proof. It follows from lemma 3 (for $k = 1$ in φ^k) by double induction: primary on $r\mathcal{D}$ and subsidiary on the number of maximal cuts (in the basis and in the inductive step of the primary induction). We always take the topmost maximal cut and apply lemma 3 to it. By successive repetition of this procedure we diminish either the rank of the proof or the number of maximal cuts in it until we obtain a proof with $r = 0$ (i.e. cut-free). □

6 Conclusion

As a result of the last section we obtained a fully analytic formalisation of (U)(I)NFL with DD, which significantly improves the result obtained for these logics in [14]. Together with the results from [17] it provides a uniform analytic characterisation of both E- and E^+-logics with DD (terminology of Troelstra and van Dalen [34]), particularly important in constructive mathematics and computer science. This uniform basis can be further used in theoretical and practical applications. In particular, these kind of sequent calculi may be used for proving interpolation theorems for respective variants of NFL and devising proof-search procedures as a basis for interactive and automated deduction. As we have mentioned in Sect. 1, theorem provers based on systems with direct formalisations of complex terms may appear more efficient than solutions based on standard languages with functional terms. These remarks apply not only to DD but to other kinds of complex terms, e.g. set abstracts commonly used in mathematical practice, but rarely exhibited in formal characterisation of set theories. For some steps in this direction see [18].

It should be emphasized that the possibility of analytic formalisation of E- and E^+-logics with DD depends strongly on the strategy of proliferation of rules for different kinds of atoms and identities. It leads to the question: is it possible to apply this approach to other kinds of logic, in particular to positive FL? It seems that in this case the answer is negative. One may observe that successful division of labour among different kinds of atoms/identities depends essentially on the validity of strictness principles characteristic for NFL. This makes the problem of improving the cut-free (but not analytic) systems for PFL with DD, introduced in [14], rather problematic. On the other hand, in case of neutral FL, strictness conditions hold not only for atoms and identities, but also for their negations. So far, a cut-free system for neutral FL with DD, on the basis of non-standard bisequent calculus (BSC), was provided in [19]. This approach is more complex and the obtained system is also non-analytic, since LL is handled by means of rules similar to (=). It is an open question, if BSC for neutral FL with DD can be improved by the application of similar strategy like the one applied to RDD in [17] and to NFL here.

Acknowledgements. I am greatly indebted to all reviewers for their valuable comments.

Disclosure of Interests. The author has no competing interests to declare that are relevant to the content of this article.

References

1. Artale, A., Mazzullo, A., Ozaki, A., Wolter, F.: On free description logics with definite descriptions. In: Proceedings of the 18th International Conference on Principles of Knowledge Representation and Reasoning, pp. 63–73, IJCAI Organization (2021)
2. Avron, A. and Lev I.: Canonical propositional Gentzen-type systems. In: Proceedings of IJCAR'01, vol. 2083, pp. 529–543, LNCS, Springer (2001)
3. Barwise, J., Etchemendy, J.: The Language of First-Order Logic. CSLI, Stanford (1991)
4. Beeson, M.: Foundations of Constructive Mathematics. Springer (1985)
5. Bencivenga, E.: Free Logics. In: Gabbay, D., Guenthner, F. (eds.) Handbook of Philosophical Logic, vol. III, pp. 373–426. Reidel Publishing Company, Dordrecht (1986)
6. Benzmüller, Ch., Scott, D.: Automating free logic in HOL, with an experimental application in category theory. J. Autom. Reas. **64**: 53–72 (2020). https://doi.org/10.1007/s10817-018-09507-7
7. Blumson, B.: Anselm's God in Isabelle/HOL URL: https://www.isa-afp.org/browser_info/current/AFP/AnselmGod/document.pdf (2020)
8. Bohrer, B., Fernández, M., Platzer, A.: dL_ι: Definite descriptions in differential dynamic logic. In: Fontaine, P. (ed.): Automated Deduction – CADE 27. Springer International Publishing, pp. 94–110 (2019). https://doi.org/10.1007/978-3-030-29436-6_6
9. Ciabattoni, A.: Automated generation of analytic calculi for logics with linearity. In: Marcinkowski, J., Tarlecki, A. (eds.) CSL 2004. LNCS, vol. 3210, pp. 503–517. Springer, Heidelberg (2004). https://doi.org/10.1007/978-3-540-30124-0_38
10. Copi, I.M.: Symbolic Logic. Oxford and IBH Publishing CO, New Delhi (1979)
11. Farmer, W.M., Guttman, J.D.: A set theory with support for partial functions. Stud. Logica. **66**(1), 59–78 (2000)
12. Feferman, S.: Definedness. Erkenntnis **43**, 295–320 (1995)
13. Gratzl, N.: A sequent calculus for a negative free logic. Stud. Logica. **96**, 331–348 (2010)
14. Indrzejczak, A.: Free definite description theory – sequent calculi and cut elimination. Logic Log. Philos. **29**(4) 505–539 (2020). https://doi.org/10.12775/LLP.2020.020

15. Indrzejczak, A.: Free logics are cut-free. Studia Logica. **109** 859–886 (2021) . https://doi.org/10.1007/s11225-020-09929-8
16. Indrzejczak, A.: Sequents and Trees. An Introduction to the Theory and Applications of Propositional Sequent Calculi. Birkhäuser (2021)
17. Indrzejczak, A.: Russellian definite description theory—a proof-theoretic approach. Rev. Symb. Logic **16**(2), 624–649 (2023). https://doi.org/10.1017/S1755020321000289
18. Indrzejczak, A.: Towards proof-theoretic formulation of the general theory of term-forming operators. In: Ramanayake, R., Urban, J. (eds.) Automated Reasoning with Analytic Tableaux and Related Methods. TABLEAUX 2023. Lecture Notes in Computer Science, vol. 14278. Springer, Cham, pp. 131–149 (2023)
19. Indrzejczak, A., Petrukhin, Y.: Bisequent calculi for neutral free logic with definite descriptions. In: Benzmüller, Ch., Otten, Y., Ramanayake, R. (eds.) Proceedings of the 5th International Workshop on Automated Reasoning in Quantified Non-Classical Logics (ARQNL 2024), pp. 48–61 (2024)
20. Indrzejczak, A., Zawidzki, M.: Tableaux for free logics with descriptions. In: Das A., Negri, S. (eds.) Automated Reasoning with Analytic Tableaux and Related Methods. Lecture Notes in Artificial Intelligence 12842, pp. 56–73, Springer, Berlin, Heidelberg (2021)
21. Kürbis, N.: A binary quantifier for definite descriptions in intuitionist negative free logic: natural deduction and normalization. Bulletin of the Section of Logic **48**(2), 81–97, (2019). https://doi.org/10.18778/0138-0680.48.2.01
22. Kürbis, N.: Proof-theory and semantics for a theory of definite descriptions. In: Das, A., Negri, S. (eds.) TABLEAUX 2021. LNCS (LNAI), vol. 12842, pp. 95–111. Springer, Cham (2021). https://doi.org/10.1007/978-3-030-86059-2_6
23. Metcalfe, G., Olivetti N., Gabbay, D: Proof Theory for Fuzzy Logics, Springer (2008)
24. Neale, S.: Descriptions. Cambridge University Press, Cambridge (1990)
25. Negri, S., von Plato, J.: Structural Proof Theory. Cambridge University Press, Cambridge (2001)
26. Neuhaus, F., Kutz, O., Righetti, G.: Free description logic for ontologists. In: K. Hammar et al. (Eds.), Proceedings of the Joint Ontology Workshops co-located with the Bolzano Summer of Knowledge (BOSK 2020), vol. 2708. Bozen-Bolzano (2020)
27. Oppenheimer, P. E., Zalta, E. N.: A computationally-discovered simplification of the ontological argument. Aust. J. Phil. **89**, 333-349 (2011). https://doi.org/10.1080/00048401003674482
28. Pavlović, E., Gratzl, N.: A more unified approach to free logics. J. Philos. Logic **50** 117-148 (2021). https://doi.org/10.1007/s10992-020-09564-7
29. Quine, W. Van O.: Methods of Logic. New York, Chicago: Holt, Rinehart and Winston (1950)
30. Russell, B.: On denoting. Mind **14** 479–494 (1905). https://doi.org/10.1093/mind/XIV.4.479
31. Scott, D.: Identity and existence in intuitionistic logic. In: M. Fourman, C. Mulvey and D. Scott (eds.) Applications of Sheaves. Springer, pp.660–696 (1979)
32. Takeuti, G.: Proof Theory. North-Holland, Amsterdam (1987)
33. Tennant, N.: Natural Logic. Edinbourgh University Press (1978)
34. Troelstra, A. S., van Dalen, D.: Constructivism in Mathematics, vol. I, North-Holland (1988)
35. Troelstra, A.S., Schwichtenberg, H.: Basic Proof Theory. Oxford University Press, Oxford (1996)

36. Whitehead, A. N., Russell, B.: Principia Mathematica vol. I. Cambridge University Press, Cambridge (1910). https://doi.org/10.1017/CBO9780511623585

From Modal Sequent Calculi to Modal Resolution

Dirk Pattinson[1(✉)], Cláudia Nalon[2], and Sourabh Peruri[3]

[1] School of Computing, The Australian National University, Canberra, Australia
dirk.pattinson@anu.edu.au

[2] Department of Computer Science, University of Brasília, Brasília, Brazil
nalon@unb.br

[3] Indian Institute of Science, Bengaluru, India
sourabhp@iisc.ac.in

Abstract. We establish a systematic correspondence between sequent and resolution calculi for a broad class of modal logics. Our main result is that soundness and completeness transfer from sequent to resolution calculi as long as cut and weakening are admissible. We first construct generative calculi that essentially import modal rules to a resolution setting, and then show how soundness and completeness transfer to absorptive calculi, where modal rules are translated into generalised resolution rules. We discuss resolution calculi that establish validity, and then introduce local clauses to generate calculi for inconsistency. Finally, for modal rules of a certain shape, we show how to construct layered resolution calculi, a technique that has so far only been established for the modal logic K. Our work directly yields new sound and complete resolution calculi, and layered resolution calculi, for a large number of modal logics.

Keywords: Modal Logics · Automated Reasoning · Resolution

1 Introduction

Computational modal logic operates along various dimensions. One concerns what we want to reason about, and determines the type and language of the logic. A wide variety of modal logics exist, including the classical modal logics such as K, T, S4, etc. [3], epistemic logics [4], doxastic logics [12], deontic logic [5], probabilistic modal logic [9], many-valued modal logics [30], conditional logic [18], game theoretic logics [26]. Each logic captures a different aspect of reasoning, and has different logical laws and primitives. A second dimension is the employed mechanics of reasoning, i.e. the structure and design of the logical system itself. Common systems include Hilbert calculi, sequent calculi, tableau methods, deep inference systems, natural deduction and resolution calculi, see e.g. [6,8,29,34] or the overview in [33]. Resolution calculi are nearly always the preferred choice for implementing automated reasoning procedures with excellent performance in practice. Nearly all entrants of the biennial competition of

C. Barrett and U. Waldmann (Eds.): CADE 2025, LNAI 15943, pp. 361–380, 2025.
https://doi.org/10.1007/978-3-031-99984-0_20

automated theorem proving systems [31] implement resolution, and resolution-based implementations of modal logic also achieve very good performance [16].

Sequent Calculi, on the other hand, are predominant in the study of meta-theoretic properties of calculi, and have been investigated for a large class of structurally different modal logics, e.g. modal and deontic logics [21], basic conditional logics [20], various probabilistic modal logics [11], epistemic logics [7].

Regardless of logic and calculus, the fundamental questions are the same: soundness, completeness, and computational complexity. Traditionally, these questions have been answered on a per-logic and per-calculus basis, leading to a fragmented understanding of the relationships between different proof systems.

In this paper, we build a systematic bridge between sequent and resolution calculi that applies to a broad class of logics. While earlier work, notably by Mints [13,14], has provided examples of such correspondences, our approach generalises these insights by establishing a formal connection that holds across a wide range of logical systems. Instead of treating each logic in isolation, we identify structural principles (the admissibility of cut and weakening) that allow for a unified treatment of proof calculi that extends both to non-monotonic modal logic and layered calculi, both of which significantly go beyond *op. cit.*

Conceptually, cut elimination emerges as the central theme. While one might expect that resolution, which inherently incorporates the cut rule, aligns more naturally with sequent calculi with cut, completeness only holds for cut-free sequent systems. This is mainly due to the fact that resolution calculi require a translation into clauses, and resolution typically does not generate new literals. Hence only calculi with the subformula property (that are, a posteriori, cut-free) generate all literals that are needed in a resolution proof. For soundness, we translate resolution proofs into sequent calculus proofs with cut, and use cut elimination to obtain equivalence with respect to the original (cut-free) system.

We translate sequent rules into two different types of resolution rules: *generative* rules that are essentially (the same) sequent calculus rules used in a resolution calculus, and *absorptive* rules that are generalisations of propositional resolution (and are closer to the spirit of resolution). For both types, we first develop a resolution calculus that characterises *validity*. This reflects the fact that semantically, the translation of a formula into clauses creates global assumptions. To construct a calculus for inconsistency, we introduce *local* clauses and obtain a calculus for both generative and absorptive rules.

The above constructions work for all (unlabelled) sequent calculi with minor conditions. For rules that adhere to a special format (step rules and propagation rules), we translate sequent calculi into *layered resolution* which reduces the non-determinism in resolution proof search [15]. We conclude with the observation that the mechanism of local clauses is unnecessary in calculi that are defined by step rules only, intuitively because clauses with a higher layer are treated as global clauses in the calculus.

Figure 1 summarises the calculi that we are considering, and their names which we will use as subscripts of the relevant entailment relation. Generative calculi use the modal rules unchanged other than a reformulation in terms of clauses. Absorptive calculi adapt the modal rules to detect inconsistency (and are arguably more in the spirit of resolution). All resolution calculi operate on clauses in normal form, and the last column indicates whether a calculus can be adapted to a layered setting, or uses local clauses.

Name	Type	Proves	Style	Clauses
SR	Sequent	Validity		
GR	Resolution	Validity	Generative	Layered
AR	Resolution	Validity	Absorptive	Layered
LGR	Resolution	Inconsistency	Generative	Local
LAR	Resolution	Inconsistency	Absorptive	Local

Fig. 1. Index of Calculi

Our technique can be applied to generate a large number of (sound and complete) resolution calculi for modal logics, including a large number of cases for which no resolution calculus had yet been discovered. For layered resolution, the only known calculus is that for the modal logic K. We re-prove its completeness, *mutatis mutandis* for a different clausal translation, while at the same time, the generality of our approach lets us automatically derive layered calculi for a large class of logics for which no such calculus was known.

Related Work. We have already mentioned Mints' work on modal resolution [13, 14]. Mints does not explicitly employ local clauses, but instead prefixes global clauses with a $\Box$-operator which effectively acts like a global modality in the logic S4. This technique is not available in other modal logics, and we solve this problem by distinguishing between local and global clauses. Moreover, our results apply to sequent calculi generically, whereas Mints exemplifies a recipe with a small number of logics. Reis and Wolzenlogel Paleo [27] analyse the complexity of translation between sequent and resolution calculi for propositional and first order logic. Modal logic is not mentioned, and hence no new modal calculi are introduced. The same applies to [10] where the equivalence of resolution and sequent calculi for deduction modulo is demonstrated. Resolution and sequent calculi for non-classical logics are also studied in [32], but again modal logic is not covered. Resolution calculi for non-monotonic logic in particular have been studied in [24, 25] where completeness is established semantically. The observation in *op.cit.* that the conditions required to obtain semantic completeness would entail cut elimination were the starting point of the present paper.

2 Preliminaries and Notation

Definition 1. A *modal similarity type* is a set Λ of modal operators with associated arities. If V is a set of variables, the set L of *formulae* over V is given by the grammar

$$\mathsf{L} \ni A, B := a \mid \neg A \mid A \wedge B \mid \heartsuit(A_1, \ldots, A_n)$$

where $a \in \mathsf{V}$ is a variable and $\heartsuit \in \Lambda$ is n-ary. In the sequel, we often deal with *sets* of formulae, and write both A, Φ and Φ, A for $\Phi \cup \{A\}$, and similarly Φ, Ψ for $\Phi \cup \Psi$ whenever $A \in \mathsf{L}$ is a formula and $\Phi, \Psi \subseteq \mathsf{L}$ are sets of formulae. Also, $\neg\Phi = \{\neg A \mid A \in \Phi\}$. Subformulae are defined in the standard way and we write $\mathsf{subf}(A)$ for the set of subformulae of a formula $A \in \mathsf{L}$, and $\mathsf{subf}(\Phi) = \bigcup\{\mathsf{subf}(A) \mid A \in \Phi\}$ if $\Phi \subseteq \mathsf{L}$ is a set of formulae. A *literal* over V is of the form a, $\neg a$, $\heartsuit(a_1, \dots, a_n)$ or $\neg\heartsuit(a_1, \dots, a_n)$ where $a, a_1, \dots, a_n \in \mathsf{V}$. The literals a and $\neg a$ are *propositional*, whereas $\heartsuit(a_1, \dots, a_n)$ and $\neg\heartsuit(a_1, \dots, a_n)$ are *modal*. Similarly, we call, a and $\heartsuit(a_1, \dots, a_n)$ *positive* whereas $\neg a$ and $\neg\heartsuit(a_1, \dots, a_n)$ are *negative*. If D is a clause, we write $\mathsf{P}(D)$ and $\mathsf{N}(D)$ for the set of positive (resp. negative) literals in D. The (classical) negation $\neg l$ of a negative literal $l = \neg a$ or $l = \neg\heartsuit(a_1, \dots, a_n)$ is a and $\heartsuit(a_1, \dots, a_n)$, respectively. A *clause* is a finite set of literals. We often write a clause $\{l_1, \dots, l_n\}$ as $l_1 \vee \dots \vee l_n$ and denote the empty clause by ϵ. We write $\mathsf{Cl}(\mathsf{V})$ for the set of clauses over a set V of variables. A *modal* (resp. *propositional*) clause is a clause consisting of modal (resp. propositional) literals only. Finally, a *substitution* is a mapping $\sigma : \mathsf{V} \to \mathsf{L}$, and we denote the simultaneous replacement of every $p \in \mathsf{V}$ by $\sigma(p)$ in a formula $A \in \mathsf{L}$ by $A\sigma$, and as usual $\Phi\sigma = \{A\sigma \mid A \in \Phi\}$ if Φ is a set of formulae.

Example 2. The set of formulae over the empty similarity type are the formulae of propositional logic. For the similarity type $\{\Box\}$ where $\Box$ is unary, we obtain the syntax of the modal logic E (and extensions, including e.g. K) [1,2]. Conditional logics [20] are captured by $\{\multimap\}$ where $\multimap$ is binary (written in infix notation). Finally, given a non-empty, finite set A of agents, the similarity type of coalition logic [26] is $\Lambda_{\mathsf{A}} = \{[C] \mid C \subseteq \mathsf{A}\}$ where each operator $[C] \in \Lambda_{\mathsf{A}}$ is unary.

Our notion of sequent and resolution calculi is mostly standard, and is summarised below. One point of note is that we are conceptualising sequents in terms of sets rather than multisets, as this will simplify their alignment with resolution, where clauses are sets (not multisets) of literals. Other than that, we mainly use calculi and notation from [33].

Definition 3 (Sequent and Resolution Calculi). A *sequent* is a pair (Γ, Δ) of finite sets of formulae, written $\Gamma \Longrightarrow \Delta$. For clauses Γ and Δ, $\mathsf{cl}(\Gamma \Longrightarrow \Delta) = \neg\Gamma \vee \Delta$ is the *clause* induced by the sequent $\Gamma \Longrightarrow \Delta$, and $\mathsf{s}(D) = \mathsf{P}(D) \Longrightarrow \mathsf{N}(D)$ is the sequent induced by the clause D.

A *modal sequent rule* is of the form $\Gamma_1 \Longrightarrow \Delta_1, \dots, \Gamma_n \Longrightarrow \Delta_n / \Gamma_0 \Longrightarrow \Delta_0$ where all Γ_i, Δ_i are clauses consisting of positive literals only, and $\Gamma_i \cup \Delta_i \subseteq \mathsf{subf}(\Gamma_0 \cup \Delta_0)$, i.e. each $l \in \Gamma_i \cup \Delta_i$ is a subformula of some $l' \in \Gamma_0 \cup \Delta_0$, for each $i = 1, \dots, n$. If R is a set of modal rules and S is a set of sequents, we write $\mathsf{S} \vdash_{\mathsf{SR}} \Sigma \Longrightarrow \Pi$ if $\Sigma \Longrightarrow \Pi$ is in the least set containing all axioms $p, \Gamma \Longrightarrow p, \Delta$, all sequents in S, and that is closed under the propositional rules,

$$\frac{A, B, \Gamma \Longrightarrow \Delta}{A \wedge B, \Gamma \Longrightarrow \Delta} \qquad \frac{\Gamma \Longrightarrow A, \Delta \quad \Gamma \Longrightarrow B, \Delta}{\Gamma \Longrightarrow A \wedge B, \Delta}$$

$$\frac{A, \Gamma \Longrightarrow \Delta}{\Gamma \Longrightarrow \neg A, \Delta} \qquad \frac{\Gamma \Longrightarrow B, \Delta}{\Gamma, \neg B \Longrightarrow \Delta}$$

and all substitution instances of modal rules

$$\frac{\Gamma_1\sigma \Longrightarrow \Delta_1\sigma \qquad \dots \qquad \Gamma_n\sigma \Longrightarrow \Delta_n\sigma}{\Gamma_0\sigma \Longrightarrow \Delta_0\sigma}$$

where $\Gamma_1 \Longrightarrow \Delta_1, \dots, \Gamma_n \Longrightarrow \Delta_n / \Gamma_0 \Longrightarrow \Delta_0 \in \mathsf{R}$ is a modal sequent rule, and $\sigma : \mathsf{V} \to \mathsf{L}$ is a substitution.

We write $\mathsf{S} \vdash_{\mathsf{SRC}} \Gamma \Longrightarrow \Delta$ and $\mathsf{S} \vdash_{\mathsf{SRCW}} \Gamma \Longrightarrow \Delta$ if in addition to the rules above, also the cut rule (C) below and, respectively, cut (C) and weakening (W)

$$(\mathsf{C})\frac{\Gamma_0 \Longrightarrow \Delta_0, A \qquad A, \Gamma_1 \Longrightarrow \Delta_1}{\Gamma_0, \Delta_0 \Longrightarrow \Gamma_1 \Delta_1} \qquad (\mathsf{W})\frac{\Gamma_0 \Longrightarrow \Delta_0}{\Gamma_0, \Gamma_1 \Longrightarrow \Delta_0, \Delta_1}$$

have been used in the derivation of $\Gamma \Longrightarrow \Delta$.

A rule $\Gamma_1 \Longrightarrow \Delta_1, \dots, \Gamma_n \Longrightarrow \Delta_n / \Gamma_0 \Longrightarrow \Delta_0$ is *admissible* in R if $\vdash_{\mathsf{SR}} \Gamma_0\sigma \Longrightarrow \Delta_0\sigma$ whenever $\vdash_{\mathsf{SR}} \Gamma_i\sigma \Longrightarrow \Delta_i\sigma$ for all $1 \leq i \leq n$ and all substitutions $\sigma : \mathsf{V} \to \mathsf{L}$.

Example 4. A large number of sequent calculi are indeed defined by modal rules in the sense of Definition 3. For purposes of presentation, we mainly follow [33] and use upper case Latin letters $A, B, \dots$ as propositional variables and upper case Greek letters $\Gamma, \Delta, \dots$ to represent contexts, that is, sequences of variables. In other words, each context $\Gamma, \Delta, \dots$ represents a finite set $\{A_1, \dots, A_n\}$ of variables, and a rule containing contexts $\Gamma, \Delta, \dots$ denotes a set of rules, where each element is given by a choice of a finite set of variables for each context.

The sequent calculus for the modal logic E consists of just the congruence rule (left) and monotone modal logic is given by the monotonicity rule (right).

$$(\mathsf{E})\frac{A \Longrightarrow B \quad B \Longrightarrow A}{\Box A, \Gamma \Longrightarrow \Box B, \Delta} \qquad (\mathsf{M})\frac{A \Longrightarrow B}{\Box A, \Gamma \Longrightarrow \Box B, \Delta}$$

Congruence is admissible in both rule sets. Another example is the set of K-rules

$$(\mathsf{K})\frac{A_1, \dots, A_n \Longrightarrow A_0}{\Box A_1, \dots, \Box A_n, \Gamma \Longrightarrow \Box A_0, \Delta} \qquad (\mathsf{T})\frac{A, \Box A, \Gamma \Longrightarrow \Delta}{\Box A, \Gamma \Longrightarrow \Delta}$$

that defines the sequent calculus for the modal logic K. The modal logic T arises by extending K with the rule T which together define a cut-free calculus.

The conditional logic CK uses a binary operator $\multimap$ (Example 2) that is congruential in the first, and normal in the second argument. A sequent calculus for this logic is given by all instances of (CK).

$$(\mathsf{CK})\frac{\{A_0 \Longrightarrow A_i \mid 1 \leq i \leq n\} \quad \{A_i \Longrightarrow A_0 \mid i \leq i \leq n\} \quad B_1, \dots, B_n \Longrightarrow B_0}{(A_1 \multimap B_1), \dots, (A_n \multimap B_n), \Gamma \Longrightarrow (A_0 \multimap B_0), \Delta}$$

One example of a rule that is often considered together with (CK) is the axiom of conditional modus ponens $(A \multimap B) \to (A \to B)$. Adding this axiom to the logic CK gives the sequent calculus given by (CK) and (MP)

$$(\mathsf{MP})\frac{B, (A \multimap B), \Gamma \Longrightarrow \Delta \qquad (A \multimap B), \Gamma \Longrightarrow A, \Delta}{(A \multimap B), \Gamma \Longrightarrow \Delta}$$

that is known as CKMP. For all the logics introduced here, and more, [22] shows that their sequent calculi (given by one-sided versions of the rules above) admits cut elimination and is sound and complete for the respective logic.

For coalition logic, we fix a set A of agents and have a unary modal operator $[C]$ for every subset $C \subseteq \mathsf{A}$ (Example 2). A (sound and complete, and cut-free) sequent calculus is given by the rules

$$(\mathsf{A})\frac{A_1, \ldots, A_n \Longrightarrow}{[C_1]A_1, \ldots, [C_n]A_n, \Gamma \Longrightarrow \Delta}$$

$$(\mathsf{B})\frac{A_1, \ldots, A_n \Longrightarrow A_0, B_1, \ldots, B_k}{[C_1]A_1, \ldots, [C_n]A_n, \Gamma \Longrightarrow [D]A_0, [N]B_1, \ldots, [N]B_k, \Delta}$$

where $N = \mathsf{A}$ is the set of all agents, the C_i are pairwise disjoint in both rules, and $C_1 \cup \cdots \cup C_n \subseteq D$ in the second rule. Completeness and cut admissibility for this sequent calculus can be found in [23].

As for all resolution calculi that we consider here, we translate formulae into clause sets. As our logics are not monotone, the translation introduces new variables that equivalently define the meaning of subformulae.

Definition 5 (Clausal Form Translation). Choose a distinct propositional variable r_A for each formula $A \in \mathsf{L}(\mathsf{V})$. The *clausal translation* of a formula $A \in \mathsf{L}$ is given inductively by

$$\begin{aligned}
\mathsf{tr}(p) &= \{\neg r_p \vee r_p\} \\
\mathsf{tr}(\neg A) &= \{r_{\neg A} \vee r_A, \neg r_{\neg A} \vee \neg r_A\} \cup \mathsf{tr}(A) \\
\mathsf{tr}(A \wedge B) &= \{\neg r_{A\wedge B} \vee r_A, \neg r_{A\wedge B} \vee r_B, \neg r_A \vee \neg r_B \vee r_{A\wedge B}\} \cup \mathsf{tr}(A) \cup \mathsf{tr}(B) \\
\mathsf{tr}(\heartsuit(\mathbf{A})) &= \{\neg r_{\heartsuit(\mathbf{A})} \vee \heartsuit(r_{\mathbf{A}}), \neg\heartsuit(r_{\mathbf{A}}) \vee r_{\heartsuit(\mathbf{A})}\} \cup \mathsf{tr}(\mathbf{A})
\end{aligned}$$

where $\mathbf{A} = (A_1, \ldots, A_n)$, $r_{\mathbf{A}} = r_{A_1} \vee \cdots \vee r_{A_n}$ and $\mathsf{tr}(\mathbf{A}) = \mathsf{tr}(A_1) \cup \cdots \cup \mathsf{tr}(A_n)$. If Γ is a set of formulae, we write $r_\Gamma = \{r_A \mid A \in \Gamma\}$, $\mathsf{tr}(\Gamma) = \{\mathsf{tr}(A) \mid A \in \Gamma\}$ and $\mathsf{tr}(\Gamma \Longrightarrow \Delta) = \mathsf{tr}(\Gamma) \cup \mathsf{tr}(\Delta)$.

The clausal translation ensures that $r_{A\wedge B} \leftrightarrow r_A \wedge r_B$, $r_{\neg A} \leftrightarrow \neg r_A$ and $r_{\heartsuit(\mathbf{A})} \leftrightarrow \heartsuit(r_{\mathbf{A}})$. For example, writing $a \to b$ for $\neg a \vee b$, $\mathsf{tr}(A \wedge B)$ contains $r_{A\wedge B} \to r_A$ and $r_{A\wedge B} \to r_B$ so that $\mathsf{tr}(A \wedge B) \vdash r_{A\wedge B} \to r_A \wedge r_B$. Modulo propositional equivalence, $r_A \wedge r_B \to r_{A\wedge B} \in \mathsf{tr}(A \wedge B)$ whence $\mathsf{tr}(A)$ derives the equivalence $r_A \wedge r_B \leftrightarrow r_{A\wedge B}$. In particular, all elements of the clausal translation are tautologies for the substitution $\sigma(r_A) = A$. As we want to show that every sequent-derivable formula is also resolution derivable from the translated sequent, we include the tautology $r_p \vee \neg r_p$ in the translation of p as in [33, Proposition 7.4.5]. Technically, this is required e.g. in the proof of Proposition 7, as $p \vee \neg p$ is clearly sequent-derivable, but without including $p \vee \neg p$ in the clausal translation, $p \vee \neg p$ would not be resolution derivable.

3 Generative Resolution Calculi

We first investigate *generative* calculi where modal rules introduce new literals. Our calculi are defined by a set of modal rules, and we prove soundness and completeness by translating between the sequent calculus and the resolution.

Definition 6 (Generative Calculus for Validity). If R is a set of modal rules and $\Phi \subseteq \mathsf{Cl}(V)$ is a set of clauses, we write $\Phi \vdash_{\mathsf{GR}} F$ if F is in the least set containing all clauses in Φ, and that is closed under resolution (left)

$$\frac{D \vee l \qquad E \vee \neg l}{D \vee E} \qquad \frac{S_1 \quad \dots \quad S_n}{\neg \Gamma_0 \tau \vee \Delta_0 \tau}$$

and all instances of modal rules (right) where $\Gamma_1 \implies \Delta_1, \dots, \Gamma_n \implies \Delta_n / \Gamma_0 \implies \Delta_0 \in \mathsf{R}$ is a modal sequent rule, $\tau : \mathsf{V} \to \mathsf{V}$ is a renaming, and $S_i \subseteq \neg \Gamma_i \tau \vee \Delta_i \tau$ is a subclause.

This calculus characterises *provability*, and we establish a correspondence between provable sequents and derivable clauses.

Proposition 7 (Generative Validity: Completeness). *If $\Gamma \implies \Delta$ is a sequent and $\vdash_{\mathsf{SR}} \Gamma \implies \Delta$, then $\mathsf{tr}(\Gamma \implies \Delta) \vdash D$ for a subclause $D \subseteq \neg r_\Gamma \vee r_\Delta$.*

For the reverse direction, we translate resolution to a sequent calculus with initial sequents (the clausal form translation), weakening and cut. This requires converting clauses back to sequents, and we use the notation from Definition 3. In a second step, we eliminate cut, weakening and the additional axioms.

Proposition 8 (Resolution to Sequent Translation). *Let R be a set of modal rules for which weakening is admissible, and let $\Phi \subseteq \mathsf{L}(\mathsf{V})$ be a set of formulae and $F \in \mathsf{Cl}(V)$ be a clause with $\mathsf{tr}(\Phi) \vdash_{\mathsf{GR}} F$. Then $\mathsf{s}(\mathsf{tr}(\Phi)) \vdash_{\mathsf{SRCW}} \mathsf{s}(F)$.*

We will apply the previous lemma to a clause F of the form $\neg r_\Gamma \vee r_\Delta$. To make the step from the derivability of $r_\Gamma \implies r_\Delta$ to that of $\Gamma \implies \Delta$, we consider the substitution $\sigma(r_A) = A$ and need to show that derivability is closed under substitution. This is mostly a standard argument by induction on the derivation, where we need admissibility of congruence to treat axioms.

Lemma 9 (Substitution). *Let congruence be admissible in R. If $\mathsf{S} \vdash_{\mathsf{SRCW}} \Gamma \implies \Delta$ and $\sigma : \mathsf{V} \to \mathsf{L}$ is a substitution, then $\mathsf{S}\sigma \vdash_{\mathsf{SRCW}} \Gamma\sigma \implies \Delta\sigma$.*

We now argue that the derivability of $\neg r_\Gamma \vee r_\Delta$ in the generative calculus gives that of $r_\Gamma \implies r_\Delta$ in the sequent calculus by Proposition 8, and by substitution (Lemma 9) we can derive $\Gamma \implies \Delta$. This derivation uses additional initial sequents that are all tautologically true, and can hence be elided. We now apply closure under cut and weakening to obtain the (cut, and weakening-free) derivability of $\Gamma \implies \Delta$.

Proposition 10 (Generative Validity: Soundness). *Suppose that the congruence rules, cut and weakening are admissible in* R. *If* $\mathsf{tr}(\Gamma \Longrightarrow \Delta) \vdash_{\mathsf{GR}} D$ *for a subclause* $D \subseteq \neg r_\Gamma \vee r_\Delta$, *then* $\vdash_{\mathsf{SR}} \Gamma \Longrightarrow \Delta$.

For single formulae, the situation is as follows.

Theorem 11 (Generative Validity). *Let* R *be a set of sequent rules that admit cut, congruence and weakening and let* $A \in \mathsf{L}(\mathsf{V})$ *be a formula. Then* $\vdash_{\mathsf{SR}} \Longrightarrow A$ *iff* $\mathsf{tr}(A) \vdash D$ *for a subclause* $D \subseteq r_A$.

We illustrate the calculus with the modal logic T.

Example 12. Let R be the set of rules containing (K) and (T) from Example 4. In the ensuing sequent calculus, the formula $A = \Box(a \wedge b) \wedge \neg a$ is inconsistent, hence its negation $\neg A$ is derivable. We give a derivation of $r_{\neg A}$ in the generative resolution calculus induced by R.

1. $\neg r_{\Box(a\wedge b)\wedge\neg a} \vee r_{\neg a} \in \mathsf{tr}(A)$
2. $\neg r_{\neg a} \vee \neg r_a \in \mathsf{tr}(A)$
3. $\neg r_{\Box(a\wedge b)\wedge\neg a} \vee \neg r_a$ (Res, 1, 2)
4. $\neg r_{\Box(a\wedge b)\wedge\neg a} \vee \neg\Box r_a$ (T, 3)
5. $\neg r_{a\wedge b} \vee r_a \in \mathsf{tr}(A)$
6. $\neg\Box r_{a\wedge b} \vee \Box r_a$ (K, 5)
7. $\neg r_{\Box(a\wedge b)\wedge\neg a} \vee \neg\Box r_{a\wedge b}$ (Res, 6, 4)
8. $\neg r_{\Box(a\wedge b)\wedge\neg a} \vee r_{\Box(a\wedge b)} \in \mathsf{tr}(A)$
9. $\neg r_{\Box(a\wedge b)\wedge\neg a}$ (Res, 7, 8)

In step (4) above, we use that – in the resolution version of a modal rule – only a subclause of a rule premiss is required to be derivable to apply the rule.

4 Absorptive Resolution Calculi for Validity

Generative calculi extend propositional resolution by almost verbatim copies of the sequent rules – the only difference is that application of modal rules just requires a subclause of each premiss, as weakening is not admissible in resolution.

Absorptive calculi re-interpret the modal rules as showing inconsistency under additional premisses. We take a modal rule with premisses $P_1, \dots, P_n$ and conclusion $A_1, \dots, A_k \Longrightarrow B_1, \dots, B_l$ to assert that $A_1, \dots, A_k, \neg B_1, \dots, \neg B_l$ are *inconsistent* under the assumption $P_1, \dots, P_n$. This gives a different version of modal resolution rules that treat this inconsistent set of literals in the same way in which standard resolution treats conflicting literals ℓ and $\neg\ell$. The inconsistency of ℓ and $\neg\ell$ is captured by the rule on the left:

$$\frac{D \vee \ell \quad E \vee \neg\ell}{D \vee E} \qquad \frac{P_1 \dots P_n \quad A_1 \vee D_1 \dots A_k \vee D_k \quad \neg B_1 \vee E_1 \dots \neg B_l \vee E_l}{D_1 \vee \dots D_k \vee E_1 \vee \dots \vee E_l}$$

The rule on the right analogously expresses that $A_1, \dots, A_k, \neg B_1, \dots, \neg B_l$ are inconsistent under the assumptions $P_1, \dots, P_n$. As the definition of the calculus is based on substitution instances of modal rules, we replace (a) the premisses P_i by subclauses of substitution instances of rule premisses, and (b) the A_i's and B_j's in the conclusion by instances of the same substitution. The formal definition of the calculus for validity is then as follows.

Definition 13 (Absorptive Calculus for Validity). If R is a set of modal rules and $\Phi \subseteq \mathsf{Cl}(V)$ is a set of clauses, we write $\Phi \vdash_{\mathsf{AR}} F$ if F is in the least set containing all clauses in Φ, that is closed under resolution (as in Definition 3) and

$$\frac{S_1 \quad \ldots \quad S_n \quad D_1 \vee A_1\tau \quad \ldots \quad D_k \vee A_k\tau \quad E_1 \vee \neg B_1\tau \quad \ldots \quad E_l \vee \neg B_l\tau}{D_1 \vee \cdots \vee D_k \vee E_1 \vee \cdots \vee E_l}$$

where $\Gamma_1 \Longrightarrow \Delta_1, \ldots, \Gamma_n \Longrightarrow \Delta_n / A_1, \ldots, A_k \Longrightarrow B_1, \ldots, B_l \in \mathsf{R}$ is a modal sequent rule, $\tau : \mathsf{V} \to \mathsf{V}$ is a renaming, and $S_j \subseteq \neg\Gamma_j\tau \vee \Delta_j\tau$ is a subclause for $j = 1, \ldots, n$. We refer to $\vdash_{\mathsf{AR}}$ as the *absorptive calculus* given by R.

Example 14. The principle for constructing absorptive calculi is best illustrated with the modal logic E. Applying Definition 13 gives the following absorptive rule (left)

$$\frac{S_1 \quad S_2 \quad D \vee \Box p \quad E \vee \neg\Box q}{D \vee E} \qquad \frac{D \vee \ell \quad E \vee \neg \ell}{D \vee E} \qquad \frac{S_1 \quad S_2}{\neg\Box p \vee \Box q}$$

(where $S_1 \subseteq \neg p \vee q$ and $S_2 \subseteq p \vee \neg q$ are subclauses) that stipulates that $\Box p$ and $\neg\Box q$ are inconsistent *under the additional assumptions* S_1 and S_2. This is identical to the standard resolution rule in the middle above, with the exception that here, ℓ and $\neg\ell$ are inconsistent without any further assumptions. Finally, the generative rule (above right) stipulates that $\neg\Box p \vee \Box q$ is valid. Given $D \vee \Box p$ and $E \vee \neg\Box q$, we can of course derive the conclusion $D \vee E$ of the absorptive rule from the conclusion $\neg\Box p \vee \Box q$ of the generative rule using two resolution steps. The reverse translation follows by instantiating $D = \neg\Box p$ and $E = \Box q$, we then need to establish derivability of (the tautologies) $\neg\Box p \vee \Box p$ and $\Box q \vee \neg\Box q$ which we get from the clausal translation.

As indicated in the example, we pick tautologies as the premisses of the absorptive rule. Their derivability follows from the definition of clausal translation.

Lemma 15. *Let* $A \in \mathsf{L}(V)$. *Then* $\mathsf{tr}(A) \vdash_{\mathsf{R}} r_A \vee \neg r_A$.

With this lemma, the completeness proof is very similar to the proof of completeness for generative calculi (Proposition 7).

Proposition 16 (Absorptive Validity: Completeness). *If* $\Gamma \Longrightarrow \Delta$ *is a sequent, and* $\mathsf{tr}(\Phi) \vdash_{\mathsf{GR}} F$, *then* $\mathsf{tr}(\Gamma \Longrightarrow \Delta) \vdash_{\mathsf{AR}} D$ *for a subclause* $D \subseteq \neg r_\Gamma \vee r_\Delta$.

Remark 17. The proof of the previous proposition shows that a stronger version of the modal rule in Definition 13 would in fact be enough for completeness: it suffices to have $D_i = \neg A_i\tau$ and $E_i = B_i\tau$. These tautologies are always derivable (Lemma 15) so could be elided which would bring us back to the generative calculus. Hence absorptive calculi allow us to find more resolution proofs as we are able to instantiate D_i and E_i with clauses other than the above.

The soundness proof imitates generative with absorptive rules as in Example 14.

Proposition 18 (Absorptive Validity: Soundness). *Let* R *be a set of modal rules,* $\Phi \subseteq \mathsf{Cl}(\mathsf{V})$, $D \in \mathsf{Cl}(V)$ *and suppose that* $\Phi \vdash_{\mathsf{AR}} D$. *Then* $\Phi \vdash_{\mathsf{GR}} D$.

We get an analogue of Proposition 10 for the absorptive calculus as consequence.

Corollary 19. *Suppose that the congruence, cut and weakening are admissible in* R, *and* $\mathsf{tr}(\Gamma \Longrightarrow \Delta) \vdash_{\mathsf{AR}} D$ *for a subclause* $D \subseteq \neg r_\Gamma \vee r_\Delta$. *Then* $\vdash_{\mathsf{SR}} \Gamma \Longrightarrow \Delta$.

For single formulae, we therefore obtain the same result that we have already reported for generative calculi (Theorem 11).

Theorem 20 (Absorptive Validity). *Let* R *be a set of sequent rules that admit cut, congruence and weakening and let* $A \in \mathsf{L}(\mathsf{V})$ *be a formula. Then* $\vdash_{\mathsf{SR}} \Longrightarrow A$ *iff* $\mathsf{tr}(A) \vdash_{\mathsf{AR}} D$ *for a subclause* $D \subseteq r_A$.

5 Resolution Calculi for Inconsistency

We now show how to construct calculi that derive the empty clause from (the clausal translation of) an inconsistent set of formulae from calculi for validity. Given a set R of modal rules, we take $A \in \mathsf{L}(\mathsf{V})$ as inconsistent if $\vdash_{\mathsf{SR}} A \Longrightarrow$.

Our approach works for both the generative and absorptive calculi introduced earlier, and we write $\vdash_{\mathsf{XR}}$ to stand for either $\vdash_{\mathsf{GR}}$ or $\vdash_{\mathsf{AR}}$.

If A inconsistent, then $\mathsf{tr}(A) \vdash_{\mathsf{XR}} D \subseteq \neg r_A$ so that $\mathsf{tr}(A) \cup \{r_A\} \vdash_{\mathsf{XR}} \epsilon$. The converse is not necessarily true, as r_A can contribute to establishing premisses of modal rules, and so prove ϵ even if A is not inconsistent. Semantically, the entailment $\vdash_{\mathsf{XR}}$ describes the global consequence relation for which the deduction lemma is false. In a possible-world semantics (e.g. using neighbourhood models [2]), the judgement $\Phi \vdash E$ would be interpreted that E is valid (at all worlds) in all models for which all clauses in Φ are valid. Hence $\mathsf{tr}(A) \cup \{r_A\} \vdash \epsilon$ only entails that there are no models that validate both $\mathsf{tr}(A)$ and r_A globally (at all worlds). Inconsistency, on the other hand, is the stronger property that r_A and $\mathsf{tr}(A)$ cannot co-exist at any world in any model.

To avoid this, we introduce a second type of clauses that we call *local* to distinguish the premisses of modal rules that (semantically speaking) need to be globally valid. Semantically, local clauses only allow propositional reasoning, which is inherently local. This allows us to establish a restricted version of the deduction lemma for propositional connectives only (Lemma 24) that allows us to conclude inconsistency if we can *locally* derive the empty clause.

We begin with an example that shows that $\mathsf{tr}(A) \cup \{r_A\} \vdash \epsilon$ does not necessarily mean that A is inconsistent.

Example 21. We demonstrate that $\mathsf{tr}(A) \cup \{r_A\} \vdash \epsilon$ does not imply that A is inconsistent. We do so with a sequent calculus that fits our framework but is completely without significance otherwise. Consider the following rules, that we refer to as left / middle / right for the purpose of this example.

$$(\mathsf{L})\frac{A \Longrightarrow B \quad B \Longrightarrow A}{\Gamma, \Box A \Longrightarrow \Box B, \Delta} \quad (\mathsf{M})\frac{A \Longrightarrow B \quad B \Longrightarrow A}{\Gamma \Longrightarrow A, \Box B, \Delta} \quad (\mathsf{R})\frac{\Longrightarrow A}{\Gamma \Longrightarrow \Box A, \Delta}$$

It is easy to see that cut and weakening are admissible. For weakening this is standard, for cut it suffices to note that all cuts between modal rule conclusions can be propagated upwards in the proof tree [22].

Consider $A = \neg\Box p$. Then A is not inconsistent, as $\not\vdash_{\mathsf{SR}} A \Longrightarrow$. This can be easily verified by applying proof rules backwards. On the other hand, we claim that $\mathsf{tr}(A) \cup \{r_A\} \vdash_{\mathsf{GR}} \epsilon$, as witnessed by the following derivation:

1. $\neg r_{\neg\Box p} \vee \neg r_{\Box p} \in \mathsf{tr}(A)$
2. $r_{\neg\Box p} \in \{r_A\}$
3. $\neg r_{\Box p}$ (Res, 1, 2)
4. $\neg\Box r_p \vee r_{\Box p} \in \mathsf{tr}(A)$
5. $\neg\Box r_p$ (Res, 3, 4)
6. $r_p \vee \neg r_p \in \mathsf{tr}(A)$
7. $r_p \vee \Box r_p$ (M, 6, 6)
8. r_p (Res, 5, 7)
9. $\Box r_p$ (R 8)
10. ϵ (Res, 5, 9)

We have written Res for the resolution rule, and M and R for the (resolution version of the) middle and right modal rule. In the proof, we can see how r_A is used, in various steps, in the derivation of a premiss of a modal rule.

We overcome this difficulty by introducing *local* clauses that block the use of the additional literal r_A in the derivation of premisses of modal rules, while still being flexible enough to derive the empty clause.

Definition 22 (Local Derivability). Let $\mathsf{lCl}(V) = \mathsf{Cl}(\mathsf{V}) \cup \{\mathsf{L}(D) \mid D \in \mathsf{Cl}(\mathsf{V})\}$. We call $\mathsf{L}(D) \in \mathsf{lCl}(\mathsf{V})$ a *local* clause. If $\Phi \subseteq \mathsf{lCl}(\mathsf{V})$ is a set of clauses and R is a set of modal rules, we put $\Phi \vdash_{\mathsf{LGR}} C$ (resp. $\Phi \vdash_{\mathsf{LAR}} C$) if C can be derived using the rules of $\vdash_{\mathsf{GR}}$ (and $\vdash_{\mathsf{AR}}$, respectively) plus the following rules

$$(\mathsf{LG})\frac{D}{\mathsf{L}(D)} \qquad (\mathsf{LRes})\frac{\mathsf{L}(D \vee \ell) \quad \mathsf{L}(E \vee \neg\ell)}{\mathsf{L}(D \vee E)}$$

that we call the *global to local* rule, and *local resolution.*

Informally speaking, a derivation in $\vdash_{\mathsf{LGR}}$ and $\vdash_{\mathsf{LAR}}$ has two phases: an initial global phase followed by a local phase. To characterise inconsistency of A, we only allow the literal r_A *locally.*

Proposition 23. *let* LXR *be one of* LGR *or* LAR, *let* $A \in \mathsf{L}(\mathsf{V})$ *be a formula and suppose that* $\vdash_{\mathsf{SR}} A \Longrightarrow$. *Then* $\mathsf{tr}(A) \cup \{\mathsf{L}(r_A)\} \vdash_{\mathsf{LXR}} \mathsf{L}(\epsilon)$.

For soundness, we need to show that $\mathsf{tr}(A) \vdash_{\mathsf{XR}} \neg r_A$ whenever $\mathsf{tr}(A) \cup \{\mathsf{L}(r_A)\} \vdash_{\mathsf{LXR}} \mathsf{L}(\epsilon)$ (and then apply the soundness theorem for $\vdash_{\mathsf{XR}}$). The following lemma allows us to eliminate the additional local (singleton) clause $\mathsf{L}(r_A)$ from the set of assumptions and is a version of the deduction lemma, anticipated earlier, that fails for global consequence (or in a calculus without local clauses). It essentially states the deduction lemma holds for individual propositional atoms *locally*: if $\Phi \cup \mathsf{L}(\ell) \vdash \mathsf{L}(D)$ then $\Phi \vdash \mathsf{L}(\neg\ell \vee D)$ where we need to re-formulate the right-hand side owing to the fact that resolution is only consequence-complete.

Lemma 24 (Dichotomy). *Let* XR *be one of* GR *of* AR *and let* Φ *be a set of clauses. Then* $\Phi \cup \mathsf{L}(\ell) \vdash_{\mathsf{LXR}} \mathsf{L}(D)$ *implies that either* $\ell \in D$ *or* $\Phi \vdash_{\mathsf{LXR}} \mathsf{L}(S)$ *for a subclause* $S \subseteq \neg\ell \vee D$.

Using dichotomy, we can now show inconsistency in case the empty clause has been derived *locally.*

Proposition 25. *Let* R *be a set of sequent rules for which weakening and cut is admissible, and let* LXR *be* LGR *or* LAR*, and let* $A \in \mathsf{L}(\mathsf{V})$. *If* $\mathsf{tr}(A) \cup \{\mathsf{L}(r_A)\} \vdash \mathsf{L}(\epsilon)$*, then* $\vdash_{\mathsf{SR}} A \Longrightarrow$.

We have a companion to Theorems 11 and 20 that treats both generative and absorptive calculi.

Theorem 26 (Generative and Absorptive Inconsistency). *Let* R *be a set of sequent rules that admit cut, congruence and weakening and let* $A \in \mathsf{L}(\mathsf{V})$. *If* $\vdash_{\mathsf{LXR}}$ *is one of* $\vdash_{\mathsf{LGR}}$ *or* $\vdash_{\mathsf{LAR}}$*, then* $\vdash_{\mathsf{SR}} A \Longrightarrow$ *iff* $\mathsf{tr}(A) \cup \{\mathsf{L}(r_A)\} \vdash_{\mathsf{LXR}} \mathsf{L}(\epsilon)$.

As the calculus for inconsistency extends the one for validity, we can extend Example 12 to obtain an example in the calculus for inconsistency.

Example 27. We consider the set R consisting of (K) and (T) as in Example 12 and show, for the same formula $A = \Box(a \wedge b) \wedge \neg a$, that $\mathsf{tr}(A) \cup \{\mathsf{L}(r_A)\} \vdash_{\mathsf{LGR}} \mathsf{L}(\epsilon)$. This is a simple matter of continuing the derivation given in Example 12.

10. $\mathsf{L}(\neg r_A)$ $(\mathsf{LG}, 9)$ 11. $\mathsf{L}(r_A) \in \{\mathsf{L}(r_A)\}$ 12. $\mathsf{L}(\epsilon)$ $(\mathsf{LRes}, 10, 11)$

Lines 1–9 of the derivation (in Example 12) use the assumptions in $\mathsf{tr}(A)$, and we have used $\mathsf{L}(r_A)$ in step 12.

6 Layered Resolution

In an unlayered calculus, any set of clauses can contribute to a (modal) resolution step. Layered calculi reduce this non-determinism by annotating every clause with a *layer* that represents the syntactic nesting depth of modal operators of a clause. Informally, the layer indicates the distance from the root node of a model, and is conceptually different to annotations in labelled tableaux that represent worlds. The layer is determined by a modified clause translation as follows:

Definition 28. A *layered clause* is of the form $i:D$ where D is a clause and $i \in \mathbb{Z}$. If Φ is a set of clauses, then $i:\Phi = \{i:D \mid D \in \Phi\}$. The *layered translation* of a formula $A \in \mathsf{L}$ at level $i \in \mathbb{Z}$ is given inductively by

$$
\begin{aligned}
\mathsf{ltr}_i(p) &= \{i:\neg r_p \vee r_p\} \\
\mathsf{ltr}_i(\neg A) &= \{i:r_{\neg A} \vee r_A, i:\neg r_{\neg A} \vee \neg r_A\} \cup \mathsf{ltr}_i(A) \\
\mathsf{ltr}_i(A \wedge B) &= \{i:\neg r_{A\wedge B} \vee r_A, i:\neg r_{A\wedge B} \vee r_B, i:\neg r_A \vee \neg r_B \vee r_{A\wedge B}\} \\
&\quad \cup \mathsf{ltr}_i(A) \cup \mathsf{ltr}_i(B) \\
\mathsf{ltr}_i(\heartsuit(\mathbf{A})) &= \{i:\neg r_{\heartsuit(\mathbf{A})} \vee \heartsuit(r_\mathbf{A}), i:\neg\heartsuit(r_\mathbf{A}) \vee r_{\heartsuit(\mathbf{A})}\} \cup \mathsf{ltr}_{i+1}(\mathbf{A})
\end{aligned}
$$

where we use the same notational conventions as in Definition 5, i.e. $\mathbf{A} = (A_1, \dots, A_n)$, $r_\mathbf{A} = r_{A_1} \vee \dots \vee r_{A_n}$ and $\mathsf{ltr}_i(\mathbf{A}) = \mathsf{ltr}_i(A_1) \cup \dots \cup \mathsf{ltr}_i(A_n)$. If Γ is a set of formulae we write $r_\Gamma = \{r_A \mid A \in \Gamma\}$ (as before), $\mathsf{ltr}_i(\Gamma) = \{\mathsf{ltr}_i(A) \mid A \in \Gamma\}$ and $\mathsf{ltr}_i(\Gamma \Longrightarrow \Delta) = \mathsf{ltr}_i(\Gamma) \cup \mathsf{ltr}_i(\Delta)$. The *stacked translation* $\mathsf{str}_i(A)$ is defined in the same way but with the last clause modified to

$$
\mathsf{str}_i(\heartsuit(\mathbf{A})) = \{i:\neg r_{\heartsuit(\mathbf{A})} \vee \heartsuit(r_\mathbf{A}), i:\neg\heartsuit(r_\mathbf{A}) \vee r_{\heartsuit(\mathbf{A})}\} \cup \mathsf{str}_{i+1}(\mathbf{A}) \cup \mathsf{str}_i(\mathbf{A})
$$

where we again use the same notational conventions as in Definition 5.

Our layered calculus permits resolution steps only when the layers match exactly. If we use the layered translation, no information is moved between layers. Intuitively, this prohibits axioms like $\Box p \to p$, and we require that all the modal rules are *step rules*. For the stacked translation, we keep the argument of the modality at the same level, so that $\Box p \to p$ can be accommodated (as a rule) as both p and $\Box p$ act at the same level. The corresponding rules are called *propagation rules*. A step rule is characterised by the fact that its premisses are purely propositional, and the conclusion is a clause composed of modal atoms only. Intuitively, a step rule describes a way to pass from a state (the premiss) to a successor (the modalised conclusion). A propagation rule similarly has a purely modal conclusion that is propagated to all premisses, but extra (modal or propositional) atoms can appear in the premisses. These extra atoms capture the interaction between states (propositional atoms) and successors (modal atoms).

Definition 29. A *step rule* is a modal sequent rule $s = \Gamma_1 \Longrightarrow \Delta_1, \dots, \Gamma_n \Longrightarrow \Delta_n / \Gamma_0 \Longrightarrow \Delta_0$ where all $\Gamma_1, \dots, \Gamma_n, \Delta_1, \dots \Delta_n$ are propositional clauses, and both Γ_0 and Δ_0 are modal clauses. A step rule s *generates* the set of modal sequent rules

$$
s^* = \{\Gamma_1 \Longrightarrow \Delta_1, \dots, \Gamma_n \Longrightarrow \Delta_n / \Gamma_0, \Sigma \Longrightarrow \Delta_0, \Pi \mid \Sigma, \Pi \subseteq \mathsf{V} \text{ finite}\}.
$$

A *propagation rule* is a modal sequent rule of the form $p = \Gamma_1 \Longrightarrow \Delta_1, \dots, \Gamma_n \Longrightarrow \Delta_n / \Gamma_0 \Longrightarrow \Delta_0$ where for $i = 1, \dots, n$, $\Gamma_0 \subseteq \Gamma_i$ and $\Delta_0 \subseteq \Delta_i$ and both Γ_0 and Δ_0 are modal clauses. A propagation rule p *generates* the set

$$
p^* = \{\Gamma_1, \Sigma \Longrightarrow \Delta_1, \Pi \dots, \Gamma_n, \Sigma \Longrightarrow \Delta_n, \Pi / \Gamma_0, \Sigma \Longrightarrow \Delta_0, \Pi \mid \Sigma, \Pi \subseteq \mathsf{V} \text{ finite}\}
$$

of modal sequent rules. A set R is *generated* by step rules (resp. by step and propagation rules) if there is a set R_0 of step rules (resp. step and propagation rules) such that $\mathsf{R} = \bigcup\{x^* \mid x \in \mathsf{R}_0\}$.

Importantly, both step rules and propagation rules are modal sequent rules, i.e. each premiss of a (step or propagation) rule is constructed from subformulae of the conclusion. The definition of step and propagation rules follows common rule shapes in the sequent calculus.

Example 30. In the rules of Example 4, all of (E), (M), (K), (CK), (A) and (B) are generated by step rules, and (T) and (MP) are generated by propagation rules. The standard sequent rule for e.g. the logic K4

$$\frac{A_1, \ldots, A_n, \Box A_1, \ldots, \Box A_n \Longrightarrow B}{\Box A_1, \ldots, \Box A_n, \Gamma \Longrightarrow \Box B, \Delta}$$

is neither generated by step or propagation rules. It is not a step rule (as there are occurrences of $\Box$ in the premiss) and not a propagation rule (as the context is not duplicated from conclusion to premiss). Indeed, we do not expect K4 to be covered by our layered calculi, as, intuitively, K4 is the modal logic of transitivity, and reasoning about transitivity requires to move information between all modal layers. This requires every clause to be labelled with every modal level, so that labels fail to restrict the applicability of resolution rules, and the labelled calculus would essentially be equivalent to the unlabelled one.

In our examples, the syntactic form of the rules easily establishes that the rule sets are generated by step, or step and propagation rules. In general, given a set of rules without any generating principles, or generated by rules that are not obviously step or propagation rules, it is an interesting open question how to (dis-)prove that the rule set is generated by step or propagation rules.

For the generative version of the layered calculus, we modify Definition 6:

Definition 31 (Layered Generative Resolution). Let R consist of step rules and propagation rules only, Φ be a set of layered clauses and $i : D$ a layered clause. Then $\Phi \vdash_{\mathsf{GR}} i : D$ if $i : D$ is in the least set containing Φ and closed under the layered versions of resolution (left) and the instances of modal rules (right)

$$\frac{i : D \vee l \qquad i : E \vee \neg l}{i : D \vee E} \qquad \frac{i' : S_1 \quad \ldots \quad i' : S_n}{i : \neg \Gamma_0 \tau \vee \Delta_0 \tau}$$

where $\Gamma_1 \Longrightarrow \Delta_1, \ldots, \Gamma_n \Longrightarrow \Delta_n / \Gamma_0 \Longrightarrow \Delta_0 \in \mathsf{R}$ is a modal sequent rule, $\tau : \mathsf{V} \to \mathsf{V}$ is a renaming, and $S_i \subseteq \neg \Gamma_i \tau \vee \Delta_i \tau$ is a subclause, and $i' = i$ for propagation rules, and $i' = i + 1$ for step rules.

We will use the layered translation ltr for rule sets that are generated by step rules only, where no information is being moved between modal levels. We use the stacked translation str for rule sets generated by step and propagation rules.

The first completeness result (step rules and layered translation) is proved as in Proposition 7 where we just need to adapt the case of the modal rule (where the layering changes). The only thing to observe here is that the definition of layered translation (Definition 28) is synchronised with the definition of layered derivability (Definition 31): the translation increases the index of the modality in the same way as the modal (step) rule.

Proposition 32 (Layered Completeness for Step Rules). *If $\Gamma \Longrightarrow \Delta$ is a sequent,* R *is generated by step rules only and* $\vdash_{\mathsf{SR}} \Gamma \Longrightarrow \Delta$*, then* $\mathsf{ltr}_0(\Gamma \Longrightarrow \Delta) \vdash_{\mathsf{GR}} 0 : D$ *for a subclause* $D \subseteq \neg r_\Gamma \vee r_\Delta$.

The completeness of layered resolution for step and propagation rules requires the modification that we have made to the layered translation to obtain the stacked translation in Definition 28. Consider for example the rule (T) from Example 4. Using induction on the derivation of $\Gamma \Longrightarrow \Delta$, the inductive hypothesis for the application of (T) is that $\mathsf{str}_i(A, \Box A, \Gamma \Longrightarrow \Delta) \vdash_{\mathsf{GR}} i : D$ whence $\mathsf{str}_i(A, \Box A, \Gamma) \vdash_{\mathsf{GR}} i : E$ by applying the resolution version of (T), for suitable clauses D and E. What is required, though, is $\mathsf{str}_i(\Box A, \Gamma) \vdash_{\mathsf{GR}} E$, and this is precisely what the stacked translation achieves, as it ensures that $\mathsf{str}_i(A, \Box A) = \mathsf{str}_i(\Box A)$. The general case is the next proposition.

Proposition 33 (Layered Completeness for Step / Propagation Rules). *If $\Gamma \Longrightarrow \Delta$ is a sequent,* R *is generated by step rules and propagation rules, and* $\vdash_{\mathsf{SR}} \Gamma \Longrightarrow \Delta$*, then* $\mathsf{str}_0(\Gamma \Longrightarrow \Delta) \vdash_{\mathsf{GR}} 0 : D$ *for a subclause* $D \subseteq \neg r_\Gamma \vee r_\Delta$.

Soundness of layered generative resolution is evident by deleting the labels.

Proposition 34. *Suppose that the congruence rules, cut and weakening are admissible in* R*, and* R *be generated by step rules and propagation rules. If* $\mathsf{ltr}_0(\Gamma \Longrightarrow \Delta) \vdash_{\mathsf{GR}} 0 : D$ *or* $\mathsf{str}_0(\Gamma \Longrightarrow \Delta) \vdash_{\mathsf{GR}} 0 : D$ *for a subclause* $D \subseteq \neg r_\Gamma \vee r_\Delta$*, then* $\vdash_{\mathsf{SR}} \Gamma \Longrightarrow \Delta$.

The above proposition also gives soundness for the layered translation together with rule sets that are generated by step and propagation rules. While this is true (layering restricts rule applicability), this combination will not be complete in general. We summarise the results of this section for the case of single formulae.

Theorem 35 (Layered Generative Validity). *Let* R *be a set of sequent rules that admit cut, congruence and weakening and let* $A \in \mathsf{L}(\mathsf{V})$ *be a formula.*

1. *If* R *is generated by step rules, then* $\vdash_{\mathsf{SR}} \Longrightarrow A$ *iff* $\mathsf{ltr}_0(A) \vdash 0 : D$
2. *If* R *is generated by step and propagation rules,* $\vdash_{\mathsf{SR}} \Longrightarrow A$ *iff* $\mathsf{str}_0(A) \vdash 0 : D$

where, in both cases, $D \subseteq r_A$ *is some subclause of* r_A.

We now add layering to the *absorptive* resolution calculus in a similar way. We modify Definition 13 as follows:

Definition 36 (Layered Absorptive Calculus for Validity). Let R be a rule set generated by step rules and propagation rules. If Φ is a set of layered clauses and $i : D$ is a layered clause, then $\Phi \vdash_{\mathsf{AR}} i : D$ if $i : D$ is in the least set that is closed under layered resolution and the layered version of propagation rules (as in Definition 31 where the layer does not change), and the rules

$$\frac{\{i+1 : S_j \mid 1 \leq j \leq n\} \quad \{i : D_j \vee A_j\tau \mid 1 \leq j \leq k\} \quad \{i : E_j \vee \neg B_j\tau \mid 1 \leq j \leq l\}}{D_1 \vee \cdots \vee D_k \vee E_1 \vee \cdots \vee E_l}$$

where $\Gamma_1 \Longrightarrow \Delta_1, \ldots, \Gamma_n \Longrightarrow \Delta_n / A_1, \ldots, A_k \Longrightarrow B_1, \ldots, B_l \in \mathsf{R}$ is (generated by) a step rule, $\tau : \mathsf{V} \to \mathsf{V}$ is a renaming, and $S_i \subseteq \neg \Gamma_i\tau \vee \Delta_i\tau$ is a subclause.

The proof of soundness and completeness for layered absorptive resolution is similar to that of non-layered generative resolution, with Lemma 15 taking the following form:

Lemma 37. *Let* $A \in \mathsf{L}(V)$ *and* $i \in \mathbb{Z}$. *Then both* $\mathsf{ltr}_i(A) \vdash_{\mathsf{AR}} i : r_A \vee \neg r_A$ *and* $\mathsf{str}_i(A) \vdash_{\mathsf{AR}} i : r_A \vee \neg r_A$.

Again, for completeness we need to show how to simulate layered generative rules with layered absorptive rules. This is as in Proposition 16, and we need to simulate generative rules with absorptive ones.

Proposition 38 (Layered Absorptive Resolution: Completeness). *Suppose that* R *is generated by step rules (step rules and propagation rules) and suppose that* $\vdash_{\mathsf{SR}} \Gamma \Longrightarrow \Delta$. *Then* $\mathsf{ltr}_i(\Gamma \Longrightarrow \Delta) \vdash_{\mathsf{AR}} i : D$ *(resp.* $\mathsf{str}_i \vdash_{\mathsf{AR}} i : D$*) for a subclause* $D \subseteq \neg r_\Gamma \vee r_\Delta$.

Again, soundness is evident by deleting the labels as in Proposition 34.

Proposition 39. *Let congruence, cut and weakening be admissible in* R, *let* R *is generated by step rules and propagation rules. If* $\mathsf{ltr}_0(\Gamma \Longrightarrow \Delta) \vdash_{\mathsf{AR}} 0 : D$ *or* $\mathsf{str}_0(\Gamma \Longrightarrow \Delta) \vdash_{\mathsf{AR}} 0 : D$ *for a subclause* $D \subseteq \neg r_\Gamma \vee r_\Delta$, *then* $\vdash_{\mathsf{SR}} \Gamma \Longrightarrow \Delta$.

The proof is identical to that of Proposition 34 but uses Corollary 19 instead of Proposition 10. Again, we have soundness and completeness for single formulae:

Theorem 40. *Suppose that* R *is generated by step rules (by step rules and propagation rules). Then* $\vdash_{\mathsf{SR}} \Longrightarrow A$ *iff* $\mathsf{ltr}_0(A) \vdash_{\mathsf{AR}} 0 : D$ *(resp.* $\mathsf{str}_0(A) \vdash_{\mathsf{AR}} 0 : D$*) for a subclause* $D \subseteq r_A$.

We turn to calculi for inconsistency. In the unlayered case, an inconsistent formula A would give $\mathsf{tr}(A) \vdash S \subseteq r_{\neg A}$ so that $\mathsf{tr}(A) \cup \{r_A\} \vdash \epsilon$. We have seen in Sect. 5 that while this is complete, it is not sound, as r_A can contribute to the derivation of a premiss of a modal rule (Example 21). To remedy this, we have introduced local clauses, and one could of course do the same here.

We do not spell out the details of this, but instead focus on a particular case where R is generated by step rules only. The interesting aspect in this case is that layering itself prevents unsoundness, i.e. we do not need to introduce local clauses. The key observation is that any derivation of a layered clause $i : D$ only uses layered clauses $j : E$ where the index $j \geq i$. As in the previous section, we let XR stand for one of AR or GR, and this allows us to prove a layered version of the Dichotomy lemma, without needing to introduce local clauses.

Lemma 41. *Let* Φ *be a set of layered clauses,* R *be generated by step rules only, and let* $i < j$. *If* D *and* E *are clauses, and* $\Phi \cup \{i : D\} \vdash_{\mathsf{XR}} j : E$, *then* $\Phi \vdash_{\mathsf{XR}} j : E$.

The proof is immediate (by induction on the derivation) from the format of the rules. This gives the following layered version of the dichotomy lemma.

Lemma 42 (Layered Dichotomy). *Suppose that* R *is generated by step rules only, let* XR *be one of* GR *of* AR *and let* Φ *be a set of labelled clauses. If* ℓ *is a propositional literal, then* $\Phi \cup \{i : \ell\} \vdash_{\mathsf{XR}} i : D$ *implies that either* $\ell \in D$ *or* $\Phi \vdash_{\mathsf{XR}} i : S$ *for a subclause* $S \subseteq \neg\ell \vee D$.

The restriction to rule sets that are generated by step rules only is necessary, as we have the following counterexample.

Example 43. Consider any rule set R, over a single modal operator $\Box$ that contains the T-rule from Example 4, such as the sequent calculus for the modal logic T. In the ensuing layered generative (say) sequent calculus, we have the following derivation:

1. $\emptyset \cup \{i : \neg p\} \vdash_{\mathsf{LGR}} i : p$ 2. $\emptyset \cup \{i : \neg p\} \vdash_{\mathsf{LGR}} i : \neg\Box p$ $(\mathsf{T}, 1)$

We do, however, not have that $\emptyset \vdash i : p \vee \neg\Box p$ (or any subclause), nor do we have that $\neg p \in \neg\Box p$ (considering the latter as a single clause).

The fact that the T-axiom is not derivable *from the empty set of clauses* is perfectly consistent with our completeness theorem. In the language using just conjunction and negation (Definition 1), the T-axiom $\Box p \to p$ becomes $A \equiv \neg(\Box p \wedge \neg p)$, and it is an easy exercise to verify that $\mathsf{str}_0(A) \vdash r_A$, as promised by Theorem 35.

We close the paper with the main theorem for layered calculi for inconsistency.

Theorem 44 (Generative and Absorptive Layered Inconsistency). *Let* R *be generated by step rules, and suppose that* R *admits cut, congruence and weakening and let* $A \in \mathsf{L}(\mathsf{V})$ *be a formula. If* $\vdash_{\mathsf{XR}}$ *is one of* $\vdash_{\mathsf{GR}}$ *or* $\vdash_{\mathsf{AR}}$, *then* $\vdash_{\mathsf{SR}} A \Longrightarrow$ *iff* $\mathsf{ltr}_0(A) \cup \{0 : r_A\} \vdash_{\mathsf{XR}} 0 : \epsilon$.

7 Conclusion and Future Work

We have shown how to generate sound and complete resolution calculi from (unlabelled) sequent systems for modal logics. Instantiating this construction, we obtain new (sound and complete) resolution calculi for a large class of modal logics, including, but by no means limited to, all the logics in Example 4. While resolution calculi for a number of extensions of K and for coalition logic are known [17,19], this is not the case e.g. for all the conditional logics as well as modal logics of probability. Open questions are both practical and theoretical. On the practical side, we need more research to modularise and combine *implementations* of various resolution systems, as well as a solid understanding of the relative efficiency of plain/labelled resolution and also different strategies (e.g. negative, ordered resolution). On the more theoretical side, we are interested in lower bounds on the size of resolution proofs, and whether the different systems p-simulate each other. Of particular interest is the question of whether the corresponding techniques for normal modal logic [28] generalise to not necessarily normal, or monotone, modal logics.

Acknowledgments. We warmly thank the referees for their exceptionally thoughtful, constructive and diligent feedback, which has greatly improved this paper.

Disclosure of Interests. The authors have no competing interests to declare that are relevant to the content of this article.

References

1. Blackburn, P., de Rijke, M., Venema, Y.: Modal Logic. Cambridge University Press (2001)
2. Chellas, B.: Modal Logic. Cambridge (1980)
3. Cresswell, M.J., Hughes, G.E.: A New Introduction to Modal Logic. Routledge, New York (1996)
4. Fagin, R., Halpern, J.Y., Moses, Y., Vardi, M.: Reasoning About Knowledge. MIT Press, Cambridge (2003)
5. Goble, L.: A proposal for dealing with deontic dilemmas. In: Lomuscio, A., Nute, D. (eds.) DEON 2004. LNCS (LNAI), vol. 3065, pp. 74–113. Springer, Heidelberg (2004). https://doi.org/10.1007/978-3-540-25927-5_7
6. Goré, R.: Tableau methods for modal and temporal logics. In: D'Agostino, M., Gabbay, D., Hähnle, R., Posegga, J. (eds.) Handbook of Tableau Methods, pp. 297–396. Kluwer (1999)
7. Greco, G., Kurz, A., Palmigiano, A.: Dynamic sequent calculus for the logic of epistemic actions and knowledge. In: Galatos, N., Kurz, A., Tsinakis, C. (eds.) Proceedings of TACL 2013. EPiC Series in Computing, vol. 25, pp. 85–87. EasyChair (2013)
8. Hawthorn, J.: Natural deduction in normal modal logic. Notre Dame J. Formal Log. **31**(2), 263–273 (1990)
9. Heifetz, A., Mongin, P.: Probabilistic logic for type spaces. Games Econom. Behav. **35**, 31–53 (2001)
10. Hermant, O.: Resolution is cut-free. J. Autom. Reason. **44**(3), 245–276 (2010)
11. Kupke, C., Pattinson, D.: On modal logics of linear inequalities. In: Beklemishev, L.D., Goranko, V., Shehtman, V.B. (eds.) Proceedings of AiML 2010, pp. 235–255. College Publications (2010)
12. Leitgeb, H., Segerberg, K.: Dynamic doxastic logic: why, how, and where to? Synthese **155**(2), 167–190 (2007)
13. Mints, G.: Gentzen-type systems and resolution rules. Part I. Propositional logic. In: COLOG-88: Proceedings of the International Conference on Computer Logic, pp. 198–231. Springer (1990)
14. Mints, G., Orevkov, V., Tammet, T.: Transfer of sequent calculus strategies to resolution for S4. In: Wansing, H. (ed.) Proof Theory of Modal Logic, pp. 17–31. Springer, Dordrecht (1996)
15. Nalon, C., Dixon, C., Hustadt, U.: Modal resolution: proofs, layers, and refinements. ACM Trans. Comput. Log. **20**(4), 23:1–23:38 (2019)
16. Nalon, C., Hustadt, U., Dixon, C.: KSP: architecture, refinements, strategies and experiments. J. Autom. Reason. **64**(3), 461–484 (2020)
17. Nalon, C., Zhang, L., Dixon, C., Hustadt, U.: A resolution-based calculus for coalition logic. J. Log. Comput. **24**(4), 883–917 (2014)
18. Nute, D.: Topics in Conditional Logic. Reidel, Boston (1980)

19. Ohlbach, H.J.: A resolution calculus for modal logics. In: Lusk, E., Overbeek, R. (eds.) CADE 1988. LNCS, vol. 310, pp. 500–516. Springer, Heidelberg (1988). https://doi.org/10.1007/BFb0012852
20. Olivetti, N., Pozzato, G.L., Schwind, C.: A sequent calculus and a theorem prover for standard conditional logics. ACM Trans. Comput. Log. **8**(4) (2007)
21. Orlandelli, E.: Sequent calculi and interpolation for non-normal modal and deontic logics. Logic Log. Philos. **30**(1), 139–183 (2020)
22. Pattinson, D., Schröder, L.: Generic modal cut elimination applied to conditional logics. In: Giese, M., Waaler, A. (eds.) Proceedings of Tableaux 2009. Lecture Notes in Artificial Intelligence, vol. 5607. Springer (2009)
23. Pattinson, D., Schröder, L.: Cut elimination in coalgebraic logics. Inf. Comput. **208**, 1447–1468 (2010)
24. Pattinson, D., Nalon, C.: Non-iterative modal resolution calculi. In: Benzmüller, C., Heule, M., Schmidt, R. (eds.) Proceedings of IJCAR 2024. Lecture Notes in Computer Science, vol. 14740, pp. 97–113. Springer (2024)
25. Pattinson, D., Nalon, C., Olivetti, N.: Resolution-based calculi for non-normal modal logics. In: Ramanayake, R., Urban, J. (eds.) Proceedings of Tableaux 2023 (2023)
26. Pauly, M.: A modal logic for coalitional power in games. J. Logic Comput. **12**(1), 149–166 (2002)
27. Reis, G., Paleo, B.W.: Complexity of translations from resolution to sequent calculus. Math. Struct. Comput. Sci. **29**(8), 1061–1091 (2019)
28. Sigley, S., Beyersdorff, O.: Proof complexity of modal resolution. J. Autom. Reason. **66**(1), 1–41 (2022)
29. Stewart, C., Stouppa, P.: A systematic proof theory for several modal logics. In: Schmidt, R.A., Pratt-Hartmann, I., Reynolds, M., Wansing, H. (eds.) Proceedings of AIML 2004, pp. 309–333. King's College Publications (2004)
30. Straccia, U.: Reasoning within fuzzy description logics. J. Artif. Intell. Res. (JAIR) **14**, 137–166 (2001)
31. Sutcliff, G.: Proceedings of the 12th IJCAR ATP System Competition (CASC-J1j) (2024). https://www.tptp.org/CASC/J12/
32. Tammet, T.: Resolution, inverse method and the sequent calculus. In: Gottlob, G., Leitsch, A., Mundici, D. (eds.) KGC 1997. LNCS, vol. 1289, pp. 65–83. Springer, Heidelberg (1997). https://doi.org/10.1007/3-540-63385-5_33
33. Troelstra, A., Schwichtenberg, H.: Basic Proof Theory. Number 43 in Cambridge Tracts in Theoretical Computer Science. Cambridge University Press (1996)
34. Wansing, H.: Sequent systems for modal logics. In: Gabbay, D.M., Guenthner, F. (eds.) Handbook of Philosophical Logic: Volume 8, pp. 61–145. Springer (2002)

A Fresh Inductive Approach to Useful Call-by-Value

Pablo Barenbaum[1,2], Delia Kesner[3(✉)], and Mariana Milicich[3]

[1] Universidad Nacional de Quilmes (CONICET), Bernal, Argentina
pbarenbaum@dc.uba.ar
[2] Instituto de Ciencias de la Computación, Universidad de Buenos Aires, Buenos Aires, Argentina
[3] Université Paris Cité, CNRS, IRIF, Paris, France
{kesner,milicich}@irif.fr

Abstract. *Useful evaluation* is an optimised evaluation mechanism for functional programming languages, introduced by Accattoli and Dal Lago. The key to useful evaluation is to represent programs with *sharing* and to implement substitution of terms only when this contributes to the progress of the computation. Initially defined in the framework of call-by-name, useful evaluation has since been extended to call-by-value. The definitions of usefulness in the literature are complex and lack inductive structure, which makes it challenging to (formally) reason about them.

In this work, we define useful call-by-value evaluation inductively, proceeding in two stages. First, we refine the well-known *Value Substitution Calculus*, so the substitution operation becomes *linear*, yielding the LCBV calculus. The two calculi are observationally equivalent. We then further refine LCBV by restricting linear substitution only when it contributes to the progress of the computation, yielding the UCBV strategy. This new substitution notion is sensitive to the surrounding evaluation context, so it is non-trivial to capture it inductively. Moreover, we formally show that the resulting UCBV is a sound and complete implementation of LCBV, optimised to implement useful evaluation.

As a further contribution, we show that the UCBV strategy can be implemented by an existing lower-level abstract machine called GLAMoUr with polynomial overhead in time. This entails, as a corollary, that UCBV is *time-invariant*, *i.e.*, that the number of reduction steps to normal form in UCBV can be used as a measure of time complexity.

Our UCBV strategy is part of the preliminary work required to develop semantic interpretations of useful evaluation, for which its inductive formulation is more suitable than the (non-inductive) existing ones.

Keywords: evaluation strategies · call-by-value · useful evaluation

1 Introduction

The λ-calculus is the foundational model behind functional programming languages and most proof assistants. Implementing them in an *efficient* way requires

C. Barrett and U. Waldmann (Eds.): CADE 2025, LNAI 15943, pp. 381–399, 2025.
https://doi.org/10.1007/978-3-031-99984-0_21

designing an evaluation mechanism that closely adheres to the operational semantics, while optimising the key operations for resource efficiency, both for time and space. This creates a significant gap between the original model and its optimised version, making it crucial to guarantee that both notions have the same *observable behaviour*.

In the λ-calculus, evaluation strategies vary, with *call-by-name* (CBN) and *call-by-value* (CBV) being two prominent examples. In both cases, efficient implementations rely on term representations with *sharing*. For example, implementations typically use environments to bind a variable to a shared subexpression, rather than textually substituting the variable by many copies of the subexpression. Formally, λ-terms with sharing can be represented with *explicit substitutions*[1] (ESs). An ES binding a variable x to an expression s is written $[x\backslash s]$, and a term t affected by such an ES is written $t[x\backslash s]$ (which some authors note "$\mathsf{let}\ x = s\ \mathsf{in}\ t$"). The expression $t[x\backslash s]$ means that all the free occurrences of x in t are bound to s, and thus s is *shared*. While the β-reduction rule of the λ-calculus is based on the meta-level substitution operation $t\{x := s\}$ that replaces all the free occurrences of x in t at once, some calculi with ESs allow replacing a *single* occurrence of a variable, such as $(x\,x)[x\backslash t] \to (t\,x)[x\backslash t]$. This finer-grained substitution operation is called **linear substitution**.

Accattoli and Dal Lago have proposed an optimised evaluation mechanism, called **useful evaluation** [6], which represents terms with ESs so that the copy of shared subterms is restricted to avoid *size explosion*. Useful evaluation has in particular been extended to *open CBV* [2,4], *i.e.*, CBV over terms that may contain free variables. This mechanism relies on two key *usefulness principles* that we call `UP1` and `UP2`. Specifically, these two principles ensure that an occurrence of a variable may be linearly substituted by an expression only if this contributes to creating a *redex*[2]. Principle `UP1` (*Sharing Structures*) ensures that terms headed by a free variable, or more precisely *structures*, such as $x\,y$, always remain shared in ESs, and are never copied. Principle `UP2` (*Substituting Abstractions for Progress*) ensures that an occurrence of a variable bound to an abstraction may be substituted only if the variable is applied to an argument. See Sect. 2 for more details.

An Inductive Approach to Useful Evaluation. It is well-known that there are two alternative ways to specify evaluation strategies. A strategy can be presented *inductively*, by providing *computation rules*, that specify how terms interact locally, and *congruence rules*, that specify when and how evaluation should focus on a subterm. Regarding congruence rules, another point of view is to rely on *evaluation contexts*, to specify the strategy at top-level.[3]

[1] See [14] for a survey on ESs.

[2] **Red**ucible **ex**pression.

[3] For example, CBN evaluation may be specified with a computation rule for β-reduction, declaring that $(\lambda x.\,t)\,s \to_{\mathsf{CBN}} t\{x := s\}$, and a congruence rule to allow evaluation to proceed on the left of an application, declaring that $t \to_{\mathsf{CBN}} t'$ implies $t\,s \to_{\mathsf{CBN}} t'\,s$. An alternative way to specify CBN evaluation is with a single top-level rule declaring that $\mathtt{N}\langle(\lambda x.\,t)\,s\rangle \to_{\mathsf{CBN}} \mathtt{N}\langle t\{x := s\}\rangle$, where $\mathtt{N}$ denotes a CBN evaluation context generated by the grammar $\mathtt{N} ::= \Diamond \mid \mathtt{N}\,t$.

It is usually easy to switch between these two points of view, because typical strategies only rely on *local* interactions. However, this is not the case with useful evaluation, which is context-sensitive, in the sense that steps involve side conditions of a *global* nature. In particular, a non-useful step can become useful when placed within a larger context. For example, the step $\mathtt{C}\langle x[x\backslash y]\rangle \to \mathtt{C}\langle y[x\backslash y]\rangle$, which substitutes x by y under a context $\mathtt{C}$, may be useful or not, depending on whether the expression $x[x\backslash y]$ is applied to an argument, and whether the variable y is (hereditarily) bound to an abstraction in $\mathtt{C}$. This makes it challenging to define useful evaluation by means of congruence rules, which are of inductive nature. As part of this work, we define an inductive specification of useful evaluation, which despite the difficulties faced, it provides several advantages, which we will discuss at the end of this paper.

Contributions. This paper defines the first inductive specification of useful evaluation. We work in the framework of open CBV. Although most functional programming languages are restricted to closed terms (forbidding free variables), working in an open setting (allowing free variables) broadens the applicability of our results. Furthermore, being able to treat the open CBV case is a prerequisite to deal in the future with other cases. For example, Grégoire and Leroy study *strong* CBV evaluation [13], motivated by the implementation of proof assistants based on dependent type theory.

In contrast to existing specifications of useful evaluation in the literature, our specification relies on *inductive* rules. To define the new strategy UCBV, we proceed in two stages. First, we recall in Sect. 3 the *Value Substitution Calculus* (VSC) [7], which is the starting point of our development. We then introduce the *linear* CBV calculus (LCBV), which refines the VSC with *linear substitution*, while remaining observationally equivalent. Moreover, LCBV implements principle UP1 but still not UP2. Second, we introduce in Sect. 4 the UCBV strategy, by refining evaluation in LCBV to also implement principle UP2. Our inductive approach to usefulness has been inspired by the definition of strong call-by-need evaluation in [8]. We also prove key operational properties of UCBV; in particular, it enjoys the diamond property—and thus confluence. In Sect. 5, we show that UCBV is indeed a useful implementation of LCBV. The relationship between the two calculi is established syntactically, by means of rewriting techniques, and relying on *partial unfolding* operation that performs *all* the substitutions assigning values to variables. The main result is that UCBV preserves the semantics of LCBV, *i.e.*, if LCBV reaches a normal form from a starting term then, UCBV reaches the same normal form, up to partial unfolding.

Finally, in Sect. 6, we show that UCBV can in turn be implemented by a lower-level abstract machine for useful CBV, namely the GLAMoUr [2,5]. This result not only connects UCBV with a preexisting notion of usefulness, but it also entails that UCBV is *time-invariant*. This means that the length of reductions to normal form can be taken as a measure of time complexity. More precisely, UCBV can be simulated by a *reasonable* cost model of computation [15] (such as a Turing machine or a RAM) with at most polynomial overhead in time.

Note. Proofs have been omitted, but they can be found in the technical report [10].

2 Preliminary Notions

In this section, we introduce the syntax used for all the calculi introduced in this work. Next, we explain the two principles UP1 and UP2 that underlie the notion of usefulness. Moreover, we recall some background notions of rewriting theory.

Syntax. Given a denumerable set of **variables** $(x, y, z, \ldots)$, the sets of **terms** $(t, s, u, \ldots)$, **substitution contexts** $(\mathtt{L}, \mathtt{L}', \ldots)$, and **values** $(v, w, \ldots)$ are given by the following grammars:

$$t ::= x \mid \lambda x.\, t \mid t\, t \mid t[x\backslash t] \qquad \mathtt{L} ::= \Diamond \mid \mathtt{L}[x\backslash t] \qquad v ::= x \mid \lambda x.\, t$$

The set of terms includes **variables**, **abstractions**, **applications**, and **closures** $t[x\backslash s]$ representing an **explicit substitution** (ES) $[x\backslash s]$ on a term t. **Free** and **bound occurrences** of variables are defined as usual, where free occurrences of x in t are bound in $t[x\backslash s]$. We write $\mathsf{fv}(t)$ and $\mathsf{fv}(\mathtt{L})$ for the set of free variables of a term and a context, respectively. Terms are considered up to *α-renaming* of bound variables. We write $t\mathtt{L}$ for the *variable-capturing* **replacement** of the hole $\Diamond$ in $\mathtt{L}$ by t. If $\mathtt{L} = \Diamond[x_1\backslash t_1] \ldots [x_n\backslash t_n]$, we write $\mathsf{dom}(\mathtt{L})$ for the set of variables that are bound by $\mathtt{L}$ at the place of the hole, that is, $\mathsf{dom}(\mathtt{L}) := \{x_1, \ldots, x_n\}$. The set of **reachable variables** of a term is defined as follows: $\mathsf{rv}(x) := \{x\}$, $\mathsf{rv}(\lambda x.\, t) := \emptyset$, $\mathsf{rv}(t\, s) := \mathsf{rv}(t) \cup \mathsf{rv}(s)$, and $\mathsf{rv}(t[x\backslash s]) := (\mathsf{rv}(t) \setminus \{x\}) \cup \mathsf{rv}(s)$. We write $t\{x := s\}$ for the *capture-avoiding* **substitution** of the free occurrences of x by s in t. Some recurring terms are the identity function $\mathtt{I} := \lambda x.\, x$ and the operator $\omega := \lambda x.\, x\, x$.

Usefulness Principles. As mentioned in the introduction, useful evaluation is motivated by the two following key *usefulness principles*:

Sharing Structures (UP1). A term is a **structure** if its *(full) unfolding*—the result of performing all the explicit substitutions by using the capture-avoiding substitution—results in an application headed by a variable, *i.e.*, of the form $x\, t_1 \ldots t_n$, where $(n \geq 0)$. For example, $(x\, x)[x\backslash y\, \mathtt{I}][y\backslash z\, z]$ is a structure, as it (fully) unfolds to $z\, z\, \mathtt{I}\, (z\, z\, \mathtt{I})$. Structures must remain *shared* in useful evaluation, as substituting a variable by a structure does not create a *function application redex*. Thus, a term like $(x\, x)[x\backslash y\, \mathtt{I}][y\backslash z\, z]$ is a normal form in useful evaluation. The notion of structure just defined is context-independent. In fact, we shall need a subtler *context-dependent* notion of structure relative to a "structure frame" (defined in Sect. 4). For instance, $x\, y$ should *not* be treated as a structure under a context that binds x to an abstraction.

Substituting Abstractions for Progress (UP2). In useful evaluation, abstractions are substituted only if they contribute to creating a function application redex, thus ensuring progress in the computation. For example, a reduction step like $x[x\backslash \mathtt{I}]\, y \to \mathtt{I}[x\backslash \mathtt{I}]\, y$ is useful, while the steps $x[x\backslash \mathtt{I}] \to \mathtt{I}[x\backslash \mathtt{I}]$ and $(t\, x)[x\backslash \mathtt{I}] \to$

$(t\,\mathtt{I})[x\backslash\mathtt{I}]$ are not, as they do not contribute to creating function application redexes. Some of these ideas can also be found in the literature on *optimal reduction* (see *e.g.*, [17]).

Background on Rewriting Theory. We now introduce some general notions of reduction that will be used in the paper. Given a **reduction system** $\mathcal{R}$, we denote by $\rightarrow_{\mathcal{R}}$ the (one-step) reduction relation associated to system $\mathcal{R}$. We write $\rightarrow_{\mathcal{R}}^{=}$ and $\rightarrow_{\mathcal{R}}^{*}$ for the reflexive and reflexive-transitive closure of $\rightarrow_{\mathcal{R}}$, and $\rightarrow_{\mathcal{R}}^{n}$ for the composition of n-steps of $\rightarrow_{\mathcal{R}}$. A term t is said to be **$\mathcal{R}$-reducible** if there is s such that $t \rightarrow_{\mathcal{R}} s$, and t is said to be **$\mathcal{R}$-irreducible**, or in **$\mathcal{R}$-normal form**, written $t \not\rightarrow_{\mathcal{R}}$, if there is no s such that $t \rightarrow_{\mathcal{R}} s$. A term t is said to be **$\mathcal{R}$-terminating** if there is no infinite $\mathcal{R}$-sequence starting at t. A term t is **$\mathcal{R}$-diamond** (or enjoys the $\mathcal{R}$-diamond property) if $t \rightarrow_{\mathcal{R}} t_0$ and $t \rightarrow_{\mathcal{R}} t_1$ with $t_0 \neq t_1$ imply there exists t' such that $t_0 \rightarrow_{\mathcal{R}} t'$ and $t_1 \rightarrow_{\mathcal{R}} t'$. A term t is **$\mathcal{R}$-confluent** if $t \rightarrow_{\mathcal{R}}^{*} t_0$ and $t \rightarrow_{\mathcal{R}}^{*} t_1$ imply there exists t' such that $t_0 \rightarrow_{\mathcal{R}}^{*} t'$ and $t_1 \rightarrow_{\mathcal{R}}^{*} t'$. A relation $\mathcal{R}$ is **terminating**, (resp. **diamond**, **confluent**) if and only if every term is $\mathcal{R}$-terminating (resp. $\mathcal{R}$-diamond, $\mathcal{R}$-confluent). Any relation verifying the diamond property is in particular confluent. Moreover, if t is confluent, then its $\mathcal{R}$-normal form, if it exists, is unique [16].

3 Linear Call-by-Value

In this section, we define the Linear CBV calculus (LCBV), a first step towards useful evaluation. LCBV fulfils principle `UP1` by keeping structures always shared, but it does not fulfil `UP2`, as it allows substituting variables by values unrestrictedly (see Sect. 2 for the definitions of `UP1` and `UP2`).

Furthermore, LCBV adapts the substitution operation in the Value Substitution Calculus (VSC) [7] to be *linear* by allowing the substitution of one occurrence of a variable at a time. We begin by explaining the difference between the (non-linear) original substitution mechanism of the VSC, and the linear substitution of LCBV. We then formally define LCBV and conclude by stating its main properties, including the observational equivalence between LCBV and VSC.

The Value Substitution Calculus. Avoiding the substitution of variables by structures is a sufficient mechanism to obtain an invariant implementation of open CBV (see *e.g.*, [4, Lemma 6]). One calculus implementing this mechanism for open terms is the VSC, which consists of two kinds of reduction steps:

Distant beta (db) steps are given by the rule $(\lambda x.\, t)\mathtt{L}\, s \rightarrow t[x\backslash s]\mathtt{L}$, where $\mathtt{L}$ denotes a list of ES, called a *substitution context*. A db-step performs a *function application* by creating an ES. For example, $(\lambda x.\, \mathtt{I})\,(y\,y)\,z \rightarrow \mathtt{I}[x\backslash y\,y]\,z \rightarrow w[w\backslash z][x\backslash y\,y]$. After the first step, the ES $[x\backslash y\,y]$ appears to block the interaction between $\mathtt{I}$ and its argument z. However, the db-rule allows an arbitrary list of ESs to occur between an abstraction and its argument, thus allowing to fire the second reduction step in the example.

Substitution steps (sv) are given by the rule $t[x\backslash v\mathtt{L}] \rightarrow t\{x := v\}\mathtt{L}$, which substitutes a variable x by a value v, *pushing outside* the substitution context $\mathtt{L}$

originally accompanying the value. For example, $(x\,x)[x\backslash\omega[y\backslash\mathtt{I}]] \to (\omega\,\omega)[y\backslash\mathtt{I}]$, where we recall that $\omega := \lambda z.\, z\,z$. The VSC implements principle UP1 because it only allows substituting variables by values (so that structures remain shared). For example, the step $(x\,x)[x\backslash z\,z] \to z\,z\,(z\,z)$ is not allowed.

Towards Linear Substitution. LCBV refines the VSC by implementing *linear substitution*, which substitutes one occurrence of a variable at a time. Linear substitution is a prerequisite—but not sufficient—to fulfil principle UP2, *i.e.*, to *fully* implement useful evaluation. Specifically, when a variable occurs multiple times in a term, substituting it with an abstraction may create a function application in some cases but not in others. For example, in the step $(z\,(\underline{x}\,y)\,\overline{x})[x\backslash\mathtt{I}] \to z\,(\mathtt{I}\,y)\,\mathtt{I}$, substituting the underlined occurrence of x by I creates a db-redex (and thus it is useful), while substituting the overlined occurrence of x by I does not contribute to creating a db-redex.

The Linear Call-by-Value Calculus. We now define the Linear CBV Calculus LCBV, which refines the VSC by implementing linear substitution. We adopt a formulation of rules based on the style of [8] that we also follow to formulate our inductive notion of useful evaluation, UCBV, in Sect. 4.

Formally, we define a family of binary relations $\overset{\circ}{\to}_{\rho}$, where $\rho \in \{\mathsf{db}, \mathsf{lsv}, \mathsf{sub}_{(x,v)}\}$ distinguishes the **step kind**, where x is a variable and v is a value such that $x \notin \mathsf{fv}(v)$. The set of **free variables** of a step kind ρ is defined as $\mathsf{fv}(\mathsf{db}) := \emptyset$, $\mathsf{fv}(\mathsf{lsv}) := \emptyset$, and $\mathsf{fv}(\mathsf{sub}_{(x,v)}) := \{x\} \cup \mathsf{fv}(v)$. The **reduction relation** $\overset{\circ}{\to}_{\rho}$ of LCBV is inductively defined as follows:

$$\frac{}{(\lambda x.\, t)\mathtt{L}\, s \overset{\circ}{\to}_{\mathsf{db}} t[x\backslash s]\mathtt{L}}\,\mathrm{DB}^{\circ} \qquad \frac{}{x \overset{\circ}{\to}_{\mathsf{sub}_{(x,v)}} v}\,\mathrm{SUB}^{\circ} \qquad \frac{t \overset{\circ}{\to}_{\mathsf{sub}_{(x,v)}} t'}{t[x\backslash v\mathtt{L}] \overset{\circ}{\to}_{\mathsf{lsv}} t'[x\backslash v]\mathtt{L}}\,\mathrm{LSV}^{\circ}$$

$$\frac{t \overset{\circ}{\to}_{\rho} t'}{t\,s \overset{\circ}{\to}_{\rho} t'\,s}\,\mathrm{APPL}^{\circ} \qquad \frac{s \overset{\circ}{\to}_{\rho} s'}{t\,s \overset{\circ}{\to}_{\rho} t\,s'}\,\mathrm{APPR}^{\circ} \qquad \frac{t \overset{\circ}{\to}_{\rho} t' \quad x \notin \mathsf{fv}(\rho)}{t[x\backslash s] \overset{\circ}{\to}_{\rho} t'[x\backslash s]}\,\mathrm{ESL}^{\circ} \qquad \frac{s \overset{\circ}{\to}_{\rho} s'}{t[x\backslash s] \overset{\circ}{\to}_{\rho} t[x\backslash s']}\,\mathrm{ESR}^{\circ}$$

We define **top-level** LCBV reduction as $\overset{\circ}{\to}_{\mathsf{top}} := \overset{\circ}{\to}_{\mathsf{db}} \cup \overset{\circ}{\to}_{\mathsf{lsv}}$. Rules DB°, SUB°, and LSV° define the three kinds of reduction steps, whereas APPL°, APPR°, ESL°, and ESR° are congruence rules, and propagate any step kind. Note that evaluation is *weak* and does not proceed under abstractions. A step of the form $t \overset{\circ}{\to}_{\mathsf{db}} s$ represents a *distant beta* step. The reduction steps $t \overset{\circ}{\to}_{\mathsf{sub}_{(x,v)}} s$ and $t \overset{\circ}{\to}_{\mathsf{lsv}} s$ constitute two kinds of *substitution* steps. In the first kind, $t \overset{\circ}{\to}_{\mathsf{sub}_{(x,v)}} s$, *one* free occurrence of x in t is substituted by v. In the second kind, $t \overset{\circ}{\to}_{\mathsf{lsv}} s$, *one* bound occurrence of x is substituted by v, provided x is bound to a term of the form $v\mathtt{L}$ by an ES; LSV° is the only rule that introduces an lsv-step. Moreover, each step substituting a bound variable ($\overset{\circ}{\to}_{\mathsf{lsv}}$) relies internally on a step that substitutes a free variable ($\overset{\circ}{\to}_{\mathsf{sub}_{(x,v)}}$). These substitution steps focus on a *single* variable occurrence, thus we say the substitution operation is *linear*.

As a technical point, note that the term s lies outside the scope of the substitution context L on the left-hand side of the db rule, and inside the scope of L on the right-hand side. In these cases, we assume that this does not cause a free variable of s to be captured by L, *i.e.* that the variables bound by L have been α-renamed in such a way that $\mathsf{fv}(s) \cap \mathsf{dom}(\mathtt{L}) = \emptyset$. For example, $(\lambda y.\, x)[x\backslash t]\, x \overset{\circ}{\to}_{\mathsf{db}} z[y\backslash x][z\backslash t]$.

Along with rule DB°, an application can be evaluated using rules APPL° and APPR°, which reduce within the left and right subterms, respectively. Since rules DB°, APPL°, and APPR° overlap, reduction is *non-deterministic.* For example:

$$x[x\backslash \mathtt{I}]\,(\mathtt{I}\,\mathtt{I}) \overset{\circ}{\leftarrow}_{\mathsf{db}} \mathtt{I}\,\mathtt{I}\,(\mathtt{I}\,\mathtt{I}) \overset{\circ}{\to}_{\mathsf{db}} \mathtt{I}\,\mathtt{I}\,x[x\backslash \mathtt{I}]$$

The congruence rules ESL° and ESR° allow reduction on the left side of a term and within the argument of an ES, respectively. These rules overlap as well. A key restriction in rule ESL° is that the variable x bound by the ES $[x\backslash s]$ must not occur free in the step kind ρ. This restriction is to avoid variable capture; for example, it ensures that a "pathological" step like $y[x\backslash z] \overset{\circ}{\to}_{\mathsf{sub}_{(y,x)}} x[x\backslash z]$ cannot be derived from the valid step $y \overset{\circ}{\to}_{\mathsf{sub}_{(y,x)}} x$.

Example 1. The following is a reduction sequence to normal form in LCBV:

$$\begin{array}{llll} & (\lambda x.\, z\, x\, (x\, y))\, \mathtt{I} \overset{\circ}{\to}_{\mathsf{db}} (z\, x\, (x\, y))[x\backslash \mathtt{I}] & \overset{\circ}{\to}_{\mathsf{lsv}} (z\, \mathtt{I}\, (x\, y))[x\backslash \mathtt{I}] & \\ \overset{\circ}{\to}_{\mathsf{lsv}} (z\, \mathtt{I}\, (\mathtt{I}\, y))[x\backslash \mathtt{I}] & \overset{\circ}{\to}_{\mathsf{db}} (z\, \mathtt{I}\, (w[w\backslash y]))[x\backslash \mathtt{I}] & \overset{\circ}{\to}_{\mathsf{lsv}} (z\, \mathtt{I}\, (y[w\backslash y]))[x\backslash \mathtt{I}] & \end{array}$$

Confluence. Despite the overlaps of some reduction rules, it is straightforward to show that *top-level* $\overset{\circ}{\to}$ reduction is confluent:

Proposition 1. *Reduction* $\overset{\circ}{\to}_{\mathsf{top}}$ *is confluent.*

Proof. The proof follows from [10, Theorem C.14].

Correspondence with the Value Substitution Calculus. We formally relate the LCBV to the VSC.

Proposition 2. *Let t be a term. Then, t terminates in* LCBV *if and only if t terminates in the* VSC.

Proof. The proof of this statement follows a standard approach using semantic tools from *(intersection) type theory.* As it falls outside the scope of this paper, we do not include the proof here. Full details can be found in [9].

In the following section, we define *useful CBV* evaluation by refining LCBV, for which we incorporate the second key principle of usefulness, *substituting abstractions for progress* (UP2).

4 Useful Call-by-Value

In this section, we refine the notion of LCBV evaluation introduced in Sect. 3, the resulting strategy is called UCBV. While preserving principle UP1, already present in LCBV, UCBV evaluation also implements principle UP2, which is non-trivial to be captured *inductively*. To achieve useful CBV evaluation, we define a family of reduction relations indexed by certain *parameters* representing the essential information from the surrounding evaluation contexts. This is the minimal data necessary to decide whether a substitution step is useful or not. Next, we give the main properties of UCBV, starting with a characterisation of normal forms (Theorem 1). Following this result, we show that UCBV satisfies the diamond property (Theorem 2), which ensures in particular that the length of a reduction sequence to normal form does not depend on the specific order of redexes chosen to reduce the terms.

Towards the Useful Call-by-Value Strategy. To implement principle UP2 in UCBV it is necessary to ensure that substitution contributes to the *progress* of the evaluation. For example, the substitution step $(x\,t)[x\backslash y][y\backslash \mathtt{I}] \to (y\,t)[x\backslash y][y\backslash \mathtt{I}]$ is (indirectly) useful because the occurrence of x is applied to an argument t, and substituting x by y then contributes to creating the underlined redex $(\underline{\mathtt{I}\,t})[x\backslash y][y\backslash \mathtt{I}]$ after one more substitution step. This motivates the need to identify *hereditary abstractions*, which intuitively include abstractions and variables hereditarily bound to abstractions, such as y in the example. Formally, let $\mathcal{A}$ be a set of variables, called an **abstraction frame**. The set of **hereditary abstractions** under $\mathcal{A}$ is written $\mathsf{HA}_{\mathcal{A}}$ and defined below:

$$\frac{}{\lambda x.\,t \in \mathsf{HA}_{\mathcal{A}}} \qquad \frac{x \in \mathcal{A}}{x \in \mathsf{HA}_{\mathcal{A}}} \qquad \frac{t \in \mathsf{HA}_{\mathcal{A}} \quad x \notin \mathcal{A}}{t[x\backslash s] \in \mathsf{HA}_{\mathcal{A}}} \qquad \frac{t \in \mathsf{HA}_{\mathcal{A}\cup\{x\}} \quad x \notin \mathcal{A} \quad s \in \mathsf{HA}_{\mathcal{A}}}{t[x\backslash s] \in \mathsf{HA}_{\mathcal{A}}}$$

The abstraction frame $\mathcal{A}$ keeps track of variables bound to hereditary abstractions. Every abstraction is a hereditary abstraction (by the first rule), while a variable is a hereditary abstraction if it appears in the abstraction frame (by the second rule). In the case of terms with ESs, the crucial point is that the bound variable x may be added to the abstraction frame only if it is bound to a hereditary abstraction (third and fourth rule). For example, $x[x\backslash \lambda y.\,y] \in \mathsf{HA}_{\mathcal{A}}$ for any $\mathcal{A}$, and $x[z\backslash w][x\backslash y] \in \mathsf{HA}_{\mathcal{A}}$ if and only if $y \in \mathcal{A}$. Note also that applications are never hereditary abstractions.

On the other hand, it is necessary to identify *structures*, which intuitively include both applied variables and variables hereditarily bound to structures. Formally, let $\mathcal{S}$ be a set of variables, called a **structure frame**. The set of **structures under** $\mathcal{S}$ is written $\mathsf{St}_{\mathcal{S}}$ and defined below:

$$\frac{x \in \mathcal{S}}{x \in \mathsf{St}_{\mathcal{S}}} \qquad \frac{t \in \mathsf{St}_{\mathcal{S}}}{t\,s \in \mathsf{St}_{\mathcal{S}}} \qquad \frac{t \in \mathsf{St}_{\mathcal{S}} \quad x \notin \mathcal{S}}{t[x\backslash s] \in \mathsf{St}_{\mathcal{S}}} \qquad \frac{t \in \mathsf{St}_{\mathcal{S}\cup\{x\}} \quad x \notin \mathcal{S} \quad s \in \mathsf{St}_{\mathcal{S}}}{t[x\backslash s] \in \mathsf{St}_{\mathcal{S}}}$$

The structure frame $\mathcal{S}$ keeps track of variables that are bound to structures. Note that no abstraction belongs to the set of structures, for any $\mathcal{S}$. An application is a structure if its left subterm is itself a structure, thus excluding db-redexes from the set of structures under any $\mathcal{S}$. Variables in the structure frame are structures as well. For terms with ESs, the intuitions behind the third and fourth rules are analogous to the corresponding ones for the predicate HA, respectively. For example, performing the substitution on the left subterm in $x[x\backslash y_1\, y_2]\, z$ does not create any db-redex, so $x[x\backslash y_1\, y_2]$ is considered a structure. Similarly, $(x\, y)[y\backslash \mathtt{I}]$ is a structure, even if y is bound to an abstraction.

The abstraction frame $\mathcal{A}$ and the structure frame $\mathcal{S}$ are assumed to be disjoint. To evaluate a term, one should always assume that $\mathsf{fv}(t) \subseteq \mathcal{A} \cup \mathcal{S}$, *i.e.*, all free variables are assumed to be bound to either a hereditary abstraction or a structure. At the top-level case, *i.e.*, when evaluating an *isolated* term t, one takes $\mathcal{A} := \emptyset$ and $\mathcal{S} := \mathsf{fv}(t)$ as starting conditions.

The Useful Call-by-Value Reduction. We can now formally define the UCBV strategy specified as a family of binary relations $\overset{\bullet}{\to}_{\rho,\mathcal{A},\mathcal{S},\mu}$, where $\rho \in \{\mathsf{db}, \mathsf{lsv}, \mathsf{sub}_{(x,v)}\}$ is a step kind, $\mathcal{A}$ is an abstraction frame, $\mathcal{S}$ is a structure frame, and $\mu \in \{@, \not@\}$ is a positional flag. The **reduction relation** $\overset{\bullet}{\to}_{\rho,\mathcal{A},\mathcal{S},\mu}$ of UCBV is inductively defined as follows:

$$\frac{}{(\lambda x.\, t)\mathtt{L}\, s \overset{\bullet}{\to}_{\mathsf{db},\mathcal{A},\mathcal{S},\mu} t[x\backslash s]\mathtt{L}}\ \text{DB}^\bullet \qquad \frac{}{x \overset{\bullet}{\to}_{\mathsf{sub}_{(x,v)},\mathcal{A}\cup\{x\},\mathcal{S},@} v}\ \text{SUB}^\bullet$$

$$\frac{t \overset{\bullet}{\to}_{\mathsf{sub}_{(x,v)},\mathcal{A}\cup\{x\},\mathcal{S},\mu} t' \quad x \notin \mathcal{A}\cup\mathcal{S} \quad v\mathtt{L} \in \mathsf{HA}_{\mathcal{A}}}{t[x\backslash v\mathtt{L}] \overset{\bullet}{\to}_{\mathsf{lsv},\mathcal{A},\mathcal{S},\mu} t'[x\backslash v]\mathtt{L}}\ \text{LSV}^\bullet$$

$$\frac{t \overset{\bullet}{\to}_{\rho,\mathcal{A},\mathcal{S},@} t'}{t\, s \overset{\bullet}{\to}_{\rho,\mathcal{A},\mathcal{S},\mu} t'\, s}\ \text{APPL}^\bullet \qquad \frac{t \in \mathsf{St}_{\mathcal{S}} \quad s \overset{\bullet}{\to}_{\rho,\mathcal{A},\mathcal{S},\not@} s'}{t\, s \overset{\bullet}{\to}_{\rho,\mathcal{A},\mathcal{S},\mu} t\, s'}\ \text{APPR}^\bullet$$

$$\frac{s \overset{\bullet}{\to}_{\rho,\mathcal{A},\mathcal{S},\not@} s'}{t[x\backslash s] \overset{\bullet}{\to}_{\rho,\mathcal{A},\mathcal{S},\mu} t[x\backslash s']}\ \text{ESR}^\bullet$$

$$\frac{t \overset{\bullet}{\to}_{\rho,\mathcal{A}\cup\{x\},\mathcal{S},\mu} t' \quad s \in \mathsf{HA}_{\mathcal{A}} \quad x \notin \mathcal{A}\cup\mathcal{S} \quad x \notin \mathsf{fv}(\rho)}{t[x\backslash s] \overset{\bullet}{\to}_{\rho,\mathcal{A},\mathcal{S},\mu} t'[x\backslash s]}\ \text{ESLA}^\bullet$$

$$\frac{t \overset{\bullet}{\to}_{\rho,\mathcal{A},\mathcal{S}\cup\{x\},\mu} t' \quad s \in \mathsf{St}_{\mathcal{S}} \quad x \notin \mathcal{A}\cup\mathcal{S} \quad x \notin \mathsf{fv}(\rho)}{t[x\backslash s] \overset{\bullet}{\to}_{\rho,\mathcal{A},\mathcal{S},\mu} t'[x\backslash s]}\ \text{ESLS}^\bullet$$

Note that each UCBV step is also a LCBV step, *i.e.*, $\overset{\bullet}{\to}_{\rho,\mathcal{A},\mathcal{S},\mu} \subseteq \overset{\circ}{\to}_{\rho}$. Also, the reduction relation defined above is **non-erasing**: if $t \overset{\bullet}{\to}_{\rho,\mathcal{A},\mathcal{S},\mu} t'$ with $\rho \in \{\mathsf{db}, \mathsf{lsv}\}$, then $\mathsf{fv}(t) = \mathsf{fv}(t')$. As in the previous section, rules DB$^\bullet$, SUB$^\bullet$, and LSV$^\bullet$ introduce the three possible step kinds, while all other cases (APPL$^\bullet$, APPR$^\bullet$, ESLA$^\bullet$, ESLS$^\bullet$, and ESR$^\bullet$) are congruence rules for steps of an arbitrary step kind ρ. Reduction is *weak* since there are no rules to evaluate under abstractions.

Rule DB$^\bullet$ performs a function application step, identical to rule DB$^\circ$ in LCBV. Steps of the form $t \overset{\bullet}{\to}_{\mathsf{sub}_{(x,v)},\mathcal{A},\mathcal{S},\mu} s$ and $t \overset{\bullet}{\to}_{\mathsf{lsv},\mathcal{A},\mathcal{S},\mu} s$ represent two different kinds of *substitution steps*, as in LCBV: the former substitutes *one* free occurrence of a variable, while the latter substitutes *one* bound occurrence. Only rule LSV$^\bullet$

creates an lsv-step. Each application of rule $\textsc{lsv}^\bullet$ relies internally on a $\mathsf{sub}_{(x,v)}$-step, where v must be a hereditary abstraction, a restriction not required in rule $\textsc{lsv}^\circ$ rule in $\textsc{lcbv}$, but that it is crucial to implement principle $\mathsf{UP2}$ (*substituting abstractions for progress*).

Substituting a free variable in a term t using rule $\textsc{sub}^\bullet$ is only possible when t is in an applied position because this ensures the progress of the computation. The following example shows an instance of the $\textsc{sub}^\bullet$ rule:

$$\dfrac{\dfrac{\dfrac{}{x \xrightarrow{\bullet}_{\mathsf{sub}_{(x,\mathtt{I})},\{x\},\{z\},@} \mathtt{I}}\ \textsc{sub}^\bullet \qquad \mathtt{I}[y\backslash z] \in \mathsf{HA}_\emptyset}{x[x\backslash \mathtt{I}[y\backslash z]] \xrightarrow{\bullet}_{\mathsf{lsv},\emptyset,\{z\},@} \mathtt{I}[x\backslash \mathtt{I}][y\backslash z]}\ \textsc{lsv}^\bullet}{x[x\backslash \mathtt{I}[y\backslash z]]w \xrightarrow{\bullet}_{\mathsf{lsv},\emptyset,\{z\},\not{@}} \mathtt{I}[x\backslash \mathtt{I}][y\backslash z]w}\ \textsc{appl}^\bullet$$

The congruence rules $\textsc{appl}^\bullet$ and $\textsc{appr}^\bullet$ perform reduction on the application constructor. Rule $\textsc{appr}^\bullet$ additionally requires the left subterm of the application to be a structure, avoiding a possible overlap with rule $\textsc{db}^\bullet$. Still, rules $\textsc{appl}^\bullet$ and $\textsc{appr}^\bullet$ overlap, so reduction is non-deterministic, like in $\textsc{lcbv}$. For example:

$$x\,y[y\backslash \mathtt{I}]\,(\mathtt{I}\,\mathtt{I}) \xleftarrow{\bullet}_{\mathsf{db},\emptyset,\{x\},\not{@}} x\,(\mathtt{I}\,\mathtt{I})\,(\mathtt{I}\,\mathtt{I}) \xrightarrow{\bullet}_{\mathsf{db},\emptyset,\{x\},\not{@}} x\,(\mathtt{I}\,\mathtt{I})\,y[y\backslash \mathtt{I}]$$

The congruence rules $\textsc{esr}^\bullet$, $\textsc{esla}^\bullet$, and $\textsc{esls}^\bullet$ apply to closures. Rule $\textsc{esr}^\bullet$ allows reducing the argument of any ESs, while rules $\textsc{esla}^\bullet$ and $\textsc{esls}^\bullet$ allow reduction of the left side of the closure under specific conditions: $\textsc{esla}^\bullet$ (resp. $\textsc{esls}^\bullet$) applies only if the substitution argument is a hereditary abstraction (resp. a structure). Note that rules $\textsc{esla}^\bullet$ and $\textsc{esls}^\bullet$ force reducing the argument s of a closure $t[x\backslash s]$ until it becomes "stuck", after which evaluation can proceed to the body t. This behaviour aligns with a CBV strategy, covering all cases in terminating terms, as every terminating term is eventually either a hereditary abstraction or a structure ([10, Lemma B.4]). These rules also enforce that the variable x bound by the ES $[x\backslash s]$ does not occur free in the step kind ρ, as in rule $\textsc{esl}^\circ$ in Sect. 3. This restriction prevents variable capture in steps like $y[x\backslash \mathtt{I}] \xrightarrow{\bullet}_{\mathsf{sub}_{(y,x)},\{y\},\emptyset,@} x[x\backslash \mathtt{I}]$. Note that there is a possible overlap between rule $\textsc{esr}^\bullet$ and rules $\textsc{esla}^\bullet$ and $\textsc{esls}^\bullet$.

A term t is $(\rho, \mathcal{A}, \mathcal{S}, \mu)$**-reducible** if there exists a term t' such that $t \xrightarrow{\bullet}_{\rho,\mathcal{A},\mathcal{S},\mu} t'$. A term t belongs to the set $\mathsf{Irred}^\bullet_{\mathcal{A},\mathcal{S},\mu}$ if t is not $(\rho, \mathcal{A}, \mathcal{S}, \mu)$-reducible.

Hereditary abstractions and structures show distinct and disjoint behaviours within $\textsc{ucbv}$, which are put in evidence through the distinction between abstraction frames and structure frames. An abstraction frame $\mathcal{A}$ and a structure frame $\mathcal{S}$ are said to verify the **correctness property** for t, written $\mathsf{cp}(\mathcal{A}, \mathcal{S}, t)$, if $\mathcal{A} \cap \mathcal{S} = \emptyset$ and $\mathsf{fv}(t) \subseteq \mathcal{A} \cup \mathcal{S}$. This property is implicitly assumed in theorems and lemmas, *i.e.*, whenever we write $t \xrightarrow{\bullet}_{\rho,\mathcal{A},\mathcal{S},\mu}$, we always keep $\mathsf{cp}(\mathcal{A}, \mathcal{S}, t)$ as an invariant. Note that $\mathsf{cp}(\emptyset, \mathsf{fv}(t), t)$ always holds, so for a top-level term t, we may take $\mathcal{A} := \emptyset$ and $\mathcal{S} := \mathsf{fv}(t)$.

Example 2. The following is an UCBV reduction sequence to normal form:

$$\begin{array}{rl} & (\lambda x.\, z\, x\, (x\, y))\, \mathtt{I} \overset{\bullet}{\to}_{\mathsf{db},\emptyset,\{z,y\},\not@} (z\, x\, (x\, y))[x\backslash\mathtt{I}] \\ \overset{\bullet}{\to}_{\mathsf{lsv},\emptyset,\{z,y\},\not@} & (z\, x\, (\mathtt{I}\, y))[x\backslash\mathtt{I}] \overset{\bullet}{\to}_{\mathsf{db},\emptyset,\{z,y\},\not@} (z\, x\, (w[w\backslash y]))[x\backslash\mathtt{I}] \end{array}$$

Compare this reduction sequence with the corresponding evaluation of the same term in LCBV (Example 1). In UCBV, the leftmost occurrence of x and the occurrence of w are not substituted, because these substitutions would not satisfy principle UP2: they do not contribute to creating a db-redex.

As discussed in Sect. 1, useful evaluation is *context-sensitive*, as the context surrounding a term determines whether a step is useful or not. For instance, the term $t = x[x\backslash\mathtt{I}]$ is already in normal form in UCBV, as substituting x by $\mathtt{I}$ is not useful, because it does not create a db-redex. However, if t is located to the left of an application, such as in $x[x\backslash\mathtt{I}]\,(y\,\mathtt{I})$, the substitution of x by $\mathtt{I}$ becomes useful, and yields the following reduction sequence:

$$x[x\backslash\mathtt{I}]\,(y\,\mathtt{I}) \overset{\bullet}{\to}_{\mathsf{lsv},\emptyset,\{y\},\not@} \mathtt{I}[x\backslash\mathtt{I}]\,(y\,\mathtt{I}) \overset{\bullet}{\to}_{\mathsf{db},\emptyset,\{y\},\not@} z[z\backslash y\,\mathtt{I}][x\backslash\mathtt{I}]$$

Conversely, a useful step like $(x\,s)[x\backslash\mathtt{I}] \overset{\bullet}{\to}_{\mathsf{lsv},\emptyset,\emptyset,\not@} (\mathtt{I}\,s)[x\backslash\mathtt{I}]$ may not be allowed if the term is located below a context such as $\lambda y.\,\Diamond$; in fact, note that $\lambda y.\,(x\,s)[x\backslash\mathtt{I}]$ cannot be reduced.

To conclude this section, we show some properties of UCBV beginning with an inductive characterisation of the set of normal forms:

Theorem 1 (Characterisation of Normal Forms). *The set of irreducible terms* $\mathsf{Irred}^{\bullet}_{\mathcal{A},\mathcal{S},\mu}$ *is exactly the set* $\mathsf{NF}^{\bullet}_{\mathcal{A},\mathcal{S},\mu}$ *inductively defined as:*

$$\frac{x \in \mathcal{A} \Rightarrow \mu = \not@}{x \in \mathsf{NF}^{\bullet}_{\mathcal{A},\mathcal{S},\mu}}\,\text{NF-VAR}^{\bullet} \qquad \frac{}{\lambda x.\, t \in \mathsf{NF}^{\bullet}_{\mathcal{A},\mathcal{S},\not@}}\,\text{NF-LAM}^{\bullet}$$

$$\frac{t \in \mathsf{NF}^{\bullet}_{\mathcal{A},\mathcal{S},@} \quad s \in \mathsf{NF}^{\bullet}_{\mathcal{A},\mathcal{S},\not@}}{t\, s \in \mathsf{NF}^{\bullet}_{\mathcal{A},\mathcal{S},\mu}}\,\text{NF-APP}^{\bullet}$$

$$\frac{t \in \mathsf{NF}^{\bullet}_{\mathcal{A}\cup\{x\},\mathcal{S},\mu} \quad s \in \mathsf{NF}^{\bullet}_{\mathcal{A},\mathcal{S},\not@} \quad s \in \mathsf{HA}_{\mathcal{A}}}{t[x\backslash s] \in \mathsf{NF}^{\bullet}_{\mathcal{A},\mathcal{S},\mu}}\,\text{NF-ESA}^{\bullet}$$

$$\frac{t \in \mathsf{NF}^{\bullet}_{\mathcal{A},\mathcal{S}\cup\{x\},\mu} \quad s \in \mathsf{NF}^{\bullet}_{\mathcal{A},\mathcal{S},\not@} \quad s \in \mathsf{St}_{\mathcal{S}}}{t[x\backslash s] \in \mathsf{NF}^{\bullet}_{\mathcal{A},\mathcal{S},\mu}}\,\text{NF-ESS}^{\bullet}$$

Proof. See [10, Corollary B.11].

UCBV enjoys a strong form of confluence, namely the diamond property.

Theorem 2 (Diamond Property). *Let* $t \overset{\bullet}{\to}_{\rho_1,\emptyset,\mathcal{S},\not@} t_1$ *and* $t \overset{\bullet}{\to}_{\rho_2,\emptyset,\mathcal{S},\not@} t_2$, *where* $t_1 \neq t_2$, *and* $\rho_1, \rho_2 \in \{\mathsf{db}, \mathsf{lsv}\}$, *and* $\mathcal{S} = \mathsf{fv}(t)$. *Then, there exists a term* t' *such that* $t_1 \overset{\bullet}{\to}_{\rho_2,\emptyset,\mathcal{S},\not@} t'$ *and* $t_2 \overset{\bullet}{\to}_{\rho_1,\emptyset,\mathcal{S},\not@} t'$.

Proof. The proof follows [10, Proposition B.3 and Proposition B.10].

This result has two consequences:

Corollary 1. *Any two reduction sequences to normal form in* UCBV *have the same number of* db *and* lsv*-steps.*

As with LCBV, *confluence* of UCBV holds only for the *top-level* step kinds db and lsv. Let $\xrightarrow{\bullet}_{\mathsf{top},\mathcal{S}} := \xrightarrow{\bullet}_{\mathsf{db},\emptyset,\mathcal{S},\not\emptyset} \cup \xrightarrow{\bullet}_{\mathsf{lsv},\emptyset,\mathcal{S},\not\emptyset}$ denote the top-level UCBV reduction, then:

Corollary 2. *The reduction* $\xrightarrow{\bullet}_{\mathsf{top},\mathcal{S}}$ *is confluent.*

5 Relating Linear and Useful Call-by-Value

This section formally relates LCBV and UCBV, defined respectively in Sects. 3 and 4. We show that *usefulness* in UCBV is a (complete) restriction of LCBV: UCBV evaluates to *equivalent* normal forms while omitting certain substitution steps, specifically those that do not contribute to the creation of db-redexes.

Simulating LCBV with UCBV is straightforward, as each UCBV step is also a LCBV step, as we mention in Sect. 4. However, relating both calculi in the opposite direction is much more delicate, since not all LCBV steps are useful: UCBV disallows some substitution steps that LCBV allows. For example, the step $t = (x\,y)[y\backslash\mathtt{I}] \xrightarrow{\circ} (x\,\mathtt{I})[y\backslash\mathtt{I}] = s$ is not useful. Indeed, t is a normal form in UCBV, whereas in LCBV it is a redex whose normal form is s.

Although normal forms differ between the two formalisms, they are *structurally equivalent*, as LCBV evaluates terms further than UCBV. To relate them precisely, we restrict the standard notion of unfolding to a subtler one. Indeed, recall that in calculi with ESs the (full) unfolding of a term is an operation that performs *all* substitutions. In this section, however, the notion of unfolding must be defined in a controlled way. For example, (fully) unfolding the term $x[x\backslash\mathtt{I}]$, which is a normal form in UCBV, yields the corresponding normal form $\mathtt{I}[y\backslash\mathtt{I}]$ in LCBV. Yet the new notion of the unfolding operation will not need to unfold *all* ESs. For example, in LCBV, $(\lambda x.\,y)[y\backslash\mathtt{I}]$ is not unfolded to $(\lambda x.\,\mathtt{I})[y\backslash\mathtt{I}]$ (due to weak evaluation), and $x[x\backslash y\,y]$ is not unfolded to $(y\,y)[x\backslash y\,y]$ (since variables are never substituted by structures). Intuitively, the new notion of the unfolding operation selectively performs only those substitutions on *reachable* variables bound to values, which is why this new operation is called *partial unfolding*.

The remainder of this section is organised as follows. We first define the partial unfolding of a term t. We then relate LCBV and UCBV via two technical results (Proposition 3), showing that (i) the partial unfolding of normal forms in UCBV always yields a normal form in LCBV, and (ii) redexes in UCBV remain reducible in LCBV.

Partial Unfolding. By Proposition 1 we know that $\xrightarrow{\circ}_{\mathsf{lsv}}$ is confluent. Moreover, $\xrightarrow{\circ}_{\mathsf{lsv}}$ can be shown to be terminating [10, Corollary C.15]. As a consequence, any term t has a unique $\xrightarrow{\circ}_{\mathsf{lsv}}$-normal form.

Relying on the previous observation, we define the **partial unfolding** of a term t, written $t^{\downarrow}$, as the unique $\overset{\circ}{\to}_{\mathsf{lsv}}$-normal form of t. For instance, one has $x[x\backslash y\,y][y\backslash \mathtt{I}]^{\downarrow} = (\mathtt{I}\,\mathtt{I})[x\backslash \mathtt{I}\,\mathtt{I}][y\backslash \mathtt{I}]$. Note that all the ESs in the original term remain on the resulting term and that some occurrences of variables are not substituted, because the occurrence may be below an abstraction, as in $((\lambda y.\, x)\, x)[x\backslash \mathtt{I}]^{\downarrow} = ((\lambda y.\, x)\, \mathtt{I})[x\backslash \mathtt{I}]$, or because the variable may be bound to a structure, as in $(x\,x)[x\backslash z\,z]^{\downarrow} = (x\,x)[x\backslash z\,z]$.

Relating Reduction Steps and Normal Forms. We now formally state the existing relation between LCBV and UCBV. Our goal is to show that UCBV simulates LCBV while reaching equivalent normal forms, up to partial unfolding. To do this, we state a proposition, consisting of two parts: (1) the partial unfolding of a useful normal form is a linear normal form, and (2) the partial unfolding of a reducible term in UCBV is either a db-redex in LCBV or an abstraction in an applied position. This second condition justifies the name "useful" in UCBV because it implies that any substitution step in the strategy must contribute to the creation of a db-redex (see Sect. 1).

Recall that $\overset{\circ}{\to}_{\mathsf{top}}$ and $\overset{\bullet}{\to}_{\mathsf{top},\mathcal{S}}$ denote top-level LCBV and UCBV reduction. The following proposition links LCBV and UCBV reductions at the top-level case:

Proposition 3 (Soundness and Completeness). *Let t be a term and $\mathcal{S} = \mathsf{fv}(t)$. Then:*

1. *If t is $\overset{\bullet}{\to}_{\mathsf{top},\mathcal{S}}$-irreducible, then $t^{\downarrow}$ is $\overset{\circ}{\to}_{\mathsf{top}}$-irreducible.*
2. *If $t \overset{\bullet}{\to}_{\mathsf{top},\mathcal{S}} t'$, then there exists t'' such that $t^{\downarrow} \overset{\circ}{\to}_{\mathsf{db}} t''$.*

Proof. The proof follows from [10, Proposition C.25], as it is a particular case of such proposition.

To illustrate statement 1, $(x\,y)[y\backslash \mathtt{I}]$ is $\overset{\bullet}{\to}_{\mathsf{top},\{x\}}$-irreducible, and its partial unfolding is $(x\,\mathtt{I})[y\backslash \mathtt{I}]$, which is $\overset{\circ}{\to}_{\mathsf{top}}$-irreducible. As an example of statement 2, consider the lsv-step $t = (x\,y)[x\backslash \mathtt{I}] \overset{\bullet}{\to}_{\mathsf{top},\{y\}} (\mathtt{I}\,y)[x\backslash \mathtt{I}] = t' = t^{\downarrow}$; note that $t' \overset{\circ}{\to}_{\mathsf{db}} x_1[x_1\backslash x][y\backslash \mathtt{I}]$. From these results, we conclude:

Corollary 3. *A term t is $\overset{\bullet}{\to}_{\mathsf{top},\mathsf{fv}(t)}$-irreducible if and only if $t^{\downarrow}$ is $\overset{\circ}{\to}_{\mathsf{top}}$-irreducible.*

6 Useful Call-by-Value is Invariant

In this section, we relate our UCBV strategy to an existing definition of usefulness in the literature, namely, to the GLAMoUr abstract machine [2]. As a consequence, we obtain that UCBV is *time-invariant, i.e.*, that the number of reduction steps to normal form can be used as a measure of time complexity.

The main result of this section is Theorem 3, stating that reduction in UCBV can be implemented by the GLAMoUr abstract machine with *linear* overhead in time. The key property to prove this implementation result is Proposition 4, which embeds the GLAMoUr abstract machine within UCBV.

Informal Discussion. The definitions and proofs to embed the GLAMoUr abstract machine in UCBV follow well-known methodologies (*e.g.* [1,2,4]). In particular, we first define a *decoding* function that maps each state s of the GLAMoUr machine to a term $\{\!\!\{s\}\!\!\}$ with ESs. As a second step, one would like to show that each transition step $s \rightsquigarrow s'$ in the GLAMoUr can be simulated by the UCBV strategy in at most one step, *i.e.* $\{\!\!\{s\}\!\!\} \xrightarrow{\bullet}^{=} \{\!\!\{s'\}\!\!\}$.[4] It is well-known that this does not suffice in general, because abstract machines usually keep the *code* (a term without ESs) an the *environment* (a list of ESs) as independent components, while the UCBV strategy allows ESs to be scattered throughout the term. This means that one can only prove a slightly weaker simulation result, namely that $\{\!\!\{s\}\!\!\} \xrightarrow{\bullet}^{=} t$ for some term t that differs from $\{\!\!\{s'\}\!\!\}$ only in the positions of some of the ESs.

To bridge this gap, we define a notion of *structural equivalence* between terms $t \equiv s$ that allows ESs to float around. The simulation result then shows that each transition $s \rightsquigarrow s'$ can be simulated by the UCBV strategy in at most one step *up to structural equivalence*, *i.e.* that $\{\!\!\{s\}\!\!\} \xrightarrow{\bullet}^{=} \equiv \{\!\!\{s'\}\!\!\}$.

Finally, to simulate the GLAMoUr with UCBV, one would also need to show that structural equivalence is a strong bisimulation with respect to the UCBV strategy, *i.e.* that if $t \equiv s$ then every UCBV step $t \xrightarrow{\bullet} t'$ can be simulated by a corresponding step $s \xrightarrow{\bullet} s'$ such that $t' \equiv s'$. Unfortunately, this result fails. Indeed, structural equivalence should allow commuting an ES with an application, *i.e.* $t[x\backslash u]\, s \equiv (t\, s)[x\backslash u]$ provided that $x \notin \mathsf{fv}(s)$. But a reduction step on the right-hand side: $t[x\backslash u]\, s \xrightarrow{\bullet} t[x\backslash u]\, s'$ cannot always be simulated by a reduction step on the left-hand side: $(t\, s)[x\backslash u] \xrightarrow{\bullet} (t\, s')[x\backslash u]$. The problem is that the UCBV strategy only allows to reduce inside the body of a closure ($t\, s$ in the example) when the argument u is *rigid*, *i.e.* a structure or a hereditary abstraction.

To resolve this, we technically need to impose an invariant on terms, requiring that the arguments of ESs always be rigid. This invariant is obviously satisfied by any initial term without ESs. Moreover, having this invariant ensures that in the equivalence $t[x\backslash u]\, s \equiv (t\, s)[x\backslash u]$ the argument u is rigid, and thus a reduction step internal to s on the right-hand side can be simulated by a reduction step on the left-hand side. Furthermore, to ensure that reduction preserves this invariant, we need to restrict to a subrelation of the UCBV strategy, $\xrightarrow{\blacktriangle}_{\rho,\mathcal{A},\mathcal{S},\mu} \subseteq \xrightarrow{\bullet}_{\rho,\mathcal{A},\mathcal{S},\mu}$, that we dub *stable reduction*. With these ingredients, we can show that each transition in the GLAMoUr machine can be simulated by at most one *stable* reduction step in UCBV, up to structural equivalence.

Stable Terms and Stable Reduction. Given an abstraction frame $\mathcal{A}$ and a structure frame $\mathcal{S}$, a term t is said to be **rigid** under $(\mathcal{A}, \mathcal{S})$ if $t \in \mathsf{HA}_{\mathcal{A}}$ or $t \in \mathsf{St}_{\mathcal{S}}$. In UCBV, evaluating a closure $t[x\backslash s]$ with abstraction frame $\mathcal{A}$ and structure frame $\mathcal{S}$ proceeds in t only when the argument s is rigid under $(\mathcal{A}, \mathcal{S})$. To better align with low-level abstract machines, we define the set of **stable terms** under $(\mathcal{A}, \mathcal{S})$ as those in which every ES argument is rigid. We also introduce **stable**

[4] We omit the parameters for $\xrightarrow{\bullet}$ in this informal discussion.

reduction $\xrightarrow{\blacktriangle}_{\rho,\mathcal{A},\mathcal{S},\mu}$, such that $\xrightarrow{\blacktriangle}_{\rho,\mathcal{A},\mathcal{S},\mu} \subseteq \xrightarrow{\bullet}_{\rho,\mathcal{A},\mathcal{S},\mu}$. Sometimes we write $\xrightarrow{\blacktriangle}$ if the parameters are clear from the context. Stable reduction forces arguments of applications to be rigid before reduction proceeds. Thus in this setting, rule $\text{APPL}^{\bullet}$ permits evaluating the head of an application $t\,s$ only if s is rigid, and rule $\text{DB}^{\bullet}$ allows to contract a db-redex only if its argument is rigid. Stable reduction preserves stable terms and enjoys the diamond property.

The GLAMoUr Abstract Machine. We start by briefly recalling the syntax of the GLAMoUr. Full details on the GLAMoUr transitions and the remaining definitions can be found in [2,4,10].

The syntax of the GLAMoUr is given by the following grammar, defining **states** $(s, s', \ldots)$, **dumps** $(D, D', \ldots)$, **stacks** $(\pi, \pi', \ldots)$, **stack items** $(\phi, \psi, \ldots)$, and **environments** $(E, E', \ldots)$:

$$\begin{array}{ll} s ::= (D, \mathbf{t}, \pi, E) & D ::= \epsilon \mid D : (\mathbf{t}, \pi) \\ \pi ::= \epsilon \mid \phi^l : \pi & \phi ::= \mathbf{t} \mid (\mathbf{t}, \pi) \\ E ::= \epsilon \mid [x \backslash \phi^l] : E & \end{array}$$

where $l \in \{\mathbb{A}, \mathbb{S}\}$ are **labels** decorating stack items. Here, **codes** $(\mathbf{t}, \mathbf{s}, \ldots)$ are terms with no ESs, but they are **not** considered up to α-equivalence. By convention, labels indicate the shape of ϕ. In particular, $l = \mathbb{A}$ if and only if ϕ is of the form $\mathbf{t}$, and $l = \mathbb{S}$ if and only if ϕ is of the form $(\mathbf{t}, \pi)$. Intuitively, these labels indicate whether a stack item unfolds to a hereditary abstraction ($\mathbb{A}$) or to a structure ($\mathbb{S}$). In a state $s = (D, \mathbf{t}, \pi, E)$, the code $\mathbf{t}$ is called the **focus** of s. A state s_0 is **initial** if it is of the form $s_0 = (\epsilon, \mathbf{t}, \epsilon, \epsilon)$.

There are seven kinds of transitions in the GLAMoUr: transitions $(s \rightsquigarrow_{\mathsf{um}} s')$ for function applications, transitions $(s \rightsquigarrow_{\mathsf{ue}} s')$ for linear substitutions, and *administrative* transitions $s \rightsquigarrow_{\mathsf{c}_i} s'$ with $i \in \{1..5\}$, for changing the evaluation focus without computing. Formally, the transitions of the GLAMoUr abstract machine are:

D	$\mathbf{t}\,\mathbf{u}$	π	E	$\rightsquigarrow_{\mathsf{c}_1}$	$D : (\mathbf{t}, \pi)$	$\mathbf{u}$	ϵ	E
D	$\lambda\mathbf{x}.\,\mathbf{t}$	$\phi^l : \pi$	E	$\rightsquigarrow_{\mathsf{um}}$	D	$\mathbf{t}$	π	$[x \backslash \phi^l] : E$
$D : (\mathbf{t}, \pi)$	$\lambda\mathbf{x}.\,\mathbf{u}$	ϵ	E	$\rightsquigarrow_{\mathsf{c}_2}$	D	$\mathbf{t}$	$(\lambda\mathbf{x}.\,\mathbf{u})^{\mathbb{A}} : \pi$	E
$D : (\mathbf{t}, \pi)$	$\mathbf{x}$	π'	E	$\rightsquigarrow_{\mathsf{c}_3}$	D	$\mathbf{t}$	$(\mathbf{x}, \pi')^{\mathbb{S}} : \pi$	E
$D : (\mathbf{t}, \pi)$	$\mathbf{x}$	π'	$E_1 : [x \backslash \phi^{\mathbb{S}}] : E_2$	$\rightsquigarrow_{\mathsf{c}_4}$	D	$\mathbf{t}$	$(\mathbf{x}, \pi')^{\mathbb{S}} : \pi$	$E_1 : [x \backslash \phi^{\mathbb{S}}] : E_2$
$D : (\mathbf{t}, \pi)$	$\mathbf{x}$	ϵ	$E_1 : [x \backslash \mathbf{u}^{\mathbb{A}}] : E_2$	$\rightsquigarrow_{\mathsf{c}_5}$	D	$\mathbf{t}$	$\mathbf{x}^{\mathbb{A}} : \pi$	$E_1 : [x \backslash \mathbf{u}^{\mathbb{A}}] : E_2$
D	$\mathbf{x}$	$\phi^l : \pi$	$E_1 : [x \backslash \mathbf{u}^{\mathbb{A}}] : E_2$	$\rightsquigarrow_{\mathsf{ue}}$	D	$\mathbf{u}^{\alpha}$	$\phi^l : \pi$	$E_1 : [x \backslash \mathbf{u}^{\mathbb{A}}] : E_2$

where $\mathbf{s}^{\alpha}$ is any code α-equivalent to $\mathbf{s}$ that preserves the well-naming of the machine. Moreover, in the transition $\rightsquigarrow_{\mathsf{c}_3}$, the variable $\mathbf{x}$ does not belong to the domain of environment E. The domain of an environment E is written $\mathtt{dom}(E)$ and is defined recursively by $\mathtt{dom}(\epsilon) := \emptyset$ and $\mathtt{dom}([x \backslash \phi^l] : E') := \{x\} \cup \mathtt{dom}(E')$.

Embedding the GLAMoUr into Useful Call-by-Value. Each GLAMoUr state s can be **decoded** into a term $\{\!\{s\}\!\}$ with ESs—note that this is exactly the decoding used in [10, Subsection D.1.1]:

- Decoding of states: $\{\!\{(D, \mathbf{t}, \pi, E)\}\!\} := \{\!\{E\}\!\}\langle \{\!\{D\}\!\}\langle \{\!\{\pi\}\!\}\langle t \rangle\rangle\rangle$.

- Decoding of dumps: $\{\!\{\epsilon\}\!\} := \Diamond$ and $\{\!\{D : (\mathbf{t}, \pi)\}\!\} := \{\!\{D\}\!\}\langle\{\!\{\pi\}\!\}\langle t\Diamond\rangle\rangle$.
- Decoding of stacks: $\{\!\{\epsilon\}\!\} := \Diamond$ and $\{\!\{\phi^l : \pi\}\!\} := \{\!\{\pi\}\!\}\langle\Diamond\{\!\{\phi^l\}\!\}\rangle$.
- Decoding of codes: $\{\!\{\mathbf{t}\}\!\} := t$, where t is the α-equivalence class of $\mathbf{t}$.
- Decoding of stack items: $\{\!\{(\mathbf{t}, \pi)^l\}\!\} := \{\!\{\pi\}\!\}\langle\{\!\{\mathbf{t}\}\!\}\rangle$ and $\{\!\{\mathbf{t}^l\}\!\} := \{\!\{\mathbf{t}\}\!\}$.
- Decoding of environments: $\{\!\{\epsilon\}\!\} := \Diamond$ and $\{\!\{[x\backslash\phi^l] : E\}\!\} := \{\!\{E\}\!\}\langle\Diamond[x\backslash\{\!\{\phi^l\}\!\}]\rangle$.

As discussed before, the GLAMoUr abstract machine can be simulated in UCBV up to **structural equivalence** of terms [3], denoted $\equiv$, defined as the least equivalence relation closed by weak contexts (*i.e.*, contexts that do not enter inside abstractions) of the four following axioms:

$$\begin{array}{rlrl} t[x\backslash s][y\backslash u] &\equiv t[y\backslash u][x\backslash s] & t[x\backslash s][y\backslash u] &\equiv t[x\backslash s[y\backslash u]] \\ (t\, s)[x\backslash u] &\equiv t[x\backslash u]\, s & (t\, s)[x\backslash u] &\equiv t\, s[x\backslash u] \end{array}$$

All these axioms assume that variable-capture is avoided, for example, the first equation assumes that $x \notin \mathsf{fv}(u)$ and $y \notin \mathsf{fv}(s)$.

The main technical result of this section is the following:

Proposition 4 (GLAMoUr Simulation). *Let s be a state reachable from an initial state with focus t_0 and let $\mathcal{S}_0 := \mathsf{fv}(t_0)$. Then:*

1. *If $s \rightsquigarrow_{\mathsf{um}} s'$, then $\{\!\{s\}\!\} \xrightarrow{\blacktriangle}_{\mathsf{db}}\equiv \{\!\{s'\}\!\}$.*
2. *If $s \rightsquigarrow_{\mathsf{ue}} s'$, then $\{\!\{s\}\!\} \xrightarrow{\blacktriangle}_{\mathsf{lsv}}\equiv \{\!\{s'\}\!\}$.*
3. *If $s \rightsquigarrow_{\mathsf{c}_i} s'$, then $\{\!\{s\}\!\} = \{\!\{s'\}\!\}$, for all $i \in \{1..5\}$.*
4. *If s is $\rightsquigarrow$-irreducible, then $\{\!\{s\}\!\}$ is $\xrightarrow{\blacktriangle}$-irreducible (progress property).*

Proof. See [10, Lemma 6.1].

As a consequence, any *sequence* of GLAMoUr transitions corresponds to a *sequence* of (stable) UCBV reduction steps interleaved with equivalences. For this correspondence, we need Lemma 1, stating that $\equiv$ is a strong bisimulation with respect to $\xrightarrow{\blacktriangle}$, for ensuring a postponement property.

Lemma 1 (Strong Bisimulation). *Let t_0 and s_0 be stable terms such that $s_0 \equiv t_0$. If $t_0 \xrightarrow{\blacktriangle}_{\rho,\mathcal{A},\mathcal{S},\mu} t_1$, then there exists s_1 such that $s_0 \xrightarrow{\blacktriangle}_{\rho,\mathcal{A},\mathcal{S},\mu} s_1 \equiv t_1$.*

Proof. See [10, Lemma 6.2].

This result relies crucially on the stability notion introduced earlier in this section: if u is not stable, equivalences like $t[x\backslash s][y\backslash u] \equiv t[y\backslash u][x\backslash s]$ cannot be postponed after the (non-stable) step $t[y\backslash u][x\backslash s] \xrightarrow{\bullet} t[y\backslash u][x\backslash s']$ because rules like ESLA$^\bullet$ and ESLS$^\bullet$ cannot apply when u is not rigid.

Based on the previous results, we can now present the main result of this section: UCBV can be implemented in the GLAMoUr with bilinear overhead in time, as a function of the size of the starting term and the length of the reduction sequence to normal form.

Theorem 3 (Bilinear Simulation of UCBV). *Let t be a term with no ESs. If $t \xrightarrow{\blacktriangle}^n t'$, where t' is in normal form and s is an initial state such that $\{\!\{s\}\!\} = t$, then $s \rightsquigarrow^k s'$, where $\{\!\{s'\}\!\} \equiv t'$ and $k \in O(|t| \cdot (n+1))$.*

Proof. See [10, Theorem 6.3].

In turn, this entails that UCBV is time-invariant, *i.e.*, that it can be simulated with at most polynomial overhead by a time-invariant cost model (such as Turing machines or RAMs):

Corollary 4. *The* UCBV *strategy is time-invariant.*

7 Conclusions

This paper proposes an inductive specification of usefulness for open CBV evaluation called UCBV, that contrasts with previous notions of usefulness in CBN, CBV, and call-by-need that are non-inductive. Our specification is inspired by the definition of strong call-by-need evaluation in [8]. Although these strategies are very different, one point in common is that they crucially depend on the information of the surrounding evaluation context, reflected in the form of parameters.

We show that UCBV is sound and complete with respect to LCBV, in the sense that, given a starting term, LCBV and UCBV compute the same normal form, up to unfolding. We also show that the LCBV calculus which implements linear substitution is observationally equivalent to the VSC. Our last contribution is establishing a relation between UCBV and an existing definition of usefulness in the literature, the GLAMoUr abstract machine [2].

Benefits of an Inductive Approach. The inductive formulation of useful evaluation is the key that has enabled us to define a *semantic model* for useful open CBV. In particular, our formulation of usefulness turned out to be appropriate to be captured by a *non-idempotent intersection type system* [11,12]. Semantic models are *compositional*, in the sense that the meaning of a program is defined inductively, in terms of the meanings of its subprograms. The inductive approach that we propose in this paper allowed us to reason about its semantics in a compositional way.[5]

Another benefit of an inductive definition of useful CBV is that all the invariants of key properties become explicit, making such notion closer to being formalised along with its results in an interactive proof assistant.

Finally, we think that the techniques and tools developed in this paper could be adapted to other evaluation strategies, and in particular to other context-sensitive notions of evaluation, such as useful CBN, whose formulation is not inductive [6]. A challenging question is how to extend our specification of usefulness to *strong* CBV so that evaluation is also allowed under abstractions. This

[5] The semantic study is outside the scope of this paper, but it can be found in the associated technical report [10].

is relevant for the implementation of proof assistants based on dependent type theory, in which type checking requires to decide the definitional equality of type expressions up to full β-conversion, thus requiring strong evaluation. Even more challenging would be to adapt all this technology to call-by-need, and to call-by-push-value.

Acknowledgments. *This project has received funding from the EU Horizon 2020 research and innovation programme under the MSCA grant No 945332.*

Disclosure of Interests. The authors have no competing interests to declare that are relevant to the content of this article.

References

1. Accattoli, B., Barenbaum, P., Mazza, D.: Distilling abstract machines. In: Jeuring, J., Chakravarty, M.M.T. (eds.) Proceedings of the 19th ACM SIGPLAN International Conference on Functional Programming, Gothenburg, Sweden, 1–3 September 2014, pp. 363–376. ACM (2014)
2. Accattoli, B., Coen, C.S.: On the relative usefulness of fireballs. In: 30th Annual ACM/IEEE Symposium on Logic in Computer Science, LICS 2015, Kyoto, Japan, 6–10 July 2015, pp. 141–155. IEEE Computer Society (2015). https://doi.org/10.1109/LICS.2015.23
3. Accattoli, B., Guerrieri, G.: Open call-by-value. In: Igarashi, A. (ed.) APLAS 2016. LNCS, vol. 10017, pp. 206–226. Springer, Cham (2016). https://doi.org/10.1007/978-3-319-47958-3_12
4. Accattoli, B., Guerrieri, G.: Implementing open call-by-value. In: Dastani, M., Sirjani, M. (eds.) FSEN 2017. LNCS, vol. 10522, pp. 1–19. Springer, Cham (2017). https://doi.org/10.1007/978-3-319-68972-2_1
5. Accattoli, B., Guerrieri, G.: Abstract machines for open call-by-value. Sci. Comput. Program. **184** (2019). https://doi.org/10.1016/J.SCICO.2019.03.002
6. Accattoli, B., Lago, U.D.: Beta reduction is invariant, indeed. In: Henzinger, T.A., Miller, D. (eds.) Joint Meeting of the Twenty-Third EACSL Annual Conference on Computer Science Logic (CSL) and the Twenty-Ninth Annual ACM/IEEE Symposium on Logic in Computer Science (LICS), CSL-LICS 2014, Vienna, Austria, 14–18 July 2014, pp. 8:1–8:10. ACM (2014). https://doi.org/10.1145/2603088.2603105
7. Accattoli, B., Paolini, L.: Call-by-value solvability, revisited. In: Schrijvers, T., Thiemann, P. (eds.) FLOPS 2012. LNCS, vol. 7294, pp. 4–16. Springer, Heidelberg (2012). https://doi.org/10.1007/978-3-642-29822-6_4
8. Balabonski, T., Lanco, A., Melquiond, G.: A strong call-by-need calculus. Log. Methods Comput. Sci. **19**(1) (2023)
9. Barenbaum, P., Kesner, D., Milicich, M.: Semantic equivalence between the linear call-by-value calculus and the value substitution calculus (technical note) (2025). https://www.irif.fr/_media/users/milicich/technicalnotelcbv.pdf
10. Barenbaum, P., Kesner, D., Milicich, M.: Useful evaluation: syntax and semantics (technical report) (2025). https://arxiv.org/abs/2404.18874
11. Carvalho, D.D.: Sémantiques de la logique linéaire et temps de calcul. Ph.D. thesis, Ecole Doctorale Physique et Sciences de la Matière (Marseille) (2007)

12. Gardner, P.: Discovering needed reductions using type theory. In: Hagiya, M., Mitchell, J.C. (eds.) TACS 1994. LNCS, vol. 789, pp. 555–574. Springer, Heidelberg (1994). https://doi.org/10.1007/3-540-57887-0_115
13. Grégoire, B., Leroy, X.: A compiled implementation of strong reduction. In: Wand, M., Jones, S.L.P. (eds.) Proceedings of the Seventh ACM SIGPLAN International Conference on Functional Programming (ICFP 2002), Pittsburgh, Pennsylvania, USA, 4–6 October 2002, pp. 235–246. ACM (2002). https://doi.org/10.1145/581478.581501
14. Kesner, D.: A theory of explicit substitutions with safe and full composition. Log. Methods Comput. Sci. **5**(3) (2009). http://arxiv.org/abs/0905.2539
15. Slot, C.F., van Emde Boas, P.: On tape versus core; an application of space efficient perfect hash functions to the invariance of space. In: DeMillo, R.A. (ed.) Proceedings of the 16th Annual ACM Symposium on Theory of Computing, 30 April–2 May 1984, Washington, DC, USA, pp. 391–400. ACM (1984). https://doi.org/10.1145/800057.808705
16. Terese: Term Rewriting Systems, Cambridge Tracts in Theoretical Computer Science, vol. 55. Cambridge University Press (2003)
17. Yoshida, N.: Optimal reduction in weak-λ-calculus with shared environments. In: Proceedings of the Conference on Functional Programming Languages and Computer Architecture, FPCA 1993, pp. 243–252. Association for Computing Machinery, New York (1993). https://doi.org/10.1145/165180.165217

Machine Learning for Automated Deduction

Efficient Neural Clause-Selection Reinforcement

Martin Suda(✉)

Czech Technical University in Prague, Prague, Czech Republic
martin.suda@cvut.cz

Abstract. Clause selection is arguably the most important choice point in saturation-based theorem proving. Framing it as a reinforcement learning (RL) task is a way to challenge the human-designed heuristics of state-of-the-art provers and to instead automatically evolve—just from prover experiences—their potentially optimal replacement.

In this work, we present a neural network architecture for scoring clauses for clause selection that is powerful yet efficient to evaluate. Following RL principles to make design decisions, we integrate the network into the VAMPIRE theorem prover and train it from successful proof attempts. An experiment on the diverse TPTP benchmark finds the neurally guided prover improves over a baseline strategy, from which it initially learns—in terms of the number of in-training-unseen problems solved under a practically relevant, short CPU instruction limit—by 20%.

Keywords: Saturation-based Theorem Proving · Clause Selection · Deep Reinforcement Learning

1 Introduction

Reinforcement learning (RL) [38] is a machine learning (ML) paradigm in which an agent learns to make sequential decisions by interacting with an environment and maximizing cumulative rewards. The impressive successes of RL in board games [30] or on the Atari benchmark [23] motivate researchers to apply RL to their own domains of interest. It is exciting to have an unsupervised method search for a decision strategy unbiased by our human preconceptions, since this intuitively increases the chances of discovering brand new approaches.

In automatic theorem proving (ATP), we have seen the Monte-Carlo tree search [16] guide a connection tableaux prover [15, 42] or, more recently, proximal policy optimization [27] applied to dynamically pick clause selection queues [29] in a saturation-based prover [22]. Despite these achievements, substantial performance improvements over the state of the art have so far only been reported for systems employing the more straightforward supervised learning methods [6, 13, 32]. Moreover, the published results predominantly focus on problem sets with a common origin and encoding, such as the Mizar40 set [14], arguably more

C. Barrett and U. Waldmann (Eds.): CADE 2025, LNAI 15943, pp. 403–422, 2025.
https://doi.org/10.1007/978-3-031-99984-0_22

amenable to ML techniques than the canonical theorem proving benchmark used by the CASC [36] competition, the TPTP library [37].

In this work, we apply a policy gradient RL method [41] to train a neural-network-based clause selection heuristic for the ATP Vampire [17]. As a highly optimized system, Vampire can generate and evaluate thousands to millions of clauses within seconds. Not to impede the prover's high inference speed with the new guidance, we design a neural network architecture that is powerful yet efficient to evaluate (Sect. 4). Analyzing clause selection through the lens of RL (Sect. 3), we propose a new learning operator for iteratively improving the network's performance from successful proof attempts (Sect. 3.1). We adopt a rather counterintuitive idea in this context and ignore the concept of a state to make our agent govern a single, standalone clause selection queue (Sect. 5).

Even on the diverse TPTP benchmark, our new system is able to improve over Vampire's default strategy, from which it initially learns, by 20%. This is done in a sanitized setting (using a train/test split) and for practically relevant proving times of approximately 10s per problem. Moreover, we find that the trained neurally-guided Vampire solves more than 100 problems of rating 1.0, roughly half of which have not been recorded as proven by any system to date. Improvements of this magnitude are exceptionally rare in the literature, particularly in terms of solving previously unrecorded problems.

After the experiments (Sect. 6), the paper reviews related work (Sect. 7) and ends with a conclusion with outlooks for future work (Sect. 8). Several appendices with additional details are available as part of a preprint [35].

2 Background

In this section, we review the basic concepts related to saturation-based theorem proving and reinforcement learning.

2.1 Saturation-Based Theorem Proving

The most successful provers for first-order logic such as E [28], iProver [7], SPASS [40] or Vampire [17], are *refutational*, based on *saturation*. The former means they aim for a proof by contradiction: Given an input problem P consisting of a set of axioms $\mathcal{A}_P$ and a conjecture G_P, they start by negating the conjecture and computing an equisatisfiable clause normal form $\mathit{CNF}(\mathcal{A}_P \cup \{\neg G_P\}) = C_P$ and then set out to show that this set of clauses C_P is unsatisfiable.

During the saturation process which follows, the provers strive to compute a closure of these clauses with respect to a selected inference system $\mathcal{I}$. Saturation is most often implemented by a *given-clause algorithm*, which keeps track of inferences by working with two sets of clauses: the *active* set $\mathcal{A}$ (initially empty) and the *passive* set $\mathcal{P}$ (initialized with the input clauses). It maintains an invariant that every inference with all premises in $\mathcal{A}$ has already been performed. Iteratively, a clause C is *selected* from $\mathcal{P}$, moved to $\mathcal{A}$ (and thus *activated*), and all inferences with at least one premise being C and others coming from $\mathcal{A}$ are computed and their conclusions are added to $\mathcal{P}$.

There are several variants of the given-clause algorithm [26]. They mostly differ in how they deal with simplifications and redundancy elimination, a crucial topic for performance, but not immediately relevant for our exposition.

Clause Selection: Heuristics are employed to decide, in each iteration, which clause from $\mathcal{P}$ to select next for activation. An imagined perfect heuristic would only select clauses from the yet-to-be-discovered proof (all other selections constitute, in retrospect, a wasted effort). Such an ideal, however, must be intractable to compute as it would essentially eliminate search from the proving task. In practice, it is thus important with clause selection to carefully trade between the quality of the decisions and the computational effort spent on making them.

Provers typically implement the passive clause container as a collection of *priority queues*, each queue representing $\mathcal{P}$ sorted by a distinct *clause evaluation function* (CEF). The two most commonly used CEFs are *age* and *weight*, the first encoding a preference for older clauses and the second a preference for clauses with fewer symbols. The prover then alternates between the queues under a specified *ratio* (called the pick-given ratio in OTTER's manual [21]) and selects the best clause from the current queue in each iteration.

2.2 Reinforcement Learning

Reinforcement Learning (RL) is an optimization framework that enables an *agent* to learn an optimal decision-making *policy* through trial and error by interacting with an *environment* and receiving feedback in the form of a *reward*. In what follows, we quickly summarize the main RL concepts; we refer the interested reader to a standard textbook [38] for a thorough formal treatment.

We focus here on a conceptualization of RL via finite Markov Decision Processes (MPDs), in which time is modeled as passing in discrete steps. In each step, the agent reflects on the current *state* s of the environment and correspondingly chooses one of possible *actions* to take. One time step later, in part as a consequence of the chosen action a, the agent receives a numerical reward r and finds itself in a new state s'. This transition (including the reward) is in general stochastic, specified by a probability distribution $p(s', r \mid s, a)$.

A policy is a mapping from states to probabilities of selecting each of the available actions, denoted $\pi(a \mid s)$. A *value* $v(s)_\pi$ of a state s under a policy π is the expected *return*, i.e., the reward accumulated (optionally under discounting) over a trajectory starting at s and following π. RL optimizes a policy to maximize the expected return (from any state). Thus, aiming for a high reward in the distance can be more important than collecting mediocre rewards immediately.

3 Clause Selection Reinforcement

Let us consider a standard clause selection heuristic like the age-weight alternation, as if driven by an RL agent. Such an agent monitors the prover's state and chooses appropriate actions to reach the goal of deriving the empty clause, ideally in the smallest number of steps possible. Our idea is to use this perspective to guide our decisions about the design of a new agent for the task, backed by a neural network and learned through reinforcement from proving experiences.

One of our aims is to make sure that the new design accommodates the old heuristic as an attainable point in the space of possible solutions. This provides for a useful sanity check, as well as a good promise for the potential to go beyond the state of the art, at least as long as the computational overhead stays relatively low and there is anything new and relevant to learn from the data.

State. The environment's states arise from the actual prover states via an abstraction that forgets any information not relevant for the agent's decisions. This natural modeling step carries along the mentioned computational tradeoff: the more information the agent receives the more precise its decisions can in principle be, however, at the same time, the more expensive may the deciding become.

We can split the information relevant for clause selection into two conceptual parts: a *static* part, the problem P given as input, and an *evolving* part, consisting of any information changing during the proving process and influencing the preferences for clause selection. This second part allows the agent to have a plan: "First select a clause like this, when done go and select a clause like that".

Surprisingly, state-of-the-art provers, backed by decades of research and experimentation, mostly ignore the evolving part for clause selection.[1] Except possibly for a few bits to remember which queue to select the next clause from,[2] the state's evolution is ignored and each selection aims greedily at the best available clause. This could be mostly for efficiency reasons; after all, if the selection preferences were to change from state to state, we could no longer cheaply keep the passive set represented as an ordered queue. On a more abstract level, it is not clear how to take an advantage of the evolving state of a saturation-based prover, consisting—at its generality—of the content of the active and passive set, large and quickly growing, but otherwise rather amorphous sets of clauses.[3]

Speculations aside, we take this observation as an indication that proof planning is not a viable approach to general-purpose saturation-based proving (in its contemporary form) and bake the assumption of trivial, single-state—effectively *stateless*—environment into our design. In a nutshell, this means we will not allow the agent to change its opinion about a clause during the prover run.

Actions. At each iteration of the saturation loop, clause selection picks one of the clauses in the passive set for activation. We therefore equate the set of available actions (at a given moment) with the current content of the passive set.

[1] Static state enters the picture when selecting proving strategies or strategy schedules.

[2] Although, within the RL framework, deterministic queue alternation might best be seen as a poor man's implementation of a probabilistic choice.

[3] Perhaps in contrast to some other methods, a state in saturation-based proving might best be understood as a meta-state, representing concurrent searches for many possible proofs at once, in analogy to the state of the A^* algorithm with many open nodes, representing all the currently considered promising paths to a goal.

A slightly strange consequence of this decision—in combination with the assumption that the score of a clause (as computed by a neural network) should not change from one moment to the next—is that this single score must allow the clause to play the role of a bad decision when currently also accompanied by more promising clauses on the passive set, while at the same time being the score of the best choice when all other passive clauses look worse. We will see, however, that this mild oddity is no hurdle to learning in practice.

Reward. An essential facet of any RL environment is the reward. Since it is a priori not clear during saturation which clauses will eventually constitute the discovered proof, the ideal, most faithful-to-reality environment should intuitively only assign a non-zero reward to the final, empty-clause-deriving step. However, an agent would only have a chance to reasonably learn from such a sparse reward through massive exploration (trial and error) and value bootstrapping.[4] As we already decided not to work with states, such avenue is effectively ruled out.

We instead follow most other ML-based approaches to clause selection guidance [1,5,22] in this regard, learn from the successful proof attempts only, and assign a reward to actions retrospectively, based on which clauses end up in the discovered proof. In more detail, at every step, each passive clause C that is in fact a future proof clause gets a reward $r_C = 1$ and the remaining, non-proof clauses receive $r_C = 0$. As detailed later (cf. Sect. 3.1 below), we also subject these rewards to several forms of scaling, with the intuitive idea to give each solved problem a fair share in influencing the update of the trained network.

3.1 RL-Inspired Learning Operator

Let a *trace* of a successful proof attempt on problem P_T be a tuple

$$T = (P_T, \mathcal{C}, \mathcal{C}^+, \{\mathcal{P}_i\}_{i \in I_T}),$$

where $\mathcal{C}$ is the set of all input and derived clauses, $\mathcal{C}^+ \subseteq \mathcal{C}$ marks clauses that ended up in the found proof, and the $\mathcal{P}_i \subseteq \mathcal{C}$ are the snapshots of the content of the passive set at each iteration $i \in I_T$ of the saturation loop just before clause selection. By a *learning operator* for clause selection we mean a procedure that receives as input a set of traces $\mathcal{T}$ and a neural network $N_{\boldsymbol{\theta}}$, described by a vector of learnable parameters $\boldsymbol{\theta}$, and updates these parameters to obtain $\boldsymbol{\theta}'$, so that $N_{\boldsymbol{\theta}'}$ is now better suited for solving the problems that gave rise to $\mathcal{T}$ and ideally also generalizes well to solve other problems.

The learning operator we describe here is derived from the REINFORCE algorithm and the accompanying policy gradient theorem [41]. This algorithm is an ideal approach for directly optimizing a policy[5] using gradient descent. We

4 Bootstrapping in RL means updating estimates based on other estimates instead of waiting for the full return. It represents a solution to the *credit assignment problem*, the challenge of determining which actions were responsible for a received reward.

5 Another family of approaches, the value-based methods, work by learning (to approximate) the state value function and thus rely on meaningful (distinct) states.

avoid introducing the algorithm in its full generality (see [38] for more details) and instead immediately describe how it is reflected in our learning operator. We start by recalling a standard trick from deep RL and the key theorem.

Logits and Softmax. We assume our network $N_{\boldsymbol{\theta}}$ produces a score $N_{\boldsymbol{\theta}}(C) = l_C$, usually called the *logit*, for each available action, i.e., for each clause C from the passive set $\mathcal{P}$ in our case. The logits are to be normalized via the softmax function to yield a probability distribution[6]

$$\pi_{C,\boldsymbol{\theta}} = \mathrm{softmax}_C\big(\{l_D\}_{D\in\mathcal{P}}\big) = \frac{e^{l_C}}{\sum_{D\in\mathcal{P}} e^{l_D}}.$$

This allows us to construe the clauses' scores, at any given moment, as a stochastic clause selection policy. The stochastic aspect is an inherent part of the theory, but not a necessary component in an implementation (cf. Sect. 5.1).

Policy Gradient. Let $\alpha > 0$ be a learning step parameter. The key theorem behind REINFORCE tells us that in order to improve a policy in terms of the expected return, we should update the network parameters as in

$$\boldsymbol{\theta} \leftarrow \boldsymbol{\theta} + \alpha r_C \nabla_{\boldsymbol{\theta}} \log \pi_{C,\boldsymbol{\theta}} \tag{1}$$

i.e., in the direction of the gradient $\nabla_{\boldsymbol{\theta}} \log \pi_{C,\boldsymbol{\theta}}$ and with a magnitude proportional to the reward r_C. (REINFORCE actually uses return here, the reward accumulated over the whole trajectory starting from the current decision C, but in our effectively stateless setup this simplifies to the immediate reward.)

Our Operator. Let $\mathcal{T}$ be a set of traces and $N_{\boldsymbol{\theta}}$ our network. We treat each moment in time in each of the given traces as an independent opportunity to improve the clause evaluation function that $N_{\boldsymbol{\theta}}$ represents. This also includes the moments in which the prover selected a different clause than a future proof clause, for which the reward is 0, and thus strictly following (1) would lead to no nontrivial update. We instead always learn from all proof clauses that are on the passive set and average their contributions to the gradient.[7]

For every $T = (P_T, \mathcal{C}, \mathcal{C}^+, \{\mathcal{P}_i\}_{i\in I_T}) \in \mathcal{T}$ and every $i \in I_T$, we define the *good passive clauses at step* i as $\mathcal{P}_i^+ = \mathcal{P}_i \cap \mathcal{C}^+$ and the corresponding gradient contribution as

$$\delta_i^T = \mathrm{mean}_{C\in\mathcal{P}_i^+} \nabla_{\boldsymbol{\theta}} \log \pi_{C,\boldsymbol{\theta}}.$$

Additionally, we set $\delta^T = \mathrm{mean}_{i\in I_T} \delta_i^T$ and $\delta = \mathrm{mean}_{T\in\mathcal{T}} \delta^T$ as the contribution of a single trace and of the whole set, resp. In experiments containing more than one trace for a single problem we insist that "all problems are equal" (not to allow the more represented ones to have more strength) and instead use:

$$\delta^P = \mathrm{mean}_{T\in\mathcal{T}, P_T = P} \delta^T \quad \text{and} \quad \delta^{fair} = \mathrm{mean}_{P, \exists T\in\mathcal{T}, P_T = P} \delta^P.$$

[6] As such, the logits are dimensionless and have only relative meaning: $l_C - l_D = d$ signifies that clause C should be e^d-times more likely to get selected than clause D.

[7] This is one of the aspects in which we depart from the strict RL paradigm and are choosing a pragmatic approach instead (hence the "RL-inspired").

Iteration. We start from a randomly initialized network $N_{\boldsymbol{\theta}_0}$. We can use it to guide our prover and generate the first set of traces $\mathcal{T}_1$ to learn from, although we expect such guidance to be quite poor. A better option might be to collect traces from runs guided by an already tuned clause selection heuristic, such as the standard age-weight alternation. In any case, we then apply the operator repeatedly, building a sequence of trace sets and guiding networks $\mathcal{T}_1, N_{\boldsymbol{\theta}_1}, \mathcal{T}_2 \ldots$, where network $N_{\boldsymbol{\theta}_j}$ is used to generate the traces $\mathcal{T}_{j+1}$ for the subsequent improvement round, until an optimum performance is reached.

4 Neural Clause Evaluation

The neural network (NN) architecture proposed in this work is designed to be general-purpose and efficient to evaluate. The first property mandates *name invariance*: we do not allow the network to base its decisions on concrete symbol names as these may change meaning from one input problem to the next.[8]

One-off GNN Invocation. Previous work has established Graph Neural Networks (GNNs) as a good basis for name invariant neural formula representations [1, 11, 24]. However, GNNs are relatively expensive to evaluate and intuitively work best when given a large formula (i.e., many clauses) to evaluate at once, so that individual constituents (sub-formulas, terms, symbols) provide sufficient context for one another [4, 8]. This becomes tricky when evaluating clauses for clause selection, as the group of newly derived clauses, which need to be evaluated after each activation, varies in size and is typically relatively small.

We avoid these complications by running a GNN only once, at the beginning of the saturation process on the input problem's CNF, and have the GNN prepare name-invariant vectorial representations (so called *embeddings*) of the signature symbols and the input clauses, to be further utilized in subsequent processing.

Generalizing Age and Weight with RvNNs. The idea is to use these embeddings to seed computations of two (independent) Recursive Neural Networks (RvNN) [18]. One RvNN starts from the input clause embeddings and unrolls along the clause derivation tree (as in [31]), the other starts from the symbol embeddings and unrolls along the clause parse tree (as in [5]). In fact, it is advantageous to treat each of these trees as a directed acyclic graph (DAG), share the common subgraphs and cache the results for the already computed subgraphs.[9]

One can think of these two RvNNs as allowing the training process to generalize and improve upon the two most commonly used standard clause evaluation functions, age and weight. Clause age is essentially the depth of the derivation tree, while weight equals the number of nodes in the parse tree. As such, they

[8] For instance, in the TPTP library which we target for our experiments, each individual problem comes with its own symbol signature, and any name overlap between two problems' signatures can be considered purely coincidental.

[9] In an ATP implementing perfect term sharing, we maintain at most one fixed-size embedding per shared subterm. This shows that the overhead of the network maintenance does not increase the prover's asymptotic time (or space) complexity.

```
1 def gage_insert(cl_num:int, inf_rule:int, parents:list[int]):
2   level = max(base_level, 1 + max(height[p] for p in parents))
3   height[cl_num] = level
4   index = level - base_level
5   if len(todo_layers) == index:
6     todo_layers.append([])
7   todo_layers[index].append((cl_num, inf_rule, parents))
```

Fig. 1. Python code for inserting clause `cl_num` derived by inference rule `inf_rule` from parents `parents` for later processing by the generalized-age (`gage`) RvNN.

could in principle be learned even without the initial embeddings from the GNN. However, we hope that the network discovers much more powerful CEFs still.

Completing the Neural CEF. To complete the tower of NN modules and obtain a final score for a clause, we concatenate the embeddings from the two RvNNs with a vector of 12 easy-to-compute simple clause features. These features include the standard age and weight, the number of literals based on their polarity, the number of variable occurrences or the number of AVATAR [39] splits a clause depends on.[10] The concatenated vector is then fed to a simple fully-connected NN with one hidden layer and a single clause score output.

4.1 Note on Efficient RvNNs

The general rule for making NN computation fast is to group as many operations as possible into one high-level one, which can be vectorized (such as matrix multiplication) and executed via a single (optimized) library call. This is often obvious to do with "rectangular" or otherwise regular inputs such as images, but can be tricky with DAGs traversed by our RvNNs.

In contrast to our previous work [31,32], we strive here to maximize such grouping by postponing node evaluations as much as possible and enqueueing the pending operations into layers based on their dependencies. The essence of the idea is captured in Fig. 1 on the example of the generalized-age (`gage`) RvNN.

To understand Fig. 1, let us first explain its context and how it is initialized. The code maintains for each clause its `height`, which the input clauses have set to 0 and the derived clauses get assigned here on line 3. The main task of the shown function is to insert a new clause (along with the information of how it got derived) into the buffer `todo_layers` at the lowest possible index, so that clauses at the individual layers are independent and can be evaluated together, provided the embeddings for the lower layers have already been computed.

Thus, when later evaluating the inserted clauses, this can be done in a layer-by-layer fashion, in a single bulk operation per layer. Thereupon, `base_level` is incremented by the number of the processed layers and the `todo_layers` buffer itself is cleared. This arrangement has the property that `height` of a clause does

[10] See Appendix A of the preprint [35] for a complete list.

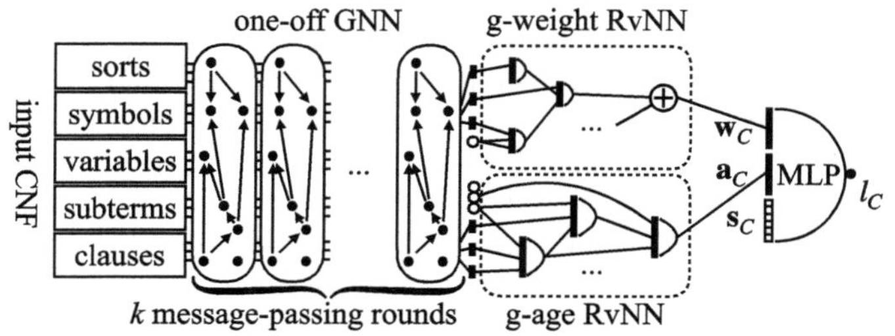

Fig. 2. Clause evaluation neural architecture. Information flows from left to right.

not need to change once set, and the code works both during inference, where many evaluations are triggered over time, and during training, where a maximal "compression" can be enjoyed and the `todo_layers` buffer is filled only once.[11]

One additional condition must, however, be met for the bulk operations to be possible, namely that there is only a single "combine" operation for our RvNN and that each node to evaluate can be represented by a fixed-size vector. In the example of our generalized-age network, we achieve this by concatenating a trainable inference rule embedding with exactly two parent embedding slots. The first slot is reserved for the embedding of the main premise and the second averages the embeddings of all the remaining premises (if present).

4.2 Architecture Details

A sketch of our architecture is shown in Fig. 2. Following it from left to right, we see how the input CNF is first turned into a graph consisting of five kinds of nodes (sort, symbol, variable, subterm, and clause nodes) and several kinds of edges. The graph it is then processed by k rounds of message-passing GNN, where k is a hyperparameter, producing embeddings for symbols and for the input clauses. The GNN is evaluated once, before saturation begins.

During saturation, the generalized-weight RvNN incrementally (on demand) produces embeddings of subterms, literals, and the derived clauses themselves, following their syntax structure. In addition to the symbol embeddings from the GNN it also uses one trainable "variable node" embedding (denoted by an empty circle in Fig. 2) to represent any variable term (i.e., we deliberately conflate distinct variables and the RvNN produces the same embedding vector for, e.g., both $r(X, Y)$ and $r(Y, X)$). The figure also highlights that a clause embedding here is obtained as a simple sum of its constituent literals' embeddings.

At the same time, the generalized-age RvNN uses the input-clause embeddings from the GNN and embeds the derived clauses by recursing along the clause derivation history. Figure 2 shows that each inner node combines the embeddings from the parents and from the used inference rule's trainable embedding (denoted by the empty circles). Thus it is possible that, e.g., a clause D derived

[11] In our experiments, the median height of the clause derivation tree was 10.

from clauses C_1 and C_2 will obtain a different embedding depending on whether it is derived by the subsumption resolution rule or by the binary resolution rule.

In the very right, Fig. 2 shows the final step of combining the embeddings from the two RvNNs with the simple clause features mentioned earlier and passing them through a fully-connected neural block (MLP). Let us spell out the mathematical details of this final step, because similar operations are also being performed within the GNN and RvNN parts (and were just not detailed here).

Let $n, m \in \mathbb{N}$ be the *embedding size* and the *expanded size* hyper-parameters, respectively. For a clause C, the final MLP receives the generalized weight and age embeddings $\mathbf{w}_C \in \mathbb{R}^n$ and $\mathbf{a}_C \in \mathbb{R}^n$, resp., and C's simple features vector $\mathbf{s}_C \in \mathbb{R}^{12}$. The single hidden layer computes

$$\mathbf{h}_C = \mathrm{ReLU}(\mathbf{W}_1 \cdot [\mathbf{w}_C, \mathbf{a}_C, \mathbf{s}_C] + \mathbf{w}_2),$$

an affine transformation with learnable tensors $\mathbf{W}_1 \in \mathbb{R}^{m\times(2n+12)}$ and $\mathbf{w}_2 \in \mathbb{R}^m$ followed by the standard activation function $\mathrm{ReLU}(\mathbf{x}) = \max(\mathbf{0}, \mathbf{x})$. And the final step is the linear $l_C = \mathbf{w}_3^T \cdot \mathbf{h}_C$, for a learnable vector $\mathbf{w}_3 \in \mathbb{R}^m$.[12]

5 Implementation

We integrated the clause-selection-guiding NN into VAMPIRE 4.9.[13] The prover's extension relies on the PyTorch 2.5 library [25] and the TorchScript bridge for interfacing the neural model trained in Python from C++. Although we initially aimed this way for zero code duplication between the Python training scripts and the invocation of the network from VAMPIRE, in the end, it was essential for good performance to duplicate the RvNN logic (cf. Sect. 4.1) in C++.[14]

5.1 Single Queue Integration

When running under neural guidance, VAMPIRE relies on a single queue ordered by the clause scores produced by the NN (the logits) to represent the passive set. While properly sampling from the corresponding softmax distribution—as suggested by the theory (cf. Sect. 3.1)—seemed too costly, adding a small amount of noise to the scores once generated turned out to be a good way to diversify the search and solve additional problems on repeated runs.

Inspired by the Gumbel-max trick [10,20], we optionally add a Gumbel noise[15] sample g_C to the score of each clause (possibly scaled by a temperature parameter). The nice property this noise has is that

$$\arg\max\big(\{l_C + g_C\}_{C\in\mathcal{P}}\big) = \mathrm{softmax}\big(\{l_C\}_{C\in\mathcal{P}}\big) \text{ (as distributions)},$$

so except for the fact that the Gumbel offsets g_C are "frozen" (i.e., not drawn fresh for each clause selection round) we achieve exactly the desired effect.

[12] Further architecture details, in particular the construction of the CNF graph and the computational details of the GNN and the RvNNs appear in Appendix B of [35].

[13] See https://github.com/quickbeam123/deepire2.0-supplementary-materials for the details on how to obtain the system and reproduce the experiments.

[14] Relying on LibTorch, the C++ distribution of PyTorch.

[15] Can be computed as $g = -\log(-\log(u))$ when sampling $u \sim \mathrm{Uniform}(0, 1)$.

5.2 Delayed Insertion Buffer

To group as many clauses as possible for a single bulk evaluation by the NN (cf. Sect. 4.1) while adhering to a principle that at the time of clause selection all passive clauses must already be assigned a score,[16] we extended VAMPIRE's passive clause container with a buffer of clauses waiting for evaluation before they can be inserted into the clause selection queue. The buffer is important for the efficient maintenance of the passive set, because often a large fraction of newly derived clauses need not be evaluated and are instead forward-simplified (or deleted through subsumption) or clause splitting triggers changes on the passive set within the AVATAR architecture [39], all before it is necessary to know the clause scores for the next clause selection step.

5.3 Iterative Improvement Loop

We use a collection of Python scripts to orchestrate 1) running VAMPIRE to collect performance data, 2) rerunning the successful proof attempts in a mode that collects traces,[17] and 3) feeding these traces to our RL-inspired learning operator (cf. Sect. 3.1) to improve the guiding NN, all in a potentially infinite loop. We use parallel processing to speed these operations as much as possible when run on a machine with multiple CPUs (but do not make use of GPUs).

We make one noteworthy departure from RL practices in step 3). Instead of performing just one gradient descent step in each loop (as REINFORCE would), we always separate a random 20% of the available traces for validation purposes and have an inner loop of training rounds use the remaining 80% of the traces to repeat gradient descent until the validation loss[18] does not improve (for 5 successive rounds). This is a standard *early stopping* regularization criterion known from supervised learning, which in our case greatly accelerates convergence.[19]

6 Experiments

We use the TPTP library [37] v9.0.0 for our experiments. TPTP is very diverse, containing problems from many domains and of various encodings collected over several decades from many sources. This poses a challenge for ML-based guiding methods as there are likely no immediate broad commonalities across the problems the learning could capitalize on. Indeed, very few successes with improving ATPs via ML have been reported in the literature for this library to date.

---

[16] Related work [11] explored postponing the evaluation of newly derived clauses until there is a certain number of them. This, however, may lead to the selection of a suboptimal clause while the current best clause is still waiting to be evaluated.

[17] This incurs a performance penalty so unlike step 1) is run without a strict time limit. We made sure there is no non-determinism that would prevent reliable reproduction.

[18] Strictly speaking, Sect. 3.1 describes gradient *ascent* with no explicitly loss. However, the role of a loss for gradient descent is in our case played by the expression $-\delta$ if understood "before the gradient operator is applied.".

[19] The single-step and iterated approach actually converge to the same fixed point [9].

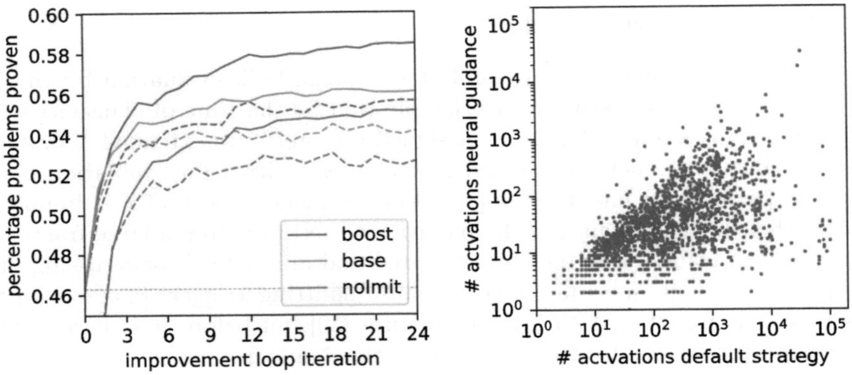

Fig. 3. Left: performance progress of three selected training sessions (test performance dashed). Right: scatter plot comparing the number of clause activations needed by the default and the neurally guided strategies, resp., on commonly solved test problems.

The first-order subset of the library consists of 19477 problems and we randomly split those into 15000 training problems and the rest, left for independent testing. For the main set of experiments we used an instruction limit[20] of 30000Mi per proof attempt, which amounts on average to 10.4s of wall clock time on our servers.[21] Unless stated otherwise, we fixed the NN parameters to: embedding size $n = 32$, expanded size $m = 256$, and $k = 8$ GNN rounds. With these parameters, the neural model takes up a bit less than 1.6MB of disk space.

We use VAMPIRE's *default strategy* both as the source of initial training traces (relying on the default clause selection heuristic, 1:1 age-weight alternation), as well as the basis for the neurally guided extension (with clause selection guided by the NN; cf. Sect. 5.1). The default strategy employs the AVATAR architecture [39] and the limited resource strategy (LRS), a version of the Otter saturation loop with a preemptive clause removal determined by an estimation of the speed of clause processing and the approaching time (instruction) limit [26]. Since delayed evaluation (cf. Sect. 5.2) is in conflict with timely LRS estimations and eager evaluation by the relatively expensive NN did not make LRS pay off anymore, we disabled LRS in the neurally guided version.

Base Experiment. The default strategy solves approximately 46.3% (6940) of the training problems. Figure 3 (left; base) shows the iterative improvement process progressing from this baseline level (marked by the horizontal gray line) to 56.2% training problems solved after 24 iterations.[22] At the same time, the test performance maxes with 54.5%, which means a 17.8% improvement over the baseline.

[20] Instruction limiting leads to more robust results than time limiting in situation (like ours) where many processes compete for the main memory (cf. Appendix A of [33]).

[21] Equipped with AMD EPYC 7513 (128 cores with 2.6GHz) and 500GHz RAM.

[22] The experiment took approximately 24 h to complete, when utilising 120 cores for the prover evaluation and trace collection and 60 cores for the training.

This shows that the trained model generalizes well from the training experience and enables VAMPIRE to solve many new problems.

Neural Guidance Cost and Quality. Around one third of the 30000Mi allotted instructions (measured over unsuccessful runs that make it past parsing and preprocessing) is on average spent by the NN: 470Mi to load a model from the disc, 1740Mi by the GNN computation, and 9420Mi on evaluating clauses during saturation. To compensate for this overhead, the trained model offers a clause selection heuristic that is very precise. In Fig. 3 (right) the neurally guided strategy needs on average 5.5-times fewer clause activations than the default one and in only 7.2% of the cases it needs more activations to solve a given problem.

"Without Imitation." In addition to the base experiment, two other training sessions have their improvement progress shown in Fig. 3 (left). The noImit experiment starts the first loop iteration from a randomly initialized network (rather than the default strategy) to generate the first set of traces. While this is arguably more a property of the TPTP library[23] than of the training method, it is interesting to see that the baseline can be improved upon even without imitating the default clause selection heuristic. However, the lower final performance suggests that the missing additional examples impair generalization.

Boost. The training session labeled in Fig. 3 (left) boost led to our current strongest guiding NN trained from the 30000Mi-limited runs. It improves in test performance by 20% over the baseline. The boost session relies on using several repeated runs of the prover to collect more training traces in each iteration,[24] and, additionally, assigns more weight in the training to (traces from) problems solved only in recent loop iterations, while the weight of problems solved repeatedly in past successive loops is gradually decreased.[25]

Architecture Ablation Experiments. We conducted several experiments to establish the performance contributions of the individual architecture building blocks (the generalized-age RvNN, the generalized-weight RvNN, and the simple features) and the influence of the hyperparameters n, m, and k. While the detailed results and several other technical details only appear in Appendix C of the preprint [35], we summarize here the main findings.

The building blocks ablation experiments are plotted in Fig. 4. (Note that a lower instruction limit 10000Mi was used here; the horizontal gray line again shows the performance of the default strategy, now under this lowered limit.) If we disable just one of the three blocks, the performance drops only mildly and the remaining two blocks are able to compensate for the missing part. We speculate

[23] In that it contains enough problems so easy that even an essentially random clause selection heuristics is able to solve them, yet sufficiently non-trivial ones that the corresponding solution traces can serve as a basis for subsequent improvement.

[24] Instead of one run, we use 5 independently seeded runs with VAMPIRE's input and internal shuffling [34] enabled and for the neurally guided runs we also add the Gumbel noise to the logits (cf. Sect. 5.1) with temperatures $\tau \in \{0, 1/27, 1/9, 1/3, 1\}$.

[25] Giving different weights to problems depending how useful they seem for the training appears to be a neat trick we plan to explore more thoroughly in future work.

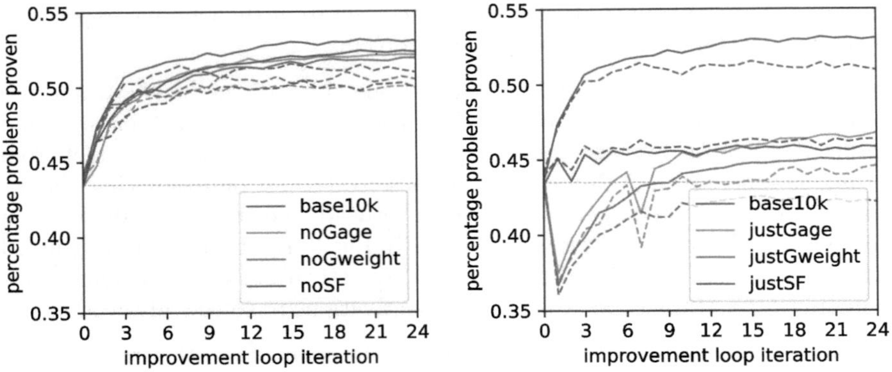

Fig. 4. Performance progress for variants of our NN architecture with a single building block disabled (left) and a single block enabled (right), compared to the same baseline (base10k) which includes all three blocks. Gage means the generalized-age RvNN, Gweight the generalized-weight RvNN and SF stands for the simple features.

that this is (in part) because the simple features bring in the standard age and weight and can thus partially act as proxies for their generalized versions. Leaving just one building block enabled, however, impairs performance substantially and the resulting NNs only barely improve over the baseline.

Reducing the embedding size ($n = 32$) or the expanded size ($m = 256$) from their respective base values leads to a noticeable decline in performance. Conversely, increasing these dimensions tends to improve results, albeit at the cost of higher computational and memory requirements for the training phase. Lastly, using $k = 8$ GNN rounds appears excessive in hindsight, as comparable performance can be achieved with only $k = 4$ rounds.

Solving Hard Problems. To check whether our neural guidance can also help VAMPIRE solve hard problems, we ran one more training session, but this time with runs limited at 100000Mi ($\sim$ 39.0 s) on the whole first-order TPTP. Note that not using a train/test split is fine here, because none of the problems we now report were solved by the seeding default strategy and so they had to be attained solely thanks to generalization. During the 30 improvement loops for which this experiment ran,[26] it solved 130 TPTP problems of rating 1.0.

A problem of TPTP rating 1.0 has the property that no known system was able to solve it during the last rating evaluation [37]. However, there are many rating 1.0 problems that had a rating smaller than 1.0 in the past. Out of our 130 problems, we found 49 that were actually never solved even once in the past.[27] This is a remarkable occurrence in the context of a single strategy improvement.

[26] Taking 12.4days to complete, while using 64 cores for the prover evaluation and trace collection and 32 cores for training.

[27] And 8 that had UNK status, so that it was not known until now whether they can be proven, or whether their conjecture is, in fact, false.

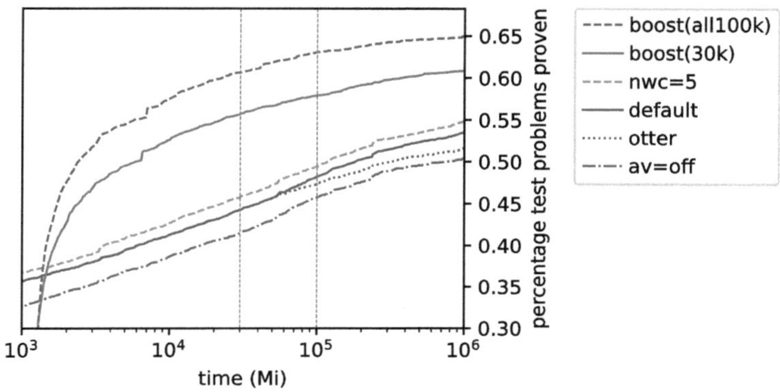

Fig. 5. Test performance cactus plot for VAMPIRE's default strategy (and three variants) and two neurally guided strategies. (Vertical lines at 30000Mi and 100000Mi.)

As a comparison with the base line, we remark that there were only two TPTP rating 1.0 problems solved by the default strategy, each solved only once out of the five randomly shuffled runs and both close to the limit of 100000Mi.

Put Into Perspective. We close this section with a *cactus plot* of Fig. 5, which shows the cumulative performance of several strategies as a function of time.[28] First to notice is that the two neurally-guided strategies, boost(all100K) and boost(30k), start solving any problems only after the 1000Mi mark, which is caused by the non-trivial start-up time of the guiding NN. boost(all100K) is the strategy presented in the previous paragraph and, as noted, has been trained also on the testing split of our problems; as such it does not constitute a fair comparison and is included only to provide a perspective. The default strategy is shown in 4 variants: default, otter (which means turning off the LRS trick), a conjecture-directed variant (nwc=5)[29] and a variant with AVATAR turned off.

We would like draw the attention to the relative sizes of the jump in performance between av=off and default and between default and boost(30k). When introduced, AVATAR came about as a major improvement in VAMPIRE's performance, now we can see a much larger jump thanks to our neural guidance.

7 Related Work

The area of machine learning for theorem proving has been developing at a rapid pace in recent years [3]. Let us, therefore, focus here only on the most related

---

[28] Another reference point, albeit not directly comparable, would be VAMPIRE's CASC mode, a schedule of many strategies selected specifically so that they complement one another, which, when run on 7 CPU cores for 120s, covers 68% of the problems.

[29] NWC stands for "non-goal weight coefficient" and means that any clause not derived from the conjecture will have its standard clause selection weight multiplied by 5.

approaches, those targeting the clause selection heuristic in saturation-based theorem proving.

Of these a prominent role is played by ENIGMA [5,11,12] and systems inspired by it [19,31,32]. Setting aside the ML technology used for now, we can single out a common *ENIGMA-style learning operator* and compare it to the one proposed in this work. While both approaches learn from successful prover runs and rely on proof clauses as their source of positive examples, ENIGMA only uses the recorded selected clauses to form the negative background (as opposed to the typically much larger set of generated clauses used here), and, moreover, it puts these clauses onto one pile, abstracting away the flow of time (while the RL-inspired operator uses each clause selection moment in the trace as an independent situation to learn from).[30] ENIGMA can be seen to already assume a reasonably strong clause selection heuristic and mainly seeks to improve upon it through the integration of the learned guidance. This is reflected in the observation that ENIGMA works best when combined with the baseline clause selection heuristic in some way (a.k.a. the "coop" mode), while the RL-inspired operator aims to provide independent guidance backed by a single clause selection queue. Interestingly, while ENIGMA trains a binary classifier whereas the RL-inspired operator relies on the policy gradient theorem, the resulting formula for gradient descent is essentially the same (negative log likelihood).

Among RL approaches, TRAIL [1] also derives its loss from policy gradient, but distinguishes itself by employing an attention mechanism to capture dependencies on the evolving state. McKeown and Sutcliffe [22] use a value-based method, but only aim to learn a meta-heuristic: an agent who picks which queue, out of the many provided by E prover [28], to selected the next clause from.

Regarding neural architectures, the use of a GNN is not novel in our context [1,11,24], but the listed approaches apply it both to the input problem as well as to the derived clauses. NIAGRA [8], a successor of TRAIL, similarly to our approach, uses a start-up invocation of a GNN of the (often large) input problem to prepare symbol embeddings to later use cheaply during saturation. Embedding of formula syntax using RvNNs was historically the first use-case of the technology [18], but more recently appeared, e.g., in ENIGMA-NG [5]. An RvNN unrolling along clause derivation history comes from Deepire [31,32].

8 Conclusion

We proposed a new neural architecture for clause selection guidance in an ATP and a learning operator for its iterative improvement inspired by RL. The architecture integrates a start-up GNN with two RvNNs, ensuring name invariance, efficiency in evaluation and strong performance thanks to access to both the clause's syntax as well as to its derivation history. The learning operator assumes no evolving state as it suggests learning a single score pre clause, but

[30] Chvalovský et al. [6] (Sect. 6.2) name this distinction *classic* vs *dynamic* data and also prefer the latter for the training, as it is closer to the situation at inference time.

draws experience independently from all the possibly many snapshots of the passive set along a successful proof attempt's trace. The resulting neural clause selection heuristic is implemented as a single standalone clause selection queue.

On problems from the TPTP library, a particularly challenging benchmark for ML-based methods due to its diverse nature, our new neural guidance improves the performance of VAMPIRE's default strategy by 20% and, moreover, allows the prover to solve many problems not previously tackled by any known ATP. To the best of our knowledge, this is a first published report of a substantial improvement by ML-based clause selection guidance on the TPTP benchmark.[31]

There are several interesting directions for future research. One of them is to experimentally compare the relative strengths of the ENIGMA-style and RL-inspired learning operators. Another is the question of transfer learning: Would guidance trained on the TPTP enable VAMPIRE to solve, e.g., more Mizar40 problems (or vice versa)? Most importantly, we are curious about the potential of the new technology for improving whole sets of theorem proving strategies and the corresponding impact on building strong strategy schedules [2], as this is the ultimate measure of an improvement's impact on the ATP users.

Acknowledgments. We thank the anonymous reviewers for their ideas for improvements. We thank Jelle Piepenbrock and Micheal Rawson for suggesting the Gumbel-max trick for cheap softmax-like sampling. The work was supported by the Czech Science Foundation project 24-12759S.

Disclosure of Interests. The authors have no competing interests to declare that are relevant to the content of this article.

References

1. Abdelaziz, I., et al.: Learning to guide a saturation-based theorem prover. IEEE Trans. Pattern Anal. Mach. Intell. **45**(1), 738–751 (2023)
2. Bártek, F., Chvalovský, K., Suda, M.: Regularization in spider-style strategy discovery and schedule construction. In: IJCAR 2024. LNCS, vol. 14739, pp. 194–213. Springer (2024)
3. Blaauwbroek, L., et al.: Learning guided automated reasoning: a brief survey. In: Logics and Type Systems in Theory and Practice - Essays Dedicated to Herman Geuvers on The Occasion of His 60th Birthday. LNCS, vol. 14560, pp. 54–83. Springer (2024)
4. Chvalovský, K., Jakubův, J., Olšák, M., Urban, J.: Learning theorem proving components. In: Das, A., Negri, S. (eds.) TABLEAUX 2021. LNCS (LNAI), vol. 12842, pp. 266–278. Springer, Cham (2021). https://doi.org/10.1007/978-3-030-86059-2_16
5. Chvalovský, K., Jakubův, J., Suda, M., Urban, J.: ENIGMA-NG: efficient neural and gradient-boosted inference guidance for E. In: Fontaine, P. (ed.) CADE 2019. LNCS (LNAI), vol. 11716, pp. 197–215. Springer, Cham (2019). https://doi.org/10.1007/978-3-030-29436-6_12

[31] In 2020 at CASC-J10, ENIGMA Anonymous [11] improved over E prover, on which it is built, by 50 problems. The details of the success, however, remain unpublished.

6. Chvalovský, K., Korovin, K., Piepenbrock, J., Urban, J.: Guiding an instantiation prover with graph neural networks. In: LPAR 2023. EPiC Series in Computing, vol. 94, pp. 112–123. EasyChair (2023)
7. Duarte, A., Korovin, K.: Implementing superposition in iProver (system description). In: Peltier, N., Sofronie-Stokkermans, V. (eds.) IJCAR 2020. LNCS (LNAI), vol. 12167, pp. 388–397. Springer, Cham (2020). https://doi.org/10.1007/978-3-030-51054-1_24
8. Fokoue, A., et al.: An ensemble approach for automated theorem proving based on efficient name invariant graph neural representations. In: IJCAI 2023, pp. 3221–3229. ijcai.org (2023)
9. Ghosh, D., Machado, M.C., Roux, N.L.: An operator view of policy gradient methods. In: NeurIPS 2020 (2020)
10. Gumbel, E.: Statistical Theory of Extreme Values and Some Practical Applications: A Series of Lectures. U.S. Government Printing Office, Applied Mathematics Series (1954)
11. Jakubův, J., Chvalovský, K., Olšák, M., Piotrowski, B., Suda, M., Urban, J.: ENIGMA anonymous: symbol-independent inference guiding machine (system description). In: Peltier, N., Sofronie-Stokkermans, V. (eds.) IJCAR 2020. LNCS (LNAI), vol. 12167, pp. 448–463. Springer, Cham (2020). https://doi.org/10.1007/978-3-030-51054-1_29
12. Jakubův, J., Urban, J.: ENIGMA: efficient learning-based inference guiding machine. In: Geuvers, H., England, M., Hasan, O., Rabe, F., Teschke, O. (eds.) CICM 2017. LNCS (LNAI), vol. 10383, pp. 292–302. Springer, Cham (2017). https://doi.org/10.1007/978-3-319-62075-6_20
13. Jakubův, J., Urban, J.: Hammering Mizar by learning clause guidance (short paper). In: ITP 2019. LIPIcs, vol. 141, pp. 34:1–34:8. Schloss Dagstuhl - Leibniz-Zentrum für Informatik (2019)
14. Kaliszyk, C., Urban, J.: Mizar 40 for mizar 40. J. Autom. Reason. **55**(3), 245–256 (2015)
15. Kaliszyk, C., Urban, J., Michalewski, H., Olšák, M.: Reinforcement learning of theorem proving. In: NeurIPS 2018, pp. 8836–8847 (2018)
16. Kocsis, L., Szepesvári, C.: Bandit based Monte-Carlo planning. In: Fürnkranz, J., Scheffer, T., Spiliopoulou, M. (eds.) ECML 2006. LNCS (LNAI), vol. 4212, pp. 282–293. Springer, Heidelberg (2006). https://doi.org/10.1007/11871842_29
17. Kovács, L., Voronkov, A.: First-order theorem proving and VAMPIRE. In: Sharygina, N., Veith, H. (eds.) CAV 2013. LNCS, vol. 8044, pp. 1–35. Springer, Heidelberg (2013). https://doi.org/10.1007/978-3-642-39799-8_1
18. Küchler, A., Goller, C.: Inductive learning in symbolic domains using structure-driven recurrent neural networks. In: Görz, G., Hölldobler, S. (eds.) KI 1996. LNCS, vol. 1137, pp. 183–197. Springer, Heidelberg (1996). https://doi.org/10.1007/3-540-61708-6_60
19. Loos, S.M., Irving, G., Szegedy, C., Kaliszyk, C.: Deep network guided proof search. In: LPAR 2017. EPiC Series in Computing, vol. 46, pp. 85–105. EasyChair (2017)
20. Maddison, C.J., Tarlow, D., Minka, T.: A* sampling. In: NIPS 2014, pp. 3086–3094 (2014)
21. McCune, W.: OTTER 3.3 reference manual. CoRR cs.SC/0310056 (2003). http://arxiv.org/abs/cs/0310056
22. McKeown, J., Sutcliffe, G.: Reinforcement learning for guiding the E theorem prover. In: FLAIRS 2023. AAAI Press (2023)
23. Mnih, V., et al.: Playing Atari with deep reinforcement learning. CoRR abs/1312.5602 (2013)

24. Olšák, M., Kaliszyk, C., Urban, J.: Property invariant embedding for automated reasoning. In: ECAI 2020. Frontiers in Artificial Intelligence and Applications, vol. 325, pp. 1395–1402. IOS Press (2020)
25. Paszke, A., et al.: Pytorch: an imperative style, high-performance deep learning library. In: Advances in Neural Information Processing Systems, vol. 32, pp. 8024–8035. Curran Associates, Inc. (2019)
26. Riazanov, A., Voronkov, A.: Limited resource strategy in resolution theorem proving. J. Symb. Comput. **36**(1–2), 101–115 (2003)
27. Schulman, J., Wolski, F., Dhariwal, P., Radford, A., Klimov, O.: Proximal policy optimization algorithms. CoRR abs/1707.06347 (2017)
28. Schulz, S., Cruanes, S., Vukmirović, P.: Faster, higher, stronger: E 2.3. In: Fontaine, P. (ed.) CADE 2019. LNCS (LNAI), vol. 11716, pp. 495–507. Springer, Cham (2019). https://doi.org/10.1007/978-3-030-29436-6_29
29. Schulz, S., Möhrmann, M.: Performance of clause selection heuristics for saturation-based theorem proving. In: Olivetti, N., Tiwari, A. (eds.) IJCAR 2016. LNCS (LNAI), vol. 9706, pp. 330–345. Springer, Cham (2016). https://doi.org/10.1007/978-3-319-40229-1_23
30. Silver, D., et al.: A general reinforcement learning algorithm that masters chess, shogi, and Go through self-play. Science **362**(6419), 1140–1144 (2018)
31. Suda, M.: Improving ENIGMA-style clause selection while learning from history. In: Platzer, A., Sutcliffe, G. (eds.) CADE 2021. LNCS (LNAI), vol. 12699, pp. 543–561. Springer, Cham (2021). https://doi.org/10.1007/978-3-030-79876-5_31
32. Suda, M.: Vampire with a brain is a good ITP hammer. In: Konev, B., Reger, G. (eds.) FroCoS 2021. LNCS (LNAI), vol. 12941, pp. 192–209. Springer, Cham (2021). https://doi.org/10.1007/978-3-030-86205-3_11
33. Suda, M.: Vampire getting noisy: Will random bits help conquer chaos? EasyChair Preprint no. 7719 (2022). https://easychair.org/publications/preprint/CSVF
34. Suda, M.: Vampire getting noisy: will random bits help conquer chaos? In: IJCAR 2022. LNCS, vol. 13385, pp. 659–667. Springer (2022)
35. Suda, M.: Efficient neural clause-selection reinforcement. CoRR abs/2503.07792 (2025). https://doi.org/10.48550/arXiv.2503.07792
36. Sutcliffe, G.: The CADE ATP system competition - CASC. AI Mag. **37**(2), 99–101 (2016)
37. Sutcliffe, G.: Stepping stones in the TPTP world. In: IJCAR 2024. LNAI, vol. 14739, pp. 30–50 (2024)
38. Sutton, R.S., Barto, A.G.: Reinforcement Learning: An Introduction. A Bradford Book, Cambridge (2018)
39. Voronkov, A.: AVATAR: the architecture for first-order theorem provers. In: Biere, A., Bloem, R. (eds.) CAV 2014. LNCS, vol. 8559, pp. 696–710. Springer, Cham (2014). https://doi.org/10.1007/978-3-319-08867-9_46
40. Weidenbach, C., Dimova, D., Fietzke, A., Kumar, R., Suda, M., Wischnewski, P.: SPASS version 3.5. In: Schmidt, R.A. (ed.) CADE 2009. LNCS (LNAI), vol. 5663, pp. 140–145. Springer, Heidelberg (2009). https://doi.org/10.1007/978-3-642-02959-2_10
41. Williams, R.J.: Simple statistical gradient-following algorithms for connectionist reinforcement learning. Mach. Learn. **8**, 229–256 (1992)
42. Zombori, Z., Urban, J., Olšák, M.: The role of entropy in guiding a connection prover. In: Das, A., Negri, S. (eds.) TABLEAUX 2021. LNCS (LNAI), vol. 12842, pp. 218–235. Springer, Cham (2021). https://doi.org/10.1007/978-3-030-86059-2_13

Learning Conjecturing from Scratch

Thibault Gauthier(✉) and Josef Urban

Czech Technical University in Prague, Prague, Czechia
email@thibaultgauthier.fr

Abstract. We develop a self-learning approach for conjecturing of induction predicates on a dataset of 14,005 problems derived from the OEIS. These problems are hard for today's SMT and ATP systems because they require a combination of inductive and arithmetical reasoning.

Starting from scratch, our approach consists of a feedback loop that iterates between (i) training a neural translator to learn the correspondence between the problems solved so far and the induction predicates useful for them, (ii) using the trained neural system to generate many new induction predicates for the problems, (iii) fast runs of the Z3 prover attempting to prove the problems using the generated predicates, (iv) using heuristics such as predicate size and solution speed on the proved problems to choose the best predicates for the next iteration of training. The algorithm discovers on its own many interesting induction predicates, ultimately solving 3,590 problems, compared to 835 problems solved by CVC5, Vampire or Z3 in 60 s.

1 Introduction: Induction, OEIS and AI Mathematicians

Proof by induction is a fundamental tool in mathematics, essential for reasoning about inductive structures such as trees, lists or integers. Efficient automation of induction is a key challenge in automated theorem proving (ATP), with direct implications for software verification and mathematical research.

A large source of induction problems is reasoning about integer sequences. The Online Encyclopedia of Integer Sequences (OEIS) [39] covers over 350,000 integer sequences from many domains, often with several proposed explanations for a sequence. Proving the equivalence of such explanations varies from easy to very hard. Some of these equivalences are open mathematical conjectures.

Recently, our program synthesis AI system [15] has generated millions of such explanations, covering more than 130,000 OEIS sequences. When a new algorithm for a particular sequence (e.g. primes) is discovered automatically by the system, it is only tested on a finite fragment of the sequence. One would however also like to automatically prove that the algorithm is equivalent to the previously known algorithms (instead of e.g. just computing pseudoprimes). Having ATPs that can routinely prove such conjectures would greatly enhance the capabilities of such autonomous AI mathematicians,[1] allowing e.g. safe optimization of the

[1] See e.g. https://t.ly/qd626 for a discussion of an AI-invented algorithm for $\sqrt[3]{2}$.

C. Barrett and U. Waldmann (Eds.): CADE 2025, LNAI 15943, pp. 423–445, 2025.
https://doi.org/10.1007/978-3-031-99984-0_23

invented algorithms by replacing slow subroutines with more efficient equivalent ones.

To measure progress in this domain, the OEIS ATP benchmark[2] citech23DBLP:confspslparspsGauthierBJU23 was recently introduced, consisting of SMT [1] problems of varying difficulty. Each problem involves proving an equivalence of two programs: a *small* program and a *fast* program, which generate the same OEIS sequence. The baseline performance of today's ATP and SMT systems measured in citech23DBLP:confspslparspsGauthierBJU23 was relatively low: of the 14,005 induction problems, unaided CVC5 (the best system) can prove 601.

1.1 Contributions

In this work we develop a self-learning approach for synthesis of instances of second-order induction which are useful for solving the OEIS problems, with the Z3 [10] SMT solver. We first give a brief overview of the task of AI-based OEIS program synthesis which motivates our work on predicate synthesis (Sect. 2). This includes the description of the OEIS ATP benchmark (Sect. 2.1) which is our problem dataset. In Sect. 3 we describe the language of the OEIS programs and explain their translation to the SMT format. This is important for understanding the kind of the SMT problems we are solving when proving equivalence of two programs and the induction predicates (i.e. conjectures used to instantiate a second-order induction axiom) that we need to invent.

Next, in Sect. 4 we introduce methods for *evaluation, selection and minimization* of the invented predicates using Z3. This is an important part of the overall system, which also decides how good our training data are and how they evolve. In Sect. 5 we design a *suitable language* for the generated induction predicates. This is used in Sect. 6 where we develop an *initial brute-force method* for generation of a set of sufficiently diverse predicates, suitable for starting the self-learning loop. Here we introduce several *pruning methods* crucial for exploring the large space of induction predicates. This includes semantic evaluation, selection of only the true predicates, fingerprinting to avoid generation of equivalent predicates, and restricting the language to the most relevant functions.

In Sect. 7, we develop our *self-learning loop* which iterates between training a neural machine translation (NMT) model [28] on previously discovered problem/solution pairs, proposing new predicates for all problems, and evaluating them with Z3. This process continuously improves the selection of predicates, which are in turn used for training, after applying our *data-augmentation* methods.

Finally, Sect. 8 evaluates the methods in several ways. Section 8.1 describes several long self-learning runs which ultimately prove **3,590** of the 14,005 problems. This also results in a strong trained NMT+ATP system that proves 3,501 problems in at most 48 s, and a large dataset of useful predicates. In Sect. 8.2 we for a comparison develop strong baseline methods which use manual heuristics

[2] https://github.com/ai4reason/oeis-atp-benchmark.

for induction. The strongest one proves 2,497 problems in 10 s, and the union of these baseline methods prove 3,285 problems. We show that union of the manual and self-learning approaches solves **4,350** problems, i.e., the feedback loop adds 1,065 problems to those solved by manual heuristics.

We analyze the problem-solving and generalization behavior of an interesting invented predicate in Sect. 8.3 and discuss further examples in Sect. 8.4.

2 From OEIS Programs to Predicate Synthesis

Our approach builds on our method for OEIS program synthesis [15]. This is a feedback loop that interleaves (i) training neural machine translation to learn the correspondence between sequences and the programs discovered so far, and (ii) proposing many new programs for each OEIS sequence by the trained neural machine translator. Starting from scratch, this loop has so far invented programs for more than 130,000 OEIS sequences. This dataset is the foundation of our benchmark, consisting of program equalities that we now aim to verify.

While our previous work focused on synthesizing *programs*, our focus here is on synthesizing *predicates* about those programs, which are then used to instantiate a second-order induction axiom. This introduces two key challenges:

1. The space of possible predicates is empirically larger than the space of programs, making the search more complex.
2. Evaluating the usefulness of predicates using Z3 is much slower than evaluating programs—taking, on average, 200 milliseconds per predicate versus less than 1 millisecond per program. We are thus able to test far fewer predicates than programs, limiting our ability to explore the broader search space.

2.1 The OEIS ATP Benchmark

Our benchmark introduced in [14] consists of SMT problems of the form $\forall x \in \mathbb{N}.\ f_{Small_s}(x) = f_{Fast_s}(x)$. Here, s is an OEIS sequence, $Small_s$ and $Fast_s$ are the smallest and fastest programs computing s discovered by our self-learning system [15,16], and f_{Small_s} and f_{Fast_s} are the SMT functions representing the $Small_s$ and $Fast_s$ programs. We will usually drop the index s and just write *Small*, *Fast*, f_{Small}, f_{Fast}. For the purpose of this work, we focus on 14,005 problems in this benchmark that were heuristically determined [14] to require induction.[3] These SMT problems include function definitions for the programs *Small* and *Fast* derived from their semantic interpretation (see Sect. 3), and the assertion $\exists c \in \mathbb{Z}.\ c \geq 0 \wedge \neg(f_{Small}(c) = f_{Fast}(c))$. Thus, if these problems are unsatisfiable then the equality holds.

Example 1.
The OEIS sequence A217 are the triangular numbers $0, 1, 3, 6, 10, 15 \ldots$ In our

[3] In [14], 16,197 problems in total were heuristically determined to require induction. We exclude here 2,192 of those problems for technical reasons.

benchmark, the $Small_{A217}$ program is $loop(X+Y, X, 0)$[4] corresponding to the mathematical formula $\sum_{k=1}^{x} k$. And our $Fast_{A217}$ program is $(X \times X + X)\ div\ 2$. The problem of determining if $Small_{A217}$ and $Fast_{A217}$ are equal is represented[5]. by the following SMT formulas[6] in our benchmark.

```
(forall ((x Int) (y Int)) (= (f x y) (+ x y)))
(forall ((x Int)) (= (g x) x))
(= h 0)
(forall ((x Int) (y Int))
  (= (u x y) (ite (<= x 0) y (f (u (- x 1) y) x))))
(forall ((x Int)) (= (v x) (u (g x) h)))
(forall ((x Int)) (= (small x) (v x)))
(forall ((x Int)) (= (fast x) (div (+ (* x x) x) 2)))
(exists ((c Int))
  (and (>= c 0) (not (= (small c) (fast c)))))
```

3 OEIS Programs

The OEIS programs in our benchmark were produced using a compact grammar, as described in [16]. In this section, we define the syntax in which these programs were written and provide formal semantics. The interpretation functions introduced are used to convert programs into SMT functions (see Sect. 3.1).

Syntax. The set $\mathbb{P}$ of programs in our language is inductively defined to be the smallest set that includes:

- first-order operators: if $A, B, C \in \mathbb{P}$ then
  $0, 1, 2, X, Y, A+B, A-B, A \times B, A\ div\ B, A\ mod\ B, cond(A, B, C) \in \mathbb{P}$.
- second-order operators: if $A, B, C, F, G \in \mathbb{P}$ then
  $loop(F, A, B)$, $loop2(F, G, A, B, C)$, $compr(F, A) \in \mathbb{P}$.

A *loop program* is a program whose top-level operator is *loop*, *loop2* or *compr*.

---

[4] Note that in $loop(X+Y, X, 0)$ the interpretation (Sect. 3) of the program $X+Y$ will be defined as f_{X+Y} where $f_{X+Y} = \lambda xy.f_{X+Y}(x,y) = \lambda xy.(f_X(x,y) + f_Y(x,y)) = \lambda xy.x+y$. So the reader can read this program as $[loop](\lambda xy.x+y, \lambda xy.x, \lambda xy.0)$ where $[loop] : (\mathbb{Z}^2 \mapsto \mathbb{Z})^3 \mapsto (\mathbb{Z}^2 \mapsto \mathbb{Z})$.

[5] The details of the translation will be given in Sect. 3.1.

[6] https://tinyurl.com/yhx239d9/A217.smt2.

Semantics. Each program P is interpreted by a (recursive) function $f_P : \mathbb{Z}^2 \mapsto \mathbb{Z}$. The interpretation f_P is recursively defined for every program P by:

$$
\begin{aligned}
& f_0(x,y) := 0,\ f_1(x,y) := 1,\ f_X(x,y) = x,\ f_Y(x,y) = y \\
& f_{A+B}(x,y) := f_A(x,y) + f_B(x,y),\ f_{A-B}(x,y) := f_A(x,y) - f_B(x,y) \\
& f_{A\times B}(x,y) := f_A(x,y) \times f_B(x,y),\ f_{A div B}(x,y) := f_A(x,y)\ div\ f_B(x,y) \\
& f_{A mod B}(x,y) := f_A(x,y)\ mod\ f_B(x,y) \\
& f_{cond(A,B,C)}(x,y) := \text{ if } f_A(x,y) \leq 0 \text{ then } f_B(x,y) \text{ else } f_C(x,y) \\
& f_{loop(F,A,B)}(x,y) = u(f_A(x,y), f_B(x,y)) \\
& \quad \text{where } u(x,y) = \text{if } x \leq 0 \text{ then } y \text{ else } f_F(u(x-1,y),x) \\
& f_{loop2(F,G,A,B,C)}(x,y) := u(f_A(x,y), f_B(x,y), f_C(x,y)) \\
& \quad \text{where } u(x,y,z) = \text{if } x \leq 0 \text{ then } y \text{ else } f_F(u(x-1,y,z), t(x-1,y,z)) \\
& \quad \text{and } t(x,y,z) = \text{if } x \leq 0 \text{ then } z \text{ else } f_G(u(x-1,y,z), t(x-1,y,z)) \\
& f_{compr(F,A)}(x,y) := u(f_A(x,y)) \\
& \quad \text{where } t(x) = \text{if } f_F(x,0) \leq 0 \text{ then } x \text{ else } t(x+1) \\
& \quad \text{and } u(x) = \text{if } x \leq 0 \text{ then } t(0) \text{ else } t(u(x-1)+1)
\end{aligned}
$$

The function $f_{compr(F,X)}(x)$ is a recursive function that returns the $(x+1)^{th}$ integer satisfying $P = \lambda x. f_F(x,0) \leq 0$. For instance, if P corresponds to a synthesized *is_prime* function, then the function $g(x) = f_{compr(is\_prime,X)}(x)$ returns the $(x+1)^{th}$ prime number. The functions *mod* (modulo) and *div* (integer division) used in these definitions follow the semantics of Standard ML [19].

Example 2. Intuitively, the program $loop(2 \times X, X, 1)$ produces the sequence $a_0 = 1, a_n = 2 \times a_{n-1}$. Similarly, the program $loop(X + Y, X, 0)$ computes the sequence $a_0 = 0, a_n = a_{n-1} + n$. Lastly, the program $loop2(X \times Y, Y, X, 1, 2)$ generates the sequence (a_n) where $(a_0, b_0) = (1, 2)$ and $(a_n, b_n) = (a_{n-1} \times b_{n-1}, b_{n-1})$.

Terminology. We classify interpretation functions into the following categories:

- *loop functions*: functions corresponding to loop programs. function $f_{loop(F,A,B)}$ is named v, the function $f_{loop2(F,G,A,B,C)}$ is named w and s is additional *loop function* associated with $loop2(F,G,A,B,C)$.
- *argument functions*: functions interpreting arguments of loop programs. Given a loop program $loop(F,A,B)$, the *update* function f_F is named f, the *bound* function f_A is named g, and the *initial value* function f_B is named h.
- *helper functions*: local recursive functions t,u within *loop functions*. For *loop2*, u computes the first component and t the second component, while in *loop* only u is used.

Additional Function s. We include an additional function s for each program $loop2(F,G,A,B,C)$ in the grammar for induction predicates. The function s is defined as:

$$s(x,y) := t(f_A(x,y), f_B(x,y), f_C(x,y))$$

This function allows proving properties about the second component of *loop2* which would otherwise require using the helper function t.[7]

3.1 Example of Our SMT Translation

We show our translation to SMT on the example of the above program $loop(X+Y, X, 0)$. To define the toplevel loop function ($f_{loop(X+Y,X,0)}$ named v below), we first create SMT definitions for the *argument functions* (f_{X+Y}, f_X, f_0, named f, g, h below). When writing SMT definitions, we omit dummy arguments, thus some of the functions become unary or nullary:

```
(forall ((x Int) (y Int)) (= (f x y) (+ x y)))
(forall ((x Int)) (= (g x) x))
(= h 0)
```

From the update function f, one can then construct the helper function u with this recursive definition:

```
(forall ((x Int) (y Int))
   (= (u x y) (ite (<= x 0) y (f (u (- x 1) y) x))))
```

For a given initial value y and a number of iterations (bound) x, this function $u(x, y)$ corresponds to the recursive sequence:

$$\{u_0, u_1, u_2, \ldots, u_x, \ldots\} = \{y, f(u_0, 1), f(u_1, 2), \ldots, f(u_{x-1}, x), \ldots\}$$

For our particular choice of f, $u(x, y) = y + \sum_{k=1}^{x} k$. To produce our final definition v, we compose u with g and h:

```
(forall ((x Int)) (= (v x) (u (g x) h)))
```

For our particular choice of f, g and h, $v(x) = u(g(x), h) = u(x, 0) = \sum_{k=1}^{x} k$.

One can similarly construct SMT definitions for *loop2* and *compr.* which match their semantic interpretation. We also number these functions based on the serial numbering of the loop constructs. e.g. $v_0, u_0, f_0, g_0, h_0, w_1, s_1, u_1, t_1, \ldots$.

Example (A108411: Powers of 3 repeated) This problem presents two ways of computing the powers of 3 repeated twice. The fast program w stores the value 3 into the second component s of the *loop2* whereas the small program v recomputes $X + X + X$ at every iteration of *loop*.

$$\underbrace{loop(\overbrace{X+X+X}^{f_0}, \overbrace{X\ div\ 2}^{g_0}, \overbrace{1}^{h_0})}_{v_0} = \underbrace{loop2(X \times Y, Y, X\ div\ 2, 1, 1+2)}_{w_1, s_1} \qquad \text{(A108411)}$$

[7] Later, we will see that this is necessary as helper functions are disallowed in our initial candidate generation step (Sect. 6).

Remark 1. Since the semantics of modulo (*mod*) and integer division (*div*) differs between Standard ML and SMT, we define the Standard ML *div* and *mod* in terms of their SMT counterpart in the preamble of each SMT problem.

3.2 Additional Axioms for Trivial Inductions

We have changed the original problems to be able to prove more equalities between programs without requiring induction. The first change is to share definitions of *loop functions* if they are syntactically equal, i.e., we now use the same name for them. Second, it is often the case that two *loop functions* v_0 and v_1, with the same loop operator (e.g. *loop*), are not syntactically equal but their helper functions are. In this case, we add an equation stating the equality between the *helper functions* u_0 and u_1. Finally, for two loops of the same kind (e.g. *loop*) we observe that if the update functions are proven equal (e.g. f_0, f_1) then the *helper functions* (e.g. u_0, u_1) must be equal. These implications (*congruences*) are added as extra axioms to our problems as they cannot be proven without induction. We will see in Sect. 8 that these simple modifications make more of the benchmark problems solvable by standard methods.

4 Candidate Selection via Proof Search

For each problem in our benchmark, we generate a list of predicates (called a *candidate*) using initially brute force (Sect. 6) and then neurally-guided generation (Sect. 7). We describe here how we determine which candidates are considered a solution for the problem and when they should be added to our set of training examples. Given a predicate Q, we produce a first-order axiom (over $\mathbb{Z}$) by instantiating the following second-order induction axiom with Q:

$$\forall P.\ ((\forall y.\ P(0,y)) \wedge (\forall xy.\ P(x,y) \Rightarrow P(x+1,y))) \Rightarrow (\forall xy.\ 0 \leq x \Rightarrow P(x,y)) \tag{Ind}$$

The condition $0 \leq x$ is omitted from the induction step, seemingly producing a weaker induction axiom. Both versions are in fact equivalent as can be seen by instantiating P by $\lambda xy.\ 0 \leq x \Rightarrow Q(x,y)$. Given a candidate (list of predicates), we create one instance of axiom Ind for each predicate in the candidate. We then append this list of axioms to the SMT problem. Finally, we call Z3 on the produced problem for 200 ms (an experimental sweet spot). If Z3 returns a proof, we refer to the candidate as a *solution* for that problem.

Minimization and Selection of Solutions. To increase the quality of our training examples (problem/solution pairs) we perform a minimization step and a selection step before using the new solutions for training. The *minimization step* repeatedly calls Z3 with subsets of the induction instances to see if any of the predicates can be removed. The *selection step* consists of keeping only the shortest solution discovered so far for each problem in our database of training examples.

Remark 2. In some of our experiments, we keep both the shortest and fastest solutions for each problem. When looking for fast solutions, the minimization step is adapted so that a predicate is removed from the solution if a proof can be found faster without the corresponding axiom for that predicate.

5 Grammar for Induction Predicates

Induction predicates are built from quantifier-free first-order formulas. Given a problem p, the set of terms $\mathbb{T}$, the set of literals $\mathbb{L}$ and the set of formulas $\mathbb{F}$ are defined to the be smallest sets such that:

- $0, 1, 2, x, y \in \mathbb{T}$.
- If $t_1, t_2 \in \mathbb{T}$ then $t_1 + t_2,\ t_1 - t_2,\ t_1 \times t_2,\ t_1\ \mathit{div}\ t_2,\ t_1\ \mathit{mod}\ t_2 \in \mathbb{T}$.
- if $t_1, t_2, t_3 \in \mathbb{T}$ then if $t_1 \leq 0$ then t_2 else $t_3 \in \mathbb{T}$.
- if f is a n-ary *function* appearing in p and $t_1, \ldots, t_n \in \mathbb{T}$ then $f(t_1, \ldots, t_n) \in \mathbb{T}$.
- if $t_1, t_2 \in \mathbb{T}$ then $t_1 = t_2,\ \neg(t_1 = t_2),\ t_1 \leq t_2, \neg(t_1 \leq t_2) \in \mathbb{L}$.
- if $l_1, l_2 \in \mathbb{L}$ and $f_1, f_2 \in \mathbb{F}$ then $l_1, l_2, f_1 \wedge f_2,\ f_1 \Rightarrow f_2 \in \mathbb{F}$.

Each formula $f[x, y]$, we associate a predicate $P = \lambda xy.\ f[x, y]$ that will be used to instantiate the induction axiom. In the rest of this paper, we omit the $\lambda xy.$ part and use the formula $f[x, y]$ to represent a predicate.

Remark 3. Early results indicate that adding quantifiers to the language of induction predicates would only help to solve a few more problems due to the practical difficulty of instantiating those quantifiers. Indeed, strong induction, which can be obtained by instantiating weak/standard induction by a quantified formula, subsumes in theory any induction over the n previous steps. However, in practice it performs worse than weak/standard induction, as shown in Sect. 8.

6 Initial Generation of Candidates

We first explain how candidates (lists of predicates) are generated in the initial phase. The predicates are generated using the grammar described in Sect. 5. This generation relies on brute-force enumeration of predicates of increasing sizes. To get interesting solutions, we use the following methods to reduce the space.

First, we only generate predicates on functions we deem the most important: *loop* functions and s functions (Sect. 3). Second, we discard equivalent terms if they are equivalent up to arithmetical reasoning. Third, we discard formulas that do not depend on the induction variable x. Fourth, we test formulas on some values and keep only the formulas that are true on all values. Thanks to these heuristics, we were able to increase the number of problems solved by these initial candidates resulting in a large enough pool of examples to train the NMT.

6.1 Initial Terms

To avoid generating many versions of the same kind of terms we define the following equivalence relation: *Equivalence for terms without loop subterms.* Two terms t_1 and t_2 are *equivalent* if they evaluate to the same value after substituting (x, y) with integers from the set $I = \{(x, y) \mid 0 \leq x < 10, -5 \leq y < 10\}$. After ordering I using the lexicographical order, the list of evaluations on I is called a *fingerprint.*

Example 3. x, $x + 0$, $x + 1 - 1$ have the same fingerprint.

Equivalence for Terms with Loop Subterms. We want to find properties of *loop functions* therefore we consider *loop functions* to be opaque functions. In practice, we do so by assigning a random fingerprint for each *loop subterm.* This fingerprint does not correspond to the real evaluation of the subterm but distinguishes it from other terms. The computation of fingerprints for terms with loop subterms then proceeds normally.

Example 4. $f(x) + 0$ and $f(x) \times 1$ have the same fingerprint but $g(x)$ and $f(x)$ do not, even if f and g compute the same function. The reason is that Z3 can prove that $f(x) + 0 = f(x) \times 1$ but might not be able to prove that $f(x) = g(x)$ without induction axioms.

We use a bottom-up approach for term generation. We first create all terms of size 1, then all the terms of size 2 and so on. During this process, if two terms are equivalent, as defined previously, we only keep the smallest one. We stop generating terms as soon as we get 1,024 terms and we call this set $\mathbb{T}_{init}$.

6.2 From Terms to Candidates

We generate candidates from terms in three stages: literals, predicates, candidates.

Literals. We generate two types of equations and inequations by randomly sampling pairs from $\mathbb{T}_{init}$. We sample 250 equations and inequations that are true on I and 250 equations and inequations that are not always false on I. This bias favors true literals. The same process is applied to produce disequalities and disinequalities forming a set $\mathbb{L}_{init}$ of 1,000 literals.

Predicates. We construct 4,000 predicates (implications or conjunctions), verified to be true on I, by sampling pairs of literals from $\mathbb{L}_{init}$.

Candidates. From these 4,000 predicates we sample 1,000 ordered subsets of size 4 to produce our initial candidate set.

7 Generating Candidates Using NMT

So far, we only generated candidates using brute-force enumeration. However, similar to OEIS program synthesis, conjecturing can be also naturally formulated as language modelling and sequence-to-sequence translation tasks. We have recently started to experiment with recurrent neural networks (RNNs) with attention [5] and transformers [46] in such symbolic settings [15,35,44,47]. In particular, a wide *beam search* using relatively small and fast encoder-decoder neural machine translation (NMT) system works surprisingly well as the learning and generative component in our OEIS program synthesis system [15].

NMT Framework, Hyperparameters, Data, Overall Loop: In this work, we train such NMT models to prune the large search space and generate relevant candidates. As in [15], we use Luong's NMT framework [27], with the hyperparameters found in [47]. In more detail, we train a 2-layer bidirectional LSTM equipped with the "scaled Luong" attention and 512 units. Depending on the experiment and the data size, we train for 2,000–14,000 steps[8]. The inference (generation of candidates) uses beam width of 240.[9] A machine learning model, such as the NMT, is trained on a set of input/output examples. In our setting, the input is a problem and the output is a solution The initial problem/solution pairs are obtained by checking candidates from the initial generation (Sect. 6). We then train the NMT on these pairs, use the trained NMT to generate new candidates, which in turn leads to new problem/solution pairs after evaluation (Sect. 4). This process can be iterated many times as seen in our experiments (Sect. 8). An interesting and important part of this process are *data augmentation* methods.

7.1 Training

Since NMT is operating on tokens, both the problem (pair of programs) and the solution are represented as token sequences. In the *split mode* (cf. Section 7.2), each problem-solution pair is decomposed into multiple problem-predicate pairs, one for each predicate in the solution. During each iteration of our self-learning loop, we train the NMT on the smallest solutions found so far. In some runs, we also add the fastest solutions.

Encoding of a Problem. We illustrate the encoding process using the problem $Small_{A217} = Fast_{A217}$ from Example 1. Understanding the exact encoding is not required for following the rest of the paper, but it is provided here for completeness. The two programs are written in prefix notation and separated by the $=$ token. To emphasize the connection between programs and functions, we insert after each loop operator a token referring to its loop function. We use the symbol $>$ to separate the problem and its solution. The encoding uses:

- lowercase letters for loop functions,

[8] This training takes 15–130 min on a low-end GPU (GTX1080 Ti, 12G RAM).
[9] The inference takes about 75 min for the 14,005 problems on the same GPU.

- uppercase letters for operators that are not loop functions,
- numerical suffixes (e.g., *a* 0, *a* 1) for argument/helper functions.

```
Problem: (loop:v0 (+ x y) x 0) = (div (+ (* x x) x) 2)
Solution: (= (+ (* x x) x) (* 2 (v0 x)))
Encoding: J a D K L K A = G D F K K K C > O D F K K K F C a K
```

Data Augmentation. We teach the NMT how to grammatically use functions that do not appear in its default training examples. To this end, we either construct extra examples or modify existing ones.

Rare Indices for Loop Functions. Problems with high number of loops are rare in our dataset. Thus, since our loops are encoded alphabetically in each problem, letter tokens such as *i* might never occur in our solutions. Yet, the token *i* might be needed to solve a problem involving at least 9 loop functions. To address this, we sometimes (10% of the time) shift function tokens by a random offset in our encoding, resulting in training data that contain such further indices.

Definition Expansion. During the initial candidate generation phase, we focused solely on producing predicates for *loop functions*. However, some induction proofs require induction predicates to be expressed in terms of *helper functions*, and incorporating *argument functions* can also be beneficial. Since our initial examples do not include helper or argument functions, we augment the training set by generating two additional variations of each problem-solution pair. This is done by randomly expanding function definitions within the solution (once for the first variation and twice for the second), thereby introducing helper and argument functions into the examples.

7.2 Neural Generation (Inference)

The potential solutions are generated by running the trained NMT in its *neural inference mode*, using each problem (i.e., a program equality) as a separate input. This is analogous to the task of neural translation of English sentences to their most statistically plausible French counterparts, but here we learn to translate from problems to their statistically most plausible induction predicates. The inference runs as 240-wide *beam search*, yielding for each problem 240 outputs. This was chosen based on prior work in a related setting [15], where it provided a good trade-off between diversity and runtime.

In the *whole mode*, we generate 240 candidates (each a list of predicates) for every problem. Each candidate is evaluated individually by Z3, which checks whether the predicates prove the original problem (see Sect. 4). Only solutions verified by Z3 and better than previous candidates in speed or size are retained to guide subsequent trainings. This allows NMT to synthesize the next predicates in the list *conditioned* on the previously generated predicates. This typically leads to good coordination and interplay between the predicates in such list [34].

In the *split mode*, 240 predicates are generated independently for each problem. To form candidate solutions, we randomly combine between 3 and 12 of these predicates to create 100 candidates, which are then evaluated by Z3. For example, if the model generates predicates $p_1, p_2, \ldots, p_{240}$, a candidate might consist of the subset $\{p_5, p_{23}, p_{87}\}$. This approach enables generating solutions with many predicates, sometimes over 300 tokens long, even though the NMT output length is limited to 60 tokens per predicate. However, since predicates are generated independently, the model does not learn which predicates naturally co-occur in the same solution.

8 Evaluation

8.1 Self-learning Runs

We have evaluated the system and its properties in four longer self-learning runs. These runs build on each other, modifying some parameters based on the previous runs. We use a machine with 36 hyperthreading CPU cores, 72 threads, 256GB RAM and 4 GPUs[10] In real time, the runs have so far taken three months, still solving new problems. This is similar to our OEIS experiment, where the self-learning loop has been solving new sequences for over two years now. The initial data were produced by the *initial (brute-force) run* (Sect. 6) using 1,000 candidates per problem. These candidates were evaluated by Z3 in approximately 9 h resulting in 762 solved problems. Figure 1 shows the evolution of the number of solved problems during each of the four self-learning runs. Each run was initialized from checkpoints in earlier run to test alternative techniques. Ideally, each run could have been restarted from scratch for maximal experimental rigor. However, this was computationally infeasible due to the substantial time and resources required to explore the vast search space of induction predicates.

Run-1: was initialized from the 762 initial solved problems. The self-learning loop ran here for 260 iterations and reached 3,128 solved problems. The learning/-generation was performed in the split mode and we only trained on the smallest solutions. Additionally, semantic evaluation was employed to remove false predicates before producing problems.[11] Each iteration involved 2 to 4 ATP runs, each on outputs produced by differently trained (2,000–14,000 steps) NMTs. In each proof attempt we randomly combine n of the 240 generated predicates, where n is randomly chosen (for each run) from the set $\{1, 2, 3, 4, 5, 6, 8, 12\}$.

Run-2: was initialized from the 3,069 problems solved at iteration 187 of *Run-1*. This run spanned 60 iterations and reached 3,331 solutions. It again used the split mode but we started to add also the fastest solutions to the training data. We also introduced data augmentation through definition expansions (Sect. 7.1) to further enlarge the training dataset, reaching approximately 40,000 examples. Two ATP runs were done per iteration, following the same approach as in *Run-1*.

[10] CPU: 2 x Intel Xeon Gold 6140 CPU @ 2.30GHz, GPU: 4 x GTX1080 Ti.
[11] This semantic filter was not included in the following runs.

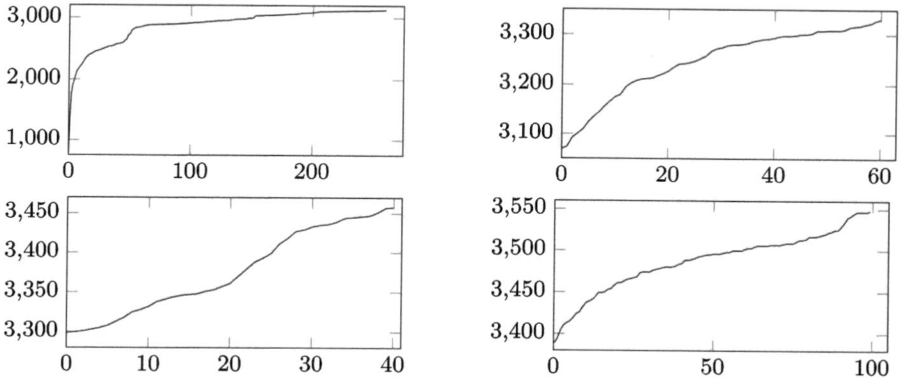

Fig. 1. Cumulative number of solved problems after x iterations in each run.(*Run-1* top-left, *Run-2* top-right, *Run-3* bottom-left, *Run-4* bottom-right)

Run-3: was initialized from the 3,299 problems solved at iteration 44 of *Run-2*. Learning/inference used the whole mode, i.e., the NMT is here learning and predicting whole candidates instead of predicates, and no random combining of predicates is done. During the learning phase, the NMT was trained on both the fastest and smallest solutions discovered but omitting data augmentation through definition expansion. The run took 40 iterations, reaching 3,458 solutions.

Run-4: was initialized from the 3,388 problems solved at iteration 23 of *Run-3*. It used the same parameters as *Run-3* with the addition of data augmentation via definition expansion. Run-4 took 99 iterations, reaching 3,548 solutions.

Further Discussion. The four runs solve in total **3,590** problems. Figure 1 shows several sudden increases in the rate at which problems are solved across the iterations. These inflections likely come from the discovery of useful induction patterns, see Sect. 8.3 and Table 2 for an example. Depending on the quality of the predictions and other factors, each (parallelized) ATP run within an iteration takes 1–3 h. This means that with the NMT learning/inference we can do about 2–8 iterations per day. Further interesting effects include: (i) As the iterations progress, the ATP runs solve more and more problems, i.e., the NMT memorizes the discovered solutions well. The record is 3,501 problems solved in iteration 98 of *Run-4*. This means that the final trained NMT+ATP system outperforms the union of all manual heuristics (Sect. 8.2) in a CPU-time comparison.[12] (ii) Solutions of a single problem can evolve a lot both in speed and size. Our system found 11 short solutions for problem A11914[13], which however differ a lot by their

[12] The CPU limit in a single run with 240 predictions is at most $240 * 0.2 = 48$ s. The NMT prediction time is negligible.

[13] https://tinyurl.com/yhx239d9/A11914.smt2.

speed. One of the longest evolutions occurred for problem A176916,[14] with 46 different solutions.

8.2 Comparison with Manual Heuristics

We compare our results with CVC5 and its induction strategy. We also measure how many problems can be solved by Z3 or CVC5 when helped by manually-selected induction axioms. Table 1 shows these results. We omit Vampire from this table because it performs poorly even with a 60-second timeout. Consequently, we do not include it in the 10-second evaluations reported here.

Table 1. Number of problems solved out of the 14,005 problems in our benchmark with a 10 s timeout. CVC5 was run with its induction strategy.

Prover	Induction over n previous terms										Str. Ind.	Total
	0	1	2	3	4	5	6	7	8	9		
Z3	333	835	2,232	2,480	2,497	2,483	2,460	2,383	2,307	2,271	401	3,099
CVC5	601	569	1,127	839	719	430	336	301	285	296	538	1,470

All these problems contain the additional axioms for trivial inductions from Sect. 3.2. The first column (0) presents problems with no instances of the induction axiom. Z3 solves 333 of those problems which is to be compared with the 7 problems Z3 could solve without the axioms for trivial inductions in [14]. Z3 and CVC5 solve together in 10 s 787 problems. If we add Vampire with its induction strategy and run it with a 60 s time limit, the systems solve jointly 835 problems. Columns (1–9) show the numbers of problems solved when we instantiate the induction axiom by the following family of predicates where $a = f_{Small}$ and $b = f_{Fast}$:

$$0 \leq x \Rightarrow a(x) = b(x) \tag{1}$$

$$0 \leq x \Rightarrow (a(x) = b(x) \wedge a(x+1) = b(x+1)) \tag{2}$$

$$0 \leq x \Rightarrow (a(x) = b(x) \wedge a(x+1) = b(x+1) \wedge a(x+2) = b(x+2)) \tag{3}$$

$$\ldots$$

The Str. Ind. column refers to the inclusion of the strong induction axiom obtained by instantiating the induction axiom used in our experiments with the predicate $\lambda xy.\ (0 \leq x \Rightarrow (\forall z.\ 0 \leq z \leq x \Rightarrow a(z) = b(z)))$.

The union of all Z3 and CVC5 runs in Table 1 solves 3,252 problems. If we additionally include the 60-second runs (including Vampire), the total number of problems solved using these **manual heuristic methods** (i.e., fixed provers

[14] https://tinyurl.com/yhx239d9/A176916.smt2.

augmented with manually crafted induction predicates) is 3,285. This is comparable to previous results from [14], but still about 305 problems fewer than what we achieve using our feedback loop with synthesized predicates.

The **union of the two approaches**, combining (i) the manual heuristics just described and (ii) the solutions found via our NMT-synthesized induction predicates and feedback loop, yields a total of **4,350** solved problems. This means that the learned approach contributes an additional **1,065** unique solutions beyond those found with manual methods alone.

8.3 Example of Influential General Discovery

One of the discoveries which produced the sudden jump at iteration 41 in *Run-1* (Table 2) is the predicate (where we dropped the loop indices):

$$s(x) = s(1) \wedge v(1+x) = w(x) + v(x) + w(x) \tag{P1}$$

This can be used to prove equalities of programs such as those for A198766:[15]

$$\underbrace{\mathit{loop}(5 \times (2+X), X, 1)}_{v} + 2 = \underbrace{\mathit{loop2}(X \times Y, Y, X, 7, 5)}_{w,s}\ \mathit{div}\ 2 \tag{Eq1}$$

Here, the left-hand side loop defines a recursive sequence $v(0) = 1$, $v(1+x) = 5v(x) + 10$. The right-hand side loop defines the sequence $(w(x))$ where $(w(0), s(0)) = (7, 5), (w(x+1), s(x+1)) = (w(x) \times s(x), s(x))$. Thus, a closed form of $w(x)$ is 7×5^x. We want to prove Eq1, i.e., $v(x) + 2 = w(x)\ \mathit{div}\ 2$. Assuming the second conjunct of P1 holds, we get:

$$\begin{aligned}
&v(1+x) - v(x) = 2w(x) \underset{v(1+x)}{\Longrightarrow} 5v(x) + 10 - v(x) = 2w(x)\\
\Longrightarrow\ &4v(x) + 10 = 2w(x) \underset{\mathit{div}\ 4}{\Longrightarrow} v(x) + (10\ \mathit{div}\ 4) = w(x)\ \mathit{div}\ 2\\
\Longrightarrow\ &v(x) + 2 = w(x)\ \mathit{div}\ 2\ \square\ \text{(this is Eq1, i.e., Q.E.D.)}
\end{aligned}$$

Similarly, the invention of predicate P1 quickly led to proofs of problems like:

$$\underbrace{\mathit{loop}(10 \times X + 4, X, 1)}_{v} = \overbrace{2 \times (\underbrace{\mathit{loop2}(X \times Y, Y, X, 2, 10)}_{w}\ \mathit{div}\ 9)}^{w'} \tag{A2278}$$

stating the equivalence of the sequences $v(0) = 1, v(x+1) = 10v(x) + 4$ and $w'(x) = 2 \times ((2 \times 10^x)\ \mathit{div}\ 9)$, and

[15] Numbers like 5 are a short notation for the expressions in our language, e.g. 1+2+2.

$$\underbrace{loop(6 \times X + 6, X, 0)}_{v} = \overbrace{2 \times (\underbrace{loop2(X \times Y, Y, X, 3, 6)}_{w}\ div\ 5)}^{w'} \qquad \text{(A105281)}$$

stating the equivalence of the sequences $v(0) = 0, v(x+1) = 6v(x) + 6$ and $w'(x) = 2 \times ((3 \times 6^x)\ div\ 5)$. An interesting property of our invented predicate P1 is its *generality* across these (and further) problems. It avoids writing explicitly large/varied numbers such as 9 or 5. Indeed, depending on the function v, the expression $v(x+1) - v(x)$ implicitly present in P1 reduces to different expressions. For instance, in the three mentioned examples, $v(x+1) - v(x)$ respectively evaluates to: $4v(x) + 10$, $9v(x) + 4$ and $5v(x) + 6$.

Table 2. Number of solutions containing the pattern $v_0(1 + x) = w_1(x) + v_0(x) + \_$ at iterations 42–51 of *Run-1*.

Iteration	42	43	44	45	46	47	48	49	50	51
Solutions	1	2	5	14	25	27	26	27	27	31

8.4 Further Examples

Example 1 A2411: Pentagonal pyramidal numbers (Gaussian sum variation).

$$\text{Problem: } \underbrace{loop(X + Y, X, 0)}_{v} \times X = (((X \times X) + X)\ div\ 2) \times X$$

$$\text{Math: } x \times \sum_{k=1}^{x} k = \frac{x \times x + x}{2} \times x \quad \text{Solution: } 0 \leq x \wedge x \times x + x = 2 \times v(x)$$

The proof requires one predicate on the *loop function* v defining $loop(X + Y, X, 0)$. We can also observe that our machine learning algorithm restricted the induction step to nonnegative integers by adding the conjunct $0 \leq x$.[16]

Example 2 A205646: empty faces in Freij's family of Hansen polytopes.
We first simplify the original problem by evaluating constant programs and reducing polynomials. The problem can then be restated as:

$$\underbrace{loop(3 \times X, X, 1)}_{v} + 16 = \underbrace{loop2(X \times Y, Y, X\ div\ 2, loop(3, x\ mod\ 2, 1), 9))}_{w,s} + 16$$

[16] None of the examples shown here were found by manually adding induction predicates.

Mathematically, the equation is $3^x + 16 = 3^{(x \ mod \ 2)} \times 9^{(x \ div \ 2)} + 16$. The fast program is saving time by computing 3^x as $3^{(x \ mod \ 2)} \times 9^{(x \ div \ 2)}$ (this is the basis of the *fast exponentiation* algorithm [9]). It stores the value of $9 = 1 + 2 \times (2 + 2)$ in the second component of the loop y to avoid recomputing it at each iteration of the loop. The solution consists of 6 predicates:

$$w(1+x) = v(1+x) \wedge w(x) = v(x), v(x) = w(x) \wedge w(1+x) = v(1+x)$$
$$x \leq w(2), x \leq w(x), s(x) = s(1), s(x+1) = s(x)$$

The first two predicates (which are equivalent) allow Z3 to prove the statement by doing an induction over the two previous steps, which is necessary and thus Z3 can perform case splitting on whether the number of iteration is even or odd. The last two predicates state that s is constant. We are not sure of the purpose of the predicates $x \leq w(2)$ and $x \leq w(x)$. Yet, we know that Z3 is not able to find a proof when these predicates are removed because the minimization step would have removed them already.

Example 3 A26532: Ratios of successive terms are $3, 2, 3, 2, 3, 2, 3, 2, \ldots$.
We prove that the two conjectured programs compute the same sequence, $a(0) = 1$ and $a(n+1) =$ if n is even then $2 \times a(n)$ else $3 \times a(n)$.

Problem: $\underbrace{loop(2 + (Y \ mod \ 2) \times X, X, 1)}_{v,u} =$

$$\underbrace{loop2(X \times Y, Y, X \ div \ 2, loop(3, X \ mod \ 2, 1), 6)}_{w,s}$$

Math: $\prod_{k=1}^{x} (2 + k \bmod 2) = 6^{\lfloor \frac{x}{2} \rfloor} \times \begin{cases} 1 & \text{if } x \bmod 2 = 0 \\ 3 & \text{otherwise} \end{cases}$

Solution: $u(1+x, 1) = w(1+x) \wedge v(x) = w(x) \wedge w(2) = s(x) \wedge s(1+x) = s(x)$

From the constructed predicate, we can infer that the proof relies on the equality holding for the two previous terms, and on the second component s of *loop2* being constant. This simple example is interesting because the sequence does not fall directly into the usual categories: polynomial, linear recurrence, (hyper)geometric.

9 Related Work

Automating inductive reasoning has been a long-standing challenge in theorem proving and software verification. Our approach is related to prior work on interactive and automated theorem provers [37] and especially their AI/ML extensions [3], and also takes inspiration from other self-learning systems.

Inductive Automated and Interactive Theorem Proving. Inductive reasoning is a key feature in ATPs, enabling proofs about recursive structures and arithmetic properties. Vampire has introduced induction techniques [18], and in particular integer induction schemes [20], that extend its first-order logic capabilities.

Similarly, CVC5 has incorporated strategies for reasoning about inductive properties [36]. Vampire and CVC5 use built-in induction mechanisms that automatically instantiate induction schemes based on patterns found in the input formula. These strategies typically rely on syntactic patterns to construct induction hypotheses, unlike our approach, which synthesizes predicates independently of the input formula's structure. This key difference allows our method to discover non-obvious or auxiliary induction lemmas that standard provers would not infer. We note that Z3 does not currently support induction. As such, its role in our experiments is to evaluate how much impact can be achieved by combining synthesized lemmas with an otherwise non-inductive solver.

Several ITPs employ techniques specifically designed for inductive proofs. For instance, Isabelle/HOL [48] and Coq [2] integrate inductive reasoning as a fundamental mechanism, with several recent systems further automating induction in Isabelle/HOL [29,30]. Rippling [4,24] and waterfall strategies [23] have been developed to systematically guide proof search by modifying goal expressions. Additionally, QuickSpeck [8,12] and HipSpec [7] have explored automated conjecturing for equational reasoning to prove properties of programs.

Self Learning. A directly related self-learning system motivating the work done here is QSynt [15,16], which however only tests the invented programs. A directly related self-learning system motivating the work done here is QSynt [15,16], which however only tests the invented programs. AI/TP metasystems such as MaLARea [42,45], ATPBoost [33], BliStr [43] and Grackle [21] are using self-learning similar to ours over large formal mathematical libraries in the context of premise selection and strategy invention. Similar self-learning has been recently introduced for internal guidance of ATPs such as rlCoP [25], E/ENIGMA [22], Vampire/Deepire [40] and iProver [6], as well as for direct neural term synthesis in instantiation proving [32]. In AlphaGoZero [38], a self-learning model learns to play Go from scratch, improving solely through self-play and feedback. DreamCoder [13], a self-learning system for program synthesis, illustrates how a mix of learning and domain specific algorithms can be used to construct program abstractions from examples. Systems like AlphaProof [11] use self-learning to address International Mathematical Olympiad problems.

Algorithmic Symbolic Approaches. In contrast to both ATPs and data-driven methods, symbolic systems such as those by Gerhold and Kauers [17], Kauers and Koutschan [26], the classical $A = B$ framework [31], and recent SMT-based approaches [41], focus on algorithmic guessing and proving of identities, particularly over special functions, recurrences, and inequalities. These works typically rely on domain-specific representations and symbolic transformations, such as hypergeometric summation or Gosper's algorithm. Our approach differs in its generality and proof targets: instead of verifying closed-form or recurrence formulas, we train models to synthesize lemmas (in the form of predicates) that help prove the equivalence between arbitrary integer programs.

10 Conclusion and Future Work

In this work, we have added instances of the second-order induction axiom to the Z3 prover to prove equalities between OEIS programs. These instances were generated using a self-learning process, ultimately allowing Z3 to prove 3,590 of the 14,005 problems. We compared our results to state-of-the-art provers for induction and arithmetical reasoning, also with heuristically added induction instances. Our approach outcompetes these methods by about 300 problems, adding 1,065 solutions. The union of all these approaches solves 4,350 problems, which is a considerable improvement over the previous state of the art in [14].

The byproducts of this work are a strong trained NMT+ATP system that proves 3,501 problems in at most 48 s and a large dataset of useful induction predicates. These can be trained on and further analyzed by humans, which we have started to do here, showing some of them to be interesting and general.

In the future, we would like to scale our approach to much larger sets of problems such as the millions of programs coming from our latest OEIS synthesis run. Furthermore, our methodology is not specific to integer induction and could be applied to other inductive datatypes. We hope to test the practicality and generality of our approach on other tasks such as the verification of loop invariants in industrial programs. Finally, we also would like to apply the approach to other forms of conjecturing such as generating instantiations of first-order quantifiers and synthesizing intermediate lemmas (cuts) to simplify large proofs.

Acknowledgments. This work was supported by the Czech Science Foundation grant no. 25-17929X, Czech Ministry of Education, Youth and Sports within the ERC CZ program under the project POSTMAN no. LL1902, and by Amazon Research Awards.

Disclosure of Interests. The authors have no competing interests to declare that are relevant to the content of this article.

References

1. Barrett, C., Stump, A., Tinelli, C., et al.: The SMT-LIB standard: version 2.0. In: Proceedings of the 8th International Workshop on Satisfiability Modulo Theories (Edinburgh, Scotland), vol. 13, p. 14 (2010)
2. Bertot, Y.: A short presentation of Coq. In: Mohamed, O.A., Muñoz, C., Tahar, S. (eds.) TPHOLs 2008. LNCS, vol. 5170, pp. 12–16. Springer, Heidelberg (2008). https://doi.org/10.1007/978-3-540-71067-7_3
3. Blaauwbroek, L., et al.: Learning guided automated reasoning: a brief survey. In: Logics and Type Systems in Theory and Practice. Lecture Notes in Computer Science, vol. 14560, pp. 54–83. Springer (2024)
4. Bundy, A., Stevens, A., van Harmelen, F., Ireland, A., Smaill, A.: Rippling: A heuristic for guiding inductive proofs. Artif. Intell. **62**(2), 185–253 (1993)
5. Chorowski, J., Bahdanau, D., Serdyuk, D., Cho, K., Bengio, Y.: Attention-based models for speech recognition. In: NIPS, pp. 577–585 (2015)
6. Chvalovský, K., Korovin, K., Piepenbrock, J., Urban, J.: Guiding an instantiation prover with graph neural networks. In: LPAR. EPiC Series in Computing, vol. 94, pp. 112–123. EasyChair (2023)

7. Claessen, K., Johansson, M., Rosén, D., Smallbone, N.: Hipspec: automating inductive proofs of program properties. In: Fleuriot, J.D., Höfner, P., McIver, A., Smaill, A. (eds.) ATx'12/WInG'12: Joint Proceedings of the Workshops on Automated Theory eXploration and on Invariant Generation, Manchester, UK, June 2012. EPiC Series in Computing, vol. 17, pp. 16–25. EasyChair (2012)
8. Claessen, K., Smallbone, N., Hughes, J.: QuickSpec: guessing formal specifications using testing. In: Fraser, G., Gargantini, A. (eds.) TAP 2010. LNCS, vol. 6143, pp. 6–21. Springer, Heidelberg (2010). https://doi.org/10.1007/978-3-642-13977-2_3
9. Cohen, H., et al.: Handbook of Elliptic and Hyperelliptic Curve Cryptography. Chapman and Hall/CRC (2005)
10. de Moura, L., Bjørner, N.: Z3: an efficient SMT solver. In: Ramakrishnan, C.R., Rehof, J. (eds.) TACAS 2008. LNCS, vol. 4963, pp. 337–340. Springer, Heidelberg (2008). https://doi.org/10.1007/978-3-540-78800-3_24
11. DeepMind. AI achieves silver-medal standard solving International Mathematical Olympiad problems. Blog post (2024). Accessed 21 Feb 2025
12. Einarsdóttir, S.H., Hajdu, M., Johansson, M., Smallbone, N., Suda, M.: Lemma discovery and strategies for automated induction. In: IJCAR (1). Lecture Notes in Computer Science, vol. 14739, pp. 214–232. Springer (2024)
13. Ellis, K., et al.: DreamCoder: bootstrapping inductive program synthesis with wake-sleep library learning. In: Freund, S.N., Yahav, E. (eds.) PLDI 2021: 42nd ACM SIGPLAN International Conference on Programming Language Design and Implementation, Virtual Event, Canada, 20–25 June 2021, pp. 835–850. ACM (2021)
14. Gauthier, T., Brown, C. E., Janota, M., Urban, J.: A mathematical benchmark for inductive theorem provers. In: Piskac, R., Voronkov, A. (eds.) LPAR 2023: Proceedings of 24th International Conference on Logic for Programming, Artificial Intelligence and Reasoning, Manizales, Colombia, 4–9 June 2023. EPiC Series in Computing, vol. 94, pp. 224–237. EasyChair (2023)
15. Gauthier, T., Olšák, M., Urban, J.: Alien coding. Int. J. Approx. Reason. **162**, 109009 (2023)
16. Gauthier, T., Urban, J.: Learning program synthesis for integer sequences from scratch. In: Williams, B., Chen, Y., Neville, J. (eds.) Thirty-Seventh AAAI Conference on Artificial Intelligence, AAAI 2023, Thirty-Fifth Conference on Innovative Applications of Artificial Intelligence, IAAI 2023, Thirteenth Symposium on Educational Advances in Artificial Intelligence, EAAI 2023, Washington, DC, USA, 7–14 February 2023, pp. 7670–7677. AAAI Press (2023)
17. Gerhold, S., Kauers, M.: A procedure for proving special function inequalities involving a discrete parameter. In: Kauers, M. (ed.) Symbolic and Algebraic Computation, International Symposium ISSAC 2005, Beijing, China, 24–27 July 2005, Proceedings, pp. 156–162. ACM (2005)
18. Hajdu, M., Kovács, L., Rawson, M., Voronkov, A.: The vampire approach to induction (short paper). In: Konev, B., Schon, C., Steen, A. (eds.) Proceedings of the Workshop on Practical Aspects of Automated Reasoning Co-located with the 11th International Joint Conference on Automated Reasoning (FLoC/IJCAR 2022), Haifa, Israel, 11–12 August 2022. CEUR Workshop Proceedings, vol. 3201. CEUR-WS.org (2022)
19. Harper, R., MacQueen, D., Milner, R.: Standard ML. University of Edinburgh, Department of Computer Science (1986)

20. Hozzová, P., Kovács, L., Voronkov, A.: Integer induction in saturation. In: Platzer, A., Sutcliffe, G. (eds.) CADE 2021. LNCS (LNAI), vol. 12699, pp. 361–377. Springer, Cham (2021). https://doi.org/10.1007/978-3-030-79876-5_21
21. Hula, J., Jakubuv, J., Janota, M., Kubej, L.: Targeted configuration of an SMT solver. In: CICM. Lecture Notes in Computer Science, vol. 13467, pp. 256–271. Springer (2022)
22. Jakubuv, J., Urban, J.: Hammering mizar by learning clause guidance. In: ITP. LIPIcs, vol. 141, pp. 34:1–34:8. Schloss Dagstuhl - Leibniz-Zentrum für Informatik (2019)
23. Jiang, Y., Papapanagiotou, P., Fleuriot, J.: Machine learning for inductive theorem proving. In: Fleuriot, J., Wang, D., Calmet, J. (eds.) AISC 2018. LNCS (LNAI), vol. 11110, pp. 87–103. Springer, Cham (2018). https://doi.org/10.1007/978-3-319-99957-9_6
24. Johansson, M., Dixon, L., Bundy, A.: Dynamic rippling, middle-out reasoning and lemma discovery. In: Siegler, S., Wasser, N. (eds.) Verification, Induction, Termination Analysis. LNCS (LNAI), vol. 6463, pp. 102–116. Springer, Heidelberg (2010). https://doi.org/10.1007/978-3-642-17172-7_6
25. Kaliszyk, C., Urban, J., Michalewski, H., Olšák, M.: Reinforcement learning of theorem proving. In: Bengio, S., Wallach, H.M., Larochelle, H., Grauman, K., Cesa-Bianchi, N., Garnett, R. (eds.) Advances in Neural Information Processing Systems 31: Annual Conference on Neural Information Processing Systems 2018, NeurIPS 2018, 3–8 December 2018, Canada, Montréal, pp. 8836–8847 (2018)
26. Kauers, M., Koutschan, C.: Guessing with little data. In: Maza, M.M., Zhi, L. (eds.) ISSAC 2022: International Symposium on Symbolic and Algebraic Computation, Villeneuve-d'Ascq, France, 4–7 July 2022, pp. 83–90. ACM (2022)
27. Luong, M.-T., Brevdo, E., Zhao, R.: Neural machine translation (seq2seq) tutorial (2017). https://github.com/tensorflow/nmt
28. Luong, M.-T., Pham, H., Manning, C.D.: Effective approaches to attention-based neural machine translation. arXiv preprint arXiv:1508.04025 (2015)
29. Nagashima, Y.: Faster smarter proof by induction in Isabelle/HOL. In: IJCAI, pp. 1981–1988. ijcai.org (2021)
30. Nagashima, Y., Xu, Z., Wang, N., Goc, D.S., Bang, J.: Template-based conjecturing for automated induction in Isabelle/HOL. In: FSEN. Lecture Notes in Computer Science, vol. 14155, pp. 112–125. Springer (2023)
31. Petkovšek, M., Wilf, H.S., Zeilberger, D.: A=B. A K Peters (1996). https://www.math.upenn.edu/~wilf/AeqB.html
32. Piepenbrock, J., Urban, J., Korovin, K., Olšák, M., Heskes, T., Janota, M.: Invariant neural architecture for learning term synthesis in instantiation proving. J. Symb. Comput. **128**, 102375 (2025)
33. Piotrowski, B., Urban, J.: ATPboost: learning premise selection in binary setting with ATP feedback. In: Galmiche, D., Schulz, S., Sebastiani, R. (eds.) IJCAR 2018. LNCS (LNAI), vol. 10900, pp. 566–574. Springer, Cham (2018). https://doi.org/10.1007/978-3-319-94205-6_37
34. Piotrowski, B., Urban, J.: Stateful premise selection by recurrent neural networks. In: LPAR. EPiC Series in Computing, vol. 73, pp. 409–422. EasyChair (2020)
35. Piotrowski, B., Urban, J., Brown, C.E., Kaliszyk, C.: Can neural networks learn symbolic rewriting? CoRR, abs/1911.04873 (2019)
36. Reynolds, A., Kuncak, V.: Induction for SMT solvers. In: D'Souza, D., Lal, A., Larsen, K.G. (eds.) VMCAI 2015. LNCS, vol. 8931, pp. 80–98. Springer, Heidelberg (2015). https://doi.org/10.1007/978-3-662-46081-8_5

37. Robinson, J.A., Voronkov, A.: Handbook of Automated Reasoning (in 2 volumes). Elsevier and MIT Press (2001)
38. Silver, D., et al.: Mastering the game of go without human knowledge. Nature **550**, 354 (2017)
39. Sloane, N.J.A.: The on-line encyclopedia of integer sequences. In: Kauers, M., Kerber, M., Miner, R., Windsteiger, W. (eds.) Calculemus/MKM -2007. LNCS (LNAI), vol. 4573, p. 130. Springer, Heidelberg (2007). https://doi.org/10.1007/978-3-540-73086-6_12
40. Suda, M.: Vampire with a brain is a good ITP hammer. In: Konev, B., Reger, G. (eds.) FroCoS 2021. LNCS (LNAI), vol. 12941, pp. 192–209. Springer, Cham (2021). https://doi.org/10.1007/978-3-030-86205-3_11
41. Uncu, A.K., Davenport, J.H., England, M.: SMT-solving induction proofs of inequalities. In: Uncu, A.K., Barbosa, H. (eds.) Proceedings of the 7th SC-Square Workshop co-located with the Federated Logic Conference, SC-Square@FLoC 2022, as a part of the 11th International Joint Conference on Automated Reasoning, IJCAR 2022, Haifa, Israel, 12 August 2022. CEUR Workshop Proceedings, vol. 3458, pp. 10–24. CEUR-WS.org (2022)
42. Urban, J.: Malarea: a metasystem for automated reasoning in large theories. In: Sutcliffe, G., Urban, J., Schulz, S. (eds.) Workshop on Empirically Successful Automated Reasoning in Large Theories (ESLART), vol. 257. CEUR-WS.org (2007)
43. Urban, J.: BliStr: the blind strategymaker. In: Gottlob, G., Sutcliffe, G., Voronkov, A. (eds.) Global Conference on Artificial Intelligence (GCAI). EPiC, vol. 36, pp. 312–319. EasyChair (2015)
44. Urban, J., Jakubův, J.: First neural conjecturing datasets and experiments. In: Benzmüller, C., Miller, B. (eds.) CICM 2020. LNCS (LNAI), vol. 12236, pp. 315–323. Springer, Cham (2020). https://doi.org/10.1007/978-3-030-53518-6_24
45. Urban, J., Sutcliffe, G., Pudlák, P., Vyskočil, J.: MaLARea SG1 - machine learner for automated reasoning with semantic guidance. In: Armando, A., Baumgartner, P., Dowek, G. (eds.) IJCAR 2008. LNCS (LNAI), vol. 5195, pp. 441–456. Springer, Heidelberg (2008). https://doi.org/10.1007/978-3-540-71070-7_37
46. Vaswani, A., et al.: Attention is all you need. In: Guyon, I., et al. (eds.) Advances in Neural Information Processing Systems 30: Annual Conference on Neural Information Processing Systems 2017, 4–9 December 2017, Long Beach, CA, USA, pp. 5998–6008 (2017)
47. Wang, Q., Kaliszyk, C., Urban, J.: First experiments with neural translation of informal to formal mathematics. In: Rabe, F., Farmer, W.M., Passmore, G.O., Youssef, A. (eds.) CICM 2018. LNCS (LNAI), vol. 11006, pp. 255–270. Springer, Cham (2018). https://doi.org/10.1007/978-3-319-96812-4_22
48. Wenzel, M., Paulson, L.C., Nipkow, T.: The Isabelle framework. In: Mohamed, O.A., Muñoz, C., Tahar, S. (eds.) TPHOLs 2008. LNCS, vol. 5170, pp. 33–38. Springer, Heidelberg (2008). https://doi.org/10.1007/978-3-540-71067-7_7

Model Checking and Quantifier Elimination

A Theorem Prover Based Approach for SAT-Based Model Checking Certification

Giulia Sindoni[1(✉)], Paolo Pasini[2(✉)], Gianpiero Cabodi[3], Paolo E. Camurati[3], Alberto Griggio[1(✉)], Marco Palena[4], Marco Roveri[5], and Stefano Tonetta[1(✉)]

[1] FBK - Fondazione Bruno Kessler, Trento, Italy
{gsindoni,griggio,tonettas}@fbk.eu
[2] DET - Dept. of Electronics and Telecommunications, Politecnico Di Torino, Turin, Italy
paolo.pasini@polito.it
[3] DAUIN - Dept. of Control and Computer Engineering, Politecnico Di Torino, Turin, Italy
{gianpiero.cabodi,paolo.camurati}@polito.it
[4] CNIT - National Inter-University Consortium for Telecommunications, Turin, Italy
marco.palena@polito.it
[5] Dept. of Information Engineering and Computer Science, University of Trento, Trento, Italy
marco.roveri@unitn.it

Abstract. In the field of formal verification, certifying proofs serve as compelling evidence to demonstrate the correctness of a model within a deductive system. These proofs can be automatically generated as a by-product of the verification process and are key artifacts for high-assurance systems. Their significance lies in their ability to be independently verified by proof checkers, which provides a more convenient approach than certifying the tools that generate them. Modern model checking algorithms adopt deductive methods and usually generate proofs in terms of inductive invariants, assuming that these apply to the original system under verification. Model checkers, though, often make use of a range of complex pre-processing simplifications and transformations to ease the verification process, which add another layer of complexity to the generation of proofs. In this paper, we present a novel approach for certifying model checking results exploiting a theorem prover and a theory of temporal deductive rules that can support various kinds of transformations and simplification of the original circuit. We implemented and experimentally evaluated our contribution on invariants generated using two state-of-the-art model checkers, nuXmv and PdTRAV, and by defining a set of rules within a theorem prover, to validate each certificate.

Keywords: Model Checking · Certificate · Safety · Invariant · Proof Checking

C. Barrett and U. Waldmann (Eds.): CADE 2025, LNAI 15943, pp. 449–467, 2025.
https://doi.org/10.1007/978-3-031-99984-0_24

1 Introduction

Adopting formal methods as a tool for certifying high-assurance and safety-critical systems calls for verification tools to being capable of providing a high level of confidence in their outcomes. Verification tools such as model checkers, are inherently complex: they rely on a variety of heuristics, transformation and simplification steps and they often exploit a variety of different techniques and algorithms in order to successfully tackle verification instances.

A model checker generally offers a straightforward "yes" or "no" answer when addressing a verification problem. However, the growing complexity of model checkers themselves has made it increasingly important to obtain certificates from the model checking process. These certificates, often in the form of deductive proofs, serve to build trust in the verification results by providing additional evidence of correctness.

The idea is for model checkers to behave similarly to SAT solvers within the SAT community. SAT solvers provide certificates that serve as proofs of unsatisfiability when a formula cannot be satisfied. These certificates enhance the trustworthiness of the solvers' outcomes, ensuring that the results can be independently verified by third parties.

For model checking, certification would involve generating deductive proofs as a by-product of the verification process [27], to be then independently verified by proof checkers, which are generally simpler to certify compared to the original proof-generating tools. The independent verification process further boosts the reliability of the results, since it can be conducted at any time outside of the model checker context.

To be effective on real-world instances, though, most model checkers adopt a range of pre-processing simplifications. For example, the model checker may compute some equivalences among variables of the original system and exploit them to reduce the model. As a result, the invariants generated by these model checkers are inductive relative to other invariants, meaning that they hold true based on the assumptions made about these other invariants. Other simplifications decompose temporally the problem: temporal decomposition first proves the invariant on the first k steps and then finds an inductive invariant that holds only after k steps [14]; phase abstraction [6] instead proves a property on subsequences defined by periodic signals. Henceforth, the generation of proofs becomes much more complex in these cases, as it requires temporal reasoning beyond the simple induction principle.

In this paper, we strive to reduce the burden of model checker developers for generating certifying proofs, by providing a proof system based on an existing theorem prover, namely PVS [29], that would build and prove theorems of the system under verification based on the information provided by a model checker. The proof system is based on a theory of temporal deductive rules for Linear-time Temporal Logic (LTL), accounting for the temporal reasoning behind simplifications. We develop strategies in PVS to prove safety properties using equivalences, temporal decomposition, and phase abstraction. This allows model checkers to generate certificates with minimal overhead – essentially outputting an inductive invariant for the simplified system along with a small amount of additional information (e.g., the bound used for temporal decomposition or the period for phase abstraction) – while delegating the proof process to the theorem prover.

We implemented and experimentally evaluated our contribution on invariants generated using two state-of-the-art model checkers, nuXmv and PdTRAV, and by defining a set of rules within PVS, to validate each certificate. The combination of two model checkers for proof generation, coupled with PVS for certification, aims at supporting the rigour and adaptability of the proposed approach.

Outline. The rest of the paper is organized as follows: Sect. 2 provides an overview of related work. Sect. 3 introduces notation and background notions. Sect. 4 describes our proposed approach at theorem prover based certification. Sect. 5 reports an evaluation of the proposed approach on industrial-level benchmarks, and Sect. 6 concludes the paper.

2 Related Work

This work leverages existing literature and further delves into the issue of certifying model checking results. This work extends on the concepts first presented in [23,24], where it was shown how to exploit the k-liveness algorithm to extend proof generation capabilities for invariant checking to cover full linear-time temporal logic (LTL) properties, with little overhead for the model checker. However, no theorem prover was used to check the proof generated by the model checker.

Among the most related works, [37] introduces a formal framework designed to certify the results of k-induction-based model checking. At the core of such a framework there is the concept of a k-witness circuit, acting as a simulation of the original circuit and including an inductive invariant that serves as a proof certificate. Such an approach is further expanded in [5], where the authors show how to simplify the approach by assuming reset functions are stratified, enabling the approach to be extended to word-level reasoning. In [38] the authors present an approach to certify temporal decomposition, and in [20], the authors present an approach to certify an extended form of phase abstraction using a generic certificate format, still relying on the construction of a witness circuit, which includes an inductive invariant property, that serves as certificate.

The main difference between our approach and [37] is that in the latter every model checker must be extended to generate a witness circuit. In our approach the model checker does not need to perform extra processing, while the proof system builds the proof for every model checker using the supported transformation. The transformation techniques have been proved once and for all as PVS lemmas. Those proofs can be checked, and they are purely symbolic manipulations done in a sequent calculus style. The proved lemmas are then used in the strategies to provide a certificate of the correctness of the fact that the property is satisfied in the corresponding model.

Moreover, [37] is explicitly limited to invariant properties only, whereas our approach can be extended to certifying liveness and general LTL properties.

Therefore, we reduce the burden of model checker developers to produce the certificates themselves. However, checking the witness circuit with a specialised model checker is more efficient compared to the certification based on an off-the-shelf theorem prover.

3 Background and Preliminaries

We operate within the framework of Boolean (propositional) logic, using the standard concepts of satisfiability, validity, interpretations, and models. We use lowercase Latin letters x, v (possibly with subscripts or primes) to denote propositional variables. Similarly, uppercase Latin letters X, V represent sets of variables. Uppercase Latin letters $F, \mathcal{I}, T$ as well as lowercase Greek letters ϕ, ψ, χ, are used to denote formulae, while uppercase Greek letters Γ and Δ represent sets of formulae. We write $F(X)$ to indicate that all variables appearing in F belong to X , which is referred to as the *support* of F. Likewise, given two disjoint sets of variables X and X', the notation $F(X, X')$ signifies that the support of F is $X \cup X'$.

3.1 Transition Systems

We take into account systems modelled by state transition structures, implicitly represented by propositional formulae. A *transition system* $\mathcal{M}$ is a triple $\langle X, \mathcal{I}, T \rangle$, where X is a set of (propositional) *state variables*, $\mathcal{I}(X)$ is a formula representing the *initial states*, and $T(X, X')$ is a formula representing the system's *transition relation*. The states of $\mathcal{M}$ are (complete) assignments to the variables in X. We denote by Σ_X the set of states. A state $s \in \Sigma_X$ is a model for a propositional formula ψ, denote by $s \models \psi(X)$, if substituting the values of s into ψ, the formula ψ evaluates to *True*. Next states, i.e., those reached after a transition, are represented as assignments to primed state variables X'. A *path* of $\mathcal{M}$ is an infinite sequence of states $s_0, s_1, \ldots$ such that $s_0 \models \mathcal{I}$, and for all $i \geq 0$ we have that $s_i, s_{i+1} \models T$. Given a path $\boldsymbol{\pi} := s_0, s_1, \ldots$ we denote with $\boldsymbol{\pi}[i]$ the state s_i.

3.2 Linear Temporal Logic

Linear Temporal Logic (LTL) was introduced by Pnueli [31] for the specification and verification of reactive systems. Formulae of LTL are constructed from a set of *propositional variables* X using the usual *logical connectives* (negation $\neg$, conjunction $\wedge$ and disjunction $\vee$) and some *temporal operators* **X** ("next time"), **F** ("eventually"), **G** ("always") and **U** ("until"). LTL formulae are interpreted in terms of paths, i.e., sequences of states of a transition system.

Given a transition system $\mathcal{M} = \langle X, \mathcal{I}, T \rangle$, a path $\boldsymbol{\pi} := s_0, s_1, \ldots$ in $\mathcal{M}$, an index i and a formula ψ over X, we define $\boldsymbol{\pi}, i \models \psi$, i.e. that $\boldsymbol{\pi}$ satisfies ψ in i, as follows:

- $\pi, i \models \top$ and $\pi, i \not\models \bot$.
- For each $p \in X$, $\pi, i \models p$ iff $\pi[i] \models p$.
- $\pi, i \models \neg\psi$ iff $\pi, i \not\models \psi$.
- $\pi, i \models \psi_1 \wedge \psi_2$ iff $\pi, i \models \psi_1$ and $\pi, i \models \psi_2$.
- $\pi, i \models \psi_1 \vee \psi_2$ iff $\pi, i \models \psi_1$ or $\pi \models \psi_2$.
- $\pi, i \models \mathbf{X}\psi$ iff $\pi, i+1 \models \psi$.
- $\pi, i \models \mathbf{F}\psi$ iff $\pi, j \models \psi$ for some $j \geq i$.
- $\pi, i \models \mathbf{G}\psi$ iff $\pi, j \models \psi$ for every $j \geq i$.
- $\pi, i \models \psi_1 \mathbf{U} \psi_2$ iff $\pi, j \models \psi_2$ for some $j \geq i$ and $\pi, k \models \psi_1$ for every $i \leq k < j$.

Other common Boolean operators have semantics that can be easily inferred from the semantics of $\neg$, $\wedge$ and $\vee$.

Finally, $\pi \models \psi$ iff $\pi, 0 \models \psi$. Given a propositional formula ϕ over X, we call the invariant checking problem, denoted by $\mathcal{M} \models \mathbf{G}(\phi)$, the problem to check $\pi \models \mathbf{G}(\phi)$ for all paths π of $\mathcal{M}$.

3.3 Model Transformations

Given a transition system $\mathcal{M}$, several pre-processing and transformation techniques may be applied before proceeding with the actual verification task. When taking into account concrete model instances, representing digital circuits, it is usual to extend the concepts previously introduced to such a context. Hardware combinational circuits, are often represented as directed acyclic graphs (DAGs), where every gate of the circuit is associated with a given Boolean function and state variables for the systems are materialized as memory elements.

Equivalence and Constant Propagation. Several pre-processing techniques rely on formulae simplifications through the identification of equivalence classes among variables. Exploiting equivalences and constants propagation one can derive a new model whose behaviour mirrors the original one. One such a technique is ternary simulation [34], that performs a symbolic simulation of the circuit using three-valued logic.

Temporal Decomposition. Temporal decomposition [14] is a technique designed to simplify a given input system by identifying and eliminating unnecessary logic associated with initialization or reset sequences within the circuit. This logic typically pertains to operations executed exclusively during the initial phases of the system's operation, and thus could be ignored when evaluating the actual behaviour of the system. The core concept revolves around estimating, or guessing, the duration of the reset sequence. Once such a length k is determined, the technique allows for the modification of the system's initial states, by replacing them with the set of states reachable within k steps, and obtaining a new model for the system. Additional simplifications might be applied alongside temporal decomposition.

Even if no additional simplifications are performed, if the property ϕ under verification is an invariant, in case of temporal decomposition, it is necessary to check whether the property holds in the first k steps as well.

Phase Abstraction. Phase abstraction [1,6] is a simplification technique that operates by detecting and removing periodic signals that exhibit clock-like behaviours and partitioning the system according to the identified phases.

Using phase abstraction, it is possible to remodel the system under verification in order to bypass difficulties that arise from managing multi-phase systems. Considering two-phase designs, the technique operates by replacing the system's transition relation with a composition of two instances of the original transitions. Additionally, it expands the property under verification to include all states reaching a safe state (with respect to the original property) in a single step.

3.4 Theorem Proving in PVS

The Prototype Verification System (PVS) [29] is a specification language integrated with a theorem prover. The PVS theorem prover is interactive, but it also supports strategy development [30] and a batch mode [26], so that proofs can be run automatically. PVS uses a sequent-style [22] proof representation. A PVS sequent is an object of the form $A_1, A_2, A_3, \ldots \vdash B_1, B_2, B_3, \ldots$, where formulae A_i make the antecedent and formulae B_j make the consequent. The sequent above asserts that "if all the A's are true, then at least one of the B's is true". Hence, the sequent means the same as: $(A_1 \wedge A_2 \wedge A_3 \ldots) \rightarrow (B_1 \vee B_2 \vee B_3 \ldots)$.

The prover builds a proof tree that starts with $\vdash A$, where A is the theorem to be established. A proof is accomplished when all the leaves are recognised as true: this occurs if any antecedent is the same as any consequent $(C, \Gamma \vdash C, \Delta)$, if any antecedent is false $(\mathit{False}, \Gamma \vdash \Delta)$, or if any consequent is true $(\Gamma \vdash \mathit{True}, \Delta)$. Other sequents can be recognised as true using more powerful inferences [35].

4 Certifying Proofs for SAT-Based Model Checking

In this section we present our approach at theorem prover based certification. Section 4.1 gives a summary of the certification process. Section 4.2 shows how to formalise the LTL logic in PVS. Section 4.3 presents a basic PVS strategy for proving invariants. Section 4.4 formalises phase abstraction as a temporal deductive rule and introduces a PVS strategy for phase abstraction. Section 4.5 presents a PVS strategy for temporal decomposition.

4.1 Certification Process

Our certification process goes through three main stages:

1. The model checking stage, where we run the model checker and we dump the invariants and any other parameter which will be required by the relevant PVS strategy. These parameters are the inductive invariant in the case of the basic strategy with no transformation (see Sect. 4.3), the inductive invariant $\hat{\chi}$ of the phase-abstracted model (see Sect. 4.4) in the case where the model

has gone through phase abstraction, and the inductive invariant ι and the natural number k (see Sect. 4.5) in the case where the model has gone through temporal decomposition.
2. The theory generation phase, where a PVS theory is generated with the relevant specification of the model $\mathcal{M}$, the property to be proved, the parameters, the claim of the main theorem and the PVS proof-script with the strategy to be run to prove the main theorem.
3. The PVS proof which generates the proof certificate. Each proof uses one of the PVS strategies presented in the next sections, and follows a consistent pattern for all invariant checking problems $\mathcal{M} \models \mathbf{G}(\phi)$. The proof consists of two key components: a *structural part* and a *proof obligations discharging part.* The structural part involves applying LTL definitions and the temporal deductive rules which we have proved *once and for all* as PVS lemmas (such as the lemmas for phase abstraction or temporal decomposition). This part remains identical regardless of the specific model and property being certified. The proof obligations discharging part focuses on proving the propositional implications at the leaves of the proof tree and it is accomplished using the PVS built-in SAT solver (PVS uses the SMT solver Yices [19]).
The critical aspect of the proof lies in this discharge of the proof obligations by Yices, as these proof steps confirm that the model $\mathcal{M}$ satisfies the necessary premises for the applied transformations lemmas, thereby validating the conclusion of $\mathcal{M} \models \mathbf{G}(\phi)$.

We remark that, alternatively to a SAT solver like Yices, purely syntactic and resolution based methods can be used at stage 3 of the process, in order to discharge the propositional implication leaves. In PVS such methods are prop or bddsimp [35], which we originally used in our strategies, and they successfully generated proof trees with trivially true sequent leaves of the form $A, \Delta \vdash A, \Gamma$. However, these purely syntactical methods exhibited the expected scalability limitations, thus the need for a SAT solver. We would also like to underline that there are SAT solvers capable of producing proofs, which could in turn be independently verified [18,21,25]. These could replace Yices, providing an additional layer of certification. While such proof producing SAT solvers are not currently available into the PVS framework, their development and incorporation represents a promising avenue for future work.

Our aim is to reduce a complex problem to a simpler one. We transform the problem of proving invariants through model checking algorithms and transformations techniques, into the verification of propositional formulae that can be discharged by a SAT solver. This represents a significant reduction in complexity, as the propositional formula handled by the SAT solver is a substantially simpler problem than the original model checking problem.

4.2 A Shallow Embedding of LTL in PVS

Previous formalisations of the Linear Temporal Logic in PVS include Pnueli's formalisation [32] and PVS-nasalib LTL library [28]. We can categorise the first approach as a shallow embedding of LTL into PVS, and the second one as a deep embedding, following the distinction drawn in [7,33]. A shallow embedding of a modal logic in PVS is a direct syntactic transformation of the logic into PVS, and it relies PVS's existing syntax and type system. On the other hand, a deep embedding defines an abstract datatype that models the syntax, and defines functions that operate on this datatype by recursion and case analysis. A deep embedding is to be preferred for proving properties *about* the logic at issue, whilst a shallow embedding should be preferred for proving properties stated *in* the logic. After some experimentation with the LTL library from [28] we realized that a shallow embedding of LTL in PVS is more efficient for our purpose. Our formalisation follows the style of the elementary shallow embedding of propositional modal logic in PVS from [33].

In the PVS theory `shallow_ltl` we declare the type *trace* as all mappings from natural numbers to states. An *LTL formula* is a function that takes a trace and a natural number, and returns a boolean PVS type (*True* or *False*), which is the truth-value of the formula at point on the trace. A *state* is an object of any type, and it is an explicit parameter of `shallow_ltl`.

```
shallow_ltl[State: TYPE+]: THEORY
BEGIN
Trace: TYPE = ARRAY[nat -> State]
ltlformula: TYPE = [Trace -> [nat -> bool]]
```

Examples of definition of propositional and LTL operators within our theory[1] follow, where P is an LTL formula.

```
NOT(P)(trace: Trace)(t: nat): bool = NOT P(trace)(t);
NEXT(P)(trace: Trace)(t: nat): bool = P(trace)(t+1);
GLOBALLY(P)(trace: Trace)(t: nat): bool = FORALL (t0: nat): t0 >= t IMPLIES P
    (trace)(t0);
```

An LTL formula P is *valid* if it is true at the initial state of any trace. A stronger notion of validity, called *global validity*, is when the formula is true at any state of any trace.

```
|=(trace:Trace, t:nat, P): bool = P(trace)(t)
valid(P): bool = FORALL (trace: Trace): |=(trace, 0, P)
valid_all(P): bool = FORALL (trace: Trace): FORALL (t: nat): |=(trace, t, P)
```

The full theory `shallow_ltl` can be found in a dedicated repository [36].

4.3 Certifying Proofs for Invariants: a Basic PVS Strategy

We are interested in the invariant checking problem $\mathcal{M} \models \mathbf{G}(\phi)$, where $\mathcal{M} = \langle X, \mathcal{I}, T \rangle$ and ϕ is a propositional formula defined over X. Following the approach from [24], in order to deal with this problem we provide a proof for

$$\mathcal{I} \wedge \mathbf{G}(T) \rightarrow \mathbf{G}(\phi) \tag{1}$$

[1] PVS allows overloading of built-in symbols. In the definition above the first `NOT` is our defined LTL operator, which creates an LTL formula and whose semantics is defined via the boolean PVS operator `NOT`.

Given a propositional formula ϕ, we say it is inductive w.r.t. the transition system if ϕ holds at the initial state, and ϕ holds in all states reachable from the states that satisfy ϕ. For these cases, a proof of 1 can be obtained using the LTL-induction rule [23]:

$$\frac{\phi \qquad \mathbf{G}(\phi \rightarrow \mathbf{X}(\phi))}{\mathbf{G}(\phi)}\ \mathrm{I}$$

One proves that $\mathcal{I} \rightarrow \phi$ and $\mathbf{G}(T) \rightarrow \mathbf{G}(\phi \rightarrow \mathbf{X}(\phi))$ so to conclude 1.

This induction rule has been formalised and proved as a `shallow_ltl` lemma of the theory `lemmas_shallow_ltl` [36]. We use this lemma within a PVS strategy for proving inductive invariants. The PVS proof tree starts with $\vdash valid(\mathcal{I} \wedge \mathbf{G}(T) \rightarrow \mathbf{G}(\phi))$ and applies PVS primitive rules as well as proved lemmas. The full strategy can be found at [36](`inductive_invariant_shallow_ltl_macro`).

However in most cases the invariant property to be proved ϕ is not necessarily inductive w.r.t. $\mathcal{M}$. Most model checkers prove these cases by generating a formula ψ that is inductive and that is stronger than ϕ, i.e. such that $\psi \rightarrow \phi$. To certify these cases, we developed a PVS strategy that takes an inductive invariant ψ as an explicit parameter (provided by the model checking phase) and uses the previously described strategy for inductive invariant as subroutine. The goal is again to provide a proof for the validity of 1. In our strategy we make of use the PVS rule `Case` which allows us to assume a formula and subsequently prove this formula to be true [35]. Thus with `Case` we assume that *i)* $\mathcal{I} \wedge \mathbf{G}(T) \rightarrow \mathbf{G}(\psi)$ is valid, and that *ii)* $\psi \rightarrow \phi$ is globally valid. Hence the strategy uses a proved lemma to infer that 1 follows from these assumptions. This concludes the *structural part* of the proof. Subsequently, it proves assumption *i* by using the strategy for proving inductive invariant, and assumption *ii* using the PVS built-in SAT solver Yices. This concludes the *proof obligations discharging part* of the proof. The full strategy can be found at [36] under the name of `general_invariant_shallow_ltl_macro` as well as an example of its application and the resulting proof for 1 applied to specific formulae for $\mathcal{I}$, T and property ϕ. This also provides an example of applying the strategy for proving inductive invariants, as the last is used as a subroutine of the former.

4.4 Phase Abstraction as a Temporal Deductive Rule

As discussed in Sect. 3.3, phase abstraction is a transformation technique that partitions the system according to identified phases. We consider two-phase abstraction, which is when the system partitions into two equivalence classes: the sets of states reachable over even and over odd time-frames. We show how phase abstraction can be formalised as a rule in LTL, and therefore the traditional proof for invariant based on the generation of an inductive invariant (discussed in Sect. 4.3) can be extended to take into account this transformation of the original system. In this way, we extend the set of LTL rules capturing transformation techniques presented in [24].

Let us define the following formulae:

$$\mathcal{I} \to \hat{\chi} \tag{2}$$

$$\mathbf{G}T \to \mathbf{G}(\hat{\chi} \to \mathbf{X}(\mathbf{X}(\hat{\chi})) \tag{3}$$

$$\mathbf{G}(\hat{\chi} \to \phi) \wedge \mathbf{G}((\hat{\chi} \wedge T) \to \mathbf{X}(\phi)) \tag{4}$$

We model phase abstraction as an LTL rule as follows, where ϕ is the invariant property of interest:

$$\frac{\mathcal{I} \to \hat{\chi} \qquad \mathbf{G}T \to \mathbf{G}(\hat{\chi} \to \mathbf{X}(\mathbf{X}(\hat{\chi})) \qquad \mathbf{G}(\hat{\chi} \to \phi) \wedge \mathbf{G}((\hat{\chi} \wedge T) \to \mathbf{X}(\phi))}{\mathcal{I} \wedge \mathbf{G}(T) \to \mathbf{G}(\phi)}\ \text{P-A}$$

Here, the formula $\hat{\chi}$ represents an inductive invariant of the phase-abstracted model, which is the model made of all states reachable over even time-frames. Premise 2 expresses that the initial condition implies $\hat{\chi}$. Premise 3 expresses that, starting from a state where $\hat{\chi}$ is true and following the transition relation, $\hat{\chi}$ holds every two steps of the original model. This makes $\hat{\chi}$ an inductive invariant of the phase-abstracted model. Finally Premise 4 expresses that $\hat{\chi}$ is not just *any* invariant of the phase-abstracted model, but it is an invariant suitable to grant a proof of the original property ϕ: ϕ holds whenever $\hat{\chi}$ holds, and starting from a state where $\hat{\chi}$ holds and looking ahead of one step, ϕ holds at the next state too. Our job is now to provide a proof of correctness of the P-A rule, so that this rule can safely be used in proofs for invariants.

In order to prove that the conclusion of our P-A rule follows from its premises we reason as follows. We define $\alpha := \hat{\chi} \vee \mathbf{X}(\hat{\chi})$. We prove that, under P-A's premises 2 and 3, α is an invariant of the original system, i.e. that $\mathcal{I} \wedge \mathbf{G}(T) \to \mathbf{G}(\alpha)$. This amounts to prove the following auxiliary lemma.

Lemma 1. $(2) \wedge (3) \to (\mathcal{I} \wedge \mathbf{G}(T) \to \mathbf{G}(\alpha))$.

The lemma above has been formalised and proved in PVS. We report a schema of the PVS proof, and we refer to [36] for the fine-grained proof.

$$\dfrac{\dfrac{\dfrac{(2)}{\mathcal{I} \to \alpha} \qquad \dfrac{(3)}{\mathbf{G}(T) \to \mathbf{G}(\alpha \to \mathbf{X}(\alpha))}}{\mathcal{I} \wedge \mathbf{G}(T) \to (\alpha \wedge \mathbf{G}(\alpha \to \mathbf{X}(\alpha)))}}{\mathcal{I} \wedge \mathbf{G}(T) \to \mathbf{G}(\alpha)}\ \text{I}$$

Finally we prove that under premise 4 and $\mathbf{G}(\alpha)$ we have $\mathbf{G}(\phi)$. Hence we conclude that $\mathcal{I} \wedge \mathbf{G}(T) \to \mathbf{G}(\phi)$.

The full formalisation and proof of the P-A rule has been done in PVS in our theory `lemmas_shallow_ltl`. The schema of the proof is as follows, and we refer to [36] for the fine-grained proof.

$$\dfrac{\dfrac{\dfrac{\text{Lemma 1}\ \dfrac{(2) \qquad (3)}{\mathcal{I} \wedge \mathbf{G}(T) \to \mathbf{G}(\alpha)} \qquad [\mathcal{I} \wedge \mathbf{G}(T)]}{\mathbf{G}(\alpha)} \qquad (4) \qquad [\mathbf{G}(T)]}{\mathbf{G}(\phi)}}{\mathcal{I} \wedge \mathbf{G}(T) \to \mathbf{G}(\phi)}$$

We intend to generalize such a proof to $k \neq 2$ as a future work, where k is the number on identified phases.

A PVS Strategy for Phase Abstraction. We propose a PVS strategy that modifies the basic strategy from Sect. 4.3 to take into account phase abstraction. The PVS proof tree starts with the goal: $\vdash valid(\mathcal{I} \wedge \mathbf{G}(T) \rightarrow \mathbf{G}(\phi))$, where $\mathcal{I}$, T and ϕ are specific formulae describing the transition system at issue and the property we need to verify. The strategy takes the formula $\hat{\chi}$, which is the inductive invariant of the phase-abstracted model, as an explicit parameter. This formula is provided by the model checking phase. We initially use the rule `Case` to introduce the three premise of P-A rule 4.4 in the sequent's assumptions. Then we apply the proved PVS lemma for phase abstraction, which formalises the rule P-A, and by some manipulation using PVS rules, we conclude the goal. This concludes the *structural part* of the proof. The rule `Case` is a branching rule and requires us to verify the truth of our assumed formulae on the other proof-branch. The developed strategy proves formulae 2, 3 and 4 for the assumed values of $\mathcal{I}$, T and $\hat{\chi}$ by applying PVS rules and expanding definitions from `shallow_ltl`, and finally invoking the Yices SAT solver. This concludes the *proof obligations discharging part* of the proof. The full strategy can be found at [36] under the name of `phase_abstraction_kis2` as well as an example of its application and the resulting proof.

4.5 Temporal Decomposition as a Temporal Deductive Rule

When using temporal decomposition (Sect. 3.3), the initial condition $\mathcal{I}$ is replaced by a condition ι that overapproximates the set of reachable states after k transitions. In [24] it is shown that this technique can be formalised as a derived LTL rule. In the following $\mathbf{X}^0(P) := P$ and $\mathbf{X}^{n+1}(P) := \mathbf{X}(\mathbf{X}^n(P))$ for all $n \geq 0$.

$$\frac{(\mathcal{I} \wedge \bigwedge_{0 \leq i < k} (\mathbf{X}^i(T))) \rightarrow \mathbf{X}^k(\iota) \quad (\mathcal{I} \wedge \bigwedge_{0 \leq i < k} (\mathbf{X}^i(T))) \rightarrow (\bigwedge_{0 \leq i < k} (\mathbf{X}^i(\phi))) \quad \mathbf{G}(\iota \wedge \mathbf{G}(T) \rightarrow \mathbf{G}(\phi))}{\mathcal{I} \wedge \mathbf{G}(T) \rightarrow \mathbf{G}(\phi)} \text{ T-D}$$

The first premise models that after k steps the condition ι is reached. The third premise models that once we are in a state of $\mathcal{M}$ where ι holds, ϕ will hold thereafter. The second premise checks that ϕ holds in the first $k-1$ steps, as for ϕ to be an invariant of original transition system it has to hold *before* ι too. The rule concludes that ϕ is an invariant of the transition system.

We have formalised and proved the T-D rule as a PVS lemma [36] within our theory `lemmas_shallow_ltl`. This enabled us to develop a PVS strategy that takes into account temporal decomposition when proving invariant properties.

A PVS Strategy for Temporal Decomposition. The PVS proof tree starts with the goal: $\vdash \mathit{valid}(\mathcal{I} \wedge \mathbf{G}(T) \rightarrow \mathbf{G}(\phi))$. The strategy takes the formula ι and the natural number k as explicit parameters. They are provided by the model checking phase. It uses the rule `Case` to introduce the three premises of T-D rule 4.5 in the sequent's assumptions. It then applies the proved PVS lemma for temporal decomposition, and by some manipulation it concludes the goal. This concludes the *structural part* of the proof. The rule `Case` is a branching rule and it requires us to verify the truth of our assumed formulae (i.e. the T-D rule's premises) on the other proof-branches. The first two premises of T-D have to be established by applying PVS rules and definitions from `shallow_ltl` and the Yices SAT solver. The third premise is an invariant claim on the temporally decomposed model $\mathcal{M}^{'} = \langle \iota, T \rangle$. So, the currently described strategy calls a version of `general_invariant_shallow_ltl_macro` (see Sect. 4.3) as a subroutine to complete the proof of this branch. This concludes the *proof obligations discharging part* of the proof. The full strategy can be found at [36] under the name `tmp_decomposition` as well as an example of its application and the resulting proof.

5 Experimental Evaluation

In this section, we present the experimental evaluation of our proposed methodology, assessing the effectiveness, efficiency, and robustness of our approach through a series of comprehensive tests run on publicly available benchmarks sets. We describe the experimental setup, including the hardware and software configurations, the datasets used, and the specific metrics considered for the evaluation. We also provide a detailed analysis of the results obtained.

Setup. We have implemented our proof generation and certification procedure on top of two model checking tools, nuXmv [15] and PdTRAV [13]. Both tools take as input a model in Aiger [4] format, and produce inductive invariants as Aiger combinational circuits expressed over the state variables of the model.We then apply a simple Python script to translate the input model and the generated invariant into a PVS theory. We make the script available (together with the rest of the our toolchain) at [36]. The Python script is relatively simple, and it can be verified through standard software verification methodologies.

We could use some certified toolchain in a future implementation to verify also these steps.

Benchmark Set. For our evaluation, we have collected a total of 105 distinct problem instances from different families, stemming from previous Hardware Model Checking Competitions (HWMCC) [2].

In order to make it possible to properly and univocally keep track of all the elements comprising the circuits under verification, we have incorporated an explicit symbol table in all chosen base model instances. Each symbol table labels the inputs, outputs, and state elements of each circuit. Such a step does not alter the nature of the benchmark at all, no elements are removed: it is just a matter of providing names to each of the circuit components.

For each of the selected benchmarks, we generated intermediate representations of the models, including possible simplification steps, if any, that were applied during the process. All benchmarks, scripts, intermediate representations, certificates, and run logs have been documented and made available for reference [36].

The set of selected benchmarks has been identified by choosing UNSAT instances that could be verified and subsequently for which an invariant could be derived, without any form of simplification and within a given time limit of 1800 seconds. We intend to expand the experimental evaluation further, as we include additional simplification strategies in the future, in order to cover a larger set of available benchmarks and to tackle harder instances.

Results. In order to evaluate our proposed approach, we implemented the described methodology within different model checking suites.

The experiments were carried out on a computer cluster, on a queue consisting of 4 nodes with identical hardware specifications. Each node is equipped with an Intel Xeon CPU 6226R processor operating at 2.9 GHz, with 32 CPU cores and 16 GB of memory. All jobs were managed by SLURM

with a memory limit of 4 GB and a wall-time limit of 1800 seconds per experimental run.

In order to keep verification and certification steps streamlined we selected a single strategy to perform the verification phase.

Specifically, we utilize our IC3 engine [9] without introducing any additional simplification steps. This approach is designed to produce a specialized invariant, which serves as a certificate. Invariants were derived from the base models, as well as from runs where either temporal decomposition or phase abstraction was used.

As a future work, we would like to extend the experimental evaluation and the set of techniques covered in order to support additional engines, such as interpolation and IGR [10], but in order to do so additional transformation techniques and simplifications steps may have to be accounted for first, as interpolants often requires additional pre-processing to enhance their usability [11,12]. Concerning nuXmv, it has been run in the same setup as described before, taking into account only its IC3 engine.

PVS experiments were conducted using PVS8.0[2] on the set of benchmarks chosen as explained above, on the same cluster and in the same setup mentioned above, with a memory limit of 8 GB and a wall-time limit of 3600 seconds per run.

---

[2] We modified the PVS Makefile configuration to increase resource allocations. The `SBCL_SPACE_SIZE` parameter was increased from 6 GB to 30 GB, and `SBCL_STACK_SIZE` was increased from 8 MB to 32 MB.

For each run we are reporting the verification time, during which the corresponding invariant/certificate has been generated as an auxiliary artifact as well as certification times for the theorem prover approach. PVS certification results are given considering type-checking times, SAT solver times and overall certification times.

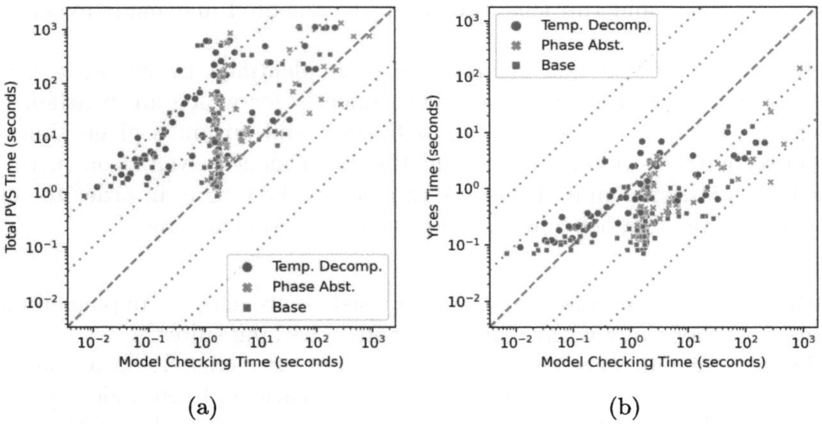

Fig. 1. Comparison between model checking verification and PVS certification times, considering overall certification times (a) and just SAT solver times (b).

Figure 1 presents preliminary results comparing the certification times of our theorem prover-based approach against model checking instances verification and invariants creation times. Figure 1a accounts for all the PVS certification contributions whereas Fig. 1b focuses on just Yices SAT solver times.

Comparing original benchmarks and invariants size in terms of number of AND-gates in their circuit based representation, shows that invariants tend to be between one and two order of magnitude smaller than the original benchmarks, as desirable.

Whilst these results demonstrate the feasibility of theorem prover-based certification, 166 out of 189 runs in total were successfully proved by PVS within the allotted time limits, they also reveal a significant performance gap between the two.

To better understand the reasons behind this performance gap, we further analysed the breakdown of execution times for different operations within PVS. We considered all runs, without distinguishing between phase abstraction runs, temporal decomposition runs and runs with no transformations. Figure 2 illustrates the total certification time divided into three components: *type-checking time*, the time spent verifying semantic constraints, determining expression types, and resolving names, *proof-checking time*, the time spent executing the actual steps of the proof strategy and *SAT solving time*, the time spent on calls to the SAT solver Yices.

This breakdown highlights that the theorem prover spends the majority of its time on type-checking, and on proof-checking operations other than the calls to Yices, and as shown in Fig. 1b, the time spent on Yices calls is usually inferior than the model checking time. To better distinguish the contribution of each series, a logarithmic scale has been used for the $y-$axis.

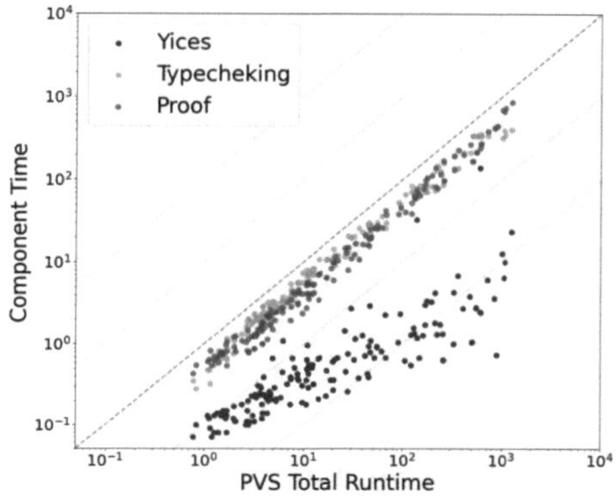

Fig. 2. Times breakdown for PVS-based runs.

Notably, the high type-checking times stem from PVS support for a rich variety of theories, which necessitates complex checks to ensure type correctness before the proof process even begins. Additionally, in our experiments, the high proof-checking times appeared to be driven more by internal bookkeeping operations and installing definitions rather than the execution of actual reasoning steps.

In conclusion, we attribute this performance gap primarily to internal bottlenecks within PVS. These inefficiencies could potentially be mitigated by an optimized, ad-hoc implementation of the theorem prover, or by engaging with the PVS maintainers to explore optimisation opportunities for our use case, or yet by adopting an alternative theorem prover with stronger support for automated proof checking rather than interactive use (LEAN [17] represents an alternative, but further exploration is needed to verify its comparative advantages). In particular, we believe that an optimized ad-hoc theorem prover could yield proof-checking times comparable to our SAT-based approach. We leave further investigation of these possibilities for future work. Nonetheless, our prototype PVS implementation and preliminary results confirm both the soundness and feasibility of our theorem prover-based approach, which can be implemented in any off-the-shelf or custom theorem prover with LTL reasoning capabilities and that requires minimal modifications to existing model checkers. Such a possibility is one of the future steps we intend to investigate as a future work.

Limitations. In this section we describe the current limitations of our prototype implementation, and the planned work to overcome these limitations.

Our certification process as it described in Sect. 4.1 currently applies transformations in isolation, but the framework provides proofs that are easily composed. This makes it possible to develop strategies that generate proofs combining multiple simplifications, such as composing phase abstraction with temporal decomposition. Proof composition among strategies is already implemented to some extent, as most strategies call the strategy for proving inductive invariants as their subroutine.

We also aim to strengthen the confidence provided by our certification process. As explained in Sect. 4.1, the proof obligation discharge component relies on the PVS SAT solver Yices. To increase trust in this fundamental part of the proof, it would be beneficial to use proof producing SAT solvers that operate with greater transparency rather than functioning as black boxes.

Finally, we already discussed in Sect. 5 the main bottlenecks observed with PVS performance and how we plan to overcome these.

6 Conclusions and Future Work

In this paper, we have presented a novel approach for certifying model checking results by exploiting a theorem prover and a theory of temporal deductive rules that can support various kinds of transformations and simplifications of the original system. We established the correctness of the model checking transformation algorithms using a theorem prover. We employed the resulting rules to provide proof certificates of the success of the model checker, thereby reducing the burden of model checker developers to produce these certificates themselves. In fact, our technique can be easily implemented on top of existing model checkers with minimal modifications.

Our experiments confirm both the soundness and feasibility of our theorem prover-based approach, but at the same time highlights the necessity to better integrate such an approach with existing theorem provers, to overcome practical limitations to their applicability.

In this paper, we presented our work on some simplification techniques, and we first tackled the problem of considering these simplifications "in isolation from each other". However, the framework provides proofs that are easily composed, and so it is a very feasible next step to consider the generation of proof that combine multiple simplifications.

We see several directions for future work, such as extending the proposed approach to include a more general take on phase abstraction, being able to support additional kind of simplifications, as well as extending the model checking strategies to derive invariants. We would also like to extend the theorem prover based certification beyond the invariant model checking problem to liveness and LTL model checking. For example, given that the k-liveness algorithm [16] has been formalised as a temporal deductive rule in [24], a natural extension of our work is to use the theorem prover based approach to formalise and prove k-liveness and implement a strategy for it. Moreover the same certifying model checking approach can be extended to other LTL model checking algorithms such as FAIR [8] and liveness-to-safety [3].

Acknowledgements. The authors would like to acknowledge the invaluable help extended by Dr. Natarajan Shankar and the whole PVS development team, for their support and insightful discussions concerning the PVS tool.

This work was supported in part by the European Union - Next Generation EU under the Italian National Recovery and Resilience Plan (NRRP), Mission 4, Component 2, Investment 1.3, CUP E13C22001870001, partnership on "Telecommunications of the Future" (PE00000001 - program "RESTART"). This work was also supported in part by SRC contract 2024-CT-3280.

A. Griggio, M. Roveri, G. Sindoni and S. Tonetta acknowledge the support of the PNRR project FAIR - Future AI Research (PE00000013), under the NRRP MUR program funded by the NextGenerationEU.

M. Roveri is also partially supported by the project MUR PRIN 2020 - RIPER - Resilient AI-Based Self-Programming and Strategic Reasoning - CUP E63C22000400001, and by the European Union under Horizon Europe Programme - Grant Agreement 101070537—CrossCon.

Discolusure of Interests. The authors have no competing interests to declare that are relevant to the content of this article.

References

1. Baumgartner, J., Heyman, T., Singhal, V., Aziz, A.: An abstraction algorithm for the verification of level-sensitive latch-based netlists. Form. Methods Syst. Des. **23**(1), 39–65 (2003)
2. Biere, A., Jussila, T.: The model checking competition web page, http://fmv.jku.at/hwmcc
3. Biere, A., Artho, C., Schuppan, V.: Liveness checking as safety checking. Electron. Notes Theor. Comput. Sci. **66**(2), 160–177 (2002)
4. Biere, A., Heljanko, K., Wieringa, S.: AIGER 1.9 and beyond. Technical Report 11/2, Institute for Formal Models and Verification, Johannes Kepler University, Altenbergerstr. 69, 4040 Linz, Austria (2011)
5. Biere, A., Yu, E., Froleyks, N.: Stratified certification for k-induction. In: Proceedings of the 22nd Conference on Formal Methods in Computer-Aided Design–FMCAD 2022, vol. 3, p. 59. TU Wien Academic Press (2022)
6. Bjesse, P., Kukula, J.: Automatic generalized phase abstraction for formal verification. In: ICCAD-2005. IEEE/ACM International Conference on Computer-Aided Design, vol. 2005, pp. 1076–1082. IEEE (2005)
7. Boulton, R.J., et al.: Experience with embedding hardware description languages in hol. In: TPCD, vol. 10, pp. 129–156 (1992)
8. Bradley, A.R., Somenzi, F., Hassan, Z., Zhang, Y.: An incremental approach to model checking progress properties. In: 2011 Formal Methods in Computer-Aided Design (FMCAD), pp. 144–153. IEEE (2011)
9. Cabodi, G., Camurati, P.E., Mishchenko, A., Palena, M., Pasini, P.: SAT solver management strategies in IC3: an experimental approach. Form. Methods Syst. Des. **50**(1), 39–74 (2017)

10. Cabodi, G., Palena, M., Pasini, P.: Interpolation with guided refinement: revisiting incrementality in SAT-based unbounded model checking. Formal Methods Syst. Des. **60**(2), 117–146 (2022)
11. Cabodi, G., Camurati, P.E., Palena, M., Pasini, P., Vendraminetto, D.: Logic synthesis for interpolant circuit compaction. IEEE Trans. Comput.-Aided Des. Integr. Circ. Syst. **38**(2), 380–384 (2018)
12. Cabodi, G., Camurati, P.E., Palena, M., Pasini, P., Vendraminetto, D.: Reducing interpolant circuit size through SAT-based weakening. IEEE Trans. Comput.-Aided Des. Integr. Circ. Syst. **39**(7), 1524–1531 (2019)
13. Cabodi, G., Nocco, S., Quer, S.: Benchmarking a model checker for algorithmic improvements and tuning for performance. Form. Methods Syst. Des. **39**(2), 205–227 (2011)
14. Case, M.L., Mony, H., Baumgartner, J., Kanzelman, R:. Enhanced verification by temporal decomposition. In: 2009 Formal Methods in Computer-Aided Design, pp. 17–24. IEEE (2009)
15. Cavada, R., et al.: The nuXmv symbolic model checker. In: Computer Aided Verification: 26th International Conference, CAV 2014, Held as Part of the Vienna Summer of Logic, VSL 2014, Vienna, Austria, 18-22 July 2014. Proceedings 26, pp. 334–342. Springer (2014)
16. Claessen, K., Sörensson, N.: A liveness checking algorithm that counts. In: 2012 Formal Methods in Computer-Aided Design (FMCAD), pp. 52–59. IEEE (2012)
17. De Moura, L., Kong, S., Avigad, J., Van Doorn, F., von Raumer, J.: The Lean theorem prover (system description). In: Automated Deduction-CADE-25: 25th International Conference on Automated Deduction, Berlin, Germany, 1-7 August 2015, Proceedings 25, pp. 378–388. Springer (2015)
18. The LeanSAT Developers. LeanSAT
19. Dutertre, B., De Moura, L.: The Yices SMT solver. **2**(2), 1–2 (2006), Tool paper athttp://yices.csl.sri.com/tool-paper.pdf
20. Froleyks, N., Yu, E., Biere, A., Heljanko, K.: Certifying phase abstraction. In: International Joint Conference on Automated Reasoning, pp. 284–303. Springer (2024)
21. Gadgil, S., Rao, A.: Saturn: experiments with SAT solvers with proofs in Lean 4, 2025. Accessed 19 May 2025
22. Gentzen, G.: Untersuchungen über das logische schließen. i. Mathematische zeitschrift, vol. 35 (1935)
23. Griggio, A., Roveri, M., Tonetta, S.: Certifying proofs for LTL model checking. In: 2018 Formal Methods in Computer Aided Design (FMCAD), pp. 1–9. IEEE (2018)
24. Griggio, A., Roveri, M., Tonetta, S.: Certifying proofs for SAT-based model checking. Formal Methods Syst. Des. **57**(2), 178–210 (2021)
25. Mohamed, A.,et al.: Lean-SMT: an SMT tactic for discharging proof goals in Lean. In: Proceedings of the 37th International Conference on Computer Aided Verification (CAV 2025) (2025)
26. Munoz, C.A.: Batch proving and proof scripting in PVS. Technical report, National Institute of Aerospace (2007)
27. Namjoshi, K.S.: Certifying model checkers. In: Computer Aided Verification: 13th International Conference, CAV 2001 Paris, France, 18–22 July 2001 Proceedings 13, pp. 2–13. Springer (2001)
28. NASA. PVS-nasalib LTL library. https://github.com/nasa/pvslib/tree/master/LTL. Accessed: 21 Feb 2025
29. Owre, S., Rushby, J.M., Shankar, N.: PVS: a prototype verification system. In: International Conference on Automated Deduction, pp. 748–752. Springer (1992)

30. Owre, S., Shankar, N.: Writing PVS proof strategies. In: Design and Application of Strategies/Tactics in Higher Order Logics (STRATA 2003), number CP-2003-212448 in NASA Conference Publication, pp. 1–15 (2003)
31. Pnueli, A.: The temporal logic of programs. In: 18th Annual Symposium on Foundations of Computer Science (SFCS 1977), pp. 46–57. IEEE (1977)
32. Pnueli, A., Arons, T.: TLPVS: a PVS-based LTL verification system. In: Verification: Theory and Practice: Essays Dedicated to Zohar Manna on the Occasion of His 64th Birthday, pp. 598–625. Springer (2003)
33. Rushby, J.: PVS embeddings of propositional and quantified modal logic. arXiv preprint arXiv:2205.06391 (2022)
34. Seger, C.-J.H., Bryant, R.E.: Formal verification by symbolic evaluation of partially-ordered trajectories. Form. Methods Syst. Des. **6**(2), 147–189 (1995)
35. Shankar, N., Owre, S., Rushby, J.M., Stringer-Calvert, D.W.: Stringer-Calvert. PVS prover guide. Computer Science Laboratory, SRI International, Menlo Park, CA, **1**, 11–12 (2001)
36. Sindoni, G., et al.: Fbk-pdt-cert25. https://gitlab.fbk.eu/gsindoni/fbk_pdt_cert25. Accessed 24 02 2025
37. Yu, E., Biere, A., Heljanko, K.: Progress in certifying hardware model checking results. In: Computer Aided Verification: 33rd International Conference, CAV 2021, Virtual Event, 20–23 July 2021, Proceedings, Part II 33, pp. 363–386. Springer (2021)
38. Yu, E., Froleyks, N., Biere, A., Heljanko, K.: Towards compositional hardware model checking certification. In: 2023 Formal Methods in Computer-Aided Design (FMCAD), pp. 1–11. IEEE (2023)

Infinite State Model Checking by Learning Transitive Relations

Florian Frohn(✉) and Jürgen Giesl(✉)

RWTH Aachen University, Aachen, Germany
{florian.frohn,giesl}@informatik.rwth-aachen.de

Abstract. We propose a new approach for proving safety of infinite state systems. It extends the analyzed system by *transitive relations* until its *diameter* D becomes finite, i.e., until constantly many steps suffice to cover all reachable states, irrespective of the initial state. Then we can prove safety by checking that no error state is reachable in D steps. To deduce transitive relations, we use *recurrence analysis*. While recurrence analyses can usually find conjunctive relations only, our approach also discovers disjunctive relations by combining recurrence analysis with *projections*. An empirical evaluation of the implementation of our approach in our tool LoAT shows that it is highly competitive with the state of the art.

1 Introduction

We consider relations defined by SMT formulas over two disjoint vectors of *pre-* and *post-variables* $\mathbf{x}$ and $\mathbf{x}'$. Such *relational formulas* can easily represent *transition systems* (TSs), linear *Constrained Horn Clauses* (CHCs), and *control-flow automata* (CFAs).[1] Thus, they subsume many popular intermediate representations used for verification of systems specified in more expressive languages.

In contrast to, e.g., source code, relational formulas are unstructured. However, source code may be unstructured, too (e.g., due to gotos), so being independent from the structure of the input makes our approach broadly applicable.

Example 1 (Running Example). Let $\tau := \tau_{\mathsf{inc}} \vee \tau_{\mathsf{dec}}$ with:

$$w \doteq 0 \wedge x' \doteq x + 1 \wedge y' \doteq y + 1 \qquad (\tau_{\mathsf{inc}})$$

$$w' \doteq w \wedge w \doteq 1 \wedge x' \doteq x - 1 \wedge y' \doteq y - 1 \qquad (\tau_{\mathsf{dec}})$$

We use "$\doteq$" for equality in relational formulas. The formula τ defines a relation $\rightarrow_\tau$ on $\mathbb{Z} \times \mathbb{Z} \times \mathbb{Z}$ by relating the non-primed pre-variables with the primed post-variables. So for all $v_w, v_x, v_y, v'_w, v'_x, v'_y \in \mathbb{Z}$, we have $(v_w, v_x, v_y) \rightarrow_\tau (v'_w, v'_x, v'_y)$ iff $[w/v_w, x/v_x, y/v_y, w'/v'_w, x'/v'_x, y'/v'_y]$ is a model of τ. Let the set of *error states* be given by $\psi_{\mathsf{err}} := w \doteq 1 \wedge x \leq 0 \wedge y > 0$.

[1] To this end, it suffices to introduce one additional variable that represents the control-flow location (for TSs and CFAs) or the predicate (for linear CHCs).

C. Barrett and U. Waldmann (Eds.): CADE 2025, LNAI 15943, pp. 468–489, 2025.
https://doi.org/10.1007/978-3-031-99984-0_25

With the *initial states* $\psi_{\mathsf{init}} := x \doteq 0 \wedge y \doteq 0$ this example[2] is challenging for existing model checkers: Neither the default configuration of Z3/Spacer [29, 36], nor Golem's [4] implementation of Spacer, LAWI [35], IMC [34], TPA [8], PDKIND [27], or predicate abstraction [25] can prove its safety. In contrast, all of these techniques can prove safety with the more general initial states $\psi_{\mathsf{init}} := x \doteq y$. As all of them are based on *interpolation*, the reason might be that the inductive invariant $x \doteq y$ is now a subterm of ψ_{init}, so it is likely to occur in interpolants. However, this explanation is insufficient, as all techniques fail again for $\psi_{\mathsf{init}} := x \doteq y \wedge y \doteq 0$.

This illustrates a well-known issue of interpolation-based verification techniques: They are highly sensitive to minor changes of the input or the underlying interpolating SMT solver (e.g., [31, p. 102]). So while they can often solve difficult problems quickly, they sometimes fail for easy examples like the one above.

In another line of research, *recurrence analysis* has been used for software verification [14,28]. Here, the idea is to extract recurrence equations from loops and solve them to summarize the effect of arbitrarily many iterations. While recurrence analysis often yields very precise summaries for loops without branching, these summaries are conjunctive. However, for loops with branching, disjunctive summaries are often important to distinguish the branches.

In this work, we embed recurrence analysis into *bounded model checking* (BMC) [3], resulting in a robust, competitive model checking algorithm. To find disjunctive summaries, we exploit the structure of the relational formula to partition the state space on the fly via *model based projection* [29] (which approximates quantifier elimination), and a variation of recurrence analysis called *transitive projection*.

Our approach is inspired by ABMC [19], which combines BMC with *acceleration* [5,15,30]. ABMC uses *blocking clauses* to speed up the search for counterexamples, but they turned out to be of little use for this purpose. Instead, they enable ABMC to prove safety of certain challenging benchmarks. This motivated the development of our novel dedicated algorithm for proving safety via BMC and blocking clauses. See Sect. 5 for a detailed comparison with ABMC.

Overview. We start with an informal explanation of our approach. Given a relational formula τ, one can prove safety with BMC by unrolling its transition relation $\rightarrow_\tau$ D times, where D is the *diameter* [3]. So D is the "longest shortest path" from an initial to some other state, or more formally:

$$D := \sup_{\mathbf{v}' \text{ is reachable from an initial state}} \left(\min\{i \in \mathbb{N} \mid \mathbf{v} \text{ is an initial state}, \mathbf{v} \rightarrow_\tau^i \mathbf{v}'\}\right)$$

So every reachable state can be reached in $\leq D$ steps. Hence, if BMC finds no counterexample in D steps, the system is safe. Our new algorithm *Transitive Relation Learning* (TRL) exploits this observation by iteratively constructing an SMT problem such that its unsatisfiability implies that the diameter has been

[2] extra-small-lia/bouncy_symmetry from the CHC competition.

reached (see the end of this section for more details). For infinite state systems, D is rarely finite: Consider the relational formula (1) with the initial state $x \doteq 0$.

$$x' \doteq x + 1 \qquad (1) \qquad\qquad n > 0 \land x' \doteq x + n \qquad (2)$$

Then $k \in \mathbb{N}$ steps are needed to reach a state with $x \doteq k$. So D is infinite, i.e., the diameter cannot be used to prove safety directly.

The core idea of TRL is to "enlarge" τ to decrease its diameter (even though TRL never computes the diameter explicitly). To this end, our approach "adds" transitive relations to τ, which will be called *learned relations* in the sequel. For (1), TRL would learn the relational formula (2). Then the diameter of (1) $\lor$ (2) is 1, as a state with $x \doteq k$ can be reached in 1 step by setting n to k. Transitive relations are particularly suitable for decreasing the diameter, as they allow us to ignore runs where the same learned relation is used twice in a row. TRL exploits this by adding assertions to the corresponding SMT problem that prevent consecutive uses of the same learned relation.

This raises the questions *when* and *how* new relations should be learned. Regarding the "when", our approach unrolls the transition relation, just like BMC. Thereby, it looks for *loops* and learns a relation when a new loop is encountered. However, as we analyze unstructured systems, the definition of a "loop" is not obvious. Details will be discussed in Sect. 3.2.

Regarding the "how", TRL ensures that we have a *model* for the loop, i.e., a valuation σ_{loop} that corresponds to an evaluation of the loop body. Then given a loop τ_{loop} and a model σ_{loop}, apart from transitivity we only require two more properties for a learned relation $\rightarrow_\pi$. First, the evaluation that corresponds to σ_{loop} must also be possible with $\rightarrow_\pi$. This ensures that TRL makes "progress", i.e., that we do not unroll the same loop with the same model again. Second, the following set must be finite:

$$\{\pi \mid \sigma_{\mathsf{loop}} \text{ is a model of } \tau_{\mathsf{loop}}, \rightarrow_\pi \text{ is learned from } \tau_{\mathsf{loop}} \text{ and } \sigma_{\mathsf{loop}}\}$$

So TRL only learns finitely many relations from a given loop τ_{loop}. While TRL may diverge (Remark 23), this "usually" ensures termination in practice.

Apart from these restrictions, we have lots of freedom when computing learned relations, as "enlarging" τ (i.e., adding disjuncts to τ) is *always* sound for proving safety. The *transitive projection* that we use to learn relations (see Sect. 4) heavily exploits this freedom. It modifies the recurrence analysis from [14] by replacing expensive operations – convex hulls and polyhedral projections – by a cheap variation of *model based projection* [29]. While convex hulls and polyhedral projections are over-approximations (for integer arithmetic), model based projections under-approximate. This is surprising at first, but the justification for using under-approximations is that, as mentioned above, "enlarging" τ is always sound.

Without our modifications, recurrence analysis over-approximates, so we "mix" over- and under-approximations. Thus, learned relations are *not* under-approximations, so TRL cannot prove unsafety and returns `unknown` if it fails to prove unreachability of the error states.

Learned relations may reduce the diameter, but computing the diameter is difficult. Instead, TRL adds *blocking clauses* to the SMT encoding that force the SMT solver to prefer learned relations over loops. Then unsatisfiability implies that the diameter has been reached, so that safe can be returned.

For our example (1), once (2) has been learned, it is preferred over (1). As (2) must not be used twice in a row, the corresponding SMT problem becomes unsatisfiable after adding a blocking clause that blocks (1) for the 1st step, and one that blocks (1) for the 2nd step. Since we check for reachability of error states after every step, this implies safety.

Outline. After introducing preliminaries in Sect. 2, we present our new algorithm TRL in Sect. 3. As TRL builds upon *transitive projections*, we show how to implement such a projection for linear integer arithmetic in Sect. 4. Finally, in Sect. 5 we discuss related work and evaluate our approach empirically.

2 Preliminaries

We assume familiarity with basics of first-order logic [13]. $\mathcal{V}$ is a countably infinite set of variables and $\mathcal{A}$ is a first-order theory with signature Σ and carrier $\mathcal{C}$. For each entity e, $\mathcal{V}(e)$ is the set of variables that occur in e. $\mathsf{QF}(\Sigma)$ denotes the set of all quantifier-free first-order formulas over Σ, and $\mathsf{QF}_\wedge(\Sigma)$ only contains conjunctions of Σ-literals. $\top$ and $\bot$ stand for "true" and "false", respectively.

Given $\psi \in \mathsf{QF}(\Sigma)$ with $\mathcal{V}(\psi) = \mathbf{y}$, we say that ψ is $\mathcal{A}$-*valid* (written $\models_\mathcal{A} \psi$) if every model of $\mathcal{A}$ satisfies the universal closure $\forall \mathbf{y}.\ \psi$ of ψ. A partial function $\sigma : \mathcal{V} \rightharpoonup \mathcal{C}$ is called a *valuation*. If $\mathcal{V}(\psi) \subseteq \mathrm{dom}(\sigma)$ and $\models_\mathcal{A} \sigma(\psi)$, then σ is an $\mathcal{A}$-*model* of ψ (written $\sigma \models_\mathcal{A} \psi$). Here, $\sigma(\psi)$ results from ψ by instantiating all variables according to σ. If ψ has an $\mathcal{A}$-model, then ψ is $\mathcal{A}$-*satisfiable*. If $\sigma(\psi)$ is $\mathcal{A}$-satisfiable (but not necessarily $\mathcal{V}(\psi) \subseteq \mathrm{dom}(\sigma)$), then we say that ψ is $\mathcal{A}$-*consistent* with σ. We write $\psi \models_\mathcal{A} \psi'$ for $\models_\mathcal{A} \psi \implies \psi'$, and $\psi \equiv_\mathcal{A} \psi'$ means $\models_\mathcal{A} \psi \iff \psi'$. In the sequel, we omit the subscript $\mathcal{A}$, and we just say "valid", "model", "satisfiable", and "consistent". We assume that $\mathcal{A}$ is complete (i.e., $\models \psi$ or $\models \neg\psi$ holds for every closed formula over Σ) and that $\mathcal{A}$ has an effective quantifier elimination procedure (i.e., quantifier elimination is computable).

We write $\mathbf{x}$ for sequences and x_i is the ith element of $\mathbf{x}$, where x_1 denotes the first element. We use "::" for concatenation of sequences, where we identify sequences of length 1 with their elements, so, e.g., $x :: \mathbf{x} = [x] :: \mathbf{x}$.

Let $d \in \mathbb{N}$ be fixed, and let $\mathbf{x}, \mathbf{x}' \in \mathcal{V}^d$ be disjoint vectors of pairwise different variables, called the *pre-* and *post-variables*. All other variables are *extra variables*. Each $\tau \in \mathsf{QF}(\Sigma)$ induces a *transition relation* $\to_\tau$ on *states*, i.e., elements of $\mathcal{C}^d$, where $\mathbf{v} \to_\tau \mathbf{v}'$ iff $\tau[\mathbf{x}/\mathbf{v}, \mathbf{x}'/\mathbf{v}']$ is satisfiable. Here, $[\mathbf{x}/\mathbf{v}, \mathbf{x}'/\mathbf{v}']$ maps $x_i^{(\prime)}$ to $v_i^{(\prime)}$.

We call $\tau \in \mathsf{QF}(\Sigma)$ a *relational formula* if we are interested in τ's induced transition relation. *Transitions* are conjunctive relational formulas without extra variables (i.e., conjunctions of literals over pre- and post-variables). We sometimes identify τ with $\to_\tau$, so we may call τ a relation.

Algorithm 1: TRL – Input: a safety problem $\mathcal{T} = (\psi_{\mathsf{init}}, \tau, \psi_{\mathsf{err}})$

1 $b \leftarrow 0$; $\boldsymbol{\pi} \leftarrow [\tau]$; BLOCKED $\leftarrow \varnothing$
2 $\mathsf{add}(\mu_1(\psi_{\mathsf{init}}))$ `// encode the initial states`
3 **while** $\top$ `// main loop`
4 b++; $\mathsf{push}()$; $\mathsf{add}(\mu_b(\psi_{\mathsf{err}}))$ `// encode the error states`
5 **if** $\mathsf{check\_sat}()$ **do return** $\mathsf{unknown}$ **else** $\mathsf{pop}()$ `// check their reachability`
6 $\mathsf{push}()$ `// add backtracking point`
7 **if** $b > 1$ **do** $\mathsf{add}(\overset{(b)}{x}_{\mathsf{id}} \doteq 1 \vee \overset{(b)}{x}_{\mathsf{id}} \not\doteq \overset{(b-1)}{x}_{\mathsf{id}})$ `// encode transitivity`
8 $\mathsf{add}(\mu_b(\bigvee_{n=1}^{|\boldsymbol{\pi}|}(\pi_n \wedge x_{\mathsf{id}} \doteq n)))$ `// encode` $\to_\tau$ `and learned relations`
9 $\mathsf{add}(\bigwedge_{(b,\pi) \in \text{BLOCKED}} \pi)$ `// add blocking clauses for this b`
10 **if** $\neg\mathsf{check\_sat}()$ **do return** safe `// check if the search space is exhausted`
11 $\sigma \leftarrow \mathsf{model}()$; $\boldsymbol{\tau} \leftarrow \mathsf{trace}_b(\sigma, \boldsymbol{\pi})$ `// build trace from current model`
12 **if** $[\tau_s, \ldots, \tau_{s+\ell-1}]$ *is a loop* **do** `// search loop`
13 $\sigma_{\mathsf{loop}} \leftarrow [x/\sigma(\mu_{s,\ell}(x)) \mid x \in \mathbf{x} \cup \mathbf{x}']$ `// build the valuation for the loop`
14 **if** *no* $\pi \in \mathsf{tail}(\boldsymbol{\pi})$ *is consistent with* σ_{loop} **do** `// redundancy check`
15 $\tau_{\mathsf{loop}} \leftarrow \mu_{s,\ell}^{-1}(\bigwedge_{i=s}^{s+\ell-1} \mu_i(\tau_i))$ `// build the loop`
16 $\boldsymbol{\pi} \leftarrow \boldsymbol{\pi} :: \mathsf{tp}(\tau_{\mathsf{loop}}, \sigma \circ \mu_{s,\ell})$ `// learn relation`
17 let $\pi \in \mathsf{tail}(\boldsymbol{\pi})$ and $\overline{\sigma} \supseteq \sigma_{\mathsf{loop}}$ s.t. $\overline{\sigma} \models \pi$ `// pick suitable learned relation`
18 BLOCKED.$\mathsf{add}(s + \ell - 1, \mathsf{blocking\_clause}(s, \ell, \pi, \overline{\sigma}))$ `// block the loop`
19 **while** $b > s$ { $\mathsf{pop}()$; b-- } `// backtrack to the start of the loop`

A τ*-run* is a sequence $\mathbf{v}_1 \to_\tau \ldots \to_\tau \mathbf{v}_k$. A *safety problem* $\mathcal{T}$ is a triple $(\psi_{\mathsf{init}}, \tau, \psi_{\mathsf{err}}) \in \mathsf{QF}(\Sigma) \times \mathsf{QF}(\Sigma) \times \mathsf{QF}(\Sigma)$ where $\mathcal{V}(\psi_{\mathsf{init}}) \cup \mathcal{V}(\psi_{\mathsf{err}}) \subseteq \mathbf{x}$. It is *unsafe* if there are $\mathbf{v}, \mathbf{v}' \in \mathcal{C}^d$ such that $[\mathbf{x}/\mathbf{v}] \models \psi_{\mathsf{init}}$, $\mathbf{v} \to_\tau^* \mathbf{v}'$, and $[\mathbf{x}/\mathbf{v}'] \models \psi_{\mathsf{err}}$.

Throughout the paper, we use c, d, e, k, ℓ, s for integer constants (where d always denotes the size of $\mathbf{x}$, and s and ℓ always denote the start and length of a loop); $\mathbf{v}$ for states; w, x, y for variables; τ, π for relational formulas; σ, θ for valuations; and μ for variable renamings.

3 Transitive Relation Learning

In this section, we present our novel model checking algorithm *Transitive Relation Learning* (TRL) in detail, see Algorithm 1. Here, for all $i, j \in \mathbb{N}_+ = \mathbb{N} \setminus \{0\}$ we define $\mu_{i,j}(x') := \overset{(i+j)}{x}$ if $x' \in \mathbf{x}'$ and $\mu_{i,j}(x) := \overset{(i)}{x}$, otherwise. So in particular, we have $\mu_{i,j}(\mathbf{x}) = \overset{(i)}{\mathbf{x}}$ and $\mu_{i,j}(\mathbf{x}') = \overset{(i+j)}{\mathbf{x}}$, where we assume that $\overset{(1)}{\mathbf{x}}, \overset{(2)}{\mathbf{x}}, \ldots \in \mathcal{V}^d$ are disjoint vectors of pairwise different fresh variables. Intuitively, the variables $\overset{(i)}{\mathbf{x}}$ represent the ith state in a run, and applying $\mu_{i,j}$ to a relational formula yields a formula that relates the ith and the $(i+j)^{th}$ state of a run. For convenience, we define $\mu_i := \mu_{i,1}$ for all $i \in \mathbb{N}_+$, i.e., $\mu_i(\mathbf{x}) = \overset{(i)}{\mathbf{x}}$ and $\mu_i(\mathbf{x}') = \overset{(i+1)}{\mathbf{x}}$. As in SMT-based BMC, TRL uses an incremental SMT solver to unroll the transition relation step by step (Line 8), but in contrast to BMC, TRL infers *learned relations* on the fly (Line 16). The *input formula* τ as well as all learned relations are stored in $\boldsymbol{\pi}$. Before each unrolling, we set a backtracking point with the command push and add a suitably variable-renamed version of the description of the error states to the SMT problem (i.e., to the state of the underlying SMT solver) in Line 4. Then the command check_sat checks for reachability of error states, and the command pop removes all formulas from the SMT problem that have been added since the last invocation of push (Line 5), i.e., it removes the encoding of the error states (unless the check succeeds, so that TRL fails). For each unrolling, suitably variable renamed variants of $\boldsymbol{\pi}$'s elements are added to the underlying SMT problem with the command add in Line 8. If no error state is reachable after $b-1$ steps, but the transition relation cannot be unrolled b times (i.e., the SMT problem that corresponds to the b-fold unrolling is unsatisfiable), then the diameter of the analyzed system (including learned relations) has been reached, and hence safety has been proven (Line 10).

The remainder of this section is structured as follows: First, Sect. 3.1 introduces *conjunctive variable projections* that are used to compute the *trace* (Line 11 of Algorithm 1). Next, Sect. 3.2 defines *loops* and discusses how to find *non-redundant loops* that are suitable for learning new relations (Lines 12 to 15). Then, Sect. 3.3 introduces *transitive projections* that are used to learn relations (Lines 7 and 16). Finally, Sect. 3.4 presents *blocking clauses*, which ensure that learned relations are preferred over other (sequences of) transitions (Lines 9 and 17 to 19).

3.1 Conjunctive Variable Projections and Traces

To decide when to learn a new relation, TRL inspects the *trace* (Lines 11 and 12). The trace is a sequence of transitions induced by the formulas that have been added to the SMT problem while unrolling the transition relation, and by the current model (Line 11). To compute them, we use *conjunctive variable projections*, which are like *model based projections* [29], but always yield conjunctions.

Definition 2 (Conjunctive Variable Projection). *A function*

$$\mathsf{cvp} : \mathsf{QF}(\Sigma) \times (\mathcal{V} \rightharpoonup \mathcal{C}) \times 2^{\mathcal{V}} \to \mathsf{QF}(\Sigma)$$

is called a conjunctive variable projection *if*

1. $\sigma \models \mathsf{cvp}(\tau, \sigma, X)$
2. $\mathsf{cvp}(\tau, \sigma, X) \models \tau$
3. $\{\mathsf{cvp}(\tau, \theta, X) \mid \theta \models \tau\}$ *is finite*
4. $\mathcal{V}(\mathsf{cvp}(\tau, \sigma, X)) \subseteq X \cap \mathcal{V}(\tau)$
5. $\mathsf{cvp}(\tau, \sigma, X) \in \mathsf{QF}_{\wedge}(\Sigma)$

for all $\tau \in \mathsf{QF}(\Sigma)$*,* $X \subseteq \mathcal{V}$*, and* $\sigma \models \tau$*. We abbreviate* $\mathsf{cvp}(\tau, \sigma, \mathbf{x} \cup \mathbf{x}')$ *by* $\mathsf{cvp}(\tau, \sigma)$.

So like model based projection, cvp under-approximates quantifier elimination by projecting to the variables X (by (2) and (4)). To do so, it implicitly performs a finite case analysis (by (3)), which is driven by the model σ (by (1)). In contrast to model based projections, cvp always yields conjunctions (by (5)). Note that by (1), $\mathsf{cvp}(\tau, \sigma, X)$ may only contain variables from $\mathrm{dom}(\sigma)$.

Remark 3 (cvp *and* mbp). Conjunctive variable projections are obtained by combining a model based projection mbp (which satisfies Definition 2 (1–4)) with *syntactic implicant projection* sip [18]. To see how to compute mbp for linear integer arithmetic, recall that Cooper's method for quantifier elimination [11] essentially maps $\exists \mathbf{y}.\ \tau$ to a disjunction of formulas of the form $\tau[\mathbf{y}/\mathbf{t}]$, where the variables $\mathbf{y}$ do not occur in the terms $\mathbf{t}$. Instead, mbp just computes one of these disjuncts, which is satisfied by the provided model. For $\mathsf{sip}(\tau, \sigma)$, one computes the conjunction of all literals of τ's negation normal form that are satisfied by σ. Then $\mathsf{cvp}(\tau, \sigma) := \mathsf{sip}(\mathsf{mbp}(\tau, \sigma), \sigma)$.

Remark 4 (cvp *and Quantifier Elimination*). Definition 2 (1–4) imply

$$\exists \mathbf{y}.\ \tau \ \equiv \ \bigvee_{\sigma \models \tau} \mathsf{cvp}(\tau, \sigma) \qquad \text{where } \mathbf{y} \text{ are } \tau\text{'s extra variables.}$$

So cvp yields a quantifier elimination procedure qe which maps $\exists \mathbf{y}.\ \tau$ to *res*:

$$\mathit{res} \leftarrow \bot; \qquad \textbf{while}\, \tau \text{ \textit{has a model} } \sigma\ \{\mathit{res} \leftarrow \mathit{res} \vee \mathsf{cvp}(\tau, \sigma); \qquad \tau \leftarrow \tau \wedge \neg\mathsf{cvp}(\tau, \sigma)\}$$

But for a single model σ, $\mathsf{cvp}(\tau, \sigma)$ under-approximates quantifier elimination.

So $\mathsf{cvp}(\tau, \sigma)$ just computes one disjunct of $\mathsf{qe}(\exists \mathbf{y}.\ \tau)$ which is satisfied by σ. However, like model based projection, cvp can be implemented efficiently for many theories with effective, but very expensive quantifier elimination procedures.

Example 5 (cvp). Consider the following formula $\tilde{\tau}$:

$$((w \doteq 0 \wedge \overset{(2)}{x} \doteq x{+}1 \wedge \overset{(2)}{y} \doteq y{+}1) \vee (\overset{(2)}{w} \doteq w \wedge w \doteq 1 \wedge \overset{(2)}{x} \doteq x{-}1 \wedge \overset{(2)}{y} \doteq y{-}1)) \wedge$$
$$((\overset{(2)}{w} \doteq 0 \wedge x' \doteq \overset{(2)}{x}{+}1 \wedge y' \doteq \overset{(2)}{y}{+}1) \vee (w' \doteq \overset{(2)}{w} \wedge \overset{(2)}{w} \doteq 1 \wedge x' \doteq \overset{(2)}{x}{-}1 \wedge y' \doteq \overset{(2)}{y}{-}1))$$

It encodes two steps with Example 1, where $\overset{(2)}{\mathbf{x}} = [\overset{(2)}{w}, \overset{(2)}{x}, \overset{(2)}{y}]$ represents the values after one step. In Line 11, Algorithm 1 might find a run like $\sigma(\overset{(1)}{\mathbf{x}}) \to_\tau \sigma(\overset{(2)}{\mathbf{x}}) \to_\tau \sigma(\overset{(3)}{\mathbf{x}})$ for

$$\sigma := [\overset{(1)}{w}/\overset{(1)}{x}/\overset{(1)}{y}/0,\ \ \overset{(2)}{w}/\overset{(2)}{x}/\overset{(2)}{y}/1,\ \ \overset{(3)}{w}/1,\ \overset{(3)}{x}/\overset{(3)}{y}/0].$$

Here, $[w/x/y/c, \ldots]$ abbreviates $[w/c, x/c, y/c, \ldots]$. Then the variable renaming $\mu_{1,2}$ allows us to instantiate the pre- and post-variables by the first and last state, resulting in the following model of $\tilde{\tau}$:

$$\tilde{\sigma} := \sigma \circ \mu_{1,2} = \sigma \cup [w/x/y/0,\ \ w'/1, x'/y'/0] \quad \text{where } (\sigma \circ \mu_{1,2})(x) = \sigma(\mu_{1,2}(x))$$

To get rid of $\overset{(2)}{w}, \overset{(2)}{x}, \overset{(2)}{y}$, one could compute $\mathsf{qe}(\exists \overset{(2)}{w}, \overset{(2)}{x}, \overset{(2)}{y}.\ \tilde{\tau})$, resulting in:

$$\begin{aligned} & w \doteq 0 \wedge x' \doteq x + 2 \wedge y' \doteq y + 2 && (\mathsf{inc}) \\ \vee\, & w \doteq 0 \wedge w' \doteq 1 \wedge x' \doteq x \wedge y' \doteq y && (\mathsf{eq}) \\ \vee\, & w \doteq 1 \wedge w' \doteq 1 \wedge x' \doteq x - 2 \wedge y' \doteq y - 2. && (\mathsf{dec}) \end{aligned}$$

Instead, we may have $\mathsf{cvp}(\tilde{\tau}, \tilde{\sigma}) = (\mathsf{eq})$, as $\tilde{\sigma} \models (\mathsf{eq})$.

Intuitively, a relational formula τ describes how states can change, so it is composed of many different cases. These cases may be given explicitly (by disjunctions) or implicitly (by extra variables, which express non-determinism). Given a model σ of τ that describes a *concrete* change of state, cvp computes a description of the corresponding case. Computing *all* cases amounts to eliminating all extra variables and converting the result to DNF, which is impractical.

When unrolling the transition relation in Line 8 of Algorithm 1, we identify each relational formula π_n with its index n in the sequence $\boldsymbol{\pi}$. To this end, we use a fresh variable x_{id}, and our SMT encoding forces $\overset{(i)}{x}_{\mathsf{id}}$ to be the identifier of the relation that is used for the ith step. Similarly to [19], the *trace* is the sequence of transitions that results from applying cvp to the unrolling of the transition relation that is constructed by Algorithm 1 in Line 8. So a trace is a sequence of transitions that can be applied subsequently, starting in an initial state.

Definition 6 (Trace). *Let $\boldsymbol{\pi}$ be a sequence of relational formulas, let*

$$\sigma \models \bigwedge_{i=1}^{b} \mu_i \left(\bigvee_{n=1}^{|\boldsymbol{\pi}|} (\pi_n \wedge x_{\mathsf{id}} \doteq n) \right) \qquad \textit{where } b \in \mathbb{N}_+, \tag{3}$$

and let $\mathsf{id}(i) := \sigma(\overset{(i)}{x}_{\mathsf{id}})$. *Then the* trace induced by σ *is*

$$\mathsf{trace}_b(\sigma, \boldsymbol{\pi}) := [\mathsf{cvp}(\pi_{\mathsf{id}(i)}, \sigma \circ \mu_i)]_{i=1}^{b}.$$

Recall that μ_i renames $\mathbf{x}$ and $\mathbf{x}'$ into $\overset{(i)}{\mathbf{x}}$ and $\overset{(i+1)}{\mathbf{x}}$, and $\mathsf{id}(i) = \sigma(\overset{(i)}{x}_{\mathsf{id}})$ is the index of the relation from $\boldsymbol{\pi}$ that is used for the ith step. So each model σ of (3) corresponds to a run $\sigma(\mu_1(\mathbf{x})) \longrightarrow_{\pi_{\mathsf{id}(1)}} \cdots \longrightarrow_{\pi_{\mathsf{id}(b-1)}} \sigma(\mu_b(\mathbf{x})) \longrightarrow_{\pi_{\mathsf{id}(b)}} \sigma(\mu_b(\mathbf{x}'))$, and the trace induced by σ contains the transitions that were used in this run.

Example 7 (Trace). Consider the extension of σ from Example 5 with $[\overset{(1)}{x}_{\mathsf{id}}/1,\ \overset{(2)}{x}_{\mathsf{id}}/1]$:

$$\sigma := [\overset{(1)}{w}/\overset{(1)}{x}/\overset{(1)}{y}/0, \overset{(1)}{x}_{\mathsf{id}}/1,\quad \overset{(2)}{w}/\overset{(2)}{x}/\overset{(2)}{y}/\overset{(2)}{x}_{\mathsf{id}}/1,\quad \overset{(3)}{w}/1, \overset{(3)}{x}/\overset{(3)}{y}/0]$$

Thus, $\mathsf{id}(1) = \sigma(\overset{(1)}{x}_{\mathsf{id}}) = 1$, $\mathsf{id}(2) = \sigma(\overset{(2)}{x}_{\mathsf{id}}) = 1$, and $\pi_{\mathsf{id}(1)} = \pi_{\mathsf{id}(2)} = \pi_1 = \tau$. Then

$$\begin{aligned} &\mathsf{trace}_2(\sigma, [\tau, \tau]) = [\mathsf{cvp}(\tau, \sigma \circ \mu_1), \mathsf{cvp}(\tau, \sigma \circ \mu_2)] \\ &= [\mathsf{cvp}(\tau, [w/x/y/0,\ w'/x'/y'/1]), \mathsf{cvp}(\tau, [w/x/y/1,\ w'/1, x'/y'/0])] = [\tau_{\mathsf{inc}}, \tau_{\mathsf{dec}}]. \end{aligned}$$

3.2 Loops

As $\boldsymbol{\pi}$ only gives rise to finitely many transitions, the trace is bound to contain *loops*, eventually (unless Algorithm 1 terminates beforehand).

Definition 8 (Loop). *A sequence of transitions $\tau_1, \ldots, \tau_k$ is called a* loop *if there are $\mathbf{v}_0, \ldots, \mathbf{v}_{k+1} \in \mathcal{C}^d$ such that $\mathbf{v}_0 \longrightarrow_{\tau_1} \cdots \longrightarrow_{\tau_k} \mathbf{v}_k \longrightarrow_{\tau_1} \mathbf{v}_{k+1}$.*

Intuitively, these loops are the reason why BMC may diverge. To prevent divergence, TRL learns a new relation when a loop is detected (Line 12).

Remark 9 (Finding Loops). Loops can be detected by SMT solving. A cheaper way is to look for duplicates on the trace, but then loops are found "later", as a trace $[\ldots, \pi, \pi, \ldots]$ is needed to detect a loop π, but one occurrence of π is insufficient. As a trade-off between precision and efficiency, our implementation uses an approximation based on *dependency graphs* [19]. More precisely, our implementation maintains a graph $\mathcal{G}$ whose nodes are transitions, and it adds an edge between two transitions if they occur subsequently on the trace at some point. Then it considers a subsequence $\tau_i, \ldots, \tau_j$ of the trace to be a potential loop if $\mathcal{G}$ contains an edge from τ_j to τ_i.

Remark 10 (Disregarding "Learned" Loops). One should disregard "loops" consisting of a single *learned transition*, i.e., a transition that results from applying cvp to some $\pi \in \mathsf{tail}(\boldsymbol{\pi})$, where $\mathsf{tail}(\tau :: \boldsymbol{\pi}') := \boldsymbol{\pi}'$. Here, $\mathsf{tail}(\boldsymbol{\pi})$ contains all learned relations, as the first element of $\boldsymbol{\pi}$ is the input formula τ. The reason is that our goal is to deduce transitive relations, but learned relations are already transitive. In the sequel, we assume that the check in Line 12 fails for such loops.

If there are several choices for s and ℓ in Line 12, then our implementation only considers loops of minimal length and, among those, it minimizes s.

Example 11 (Detecting Loops). Consider the following model for τ from Example 1.

$$\sigma := [\overset{(1)}{w} / \overset{(1)}{x} / \overset{(1)}{y} /0, \overset{(1)}{x}_{\mathsf{id}}/1, \quad \overset{(2)}{w}/0, \overset{(2)}{x} / \overset{(2)}{y} /1]$$

Then $\mathsf{trace}_1(\sigma, [\tau]) = [\tau_{\mathsf{inc}}]$. As τ_{inc} is a loop,[3] this causes TRL to learn a relation like the following one (see Sect. 3.3 for details).

$$w \doteq 0 \land x' > x \land x' - x \doteq y' - y \qquad (\tau_{\mathsf{inc}}^{+})$$

TRL only learns relations from loops that are *non-redundant* w.r.t. all relations that have been learned before [18].

Definition 12 (Redundancy). *If* $\to_\tau \subseteq \to_{\tau'}$, *then* τ *is* redundant *w.r.t.* τ'.

Example 13 The relation τ_{inc} is redundant w.r.t. τ_{inc}^{+}, but τ_{dec} is not.

Line 14 uses a sufficient criterion for non-redundancy: If all learned relations are falsified by the values before and after the loop, then $\tau_s, \ldots, \tau_{s+\ell-1}$ cannot be simulated by a previously learned relation, so it is non-redundant and we learn a new relation. The values before and after the loop are obtained from the

---

[3] Depending on the technique that is used to detect loops, an actual implementation might require one more unrolling of $\to_\tau$ to obtain the trace $[\tau_{\mathsf{inc}}, \tau_{\mathsf{inc}}]$ in order to detect the loop τ_{inc}, see Remark 9.

current model σ by setting $\mathbf{x}$ to $\sigma(\overset{(s)}{\mathbf{x}})$ and $\mathbf{x}'$ to $\sigma(\overset{(s+\ell)}{\mathbf{x}})$, i.e., we use $\sigma \circ \mu_{s,\ell}$ in Line 13.

To learn a new relation, we first compute the relation

$$\tau_{\mathsf{loop}} := \mu_{s,\ell}^{-1}(\varphi_{\mathsf{loop}}) \qquad \text{where} \qquad \varphi_{\mathsf{loop}} := \bigwedge_{i=s}^{s+\ell-1} \mu_i(\tau_i) \tag{4}$$

of the loop in Line 15, where $\mu_{s,\ell}^{-1}$ is the inverse of $\mu_{s,\ell}$. So in Example 11, we have $\sigma \circ \mu_{1,1} \supseteq [w/x/y/0,\ w'/0, x'/y'/1]$ and $\tau_{\mathsf{loop}} := \mu_{1,1}^{-1}(\mu_1(\tau_{\mathsf{inc}})) = \tau_{\mathsf{inc}}$ as $s = \ell = 1$. So $\sigma \circ \mu_{s,\ell}$ indeed corresponds to one evaluation of the loop, as $\sigma \circ \mu_{s,\ell} \models \tau_{\mathsf{loop}}$.

To see that τ_{loop} is also the desired relation in general, note that φ_{loop} is the conjunction of the transitions that constitute the loop, where all variables are renamed as in Line 8 of Algorithm 1, i.e., in such a way that the post-variables of the ith step are equal to the pre-variables of the $(i+1)^{th}$ step. So we have $\sigma \models \varphi_{\mathsf{loop}}$ and thus $\sigma \circ \mu_{s,\ell} \models \tau_{\mathsf{loop}}$. Hence, we can use τ_{loop} and $\sigma \circ \mu_{s,\ell}$ to learn a new relation via so-called *transitive projections* in Line 16.

3.3 Transitive Projections

We now define *transitive projections* that approximate transitive closures of loops. As explained in Sect. 1, we do not restrict ourselves to under- or over-approximations, but we allow "mixtures" of both. Analogously to cvp, transitive projections perform a finite case analysis that is driven by the provided model σ.

Definition 14 (Transitive Projection). *A function*

$$\mathsf{tp} : \mathsf{QF}(\Sigma) \times (\mathcal{V} \rightharpoonup \mathcal{C}) \to \mathsf{QF}(\Sigma)$$

is called a transitive projection *if the following holds for all transitions $\tau \in \mathsf{QF}(\Sigma)$ and all $\sigma \models \tau$:*

1. *$\mathsf{tp}(\tau, \sigma)$ is consistent with σ*
2. *$\{\mathsf{tp}(\tau, \theta) \mid \theta \models \tau\}$ is finite*
3. *$\to_{\mathsf{tp}(\tau,\sigma)}$ is transitive*

Clearly, the specifics of tp depend on the underlying theory. Our implementation of tp for quantifier-free linear integer arithmetic is explained in Sect. 4.

*Example 15 (*tp*).* For Example 1, $\tau_{\mathsf{ti}} := x' - x \doteq y' - y$ over-approximates the transitive closure $\to_\tau^+$. Such over-approximations are also called *transition invariants* [38]. With τ_{ti}, one can prove safety for any ψ_{init} with $\psi_{\mathsf{init}} \models x \doteq y$, as then $\psi_{\mathsf{init}} \wedge \tau_{\mathsf{ti}} \models x' \doteq y'$, which shows that no error state with $w \doteq 1 \wedge x \leq 0 \wedge y > 0$ is reachable.

By using cvp, TRL instead considers τ_{inc} and τ_{dec} separately and learns

$$\mathsf{tp}(\tau_{\mathsf{inc}}, \sigma_{\mathsf{inc}}) := w \doteq 0 \wedge x' > x \wedge x' - x \doteq y' - y \tag{τ_{inc}^+}$$

$$\mathsf{tp}(\tau_{\mathsf{dec}}, \sigma_{\mathsf{dec}}) := w' \doteq w \wedge w \doteq 1 \wedge x' < x \wedge x' - x \doteq y' - y \tag{τ_{dec}^+}$$

if $\sigma_{\mathsf{inc}} \models \tau_{\mathsf{inc}}$ and $\sigma_{\mathsf{dec}} \models \tau_{\mathsf{dec}}$. In this way, Algorithm 1 can learn disjunctive relations like $\tau_{\mathsf{inc}}^{+} \vee \tau_{\mathsf{dec}}^{+}$, even if tp only yields conjunctive relational formulas (which is true for our current implementation of tp – see Sect. 4 – but not enforced by Definition 14).

In contrast to conjunctive variable projections, $\mathsf{tp}(\tau,\sigma)$ may contain extra variables that do not occur in τ (which will be exploited in Sect. 4). Hence, instead of $\sigma \models \mathsf{tp}(\tau,\sigma)$ we require consistency with σ, i.e., $\sigma(\mathsf{tp}(\tau,\sigma))$ must be satisfiable.

Remark 16 (Properties of tp*).* Due to Definition 14 (1), our definition of tp implies

$$\tau \models \exists \mathbf{y}.\ \bigvee_{\sigma\models\tau} \mathsf{tp}(\tau,\sigma), \quad \text{and thus,} \quad \rightarrow_\tau \subseteq \bigcup_{\sigma\models\tau} \rightarrow_{\mathsf{tp}(\tau,\sigma)},$$

where $\mathbf{y}$ are the extra variables of $\bigvee_{\sigma\models\tau} \mathsf{tp}(\tau,\sigma)$. However, Definition 14 does *not* ensure $\rightarrow_\tau^+ \subseteq \bigcup_{\sigma\models\tau} \rightarrow_{\mathsf{tp}(\tau,\sigma)}$. So there is no guarantee that tp covers $\rightarrow_\tau^+$ entirely, i.e., tp cannot be used to compute transition invariants, in general. Definition 14 does not ensure $\rightarrow_\tau^+ \supseteq \bigcup_{\sigma\models\tau} \rightarrow_{\mathsf{tp}(\tau,\sigma)}$ either, as $\mathsf{tp}(\tau,\sigma)$ does not imply $\sigma(\mathbf{x}) \rightarrow_\tau^+ \sigma(\mathbf{x}')$.

Example 17. To see that tp computes no over- or under-approximations, let

$$\tau := x' \doteq x + 1 \wedge y' \doteq y + x.$$

Then for all $\sigma \models \tau$, we might have:

$$\mathsf{tp}(\tau,\sigma) = \begin{cases} x \geq 0 \wedge x' > x \wedge y' \geq y, & \text{if } \sigma(x) \geq 0 \\ x < 0 \wedge x' > x \wedge y' < y, & \text{if } \sigma(x) < 0 \end{cases}$$

However, $(x \geq 0 \wedge x' > x \wedge y' \geq y) \vee (x < 0 \wedge x' > x \wedge y' < y)$ is not an over-approximation of $\rightarrow_\tau^+$ (i.e., $\rightarrow_\tau^+ \not\subseteq \bigcup_{\sigma\models\tau} \rightarrow_{\mathsf{tp}(\tau,\sigma)}$), as we have, e.g.,

$$(-1,0) \rightarrow_\tau (0,-1) \rightarrow_\tau (1,-1) \rightarrow_\tau (2,0), \qquad \text{but} \qquad (-1,0) \not\rightarrow_{\mathsf{tp}(\tau,\sigma)} (2,0)$$

for all $\sigma \models \tau$. Moreover, we also have $\rightarrow_\tau^+ \not\supseteq \bigcup_{\sigma\models\tau} \rightarrow_{\mathsf{tp}(\tau,\sigma)}$, since

$$(-1,0) \rightarrow_{\mathsf{tp}(\tau,\sigma)} (10,-20), \qquad \text{but} \qquad (-1,0) \not\rightarrow_\tau^+ (10,-20)$$

if $\sigma(x) < 0$. In contrast to $\mathsf{tp}(\tau,\sigma)$, linear over-approximations for $\rightarrow_\tau^+$ like $x' > x$ cannot distinguish whether y increases or decreases.

As TRL proves safety via *blocking clauses* (Sect. 3.4) that only block steps that are covered by learned relations, the fact that tp does not yield over-approximations does not affect soundness. However, it may cause divergence (Remark 23).

Recall that our SMT encoding forces $\overset{(i)}{x}_{\mathsf{id}}$ to be the identifier of the relation that is used for the ith step (Line 8). To exploit transitivity of tp, we add the constraint $\overset{(b)}{x}_{\mathsf{id}} \doteq 1 \vee \overset{(b)}{x}_{\mathsf{id}} \not\doteq \overset{(b-1)}{x}_{\mathsf{id}}$ in Line 7, so that learned relations (with index > 1) are not used several times in a row, since this is unnecessary for transitive relations.

3.4 Blocking Clauses

In Line 17, we are guaranteed to find a learned relation π which is consistent with σ_{loop}: If our sufficient criterion for non-redundancy in Line 14 failed, then the existence of π is guaranteed. Otherwise, we learned a new relation π in Line 16 which is consistent with $\sigma_{\mathsf{loop}} \subseteq \sigma \circ \mu_{s,\ell}$ by definition of tp. Thus, we can use π and a model $\overline{\sigma} \supseteq \sigma_{\mathsf{loop}}$ of π to record a *blocking clause* in Line 18.

Definition 18 (Blocking Clauses). *Consider a relational formula π, and let $\overline{\sigma}$ be a model of π. We define:*

$$\mathsf{blocking\_clause}(s, \ell, \pi, \overline{\sigma}) := \begin{cases} \mu_{s,\ell}(\neg \mathsf{cvp}(\pi, \overline{\sigma})) \vee \overset{(s)}{x}_{\mathsf{id}} > 1, & \textit{if } \ell = 1 \\ \mu_{s,\ell}(\neg \mathsf{cvp}(\pi, \overline{\sigma})), & \textit{if } \ell > 1 \end{cases}$$

Here, s and ℓ are natural numbers such that $[\tau_i]_{i=s}^{s+\ell-1}$ is a (possibly) redundant loop on the trace. Blocking clauses exclude models that correspond to runs

$$\mathbf{v}_1 \rightarrow_{\tau_1} \cdots \rightarrow_{\tau_{s-1}} \mathbf{v}_s \rightarrow_{\tau_s} \cdots \rightarrow_{\tau_{s+\ell-1}} \mathbf{v}_{s+\ell} \tag{5}$$

where $\mathbf{v}_s \rightarrow_\pi \mathbf{v}_{s+\ell}$. Intuitively, if $\ell = 1$ then $\mathsf{blocking\_clause}(s, \ell, \pi, \overline{\sigma})$ states that one may still evaluate $\mathbf{v}_s$ to $\mathbf{v}_{s+\ell}$, but one has to use a learned transition. If $\ell > 1$, then $\mathsf{blocking\_clause}(s, \ell, \pi, \overline{\sigma})$ states that one may still evaluate $\mathbf{v}_s$ to $\mathbf{v}_{s+\ell}$, but not in ℓ steps. More precisely, blocking clauses take into account that

$$\mathbf{v}_1 \rightarrow_{\tau_1} \cdots \rightarrow_{\tau_{s+\ell-2}} \mathbf{v}_{s+\ell-1} \quad (6) \qquad \text{and} \qquad \mathbf{v}_1 \rightarrow_{\tau_1} \cdots \rightarrow_{\tau_{s-1}} \mathbf{v}_s \rightarrow_\pi \mathbf{v}_{s+\ell} \quad (7)$$

must not be blocked to ensure that $\mathbf{v}_2, \ldots, \mathbf{v}_{s+\ell}$ remain reachable. For the former, note that blocking clauses affect the suffix $\mathbf{v}_s \rightarrow_{\tau_s} \cdots \rightarrow_{\tau_{s+\ell-1}} \mathbf{v}_{s+\ell}$ of (5) (as they contain $\mu_{s,\ell}(\neg \mathsf{cvp}(\pi, \overline{\sigma}))$), but not (6), so $\mathbf{v}_2, \ldots, \mathbf{v}_{s+\ell-1}$ remain reachable.

Regarding (7), note that (5) corresponds to one unrolling of the loop (without using the newly learned relation π). In contrast, (7) simulates one unrolling of the loop using the new relation π. To see that our blocking clauses prevent the sequence (5), but not the sequence (7), first consider the case $\ell > 1$. Then (7) is not affected by the blocking clause, as it requires less than $s + \ell$ steps. If $\ell = 1$, then the loop that needs to be blocked is a single *original transition* (i.e., a transition that results from applying cvp to τ) due to Remark 10. So $\overset{(s)}{x}_{\mathsf{id}} > 1$ is falsified by (5), as τ_s is an original transition, i.e., using it for the sth step implies $\overset{(s)}{x}_{\mathsf{id}} \doteq 1$. However, $\overset{(s)}{x}_{\mathsf{id}} > 1$ is satisfied by (7), as π is a learned transition, so using it implies $\overset{(s)}{x}_{\mathsf{id}} > 1$.

Remark 19 (Extra Variables and Negation). In Definition 18, cvp is used to project π according to the model $\overline{\sigma}$. In this way, negation has the intended effect, i.e.,

$$[\mathbf{x}/\mathbf{v}, \mathbf{x}'/\mathbf{v}'] \models \neg \mathsf{cvp}(\ldots) \qquad \text{iff} \qquad \mathbf{v} \not\rightarrow_{\mathsf{cvp}(\ldots)} \mathbf{v}',$$

as $\mathsf{cvp}(\ldots)$ has no extra variables. To see why this is important here, consider the relation $\tau := n > 0 \land x' \doteq x + n$, where n is an extra variable. Then $0 \to_\tau 1$, but

$$\neg\tau[x/0, x'/1] = (n \leq 0 \lor x' \not\doteq x + n)[x/0, x'/1] = n \leq 0 \lor 1 \not\doteq n$$

is satisfiable, so $\neg\tau$ is not a suitable characterization of $\not\to_\tau$. The reason is that n is implicitly existentially quantified in τ. So to characterize $\not\to_\tau$, we have to negate $\exists n.\ \tau$ instead of τ, resulting in $\forall n.\ n \leq 0 \lor x' \not\doteq x + n$. Then, as desired,

$$(\forall n.\ n \leq 0 \lor x' \not\doteq x + n)[x/0, x'/1] = \forall n.\ n \leq 0 \lor 1 \not\doteq n$$

is invalid. To avoid quantifiers, we eliminate extra variables via cvp instead.

In Line 18, a pair consisting of $s + \ell - 1$ and the blocking clause is added to BLOCKED. The first component means that the blocking clause has to be added to the SMT encoding when the transition relation is unrolled for the $(s+\ell-1)^{th}$ time, i.e., when $b = s+\ell-1$. So blocking clauses are added to the SMT encoding "on demand" (in Line 9) to block loops that have been found on the trace at some point. Afterwards, TRL backtracks to the last step before the loop in Line 19.

Remark 20 (Adding Blocking Clauses). To see why blocking clauses must only be added to the SMT encoding in the $(s + \ell - 1)^{th}$ unrolling, assume $\pi \equiv \top$. Then, e.g., $\mathsf{blocking\_clause}(1, 2, \pi, \overline{\sigma}) \equiv \bot$. This means that unrolling the transition relation twice is superfluous, as every state can be reached in a single step with π, so the diameter is 1. But after learning π when $b = 2$ and backtracking to $b = 0$, adding such a blocking clause too early (e.g., before the first unrolling of the transition relation) would *immediately* result in an unsatisfiable SMT problem.

Example 21 (Blocking Redundant Loops). Consider the model

$$\sigma := [\overset{(1)}{w}/\overset{(1)}{x}/\overset{(1)}{y}/0, \overset{(1)}{x}_{\mathsf{id}}/2, \quad \overset{(2)}{w}/0, \overset{(2)}{x}/\overset{(2)}{y}/2, \overset{(2)}{x}_{\mathsf{id}}/1, \quad \overset{(3)}{x}/\overset{(3)}{y}/3]$$

and assume that TRL has already learned the relation τ_{inc}^{+} (i.e., $\boldsymbol{\pi} = [\tau, \tau_{\mathsf{inc}}^{+}]$). Moreover, assume that the trace is $[\tau_{\mathsf{inc}}^{+}, \tau_{\mathsf{inc}}]$, so that TRL detects the loop τ_{inc}. To check for non-redundancy, we instantiate the pre- and post-variables in τ_{inc}^{+} according to σ, taking the renaming μ_2 into account (note that here $s = 2$, $\ell = 1$, and $\mu_{s,\ell} = \mu_{2,1} = \mu_2$):

$$\sigma(\mu_2(\tau_{\mathsf{inc}}^{+})) = \tau_{\mathsf{inc}}^{+}[w/0, x/y/2, x'/y'/3] \equiv \top.$$

So our sufficient criterion for non-redundancy fails, as τ_{inc} is indeed redundant w.r.t. τ_{inc}^{+}. Thus, TRL records that the following blocking clause has to be added for the second unrolling (i.e., when $b = s + \ell - 1 = 2$).

$$\mu_{s,\ell}(\neg \mathsf{cvp}(\tau_{\mathsf{inc}}^{+}, \overline{\sigma})) \vee \overset{(s)}{x}_{\mathsf{id}} > 1 \;=\; \mu_{s,\ell}(\neg \tau_{\mathsf{inc}}^{+}) \vee \overset{(s)}{x}_{\mathsf{id}} > 1 \;\; \text{(as } \tau_{\mathsf{inc}}^{+} \text{ is a transition)}$$
$$= \mu_2(\neg(w \doteq 0 \wedge x' > x \wedge x' - x \doteq y' - y)) \vee \overset{(2)}{x}_{\mathsf{id}} > 1$$
$$\equiv (w \not\doteq 0 \vee x' \leq x \vee x' - x \not\doteq y' - y)[w/\overset{(2)}{w}, x/\overset{(2)}{x}, y/\overset{(2)}{y}, x'/\overset{(3)}{x}, y'/\overset{(3)}{y}] \vee \overset{(2)}{x}_{\mathsf{id}} > 1$$
$$= \overset{(2)}{w} \not\doteq 0 \vee \overset{(3)}{x} \leq \overset{(2)}{x} \vee \overset{(3)}{x} - \overset{(2)}{x} \not\doteq \overset{(3)}{y} - \overset{(2)}{y} \vee \overset{(2)}{x}_{\mathsf{id}} > 1$$

As this blocking clause is falsified by σ, it prevents TRL from finding the same model again after backtracking in Line 19, so that TRL makes progress.

The following theorem states that our approach is sound.

Theorem 22. *If TRL($\mathcal{T}$) returns* safe, *then $\mathcal{T}$ is safe.*

Proof (Sketch). The key idea of the proof, which works by induction over the length of runs, is to show that blocking clauses do not prevent us from reaching all reachable states. See [20] for the full proof.

Remark 23 (Termination). In general, Algorithm 1 does not terminate, since tp decomposes the relation into finitely many cases and approximates their transitive closures independently, but $\rightarrow_{\tau_{\mathsf{loop}}}^{+} \subseteq \bigcup_{\sigma \models \tau_{\mathsf{loop}}} \rightarrow_{\mathsf{tp}(\tau_{\mathsf{loop}}, \sigma)}$ is not guaranteed (Remark 16). To see why this may prevent termination, consider a loop τ_{loop} and assume that there are reachable states $\mathbf{v}, \mathbf{v}'$ with $\mathbf{v} \rightarrow_{\tau_{\mathsf{loop}}}^{+} \mathbf{v}'$, but $\mathbf{v} \not\rightarrow_{\mathsf{tp}(\tau_{\mathsf{loop}}, \sigma)} \mathbf{v}'$ for all models σ of τ_{loop}. Then TRL may find a model that corresponds to a run from $\mathbf{v}$ to $\mathbf{v}'$. Unless $\mathbf{v}$ can be evaluated to $\mathbf{v}'$ with another learned transition $\pi \notin \{\mathsf{tp}(\tau_{\mathsf{loop}}, \sigma) \mid \sigma \models \tau_{\mathsf{loop}}\}$ by coincidence, this loop cannot be blocked and TRL learns a new relation. Thus, TRL may keep learning new relations as long as there are loops whose transitive closure is not yet covered by learned relations.

As the elements of $\{\mathsf{tp}(\tau, \sigma) \mid \sigma \models \tau\}$ are independent of each other, a more "global" view may help to enforce convergence. We leave that to future work.

Example 24 (Example 1 *Finished).* After learning τ_{dec}^{+} and τ_{inc}^{+}, the underlying SMT problem becomes unsatisfiable when $b = 3$ after adding appropriate blocking clauses, so that τ_{dec}^{+} and τ_{inc}^{+} are preferred over τ_{dec} and τ_{inc}. The reason is that τ_{dec}^{+} and τ_{inc}^{+} must not be used twice in a row due to Line 7 of Algorithm 1, and τ_{inc}^{+} cannot be used after τ_{dec}^{+}, as it requires $w \doteq 0$, but τ_{dec}^{+} sets w to 1. Thus, Algorithm 1 returns safe. See [20] for a detailed run of Algorithm 1 on Example 1.

4 Implementing tp for Linear Integer Arithmetic

We now explain how to compute transitive projections for quantifier-free linear integer arithmetic via recurrence analysis. As in SMT-LIB [2], in our setting linear integer arithmetic also features (in)divisibility predicates of the form $e|t$

(or $e \nmid t$) where $e \in \mathbb{N}_+$ and t is an integer-valued term. Then we have $\sigma \models e|t$ iff $\sigma(t)$ is a multiple of e, and $\sigma \models e \nmid t$, otherwise.

The technique that we use is inspired by the recurrence analysis from [14]. However, there are some important differences. The approach from [14] computes convex hulls to over-approximate disjunctions by conjunctions, and it relies on polyhedral projections. In our setting, we always have a suitable model at hand, so that we can use cvp instead. Hence, our recurrence analysis can be implemented more efficiently.[4] Additionally, our recurrence analysis can handle divisibility predicates, which are not covered in [14].

On the other hand, [14] yields an over-approximation of the transitive closure of the given relation, whereas our approach performs an implicit case analysis (via cvp) and only yields an over-approximation of the transitive closure of one out of finitely many cases.

Moreover, the recurrence analysis from [14] also discovers non-linear relations, and then uses linearization techniques to eliminate them. For simplicity, our recurrence analysis only derives linear relations so far. However, just like [14], we could also derive non-linear relations and linearize them afterwards. Apart from these differences, our technique is analogous to [14].

In the sequel, let τ and $\sigma \models \tau$ be fixed. Our implementation of $\mathsf{tp}(\tau, \sigma)$ first searches for *recurrent literals*, i.e., literals of the form[5]

$$t \bowtie 0 \text{ or } e|t \quad \text{where} \quad t = \sum_{x \in \mathbf{x}} c_x \cdot (x' - x) + c, \ \bowtie \in \{\leq, \geq, <, >, \doteq\}, \text{ and } c_x, c \in \mathbb{Z}.$$

Hence, these literals provide information about the change of values of variables. To find such literals, we introduce a fresh variable x_δ for each $x \in \mathbf{x}$, and we conjoin $x_\delta \doteq x' - x$ to τ, i.e., we compute

$$\tau_{\wedge\delta} := \tau \wedge \bigwedge_{x \in \mathbf{x}} x_\delta \doteq x' - x.$$

So the value of x_δ corresponds to the change of x when applying τ. Next, we use cvp to eliminate all variables but $\{x_\delta \mid x \in \mathbf{x}\}$ from $\tau_{\wedge\delta}$, resulting in τ_δ. More precisely, we have

$$\tau_\delta := \mathsf{cvp}(\tau_{\wedge\delta}, \quad \sigma \uplus [x_\delta / \sigma(x' - x) \mid x \in \mathbf{x}], \quad \{x_\delta \mid x \in \mathbf{x}\}).$$

[4] The *double description method*, which is popular for computing polyhedral projections and convex hulls, and other state-of-the-art approaches have exponential complexity [7,39]. See [23] for an easily accessible discussion of the complexity of the double description method. In contrast, combining the model based projection from [29] with syntactic implicant projection [18] yields a polynomial time algorithm for cvp.

[5] W.l.o.g., we assume that literals are never negated, as we can negate the corresponding (in)equalities or divisibility predicates directly instead. Furthermore, in our implementation, we replace disequalities $s \not\doteq t$ with $s > t \vee s < t$ and eliminate the resulting disjunction via cvp to obtain a transition without disequalities.

Finally, to obtain a formula where all literals are recurrent, we replace each x_δ by its definition, i.e., we compute

$$\tau_{\mathsf{rec}} := \tau_\delta[x_\delta/x' - x \mid x \in \mathbf{x}].$$

Example 25 (Finding Recurrent Literals). Consider the transition τ_{dec}. We first construct the formula

$$\tau_{\wedge\delta} := \tau_{\mathsf{dec}} \wedge w_\delta \doteq w' - w \wedge x_\delta \doteq x' - x \wedge y_\delta \doteq y' - y.$$

Then for any model $\sigma \models \tau_{\mathsf{dec}}$, we get[6]

$$\begin{aligned} \tau_\delta &:= \mathsf{cvp}(\tau_{\wedge\delta}, \quad \sigma \uplus [w_\delta/0,\ x_\delta/{-1},\ y_\delta/{-1}], \quad \{w_\delta, x_\delta, y_\delta\}) \\ &= w_\delta \doteq 0 \wedge x_\delta \doteq -1 \wedge y_\delta \doteq -1. \end{aligned}$$

Next, replacing w_δ, x_δ, and y_δ with their definition results in

$$\begin{aligned} \tau_{\mathsf{rec}} &:= w' - w \doteq 0 \wedge x' - x \doteq -1 \wedge y' - y \doteq -1 \\ &\equiv w' - w \doteq 0 \wedge x' - x + 1 \doteq 0 \wedge y' - y + 1 \doteq 0. \end{aligned}$$

Then the construction of $\mathsf{tp}(\tau, \sigma)$ proceeds as follows:

- $\mathsf{tp}(\tau, \sigma)$ contains the literal $n > 0$, where $n \in \mathcal{V}$ is a fresh extra variable
- for each literal $\sum_{x \in \mathbf{x}} c_x \cdot (x' - x) + c \bowtie 0$ of τ_{rec}, $\mathsf{tp}(\tau, \sigma)$ contains the literal $\sum_{x \in \mathbf{x}} c_x \cdot (x' - x) + n \cdot c \bowtie 0$
- for each literal $e \mid \sum_{x \in \mathbf{x}} c_x \cdot (x' - x) + c$ of τ_{rec}, $\mathsf{tp}(\tau, \sigma)$ contains the literal $e \mid \sum_{x \in \mathbf{x}} c_x \cdot (x' - x) + n \cdot c$

Intuitively, the extra variable n can be thought of as a "loop counter", i.e., when n is instantiated with some constant k, then the literals above approximate the change of variables when $\to_\tau$ is applied k times.

Example 26 (Computing tp *(1)).* Continuing Example 25, $\mathsf{tp}(\tau_{\mathsf{dec}}, \sigma)$ contains the literals

$$\begin{aligned} & n > 0 \wedge w' - w + n \cdot 0 \doteq 0 \wedge x' - x + n \cdot 1 \doteq 0 \wedge y' - y + n \cdot 1 \doteq 0 \\ \equiv\ & n > 0 \wedge w' \doteq w \wedge x' \doteq x - n \wedge y' \doteq y - n \end{aligned}$$

for any model $\sigma \models \tau_{\mathsf{dec}}$. Note that in our example, this formula precisely characterizes the change of the variables after n iterations of $\to_{\tau_{\mathsf{dec}}}$. To simplify the formula above, we can propagate the equality $n = x - x'$, resulting in:

$$\begin{aligned} & x - x' > 0 \wedge w' \doteq w \wedge y' \doteq y - x + x' \\ \equiv\ & w' \doteq w \wedge x' < x \wedge x' - x \doteq y' - y \end{aligned} \tag{8}$$

[6] In the case of τ_{dec}, we obtain the same formula τ_δ for *every* model $\sigma \models \tau_{\mathsf{dec}}$, as variables can simply be eliminated by propagating equalities.

Compared to τ^+_{dec}, (8) lacks the literal $w \doteq 1$. To incorporate information about the pre- and post-variables (but not about their relation) we conjoin $\mathsf{cvp}(\tau, \sigma, \mathbf{x})$ and $\mathsf{cvp}(\tau, \sigma, \mathbf{x}')$ to $\mathsf{tp}(\tau, \sigma)$.

Example 27 (Computing tp *(2)).* We finish Example 26 by conjoining

$$\mathsf{cvp}(\tau_{\mathsf{dec}}, \sigma, \{w, x, y\}) = w \doteq 1 \qquad \text{and} \qquad \mathsf{cvp}(\tau_{\mathsf{dec}}, \sigma, \{w', x', y'\}) = w' \doteq 1$$

to (8), resulting in:

$$w' \doteq w \land x' < x \land x' - x \doteq y' - y \land w \doteq 1 \land w' \doteq 1 \quad \equiv \quad \tau^+_{\mathsf{dec}}$$

Example 28 (Divisibility). To see how tp can handle divisibility predicates, consider the transition

$$\tau := 2|x \land 3|x' - x + 1.$$

Then our approach identifies the recurrent literal $\tau_{\mathsf{rec}} = 3|x' - x + 1$, so that $\mathsf{tp}(\tau, \sigma)$ contains the literal $3|x' - x + n$. To see why we conjoin this literal to $\mathsf{tp}(\tau, \sigma)$, note that $3|x' - x + 1$ and $3|x' - x + n$ are equivalent to $x' - x + 1 \equiv_3 0$ and $x' - x + n \equiv_3 0$, respectively, where "$\equiv_3$" denotes congruence modulo 3. So $e \to^n_\tau e'$ implies $e' - e + n \equiv_3 0$, just like $e \to^n_\pi e'$ implies $e' - e + n = 0$ for $\pi := x' - x + 1 \doteq 0$. Moreover, we have $\mathsf{cvp}(\tau, \sigma, \mathbf{x}) = 2|x$, and thus

$$\mathsf{tp}(\tau, \sigma) = n > 0 \land 3|x' - x + n \land 2|x.$$

We refer to [20] for the straightforward proof of the following theorem:

Theorem 29 (Correctness of tp). *The function* tp *as defined above is a transitive projection.*

5 Related Work and Experiments

Related Work. For reasons of space, we only discuss the most important related work and refer to [20] for more details. Most state-of-the-art infinite state model checking algorithms use *interpolation* [8,26,27,29,31,34,35,42]. As discussed in Sect. 1, these techniques are very powerful, but also fragile. In contrast, robustness of TRL depends on the underlying transitive projection. Our implementation for linear integer arithmetic is a variation of the recurrence analysis from [14], which is very robust in our experience. In particular, our recurrence analysis does not require an SMT solver.

Currently, the most powerful model checking algorithm is *Spacer with global guidance* (GSpacer). In GSpacer, interpolation is optional, and thus it is more robust than Spacer (without global guidance) and other interpolation-based techniques. GSpacer is part of the IC3/PDR family of model checking algorithms [6], which differ fundamentally from BMC-based approaches like TRL: The latter unroll the transition relation, whereas GSpacer and other variants of IC3/PDR for infinite state systems prove global properties by combining local reasoning about a single step with techniques like induction, interpolation, or global guidance.

Many techniques for program verification use *transition invariants* or related concepts like *loop summarization* or *acceleration* [1,5,14,18,19,32,33,37,41]. All of them rely on over- or under-approximations, whereas TRL can use both.

TRL has been inspired by ABMC [19], which is also restricted to under-approximations and thus weaker for proving safety. However, ABMC is currently one of the most powerful techniques for proving unsafety. Other important conceptual differences include TRL's use of: blocking clauses on demand; model based projection, which cannot be used by ABMC, as acceleration yields formulas in theories without quantifier elimination; backtracking, which is useful for proving safety as it keeps the SMT problem small, but it would slow down the discovery of counterexamples in ABMC.

Our tool LoAT also implements ADCL [18], which embeds acceleration into a depth-first search for counterexamples (whereas ABMC and TRL perform breadth-first search). Thus, TRL is conceptually closer to ABMC, and for proving unsafety, ABMC is superior to ADCL (see [19]). However, as witnessed by the results of the annual *Termination Competition* [24], ADCL is currently the most powerful technique for proving non-termination of transition systems (see [17]).

Experiments. We implemented TRL in our tool LoAT [16], which is available on Github [22] and uses the SMT solvers Yices [12] and Z3 [36]. We evaluated it on all linear CHCs from the CHC competitions '23 and '24 [9] (excluding duplicates), resulting in 626 problems from applications like verification of C, Rust, and Java.

We compared 14 techniques of leading CHC solvers:

LoAT's implementations of TRL (LoAT TRL), ABMC [19], and *k-induction* [40].
Z3 4.13.3 [36] Z3's implementations of the Spacer [29] (Z3 Spacer) and GSpacer [31] (Z3 GSpacer) algorithms, and of BMC.
Golem 0.6.2 [4] Golem's implementations of *transition power abstraction* [8], *interpolation based model checking* [34] (Golem IMC), *lazy abstraction with interpolants* [35], *predicate abstraction/CEGAR* [10,25], *property directed k-induction* [27] (Golem PDKIND), Spacer (Golem Spacer), and BMC.
Eldarica 2.1 [26] Eldarica's implementation of predicate abstraction/CEGAR.

We ran our experiments on CLAIX-2023-HPC nodes of the RWTH University High Performance Computing Cluster with a memory limit of 10560 MiB ($\approx$ 11GB) and a timeout of 300 s per example. Here, we report on the results of the seven best configurations, and we refer to [20,21] for more details. Note that our implementation can also prove unsafety, by using the *acceleration technique* from [15] instead of transitive projections, see [20] for details.

	✓	safe		unsafe	
		✓	!	✓	!
LoAT TRL	386	267	24	119	22
Z3 GSpacer	373	287	18	86	4
Golem Spacer	340	231	–	109	–
Z3 Spacer	339	236	–	103	–
Golem IMC	318	215	2	103	2
Golem PDKIND	315	224	2	91	2
Eldarica	298	219	8	79	0

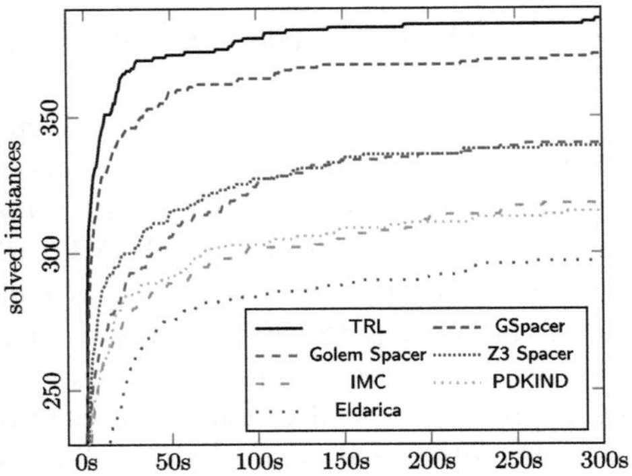

In the table above, the first column marked with ✓ contains the number of solved instances (i.e., all remaining instances could not be solved by the respective configuration), and the columns with ! show the number of examples that could only be solved by the corresponding configuration. Such a comparison only makes sense if just one implementation of each algorithm is considered, so here we disregarded Z3 Spacer and Golem Spacer (as GSpacer is a variant of Spacer).

The table shows that TRL is highly competitive: Overall, it solves the most instances, and only GSpacer can prove safety more often. More importantly, TRL finds many unique proofs, i.e., it is orthogonal to existing model checking algorithms, and hence it improves the state of the art.

The plot on the right shows how many instances were solved within 300 s. It shows that TRL is also highly competitive in terms of runtime.

6 Conclusion

We presented *Transitive Relation Learning (TRL)*, a powerful model checking algorithm for infinite state systems. TRL adds transitive relations to the analyzed system until its *diameter* (the number of steps that is required to cover all reachable states) becomes finite, which facilitates a safety proof. As it does not search for invariants, TRL does not need interpolation, which is in contrast to most state-of-the-art techniques. Nevertheless, our evaluation shows that TRL is highly competitive. Moreover, not using interpolation allows us to avoid the well-known fragility of interpolation-based approaches.

In future work, we plan to support other theories like reals, bitvectors, and arrays, and we will investigate an extension to temporal verification.

Disclosure of Interests. The authors have no competing interests to declare that are relevant to the content of this article.

References

1. Bardin, S., Finkel, A., Leroux, J., Schnoebelen, P.: Flat acceleration in symbolic model checking. In: ATVA 2005, pp. 474–488. LNCS 3707 (2005). https://doi.org/10.1007/11562948_35

2. Barrett, C., Fontaine, P., Tinelli, C.: The satisfiability modulo theories library (SMT-LIB). www.SMT-LIB.org (2016)
3. Biere, A., Cimatti, A., Clarke, E.M., Strichman, O., Zhu, Y.: Bounded model checking. Adv. Comput. **58**, 117–148 (2003). https://doi.org/10.1016/S0065-2458(03)58003-2
4. Blicha, M., Britikov, K., Sharygina, N.: The Golem Horn solver. In: CAV 2023, pp. 209–223. LNCS 13965 (2023). https://doi.org/10.1007/978-3-031-37703-7_10
5. Bozga, M., Iosif, R., Konečný, F.: Fast acceleration of ultimately periodic relations. In: CAV 2010, pp. 227–242. LNCS 6174 (2010). https://doi.org/10.1007/978-3-642-14295-6_23
6. Bradley, A.R.: SAT-based model checking without unrolling. In: VMCAI 2011, pp. 70–87. LNCS 6538 (2011). https://doi.org/10.1007/978-3-642-18275-4_7
7. Bremner, D.: Incremental convex hull algorithms are not output sensitive. Discret. Comput. Geom. **21**(1), 57–68 (1999). https://doi.org/10.1007/PL00009410
8. Britikov, K., Blicha, M., Sharygina, N., Fedyukovich, G.: Reachability analysis for multiloop programs using transition power abstraction. In: FM 2024, pp. 558–576. LNCS 14933 (2024). https://doi.org/10.1007/978-3-031-71162-6_29
9. CHC Competition, https://chc-comp.github.io
10. Clarke, E.M., Grumberg, O., Jha, S., Lu, Y., Veith, H.: Counterexample-guided abstraction refinement. In: CAV 2000, pp. 154–169. LNCS 1855 (2000). https://doi.org/10.1007/10722167_15
11. Cooper, D.C.: Theorem proving in arithmetic without multiplication. Mach. Intell. **7**, 91–99 (1972)
12. Dutertre, B.: Yices 2.2. In: CAV 2014, pp. 737–744. LNCS 8559 (2014). https://doi.org/10.1007/978-3-319-08867-9_49
13. Enderton, H.B.: A Mathematical Introduction to Logic. Academic Press (1972)
14. Farzan, A., Kincaid, Z.: Compositional recurrence analysis. In: FMCAD 2015, pp. 57–64 (2015). https://doi.org/10.1109/FMCAD.2015.7542253
15. Frohn, F.: A calculus for modular loop acceleration. In: TACAS 2020, pp. 58–76. LNCS 12078 (2020). https://doi.org/10.1007/978-3-030-45190-5_4
16. Frohn, F., Giesl, J.: Proving non-termination and lower runtime bounds with LoAT (system description). In: IJCAR 2022, pp. 712–722. LNCS 13385 (2022). https://doi.org/10.1007/978-3-031-10769-6_41
17. Frohn, F., Giesl, J.: Proving non-termination by acceleration driven clause learning. In: CADE 2023, pp. 220–233. LNCS 14132 (2023). https://doi.org/10.1007/978-3-031-38499-8_13
18. Frohn, F., Giesl, J.: ADCL: acceleration driven clause learning for constrained Horn clauses. In: SAS 2023, pp. 259–285. LNCS 14284 (2023). https://doi.org/10.1007/978-3-031-44245-2_13
19. Frohn, F., Giesl, J.: Integrating loop acceleration into bounded model checking. In: FM 2024, pp. 73–91. LNCS 14933 (2024). https://doi.org/10.1007/978-3-031-71162-6_4
20. Frohn, F., Giesl, J.: Infinite state model checking by learning transitive relations. CoRR **abs/2502.04761** (2025). https://doi.org/10.48550/arXiv.2502.04761
21. Frohn, F., Giesl, J.: Evaluation of "Infinite State Model Checking by Learning Transitive Relations" (2025), https://loat-developers.github.io/trl-eval/
22. Frohn, F., Giesl, J.: LoAT website, https://loat-developers.github.io/LoAT/
23. Genov, B.: The convex hull problem in practice: improving the running time of the double description method. Ph.D. thesis, Bremen University, Germany (2015), https://media.suub.uni-bremen.de/handle/elib/833

24. Giesl, J., Rubio, A., Sternagel, C., Waldmann, J., Yamada, A.: The termination and complexity competition. In: TACAS 2019, pp. 156–166. LNCS 11429 (2019). https://doi.org/10.1007/978-3-030-17502-3_10
25. Graf, S., Saïdi, H.: Construction of abstract state graphs with PVS. In: CAV 1997, pp. 72–83. LNCS 1254 (1997). https://doi.org/10.1007/3-540-63166-6_10
26. Hojjat, H., Rümmer, P.: The Eldarica Horn solver. In: FMCAD 2018, pp. 1–7 (2018). https://doi.org/10.23919/FMCAD.2018.8603013
27. Jovanovic, D., Dutertre, B.: Property-directed k-induction. In: FMCAD 2016, pp. 85–92 (2016). https://doi.org/10.1109/FMCAD.2016.7886665
28. Kincaid, Z., Breck, J., Boroujeni, A.F., Reps, T.W.: Compositional recurrence analysis revisited. In: PLDI 2017, pp. 248–262 (2017). https://doi.org/10.1145/3062341.3062373
29. Komuravelli, A., Gurfinkel, A., Chaki, S.: SMT-based model checking for recursive programs. Formal Methods Syst. Des. **48**(3), 175–205 (2016). https://doi.org/10.1007/s10703-016-0249-4
30. Konečný, F.: PTIME computation of transitive closures of octagonal relations. In: TACAS 2016, pp. 645–661. LNCS 9636 (2016). https://doi.org/10.1007/978-3-662-49674-9_42
31. Krishnan, H.G.V., Chen, Y., Shoham, S., Gurfinkel, A.: Global guidance for local generalization in model checking. In: CAV 2020, pp. 101–125. LNCS 12225 (2020). https://doi.org/10.1007/978-3-030-53291-8_7
32. Kroening, D., Sharygina, N., Tonetta, S., Tsitovich, A., Wintersteiger, C.M.: Loop summarization using state and transition invariants. Formal Methods Syst. Des. **42**(3), 221–261 (2013). https://doi.org/10.1007/S10703-012-0176-Y
33. Kroening, D., Lewis, M., Weissenbacher, G.: Proving safety with trace automata and bounded model checking. In: FM 2015, pp. 325–341. LNCS 9109 (2015). https://doi.org/10.1007/978-3-319-19249-9_21
34. McMillan, K.L.: Interpolation and SAT-based model checking. In: CAV 2003, pp. 1–13. LNCS 2725 (2003). https://doi.org/10.1007/978-3-540-45069-6_1
35. McMillan, K.L.: Lazy abstraction with interpolants. In: CAV 2006, pp. 123–136. LNCS 4144 (2006). https://doi.org/10.1007/11817963_14
36. de Moura, L., Bjørner, N.: Z3: An efficient SMT solver. In: TACAS 2008, pp. 337–340. LNCS 4963 (2008). https://doi.org/10.1007/978-3-540-78800-3_24
37. Pimpalkhare, N., Kincaid, Z.: Semi-linear VASR for over-approximate semi-linear transition system reachability. In: RP 2024, pp. 154–166. LNCS 15050 (2024). https://doi.org/10.1007/978-3-031-72621-7_11
38. Podelski, A., Rybalchenko, A.: Transition invariants. In: LICS 2004, pp. 32–41 (2004). https://doi.org/10.1109/LICS.2004.1319598
39. Promies, V., Ábrahám, E.: A divide-and-conquer approach to variable elimination in linear real arithmetic. In: FM 2024, pp. 131–148. LNCS 14933 (2024). https://doi.org/10.1007/978-3-031-71162-6_7
40. Sheeran, M., Singh, S., Stålmarck, G.: Checking safety properties using induction and a SAT-solver. In: FMCAD 2000, pp. 108–125. LNCS 1954 (2000). https://doi.org/10.1007/3-540-40922-X_8
41. Silverman, J., Kincaid, Z.: Loop summarization with rational vector addition systems. In: CAV 2019, pp. 97–115. LNCS 11562 (2019). https://doi.org/10.1007/978-3-030-25543-5_7
42. Solanki, M., Chatterjee, P., Lal, A., Roy, S.: Accelerated bounded model checking using interpolation based summaries. In: TACAS 2024, pp. 155–174. LNCS 14571 (2024). https://doi.org/10.1007/978-3-031-57249-4_8

Relatively Complete and Efficient Partial Quantifier Elimination

Estifanos Getachew(✉), Arie Gurfinkel, and Richard Trefler

University of Waterloo, Waterloo, Canada
{esgetach,agurfink,trefler}@uwaterloo.ca

Abstract. Quantifier elimination is used in various automated reasoning tasks, including quantified SMT solving, exists/forall solving, program synthesis, model checking, and constrained Horn clause (CHC) solving. Complete quantifier elimination, however, is computationally intractable for many theories. The recent algorithm QEL shows a promising approach to approximate quantifier elimination, which has resulted in improvements in solver performance. QEL performs partial quantifier elimination with a completeness guarantee that depends on a certain semantic property of the given formula. Considerably generalizing the previous approach, we identify a subclass of *local theories* in which *partial quantifier elimination* can be performed efficiently. We present $\mathcal{T}$-QEL a parametrized polynomial time algorithm that is a sound extension of QEL and is relatively complete for this class of theories. The algorithm utilizes the proof theoretic characterization of the theories, which is based on *restricted derivations*. Finally, we prove for $\mathcal{T}$-QEL, soundness in general, and relative completeness with respect to the identified class of theories.

1 Introduction

Several automated reasoning tasks, including quantified SMT solving [1], exists/forall solving [3,4], program synthesis [17], model checking [9,15], and CHC solving [22] utilize quantifier elimination. Regardless, the intractability of complete quantifier elimination procedures, see e.g. [2,12,16], poses a challenge. As a result, solvers often use some form of an approximate technique. An interesting example of this, is the algorithm QEL proposed in [8], that resulted in significant performance improvements in Z3 [19] and the CHC solver Spacer [15].

The problem QEL solves can be formulated as a *partial quantifier elimination* problem. In particular, for any formula of the form $\exists \bar{x}\, \varphi(\bar{x})$, where $\varphi(\bar{x})$ is a conjunction of literals, QEL computes a quantifier free $\psi(\bar{y})$ whose free variables are among the x_i and its existential closure, $\exists \bar{y}\, \psi(\bar{y})$, is equivalent to $\exists \bar{x}\, \varphi(\bar{x})$. This can be seen as a relaxation of (complete) quantifier elimination, in which we allow some of the quantified variables to remain. An important property of QEL

This work was supported, in part, by Individual Discovery Grants from the Natural Sciences and Engineering Research Council of Canada.

C. Barrett and U. Waldmann (Eds.): CADE 2025, LNAI 15943, pp. 490–507, 2025.
https://doi.org/10.1007/978-3-031-99984-0_26

is that it is *relatively complete* for the theory of equality (with free functions), $\mathcal{T}_{eq}$; that is, QEL guarantees to eliminate a variable x_i if x_i has an entailed ground definition—i.e., $\varphi(\bar{x}) \models x_i \approx s$ for some *arbitrary* ground term s.

Despite this, QEL only deals with formulas in the language of $\mathcal{T}_{eq}$, and consequently, its completeness guarantees are restricted to just $\mathcal{T}_{eq}$. We take a theoretical direction, and investigate for which other theories we can *efficiently* generalize QEL while maintaining *relative completeness* with respect to the theories. In particular, we explore theories in which we can do so in polynomial time. We use the notion of *locality* [7,10] of a theory to identify theories in which we can perform partial quantifier elimination efficiently. Using the proof theoretic characterization of the theories, we present $\mathcal{T}$-QEL, a generalization of QEL.

The notion of *locality* in theories was first introduced by Givan and McAllester in [10,11,18]. They considered locality of theories in the context of First Order Logic (FOL) without equality. They gave a proof theoretic account of locality based on the concept of confining deductions to the subterms of an input formula. Ganzinger in [7] considers locality in the context of FOL with equality and gives a semantic characterization of local (equational) theories. We adopt some results due to Ganzinger [7], to lift the proof theoretic characterization of locality by Givan and McAllester to FOL with equality. We then base our algorithm $\mathcal{T}$-QEL on this *proof theoretic characterization.*

The reason we are interested in locality is that the uniform word problem for local theories is *polynomial time* decidable [7]. That is, given a ground Horn clause C and a local theory (locally) axiomatized by a finite set of Horn clauses Φ, we can decide entailment from the theory, $\Phi \models C$, in polynomial time. This is central to generalizing QEL to other theories in polynomial time.

Another central issue that arises, when trying to generalize QEL, is the problem of deciding whether in the theory $\mathcal{T}$, there is an entailed ground definition from a conjunction of literals φ. That is, given a free variable x of φ deciding whether for some *arbitrary* ground term s, $\varphi \models_{\mathcal{T}} x \approx s$. The problem is complicated by the fact that s is potentially an arbitrary term, not necessarily occurring in φ. Since we are working in a countable language, however, if $\mathcal{T}$ has a decision procedure for its quantifier free fragment, there is the following (rather naive) semi-decision procedure: enumerate the ground terms $s_0, s_1, \ldots$ and for each s_i, check whether $\varphi \wedge x \not\approx s_i$ is $\mathcal{T}$-unsatisfiable, if so replace, in φ, x by s_i. Clearly, this is sound, but potentially non-terminating.

A way to deal with this potentially non-terminating behavior, is to reduce the search space for ground definitions to a finite one. Specifically, we introduce the finite notion of being a *constructively ground term* with respect to a theory $\mathcal{T}$ and a conjunction of literals φ. We then give a definition for a subclass of local theories[1], which we call *locally ground theories*, based on this concept. It is worth noting that the constructively ground terms can be computed in polynomial time.

Interestingly, several important theories shown in the literature to exhibit *locality* properties are also *locally ground.* In particular, we show the theories

[1] Strictly speaking, we are considering an extended notion of *locality* from [7].

listed below to be locally ground; for each of these theories, we include in our signature a countable set of free/uninterpreted function and constant symbols: **(i)** The theory of recursively defined data structures $\mathcal{T}_{rd}$; **(ii)** the theory of partial orders $\mathcal{T}_{po}$; **(iii)** the theory $\mathcal{T}_{mo}$, where some functions are axiomatized as monotone with respect to the partial order $\leq$; and **(iv)** the theory of equality $\mathcal{T}_{eq}$.

Finally, building on the ideas discussed above, we present the partial quantifier elimination algorithm $\mathcal{T}$-QEL. $\mathcal{T}$-QEL is a sound extension of QEL that utilizes the concepts of restricted derivations and constructively ground terms to solve the partial quantifier elimination problem in polynomial time for the locally ground theories. We prove, for $\mathcal{T}$-QEL, soundness in general and relative completeness for the locally ground theories.

Applications Beyond Locally Ground Theories. The algorithm $\mathcal{T}$-QEL can be used as a partial quantifier elimination algorithm for theories that might not necessarily be locally ground. Even for theories such as Linear Integer Arithmetic and Linear Real Arithmetic—where (complete) quantifier elimination is available—we can abstract away the semantics of the functions $+$ and $\times$ as simply monotonic and free (uninterpreted) functions respectively and keep the semantics of $\leq$ as a partial order. This abstraction allows us to use $\mathcal{T}$-QEL as a potentially efficient preprocessing step to partially eliminate quantified variables before performing the more expensive quantifier elimination algorithms of the theories.

Contributions. The contributions of this paper can be summarized as follows.

- We identify a subclass of local theories, called *locally ground theories*, in which partial quantifier elimination can be done in polynomial time.
- We show several important theories to be locally ground.
- We give a *polynomial time algorithm* by lifting the proof theoretic characterization due to Givan and McAllester to FOL with equality.
- We prove for the algorithm $\mathcal{T}$-QEL *soundness* in general, and *relative completeness* with respect to the locally ground theories.

2 Basic Notions and Notation

First Order Logic [5]. We assume the usual concepts from First order logic (FOL) with equality such as model, satisfaction, logical consequence, and a theory, as presented in e.g. [5,6]. We briefly summarize the notation used here.

For a given signature Σ, we take a Σ-structure $\mathfrak{A}$ to be a tuple (A, I) where A is the universe, and I is a mapping that assigns each k-ary function and predicate symbol, f and P, a k-ary operation and relation, $f^{\mathfrak{A}}$ and $P^{\mathfrak{A}}$, on A. We use $\mathcal{V}$ to denote the set of all variables, and take a Σ-interpretation, $\mathcal{I}$, to be a tuple ($\mathfrak{A}$, α) of a Σ-structure $\mathfrak{A}$ and a variable assignment $\alpha : \mathcal{V} \rightarrow A$. We denote by $t^{\mathcal{I}}$ the interpretation of the term t under $\mathcal{I}$. We use the notation $\mathrm{FV}(\varphi)$ to denote the set of free variables of the formula φ. Given a conjunction of literals φ, we use Γ_φ for the set containing exactly the positive literals of φ.

For a given term t, we let S_t be the set consisting of the subterms of t, i.e., $S_t = \{x\}$ if t is some variable x, and $S_t = \{t\} \cup \bigcup S_{t_i}$ if t is $f(t_1, \ldots, t_n)$. We extend the definition to S_φ and S_Φ for a Σ-formula φ and a set of Σ-formulas Φ, in the expected way. We denote by Σ^F the set of all function symbols in Σ, and by Σ^T the set of all terms generated from Σ. Given a function $\lambda : \mathcal{P}(\Sigma^T) \to \mathcal{P}(\Sigma^T)$ we adopt the notation S_φ^λ to denote the set $\lambda(S_\varphi)$ assigned to S_φ.

Say that a subterm set Ψ is closed under the subterm relation, if, for all $t \in \Psi$ all the subterms of t are in Ψ. We say that a binary relation R on a subterm set Ψ is *a congruence relation* if it is an equivalence relation and whenever $t_i \, R \, s_i$ and $f(t_1, \ldots, t_n), f(s_1, \ldots, s_n) \in \Psi$ we have $f(t_1, \ldots, t_n) \, R \, f(s_1, \ldots, s_n)$.

We take a theory $\mathcal{T}$ to be a set of Σ-sentences that is closed under logical consequence. Note that, for a given set of sentences (axioms) Φ, the consequences of Φ, denoted by $\mathrm{Cn}\,\Phi = \{\varphi \mid \Phi \models \varphi\}$, is a theory. Say that φ is $\mathcal{T}$-satisfiable if there is a model of $\mathcal{T}$ that is also a model of φ. We use the notation $\models_\mathcal{T}$ to denote logical consequence in the theory $\mathcal{T}$.

Horn Theories and Direct Products [14]. We use the term basic Horn clause for formulas of the form $\bigwedge \psi_i \to \psi$, where ψ_i, ψ are atoms, to distinguish them from (universal) Horn clauses $\forall \bar{x} \, (\bigwedge \psi_i \to \psi)$. Given a non-empty index set I and a family of Σ-structures $(\mathfrak{A}_i)_{i \in I}$, we use the notation $\Pi_{i \in I} \, \mathfrak{A}_i$ for the *direct product (product)* of the given family of structures. For background on direct products of models of Horn theories and products in general, see Ch. 9 of [14].

Egraphs [8,20]. An egraph is a well-known data structure to compactly represent a set of terms and an equivalence relation on those terms [20]. We assume that graphs have an ordered successor relation and use $n[i]$ to denote the ith successor (child) of a node n. We denote by $deg(n)$, the out degree of a node n, i.e., the number of edges leaving n.

Definition 1. *(Egraph [8]) For a given signature Σ, an egraph is a tuple $G = \langle N, E, L, root \rangle$, where*

(a) $\langle N, E \rangle$ is a directed acyclic graph (possibly multigraph).
(b) $L : N \to \Sigma^F \cup \mathcal{V}$ labels nodes by function and variable symbols s.t. nodes labelled by variables are leaves, and $deg(n) = k$ if n is labelled by a k-ary function symbol f.
(c) $root : N \to N$ maps a node to its representative such that the relation $\rho_{root} := \{ (n, n') \mid root(n) = root(n') \}$ is closed under congruence w.r.t. root. That is, $(n, n') \in \rho_{root}$ whenever $L(n) = L(n')$, $deg(n) = deg(n') > 0$, and for $1 \le i \le deg(n)$, $(n[i], n'[i]) \in \rho_{root}$.

Given an egraph G, we let $term_G : N \to \Sigma^T$ be the function that maps nodes to their corresponding terms in the expected way. We assume the terms of different nodes are different (i.e., *term* is injective) and denote by n_t the node whose term is t. We denote by *egraph*(φ) the egraph of φ built by the standard procedure given in [20], see Sect. 2 of [8] for more.

3 Overview

Intuitively, $\mathcal{T}$-QEL, the algorithm presented in Sect. 5, is based on the following observation: for any formula of the form $\exists x\, \varphi$, if $\varphi \models_{\mathcal{T}} x \approx s$ for some *arbitrary* ground term s, then $\models_{\mathcal{T}} \exists x\, \varphi \leftrightarrow \varphi[x/s]$. Hence, effectively eliminating the quantified variable x. As discussed in the introduction, we want to do this in *polynomial time*, and we want to maintain *relative completeness*—that is, we want to eliminate every variable that has an entailed ground definition. We illustrate our approach in the following example.[2]

Example 1. Fix a signature $\Sigma_{po} = (\Sigma^F, \{\leq\})$, where Σ^F contains countably many free function and constant symbols, and let $\mathcal{T}_{po}$ be the theory of partial orders in this signature. That is, $\leq$ is reflexive, transitive, and antisymmetric. Now consider the formula $\exists \bar{x}\, \varphi(\bar{x})$, where

$$\varphi(\bar{x}) := x_1 \approx f(c) \land f(x_2) \approx g(x_1) \land x_3 \leq g(f(x_2)) \land g(f(x_2)) \leq x_3$$

and c, f, g are free constant and function symbols. It is straightforward to see that x_1 has an entailed ground definition, however, it is not so clear for x_2 and x_3. In fact, note for the term $g(g(f(c)))$, which is not a subterm of φ, we have $\varphi(\bar{x}) \models_{\mathcal{T}_{po}} x_3 \approx g(g(f(c)))$; this would be completely missed by QEL. It is essential that we detect such entailments to guarantee relative completeness. We proceed as follows:
Compute the Partition $S_\varphi/{\sim}$ of the Subterms. Let $\sim$ be the congruence relation defined on the subterm set of φ, S_φ, as: $t_1 \sim t_2$ iff $\varphi \models_{\mathcal{T}_{po}} t_1 \approx t_2$. Then, note that the quotient set

$$S_\varphi/{\sim} = \{\{x_1, f(c)\}, \{c\}, \{x_2\}, \{f(x_2), g(x_1)\}, \{x_3, g(f(x_2))\}\}$$

represents terms which are equivalent under *every* model of φ and $\mathcal{T}_{po}$. Here is where the locality of the theories is crucial, to compute the partition in polynomial time. Let us use the notation $[t]$ to refer to the equivalence classes in $S_\varphi/{\sim}$, e.g. $[x_1] = \{x_1, f(c)\}$.
Construct a Ground Term. Next, we pick for each equivalence class in $S_\varphi/{\sim}$ (if we can) a *representative* term that is either *already* ground or can be transformed via substitution of equivalent terms into an *equivalent* ground term. For the class $[x_1]$ we pick $f(c)$, for the class $[c]$ we pick c, and the class $[x_2]$ does not contain such a term. For the class $[f(x_2)]$, we note that $x_1 \sim f(c)$ and hence by functional congruence we know $\varphi \models_{\mathcal{T}_{po}} g(x_1) \approx g(f(c))$, thus we pick $g(x_1)$. With similar reasoning, we can see $\varphi \models_{\mathcal{T}_{po}} g(f(x_2)) \approx g(g(f(c)))$, hence we pick $g(f(x_2))$ for the class $[x_3]$. Interestingly, if a variable has *any* entailed ground definition, its equivalence class will contain such a *constructively* ground term.
Eliminate by Substitution. Finally, we note that $\varphi(\bar{x})$ is equivalent (in $\mathcal{T}_{po}$) with the following formula: $f(c) \approx f(c) \land f(x_2) \approx g(f(c)) \land g(g(f(c))) \leq$

[2] The intuitive explanation presented here slightly differs from the presentation of $\mathcal{T}$-QEL in Sect. 5. See the explanation for Algorithm 1($\mathcal{T}$-QEL) provided in Sect. 5.

$g(g(f(c))) \wedge g(g(f(c))) \leq g(g(f(c)))$. Which we obtained by simply replacing each variable and representative with their equivalent ground formula we inferred in the above step. Hence, we output the formula $\exists x_2\, f(x_2) \approx g(f(c)) \wedge g(g(f(c))) \leq g(g(f(c)))$ after removing redundant atoms.

Representation of $S_\varphi/\!\sim$ on an Egraph. Egraphs give us a compact way to represent congruence relations. For local theories such as $\mathcal{T}_{po}$, representing the partition $S_\varphi/\!\sim$ amounts to saturating the egraph with implied atoms that are formed over the subterms of φ. Locality here allows us to consider only those atoms whose subterms are already in φ. We formalize this notion in Sect. 5.

4 Locally Ground Theories

In this section, we define a subclass of local theories in which the search space for entailed ground definitions—i.e., entailments of the form $\varphi(\bar{x}) \models_\mathcal{T} x_i \approx s$, where s is an arbitrary ground term—is reduced to a finite space. We introduce the notion of being a *constructively ground term* with respect to a conjunction of literals φ and a theory $\mathcal{T}$. We give a definition for the *locally ground theories* based on this notion.

We adopt here the notion of a *restricted derivation* on which the definition of local theories (in FOL without equality) [10] is based. As we are working with theories in the context of FOL with equality, however, we consider the equality axioms in our definition. We use Φ_{eq} to denote the set of equality axioms (i.e., reflexivity, symmetry, transitivity, functional and relational congruence).

A local theory in FOL with equality [7] is a theory that is axiomatized by some finite set of (universal) Horn clauses Φ such that for any basic Horn clause ψ, $\Phi \models \psi$ iff $\Phi[S_\psi] \models \psi$, where $\Phi[S_\psi]$ is the set consisting of instances of Φ whose subterms are all in S_ψ.[3,4] We say Φ is a local axiomatization of $\mathcal{T}$. To motivate the definition of restricted derivations in FOL with equality, we restate, in the terminology of this paper, a result by Ganzinger.

Theorem 2. *(Ganzinger [7]). The set of Horn clauses Φ is a local axiomatization of $\mathcal{T}$ in FOL with equality iff $\Phi \cup \Phi_{eq}$ is a local axiomatization of $\mathcal{T}$ in FOL without equality. That is, for any basic Horn clause ψ the following are equivalent:*

(i) $\Phi \models \psi$ iff $\Phi[S_\psi] \models \psi$.
(ii) $\Phi \cup \Phi_{eq} \models_{neq} \psi$ iff $(\Phi \cup \Phi_{eq})[S_\psi] \models_{neq} \psi$.

where $\models_{neq}$ denotes logical consequence in FOL without equality.

This along with the characterization of local theories in FOL without equality given by Givan and McAllester in [10] motivates the proof theoretic definition we

[3] Note that, only ground formulas are considered in [7,10]. It is straightforward to adopt the results to formulas with free variables, as is done here, by observing for any quantifier free $\varphi(\bar{x})$, we have $\models \varphi(\bar{x})$ iff $\models \varphi[x_i/c_{x_i}]$, where c_{x_i} are fresh constants.

[4] For ease of presentation, we assume no ground terms occur in the axioms Φ.

adopt below. We note here that, the definition of locality we give below subsumes the original notion of *locality* given in [7,10], as we are restricting the terms that appear in the derivations to a (polynomially) *extended subterm set.* Note that the uniform word problem is still polynomial time decidable.

In particular, let $\lambda : \mathcal{P}(\Sigma^T) \to \mathcal{P}(\Sigma^T)$ be a map associating with each set S of terms a set $\lambda(S)$ of terms. We further require λ be computable on finite inputs S. For a given φ, recall we use the notation S_φ^λ to denote the set $\lambda(S_\varphi)$ assigned to S_φ. Call such a function λ, *proper*, if for each formula φ, *(i)* $S_\varphi \subseteq S_\varphi^\lambda$, *(ii)* the size of S_φ^λ is polynomial in $|S_\varphi|$ and *(iii)* S_φ^λ is closed under the subterm relation.

Definition 3. *(Restricted Derivation). Let $\Gamma \cup \{\theta\}$ be a set of atoms, and λ a proper function, then, a restricted derivation of θ from Γ using the axioms Φ, is θ if $\theta \in \Gamma$ and otherwise is a sequence of atomic formulas $\theta_1, \ldots, \theta_n$ s.t. θ_n is θ and we have for each θ_i* ***(i)*** *$S_{\theta_i} \subseteq S_\varphi^\lambda$ and,* ***(ii)*** *there exists a Horn clause $\forall \bar{x}\,(\psi_1 \wedge \cdots \wedge \psi_k \to \psi) \in \Phi \cup \Phi_{eq}$ and a substitution σ such that θ_i is $\psi\sigma$ and each $\psi_j\sigma$ is either in Γ or appears earlier in the derivation.*

Write $\Gamma \cup \Phi \Vdash^\lambda \theta$ if there exists a restricted derivation of θ from Γ using Φ and λ. Then, we say a theory $\mathcal{T}$ is *a local theory* if it can be axiomatized by a finite set of Horn clauses Φ, and there is a proper function λ, such that $\Gamma \cup \Phi \vdash \theta$ iff $\Gamma \cup \Phi \Vdash^\lambda \theta$. Where $\vdash$ is the provability relation for some proof system that is sound and complete for FOL with equality—i.e., $\Gamma \vdash \theta$ iff $\Gamma \models \theta$—as is done in [10]. It is clear to see that, if we fix λ to be the identity on $\mathcal{P}(\Sigma^T)$ the original notion of locality is recovered. In what follows we will simply write $\Vdash$ and omit λ when it is clear from context.

We now introduce the finite notion of being a *constructively ground term* with respect to some given conjunction of literals and a theory. Constructively ground terms are terms which might not be ground themselves, but can be transformed into an equivalent ground term in polynomial time using the (extended) subterm set of φ.

More formally, let φ be a conjunction of literals, $\mathcal{T}$ a theory, and λ a proper function. We let $\sim_{\mathcal{T},\lambda}^\varphi$ be the equivalence relation defined on S_φ^λ, such that $t \sim_{\mathcal{T},\lambda}^\varphi s$ iff $\varphi \models_\mathcal{T} t \approx s$. Note that $\sim_{\mathcal{T},\lambda}^\varphi$ is a congruence relation on S_φ^λ. We denote by $[t]_{\mathcal{T},\lambda}^\varphi$ the equivalence class of t induced by $\sim_{\mathcal{T},\lambda}^\varphi$. We simply write $\sim$ and $[-]$, when φ, $\mathcal{T}$, and λ are clear from the context.

We now give a recursive definition for the constructively ground terms. A term $t \in S_\varphi^\lambda$ is *constructively ground (c-ground)* if either **(i)** t is a ground term, or, **(ii)** t is $f(t_1, \ldots, t_n)$ and for each t_i, $[t_i] = [r_i]$ for some c-ground term r_i. We say that the equivalence class of t, $[t]$, is *ground* if it contains a c-ground term.

Definition 4. *(Locally Ground Theory). Call a theory $\mathcal{T}$ locally ground, if there exists a proper function λ such that $\mathcal{T}$ is a local theory with λ, and for any $\mathcal{T}$-satisfiable conjunction of literals φ and t a subterm of φ, whenever $\varphi \models_\mathcal{T} t \approx s$ for an arbitrary ground term s, we have $[t]_{\mathcal{T},\lambda}^\varphi$ is ground.*

The additional condition in the definition of locally ground theories allows us to limit our attention to the c-ground terms. We state the following variant of McKinsey's lemma for theories axiomatized by Horn clauses. This will help us ignore the negative literals when considering the logical consequences of a (satisfiable) conjunction of literals, as shown in Corollary 6. The proof involves noting that models of Horn formulas are closed under direct products. Other similar formulations of McKinsey's lemma can be found in [13,14].

Lemma 5. *(McKinsey's lemma). Let $\Phi(\bar{x})$ be a set consisting of universal and basic Horn clauses, and $\Psi(\bar{x})$ be a set of atoms. If $\Phi(\bar{x}) \models \bigvee \Psi(\bar{x})$ then $\Phi(\bar{x}) \models \psi$ for some $\psi \in \Psi(\bar{x})$.*

Corollary 6. *Let $\mathcal{T}$ be a theory axiomatized by a set of universal Horn clauses Φ and $\varphi(\bar{x})$ be a $\mathcal{T}$-satisfiable conjunction of literals, $\bigwedge \varphi_i \wedge \bigwedge \neg\psi_i$, where each φ_i and ψ_i is an atom. Then, if $\varphi(\bar{x}) \models_{\mathcal{T}} \psi(\bar{x})$ for some atom $\psi(\bar{x})$, we have $\bigwedge \varphi_i \models_{\mathcal{T}} \psi(\bar{x})$.*

4.1 Partial Orders

We take as our working signature $\Sigma_{po} = (\Sigma^F, \{\leq\})$ where Σ^F contains countably many function and constant symbols. Now take as axioms for $\mathcal{T}_{po}$, the set Φ_{po}, containing the following Horn clauses.

$\forall x$	$x \leq x$	(Reflexivity)
$\forall x \forall y \forall z$	$x \leq y \wedge y \leq z \rightarrow x \leq z$	(Transitivity)
$\forall x \forall y$	$x \leq y \wedge y \leq x \rightarrow x \approx y$	(Antisymmetry)

The proof given below for $\mathcal{T}_{po}$ can be adapted to show other theories to be locally ground. Specifically, it can be easily adapted for the theory $\mathcal{T}_{eq}$ axiomatized by the empty set of axioms (i.e., EUF) as well as for the theory of *Recursively Defined Data Structures* [21] as shown in Sect. 4.2. Moreover, $\mathcal{T}_{po}$ remains locally ground if we extend it by adding axioms expressing monotonicity of some functions.

In this section, we take λ_p to be the identity on $\mathcal{P}(\Sigma^T_{po})$. Moreover, we simply write $\sim$ and $[-]$ in place of $\sim^{\varphi}_{\mathcal{T}_{po},\lambda_p}$ and $[t]^{\varphi}_{\mathcal{T}_{po},\lambda_p}$, when there is no ambiguity.

Lemma 7. *For a given $\mathcal{T}_{po}$-satisfiable conjunction of literals φ, there exists a model, $\mathcal{I}_p = (\mathfrak{A}_p, \alpha_p)$, of $\mathcal{T}_{po}$ such that $\mathcal{I}_p \models_{\mathcal{T}_{po}} \varphi$, and satisfies the following properties:*

(i) The universe $A_p = (S_\varphi/{\sim}) \cup \{\zeta\}$, where $\zeta \notin (S_\varphi/{\sim})$.
(ii) For every term t in S_φ, $t^{\mathcal{I}_p} = [t]$.
(iii) For any ground *term s, $s^{\mathcal{I}_p} \neq \zeta$ implies $s^{\mathcal{I}_p} = [r]$, for some c-ground term $r \in S_\varphi$.*

We defer the proof of Lemma 7 and proceed to show that $\mathcal{T}_{po}$ is a locally ground theory. After which we present a proof of the lemma.

Theorem 8. *The theory of partial orders, $\mathcal{T}_{po}$, is a locally ground theory.*

Proof. The locality of $\mathcal{T}_{po}$ follows from Theorem 2 in [24], by noting that every weak partial model of its axioms, Φ_{po}, weakly embeds into a total model of Φ_{po}. What remains to show is that $\mathcal{T}_{po}$ satisfies condition (ii) in the definition of locally ground theories. Towards showing this, assume φ is a $\mathcal{T}_{po}$-satisfiable conjunction of literals, t a subterm of φ, and s an arbitrary ground term. Note that s is not necessarily in S_φ. Now, assume $\varphi \models_{\mathcal{T}_{po}} t \approx s$ for some arbitrary ground term s. By Lemma 7, $\mathcal{I}_p$ is a model of φ and $\mathcal{T}_{po}$, hence $t^{\mathcal{I}_p} = s^{\mathcal{I}_p}$. By (ii) in Lemma 7, $t^{\mathcal{I}_p} = [t] = s^{\mathcal{I}_p}$ and hence $s^{\mathcal{I}_p} \neq \zeta$. Thus, by (iii) in lemma 7, $s^{\mathcal{I}_p} = [r]$ for some c-ground term r, and hence $[t]$ is ground. □

Proof. (of Lemma 7) construct the model $\mathcal{I}_p = (\mathfrak{A}_p, \alpha_p)$, as follows.

(i) Set the domain A_p to be $(S_\varphi/{\sim}) \cup \{\zeta\}$, where $\zeta \notin S_\varphi/{\sim}$.
(ii) For each n-ary function symbol f and $a_1, \ldots, a_n \in A_p$, $f^{\mathfrak{A}_p}(a_1, \ldots, a_n) = [f(s_1, \ldots, s_n)]$ if $\exists\, \bar{s}, f(s_1, \ldots, s_n) \in S_\varphi$ and $\forall i, a_i = [s_i]$; otherwise $f^{\mathfrak{A}_p}(a_1, \ldots, a_n) = \zeta$.
(iii) For the binary predicate symbol $\leq$, (a) $\zeta \leq^{\mathfrak{A}_p} \zeta$, and (b) for any $t_1, t_2 \in S_\varphi$, $[t_1] \leq^{\mathfrak{A}_p} [t_2]$ iff $\Gamma_\varphi \cup \Phi_{po} \Vdash t_1 \leq t_2$.[5]

Finally, set $\mathcal{I}_p = (\mathfrak{A}_p, \alpha_p)$, where the variable assignment $\alpha_p : \mathcal{V} \to A_p$ is defined as $\alpha_p(x) = [x]$ if $x \in S_\varphi$, and otherwise $\alpha_p(x) = \zeta$.

We note here, as $\sim$ is a congruence relation, that each n-ary function $f^{\mathfrak{A}_p}$ and the binary relation $\leq^{\mathfrak{A}_p}$ are well-defined. We proceed to show that $\mathcal{I}_p$ satisfies conditions *(ii)* and *(iii)* outlined in Lemma 7. We can use induction on $t \in S_\varphi$ to see that for each subterm t of φ, $t^{\mathcal{I}_p} = [t]$, hence $\mathcal{I}_p$ satisfies condition *(ii)*.

To see that $\mathcal{I}_p$ satisfies condition *(iii)*, we proceed by induction on t. If $t = c$ for some constant symbol c, then either c is in S_φ and so by definition $c^{\mathcal{I}} = [c]$ or $c \notin S_\varphi$ and $c^{\mathcal{I}} = \zeta$. Otherwise, let t be the term $f(t_1, \ldots, t_n)$ and assume $t^{\mathcal{I}_p} \neq \zeta$. Then, by definition, we have each $t_i^{\mathcal{I}_p} = [u_i]$ for some u_i in S_φ. Now, note that as each t_i is ground and each $t_i^{\mathcal{I}_p}$ is different from ζ, we have by the inductive hypothesis $[u_i] = [r_i]$ for some constructively ground term r_i. Moreover, by definition $t^{\mathcal{I}_p} = f^{\mathfrak{A}_p}([u_1], \ldots, [u_n]) = [f(s_1, \ldots, s_n)]$ for some s_i in $[u_i]$. Hence, $[s_i]$, which is equal to $[u_i]$, contains the c-ground term r_i. Therefore, the term $f(s_1, \ldots, s_n)$ is a constructively ground term and the conclusion follows.

Finally, we show that $\mathcal{I}_p$ is a model of both $\mathcal{T}_{po}$ and φ. Note that, for any t_1, t_2 in S_φ, we have by Corollary 6 and the fact that Φ_{po} is a local axiomatization of $\mathcal{T}_{po}$, $[t_1] \leq^{\mathfrak{A}_p} [t_2]$ iff $\varphi \models_{\mathcal{T}_{po}} t_1 \leq t_2$. Hence, $\leq^{\mathfrak{A}_p}$ is reflexive, transitive, and antisymmetric on A_p. Therefore, $\mathcal{I}_p \models \Phi_{po}$, and thus is a model of $\mathcal{T}_{po}$. Next, to see that $\mathcal{I}_p$ satisfies φ, recall that φ is a $\mathcal{T}$-satisfiable conjunction of literals, φ_i, of the form $t_i \approx u_i$ or $r_i \leq s_i$ or their negations. Then, observe that $\mathcal{I}_p \models \varphi_i$, by noting $\varphi \models_{\mathcal{T}_{po}} \varphi_i$, and that for each $t \in S_\varphi$, $t^{\mathcal{I}_p} = [t]$. Therefore, it follows $\mathcal{I}_p \models_{\mathcal{T}_{po}} \varphi$. □

The construction is motivated by Shostak's decision procedure [23] for the quantifier free fragment of the theory of equality. However, unlike [23] we don't use the entire Herbrand universe, and simply interpret/map terms to their equivalence classes under $\sim$.

[5] Equivalently, $[t_1] \leq^{\mathfrak{A}_p} [t_2]$ iff $\varphi \models_{\mathcal{T}_{po}} t_1 \leq t_2$.

4.2 Recursively Defined Data Structures

We now show that the theory of Recursively Defined Data Structures, $\mathcal{T}_{rd}$, [21] without the acyclicity axioms is locally ground. We take as our working signature $\Sigma_{rd} = (\Sigma^F \cup \{ cr, sr_1, \ldots, sr_k \}, \varnothing)$ where Σ^F contains countably many function and constant symbols, and cr and sr_i are intended to denote the k-ary constructor and unary selector functions respectively. Take as axioms for $\mathcal{T}_{rd}$, the set Φ_{rd}, containing the following Horn clauses:

$$\forall x\; cr(sr_1(x), \ldots, sr_k(x)) \approx \mathrm{x} \qquad \text{(Construction)}$$
$$\forall \bar{x}\; sr_i(cr(x_1, \ldots, x_k)) \approx x_i \quad \text{for } i = 1, \ldots, k \qquad \text{(Selection)}$$

The approach we take in showing that $\mathcal{T}_{rd}$ is a locally ground theory is similar to the approach we took in Sect. 4.1. Following Oppen's method in [21], we construct an infinite model of $\mathcal{T}_{rd}$. Let $\lambda_r : \mathcal{P}(\Sigma^T_{rd}) \to \mathcal{P}(\Sigma^T_{rd})$ be the function such that for each $S \in \mathcal{P}(\Sigma^T_{rd})$,

$$\lambda_r(S) = S \cup \bigcup_{t \in S} \{ sr_i(t), cr(sr_1(t), \ldots, sr_k(t)) \}$$

Note that λ_r is a *proper* function. For the rest of the section, we simply write $\sim$ and $[-]$ in place of $\sim^{\varphi}_{\mathcal{T}_{rd},\lambda_r}$ and $[t]^{\varphi}_{\mathcal{T}_{rd},\lambda_r}$, when there is no ambiguity. Recall that we use $S^{\lambda_r}_{\varphi}$ as a shorthand for $\lambda_r(S_\varphi)$.

Lemma 9. *For a given $\mathcal{T}_{rd}$-satisfiable conjunction of literals φ, there exists a model, $\mathcal{I}_r = (\mathfrak{A}_r, \alpha_r)$, of $\mathcal{T}_{rd}$ such that $\mathcal{I}_r \models_{\mathcal{T}_{rd}} \varphi$, and satisfies the following properties:*

(i) The set $S^{\lambda_r}_{\varphi}/\sim$ is a subset of the universe A_r.
(ii) For every term t in S_φ, $t^{\mathcal{I}_r} = [t]$.
(iii) For any ground *term s, $s^{\mathcal{I}_r} \in Z$. Where Z is a set such that each element of Z that is an equivalence class is ground—i.e., for all $[t] \in Z \cap S^{\lambda_r}_{\varphi}/\sim$, $[t]$ is ground.*

We defer the proof of Lemma 9 and proceed to show that $\mathcal{T}_{rd}$ is a locally ground theory. After which we present a proof of the lemma.

Theorem 10. *The theory of recursively defined data structures, $\mathcal{T}_{rd}$, is a locally ground theory.*

Proof. It can be seen for any basic Horn clause ψ that $\Phi_{rd} \models \psi$ iff $\Phi_{rd}[S^{\lambda_r}_{\psi}] \models \psi$. Hence, $\mathcal{T}_{rd}$ satisfies condition (i). What remains to show is that $\mathcal{T}_{rd}$ satisfies condition (ii) in the definition of locally ground theories. Towards showing this, assume φ is a $\mathcal{T}_{rd}$-satisfiable conjunction of literals, $t \in S_\varphi$ a subterm of φ, and s an arbitrary ground term. Now, assume that $\varphi \models_{\mathcal{T}_{rd}} t \approx s$. Then, by Lemma 9, we have $\mathcal{I}_r \models_{\mathcal{T}_{rd}} t \approx s$, hence $t^{\mathcal{I}_r} = s^{\mathcal{I}_r}$. By (ii) in Lemma 9, $t^{\mathcal{I}_r} = [t] = s^{\mathcal{I}_r}$, moreover, by (iii) in Lemma 9, $s^{\mathcal{I}_r} \in Z$. Hence, by definition of Z, $[t]$ is ground.
□

Proof. (of Lemma 9). Construct the model, $\mathcal{I}_r = (\mathfrak{A}_r, \alpha_r)$, as follows. First define for each $n \geq 0$, the sets A_n, the partial functions cr_n and $sr_{i,n}$ for each $i \in \{1, \ldots, k\}$.

(i) Let $A_0 = (S_\varphi^{\lambda_r}/\sim) \cup \{\zeta\}$, where $\zeta \notin S_\varphi^{\lambda_r}/\sim$.
(ii) Define the partial function cr_0 on A_0 as follows: $cr_0(a_1, \ldots, a_k) = [cr(t_1, \ldots, t_k)]$ if $\exists \bar{t}, cr(t_1, \ldots, t_k) \in S_\varphi^{\lambda_r}$ s.t. $\forall i, a_i = [t_i]$; otherwise $cr_0(a_1, \ldots, a_k)$is undefined.
(iii) For $i = 1, \ldots, k$, define the partial functions $sr_{i,0}$ on A_0 as follows: $sr_{i,0}(a) = [sr_i(t)]$ if $\exists t, sr_i(t) \in S_\varphi^{\lambda_r}$ and $a = [t]$; otherwise $sr_{i,0}(a)$ is undefined.

We now keep extending the domains of cr_0 and $sr_{i,0}$. For each $n > 0$,

(i) Let $S_{n-1} = \{\zeta_1^a, \ldots, \zeta_k^a \mid a \in (A_{n-1} \backslash \mathrm{dom}\, sr_{i,n-1}) \text{ and } \zeta_i^a \notin (A_{n-1} \cup A_{n-1}^k)\}$
(ii) Let $A_n = A_{n-1} \cup (A_{n-1}^k \backslash \mathrm{dom}\, cr_{n-1}) \cup S_{n-1}$.
(iii) Define cr_n to be a partial function on A_n that is an extension of cr_{n-1}, such that for each $\bar{b} = (b_1, \ldots, b_k) \in A_n^k \backslash \mathrm{dom}\, cr_{n-1}$: $cr_n(\bar{b}) = \bar{b} \text{ if } \bar{b} \in A_{n-1}^k \backslash \mathrm{dom}\, cr_{n-1}$; otherwise $cr_n(\bar{b}) = a \text{ if } \bar{b} = (\zeta_1^a, \ldots, \zeta_k^a)$; and finally, $cr_n(\bar{b})$ is undefined for every other case.
(iv) Similarly, for $i = 1, \ldots, k$, define the partial function $sr_{i,n}$ on A_n, that is an extension of $sr_{i,n-1}$, such that, for all $a \in A_n \backslash \mathrm{dom}\, sr_{i,n-1}$: $sr_{i,n}(a) = \zeta_i^a$ if $a \in A_{n-1} \backslash \mathrm{dom}\, sr_{i,n-1}$; otherwise $sr_{i,n}(a) = a_i$ if $a = (a_1, \ldots, a_k) \in A_{n-1}^k \backslash \mathrm{dom}\, cr_{n-1}$; and finally $sr_{i,n}(a)$ is undefined for every other case.

Note that both cr_n and $sr_{i,n}$ are total on A_{n-1}. We now construct the interpretation $\mathcal{I}_r = (\mathfrak{A}_r, \alpha_r)$ as follows.

(i) Set the universe $A_r = \bigcup_{n<\omega} A_n$.
(ii) For the function symbol, cr, and the k-tuple $\bar{a} = (a_1, \ldots, a_k)$ in $(A_r)^k$, $cr^{\mathfrak{A}_r}(a_1, \ldots, a_k) = cr_n(a_1, \ldots, a_k)$, for the least index n, s.t. $\bar{a} \in \mathrm{dom}\, cr_n$.
(iii) Similarly, for each selector function symbol sr_i, and $a \in A_r$, $sr_i^{\mathfrak{A}_r}(a) = sr_{i,n}(a)$, for the least index n, such that $a \in dom\, sr_n$.
(iv) For each k-ary function symbol $f \in \Sigma^F$ and $a_1, \ldots, a_k$ in A_r, $f^{\mathfrak{A}_r}(a_1, \ldots, a_k) = [f(s_1, \ldots, s_k)]$ if $\exists \bar{s},\ f(s_1, \ldots, s_k) \in S_\varphi$ and $\forall i, a_i = [s_i]$; and otherwise $f^{\mathfrak{A}_r}(a_1, \ldots, a_k) = \zeta$.

Finally, define the variable assignment $\alpha_r : \mathcal{V} \to A_r$, as follows $\alpha_r(x) = [x]$ if $x \in S_\varphi^{\lambda_r}$ and $\alpha_r(x) = \zeta$ otherwise. We note that all the functions above are total on A_r. Moreover, as $\sim$ is a congruence relation, the functions are well-defined. Now, to see that $\mathcal{I}_r \models_{\mathcal{T}_{rd}} \varphi$, we first observe, using induction similar to the proof given in [21] the following:
1. If $a \in \mathrm{dom}\, sr_{i,n}$ then $\bar{b} = (sr_{1,n}(a), \ldots, sr_{k,n}(a)) \in \mathrm{dom}\, cr_n$, and $cr_n(\bar{b}) = a$.
2. If $\bar{a} = (a_1, \ldots, a_k) \in \mathrm{dom}\, cr_n$ then $sr_{i,n}(cr_n(a_1, \ldots, a_k)) = a_i$.

Hence, the properties 1 and 2 above hold for the functions $cr^{\mathfrak{A}}$ and $sr_i^{\mathfrak{A}}$ and $\mathcal{I}_r \models \mathcal{T}_{rd}$. Furthermore, we can see by induction on each $t \in S_\varphi$ that $t^{\mathcal{I}_r} = [t]$, and hence for each positive literal $t_1 \approx t_2$ occurring in φ, $\mathcal{I}_r \models t_1 \approx t_2$. Additionally, as φ is $\mathcal{T}_{rd}$-satisfiable, we have for each negative literal $t_1 \not\approx t_2$ in φ, $[t_1] \neq [t_2]$ and hence $\mathcal{I}_r \models t_1 \not\approx t_2$. Thus, $\mathcal{I}_r \models_{\mathcal{T}_{rd}} \varphi$.

We now proceed to show that $\mathcal{I}_r$ satisfies the conditions $(i) - (iii)$ given in Lemma 9. Note $A_0 \subseteq A_r$, hence, $\mathcal{I}_r$ satisfies condition (i). It is also straightforward to see by induction on $t \in S_\varphi$, that $t^{\mathcal{I}_r} = [t]$, hence $\mathcal{I}_r$ satisfies condition (ii). To see $\mathcal{I}_r$ satisfies condition (iii), let $Z = \bigcup_{n<\omega} Z_n$ where Z_n is defined as:

$$Z_0 = \{\,\zeta\,\} \cup \{\,[t] \in S_\varphi^{\lambda_r}/\!\sim \mid [t] \text{ is ground}\,\} \text{ and for } n > 0,$$

$$Z_n = Z_{n-1} \cup (Z_{n-1}^k \backslash \text{dom } cr_{n-1}) \cup \bigcup_{\zeta_i^a \in S_{n-1}} \{\,\zeta_i^a \mid a \in Z_{n-1}\,\}$$

Note that for every $[t] \in Z \cap S_\varphi^{\lambda_r}/\!\sim$, $[t]$ is ground. Now, let s be a ground term, we show by induction on s that $s^{\mathcal{I}_r} \in Z$. It suffices to show $s^{\mathcal{I}_r} \in Z_n$ for some n. For the base case, if $s = c$ for some constant c, then $s^{\mathcal{I}_r}$ is $[c]$ if $c \in S_\varphi$ and ζ otherwise, in both cases $s^{\mathcal{I}_r} \in Z_0$. Otherwise, if $s = f(t_1, \ldots, t_n)$ for some $f \in \Sigma^F$, the argument is the same as in Lemma 7. For the case $s = sr_i(t_1)$, let $a = t_1^{\mathcal{I}_r}$, then, we have by the inductive hypothesis, $a \in Z$. Let n be the least index such that $a \in \text{dom } sr_{i,n}$, we proceed by induction on n. First, note that for any $n \geq 0$, we have $Z \cap A_n \subseteq Z_n$. Hence, for the base case, $n = 0$, we have $a = [t]$ for some ground class $[t]$, and $s^{\mathcal{I}_r} = sr_{i,0}([t]) = [sr_i(t)]$. Hence, $s^{\mathcal{I}_r} \in Z_0$ as $sr_i(t)$ is c-ground. For $n > 0$, we have either $a \in A_{n-1} \backslash \text{dom } sr_{i,n-1}$ in which case $s^{\mathcal{I}_r} = sr_{i,n}(a) = \zeta_i^a$ and hence $s^{\mathcal{I}_r} \in Z_n$, or $a = (a_1, \ldots, a_k) \in A_{n-1}^k \backslash \text{dom } cr_{n-1}$ and $sr_{i,n}(a) = a_i \in Z_{n-1}$.

Similarly, for the case $s = cr(t_1, \ldots, t_k)$ we have by the induction hypothesis, $t_i^{\mathcal{I}_r} \in Z_{n_i}$. Let n be the least index such that $\bar{b} = (t_1^{\mathcal{I}_r}, \ldots, t_k^{\mathcal{I}_r}) \in \text{dom } cr_n$, we proceed by induction on n. For $n = 0$, we can use a similar argument to the case $s = sr_i(t_1)$. For the inductive case, we have either $\bar{b} \in A_{n-1}^k \backslash \text{dom } cr_{n-1}$, in which case $s^{\mathcal{I}_r} = cr_n(\bar{b}) = \bar{b}$, and hence $s^{\mathcal{I}_r} \in Z_n$, or $\bar{b} = (\zeta_1^a, \ldots, \zeta_k^a)$, and $s^{\mathcal{I}_r} = cr_n(\bar{b}) = a \in Z_{n-1}$. □

5 Partial Quantifier Elimination

In this section, we consider the *partial quantifier elimination* problem and give an efficient algorithm, $\mathcal{T}$-QEL, that is relatively complete for the locally ground theories. In particular, we consider the following problem: given a theory $\mathcal{T}$ and a formula $\exists \bar{x}\, \varphi(\bar{x})$, where $\varphi(\bar{x})$ is a conjunction of literals, over the signature Σ, find a quantifier free Σ formula $\psi(\bar{y})$ such that: **(i)** $\models_{\mathcal{T}} \exists \bar{x}\, \varphi(\bar{x}) \leftrightarrow \exists \bar{y}\, \psi(\bar{y})$ **(ii)** $\text{FV}(\psi) \subseteq \text{FV}(\varphi)$ and **(iii)** for all $x \in \text{FV}(\varphi)$, if x has an entailed ground definition (i.e., $\varphi \models_{\mathcal{T}} x \approx s$ with s an arbitrary ground term), then $x \notin \text{FV}(\psi)$.

In essence, we have reduced the number of quantified variables that have entailed ground definitions from φ. We call ψ a *quantifier reduction* of $\exists \bar{x}\, \varphi(\bar{x})$ if it satisfies (i) and (ii). We say a procedure is *relatively complete* if for every input, it computes a quantifier free formula satisfying (iii). For the rest of the section, we fix a locally ground theory $\mathcal{T} = \text{Cn}\,\Phi$. Moreover, for simplicity of presentation, we take λ to be the identity on $\mathcal{P}(\Sigma^{\mathcal{T}})$.

Egraphs give us a compact way of representing congruence relations. In what follows, we describe a construction of a certain egraph, G^*, which we call *the completion* of the egraph of φ. The goal of the construction is to represent the partition $S_\varphi/{\sim}$ induced by the congruence relation $\sim$ on top of an egraph. For locally ground theories, this allows us to efficiently search the equivalence classes in $S_\varphi/{\sim}$ for the constructively ground terms. Finally, we utilize QEL to extract an equivalent formula from the egraph G^*.

Intuitively, our construction saturates the egraph of φ with implied atoms. That is, we pick an instance of an axiom $\psi_1 \wedge \cdots \wedge \psi_k \rightarrow \theta$, for which all ψ_i are represented (i.e., exist) in the egraph, after which we add θ to the egraph. We stop when no new atoms are added. Locality here allows us to restrict to instances of axioms whose subterms are already in φ. We formalize this notion in the rest of the section, and use it to give proofs of soundness and relative completeness for our algorithm $\mathcal{T}$-QEL.

We refer to intermediate graphs arising from the construction that might not satisfy the congruence condition 1 in the definition of egraphs, as *partial egraphs.* For simplicity of presentation, we follow [8] and allow labelling nodes with predicate symbols and introduce the fresh constant symbols $\top$ and $\bot$.

Definition 11. *(Representability). Given a (partial) egraph, $G = (N, E, L, root)$, say that a literal γ over the subterms of φ is representable in G if either **(i)** γ is $t_1 \approx t_2$, and $root(n_{t_1}) = root(n_{t_2})$, or **(ii)** γ is $t_1 \not\approx t_2$, and for some node w in N labelled with $\not\approx$, we have $w[i] = n_{t_i}$, or **(iii)** γ is $P(t_1, \ldots, t_k)$ or $\neg P(t_1, \ldots, t_k)$, and for some node w in N labelled with P, we have $w[i] = n_{t_i}$, and $root(w) = n_\top$ if γ is positive and $root(w) = n_\bot$ otherwise.*

Let $G_0 = egraph(\varphi)$, and for $k > 0$, form G_k from G_{k-1} by instantiating the axioms on the nodes of G_{k-1}. More formally, let $\psi \in \Phi \cup \Phi_{eq}$ be an axiom of the form $\forall \bar{x}\,(\psi_1 \wedge \cdots \wedge \psi_m \rightarrow P(t_1, \ldots, t_n))$ where each ψ_i is an atom and P is different from the equality symbol, then let $\Pi_k^\psi = \{\, \bar{u} \in N_{k-1}^n \mid term(u_j) = t_j\sigma$ and each $\psi_i\sigma$ is representable in G_{k-1} for some substitution $\sigma \,\}$ and $\Pi_k = \bigcup \{\, (\bar{u}, P) \mid \bar{u} \in \Pi_k^\psi \,\}$ for some ψ of the above form . Then, form $G_k = (N_k, E_k, L_k, root_k)$ as follows:

(a) $N_k = N_{k-1} \cup \{\, w_{(\bar{u},\,P)} \mid (\bar{u}, P) \in \Pi_k \,\}$
(b) $L_k = L_{k-1} \cup \{\, (w_{(\bar{u},\,P)}, P) \mid w_{(\bar{u},\,P)} \in N_k \backslash N_{k-1} \,\}$
(c) $E_k = E_{k-1} \cup \{\, (w_{(\bar{u},\,P)}, u_i) \mid w_{(\bar{u},\,P)} \in N_k \backslash N_{k-1}$ and $u_i \in \bar{u} \,\}$ and set the order of the children as $w_{\bar{u}}[i] = u_i$.

To complete the construction of G_k we now consider an equality that arises as a result of adding new nodes/atoms. Equality is handled by merging the equivalence classes of any two nodes that are inferred to be equal at this stage. We define Δ_k^ψ in a similar way we defined Π_k^ψ. Let $\psi \in \Phi \cup \Phi_{eq}$ be an axiom of the form $\forall \bar{x}(\psi_1 \wedge \cdots \wedge \psi_m \rightarrow t_1 \approx t_2)$,

Algorithm 1. $\mathcal{T}$-QEL : An extension of QEL that utilizes theories.

Input: $\exists\bar{x}\,\varphi(\bar{x})$, where $\varphi(\bar{x})$ is a conjunction of literals; Φ a set of axioms.
Output: a quantifier reduction of $\exists\bar{x}\,\varphi(\bar{x})$ in the theory $\mathcal{T} := Cn\,\Phi$.

1: $G \leftarrow egraph(\varphi)$
2: $G \rightsquigarrow_{\Phi} G^*$
3: $\beta \leftarrow G^*.find\_defs()$
4: $core \leftarrow G^*.find\_core(\beta)$
5: **return** $G^*.to\_formula(\beta, N^*\backslash core)$

where each ψ_i is an atom. Then let $\Delta_k^{\psi} = \{\bar{u} \in N_{k-1}^2 \mid term(u_j) = t_j\sigma$ and each $\psi_i\sigma$ is representable in G_{k-1} for some substitution $\sigma\}$

Let $\Delta_k = \bigcup \Delta_k^{\psi}$ and let $(u_1, v_1), \ldots, (u_r, v_r) \in \Delta_k$ be an enumeration of the elements of Δ_k. Now we iteratively merge the equivalence classes of each u_i with that of v_i, by setting the root of each u in the class of u_i to that of v_i. Let $root_k^0 = root_{k-1}$ and for $1 \leq i \leq r$ define $root_k^i : N_k \to N_k$, for all $u \in N_k$ as:

$$root_k^i(u) = n_\top \text{ if } u \in N_k \backslash N_{k-1}, \text{ otherwise } root_k^i(u) = root_k^{i-1}(v_i) \text{ if } root_k^{i-1}(u) = root_k^{i-1}(u_i), \text{ and otherwise } root_k^i(u) = root_k^{i-1}(u).$$

Finally, define $root_k = root_k^r$. This concludes the construction of G_k.

For a (partial) egraph G, let $\mathcal{X}_G = \{\ \gamma \mid \gamma$ is an atom representable in $G\}$. Then, let ℓ be the least index such that $\mathcal{X}_{G_\ell} = \mathcal{X}_{G_{\ell+1}}$, and let $G^* = G_\ell$. We use the notation $G \rightsquigarrow_{\Phi} G^*$ to denote the construction above. Below, we show that the maximum number of steps for the construction, is polynomial in $|S_\varphi|$. Hence, giving us an overall polynomial time algorithm.

Lemma 12. *The construction $G \rightsquigarrow_{\Phi} G^*$ takes at most $\mathcal{O}(|S_\varphi|^m)$ steps, where m is the maximum arity of the predicates occurring in the axioms and in φ.*

Our algorithm $\mathcal{T}$-QEL is presented in Algorithm 1. $\mathcal{T}$-QEL takes as input the axioms Φ of the theory and a formula $\exists\bar{x}\,\varphi(\bar{x})$. The full details of all the steps (except step 2) are discussed in [8]. Regardless, we will go ahead and provide a brief explanation of each of the steps.

In step 1, the egraph of φ is constructed using the standard procedure. Then, in step 2, we represent the partition $S_\varphi/{\sim}$ of the subterms induced by $\sim$ on the egraph. We note here that once $S_\varphi/{\sim}$ has been represented, the newly added predicate symbols don't serve any purpose and can be removed from the egraph. In step 3, a function β that picks a representative node (term) from each equivalence class is computed. Step 4 identifies a subset of nodes (terms) that must be considered in the output. Finally, step 5 extracts a formula from the egraph using β and *core*.

We now proceed to show that the partition $S_\varphi/{\sim}$ is represented on the egraph G^*. First, we prove the following Lemma.

Lemma 13. *(Representability lemma). Let $\mathcal{T}$ be a locally ground theory axiomatized by Φ, φ a $\mathcal{T}$-satisfiable conjunction of literals, G^* the completion of the* *egraph*(φ), *and* γ *an atom such that* $S_\gamma \subseteq S_\varphi$, *then* $\varphi \models_{\mathcal{T}} \gamma$ *iff* γ *is representable in* G^*.

Proof. ($\implies$) To show representability in G^* we show that γ is representable in some G_k. The conclusion follows as for any $k \geq 0$, $\mathcal{X}_{G_k} \subseteq \mathcal{X}_{G_\ell}$. Now assume $\varphi \models_{\mathcal{T}} \gamma$, then by Corollary 6, we have $\bigwedge \varphi_i \models_{\mathcal{T}} \gamma$ hence for some proof calculus that is sound and complete for FOL($\approx$) we have $\Gamma_\varphi \cup \Phi \vdash \gamma$. By definition of locality we have a restricted derivation, $\theta_1, \ldots, \theta_d$, of γ. If γ is in Γ_φ then the conclusion follows trivially. For the case it does not, we proceed by induction on the length of the derivation. For $d = 1$, we have for some clause $\psi \in \Phi \cup \Phi_{eq}$ of the form $\forall \bar{x}\,(\psi_1 \wedge \cdots \wedge \psi_n \rightarrow \theta)$ and substitution σ, $\theta\sigma$ is γ and each $\psi_i\sigma$ is in Γ_φ. Hence, each $\psi_i\sigma$ is representable in G_0 by the way the *egraph*(φ) is constructed. Now, if γ is $P(t_1, \ldots, t_n)$, different from an equality atom, then there exists nodes $\bar{u} \in \Pi_1^\psi$ and $w_{(\bar{u},\,P)} \in N_1$ such that $w_{\bar{u}}$ is labelled with P and $w_{(\bar{u},\,P)}[i] = n_{t_i}$. Hence, $P(t_1, \ldots, t_n)$ is representable in G_1. Otherwise, γ is an equality atom and there exists $(u_1, u_2) \in \Delta_1^\psi$ with $term(u_i) = t_i$. Let (u_1, u_2) be the jth element $(u_j, v_j) \in \Delta_k$ in the enumeration given during the construction of G_1. Then we have merged the equivalence classes of u_j and v_j in G_1. More precisely, we have $root_1^j(u_j) = root_1^j(v_j)$ and it can be shown by induction that for all $m \geq j$, $root_1^m(u_j) = root_1^m(v_j)$, hence $root_1(u_j) = root_1(v_j)$ and therefore $t_1 \approx t_2$ is representable in G_1. In both cases we have shown γ is representable in G_1. For the inductive step we have for some clause $\forall \bar{x}(\psi_1 \wedge \cdots \wedge \psi_n \rightarrow \psi)$ and substitution σ, $\psi\sigma$ is γ , and either $\psi_i\sigma \in \Gamma_\varphi$ in which case $\psi_i\sigma$ is representable in G_0 or $\psi_i\sigma$ occurs earlier in the derivation. In the later case, we have by the inductive hypothesis $\psi_i\sigma$ is representable in some G_{k_i}. Let $k = max\{\, k_i \,\}$, then, as $\mathcal{X}_{G_{k_i}} \subseteq \mathcal{X}_{G_k}$, we have each $\psi_i\sigma$ is representable in G_k. It follows then $\psi\sigma$ which is γ is representable in G_{k+1}.

($\impliedby$) Let $k \leq \ell$ be the least index s.t. γ is representable in G_k. We proceed by induction on k. For $k = 0$, note that γ is representable in $G_0 =$ *egraph*(φ) hence $\varphi \models_{\mathcal{T}} \gamma$. Now, for the inductive step, if γ is $P(t_1, \ldots, t_n)$ that is different from an equality atom, then there are nodes $\bar{u} \in \Pi_k^\psi$ and $w_{(\bar{u},\,P)} \in N_k \backslash N_{k-1}$ for some $\psi \in \Phi \cup \Phi_{eq}$ where ψ is of the form $\forall \bar{x}(\psi_1 \wedge \cdots \wedge \psi_n \rightarrow P(t'_1, \ldots, t'_n))$ and $term(u_i) = t'_i\sigma = t_i$ for some substitution σ. Moreover, each $\psi_i\sigma$ is representable in G_{k-1}. By the inductive hypothesis we have $\varphi \models_{\mathcal{T}} \psi_i\sigma$ hence, $\varphi \models_{\mathcal{T}} P(t'_1, \ldots, t'_n)\sigma$, and thus $\varphi \models_{\mathcal{T}} P(t_1, \ldots, t_n)$ as required. Otherwise, γ is an equality atom, $t_1 \approx t_2$, and we have $(u_1, u_2) \in \Delta_k^\psi$ for some axiom ψ of the form $\forall \bar{x}\,(\psi_1 \wedge \cdots \wedge \psi_n \rightarrow t'_1 \approx t'_2)$ s.t. $term(u_i) = t'_i\sigma$, (u_1, u_2) is the jth element,(u_j, v_j), in the enumeration of Δ_k and $root_k^j(n_{t_1}) = root_k^j(u_j)$ and $root_k^j(n_{t_2}) = root_k^j(v_j)$. It can be shown by induction on j and the induction hypothesis that $\varphi \models_{\mathcal{T}} t'_i\sigma \approx t_i$. Furthermore, each $\psi_i\sigma$ is representable in G_{k-1} and hence by the inductive hypothesis $\varphi \models_{\mathcal{T}} \psi_i\sigma$. Therefore, $\varphi \models_{\mathcal{T}} (t'_1 \approx t'_2)\sigma$ and hence $\varphi \models_{\mathcal{T}} t_1 \approx t_2$ by transitivity. □

It follows then the class of a node, $\rho_{root^*}(n_t)$, that emerges in G^* corresponds to the class of its term $[t]^{\varphi}_{\mathcal{T},\lambda}$ that is induced by $\sim^{\varphi}_{\mathcal{T},\lambda}$ on the subterm set of φ.

This is essential as G^* faithfully represents the partition $S_\varphi/\sim^\varphi_{\mathcal{T},\lambda}$, and hence allows for searching of the constructively ground terms.

Corollary 14. *Assume $\mathcal{T}$ is a locally ground theory and φ a $\mathcal{T}$-satisfiable conjunction of literals. Then, for any subterms $t, s \in S_\varphi$, $t \sim^\varphi_{\mathcal{T},\lambda} s$ iff $root^*(n_t) = root^*(n_s)$.*

Theorem 15. *(Soundness and Relative Completeness). Let $\mathcal{T}$ be a locally ground theory axiomatized by Φ and $\varphi(\bar{x})$ a $\mathcal{T}$-satisfiable conjunction of literals. Then,*

(a) The result of $\mathcal{T}$-QEL($\exists \bar{x}\, \varphi(\bar{x})$, Φ) is a quantifier reduction of $\exists \bar{x}\, \varphi(\bar{x})$.
(b) The algorithm $\mathcal{T}$-QEL is relatively complete for $\mathcal{T}$.

6 Conclusion and Future Work

We identified a subclass of local theories, called *locally ground theories*, in which we can perform partial quantifier elimination efficiently while maintaining relative completeness. By lifting the proof theoretic characterization of locality to FOL with equality, we gave the polynomial time algorithm, $\mathcal{T}$-QEL. We showed that $\mathcal{T}$-QEL is sound in general and relatively complete for the locally ground theories. We showed several theories, which were previously shown to exhibit locality properties, were also locally ground. For future work, it would be interesting to see how relative completeness is preserved for other theories and under combination of theories. Moreover, we leave for future work investigating the potential applications as an efficient preprocessing step for arithmetical theories.

Disclosure of Interest. The authors have no competing interests to declare that are relevant to the content of this article.

References

1. Bjørner, N.S., Janota, M.: Playing with quantified satisfaction. LPAR (short papers) **35**, 15–27 (2015)
2. Davenport, J.H., Heintz, J.: Real quantifier elimination is doubly exponential. J. Symb. Comput. **5**(1–2), 29–35 (1988)
3. Dutertre, B.: Yices 2.2. In: Biere, A., Bloem, R. (eds.) Computer Aided Verification - 26th International Conference, CAV 2014, Held as Part of the Vienna Summer of Logic, VSL 2014, Vienna, Austria, July 18-22, 2014. Proceedings. LNCS, vol. 8559, pp. 737–744. Springer (2014). https://doi.org/10.1007/978-3-319-08867-9_49
4. Dutertre, B.: Solving exists/forall problems with yices. In: Workshop on Satisfiability Modulo Theories (2015)
5. Enderton, H.B.: A Mathematical Introduction to Logic. Harcourt/Academic Press, Burlington, MA, 2nd edn. (2001)
6. Fitting, M.: First-Order Logic and Automated Theorem Proving, Second Edition. Graduate Texts in Computer Science, Springer (1996). https://doi.org/10.1007/978-1-4612-2360-3

7. Ganzinger, H.: Relating semantic and proof-theoretic concepts for polynomial time decidability of uniform word problems. In: Proceedings 16th Annual IEEE Symposium on Logic in Computer Science, pp. 81–90. IEEE (2001)
8. Garcia-Contreras, I., Hari Govind, V.K., Shoham, S., Gurfinkel, A.: Fast approximations of quantifier elimination. In: Computer aided verification. Part II, Lecture Notes in Comput. Sci., vol. 13965, pp. 64–86. Springer (2023). https://doi.org/10.1007/978-3-031-37703-7_4
9. Ghilardi, S., Ranise, S.: MCMT: A model checker modulo theories. In: Giesl, J., Hähnle, R. (eds.) IJCAR 2010. LNCS (LNAI), vol. 6173, pp. 22–29. Springer, Heidelberg (2010). https://doi.org/10.1007/978-3-642-14203-1_3
10. Givan, R., Mcallester, D.: Polynomial-time computation via local inference relations. ACM Trans. Comput. Logic (TOCL) **3**(4), 521–541 (2002)
11. Givan, R., McAllester, D.A.: New results on local inference relations. In: Nebel, B., Rich, C., Swartout, W.R. (eds.) Proceedings of the 3rd International Conference on Principles of Knowledge Representation and Reasoning (KR 1992). Cambridge, MA, USA, October 25-29, 1992, pp. 403–412. Morgan Kaufmann (1992)
12. Haase, C., Krishna, S.N., Madnani, K., Mishra, O.S., Zetzsche, G.: An efficient quantifier elimination procedure for presburger arithmetic. In: Bringmann, K., Grohe, M., Puppis, G., Svensson, O. (eds.) 51st International Colloquium on Automata, Languages, and Programming, ICALP 2024, July 8-12, 2024, Tallinn, Estonia. LIPIcs, vol. 297, pp. 142:1–142:17. Schloss Dagstuhl - Leibniz-Zentrum für Informatik (2024). https://doi.org/10.4230/LIPIcs.ICALP.2024.142
13. Hodges, W.: Logical features of Horn clauses. In: Handbook of logic in artificial intelligence and logic programming, vol. 1, pp. 449–503. Oxford Sci. Publ., Oxford Univ. Press, New York (1993)
14. Hodges, W.: Model Theory. Encyclopedia of Mathematics and its Applications 42, Cambridge University Press, 1 edn. (1993)
15. Komuravelli, A., Gurfinkel, A., Chaki, S.: SMT-based model checking for recursive programs. In: Biere, A., Bloem, R. (eds.) CAV 2014. LNCS, vol. 8559, pp. 17–34. Springer, Cham (2014). https://doi.org/10.1007/978-3-319-08867-9_2
16. Kroening, D., Strichman, O.: Decision Procedures - An Algorithmic Point of View, Second Edition. Texts in Theoretical Computer Science. An EATCS Series, Springer (2016). https://doi.org/10.1007/978-3-662-50497-0
17. Kuncak, V., Mayer, M., Piskac, R., Suter, P.: Complete functional synthesis. In: Zorn, B.G., Aiken, A. (eds.) Proceedings of the 2010 ACM SIGPLAN Conference on Programming Language Design and Implementation, PLDI 2010, Toronto, Ontario, Canada, June 5-10, 2010, pp. 316–329. ACM (2010). https://doi.org/10.1145/1806596.1806632
18. McAllester, D.A.: Automatic recognition of tractability in inference relations. J. ACM **40**(2), 284–303 (1993). https://doi.org/10.1145/151261.151265
19. de Moura, L.M., Bjørner, N.S.: Z3: an efficient SMT solver. In: Ramakrishnan, C.R., Rehof, J. (eds.) Tools and Algorithms for the Construction and Analysis of Systems, 14th International Conference, TACAS 2008, Held as Part of the Joint European Conferences on Theory and Practice of Software, ETAPS 2008, Budapest, Hungary, March 29-April 6, 2008. Proceedings. LNCS, vol. 4963, pp. 337–340. Springer (2008). https://doi.org/10.1007/978-3-540-78800-3_24
20. Nelson, G., Oppen, D.C.: Fast decision algorithms based on union and find. In: 18th Annual Symposium on Foundations of Computer Science (Providence, R.I., 1977), pp. 114–119. IEEE, Long Beach, CA (1977)
21. Oppen, D.C.: Reasoning about recursively defined data structures. J. ACM **27**(3), 403–411 (1980). https://doi.org/10.1145/322203.322204

22. Riley, D., Fedyukovich, G.: Multi-phase invariant synthesis. In: Roychoudhury, A., Cadar, C., Kim, M. (eds.) Proceedings of the 30th ACM Joint European Software Engineering Conference and Symposium on the Foundations of Software Engineering, ESEC/FSE 2022, Singapore, Singapore, November 14-18, 2022, pp. 607–619. ACM (2022). https://doi.org/10.1145/3540250.3549166
23. Shostak, R.E.: An algorithm for reasoning about equality. Commun. ACM **21**(7), 583–585 (1978)
24. Sofronie-Stokkermans, V.: Hierarchic reasoning in local theory extensions. In: Nieuwenhuis, R. (ed.) CADE 2005. LNCS (LNAI), vol. 3632, pp. 219–234. Springer, Heidelberg (2005). https://doi.org/10.1007/11532231_16

Saturation

Computing Witnesses Using the SCAN Algorithm

Fabian Achammer[1(✉)], Stefan Hetzl[1], and Renate A. Schmidt[2]

[1] Institute for Discrete Mathematics and Geometry, TU Wien, Vienna, Austria
{fabian.achammer,stefan.hetzl}@tuwien.ac.at
[2] Department of Computer Science, University of Manchester, Manchester, UK
renate.schmidt@manchester.ac.uk

Abstract. Second-order quantifier-elimination is the problem of finding, given a formula with second-order quantifiers, a logically equivalent first-order formula. While such formulas are not computable in general, there are practical algorithms and subclasses with applications throughout computational logic. One of the most prominent algorithms for second-order quantifier elimination is the SCAN algorithm which is based on saturation theorem proving. In this paper we show how the SCAN algorithm on clause sets can be extended to solve a more general problem: namely, finding an instance of the second-order quantifiers that results in a logically equivalent first-order formula. In addition we provide a prototype implementation of the proposed method. This work paves the way for applying the SCAN algorithm to new problems in application domains such as modal correspondence theory, knowledge representation, and verification.

Keywords: Second-order quantifier elimination · SCAN algorithm · Formula equations · Saturation theorem proving

1 Introduction

Second-order quantifier elimination (SOQE) [23,24] is the problem of, given a formula with second-order quantifiers $\exists \overline{X}\, \varphi$ where φ is first-order, find a first-order formula ψ such that

$$\exists \overline{X}\, \varphi \equiv \psi.$$

For example, one can show that $\Phi = \exists X\, (X(a) \wedge \forall u\, (X(u) \to B(u)))$ is equivalent to $B(a)$. An algorithm for eliminating existential quantifiers can be used to eliminate universal quantifiers by writing $\forall \overline{X}$ as $\neg \exists \overline{X} \neg$.

SOQE is an important topic in logic, automated reasoning and artificial intelligence that has real-world applications in diverse areas. It has been used to automate correspondence theory for modal logic [23], which has led to new attention and results in correspondence theory of various algebras and logics [9,11,12,26]. SOQE can be used to transform a knowledge base (or set of formulas, given by φ) into a restricted view ψ of the knowledge base in which

C. Barrett and U. Waldmann (Eds.): CADE 2025, LNAI 15943, pp. 511–531, 2025.
https://doi.org/10.1007/978-3-031-99984-0_27

all occurrences of the predicate symbols $\overline{X}$ have been eliminated. This reduction has also been referred to as forgetting [37] or projection and studied in the form of uniform interpolation or strongest necessary condition in knowledge representation [13,16,22,32–34] and answer set programming [20,25]. Forgetting offers solutions to several important applications and manipulations of ontologies: ontology extraction, ontology creation, reuse and comparison, and abductive reasoning [10,36,38,39]. In automated reasoning an application of SOQE is (predicate) symbol elimination [23,29,31,44]. Another very promising application domain is agent communication, requiring knowledge sharing among agents [17,47].

Two prominent approaches to computing SOQE-solutions are the SCAN algorithm introduced in [23] and the DLS algorithm introduced in [14] and extended in [15,41]. SCAN is based on the idea of computing all logical consequences of $\exists\overline{X}\,\varphi$ and omit those formulas that contain predicate variables from $\overline{X}$. It transforms the first-order part φ into clausal normal form and computes the closure under a constraint resolution calculus, performing inferences only on $\overline{X}$-literals. During this process clauses with $\overline{X}$-literals for which sufficiently many inferences have been performed are deleted [21,43]. If the algorithm terminates, it returns a set of first-order consequences which is logically equivalent $\exists\overline{X}\,\varphi$. Reverse Skolemization might be applied, if during the clause form transformation Skolemization was performed. SCAN has been shown complete for computing frame correspondence properties for the class of modal Sahlqvist axioms [26]. The SCAN algorithm is closely related to hierarchic superposition [4,5].

The other prominent approach, the DLS algorithm, is based on a result of Ackermann [2]. Known as Ackermann's Lemma, it states a condition under which a predicate variable is eliminable from a second-order formula $\exists X\varphi$. The idea of the DLS algorithm is to use equivalence preserving operations to bring the problem into a form where Ackermann's Lemma is applicable.

In this paper we are interested in a more general problem which we call *witnessed second-order quantifier elimination (WSOQE)*: Given a formula $\exists\overline{X}\,\varphi$ with first-order φ, find first-order predicates (formulas) $\overline{\alpha}$ satisfying this *WSOQE-condition*

$$\exists\overline{X}\,\varphi \equiv \varphi[\overline{X} \leftarrow \overline{\alpha}]. \qquad (*)$$

That is, the goal is to find a first-order instantiation $\overline{\alpha}$ (in the same language as φ) of variables $\overline{X}$ such that an equivalent first-order formula is obtained. We call $\overline{\alpha}$ a *WSOQE-witness for* $\exists\overline{X}\,\varphi$. Recall that the second-order formula Φ from the beginning of the introduction is equivalent to $B(a)$. One can check that $\alpha = \lambda u.u \simeq a$ and $\beta = \lambda u.B(u)$ are WSOQE-witnesses for Φ.

The contribution of this paper is an algorithm to solve WSOQE and compute such witnesses. Our algorithm, called *WSCAN*, is an extension of the SCAN algorithm with a post-processing step which extracts a witness from the derivation of a terminating SCAN run. The witness construction proceeds in a bottom-up way, computing iteratively from a witness at derivation step i a witness for step $i-1$. A prototype has been implemented in version 2.18.1 of the GAPT software package [19]. In addition to solving the more general WSOQE problem, the concepts introduced in this paper provide a new correctness proof for the SCAN algorithm.

The WSOQE problem bridges the gap between SOQE and another important problem, namely, *solving formula equations (FEQ)*: Given an input formula $\exists\overline{X}\,\varphi$, where φ is first-order find a tuple $\overline{\alpha}$ of first-order predicates such that

$$\models \varphi[\overline{X} \leftarrow \overline{\alpha}].$$

Since the earlier example Φ is not valid it does not have an FEQ-solution. However, one can check that the witnesses α and β from above are FEQ-solutions for the modified formula $\Phi' = \exists X\,(B(a) \rightarrow (X(a) \wedge \forall u\,(X(u) \rightarrow B(u))))$.

Going back to studies in the 19th century by [46], solving formula equations is one of the oldest and most central problems of logic. The book [45] comprehensively considers the problem in the setting of Boolean algebra. Solving Boolean equations is closely related to Boolean unification, a subject of thorough study in computer science, see, e.g., [40] for a survey. The generalization of this problem from propositional to first-order logic has been made explicit as early as [6,7].

Today, FEQ is the central problem underlying several areas of computational logic, even though this is often not made explicit. For example, solving constrained Horn clauses [8], a popular formalism in verification, is a restriction of FEQ, with the existentially quantified variables representing unknown loop invariants in applications of software verification. More generally, the problem of inductive theorem proving, e.g., in Peano arithmetic, can be formulated as a restriction of FEQ, where the predicate variables stand for the unknown induction formulas. One can naively solve FEQ for $\exists\overline{X}\,\varphi$ by enumerating all first-order predicates $\overline{\alpha}$ and checking whether $\varphi[\overline{X} \leftarrow \overline{\alpha}]$ is valid by using, e.g., a first-order theorem prover.

An algorithm for WSOQE, like the one we introduce in this paper, can be used to solve both SOQE and FEQ: A WSOQE-witness $\overline{\alpha}$ satisfies (*) and therefore $\varphi[\overline{X} \leftarrow \overline{\alpha}]$ solves SOQE for $\exists\overline{X}\,\varphi$. However, note that WSOQE is not complete for SOQE as there are formulas that have a SOQE-solution, but no WSOQE-witness (see Sect. 7 for such an example). Furthermore, if one has a WSOQE-witness $\overline{\alpha}$ for $\exists\overline{X}\,\varphi$ one can determine whether it is an FEQ-solution for $\exists\overline{X}\,\varphi$ by checking whether $\varphi[\overline{X} \leftarrow \overline{\alpha}]$ is valid which can be done with a first-order theorem prover. The use of solutions to WSOQE for solving SOQE or FEQ is widespread in the literature: it is the basis of Ackermann's Lemma [2], which provides the foundation for the DLS algorithm [14] for SOQE. It is central for the decidability of quantifier-free Boolean unification with predicates [18] and for the fixed-point theorem for Horn formula equations of [27,28]. Solutions to WSOQE are called ELIM-witnesses in [48].

The paper is organized as follows. In Sect. 2 we introduce some necessary notation. Section 3 describes the SCAN algorithm. We present our method of extracting witnesses from SCAN derivations in Sect. 4. Section 5 provides conditions under which these SCAN derivations guarantee first-order witnesses. The prototype implementation of our method is outlined in Sect. 6. Section 7 discusses limitations of our method and outlines avenues for future work. Full proofs of all results and further examples are given in the appendix of the extended preprint of this paper [1]

2 Preliminaries

We assume familiarity with classical second-order and first-order logic with equality, the usual Tarskian semantics and first-order clause logic, and use standard notation for the connectives, semantic entailment and logical equivalence. Two formulas (of first- or second-order logic) are called *(logically) equivalent*, if they have the same Tarski models. We assume a language with equality $\simeq$ and countably many individual variables $u, v, w, \ldots$, predicate variables $X, Y, Z, \ldots$, individual constant symbols $a, b, c, \ldots$, function symbols $f, g, h, \ldots$ and predicate symbols $A, B, \ldots$. We denote terms by $t, s, r \ldots$, formulas by $\varphi, \psi, \ldots$, literals by $L, L', \ldots$, clauses by $C, C', \ldots$ and clause sets by $N, N', \ldots$. A literal L is called an $\overline{X}$-literal, if $L = Y(\overline{t})$ or $L = \neg Y(\overline{t})$ for some predicate variable Y in $\overline{X}$ and terms $\overline{t}$. The dualization of a literal L is denoted by $L^{\perp}$ and defined as $\neg X(\overline{t})$ if $L = X(\overline{t})$ and $X(\overline{t})$, if $L = \neg X(\overline{t})$.

When a clause set is used in the context of a formula we mean the first-order universal closure of its corresponding conjunctive normal form. We will sometimes use infinite conjunctions and disjunctions.

The set of *basic expressions* is the union of the set of terms, formulas, clauses and clause set. The set of *expressions* is the smallest set containing the basic expressions that is closed under λ-abstraction, i.e., if E is an expression and u is an individual variable, then $\lambda u.E$ is an expression.

Given expressions $E_1, \ldots, E_n$ we write $\overline{E}$ for the tuple $(E_1, \ldots, E_n)$. If $\overline{u} = (u_1, \ldots, u_n)$ is a tuple of first-order variables and E an expression, we write $\lambda\overline{u}.E$ for the expression $\lambda u_1. \ldots \lambda u_n.E$. For tuples of terms $\overline{t} = (t_1, \ldots, t_n)$ and $\overline{s} = (s_1, \ldots, s_n)$ we write $\overline{t} \simeq \overline{s}$ for $t_1 \simeq s_1 \wedge \cdots \wedge t_n \simeq s_n$ and $\overline{t} \not\simeq \overline{s}$ for $t_1 \not\simeq s_1 \vee \cdots \vee t_n \not\simeq s_n$. If we consider an expression $E(\overline{u})$, where $\overline{u}$ is a tuple of first-order variables (or constants), and $\overline{t}$ is a tuple of terms with the same length as $\overline{u}$, then $E(\overline{t})$ denotes the simultaneous substitution of the free variables (or constants) $\overline{u}$ in E by $\overline{t}$. Additionally, using $E(\overline{u})$ implies that all free variables of E are among those in $\overline{u}$. A *predicate expression* α is an expression of the form $\lambda\overline{u}.\varphi$ where φ is a formula. If φ is first-order, we call α a *first-order predicate*. Predicate expressions $\alpha = \lambda\overline{u}.\varphi(\overline{u})$ and $\beta = \lambda\overline{u}.\psi(\overline{u})$ are *equivalent (in symbols $\alpha \equiv \beta$)* if $\models \forall\overline{u}\,(\varphi(\overline{u}) \leftrightarrow \psi(\overline{u}))$.

Let E be an expression. For $1 \leq i \leq d$, let X_i be a predicate variable and $F_i = \lambda\overline{u_i}.\varphi_i(\overline{u_i})$ be a predicate expression of the same arity. Then we denote by $E[X_1 \leftarrow F_1, \ldots, X_d \leftarrow F_d]$ (abbreviated as $E[\overline{X} \leftarrow \overline{F}]$) the expression resulting from E by simultaneously replacing all occurrences $X_i(\overline{t})$ in E by $\varphi_i(\overline{t})$.

For terms $\overline{t} = (t_1, \ldots, t_n)$ and $\overline{s} = (s_1, \ldots, s_n)$ a substitution σ is called a *unifier* of $\overline{t}$ and $\overline{s}$, if $t_i\sigma = s_i\sigma$ for all $i \in \{1, \ldots, n\}$. A unifier σ of $\overline{t}$ and $\overline{s}$ is called a *most general unifier* of $\overline{t}$ and $\overline{s}$, if for all unifiers τ of $\overline{t}$ and $\overline{s}$ there exists a substitution ρ such that $\tau = \sigma\rho$.

3 The SCAN Algorithm

The SCAN algorithm takes as input a formula $\exists\overline{X}\,\varphi$, where φ is first-order and then transforms φ into its clausal normal form N, which might include a Skolemization step. Next, N is saturated by a *purification* process: SCAN picks a clause C and a designated $\overline{X}$-literal $L \in C$. All non-redundant constraint resolution inferences (defined below) between C (on that literal L) and the rest of the clauses are performed. In addition constraint factoring inferences (defined below) on C, constraint elimination and redundancy criteria are used to simplify the resulting clauses. If all non-redundant inferences have been generated, C is deleted from the clause set and the process is repeated with a new clause and designated $\overline{X}$-literal. This process might not terminate, but if we reach a point where no clause contains an $\overline{X}$-literal the result is a clause set N^* such that $\exists\overline{X}\,N \equiv N^*$. SCAN attempts to reverse the Skolemization step from the beginning, if performed, and returns a first-order formula logically equivalent to $\exists\overline{X}\,\varphi$. As we present our results for clause sets, we do not deal with reverse Skolemization.

Note that during the purification process, SCAN not only chooses a clause, but also a literal within this clause. To give a name to this concept we introduce the notion of *pointed clause* (in analogy to *pointed sets* in mathematics):

Definition 1. *Let L be a literal and C a clause. A* pointed clause *P is a clause $\underline{L} \vee C$, in which the literal L in $L \vee C$ is underlined. We call L the* designated literal *of P. If L is an X-literal, then we say P is an X*-pointed *clause.*

We fix an existential prefix of predicate variables $\overline{X}$. The inference rules on clauses used in the SCAN algorithm are:

Constraint resolution:

$$\frac{C \vee L(\overline{t}) \qquad C' \vee L(\overline{s})^{\perp}}{\overline{t} \not\approx \overline{s} \vee C \vee C'}\ \text{Res}$$

where L is an $\overline{X}$-literal and w.l.o.g. $C \vee L(\overline{t})$ and $C' \vee L(\overline{s})^{\perp}$ are assumed to be variable-disjoint. The clause $\overline{t} \not\approx \overline{s} \vee C \vee C'$ is called the *resolvent* of this inference.

Constraint factoring:

$$\frac{C \vee L(\overline{t}) \vee L(\overline{s})}{\overline{t} \not\approx \overline{s} \vee C \vee L(\overline{t})}\ \text{Fac}$$

where L is an $\overline{X}$. The clause $\overline{t} \not\approx \overline{s} \vee C \vee L(\overline{t})$ is called the *factor* of this inference.

Constraint elimination:

$$\frac{\overline{t} \not\approx \overline{s} \vee C}{C\sigma}\ \text{ConstrElim}$$

where σ is a most general unifier of $\overline{t}$ and $\overline{s}$.

Our method does not depend on the specific choice of redundancy criteria, as long as the notion of redundancy is (i) *compatible with entailment*: If a clause C

is redundant in a clause set N, then $\models N \rightarrow C$ and (ii) *equivalence-preserving*: If N/N' is a redundancy elimination step, then $N \equiv N'$. Common redundancy criteria such as tautology deletion, subsumption deletion, constraint elimination and condensing (replacing a clause by a minimal subclause that subsumes it) all satisfy these properties.

We now give a calculus for the saturation process of SCAN:

Definition 2. *We denote by* $\mathcal{C}$ *the* constraint resolution calculus *operating on clause sets with the following derivation steps:*

Inference:
$$\frac{N}{N \cup \{C\}}\, I$$

for $I \in \{\text{Res}, \text{Fac}, \text{ConstrElim}\}$ *if* $\dfrac{C_1 \cdots C_n}{C}\, I$ *is one of the inferences from above and* $C_1, \ldots, C_n \in N$.

Redundancy elimination:
$$\frac{N}{N'}\, \text{RedElim}$$

if $N' = N \setminus \{C\}$ *with* $C \in N$ *and* C *is redundant in* N.

Extended purity deletion:
$$\frac{N}{N \setminus \{C \in N \mid C \textit{ contains } X\}}\, \text{ExtPurDel}_X^p$$

for $p \in \{+, -\}$, *where* X *is a predicate variable if every clause in* N *containing* X *contains* X *with polarity* p.

Purified clause deletion:
$$\frac{N \uplus \{P\}}{N}\, \text{PurDel}_P,$$

if P *is an* X*-pointed clause, where* X *is a predicate variable and every resolvent of* P *with a clause from* N *is redundant in* N*. We call* P the pointed clause *of this purified clause deletion step and also say that* P is purified in N*. By* purification of P *we refer to the process of adding resolvents between* P *and* N *until* P *is purified in* N *followed by the application of* PurDel_P.

One can show that $\mathcal{C}$ preserves equivalence with respect to existential quantification which shows that SCAN is correct:

Proposition 3. *If* N/N' *is a* $\mathcal{C}$*-derivation step, then* $\exists \overline{X}\, N \equiv \exists \overline{X}\, N'$.

We record the derivation steps performed during the saturation process using the following definition:

Definition 4. *Let* $D := (D_i)_{1 \leq i \leq m}$ *be a finite sequence of* $\mathcal{C}$*-derivation steps and let* N, N' *be clause sets. We inductively define the concept of a* $\mathcal{C}$-derivation from N with conclusion N' *by: (i) the empty sequence is a* $\mathcal{C}$*-derivation from* N

with conclusion N *and (ii) if* $D = (D_i)_{1 \leq i \leq m}$ *is a* $\mathcal{C}$*-derivation from* N *with conclusion* N' *and* D_{m+1} *is a* $\mathcal{C}$*-derivation step from* N' *to* N''*, then* $(D_i)_{1 \leq i \leq m+1}$ *is a* $\mathcal{C}$*-derivation from* N *with conclusion* N''*.*

We say D is a $\mathcal{C}$-derivation from N, *if* D *is a* $\mathcal{C}$*-derivation from* N *with conclusion* N' *for some clause set* N'*. We assume the* D_i *contain enough information so that* N' *is uniquely determined by* D *and* N *so we call* N' the conclusion of D from N. *For a* $\mathcal{C}$*-derivation* D *from* N *we define the sequence* $N(D) := (N(D)_i)_{0 \leq i \leq m}$ *of intermediate clause sets in which* $N(D)_i$ *is defined to be the conclusion of the* $\mathcal{C}$*-derivation* $(D_j)_{1 \leq j \leq i}$ *from* N*. For a tuple of predicate variables* $\overline{X}$ *we say* D is $\overline{X}$-eliminating from N *if the conclusion of* D *from* N *contains no predicate variables from* $\overline{X}$*. A pointed clause* P *is* purified in D *if there is a derivation step* D_i *with* $D_i = \mathrm{PurDel}_P$*.*

Example 5. Consider the clause set N with the clauses

$$(1)\ B(a,v) \qquad (2)\ X(a) \qquad (3)\ B(u,v) \vee \neg X(u) \vee X(v) \qquad (4)\ \neg X(c)$$

and suppose we want to eliminate X. We denote clauses by their numbers, e.g., 1 refers to clause $B(a,v)$. Pointed clauses are referred to by dot notation, e.g., 3.2 refers to the pointed clause $B(u,v) \vee \underline{\neg X(u)} \vee X(v)$. Applying SCAN, some resolvents from N are

$$(5)\ a \not\approx u \vee B(u,v) \vee X(v) \quad (2 \text{ with } 3) \quad \text{and} \quad (6)\ a \not\approx c \qquad (2 \text{ with } 4)$$

Note that clause 5 is semantically entailed by clause 1 because 1 subsumes 5 after constraint elimination. Let D be this derivation:

$$\cfrac{\cfrac{\cfrac{\{1,2,3,4\}}{\{1,2,3,4,6\}}\ \mathrm{Res}_{2.1,4.1}}{\{1,3,4,6\}}\ \mathrm{PurDel}_{2.1}}{\{1,6\}}\ \mathrm{ExtPurDel}_{\overline{X}}$$

The subscripts in Res indicate the corresponding resolution premises. Note that the pointed clause 2.1 is purified in $\{1,3,4,6\}$ since 5, the resolvent of 2 with 4, is redundant in $\{1,3,4,6\}$. Thus the $\mathrm{PurDel}_{2.1}$ step is applicable to $\{1,2,3,4,6\}$. As $\{1,6\}$ does not contain X, we have that D is an X-eliminating derivation.

4 Witness Extraction from SCAN Derivations

In this section we introduce the WSCAN algorithm ('W' for witness), as an extension of SCAN on clause sets by providing a witness for the second-order quantifier elimination on termination. At first we also consider solutions to WSOQE that are not necessarily first-order and give them a name: A tuple of predicate expressions $\overline{\alpha}$ is called an *elimination witness*, or simply a *witness for* $\exists \overline{X}\, \varphi$, if it satisfies the WSOQE-condition $(*)$ for $\exists \overline{X}\, \varphi$.

An illustration of how WSCAN works is given in the following diagram:

$$\begin{array}{ccccccc} N = N(D)_0 & \xrightarrow{D_1} & N(D)_1 & \xrightarrow{D_2} & \ldots\ N(D)_{m-1} & \xrightarrow{D_m} & N(D)_m \\ \overline{\mathrm{wit}(D)} = \overline{\mathrm{wit}_0(D)} & \xleftarrow{T_{D_1}} & \overline{\mathrm{wit}_1(D)} & \xleftarrow{T_{D_2}} & \ldots\ \overline{\mathrm{wit}_{m-1}(D)} & \xleftarrow{T_{D_m}} & \overline{\mathrm{wit}_m(D)} \end{array}$$

We start by saturating a given clause set N using the derivation steps of the calculus and collect them in a derivation $D = (D_i)_{1 \le i \le m}$. If saturation terminates we construct a witness $\overline{\mathrm{wit}(D)}$ for $\exists \overline{X}\, N$. To this aim we iteratively compute witnesses $\overline{\mathrm{wit}_i(D)}$ for $\exists \overline{X}\, N(D)_i$ for all $0 \le i \le m$ starting from the back with $\overline{\mathrm{wit}_m(D)}$. Since D resulted from saturating the input clause set N we have that $N(D)_m$, i.e., the conclusion of D from N, contains none of the variables in $\overline{X}$, otherwise a $\mathcal{C}$-derivation step would be applicable. We now need an initial witness $\overline{\mathrm{wit}_m(D)}$ for $N(D)_m$. Since $N(D)_m$ does not contain any of the variables of $\overline{X}$ choosing for $\overline{\mathrm{wit}_m(D)}$ any tuple of predicate expressions (compatible with the arities of $\overline{X}$) produces a witness. We then iteratively transform witness $\overline{\mathrm{wit}_i(D)}$ of $N(D)_i$ to a witness $\overline{\mathrm{wit}_{i-1}(D)}$ of $N(D)_{i-1}$ using an operation T_{D_i}. Finally, the tuple of predicates $\overline{\mathrm{wit}_0(D)}$ is a witness for $\exists \overline{X}\, N$.

We now want to define the transformation T_S for the different derivation steps S in $\mathcal{C}$. It has to satisfy the following property:

Lemma 6 (Witness preservation lemma). *If S is a $\mathcal{C}$-derivation step from N to N' and $\overline{\alpha}$ is a witness for $\exists \overline{X}\, N'$, then $T_S(\overline{\alpha})$ is a witness for $\exists \overline{X}\, N$.*

Before we give the formal definition of T_S, we give some intuition on how to satisfy Lemma 6. For $S \in \{\mathrm{Res}, \mathrm{Fac}, \mathrm{ConstrElim}, \mathrm{RedElim}\}$ we have $N \equiv N'$. Therefore we can use the same witness, i.e., we set $T_S(\overline{\alpha}) = \overline{\alpha}$. If we have $S = \mathrm{ExtPurDel}^+_X$ we see that $N' \equiv N[X \leftarrow \lambda\overline{u}.\top]$ since every clause in N that contains X has a positive occurrence of X, making those clauses logically equivalent to $\top$ under $[X \leftarrow \lambda\overline{u}.\top]$. If $\overline{\alpha}$ is a witness for $\exists \overline{X}\, N'$, then setting the X-component of $\overline{\alpha}$ to $\lambda\overline{u}.\top$ and leaving the other components the same results in a witness for N. Similarly, if $S = \mathrm{ExtPurDel}^-_X$ we set the X-component of $T_S(\overline{\alpha})$ to X to $\lambda\overline{u}.\bot$. Then $N' \equiv N[X \leftarrow \lambda\overline{u}.\bot]$.

Defining the transformation T_S for $S = \mathrm{PurDel}_P$ needs a bit of groundwork. A central piece is the resolution closure of a clause set with respect to a pointed clause:

Definition 7. *Let P be a pointed clause with designated literal L and let N be a clause set. We define $\mathrm{Res}_P(N)$ to be the smallest set such that (i) $N \subseteq \mathrm{Res}_P(N)$, and (ii) if $C \in \mathrm{Res}_P(N)$ and R is a resolvent between C and P upon L, then $R \in \mathrm{Res}_P(N)$.*

For a clause C we define the abbreviation $\mathrm{Res}_P(C) := \mathrm{Res}_P(\{C\})$ and for a literal L we set $\mathrm{Res}_P(L) := \mathrm{Res}_P(\{L\})$.

Furthermore for $P = \underline{L(\overline{t})} \vee C_P$ we define the set $\mathrm{ResU}_P(\overline{c}) := \mathrm{Res}_P(L(\overline{c})^\perp)$, where $\overline{c}$ is a tuple of fresh constants. The 'U' stands for unit and signifies that we consider the resolution closure with respect to P starting with a unit clause dual to the designated literal of P.

To simplify the presentation of the set $\mathrm{Res}_P(N)$ we often tacitly replace it by a logically equivalent clause set, for example by replacing a clause $C \in \mathrm{Res}_P(N)$ by a logically equivalent clause C', which results from C by constraint elimination.

Some examples of $\mathrm{ResU}_P(\overline{c})$ are given in the following:

Example 8. Let $P = \underline{X(a)}$, then we have $\mathrm{ResU}_P(c) = \{\neg X(c), a \not\simeq c\}$ and for $P' = \underline{\neg X(a)} \vee \neg X(b)$ we get $\mathrm{ResU}_{P'}(c) = \{X(c), a \not\simeq c \vee \neg X(b)\}$.

For $P'' = B(u,v) \vee \underline{\neg X(u)} \vee X(v)$ we get an infinite set:

$$\begin{aligned}\mathrm{ResU}_{P''}(c) = \{&X(c),\ B(c,v) \vee X(v),\\ &B(c,v) \vee B(v,v') \vee X(v'),\\ &B(c,v) \vee B(v,v') \vee B(v',v'') \vee X(v''), \dots\}.\end{aligned}$$

In the definition of the clause set $\mathrm{ResU}_P(\overline{c})$ we use a tuple of constants $\overline{c}$ instead of variables as we want to avoid the implicit universal quantification over the clauses for these placeholders. These constants are intended as arguments for a predicate expression pResU_P ('p' for predicate) given by:

Definition 9. *Let P be an X-pointed clause. We set*

$$\mathrm{pResU}_P := \begin{cases} \lambda\overline{u}. \bigwedge_{C'(\overline{c},\overline{v}) \in \mathrm{ResU}_P(\overline{c})} \forall\overline{v}\, C'(\overline{u},\overline{v}) & \text{if } P = \underline{\neg X(\overline{t})} \vee C \text{ and}\\ \lambda\overline{u}. \bigvee_{C'(\overline{c},\overline{v}) \in \mathrm{ResU}_P(\overline{c})} \exists\overline{v}\, \neg C'(\overline{u},\overline{v}) & \text{if } P = \underline{X(\overline{t})} \vee C, \end{cases}$$

where $\overline{u}$ is a tuple of fresh variables of the same size as $\overline{c}$.

Example 10. For $P = \underline{X(a)}$ and $P' = \underline{\neg X(a)} \vee \neg X(b)$ as in Example 8 we get $\mathrm{pResU}_P = \lambda u.X(u) \vee u \simeq a$ and $\mathrm{pResU}_{P'} = \lambda u.X(u) \wedge (u \not\simeq a \vee \neg X(b))$. If $\mathrm{ResU}_P(\overline{c})$ is infinite, as for P'' of Example 8, then pResU_P is an infinite predicate expression.

A crucial property of pResU_P is the following:

Lemma 11. *Let P be an X-pointed clause and let C be a clause. Then we have $\models P[X \leftarrow \mathrm{pResU}_P]$ and $\models \mathrm{Res}_P(C) \rightarrow C[X \leftarrow \mathrm{pResU}_P]$.*

A way to view this lemma is (i) $X \leftarrow \mathrm{pResU}_P$ is always a satisfying assignment for P and (ii) $X \leftarrow \mathrm{pResU}_P$ is a satisfying assignment for C, given that there is an assignment of X that satisfies all clauses in $\mathrm{Res}_P(C)$ (note that X can occur freely in $\mathrm{Res}_P(C)$ and pResU_P). The reader might gain an intuition for the lemma by applying it to the pointed clauses from the previous example.

Using Lemma 11 we can show the witness preservation lemma (Lemma 6) for purified clause deletion steps using pResU_P:

Lemma 12. *Let N be a clause set, let P be X_i-pointed and purified in N and suppose $\overline{\alpha} = (\alpha_1, \dots, \alpha_d)$ is a witness for $\exists\overline{X}\, N$. Then a witness for $\exists\overline{X}\, (N \cup \{P\})$ is given by $(\alpha_1, \dots, \alpha_{i-1}, \mathrm{pResU}_P[\overline{X} \leftarrow \overline{\alpha}], \alpha_{i+1}, \dots, \alpha_d)$.*

Proof sketch. To avoid notational overhead we give a proof sketch under the simplifying assumption $d = 1$, i.e., we only consider a single variable X.

To show that $\alpha_P := \mathrm{pResU}_P[X \leftarrow \alpha]$ is a witness for $N_P := N \cup \{P\}$ we need to show that both directions of the WSOQE-condition $(*)$ hold. The direction $\models N_P[X \leftarrow \alpha_P] \rightarrow \exists X\, N_P$ holds as α_P is an instance of the existential quantifier. Now it suffices to show $\models \exists X\, N_P \rightarrow N_P[X \leftarrow \alpha_P]$. Since $N \subseteq N_P$ we have $\models \exists X\, N_P \rightarrow \exists X\, N$ and because α is a witness for $\exists X\, N$ we have $\models \exists X\, N \rightarrow N[X \leftarrow \alpha]$. It remains to show $\models N[X \leftarrow \alpha] \rightarrow N_P[X \leftarrow \alpha_P]$. We reduce this to $\models P[X \leftarrow \alpha_P]$ and $\models N[X \leftarrow \alpha] \rightarrow C[X \leftarrow \alpha_P]$ for all $C \in N$.

Using the first statement of Lemma 11 we get $\models P[X \leftarrow \mathrm{pResU}_P]$. Applying the substitution which sends X to α results in $\models P[X \leftarrow \mathrm{pResU}_P][X \leftarrow \alpha]$. Note that applying $[X \leftarrow \alpha]$ after $[X \leftarrow \mathrm{pResU}_P]$ is the same as applying $[X \leftarrow \mathrm{pResU}_P[X \leftarrow \alpha]]$. Thus $\models P[X \leftarrow \alpha_P]$.

To show $\models N[X \leftarrow \alpha] \rightarrow C[X \leftarrow \alpha_P]$ we use that P is purified in N to get that all clauses in $\mathrm{Res}_P(N)$, and in particular all clauses in $\mathrm{Res}_P(C) \subseteq \mathrm{Res}_P(N)$, are redundant in N. Therefore $\models N \rightarrow \mathrm{Res}_P(C)$ and we can apply the second statement of Lemma 11 to get $\models N \rightarrow C[X \leftarrow \mathrm{pResU}_P]$. Again, applying $[X \leftarrow \alpha]$ results in the desired statement $\models N[X \leftarrow \alpha] \rightarrow C[X \leftarrow \alpha_P]$.

We now give the formal definition of the witness transformation:

Definition 13. *Let S be a $\mathcal{C}$-derivation step and let $\overline{X} = (X_1, \ldots, X_d)$ be a tuple of predicate variables. For $1 \leq i \leq d$, let $\overline{u_i}$ be a tuple of distinct variables, the size of which is the arity of X_i. Also, let $\overline{\alpha} = (\alpha_1, \ldots, \alpha_d)$ be a tuple of predicate expressions such that α_i has the same arity as X_i for $1 \leq i \leq d$. We define the predicate expression $T_S(\overline{\alpha})$ by a case distinction on S as follows:*

$$
\begin{aligned}
T_S(\overline{\alpha}) &:= \overline{\alpha} \text{ for } S \in \{\mathrm{Res}, \mathrm{Fac}, \mathrm{ConstrElim}, \mathrm{RedElim}\}, \\
T_{\mathrm{ExtPurDel}^+_{X_i}}(\overline{\alpha}) &:= (\alpha_1, \ldots, \alpha_{i-1}, \lambda\overline{u_i}.\top, \alpha_{i+1}, \ldots, \alpha_d), \\
T_{\mathrm{ExtPurDel}^-_{X_i}}(\overline{\alpha}) &:= (\alpha_1, \ldots, \alpha_{i-1}, \lambda\overline{u_i}.\bot, \alpha_{i+1}, \ldots, \alpha_d), \text{ and} \\
T_{\mathrm{PurDel}_P}(\overline{\alpha}) &:= (\alpha_1, \ldots, \alpha_{i-1}, \mathrm{pResU}_P[\overline{X} \leftarrow \overline{\alpha}], \alpha_{i+1}, \ldots, \alpha_d), \\
&\quad \text{if } P \text{ is } X_i\text{-pointed.}
\end{aligned}
$$

Above we explained why the witness preservation lemma holds for these $T_S(\overline{\alpha})$. We now construct witnesses iteratively given a $\mathcal{C}$-derivation $(D_i)_{1 \leq i \leq m}$ starting from the back:

Definition 14. *Let $N(X_1, \ldots, X_d)$ be a clause set and let $D = (D_i)_{1 \leq i \leq m}$ be a $\mathcal{C}$-derivation from N. For $1 \leq i \leq d$ let W_i be a predicate variable with the same arity as X_i. We inductively define a tuple $\overline{\mathrm{wit}_i(D)}$ of predicate expressions, for $0 \leq i \leq m$, starting with $\overline{\mathrm{wit}_m(D)}$ as the base case by*

$$
\overline{\mathrm{wit}_m(D)} := (W_1, \ldots, W_d) \quad \text{and} \quad \overline{\mathrm{wit}_{i-1}(D)} := T_{D_i}(\overline{\mathrm{wit}_i(D)}).
$$

Finally, the witness for $\exists \overline{X}\, N$ is given by $\overline{\mathrm{wit}(D)} := \overline{\mathrm{wit}_0(D)}$.

If $D = (D_i)_{1 \leq i \leq m}$ is an $\overline{X}$-eliminating $\mathcal{C}$-derivation from N, the conclusion of D does not contain any of the predicate variables in $\overline{X}$. Thus, any tuple of predicate expressions (compatible with the arities in $\overline{X}$) provides a witness for the conclusion of D. The predicate variables W_i in the above definition serve as placeholders for this arbitrary choice of witness and any instantiation of these predicate variables provides a witness. We call W_i the *witness parameter corresponding to* X_i. The $\overline{\mathrm{wit}_i(D)}$ are witnesses for the intermediate clause sets $N(D)_i$ which can be proved by an inductive argument on the length of D using Lemma 6.

Our main result is:

Theorem 15. *If D is an $\overline{X}$-eliminating $\mathcal{C}$-derivation from N, then $\overline{\mathrm{wit}(D)}$ is a witness for $\exists\overline{X}\,N$.*

Here is an example illustrating the algorithm:

Example 16. Remember the clause set N from Example 5:

$$(1)\ B(a,v) \qquad (2)\ X(a) \qquad (3)\ B(u,v) \vee \neg X(u) \vee X(v) \qquad (4)\ \neg X(c)$$

and suppose we want to find a witness for X. Some resolvents from N are

$$(5)\ a \not\simeq u \vee B(u,v) \vee X(v) \quad \text{(2 with 3)} \quad \text{and} \quad (6)\ a \not\simeq c \qquad \text{(2 with 4)}.$$

Also recall the derivation D:

$$\begin{array}{cl} \{1,2,3,4\} & \\ \hline & \mathrm{Res}_{2.1,4.1} \\ \{1,2,3,4,6\} & \\ \hline & \mathrm{PurDel}_{2.1} \\ \{1,3,4,6\} & \\ \hline & \mathrm{ExtPurDel}_{\overline{X}} \\ \{1,6\} & \end{array}$$

In computing $\mathrm{wit}_i(D)$, we freely use equivalences of the form $\bot \vee \varphi \equiv \varphi$, $\top \wedge \varphi \equiv \varphi$ and $\neg\neg\varphi \equiv \varphi$ as well as commutativity and associativity of $\wedge$ and $\vee$ to simplify the constructed witnesses. We use W_X to denote the witness parameter corresponding to X. The steps to construct $\mathrm{wit}(D)$ are:

i	$N(D)_i$	D_{i+1}	$T_{D_{i+1}}(\alpha)$	$\mathrm{wit}_i(D)$
3	$\{1,6\}$	–	–	W_X
2	$\{1,3,4,6\}$	$\mathrm{ExtPurDel}_{\overline{X}}$	$\lambda u.\bot$	$\lambda u.\bot$
1	$\{1,2,3,4,6\}$	$\mathrm{PurDel}_{2.1}$	$\mathrm{pResU}_{2.1}[X \leftarrow \alpha]$	$\lambda u.u \simeq a$
0	$\{1,2,3,4\}$	$\mathrm{Res}_{2.1,4.1}$	α	$\lambda u.u \simeq a$

Note that $\mathrm{ResU}_{2.1}(d) = \{\neg X(d), d \not\simeq a\}$ and thus $\mathrm{pResU}_{2.1} = \lambda u.X(u) \vee u \simeq a$. Therefore $\mathrm{wit}(D) = \lambda u.u \simeq a$ is a WSOQE-witness for $\exists X\,N$.

5 First-Order Witnesses

At this point it is not clear that the components of $\overline{\mathrm{wit}(D)}$ are always first-order predicates as the expression pResU_P can be infinite. In fact, there are $\overline{X}$-eliminating derivations where the predicate expressions in $\overline{\mathrm{wit}(D)}$ are not equivalent to first-order predicates. This can be avoided, if for all purified clauses P in D there are first-order predicates F_P equivalent to pResU_P:

Definition 17. *Let D be a $\mathcal{C}$-derivation from N. Let F be a mapping that assigns to all purified pointed clauses P of D a first-order predicate F_P with* $\mathrm{pResU}_P \equiv F_P$. *Then F is called a* first-order annotation for D. *In that case, denote by $\overline{\mathrm{wit}(D, F)}$ the tuple of first-order predicate expressions resulting from $\overline{\mathrm{wit}(D)}$ where every occurrence of* pResU_P *is replaced by F_P.*

Now the first-order version of our main result is:

Corollary 18. *If D is an $\overline{X}$-eliminating $\mathcal{C}$-derivation from N and F is a first-order annotation for D, then $\overline{\mathrm{wit}(D, F)}$ is a first-order witness for $\exists\overline{X}\, N$.*

To find such a first-order annotation F we compute for all purified pointed clauses P a finite clause set N_P logically equivalent to $\mathrm{ResU}_P(\overline{c})$. Then replacing $\mathrm{ResU}_P(\overline{c})$ by N_P in the definition of pResU_P results in a first-order predicate expression F_P equivalent to pResU_P. We use SCAN's purification process to find such finite clause sets N_P: Let $P = \underline{L(\overline{t})} \vee C$. Start with the clause set $\{L(\overline{c})^{\perp}\}$ and saturate it with respect to constraint resolution with P. In addition we use constraint and redundancy elimination to simplify the intermediate clause sets. If at some point all constraint resolvents of the clause set with P are redundant, we obtain a finite clause set N_P which is logically equivalent to $\mathrm{ResU}_P(\overline{c})$. However, this process might not terminate as is the case for P'' from Example 8. Thus it is unclear whether computing a first-order annotation F is always possible.

To get a concrete strategy for constructing $\mathcal{C}$-derivations where Corollary 18 is applicable we direct our search to a decidable property which is sufficient to guarantee first-order annotations. One such property is:

Definition 19. *An X-pointed clause P is called* one-sided *if X occurs only positively or only negatively in P. A $\mathcal{C}$-derivation D is called* one-sided *if all purified pointed clauses in D are one-sided (not necessarily with the same polarity).*

Derivation D in Example 16 is one-sided as its only purified pointed clause 2.1 is one-sided. In general, if $P = \underline{L(\overline{t})} \vee C$ is one-sided, then we have $\mathrm{ResU}_P(\overline{c}) = \{L(\overline{c})^{\perp}, \overline{t} \not\simeq \overline{c} \vee C\}$, i.e., $\mathrm{ResU}_P(\overline{c})$ is finite. Thus $P \mapsto \mathrm{pResU}_P$ is a first-order annotation for one-sided $\mathcal{C}$-derivations. One-sidedness of a pointed clause P is not necessary for the existence of a first-order predicate equivalent to pResU_P, e.g., for $P = \underline{\neg X(u, v)} \vee X(v, u)$ we have $\mathrm{ResU}_P(c, d) \equiv \{X(c, d), X(d, c)\}$, therefore $F_P = \lambda u \lambda v. X(u, v) \wedge X(v, u)$ satisfies $F_P \equiv \mathrm{pResU}_P$.

As a special case of Corollary 18 we get:

Corollary 20. *If D is a one-sided $\overline{X}$-eliminating $\mathcal{C}$-derivation from N, then $\overline{\mathrm{wit}(D)}$ is a first-order witness for $\exists\overline{X}\, N$.*

Since one-sidedness is a decidable property, this suggests a strategy to construct $\overline{X}$-eliminating $\mathcal{C}$-derivations which induce WSOQE-witnesses: Run SCAN in such a way that only one-sided pointed clauses P are purified. If SCAN terminates, the resulting derivation will also be one-sided, ensuring a first-order witness $\overline{\mathrm{wit}(D)}$. However, it is open whether this affects completeness of the calculus (see Problem 21).

Furthermore for one-sided $\overline{X}$-eliminating derivations D one can show a tight exponential upper bound on the size of $\overline{\text{wit}(D)}$ in terms of the length of D. If every purified pointed clause in D contains at most one $\overline{X}$-literal, the bound is even linear.

6 Implementation

The presented method is implemented in the Scala programming language [42] as part of the General Architecture for Proof Theory (GAPT) software package [19] which provides useful data structures to develop algorithms in computational logic, including terms, formulas and clauses. The prototype is available in version 2.18.1 of GAPT (https://www.logic.at/gapt/release_archive.html). Section 8.4 of the GAPT user manual details how to use the prototype.

To evaluate our witness construction method we have implemented the SCAN algorithm which, in addition to finding a logically equivalent first-order clause set, provides a $\mathcal{C}$-derivation which is then used by our method to extract a witness.

The saturation loop proceeds by picking a pointed clause $P = \underline{L(\overline{t})} \vee C$ from the active clause set and performs purification, i.e., adds all non-redundant resolvents between P and the rest of the clause set while eagerly applying constraint elimination, tautology deletion, subsumption deletion, as well as inferring all non-redundant constraint factors of newly added clauses. Once P is purified, it is deleted from the active clause set. Since this process might not terminate we provide parameters that limit the inferences to be performed. If the input clause set is not saturated within this limit the procedure reports an error. Since one-sided derivations guarantee first-order witnesses, we also provide an option to only apply the purification process to one-sided pointed clauses. During the saturation process all performed steps are stored in a $\mathcal{C}$-derivation, modelled as the initial clause set together with a list of $\mathcal{C}$-derivation steps.

The choice of pointed clause determines the outcome of the saturation process. Different choices can lead to termination or non-termination. This also affects which $\mathcal{C}$-derivations are found. To find all possible $\mathcal{C}$-derivations from a given clause set, we have implemented backtracking on top of the saturation process to be able to get $\mathcal{C}$-derivations based on the different choices of pointed clauses. This backtracking can be performed on-demand, and allows to find multiple derivations and therefore multiple witnesses.

The witness extraction method recurses on the produced $\mathcal{C}$-derivation following Definition 14. We implemented T_S according to Definition 13 where pResU_P is computed by using the same purification process as described above, but starting with the clause set consisting of the single literal $L(\overline{c})^{\perp}$. This means we also use redundancy criteria and constraint factoring inferences to simplify the clause set $\text{ResU}_P(\overline{c})$. Since pResU_P is potentially infinite we also provide parameters that limit the inference steps performed in its computation. If the witness computation succeeds, it returns a substitution that maps the eliminated symbols to the computed first-order witness predicates.

Our prototype implementation has been tested on 26 examples from the file `examples/predicateEliminationProblems.scala` included in GAPT 2.18.1. These examples were either created by us or selected from the literature and possibly modified. Tests were run using the GAPT shell with the Azul Zulu Java JDK 21.0.2 on a MacBook Pro with an M2 Pro CPU and 32GB RAM. We run the `wscan` method with default parameters, measuring execution time, input clause set size, and resulting witness size (if found). We measure the size of a literal by the number of non-logical symbols it contains. The size of a clause is given by the sum of the sizes of its literals and the size of a clause set is given by the sum of the sizes of its clauses. The size of a witness is measured by the number of logical and non-logical symbols it contains. See the `wscanTest` method in the file `examples/predicateEliminationProblems.scala` for the exact test protocol.

The results are the following: The input size ranged from 2 to 177 with an average of 21.58. For 21 of the 26 examples a witness could be computed. In the remaining five cases a user-set timeout based on the number of derivation steps was reached without finding a derivation. For the 21 terminating examples the running times ranged from 0.03 milliseconds to 150.60 milliseconds with an average of 14.96 milliseconds. The witness sizes ranged from 0 (this example had no second-order quantifiers) to 220 with an average of 21.50.

We have not optimized our implementation for large clause sets. Furthermore, we are not aware of a sufficiently large database of examples to test our method on. This means a thorough empirical evaluation is left as future work.

7 Discussion and Future Work

Constructing Multiple Witnesses. Different $\mathcal{C}$-derivations can result in different, non-equivalent witnesses. Thus one can use our method to construct multiple witnesses for a given input clause set. As already mentioned, to get different $\mathcal{C}$-derivations our prototype performs backtracking on different choices of pointed clauses in the purification process of SCAN.

Another approach to finding multiple witnesses would be to instantiate the free predicate variables $W_1, \ldots, W_d$ in the definition of $\text{wit}(D)$. These are contained in the witness if D does not use extended purity deletion.

In practice certain witnesses might be preferred over others, e.g., based on size. Accounting for additional constraints like these when constructing witnesses is an avenue for future work.

Limitations for Finding Witnesses. The original SCAN algorithm uses Skolemization if the input formula is not in clause form and after the saturation process tries to undo the Skolemization to find a logically equivalent first-order formula. While reverse Skolemization is undecidable in general, it does work in some cases, for example, if the input formula has the form $\exists \overline{u}\, \varphi$ where φ is quantifier-free. We discuss such an example where the SCAN algorithm terminates and finds a SOQE-solution, but where no WSOQE-witness exists.

The input formula is $\Phi = \exists X\, \exists u\, \exists v\, (X(u) \wedge \neg X(v))$. Skolemization of the first-order part yields the clause set $N = \{X(a), \neg X(b)\}$ with Skolem constants a and b. An X-eliminating $\mathcal{C}$-derivation from N is given by $D =$

$$\cfrac{\cfrac{\cfrac{\{X(a), \neg X(b)\}}{\{X(a), \neg X(b), a \not\simeq b\}}\ \mathrm{Res}_{\underline{X(a), \neg X(b)}}}{\{\neg X(b), a \not\simeq b\}}\ \mathrm{PurDel}_{\underline{X(a)}}}{\{a \not\simeq b\}}\ \mathrm{ExtPurDel}^{-}_{\overline{X}}$$

The original SCAN algorithm now reverses the Skolemization on the resulting formula $a \not\simeq b$, to get the logically equivalent formula $\exists u\, \exists v\, u \not\simeq v$, i.e., we have $\Phi \equiv \exists u\, \exists v\, u \not\simeq v$. The computed witness $\mathrm{wit}(D) = \mathrm{pResU}_{\underline{X(a)}}[X \leftarrow \lambda u.\bot]$ is equivalent to $\lambda u.u \simeq a$. However, this witness contains a Skolem constant which is not in the language of the input formula. In fact, no WSOQE-witness exists in the input language: Assume Φ had a WSOQE-witness $\alpha = \lambda u.\varphi(u)$. Then α is a first-order predicate in the empty language and in every structure $\mathcal{M}$ it defines the subset $\alpha^{\mathcal{M}}$ given by $\{m \in M \mid \mathcal{M} \models \varphi(u)\}$. For every two-element model $\mathcal{M} = \{m_1, m_2\}$ we have $\mathcal{M} \models \exists X\, \exists u\, \exists v\, (X(u) \wedge \neg X(v))$. Since α is a witness we get $\mathcal{M} \models \exists u\, \exists v\, (\varphi(u) \wedge \neg\varphi(v))$. Thus $\alpha^{\mathcal{M}}$ is neither the empty set nor the whole set M. However, in the empty language the only first-order parameter-free definable sets in a structure $\mathcal{M}$ are the empty set and M itself, see [30, Theorem 2.1.2], which is a contradiction.

This shows a fundamental limitation for finding witnesses, even if SOQE-solutions exist. For practical applications it would be useful to add Skolemization and reverse Skolemization steps to the implementation and investigate classes of formulas where witness construction succeeds in the presence of Skolemization.

Quantifier Alternations. We have discussed the WSOQE problem in the context of existential quantifiers, but one can also consider the dual problem for universal quantifiers: Given a formula $\forall \overline{X}\, \varphi$ with first-order φ, find first-order predicates $\overline{\alpha}$ such that

$$\forall \overline{X}\, \varphi \equiv \varphi[\overline{X} \leftarrow \overline{\alpha}].$$

One can reduce this problem to the existential case since for all first-order predicates $\overline{\alpha}$ we have $\forall \overline{X}\, \varphi \equiv \varphi[\overline{X} \leftarrow \overline{\alpha}]$ if and only if $\exists \overline{X}\, \neg\varphi \equiv \neg\varphi[\overline{X} \leftarrow \overline{\alpha}]$ by writing $\forall \overline{X}$ as $\neg\exists \overline{X}\, \neg$. This way, one can solve the problem for an arbitrary quantifier prefix by successively eliminating alternating blocks of existential and universal quantifiers starting with the innermost block.

While the reduction above works if one has a general WSOQE method that can handle any input formula, our submission only works when the input is a clause set, i.e., the domain variables are universally quantified. The above reduction introduces a negation on the input formula, meaning that we now have to deal with existential quantifiers on the domain variables as well, e.g., via Skolemization. However, as stated before there are fundamental limitations when introducing Skolemization. For input formulas where the first-order part is quantifier-free our method is applicable though.

Completeness of One-Sided $\overline{X}$-Eliminating Derivations. To ensure that SCAN produces a one-sided derivation, if terminating, one can restrict the application of PurDel_P to one-sided P. However, this might restrict the number of clause sets for which an $\overline{X}$-eliminating derivation can be found. It is open whether one-sided $\overline{X}$-eliminating derivations are complete in this sense:

Problem 21. *If there is an $\overline{X}$-eliminating $\mathcal{C}$-derivation from N, is there always a one-sided $\overline{X}$-eliminating $\mathcal{C}$-derivation from N?*

A positive answer would justify using the strategy of restricting PurDel_P to one-sided P during a run of the SCAN algorithm which, if terminating, guarantees a first-order witness by Corollary 20.

Computing Witnesses with DLS(*). As this work extends a known algorithm for solving SOQE to solve the more general WSOQE problem, the question arises whether other algorithms like DLS [14] and DLS* [15,41] can be equally modified to solve WSOQE and how the resulting witnesses compare.

Improvement of Ackermann's Lemma. Ackermann's Lemma provides a method for solving WSOQE as well. On clause sets, our method is an improvement on Ackermann's Lemma in the following sense: If Ackermann's Lemma applies to $\exists X\, N$, then there is a one-sided $\mathcal{C}$-derivation D from N, such that $\text{wit}(D)$ is equivalent to the witness produced by Ackermann's Lemma. Furthermore our method can construct a witness for Example 16 where Ackermann's Lemma is not applicable. This result makes no claim about whether our method improves on other Ackermann-based algorithms, such as DLS and DLS*, since they employ other transformation steps besides the application of Ackermann's Lemma.

Equality Reasoning. A desirable extension is an implementation with equality reasoning. The original SCAN algorithm works in the presence of equality [4], so we expect the witness construction to carry over to first-order logic with equality.

Solving FEQ. As discussed in the Introduction, any WSOQE algorithm can be applied to solving formula equations, by appending a validity check with a first-order theorem prover. In some cases our method can skip the additional validity check: If SCAN terminates with the empty set (which implies that $\exists \overline{X}\, N$ is valid) and the resulting derivation is one-sided, the witness found is also a solution to the FEQ problem. However, SCAN might output a valid clause set which is not the empty set, in which case a validity check is still required to solve FEQ.

This opens the door to apply this method in Boolean unification (which is a restriction of FEQ to nullary predicate variables) and in the context of software verification for solving sets of constrained Horn clauses [8].

Application to Forgetting. Methods for computing forgetting solutions and uniform interpolants have been developed for description logics and modal logics [3, 33–35]. For applications, e.g., knowledge processing, agent applications and Boolean unification, the possibility of extending these to compute also witnesses for eliminated variables would be attractive. Using a WSOQE-solution instead of a SOQE-solution has the advantage that the structure of the existing knowledge base is left largely intact. Functionality to return witnesses could provide a promising avenue to develop methods for such applications, but such development is subject to future work.

Expressivity. Investigating SOQE, and related problems, e.g., uniform interpolation, one quickly encounters expressibility challenges. These carry over to WSOQE, as we have seen in this paper, but also to FEQ and Boolean unification as a special instance of FEQ. However, applications might be able to cope with language extensions, e.g., the extent to which infinite witnesses can be expressed using fixpoints is worth investigating. Enhancing the expressivity of the target language might increase success rates.

8 Conclusion

We introduced WSCAN, an extension of the SCAN algorithm on clause sets, to compute witnesses for existential second-order quantifiers, thereby solving the more general WSOQE-problem. Given an $\overline{X}$-eliminating derivation D from a clause set N we can produce a witness for $\exists \overline{X}\, N$. That witness might be infinite in general, but if in addition all purified pointed clauses of D have a certain finiteness property, like one-sidedness, we can guarantee that the witness is first-order. To the best of our knowledge there are currently no other WSOQE-algorithms applicable to arbitrary clause sets. This work paves the way to new applications of the SCAN algorithm in a variety of different areas, ranging from modal correspondence theory and knowledge representation to verification.

On a more abstract level, we see this work as a contribution to bridging the gap between second-order quantifier elimination (SOQE) and solving formula equations (FEQ) which will be of interest to the respective communities investigating these problems. SOQE has been studied mostly in the context of modal logic, description logics, knowledge representation and answer set programming. On the other hand, FEQ is studied (usually in different formalisms and under different names) in the verification and automated (inductive) theorem proving communities. We believe that the complex of problems consisting of SOQE, WSOQE, and FEQ provides a suitable *common logical foundation* for work that is done on all of these topics, as has also been observed in [48]. This perspective not only allows to relate these, at first sight different, problems to one another on a logical level, but also stimulates a cross-fertilization in terms of practical solution ideas, techniques, and algorithms.

Acknowledgements. We thank the anonymous reviewers for many helpful comments that led to an improvement of the presentation of this paper.

Furthermore we thank Luke Sanderson who dockerfied the original version of SCAN with help from the University of Manchester Open Source Software Club.

This research was funded in part by the Austrian Science Fund (FWF) 10.55776/P35787.

Disclosure of Interests. The authors have no competing interests to declare that are relevant to the content of this article.

References

1. Achammer, F., Hetzl, S., Schmidt, R.A.: Computing witnesses using the SCAN algorithm (Extended Preprint) (2025). Preprint at https://achammer.dev/research/cade2025-extended-preprint
2. Ackermann, W.: Untersuchungen über das Eliminationsproblem der mathematischen Logik. Math. Ann. **110**(1), 390–413 (1935). https://doi.org/10.1007/BF01448035
3. Alassaf, R., Schmidt, R.A., Sattler, U.: Saturation-based uniform interpolation for multi-modal logics. In: Fernández-Duque, D., Palmigiano, A., Pinchinat, S. (eds.) Advances in Modal Logic, vol. 14, pp. 37–58. College Publications, London (2022). http://www.aiml.net/volumes/volume14
4. Bachmair, L., Ganzinger, H., Waldmann, U.: Refutational theorem proving for hierarchic first-order theories. Appl. Algebra Eng. Commun. Comput. **5**, 193–212 (1994). https://doi.org/10.1007/BF01190829
5. Baumgartner, P., Waldmann, U.: Hierarchic superposition revisited. In: Lutz, C., Sattler, U., Tinelli, C., Turhan, A., Wolter, F. (eds.) Description Logic, Theory Combination, and All That. LNCS, vol. 11560, pp. 15–56. Springer (2019). https://doi.org/10.1007/978-3-030-22102-7_2
6. Behmann, H.: Das Auflösungsproblem in der Klassenlogik. Archiv für mathematische Logik und Grundlagenforschung **1**(1), 17–29 (1950). https://doi.org/10.1007/BF01976313, first of two parts
7. Behmann, H.: Das Auflösungsproblem in der Klassenlogik. Archiv für mathematische Logik und Grundlagenforschung **1**(2), 33–51 (1951). https://doi.org/10.1007/BF01982011, second of two parts
8. Bjørner, N., Gurfinkel, A., McMillan, K.L., Rybalchenko, A.: Horn clause solvers for program verification. In: Beklemishev, L.D., Blass, A., Dershowitz, N., Finkbeiner, B., Schulte, W. (eds.) Fields of Logic and Computation II - Essays Dedicated to Yuri Gurevich on the Occasion of His 75th Birthday. LNCS, vol. 9300, pp. 24–51. Springer (2015). https://doi.org/10.1007/978-3-319-23534-9_2
9. Brink, C., Gabbay, D.M., Ohlbach, H.J.: Towards automating duality. Comput. Math. Appl. **29**(2), 73–90 (1995)
10. Chen, J., Alghamdi, G., Schmidt, R.A., Walther, D., Gao, Y.: Ontology extraction for large ontologies via modularity and forgetting. In: Kejriwal, M., Szekely, P.A., Troncy, R. (eds.) Proceedings of the 10th International Conference on Knowledge Capture (K-CAP 1919), pp. 45–52. ACM (2019).https://doi.org/10.1145/3360901.3364424
11. Conradie, W., Goranko, V., Vakarelov, D.: Algorithmic correspondence and completeness in modal logic: I. The core algorithm SQEMA. Logical Methods Comput. Sci. **2**(1:5), 1–26 (2006)

12. Conradie, W., Ghilardi, S., Palmigiano, A.: Unified correspondence. In: Baltag, A., Smets, S. (eds.) Johan van Benthem on Logic and Information Dynamics, pp. 933–975. Springer (2014). https://doi.org/10.1007/978-3-319-06025-5_36
13. Delgrande, J.P.: A knowledge level account of forgetting. J. Artif. Intell. Res. **60**, 1165–1213 (2017). https://doi.org/10.1613/JAIR.5530
14. Doherty, P., Lukaszewicz, W., Szalas, A.: Computing circumscription revisited: a reduction algorithm. J. Autom. Reason. **18**(3), 297–336 (1997). https://doi.org/10.1023/A:1005722130532
15. Doherty, P., Łukaszewicz, W., Szałas, A.: General domain circumscription and its effective reductions. Fund. Inform. **36**(1), 23–55 (1998). https://doi.org/10.3233/FI-1998-3612
16. Doherty, P., Lukaszewicz, W., Szalas, A.: Computing strongest necessary and weakest sufficient conditions of first-order formulas. In: Nebel, B. (ed.) Proceedings of the Seventeenth International Joint Conference on Artificial Intelligence (IJCAI 2001), pp. 145–154. Morgan Kaufmann (2001)
17. Doherty, P., Szałas, A.: On the correspondence between approximations and similarity. In: Tsumoto, S., Słowiński, R., Komorowski, J., Grzymała-Busse, J.W. (eds.) RSCTC 2004. LNCS (LNAI), vol. 3066, pp. 143–152. Springer, Heidelberg (2004). https://doi.org/10.1007/978-3-540-25929-9_16
18. Eberhard, S., Hetzl, S., Weller, D.: Boolean unification with predicates. J. Log. Comput. **27**(1), 109–128 (2017). https://doi.org/10.1093/logcom/exv059
19. Ebner, G., Hetzl, S., Reis, G., Riener, M., Wolfsteiner, S., Zivota, S.: System description: GAPT 2.0. In: Olivetti, N., Tiwari, A. (eds.) IJCAR 2016. LNCS (LNAI), vol. 9706, pp. 293–301. Springer, Cham (2016). https://doi.org/10.1007/978-3-319-40229-1_20
20. Eiter, T., Kern-Isberner, G.: A brief survey on forgetting from a knowledge representation and reasoning perspective. Künstliche Intell. **33**(1), 9–33 (2019). https://doi.org/10.1007/S13218-018-0564-6
21. Engel, T.: Quantifier elimination in second-order predicate logic. Diplomarbeit, Fachbereich Informatik, Univ. des Saarlandes, Saarbrücken, Germany (1996)
22. Férée, H., van der Giessen, I., van Gool, S., Shillito, I.: Mechanised uniform interpolation for modal logics K, GL, and ISL. In: Benzmüller, C., Heule, M.J.H., Schmidt, R.A. (eds.) Automated Reasoning (IJCAR 2024). LNCS, vol. 14740, pp. 43–60. Springer (2024). https://doi.org/10.1007/978-3-031-63501-4_3
23. Gabbay, D., Ohlbach, H.J.: Quantifier elimination in second order predicate logic. S. Afr. Comput. J. **7**, 35–43 (1992)
24. Gabbay, D.M., Schmidt, R.A., Szałas, A.: Second-Order Quantifier Elimination. College Publications (2008)
25. Gonçalves, R., Knorr, M., Leite, J.: Forgetting in answer set programming: a survey. Theory Pract. Log. Program. **23**(1), 111–156 (2023). https://doi.org/10.1017/S1471068421000570
26. Goranko, V., Hustadt, U., Schmidt, R.A., Vakarelov, D.: SCAN is complete for all Sahlqvist formulae. In: Berghammer, R., Möller, B., Struth, G. (eds.) RelMiCS 2003. LNCS, vol. 3051, pp. 149–162. Springer, Heidelberg (2004). https://doi.org/10.1007/978-3-540-24771-5_13
27. Hetzl, S., Kloibhofer, J.: A fixed-point theorem for Horn formula equations. In: Hojjat, H., Kafle, B. (eds.) 8th Workshop on Horn Clauses for Verification and Synthesis (HCVS). Electronic Proceedings in Theoretical Computer Science, vol. 344, pp. 65–78. Open Publishing Association (2021). https://doi.org/10.4204/EPTCS.344.5

28. Hetzl, S., Kloibhofer, J.: An abstract fixed-point theorem for Horn formula equations (Abstract). In: Schmidt, R.A., Wernhard, C., Zhao, Y. (eds.) Proceedings of the Second Workshop on Second-Order Quantifier Elimination and Related Topics (SOQE). CEUR Workshop Proceedings, vol. 3009, pp. 59–60. CEUR-WS.org (2021)
29. Hoder, K., Kovács, L., Voronkov, A.: Interpolation and symbol elimination in vampire. In: Giesl, J., Hähnle, R. (eds.) IJCAR 2010. LNCS (LNAI), vol. 6173, pp. 188–195. Springer, Heidelberg (2010). https://doi.org/10.1007/978-3-642-14203-1_16
30. Hodges, W.: A Shorter Model Theory. Cambridge University Press (1997)
31. Khasidashvili, Z., Korovin, K.: Predicate elimination for preprocessing in first-order theorem proving. In: Creignou, N., Le Berre, D. (eds.) SAT 2016. LNCS, vol. 9710, pp. 361–372. Springer, Cham (2016). https://doi.org/10.1007/978-3-319-40970-2_22
32. Konev, B., Walther, D., Wolter, F.: Forgetting and uniform interpolation in large-scale description logic terminologies. In: Boutilier, C. (ed.) Proceedings of the 21st International Joint Conference on Artificial Intelligence (IJCAI 2009), pp. 830–835 (2009). http://ijcai.org/papers09/Papers/IJCAI09-142.pdf
33. Koopmann, P., Schmidt, R.A.: Forgetting concept and role symbols in $\mathcal{ALCH}$-ontologies. In: McMillan, K., Middeldorp, A., Voronkov, A. (eds.) LPAR 2013. LNCS, vol. 8312, pp. 552–567. Springer, Heidelberg (2013). https://doi.org/10.1007/978-3-642-45221-5_37
34. Koopmann, P., Schmidt, R.A.: Uniform interpolation of $\mathcal{ALC}$-ontologies using fixpoints. In: Fontaine, P., Ringeissen, C., Schmidt, R.A. (eds.) FroCoS 2013. LNCS (LNAI), vol. 8152, pp. 87–102. Springer, Heidelberg (2013). https://doi.org/10.1007/978-3-642-40885-4_7
35. Koopmann, P., Schmidt, R.A.: Uniform interpolation and forgetting for $\mathcal{ALC}$ ontologies with aboxes. In: Bonet, B., Koenig, S. (eds.) Proceedings of the Twenty-Ninth AAAI Conference on Artificial Intelligence (AAAI-2015), pp. 175–181. AAAI Press (2015)
36. Koopmann, P., Del-Pinto, W., Tourret, S., Schmidt, R.A.: Signature-based abduction for expressive description logics. In: Calvanese, D., Erdem, E., Thielscher, M. (eds.) Proceedings of the 17th International Conference on Principles of Knowledge Representation and Reasoning (KR 2020), pp. 592–602. AI Press (2020). https://doi.org/10.24963/kr.2020/59
37. Lin, F., Reiter, R.: Forget it!. In: Presented at the AAAI Fall Symposium on Relevance, New Orleans (1994)
38. Liu, Z., Lu, C., Alghamdi, G., Schmidt, R.A., Zhao, Y.: Tracking semantic evolutionary changes in large-scale ontological knowledge bases. In: Demartini, G., Zuccon, G., Culpepper, J.S., Huang, Z., Tong, H. (eds.) CIKM 2021: The 30th ACM International Conference on Information and Knowledge Management, pp. 1130–1139. ACM (2021). https://doi.org/10.1145/3459637.3482307
39. Ludwig, M., Konev, B.: Practical uniform interpolation and forgetting for ALC tboxes with applications to logical difference. In: Baral, C., De Giacomo, G., Eiter, T. (eds.) Principles of Knowledge Representation and Reasoning (KR 2014). AAAI Press (2014)
40. Martin, U., Nipkow, T.: Boolean unification - The story so far. J. Symb. Comput. **7**(3–4), 275–293 (1989). https://doi.org/10.1016/S0747-7171(89)80013-6
41. Nonnengart, A., Szałas, A.: A fixpoint approach to second-order quantifier elimination with applications to correspondence theory. In: Orłowska, E. (ed.) Logic at

Work: Essays Dedicated to the Memory of Helena Rasiowa, Studies in Fuzziness and Soft Computing, vol. 24, pp. 307–328. Springer (1998)
42. Odersky, M., et al.: An overview of the Scala programming language (2004). https://infoscience.epfl.ch/handle/20.500.14299/214698
43. Nonnengart, A., Ohlbach, H.J., Szałas, A.: Elimination of predicate quantifiers. In: Ohlbach, H.J., Reyle, U. (eds.) Logic, Language and Reasoning. Trends in Logic, vol. 5, pp. 149–171. Springer, Dordrecht (1999). https://doi.org/10.1007/978-94-011-4574-9_9
44. Peuter, D., Sofronie-Stokkermans, V.: Symbol elimination and applications to parametric entailment problems. In: Konev, B., Reger, G. (eds.) FroCoS 2021. LNCS (LNAI), vol. 12941, pp. 43–62. Springer, Cham (2021). https://doi.org/10.1007/978-3-030-86205-3_3
45. Rudeanu, S.: Boolean Functions and Equations. North-Holland (1974)
46. Schröder, E.: Vorlesungen über die Algebra der Logik, vol. 1. Teubner (1890)
47. Toluhi, D., Schmidt, R.A., Parsia, B.: Concept description and definition extraction for the ANEMONE system. In: Alechina, N., Baldoni, M., Logan, B. (eds.) Engineering Multi-Agent Systems (EMAS 2021), Revised Selected Papers. LNCS, vol. 13190, pp. 352–372. Springer (2021).https://doi.org/10.1007/978-3-030-97457-2_20
48. Wernhard, C.: The Boolean solution problem from the perspective of predicate logic. In: Dixon, C., Finger, M. (eds.) FroCoS 2017. LNCS (LNAI), vol. 10483, pp. 333–350. Springer, Cham (2017). https://doi.org/10.1007/978-3-319-66167-4_19

Partial Redundancy in Saturation

Márton Hajdu[1(✉)], Laura Kovács[1], and Andrei Voronkov[2,3]

[1] TU Wien, Vienna, Austria
marton.hajdu@tuwien.ac.at
[2] University of Manchester, Manchester, UK
[3] EasyChair, Manchester, UK

Abstract. Redundancy elimination is one of the crucial ingredients of efficient saturation-based proof search. We strengthen redundancy elimination by introducing a new notion of redundancy, based on *partial clauses* and *redundancy formulas*. The new notion allows us to recognize redundant clauses and inferences that cannot be recognized by standard redundancy elimination criteria. In a way, our notion blurs the distinction between redundancy at the level of inferences and redundancy at the level of clauses. We present a superposition calculus PaRC on partial clauses and prove that it is refutationally complete. We discuss the implementation of the calculus in the theorem prover VAMPIRE. Our experiments show the power of the new approach: we were able to solve 24 TPTP problems not previously solved by any prover, including previous versions of VAMPIRE.

1 Introduction

Modern theorem provers for first-order logic with equality use variants of the *superposition calculus* [39,30,6]. A key ingredient in superposition reasoning is the use of *simplification orders* on terms and clauses. Efficiency is achieved using a powerful concept of *redundancy*: a clause that is a logical consequence of smaller clauses in the search space can be removed from the search space. While checking whether a clause is redundant is undecidable, there are special cases, such as subsumption, which are easy to check and are widely used. The efficiency of superposition is evidenced by the practical performance of saturation-based provers, including E [40], VAMPIRE [26], and iProver [24].

C. Barrett and U. Waldmann (Eds.): CADE 2025, LNAI 15943, pp. 532–551, 2025.
https://doi.org/10.1007/978-3-031-99984-0_28

In this paper, we propose a powerful generalization of standard redundancy, called *partial redundancy*. In a nutshell, the idea is as follows.

Standard completeness proofs of superposition calculi with redundancy are carried out by studying the behavior of the set of ground instances of clauses in the search space [30]. A superposition inference with a premise C may produce a clause that makes some set S of ground instances of C redundant. If S is the set C^* of *all* ground instances of C, then C itself becomes redundant and can be removed. This property is used in standard redundancy criteria, for example, demodulation.

Interestingly, when S does not cover all ground instances of C, the fact that S is redundant can still be used. Suppose that we performed n inferences with C, making subsets $S_1, \ldots, S_n$ of C^* redundant. Then

1. If $C^* \subseteq S_1 \cup \ldots \cup S_n$, then C is redundant.
2. Suppose that we have an inference where (i) C is a premise; (ii) a substitution σ is applied to this premise in the inference, and (iii) $(C\sigma)^* \subseteq S_1 \cup \ldots \cup S_n$. Then this inference is redundant, too.

To capture this idea, we attach to each clause C a *redundancy formula*, which can be true or false on ground instances of C, or, equivalently, substitutions grounding for C. This formula expresses the fact that all ground instances of C that satisfy R are redundant. A *partial clause* $C\backslash R$ is a clause with a redundancy formula attached to it. Then (1) and (2) above become new redundancy criteria: one on clauses and one on inferences. Neither of these criteria has been used before.

To make this idea work, we need several ingredients:

1. a suitable collection of predicates that can be used in redundancy formulas;
2. an algorithm for checking that a redundancy formula is valid (if it is, C is redundant);
3. an algorithm for determining redundancy in inferences.

Note that neither algorithm has to be complete: we can implement sufficient conditions instead.

Motivating example. Let us illustrate our work with the following example. Consider binary function symbols f and h, a unary function symbol g, and constants a and b. Let $\succ$ denote a Knuth-Bendix simplification order [23] with constant weight function and precedence $f \gg g \gg h$. Let C be the clause $f(g(y), y) \approx g(h(x, y))$. The sides of the equation in C are incomparable w.r.t. $\succ$, so standard superposition reasoning has to consider both orientations of this equation. For example, for an arbitrary substitution σ that grounds C, superposition orients the equation in C right-to-left only if $x\sigma \succ y\sigma$ holds. Now, consider the clause $h(z, u) \approx h(u, z)$ and the following inference:

$$\frac{h(z,u) \approx h(u,z) \quad f(g(y),y) \approx g(h(x,y))}{f(g(y),y) \approx g(h(y,x))}$$

We can easily show that in the presence of $h(z,u) \approx h(u,z)$ and $f(g(y),y) \approx g(h(y,x))$, the right-to-left orientation of the equation in C is not needed anymore, since all instances $C\sigma$ s.t. $x\sigma \succ y\sigma$ are now redundant. In this case, we replace C with the partial clause $C \setminus x \succ y$ in the search space. As the right-to-left orientation of the equation in C is not needed anymore (item 2 above), we can simply remove the right-hand side of this equation from all term indices, avoiding potentially thousands of unnecessary inferences. ❑

Contributions. We extend superposition with *partial redundancy* by attaching redundancy formulas to clauses. Further,

1. We introduce the *partial redundancy calculus* PaRC using partial clauses and redundancy formulas (Section 3). We prove soundness and refutational completeness in Sections 4–5.
2. We demonstrate the strength of PaRC by introducing a generalization of demodulation (Section 6). We show that PaRC significantly reduces the number of superposition inferences performed during proof search.
3. We implemented PaRC in VAMPIRE and show that we could solve very hard problems that no other prover was able to solve before (Section 7).

2 Preliminaries

We work in standard *first-order logic with equality*, where equality is denoted by $\approx$. We use variables x, y, z, u, v, w and terms s, t, l, r, all possibly with indices. A literal is an unordered pair of terms with polarity, i.e., an equality $s \approx t$ or a disequality $s \not\approx t$. We write $s \dot{\approx} t$ for either an equality or a disequality. A *clause* is a multiset of literals. We denote clauses by B, C, D and reserve $\square$ for the *empty clause* that is logically equivalent to $\bot$.

An *expression* E is a term, literal, or clause. We also consider redundancy formulas and partial clauses to be expressions, introduced later (Section 3). An expression is called *ground* if it contains no variables. The set of all ground instances of an expression E is denoted E^*. We write $E[s]$ to state that the expression E contains a distinguished occurrence of the term s at some position. Further, $E[s \mapsto t]$ denotes that this occurrence of s is replaced with t; when s is clear from the context, we simply write $E[t]$. We say that t is a *subterm* of $s[t]$, denoted by $t \trianglelefteq s[t]$; and a *strict subterm* if additionally $t \neq s[t]$, denoted by $t \triangleleft s[t]$.

A *substitution* σ is a mapping from variables to terms, such that the set of variables $\{x \mid \sigma(x) \neq x\}$ is finite. We denote substitutions by θ, σ, ρ, μ, η. The application of a substitution θ on an expression E is denoted $E\theta$. A substitution θ is called *grounding for an expression* E if $E\theta$ is ground. A substitution θ is *more general* than a substitution σ if $\theta\eta = \sigma$ for some substitution η. A substitution θ is a *unifier* of two terms s and t if $s\theta = t\theta$, and is a *most general unifier (mgu)*, denoted $\mathsf{mgu}(s,t)$, if for every unifier η of s and t, there exists a substitution μ s.t. $\eta = \theta\mu$. We assume that the mgus are idempotent [2].

A binary relation $\rightarrow$ over the set of terms is a *rewrite relation* if (i) $l \rightarrow r \Rightarrow l\theta \rightarrow r\theta$ and (ii) $l \rightarrow r \Rightarrow s[l] \rightarrow s[r]$ for any term l, r, s and substitution θ. We write $\leftarrow$ to denote the inverse of $\rightarrow$. We call an ordered pair $l \rightarrow r$ a *rewrite rule* if (i) l is not a variable and (ii) l contains all variables that occur in r. A *rewrite system* R is a set of rewrite rules. We denote by $\rightarrow_R$ the smallest rewrite relation that contains R. A term l is *irreducible* in R if there is no r s.t. $l \rightarrow r \in R$. A *rewrite ordering* is a strict (irreflexive) rewrite relation. A *reduction ordering* is a well-founded rewrite ordering. We consider reduction orderings which are total on ground terms, that is, they satisfy $s \rhd t \Rightarrow s \succ t$; such orderings are also called *simplification orders*.

We use the standard definition of a *bag extension* of an ordering [15]. An ordering $\succ$ on terms induces an ordering on literals by identifying $s \approx t$ with the multiset $\{s, t\}$ and $s \not\approx t$ with the multiset $\{s, s, t, t\}$, and using the bag extension of $\succ$. We denote this induced ordering on literals also with $\succ$. Likewise, the ordering $\succ$ on literals induces the ordering on clauses by using the bag extension of $\succ$. Again, we denote this induced ordering on clauses also with $\succ$. The induced relations $\succ$ on literals and clauses are well-founded (resp. total) if the original relation $\succ$ on terms is too. In examples used in this paper, we assume a Knuth Bendix order (KBO) with constant weight [23].

Many first-order theorem provers work with clauses [40,24,26]. Let S be a set of clauses. An inference system $\mathcal{I}$ is a set of inference rules of the form

$$\frac{C_1 \quad \ldots \quad C_n}{C},$$

where $C_1, \ldots, C_n$ are the *premises* and C is the *conclusion* of the inference. We also use the notation $C_1, \ldots, C_n \rightarrow C$ for inferences. The inference rule is *sound* if its conclusion is the logical consequence of its premises, that is $C_1, \ldots, C_n \models C$. An inference system $\mathcal{I}$ is *sound* if all its inferences are sound. An inference system $\mathcal{I}$ is *refutationally complete* if, for every unsatisfiable clause set S, there is a derivation of the empty clause in $\mathcal{I}$.

3 The Partial Redundancy Calculus

We introduce the notion of *partial redundancy* and describe a general calculus, called PaRC, based on it. Soundness and completeness of PaRC are proved in Sections 4–5.

Let us first define the key notions of redundancy formulas and partial clauses. We assume to have a finite signature Σ consisting of function symbols and having at least one constant. As usual, the *term algebra* over Σ, denoted by $T(\Sigma)$, is the algebra with the universe consisting of the ground terms built from symbols in Σ and having Σ as the signature, such that the interpretation of every ground term t in $T(\Sigma)$ is t itself. We will consider *extensions of* $T(\Sigma)$ *by a finite set* $\mathcal{R}$ *of predicate symbols*, each one having a fixed interpretation. We will denote these extensions by $T_{\mathcal{R}}(\Sigma)$ and have their interpretations as *redundancy relations*.

Let us assume that we have a simplification order $\succ$ on terms. We consider $\succ$ to be a redundancy relation and assume that $\mathcal{R}$ contains the symbol $\succ$ interpreted as this simplification order. In general, we can also consider redundancy relations different from orderings. For the moment, we will leave the choice of suitable redundancy relations open. In a way, $T_{\mathcal{R}}(\Sigma)$ is a Herbrand interpretation, with the difference that relations in it are not taken from clauses.

Definition 1 (Redundancy Formula and Partial Clause). A *redundancy formula* R is an arbitrary first-order formula of $T_{\mathcal{R}}(\Sigma)$. A *partial clause* is an expression $C \setminus R$, where C is a clause and R a redundancy formula whose free variables occur in C. If σ is a substitution and R a redundancy formula, we write $\sigma \models R$ if every ground instance of $R\sigma$ is true in $T_{\mathcal{R}}(\Sigma)$. We write $\sigma \not\models R$ if $\sigma \models R$ does not hold. ❏

An example of a redundancy formula is $f(x) \succ y \vee y = x$. Note that we can use equality $=$ in redundancy formulas as in this example. In the sequel, we denote redundancy formulas by R, and partial clauses by $\mathcal{C}$ and $\mathcal{D}$, possibly with indices. We sometimes write C instead of $C \setminus \bot$. Logically, a partial clause $C \setminus R$ is the same as C. The intuitive semantics of partial clauses come from their use in saturation: when a partial clause $C \setminus R$ occurs in a search space, we know that all ground instances of C that satisfy R are redundant in this search space.

Let us introduce some abbreviations for redundancy formulas. Let s, t and l be terms. We will write $s \neq t$ for $\neg(s = t)$; $s \succeq t$ for $s \succ t \vee s = t$. If $s \mathrel{\dot{\approx}} t$ is an equality literal, we write $(s \mathrel{\dot{\approx}} t) \succ l$ for $s \succ l \vee t \succ l$ and $(s \mathrel{\dot{\approx}} t) \succeq l$ for $s \succeq l \vee t \succeq l$. If C is a clause $L_1 \vee \ldots \vee L_n$, we write $C \succ l$ for $L_1 \succ l \vee \ldots \vee L_n \succ l$, and $C \succeq l$ for $L_1 \succeq l \vee \ldots \vee L_n \succeq l$. We assume a literal selection function satisfying the standard condition on $\succ$ and underline selected literals.

Our Partial Redundancy Calculus (PaRC), dealing with partial clauses, is displayed in Figure 1.

4 Saturation with PaRC

This section explains how saturation algorithms work on partial clauses and concludes the completeness of PaRC. We assume a fixed signature Σ.

Definition 2 (Redundant Clause). A ground clause D is *redundant w.r.t. a set of clauses* S, if there are clauses $C_1, \ldots, C_n \in S$ s.t. $C_1, \ldots, C_n \models D$ and $D \succ C_i$ for all $1 \leq i \leq n$. ❏

Let C be a clause. Then C^* denotes the set of all ground instances of C. For a set S of clauses, the set S^* is defined as $\bigcup_{C \in S} C^*$.

Definition 3 (Saturation). A *saturation* $\mathbb{S}$ is a sequence of sets of partial clauses $S_0, S_1, \ldots$, such that S_0 is a set of partial clauses of the form $C \setminus \bot$, and for each i, we have one of the following cases:

1. S_{i+1} is obtained by adding to S_i the conclusion of a PaRC inference with premises in S_i. We then say that we *apply this inference at the step* S_{i+1}.

$$(\mathsf{Sup})\ \frac{\underline{l \approx r} \vee C_1 \setminus R_1 \quad \underline{s[l'] \mathrel{\dot{\approx}} t} \vee C_2 \setminus R_2}{(s[r] \mathrel{\dot{\approx}} t \vee C_1 \vee C_2)\sigma} \quad \text{where} \quad \begin{array}{l} (1)\ \sigma = \mathsf{mgu}(l, l') \\ (2)\ l' \text{ is not a variable} \\ (3)\ \sigma \not\models r \succeq l \\ (4)\ \sigma \not\models t \succeq s[l'] \\ (5)\ \sigma \not\models C_1 \succeq l \\ (6)\ \sigma \not\models C_2 \succeq s[l'] \text{ (if} \\ \qquad s[l'] \mathrel{\dot{\approx}} t \text{ is positive)} \\ (7)\ \sigma \not\models R_1 \\ (8)\ \sigma \not\models R_2 \end{array}$$

$$(\mathsf{EqRes})\ \frac{\underline{s \not\approx t} \vee C \setminus R}{C\sigma} \quad \text{where} \quad \begin{array}{l} (1)\ \sigma = \mathsf{mgu}(s, t) \\ (2)\ \sigma \not\models R \end{array}$$

$$(\mathsf{EqFac})\ \frac{\underline{s \approx t} \vee \underline{s' \approx t'} \vee C \setminus R}{(s \approx t \vee t \not\approx t' \vee C)\sigma} \quad \text{where} \quad \begin{array}{l} (1)\ \sigma = \mathsf{mgu}(s, s') \\ (2)\ \sigma \not\models t \succeq s \\ (3)\ \sigma \not\models t' \succ t \\ (4)\ \sigma \not\models C \succ s \\ (5)\ \sigma \not\models R \end{array}$$

Fig. 1. The PaRC calculus.

2. S_{i+1} is obtained from S_i by changing a partial clause $C \setminus R_1$ to $C \setminus R_1 \vee R_2$, such that for every substitution θ grounding for C, if $\theta \models R_2$, then $C\theta$ is redundant w.r.t. S_i^*.

We call clauses in S_0 the *initial clauses* of this saturation. We also refer to steps that apply an inference as *inference steps* and steps that update redundancy formulas as *redundancy steps.* ❑

To prove the completeness of PaRC, we introduce notions of fairness and persistent ground clauses, which are modifications of similar notions used in completeness proofs of superposition calculi [30]. In the sequel, we assume that $\mathbb{S}$ is a saturation $S_0, S_1, \ldots$ and denote by S_ω the set $\bigcup_{i \geq 0} S_i$. Let $C \setminus R$ be a partial clause and S a set of partial clauses. We define

$$(C \setminus R)^{\circledast} \overset{\mathsf{def}}{=} \{C\theta \mid C\theta \text{ is ground and } \theta \not\models R\};$$
$$S^{\circledast} \overset{\mathsf{def}}{=} \textstyle\bigcup_{C \in S} C^{\circledast}.$$

Definition 4 (Limit and Persistent Clause). The *limit* of a saturation $\mathbb{S}$ is the set of ground clauses $\bigcup_{i \geq 0} \bigcap_{j \geq i} S_j^{\circledast}$. We call a ground clause C *persistent* if C belongs to the limit. ❑

It is not hard to argue that a ground clause C is persistent if and only if there exists $i \geq 0$ such that for all $j \geq i$ we have $C \in S_j^{\circledast}$.

Definition 5 (Fair Saturation). A saturation $\mathbb{S}$ is *fair* if it has the following property. Suppose that

1. $D_1, \dots, D_n$ are persistent ground clauses;
2. there exists an inference $C_1 \setminus R_1, \dots, C_n \setminus R_n \to C\sigma$ and a substitution ρ such that for all $i = 1, \dots, n$ we have that $D_i = C_i\sigma\rho$.

Then $\mathbb{S}$ contains a step i such that $C\sigma \setminus \bot \in S_i$. ❑

Note that our notion of fairness is not a standard one: it reflects the fact that the redundancy formula attached to a clause C may change when we apply redundancy steps. Indeed, we can have a partial clause $C \setminus R_1$ that can be replaced by $C \setminus R_1 \vee R_2$, then replaced by $C \setminus R_1 \vee R_2 \vee R_3$, and so on. Our notion of fairness requires that we apply the rule to *some* of these partial clauses, but not necessarily to $C \setminus R_1$.

Our goal is to prove the soundness and completeness of the PaRC calculus.

Theorem 1 (Completeness). Let $\mathbb{S}$ be a fair saturation $S_0, S_1, \dots$. Then, S_0 is unsatisfiable if and only if the empty partial clause $\square \setminus \bot$ occurs in S_i for some i.

We will not give a full proof of Theorem 1, as it repeats standard completeness proof arguments. Instead, we give the sketch of the proof and consider a few representative cases in detail (Section 5), to illustrate how we deal with redundancy formulas and a slightly non-standard notion of fairness.[4]

5 Model Construction

We start this section by proving the soundness of PaRC.

Definition 6. Let C be a clause and S a set of partial clauses. We say that C *occurs in* S, or that S *contains* C (denoted by $C \hat{\in} S$) if there exists a redundancy formula R such that $(C \setminus R) \in S$. ❑

Lemma 1 (Soundness). Let C be a clause such that $C \hat{\in} S_\omega$. Then C is a logical consequence of the clauses in S_0. Hence, if $\square \hat{\in} S_\omega$, then S_0 is unsatisfiable.

To prove completeness (Theorem 1), we introduce several properties.

Lemma 2. If a ground clause C is redundant with respect to S_i^*, then for all $j \geq i$, this clause is redundant with respect to S_j^* and also with respect to $S_j^{\circledast}$.

Note that, as a consequence, a ground clause is redundant w.r.t. S_j^* if and only if it is redundant with respect to $S_j^{\circledast}$, for all $j = 0, 1, \dots$.

Definition 7 (Trace). The *trace* of a ground clause C is any finite set $\{C_1, \dots, C_n\}$ of persistent clauses such that $C_1, \dots, C_n \models C$ and, for all $i = 1, \dots, n$, we have $C \succeq C_i$. ❑

Let us prove that every ground instance of every clause in S_ω has a trace.

[4] Detailed proofs can be found in the extended version of this paper [20].

Lemma 3. Suppose that $C \mathrel{\hat{\in}} S_\omega$ and θ is a substitution grounding for C. Then $C\theta$ has a trace.

Lemma 4. Suppose that $(C \setminus R) \in S_i$, θ is a substitution grounding for C and $\theta \models R$. Then $C\theta$ is redundant w.r.t. S_i^*.

Now, as usual in completeness proofs, we will build an interpretation for the set of partial clauses S_ω by well-founded induction on the relation $\succ$ on terms and prove that this interpretation satisfies all persistent ground clauses.

We assume familiarity with standard notions of rewrite systems. Let I be a convergent ground rewrite system on terms of the signature Σ. We can consider I also as a first-order interpretation (or a factor-algebra of $T(\Sigma)$) by defining $I \models s \approx t$ if and only if s and t have the same normal form in I.

To define the model of S_ω, for each ground term l, we define two convergent rewrite systems I_l and $I_{\prec l}$. First, we set

$$I_{\prec l} \stackrel{\mathsf{def}}{=} \bigcup_{\{r \mid l \succ r\}} I_r.$$

We next define I_l using $I_{\prec l}$. Suppose that l is irreducible in $I_{\prec l}$ and there exist a partial clause $(\underline{l_1 \approx r_1} \vee C \setminus R) \in S_\omega$ and a substitution θ grounding for this clause such that

1. $l_1\theta = l$;
2. $l_1\theta \succ r_1\theta$;
3. $l_1\theta \succ C\theta$;
4. $\theta \not\models R$;
5. $I_{\prec l} \not\models C\theta$.

Then, we let $I_l \stackrel{\mathsf{def}}{=} I_{\prec l} \cup \{l \to r_1\theta\}$. If there is more than one partial clause $\underline{l_1 \approx r_1} \vee C \setminus R$ and substitution θ with this property, we can select an arbitrary one. In all other cases, we let $I_l \stackrel{\mathsf{def}}{=} I_{\prec l}$. Finally, we define

$$I_\omega \stackrel{\mathsf{def}}{=} \bigcup_l I_l.$$

Let us note some properties of this construction. They are used in many completeness proofs of variants of the superposition calculus (and are straightforward), so we will not prove them. In these properties, l, s, t are ground terms and C is a ground clause:

1. I_ω is non-overlapping and terminating, and so it is convergent.
2. Let $s \succ t$. Suppose that for every term r occurring in C, we have $t \succeq r$. Then $I_s \models C$ if and only if $I_t \models C$.
3. Suppose that for every term r occurring in C, we have $l \succeq r$. Then $I_\omega \models C$ if and only if $I_l \models C$.
4. Let $s \succ t$. Then t is irreducible in I_t if and only if t is irreducible in I_s and if and only if t is irreducible in I_ω.

5. If $s \succ t$ and s is irreducible w.r.t. I_ω, then $I_\omega \models s \not\simeq t$.

Let us now give a useful property of persistent clauses.

Lemma 5. Suppose that C is a ground clause, $C \in S_i^*$, and $I_\omega \not\models C$. Then there exists a persistent ground clause D such that $C \succeq D$ and $I_\omega \not\models D$.

We are now ready to conclude the completeness of PaRC with the following lemma.

Lemma 6. For every persistent ground clause B, we have $I_\omega \models B$.

Proof. We prove by induction on the ordering $\succ$ on clauses. By contradiction, suppose that this is not the case, then there is a persistent clause false in I_ω. Since $\succ$ is well-founded, then there is a persistent clause B that is minimal among persistent clauses false in I_ω.

We prove that this is impossible by finding a persistent clause that is false in I_ω and smaller than B. Here, we only prove a few representative cases. The full proof can be found in the extended version of this paper [20].

Case 1. *There is a step i, a partial clause $C \setminus R \in S_i$ and a ground substitution θ such that $C\theta = B$ and $\theta \models R$.*

By Lemma 4, we have that B is redundant in S_i^*. By Lemma 5, there exists a ground persistent clause D such that $B \succeq D$ and $I_\omega \not\models D$. Note that B is different from D since B is redundant, hence we have $B \succ D$. Thus, we have found a persistent false clause smaller than B.

Case 2. *B has the form $\underline{s' \not\simeq s'} \vee C'$.*

Note that in this case, we also have $I_\omega \not\models C'$. Since B is a ground instance of a clause occurring in the saturation, there exists a step i, a partial clause $(\underline{s \not\simeq t} \vee C \setminus R) \in S_i$, and a ground substitution θ such that $s\theta = t\theta = s'$ and $C\theta = C'$. Note that s and t are unifiable. Let $\sigma = \mathsf{mgu}(s, t)$. Since the saturation is fair, it has a step j, where the following rule is applied:

$$\frac{\underline{s \not\simeq t} \vee C \setminus R'}{C\sigma}\ (\mathsf{EqRes})$$

Note that by $\theta \not\models R'$ (since Case 1 does not apply), we also have $\sigma \not\models R'$ and side condition (2) of EqRes is satisfied. We have that $(C\sigma \setminus \bot) \in S_j$. But C' is a ground instance of $C\sigma$, so $C' \in S_j^*$. Using $I_\omega \not\models C'$ and Lemma 5, there exists a persistent ground clause D such that $C' \succeq D$ and $I_\omega \not\models D$. Note that we have $B \succ D$, so we have found a persistent false clause smaller than B.

Case 3. *B has the form $\underline{s' \not\simeq t'} \vee C'$.*

W.l.o.g. $s' \succ t'$. Since B is a ground instance of a clause occurring in the saturation, there exists a step i, a partial clause $(s \not\simeq t \vee C \setminus R_2) \in S_i$, and a ground substitution θ_2 such that $s\theta_2 = s'$, $t\theta_2 = t'$ and $C\theta_2 = C'$.

Subcase 3.1. *s' is irreducible in I_ω.*

In this case, $I_\omega \models s' \not\approx t'$ contradicts the assumption that $I_\omega \not\models B$.

Subcase 3.2. *s' is reducible in I_ω.*

In this case, s' contains a subterm l' such that for some ground term r', we have $(l' \to r') \in I_\omega$. Now B has the form $\underline{s'[l'] \not\approx t'} \vee C'$. Since $(l' \to r') \in I_\omega$, by construction we have that l' is irreducible in $I_{\prec l'}$ and there exist a partial clause $(\underline{l_1 \approx r_1} \vee C_1 \setminus R_1) \in S_\omega$ and a substitution θ_1 grounding for this clause such that $l_1\theta_1 = l'$, $l_1\theta_1 \succ r_1\theta_1$, $l_1\theta_1 \succ C_1\theta_1$, $\theta_1 \not\models R_1$ and $I_{\prec l'} \not\models C_1\theta_1$.

As usual, we assume that clauses have pairwise disjoint sets of variables, and we can define a substitution θ as a union of θ_1 and θ_2. Then θ will satisfy all properties we used for θ_1 and θ_2 above.

Suppose that there is a variable x in s such that $x\theta$ contains an occurrence of l'. Let θ' be a substitution identical to θ except that it maps x to the normal form of $x\theta$ in I_ω. Since for all variables y we have $y\theta \succeq y\theta'$ and $x\theta \succ x\theta'$, we also have $B = (s \not\approx t \vee C)\theta \succ (s \not\approx t \vee C)\theta'$. Note that $(s \not\approx t \vee C)\theta$ and $(s \not\approx t \vee C)\theta'$ are equivalent in I_ω, so $I_\omega \not\models (s \not\approx t \vee C)\theta'$. By Lemma 5, there is a persistent ground clause D such that $(s \not\approx t \vee C)\theta' \succeq D$ and $I_\omega \not\models D$. But then we also have $(s \not\approx t \vee C)\theta \succ D$, and therefore we have found a false persistent clause smaller than B.

Otherwise, there must be a subterm l in s such that $l\theta = l'$. Note that l and l_1 are unifiable. Let $\sigma = \mathsf{mgu}(l, l_1)$. Since the saturation is fair, it has a step j, where the following rule is applied:

$$\frac{\underline{l_1 \approx r_1} \vee C_1 \setminus R'_1 \quad \underline{s[l] \not\approx t} \vee C \setminus R'_2}{(s[r_1] \not\approx t \vee C_1 \vee C)\sigma}\ (\mathsf{Sup})$$

Conditions (3) and (5) of Sup are satisfied due to $l_1\theta_1 \succ r_1\theta_1$ and $l_1\theta_1 \succ C_1\theta_1$. Condition (4) of Sup is satisfied due to $s' \succ t'$. By assumption, we have $\theta \not\models R'_1$ and $\theta \not\models R'_2$, satisfying conditions (7) and (8) of Sup.

We have that $((s[r_1] \not\approx t \vee C_1 \vee C)\sigma \setminus \bot) \in S_j$. The ground clause $s'[r'] \not\approx t' \vee C'_1 \vee C'$ is an instance of $(s[r_1] \not\approx t \vee C_1 \vee C)\sigma$, so we have $(s'[r'] \not\approx t' \vee C'_1 \vee C') \in S^*_j$. It is also not hard to argue that $I_\omega \not\models s'[r'] \not\approx t' \vee C'_1 \vee C'$. Using this and Lemma 5, there exists a persistent ground clause D such that $(s'[r'] \not\approx t' \vee C'_1 \vee C') \succeq D$ and $I_\omega \not\models D$. Finally, we note that $B \succ (s'[r'] \not\approx t' \vee C'_1 \vee C')$, hence we have $B \succ D$, so we have found a persistent false clause smaller than B. ❑

6 PaRC Demodulation and Examples

In this section, we demonstrate how the PaRC calculus works and adapt some standard simplifications.

Definition 8 (Admissible Redundancy Formula). Let S be a set of partial clauses, C a clause, and R a redundancy formula. We say that R is *admissible for S and C*, if for every substitution σ grounding for C, if $\sigma \models R$, then $C\sigma$ is redundant w.r.t. S^*. ❑

Note that the definition of redundancy steps in saturation requires R_2 to be admissible for S_i and C. Let us now introduce a redundancy step that generalizes the standard simplifying inference *demodulation*.

Lemma 7. Let $S_0, \ldots, S_i$ be a saturation s.t. the step S_i applies an inference of the form

$$\frac{l \approx r \setminus R_1 \quad C[l'] \setminus R_2}{C[r]\sigma},$$

where $\sigma = \mathsf{mgu}(l, l')$. Consider the following redundancy formula:

$$R \stackrel{\text{def}}{=} \exists \bar{y}. \left(l = l' \land l \succ r \land C[l'] \succ l\right),$$

where $\bar{y}$ contains all free variables occurring in l and r but not in $C[l']$. Then R is admissible for S_i and $C[l']$.

We call a redundancy step that adds the redundancy formula R to $C[l'] \setminus R_2$ from Lemma 7 a *demodulation step.* Note that the first two conjuncts $l = l'$ and $l \succ r$ in R ensure that the existential quantifier can be eliminated. In our examples, we will use binary symbols f and h, a unary symbol g, constants a and b, and assume that $\succ$ is a KBO with precedence $f \gg g \gg h$ and a constant weight function.

Let us first illustrate a saturation simulating a standard demodulation inference with a demodulation step. The first example shows a saturation that results in a partially redundant clause.

Example 1. We show a saturation below, where each box contains clauses from a saturation step.

S_0		S_1		S_2	
1.	$f(a, b) \approx b$	1.	$f(a, b) \approx b$	1.	$f(a, b) \approx b$
2.	$f(a, y) \approx g(y)$	2.	$f(a, y) \approx g(y)$	2.	$f(a, y) \approx g(y)$
3.	$g(f(x, b)) \not\approx a$	3.	$g(f(x, b)) \not\approx a$	3.	$g(f(x, b)) \not\approx a \setminus x = a$
		4.	$g(g(b)) \not\approx a$	4.	$g(g(b)) \not\approx a$

We obtain S_1 by adding to S_0 the conclusion of the following superposition into clause 3 with clause 2:

$$\frac{f(a, y) \approx g(y) \quad g(f(x, b)) \not\approx a}{g(g(b)) \not\approx a}$$

We apply a demodulation step, generating the following redundancy formula based on the above inference:

$$\exists y. f(a, y) = f(x, b) \land f(a, y) \succ g(y) \land (g(f(x, b)) \not\approx a) \succ f(a, y)$$

The first conjunct of R simplifies to $a = x \land y = b$, so we can eliminate the quantifier to simplify the formula to:

$$x = a \land f(a, b) \succ g(b) \land (g(f(a, b)) \not\approx a) \succ f(a, b)$$

The second conjunct is true, and the third conjunct is $g(f(a,b)) \succ f(a,b) \lor a \succ f(a,b)$, which is also true. Hence, S_2 is a demodulation step adding the redundancy formula $x = a$ to $g(f(x,b)) \not\approx a$. Consider the following superposition in S_2 with clause 1 into clause 3:

$$\frac{f(a,b) \approx b \quad g(f(x,b)) \not\approx a \setminus x = a}{g(b) \not\approx a}$$

The unifier of the inference is $\sigma = \{x \mapsto a\}$, and the inference is not performed due to condition (4) of Sup, as $\sigma \models x = a$. We conclude this example by noting that the clause $g(b) \not\approx a$ can still be derived, by superposing with clause 1 into clause 2, and then superposing with the resulting clause into clause 4. ❑

The next example shows that PaRC can detect redundant *orientations* of equations.

Example 2. Consider the following saturation:

S_0			S_2	
1.	$h(z,u) \approx h(u,z)$		1.	$h(z,u) \approx h(u,z)$
2.	$f(g(y),y) \approx g(h(x,y))$	...	2.	$f(g(y),y) \approx g(h(x,y)) \setminus x \succ y$
			3.	$f(g(y),y) \approx g(h(y,x))$

We first obtain S_1 by performing the following superposition:

$$\frac{h(z,u) \approx h(u,z) \quad f(g(y),y) \approx g(h(x,y))}{f(g(y),y) \approx g(h(y,x))}$$

Then, we perform a demodulation step with the following redundancy formula:

$$\exists z,u.\, h(z,u) = h(x,y) \land h(z,u) \succ h(u,z) \land (f(g(y),y) \approx g(h(x,y))) \succ h(z,u)$$

This simplifies to $x \succ y$, which we add to clause 2 in S_1 to obtain S_2. The two sides of the equation in clause 2 are incomparable, so it is possible to perform superpositions into both sides and with both orientations of the equation in S_0 and S_1.

However, for any substitution σ s.t. $\sigma \models g(h(x,y)) \succ f(g(y),y)$, we also have $\sigma \models x \succ y$. Hence, when using clause 2 oriented right-to-left in a Sup inference in S_2,

1. if clause 2 is the left premise, then either condition (3) or (7) of Sup is violated, and
2. if clause 2 is the right premise, then either condition (4) or (8) of Sup is violated.

For example, we skip the following superposition with clause 2 into itself in S_2:

$$\frac{f(g(y),y) \approx g(h(x,y)) \quad f(g(y),y) \approx g(h(x,y))}{f(f(g(y),y),h(x,y)) \approx g(h(z,h(x,y)))}$$

❏

For the next example, we use the following lemma.

Lemma 8. Let $S_0, \ldots, S_i$ be a saturation s.t. there is a clause $C \setminus R$ in S_i and for each substitution θ grounding for $C \setminus R$, either $\sigma \models R$, or $\sigma \models s = t$ for some equation $s \approx t$ in C. Then $\top$ is admissible for S_i and $C \setminus R$.

The next example illustrates ground joinability [17] using PaRC.

Example 3. Consider the following saturation:

S_0			S_2	
1.	$f(z,u) \approx f(u,z)$	...	1.	$f(z,u) \approx f(u,z)$
2.	$g(f(x,a)) \approx g(f(a,x))$		2.	$g(f(x,a)) \approx g(f(a,x)) \setminus x \succ a$
			3.	$g(f(a,x)) \approx g(f(a,x))$

We perform the following superposition to obtain S_1:

$$\frac{f(z,u) \approx f(u,z) \quad g(f(x,a)) \approx g(f(a,x))}{g(f(a,x)) \approx g(f(a,x))}$$

S_2 is then obtained by adding $x \succ a$ to clause 2 using Lemma 7. We continue with the following clause sets:

S_3			S_5	
1.	$f(z,u) \approx f(u,z)$	...	1.	$f(z,u) \approx f(u,z)$
2.	$g(f(x,a)) \approx g(f(a,x)) \setminus x \succ a$		2.	$g(f(x,a)) \approx g(f(a,x)) \setminus x \succ a \vee a \succ x$
3.	$g(f(a,x)) \approx g(f(a,x)) \setminus \top$		3.	$g(f(a,x)) \approx g(f(a,x)) \setminus \top$
			4.	$g(f(x,a)) \approx g(f(x,a))$

For clause 3 in S_2, we have $\sigma \models g(f(a,x)) = g(f(a,x))$ for any substitution σ, so we change the redundancy formula of clause 3 to $\top$ by Lemma 8 to obtain S_3. We perform a similar superposition as the first and attach corresponding constraints to obtain S_5. Finally, we change the redundancy formulas of both clauses 2 and 4 to $\top$, again by Lemma 8. Hence, we obtain a clause set where all clauses except for clause 1 have redundancy formulas $\top$ and are identified as redundant. ❏

7 Implementation and Evaluation

Implementation. We implemented a variant of saturation in the VAMPIRE prover [26] to demonstrate the applicability of the PaRC calculus. Our implementation uses a standard saturation algorithm and partial clauses as follows:

1. At the beginning of saturation, every clause C is initialized as $C \setminus \bot$.
2. We perform PaRC inferences instead of standard superposition inferences, and as usual, skip inferences whose side conditions are violated.
3. If a PaRC inference is performed, we apply a redundancy step similar to demodulation steps (Section 6) and add a redundancy formula to the main premise of the inference.

We note that the added redundancy formulas might be slightly different from the one used in demodulation steps, corresponding to various demodulation variants used in VAMPIRE, controlled by options.

Fully checking PaRC side conditions from Figure 1 and handling redundancy formulas can be expensive. Our implementation uses several sufficient conditions to check these. Namely, we always checks side conditions (1)–(6) of Sup inferences, side condition (1) of EqRes inferences and side conditions (1)–(4) of EqFac inferences. Additionally, when adding redundancy formulas to partial clauses, we simplify these redundancy formulas, similarly to the examples of Section 6.

We introduce the following Boolean options in VAMPIRE to control PaRC:

1. The option `-crc` toggles checking *all* side conditions of the PaRC inferences, as well as attaching redundancy formulas to clauses when they contain tautological ordering constraints.
2. The option `-croc` depends on `-crc` being enabled, and allows adding redundancy formulas with non-tautological ordering constraints.
3. The option `-crs` depends on `-croc` being enabled, and toggles a more expensive case analysis on non-tautological ordering constraints, as in Examples 2 and 3.

Our implementation in VAMPIRE requires less than a thousand lines of code[5], as it utilizes existing efficient data structures: *code trees* [37] for checking equality constraints and *term ordering diagrams* for checking ordering constraints [19].

Experimental Setup. Our experiments used benchmarks from version 8.2.0 of the TPTP library [41], and were run using AMD Epyc 7502 2.5GHz processors and 1TB RAM. Each benchmark ran with a single core and 16GB of memory.

For our evaluation, we used a Spider-style strategy discovery [9]. This approach takes a set of problems (the *training set*), discovers sets of options (*strategies*) that solve these problems, and finds a sequence of strategies (*schedule*) that solves most of these problems given an instruction limit. Our training set consists of 5000 randomly selected CNF problems with equality from TPTP. The strategy discovery phase lasted 7 days, and the strategies collected solved 3300 of the 5000 problems. The collected strategies were then used to create two schedules[6] that greedily cover as many problems as possible:

1. the `baseline` schedule contains 285 strategies, all of them with `-crc`, `-croc` and `-crs` disabled,

[5] `https://github.com/vprover/vampire/tree/7deb7a5e2f08674992b6`

[6] `https://gist.github.com/mezpusz/cf07dbda3ee0c5eabebf391254222a70`

Table 1. Results for running the `baseline` and `modified` schedules for 300 seconds on the training and test sets.

set	number of benchmarks	`baseline`			`modified`		
		solved	uniques	avg.rating of uniques	solved	uniques	avg.rating of uniques
training	5000	3216	22	0.82	3269	75	0.88
test	15530	11612	94	0.61	11624	106	0.70
total	20530	14828	116	0.65	14893	181	0.77

Table 2. 16 highest-rated problems in the training and test sets, respectively, solved by the `modified` schedule and not solved by the `baseline` schedule. Problems with `Unknown` status are marked with †, the rest of the problems have status `Theorem/Unsatisfiable`.

Training set				Test set			
Problem	Rating	Problem	Rating	Problem	Rating	Problem	Rating
CAT030+3†	1.0	REL040+3	1.0	HAL001+1	0.94	ALG232+4	1.0
KLE130+1	1.0	REL040+4	1.0	LCL275-3	0.94	CAT030+2†	1.0
KLE156+2	1.0	REL040-4	1.0	NUN075+1	0.94	HWV088_1	1.0
LCL148-1	1.0	SET368-6	1.0	CSR036-10	0.95	ITP265_3	1.0
NUM090-1	1.0	SET546-6	1.0	LCL775-1	0.95	ITP285_4	1.0
NUM636+4	1.0	SEU443+2	1.0	REL040-3	0.95	ITP382_1	1.0
NUM660+4	1.0	SWV276-1	1.0	SET039-3	0.95	LAT368+1	1.0
NUM786+4	1.0	SWV978-1	1.0	LAT357+2	0.97	LCL646+1.015	1.0

2. the `modified` schedule has 342 strategies, containing 100 strategies with `-crc` enabled, 29 strategies with `-croc`, and 13 strategies with `-crs`.

We selected a *test set* to test the `baseline` and `modified` schedules. This set consists of selected TPTP benchmarks that are not in the training set and do not yield immediate errors (for example, higher-order benchmarks). We ran both schedules on the training set and the test set, with a 300-second timeout. Note that neither of the two schedules is fully executed within 300 seconds.

Our results are summarized in Table 1. The `modified` schedule solved 65 more problems, 53 in the training set and 12 in the test set. There were overall 181 unique solutions by the `modified` schedule. We show the 16 highest-ranking uniques solved in the two sets in Table 2.

We show more detailed statistics regarding PaRC inferences of `modified` runs in Table 3. The table displays for each option the distribution of ratios n/m for successful strategy runs with at least one PaRC inference performed, where n is the number of discarded PaRC inferences due to the corresponding option being enabled, and m is the number of performed PaRC inferences within that run. For example, there were 1313 successful strategy runs where `-crc` was enabled and at least one PaRC inference was performed, 514 of them did not discard any PaRC inferences, while 21 discarded more than 1.6 times more PaRC inferences than they performed.

Below, we list some benchmarks that `baseline` failed to solved, but `modified` succeeded by using our new techniques:

Table 3. Distribution of ratios n/m for successful strategy runs with at least one PaRC inference performed, where n is the number discarded PaRC inferences due to the corresponding option being enabled (`-crc`, `-croc` or `-crs`), and m is the number of performed PaRC inferences within that run.

option	total	0	(0,0.1]	(0.1,0.2]	(0.2,0.4]	(0.4,0.8]	(0.8,1.6]	> 1.6
`-crc`	1313	514	433	109	97	95	44	21
`-croc`	194	119	47	8	20	4	0	0
`-crs`	44	25	11	2	1	3	2	0

- `LAT243-1` (rating 0.73) was solved by performing only 22,533 inferences and discarding 238,768 inferences due to `-crc`,
- `GRP177-1` (rating 0.95) was solved by performing 59,243 inferences and discarding 45,839 and 39,516 inferences due to `-crc` and `-croc`, respectively,
- `SWV021-10` (rating 0.67) was solved by performing only 11 inferences and discarding 18, 2 and 17 inferences due to `-crc`, `-croc` and `-crs`, respectively.

To summarize, our evaluation shows that our initial implementation of the PaRC calculus is complementary to standard superposition reasoning, and it solves many problems that could not be solved without PaRC reasoning.

8 Related work

Model construction [5] is utilized in the majority of refutational completeness proofs for superposition-based calculi. Other notable approaches include forcing [34], semantic trees [22], and using closures for basic superposition [8] and closure redundancy [17]. Model construction has been used for proving completeness of higher-order superposition [10], and it has several formalizations [16,35]. Standard redundancy and static and dynamic completeness have been discussed in detail in [7,42]. Our work proves static and dynamic completeness of PaRC at the same time, using a slightly non-standard notion of fairness and a derivation process that is based on redundancy formulas. Using redundancy formulas circumvents the need to separate redundancy for clauses and inferences, simplifying some reasoning in the proof.

Constraints in first-order reasoning are mainly used to characterize subsets of ground instances of non-ground clauses [18]. Unification constraints serve various purposes, from restricting the search space by implementing basicness restrictions [8,32,28,22] or dealing with infinitary unifiers [11,10], to separating first-order and theory reasoning [36]. Ordering constraints also enforce and strengthen ordering rewriting [33] and are implicitly used in ground joinability and reducibility [17,1,27]. Our redundancy formulas in PaRC contain predicates similar to unification and ordering constraints. PaRC differs from other constrained systems in that redundancy formulas are not inherited, and they are compatible with standard redundancy elimination. This is due to the semantics of redundancy formulas, as they correspond to clauses on the ground level that are known to be redundant. Various algorithms and specialized data structures have been proposed to solve ordering constraints [12,25,31,13,29,38]. Common axiomatizations, such as associativity-commutativity (AC), enjoy more specialized handling [14,1].

More sophisticated restrictions on superposition inferences are special cases of connectedness [3] and ground connectedness [17]. These include, for example, blocking [4], compositeness [21] and general superposition [43,44]. Our framework generalizes such case analysis-based redundancy detection approaches since (partial) case analyses can be expressed as redundancy formulas. We note that our partial redundancy method is not limited to unification and ordering predicates.

9 Conclusion

We introduce partial redundancy to restrict quantified equational reasoning while retaining refutational completeness and full simplifications, resulting in the PaRC calculus. Our framework yields an alternative characterization of standard redundancy notions, using redundancy formulas, and opens up a new research direction in redundancy criteria. We implemented a variant of the PaRC calculus in the superposition theorem prover VAMPIRE. Our evaluation demonstrates that partial redundancy is efficient and complements current techniques. Future work includes finding new ways to apply our framework within first-order reasoning and beyond, such as theories and higher-order logic. Developing tighter integration in saturation and designing more efficient data structures that fit our constraint-solving purposes better is also a future work.

Acknowledgements. We are grateful to Martin Suda for his help in strategy discovery and building the portfolio schedules. This research was funded in whole or in part by the ERC Consolidator Grant ARTIST 101002685, the ERC Proof of Concept Grant LEARN 101213411, the TU Wien Doctoral College SecInt, the FWF SpyCoDe Grant 10.55776/F85, the WWTF grant ForSmart 10.47379/ICT22007, and the Amazon Research Award 2023 QuAT.

Disclosure of Interests. The authors have no competing interests to declare that are relevant to the content of this article.

References

1. Avenhaus, J., Hillenbrand, T., Löchner, B.: On Using Ground Joinable Equations in Equational Theorem Proving. Journal of Symbolic Computation (2003). https://doi.org/10.1016/S0747-7171(03)00024-5
2. Baader, F., Nipkow, T.: Equational problems. In: Term Rewriting and All That, chap. 4. Cambridge University Press (1998). https://doi.org/10.1017/CBO9781139172752
3. Bachmair, L.: Canonical Equational Proofs. Progress in theoretical computer science, Birkhäuser (1991). https://doi.org/10.1007/978-1-4684-7118-2

4. Bachmair, L., Dershowitz, N.: Critical Pair Criteria for Completion. Journal of Symbolic Computation (1988). https://doi.org/10.1016/S0747-7171(88)80018-X
5. Bachmair, L., Ganzinger, H.: On restrictions of ordered paramodulation with simplification. In: CADE (1990). https://doi.org/10.1007/3-540-52885-7_105
6. Bachmair, L., Ganzinger, H.: Equational Reasoning in Saturation-Based Theorem Proving. In: Automated Deduction: A Basis for Applications, vol. I, chap. 11. Springer (1998). https://doi.org/10.1007/978-94-017-0437-3
7. Bachmair, L., Ganzinger, H.: Resolution Theorem Proving. In: Handbook of Automated Reasoning, pp. 19–99. Elsevier and MIT Press (2001). https://doi.org/10.1016/B978-044450813-3/50004-7
8. Bachmair, L., Ganzinger, H., Lynch, C., Snyder, W.: Basic Paramodulation. Information and Computation (1995). https://doi.org/10.1006/inco.1995.1131
9. Bártek, F., Chvalovský, K., Suda, M.: Regularization in Spider-Style Strategy Discovery and Schedule Construction. In: IJCAR (2024). https://doi.org/10.1007/978-3-031-63498-7_12
10. Bentkamp, A., Blanchette, J., Tourret, S., Vukmirović, P.: Superposition for Full Higher-order Logic. In: CADE (2021). https://doi.org/10.1007/978-3-030-79876-5_23
11. Bhayat, A., Schoisswohl, J., Rawson, M.: Superposition with Delayed Unification. In: CADE (2023). https://doi.org/10.1007/978-3-031-38499-8_2
12. Comon, H.: Solving Symbolic Ordering Constraints. International Journal of Foundations of Computer Science (1990). https://doi.org/10.1142/S0129054190000278
13. Comon, H., Narendran, P., Nieuwenhuis, R., Rusinowitch, M.: Deciding the confluence of ordered term rewrite systems. ACM TOCL (2003). https://doi.org/10.1145/601775.601777
14. Comon, H., Nieuwenhuis, R., Rubio, A.: Orderings, AC-Theories and Symbolic Constraint Solving (Extended Abstract). In: Annual IEEE Symposium on Logic in Computer Science (1995). https://doi.org/10.1109/LICS.1995.523272
15. Dershowitz, N., Manna, Z.: Proving Termination with Multiset Orderings. Communications of the ACM (1979). https://doi.org/10.1145/359138.359142
16. Desharnais, M., Toth, B., Waldmann, U., Blanchette, J., Tourret, S.: A Modular Formalization of Superposition in Isabelle/HOL. In: ITP (2024). https://doi.org/10.4230/LIPIcs.ITP.2024.12
17. Duarte, A., Korovin, K.: Ground Joinability and Connectedness in the Superposition Calculus. In: IJCAR (2022). https://doi.org/10.1007/978-3-031-10769-6_11
18. Ganzinger, H., Nieuwenhuis, R.: Constraints and Theorem Proving, p. 159–201. Springer Berlin Heidelberg (2001). https://doi.org/10.1007/3-540-45406-3_4
19. Hajdu, M., Coutelier, R., Kovács, L., Voronkov, A.: Term Ordering Diagrams (extended) (2025). https://doi.org/10.48550/arXiv.2505.22181
20. Hajdu, M., Kovács, L., Voronkov, A.: Partial Redundancy in Saturation (extended) (2025). https://doi.org/10.48550/arXiv.2505.22213
21. Kapur, D., Musser, D.R., Narendran, P.: Only Prime Superpositions Need be Considered in the Knuth-Bendix Completion Procedure. Journal of Symbolic Computation (1988). https://doi.org/10.1016/S0747-7171(88)80019-1
22. Kirchner, C., Kirchner, H., Rusinowitch, M.: Deduction with Symbolic Constraints. Research report, INRIA (1990), `https://www.researchgate.net/publication/245850515`
23. Knuth, D.E., Bendix, P.B.: Simple Word Problems in Universal Algebras. In: Automation of Reasoning: 2: Classical Papers on Computational Logic 1967–1970. Springer (1983). https://doi.org/10.1007/978-3-642-81955-1_23

24. Korovin, K.: iProver — An Instantiation-Based Theorem Prover for First-Order Logic (System Description). In: IJCAR (2008). https://doi.org/10.1007/978-3-540-71070-7_24
25. Korovin, K., Voronkov, A.: Knuth-Bendix Constraint Solving Is NP-Complete. In: ICALP (2001). https://doi.org/10.1007/3-540-48224-5_79
26. Kovács, L., Voronkov, A.: First-Order Theorem Proving and Vampire. In: CAV (2013). https://doi.org/10.1007/978-3-642-39799-8_1
27. Löchner, B.: A Redundancy Criterion Based on Ground Reducibility by Ordered Rewriting. In: IJCAR (2004). https://doi.org/10.1007/978-3-540-25984-8_2
28. Lynch, C., Snyder, W.: Redundancy Criteria for Constrained Completion. In: RTA (1993). https://doi.org/10.1007/978-3-662-21551-7_2
29. Löchner, B.: Things to Know when Implementing KBO. Journal of Automated Reasoning (2006). https://doi.org/10.1007/s10817-006-9031-4
30. Nieuwenhuis, R., Rubio, A.: Paramodulation-Based Theorem Proving. In: Handbook of Automated Reasoning, chap. 7. Elsevier and MIT Press (2001). https://doi.org/10.1016/B978-044450813-3/50009-6
31. Nieuwenhuis, R.: Simple LPO constraint solving methods. Information Processing Letters (1993). https://doi.org/10.1016/0020-0190(93)90226-Y
32. Nieuwenhuis, R., Rubio, A.: Basic Superposition is Complete. In: ESOP (1992). https://doi.org/10.1007/3-540-55253-7_22
33. Nieuwenhuis, R., Rubio, A.: Theorem Proving with Ordering and Equality Constrained Clauses. Journal of Symbolic Computation (1995). https://doi.org/10.1006/jsco.1995.1020
34. Pais, J., Peterson, G.E.: Using forcing to prove completeness of resolution and paramodulation. Journal of Symbolic Computation (1991). https://doi.org/10.1016/S0747-7171(08)80130-7
35. Peltier, N.: A variant of the superposition calculus. Archive of Formal Proofs (September 2016), `https://isa-afp.org/entries/SuperCalc.html`
36. Reger, G., Suda, M., Voronkov, A.: Unification with Abstraction and Theory Instantiation in Saturation-Based Reasoning. In: TACAS (2018). https://doi.org/10.1007/978-3-319-89960-2_1
37. Riazanov, A., Voronkov, A.: Partially adaptive code trees. In: Logics in Artificial Intelligence (2000). https://doi.org/10.1007/3-540-40006-0_15
38. Riazanov, A., Voronkov, A.: Efficient Checking of Term Ordering Constraints. In: CADE (2004). https://doi.org/10.1007/978-3-540-25984-8_3
39. Robinson, G., Wos, L.: Paramodulation and Theorem-Proving in First-Order Theories with Equality, p. 298–313. Springer Berlin Heidelberg, Berlin, Heidelberg (1983). https://doi.org/10.1007/978-3-642-81955-1_19
40. Schulz, S., Cruanes, S., Vukmirović, P.: Faster, Higher, Stronger: E 2.3. In: CADE (2019). https://doi.org/10.1007/978-3-030-29436-6_29
41. Sutcliffe, G.: Stepping Stones in the TPTP World. In: IJCAR (2024). https://doi.org/10.1007/978-3-031-63498-7_3
42. Waldmann, U., Tourret, S., Robillard, S., Blanchette, J.: A Comprehensive Framework for Saturation Theorem Proving. Journal of Automated Reasoning (2022). https://doi.org/10.1007/S10817-022-09621-7
43. Zhang, H., Kapur, D.: Consider only General Superpositions in Completion Procedures. In: RTA (1989). https://doi.org/10.1007/3-540-51081-8_129
44. Zhang, H., Kapur, D.: Unnecessary Inferences in Associative-Commutative Completion Procedures. In: Mathematical Systems Theory (1990). https://doi.org/10.1007/BF02090774

Term Ordering Diagrams

Márton Hajdu[1(✉)], Robin Coutelier[1], Laura Kovács[1], and Andrei Voronkov[2,3]

[1] TU Wien, Vienna, Austria
marton.hajdu@tuwien.ac.at
[2] University of Manchester, Manchester, UK
[3] EasyChair, Manchester, UK

Abstract. The superposition calculus for reasoning in first-order logic with equality relies on simplification orderings on terms. Modern saturation provers use the Knuth-Bendix order (KBO) and the lexicographic path order (LPO) for discovering redundant clauses and inferences. Implementing term orderings is, however, challenging. While KBO comparisons can be performed in linear time and LPO checks in quadratic time, using the best-known algorithms for these orders is not enough. Indeed, our experiments show that for some examples, term ordering checks may use about 98% of the overall proving time. The reason for this is that some equalities that cannot be ordered can become ordered after applying a substitution (post-ordered), and we have to check for post-ordering repeatedly for the same equalities. In this paper, we show how to improve post-ordering checks by introducing a new data structure called *term ordering diagrams*, in short TODs, which creates an index for these checks. We achieve efficiency by lazy modifications of the index and by storing and reusing information from previously performed checks to speed up subsequent checks. Our experiments demonstrate the efficiency of TODs.

1 Introduction

Superposition-based theorem provers commonly use simplification orderings on terms to restrict their search space [17]. All top performing provers from the last CASC competitions [25] – Vampire [11], iProver [8], E [23], and Zipperposition [28] – use the Knuth-Bendix order (KBO) [7] and some also use the lexicographic path order (LPO) [6]. There is a linear-time KBO algorithm [15] and a quadratic-time LPO algorithm [18], so implementing ordering comparisons does not seem to be challenging.

We denote by $\succ$ the simplification order used by the superposition calculus, and we call an *ordering comparison* the operation of checking whether $s \succ t$ holds for two terms s and t. Although there are very efficient algorithms for ordering comparison, surprisingly, it can easily take up a significant part of a theorem prover's running time. For example, ordering comparison is required in the following frequently used inference rule called *demodulation*:

C. Barrett and U. Waldmann (Eds.): CADE 2025, LNAI 15943, pp. 552–569, 2025.
https://doi.org/10.1007/978-3-031-99984-0_29

$$\frac{l \approx r \qquad C[l\sigma]}{C[r\sigma]} \quad \text{where} \quad \begin{array}{l}(1)\ l\sigma \succ r\sigma,\\ (2)\ C[l\sigma] \succ (l \simeq r)\sigma,\end{array}$$

between a unit clause consisting of an equality $l \approx r$ and a clause $C[l\sigma]$ containing a subterm $l\sigma$, where σ is a substitution. We can remove the right premise $C[l\sigma]$ after applying this rule, so demodulation is very valuable for keeping the search space smaller.

Post-ordering checks with unordered equalities. Demodulation is applied only when the side condition $l\sigma \succ r\sigma$ is satisfied. Based on properties of simplification orders, this side condition always holds when $l \succ r$. A more challenging case is when $l \not\succ r$ and $r \not\succ l$ (we say that $l \approx r$ is *unordered*), and we repeatedly apply demodulation with the same left premise $l \approx r$ and different right premises. We call the comparison of $l\sigma$ and $r\sigma$ a *post-ordering check* to emphasize that $l \approx r$ is not pre-ordered. The number of required post-ordering checks can be very large. For example, if we have a unit equality problem (which is not unusual in algebraic reasoning) and generate 10^6 clauses, the number of demodulation inferences can be of the order of 10^{12}. Even if only 1% of all equalities are unordered, we still can have 10^{10} post-ordering comparisons. Further, while KBO has a linear time algorithm [15], it still takes a significant time compared to other algorithms used by a theorem prover (such as matching or unification). Improving post-ordering checks could thus further improve equational reasoning.

Equality retrieval with post-ordering checks. This paper focuses on retrieving equalities that become ordered after applying a substitution. This is used in implementing the superposition and demodulation rules, after the retrieval of candidate equalities of the form $l \approx r$, for applying these rules with the same left-hand side l. This can be formulated as the following problem.

THE POST-ORDERING PROBLEM

Given a finite set $\mathcal{E}$ of unordered equalities $l \approx r_1, \ldots, l \approx r_n$ with the same left-hand side and a substitution σ, *retrieve* from $\mathcal{E}$ equalities that satisfy $l\sigma \succ r_i\sigma$.

We can be interested in retrieving one, some, or all equalities. When this problem is used in demodulation, one normally first uses an index that retrieves a term l, and only then unordered equalities $l \approx r_1, \ldots, l \approx r_n$ that form the set $\mathcal{E}$. In this case, all equalities in $\mathcal{E}$ have the same left-hand side. We assume that the same set $\mathcal{E}$ of equalities can be repeatedly used for retrieval, interleaved with operations of adding new equalities to $\mathcal{E}$ or removing existing equalities from it. As such, the post-ordering problem becomes a *term indexing problem* [24], where the substitution σ is a *query substitution*.

Motivating Example. Let us illustrate the post-ordering problem using a KBO with a constant weight function. Let l and r_1 denote the terms $f(x, y)$ and $f(y, x)$, respectively, and let $l \approx r_1$ be an equality. Given a substitution σ, checking whether $l\sigma \succ r_1\sigma$ holds involves computing term weights and comparing symbol precedences of $f(x, y)\sigma$ and $f(y, x)\sigma$ recursively. Some of these operations are, however, independent of the substitution σ applied. For example, the weight of

$f(x,y)\sigma$ is the same as the weight of $f(y,x)\sigma$ independently of σ, so the weight check can be dropped. Simple analysis shows that checking $l\sigma \succ r_1\sigma$ can be simplified to an *equivalent* ordering check $x\sigma \succ y\sigma$. Note that this analysis has to be performed only once, so all consequent checks of $f(x,y)\sigma' \succ f(y,x)\sigma'$ for any substitution σ' can be immediately reduced to checking $x\sigma' \succ y\sigma'$.

We can do even better when we perform several consecutive checks. For example, suppose that we retrieve equalities in the same order and the next equality after $f(x,y) \approx f(y,x)$ is $f(x,y) \approx f(x,x)$. Then, if during the first check we established $y\sigma \succ x\sigma$, we can immediately conclude $f(x,y)\sigma \succ f(x,x)\sigma$.

Our contributions. This paper is based on ideas explained in the example above: (i) simplify ordering checks using the definition of KBO or LPO, and (ii) use the previous computation history to get rid of redundant checks. We bring the following contributions.

- We introduce a new data structure, called the *term ordering diagram (TOD)*, in Section 3.
- We describe TOD transformations in Section 4. These transformations use KBO/LPO properties and produce equivalent, yet more efficient TODs. [4]
- We propose an equality retrieval algorithm in Section 5 for solving the post-ordering problem using TODs. To the best of our knowledge, our work provides the first algorithm for efficiently solving post-ordering checks. It is also the first paper discussing runtime specialization of LPO checks, previously used for KBO ordering checks in [22] and earlier in [27,21] for other operations.
- We evaluate our work by implementing term ordering diagrams in VAMPIRE and report on our results in Section 6. The use of TODs in forward demodulation, that is, demodulation applied to newly generated clauses from previously stored unit equalities [11], has significantly contributed to VAMPIRE's success in the unit equality division (UEQ) of the CASC competition [25] in 2024.

2 Preliminaries

We work with a fixed signature $\mathcal{F}$ consisting of a finite set of *function symbols* with associated arities and consider an alphabet of *variables* $\mathcal{V}$; variables are not part of the signature. *Function symbols* are denoted by f, g, and variables by x, y, possibly with indices. *Terms* are defined in the standard way over $\mathcal{F} \cup \mathcal{V}$; variable-free terms are called *ground*. A *substitution* σ is a mapping from variables to terms, such that the set $\{x \mid \sigma(x) \neq x\}$ of variables is finite. We call a *simplification ordering* any ordering $\succ$ on terms that is

(1) *well-founded*: there is no infinite decreasing chain of terms $s_1 \succ s_2 \succ \ldots$,
(2) *stable under substitutions*: if $s \succ t$ then $s\sigma \succ t\sigma$,

[4] Detailed proofs can be found in the extended version of this paper [5].

(3) *monotonic*: for $f \in \mathcal{F}$ and terms $s_1, \ldots, s_n, s, t$ such that $s \succ t$, we have $f(s_1, \ldots, s_{i-1}, s, s_i, \ldots, s_n) \succ f(s_1, \ldots, s_{i-1}, t, s_i, \ldots, s_n)$,
(4) satisfies the *subterm property*: if t is a proper subterm of s, then $s \succ t$.

A *precedence relation*, denoted by $\gg$, is a total order on the signature $\mathcal{F}$. Given a precedence relation, a *weight function* is a function w from $\mathcal{F}$ to non-negative integers such that (i) $w(c) > 0$ for all constants c and (ii) if $w(f) = 0$ and f is unary, then f is the greatest element w.r.t. $\gg$. We will refer to $w(f)$ as the *weight* of f. We denote by w_0 the smallest weight of constants. For $p \in \mathcal{F} \cup \mathcal{V}$, we write $|t|_p$ to denote the *number of occurrences* of a variable or a symbol p in a term t. For example, $|f(x,x)|_f = 1$, $|f(x,x)|_x = 2$ and $f(x,x)_y = 0$. Let $\mathcal{P}(\mathcal{V})$ be the set of linear expressions over $\mathcal{V}$ with integer coefficients. The *weight of a term* t, denoted by $|t|$, is a linear expression in $\mathcal{P}(\mathcal{V})$ defined as:

$$|t| \stackrel{\mathsf{def}}{=} \sum_{f \in \mathcal{F}} |t|_f \cdot w(f) + \sum_{x \in \mathcal{V}} |t|_x \cdot x$$

A substitution σ can also be considered as a mapping from linear expressions to linear expressions, as follows:

$$\sigma(\alpha_0 + \alpha_1 \cdot x_1 + \ldots + \alpha_n \cdot x_n) \stackrel{\mathsf{def}}{=} \alpha_0 + \alpha_1 \cdot |x_1\sigma| + \ldots + \alpha_n \cdot |x_n\sigma|.$$

For example, if $w(f) = 2$, $w(a) = 1$ and $\sigma = \{x \mapsto a\}$, then $|f(x,x)| = 2 \cdot x + 2$ and $\sigma(|f(x,x)|) = \sigma(2 \cdot x + 2) = 2 \cdot |x\sigma| + 2 = 4$. It is not hard to argue that $|t\sigma|$ $= \sigma(|t|)$. Let $e \in \mathcal{P}(\mathcal{V})$ be a linear expression. We call a substitution σ *grounding* for e if $\sigma(e)$ does not contain variables and $|x\sigma| \geq w_0$ for all $x \in \mathcal{V}$ such that $|x\sigma|$ is a constant. We write $e > 0$ if $\sigma(e) > 0$ for all grounding substitutions σ for e. We write $e \gtrsim 0$ if $\sigma(e) \geq 0$ for all grounding substitution σ for e.

The *Knuth-Bendix order (KBO)*, denoted by $\succ_{\mathsf{kbo}}$, is parameterized by a precedence relation $\gg$ and a weight function w. For terms s, t, we have $s \succ_{\mathsf{kbo}} t$ if:

(K1) $|s| - |t| > 0$, or
(K2) $|s| - |t| \gtrsim 0$, $s = f(s_1, ..., s_n)$, $t = g(t_1, ..., t_m)$ and $f \gg g$, or
(K3) $|s| - |t| \gtrsim 0$, $s = f(s_1, ..., s_n)$, $t = f(t_1, ..., t_n)$ and there exists $1 \leq i \leq n$ such that $s_i \succ_{\mathsf{kbo}} t_i$ and $s_j = t_j$ for all $1 \leq j < i$.

The *lexicographic path order (LPO)*, denoted by $\succ_{\mathsf{lpo}}$, is parameterized by a precedence relation $\gg$. Let s, t be terms with $s = f(s_1, ..., s_n)$. We write $s \succ_{\mathsf{lpo}} t$ if:

(L1) $t = f(t_1, ..., t_n)$ and there exists $1 \leq i \leq n$ s.t. $s_j = t_j$ for $1 \leq j < i$, $s_i \succ_{\mathsf{lpo}} t_i$, and $s \succ_{\mathsf{lpo}} t_k$ for $i < k \leq n$, or
(L2) $t = g(t_1, ..., t_m)$, $f \gg g$ and $s \succ_{\mathsf{lpo}} t_i$ for $1 \leq i \leq m$, or
(L3) $s_i \succeq_{\mathsf{lpo}} t$ for some $1 \leq i \leq n$.

It is known that every instance of LPO and KBO is a simplification order.

3 Term Ordering Diagram – TOD

To solve the post-ordering problem, we introduce the *term ordering diagram (TOD)* data structure (Definition 1). For retrieving equalities using TODs, we will need the following two operations on substitutions.

1. Given two terms s and t, compare $s\sigma$ and $t\sigma$ using $\succ$. We call the expression $s >^? t$ a *term comparison*. We consider a substitution σ as a mapping from term comparisons to the set of values $\{>, =, \not\gtrsim\}$, as follows:

$$\sigma(s >^? t) \stackrel{\text{def}}{=} \begin{cases} >, & \text{if } s\sigma \succ t\sigma, \\ =, & \text{if } s\sigma = t\sigma, \\ \not\gtrsim, & \text{otherwise.} \end{cases}$$

2. Given a linear expression e, check the sign of the linear expression $\sigma(e)$. We call the expression $e \geq^? 0$ a *positivity check*. We consider a substitution σ as a mapping from positivity checks to the set of values $\{>, \geq, \not\gtrsim\}$, as follows:

$$\sigma(e \geq^? 0) \stackrel{\text{def}}{=} \begin{cases} >, & \text{if } \sigma(e) > 0, \\ \geq, & \text{if } \sigma(e) \gtrsim 0, \\ \not\gtrsim, & \text{otherwise.} \end{cases}$$

   Note that positivity checks are only defined for KBO.

Before defining TODs, we illustrate how we solve the post-ordering problem.

Example 1. Let σ be a query substitution and $l \stackrel{\text{def}}{=} f(x, y)$, $r_1 \stackrel{\text{def}}{=} f(y, x)$ be terms. The rooted directed graph of Figure 1(a) illustrates the two key operations for retrieving the equality $l \approx r_1$ if $f(x, y)\sigma \succ f(y, x)\sigma$ holds. We first evaluate the *term comparison* $f(x, y) >^? f(y, x)$ in the top node. If $\sigma(f(x, y) >^? f(y, x))$ evaluates to $>$, the computation proceeds to the bottom node, which contains the equality $l \approx r_1$, which is then included in the result of the retrieval.

The evaluation of $\sigma(f(x, y) >^? f(y, x))$ in Figure 1(a) uses KBO, which in turn computes the linear expression $|f(x, y)| - |f(y, x)|$, performs a *positivity check* and proceeds with one of the subcases (K1)–(K3). The linear expression is 0 as both terms have the same number of f, x, and y symbols. Hence, the positivity check always results in $\geq$, which rules out subcase (K1). Similarly, (K2) is violated, as $f(x, y)$ and $f(y, x)$ both have f as top-most symbol.

Note that (K1) and (K2) are not applicable *regardless of the query substitution* σ, hence we can simplify $f(x, y)\sigma \succ f(y, x)\sigma$ into $(x \succ y \vee (x = y \wedge y \succ x))\sigma$. As $(x = y \wedge y \succ x)\sigma$ is false, this further simplifies into $(x \succ y)\sigma$. The term comparison $f(x, y) >^? f(y, x)$ of Figure 1(a) is thus turned into the (cheaper) term comparison $x >^? y$ shown in Figure 1(b).

Let us now consider an additional equality $l \approx r_2$, with $r_2 \stackrel{\text{def}}{=} f(x, x)$. Figure 1(c) displays the steps of retrieving $l \approx r_2$ if $f(x, y)\sigma \succ f(x, x)\sigma$ holds. Similarly to Figure 1(a), the *term comparison* $f(x, y) >^? f(x, x)$ is simplified using KBO properties into $(y - x > 0 \vee (y - x \gtrsim 0 \wedge y \succ x))\sigma$.

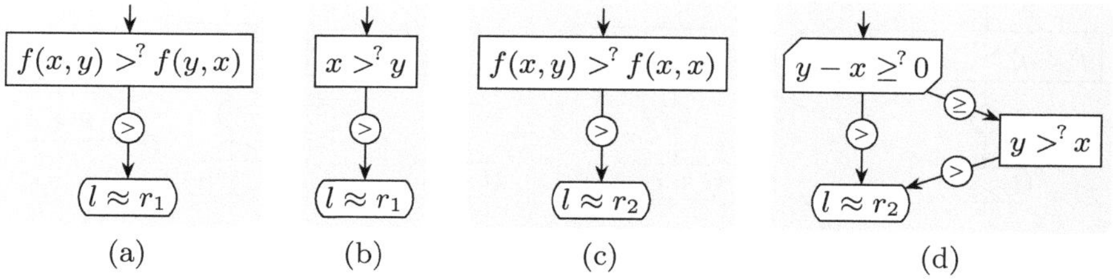

Fig. 1. Equality retrievals, where $l \stackrel{\text{def}}{=} f(x, y)$, $r_1 \stackrel{\text{def}}{=} f(y, x)$ and $r_2 \stackrel{\text{def}}{=} f(x, x)$. (a) and (b) show retrieval of $l \approx r_1$, where (a) contains a term comparison $l >^? r_1$ and (b) is a simplified version of (a) with term comparison $x >^? y$. Further, (c) and (d) show retrieval of $l \approx r_2$, where (c) contains term comparison $l >^? r_2$ and (d) is a simplified version of (c) with a positivity check $y - x \geq^? 0$ and term comparison $y >^? x$.

The simplified computation is depicted in Figure 1(d), where we first perform a *positivity check* $y - x \geq^? 0$, corresponding to deciding which of $\sigma(y - x) > 0$ or $\sigma(y - x) \gtrsim 0$ hold in the above formula, then performing at most one more term comparison. The computation of Figure 1(d) is more efficient than the one in Figure 1(c) because we avoid the computation of the linear expression $|f(x, y)| - |f(x, x)|$ and as well as some intermediate term comparisons. ❑

Example 1 shows that interleaving term comparisons and positivity checks can simplify, and hence speed up, term ordering checks. Let us now give formal definitions. We will use standard graph-theoretic notions related to directed acyclic graphs (dags), trees, and paths in a graph.

Definition 1 (Term Ordering Diagram – TOD). A *term ordering diagram* (TOD) is a directed acyclic graph $\mathcal{T}$ which contains five kinds of nodes:

(1) A single *root node*, so that every node is reachable from the root node. The root node has one outgoing edge.
(2) A single *exit node*, reachable from every node.
(3) A *term comparison node* is labeled by a term comparison $s >^? t$ and has three outgoing edges, labeled by $>$, $=$, and $\not\geq$.
(4) A *positivity check node* is labeled by a positivity check $e \geq^? 0$ and has three outgoing edges, labeled by $>$, $\geq$, and $\not\geq$.
(5) A *success node* is labeled by an equality $l \approx r$ and has one outgoing edge.❑

We collectively refer to the term comparison nodes and positivity check nodes as *evaluation nodes*. The idea is that we evaluate the substitution in these nodes and follow the node label resulting from the evaluation. Note that the exit node and its incoming edges are usually omitted when displaying a TOD (as in Figure 1). To retrieve equalities towards solving the post-ordering problem, we traverse a TOD as follows.

Definition 2 (TOD Traversal). Let σ be a query substitution and $\mathcal{T}$ a TOD. The $\mathcal{T}$ *traversal for* σ is the path in $\mathcal{T}$ from its root to its exit node so that:

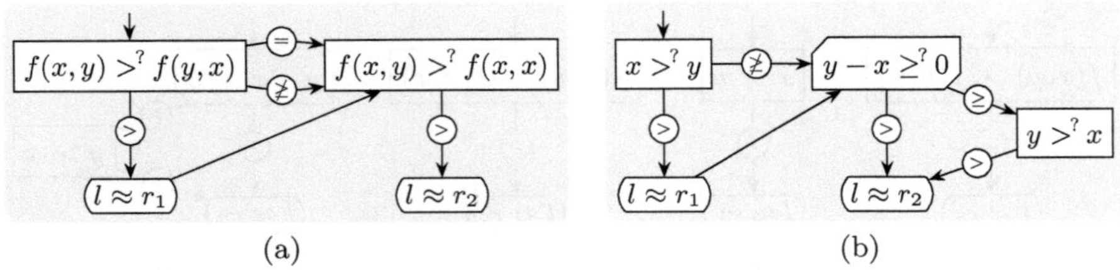

Fig. 2. Retrieving multiple equalities, where $l \stackrel{\text{def}}{=} f(x,y)$, $r_1 \stackrel{\text{def}}{=} f(y,x)$ and $r_2 \stackrel{\text{def}}{=} f(x,x)$.

(1) If the path contains a term comparison node labeled by $s >^? t$, then the path also contains the outgoing edge of this node labeled by $\sigma(s >^? t)$.
(2) If the path contains a positivity check node labeled by $e \geq^? 0$, then the path also contains the outgoing edge of this node labeled by $\sigma(e \geq^? 0)$.

The *success set of the $\mathcal{T}$ traversal for σ* is the set of labels of all success nodes on this path; we also refer to it as *the success set of σ in $\mathcal{T}$*. For any non-exit node in a traversal, we refer to its *next edge* and *next node*.

For a node n labeled by c, where c is either a term comparison or a positivity check, we say that the node n *forces an edge label* ℓ, if for every query substitution σ, if the $\mathcal{T}$ traversal for σ reaches n, then $\sigma(c) = \ell$. ❑

We use a TOD to perform term ordering checks only when it is necessary. Key to this are TOD transformations (Section 4): given a TOD $\mathcal{T}_1$, we transform $\mathcal{T}_1$ into an equivalent TOD $\mathcal{T}_2$, so that $\mathcal{T}_2$ can be traversed faster, making ordering checks cheaper. The efficiency gain in $\mathcal{T}_2$ traversal comes by replacing $\mathcal{T}_1$ checks with less expensive ones or removing redundant checks of $\mathcal{T}_1$. Importantly, our TOD transformations on $\mathcal{T}_1$ are performed while we traverse $\mathcal{T}_1$ for a specific query substitution, as shown in Example 2.

Example 2. Consider again $l \stackrel{\text{def}}{=} f(x,y)$, $r_1 \stackrel{\text{def}}{=} f(y,x)$ and $r_2 \stackrel{\text{def}}{=} f(x,x)$. Let σ be a query substitution. Figure 2(a) shows the sequence of steps for retrieving $l \approx r_1$ if $(l \succ r_1)\sigma$, and then retrieving $l \approx r_2$ if $(l \succ r_2)\sigma$. Similarly to Figures 1(a) and (c), we can modify Figure 2(a) into its more efficient version displayed in Figure 2(b). However, in Figure 2(b) we implement stronger TOD modifications: in the (second) retrieval of $l \approx r_2$ we use information from the (first) retrieval of $l \approx r_1$. For example, if $x\sigma = y\sigma$, the evaluation of $x >^? y$ in Figure 2(b) results in neither $l \approx r_1$ nor $l \approx r_2$ retrieved. This evaluation is more efficient compared to its equivalent version in Figure 2(a) where both $f(x,y) >^? f(y,x)$ and $f(x,y) >^? f(x,x)$ have to be evaluated to obtain the same result. ❑

Examples 1–2 show that *we transform a TOD while we are traversing it.* This is done for two reasons. (i) First, term comparisons may involve expensive computations, for example, when we deal with linear expressions (as shown in Example 1). When we compute a linear expression, we modify the TOD to have a corresponding positivity check node, so that on the next traversal, if we reach the same node, we do not compute the linear expression again. (ii) Second, our

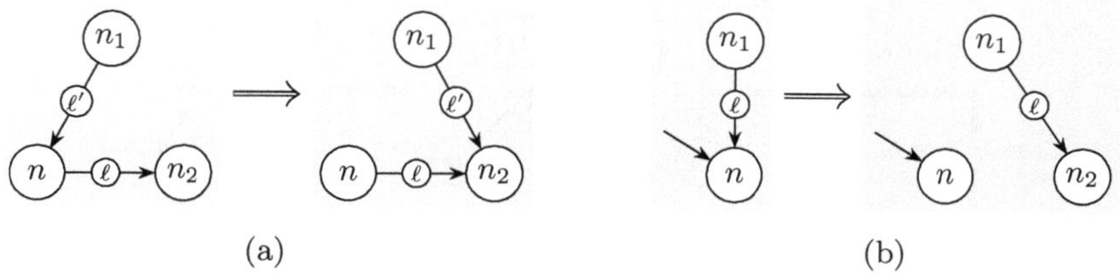

Fig. 3. Generic transformations on TODs: (a) *redundant node removal*, where node n forces label ℓ; and (b) *node replication*, where n_2 is an exact copy of a non-exit node n that has multiple incoming edges.

transformations are *lazy* – we only modify nodes in a TOD when we reach them during traversal. The reason for this is that modifying TODs is expensive due to KBO/LPO checks; hence, these modifications should not be performed for nodes that will never be visited. Despite modifying TODs, we do not change their semantics: our TOD transformations (Section 4) yield equivalent TODs.

Definition 3 (TOD Equivalence). Two TODs $\mathcal{T}_1$ and $\mathcal{T}_2$ are *equivalent* if for every substitution σ, the success sets of σ in $\mathcal{T}_1$ and $\mathcal{T}_2$ coincide. ❑

4 TOD Transformations

We explain our TOD transformations via a sequence of subgraph replacements and show how TOD equivalences are preserved. Replacements are performed while visiting specific nodes n in the TOD, depending on the node label. As such, some replacements are *specific to KBO/LPO* constraints (Figures 4–5), whereas others are *generic* (Figure 3), independent of the ordering. Figure 3 summarizes our generic TOD transformations, as detailed below:

- Figure 3(a) corresponds to a *redundant node removal*, where n forces ℓ. Simply removing nodes might violate TOD properties: as n may have no incoming edges, the existence of a single root node in a TOD is not fulfilled. In such cases, we also remove n from the TOD. Generally, if a redundant node removal introduces a node with no incoming edges, we repeatedly remove such nodes.
- Figure 3(b) shows a *node replication*, where n is a non-exit node with multiple incoming edges and n_2 is the exact copy of n with the same outgoing edges.

Our *KBO and LPO transformations* on TODs are shown Figures 4 and 5, respectively. Here, we denote by s a term $f(s_1, \ldots, s_k)$, also written as $f(\bar{s})$, with $k \geq 0$. Similarly, t is a term $g(t_1, \ldots, t_m)$, also written as $g(\bar{t})$, with $m \geq 0$. Note that in Figure 5, if $f \gg g$ and $m = 0$, the node n_1 replaces the top node; conversely, in case of $g \gg f$ and $k = 0$, the node n_3 replaces the top node; finally, if $f = g$ and $k = 0$, then the node n_2 replaces the top node.

Theorem 1 (Correctness of TOD Transformations). *(1) Every sequence of TOD transformations terminates. (2) Every TOD transformation of Figures 3–5 preserves TOD equivalence.*

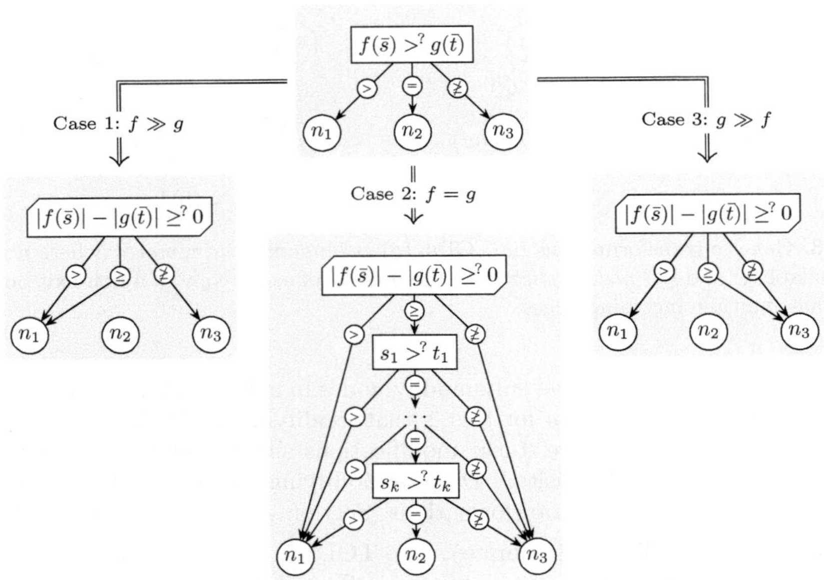

Fig. 4. KBO transformations on TODs.

Proof. (1) For proving *termination*, we introduce a well-founded order on TODs and show that every transformation replaces a TOD by a smaller one. In the proof, we use (well-founded) finite multiset extensions of (well-founded) orders.

We first introduce a mapping μ from nodes to finite multisets of terms as:

(i) If n is a term comparison node $s >^? t$, then $\mu(n)$ is the multiset $\{s, t\}$.
(ii) For any other node n, we define $\mu(n)$ to be the empty multiset.

Let us also define an order $>_\mu$ on nodes as follows: $n_2 >_\mu n_1$ if $\mu(n_2)$ is greater than $\mu(n_1)$ in the multiset extension of the order $\succ$ on terms. Note that $>_\mu$ is well-founded, since μ embeds it in the multiset extension of a well-founded order.

For every path π in a TOD, we denote by $\mu(\pi)$ the multiset consisting of elements $\mu(n)$ for all nodes n in π. We define an ordering, also denoted by $>_\mu$, on paths as follows: $\pi_2 >_\mu \pi_1$ if $\mu(\pi_2)$ is greater than $\mu(\pi_1)$ in the multiset extension of the order $>_\mu$ on nodes. Again, $>_\mu$ is well-founded, since it can be embedded to the multiset extension of a well-founded order.

Finally, for a TOD $\mathcal{T}$, we denote by $\mu(\mathcal{T})$ the multiset consisting of all multisets $\mu(\pi)$, where π is a path from the root node in $\mathcal{T}$. We also define an ordering $>_\mu$ on TODs by letting $\mathcal{T}_2 >_\mu \mathcal{T}_1$ if $\mu(\mathcal{T}_2) > \mu(\mathcal{T}_1)$. Using the same arguments as before, we conclude that $>_\mu$ on TODs is well-founded, too.

For every transformation apart from node replication that changes a TOD $\mathcal{T}$ to a TOD $\mathcal{T}'$, we have that $\mathcal{T} >_\mu \mathcal{T}'$, which implies termination. The proof is by routine inspection of transformations. For example for the case $f = g$ of the LPO transformations (last transformation of Figure 5), we replace a path with a term

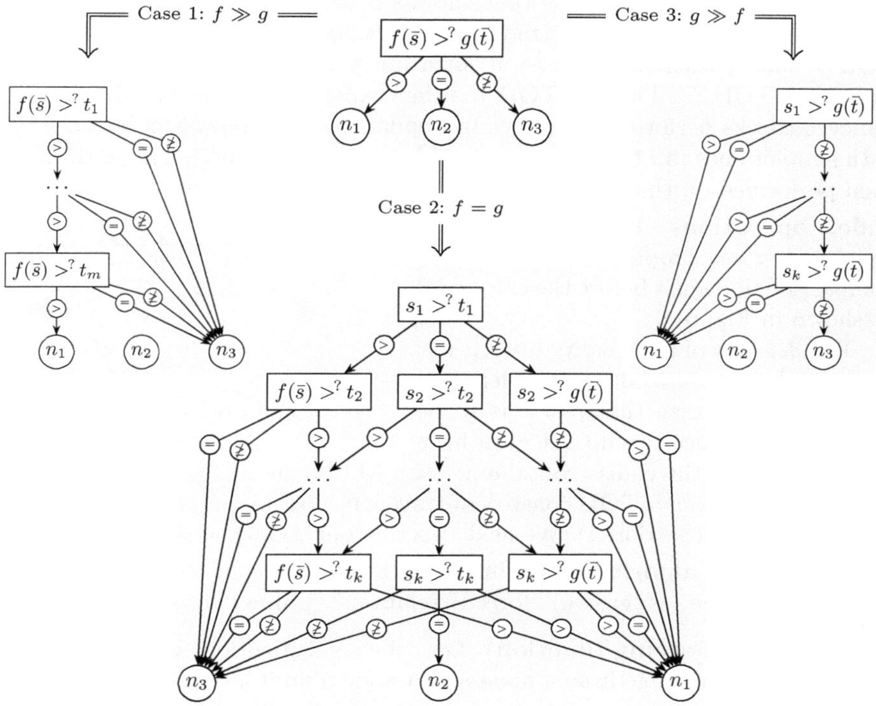

Fig. 5. LPO transformations on TODs.

comparison node $f(\bar{s}) >^? f(\bar{t})$ by a finite number of paths, so that every new term comparison node on these paths contains a comparison of a pair of terms strictly smaller in the multiset order than the multiset $\{f(\bar{s}), f(\bar{t})\}$. Another example is the redundant node removal of Figure 3. This transformation replaces on some paths nodes n_1, n, n_2 by n_1, n_2, which results in a smaller multiset.

Finally, we note that node replication results in a TOD containing exactly the same multiset of paths, but it can only be applied a finite number of times. *(2) TOD equivalence.* The TOD transformations of Figure 4–5 preserve TOD equivalence by properties of KBO/LPO. Redundant node removal in Figure 3(a) ensures equivalence by the "forces" relation (Definition 2). Node replication in Figures 3(b) preserves equivalence since the set of TOD paths does not change. ❑

5 TOD Retrieval and Maintenance

TOD is a data structure intended to be an index [24] for retrieval of equalities, which become ordered by the query substitution. In this section, we describe the three main operations on the TOD index: *insertion, deletion, and retrieval.* An interesting feature of TODs is that the main modifications of them occur not during insertion but during retrieval. As mentioned in Section 3, we modify the TOD $\mathcal{T}$ lazily, when we traverse it for a query substitution σ, resulting in an equivalent TOD $\mathcal{T}'$. The new TOD $\mathcal{T}'$ is less expensive to traverse, since it either removes checks performed at nodes (redundant node removal) or replaces them with simpler ones (all transformations of Figures 4–5). Subsequent retrievals are then performed on the TOD $\mathcal{T}'$ instead of $\mathcal{T}$.

Index operations. The *insertion* of an equality $l \approx r$ is simple: we insert a term comparison node just before the exit node, as shown in Figure 6.

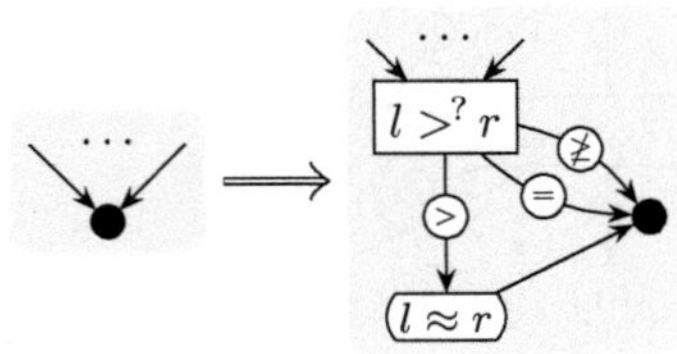

Fig. 6. Insertion of $l \approx r$

The *deletion* of an equality $l \approx r$ is not performed. Instead of doing the deletion, we simply memorize that $l \approx r$ is to be deleted. In practice, we do not even have to do this, since the clause containing $l \approx r$ will be marked as deleted anyhow.

A *retrieval* from a TOD consists of traversal, possibly interleaved with TOD transformations (Section 4). We next describe our TOD retrieval algorithm.

TOD retrieval algorithm. We introduce a notion meant to capture sufficient conditions for the (expensive) "forced" relation [5] , in extension of Definition 2.

Definition 4 (Forcing function). Let σ be a substitution. We call a path π a *σ-path*, if for every edge from a node n to a node n' in it labeled by ℓ, (1) if n is a term comparison node $s >^? t$, then $\sigma(s >^? t) = \ell$, and (2) if n is a positivity check node $e \geq^? 0$, then $\sigma(e \geq^? 0) = \ell$. We call a partial function F from paths to edge labels a *forcing function* if it has the following property. For every substitution σ and every σ-path $\pi = n_0, \ldots, n_i, n_{i+1}$ from the root, if $F(n_0, \ldots, n_i) = \ell$, then the edge in π from n_i to n_{i+1} is labeled with ℓ. ❑

Our retrieval algorithm is parametrized by a forcing function F. During the retrieval, we mark some nodes *visited.* Once a node n is marked visited, the path from the root to n will never change. Initially, all nodes in a TOD are unvisited. Let $\mathcal{T}$ be a TOD and σ a substitution. The traversal starts in the successor of the root node and repeatedly applies steps shown in Figure 7. When we describe the steps, we assume that during the traversal we already followed a path $\pi = n_0, n_1, \ldots, n_k, n$ leading to the current node n.

Let us now establish some properties of the algorithm, proving its correctness.

Lemma 1. *If n is a visited node, there is a single path from the root to n.*

Proof. When we make a node visited at step 3c of Figure 7, by induction we can assume that n_k already has this property. Since after this step there is only one edge to n, and this edge is from n_k, n satisfies this property. None of the other steps adds an incoming edge to a visited node or changes the content of a visited node, so $n_0, \ldots, n_k, n$ remains the only path to n. ❑

[5] We discuss forcing functions implemented in VAMPIRE in the extended version of this paper [5].

1. If n is the exit node, we terminate and return the success set of σ for $\mathcal{T}$ (the set of all non-deleted equalities in success nodes visited during the traversal).
2. If n is a success node, we set n to the successor node of n. Alternatively, if we are interested in only one candidate, we can terminate once we reach the first success node with a non-deleted equality.
3. Let n be an unvisited evaluation node. If n has more than one incoming edge, we first apply node replication so that the only incoming edge to n is from n_k. Then,
   (a) If $F(\pi) = \ell$, we apply the transformation of Figure 3 (a).
   (b) If any of the transformations of Figures 4 and 5 applies to n, we apply this transformation.
   (c) Otherwise, we mark n visited.
4. If n is a visited term comparison node containing $s >^? t$, we follow the edge $\sigma(s >^? t)$ from n.
5. If n is a visited positivity check node containing $e \geq^? 0$, we follow the edge $\sigma(e \geq^? 0)$ from n.

Fig. 7. Retrieval algorithm steps.

Lemma 2. *Step 3a of Figure 7 transforms the TOD into an equivalent one.*

Proof. By Lemma 1, there is only one path from the root to n. By Definition 4, it follows that n forces ℓ, so this step is a special case of redundant mode removal from Figure 3(a), which preserves TOD equivalence by Theorem 1. ❑

Lemma 3 (Termination). *The retrieval algorithm terminates.*

Proof. Straightforward by Lemma 2 and Theorem 1. Indeed, all transformations made during the retrieval are special cases of TOD transformations, so we can only make a finite number of them. All other steps of the algorithm either change the current node to its successor in the TOD or mark an unvisited node as visited. Since any TOD is a dag, we can only make a finite number of such steps. ❑

Lemma 4 (Correctness). *The TOD $\mathcal{T}'$ resulting from the retrieval is equivalent to the TOD $\mathcal{T}$ before the retrieval.*

Proof. By Lemma 2, step 3a of Figure 7 is a special case of redundant node removal. All other transformations in Figure 7 are special cases of TOD transformations, which preserve equivalence by Theorem 1. ❑

Example 3. Consider the TOD in Figure 1(a). We perform retrieval on this TOD using a KBO with constant weight function and a query substitution σ such that $x\sigma = y\sigma$. The retrieval steps are shown in Figure 8. Initially, all nodes in the TOD are unvisited. We highlight the path up to the current node in each sub-diagram with blue, and denote visited nodes with a red striped background. Note that the last node on the blue path is the current node n from the algorithm.

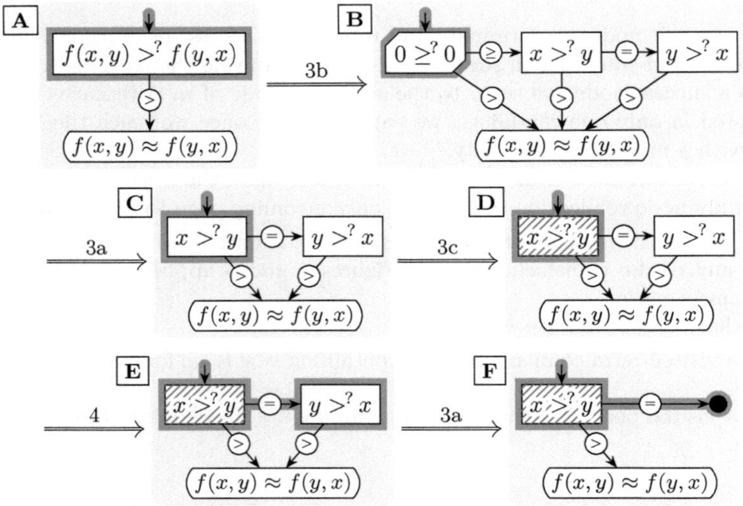

Fig. 8. Retrieval with a query substitution σ such that $x\sigma = y\sigma$.

1. Starting with sub-diagram **A** of Figure 8, we use step 3b, applying case 2 of the KBO transformations (see Figure 4).
2. In sub-diagram **B**, for the current path π we have that $F(\pi)$ equals $\geq$, so we apply redundant node removal (step 3a).
3. In sub-diagram **C**, the current node does not admit any transformations, so we mark it visited (step 3c).
4. In sub-diagram **D**, $\sigma(x >^? y)$ is $=$, so we follow the edge labeled $=$ (step 4).
5. In sub-diagram **E**, for the current path π we get that $F(\pi)$ equals $=$, due to $\sigma(x >^? y)$ being $=$. We apply redundant node removal and get to the exit node denoted explicitly with a black disc (step 3a).
6. In sub-diagram **F**, we return from the retrieval with no equalities (step 1).

Suppose that, before further traversals, we insert the equality $f(x,y) \approx f(x,x)$ into the TOD in sub-diagram **F** of Figure 8. The resulting TOD is shown in sub-diagram **G** of Figure 9, with a new term comparison node labeled $f(x,y) >^? f(x,x)$ and a new success node labeled $f(x,y) \approx f(x,x)$. The $>$ edge of the new term comparison node is connected to the new success node. The $=$ and $\not\geq$ edges of the new term comparison node, and the outgoing edge of the success node are connected to a new exit node (not shown). We traverse the TOD in sub-diagram **G** with a query substitution σ such that $x\sigma \succ y\sigma$.

1. Starting from sub-diagram **G** of Figure 9, we follow the edge $>$ (step 4), mark the success node labeled $f(x,y) \approx f(y,x)$ visited (step 3c) and follow its outgoing edge (step 2).
2. In sub-diagram **H**, we apply Case 2 of the KBO transformations (step 3b) and mark the current node labeled $y - x \geq^? 0$ visited (step 3c).

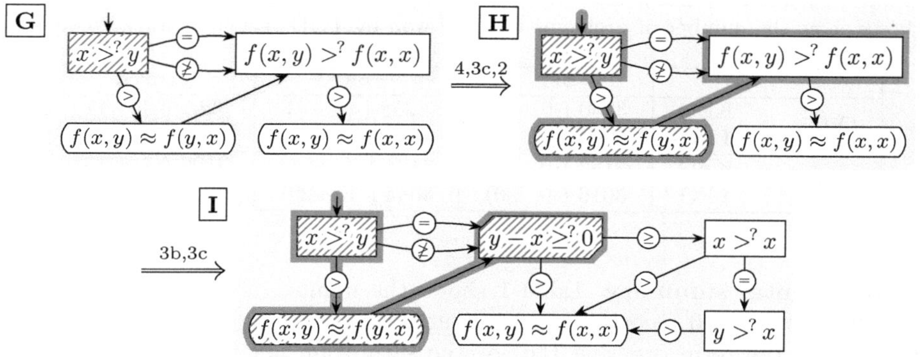

Fig. 9. Result of insertion of $f(x,y) \approx f(x,x)$ into the TOD of in sub-diagram **F** of Figure 8, and retrieval steps from top-left TOD with query substitution σ s.t. $x\sigma \succ y\sigma$.

3. In sub-diagram **I**, we follow the $\not\geq$ edge of the current node (step 5) and get to the exit node.
4. We exit with a single equality $f(x,y) \approx f(y,x)$ (step 1). ❑

6 Evaluation

We implemented our equality retrieval approach using TOD in Vampire.

Prover setup. We considered twelve configurations of Vampire options for reasoning using TOD, by taking Discount [2] or Otter [16] as saturation algorithm (`-sa discount/otter`), KBO or LPO as term order (`-to kbo/lpo`), and TOD variants using the new option `-fdtod` with values `off/on/shared` [6] for using TODs in forward demodulation, where:

(1) `off` does not use TODs,
(2) `on` uses a separate TOD for each forward demodulator (see e.g. Figure 1),
(3) `shared` uses a shared TOD for each set of forward demodulators with the same left-hand side (see e.g. Figure 2).

Benchmarks. We used version 8.2.0 of the TPTP library [26], which contains 25474 problems. We ignored problems where TODs are not used at all, resulting in 9310 problems used for evaluation.

Hardware. We used compute nodes with AMD Epyc 7502 2.5GHz processors and 1TB RAM. Each benchmark run relied on a single core and 16GB of memory.

[6] The option values `on` and `shared` are implemented in the `master` and `term-ordering-diagrams` branches of Vampire, respectively.

Table 1. Number of problems solved by VAMPIRE within 60s. The numbers in parentheses show the number of problems lost and won by TOD variants compared to `off`.

		`off`	`on`	`shared`
Otter	KBO	3250 (-0, +0)	3258 (-0, +8)	3261 (-0, +11)
	LPO	3064 (-0, +0)	3083 (-1, +20)	3092 (-2, +30)
Discount	KBO	3182 (-0, +0)	3194 (-1, +13)	3196 (-1, +15)
	LPO	3016 (-0, +0)	3044 (-1, +29)	3058 (-1, +43)

Experimental summary. Table 1 shows the number of problems solved by VAMPIRE with a 60 seconds timeout. Our approach using TODs is better, regardless of the term ordering (`to`) or the saturation algorithm (`sa`). Further, VAMPIRE `shared` proves theorems significantly faster than `off`.[7]

Experiments using TODs seem to reach the memory limit in more instances than without TODs. For example in `-sa otter -to lpo`, 44 problems reach a memory limit with `shared`, whereas only 14 do so when TODs are `off`. However, VAMPIRE `-fdtod off` hits some difficult ordering checks and is unable to generate huge clauses that consume a lot of memory.

Table 2 shows the proportion of machine instructions spent on forward demodulation and on entire runs, showcasing that we reduce the solving time of the post-ordering problem. We used an instruction limit of 200×10^9 (approximately 60 seconds). We highlight the subset of results from Table 2 for problems in the UEQ (unit equality) category of TPTP in Table 3. Post-ordering checks in this category generally take up a more significant proportion of instructions. In some cases, when using LPO without TODs, these checks even dominate the number of instructions.

7 Related Work and Conclusion

We introduce the term ordering diagram (TOD) index to improve the efficiency of term ordering checks. Our evaluation using VAMPIRE shows significant improvement over naive term ordering checks.

Decidability and complexity of problems related to KBO and LPO are studied in [18,9,10,20], complemented by efficient implementations [15,22,13]. In particular, in [22] each KBO ordering check is runtime specialized individually in one step. We improve upon this by preprocessing ordering checks completely lazily. Additionally, TODs allow algorithm specialization for an arbitrary number of sequential ordering checks, including also for LPO. The open problem 9 of [19] is a generalization of the post-ordering problem. Confluence trees, developed to decide ground confluence of equational systems [1], are similar to TODs. Confluence trees have also been adapted to ground reducibility checking [12]. Shared rewriting avoids the post-ordering problem by caching the results of demodulations in shared terms [14]. Similarly to term indexing structures, the efficiency

[7] A more detailed evaluation can be found in the extended version of this paper [5].

Table 2. Number of instructions spent on post-ordering checks and forward demodulation compared to total instruction count. The first column describes the options, and the next three display the number of instructions performed on parts of VAMPIRE. Columns 5–6 list the percentage of instructions spent on post-ordering checks and forward demodulation, and the last column gives the number of forward demodulations.

Options			# of instructions $\times 10^{12}$			Ratio to total		# of $\times 10^6$
			PostOrd.	Fw dem.	Total	PostOrd.	Fw dem.	Fw dem.
Otter	KBO	off	73	174	1258	5.8%	13.9%	2598
		on	34	142	1256	2.7%	11.3%	2714
		shared	18	116	1255	1.4%	9.2%	2813
	LPO	off	259	362	1292	20.0%	28.0%	1922
		on	154	279	1286	12.0%	21.7%	2064
		shared	98	213	1284	7.7%	16.6%	2238
Discount	KBO	off	91	314	1272	7.2%	24.7%	3044
		on	45	281	1258	3.6%	22.4%	3279
		shared	37	272	1269	3.0%	21.4%	3520
	LPO	off	214	417	1301	16.5%	32.1%	2376
		on	115	354	1283	8.9%	27.6%	2768
		shared	86	330	1294	6.7%	25.5%	3228

of term ordering diagrams is based on sharing information in indexed elements. However, the insertion retrieval operations for term ordering diagrams are done lazily, necessitated by the more expensive ordering comparison operations they support. To the best of our knowledge, our TOD approach gives the first algorithmic solution to efficient post-ordering checks.

Further work includes applying TODs to, for example, backward demodulation, constrained superposition, subsumption demodulation [4], ground reducibility [12], or ground joinability [3]. Extending our framework to other simplification orders, such as the weighted path order (WPO) [29], is another task for the future.

Acknowledgements. This research was funded in whole or in part by the ERC Consolidator Grant ARTIST 101002685, the ERC Proof of Concept Grant LEARN 101213411, the TU Wien Doctoral College SecInt, the FWF SpyCoDe Grant 10.55776/F85, the WWTF grant ForSmart 10.47379/ICT22007, and the Amazon Research Award 2023 QuAT.

Disclosure of Interests. The authors have no competing interests to declare that are relevant to the content of this article.

References

1. Comon, H., Narendran, P., Nieuwenhuis, R., Rusinowitch, M.: Deciding the confluence of ordered term rewrite systems. ACM TOCL (2003). https://doi.org/10.1145/601775.601777

Table 3. Number of instructions spent on post-ordering checks and forward demodulation compared to total instruction count, within UEQ problems (1456 problems).

Options			# of instructions $\times 10^{12}$			Ratio to total		# of $\times 10^6$
			PostOrd.	Fw dem.	Total	PostOrd.	Fw dem.	Fw dem.
Otter	KBO	off	23.6	37.9	101.0	23.4%	37.6%	295.3
		on	10.8	28.1	100.3	10.8%	28.0%	342.4
		shared	5.1	18.8	99.9	5.1%	18.8%	382.9
	LPO	off	58.4	69.0	113.2	51.6%	60.9%	130.3
		on	33.9	50.6	110.0	30.8%	46.0%	158.2
		shared	20.0	34.1	111.2	18.0%	30.6%	215.5
Discount	KBO	off	26.8	70.3	112.6	23.8%	62.5%	726.5
		on	15.4	65.1	111.8	13.8%	58.3%	815.1
		shared	11.6	60.2	111.7	10.4%	54.0%	919.5
	LPO	off	63.0	95.2	121.5	51.8%	78.4%	420.3
		on	39.0	85.3	119.5	32.6%	71.4%	567.1
		shared	28.9	77.4	119.4	24.2%	64.8%	732.0

2. Denzinger, J., Kronenburg, M., Schulz, S.: DISCOUNT - A Distributed and Learning Equational Prover. Journal of Automated Reasoning (1997). https://doi.org/10.1023/A:1005879229581
3. Duarte, A., Korovin, K.: Ground Joinability and Connectedness in the Superposition Calculus. In: IJCAR (2022). https://doi.org/10.1007/978-3-031-10769-6_11
4. Gleiss, B., Kovács, L., Rath, J.: Subsumption Demodulation in First-Order Theorem Proving. In: IJCAR (2020). https://doi.org/10.1007/978-3-030-51074-9_17
5. Hajdu, M., Coutelier, R., Kovács, L., Voronkov, A.: Term Ordering Diagrams (extended) (2025). https://doi.org/10.48550/arXiv.2505.22181
6. Kamin, S., Lévy, J.J.: Two generalizations of the recursive path ordering. Unpublished manuscript (1980)
7. Knuth, D.E., Bendix, P.B.: Simple Word Problems in Universal Algebras. In: Automation of Reasoning 2. Springer (1983). https://doi.org/10.1007/978-3-642-81955-1_23
8. Korovin, K.: iProver — An Instantiation-Based Theorem Prover for First-Order Logic (System Description). In: IJCAR (2008). https://doi.org/10.1007/978-3-540-71070-7_24
9. Korovin, K., Voronkov, A.: Knuth-Bendix Constraint Solving Is NP-Complete. In: ICALP (2001). https://doi.org/10.1007/3-540-48224-5_79
10. Korovin, K., Voronkov, A.: Orienting rewrite rules with the Knuth–Bendix order. Information and Computation (2003). https://doi.org/10.1016/S0890-5401(03)00021-X
11. Kovács, L., Voronkov, A.: First-Order Theorem Proving and Vampire. In: CAV. pp. 1–35 (2013). https://doi.org/10.1007/978-3-642-39799-8_1
12. Löchner, B.: A Redundancy Criterion Based on Ground Reducibility by Ordered Rewriting. In: CADE (2004). https://doi.org/10.1007/978-3-540-25984-8_2
13. Löchner, B.: Things To Know When Implementing LPO. International Journal on Artificial Intelligence Tools (2006). https://doi.org/10.1142/S0218213006002564
14. Löchner, B., Schulz, S.: An Evaluation of Shared Rewriting. In: IWIL (2001), `https://www.researchgate.net/publication/229079124`

15. Löchner, B.: Things to Know when Implementing KBO. Journal of Automated Reasoning (2006). https://doi.org/10.1007/s10817-006-9031-4
16. McCune, W., Wos, L.: Otter - the CADE-13 competition incarnations. Journal of Automated Reasoning (1997). https://doi.org/10.1023/A:1005843632307
17. Nieuwenhuis, R., Rubio, A.: Paramodulation-Based Theorem Proving. In: Handbook of Automated Reasoning, chap. 7. Elsevier and MIT Press (2001). https://doi.org/10.1016/B978-044450813-3/50009-6
18. Nieuwenhuis, R.: Simple LPO constraint solving methods. Information Processing Letters (1993). https://doi.org/10.1016/0020-0190(93)90226-Y
19. Nieuwenhuis, R.: Invited Talk: Rewrite-Based Deduction and Symbolic Constraints. In: CADE (1999). https://doi.org/10.1007/3-540-48660-7_28
20. Nieuwenhuis, R., Rivero, J.M.: Practical Algorithms for Deciding Path Ordering Constraint Satisfaction. Information and Computation (2002). https://doi.org/10.1006/inco.2002.3146
21. Riazanov, A., Voronkov, A.: Partially Adaptive Code Trees. In: JELIA (2000). https://doi.org/10.1007/3-540-40006-0_15
22. Riazanov, A., Voronkov, A.: Efficient Checking of Term Ordering Constraints. In: CADE (2004). https://doi.org/10.1007/978-3-540-25984-8_3
23. Schulz, S., Cruanes, S., Vukmirović, P.: Faster, Higher, Stronger: E 2.3. In: CADE (2019). https://doi.org/10.1007/978-3-030-29436-6_29
24. Sekar, R., Ramakrishnan, I., Voronkov, A.: Term Indexing. In: Handbook of Automated Reasoning, chap. 26. MIT Press (2001). https://doi.org/10.1016/B978-044450813-3/50028-X
25. Sutcliffe, G.: The CADE ATP System Competition - CASC. AI Magazine (2016). https://doi.org/10.1609/aimag.v37i2.2620
26. Sutcliffe, G.: Stepping Stones in the TPTP World. In: IJCAR (2024). https://doi.org/10.1007/978-3-031-63498-7_3
27. Voronkov, A.: The anatomy of Vampire: Implementing bottom-up procedures with code trees **15**(2), 237–265 (1995)
28. Vukmirovic, P., Bentkamp, A., Blanchette, J., Cruanes, S., Nummelin, V., Tourret, S.: Making Higher-Order Superposition Work. Journal of Automated Reasoning (2022). https://doi.org/10.1007/s10817-021-09613-z
29. Yamada, A., Kusakari, K., Sakabe, T.: A unified ordering for termination proving. Science of Computer Programming (2015). https://doi.org/10.1016/j.scico.2014.07.009

Equational Reasoning

Exploiting Instantiations from Paramodulation Proofs in Isabelle/HOL

Lukas Bartl[1(✉)], Jasmin Blanchette[2], and Tobias Nipkow[3]

[1] Universität Augsburg, Augsburg, Germany
lukas.bartl@uni-a.de
[2] Ludwig-Maximilians-Universität München, Munich, Germany
jasmin.blanchette@ifi.lmu.de
[3] Technische Universität München, Munich, Germany
nipkow@in.tum.de

Abstract. Metis is an ordered paramodulation prover built into the Isabelle/HOL proof assistant. It attempts to close the current goal using a given list of lemmas. Typically these lemmas are found by Sledgehammer, a tool that integrates external automatic provers. We present a new tool that analyzes successful Metis proofs to derive variable instantiations. These increase Sledgehammer's success rate, improve the speed of Sledgehammer-generated proofs, and help users understand why a goal follows from the lemmas.

Keywords: instantiations · paramodulation · Isabelle/HOL · Sledgehammer

1 Introduction

Sledgehammer [31] is undoubtedly one of the interactive proof assistant Isabelle/HOL's [27] most popular components. This component gives Isabelle access to many external automatic theorem provers (ATPs), which can mechanize routine proofs [12, 16]. When the user invokes Sledgehammer on a proposition to be proved, it performs the following steps:

1. It invokes a number of external ATPs with the goal and the background library of *facts* (definitions, lemmas, theorems, etc.); this involves translating the goal and facts from higher-order logic to the ATPs' logics.
2. For any proof that is found, the used facts are extracted from it and the internal prover *Metis* [20], based on ordered paramodulation, is invoked to reconstruct an Isabelle proof based on this list of facts only.

This paper is about obtaining and exploiting the instantiations of the facts used in the proofs. Our motivation is that using instantiated facts

C. Barrett and U. Waldmann (Eds.): CADE 2025, LNAI 15943, pp. 573–593, 2025.
https://doi.org/10.1007/978-3-031-99984-0_30

- can speed up proof reconstruction (and even turn timeouts into successes);
- can improve readability of proofs for humans; and
- can lead to simpler proofs.

Example 1. We start with a simple example where we believe human readability is improved. We work in a linear order with $\bot$ and $\top$. Sledgehammer proves that in the context of the facts

$$\top \not< x \ (1) \qquad x \neq \bot \leftrightarrow \bot < x \ (2)$$

the assumption $\bot \not< \top$ implies $\mathtt{a} = \mathtt{b}$, where $\mathtt{a}$ and $\mathtt{b}$ are arbitrary constants. Why is that? It turns out that the following instantiations are used:

$$\top \not< \mathtt{a} \ (1\mathtt{a}) \qquad \top \not< \mathtt{b} \ (1\mathtt{b})$$
$$\mathtt{a} \neq \bot \leftrightarrow \bot < \mathtt{a} \ (2\mathtt{a}) \qquad \mathtt{b} \neq \bot \leftrightarrow \bot < \mathtt{b} \ (2\mathtt{b}) \qquad \top \neq \bot \leftrightarrow \bot < \top \ (2\top)$$

Clearly $\bot \not< \top$ implies $\bot = \top$ via (2$\top$). This implies $\bot \not< \mathtt{a}$ and $\bot \not< \mathtt{b}$ via (1$\mathtt{a}$) and (1$\mathtt{b}$). Now we obtain $\mathtt{a} = \bot$ and $\mathtt{b} = \bot$ via (2$\mathtt{a}$) and (2$\mathtt{b}$), and thus $\mathtt{a} = \mathtt{b}$. Although this deduction still needs some thought, we believe that it is far simpler than if we had to work out the derivation from (1) and (2) alone.

This paper is structured as follows. Section 2 presents the necessary background about Isabelle, Sledgehammer, and Metis. Section 3 presents further introductory examples. The core of the paper is in Sect. 4, which explains how to obtain the instantiations used during a Metis proof and translate them into instantiations of the corresponding Isabelle facts. Section 5 explains how Sledgehammer was extended to cooperate with the extended Metis prover. Section 6 presents our empirical evaluation of how instantiations improve the performance of Sledgehammer. We end with related work and the conclusion.

Our extensions are available as part of Isabelle starting with version 2025.[1] They are documented in the Sledgehammer user's manual [5]. The raw data for our evaluation is available online.[2]

2 Background

Isabelle. Isabelle/HOL [27,41] is a proof assistant for polymorphic higher-order logic enriched with type classes [34]. It is written primarily in Standard ML. It has an inference kernel through which all logical inferences must go to be deemed acceptable. At the user level, notations largely follow mathematical practice.

Sledgehammer. The Sledgehammer tool [31] consists of six main components:

1. The *relevance filter* (or "premise selector") heuristically selects a subset of the available facts as likely relevant to the current goal. Typically, hundreds of

[1] https://isabelle.in.tum.de/website-Isabelle2025/.
[2] https://nekoka-project.github.io/pubs/instantiations_data.zip.

facts can be chosen without overwhelming ATPs. Sledgehammer includes two relevance filters [8, 23], which can be combined.

2. The *translation module* constructs an ATP problem from the selected facts and the current goal, translating Isabelle's polymorphic higher-order logic to the ATP's logic [7, 22].
3. The ATP tries to prove the problem. Actually, multiple ATPs can be run in parallel. Commonly used ATPs include cvc5 [3], E [39], Leo-III [35], SPASS [10], Vampire [4], veriT [13], Z3 [25], and Zipperposition [38].
4. If one or more ATPs find a proof, the *proof minimization module* repeatedly invokes each ATP with subsets of the facts referenced in the respective proof, trying to reduce the number of dependencies and speed up the next steps.
5. The *proof reconstruction module* transforms each ATP proof into a textual Isabelle proof. Reconstruction means that Sledgehammer and the ATP need not be trusted. Typically, the structure of the ATP proof is discarded, and the Isabelle proof consists of a single proof method (often *metis*) invoked with the facts referenced in the ATP proof. Detailed Isabelle proofs, or Isar proofs [40], are available as an experimental feature [6].
6. For each ATP proof, the *preplay module* tries out various proof methods before they are presented to the user. If several methods succeed, the fastest one is chosen [6].

As an example, suppose Sledgehammer selects 512 facts $f_1, \ldots, f_{512}$ and passes them, along with the goal, to E. Then E finds a proof involving three facts, f_{10}, f_{73}, and f_{359}, and minimization reduces this list to two: f_{10} and f_{359}. By trial and error (and preplaying), Sledgehammer determines that the proof method *metis* with f_{10} and f_{359} as arguments solves the Isabelle goal in 23 ms, and no other proof method succeeds, so this *metis* call is suggested to the user.

The Metis ATP. Metis [20] is an ATP for untyped first-order logic with equality written in Standard ML. It is based on ordered paramodulation, a variant of superposition [2]. Although Metis was developed as a standalone program, it is also incorporated in Isabelle's source code, so that it is always available.

Thanks to its calculus, Metis is reasonably performant, although it cannot compete with state-of-the-art superposition provers such as Vampire [36]. Metis's main strengths are the readability of its source code and the simplicity and fine granularity of its proof format. Proofs are expressed using the following six inference rules:

$$\frac{}{C}\ \textsc{Axiom} \qquad \frac{}{A \vee \neg A}\ \textsc{Assume} \qquad \frac{C}{C\sigma}\ \textsc{Subst}$$

$$\frac{}{t = t}\ \textsc{Refl} \qquad \frac{}{s \neq t \vee \neg L[s]_p \vee L[t]_p}\ \textsc{Equality} \qquad \frac{C \vee A \quad \neg A \vee D}{C \vee D}\ \textsc{Resolve}$$

Notice that substitution is captured by the explicit SUBST rule instead of being part of RESOLVE. Moreover, all equality reasoning is reduced to REFL and EQUALITY. For proof search, Metis relies on a more efficient calculus that performs ordered paramodulation, but the proofs are then translated to the above fine-granular rules.

The *metis* Proof Method. Isabelle's *metis* (with a lowercase m) proof method [32] builds on the Metis (with an uppercase M) ATP to provide general-purpose proof automation. The *metis* proof method takes a list of facts as argument and translates them, together with the current goal, from polymorphic higher-order logic to untyped first-order logic. The resulting *axiom clauses* are then introduced in the proof attempt using the AXIOM rule. The translation uses the same techniques (and the same code) as Sledgehammer. Next, *metis* invokes the Metis ATP, and if Metis finds a proof, it is reconstructed step by step using Isabelle's inference kernel, so that the goal becomes an Isabelle theorem. A *metis* call is considered successful if the Metis ATP found a proof and Isabelle reconstructed it.

Since it may be hard for the user to determine which facts are necessary for a proof, in practice *metis* is almost always used in conjunction with Sledgehammer.

3 Examples

Before we study our *metis* and Sledgehammer extensions in detail, we take a look at a few examples that illustrate how instantiating facts can not only improve readability but also speed up proof reconstruction and lead to simpler proofs. The final example demonstrates how more complex terms are displayed.

Example 2. We present a goal from the *Archive of Formal Proofs* [9], where instantiating facts substantially speeds up the proof and turns a timeout into a success. This example stems from a formalization of Tarski's axioms for Euclidean geometry [15]. The lemma *cong_mid2__cong* states the following property, where `Cong` denotes the congruence relation and `Midpoint` states that a point lies exactly in the middle of two other points:

$$\texttt{Midpoint M A B} \longrightarrow \texttt{Midpoint M}' \texttt{ A}' \texttt{ B}' \longrightarrow \texttt{Cong A M A}' \texttt{ M}' \longrightarrow \texttt{Cong A B A}' \texttt{ B}'$$

When invoking Sledgehammer on a modern laptop for this goal, the external ATP cvc5 [3] finds a proof using the facts *cong_inner_transitivity*, *l2_l1_b*, *midpoint_bet*, and *midpoint_cong*. However, *metis* times out; i.e., it fails to find a proof derived from these facts within 1 s. After inferring the instantiations and instantiating the facts, though, *metis* successfully solves the goal in 50 ms. The instantiations are simple: Each free variable in the facts is replaced by one of $\texttt{M}, \texttt{A}, \texttt{B}, \texttt{M}', \texttt{A}', \texttt{B}'$. The facts *midpoint_bet* and *midpoint_cong* each have two different instantiations and thus appear twice in the resulting Isabelle proof, which may also improve readability.

Example 3. Instantiating facts not only speeds up *metis* but also leads to simpler and more readable proofs. Suppose that we want to prove the goal $0 < \mathtt{i} \longrightarrow \mathtt{x} \leq \mathtt{x}^{\mathtt{i}}$ for natural numbers $\mathtt{i}, \mathtt{x}$. When invoking Sledgehammer on a modern laptop, the external ATP veriT [13] finds a proof including the following facts, where `Suc` returns the successor of its argument:

$$\begin{aligned} 1 = \mathtt{Suc}\ 0 &\quad (\mathit{nat\_1}) \\ a \leq 0 \longrightarrow a = 0 &\quad (\mathit{bot\_nat\_0.extremum\_uniqueI}) \\ m \not\leq n \longleftrightarrow \mathtt{Suc}\ n \leq m &\quad (\mathit{not\_less\_eq\_eq}) \\ 1 \leq a \longrightarrow 0 < n \longrightarrow a \leq a^n &\quad (\mathit{self\_le\_power}) \\ 0 \leq a \longrightarrow 0 \leq a^n &\quad (\mathit{zero\_le\_power}) \end{aligned}$$

The *metis* method can solve the goal with these facts in 82 ms. However, after inferring the instantiations and instantiating the facts, *metis* needs only 41 ms to solve the goal, and the *auto* [29] proof method is even faster, needing only 7 ms. Additionally, *auto* requires only the following two instantiated facts:

$$\begin{aligned} \mathtt{x} \not\leq 0 \longleftrightarrow \mathtt{Suc}\ 0 \leq \mathtt{x} &\quad (\mathit{not\_less\_eq\_eq}\ \text{with}\ \{m \mapsto \mathtt{x}, n \mapsto 0\}) \\ 1 \leq \mathtt{x} \longrightarrow 0 < \mathtt{i} \longrightarrow \mathtt{x} \leq \mathtt{x}^{\mathtt{i}} &\quad (\mathit{self\_le\_power}\ \text{with}\ \{a \mapsto \mathtt{x}, n \mapsto \mathtt{i}\}) \end{aligned}$$

By contrast, *auto* fails to find a proof derived from these facts without instantiations. The Isabelle proof using *auto* is simpler and more readable than the *metis* proof, since trivial facts were eliminated. This helps the user focus on the relevant facts when trying to understand the proof.

Example 4. In the preceding examples, the instantiations were simple, with each free variable being replaced by a single symbol. There are also proofs where instantiations are more complex, possibly involving λ-abstractions and quantified variables. Consider the goal

$$\mathtt{surj}\ (\lambda n.\ \mathtt{g}\ (\mathtt{Suc}\ n)) \longrightarrow (\exists m.\ \mathtt{P}\ (\mathtt{Suc}\ (\mathtt{g}\ m))) \longrightarrow (\exists n.\ \mathtt{P}\ (\mathtt{g}\ (\mathtt{Suc}\ n)))$$

where `surj` states that a function is surjective. We have the fact $\mathtt{surj}\ f \longrightarrow (\exists x.\ f\ x = y)$ at our disposal. Our *metis* extension suggests instantiating f with $\lambda c.\ \mathtt{g}\ (\mathtt{Suc}\ c)$ and y with $\mathtt{Suc}\ (\mathtt{g}\ \_)$ in the fact. Notice that bound variables can be renamed in the inferred instantiations (here, n became c). Additionally, '_'—which corresponds to a fresh free variable—can appear as a placeholder for quantified variables (e.g., m), since there is no way to refer to them.

4 Instantiations from Metis Proofs

We extend the *metis* proof method so that it infers the instantiations of facts used in a proof and suggests them to the user. This extension is executed after a successful *metis* proof, provided that the *metis_instantiate* option is enabled.

Inference of Instantiations for Metis Proofs. To infer the instantiations of the Isabelle facts, we first infer the instantiations of the Metis clauses. These are the substitutions that were applied to the axiom clauses in the Metis proof.

Definition 1. A *Metis theorem* θ is recursively defined as a triple $(C, r, \bar{\theta})$ consisting of a Metis clause C, an inference rule r, and a list of Metis theorems $\bar{\theta}$, where C is derived directly from $\bar{\theta}$ using the rule r. A *Metis proof* is a Metis theorem for the empty clause, denoted by `False`.

Definition 2. A *Metis substitution* $\sigma = \{x_1 \mapsto t_1, \ldots, x_n \mapsto t_n\}$ is a partial function from Metis variable names to Metis terms. The *composition* of two substitutions $\sigma_1 \circ \sigma_2$ first applies σ_2 and then σ_1, so that $C(\sigma_1 \circ \sigma_2) = (C\sigma_2)\sigma_1$.

Definition 3. The function $\text{infer}(\theta, \sigma)$ returns a list of pairs (C, σ'), where C is an axiom clause in the Metis theorem θ and σ' is the applied substitution. The argument σ is used as an accumulator and is initialized to $\varnothing$ for a Metis proof. The function is defined recursively as follows:

$$\text{infer}((C, r, []), \sigma) = \begin{cases} [(C, \sigma)] & \text{if } r = \textsc{Axiom} \\ [] & \text{otherwise} \end{cases}$$
$$\text{infer}((C, \textsc{Subst}, [\theta]), \sigma) = \text{infer}(\theta, \sigma \circ \sigma')$$
$$\text{infer}((C, \textsc{Resolve}, [\theta_1, \theta_2]), \sigma) = \text{infer}(\theta_1, \sigma) \mathbin{@} \text{infer}(\theta_2, \sigma)$$

where σ' in the second equation is the substitution carried by the Subst inference rule on the left, and @ in the third equation denotes list concatenation.

Example 5. Suppose that we want to prove the goal $1 < \texttt{Suc (Suc x)}$ on natural numbers from the following facts:

$$m < n \longrightarrow \texttt{Suc}\ m < \texttt{Suc}\ n \qquad \texttt{Suc}\ 0 = 1 \qquad 0 < \texttt{Suc}\ n$$

We translate the goal and the facts into first-order logic by using the predicate symbol `less` for $<$. Metis finds the following proof:

(1) Axiom: $\neg\texttt{less}(1, \texttt{Suc}(\texttt{Suc}(\texttt{x})))$
(2) Axiom: $\neg\texttt{less}(m, n) \lor \texttt{less}(\texttt{Suc}(m), \texttt{Suc}(n))$
(3) Subst from (2) using $\sigma = \{m \mapsto 0, n \mapsto y\}$:
$\neg\texttt{less}(0, y) \lor \texttt{less}(\texttt{Suc}(0), \texttt{Suc}(y))$
(4) Axiom: $\texttt{Suc}(0) = 1$
(5) Equality: $\texttt{Suc}(0) \neq 1 \lor \neg\texttt{less}(\texttt{Suc}(0), \texttt{Suc}(y)) \lor \texttt{less}(1, \texttt{Suc}(y))$
(6) Resolve from (4) and (5): $\neg\texttt{less}(\texttt{Suc}(0), \texttt{Suc}(y)) \lor \texttt{less}(1, \texttt{Suc}(y))$
(7) Resolve from (3) and (6): $\neg\texttt{less}(0, y) \lor \texttt{less}(1, \texttt{Suc}(y))$
(8) Subst from (7) using $\sigma = \{y \mapsto \texttt{Suc}(\texttt{x})\}$:
$\neg\texttt{less}(0, \texttt{Suc}(\texttt{x})) \lor \texttt{less}(1, \texttt{Suc}(\texttt{Suc}(\texttt{x})))$
(9) Resolve from (1) and (8): $\neg\texttt{less}(0, \texttt{Suc}(\texttt{x}))$

(10) Axiom: $\texttt{less}(0, \texttt{Suc}(n))$
(11) Subst from (10) using $\sigma = \{n \mapsto \texttt{x}\}$: $\texttt{less}(0, \texttt{Suc}(\texttt{x}))$
(12) Resolve from (9) and (11): $\texttt{False}$

We can now infer the substitutions that were applied to the axiom clauses:

$$\begin{aligned}
\text{infer}(12, \varnothing) &= \text{infer}(1, \varnothing) \mathbin{@} \text{infer}(2, \{y \mapsto \texttt{Suc}(\texttt{x})\} \circ \{m \mapsto 0,\ n \mapsto y\}) \\
&\quad \mathbin{@} \text{infer}(4, \{y \mapsto \texttt{Suc}(\texttt{x})\}) \mathbin{@} \text{infer}(5, \{y \mapsto \texttt{Suc}(\texttt{x})\}) \\
&\quad \mathbin{@} \text{infer}(10, \{n \mapsto \texttt{x}\}) \\
&= \text{infer}(1, \varnothing) \mathbin{@} \text{infer}(2, \{y \mapsto \texttt{Suc}(\texttt{x}),\ m \mapsto 0,\ n \mapsto \texttt{Suc}(\texttt{x})\}), \\
&\quad \mathbin{@} \text{infer}(4, \{y \mapsto \texttt{Suc}(\texttt{x})\}) \mathbin{@} [] \mathbin{@} \text{infer}(10, \{n \mapsto \texttt{x}\}) \\
&= [(\neg\texttt{less}(1, \texttt{Suc}(\texttt{Suc}(\texttt{x}))), \varnothing), \\
&\quad (\neg\texttt{less}(m, n) \lor \texttt{less}(\texttt{Suc}(m), \texttt{Suc}(n)), \\
&\quad\ \{y \mapsto \texttt{Suc}(\texttt{x}),\ m \mapsto 0,\ n \mapsto \texttt{Suc}(\texttt{x})\}), \\
&\quad (\texttt{Suc}(0) = 1, \{y \mapsto \texttt{Suc}(\texttt{x})\}), (\texttt{less}(0, \texttt{Suc}(n)), \{n \mapsto \texttt{x}\})]
\end{aligned}$$

Given a Metis proof θ, the call infer$(\theta, \varnothing)$ yields a list of pairs (C, σ), where C is an axiom clause and σ is the applied substitution. If the proof is retried, the *instantiated axiom clauses*—i.e., the list of all clauses $C\sigma$ corresponding to the pairs (C, σ)—can be used instead of the original axiom clauses to restrict the search space and speed up Metis. After instantiation, a Metis proof is still possible:

Theorem 1. *A Metis proof θ can be transformed into a new Metis proof derived from the instantiated axiom clauses (defined above). The new Metis proof does not involve the* Subst *inference rule and uses at most as many proof steps as θ.*

The proof is by induction on the structure of the Metis proof θ. It proceeds by instantiating the clauses in θ with infer's current accumulator value and removing Subst inference steps. Because clauses are sets and not multisets of literals, instantiation can shorten clauses by unifying literals. This can result in the elimination of resolution steps and thereby entire subproofs.

Proof. We annotate each Metis theorem in θ with infer's current accumulator value using the call annotate$(\theta, \varnothing)$, defined as follows:

$$\begin{aligned}
\text{annotate}((C, r, []), \sigma) &= (C, r, [], \sigma) \\
\text{annotate}((C, \textsc{Subst}, [\theta']), \sigma) &= (C, \textsc{Subst}, [\text{annotate}(\theta', \sigma \circ \sigma')], \sigma) \\
\text{annotate}((C, \textsc{Resolve}, [\theta_1, \theta_2]), \sigma) &= (C, \textsc{Resolve}, \\
&\qquad [\text{annotate}(\theta_1, \sigma), \text{annotate}(\theta_2, \sigma)], \sigma)
\end{aligned}$$

where σ' is again the substitution carried by the Subst inference rule.

It suffices to show that each annotated Metis theorem $(C, r, \bar{\theta}, \sigma)$ contained in annotate$(\theta, \varnothing)$ can be transformed into a new Metis theorem $(C', r', \bar{\theta}')$ such that $C' \subseteq C\sigma$ holds (with $C' = C\sigma$ for axiom clauses), SUBST inference steps are removed, and no new proof step is introduced. Since $C' \subseteq \texttt{False}\,\varnothing$ implies $C' = \texttt{False}$, the whole Metis proof θ is transformed into a new Metis proof. By the definitions of the infer and annotate functions, $C' = C\sigma$ for axiom clauses implies that the new Metis proof is derived from the instantiated axiom clauses.

Assume that we have an annotated Metis theorem $(C, r, \bar{\theta}, \sigma)$ contained in annotate$(\theta, \varnothing)$. We prove the proposition by induction on the inference rule r. In the base case, r has no premises, so $\bar{\theta} = []$ and r is one of AXIOM, ASSUME, REFL, and EQUALITY. We construct the new Metis theorem $(C', r', \bar{\theta}') = (C\sigma, r, [])$ so that $C' = C\sigma \subseteq C\sigma$ holds.

If $r =$ SUBST, we have $\bar{\theta} = [\theta_1]$, where $\theta_1 = (C_1, r_1, \bar{\theta}_1)$, and $C = C_1\sigma'$, where σ' is the substitution carried by the SUBST inference rule. Inductively, we can transform annotate$(\theta_1, \sigma \circ \sigma')$ into a new Metis theorem $\theta' = (C', r', \bar{\theta}')$ with $C' \subseteq C_1(\sigma \circ \sigma')$. Using $C_1(\sigma \circ \sigma') = (C_1\sigma')\sigma = C\sigma$, we can deduce $C' \subseteq C\sigma$, so we use θ' as the new Metis theorem and remove the substitution step.

If $r =$ RESOLVE, then $\bar{\theta} = [\theta_1, \theta_2]$, where $\theta_1 = (C_1, r_1, \bar{\theta}_1)$, $\theta_2 = (C_2, r_2, \bar{\theta}_2)$, $C_1 = D \vee A$, $C_2 = \neg A \vee E$, and $C = D \vee E$. Inductively, we can transform annotate(θ_1, σ) into a new Metis theorem $\theta'_1 = (C'_1, r'_1, \bar{\theta}'_1)$ with $C'_1 \subseteq C_1\sigma$ and annotate(θ_2, σ) into $\theta'_2 = (C'_2, r'_2, \bar{\theta}'_2)$ with $C'_2 \subseteq C_2\sigma$. Since instantiation can shorten clauses, we distinguish between two cases: In the first case, $A\sigma$ is contained in the clauses C'_1 and C'_2, so we obtain D' and E', where $C'_1 = D' \vee A\sigma$ and $C'_2 = \neg\, A\sigma \vee E'$. Then we can construct the new Metis theorem $(C', r', \bar{\theta}') = (D' \vee E', \text{RESOLVE}, [\theta'_1, \theta'_2])$ and $C' \subseteq C\sigma$ holds since $D' \vee E' \subseteq D\sigma \vee E\sigma = C\sigma$. In the second case, we find $\theta' = (C', r', \bar{\theta}') \in \{\theta'_1, \theta'_2\}$ such that C' does not contain $A\sigma$. Then $C' \subseteq C\sigma$ holds, and we can use θ' as the new Metis theorem, thereby removing the resolution step as well as the other subproof.

Translation of Metis Terms to Isabelle Terms. Once the instantiations of the Metis clauses have been inferred, a *translation procedure* converts the contained Metis terms into Isabelle terms that can be presented to the user.

The list obtained from the infer function is filtered to include only those pairs (C, σ) where the Metis clause C is derived from an Isabelle fact φ, and not from the negated goal. The procedure then continues to translate only Metis terms t of substitution elements $(x \mapsto t) \in \sigma$ where the Metis variable x occurs in C and corresponds to a free variable in φ. There may be other Metis variables, including those corresponding to type variables or quantified variables. The direct instantiation of type variables is seldom useful, since types can be inferred from the instantiated terms. Metis variables that correspond to quantified Isabelle variables may emerge during clausification; however, since these are bound in Isabelle, there is no way to refer to them.

The translation procedure must decode constructs that are introduced by the translation from polymorphic higher-order logic to untyped first-order logic in *metis*. This decoding uses the same code as the proof reconstruction in *metis* [32], where Metis terms emerge during reconstruction of the SUBST inference rule. The introduced constructs include the encoding of Isabelle symbols using Metis constants, the encoding of free variables using Metis variables, and the encoding of partial application using a distinguished binary symbol app [22]. For example, map f and map f xs might be translated to app(map, f) and app(app(map, f), xs), where map and f are Metis constants and xs is a Metis variable. While decoding these constructs is straightforward, decoding the type information (for which there are several encodings [7]) was considered too complicated for proof reconstruction in *metis*, so type inference is used instead [32].

The resulting Isabelle terms may still contain *Skolem terms* and encodings of *λ-abstractions*. Such *metis*-internal constructs may not appear in terms suggested to the user. Thus our translation procedure must eliminate them.

Skolem terms are eliminated by replacing them with a *wildcard*, which is displayed as '_' and corresponds to a fresh free variable (as demonstrated in Example 4). Consequently, the instantiated facts may still contain free variables, for which Metis must substitute the corresponding Skolem terms. It does not suffice to simply replace the Skolem symbols with '_'; their arguments must also be removed. This is necessary because the arity of Skolem symbols can change due to the instantiation of facts. For example, the Skolem symbol introduced for $\exists y.\ x < y$ depends on x and therefore requires an argument, whereas the Skolem symbol for the instance $\exists y.\ 0 < y$ does not require any argument.

The *metis* proof method encodes λ-abstractions using either SKBCI combinators [37] or λ-lifted supercombinators [19]. To eliminate these combinators, the translation procedure replaces them with their definition, followed by a $\beta\eta$-reduction of the resulting terms. For example, the term $\lambda x.\ 0$ is encoded as K 0, where K a b $= a$. When the translation procedure detects the term K 0 1, it replaces K with $\lambda a.\ \lambda b.\ a$ and produces the term 0 after β-reduction. If λ-abstractions remain after $\beta\eta$-reduction, the bound variables may have different names than in the original λ-abstractions (as demonstrated in Examples 4 and 7), but this is not a problem since Isabelle equates terms up to α-equivalence.

In the final step of the translation procedure, all remaining free variables (i.e., all free variables occurring in the Isabelle terms and all uninstantiated variables in the clauses) are instantiated with the Isabelle polymorphic constant undefined, which provides a witness for every type's inhabitedness. These variables emerge when the proof was possible without concrete terms. For example, a $=$ b can be derived from $x +$ a $= x +$ b without choosing a value for x. Instantiation of such variables is sensible, since it restricts the search space, but users can prevent this behavior by disabling the *metis_instantiate_undefined* option, in which case the variables are replaced by '_'.

Instantiation of Isabelle Facts. The translation procedure yields a list of Isabelle facts and instantiations of their free variables. A single fact may possess multiple instantiations if it is used multiple times in the proof. To reduce the number of instantiations and to avoid duplicates, we merge instantiations whenever possible:

Definition 4. A *(variable) instantiation* $\{x_1 \mapsto t_1, \ldots, x_n \mapsto t_n\}$ for an Isabelle fact φ is a partial function from variable names to Isabelle terms in which all variable names $x_1, \ldots, x_n$ occur in φ as free variables. Two instantiations ι_1, ι_2 for the same fact φ can be *merged* into $\iota_1 \cup \iota_2$ if $\iota_1(x)$ equals $\iota_2(x)$ up to α-equivalence for all shared variable names $x \in \text{dom}(\iota_1) \cap \text{dom}(\iota_2)$.

Merging can be used to avoid duplicates, since every instantiation can be merged with itself. Conversely, if two instantiations stem from the same clause C and can be merged, they are equal up to α-equivalence. This is because the translation procedure considers only variables occurring in C, and all uninstantiated variables of C are instantiated with `undefined` or '_'. As a result, the domains of the instantiations are exactly the variable names occurring in C that correspond to a free variable in the fact.

By the above argument, if different instantiations can be merged, they must stem from different clauses. In practice, *metis* will still succeed with the merged instantiation, since the clausifier will split the instantiated fact into the instantiated clauses again. Consequently, merging does not lose information.

Example 6. Consider the following Isabelle fact φ:

$$\text{even } n \longrightarrow 0 \leq x^n \wedge (-y)^n = y^n$$

The clausifier splits it into two clauses. Suppose that both clauses are used in a *metis* proof and we inferred the instantiations $\iota_1 = \{x \mapsto \texttt{a},\ n \mapsto 2\}$ and $\iota_2 = \{y \mapsto \texttt{b},\ n \mapsto 2\}$. Since the variable name n is mapped to the same term in both instantiations, these can be merged to $\iota_1 \cup \iota_2 = \{x \mapsto \texttt{a},\ y \mapsto \texttt{b},\ n \mapsto 2\}$. By instantiating φ with $\iota_1 \cup \iota_2$, we obtain the following new fact:

$$\text{even } 2 \longrightarrow 0 \leq \texttt{a}^2 \wedge (-\texttt{b})^2 = \texttt{b}^2$$

If *metis* is invoked again using this fact instead of the original fact, the clausifier will again split it into the two clauses, instantiated with ι_1 and ι_2, respectively.

Since we use type inference instead of reconstructing type information, the translation procedure may produce Isabelle terms with overly generic types. Given that types can be displayed in Isabelle (e.g., using the *show_types* option) and overly generic types can prevent the folding of abbreviations, we attempt to concretize the types of the terms of a variable instantiation ι for a fact φ. We achieve this through type unification [28]: The types of the terms of ι are unified with the types of the corresponding variables in φ, and the unifier is then applied to all the types contained in the terms of ι. It is crucial to find a single unifier for the entire instantiation ι, since the same type variable may appear in multiple types of the free variables in φ, and they must be synchronized.

Finally, if instantiations have been found, *metis* suggests that the user replaces the current *metis* call with a new call using the instantiated facts. Each instantiated fact is displayed by its name together with an annotation that specifies to instantiate it with the terms of the corresponding instantiation. If there are multiple instantiations of a single fact, the fact is displayed multiple times. By replacing the call, the user may get a more readable and faster proof.

5 Sledgehammer Extension

Since *metis* calls are usually generated by Sledgehammer, we also extend Sledgehammer's proof reconstruction module to enable direct generation of proofs with instantiated facts. By using Sledgehammer's preplay module, this extension can not only generate faster and more readable proofs but also transform timeouts into successes as well as produce simpler proofs using other proof methods than *metis*.

Preplay with Instantiations. Sledgehammer's proof reconstruction is started after an external ATP has found and minimized a proof. The facts referenced in the ATP proof are then used to generate an Isabelle proof. The *metis* extension we presented in Sect. 4 can now be invoked to infer the instantiations of these facts. To do so, *metis* must first succeed—both the Metis proof (for inferring the instantiations) and the reconstruction in Isabelle (for ensuring that the instantiations are type-correct, if an unsound type encoding was used) are essential.

After instantiating the facts, Sledgehammer's preplay tries out the proof with the instantiated facts. Even though *metis* has already found a proof, this is beneficial for a number of reasons:

1. The preplay module includes an additional minimization tool that repeatedly invokes a successful proof method with subsets of the facts. Its purpose is to reduce the number of facts and thereby simplify the generated Isabelle proof. Instantiated facts might be redundant and, consequently, can be eliminated by this minimization. Consider the goal $\mathtt{a} < -\mathtt{b} \longleftrightarrow \mathtt{b} < -\mathtt{a}$ and the fact $x < -y \longleftrightarrow y < -x$. This fact is translated to two Metis clauses, corresponding to the two implications $x < -y \longrightarrow y < -x$ and $y < -x \longrightarrow x < -y$. Since both clauses are equal up to the naming of variables, Metis uses only the first one to prove both directions of the goal. Accordingly, the instantiations $\{x \mapsto \mathtt{a},\, y \mapsto \mathtt{b}\}$ and $\{x \mapsto \mathtt{b},\, y \mapsto \mathtt{a}\}$ are inferred, resulting in two instantiated facts. Since only one of these is necessary, the minimization tool removes one of them.
2. Via a mechanism called *try0*, preplay tries a variety of proof methods [6], including multiple *metis* calls with different options (describing the encoding of types and λ-abstractions) and other standard proof methods, such as *simp* [26], *blast* [30], and *auto* [29]. This can result in even faster Isabelle proofs, since other proof methods are frequently faster than *metis* but sometimes require instantiated facts to find any proof at all (as demonstrated in Example 3). Additionally, Isabelle proofs resulting from methods such as *simp*, *blast*, and *auto* are often simpler and more readable, since they do not require the user to provide all the necessary facts for the proof. Minimization removes the facts that are irrelevant for these proof methods.
3. According to Theorem 1, a new Metis proof derived from the instantiated Metis clauses is possible. However, this does not necessarily extend to Isabelle proofs using *metis*. A new *metis* proof using the instantiated Isabelle facts may

not be possible, since their encoding is not guaranteed to produce the same Metis clauses again. This is mostly due to $\beta\eta$-conversion (as demonstrated in Example 7). This rarely happens in practice but is nonetheless one reason to preplay the new *metis* proof.

During preplay, each proof method is executed for a predetermined duration (called the *preplay time limit*, which defaults to 1 s). The instantiation of facts often speeds up proofs, possibly turning timeouts into successes. However, in order to instantiate the facts, *metis* must first succeed. Consequently, the *metis* call used to infer the instantiations is given more time than the proof methods during preplay. More precisely, it is executed for five times the preplay time limit (i.e., 5 s by default).

An alternative would be to increase the preplay time limit in the first place. However, this would work less well in practice, because users typically insert the generated proofs directly into the Isabelle proof text. Given that these are re-executed each time the text is processed, multiple slow proofs could substantially increase the overall processing time.

Our Sledgehammer extension can be controlled through the three-valued Sledgehammer option *instantiate*. If this option is set to *false*, the extension is disabled. If the option is set to *true*, *metis* is started with the *metis_instantiate* option enabled directly after an ATP has found and minimized a proof, at the beginning of Sledgehammer's proof reconstruction module. In most cases, this leads to Isabelle proofs with instantiated facts; otherwise, a proof without instantiations is displayed. The latter case may occur if *metis* is unable to find a proof (but, e.g., *auto* is able to), the proof does not use any facts, or there are no instantiations (e.g., if the facts contain no free variables).

Finally, if the option is set to *smart*, the instantiation of facts is started only if preplay failed (i.e., no proof method was successful within the preplay time limit). If the instantiation was successful, preplay is invoked once more with the instantiated facts, as usual. Therefore, Isabelle proofs with instantiated facts are displayed only if *metis* takes more time than the preplay time limit to prove the goal from the original facts and instantiation can speed up the proof so that it takes less time than the preplay time limit (as demonstrated in Example 2).

Although setting the option to *true* leads to faster, simpler, and more readable proofs, it is too disruptive. Most users, most of the time, are satisfied with uninstantiated facts, which are less verbose. They are pleased if they occasionally get a proof with instantiated facts that would have failed otherwise. Therefore, we make *smart* the default.

Extensionality for Metis. Extensionality states that two functions are equal if they yield the same results for the same arguments. In Isabelle, extensionality is a basic axiom called *ext*:

$$(\forall x.\ f\ x = g\ x) \longrightarrow f = g$$

Since Metis targets first-order logic, it is unaware of this principle. Instead, *ext* must be passed to *metis* (which uses a first-order encoding) when extensionality is required. Since this enlarges the search space, this is not done by default.

However, the need for extensionality can change as facts are instantiated. In other words, *ext* may not be necessary for a proof derived from the original facts, but it may be necessary for a proof derived from the instantiated facts, and vice versa. This phenomenon is mostly due to Isabelle's application of $\beta\eta$-conversion.

Example 7. Recall the fact $\texttt{surj}\ f \longrightarrow (\exists x.\ f\ x = y)$, and suppose that we want to prove the following goal:

$$\texttt{surj}\ (\lambda x.\ \lambda y.\ \texttt{g}\ y\ x) \longrightarrow (\forall x.\ \texttt{P}\ (\lambda y.\ \texttt{g}\ y\ x)) \longrightarrow \texttt{P}\ \texttt{h}$$

To encode the λ-abstractions, we use λ-lifting [19] and thus introduce a new supercombinator $\texttt{A}$ with the definition $\texttt{A}\ a\ b = \texttt{g}\ b\ a$, leading to a new goal:

$$\texttt{surj}\ \texttt{A} \longrightarrow (\forall x.\ \texttt{P}\ (\texttt{A}\ x)) \longrightarrow \texttt{P}\ \texttt{h}$$

We invoke *metis*, which infers that f should be instantiated with $\texttt{A}$ and y should be instantiated with $\texttt{h}$. As described in Sect. 4, $\texttt{A}$ is replaced by $\lambda a.\ \lambda b.\ \texttt{g}\ a\ b$ again, resulting in the following instantiated fact:

$$\texttt{surj}\ (\lambda a.\ \lambda b.\ \texttt{g}\ b\ a) \longrightarrow (\exists x.\ (\lambda b.\ \texttt{g}\ b\ x) = \texttt{h})$$

Notice that Isabelle applied β-reduction, resulting in the modified λ-abstraction $\lambda b.\ \texttt{g}\ b\ x$. If we attempt a proof with *metis* and λ-lifting again, this λ-abstraction will be encoded as another supercombinator $\texttt{B}$ with the definition $\texttt{B}\ a = \texttt{g}\ a\ \texttt{sk}$, where $\texttt{sk}$ is the Skolem constant introduced for the existentially quantified variable x. Using $\texttt{A}$'s and $\texttt{B}$'s definitions, Metis can prove that $\texttt{A}\ \texttt{sk}\ z = \texttt{B}\ z$ for every z, but extensionality is needed to conclude that $\texttt{A}\ \texttt{sk} = \texttt{B}$ and thus to exchange the two terms and prove the goal. Therefore, *metis* can prove the goal from the instantiated fact only if we add the fact *ext*.

Thus, *ext* may be necessary for a proof derived from the instantiated facts. Conversely, if $\beta\eta$-conversion eliminates λ-abstractions, *ext* might be unnecessary for a proof derived from the instantiated facts even though it is needed for a proof derived from the original facts. Therefore, we also extend the preplay module so that a few *metis* calls with the additional fact *ext* are tried after other proof methods have failed, including multiple *metis* calls with different options. These new *metis* calls use λ-lifting as the encoding of λ-abstractions, since λ-lifting benefits more from *ext* than the `SKBCI` combinators [22].

The *metis* calls with the fact *ext* are also useful regardless of instantiations, since some ATPs, such as Zipperposition [38], are based on higher-order logic and already include extensionality. As a result, their proofs do not need *ext*, and proof reconstruction might be unsuccessful without the new *metis* calls.

6 Evaluation

Our empirical evaluation is based on the repository revision d3c0734059ee (October 25, 2024) of Isabelle and 4082096ade5a (October 25, 2024) of the *Archive of Formal Proofs* [9].

Setup. We performed the evaluation using the Slurm batch system [21] on the computer resources of the Institute for Informatics at Ludwig-Maximilians-Universität München. We requested 32 GiB of RAM and 8 logical processors (CPU threads). Given that not all Sledgehammer steps and ATPs are deterministic and time limits are used, the results are not entirely reproducible. To increase reproducibility, we used a fresh Isabelle installation and reset the state of the learning-based relevance filter MaSh [8] before each evaluation run.

We used the testing and evaluation tool Mirabelle [16], which is included in Isabelle. Mirabelle applies a selected *action* to each selected *goal*. We used the same 50 *Archive* entries as Desharnais et al. [16], from which we randomly selected 100 goals per entry, resulting in a total of 5 000 goals. As the action, we invoked Sledgehammer with several options:

- The *try0* option was disabled so that Sledgehammer's preplay exclusively tried *metis*. This was done to test *metis* extensively, since we extended this proof method, and to keep the evaluation feasible in reasonable time, since other proof methods frequently caused the Isabelle process to abort for technical reasons.
- The *provers* option for specifying the external ATPs was set to use the high-performance [16] superposition provers E, Vampire, and Zipperposition. We excluded satisfiability-modulo-theories (SMT) solvers since these support theories, such as linear arithmetic, that are not built into *metis*.
- The *strict* option was enabled to force the use of sound type encodings for the external ATPs to produce type-correct proofs that should be reconstructable.

We performed two evaluation runs, with Sledgehammer's *instantiate* option set to *smart* in the first run and to *true* in the second run. From the Mirabelle output of each run, we extracted the number of successful Isabelle proofs with and without instantiations, the average execution times of Sledgehammer and *metis*, and the kinds of *metis* calls used in the generated Isabelle proofs. With this information, we try to answer the following research questions:

1. Is it possible to reconstruct additional proofs by instantiating the facts, and in how many cases is a proof derived from the instantiated facts impossible?
2. What are the advantages of enabling Sledgehammer's *instantiate* option? That is, how often are Isabelle proofs with instantiated facts actually presented to users, how much longer do Sledgehammer executions take, and how much faster are Isabelle proofs?
3. What do Sledgehammer-generated *metis* calls look like after instantiating the facts, and what are the benefits of adding the fact *ext*?

Results. We consider only Sledgehammer invocations where an external ATP has found a proof. Sledgehammer's proof reconstruction module initially attempts to generate a *one-line proof* consisting of a single proof method invoked with facts, which can now have instantiations thanks to our extensions. If this attempt is unsuccessful, Sledgehammer tries to transform the ATP proof into an Isar proof [6]. If this also fails, the proof reconstruction is considered to have *failed*. The number of occurrences of each of these outcomes in each evaluation run is shown in Table 1.

Table 1. Proof reconstruction for Sledgehammer invocations yielding ATP proofs

Evaluation run	One-line proofs		Isar proofs	Failed	Total
	W/o inst.	With inst.			
1 (*instantiate* = *smart*)	3 128	44	37	164	3 373
2 (*instantiate* = *true*)	805	2 349	45	159	3 358

In the first evaluation run, there were a total of 3 373 Sledgehammer invocations yielding ATP proofs. Whereas 3 128 ATP proofs (92.7%) were reconstructed directly as one-line proofs without instantiations, 44 additional ATP proofs (1.3%) could be reconstructed by instantiating the facts and thereby speeding up the *metis* proofs. This number may seem low, but this corresponds to 18.0% of cases where there was no one-line proof before. The remaining 6.0% of ATP proofs could not be reconstructed as one-line proofs. This number may seem alarmingly high, but detailed Isar proofs were available in 1.1% of the cases, and in practice the *try0* option is usually enabled, which leads to further proof methods being tried in addition to *metis*. We note that our approach brings similar benefits to Sledgehammer's success rate as Isar proof reconstruction.

In the second evaluation run, there were a total of 3 358 Sledgehammer invocations with ATP proofs. In 2 349 cases (70.0%), Sledgehammer suggested a one-line proof with instantiated facts. In 805 cases (24.0%), Sledgehammer suggested a one-line proof without instantiated facts. The raw evaluation data reveals that in most of these cases, the proof did not use any facts or there were no instantiations.

However, sometimes the instantiations were successfully inferred, but preplay failed to generate a *metis* proof derived from the instantiated facts. According to the raw data, there were 5 such cases (0.1%) in the first evaluation run and 18 (0.5%) in the second. There are several reasons for this, including the following:

- The instantiations did not speed up the *metis* proof enough to take less time than the preplay time limit. The instantiations could have even prolonged the proof, since they modify the problem and could affect Metis's heuristics.
- Isabelle's extremely flexible syntax allows ambiguities and does not guarantee that all terms can be parsed back [6].

Table 2 shows the average execution times of Sledgehammer invocations that successfully generated a one-line *metis* proof. The average execution time of Sledgehammer increased by 312 ms (+0.9%) from the first to the second evaluation run, which can be explained by the additional time required for instantiating

Table 2. Average execution times for a one-line proof

Evaluation run	Sledgehammer	Generated *metis* proof
1 (*instantiate* = *smart*)	34 185 ms	221 ms
2 (*instantiate* = *true*)	34 497 ms	137 ms

facts. However, this did not have a substantial impact on the overall duration of an average Sledgehammer execution. By contrast, the average execution time of *metis* decreased by 84 ms (−38.0%), indicating that the instantiation of facts markedly speeds up proofs. Notice that in about 25% of cases (805 and 44 in Table 1), the *metis* calls generated in the two evaluation runs were both without or both with instantiations. Consequently, for the remaining 75% of cases, it can be deduced that the average execution time decreases by more than 38%. If those proofs are inserted into an Isabelle proof text, this improvement applies every time the text is processed. In particular, every one of the frequent regression tests of the *Archive of Formal Proofs* with its more than 90 000 *metis* calls could benefit.

In Sledgehammer's preplay, a series of *metis* calls are tried, each involving different options that describe the encoding of types and λ-abstractions. Initially, the default options (type encoding `a` [7] and `SKBCI` combinators [37]) are tested, resulting in a standard *metis* call. If this fails, Sledgehammer tries multiple alternative options, selecting the fastest *metis* call with options. If this also fails, Sledgehammer tries the new *metis* calls with the additional fact *ext*. The number of occurrences of each of these kinds of *metis* calls in one-line proofs in each evaluation run is shown in Table 3.

Table 3. Kinds of *metis* calls in one-line proofs

Evaluation run	Standard *metis*	With options	With *ext*	Total
1 (*instantiate* = *smart*)	2 801	318	53	3 172
2 (*instantiate* = *true*)	3 008	110	36	3 154

The number of standard *metis* calls increased from the first evaluation run (88.3%) to the second (95.4%). This observation suggests that Metis's proof search becomes more efficient after the instantiation of facts, since special encodings are needed less often. Moreover, adding *ext* was effective, since it was used in 1.7% and 1.1% of the proofs, respectively, which would have failed otherwise.

Regarding our research question 1, the results show that Sledgehammer can reconstruct additional one-line proofs by instantiating the facts, and that a proof derived from the instantiated facts is almost always possible. Regarding question 2, we observe that enabling Sledgehammer's *instantiate* option leads to proofs with instantiations in 70% of the cases, which may help users understand the generated proofs. Sledgehammer executions also take a bit longer, but the execution time of the generated Isabelle proofs is substantially reduced, which is much more important. Regarding question 3, we see that there are more standard *metis* calls without options after instantiating the facts and that adding the fact *ext* brings similar benefits to Sledgehammer's success rate as instantiating facts.

7 Related Work

The Metis ATP [20], on which our work is based, was developed by Hurd with the goal of integrating it into the HOL proof assistant [18]. Metis was integrated in Isabelle by Paulson and Susanto [32]. Metis's fine-grained proofs were particularly useful to us. Beyond the HOL and Isabelle integrations, there is also a Metis proof checker in Agda developed by Prieto-Cubides and Sicard-Ramírez [33].

Our tool joins the ranks of various proof analysis tools. The GAPT (General Architecture for Proof Theory) framework by Ebner et al. [17] consists of data structures, algorithms, parsers, and more, with the aim of supporting proof theory applications and ATPs. Other proof-manipulating frameworks are ProofCert by Miller and colleagues [14,24] and Dedukti by Dowek and colleagues [1,11].

Our work is also loosely related to the experimental reconstruction of ATP proofs as detailed Isabelle proofs, or Isar proofs [40], by Blanchette et al. [6].

8 Conclusion

We extended Isabelle's *metis* proof method and the Sledgehammer tool to infer variable instantiations from proofs and present them to users. This speeds up Sledgehammer's proof reconstruction and increases its success rate. It also helps users to understand the proof without inspecting all of its details.

We see three main directions for future work. First, we could provide type annotations when parsing of the instantiations is ambiguous. Second, we could provide instantiations not only for one-line proofs but also for individual steps in detailed Isar proofs. Third, we could extend the approach to more ATPs in order to obtain variable instantiations even when *metis* without instantiations fails. The superposition provers E, SPASS, Vampire, and Zipperposition are difficult to integrate, because they fail to preserve the connection between the variables before and after clausification. The *metis* proof method's clausifier, by contrast, preserves variable names. As for SMT solvers, some of them, including cvc5, can be asked to output the instantiations they needed to show unsatisfiability. Then there is no need to analyze the proofs to infer the instantiations.

Acknowledgments. We thank Xavier Généreux, Elisabeth Lempa, Jannis Limperg, Kirstin Peters, Mark Summerfield, and the anonymous reviewers for suggesting various textual improvements. Blanchette's research was cofunded by the European Union (ERC, Nekoka, 101083038). Views and opinions expressed are however those of the authors only and do not necessarily reflect those of the European Union or the European Research Council. Neither the European Union nor the granting authority can be held responsible for them.

Disclosure of Interests. The authors have no competing interests to declare that are relevant to the content of this paper.

References

1. Assaf, A., et al.: Dedukti: a logical framework based on the $\lambda\Pi$-calculus modulo theory. CoRR abs/2311.07185 (2023). https://doi.org/10.48550/ARXIV.2311.07185
2. Bachmair, L., Ganzinger, H.: On restrictions of ordered paramodulation with simplification. In: Stickel, M.E. (ed.) CADE 1990. LNCS, vol. 449, pp. 427–441. Springer, Heidelberg (1990). https://doi.org/10.1007/3-540-52885-7_105
3. Barbosa, H., et al.: cvc5: a versatile and industrial-strength SMT solver. In: TACAS 2022, Part I. LNCS, vol. 13243, pp. 415–442. Springer, Cham (2022). https://doi.org/10.1007/978-3-030-99524-9_24
4. Bhayat, A., Suda, M.: A higher-order Vampire (short paper). In: Benzmüller, C., Heule, M.J.H., Schmidt, R.A. (eds.) IJCAR 2024, Part I. LNCS, vol. 14739, pp. 75–85. Springer, Heidelberg (2024). https://doi.org/10.1007/978-3-031-63498-7_5
5. Blanchette, J.: Hammering away: a user's guide to Sledgehammer for Isabelle/HOL (2025). https://isabelle.in.tum.de/website-Isabelle2025/dist/Isabelle2025/doc/sledgehammer.pdf
6. Blanchette, J.C., Böhme, S., Fleury, M., Smolka, S.J., Steckermeier, A.: Semi-intelligible Isar proofs from machine-generated proofs. J. Autom. Reason. **56**(2), 155–200 (2016). https://doi.org/10.1007/S10817-015-9335-3
7. Blanchette, J.C., Böhme, S., Popescu, A., Smallbone, N.: Encoding monomorphic and polymorphic types. Log. Meth. Comput. Sci. **12**(4) (2016). https://doi.org/10.2168/LMCS-12(4:13)2016
8. Blanchette, J.C., Greenaway, D., Kaliszyk, C., Kühlwein, D., Urban, J.: A learning-based fact selector for Isabelle/HOL. J. Autom. Reason. **57**(3), 219–244 (2016). https://doi.org/10.1007/s10817-016-9362-8
9. Blanchette, J.C., Haslbeck, M., Matichuk, D., Nipkow, T.: Mining the archive of formal proofs. In: Kerber, M., Carette, J., Kaliszyk, C., Rabe, F., Sorge, V. (eds.) CICM 2015. LNCS (LNAI), vol. 9150, pp. 3–17. Springer, Cham (2015). https://doi.org/10.1007/978-3-319-20615-8_1
10. Blanchette, J.C., Popescu, A., Wand, D., Weidenbach, C.: More SPASS with Isabelle: superposition with hard sorts and configurable simplification. In: Beringer, L., Felty, A. (eds.) ITP 2012. LNCS, vol. 7406, pp. 345–360. Springer, Heidelberg (2012). https://doi.org/10.1007/978-3-642-32347-8_24
11. Blot, V., Dowek, G., Traversié, T., Winterhalter, T.: From rewrite rules to axioms in the $\lambda\Pi$-calculus modulo theory. In: Kobayashi, N., Worrell, J. (eds.) FoSSaCS 2024, Part II. LNCS, vol. 14575, pp. 3–23. Springer, Heidelberg (2024). https://doi.org/10.1007/978-3-031-57231-9_1

12. Böhme, S., Nipkow, T.: Sledgehammer: judgement day. In: Giesl, J., Hähnle, R. (eds.) IJCAR 2010. LNCS, vol. 6173, pp. 107–121. Springer, Heidelberg (2010). https://doi.org/10.1007/978-3-642-14203-1_9
13. Bouton, T., Caminha B. de Oliveira, D., Déharbe, D., Fontaine, P.: veriT: an open, trustable and efficient SMT-solver. In: Schmidt, R.A. (ed.) CADE 2009. LNCS (LNAI), vol. 5663, pp. 151–156. Springer, Heidelberg (2009). https://doi.org/10.1007/978-3-642-02959-2_12
14. Chihani, Z., Miller, D., Renaud, F.: A semantic framework for proof evidence. J. Autom. Reason. **59**(3), 287–330 (2017). https://doi.org/10.1007/S10817-016-9380-6
15. Coghetto, R.: Tarski's Parallel Postulate implies the 5th Postulate of Euclid, the Postulate of Playfair and the original Parallel Postulate of Euclid. Archive of Formal Proofs (2021). https://isa-afp.org/entries/IsaGeoCoq.html
16. Desharnais, M., Vukmirović, P., Blanchette, J., Wenzel, M.: Seventeen provers under the hammer. In: Andronick, J., de Moura, L. (eds.) ITP 2022, pp. 8:1–8:18. Schloss Dagstuhl – Leibniz-Zentrum für Informatik (2022). https://doi.org/10.4230/LIPIcs.ITP.2022.8
17. Ebner, G., Hetzl, S., Reis, G., Riener, M., Wolfsteiner, S., Zivota, S.: System description: GAPT 2.0. In: Olivetti, N., Tiwari, A. (eds.) IJCAR 2016. LNCS (LNAI), vol. 9706, pp. 293–301. Springer, Cham (2016). https://doi.org/10.1007/978-3-319-40229-1_20
18. Gordon, M.J.C.: Introduction to the HOL system. In: Archer, M., Joyce, J.J., Levitt, K.N., Windley, P.J. (eds.) TPHOLs 1991, pp. 2–3. IEEE Computer Society (1991). https://ieeexplore.ieee.org/document/596265
19. Hughes, R.J.M.: Super-combinators: a new implementation method for applicative languages. In: LFP 1982, pp. 1–10. ACM Press (1982). https://doi.org/10.1145/800068.802129
20. Hurd, J.: First-order proof tactics in higher-order logic theorem provers. In: Archer, M., Vito, B.D., Muñoz, C. (eds.) Design and Application of Strategies/Tactics in Higher Order Logics, pp. 56–68. No. NASA/CP-2003-212448 in NASA Technical Reports, September 2003. https://www.gilith.com/papers/metis.pdf
21. Jette, M.A., Wickberg, T.: Architecture of the Slurm workload manager. In: Klusáček, D., Corbalán, J., Rodrigo, G.P. (eds.) JSSPP 2023, pp. 3–23. Springer, Heidelberg (2023). https://doi.org/10.1007/978-3-031-43943-8_1
22. Meng, J., Paulson, L.C.: Translating higher-order clauses to first-order clauses. J. Autom. Reason. **40**(1), 35–60 (2007). https://doi.org/10.1007/s10817-007-9085-y
23. Meng, J., Paulson, L.C.: Lightweight relevance filtering for machine-generated resolution problems. J. App. Log. **7**(1), 41–57 (2009). https://doi.org/10.1016/J.JAL.2007.07.004
24. Miller, D.: Foundational proof certificates: making proof universal and permanent. In: Momigliano, A., Pientka, B., Pollack, R. (eds.) LFMTP 2013, pp. 1–2. ACM (2013). https://doi.org/10.1145/2503887.2503894
25. de Moura, L., Bjørner, N.: Z3: an efficient SMT solver. In: Ramakrishnan, C.R., Rehof, J. (eds.) TACAS 2008. LNCS, vol. 4963, pp. 337–340. Springer, Heidelberg (2008). https://doi.org/10.1007/978-3-540-78800-3_24
26. Nipkow, T.: Equational reasoning in Isabelle. Sci. Comput. Prog. **12**(2), 123–149 (1989). https://doi.org/10.1016/0167-6423(89)90038-5
27. Nipkow, T., Wenzel, M., Paulson, L.C. (eds.): Isabelle/HOL. LNCS, vol. 2283. Springer, Heidelberg (2002). https://doi.org/10.1007/3-540-45949-9
28. Nipkow, T., Prehofer, C.: Type reconstruction for type classes. J. Funct. Prog. **5**(2), 201–224 (1995). https://doi.org/10.1017/S0956796800001325

29. Paulson, L.C. (ed.): Isabelle. LNCS, vol. 828. Springer, Heidelberg (1994). https://doi.org/10.1007/BFb0030541
30. Paulson, L.C.: A generic tableau prover and its integration with Isabelle. J. Univ. Comput. Sci. **5**(3), 73–87 (1999). https://doi.org/10.3217/jucs-005-03-0073
31. Paulson, L.C., Blanchette, J.C.: Three years of experience with Sledgehammer, a practical link between automatic and interactive theorem provers. In: Sutcliffe, G., Schulz, S., Ternovska, E. (eds.) IWIL 2010. EPiC Series in Computing, vol. 2, pp. 1–11. EasyChair (2012). https://doi.org/10.29007/36dt
32. Paulson, L.C., Susanto, K.W.: Source-level proof reconstruction for interactive theorem proving. In: Schneider, K., Brandt, J. (eds.) TPHOLs 2007. LNCS, vol. 4732, pp. 232–245. Springer, Heidelberg (2007). https://doi.org/10.1007/978-3-540-74591-4_18
33. Prieto-Cubides, J., Sicard-Ramírez, A.: Proof-reconstruction in type theory for propositional logic. https://raw.githubusercontent.com/jonaprieto/athena/master/pubs/paper/paper.pdf
34. Roßkopf, S., Nipkow, T.: A formalization and proof checker for Isabelle's metalogic. J. Autom. Reason. **67**(1), 1 (2023). https://doi.org/10.1007/s10817-022-09648-w
35. Steen, A., Benzmüller, C.: The higher-order prover Leo-III. In: Galmiche, D., Schulz, S., Sebastiani, R. (eds.) IJCAR 2018. LNCS (LNAI), vol. 10900, pp. 108–116. Springer, Cham (2018). https://doi.org/10.1007/978-3-319-94205-6_8
36. Sutcliffe, G.: The CADE-23 automated theorem proving system competition–CASC-23. AI Commun. **25**(1), 49–63 (2012). https://doi.org/10.3233/AIC-2012-0512
37. Turner, D.A.: A new implementation technique for applicative languages. Softw. Pract. Exper. **9**(1), 31–49 (1979). https://doi.org/10.1002/spe.4380090105
38. Vukmirović, P., Bentkamp, A., Blanchette, J., Cruanes, S., Nummelin, V., Tourret, S.: Making higher-order superposition work. In: Platzer, A., Sutcliffe, G. (eds.) CADE-28. LNCS, vol. 12699, pp. 415–432. Springer, Heidelberg (2021). https://doi.org/10.1007/S10817-021-09613-Z
39. Vukmirović, P., Blanchette, J., Schulz, S.: Extending a high-performance prover to higher-order logic. In: Sankaranarayanan, S., Sharygina, N. (eds.) TACAS 2023, Part II. LNCS, vol. 13994, pp. 111–129. Springer, Heidelberg (2023). https://doi.org/10.1007/978-3-031-30820-8_10
40. Wenzel, M.: Isar—a generic interpretative approach to readable formal proof documents. In: Bertot, Y., Dowek, G., Théry, L., Hirschowitz, A., Paulin, C. (eds.) TPHOLs 1999. LNCS, vol. 1690, pp. 167–183. Springer, Heidelberg (1999). https://doi.org/10.1007/3-540-48256-3_12
41. Wenzel, M.: Isabelle/Isar—A Versatile Environment for Human-Readable Formal Proof Documents. Ph.D. thesis, Institut für Informatik, Technische Universität München (2002). http://tumb1.biblio.tu-muenchen.de/publ/diss/in/2002/wenzel.pdf

Computing Ground Congruence Classes

Hendrik Leidinger[1,2(✉)] and Christoph Weidenbach[1]

[1] Max Planck Institute for Informatics, Saarland Informatics Campus, Saarbrücken, Germany
hleiding@mpi-inf.mpg.de
[2] Graduate School of Computer Science, Saarbrücken, Germany

Abstract. Congruence closure on ground equations is a well-established and efficient algorithm for deciding ground equalities. It constructs an explicit representation of ground equivalence classes based on a given set of input equations, allowing ground equalities to be decided by membership. In many applications, these ground equations originate from grounding non-ground equations.

We propose an algorithm that directly computes a non-ground representation of ground congruence classes for non-ground equations. Our approach is sound and complete with respect to the corresponding ground congruence classes. Experimental results demonstrate that computing non-ground congruence classes often outperforms the classical ground congruence closure algorithm in efficiency.

Keywords: Congruence Closure · Equational Reasoning · First-Order Automated Reasoning

1 Introduction

Equational logic is widely used in almost all aspects of formal reasoning about systems. Given a set of non-ground equations, in order to apply congruence closure (CC) [11] the non-ground equations must be grounded first. Then after applying CC to the grounded equations, ground equalities can be decided by testing membership in the generated congruence classes. CC is in particular useful compared to ground completion [17], if many different ground equalities are tested, in particular, with respect to the same set of input equations. For CC testing an equality amounts to a membership test, for completion normal forms need to be computed. If the starting point for reasoning is a set of first-order equations with variables, then applying CC amounts to grounding the set of equations by a set $\mathcal{M}$ of ground terms resulting in an exponential blow-up in $|\mathcal{M}|$. In this paper we introduce CC($\mathcal{X}$) that prevents the a priori exponential blow-up by grounding and operates on the original equations. Still CC($\mathcal{X}$) ensures that any congruence class it derives has ground instances in $\mathcal{M}$.

In CC($\mathcal{X}$) a (congruence) class is a set of *constrained terms*, also called a *constrained class*. A constraint is a conjunction of checks resembling membership

C. Barrett and U. Waldmann (Eds.): CADE 2025, LNAI 15943, pp. 594–613, 2025.
https://doi.org/10.1007/978-3-031-99984-0_31

conditions and of the form $t \in \mathcal{M}$, where t is a possibly non-ground term and $\mathcal{M}$ is a set of ground terms. When presenting CC($\mathcal{X}$) we assume $\mathcal{M}$ to be finite. For example, such a set of ground terms can either be explicitly represented by enumerating the considered ground terms (as done in SMT) or implicitly through an ordering that always guarantees only finitely many smaller ground terms given some upper bound ground term. The *constraint* restricts the number of ground instances of the *constrained term* to those in $\mathcal{M}$. CC($\mathcal{X}$) creates a solution for the whole ground input space $\mathcal{M}$. It consists of two main rules *Merge* and *Deduction* to build up the congruence classes that are generalizations of the Merge and Deduction rule from CC. *Merge* creates a new class by unifying two terms in different classes and applying this unifier to the Union of these two classes. *Deduction* creates a new class by simultaneously unifying the arguments of two terms with the same top symbol in different classes with terms in the same class. Termination is guaranteed by an effective subsumption test between two classes and the fact that all terms are constrained by $\mathcal{M}$.

As an example, consider the equations $g(x) \approx h(x), h((h(y))) \approx f((h(y)))$ and $\mathcal{M} = \{g(x), h(x), f(x), f((h(x))), h(h(x)), g(h(x)), g(g(x)), h(g(x)), f(g(x)) \mid x \in \{t_1, ..., t_n\},\ t_i \text{ground, symbols } f, g, h \text{ do not occur in } t_i\}$. Initially CC($\mathcal{X}$) creates the classes:

$$\{g(x), h(x) \parallel g(x), h(x)\}, \{h(h(y)), f(h(y)) \parallel h(h(y)), f(h(y))\}$$

where the left-hand side of the $\parallel$ operator is the set of constraints and the right-hand side is the set of terms. The set $\mathcal{M}$ of ground terms is fixed, therefore for readability we simply write, e.g., $\{g(x), h(x) \parallel g(x), h(x)\}$ instead of $\{g(x) \in \mathcal{M}, h(x) \in \mathcal{M} \parallel g(x), h(x)\}$ and use the notation $\{\Gamma \parallel s_1 \ldots, s_n\}$ to denote that the constraint Γ holds for all terms. CC($\mathcal{X}$) can now merge the classes $\{g(x), h(x) \parallel g(x), h(x)\}$ and $\{h(h(y)), f(h(y)) \parallel h(h(y)), f(h(y))\}$ by unifying $h(x)$ with $h(h(y))$. So we get $\{g(h(y)), h(h(y)), f(h(y)) \parallel g(h(y)), h(h(y)), f(h(y))\}$. The new class subsumes the second merged class, so it can be deleted. Now we can apply three times Deduction with one of the implicitly available single term classes $\{f(y) \parallel f(y)\}$, $\{g(y) \parallel g(y)\}$ and $\{h(y) \parallel h(y)\}$ and the class $\{g(x), h(x) \parallel g(x), h(x)\}$ to create the new class $\{f(g(x)), f(h(x)) \parallel f(g(x)), f(h(x))\}$. Repeating this procedure for the other two single-term classes we get $\{g(g(x)), g(h(x)) \parallel g(g(x)), g(h(x))\}$ and $\{h(g(x)), h(h(x)) \parallel h(g(x)), h(h(x))\}$. All these classes can now be merged step by step with the first merged class, whereby the involved classes are always subsumed by the new class. The final result is now:

$$\begin{gathered}\{g(x), h(x) \parallel g(x), h(x)\},\\ \{g(h(y)), g(g(y)), h(h(y)), h(g(y)), f(g(y)), f(h(y)) \parallel\\ g(h(y)), g(g(y)), h(h(y)), h(g(y)), f(g(y)), f(h(y))\}\end{gathered}$$

Comparing the application of CC($\mathcal{X}$) with CC, grounding with $\mathcal{M}$ leads to multiple copies of the involved classes if the number of ground terms is at least higher than one and even if the ground terms t_i do not contain the function symbols f, g, h. For example, if the t_i represent 8 different constants, ground congruence closure would create a total number of 16 classes, whereas in CC($\mathcal{X}$)

the number of classes is independent of the number of constants in this example. In Sect. 5 we will show that CC($\mathcal{X}$) typically outperforms CC.

Related Work: To the best of our knowledge, the only algorithm that is similar to ours is Joe Hurd's Congruence Classes with Logic Variables [15]. The algorithm creates a set of classes, where each class consists of multiple, possibly non-ground terms. It incrementally finds all matchers between all pairs of classes and applies these matchers to extend these classes. Therefore, in order to test equality of two terms they need to be added and the algorithm restarted. The size of terms is not constrained by the algorithm so it may diverge. There is no notion of redundancy. The semantics of the classes is with respect to an infinite signature. In contrast, we generate a complete classification of all considered ground terms, i.e., testing equality of two terms means testing membership in the same class. Due to a notion of redundancy, our algorithm always terminates (Lemma 20), and it is implemented (Sect. 4).

There are two potential applications of CC($\mathcal{X}$) in existing frameworks: SMT (Satisfiability Modulo Theory) and SCL(EQ) (Simple Clause Learning in first-order logic with equality). Satisfiability modulo theory (SMT) [14,26] solvers (e.g., [2,7,9,12,22]) make use of congruence closure (CC) [11,23,29]. It is well suited as an incremental algorithm that decides the validity of ground equations and is able to find a small subset of input equations that serves as a proof, all in time $\mathcal{O}(n\, log(n))$ [25]. Typical applications consider a set of first-order equations with variables plus further theories. For SMT solvers many techniques have been invented to instantiate non-ground input equations [3,27,28] in order to make them applicable to CC. With CC($\mathcal{X}$) the grounding could be postponed allowing reasoning modulo a larger set of grounding terms.

SCL(EQ) (Simple Clause Learning over Equations) [18] is a complete calculus for first-order logic with equality that only learns non-redundant clauses. Similar to CDCL (Conflict Driven Clause Learning) [5,16,21,30,32] it builds an explicit model assumption (trail) of ground literals where ground instances are finitely limited by some ground term β with respect to an ordering. Clauses are evaluated with respect to a trail. CC($\mathcal{X}$) can be immediately applied by not grounding the equations but reasoning modulo a set of ground terms smaller than β.

For uniform word problems [10] CC(X) can be used as an alternative semi-decision procedure by iteratively increasing the set of considered ground terms. It may also provide a priori guarantees, e.g., if there is a depth bound on the overall set of ground terms that need to be considered. Whenever the overall set of ground terms to be considered is finite CC(X) turns into a decision procedure due to soundness, Lemma 19, completeness, Lemma 21, and termination, Lemma 20.

The rest of the paper is organized as follows. Section 2 provides the necessary technical background notions needed for the development of our algorithm. Section 3 presents our new calculus including examples and proofs for soundness, Lemma 19, completeness, Lemma 21, and termination, Lemma 20. Section 4 presents refinements of the calculus towards an implementation. Section 5 compares the performance of CC($\mathcal{X}$) with CC by experiments. All experiments can be reproduced by the provided supplementary material. Section 6 concludes the paper. An extended version contains additional examples, proofs and pseudo code of our implementation and is available on arXiv [19].

2 Preliminaries

We assume a standard first-order language with equality and over a finite set of function symbols Ω, where the only predicate symbol is equality $\approx$. We assume that Ω contains at least one constant and one non-constant function symbol. t, s, l, r are terms from $\mathcal{T}(\Omega, \mathcal{X})$ for an infinite set of variables $\mathcal{X}$; f, g, h function symbols from Ω; a, b, c constants from Ω and x, y, z variables from $\mathcal{X}$. The function vars returns all variables of a term. The function $\#(x, t)$ returns the number of occurrences of a variable x in t.

By $\sigma, \tau, \delta, \mu$ we denote substitutions. Let σ be a substitution, then its finite domain is defined as $\operatorname{dom}(\sigma) := \{x \mid x\sigma \neq x\}$ and its codomain is defined as $\operatorname{cdom}(\sigma) = \{t \mid x\sigma = t, x \in \operatorname{dom}(\sigma)\}$. We extend their application to terms and sets of terms in the usual way. A term, equation is *ground* if it does not contain any variable. A substitution σ is *ground* if $\operatorname{cdom}(\sigma)$ is ground. A substitution σ is *grounding* for a term t, equation $s \approx t$ if $t\sigma$, $(s \approx t)\sigma$ is ground, respectively. The function gnd returns the set of all ground instances of a term, equation or sets thereof. The function mgu denotes the most general unifier of two terms, two equations, respectively. We assume that mgus do not introduce fresh variables and that they are idempotent. The size of a term t (equation E) is denoted by $\operatorname{size}(t)$ ($\operatorname{size}(E)$), which is the number of symbols in t (E).

Let $\preceq$ be a total quasi-ordering on ground terms where the strict part is well-founded. The ordering is lifted to the non-ground case via instantiation: we define $t \preceq s$ if for all grounding substitutions σ it holds $t\sigma \preceq s\sigma$. Given a ground term β then $\operatorname{gnd}_{\preceq\beta}$ computes the set of all ground instances of a term, equation, or sets thereof where all ground terms are smaller or equal to β with respect to $\preceq$. Analogously, for a set of ground terms $\mathcal{M}$, we define $\operatorname{gnd}_{\mathcal{M}}$ as the set of ground instances of a term, equation or sets thereof where all ground terms are in $\mathcal{M}$. By $\mathcal{T}_{\preceq\beta}(\Omega, \emptyset)$ or just $\mathcal{T}_{\preceq\beta}$ we denote the set of all ground terms $\preceq \beta$.

We rely on standard first-order semantics and in particular write $E \models s \approx t$ if any model of the implicitly universally quantified equations in E is also a model for the ground equation $s \approx t$.

Let E be a set of equations over $T(\Omega, \mathcal{X})$ where all variables are implicitly universally quantified. The well-known inference system of equational logic comprises the following rules [1]

Reflexivity $E \Rightarrow_{\mathrm{EQ}} E \cup \{t \approx t\}$
provided t is a term.

Symmetry $E \cup \{t \approx t'\} \Rightarrow_{\mathrm{EQ}} E \cup \{t \approx t', t' \approx t\}$

Transitivity $E \cup \{t \approx t', t' \approx t''\} \Rightarrow_{\mathrm{EQ}} E \cup \{t \approx t', t' \approx t'', t \approx t''\}$

Congruence $E \cup \{t_1 \approx t'_1, ..., t_n \approx t'_n\} \Rightarrow_{\mathrm{EQ}} E \cup \{t_1 \approx t'_1, ..., t_n \approx t'_n, f(t_1, ..., t_n) \approx f(t'_1, ..., t'_n)\}$

Instance $E \cup \{t \approx t'\} \Rightarrow_{\mathrm{EQ}} E \cup \{t \approx t, t\sigma \approx t'\sigma\}$

provided σ is a substitution.
and by Bikhoff's Theorem [1] we get for two ground terms $t, s : E \models s \approx t$ iff $E \Rightarrow^*_{\text{EQ}} \{t, s\} \cup E'$. We will base our completeness proof, Lemma 21, on $\Rightarrow_{\text{EQ}}$.

Congruence Closure [11,23,29] is an algorithm for deciding satisfiability of ground equations. We present the abstract version of congruence closure as described by Fontaine [13] and based on the algorithm by Nelson and Oppen [23]. The initial state is (Π, E), where Π is a partition of all ground subterms of terms in E, such that every term is in its own class, and E is the set of ground equations. The algorithm consists of the following three inference rules.

Delete $(\{A\} \cup \Pi, E \cup \{s \approx t\}) \Rightarrow_{\text{CC}} (\{A\} \cup \Pi, E)$
provided $\{s, t\} \subseteq A$.

Merge $(\{A, B\} \cup \Pi, E \cup \{s \approx t\}) \Rightarrow_{\text{CC}} (\{A \cup B\} \cup \Pi, E)$
provided $s \in A$, $t \in B$ and $A \neq B$.

Deduction $(\{A, B\} \cup \Pi, E) \Rightarrow_{\text{CC}} (\{A, B\} \cup \Pi, E \cup \{f(s_1, ..., s_n) \approx f(t_1, ..., t_n)\})$
provided $f(s_1, ..., s_n) \in A$, $f(t_1, ..., t_n) \in B$, $A \neq B$ and for each i, there exists a $D_i \in \{A, B\} \cup \Pi$ such that $\{s_i, t_i\} \in D_i$ and $f(s_1, ..., s_n) \approx f(t_1, ..., t_n) \notin E$.

The algorithm terminates if no rule is applicable anymore. The resulting set Π represents the set of congruence classes.

3 CC($\mathcal{X}$): Non-ground Congruence Closure

We now present our calculus in full detail. Throughout this section we assume a finite set $\mathcal{M}$ of ground terms and a finite set E of possibly non-ground equations.

Definition 1. *A* constrained term *$\Gamma \parallel s$ is a term s with a constraint Γ. The* constraint *Γ is a conjunction of atoms $t \in \mathcal{M}$. A substitution σ is* grounding *for a constraint term $\Gamma \parallel s$ if $\Gamma\sigma$ and $s\sigma$ are ground.*

The constraint Γ restricts the possible ground instances of the term s to those instances $s\sigma$ such that $\Gamma\sigma$ evaluates to true. If it is clear from the context, we omit the $\in \mathcal{M}$ and just write the left-hand side of the operation. A constraint class is a set of constraint terms. We distinguish between separating and free variables, where a separating variable occurs in all terms within the class whereas a free variable does not.

Definition 2 (Congruence Class). *A* congruence class *or simply class is a finite set of constraint terms $\Gamma \parallel s$. Let $A = \{\Gamma_1 \parallel s_1, ..., \Gamma_n \parallel s_n\}$ be a class. The set of* separating *variables X of A is defined as $X = \text{vars}(s_1) \cap ... \cap \text{vars}(s_n)$. The set of* free *variables Y of A is defined as $Y = (vars(s_1) \cup ... \cup vars(s_n)) \setminus X$. A substitution is* grounding *for A if it is grounding for all constraint terms $\Gamma_i \parallel s_i$.*

If the terms in a congruence class all have the same constraint then we use $\{\Gamma \parallel s_1, ..., s_n\}$ as a shorthand for $\{\Gamma \parallel s_1, ..., \Gamma \parallel s_n\}$. For example, with all shorthands we can now write $\{g(x), h(x) \parallel g(x), h(x)\}$ instead of $\{g(x) \in \mathcal{M}, h(x) \in \mathcal{M} \parallel g(x), g(x) \in \mathcal{M}, h(x) \in \mathcal{M} \parallel h(x)\}$. In the calculus later on the constraints of each term within a class are always the same. Variables in a class can always be renamed.

Definition 3. *Let* $A = \{\Gamma_1 \parallel s_1, ..., \Gamma_n \parallel s_n\}$ *be a class and* μ *a substitution. We define* $A\mu$ *as* $\{\Gamma_1\mu \parallel s_1\mu, ..., \Gamma_n\mu \parallel s_n\mu\}$. *In particular, if* μ *is grounding for* A *we overload its application by* $A\mu = \{s\mu \mid (\Gamma \parallel s \in A \text{ and } \Gamma\mu \text{ true})\}$.

The semantics of a congruence class with variables is defined by creating a mapping to the corresponding ground classes. It is important to distinguish between separating and free variables here. Separating variables divide the non-ground class into several ground classes.

Definition 4 (Congruence Class Semantics). *Let* A *be a congruence class. Let* X *be the separating variables of* A. *Then the set* $\text{gnd}'(A)$ *is defined as:*

$$\bigcup_{\substack{\sigma \text{ ground,} \\ \text{dom}(\sigma)=X}} \{\{(\Gamma\sigma \parallel s\sigma) \mid (\Gamma \parallel s) \in A \text{ and } \Gamma\sigma \text{ satisfiable}\}\}$$

and the set $\text{gnd}(A)$ *is defined as:*

$$\bigcup_{B \in \text{gnd}'(A)} \Big\{ \bigcup_{\sigma \text{ grounding for } B} \{s\sigma \mid (\Gamma \parallel s) \in B \text{ and } \Gamma\sigma \text{ true}\}\Big\}$$

Example 5. Assume $\Omega = \{g, h, a, b\}$, $\mathcal{M} = \{g(a), g(b), h(a), h(b)\}$ and classes $A = \{g(x), h(x) \parallel g(x), h(x)\}, B = \{g(x), h(y) \parallel g(x), h(y)\}$. Then:

$$\text{gnd}(A) = \{\{g(a), h(a)\}, \{g(b), h(b)\}\} \text{ and } \text{gnd}(B) = \{\{g(a), h(a), g(b), h(b)\}\}$$

Definition 6 (Normal Class). *Let* A *be a class. The* normal *class* $\text{norm}(A)$ *is defined as* $\{(\Gamma \wedge \Gamma\sigma \parallel s) \mid (\Gamma \parallel s) \in A\} \cup \{(\Gamma \wedge \Gamma\sigma \parallel s\sigma) \mid (\Gamma \parallel s) \in A$ *and* s *contains free variables*$\}$ *for a renaming* σ *on the free variables introducing only fresh variables.*

A class can be turned into a normal class by generating exactly one renamed copy for all constrained terms containing free variables. The motivation for normal classes is of technical nature. CC($\mathcal{X}$) rules always operate on two terms out of a class. In case of terms with variables the two terms may be actually instances of the same term from the class. This can only happen for terms with free variables. By introducing one renamed copy for such terms, the style of CC($\mathcal{X}$)rules is preserved and the rules do not need to distinguish between free and separated variables. For example, the class $A = \{g(x), h(y) \parallel g(x), h(y)\}$ contains all ground terms build with top-symbols g and h. So for a CC($\mathcal{X}$) step picking $g(a)$ and $g(b)$ out of the class the term $g(x)$ needs to be instantiated with two different constants. By using renamed copies $\text{norm}(A) = \{g(x), g(x'), h(y), h(y') \parallel g(x), g(x'), h(y), h(y')\}$ this technical issue is removed. Obviously, $\text{gnd}(A) = \text{gnd}(\text{norm}(A))$, holding for all classes and their normal counterparts.

Definition 7 (Subsumption). *A class* B *subsumes another class* A *if for all* $A' \in \text{gnd}(A)$ *there exists a* $B' \in \text{gnd}(B)$ *such that* $A' \subseteq B'$.

The following definitions and lemmas prepare termination, Lemma 20. We show that we cannot create infinitely many classes restricted by $\mathcal{M}$ such that each new class is not subsumed by any existing class, guaranteeing termination.

Definition 8. *Let $A = \{\Gamma_1 \parallel s_1, ..., \Gamma_n \parallel s_n\}$ be a class. A is constrained by $\mathcal{M}$ (or $\mathcal{M}$-constrained) iff $(s_i \in \mathcal{M}) \in \Gamma_i$ for all $1 \leq i \leq n$.*

Lemma 9. (Constraint Semantics matches $\mathcal{M}$). *Let A be a $\mathcal{M}$-constrained class. Then* $\text{gnd}(A) \in \mathcal{P}(\mathcal{M})$*, the powerset of $\mathcal{M}$.*

Lemma 10 (Constraint Semantics matches $\mathcal{M}$). *There exists no infinite chain of (possibly non-ground) $\mathcal{M}$-constrained classes $A_0, A_1, ...$ such that for all $i \geq 0$, A_i is not subsumed by any $B \in \{A_0, ..., A_{i-1}\}$.*

Definition 11. *Let $A = \{\Gamma_1 \parallel s_1, ..., \Gamma_n \parallel s_n\}$ be a class. The set $vars(A)$ is defined as $\bigcup_{1 \leq i \leq n} (\bigcup_{t \in \Gamma_i} vars(t)) \cup vars(s_i)$.*

A *state* of $\text{CC}(\mathcal{X})$ is a finite set of congruence classes. For a state $\Pi = \{A_1, ..., A_n\}$ we define $\text{gnd}(\Pi) = \text{gnd}(A_1) \cup ... \cup \text{gnd}(A_n)$. For any state Π and classes $\{A, B\} \subseteq \Pi$ with $A \neq B$, we assume that $vars(A) \cap vars(B) = \emptyset$. This can always be achieved by renaming the variables of the classes. Now given a set of equations E, where $\text{gnd}_{\mathcal{M}}(s \approx t) \neq \emptyset$ for all $s \approx t \in E$ the initial state of $\text{CC}(\mathcal{X})$ is

$$\begin{aligned}\Pi = &\{\{s \in \mathcal{M} \wedge t \in \mathcal{M} \parallel s, s \in \mathcal{M} \wedge t \in \mathcal{M} \parallel t\} \mid s \approx t \in E\} \cup \\ &\{\{f_i(x_{1_i}, \ldots, x_{k_i}) \in \mathcal{M} \parallel f_i(x_{1_i}, \ldots, x_{k_i})\} \mid f_i \in \Omega\}\end{aligned}$$

In particular, the linear single term classes $f_i(x_{1_i}, \ldots, x_{k_i})$ are needed for technical reasons. They enable the Deduction rule to build terms that are not contained in E as a subterm but are contained in $\mathcal{M}$.

Definition 12 (Π -closed). *We call a set $\mathcal{M}$ of ground terms Π-*closed *for a ground term t and a set of congruence classes Π, if for all (sub)terms s occurring in Π and all grounding substitutions σ for s we have if $s\sigma \in \mathcal{M}$ then $s\delta \in \mathcal{M}$ for all δ where if $x\sigma \neq x\delta$ for some variable x, then $x\delta = t$.*

The ground term set $\mathcal{M}$ from the introduction is *Π-closed* with respect to $\{g(x) \parallel g(x)\}, \{h(x) \parallel h(x)\}, \{f(x) \parallel f(x)\}, \{g(x), h(x) \parallel g(x), h(x)\}, \{h(h(y)), f(h(y)) \parallel h(h(y)), f(h(y))\}$ for any of the constants. We need this property for our soundness proof, in particular Lemma 17. The property guarantees that the rules do not generate classes that have no meaning in $\mathcal{M}$. From now on we assume that $\mathcal{M}$ is always *Π-closed* for some ground term $t \in M$. We present our algorithm in the form of two abstract rewrite rules:

Merge $\Pi \cup \{A, B\} \Rightarrow_{\text{CC}(\mathcal{X})} \Pi \cup \{A, B, (A' \cup B')\mu\}$
provided $\text{norm}(A) = \{\Gamma_1 \parallel s_1, ..., \Gamma_n \parallel s_n\}$, $\text{norm}(B) = \{\Delta_1 \parallel t_1, ..., \Delta_n \parallel t_n\}$, there exist $(\Gamma \parallel s) \in A, (\Delta \parallel t) \in B$ and μ such that $\mu = mgu(s, t)$, $A' =$

$\{\Gamma_1 \wedge \Gamma \wedge \Delta \parallel s_1, ..., \Gamma_n \wedge \Gamma \wedge \Delta \parallel s_n\}$, $B' = \{\Delta_1 \wedge \Gamma \wedge \Delta \parallel t_1, ..., \Delta_n \wedge \Gamma \wedge \Delta \parallel t_n\}$, there exists no $A'' \in \Pi \cup \{A, B\}$ such that $(A' \cup B')\mu$ is subsumed by A''.

The rule *Merge* takes as input two classes where a term in the first class is unifiable with a term in the second class. The result is the union of their normal classes with the unifier applied. For termination it is crucial to check if there exists a class that subsumes the newly generated class. Note that the *Merge* rule can be seen as a generalization of the *Merge* rule in $\Rightarrow_{\text{CC}}$. We do not explicitly require the constraint of the newly generated class to be satisfiable, if it is not, the class is empty and subsumed by any other class.

Deduction. $\Pi \cup \{A, B\} \quad \Rightarrow_{\text{CC}(\mathcal{X})} \quad \Pi \cup \{A, B, \{\Gamma' \parallel f(s'_1, ..., s'_n), \Gamma' \parallel f(t'_1, ..., t'_n)\}\mu\}$
provided $\Gamma \parallel f(s_1, ..., s_n) \in A$, $\Delta \parallel f(t_1, ..., t_n) \in B$, and for each $0 < i \leq n$, there exists a $D_i \in \Pi$ such that $\Gamma_i \parallel s'_i \in \text{norm}(D_i)$, $\Delta_i \parallel t'_i \in \text{norm}(D_i)$, μ is a simultaneous mgu of $f(s'_1, ..., s'_n) = f(s_1, ..., s_n)$ and $f(t'_1, ..., t'_n) = f(t_1, ..., t_n)$, $\Gamma' = \Gamma \wedge \Delta \wedge \Gamma_1 \wedge ... \wedge \Gamma_n \wedge \Delta_1 \wedge ... \wedge \Delta_n$, there exists no $A' \in \Pi \cup \{A, B\}$ such that $\{\Gamma' \parallel f(s'_1, ..., s'_n), \Gamma' \parallel f(t'_1, ..., t'_n)\}\mu$ is subsumed by A'.

The rule *Deduction* creates a new class if there exist terms with the same top symbol in two different (copies of) classes such that their arguments are unifiable with terms that are in the same class. Again *Deduction* is a generalization of the *Deduction* rule from $\Rightarrow_{\text{CC}}$. Note, that in *Merge* and *Deduction* A and B can be identical. In this case we assume the consideration of a renamed copy. Furthermore, in both rules we inherit all parent constraints for the new class. Using this invariant, we could also represent each class by a single constraint that is not dedicated to a term. We do not do so in order to get a nicer representation, the way constraints are composed depending on the term they belong to. Our way of constraint composition can also result in constraints containing variables that do not occur in any term of the class anymore. We'll take care of these constraints in Sect. 5.

Example 13. Suppose we have the following equations: $g(x) \approx a$, $h(y) \approx a$, $g(h(z)) \approx h(h(z))$ and Ω consists only of symbols occuring in these equations. Further assume that $\mathcal{M}$ is chosen in such a way that the following classes have at least one non-empty ground instance. Initially, without single term classes, we have one class for each equation:

$$\Pi = \{\{g(x), a \parallel g(x), a\}, \{h(y), a \parallel h(y), a\}, \{g(h(z)), h(h(z)) \parallel g(h(z)), h(h(z))\}\}$$

Merge could now be applied to the last class and the second class (Note that Merge is applied to the normal counterparts of the input classes) to create the new class: $\{g(h(z)), h(h(z)), h(y), a \parallel g(h(z)), h(h(z)), h(y), a\}$. Another Merge operation to this new class and the first class results in:

$$\{g(h(z)), h(h(z)), a, h(y), g(x) \parallel g(h(z)), h(h(z)), a, h(y), g(x)\}$$

This class subsumes all other classes, for example with our implicit representation of $\mathcal{M}$ by an ordering and a maximum term β as described in more detail in

Sect. 5. So this would be the final result. Note that this result is independent of the chosen maximum term β. No matter how large β is the result of the calculus is always the same (assuming that β allows for the initial classes).

Note that a large number of redundant classes can be created. While these redundant classes affect neither soundness nor completeness getting rid of redundant classes is essential for an efficient implementation. To this end we introduce a Subsumption rule that has precedence over all other rules.

Subsumption. $\Pi \cup \{A, B\} \Rightarrow_{\mathrm{CC}(\mathcal{X})} \Pi \cup \{B\}$
provided B subsumes A.

Note, that despite this subsumption rule, $\mathrm{CC}(\mathcal{X})$ does not always guarantee fewer or equally many Congruence Classes than CC. Consider the following example.

Example 14. Let $f(a) \approx h(a), g(a) \approx h(a), f(b) \approx h(b), g(b) \approx h(b), f(x) \approx g(x), a \approx f(a), b \approx f(b)$ be some input equations. Further assume

$$\mathcal{M} = \{f(a), g(a), h(a), f(b), g(b), h(b), a, b\}$$

Initially $\mathrm{CC}(\mathcal{X})$ contains a class for the terms in each equation. Note, that Subsumption is not applicable in this state. Now, multiple Merge operations are possible, but no matter in which sequence they are applied the result is always

$$\{\{f(a), h(a), g(a), a \parallel f(a), h(a), g(a), a\}, \{f(b), h(b), g(b), b \parallel f(b), h(b), g(b), b\},$$
$$\{f(x), g(x) \parallel f(x), g(x)\}\}$$

Subsumption is not applicable to this set of classes. In ground congruence closure, however, we only get two classes:

$$\{\{f(a), h(a), g(a), a\}, \{f(b), h(b), g(b), b\}\}$$

The following example shows that Merge also has to be applied to two instances of the same class.

Example 15. Assume initial classes (without single term classes):

$$\Pi = \{\{f(x, y), g(x, y) \parallel f(x, y), g(x, y)\},$$
$$\{f(x, y), g(y, x) \parallel f(x, y), g(y, x)\}\}$$

and $\mathcal{M} = \{f(a, b), f(b, a), g(a, b), g(b, a)\}$ which is extended to a Π-closed set by Definition 12. Now we can merge the classes by unifying $f(x, y)$:

$$\{f(x, y), g(x, y), g(y, x) \parallel f(x, y), g(x, y), g(y, x)\}$$

Now it could be the case that the new class subsumes both initial classes and they are removed from the set of classes as a consequence. This means that no further Merge operations with the original classes are possible. Therefore, to get the final result, we have to merge this new class with itself by unifying $g(x, y)$ and $g(y, x)$ to get:

$$A = \{f(x, y), g(x, y), g(y, x), f(y, x) \parallel$$
$$f(x, y), g(x, y), g(y, x), f(y, x)\}$$

Otherwise, e.g. $\{f(a, b), f(b, a)\} \not\subseteq A'$ for all $A' \in gnd(A)$.

We will now prove termination, soundness and completeness. We start with soundness.

Lemma 16 (Normal Classes). *Let A be a class. There exists a $A' \in gnd(A)$ s.t. for all s, t: $\{s, t\} \subseteq A'$ iff there exists a substitution σ' such that $\{s, t\} \subseteq norm(A)\sigma'$.*

Lemma 17 (Ground Testing). *Let Π be a set of classes. Assume that $\mathcal{M}$ is Π-closed for the term α. Let $A \in \Pi$ be a class where all constraints are the same, X separating variables, Y free variables of A and $gnd_{\mathcal{M}}(E) \models s\sigma \approx t\sigma$ for all $\{s\sigma, t\sigma\} \subseteq A\sigma$ and grounding σ. Then for all $\Gamma \parallel s \in A$ we have $gnd_{\mathcal{M}}(E) \models s\sigma\delta \approx s\sigma\delta'$ for all $\sigma : X \to \mathcal{T}(\Omega, \emptyset)$, $\delta : Y \to \mathcal{T}(\Omega, \emptyset)$ and $\delta' = \{y \mapsto \alpha \mid y \in Y\}$, where $\alpha \in \mathcal{M}$, $\Gamma\sigma\delta$ satisfiable.*

Corollary 18. *Let A be a class where all constraints are the same, and $gnd_{\mathcal{M}}(E) \models s\sigma \approx t\sigma$ for all $\{s\sigma, t\sigma\} \subseteq A\sigma$ and grounding σ. Then $gnd_{\mathcal{M}}(E) \models s\sigma \approx t\sigma$ for all $\{s\sigma, t\sigma\} \subseteq norm(A)\sigma$ and grounding σ.*

Lemma 19 ($\Rightarrow_{\mathrm{CC}(\mathcal{X})}$ is sound). *For any run of $\Rightarrow_{CC(\mathcal{X})}$, any state Π' in this run and for all terms s, t and grounding substitution σ such that there exists a class $A \in \Pi'$ such that $\{\Gamma \parallel s, \Delta \parallel t\} \subseteq norm(A)$, $\Gamma\sigma$ and $\Delta\sigma$ satisfiable, it holds that* $\mathrm{gnd}_{\mathcal{M}}(E) \models s\sigma \approx t\sigma$.

Proof. (Idea) By induction on the state Π within a $\mathrm{CC}(\mathcal{X})$ derivation and a case analysis for the different rules preserving soundness of the state Π.

Lemma 20 ($\Rightarrow_{\mathrm{CC}(\mathcal{X})}$.is Terminating). *For any run of $\Rightarrow_{CC(\mathcal{X})}$ we reach a state, where no rule of $\Rightarrow_{CC(\mathcal{X})}$ is applicable anymore.*

Proof. (Idea) By Lemma 10 there are only finitely many possible $\mathcal{M}$-constrained classes that are not subsumed. *Merge* and *Deduction* only create classes that are not subsumed. *Subsumption* only removes classes that are subsumed.

Lemma 21 ($\Rightarrow_{\mathrm{CC}(\mathcal{X})}$.is Complete). *Let Π be the result of a run of $\Rightarrow_{CC(\mathcal{X})}$ such that no rule of $\Rightarrow_{CC(\mathcal{X})}$ is applicable anymore. Then for all $\{s, t\} \subseteq \mathcal{M}$ such that* $\mathrm{gnd}_{\mathcal{M}}(E) \models s \approx t$ *there exists a class $A \in \Pi$, $\{\Gamma \parallel s', \Delta \parallel t'\} \subseteq norm(A)$ and grounding substitution σ such that $s'\sigma = s$ and $t'\sigma = t$ and $\Gamma\sigma, \Delta\sigma$ satisfiable.*

Proof. (Idea) We show by induction that for any sequence of applications of $\Rightarrow_{EQ}$ there exists a sequence of applications of $\Rightarrow_{\mathrm{CC}(\mathcal{X})}$ such that the results are semantically equivalent by case analysis for the different rules of $\Rightarrow_{EQ}$.

4 Towards Implementation

In the following, we describe refinements and optimizations of the CC($\mathcal{X}$) calculus towards an implementation. We start with a simplification of the Deduction rule. It suffices to use only the single term classes for A and B in the Deduction rule.

Lemma 22 (Deduction with Single Term Classes). *Assume a state Π such that Deduction is applicable for some $\{A, B\} \subseteq \Pi$ and $\Gamma \parallel f(s_1, ..., s_n) \in A, \Delta \parallel f(t_1, ..., t_n) \in B$. Let μ be the resulting simultaneous mgu and $\{\Gamma_i \parallel s_i', \Delta_i \parallel t_i'\} \subseteq norm(D_i)$ for all $1 \leq i \leq n$ such that $\{\Gamma' \parallel f(s_1', ..., s_n'), f(t_1', ..., t_n')\}\mu$ is the resulting new class. Then Deduction is applicable for two variable disjoint copies of the single term class $\{f(x_1, ..., x_n) \parallel f(x_1, ..., x_n)\}$.*

It is easy to see that the class created by the single term class is always more general than the other classes that can be created by Deduction.

A naive implementation of Subsumption, Definition 7, by ground instantiation results in a practically intractable procedure. Therefore, it is approximated by the below subsumption by matching rule that does not need ground instantiation and is practically tractable, see Sect. 5.

Definition 23 (Subsumption by Matching) *Let A, B be classes. Let X be the separating variables of B and Y the free variables of B. B subsumes A by matching iff there exists a substitution $\sigma : X \to \mathcal{T}(\Omega, vars(A))$ that maps every variable in X, such that for every $\Gamma \parallel t \in A$ there is a $\tau : Y \to \mathcal{T}(\Omega, vars(A))$ and $(\Delta \parallel s)\sigma \in B\sigma$ such that $t = s\sigma\tau$ and $\forall\delta.(\Gamma\delta \to \exists\delta'.\Delta\sigma\tau\delta\delta')$.*

Lemma 24. *Let A, B be classes. If B subsumes A by matching then B subsumes A.*

The converse of Lemma 24 does not hold. Consider symbols f, g, a, b, $\mathcal{M} = \{a, b, f(a), f(b), g(a), g(b)\}$ and classes $A = \{f(x), g(a), g(b) \parallel f(x), g(a), g(b)\}$ and $B = \{f(a), f(b), g(x) \parallel f(a), f(b), g(x)\}$. Then neither A subsumes B nor B subsumes A by subsumption by matching, although $gnd(A) = gnd(B)$. However, in Sect. 5 we show that the subsumption by matching rule performs nicely in practice.

To keep the number of constrained terms within classes small, we also need a new condensation rule:

Condensation. $\Pi \cup \{\{\Gamma_1 \parallel s_1, ..., \Gamma_n \parallel s_n\}\} \Rightarrow_{\mathrm{CC}(\mathcal{X})} \Pi \cup \{\{\Gamma_1 \parallel s_1, ..., \Gamma_{j-1} \parallel s_{j-1}, \Gamma_{j+1} \parallel s_{j+1}, ..., \Gamma_n \parallel s_n\}\delta\}$
provided there exists indices i, j and a matcher δ such that $s_i\delta = s_j$, $\{\Gamma_1 \parallel s_1, ..., \Gamma_{j-1} \parallel s_{j-1}, \Gamma_{j+1} \parallel s_{j+1}, ..., \Gamma_n \parallel s_n\}\delta$ subsumes $\{\Gamma_1 \parallel s_1, ..., \Gamma_n \parallel s_n\}$.

For example, the Condensation rule would reduce the class $\{f(x), f(y), f(z) \parallel f(x), f(y), f(z)\}$ to $\{f(x), f(y) \parallel f(x), f(y)\}$. Condensation together with subsumption by matching ensures termination, because the number of separating variables is bounded. Condensation is an example where we could improve the performance of our implementation. It can be implemented without additional memory consumption, however, our current implementation copies the class, modifies it and then checks subsumption.

To keep the number of full subsumption checks to a minimum, we have also implemented fast pre-filtering techniques. It turns out that it is more efficient to first check whether for each term in the instance class there is a term in the general class that matches this term.

Corollary 25. *Let A, B be two classes. If there exists a $\Gamma \parallel t \in A$ such that there exists no $\Delta \parallel s \in B$ and no matcher δ such that $s\delta = t$, then A is not subsumed by B.*

We use bit vectors to track the number of occurrences of top symbols of terms within a class to check the above filter. For each symbol we store in one bit whether there are 0, 1 or more terms in the class that contain this symbol as a top symbol, where $[0]_{10} = [0]_2, [1]_{10} = [1]_2$. For two bit vectors $\mathcal{V}_0$ of a general and $\mathcal{V}_1$ of an instance class we compute NOT($\mathcal{V}_0$) AND $\mathcal{V}_1$, where NOT and AND are bitwise operators. Note that classes containing a variable term must be excluded from this check.

5 Evaluation

The first step for an actual implementation and evaluation is to choose a representation for the set of ground terms $\mathcal{M}$. This could be through an explicit representation of the ground terms, e.g., by indexing [24] or an implicit representation, e.g., by an upper bound with respect to an ordering. For our evaluation we choose the latter, in particular we define the set $\mathcal{M}$ with respect to the ordering $\preceq$ that simply counts the number of symbols. Given a finite signature and a finite set of variables and a ground term β, there are only finitely many different ground terms smaller than β, denoted by $\mathcal{T}_{\preceq\beta}$ and we define $\mathcal{M} = \mathcal{T}_{\preceq\beta}$. More formally, let s, t be two terms. Then $s \preceq t$ if $\text{size}(s) \leq \text{size}(t)$. Now $t \in \mathcal{M}$ iff $t \in \mathcal{T}_{\preceq\beta}$ iff $t \preceq \beta$. The ground term set $\mathcal{M}$ defined this way is Π-closed with respect to any set of congruence classes and the constants in M, because the constants are minimal in the symbol order.

Solving $\preceq$-constraints is equivalent to solving linear integer arithmetic constraints. Note that a constraint Γ is satisfiable iff it is satisfiable without applying any substitution, because variables and constants are the smallest terms in the symbol count order. Regarding the implication $\forall\delta.(\Gamma\delta \rightarrow \exists\delta'.\Delta\sigma\tau\delta\delta')$, see Definition 23, the quantifier alternation can be removed, so $\forall\delta.(\Gamma\delta \rightarrow \exists\delta'.\Delta\sigma\tau\delta\delta')$ holds iff $\forall\delta.(\Gamma\delta \rightarrow \Delta\sigma\tau\delta)$ holds. This is due to the fact that there exists such a δ' in the symbol count order iff all variables are replaced by a smallest term. But again, according to the definition of the symbol count order, the variable is already a smallest term.

Definition 26 (LIA Constraint Abstraction). *Let $t \preceq \beta$ be a constraint. Let $vars(t) = \{x_1, ..., x_n\}$. Then* $\text{lic}(t \preceq \beta) = x_1 \geq 1 \wedge ... \wedge x_n \geq 1 \wedge \#(x_1, t) * x_1 + ... + \#(x_n, t) * x_n \leq \text{size}(\beta) - (\text{size}(t) - \sum_{1 \leq i \leq n} \#(x_i, t))$ *is the linear arithmetic constraint of $t \preceq \beta$.*

Lemma 27 (Correctness LIA Constraint Abstraction). *Let $t \preceq \beta$ be a constraint, $vars(t) = \{x_1, ..., x_n\}$.*

1. *For any ground substitution $\sigma = \{x_i \mapsto s_i \mid 1 \leq i \leq n\}$: if $t\sigma \preceq \beta$ is true then $\text{lic}(t \preceq \beta)\{x_i \mapsto \text{size}(s_i) \mid 1 \leq i \leq n\}$ is true.*
2. *For any substitution $\sigma = \{x_i \mapsto k_i \mid 1 \leq i \leq n, k_i \in \mathbb{N}\}$: if $\text{lic}(t \preceq \beta)\sigma$ is true then $t\delta \preceq \beta$ is true for all $\delta = \{x_i \mapsto s_i \mid 1 \leq i \leq n\}$ where all s_i are ground, and $\text{size}(s_i) = k_i$.*

Lemma 28 (LIA Quantifier Elimination). *Let β be a ground term and $\Gamma_1 = \{s_1 \preceq \beta \wedge ... \wedge s_n \preceq \beta\}$ and $\Gamma_2 = \{t_1 \preceq \beta \wedge ... \wedge t_m \preceq \beta\}$ be two constraints. Then $\forall\sigma.(\Gamma_1\sigma \rightarrow \exists\sigma'.\Gamma_2\sigma\sigma')$ iff $\text{lic}(s_1 \preceq \beta) \wedge ... \wedge \text{lic}(s_n \preceq \beta) \rightarrow \text{lic}(t_1 \preceq \beta) \wedge ... \wedge \text{lic}(t_m \preceq \beta)$.*

Thus checking if a $\preceq$-constraint Γ models a $\preceq$-constraint Γ' reduces to a linear integer arithmetic implication test. We make use of the linear arithmetic solver implemented in SPASS-SATT [8].

Before creating a new class we rename all involved classes and then apply *Merge* or *Deduction*. Especially, after application of *Deduction* the new class may contain variables in a constraint that do not occur in any of the class terms. Subsequent merges then continuously increases the number of constraints and variables. Fortunately, only one extra variable is needed.

Lemma 29. *Let $A = \{\Gamma \parallel s_1, ..., s_n\}$ be a class. Let $Y = vars(\Gamma) \setminus (vars(s_1) \cup ... \cup vars(s_n))$ be the variables occurring in Γ but not in $s_1, ..., s_n$. Let $\sigma : Y \rightarrow \{y'\}$ for some fresh variable $y' \in \mathcal{X}$. Then A subsumes $A\sigma$ and $A\sigma$ subsumes A.*

With regard to reducing the number of constraints as seen in Lemma 29 we can further reduce the number of constraints in our specific case of $\preceq$ by removing terms that have the same variable occurrences and are smaller or equal to some other term in the constraint according to $\preceq$, e.g. $f(x)$ can be removed if $f(g(x))$ already exists.

We process classes using a *worked-off* and *usable* queue. Initially the *worked-off* queue contains all single-term classes and *usable* contains the initial classes that are created from the input equations. In each loop we select a class from the *usable* queue, perform all possible *Merge* and *Deduction* steps on it and add the class to the *worked-off* queue afterwards if not subsumed. Newly created classes are added to the usable queue.

Finally, we record whether merge or subsumption checks have already been applied on classes. To find candidates for the subsumption rule we maintain an index for each term in which classes it occurs. General terms are retrieved by a discrimination tree index, unifiable terms and instances of a term by a path index [20].

We evaluated our algorithm on all unit equality (UEQ) problems from TPTP-v8.2.0 [31]. From each problem we created two benchmark problems: one with all inequations removed and the other by turning inequations into equations. We choose two fixed nesting depths of 6 and 8 in order to construct

β. It is constructed by nesting all function symbols in one argument up to the chosen depth and filling all other arguments with a constant. E.g., with function symbols $a/0$,$f/1$,$g/2$,$h/1$,$i/2$ and nesting depth 4 we create the term $\beta = i(h(g(f(a), a)), a)$. Then the size of all terms is limited to 7 symbols.

We created another evaluation on the SMT-LIB UF non-incremental problems (release 2024) [4] for a nesting depth of 2 without those examples that use the distinct operator. In order to make these examples available for untyped congruence closure, we carried out various pre-processing steps: we expanded let operators, removed the typing and quantifiers, coded predicates as equations and did a CNF transformation. We then selected the first equational literal in each clause that contained at least one variable, excluding equations of the form $x \approx y$, $x \approx t$, or $t \approx x$, as input for CC($\mathcal{X}$). If no such literal was found, we instead chose the first ground literal and skipped the clause if this literal was also absent. We skipped the above mentioned equations because there existence typically resulted in trivial problems in the case of CC($\mathcal{X}$), partly because the typing was removed.

We compared the performance of our algorithm to the performance of a CC implementation based on the implementation in the veriT solver [6]. The resulting benchmark problems turn out to be challenging for both algorithms.

CC($\mathcal{X}$) provides a solution to the entire ground input space smaller than β. Therefore, for the comparison of the two algorithms, we feed all ground terms smaller than β into CC. CC($\mathcal{X}$) also provides a solution to the entire ground input space. We skip all examples where no equation has ground instances $\preceq \beta$.

Experiments for the UEQ problems are performed on a Debian Linux server running AMD EPYC 7702 64-core CPUs with 3.35 GHz and a total memory of 2 TB and for the SMT examples they were performed on AMD EPYC 9754 128-Core Processors with 3.1 Ghz and a total memory of 2.2 TB. The time limit for each test is 30 min. The results of all runs as well as all input files and binaries can be found at https://nextcloud.mpi-klsb.mpg.de/index.php/s/ttjj3tDBebgtmHj for the UEQ problems and at https://nextcloud.mpi-klsb.mpg.de/index.php/s/769Ca7Dc9Ck88pi for the UF problems.

For a nesting depth of 6 on the UEQ problems, CC($\mathcal{X}$) terminates on 519 and CC on 457 of the 2900 problems. CC($\mathcal{X}$) is faster on 474 problems and CC on 172. CC($\mathcal{X}$) terminated on 189 examples where CC timed out, and CC terminated on 127 examples where CC($\mathcal{X}$) timed out.

Figure 1a shows the results of all terminating test cases for the runtime and Fig. 1b shows the results for the number of classes. The performance of CC($\mathcal{X}$) currently drops if there are many different variables. This is mainly due to the current implementation of the redundancy checks. Concerning the number of classes, the number of classes generated by CC($\mathcal{X}$) is significantly smaller than the number in CC for almost all examples. Examples where this does not hold are border cases, i.e., they only contain few equations or contain only one constant.

For a nesting depth of 8 on the UEQ problems, 299 of 2900 problems terminate in CC($\mathcal{X}$) and 102 in CC. CC($\mathcal{X}$) is faster in 294 terminating examples

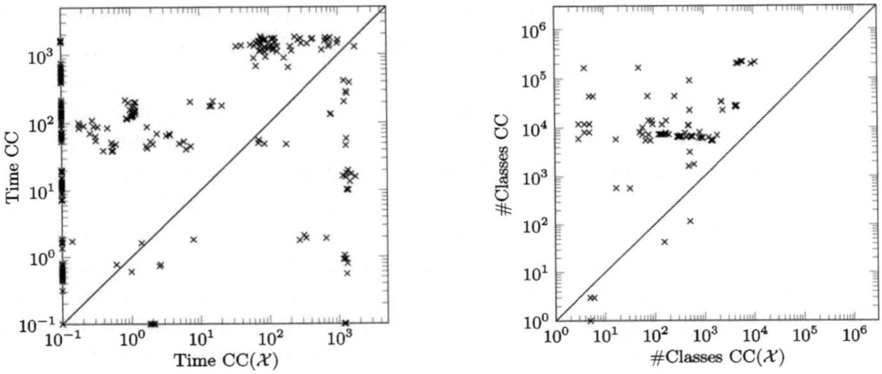

(a) Comparison of the runtime of CC and CC($\mathcal{X}$).

(b) Comparison of the number of classes of CC and CC($\mathcal{X}$).

Fig. 1. Benchmark results for a nesting depth of 6.

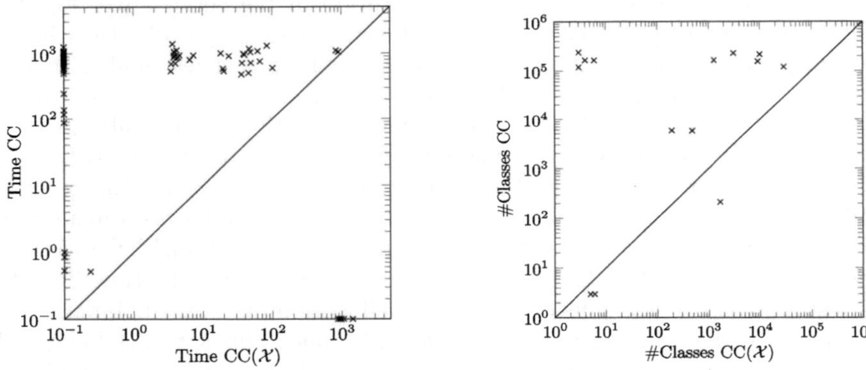

(a) Comparison of the runtime of CC and CC($\mathcal{X}$).

(b) Comparison of the number of classes of CC and CC($\mathcal{X}$).

Fig. 2. Benchmark results for a nesting depth of 8.

and CC in 24. CC($\mathcal{X}$) terminated on 216 examples where CC timed out and CC terminated on 19 examples where CC($\mathcal{X}$) timed out.

Figure 2a shows the results of all terminating test cases for the runtime and Fig. 2b shows the results for the number of classes. CC($\mathcal{X}$) is particularly advantageous with a large β, where the number of ground equations become very large. The number of classes are again significantly smaller than in CC, except for the already mentioned border case examples.

For a nesting depth of 2 on the SMT examples, 1123 of 7516 problems terminate in CC($\mathcal{X}$) and only 561 in CC. CC($\mathcal{X}$) is faster in 886 terminating examples and CC in 277. CC($\mathcal{X}$) terminated on 839 examples where CC timed out and

CC terminated on 40 examples where CC($\mathcal{X}$) timed out. The significantly better performance of CC($\mathcal{X}$) is mainly due to the fact that the problems in the SMT-LIB contain considerably more symbols, which creates a huge number of ground equations even for small nesting depth sizes.

Figure 3a shows the results of all terminating test cases for the runtime and Fig. 3b shows the results for the number of classes. Here, we can see that CC($\mathcal{X}$) is already advantageous with a small β. The number of classes are again smaller in all cases.

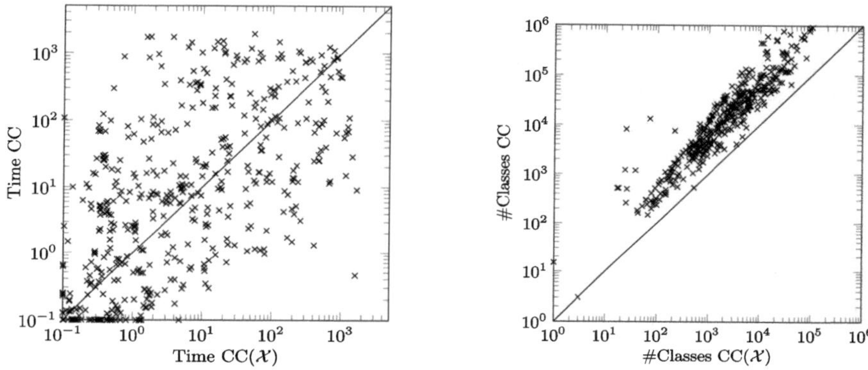

(a) Comparison of the runtime of CC and CC($\mathcal{X}$).

(b) Comparison of the number of classes of CC and CC($\mathcal{X}$).

Fig. 3. Benchmark results for a nesting depth of 2 on the SMT UF examples.

Nesting Depth	Average				Median			
	Time		#Classes		Time		#Classes	
	CC($\mathcal{X}$)	CC	CC($\mathcal{X}$)	CC	CC($\mathcal{X}$)	CC	CC($\mathcal{X}$)	CC
6	155	352.38	1199	55436	0.06	57.2	107	11819
8	94.14	720.52	2844	145705	0.001	795.73	6	165145
2-SMT	83.26	128.11	7731	102024	2.27	5.68	2093	14958

The following table shows the average and median time and number of classes of examples terminating in both CC($\mathcal{X}$) and CC for nesting depth 6, 8 and 2 in the SMT case. For the UEQ examples, one can see that CC($\mathcal{X}$) is significantly faster on average and produces only a fraction of the classes of the ground CC. The difference is even stronger when looking at the median. Here CC($\mathcal{X}$) only needs 1 s or less for half of all terminating examples whereas CC needs more than ten minutes. In the SMT case, the numbers are slightly worse, but CC($\mathcal{X}$) still only takes half the time both on average and on median and produces significantly fewer classes.

6 Discussion and Conclusion

We presented the new calculus non-ground congruence closure (CC($\mathcal{X}$)). It takes as input non-ground equations and computes the corresponding congruence classes with respect to a finite set of ground terms $\mathcal{M}$. The algorithm is sound, complete, and terminating due to a notion of redundancy and the implicit, finite ground input space. We implemented redundancy concepts, e.g., by introducing filters to expensive checks such as subsumption. The resulting implementation of CC($\mathcal{X}$) outperforms CC in the vast majority of benchmark examples taken from the TPTP [31] and SMT-LIB [4].

Still there is room for further improvement. From an implementation point of view, as already mentioned, *Condensation* modifies a copy of the class and checks for subsumption. In the *Merge* and *Deduction* rules, the number of copies of classes is also higher than necessary, especially when the generated class is subsumed. For some border cases CC outperforms CC($\mathcal{X}$). Extending $\Rightarrow_{\mathrm{CC}(\mathcal{X})}$ to cope with input equations with only a few constants or few equations is a further line of research. Already now CC($\mathcal{X}$) can decide shallow equational classes, where the only arguments to functions are variables. This is independently of β and due to our notion of redundancy.

Equality checking between ground terms amounts to instance finding in a particular class, once the congruence closure algorithm is finished, both for CC and CC($\mathcal{X}$) where for the latter this has to be done modulo matching. Checking the equality of non-ground terms is much more involved both for CC($\mathcal{X}$) and CC. This is mainly due to the fact that we consider a finite signature. If two non-ground terms are not in the same class this does not actually mean that they are not equal, since it could be the case that all ground instances of these terms are in the same class.

In general, CC($\mathcal{X}$) outperforms CC if the number of different variables in equations is smaller than the number of ground terms to be considered. The other way round, if there are many variables but only a few ground terms to consider, then running CC is beneficial. This situation can be easily checked in advance, so CC($\mathcal{X}$) can be selected on problems where CC will fail extending the overall scope of applicability.

Disclosure of Interests. The authors have no competing interests to declare that are relevant to the content of this paper.

References

1. Baader, F., Nipkow, T.: Term Rewriting and All That. Cambridge University Press (1998)
2. Barbosa, H., et al.: cvc5: a versatile and industrial-strength SMT solver. In: Fisman, D., Rosu, G. (eds.) Tools and Algorithms for the Construction and Analysis of Systems - 28th International Conference, TACAS 2022, Held as Part of the European Joint Conferences on Theory and Practice of Software, ETAPS 2022, Munich, Germany, 2–7 April 2022, Proceedings, Part I. LNCS, vol. 13243, pp. 415–442. Springer (2022)

3. Barbosa, H., Fontaine, P., Reynolds, A.: Congruence closure with free variables. In: Legay, A., Margaria, T. (eds.) TACAS 2017. LNCS, vol. 10206, pp. 214–230. Springer, Heidelberg (2017). https://doi.org/10.1007/978-3-662-54580-5_13
4. Barrett, C., Fontaine, P., Tinelli, C.: The Satisfiability Modulo Theories Library (SMT-LIB) (2016). www.SMT-LIB.org
5. Biere, A., Heule, M., van Maaren, H., Walsh, T. (eds.): Handbook of Satisfiability. Frontiers in Artificial Intelligence and Applications, vol. 185. IOS Press (2009)
6. Bouton, T., Caminha B. de Oliveira, D., Déharbe, D., Fontaine, P.: veriT: an open, trustable and efficient SMT-solver. In: International Conference on Automated Deduction, pp. 151–156. Springer (2009)
7. Bouton, T., Caminha B. de Oliveira, D., Déharbe, D., Fontaine, P.: veriT: an open, trustable and efficient SMT-solver. In: Schmidt, R.A. (ed.) CADE 2009. LNCS (LNAI), vol. 5663, pp. 151–156. Springer, Heidelberg (2009). https://doi.org/10.1007/978-3-642-02959-2_12
8. Bromberger, M., Fleury, M., Schwarz, S., Weidenbach, C.: SPASS-SATT - A CDCL(LA) solver (2019)
9. Cimatti, A., Griggio, A., Schaafsma, B.J., Sebastiani, R.: The MathSAT5 SMT solver. In: Piterman, N., Smolka, S.A. (eds.) Tools and Algorithms for the Construction and Analysis of Systems - 19th International Conference, TACAS 2013, Held as Part of the European Joint Conferences on Theory and Practice of Software, ETAPS 2013, Rome, Italy, 16–24 March 2013. Proceedings. vol. 7795, pp. 93–107. Springer, Heidelberg (2013)
10. Dershowitz, N., Plaisted, D.A.: Rewriting, Chap. 9. In: Robinson, A., Voronkov, A. (eds.) Handbook of Automated Reasoning, vol. I, pp. 535–610. Elsevier (2001)
11. Downey, P.J., Sethi, R., Tarjan, R.E.: Variations on the common subexpression problem. J. ACM **27**(4), 758–771 (1980)
12. Dutertre, B.: Yices 2.2. In: Biere, A., Bloem, R. (eds.) Computer-Aided Verification (CAV'2014). LNCS, vol. 8559, pp. 737–744. Springer, July 2014
13. Fontaine, P.: Techniques for verification of concurrent systems with invariants. Ph.D. thesis, Institut Montefiore, Université de Liege, Belgium (2004)
14. Ganzinger, H., Hagen, G., Nieuwenhuis, R., Oliveras, A., Tinelli, C.: DPLL(T): fast decision procedures. In: Alur, R., Peled, D.A. (eds.) CAV 2004. LNCS, vol. 3114, pp. 175–188. Springer, Heidelberg (2004). https://doi.org/10.1007/978-3-540-27813-9_14
15. Hurd, J.: Congruence classes with logic variables. Log. J. IGPL **9**(1), 53–69 (2001)
16. Bayardo, R.J., Schrag, R.: Using CSP look-back techniques to solve exceptionally hard SAT instances. In: Freuder, E.C. (ed.) Proceedings of the Second International Conference on Principles and Practice of Constraint Programming, Cambridge, Massachusetts, USA, 19–22 August 1996. LNCS, vol. 1118, pp. 46–60. Springer (1996)
17. Knuth, D.E., Bendix, P.B.: Simple word problems in universal algebras. In: Leech, I. (ed.) Computational Problems in Abstract Algebra, pp. 263–297. Pergamon Press (1970)
18. Leidinger, H., Weidenbach, C.: SCL(EQ): SCL for first-order logic with equality. J. Autom. Reason. **67**(3), 22 (2023)
19. Leidinger, H., Weidenbach, C.: Non-ground congruence closure. CoRR abs/2412.10066 (2024)
20. McCune, W.: Experiments with discrimination-tree indexing and path indexing for term retrieval. J. Autom. Reason. **9**(2), 147–167 (1992)

21. Moskewicz, M.W., Madigan, C.F., Zhao, Y., Zhang, L., Malik, S.: Chaff: engineering an efficient SAT solver. In: 2001 Proceedings of the Design Automation Conference, pp. 530–535. ACM (2001)
22. Ramakrishnan, C.R., Rehof, J. (eds.): TACAS 2008. LNCS, vol. 4963. Springer, Heidelberg (2008). https://doi.org/10.1007/978-3-540-78800-3
23. Nelson, G., Oppen, D.C.: Fast decision procedures based on congruence closure. J. ACM **27**(2), 356–364 (1980)
24. Nieuwenhuis, R., Hillenbrand, T., Riazanov, A., Voronkov, A.: On the evaluation of indexing techniques for theorem proving. In: Goré, R., Leitsch, A., Nipkow, T. (eds.) IJCAR 2001, LNCS, vol. 2083, pp. 257–271. Springer, Heidelberg (2001). https://doi.org/10.1007/3-540-45744-5_19
25. Nieuwenhuis, R., Oliveras, A.: Fast congruence closure and extensions. Inf. Comput. **205**(4), 557–580 (2007)
26. Nieuwenhuis, R., Oliveras, A., Tinelli, C.: Solving SAT and SAT modulo theories: from an abstract Davis-Putnam-Logemann-Loveland procedure to DPLL(T). J. ACM **53**, 937–977 (2006)
27. Reynolds, A., Barbosa, H., Fontaine, P.: Revisiting enumerative instantiation. In: Beyer, D., Huisman, M. (eds.) Tools and Algorithms for the Construction and Analysis of Systems - 24th International Conference, TACAS 2018, Held as Part of the European Joint Conferences on Theory and Practice of Software, ETAPS 2018, Thessaloniki, Greece, 14–20 April 2018, Proceedings, Part II. LNCS, vol. 10806, pp. 112–131. Springer, Heidelberg (2018)
28. Reynolds, A., Tinelli, C., de Moura, L.: Finding conflicting instances of quantified formulas in SMT. In: 2014 Formal Methods in Computer-Aided Design (FMCAD), pp. 195–202 (2014). https://doi.org/10.1109/FMCAD.2014.6987613
29. Shostak, R.E.: Deciding combinations of theories. J. ACM **31**(1), 1–12 (1984)
30. Silva, J.P.M., Sakallah, K.A.: GRASP - a new search algorithm for satisfiability. In: International Conference on Computer Aided Design, ICCAD, pp. 220–227. IEEE Computer Society Press (1996)
31. Sutcliffe, G.: The TPTP problem library and associated infrastructure - from CNF to TH0, TPTP v6.4.0. J. Autom. Reason. **59**(4), 483–502 (2017)
32. Weidenbach, C.: Automated reasoning building blocks. In: Meyer, R., Platzer, A., Wehrheim, H. (eds.) Correct System Design - Symposium in Honor of Ernst-Rüdiger Olderog on the Occasion of His 60th Birthday, Oldenburg, Germany, 8–9 September 2015. Proceedings. LNCS, vol. 9360, pp. 172–188. Springer, Heidelberg (2015)

Anti-pattern Templates

Jan Otop(✉)

Institute of Computer Science, University of Wrocław,Wrocław, Poland
jan.otop@uwr.edu.pl

Abstract. We introduce anti-pattern templates, which extend both anti-pattern matching by abstracting ground terms to variables, and unification by negative constraints. For anti-pattern templates, we study the satisfiability problem, which asks whether a given template can be instantiated to a valid anti-pattern matching instance. We show that the satisfiability problem for anti-pattern templates is NP-complete, but it becomes tractable if the number of negation symbols is bounded. Next, we consider anti-pattern templates modulo an equational theory and discuss its relations with other variants of equational frameworks with negative constraints. In particular, we conclude that the satisfiability problem for anti-pattern templates considered modulo associativity becomes undecidable, while it is decidable modulo associativity and commutativity.

Keywords: pattern matching · satisfiability · unification · equational reasoning

1 Introduction

Anti-patterns have been introduced as an extension of patterns for structured data with negative constraints [5,11]. The main idea is to extend terms built over a signature of functional symbols with an auxiliary unary symbol $\urcorner$ representing the complement. E.g. while pattern $f(X, X)$ matches to all terms with the head symbol f and both arguments of f equal, pattern $\urcorner f(X, X)$ matches to terms that do not match to $f(X, X)$, i.e., terms that either have the head symbol different than f or the head symbol is f but arguments are different.

Anti-patterns have been introduced primarily to extend the expression power of pattern matching in programming languages. A prototype of pattern matching with anti-patterns has been implemented in TOM language [3]. Other applications include symbolic computations and querying structured data. The main advantages of anti-pattern matching are intuitive semantics and an efficient matching algorithm. While research has been focused on algorithms for solving anti-pattern matching [5,11], reasoning about anti-patterns as prime objects has not been addressed. We discuss two cases motivating this approach.

Consider a query expressed with anti-patterns. While solving anti-pattern matching against any particular item from a dataset is efficient, iterating over

C. Barrett and U. Waldmann (Eds.): CADE 2025, LNAI 15943, pp. 614–631, 2025.
https://doi.org/10.1007/978-3-031-99984-0_32

the whole dataset may be expensive. Especially, if the expression involving anti-patterns matches no items at all, and hence there is no need to iterate over the dataset. A less extreme example would be an expression, which matches to a specific subset of the dataset; in such a case it is beneficial to preprocess the expression to compute its overapproximation, and iterate only over a fraction of the dataset using an index structure [18].

In rule-based programming languages, anti-pattern rules can be combined into complex expressions, which in turn is prone to errors. Checking whether given anti-pattern rules are irredundant, i.e., there are no unreachable parts of the rule list, is a good sanity check as redundant rules are likely incorrect and require revision. This is the first step towards verification of anti-pattern rules.

However, anti-pattern matching has been defined exclusively between anti-patterns and ground terms. Therefore, in order to pose questions about non-emptiness of the answer set or irredundancy of rules, we have to generalize anti-pattern matching expressions by turning matched terms into variables. For the resulting expressions, called *anti-pattern templates*, we study the satisfiability problem, which essentially asks, whether a given template can be instantiated to a satisfied anti-pattern matching expression. Therefore, the satisfiability problem can be regarded as a generalization of anti-pattern matching. In particular, the above two cases, non-emptiness of the answer set or irredundancy of rules, are instances of the satisfiability question for anti-pattern templates.

Contributions. We introduce anti-pattern templates, which are Boolean combinations of expressions $s \stackrel{?}{=} X$, where s is an anti-pattern and X is a variable. We focus on the satisfiability problem for anti-pattern templates, which asks whether a given anti-pattern template can be instantiated to a valid anti-pattern matching expression. Our main contributions are as follows:

- We establish NP-completeness of the satisfiability problem. Furthermore, NP-hardness holds even for conjunctions of two expressions $s_1 \stackrel{?}{=} X \wedge s_2 \stackrel{?}{=} X$.
- We identify subclasses of anti-pattern templates for which the satisfiability problem becomes tractable.
- We define anti-pattern templates modulo an equational theory and compare satisfiability of anti-pattern templates with other frameworks combining equational reasoning with negative constrains: disunification and the complement problem.
- Finally, we conclude that in presence of (binary) free function symbols, the satisfiability problem for anti-pattern templates modulo **AC** is decidable.

Paper Organization. This paper is a revised and substantially extended version of a workshop paper [16]. It builds on top of [5,11]. In Sect. 2 we introduce notions used throughout the paper along with the notions of anti-terms and anti-patterns from [5,11]. In Sect. 3, we present the original contributions: anti-pattern templates and the study of the satisfiability problem for anti-pattern templates. Finally, in Sect. 4 we discuss anti-pattern templates modulo an equational theory and related problems.

2 Preliminaries

Functional Symbols and Variables. A signature $\mathcal{F}$ is a set of function symbols, where every function symbol has assigned a unique arity, which is non-negative. Function symbols of arity 0 are called *constants* and denoted with letters $a, b, c, \ldots$, while function symbols of positive arity are denoted with letters $f, g, h, \ldots$. We consider a countable set of variables denoted with capital letters $X, Y, Z, \ldots$. We assume that all signatures that we consider contain at least one constant and at least one symbol of arity at least 1.

Terms. A set of terms over a signature $\mathcal{F}$ and a set of variables $\mathcal{V}$, denoted by $\mathcal{T}(\mathcal{F}, \mathcal{V})$, is the least set containing $\mathcal{V}$ such that for every function symbol f of arity $k \geq 0$, if $t_1, \ldots t_k \in \mathcal{T}(\mathcal{F}, \mathcal{V})$, then $f(t_1, \ldots, t_k)$ belongs to $\mathcal{T}(\mathcal{F}, \mathcal{V})$. Therefore, every term is either a variable or it is of the form $f(t_1, \ldots, t_k)$, where $k \geq 0$. We define the head symbol $\mathsf{hd}(t)$ as $\mathsf{hd}(X) = X$, if $t = X$, and $\mathsf{hd}(f(t_1, \ldots, t_k)) = f$.

Ground Terms. A term $t \in \mathcal{T}(\mathcal{F}, \mathcal{V})$ is *ground* if it belongs to $\mathcal{T}(\mathcal{F}, \emptyset)$. We will denote the set of all ground terms over $\mathcal{F}$ with $\mathcal{T}(\mathcal{F})$. Since we consider signatures with at least one constant and at least one non-constant symbol, the set of ground terms is infinite.

The Size of Terms. The size of a term t, denoted by $\|t\|$, is defined as $\|t\| = 1$, if t is a variable, and otherwise, if $t = f(t_1, \ldots, t_k)$, where $k \geq 0$, $\|t\| = 1 + \sum_{i=1}^{k} \|t_i\|$.

Positions and Subterms. A *position* in a term is a sequence of natural numbers with ϵ denoting the empty sequence. For a term t, we define the set of *positions* $\mathsf{Pos}(t)$ in t as $\{\epsilon\}$ if t is a constant or a variable. Otherwise, if $t = f(t_1, \ldots, t_k)$ and $k \geq 1$, then $\mathsf{Pos}(t) = \{\epsilon\} \cup \{i \cdot p \mid 1 \leq i \leq k \text{ and } p \in \mathsf{Pos}(t_i)\}$, where $i \cdot p$ is the result of prepending i to the sequence p. A *subterm* of t at a position p, denoted by $t_{|p}$, is defined as follows: if $p = \epsilon$, then $t_{|p} = t$, otherwise, if $p = i \cdot p' \in \mathsf{Pos}(t)$ and $t = \mathrm{f}(t_1, \ldots, t_k)$, the subterm at the position p is the subterm of t_i at the position p', i.e., $f(t_1, \ldots, t_k)_{|i \cdot p'} = t_{i|p'}$. E.g. for $t = f(g(a), g(g(b)))$, the subterms of t at the positions $\epsilon, (2), (2,1), (2,1,1)$ are resp. t, $\mathrm{g}(\mathrm{g}(b)), g(b)$ and b.

Substitutions. A function σ from variables $\mathcal{V}_1 \subseteq \mathcal{V}$ into terms $\mathcal{T}(\mathcal{F}, \mathcal{V})$ is called a substitution. Every substitution σ can be uniquely extended to a function $\widehat{\sigma}$ from $\mathcal{T}(\mathcal{F}, \mathcal{V})$ to $\mathcal{T}(\mathcal{F}, \mathcal{V})$ as follows: for every $t \in \mathcal{T}(\mathcal{F}, \mathcal{V})$, (a) if $t = X \in \mathrm{dom}(\sigma)$, then $\widehat{\sigma}(X) = \sigma(X)$, (b) if $t = X$ is a variable, but it does not belong to $\mathrm{dom}(\sigma)$, then $\widehat{\sigma}(X) = X$, and (c) if $t = f(t_1, \ldots, t_k)$ for $f \in \Sigma$ of arity $k \geq 0$, then $\widehat{\sigma}(t) = f(\widehat{\sigma}(t_1), \ldots, \widehat{\sigma}(t_k))$. Since $\widehat{\sigma}$ is uniquely defined, we will abuse the notation and refer to it as a substitution and we will denote it by σ. The term $\sigma(t)$ is called an *instance* of t. An expression $X_1 \mapsto t_1, \ldots, X_k \mapsto t_k$ denotes the substitution σ with $\mathrm{dom}(\sigma) = \{X_1, \ldots, X_k\}$ such that for $i \in \{1, \ldots, k\}$ we have $\sigma(X_i) = t_i$.

2.1 Anti-terms: Syntax and Semantics

The set of *anti-terms* over a signature $\mathcal{F}$ and a set of variables $\mathcal{V}$, denoted by $\mathcal{AT}(\mathcal{F},\mathcal{V})$ is the set $\mathcal{T}(\mathcal{F}\cup\{\urcorner\},\mathcal{V})$, where $\urcorner$ is a fresh unary function symbol not in $\mathcal{F}$. An anti-term s is *proper* if it contains the $\urcorner$ symbol, and hence $s \in \mathcal{AT}(\mathcal{F},\mathcal{V}) \setminus \mathcal{T}(\mathcal{F},\mathcal{V})$. Since an anti-term is syntactically a term over $\mathcal{F}\cup\{\urcorner\}$, the notions of the size, a position and a subterm extend straightforwardly to anti-terms. In contrast, semantics of $\urcorner$ is different than other function symbols, and it changes the definition of free variables.

Free Variables in Anti-terms. For an anti-term t, we define $\mathsf{FVars}(t)$, the set of free variables of t: $\mathsf{FVars}(t) = \{t\}$ if t is a variable, $\mathsf{FVars}(\urcorner t) = \emptyset$, and $\mathsf{FVars}(f(t_1,\ldots,t_k)) = \bigcup_{1\le i\le k} \mathsf{FVars}(t_i)$. E.g. $\mathsf{FVars}(\urcorner\urcorner f(X,\urcorner f(X,Y))) = \emptyset$, while $\mathsf{FVars}(f(X,\urcorner f(X,Y))) = \{X\}$.

Substitutions on Anti-terms. Substitutions on anti-terms are defined analogously to substitutions over terms; they substitute variables with terms (not anti-terms). Instead of disabling substitutions over non-free variables, as it has been defined in [5,11], we consider variables in the domain of a substitution as *free* from the context. E.g. for $s = f(X,\urcorner f(X,Y))$ the variable Y is not free, but we explicitly allow substitutions to act on Y. It will be useful later on to consider some variables non-free in a particular anti-term as free anyway.

Grounding Substitutions on Anti-terms. A substitution σ is *grounding* for an anti-term s if $\mathsf{FVars}(s) \subseteq \mathrm{dom}(\sigma)$ and all terms $\sigma(X)$ are ground terms.

The Ground-Term Semantics of Anti-terms. Consider $t \in \mathcal{AT}(\mathcal{F},\mathcal{V})$. First, assume that t is ground, i.e., $\mathsf{FVars}(t) = \emptyset$. If $t = f(t_1,\ldots,t_k)$, then the *ground-term semantics* $[\![t]\!]$ of t is defined as $[\![t]\!] = \{f(s_1,\ldots,s_k) \mid s_1 \in [\![t_1]\!],\ldots,s_k \in [\![t_k]\!]\}$. Otherwise, if $t = \urcorner s$, then $[\![t]\!] = \mathcal{T}(\mathcal{F}) \setminus [\![s]\!]$. Note that the set of free variables of s may be non-empty. Second, if t is not a ground anti-term, i.e., $\mathsf{FVars}(t) \neq \emptyset$, then $[\![t]\!] = \bigcup\{[\![\sigma(t)]\!] \mid \sigma$ is grounding for t and $\mathrm{dom}(\sigma) = \mathsf{FVars}(t)\}$. Note that we only instantiate variables that are free in t alone. Observe that if t is a term, then $[\![t]\!]$ is the set of all ground instances of t, that is, we have $[\![t]\!] = \{\sigma(t) \mid \sigma$ is a grounding substitution for $t\}$. In particular, if t is a ground term, then $[\![t]\!] = \{t\}$.

Example 1. We explain the ground-term semantics with examples:

- $[\![f(X,Y)]\!] = \{f(t,s) \mid t,s \in \mathcal{T}(\mathcal{F})\}$, the set of all ground terms with the head symbol f, where the variables X and Y can be instantiated independently to any ground term,
- $[\![f(X,X)]\!] = \{f(t,t) \mid t \in \mathcal{T}(\mathcal{F})\}$
- $[\![f(X,\urcorner X)]\!] = \{f(t,s) \mid t,s \in \mathcal{T}(\mathcal{F}) \wedge t \neq s\}$ as X is free in $f(X,\urcorner X)$,
- $[\![\urcorner f(X,\urcorner Y)]\!] = \mathcal{T}(\mathcal{F})$ as $\urcorner f(X,\urcorner Y)$ has no free variables and hence we have $[\![\urcorner Y]\!] = \emptyset$ and $[\![f(X,\urcorner Y)]\!] = \emptyset$, and
- $[\![s]\!] = [\![\urcorner\urcorner s]\!]$, which has been shown in [5].

Even though $[\![s]\!] = [\![\urcorner\urcorner s]\!]$, anti-terms s and $\urcorner\urcorner s$ are not equivalent. Note that in general $\mathsf{FVars}(s) \supsetneq \mathsf{FVars}(\urcorner\urcorner s)$, and hence a grounding substitution σ for $\urcorner\urcorner s$ need not be grounding for s.

We discuss another example, which explains how to express some form of disjunction with anti-terms.

Example 2. Consider ground terms $t_1, t_2 \in \mathcal{T}(\mathcal{F})$ and an anti-term $\urcorner f(\urcorner t_1, \urcorner t_2)$. Since t_1 is a ground term, we have $[\![\urcorner t_1]\!] = \mathcal{T}(\mathcal{F}) \setminus \{t_1\}$. Next, consider the semantics of $f(\urcorner t_1, \urcorner t_2)$. By applying the definition to $\urcorner t_1$ and $\urcorner t_2$, we have $[\![f(\urcorner t_1, \urcorner t_2)]\!] = \{f(s_1, s_2) \mid s_1, s_2 \in \mathcal{T}(\mathcal{F}) \wedge s_1 \neq t_1 \wedge s_2 \neq t_2\}$, i.e., all ground terms of the form $f(s_1, s_2)$ except for $f(t_1, t_2)$. Finally, semantics of $\urcorner f(\urcorner t_1, \urcorner t_2)$ is the set of ground terms except for terms from $[\![f(\urcorner t_1, \urcorner t_2)]\!]$, i.e., $\{s \mid \mathsf{hd}(s) \neq f\} \cup \{f(s_1, s_2) \mid s_1, s_2 \in \mathcal{T}(\mathcal{F}) \wedge (s_1 = t_1 \vee s_2 = t_2)\}$. Interestingly, it is possible to express a form of disjunction $s_1 = t_1 \vee s_2 = t_2$, which will be exploited later.

2.2 Anti-pattern Matching and Matching Systems

Consider a signature $\mathcal{F}$. Given an anti-term $s \in \mathcal{AT}(\mathcal{F}, \mathcal{V})$ and a ground term $t \in \mathcal{T}(\mathcal{F})$, a *matching equation* is an expressions of the form $s \preccurlyeq t$. The matching equation $s \preccurlyeq t$ has a solution if $t \in [\![s]\!]$, and a solution is a grounding substitution σ for s such that $t \in [\![\sigma(s)]\!]$(it is possible that $t \neq \sigma(s)$, as the latter is a ground anti-term). Note that the ground-term semantics of $[\![s]\!]$ implies that $t \in [\![s]\!]$ if and only if there is a grounding substitution such that $t \in [\![\sigma(s)]\!]$.

A (quantifier-free) matching system S is a Boolean combination of equations $s \preccurlyeq t$. The set of free variables in S is the union of all free variables over all anti-terms from S. E.g. in $(\urcorner Y \preccurlyeq a) \wedge (f(Y,Y) \preccurlyeq f(a,a))$, variable Y is free. While matching systems in [5] allow explicit quantifiers over variables, we consider only Boolean combinations of matching equations.

The system S has a solution if there is a grounding substitution σ such that the following Boolean formula φ_S is true. We substitute in S every equation by its truth value, i.e., every equation $s \preccurlyeq t$ from S satisfying $t \in [\![\sigma(s)]\!]$ is substituted by $\top$, while every $s \preccurlyeq t$ satisfying $t \notin [\![\sigma(s)]\!]$ is substituted by $\bot$. The resulting expression φ_S is a Boolean combination of $\top$ and $\bot$. E.g. the system $(\urcorner Y \preccurlyeq a) \wedge (f(Y,Y) \preccurlyeq \mathrm{f}(a,a))$ has no solutions as $f(Y,Y) \preccurlyeq f(a,a)$ implies that $Y \mapsto a$, and $\urcorner a \preccurlyeq a$ does not hold. Still, the substitution $Y \mapsto a$ is applied to $\urcorner Y$ even though $\mathsf{FVars}(\urcorner Y) = \emptyset$, but Y is free in the whole system.

A matching system is *conjunctive* if it is a conjunction of equations $s \preccurlyeq t$. It has been shown in [5, Theorem 21] that for a conjunctive matching system S one of the following three conditions holds: (a) S has no solutions,(b) S has the unique solution, which is a grounding substitution, or (c) S is satisfied by an empty substitution. Therefore, to solve a conjunctive matching system, it suffices to solve each equation separately and check whether the solutions are consistent.

3 Anti-pattern Templates

In this section, we define and study the satisfiability problem for *anti-pattern templates*. Anti-pattern templates arise from (quantifier-free) matching systems by abstracting matched ground terms to (template) variables.

Anti-pattern Templates. We define *anti-pattern templates* (APTs) as follows. An *atomic* APT over $\mathcal{F}$ is an expression of the form $s \stackrel{?}{=} X$, where $s \in \mathcal{AT}(\mathcal{F}, \mathcal{V})$ is an anti-term and $X \in \mathcal{V}$ is a *template* variable. An APT is a Boolean combination of atomic APTs, while a *conjunctive* APT is a conjunction of atomic APTs. We do not consider explicit quantifiers over variables. The size of an APT T, denoted by $\|T\|$, is the sum of values $\|s\| + 1$ over all atomic APTs $s \stackrel{?}{=} X$ from T.

Free Variables. For an atomic APT $s \stackrel{?}{=} X$, we define the set of free variables $\mathsf{FVars}(s \stackrel{?}{=} X) = \mathsf{FVars}(s) \cup \{X\}$. For an APT T, we define $\mathsf{FVars}(T)$ as the union of the sets of free variables over atomic APTs from T.

Grounding Substitutions. A substitution σ defined over a subset of $\mathsf{FVars}(T)$ is *grounding* for T if for every APT $s \stackrel{?}{=} X$ from T we have $\sigma(s)$ is a ground anti-term and $\sigma(X)$ is a ground term. Every (quantifier-free) matching system can be obtained from some APT by applying a grounding substitution restricted to template variables and changing relation $\stackrel{?}{=}$ to $\preccurlyeq$.

Substitutions Satisfying Templates. An atomic APT $s \stackrel{?}{=} X$ is satisfied by a substitution σ if and only if (a) σ is grounding for $s \stackrel{?}{=} X$, and (b) $\sigma(X) \in [\![\sigma(s)]\!]$. A substitution σ satisfies an APT T if and only if (a) σ is grounding for T, and (b) the Boolean formula $\varphi_{T,\sigma}$, which is obtained from T by substituting atomic APTs $s \stackrel{?}{=} X$ satisfied by σ with $\top$, and the ones unsatisfied by σ with $\bot$, is true.

Definition 3. The *satisfiability* problem for APTs over $\mathcal{F}$ asks, given an APT T, whether there is a (grounding) substitution σ for T that satisfies T.

Note that the signature is an important parameter of the satisfiability problem. Observe that the APT $\urcorner(f(Z)) \stackrel{?}{=} X \wedge \urcorner a \stackrel{?}{=} X$ is unsatisfiable over the signature $\{f, a\}$, but it is satisfiable if there are other function symbols.

Example 4. We illustrate the notion of satisfying substitutions with examples.

- While $\urcorner(f(Z)) \stackrel{?}{=} X \wedge \urcorner a \stackrel{?}{=} X$ is unsatisfiable over $\{f, a\}$, the template T_1 defined as $\left(\urcorner(f(Z)) \stackrel{?}{=} X\right) \wedge \left(\urcorner a \stackrel{?}{=} X\right) \wedge \left(\urcorner a \stackrel{?}{=} Z\right)$ is satisfiable over $\{f, a\}$ as Z becomes free; for instance $X \mapsto f(a), Z \mapsto f(a)$ satisfies T_1.
- Consider T_2 defined as

$$\left(f(Y_1) \stackrel{?}{=} X_1 \vee h(Y_1) \stackrel{?}{=} X_1\right) \wedge \left(g(\urcorner f(Z), X_1) \stackrel{?}{=} X_2\right) \wedge \left(g(Y_2, Y_2) \stackrel{?}{=} X_2\right)$$

The variables X_1, X_2, Y_1, Y_2 are free, while Z is not. Any substitution σ satisfying T_2 also satisfies $\sigma(X_1) = \sigma(Y_2)$ and $\mathsf{hd}(\sigma(Y_2)) \neq f$. A substitution σ defined by $Y_1 \mapsto a, Y_2 \mapsto h(a), X_1 \mapsto h(a), X_2 \mapsto g(h(a), h(a))$ satisfies T_2. The Boolean formula $\varphi_{T_2,\sigma}$ equals $(\bot \vee \top) \wedge \top \wedge \top$ is true.

- Consider T_3 resulting from T_2 by equating Y_1, Y_2 to Y, i.e., T_3 defined as

$$\left(f(Y) \stackrel{?}{=} X_1 \vee h(Y) \stackrel{?}{=} X_1)\right) \wedge \left(\urcorner g(f(Z), X_1) \stackrel{?}{=} X_2\right) \wedge \left(g(Y, Y) \stackrel{?}{=} X_2\right)$$

Then, any substitution satisfying T_3 satisfies $\sigma(Y) = \sigma(X_1)$, and hence $\sigma(Y)$ is equal to $\sigma(f(Y))$ or $\sigma(h(Y))$. Therefore, T_3 is not satisfiable. However, consider a substitution defined only on template variables X_1, X_2 such that $X_1 \mapsto h(a), X_2 \mapsto g(h(a), h(a))$. The expression $\sigma(T_3)$ equals $\left(f(Y) \stackrel{?}{=} h(a) \vee h(Y) \stackrel{?}{=} h(a)\right) \wedge \left(\urcorner g(f(Z), h(a)) \stackrel{?}{=} g(h(a), h(a))\right) \wedge g(Y, Y) \stackrel{?}{=} g(h(a), h(a))$. Observe that all atomic APTs from T_3 except for $f(Y) \stackrel{?}{=} X_1$ are separately satisfied by $X_1 \mapsto h(a), X_2 \mapsto g(h(a), h(a))$. It shows that a satisfying substitution has to be defined on all free variables, not only on template variables.

3.1 Hardness of the Satisfiability Problem

We show that the *satisfiability* problem for conjunctive APTs is NP-hard. Recall the ground-term semantics of the anti-term $\urcorner f(\urcorner t_1, \urcorner t_2)$ discussed in Example 2. Observe that $[\![\urcorner f(\urcorner t_1, \urcorner t_2)]\!] \cap [\![f(Y, Y)]\!] = \{f(t_1, t_1), f(t_2, t_2)\}$, and hence the conjunctive APT $(\urcorner f(\urcorner t_1, \urcorner t_2) \stackrel{?}{=} X) \wedge (f(Y, Y) \stackrel{?}{=} X)$ has exactly two solutions $X \mapsto f(t_1, t_1)$ and $X \mapsto f(t_2, t_2)$. We extend this idea to construct a reduction of the 3-SAT problem to the satisfiability problem for conjunctive APTs.

Lemma 5. *The satisfiability problem for conjunctive APTs is NP-hard.*

Proof. Let $\mathcal{F} = \{f, g, \top, \bot\}$, where f has arity 8, g has arity 3 and $\top, \bot$ are constants. Given a formula $\varphi = \bigwedge_{i=1}^{k} C_i$ in 3-CNF over propositional variables $z_1, \ldots, z_l$, we define a conjunctive APT T_φ such that φ is satisfiable if and only if T_φ is satisfiable.

Let $\mathcal{V} = \{Z_j \mid j \in \{1, \ldots, l\}\} \cup \{X_i \mid i \in \{1, \ldots, k\}\}$. Consider a clause C_i from φ over propositional variables z_a, z_b, z_c where $a, b, c \in \{1, \ldots, l\}$ and $a \leq b \leq c$. The clause C_i has three literals and hence there are at most 8 assignments from $\{z_a, z_b, z_c\}$ to $\{\top, \bot\}$, which satisfy C_i. Let $\tau_1, \ldots, \tau_8$ be all such assignments (with repetitions if necessary). We define T_i as the conjunction of the following two atomic APTs:

$$\urcorner f(\urcorner g(\tau_1(z_a), \tau_1(z_b), \tau_1(z_c)), \ldots, \urcorner g(\tau_8(z_a), \tau_8(z_b), \tau_8(z_c))) \stackrel{?}{=} X_i$$
$$f(g(Z_a, Z_b, Z_c), \ldots, g(Z_a, Z_b, Z_c)) \stackrel{?}{=} X_i$$

Finally, we define T_φ as the conjunction of $T_1, \ldots, T_k$. Note that we refer to propositional variables with lowercase letters, while variables from $\mathcal{V}$ are denoted with capital letters.

Consider a substitution σ satisfying the conjunctive APT T_φ. Reasoning as in Example 2, we observe that for every $i \in \{1, \ldots, k\}$ we have

$$\sigma(X_i) = f(g(\tau_m(z_a), \tau_m(z_b), \tau_m(z_c)), \ldots, g(\tau_m(z_a), \tau_m(z_b), \tau_m(z_c)))$$

where z_a, z_b, z_c are propositional variables from C_i and τ_m is an assignment satisfying the clause C_i. Since all partial substitutions agree on variables $Z_1, \ldots, Z_l$, the assignment $z_j \mapsto \sigma(Z_j)$ satisfies φ.

Conversely, suppose that we have an assignment τ satisfying φ. We define the substitution σ such that $\sigma(Z_j) = \tau(z_j)$ and for every clause C_i with propositional variables z_a, z_b, z_c with $a \le b \le c$, we put

$$\sigma(X_i) = f(g(\tau(z_a), \tau(z_b), \tau(z_c)), \ldots, g(\tau(z_a), \tau(z_b), \tau(z_c)))$$

One can check that σ satisfies T_φ. □

We have presented the hardness proof in detail to discuss parameters, which make the problem tractable. First, observe that atomic APTs of the form $t \stackrel{?}{=} X$ such that t does not contain the $\urcorner$ symbol, i.e., $t \in \mathcal{T}(\mathcal{F}, \mathcal{V})$, can be eliminated by applying standard unification, and hence we focus on proper anti-terms that contain at least one $\urcorner$ symbol. All proper anti-terms in T_φ are ground of bounded depth. Therefore, any restrictions regarding occurrence of variables in anti-terms would not affect the worst-case complexity of the satisfiability problem.

There is a bounded number of different proper anti-terms produced by the reduction. However, while multiple occurrences of ground terms can be eliminated by substituting them with a fresh variable X and stating $t \stackrel{?}{=} X$, this is not possible with anti-terms. E.g. $\urcorner a \stackrel{?}{=} X_1 \wedge \urcorner a \stackrel{?}{=} X_2$ state that each X_1 and X_2 can be instantiated to any ground term different than the constant a, but not necessarily the same term, and hence it does not entail $X_1 \stackrel{?}{=} X_2$.

Another possible parameter is the number of conjuncts, which is unbounded in the conjunctive APTs produced by the reduction. Indeed, for a single conjunct, the satisfiability problem is tractable.

Lemma 6. *The satisfiability problem for atomic APTs can be decided in polynomial time.*

However, conjunction of any number of atomic APTs can be transformed to a conjunction of just two atomic APTs provided that the signature contains h of arity greater then 1. Assume for simplicity that h is binary. Then, any three conjuncts $t_1 \stackrel{?}{=} X_1 \wedge t_2 \stackrel{?}{=} X_2 \wedge t_3 \stackrel{?}{=} X_3$ can be transformed to two conjuncts $f(t_1, f(t_2, t_3)) \stackrel{?}{=} X \wedge f(X_1, f(X_2, X_3)) \stackrel{?}{=} X$. Similarly, any number of conjuncts can be reduced to two.

Corollary 7. *The satisfiability problem for conjunctive APTs with two conjuncts is* NP*-hard.*

Note that in the proposed transformation, the number of occurrences the $\urcorner$ symbol does not change. In Sect. 3.3, we show that bounding the number of occurrences of the $\urcorner$ symbol in conjunctive APTs makes the satisfiability problem tractable.

3.2 Conjunctive Anti-pattern Templates

To show that the satisfiability problem for conjunctive APTs can be solved in non-deterministic polynomial time, we define a *solved form* for conjunctive APTs and show that the satisfiability problem for conjunctive APTs in a solved form can be decided in polynomial time. Next, we present rules that simplify conjunctive APTs toward a solved form, i.e., the rules reduce size of anti-terms containing the $\urcorner$ symbol and make APTs closer to a solved form. We show that APTs, which are not in a solved form already, can be transformed to other templates. Furthermore, any sequence of transformations starting from a conjunctive APT T is bounded by the size of T. However, for some atomic APTs multiple transformation rules can be applied; thus, the transformation is non-deterministic. An incorrect choice may transform satisfiable templates into unsatisfiable, but not vice versa. Finally, we show that for every satisfiable conjunctive APT there is a sequence of transformations leading to a satisfiable template in a solved form.

Definition 8. A conjunctive APT T is in a *solved form* if and only if for every atomic APT $s \stackrel{?}{=} X$ from T either s is of the form $\urcorner Y$, where Y is a variable, or s does not contain the $\urcorner$ symbol, i.e., it is a term.

We show that for a conjunctive APT in a solved form a satisfying substitution can be constructed via applying unification on the part that does not contain $\urcorner$. Such a substitution either satisfies all templates $\urcorner Y \stackrel{?}{=} X$, or no solution exists.

Lemma 9. *The satisfiability problem is decidable in polynomial time for conjunctive APTs in a solved form.*

Proof. A given conjunctive APT T in a solved form can be partitioned into T_1 and T_2, where T_1 consists of expressions of the form $\urcorner Y \stackrel{?}{=} X$, and T_2 consists of expressions of the form $s \stackrel{?}{=} X$, where s is a term.

The algorithm works as follows. First, it checks whether T_1 contains $\urcorner Y \stackrel{?}{=} X$ such that $Y \notin \mathsf{FVars}(T)$. If it does, the algorithm returns the answer *unsatisfiable* as $[\![\urcorner Y]\!] = \emptyset$. Next, it considers T_2 as an instance of the standard unification problem, and it finds (in polynomial time) the most general unifier Θ [2]. If the unifer Θ does not exist, it returns the answer *unsatisfiable.* Finally, it checks for all atomic APTs $\urcorner Y \stackrel{?}{=} X$ from T_1, whether $\Theta(Y) \neq \Theta(X)$. If there is $\urcorner Y \stackrel{?}{=} X$ from T_1 with $\Theta(Y) = \Theta(X)$, it returns the answer *unsatisfiable.* Otherwise, it returns the answer *satisfiable.* □

We introduce simplification rules, which transform any conjunctive APT into a template in a solved form. The following four rules transform a conjunctive

APT T_1 of the form $T \wedge t \stackrel{?}{=} X$ into T_2 of the form $T \wedge T'$, where T' is a simpler APT (we discuss the measure of simplicity later). We define the transformation relation $\longrightarrow$ as follows.

- **(Decompose)** If t is of the form $f(t_1, \ldots, t_k)$, where $k \geq 1$ and at least one of the anti-terms $t_1, \ldots, t_k$ is a proper anti-term, then

$$T \wedge f(t_1, \ldots, t_k) \stackrel{?}{=} X \longrightarrow T \wedge f(X_1, \ldots, X_k) \stackrel{?}{=} X \wedge \bigwedge_{i=1}^{k} t_i \stackrel{?}{=} X_i$$

  where $X_1, \ldots, X_k$ are fresh variables w.r.t. T_1.
- **(Clash)** If t is of the form $\urcorner f(t_1, \ldots, t_k)$, where f can be a constant, then

$$T \wedge \urcorner f(t_1, \ldots, t_k) \stackrel{?}{=} X \longrightarrow T \wedge g(X_1, \ldots, X_p) \stackrel{?}{=} X$$

  where $f \neq g$, the symbol g can be a constant, and $X_1, \ldots, X_p$ are fresh variables.
- **(Push-i)** If t is of the form $\urcorner f(t_1, \ldots, t_k)$, where $0 < i \leq k$, then

$$T \wedge \urcorner f(t_1, \ldots, t_k) \stackrel{?}{=} X \longrightarrow T \wedge f(X_1, \ldots, X_k) \stackrel{?}{=} X \wedge \urcorner t_i \stackrel{?}{=} X_i$$

  where $X_1, \ldots, X_p$ are fresh variables.
- **(Cancel)** If t is of the form $\urcorner\urcorner s \stackrel{?}{=} X$, then

$$T \wedge \urcorner\urcorner s \stackrel{?}{=} X \longrightarrow T \wedge s \stackrel{?}{=} X$$

Observe that unless an atomic APT $t \stackrel{?}{=} X$ is in a solved form, at least one rule is applicable, i.e., there is T' such that $t \stackrel{?}{=} X \longrightarrow T'$. Furthermore, the relation $\longrightarrow$ is terminating, i.e., for every conjunctive APT T, the sequence $T = T_0 \longrightarrow T_1 \ldots$ is finite and bounded linearly in $\|T\|$. To see that, consider the measure $\|T\|^-$, the *negative size* of T, which is the size of subanti-terms occurring below some $\urcorner$ symbol. E.g. $\|g(\urcorner s) \stackrel{?}{=} X \wedge f(X_1, X_2, \urcorner\urcorner t) \stackrel{?}{=} X\|^- = \|s\| + \|\urcorner t\|$. Formally, for an anti-term s, if $s = \urcorner s'$, then $\|s\|^- = \|s'\|$, i.e., it is the size of s'. Otherwise, if $s = f(s_1, \ldots, s_k)$ with $k > 0$, then $\|s\|^- = \sum_{i=1}^{k} \|s_i\|^-$, and $\|s\|^- = 0$ if s is a constant or a variable. Finally, it extends to conjunctive APT as follows: $\|s \stackrel{?}{=} X\|^- = \|s\|^-$ and $\|T_1 \wedge \ldots \wedge T_k\|^- = \sum_{i=1}^{k} \|T_i\|^-$.

We observe that all of the above transformation rules decrease the negative size, while the size increases by at most constant depending on the signature only. In consequence, we have:

Lemma 10. *Let T be a conjunctive* APT *over the signature $\mathcal{F}$ and let p be the maximal arity over symbols from $\mathcal{F}$. Any sequence of transformations $T = T_0 \longrightarrow T_1 \ldots$ has a finite length bounded by $\|T\|^-$, the last element T_k is in a solved form, and for every $i \in \{0, \ldots, k\}$, the size $\|T_i\|$ is bounded by $\|T\| + 2 \cdot i \cdot p$.*

Observe that rules **(Clash)** and **(Push-i)** are overlapping (and **(Push-i)** for different i's). Furthermore, if one rule is applied at the considered position, the other rules are blocked. This eliminates possible counterparts of confluency, which makes rewriting systems convergent. In summary, presented rules are *non-deterministic* and the choice of rules is important.

To state correctness of the transformation $\longrightarrow$ we need to factor in its non-determinism. We show that all presented rules transform unsatisfiable APTs into unsatisfiable templates (preserve unsatisfiablity), and there is always at least one choice of a rule to preserve satisfiability.

Lemma 11. *Let T_1 be a conjunctive* APT*. (1) If $T_1 \longrightarrow T_2$, and T_2 is satisfiable, then T_1 is satisfiable as well. (2) If T_1 is satisfiable and not in a solved form, then there is T_2 such that $T_1 \longrightarrow T_2$ and T_2 is satisfiable.*

Lemmas 10 and 11 imply that a conjunctive APT T is satisfiable if and only if there exists a sequence $T = T_0 \longrightarrow T_1 \longrightarrow \ldots \longrightarrow T_m$ such that T_m is satisfiable and in a solved form. Furthermore, due to Lemma 10 the overall size of such a sequence is polynomially bounded in $\|T\|$. Finally, satisfiability of T_m in a solved form can be decided in polynomial time (Lemma 9). In consequence, the satisfiability problem for conjunctive APTs is in NP, which together with Lemma 5 stating NP-hardness of the problem gives us:

Theorem 12. *The satisfiability problem for conjunctive* APTs *is* NP*-complete.*

The matching problem for anti-patterns can be solved in polynomial time. However, if anti-patterns are to be used as a query language, running exponential-time satisfiablity check of an APT before executing matching against a big dataset may still be beneficial. Especially, if the base in the exponent is low.

3.3 Bounded Conjunctive Anti-pattern Templates

We show that satisfiability of conjunctive APTs with bounded number of the $\urcorner$ symbols is tractable. Therefore, the number of the $\urcorner$ symbols is the crucial parameter determining complexity of the satisfiability problem.

Definition 13. A conjunctive APT T is m-negation bounded if there are at most m occurrences of the symbol $\urcorner$ in T.

Consider an atomic APT $\urcorner s \stackrel{?}{=} X$, where s is a term. This template can be reduced to a solved form by a sequence of **(Push-i)** rules, which terminates with a template containing $\urcorner Y \stackrel{?}{=} Z$ with Y being a variable from s, or a sequence of **(Push-i)** rules and the final application of **(Clash)** rule. While the sequence of reductions involves a non-deterministic pick at each step, the overall number of possible outcomes for $\urcorner s \stackrel{?}{=} X$ is bounded by the number of positions in s, corresponding to the sequence of applied **(Push-i)** rules, multiplied by the number of symbols in the signature corresponding to the last rule **(Clash)**.

For an atomic APT $f(\urcorner t_1, \urcorner t_2) \stackrel{?}{=} X$, the number of possible outcomes is bounded by the product of the possible outcomes for $\urcorner t_1 \stackrel{?}{=} X_1$ and for $\urcorner t_2 \stackrel{?}{=} X_2$. We combine these two observations to show that for any fixed m, the satisfiability problem for conjunctive APTs is solvable in polynomial time.

Theorem 14. *For every m, the satisfiability problem for m-negation bounded conjunctive APTs is decidable in polynomial time.*

Proof. We define the potential $\mathbf{\Phi}(T)$ of a conjunctive APT as follows. Consider the set of positions of the $\urcorner$ symbol $\mathsf{Pos}_{\urcorner}(t) = \{p \in \mathsf{Pos}(t) \mid \mathsf{hd}(t_{|p}) = \urcorner\}$. First, for an anti-term t, we define $\mathbf{\Phi}(t) = 1$, if t does not contain the symbol $\urcorner$, and otherwise $\mathbf{\Phi}(t) = \prod_{p \in \mathsf{Pos}_{\urcorner}(t)} |\mathcal{F}| \cdot |\mathsf{Pos}(t_{|p \cdot 1})|$, where $t_{|p \cdot 1}$ is a sub(anti)term directly under the position p of an occurrence of $\urcorner$. For an atomic APT $t \stackrel{?}{=} X$, we define $\mathbf{\Phi}(t \stackrel{?}{=} X) = \mathbf{\Phi}(t)$. Finally, for a conjunctive APT $T = T_1 \wedge \ldots \wedge T_k$, where each T_i is an atomic APT, we put $\mathbf{\Phi}(T) = \prod_{i=1}^{k} \mathbf{\Phi}(T_i)$. E.g. $\mathbf{\Phi}(\urcorner f(\urcorner c_1, c_2)) = |\mathcal{F}| \cdot |\mathsf{Pos}(f(c_1, c_2))| \cdot |\mathcal{F}| \cdot |\mathsf{Pos}(c_1)| = 3 \cdot |\mathcal{F}|^2$.

We show the following condition (*) about the potential. For a conjunctive APT S, if $S_1, \ldots, S_k$ are all successors w.r.t. $\longrightarrow$, then (*) $\mathbf{\Phi}(S) \geq \sum_{i=1}^{k} \mathbf{\Phi}(S_i)$. Having shown that, we conclude that for every T, if $T_1, \ldots, T_n$ of all conjunctive APTs in a solved form such that T can be transformed in many steps to T_i, then $\mathbf{\Phi}(T) \geq \sum_{i=1}^{n} \mathbf{\Phi}(T_i)$. Since the potential is always greater or equal to 1, there are at most $\mathbf{\Phi}(T)$ outcomes of the transformation $\longrightarrow$. Now, if there are m occurrences of the $\urcorner$ symbol in T, the potential $\mathbf{\Phi}(T)$ is bounded by $(|\mathcal{F}| \cdot |T|)^m$, i.e., it is polynomially bounded. Therefore, we can enumerate in polynomial time all such T_i, and check for each of them in polynomial time whether it is satisfiable. Thus, the result follows.

It remains to show condition (*). Since the potential is multiplicative, i.e., $\mathbf{\Phi}(T_1 \wedge T_2) = \mathbf{\Phi}(T_1) \cdot \mathbf{\Phi}(T_2)$, it suffices to show (*) for atomic templates only. It can be verified for each transformation separately. □

3.4 General APTs

We briefly discuss how to solve the satisfiability problem for all APTs, which are any Boolean combinations of atomic APTs.

Consider an APT T. Let φ_T be a Boolean formula resulting from replacing each atomic APT T_i from T with a propositional variable x_i. If φ_T is satisfiable, then it has a satisfiable conjunctive implicant ψ, which corresponds to a satisfying assignment. We construct a conjunctive APT T_ψ from ψ as the conjunction of T_i that correspond to literals x_i from ψ, and the conjunction of *negated* atomic APTs T_i that correspond to literals $\neg x_i$ from ψ, where negated atomic APT $t \stackrel{?}{=} X$

is defined as $\urcorner t \stackrel{?}{=} X$. Observe that if T is satisfiable, then T_ψ is satisfiable for some implicant ψ.

In summary, to decide the satisfiability problem of a given APT, it suffices to non-deterministically pick a conjunctive APT corresponding to an implicant and check its satisfiability, which can be done in non-deterministic polynomial time.

Corollary 15. *The satisfiability problem for all APTs is* NP*-complete.*

Remark 16. The satisfiability problem for APTs is NP-hard even if the $\urcorner$ symbol does not occur at all. The SAT problem reduces to the satisfiability problem over $\mathcal{F}$ consisting of just two constants $\top, \bot$; given a propositional formula φ in CNF, we define an APT T_φ by substituting each positive literal x with $\top \stackrel{?}{=} X$, while the literals $\neg x$ are substituted with $\bot \stackrel{?}{=} X$. There is a direct correspondence between satisfying assignment for φ and solutions to T_φ.

4 Anti-pattern Templates Modulo Theory

In this section we consider APTs modulo an equational theory E. In context of equational theories, we compare the expressive power of APTs with other frameworks combining symbolic equations and negative constraints: disunification and the complement problem. These frameworks do not involve anti-terms as they express negative constraints with other means. As a consequence, we show that, under mild assumptions, the satisfiability problem for conjunctive APTs remains decidable under presence of associative and commutative symbols.

4.1 Term Algebra Modulo an Equational Theory

Equational Theories. Consider a finite set E of term equations over $\mathcal{F}(E) \subseteq \mathcal{F}$. We define a binary relation $=_E$ on terms $\mathcal{T}(\mathcal{F}, \mathcal{V})$ as the least *equivalence* relation containing E that is

- *closed under substitutions*, i.e., if $s =_E t$, then for every substitution σ we have $\sigma(s) =_E \sigma(t)$, and
- a *congruence*, i.e., for all $f \in \mathcal{F}$ and for all terms $s_1, t_1, \ldots, s_k, t_k$, where k is the arity of f, if $s_1 =_E t_1, \ldots, s_k =_E t_k$, then $f(s_1, \ldots, s_k) =_E f(t_1, \ldots, t_k)$.

We focus on two important equational theories:

- **associativity** (**A**): for all $f \in \mathcal{F}(E)$ we have $f(X, f(Y, Z)) = f(f(X, Y), Z)$.
- **associativity and commutativity** (**AC**): the identities defined by **A** and for all $f \in \mathcal{F}(E)$ we have the identity $f(X, Y) = f(Y, X)$.

4.2 E-unification

The unification problem over a signature $\mathcal{F}$ modulo E (called E-unification) is to find, given a set of equations $\Gamma = \{s_1 \stackrel{?}{=} t_1, \ldots, s_n \stackrel{?}{=} t_n\}$ over $\mathcal{F}$, a substitution σ such that for every i we have $\sigma(s_i) =_E \sigma(t_i)$. Such a substitution is called an *unifier* (also called an E-unifier) and the set of equations having a unifier is *unifiable.*

Unifiers can be compared with respect to their generality. Consider a set of equations Γ and let $\mathcal{V}$ be the variables from Γ. We say that a unifier σ_1 is more general than σ_2 modulo E on $\mathcal{V}$ if σ_2 can be obtained by instantiating σ_1, i.e., there is σ_3 such that for all $X \in \mathcal{V}$ we have $\sigma_2(X) =_E \sigma_3(\sigma_1(X))$. A set $\mathcal{C}$ is a *minimal complete set of unifiers* of Γ modulo E if and only if (1) every element of $\mathcal{C}$ is a unifier of Γ modulo E, (2) for every unifier σ_1 of Γ modulo E, there is a more general unifier from $\mathcal{C}$ modulo E on $\mathcal{V}$ from Γ, and (3) removal of any element from $\mathcal{C}$ violates (2).

There are various *unification types* depending on E. In the base case $E = \emptyset$, unification is *unitary,* i.e., any unifiable set of equations has the most general unifier Θ. Unification modulo **AC** is *finitary,* i.e., any unifiable set of equations has a minimal complete set of unifiers modulo **AC**, but it need not have the most general unifier. E.g. $f(X,Y) \stackrel{?}{=} f(a, f(b,c))$ with f being **AC** has 6 ground unifiers with are incomparable in generality. For instance, $X \mapsto a, Y \mapsto f(b,c)$, and $X \mapsto c, Y \mapsto f(b,a)$, are incomparable unifiers modulo **AC**. Finally, unification modulo **A** is *infinitary,* i.e., there are sets of equations having only infinite minimal complete set of unifiers modulo **A** [2].

As in the case of the satisfiability problem for APTs, complexity and the unification type depend on the signature. There are three variants of E-unification: *elementary* E-unification, if $\mathcal{F} = \mathcal{F}(E)$, i.e., only symbols that appear in E are allowed in the equations and unifiers, E-unification *with constants,* if $\mathcal{F}$ consists of $\mathcal{F}(E)$ and constant symbols, and *general* E-unification, if $\mathcal{F} \supseteq \mathcal{F}(E)$ and there are no other restrictions on $\mathcal{F}$.

4.3 Equational Frameworks with Negation

We briefly introduce the disunification problem and the complement problem and discuss their relation.

Disunification. The disunification problem over the signature $\mathcal{F}$ modulo E is to find, given a set of term equations $\{s_1 \stackrel{?}{=} t_1, \ldots, s_n \stackrel{?}{=} t_n\}$ and a set of term disequations $\{u_1 \stackrel{?}{\neq} v_1, \ldots, u_m \stackrel{?}{\neq} v_m\}$ over $\mathcal{F}$, a substitution σ, such that for every $i \in \{1, \ldots, n\}$ we have $\sigma(s_i) =_E \sigma(t_i)$, and for every $j \in \{1, \ldots, m\}$ we have $\sigma(u_j) \neq_E \sigma(v_j)$.

Disunification has been intensively studied [7]. In particular, it has been established that disunification modulo **AC** is NP-complete [6]. For associativity, there has been established a (non-deterministic) reduction of disunification modulo **A** to unification modulo **A** [1]. The latter is known as *word equations* and it is PSPACE-complete [10,17]. It follows that the disunification problem modulo **A** is PSPACE-complete as well.

The Complement Problem. The complement problem over the signature $\mathcal{F}$ modulo E is to find, given a term $s \in \mathcal{T}(\mathcal{F}, \mathcal{V})$ and a set of terms $\{t_1, \ldots, t_k\}$ from $\mathcal{T}(\mathcal{F}, \mathcal{V})$, a substitution σ such that $\sigma(s)$ is a ground term not equal modulo E to an instance of any of the terms $t_1, \ldots, t_k$ modulo E, i.e., for $i \in \{1, \ldots, k\}$ we have $\sigma(s) \notin [\![t_i]\!]_E$.

The complement problem has applications in various areas including inductive learning, conditional rewriting, algebraic specifications and knowledge representation [9,14,15]. The complement problem modulo **AC** is decidable [12], while it is undecidable modulo **A** [13].

Disunification and the complement problem may seem superficially similar, but the disunification problem modulo **A** is PSPACE-complete whereas the complement problem modulo **A** is undecidable. The difference between these problems is perhaps best explained by translating them to first order logic over the term algebra modulo E. The disunification problem translates to the formula

$$\exists \vec{x} \bigwedge_i s_i[\vec{x}] = t_i[\vec{x}] \wedge \bigwedge_i u_i[\vec{x}] \neq v_i[\vec{x}]$$

whereas the complement problem translates to the formula

$$\exists \vec{x} \forall \vec{y} \bigwedge_i s[\vec{x}] \neq t_i[\vec{y}]$$

4.4 Comparing APT with Other Equational Frameworks

We consider variants of anti-patterns and APTs defined modulo E by replacing equality $=$ with equality modulo $=_E$. For an anti-term s we consider its ground-term semantics modulo E defined as $[\![s]\!]_E = \{t \in \mathcal{T}(\mathcal{F}) \mid s' \in [\![s]\!] \wedge t =_E s'\}$. Then, we define accordingly the counterparts modulo E of anti-pattern matching, APTs and the satisfiability problem.

Now, we relate the satisfiability problem for conjunctive APTs with the disunification problem and the complement problem. While the satisfiability problem is a decision problem, disunification and the complement problem are function problems returning a substitution. To relate them, we consider their decision variants, i.e., the questions whether there exists any substitution satisfying the requirements.

Lemma 17. *For every finite set of identities E and a signature $\mathcal{F}$, the (decision variants of) disunification problem over $\mathcal{F}$ modulo E and the complement problem over $\mathcal{F}$ modulo E reduce in polynomial time to the satisfiability problem for conjunctive APTs over $\mathcal{F}$ modulo E.*

While Lemma 17 states only a weak link, the reductions actually show that sets of solutions to the disunification problem (resp. the complement problem) and the set of substitutions satisfying the APT from the reduction are equal.

The decision variant of the complement problem modulo **A** has been show to be undecidable [13]. This result together with Lemma 17 gives us:

Corollary 18. *The satisfiability problem for conjunctive* APTs *modulo* **A** *is undecidable.*

We conclude with the converse reduction to the one from Lemma 17. This reduction need not be polynomial nor many-one, but it is sufficient to show conditional decidability.

Lemma 19. *Assume that the signature $\mathcal{F}$ contains a free function symbol (not occurring in E) of arity at least 2. Let E be a finite set of identities such that (1) general E-unification over $\mathcal{F}$ is unitary or finitary, and there is an effective algorithm computing a minimal complete set of unifiers and (2) the complement problem over $\mathcal{F}$ modulo E is decidable. Then, the satisfiability problem for conjunctive* APTs *over $\mathcal{F}$ modulo E is decidable.*

The proof of Lemma 19 consists of three steps. First, a conjunctive APT is transformed to two sets of equations: positive without $\urcorner$ and negative with $\urcorner$ on the top position only. Next, the positive part is solved using E-unification over $\mathcal{F}$. We compute a finite complete set of unifiers, non-deterministically pick one unifier, and apply it to the negative part. This gives us an intermediate problem, which can be considered as the *simultaneous* complement problem modulo E. It is to decide whether, given terms $s_1, \ldots, s_k \in \mathcal{T}(\mathcal{F}, \mathcal{V}_1)$ and $t_1, \ldots, t_k \in \mathcal{T}(\mathcal{F}, \mathcal{V}_2)$ over disjoint sets of variables $\mathcal{V}_1$ and $\mathcal{V}_2$, there is a substitution σ such that for $i \in \{1, \ldots, k\}$ we have $\sigma(s_i) \notin [\![t_i]\!]_E$. This is a generalization of the complement problem, in which s_i are equal. However, using a free function symbol, we can transform it to the complement problem with a single pair s, t.

As a consequence of Lemma 19 we get decidability of the satisfiability problem for conjunctive APTs modulo **AC** in presence of free function symbols. Unification modulo **AC** is finitary and a set of most general unifiers is computable [8]. Furthermore, the complement problem modulo **AC** is decidable [12]. These two results and Lemma 19 imply the following:

Corollary 20. *Assume that $\mathcal{F}$ contains a non-AC function symbol g of arity at least 2. Then, the satisfiability problem for conjunctive* APTs *over $\mathcal{F}$ modulo* **AC** *is decidable.*

The case of $\mathcal{F}$ consisting of only AC symbols, unary symbols and constants remains open. There are two possible approaches to tackle this problem. One is to focus on this case, as it rather restricted. Another is to work on the simultaneous complement problem modulo **AC** as described above.

5 Conclusions and Future Work

We have introduced anti-pattern templates, which generalize anti-pattern matching by abstracting matched ground terms to variables. Furthermore, we have adapted related notions, such as free variables, to the new framework, which would not be possible with anti-pattern matching.

This allowed us to consider validity of anti-pattern templates expressed via the satisfiability problem; an anti-pattern template is valid if it can be instantiated to some satisfied (anti-pattern) matching system. While the satisfiability problem for anti-pattern templates is NP-complete in general, we have identified the number of the $\urcorner$ symbols as the key parameter determining the complexity over conjunctive anti-pattern templates. Finally, we have discussed anti-pattern templates modulo equational theories. We have observed a significant complexity jump compared to anti-pattern matching; anti-pattern matching modulo associativity is decidable in NEXPTIME, but the satisfiablity problem for anti-pattern templates is undecidable. On the positive side, under mild assumptions, the satisfiablity problem for anti-pattern templates modulo associativity and commutativity is decidable, and establishing exact complexity is left as future work.

Anti-pattern templates provide an intuitive means to express negative constraints. An interesting future work would be to apply anti-pattern templates to rewriting with membership conditions [4,19].

Acknowledgments. We thank the anonymous reviewers for their detailed and constructive comments on this paper.

This work was supported by the National Science Centre (NCN), Poland under grant 2024/53/B/ST6/01620.

Disclosure of Interests. The author has no competing interests to declare that are relevant to the content of this article.

References

1. Baader, F., Schulz, K.U.: Combination techniques and decision problems for disunification. Theor. Comput. Sci. **142**(2), 229–255 (1995). https://doi.org/10.1016/0304-3975(94)00277-0
2. Baader, F., Snyder, W.: Unification theory. In: Handbook of Automated Reasoning (in 2 volumes), pp. 445–532. MIT Press (2001). https://doi.org/10.1016/B978-044450813-3/50010-2
3. Balland, E., Brauner, P., Kopetz, R., Moreau, P.-E., Reilles, A.: Tom: piggybacking rewriting on Java. In: Baader, F. (ed.) RTA 2007. LNCS, vol. 4533, pp. 36–47. Springer, Heidelberg (2007). https://doi.org/10.1007/978-3-540-73449-9_5
4. Bouhoula, A., Jouannaud, J., Meseguer, J.: Specification and proof in membership equational logic. Theor. Comput. Sci. **236**(1–2), 35–132 (2000). https://doi.org/10.1016/S0304-3975(99)00206-6
5. Cirstea, H., Kirchner, C., Kopetz, R., Moreau, P.: Anti-patterns for rule-based languages. J. Symb. Comput. **45**(5), 523–550 (2010). https://doi.org/10.1016/J.JSC.2010.01.007
6. Comon, H.: Unification et disunification: théorie et applications. (Unification and disunification in free algebras and in initial algebras : theory and applications). Ph.D. thesis, Grenoble Institute of Technology, France (1988). https://tel.archives-ouvertes.fr/tel-00331263
7. Comon, H.: Disunification: a survey. In: Computational Logic - Essays in Honor of Alan Robinson, pp. 322–359 (1991)

8. CADE 1984. LNCS, vol. 170. Springer, New York (1984). https://doi.org/10.1007/978-0-387-34768-4_30
9. Fernández, M.: AC complement problems: satisfiability and negation elimination. J. Symb. Comput. **22**(1), 49–82 (1996). https://doi.org/10.1006/JSCO.1996.0041
10. Jez, A.: Recompression: a simple and powerful technique for word equations. In: STACS 2013. LIPIcs, vol. 20, pp. 233–244. Schloss Dagstuhl - Leibniz-Zentrum für Informatik (2013). https://doi.org/10.4230/LIPICS.STACS.2013.233
11. Kirchner, C., Kopetz, R., Moreau, P.: Anti-pattern matching modulo. In: Language and Automata Theory and Applications, Second International Conference, LATA 2008, Tarragona, Spain, 13–19 March 2008. Revised Papers, pp. 275–286 (2008). https://doi.org/10.1007/978-3-540-88282-4_26
12. Kounalis, E., Lugiez, D., Pottier, L.: A solution of the complement problem in associative-commutative theories. In: MFCS 1991, pp. 287–297 (1991). https://doi.org/10.1007/3-540-54345-7_72
13. Kucherov, G., Rusinowitch, M.: Undecidability of ground reducibility for word rewriting systems with variables. Inf. Process. Lett. **53**(4), 209–215 (1995). https://doi.org/10.1016/0020-0190(94)00188-5
14. Lassez, J., Maher, M.J., Marriott, K.: Elimination of negation in term algebras. In: Mathematical Foundations of Computer Science 1991, 16th International Symposium, MFCS 1991, Kazimierz Dolny, Poland, 9–13 September 1991, Proceedings, pp. 1–16 (1991). https://doi.org/10.1007/3-540-54345-7_44
15. Lugiez, D., Moysset, J.L.: Complement problems and tree automata in AC-like theories. In: STACS 1993, pp. 515–524 (1993). https://doi.org/10.1007/3-540-56503-5_51
16. Otop, J.: Unification of anti-terms. In: UNIF 2011, pp. 9–14 (2011)
17. Plandowski, W.: Satisfiability of word equations with constants is in PSPACE. J. ACM **51**(3), 483–496 (2004). https://doi.org/10.1145/990308.990312
18. Ramakrishnan, I.V., Sekar, R., Voronkov, A.: Term indexing. In: Handbook of Automated Reasoning (in 2 volumes), pp. 1853–1964. MIT Press (2001). https://doi.org/10.1016/B978-044450813-3/50028-X
19. Toyama, Y.: Confluent term rewriting systems with membership conditions. In: Conditional Term Rewriting Systems, pp. 228–241 (1987). https://doi.org/10.1007/3-540-19242-5_17

Equational Reasoning Modulo Commutativity in Languages with Binders

Ali K. Caires-Santos[1(✉)], Maribel Fernández[2], and Daniele Nantes-Sobrinho[1,3]

[1] University of Brasília, Brasília, Brazil
A.K.C.R.Santos@mat.unb.br, dnantes@unb.br
[2] King's College London, London, UK
maribel.fernandez@kcl.ac.uk
[3] Imperial College London, London, UK

Abstract. Many formal languages include binders as well as operators that satisfy equational axioms, such as commutativity. Here we consider the nominal language, a general formal framework which provides support for the representation of binders, freshness conditions and α-renaming. Rather than relying on the usual freshness constraints, we introduce a nominal algebra which employs permutation fixed-point constraints in α-equivalence judgements, seamlessly integrating commutativity into the reasoning process. We establish its proof-theoretical properties and provide a sound and complete semantics in the setting of nominal sets. Additionally, we propose a novel algorithm for nominal unification modulo commutativity, which we prove terminating and correct. By leveraging fixed-point constraints, our approach ensures a finitary unification theory, unlike standard methods relying on freshness constraints. This framework offers a robust foundation for structural induction and recursion over syntax with binders and commutative operators, enabling reasoning in settings such as first-order logic and the π-calculus.

Keywords: Languages with binders · Unification · Equational theories

1 Introduction

In computer science and logic, formal languages abstract away concrete syntax details, focusing on abstract syntax to capture structural properties. However, conventional abstract syntax falls short for languages with variable-binding constructs. The formalisation of languages with binding is challenging and requires specialised tools: one of the aims of the POPLMark challenge [8] was to explore and compare methods for the formalisation of binding operators. Many different techniques were proposed to address the challenge, for example, the approach based on higher-order abstract syntax (HOAS) is described in the survey [18] by Felty et al. Here we follow the nominal approach, introduced by Gabbay and Pitts [23]: Binders are specified using an abstraction construct of the form $[a]t$, where a is a name and t an arbitrary expression (read "abstract a in t").

C. Barrett and U. Waldmann (Eds.): CADE 2025, LNAI 15943, pp. 632–652, 2025.
https://doi.org/10.1007/978-3-031-99984-0_33

Nominal syntax [23] makes a distinction between *names* $a, b, \ldots$ (also called atoms), which can be abstracted but cannot be substituted, and *(meta-)variables* $X, Y, \ldots$ (also called *unkowns*), which can be substituted but not abstracted. The α-equivalence relation $\approx_\alpha$ is defined using the notion of support, or equivalently, the notion of freshness, a concept that generalises the idea of an atom not being free in a term: a is *fresh* for t, written $a\#t$, if a is not in the support of t.

More generally, in languages where operators are subject to equational axioms E, such as associativity (A) and commutativity (C), the equivalence relation of interest is generated by α and E. A well-known example is first-order logic with $\forall$ and $\exists$ quantifiers and conjunction and disjunction connectives; similarly, in Milner's π-calculus expressions are considered modulo a structural congruence. Effective reasoning techniques for such languages are essential, particularly when proving properties about them in a proof assistant. A common subproblem in this context is solving unification problems—finding the appropriate *substitution* that equates two expressions—when applying lemmas in automated proofs.

Although unification of first-order terms modulo commutativity is decidable and finitary, and nominal unification is unitary (every solvable problem has a unique most general unifier), unification modulo α and C is not finitary if solutions are expressed using substitutions and freshness contexts [5]. This motivated the study of a version of nominal syntax where the α-equivalence relation is specified using permutation fixed-point constraints $\pi \curlywedge t$ (read "π fixes t)" instead of freshness constraints [6]. However, the derivation relation defined in [6] is sound for strong nominal algebras [25,33] only (that is, the carriers should be strong nominal sets). Soundness with respect to the standard nominal set models was proved only for a restricted calculus in [10].

Contributions. The system presented in this paper is a generalisation of the latter in two ways: judgements here can include arbitrary fixed point constraints in contexts, and equational axioms are taken into account, making the system more expressive while maintaining soundness for standard nominal set models. Devising a proof system for general fixed point judgements that is sound and complete is challenging; the difficulty lies in the variable rule, which needs to be sufficiently powerful to derive all the valid judgements, but only those that are valid in all nominal set models. A key idea to obtain soundness and completeness with respect to standard nominal set semantics is to analyse the permutation cycles in fixed-point assumptions.

We also study satisfiability of equality constraints: we show that nominal unification is decidable and unitary if $E = \emptyset$, and it is finitary if Commutativity axioms are included. More precisely, we provide a unification algorithm specified as a set of simplification rules on unification problems, which we show terminating and correct. The normal forms of the simplification system consist of a finite set (Υ) of fixed-point constraints and a substitution. The algorithm outputs a most general solution of the form (Υ, σ) if $E = \emptyset$ and a finite complete set of solutions of the form (Υ_i, σ_i) if $E =$ C. Having a finitary theory is important in practice, for example to design programming languages and theorem provers that support binders and equational axioms, to specify completion procedures for rewriting modulo α and E, etc. A notable feature of our unification algorithm is its treatment of computed *substitutions*: it ensures that meta-variables are instantiated while maintaining stability under renaming of bound names—preserving consistency when fresh names are introduced during computation (see Remark 1).

An extended version with all the proofs is available in [11].

2 Preliminaries

In this section, we introduce some basic notions and notations used throughout the paper; for more details we refer the reader to [3,19,23].

Nominal Syntax. Fix disjoint countably infinite sets $\mathbb{A} = \{a, b, c, \ldots\}$ of *atoms* or *names* and $\mathbb{V} = \{X, Y, Z, \ldots\}$ of *variables*. A *signature* Σ is a set of *term-formers* ($\mathtt{f}, \mathtt{g}, \ldots$)—disjoint from $\mathbb{A}$ and $\mathbb{V}$—where each $\mathtt{f} \in \Sigma$ has a fixed *arity* $n \geq 0$, denoted $\mathtt{f} : n$. A *finite* permutation π of atoms is a bijection $\mathbb{A} \to \mathbb{A}$ such that the set $\mathtt{dom}(\pi) := \{a \in \mathbb{A} \mid \pi(a) \neq a\}$ is finite. Write $\mathtt{id}$ for the *identity permutation*, $\pi \circ \pi'$ for the *composition* of π and π', and π^{-1} for the *inverse* of π. We use *swappings* of atoms of the form $(a\ b)$ to implement the renaming of atoms, for the purpose of α-conversion. Given two permutations π and ρ, the permutation $\pi^\rho = \rho \circ \pi \circ \rho^{-1}$ denotes the *conjugate* of π with respect to ρ.

Nominal terms are defined inductively by the following grammar:

$$s, t, u ::= a \mid \pi \cdot X \mid \mathtt{f}^{\mathtt{E}}(t_1, \ldots, t_n) \mid [a]t$$

where a is an *atom*, $\pi \cdot X$ is a *suspension* (with π acting upon substitution) where suspensions of the form $\mathtt{id} \cdot X$ will be represented simply by X, $[a]t$ denotes the *abstraction* of the atom a over the term t. Function symbols $\mathtt{f}^{\mathtt{E}}$ carry equational theory $\mathtt{E}$ (e.g., $\mathtt{C}$ for commutativity), though syntactically $\mathtt{f}^{\mathtt{E}}(t_1, ..., t_n)$ remains a nominal term. The annotation affects only semantic equality: for all terms t_1, t_2, $\mathtt{f}^{\mathtt{C}}(t_1, t_2)$ equals $\mathtt{f}^{\mathtt{C}}(t_2, t_1)$ under $\mathtt{C}$, while remaining syntactically distinct. Unannotated symbols ($\mathtt{f}^{\emptyset}$ or simply $\mathtt{f}$) are treated rigidly. The set of all nominal terms formed from a signature Σ will be denoted by $\mathbb{F}(\Sigma, \mathbb{V})$.

Write $\mathtt{Var}(-)$ and $\mathtt{Atm}(-)$ to denote the sets of all variables and all atoms occurring in the argument, respectively. A nominal term t is *ground* when it does not mention variables, i.e., when $\mathtt{Var}(t) = \emptyset$. The set of all ground terms will be denoted by $\mathbb{F}(\Sigma)$. The set of *free atoms* of a ground term g is denoted as $\mathtt{fn}(t)$ and consists of the atoms, say a, that do not occur under the scope of an abstraction $[a]$, that is, $\mathtt{fn}(a) = \{a\}, \mathtt{fn}(\mathtt{f}^{\mathtt{E}}(g_1, \ldots, g_n)) = \bigcup_{i=1}^{n} \mathtt{fn}(g_i)$, and $\mathtt{fn}([a]g) = \mathtt{fn}(g) \setminus \{a\}$. Write $t \equiv u$ for *syntactic identity* of terms.

The *object-level permutation action on terms*, denoted as $\pi \cdot t$, is defined via the homomorphic application of a permutation on the structure of the term: $\pi \cdot a \equiv \pi(a)$, $\pi \cdot (\pi' \cdot X) \equiv (\pi \circ \pi') \cdot X, \pi \cdot ([a]t) \equiv [\pi(a)](\pi \cdot t)$ and $\pi \cdot \mathtt{f}^{\mathtt{E}}(t_1, \ldots, t_n) \equiv \mathtt{f}^{\mathtt{E}}(\pi \cdot t_1, \ldots, \pi \cdot t_n)$. *Substitutions*, usually denoted by $\sigma, \delta, \ldots$, are finite mappings from variables to terms, which extend homomorphically over terms. We write Id to denote the identity substitution, $\mathtt{dom}(\sigma)$ to denote the domain of σ. Substitutions and permutations commute: $\pi \cdot (s\sigma) \equiv (\pi \cdot s)\sigma$.

Example 1. Abstractions will be used to represent binding operators (e.g. the lambda operator from the λ-calculus). Considering the signature $\Sigma = \{\mathtt{lam} : 1, \mathtt{app} : 2\}$ and treating λ-variables as atoms, λ-terms can be inductively generated by the grammar: $e ::= a \mid \mathtt{app}(e,e) \mid \mathtt{lam}([a]e)$. Note that $(a\ b) \cdot \mathtt{lam}([a]a) \equiv \mathtt{lam}([b]b)$ implements the renaming of a for b using the swapping $(a\ b)$.

Groups and Permutations. For completeness, we outline basic group and permutation concepts used in this work. This subsection can be skipped on a first reading and consulted later as a reference. A *permutation group* is a group[1] whose elements are permutations on a set with composition $\circ$ as the group operation. For $S \subseteq G$, $\langle S \rangle$ denotes the subgroup generated by S (all finite compositions of elements from S and their inverses). We work with $\mathcal{G}(\mathbb{A})$, the group of finite permutations on atoms $\mathbb{A}$, where for $B \subseteq \mathbb{A}$, $\mathcal{G}(B) = \{\pi \in \mathcal{G}(\mathbb{A}) \mid \mathtt{dom}(\pi) \subseteq B\}$. Permutations can be represented via swappings $(a\ b)$ or disjoint cycles $(a_1\ \cdots\ a_n)$. For $H, K \subseteq G$ with operation $\star$, $H \star K = \{h \star k \mid h \in H, k \in K\}$ forms a subgroup iff $H \star K = K \star H$.

Nominal Sets. A $\mathcal{G}(\mathbb{A})$-*set* $\mathscr{X}$ is a pair $(|\mathscr{X}|, \cdot)$ where $|\mathscr{X}|$ is any set and $\cdot : \mathcal{G}(A) \times |\mathscr{X}| \to |\mathscr{X}|$ is a group action satisfying: $\mathtt{id} \cdot x = x$ and $\pi \cdot (\pi' \cdot x) = (\pi \circ \pi') \cdot x$ for all $x \in |\mathscr{X}|$ and $\pi, \pi' \in \mathcal{G}(A)$. The notation $\pi \cdot_{\mathscr{X}} x$ may be used to emphasize the action on $\mathscr{X}$. For $B \subseteq \mathbb{A}$, we denote $\mathtt{pfix}(B)$ as the set of permutations that fix pointwise the elements of B, i.e. $\mathtt{pfix}(B) = \{\pi \in \mathcal{G}(\mathbb{A}) \mid \forall a \in B.\ \pi(a) = a\}$. A set $B \subseteq \mathbb{A}$ *supports* an element $x \in |\mathscr{X}|$ when for all permutations $\pi \in \mathcal{G}(\mathbb{A})$: $\pi \in \mathtt{pfix}(B) \implies \pi \cdot x = x$. Additionally, B *strongly supports* $x \in |\mathscr{X}|$ if the reverse implication holds. A *(strong) nominal set* is a $\mathcal{G}(\mathbb{A})$-set $\mathscr{X}$ all of whose elements are finitely (strongly) supported. $\mathscr{X}, \mathscr{Y}, \mathscr{Z}$ will range over nominal sets.

The *support* of an element $x \in |\mathscr{X}|$ in a nominal set $\mathscr{X}$ is defined as $\mathtt{supp}(x) = \bigcap \{B \mid B \text{ is finite and supports} x\}$, which ensures $\mathtt{supp}(x)$ is the *least* finite support of x; intuitively, it consists of all atoms "occurring" in x. This notion provides the semantics for freshness constraints in nominal sets [19,22]: when $a \notin \mathtt{supp}(x)$, we write $a \#_{\text{sem}} x$ (read "a is fresh for x").

One of the main properties of the relation $a \#_{\mathtt{sem}} x$ is the so-called *Choose-a-Fresh-Name Principle*, which says that if $x \in |\mathscr{X}|$ has a finite support, then it is always possible to choose a new atom a such that $a \#_{\mathtt{sem}} x$. Therefore, the notion of freshness provides a generative aspect of fresh atoms.

Example 2. Examples of nominal sets include: (1) the set of atoms $\mathbb{A}$ with its canonical permutation action $\pi \cdot_{\mathbb{A}} a = \pi(a)$, where each atom a satisfies $\mathtt{supp}(a) = \{a\}$; (2) the set of ground terms $\mathbb{F}(\Sigma)$ with the object-level permutation action,

[1] A *group* is a set G equipped with an operation $\star : G \times G \to G$ that satisfies four properties: closure, associativity, identity, and invertibility.

where $\mathtt{supp}(g) = \mathtt{Atm}(g)$ (the set of all atoms occurring in g). However, nominal sets are not limited to syntactic objects like atoms or terms. A key example is the permutation group $\mathcal{G}(\mathbb{A})$ itself under conjugation $\rho \cdot \pi = \rho \circ \pi \circ \rho^{-1}$, with $\mathtt{supp}(\pi) = \mathtt{dom}(\pi)$. Another example is the collection $\mathcal{P}_{\mathtt{fin}}(\mathbb{A})$ of finite subsets of $\mathbb{A}$ under the pointwise action $\pi \cdot B = \{\pi(a) \mid a \in B\}$, with $\mathtt{supp}(B) = B$.

The New И -Quantifier. The И-quantifier [23] models the quantification used when we informally write "rename x in $\lambda x.t$ to a new name". Thus, if ϕ is the description of some property of atomic names c, then $\text{И}c.\phi(c)$ holds when $\phi(c)$ holds for all but finitely many atoms c. Usually, ϕ is a predicate in higher-order logic [3] or in ZFA or FM set theory [20,23]. Let $\bar{x}$ denote the list of variables occurring in ϕ. The И-quantifier is defined as ([2] A *cofinite* subset of a set M is a subset B whose complement in M is a finite set.)([3] This is a well-known equivalence [23], Propositon 4.10)

$$\text{И}c.\ \phi(c, \bar{x}) \iff \{c \in \mathbb{A} \mid \phi(c, \bar{x})\} \text{ is cofinite}^2 \tag{1}$$

$$\iff \forall c.(c \notin \mathtt{supp}(\bar{x}) \Rightarrow \phi(c, \bar{x}))^3 \tag{2}$$

Therefore, $\text{И}c.\ (\dots)$ means "for a cofinite number of atoms c, $(\dots)$". The quantifier И allows to quantify the *generative* aspect of names. This aligns with the Choose-a-Fresh-Name Principle of the relation $\#_{\mathtt{sem}}$. The connection between these two notions is established by *Gabbay-Pitts equivalence* [3,23], which defines the freshness of an atom a for an element x in a nominal set using the new-quantifier И and a fixed-point identity as follows:

$$a \#_{\mathtt{sem}} x \iff \text{И}c.\ (a\ c) \cdot x = x. \tag{3}$$

The following equivalences will be heavily used throughout the text:

$$\begin{aligned} a \notin \mathtt{supp}(x) &\iff a \#_{\mathtt{sem}} x \\ &\iff \text{И}c.\ (a\ c) \cdot x = x \\ &\iff \{c \in \mathbb{A} \mid (a\ c) \cdot x = x\} \text{ is cofinite.} \end{aligned} \tag{4}$$

Let $\overline{c} = \{c_1, \dots, c_n\}$ be a set of atoms. We will write $\text{И}\overline{c}.\phi(\overline{c})$ as shorthand for $\text{И}c_1.\text{И}c_2.\dots\text{И}c_n.\phi(\overline{c})$. Since $\text{И}a_1.\text{И}a_2.\phi$ holds if and only if $\text{И}a_2.\text{И}a_1.\phi$ holds, then $\overline{c}$ can be interchangeably treated as either an arbitrary unordered list or a finite set of atoms. We will refer to this set as the set of И-*quantified names.*

3 Generalised Permutation Fixed-Points in Nominal Sets

In this section, we consider *generalised fixed-point identities*: a version of fixed-point identities with general И-quantified atom permutations π. That is,

$$\text{И}\overline{c}.\pi \cdot x = x,$$

where π is a finite composition of disjoint cycles, and not only swappings. For example, $\text{И}c_1, c_2, c_3.(a\ c_1\ c_2) \circ (b\ d) \cdot x = x$ is a generalised fixed-point identity.

In addition, we will split the permutation π into $\pi_{\overline{c}}$, consisting of the cycles that contain at least one И-quantified atom, and $\pi_{\neg\overline{c}}$, consisting of the cycles whose atoms are not quantified.

Example 3. Consider the generalised fixed-point identity $\text{И}\overline{c}.\pi \cdot x = x$ with $\overline{c} = c_1, c_2, c_3, c_4$ and $\pi = (a_1\ c_1\ c_2) \circ (a_2\ c_3) \circ (a_3\ a_4\ a_5) \circ (a_6\ c_4) \circ (a_7\ a_8)$. Note that π is equivalent to the permutation consisting of the composition of $\pi_{\overline{c}}$ and $\pi_{\neg\overline{c}}$: $\pi = \underbrace{(a_1\ c_1\ c_2) \circ (a_2\ c_3) \circ (a_6\ c_4)}_{\pi_{\overline{c}}} \circ \underbrace{(a_3\ a_4\ a_5) \circ (a_7\ a_8)}_{\pi_{\neg\overline{c}}}$. Interesting permutations with different behaviours are: (i) $\pi_1 = (a\ c_1) \circ (b\ c_2\ c_3\ d) \circ (f\ c_4)$, with $(\pi_1)_{\overline{c}} = \pi_1$ and $(\pi_1)_{\neg\overline{c}} = \mathtt{id}$; and (ii) $\pi_2 = (a_1\ b_1\ d_1) \circ (a_2\ b_2)$ with $(\pi_2)_{\neg\overline{c}} = \pi_2$ and $(\pi_2)_{\overline{c}} = \mathtt{id}$.

We formalise this decomposition of permutations in the following definition.

Definition 1 (Classifying Permutation Cycles). *Let π be a permutation and $\overline{c}$ a list of atoms. Define $\pi_{\overline{c}}$ as the product of disjoint cycles of π that mention atoms in $\overline{c}$, and $\pi_{\neg\overline{c}}$ as the product of disjoint cycles of π that do not mention atoms in $\overline{c}$. Define $\pi_{\overline{c}} := \mathtt{id}$ if $\overline{c} \cap \mathtt{dom}(\pi) = \emptyset$. Similarly, $\pi_{\neg\overline{c}} := \mathtt{id}$ if every disjoint cycle of π mentions at least one atom from $\overline{c}$.*

Example 4. The following illustrate some properties of splitting permutations:

1. In general, it is not true that $(\pi_1 \circ \pi_2)_{\overline{c}} = (\pi_1)_{\overline{c}} \circ (\pi_2)_{\overline{c}}$ for all permutations π_1, π_2. Take $\overline{c} = c_1$ and the permutations $\pi_1 = (a\ c_1)$ and $\pi_2 = (a\ b\ d)$. Then $\pi_1 \circ \pi_2 = (a\ b\ d\ c_1) \neq (a\ c_1) = (\pi_1)_{c_1} \circ (\pi_2)_{c_1}$.
2. In general, it is not true that $(\pi^\rho)_{\overline{c}} = (\pi_{\overline{c}})^\rho$, for all permutations π and ρ. Similarly, $(\pi^\rho)_{\neg\overline{c}} = ((\pi)_{\neg\overline{c}})^\rho$ does not hold in general. Take $\overline{c} = c_1$ and consider $\pi = (a\ b\ c_1) \circ (d\ e)$ and $\rho = (c_1\ d)$. After computing the conjugate and reorganising the cycles we obtain $(\pi^\rho)_{c_1} = (c_1\ e) \neq (a\ b\ d) = (\pi_{c_1})^\rho$. We can similarly check that $(\pi_{\neg c_1})^\rho \neq (\pi^\rho)_{\neg c_1}$.

Assuming permutations are written as compositions of disjoint cycles, the next lemma states that if $\pi \cdot x = x$ and η is a cycle in π, then if one atom of η is not in $\mathtt{supp}(x)$, none of the atoms in η are in $\mathtt{supp}(x)$. Moreover, it also states that all the permutations in the group generated by permutations that fix an element x of a nominal set, also fix x.

Lemma 1. *Let x be an element of a nominal set and $\pi, \eta_1, \ldots, \eta_n$ be permutations written as compositions of disjoint cycles.*

1. *If $\pi \cdot x = x$, η is a cycle of π and $\mathtt{dom}(\eta) - \mathtt{supp}(x) \neq \emptyset$ then $\mathtt{dom}(\eta) \cap \mathtt{supp}(x) = \emptyset$.*
2. *If $\eta_i \cdot x = x$, for all $i = 1, \ldots, n$, and $\rho \in \langle \eta_1, \ldots, \eta_n \rangle$, then $\rho \cdot x = x$.*

E.g., if $(a_1\ a_2\ a_3) \circ (a_4\ a_5) \cdot x = x$ and $a_2 \notin \mathtt{supp}(x)$, then $a_3, a_1 \notin \mathtt{supp}(x)$.

The following result generalises Pitts' equivalence (3) to any permutation π.

Lemma 2. Generalised Pitts' equivalence

1. $\text{И}\overline{c}.\ \pi \cdot x = x \iff (\text{И}\overline{c}.\pi_{\overline{c}} \cdot x = x) \wedge (\text{И}\overline{c}.\pi_{\neg\overline{c}} \cdot x = x)$.
2. $\text{И}\overline{c}.\ \pi_{\overline{c}} \cdot x = x \iff \forall \overline{c}.\ (\overline{c} \cap \mathtt{supp}(x) = \emptyset \Rightarrow \mathtt{dom}(\pi_{\overline{c}}) \cap \mathtt{supp}(x) = \emptyset)$.
3. $\text{И}\overline{c}.\ \pi_{\neg\overline{c}} \cdot x = x \iff \forall \overline{c}.\ (\overline{c} \cap \mathtt{supp}(x) = \emptyset \Rightarrow \pi_{\neg\overline{c}} \cdot x = x)$.

4 A Proof System

In this section, we introduce notions of fixed-point constraint, equality constraint and $\alpha, \mathtt{C}$-equivalence judgement, together with derivation rules (Fig. 1). Our judgements and rules are more general than the ones in [6,10,22] since we consider *general* И-quantified permutations subsuming both freshness and algebraic (here, commutative) conditions (more discussion about expressivity can be found below); as a consequence, we need only one predicate (equality, denoted $\approx_{\mathtt{C}}$) and only one set of rules to handle notions of term equality and name freshness. Before discussing the rules, we define generalised fixed-point contexts and judgements, as well as a normalisation process to refine permutations in contexts.

Definition 2. Generalised fixed-point constraint and context

1. *An* $\alpha, \mathtt{C}$-equality constraint *(or simply an* equality constraint*) is an expression of the form $t \approx_{\mathtt{C}} u$, where t and u are nominal terms.*
2. *A (generalized)* fixed-point constraint *is an $\alpha, \mathtt{C}$-equality constraint of the form $\pi \cdot t \approx_{\mathtt{C}} t$, where π is a permutation. A fixed-point constraint of the form $\pi \cdot X \approx_{\mathtt{C}} X$ is called* primitive.
3. *A (generalised)* fixed-point context *is an expression of the form $\text{И}\overline{c}.\Upsilon$, where $\overline{c} = c_1, \ldots, c_n$ and Υ is a finite set containing only primitive fixed-point constraints. For simplicity, we write $\Upsilon_{\overline{c}}$ to denote $\text{И}\overline{c}.\Upsilon$. Symbols such as $\Upsilon, \Psi, \Upsilon', \Psi'$, are used to represent fixed-point contexts.*

We will adopt the existing notation for fixed-point constraints [6] and abbreviate $\pi \cdot t \approx_{\mathtt{C}} t$ as $\pi \curlywedge_{\mathtt{C}} t$, writing primitive constraints as $\pi \curlywedge_{\mathtt{C}} X$.

Definition 3 (Judgement). *An $\alpha, \mathtt{C}$-*equivalence judgement *is an expression of the form $\text{И}\overline{c}.(\Upsilon \vdash t \approx_{\mathtt{C}} u)$ consisting of a fixed-point context $\Upsilon_{\overline{c'}}$, with $\overline{c'} \subseteq \overline{c}$, and an equality constraint $t \approx_{\mathtt{C}} u$, which may contain atoms from $\overline{c}$. We simplify the notation to $\Upsilon \vdash^{\overline{c}} t \approx_{\mathtt{C}} u$.*

Let $\Upsilon|_X := \{\pi \curlywedge_{\mathtt{C}} X \mid \pi \curlywedge_{\mathtt{C}} X \in \Upsilon\}$ and $\Upsilon_{\overline{c}}|_X := \text{И}\overline{c}.\Upsilon|_X$. We extend the notation $\mathtt{Atm}(-)$ to contexts $\Upsilon_{\overline{c}}$ (including possible vacuous quantifications). For example, $\mathtt{Atm}(\text{И}c, c_1.\{(a\ c) \curlywedge_{\mathtt{C}} X\}) = \{a, c, c_1\}$. We write $\Upsilon_{\overline{c}} \subseteq \Upsilon'_{\overline{c'}}$ when $\Upsilon \subseteq \Upsilon'$ and $\overline{c} \subseteq \overline{c'}$.

Expressivity. In the standard nominal approach using freshness constraints, contexts store only information about the freshness of atoms in (meta-)variables—they impose conditions on which atoms cannot occur free in any interpretation of the variables. Generalised fixed-point contexts are more expressive. Consider the context $\Psi_c = \text{И}c.\{(a\ c\ b) \circ (d\ e) \curlywedge_{\mathsf{C}} Z\}$. By the generalized Pitts' equivalence (see Lemma 2), this context implies two things:

1. The atoms a, b (and also c) cannot occur freely in an interpretation of Z.
2. $(d\ e) \curlywedge_{\mathsf{C}} Z$ holds, which does not force the atoms d and e to be fresh in interpretations of Z, since neither d nor e are И-quantified or occur in a cycle with a И-quantified name. For example, Z could be mapped to the term $d+e$ where $+$ is a commutative operator. In this case, a, b, and c do not occur freely in $d+e$, while d and e occur freely in $d+e$, but $(a\ c\ b)\cdot(d+e) \approx_{\mathsf{C}} d+e$ and $(d\ e)\cdot(d+e) \approx_{\mathsf{C}} d+e$.

The example above shows that generalised fixed-point contexts are a form of "hybrid context": they store more than just freshness information; they also encode relevant fixed-point constraints that cannot be reduced to freshness.

4.1 Normalisation

We can explore the properties of permutations to improve the representation of our generalized contexts. The idea is to use the properties in Lemmas 1 and 2 to transform generalized contexts into equivalent, simpler ones, using first the rule **(R1)** exhaustively and then **(R2)**: ([4]The notation $\text{И}\overline{c}.(\Upsilon, \pi \curlywedge_{\mathsf{C}} X)$ abbreviates $\text{И}\overline{c}.(\Upsilon \cup \{\pi \curlywedge_{\mathsf{C}} X\})$.)

(R1) $\text{И}\overline{c}.(\Upsilon, (\pi_{\overline{c}} \circ \pi_{\neg\overline{c}}) \curlywedge_{\mathsf{C}} X) \longrightarrow \text{И}\overline{c}.(\Upsilon, \pi_{\overline{c}} \curlywedge_{\mathsf{C}} X, \pi_{\neg\overline{c}} \curlywedge_{\mathsf{C}} X)^4$
if $\pi_{\overline{c}} \neq \mathtt{id}$ and $\pi_{\neg\overline{c}} \neq \mathtt{id}$,

(R2) $\text{И}\overline{c}.(\Upsilon, \pi_{\overline{c}} \curlywedge_{\mathsf{C}} X, (\eta_{\neg\overline{c}} \circ \pi'_{\neg\overline{c}}) \curlywedge_{\mathsf{C}} X) \longrightarrow \text{И}\overline{c}.(\Upsilon, (\pi_{\overline{c}} \circ \eta_{\neg\overline{c}}) \curlywedge_{\mathsf{C}} X, \pi'_{\neg\overline{c}} \curlywedge_{\mathsf{C}} X)$
if $\mathtt{dom}(\pi_{\overline{c}}) \cap \mathtt{dom}(\eta_{\neg\overline{c}}) \neq \emptyset$, where $\eta_{\neg\overline{c}}$ is a cycle that is disjoint from $\pi'_{\neg\overline{c}}$.

We justify our rules as follows: For rule **(R1)**: From Definition 1, it follows that given $\overline{c}$, every permutation π that is written as a product of disjoint cycles can be rewritten such that $\pi = \pi_{\overline{c}} \circ \pi_{\neg\overline{c}}$. By Lemma 2, the constraint $(\pi_{\overline{c}} \circ \pi_{\neg\overline{c}}) \curlywedge_{\mathsf{C}} X$ is equivalent to $(\pi_{\overline{c}} \curlywedge_{\mathsf{C}} X) \wedge (\pi_{\neg\overline{c}} \curlywedge_{\mathsf{C}} X)$. For rule **(R2)** the constraints on the lhs are normal forms w.r.t. **(R1)**: From $\pi_{\overline{c}} \curlywedge_{\mathsf{C}} X$ it follows that the atoms in $\pi_{\overline{c}}$ cannot occur free in the instances of X (they are not in the support of the instances of X). Since $\eta_{\neg\overline{c}}$ is a cycle that contains atoms in $\pi_{\overline{c}}$, by Lemma 1, all the atoms in the cycle must not be in the support of X. The composition $\pi_{\overline{c}} \circ \rho_{\neg\overline{c}}$ generates a new permutation $(\pi'')_{\overline{c}}$ with the atoms of $\pi_{\overline{c}}$ and $\rho_{\neg\overline{c}}$ organised as a composition of disjoint cycles.

Example 5. To illustrate **(R1)**, consider $\Psi_c = \text{И}c.\{(((a\ c) \circ (d\ e)) \curlywedge_{\mathsf{C}} Z)\}$, which reduces to $\Psi'_c = \text{И}c.\{(a\ c) \curlywedge_{\mathsf{C}} Z, (d\ e) \curlywedge_{\mathsf{C}} Z\}$ with simpler constraints. The left constraint gives information about freshness whereas the right constraint is about terms that are fixed by permutation $(d\ e)$. To illustrate (**R2**), consider the context $\Phi_c = \text{И}c.\{(a\ c) \curlywedge_{\mathtt{C}} X, (a\ b) \circ (d\ e) \curlywedge_{\mathtt{C}} X\}$. By Lemma 2, $(a\ c) \curlywedge_{\mathtt{C}} X$ alone implies that a cannot occur freely in any interpretation of X, as c is И-quantified. In contrast, when considering the constraint $(a\ b) \circ (d\ e) \curlywedge_{\mathtt{C}} X$ on its own, the names a, b, d, e may occur freely in an interpretation of X. However, when the two constraints are considered together, as in Φ_c, the scenario for the name b changes: it follows from Lemma 1 that b also cannot be free in any interpretation of X. Rule (**R2**) composes both permutations as in $(a\ c) \circ (a\ b)$ obtaining the equivalent generalized context $\Phi'_c = \text{И}c.\{(a\ b\ c) \curlywedge_{\mathtt{C}} X, (d\ e) \curlywedge_{\mathtt{C}} X\}$ where it is explicit that a and b must be fresh in all the instances of X.

Important Assumption. From now on, unless explicitly stated otherwise, we will assume that *every generalized fixed-point context, say* $\Upsilon_{\overline{c}}$*, is in normal form with respect to the exhaustive application of rules* (**R1**) *and* (**R2**).

Thus, in a normal form $\Upsilon_{\overline{c}}$ the set Υ can be split into two disjoint sets: The "freshness" part $\Upsilon^{\#} := \{\pi_{\overline{c}} \curlywedge_{\mathtt{C}} X \mid \pi \curlywedge_{\mathtt{C}} X \in \Upsilon \text{ and } \pi_{\overline{c}} = \pi\}$, and the "pure fixed-point" (but non-freshness) part $\Upsilon^{\curlywedge_{\mathtt{C}}} := \{\pi_{\neg\overline{c}} \curlywedge_{\mathtt{C}} X \mid \pi \curlywedge_{\mathtt{C}} X \in \Upsilon \text{ and } \pi_{\neg\overline{c}} = \pi\}$. For example, Φ in the generalized context Φ_c from Example 5 splits into the sets $\Phi^{\#} = \{(a\ b\ c) \curlywedge_{\mathtt{C}} X\}$ and $\Phi^{\curlywedge_{\mathtt{C}}} = \{(d\ e) \curlywedge_{\mathtt{C}} X\}$.

In the following we denote the set of all permutations occurring in the pure fixed-point part by $\mathtt{perm}(\Upsilon^{\curlywedge_{\mathtt{C}}}) := \{\pi_{\neg\overline{c}} \mid \pi_{\neg\overline{c}} \curlywedge_{\mathtt{C}} X \in \Upsilon^{\curlywedge_{\mathtt{C}}}\}$.

$$\frac{}{\Upsilon \vdash^{\overline{c}} a \approx_{\mathtt{C}} a}\ (\approx_{\mathtt{C}} \mathbf{a}) \qquad \frac{\pi'^{-1} \circ \pi \in \mathtt{P}(\Upsilon_{\overline{c}}|_X)}{\Upsilon \vdash^{\overline{c}} \pi \cdot X \approx_{\mathtt{C}} \pi' \cdot X}\ (\approx_{\mathtt{C}} \mathbf{var})$$

$$\frac{\Upsilon \vdash^{\overline{c}} t_1 \approx_{\mathtt{C}} t'_1 \quad \ldots \quad \Upsilon \vdash^{\overline{c}} t_n \approx_{\mathtt{C}} t'_n}{\Upsilon \vdash^{\overline{c}} \mathtt{f}(t_1, \ldots, t_n) \approx_{\mathtt{C}} \mathtt{f}(t'_1, \ldots, t'_n)}\ \mathtt{f} \neq \mathtt{f}^{\mathtt{C}}\ (\approx_{\mathtt{C}} \mathtt{f})$$

$$\frac{\Upsilon \vdash^{\overline{c}} s_0 \approx_{\mathtt{C}} t_i \qquad \Upsilon \vdash^{\overline{c}} s_1 \approx_{\mathtt{C}} t_{1-i}}{\Upsilon \vdash^{\overline{c}} \mathtt{f}^{\mathtt{C}}(s_0, s_1) \approx_{\mathtt{C}} \mathtt{f}^{\mathtt{C}}(t_0, t_1)}\ (\approx_{\mathtt{C}} \mathtt{f}^{\mathtt{C}}),\ i = 0, 1$$

$$\frac{\Upsilon \vdash^{\overline{c}} t \approx_{\mathtt{C}} t'}{\Upsilon \vdash^{\overline{c}} [a]t \approx_{\mathtt{C}} [a]t'}\ (\approx_{\mathtt{C}} [\mathbf{a}]) \qquad \frac{\Upsilon \vdash^{\overline{c}, c_1} (a\ c_1) \cdot t \approx_{\mathtt{C}} (b\ c_1) \cdot s}{\Upsilon \vdash^{\overline{c}} [a]t \approx_{\mathtt{C}} [b]s}\ (\approx_{\mathtt{C}} \mathbf{ab})$$

Fig. 1. Derivation rules for $\approx_{\mathtt{C}}$. The group $\mathtt{P}(\Upsilon_{\overline{c}}|_X)$ is defined in (6).

4.2 Derivation Rules for $\approx_{\mathtt{C}}$

We are now ready to present our derivation rules (Fig. 1). The rule ($\approx_{\mathtt{C}}$ **ab**) for abstraction is based in Pitts' notion of α-equivalence, which employs the

И-quantifier [3, Chapter 4, Sect. 4.2]. This approach naturally extends to a generalised form of α-equivalence over arbitrary nominal sets. Accordingly, we define the binary relation $=_\alpha$ on $\mathbb{A} \times \mathscr{X}$ by

$$(a_1, x_1) =_\alpha (a_2, x_2) \iff \text{И} c_1.(a_1\ c_1) \cdot x_1 = (a_2\ c_1) \cdot x_2, \tag{5}$$

where $=$ on the right-hand side denotes equality in $\mathscr{X}$. Hence, two abstractions $[a_1]t$ and $[a_2]s$ are α-equivalent if and only if $\text{И} c_1.(a_1\ c_1) \cdot t \approx_{\mathsf{C}} (a_2\ c_1) \cdot s$.

As expected, the commutativity rule ($\approx_{\mathsf{C}}\, \mathtt{f}^{\mathsf{C}}$) guarantees that a derivation of $\Upsilon \vdash^{\overline{c}} \mathtt{f}^{\mathsf{C}}(s_0, s_1) \approx_{\mathsf{C}} \mathtt{f}^{\mathsf{C}}(t_0, t_1)$ requires either derivations of $\Upsilon \vdash^{\overline{c}} s_0 \approx_{\mathsf{C}} t_0$ and $\Upsilon \vdash^{\overline{c}} s_1 \approx_{\mathsf{C}} t_1$, or alternatively, derivations of $\Upsilon \vdash^{\overline{c}} s_0 \approx_{\mathsf{C}} t_1$ and $\Upsilon \vdash^{\overline{c}} s_1 \approx_{\mathsf{C}} t_0$.

The rule ($\approx_{\mathsf{C}}$ **var**) for handling variables is more involved. It is inspired by Lemma 1 and Lemma 2. Applying π'^{-1} to both sides of $\pi \cdot X \approx_{\mathsf{C}} \pi' \cdot X$ yields $\pi'^{-1} \cdot (\pi \cdot X) \approx_{\mathsf{C}} X$, which simplifies to $(\pi'^{-1} \circ \pi) \cdot X \approx_{\mathsf{C}} X$. At this point, it is essential to verify whether $\pi'^{-1} \circ \pi$ belongs to the *group generated by permutations derived from the fixed-point context* $\Upsilon|_X$, denoted as $\mathtt{P}(\Upsilon_{\overline{c}}|_X)$, whose permutations are known to fix X. Here

$$\mathtt{P}(\Upsilon_{\overline{c}}|_X) := \mathcal{G}(\mathtt{Atm}(\Upsilon^{\#}_{\overline{c}}|_X)) \circ \langle \mathtt{perm}(\Upsilon^{\curlywedge_{\mathsf{C}}}|_X) \rangle, \tag{6}$$

which is a subgroup of $\mathcal{G}(\mathbb{A})$ because $\pi_1 \circ \pi_2 = \pi_2 \circ \pi_1$ holds for all $\pi_1 \in \mathcal{G}(\mathtt{Atm}(\Upsilon^{\#}_{\overline{c}}|_X))$ and all $\pi_2 \in \langle \mathtt{perm}(\Upsilon^{\curlywedge_{\mathsf{C}}}|_X) \rangle$ since π_1 and π_2 are disjoint. The inclusion of $\overline{c}$ in $\mathcal{G}(\mathtt{Atm}(\Upsilon^{\#}_{\overline{c}}|_X))$ ensures that the И-quantified atoms are not lost due to vacuous quantification. The remaining rules are standard and rely on the decomposition of the constraint over the structure of its terms.

Example 6. The judgement $\Upsilon \vdash^{c} \mathtt{f}^{\mathsf{C}}([d]X, ((a\ b) \cdot Y) \approx_{\mathsf{C}} \mathtt{f}^{\mathsf{C}}(Y, [e]X))$ is derivable, where $\Upsilon = \{(d\ e\ c) \curlywedge_{\mathsf{C}} X, (a\ b) \curlywedge_{\mathsf{C}} Y\}$:

$$\dfrac{\dfrac{\dfrac{(a\ b) \in \mathcal{G}(\{c\}) \circ \langle (a\ b) \rangle}{(a\ b) \in \mathtt{P}(\Upsilon_c|_Y)}}{\Upsilon \vdash^{c} (a\ b) \cdot Y \approx_{\mathsf{C}} Y}\,(\approx_{\mathsf{C}}\,\mathbf{var}) \qquad \dfrac{\dfrac{\dfrac{(d\ e\ c_1) \in \mathcal{G}(\{d, e, c, c_1\}) \circ \langle \emptyset \rangle}{(d\ e\ c_1) \in \mathtt{P}(\Upsilon_{c,c_1}|_X)}}{\Upsilon \vdash^{c,c_1} (d\ c_1) \cdot X \approx_{\mathsf{C}} (e\ c_1) \cdot X}\,(\approx_{\mathsf{C}}\,\mathbf{var})}{\Upsilon \vdash^{c} [d]X \approx_{\mathsf{C}} [e]X}\,(\approx_{\mathsf{C}}\,\mathbf{ab})}{\Upsilon \vdash^{c} \mathtt{f}^{\mathsf{C}}([d]X, (a\ b) \cdot Y) \approx_{\mathsf{C}} \mathtt{f}^{\mathsf{C}}(Y, [e]X)}\,(\approx_{\mathsf{C}}\,\mathtt{f}^{\mathsf{C}})$$

While the freshness approach [39] requires $a \# Y$ and $b \# Y$ to derive $(a\ b) \cdot Y \approx_{\mathsf{C}} Y$, the fixed-point calculus removes this limitation. Here, $(a\ b) \cdot Y \approx_{\mathsf{C}} Y$ is derivable without relying on any freshness assumption. Yet, if desired, it could be derived using freshness; for instance, it could be derived using the context $\text{И} c.\{(a\ b\ c) \curlywedge_{\mathsf{C}} Y\}$. This shows that the fixed-point calculus generalises and extends the freshness calculus, establishing it as proper subcalculus.

4.3 Properties

Our calculus satisfies essential structural properties, as summarised in Theorem 1. It upholds *equivariance*, ensuring that derivations remain invariant under the action of permutations, thereby preserving consistency across transformations. It also satisfies *inversion*, a useful property for inductive proofs on derivations, as it facilitates the bottom-up application of derivation rules. More significantly, and in contrast with previous fixed-point approaches [6,10], our framework enables the definition of a sound and complete semantics for commutative nominal algebra with И-quantified fixed-point constraints in nominal sets, as established in Theorem 4 below. The key insight to achieve this result lies in the ($\approx_{\mathsf{C}}$ **var**) rule, more precisely in the construction of the group $\mathtt{P}(\Upsilon_{\overline{c}}|_X)$ (see (6)), which carefully distinguishes freshness information from fixed-point behaviour.

Theorem 1 (Miscellaneous). *The following hold:*

1. *(Inversion) The derivation rules from Fig. 1 are invertible.*
2. *(Equivariance)* $\Upsilon \vdash^{\overline{c}} s \approx_{\mathsf{C}} t$ *iff* $\Upsilon \vdash^{\overline{c}} \rho \cdot s \approx_{\mathsf{C}} \rho \cdot t$, *where* ρ *is an arbitrary permutation (it could have atoms of* $\overline{c}$ *in its domain).*
3. *(Equivalence)* $\Upsilon \vdash^{\overline{c}} - \approx_{\mathsf{C}} -$ *is an equivalence relation.*
4. *(Strengthening) If* $\Upsilon, \pi \curlywedge_{\mathsf{C}} X \vdash^{\overline{c}} s \approx_{\mathsf{C}} t$ *and* $(\mathtt{dom}(\pi) \setminus \overline{c}) \cap \mathtt{Atm}(s,t) = \emptyset$, *then* $\Upsilon \vdash^{\overline{c}} s \approx_{\mathsf{C}} t$.
5. *(Weakening) If* $\Upsilon \vdash^{\overline{c}} s \approx_{\mathsf{C}} t$ *and* $\Upsilon_{\overline{c}} \subseteq \Upsilon'_{\overline{c'}}$, *then* $\Upsilon' \vdash^{\overline{c'}} s \approx_{\mathsf{C}} t$.

5 Nominal C-Unification

In this section, we present a rule-based algorithm for solving C-unification problems using fixed-point constraints, proving its termination and correctness.

5.1 Problem and Solutions

Definition 4 (Nominal C-Unification Problem). *A* (nominal) C-unification problem $\mathcal{P}_{\mathsf{C}}$ *has the form* $\text{И}\overline{c}.Pr$, *where* Pr *consists of a finite set of (unification) constraints of the form* $s \approx^?_{\mathsf{C}} t$.

Solutions for nominal C-unification problems will be expressed using pairs $\langle \Psi, \sigma \rangle_{\overline{c}}$ consisting of a generalised fixed-point context $\Psi_{\overline{c}}$ and a substitution σ, where occurrences of the atoms $\overline{c}$ in the image of σ are И-quantified. We call such σ a И-substitution, denoted as $\text{И}\overline{c}.\sigma$ or $\sigma_{\overline{c}}$. We will omit the subscript and write only σ to avoid clutter. We will come back to this later in §5.2.

Definition 5 (C-Solution/Unifier). *A* C-*unifier (*C-solution*) for a nominal* C-*unification problem* $\mathcal{P}_{\mathsf{C}} = \text{И}\overline{c}.Pr$ *is a pair* $\langle \Psi, \sigma \rangle$ *consisting of a finite set of primitive constraints* Ψ *and* σ *a substitution such that there is a finite (possibly empty) set of new atoms* $\overline{c'}$ *and* $\Psi \vdash^{\overline{c},\overline{c'}} s\sigma \approx_{\mathsf{C}} t\sigma$, *for each* $s \approx^?_{\mathsf{C}} t \in Pr$. *If no* C-*unifier* $\langle \Psi, \sigma \rangle$ *exists for* $\mathcal{P}_{\mathsf{C}}$, *the problem* $\mathcal{P}_{\mathsf{C}}$ *is* unsolvable. *We denote the set of all* C-*unifiers of* $\mathcal{P}_{\mathsf{C}}$ *by* $\mathcal{U}(\mathcal{P}_{\mathsf{C}})$.

For simplicity, we will omit C and primarily refer to C-unifiers and C-solutions of C-unification problems as unifiers and solutions, respectively. The solutions to a problem $\mathcal{P}_{\mathsf{C}}$, elements of the set $\mathcal{U}(\mathcal{P}_{\mathsf{C}})$, can be compared using the instantiation order $\lesssim$ (quasi-order) defined as follows:

Definition 6 (Instantiation order). *Given* $\langle\Psi_1,\sigma_1\rangle$ *and* $\langle\Psi_2,\sigma_2\rangle$*, we write* $\langle\Psi_1,\sigma_1\rangle \lesssim \langle\Psi_2,\sigma_2\rangle$ *when there is a finite set of atoms* $\overline{c'}$ *and a substitution* δ *such that* $\Psi_2 \vdash^{\overline{c'}} \Psi_1\delta$ *and* $\Psi_2 \vdash^{\overline{c'}} X\sigma_2 \approx_{\mathtt{C}} X\sigma_1\delta$*, for all* $X \in \mathbb{V}$*.*

For example, for $\sigma = [Y \mapsto a, X \mapsto Z]$, $\sigma' = [Y \mapsto a, X \mapsto \mathtt{f}(Y,d), Z \mapsto \mathtt{f}(Y,d)]$, we can verify that $\langle\{(a\ c) \curlywedge_{\mathtt{C}} Z\},\sigma\rangle \lesssim \langle\{(a\ c) \curlywedge_{\mathtt{C}} Z, (a\ c_1) \curlywedge_{\mathtt{C}} Y\},\sigma'\rangle$. In fact, for $\delta = [Z \mapsto \mathtt{f}(Y,d)]$:

1. $\{(a\ c) \curlywedge_{\mathtt{C}} Z, (a\ c_1) \curlywedge_{\mathtt{C}} Y\} \vdash^{c,c_1} W\sigma' \approx_{\mathtt{C}} W\sigma\delta$, for all $W \in \mathbb{V}$.
2. $\{(a\ c) \curlywedge_{\mathtt{C}} Z, (a\ c_1) \curlywedge_{\mathtt{C}} Y\} \vdash^{c,c_1} (a\ c) \curlywedge_{\mathtt{C}} Z\delta$.

Unlike nominal unification [39] (without equational theories), solvable nominal C-unification problems need not have just one most general unifier. Thus, the role of the most general unifier is taken on by a complete set of C-unifiers:

Definition 7 (Complete Set of C-unifiers). *Let* $\mathcal{P}_{\mathtt{C}}$ *be a* C*-unification problem. A* complete set of C-unifiers *of* $\mathcal{P}_{\mathtt{C}}$ *is a set of pairs* S *that satisfies*

1. $S \subseteq \mathcal{U}(\mathcal{P}_{\mathtt{C}})$;
2. *For all* $\langle\Psi,\sigma\rangle \in \mathcal{U}(\mathcal{P}_{\mathtt{C}})$ *there exists* $\langle\Phi,\sigma'\rangle \in S$ *s.t.* $\langle\Phi,\sigma'\rangle \lesssim \langle\Psi,\sigma\rangle$.

(del)	$\text{И}\overline{c}.Pr \uplus \{t \approx^?_{\mathtt{C}} t\}$	$\Longrightarrow$	$\text{И}\overline{c}.Pr$
$(\mathtt{f})$	$\text{И}\overline{c}.Pr \uplus \{\mathtt{f}(\tilde{t})_n \approx^?_{\mathtt{C}} \mathtt{f}(\tilde{t'})_n\}$	$\Longrightarrow$	$\text{И}\overline{c}.Pr \cup \{t_1 \approx^?_{\mathtt{C}} t'_1, \ldots, t_n \approx^?_{\mathtt{C}} t'_n\}$
$(\mathtt{f}^{\mathtt{C}})$	$\text{И}\overline{c}.Pr \uplus \{\mathtt{f}^{\mathtt{C}}(t_0,t_1) \approx^?_{\mathtt{C}} \mathtt{f}^{\mathtt{C}}(s_0,s_1)\}$	$\Longrightarrow$	$\begin{cases}\text{И}\overline{c}.Pr \cup \{t_0 \approx^?_{\mathtt{C}} s_0, t_1 \approx^?_{\mathtt{C}} s_1\},\\ \text{И}\overline{c}.Pr \cup \{t_0 \approx^?_{\mathtt{C}} s_1, t_1 \approx^?_{\mathtt{C}} s_0\}\end{cases}$
$([a])$	$\text{И}\overline{c}.Pr \uplus \{[a]t \approx^?_{\mathtt{C}} [a]t'\}$	$\Longrightarrow$	$\text{И}\overline{c}.Pr \cup \{t \approx^?_{\mathtt{C}} t'\}$
(ab)	$\text{И}\overline{c}.Pr \uplus \{[a]t \approx^?_{\mathtt{C}} [b]t'\}$	$\Longrightarrow$	$\text{И}\overline{c}, c_1, c_2.Pr \cup \{(a\ c_1)\cdot t \approx^?_{\mathtt{C}} (b\ c_1)\cdot t', \overline{(c_1\ c_2) \curlywedge^?_{\mathtt{C}} \mathtt{Var}(t,t')}\}$
(var)	$\text{И}\overline{c}.Pr \uplus \{\pi\cdot X \approx^?_{\mathtt{C}} \pi'\cdot X\}$	$\Longrightarrow$	$\text{И}\overline{c}.Pr \cup \{(\pi'^{-1}\circ\pi)\cdot X \approx^?_{\mathtt{C}} X\}$, if $\pi' \neq \mathtt{id}$
$(inst_1)$	$\text{И}\overline{c}.Pr \uplus \{\pi\cdot X \approx^?_{\mathtt{C}} t\}$	$\overset{[X\mapsto\pi^{-1}\cdot t]}{\Longrightarrow}$	$\text{И}\overline{c}.Pr[X \mapsto \pi^{-1}\cdot t]$, if $X \notin \mathtt{Var}(t)$
$(inst_2)$	$\text{И}\overline{c}.Pr \uplus \{t \approx^?_{\mathtt{C}} \pi\cdot X\}$	$\overset{[X\mapsto\pi^{-1}\cdot t]}{\Longrightarrow}$	$\text{И}\overline{c}.Pr[X \mapsto \pi^{-1}\cdot t]$, if $X \notin \mathtt{Var}(t)$

Fig. 2. Simplification rules for $\approx_{\mathtt{C}}$. The notation $(\tilde{t})_n$ in rule $(\mathtt{f})$ abbreviates the tuple $(t_1,\ldots,t_n)$. In rule (ab), $\overline{(c_1\ c_2) \curlywedge^?_{\mathtt{C}} \mathtt{Var}(t,t')} := \{(c_1\ c_2)\cdot X \approx^?_{\mathtt{C}} X \mid X \in \mathtt{Var}(t,t')\}$.

5.2 $\mathtt{Unif}_{\mathtt{C}}$: A Rule-Based Algorithm for C-Unification

In this subsection, we introduce a set of *simplification rules* (Fig. 2) for "solving" C-unification problems. These rules simplify problems by transforming constraints into "simpler" ones, by running the derivation rules from Fig. 1 in reverse. In the instantiation rules, $Pr\sigma$ denotes the application of the substitution σ to

Pr. The derivation rule $(\approx_{\mathtt{C}} \mathtt{f}^{\mathtt{C}})$ splits a C-unification problem into two in the simplification rule $(\mathtt{f}^{\mathtt{C}})$, with the original problem solvable if at least one of the new problems is solvable. This requires working with finite sets of C-unification problems, called *extended* C-*unification problems*, denoted as $\mathcal{M}$.

The algorithm $\mathtt{Unif}_{\mathtt{C}}$ starts with $\mathcal{M} = \{\mathcal{P}_{\mathtt{C}}\}$ and exhaustively applies simplification rules. We denote by $\langle \mathcal{M} \rangle_{\mathtt{nf}}$ the normal forms of $\mathcal{M}$ by the reduction relation $\Longrightarrow$ generated by the simplification rules. In the instantiation rules $(inst_1)$ and $(inst_2)$, we write $\stackrel{\sigma}{\Longrightarrow}$ to annotate the substitution σ that was generated by the rule.

Theorem 2 (Termination). *The relation* $\Longrightarrow$ *is terminating.*

Some constraints in $\mathcal{P}_{\mathtt{C}}$ cannot be simplified, we say that they are *reduced.* An equality constraint $s \approx_{\mathtt{C}}^{?} t$ is *reduced* if it satisfies one of the following:

- s is a suspension on a variable and t is that variable (e.g., $\pi \cdot X \approx_{\mathtt{C}}^{?} X$).
- s and t are distinct atoms (e.g. $a \approx_{\mathtt{C}}^{?} b$).
- s and t have different head symbols (e.g., $\mathtt{f}(u) \approx_{\mathtt{C}}^{?} \mathtt{g}(v)$).
- s and t have different root constructors (e.g., $[a]s' \approx_{\mathtt{C}}^{?} \mathtt{f}(t)$).
- s is a suspension on some variable, t is not a suspension, but t contains occurrences of that variable (e.g. $X \approx_{\mathtt{C}}^{?} \mathtt{f}(X, a)$).

The first form, which is a fixed-point equation, is *consistent*; the others are *inconsistent.* A problem $\mathcal{P}_{\mathtt{C}} = \mathsf{N}\overline{c}.Pr$ is *reduced* if all constraints in Pr are reduced. A problem $\mathcal{P}_{\mathtt{C}}$ is called *solvable* if its normal form $\langle \mathcal{P}_{\mathtt{C}} \rangle_{\mathtt{nf}}$ contains a reduced problem where all the constraints are consistent. In this case, we compute $\langle \mathcal{P}_{\mathtt{C}} \rangle_{\mathtt{sol}}$ as the set of pairs $\langle \Upsilon, \sigma \rangle$ where $\Upsilon = \{\pi \curlywedge_{\mathtt{C}} X \mid \pi \cdot X \approx_{\mathtt{C}}^{?} X \in \mathcal{P}'_{\mathtt{C}}$ solvable and $\mathcal{P}'_{\mathtt{C}} \in \langle \mathcal{P}_{\mathtt{C}} \rangle_{\mathtt{nf}}\}$, and σ is either Id (if no instantiation rules were used) or the composition of substitutions used throughout the simplification of a branch starting in $\mathcal{P}_{\mathtt{C}}$ and ending in $\mathcal{P}'_{\mathtt{C}}$.

Example 7. The next two problems illustrate the expressivity of our solutions:

1. For the problem $(a\ b) \cdot X \approx_{\mathtt{C}}^{?} X$, *standard* nominal unification algorithm [39] returns the pair $\langle \{a, b\#X\}, \mathtt{id} \rangle$, which fails to capture an infinite family of valid solutions including $\langle \emptyset, X \mapsto a{+}b \rangle$, $\langle \emptyset, X \mapsto \mathtt{f}(a){+}\mathtt{f}(b) \rangle, \ldots$, as these are not instances of the computed pair. The fixed-point approach resolves this limitation by computing the unifier $\langle (a\ b) \curlywedge_{\mathtt{C}} X, \mathtt{id} \rangle$, which is more general than all these solutions. Moreover, $\langle \{a, b\#X\}, \mathtt{id} \rangle$ is not lost as a solution, as it can be encoded as the pair $\langle \{(a\ b\ c) \curlywedge_{\mathtt{C}} X\}, \mathtt{id} \rangle$.
2. Consider the problem $\{[a](X \wedge Y) \approx_{\mathtt{C}}^{?} [b](Y \wedge X)\}$ where $\wedge$ represents the (commutative) symbol of conjunction. Then the algorithm computes:
   1. $\langle \{(a\ c_1\ b) \curlywedge_{\mathtt{C}} Y, (a\ c_2) \curlywedge_{\mathtt{C}} Y, (c_1\ c_2) \curlywedge_{\mathtt{C}} Y\}, [X \mapsto (b\ a\ c_1) \cdot Y] \rangle$
   2. $\langle \{(a\ b\ c_1) \curlywedge_{\mathtt{C}} X, (a\ b\ c_1) \curlywedge_{\mathtt{C}} Y, (c_1\ c_2) \curlywedge_{\mathtt{C}} X, (c_1\ c_2) \curlywedge_{\mathtt{C}} Y\}, \mathtt{id} \rangle$,

   forming a complete set of C-solutions for $\mathcal{P}_{\mathtt{C}}$. Notably, the first solution is an instance of the second via substitution $\delta = [X \mapsto Y]$.

Remark 1. Substitutions feature И-quantified names, as in $\sigma = [X \mapsto (b\,a\,c_1)\cdot Y]$. This is a desirable property that shows that solutions are stable under the choice of new names for renaming that can be done throughout computation. This is achieved using the concept of a И-substitution, which provides a systematic way to track freshness information.

The next result shows that if a C-unification problem $\mathcal{P}_{\mathtt{C}}$ is solvable, our algorithm $\mathtt{Unif}_{\mathtt{C}}$ will output $\langle\mathcal{P}_{\mathtt{C}}\rangle_{\mathtt{sol}}$ which is a complete set of solutions of $\mathcal{P}_{\mathtt{C}}$.

Theorem 3 (Correctness). *Let $\mathcal{P}_{\mathtt{C}}$ be a problem such that $\mathcal{P}_{\mathtt{C}} \overset{*}{\Longrightarrow} \langle\mathcal{P}_{\mathtt{C}}\rangle_{\mathtt{nf}}$. If $\mathcal{P}_{\mathtt{C}}$ is solvable, then the following hold:*

1. (Soundness) $\langle\mathcal{P}_{\mathtt{C}}\rangle_{\mathtt{sol}} \subseteq \mathcal{U}(\mathcal{P}_{\mathtt{C}})$.
2. (Completeness) *If $\langle\Phi,\tau\rangle \in \mathcal{U}(\mathcal{P}_{\mathtt{C}})$ then there exists $\langle\Psi,\sigma\rangle \in \langle\mathcal{P}_{\mathtt{C}}\rangle_{\mathtt{sol}}$ s.t. $\langle\Psi,\sigma\rangle \lesssim \langle\Phi,\tau\rangle$.*
   The set $\langle\mathcal{P}_{\mathtt{C}}\rangle_{\mathtt{sol}}$ is a complete set of C*-unifiers of $\mathcal{P}_{\mathtt{C}}$.*

A direct consequence of termination and correctness is that the complete set of C-unifiers of a $\mathcal{P}_{\mathtt{C}}$ is always finite.

Corollary 1. C*-unification using generalised fixed-point constraints is finitary.*

Example 8 (Resolution in αProlog). Consider the language of π-calculus defined by the grammar below [16,32]:

$$\begin{array}{lll}\textbf{(Process terms)} & p ::= 0 \mid \mathtt{tau}(p) \mid \mathtt{par}(p,q) \mid \mathtt{sum}(p,q) \mid \mathtt{match}(x,y,p) \\ & \qquad \mathtt{in}(x,[y]p) \mid \mathtt{out}(x,y,p) \mid \nu([y]p) \\ \textbf{(Actions)} & \mathtt{a} ::= \mathtt{tau\_a} \mid \mathtt{in\_a}(x,y) \mid \mathtt{fout\_a}(x,y) \mid \mathtt{bout\_a}(x,y)\end{array}$$

where $a, b, \ldots, x, y, \ldots$ are atoms for names of channels.

Consider the following fragment[2] of an αProlog program for the π-calculus:

$$\begin{array}{l}\textbf{pred}\ \mathtt{step}(\mathtt{process},\mathtt{action},\mathtt{process}). \qquad (*encodes p \xrightarrow{\mathtt{a}} p'*)\\ \mathtt{step}(\mathtt{sum}(P,Q),A,P')\ :-\ \mathtt{step}(P,A,P').\\ \mathtt{step}(\mathtt{out}(X,Y,P),\mathtt{fout\_a}(X,Y),P).\\ \mathtt{step}(\nu([y]P),A,\nu([y]P'))\ :-\ \text{И}c.(y\ c)\cdot A \approx_{\mathtt{C}} A,\ \mathtt{step}(P,A,P').\end{array}$$

These clauses describe *some* of the labelled transition rules between processes in the π-calculus. Respectively, they are describing:

$$\frac{p \xrightarrow{\mathtt{a}} p'}{\mathtt{sum}(p,q) \xrightarrow{\mathtt{a}} p'} \qquad \mathtt{out}(x,y,p) \xrightarrow{\mathtt{fout\_a}(x,y)} p \qquad \frac{p \xrightarrow{\mathtt{a}} p'\, y \notin \mathtt{Atm}(a)}{\nu([y]p) \xrightarrow{\mathtt{a}} \nu([y]p')}$$

For example, the unification algorithm is needed to answer the query

$$?-\ \mathtt{step}(\nu([x]\mathtt{sum}(\mathtt{out}(x,y,0),\mathtt{out}(z,y,0))),A,P).$$

[2] The complete program is in [16].

We can reduce this goal by backchaining against the suitably freshened rule

$$\mathtt{step}(\nu([y_1]P_1), A_1, \nu([y_1]P_1')) \coloneq \text{И} c_1.(y_1\ c_1)\cdot A_1 \approx_{\mathtt{C}} A_1,\ \mathtt{step}(P_1, A_1, P_1').$$

which unifies with the goal with

$$\langle \emptyset, [A_1 \mapsto A, P \mapsto \nu([y_1]P_1'), P_1 \mapsto \mathtt{sum}(\mathtt{out}(y_1, y, 0), \mathtt{out}(z, y, 0))]\rangle$$

This yields the subgoal

$$\text{И} c_1.(y_1\ c_1)\cdot A \approx_{\mathtt{C}} A, \mathtt{step}(\mathtt{sum}(\mathtt{out}(y_1, y, 0), \mathtt{out}(z, y, 0)), A, P_1')$$

The second is solved by backchaining against

$$\mathtt{step}(\mathtt{sum}(P_2, Q_2), A_2, P_2') \ \coloneq \mathtt{step}(P_2, A_2, P_2'),$$

producing two unifiers:

$$\langle \emptyset, [A_2 \mapsto A, P_1' \mapsto P_2', P_2 \mapsto \mathtt{out}(y_1, y, 0), Q_2 \mapsto \mathtt{out}(z, y, 0)]\rangle$$
$$\langle \emptyset, [A_2 \mapsto A, P_1' \mapsto P_2', Q_2 \mapsto \mathtt{out}(y_1, y, 0), P_2 \mapsto \mathtt{out}(z, y, 0)]\rangle.$$

This creates two subgoals:

$$G_1 = \mathtt{step}(\mathtt{out}(y_1, y, 0), A, P_2') \ \text{ and } \ G_2 = \mathtt{step}(\mathtt{out}(z, y, 0), A, P_2')$$

By backchaining G_1 against

$$\mathtt{step}(\mathtt{out}(X_1, Y_1, P_3), \mathtt{fout\_a}(X_1, Y_1), P_3),$$

produces: $\langle \emptyset, [X_1 \mapsto y_1, Y_1 \mapsto y, P_3 \mapsto 0, P_2' \mapsto 0, A \mapsto \mathtt{fout\_a}(y_1, y)]\rangle$. Solving A and P, we get $A = \mathtt{fout\_a}(y_1, y)$ and $P = \nu([y_1]0)$. However, this is not a solution as $\text{И} c_1.(y_1\ c_1)\cdot A \approx_{\mathtt{C}} A$ is not satisfied. Backchaining G_2 against the same rule produces the pair $\langle \emptyset, [X_1 \mapsto z, Y_1 \mapsto y, P_3 \mapsto 0, P_2' \mapsto 0, A \mapsto \mathtt{fout\_a}(z, y)]\rangle$. We obtain the solution $A = \mathtt{fout\_a}(z, y)$ and $P = \nu([y_1]0)$, as $\text{И} c_1.(y_1\ c_1)\cdot A \approx_{\mathtt{C}} A$ is valid.

6 Soundness and Completeness.

We outline the semantics of judgements. A *commutative nominal* Σ*-algebra* $\mathfrak{A}$ consists of: (1) a nominal set $(|\mathfrak{A}|, \cdot)$, (2) an injective equivariant[3] map $\mathtt{atom}^{\mathfrak{A}} : \mathbb{A} \to |\mathfrak{A}|$, (3) an abstraction map $\mathtt{abs}^{\mathfrak{A}} : \mathbb{A} \times |\mathfrak{A}| \to |\mathfrak{A}|$ such that $\text{И} c.(a\ c)\cdot \mathtt{abs}^{\mathfrak{A}}(a, x) = \mathtt{abs}^{\mathfrak{A}}(a, x)$ (here $=$ is the equality on $|\mathfrak{A}|$), and (4) an equivariant interpretation $f^{\mathfrak{A}}$ for each $\mathtt{f} : n$ in Σ. If every commutative symbol $\mathtt{f}^{\mathtt{C}}$ satisfies $f^{\mathtt{C},\mathfrak{A}}(x_1, x_2) = f^{\mathtt{C},\mathfrak{A}}(x_2, x_1)$, $\mathfrak{A}$ is called a *model of* $\mathtt{C}$.

[3] Given $\mathcal{G}(\mathbb{A})$-sets $\mathscr{X}, \mathscr{Y}$, call a map $f : |\mathscr{X}| \to |\mathscr{Y}|$ *equivariant* when $\pi \cdot f(x) = f(\pi \cdot x)$ for all $\pi \in \mathcal{G}(\mathbb{A})$ and $x \in |\mathscr{X}|$.

A valuation ς maps unknowns to elements of $|\mathfrak{A}|$. Terms $t \in \mathbb{F}(\Sigma, \mathbb{V})$ are interpreted inductively by the mapping $[\![\cdot]\!]_\varsigma^{\mathfrak{A}}$, as follows:

$$
\begin{array}{rlrl}
[\![a]\!]_\varsigma^{\mathfrak{A}} &= a^{\mathfrak{A}} & & \\
[\![[a]t]\!]_\varsigma^{\mathfrak{A}} &= \mathtt{abs}^{\mathfrak{A}}(a, [\![t]\!]_\varsigma^{\mathfrak{A}}) & [\![\pi \cdot X]\!]_\varsigma^{\mathfrak{A}} &= \pi \cdot \varsigma(X) \\
[\![\mathtt{f}^{\mathtt{C}}(t_1, t_2)]\!]_\varsigma^{\mathfrak{A}} &= f^{\mathtt{C},\mathfrak{A}}([\![t_1]\!]_\varsigma^{\mathfrak{A}}, [\![t_2]\!]_\varsigma^{\mathfrak{A}}) & [\![\mathtt{f}(t_1, \ldots, t_n)]\!]_\varsigma^{\mathfrak{A}} &= f^{\mathfrak{A}}([\![t_1]\!]_\varsigma^{\mathfrak{A}}, \ldots, [\![t_n]\!]_\varsigma^{\mathfrak{A}})
\end{array}
$$

We say $[\![\Upsilon_{\overline{c}}]\!]_\varsigma^{\mathfrak{A}}$ is *valid* if $\mathsf{N}\overline{c}.\pi \cdot [\![X]\!]_\varsigma^{\mathfrak{A}} = [\![X]\!]_\varsigma^{\mathfrak{A}}$ for every $\pi \curlywedge_{\mathtt{C}} X \in \Upsilon$. A judgement $\Upsilon \vdash^{\overline{c}} t \approx_{\mathtt{C}} u$ is *valid* if $[\![\Upsilon_{\overline{c}}]\!]_\varsigma^{\mathfrak{A}}$ being valid implies $[\![t]\!]_\varsigma^{\mathfrak{A}} = [\![u]\!]_\varsigma^{\mathfrak{A}}$, for all valuations ς. We write $\Upsilon \vDash^{\overline{c}} t \approx_{\mathtt{C}} u$ when $\Upsilon \vdash^{\overline{c}} t \approx_{\mathtt{C}} u$ is valid for all models of $\mathtt{C}$.

Example 9. Let $\mathfrak{A} = \mathcal{P}_{\mathtt{fin}}(\mathbb{A})$ with $\mathtt{atom}^{\mathfrak{A}}(a) = a$, $\mathtt{abs}^{\mathfrak{A}}(a, S) = S \setminus a$, and $f^{\mathfrak{A}}(S_1, \ldots, S_n) = \bigcap_i S_i$ for each $\mathtt{f}:n$ in Σ. Then $\mathfrak{A}$ is a model of $\mathtt{C}$.

Soundness and completeness hold for our proof system relative to the semantics. In contrast to prior work, the rule ($\approx_{\mathtt{C}}$ **var**) now relies on the subgroup $\mathtt{P}(\Upsilon_{\overline{c}}|_X)$, allowing for full completeness.

Theorem 4. *For any $\Upsilon_{\overline{c}}, t, u$, the following hold:*

1. *(Soundness) If $\Upsilon \vdash^{\overline{c}} t \approx_{\mathtt{C}} u$ then $\Upsilon \vDash^{\overline{c}} t \approx_{\mathtt{C}} u$.*
2. *(Completeness) If $\Upsilon \vDash^{\overline{c}} t \approx_{\mathtt{C}} u$ then $\Upsilon \vdash^{\overline{c}} t \approx_{\mathtt{C}} u$.*

7 Related Work

Gabbay and Mathijssen [22] define a sound and complete proof system for nominal algebra, where derivation rules are subject to freshness conditions, and they provide a semantics in the class of nominal sets. Nominal sets provide an absolute denotation for first-order logic [21], have recently been extended to predicate logic [17], and offer a semantic interpretation for probabilistic programming languages over graphs [2].

Applications of nominal techniques in languages where operators satisfy equational axioms were studied in various contexts, using freshness constraints in the definition of α-equivalence, e.g.: to specify syntactic reasoning algorithms to show properties of program transformations on higher-order expressions in call-by-need functional languages, taking into account, e.g., `letrec` constructs [36]; in theorem proving, due to nominal logic's equivariance property, a different form of unification, called equivariant unification, was investigated [14]; applications in theorem proving and rewrite-based programming languages also require the use of $\mathtt{A}$ and/or $\mathtt{C}$ operators [29]. However, existing nominal unification algorithms for such settings typically yield infinite solutions [4,5]. The finitary algorithm developed here opens the path for extensions of programming languages such as αProlog [15], building commutativity into the unification algorithm.

Regarding alternative approaches to syntax with binders, the well-known higher-order abstract syntax (HOAS) [34] plays an important role. Higher-order unification, which is based on HOAS, has many applications, including type checking [28] and automatic theorem proving in higher-order logics [31]. While elegant and concise, general higher-order unification is undecidable [24], and practical implementations often rely on restricted fragments, such as Miller's higher-order pattern unification [30], which is decidable.

In this context, the higher-order approach can benefit from nominal techniques. Although nominal methods form a theoretical framework of their own, they also offer insights into higher-order patterns. Notably, Cheney shows that higher-order pattern unification can be reduced to nominal unification. Conversely, Levy and Villaret [26] show that nominal unification can be reduced to higher-order pattern unification. This demonstrates that nominal logic offers not only comparable expressive power but also a more first-order-flavoured framework that is close to the one used in textbooks and informal descriptions.

Other approaches to representing binders, beyond the already-mentioned HOAS, include the $\lambda\sigma$-calculus [1] and the locally nameless representation [12]. The $\lambda\sigma$-calculus is based on explicit capture-avoiding substitutions. However, a significant drawback is that it does not support reasoning about open terms, as it lacks confluence when applied to terms with meta-variables. Handling meta-variables effectively is essential for reasoning about binders in proof assistants, such as AutoSubst2 [37], which provides support for formalising metatheory in Rocq (formely known as Coq). It is based on the $\lambda\sigma$-calculus and could benefit from an alternative approach to computing substitutions for meta-variables—one that systematically accounts for the required renamings.

Recent investigations have explored the implementation of the simply typed lambda calculus in both Rocq [13] and Lean [40], using the locally nameless representation combined with cofinite quantification. Our approach, which employs quantified fixed-point constraints using the И-quantifier aligns with this cofinite style. This suggests that nominal reasoning based on fixed-points may offer a complementary alternative for representing and verifying binding structures in proof assistants. Nominal Isabelle also stands out, building on its well-established support for nominal reasoning (including general bindings and α-equivalence) since [38] and more recent advances in implementing nominal techniques for strong rule induction principles respecting Barendregt's convention [9] and recursion principles for bindings [35].

While our use of permutation fixed-point constraints introduces a different style of reasoning compared to HOAS or traditional nominal approaches based on freshness, we emphasise that the permutation groups involved are finite and explicitly generated, making the associated computations practical. In particular, membership in such groups—a key operation in our framework—can be decided in polynomial time [27]. Alternatively, this check can be performed using tools such as GAP or Mathematica, which offer efficient implementations for permutation group operations.

8 Conclusion

We introduced a novel framework for equational reasoning modulo commutativity in languages with binders, using nominal techniques with (И-quantified) permutation fixed-point constraints. This approach integrates commutativity into α-equivalence reasoning without relying on freshness constraints, ensuring soundness and completeness with respect to nominal set semantics.

Additionally, we proposed a terminating and correct C-unification algorithm that provides finite complete sets of solutions, addressing a key limitation of previous methods that relied on freshness constraints and could yield infinite solution sets. These results establish a solid foundation for reasoning about syntax with binding and equational properties, with potential applications in theorem proving, programming language semantics, and automated reasoning systems.

Future work includes extending our approach to broader equational theories, e.g. integrating associativity along commutativity, and exploring practical implementations in verification tools. For instance, PVS could be a natural choice, as it already supports mechanised nominal AC-matching [7] and nominal C-unification [5].

Acknowledgements. Research reported in this paper is partially funded by CAPES and the EPSRC Fellowship 'VeTSpec: Verified Trustworthy Software Specification' (EP/R034567/1).

Disclosure of Interests. The authors declare they have no competing interests (financial or non-financial) to declare that are relevant to the content of this article.

References

1. Abadi, M., Cardelli, L., Curien, P., Lévy, J.: Explicit substitutions. J. Funct. Program. **1**(4), 375–416 (1991). https://doi.org/10.1017/S0956796800000186
2. Ackerman, N., et al.: Probabilistic programming interfaces for random graphs: Markov categories, graphons, and nominal sets. Proc. ACM Program. Lang. **8**(POPL) (2024). https://doi.org/10.1145/3632903
3. Pitts, A.M.: Nominal Sets: Names and Symmetry in Computer Science. Cambridge Tracts in Theoretical Computer Science. Cambridge University Press (2013). https://doi.org/10.1017/CBO9781139084673
4. Ayala-Rincón, M., de Carvalho-Segundo, W., Fernández, M., Nantes-Sobrinho, D.: On solving nominal fixpoint equations. In: Dixon, C., Finger, M. (eds.) FroCoS 2017. LNCS (LNAI), vol. 10483, pp. 209–226. Springer, Cham (2017). https://doi.org/10.1007/978-3-319-66167-4_12
5. Ayala-Rincón, M., de Carvalho-Segundo, W., Fernández, M., Silva, G.F., Nantes-Sobrinho, D.: Formalising nominal C-unification generalised with protected variables. Math. Struct. Comput. Sci. **31**(3), 286–311 (2021). https://doi.org/10.1017/S0960129521000050
6. Ayala-Rincón, M., Fernández, M., Nantes-Sobrinho, D.: On nominal syntax and permutation fixed points. Log. Meth. Comput. Sci. **16**(1), 19:1–19:36 (2020). https://doi.org/10.23638/LMCS-16(1:19)2020
7. Ayala-Rincón, M., Fernández, M., Silva, G.F., Kutsia, T., Nantes-Sobrinho, D.: Nominal AC-matching. In: Dubois, C., Kerber, M. (eds.) Intelligent Computer Mathematics - 16th International Conference, CICM 2023, Cambridge, UK, 5–8 September 2023, Proceedings, vol. 14101, pp. 53–68. Springer, Cham (2023). https://doi.org/10.1007/978-3-031-42753-4_4

8. Aydemir, B.E., et al.: Mechanized metatheory for the masses: the PoplMark challenge. In: Hurd, J., Melham, T. (eds.) TPHOLs 2005. LNCS, vol. 3603, pp. 50–65. Springer, Heidelberg (2005). https://doi.org/10.1007/11541868_4
9. van Brügge, J., McKinna, J., Popescu, A., Traytel, D.: Barendregt convenes with Knaster and Tarski: strong rule induction for syntax with bindings. Proc. ACM Program. Lang. **9**(POPL), 1687–1718 (2025). https://doi.org/10.1145/3704893
10. Caires-Santos, A.K., Fernández, M., Nantes-Sobrinho, D.: Strong nominal semantics for fixed-point constraints. Electron. Notes Theoret. Inf. Comput. Sci. **4**, 6 (2024). Proceedings of MFPS XL. https://entics.episciences.org/14777
11. Caires-Santos, A.K., Fernández, M., Nantes-Sobrinho, D.: Equational reasoning modulo commutativity in languages with binders (extended version) (2025). https://arxiv.org/abs/2502.19287
12. Charguéraud, A.: The locally nameless representation. J. Autom. Reason. **49**(3), 363–408 (2012). https://doi.org/10.1007/s10817-011-9225-2
13. Charguéraud, A.: LN: locally nameless library. https://www.chargueraud.org/softs/ln/
14. Cheney, J.: Equivariant unification. J. Autom. Reason. **45**(3), 267–300 (2010). https://doi.org/10.1007/s10817-009-9164-3
15. Cheney, J., Urban, C.: αProlog: a logic programming language with names, binding and α-equivalence. In: Demoen, B., Lifschitz, V. (eds.) ICLP 2004. LNCS, vol. 3132, pp. 269–283. Springer, Heidelberg (2004). https://doi.org/10.1007/978-3-540-27775-0_19
16. Cheney, J., Urban, C.: Nominal logic programming. ACM Trans. Program. Lang. Syst. **30**(5) (2008). https://doi.org/10.1145/1387673.1387675
17. Dowek, G., Gabbay, M.J.: Nominal semantics for predicate logic: algebras, substitution, quantifiers, and limits (2023). https://arxiv.org/abs/2312.16487
18. Felty, A.P., Momigliano, A., Pientka, B.: The next 700 challenge problems for reasoning with higher-order abstract syntax representations - part 2 - a survey. J. Autom. Reason. **55**(4), 307–372 (2015). https://doi.org/10.1007/s10817-015-9327-3
19. Gabbay, M.J.: Nominal algebra and the HSP theorem. J. Log. Comput. **19**(2), 341–367 (2009). https://doi.org/10.1093/logcom/exn055
20. Gabbay, M.J.: Foundations of nominal techniques: logic and semantics of variables in abstract syntax. Bull. Symb. Log. **17**(2), 161–229 (2011). https://doi.org/10.2178/bsl/1305810911
21. Gabbay, M.J.: Semantics out of context: nominal absolute denotations for first-order logic and computation. J. ACM **63**(3), 25:1–25:66 (2016). https://doi.org/10.1145/2700819
22. Gabbay, M.J., Mathijssen, A.: Nominal (universal) algebra: equational logic with names and binding. J. Log. Comput. **19**(6), 1455–1508 (2009). https://doi.org/10.1093/logcom/exp033
23. Gabbay, M.J., Pitts, A.M.: A new approach to abstract syntax with variable binding. Formal Aspects Comput. **13**(3-5), 341–363 (2002). https://doi.org/10.1007/s001650200016
24. Goldfarb, W.D.: The undecidability of the second-order unification problem. Theoret. Comput. Sci. **13**(2), 225–230 (1981). https://doi.org/10.1016/0304-3975(81)90040-2
25. Kurz, A., Petrisan, D., Velebil, J.: Algebraic theories over nominal sets. CoRR abs/1006.3027 (2010). http://arxiv.org/abs/1006.3027
26. Levy, J., Villaret, M.: Nominal unification from a higher-order perspective. ACM Trans. Comput. Logic **13**(2) (2012). https://doi.org/10.1145/2159531.2159532

27. Luks, E.: Permutation groups and polynomial-time computation. DIMACS Ser. Discrete Math. Theoret. Comput. Sci. **11** (1993). https://doi.org/10.1090/dimacs/011/11
28. Mazzoli, F., Abel, A.: Type checking through unification (2016). https://arxiv.org/abs/1609.09709
29. Meseguer, J.: Inductive reasoning with equality predicates, contextual rewriting and variant-based simplification. J. Log. Algebraic Meth. Program. **144**, 101036 (2025). https://doi.org/10.1016/j.jlamp.2025.101036
30. Miller, D.: A logic programming language with lambda-abstraction, function variables, and simple unification. J. Logic Comput. **1**(4), 497–536 (1991). https://doi.org/10.1093/logcom/1.4.497
31. Miller, D., Nadathur, G.: Programming with Higher-Order Logic. Cambridge University Press, Cambridge (2012)
32. Milner, R., Parrow, J., Walker, D.: A calculus of mobile processes, I. Inf. Comput. **100**(1), 1–40 (1992). https://www.sciencedirect.com/science/article/pii/0890540192900084
33. Murawski, A.S., Tzevelekos, N.: Nominal game semantics. Found. Trends Program. Lang. **2**(4), 191–269 (2016). https://doi.org/10.1561/2500000017
34. Pfenning, F., Elliott, C.: Higher-order abstract syntax. SIGPLAN Not. **23**(7), 199–208 (1988). https://doi.org/10.1145/960116.54010
35. Popescu, A.: Nominal recursors as epi-recursors. Proc. ACM Program. Lang. **8**(POPL), 425–456 (2024). https://doi.org/10.1145/3632857
36. Schmidt-Schauß, M., Kutsia, T., Levy, J., Villaret, M., Kutz, Y.: Nominal unification and matching of higher order expressions with recursive let. Fundam. Informaticae **185**(3), 247–283 (2022). https://doi.org/10.3233/FI-222110
37. Stark, K., Schäfer, S., Kaiser, J.: Autosubst 2: reasoning with multi-sorted de Bruijn terms and vector substitutions. In: Mahboubi, A., Myreen, M.O. (eds.) Proceedings of the 8th ACM SIGPLAN International Conference on Certified Programs and Proofs, CPP 2019, Cascais, Portugal, 14–15 January 2019, pp. 166–180. ACM (2019). https://doi.org/10.1145/3293880.3294101
38. Urban, C., Kaliszyk, C.: General bindings and alpha-equivalence in nominal Isabelle. Logical Meth. Comput. Sci. **8**(2), 14 (2012). https://doi.org/10.2168/LMCS-8(2:14)2012
39. Urban, C., Pitts, A.M., Gabbay, M.J.: Nominal unification. Theor. Comput. Sci. **323**(1–3), 473–497 (2004). https://doi.org/10.1016/j.tcs.2004.06.016
40. Uskuplu, E.: Formalizing locally nameless syntax with Cofinite quantification. Presented at the 4th Workshop on the Implementation of Type Systems (WITS 2025), co-located with POPL 2025, January 2025

Non-classical Logics

Uniform Interpolation and Forgetting for Large-Scale Ontologies with Application to Semantic Difference in SNOMED CT

Yizheng Zhao[1,2(✉)], Junyi Zhang[1,2], and Renate A. Schmidt[3]

[1] National Key Laboratory for Novel Software Technology, Nanjing University, Nanjing, China
zhaoyz@nju.edu.cn
[2] School of Artificial Intelligence, Nanjing University, Nanjing, China
[3] Department of Computer Science, The University of Manchester, Manchester, UK

Abstract. In this paper, we present a practical method for computing uniform interpolation and forgetting in $\mathcal{ELIH}$-ontologies, addressing fundamental operations critical for detecting semantic differences in ontology evolution. Our method extends previous work to accommodate inverse roles while maintaining soundness and termination guarantees. Empirical evaluation across industry benchmarks from Oxford ISG and NCBO BioPortal demonstrates 100% success rates with notable improvements in computational efficiency compared to state-of-the-art systems. The practical impact of our method has been validated through application to SNOMED CT, the world's largest clinical terminology supporting healthcare information systems globally. This enables terminologists and developers to systematically track semantic differences, detect unintended consequences, and validate change safety across SNOMED CT releases.

1 Introduction

Ontologies [39] establish a vocabulary of *terms* (often known as the *signature* of the ontology) specific to a subject domain, and define the meaning of the terms through logical statements. These terms comprise *classes* (sets of instances sharing common properties) and *relationships* (binary relations between classes and their instances). Through set-theoretic interpretations [36], ontologies acquire formal semantics that enable machine processing and automated reasoning. Modern ontologies are formalized in the *Web Ontology Language* (OWL) [1] based on *Description Logics* (DLs) [2]—a family of knowledge representation formalisms where classes and relationships are termed *concepts* and *roles*, respectively.

SNOMED CT [38] maintained by SNOMED International,[1] serves as a comprehensive clinical terminology that underpins healthcare delivery worldwide.

Y. Zhao and J. Zhang—Contributed equally to this work.

[1] https://www.snomed.org/

C. Barrett and U. Waldmann (Eds.): CADE 2025, LNAI 15943, pp. 655–675, 2025.
https://doi.org/10.1007/978-3-031-99984-0_34

Formalized in OWL 2 [9], SNOMED CT comprises over 350,000 clinical concepts with a similar number of logical axioms that establish their precise semantics. Several other major healthcare ontologies complement SNOMED CT: *NCIt* [37] provides reference terminology for cancer-related diseases and findings; the *Gene Ontology* (GO) [40] enables consistent description and querying of gene products across databases; and *GALEN* [34] offers comprehensive terminology for surgical procedures. These ontologies have been widely used in healthcare sectors and related research areas, supporting standardized concept codes and interoperability among clinical information systems.

SNOMED CT sustains currency through regular updates to its International edition, with monthly releases incorporating additions of new terms, retirement of obsolete ones, and refinements to existing definitions. These revisions occur at considerable scale: between January 2015 and January 2016, SNOMED CT underwent approximately 192,000 content modifications [46]. Even minor definitional modifications can have far-reaching implications for concept and relationship hierarchies, making their semantic impact challenging to assess fully. Therefore, quality assurance (QA) becomes crucial. QA in ontology evolution focuses on two key aspects:

- Structural changes: These involve modifications to the ontology's structure, captured through the notion of *structural difference* [32]. This aspect treats ontologies as structured objects and characterizes changes through basic operations such as concept addition or axiom removal.
- Semantic changes: These reflect differences in the meaning of terms between ontology versions, which include differences in both explicitly stated and implicitly derived axioms.

While tools like Protégé [12,30], SWOOP [13], OntoView [14], PROMPTDIFF [32], and OBO-Edit [6] effectively track structural changes, the field lacks practical methods and tools for detecting *semantic* changes. Two major challenges complicate this task:

- The difficulty of identifying implicit information: Semantic changes include not just explicit modifications but also their logical implications, which are in general not immediately visible.
- Signature inconsistency: When new releases of ontology introduce new terms or remove existing ones, comparing their semantic content becomes complicated.

To address these challenges, the notion of semantic change between ontologies $\mathcal{O}_1$ and $\mathcal{O}_2$ as axioms entailed by one but not the other has been defined in [15]. Computing these differences requires:

- Unifying the signatures of both versions while preserving their meaning;
- Identifying all entailed axioms (both explicitly stated and implicitly inferred);
- Isolating from these axioms the semantic differences important for the user/use case/application.

Related Work

Konev et al. [15] introduced the use of *Uniform Interpolation* (UI) [5,10,28,33,41] as a formal mechanism for unifying ontology signatures and finding finite representations of semantic differences. UI is a non-standard reasoning service that aims to project an ontology down to a sub-signature, i.e., given an ontology using a specific signature, and a subset Σ of 'relevant names' of that signature, the aim is to compute an ontology, namely a *uniform interpolant*, that employs only the relevant names while preserving the semantics of the relevant names in the absence of the other names. This process typically requires deriving a large number of new axioms to maintain semantic preservation, as original axioms may lose meaning when definitional terms are excluded from the specified signature. Moreover, computing uniform interpolants is computationally expensive and may not terminate [28]. Despite these challenges, with UI there is the possibility to compress representations of the semantic difference by focusing on the strongest entailments rather than exhaustively computing all logical entailments of one version not entailed by the other. The complete set of logical entailments can be derived from the deductive closure of these strongest entailments.[2]

However, UI poses a significant computational challenge: uniform interpolants may not exist for the DL $\mathcal{ELH}$ or $\mathcal{ALC}$ [16] with existence of finite representations of the strongest entailments being the main problem. Moreover, existence checking is ExpTime-complete for $\mathcal{ELH}$ [26] and 2ExpTime-complete for $\mathcal{ALC}$ [28]. Size complexity is also substantial: as shown in [31], when finite uniform interpolants exist, their minimal size can be triple exponential in the size of the input ontology. For example, uniform interpolants can grow exponentially in DL-Lite [18] and triple exponentially in $\mathcal{ALC}$ [28] and $\mathcal{EL}$ [31]. Even for propositional logic, polynomial-size uniform interpolants are not guaranteed [23].

Several methods have been developed to implement UI. The NUI tool [17] uses a recursive algorithm for computing instance Σ-interpolants, but its effectiveness diminishes with larger interpolation signatures—when tested on SNOMED CT (January 2005), success rates dropped from 93% for $|\Sigma| = 2000$ to 59.5% for $|\Sigma| = 5000$, making it impractical for modern ontologies where $|\Sigma|$ can be very large [25]. Other tools like Lethe [20], UI-Fame [43,46], and the method developed by [25,44,45] employ forgetting-based procedures. However, these methods face at least one of the following key limitations:

- They are designed for more expressive DLs than $\mathcal{ELIH}$ (which is commonly used in large-scale ontologies), producing uniform interpolants with constructs outside of $\mathcal{ELIH}$'s expressivity.
- They exhibit substantial computational inefficiency when processing industrial-scale ontologies [4,20].

[2] In the context of logical statements, a set $\mathcal{O}$ of statements is *deductively closed* if it contains every statement ϕ that can be logically deduced from $\mathcal{O}$, i.e., $\mathcal{O} \models \phi$ implies $\phi \in \mathcal{O}$. The deductive closure of $\mathcal{O}$ is its smallest superset that is deductively closed.

Our Contributions

In this paper, we present a practical method for computing uniform interpolants of $\mathcal{ELIH}$-ontologies, extending previous work of [24] to accommodate SNOMED CT's recent adoption of inverse roles ($\mathcal{I}$). Our method is based on an optimized forgetting procedure that systematically eliminates non-relevant names from ontology $\mathcal{O}$ (i.e., those in $\mathsf{sig}(\mathcal{O}) \setminus \Sigma$) while preserving the semantics within the interpolation signature Σ. This method is terminating and sound, offering a principled solution to tackling the computational challenges inherent for UI and forgetting, and addressing the need for efficient semantic difference detection. The method is however not complete, because UI is undecidable for $mathcalEL$ and $\mathcal{ELIH}$. The expressivity does not help solve examples with problematic recursive axioms but results show that success rates and performance are good compared to other UI tools. Moreover, modeling guidelines of SNOMED International do not allow recursive definitions which are problematic for UI methods as they can lead to infinite solutions which cannot be expressed in $\mathcal{ELIH}$ without the use of auxiliary concept names.

Extensive empirical evaluation using our prototype implementation demonstrates exceptional performance, achieving 100% success rates across two comprehensive ontology corpora derived from Oxford ISG and NCBO BioPortal, which are the established benchmarks in the field. When compared to LETHE, the current state-of-the-art UI system for expressive DLs, our method exhibits superior performance in terms of success rates and substantial improvements in both computational efficiency and memory utilization. A case study analyzing 20 consecutive releases of SNOMED CT, currently the largest biomedical ontology in clinical deployment, demonstrates our method's capacity to overcome the inherent scalability limitations of UI and forgetting. This advancement enables the identification of semantic modifications across large-scale ontologies, providing users a new mechanism for ontology evolution and enabling knowledge-preserving data and service migration processes.

2 Preliminaries

In this section, we introduce the underlying language $\mathcal{ELIH}$ and illustrate some basic notions used throughout this paper. Based on them, we formalize the notions of *UI* (*forgetting*) and *semantic difference.*

2.1 The Description Logic $\mathcal{ELIH}$

Let $\mathsf{N_C}$ and $\mathsf{N_R}$ be pairwise disjoint, countably infinite sets of *concept names* and *role names*, respectively. *Roles* in $\mathcal{ELIH}$ can be a role name $\mathsf{r} \in \mathsf{N_R}$ or the inverse r^- of a role name r. *Concepts* in $\mathcal{ELIH}$ are inductively defined by the following syntax rule:

$$C, D \longrightarrow \top \mid A \mid C \sqcap D \mid \exists R.C$$

where $A \in \mathsf{N_C}$, C, D range over concepts, and R over role names and inverse roles. We distinguish between *atomic* concepts (concept names A in $\mathsf{N_C}$) and *complex* concepts (all others). An *$\mathcal{ELIH}$-ontology* $\mathcal{O}$ is a finite set of axioms in the following forms:

Concept Inclusions (CIs): $C \sqsubseteq D$ Role Inclusions (RIs): $R \sqsubseteq S$

where C and D are concepts, and R and S are role names or inverse roles. We denote concept equivalence $C \equiv D$ as an abbreviation for the pair of CIs $C \sqsubseteq D$ and $D \sqsubseteq C$ (analogously for role equivalence $R \equiv S$). Throughout this paper, we assume w.l.o.g. that an $\mathcal{ELIH}$-ontology contains only CIs and RIs. We define an occurrence of a (concept/role) name as *positive* in an axiom if it occurs at the right-hand side of $\sqsubseteq$ and as *negative* if on the left-hand side.

The semantics of $\mathcal{ELIH}$ is defined using an *interpretation* $\mathcal{I} = \langle \Delta^\mathcal{I}, \cdot^\mathcal{I} \rangle$, where $\Delta^\mathcal{I}$ is a nonempty set, called the *domain of the interpretation*, and $\cdot^\mathcal{I}$ is the *interpretation function* that maps every concept name $A \in \mathsf{N_C}$ to a subset $A^\mathcal{I} \subseteq \Delta^\mathcal{I}$, and every role name $r \in \mathsf{N_R}$ to a binary relation $r^\mathcal{I} \subseteq \Delta^\mathcal{I} \times \Delta^\mathcal{I}$. The interpretation function $\cdot^\mathcal{I}$ is inductively extended to other concepts as follows:

$$\top^\mathcal{I} = \Delta^\mathcal{I} \qquad (C \sqcap D)^\mathcal{I} = C^\mathcal{I} \cap D^\mathcal{I}$$
$$(\exists R.C)^\mathcal{I} = \{x \in \Delta^\mathcal{I} \mid \exists y.(x, y) \in R^\mathcal{I} \wedge y \in C^\mathcal{I}\}$$
$$(R^-)^\mathcal{I} = \{(y, x) \in \Delta^\mathcal{I} \times \Delta^\mathcal{I} \mid (x, y) \in R^\mathcal{I}\}$$

And to axioms as follows:

- A CI $C \sqsubseteq D$ holds in $\mathcal{I}$ (written $\mathcal{I} \models C \sqsubseteq D$) iff $C^\mathcal{I} \subseteq D^\mathcal{I}$.
- An RI $R \sqsubseteq S$ holds in $\mathcal{I}$ (written $\mathcal{I} \models R \sqsubseteq S$) iff $R^\mathcal{I} \subseteq S^\mathcal{I}$.

An interpretation $\mathcal{I}$ is a *model* of ontology $\mathcal{O}$ (written $\mathcal{I} \models \mathcal{O}$) iff every axiom in $\mathcal{O}$ holds in $\mathcal{I}$. We say that an axiom α is *entailed* by $\mathcal{O}$ or a *logical entailment* of $\mathcal{O}$ (written $\mathcal{O} \models \alpha$) iff α holds in every model of $\mathcal{O}$. An ontology $\mathcal{O}_1$ is *entailed* by $\mathcal{O}_2$ (written $\mathcal{O}_2 \models \mathcal{O}_1$) iff every model of $\mathcal{O}_2$ is also a model of $\mathcal{O}_1$.

A *signature* $\Sigma \subseteq \mathsf{N_C} \cup \mathsf{N_R}$ is a finite set of concept and role names. For any syntactic object X (concept, CI, axiom, or ontology), we define:

- $\mathsf{sig_C}(X)$: the set of concept names in X
- $\mathsf{sig_R}(X)$: the set of role names in X
- $\mathsf{sig}(X)$: $\mathsf{sig_C}(X) \cup \mathsf{sig_R}(X)$

For any signature Σ, a syntactic object X is called a Σ-object if $\mathsf{sig}(X) \subseteq \Sigma$ (e.g., Σ-concept, Σ-CI, Σ-axiom). For any name $S \in \mathsf{N_C} \cup \mathsf{N_R}$, a syntactic object X is called an S-object if $A \in \mathsf{sig}(X)$.

2.2 UI-Based Semantic Difference

Definition 1 (Semantic Difference for $\mathcal{ELIH}$). *For any two $\mathcal{ELIH}$-ontologies $\mathcal{O}_1$ and $\mathcal{O}_2$ and a signature $\Sigma \subseteq \mathsf{sig}(\mathcal{O}_1) \cap \mathsf{sig}(\mathcal{O}_2)$, the* semantic difference *$\mathit{Diff}_\Sigma(\mathcal{O}_1, \mathcal{O}_2)$ comprises all $\mathcal{ELIH}$-axioms α satisfying:*

$$\mathsf{sig}(\alpha) \subseteq \Sigma, \qquad \mathcal{O}_2 \models \alpha, \qquad \text{and} \qquad \mathcal{O}_1 \not\models \alpha.$$

An axiom α satisfying these conditions is called a witness *of the difference.*

As noted before, the notion of semantic difference requires a unified signature basis for comparison between ontology versions. This unification can be achieved through UI, which we formally define it here for $\mathcal{ELIH}$-ontologies.

Definition 2 (UI for $\mathcal{ELIH}$). *For any $\mathcal{ELIH}$-ontology $\mathcal{O}$ and an* interpolation signature *$\Sigma \subseteq \mathsf{sig}(\mathcal{O})$, an $\mathcal{ELIH}$-ontology $\mathcal{V}$ is a* uniform Σ-interpolant *of $\mathcal{O}$ if it satisfies:*

1. *$\mathsf{sig}(\mathcal{V}) \subseteq \Sigma$, and*
2. *$\mathcal{V} \models \alpha$ iff $\mathcal{O} \models \alpha$, for every $\mathcal{ELIH}$-axiom α such that $\mathsf{sig}(\alpha) \subseteq \Sigma$.*

This makes $\mathcal{V}$ the *strongest Σ-entailment of* $\mathcal{O}$, meaning that for any ontology $\mathcal{V}'$ with $\mathcal{O} \models \mathcal{V}'$ and $\mathsf{sig}(\mathcal{V}') \subseteq \Sigma$, we have that $\mathcal{V} \models \mathcal{V}'$. Uniform interpolants are unique up to equivalence: any two uniform Σ-interpolants $\mathcal{V}_1$ and $\mathcal{V}_2$ of $\mathcal{O}$ are semantically equivalent.

We use the notation $\mathsf{Diff}_\Sigma(\mathcal{O}_1, \mathcal{O}_2)$ to denote the semantic difference between ontologies $\mathcal{O}_1$ and $\mathcal{O}_2$ w.r.t. the signature $\Sigma \subseteq \mathsf{sig}(\mathcal{O}_1) \cap \mathsf{sig}(\mathcal{O}_2)$. Each axiom in this set constitutes a *witness* of $\mathsf{Diff}_\Sigma(\mathcal{O}_1, \mathcal{O}_2)$, representing a Σ-entailment of $\mathcal{O}_2$ not entailed by $\mathcal{O}_1$. While an empty difference (i.e., $\mathsf{Diff}_\Sigma(\mathcal{O}_1, \mathcal{O}_2) = \emptyset$) implies semantic equivalence over Σ, a non-empty difference typically yields an infinite witness set [25]. To address this, we introduce *UI-based semantic difference*, which provides a possibly finite representation of the witness set while generalizing the standard notion.

Definition 3 (UI-based Semantic Difference for $\mathcal{ELIH}$). *For any $\mathcal{ELIH}$-ontologies $\mathcal{O}_1$ and $\mathcal{O}_2$ and a signature $\Sigma \subseteq \mathsf{sig}(\mathcal{O}_1) \cap \mathsf{sig}(\mathcal{O}_2)$, the* UI-based semantic difference *$\mathsf{UI\text{-}Diff}_\Sigma(\mathcal{O}_1, \mathcal{O}_2)$ comprises all $\mathcal{ELIH}$-axioms α satisfying:*

1. *$\mathsf{sig}(\alpha) \subseteq \Sigma$,*
2. *$\alpha \in \mathcal{V}_2$, where $\mathcal{V}_2$ is a uniform Σ-interpolant of $\mathcal{O}_2$, and*
3. *$\mathcal{O}_1 \not\models \alpha$.*

Each such axiom α is termed a UI-witness.

UI witnesses have two key properties: (i) Every UI-witness is also a witness, i.e., $\mathsf{UI\text{-}Diff}_\Sigma(\mathcal{O}_1, \mathcal{O}_2) \subseteq \mathsf{Diff}_\Sigma(\mathcal{O}_1, \mathcal{O}_2)$, because $\mathcal{V}_2$ contains only entailments of $\mathcal{O}_2$, and (ii) $\mathsf{UI\text{-}Diff}_\Sigma(\mathcal{O}_1, \mathcal{O}_2)$ denotes a possibly finite representation of $\mathsf{Diff}_\Sigma(\mathcal{O}_1, \mathcal{O}_2)$, as all witnesses can in principle be derived from the deductive closure of $\mathcal{V}_2$. The computation of $\mathsf{UI\text{-}Diff}_\Sigma(\mathcal{O}_1, \mathcal{O}_2)$ follows a two-step procedure:

1. Compute uniform Σ-interpolant $\mathcal{V}_2$ of $\mathcal{O}_2$ using a UI tool,
2. Identify axioms $\alpha \in \mathcal{V}_2$ that are not entailed by $\mathcal{O}_1$ using a DL reasoner.

We notice that $\mathsf{UI\text{-}Diff}_\Sigma(\mathcal{O}_1, \mathcal{O}_2)$ captures both *information gain* from $\mathcal{O}_1$ to $\mathcal{O}_2$ and *information loss* from $\mathcal{O}_2$ to $\mathcal{O}_1$ over Σ.

2.3 Duality of UI and Forgetting

Uniform interpolants can be computed via forgetting [21, 47]—a procedure that eliminates non-Σ names from an ontology while preserving all logical entailments within the remaining names [20, 22, 25, 42].

Definition 4 (Forgetting for $\mathcal{ELIH}$). *For any $\mathcal{ELIH}$ ontology $\mathcal{O}$ and a* forgetting signature $\mathcal{F} \subseteq \mathsf{sig}(\mathcal{O})$, *an $\mathcal{ELIH}$-ontology $\mathcal{V}$ is a* result of forgetting $\mathcal{F}$ from $\mathcal{O}$ *if:*

1. $\mathsf{sig}(\mathcal{V}) \subseteq \mathsf{sig}(\mathcal{O}) \setminus \mathcal{F}$, *and*
2. $\mathcal{V} \models \alpha$ *iff* $\mathcal{O} \models \alpha$, *for any $\mathcal{ELIH}$-axiom α such that* $\mathsf{sig}(\alpha) \subseteq \mathsf{sig}(\mathcal{O}) \setminus \mathcal{F}$.

UI and forgetting exhibit a duality: $\mathcal{V}$ is a uniform Σ-interpolant of $\mathcal{O}$ precisely when $\mathcal{V}$ results from forgetting the complementary signature $\mathcal{F} = \mathsf{sig}(\mathcal{O}) \setminus \Sigma$ from $\mathcal{O}$. When computing $\mathsf{UI\text{-}Diff}_{\Sigma}(\mathcal{O}_1, \mathcal{O}_2)$, we have $\mathcal{F} = \mathsf{sig}(\mathcal{O}_2) \setminus \mathsf{sig}(\mathcal{O}_1)$.

3 Normalization of $\mathcal{ELIH}$-Ontologies

Given an $\mathcal{ELIH}$-ontology $\mathcal{O}$ and a forgetting signature $\mathcal{F}$, our method computes the forgetting result through iterative elimination of individual names from $\mathcal{F}$. This elimination process is realized by two independent specialized calculi that operate on distinct normal forms specifically designed for $\mathcal{ELIH}$-ontologies. In the subsequent definitions, A denotes an arbitrary concept name in $\mathsf{N_C}$, and r an arbitrary role name in $\mathsf{N_R}$. The normal forms are defined relative to these elimination targets, ensuring that the syntactic structure facilitates the application of the corresponding inference rules.

3.1 A-Normal Form (A-NF)

Definition 5 (A-Normal Form). *A CI is in* A-normal form *(or* A-NF*) if it has one of the forms: (I) $C \sqsubseteq \mathsf{A}$, (II) $C \sqsubseteq \exists R.(\mathsf{A} \sqcap D)$, (III) $\mathsf{A} \sqcap C \sqsubseteq D$, and (IV) $C \sqcap \exists R.(\mathsf{A} \sqcap D) \sqsubseteq E$, where (i) R is a role name or an inverse role, and (ii) C, D, and E are concepts not containing A. An $\mathcal{ELIH}$-ontology $\mathcal{O}$ is in* A-NF *if every* A-*CI in $\mathcal{O}$ is in A-NF.*

An $\mathcal{ELIH}$-ontology $\mathcal{O}$ can be transformed into A-NF through exhaustive application of the normalization rules NR1 – NR5 to each A-CI in $\mathcal{O}$ not already in A-NF. Let X, Y, Y_1, and Y_2 denote concepts, and let Z be a 'definer', i.e., a newly introduced concept name that serves as an abbreviation for complex concepts during normalization.

NR1 For each instance of $X \sqsubseteq Y_1 \sqcap Y_2$, replace with $X \sqsubseteq Y_1$ and $X \sqsubseteq Y_2$ if A occurs in Y_1 or Y_2;
NR2 For each instance of $X \sqsubseteq Y$ with multiple occurrences of A, replace C with a new definer $Z \in \mathsf{N_C}$, and add $C \sqsubseteq Z$ to $\mathcal{O}$ if X contains a concept of the form $\exists R.C$ at surface level with $\mathsf{A} \in \mathsf{sig}(C)$;

NR3 For each instance of $X \sqsubseteq Y$ with multiple occurrences of A, replace C with a new definer $Z \in \mathsf{N_C}$, and add $Z \sqsubseteq C$ to $\mathcal{O}$ if Y contains a concept of the form $\exists R.C$ at surface level with $\mathsf{A} \in \mathsf{sig}(C)$;
NR4 For each instance of $X \sqsubseteq Y$ with a single occurrence of A, replace C with a new definer $Z \in \mathsf{N_C}$, and add $C \sqsubseteq Z$ to $\mathcal{O}$ if X contains a concept of the form $\exists R.C$ at surface level with $\mathsf{A} \in \mathsf{sig}(C)$ but $C \neq \mathsf{A} \sqcap D$ (per A-NF VI);
NR5 For each instance of $X \sqsubseteq Y$ with a single occurrence of A, replace C with a new definer $Z \in \mathsf{N_C}$, and add $Z \sqsubseteq C$ to $\mathcal{O}$ if Y contains a concept of the form $\exists R.C$ at surface level with $\mathsf{A} \in \mathsf{sig}(C)$ but $C \neq \mathsf{A} \sqcap D$ (per A-NF II).

Lemma 6. *Let $\mathcal{O}$ be an $\mathcal{ELIH}$-ontology and $\mathcal{O}'$ a normalized ontology obtained from $\mathcal{O}$ using NR1 – NR5. Then we have*

$$\mathcal{O} \models \alpha \textit{ iff } \mathcal{O}' \models \alpha,$$

for any $\mathcal{ELIH}$-axiom α such that $\mathsf{sig}(\alpha) \subseteq \mathsf{sig}(O)$.

Lemma 6 shows that the A-NF transformations are semantically conservative, preserving all original logical entailments while potentially introducing new vocabulary for structural purposes.

3.2 r-Normal Form (r-NF)

Definition 7 (r-Normal Form). *A CI or an RI is in* r-normal form *(or* r-NF*) if it has one of the forms: (I) $C \sqsubseteq \exists \mathsf{r}.D$, (II) $C \sqsubseteq \exists \mathsf{r}^-.D$, (III) $C \sqcap \exists \mathsf{r}.D \sqsubseteq E$, (IV) $C \sqcap \exists \mathsf{r}^-.D \sqsubseteq E$, (V) $S \sqsubseteq \mathsf{r}$, (VI) $S \sqsubseteq \mathsf{r}^-$, (VII) $\mathsf{r} \sqsubseteq S$, and (VIII) $\mathsf{r}^- \sqsubseteq S$, where (i) $\mathsf{r} \in \mathsf{N_R}$, (ii) S is a role name or an inverse role, and (iii) C, D, and E are concepts not containing* r. *An $\mathcal{ELIH}$-ontology $\mathcal{O}$ is in* r-NF *if every* r*-CI and* r*-RI in $\mathcal{O}$ is in r-NF.*

An $\mathcal{ELIH}$-ontology $\mathcal{O}$ can be transformed into r-NF through exhaustive application of the normalization rules NR6 – NR10 to each r-CI in $\mathcal{O}$ not already in A-NF. We notice that any r-RI is already in r-NF.

NR1 For each instance of $X \sqsubseteq Y_1 \sqcap Y_2$, replace with $X \sqsubseteq Y_1$ and $X \sqsubseteq Y_2$ if A occurs in Y_1 or Y_2;
NR2 For each instance of $X \sqsubseteq Y$ with multiple occurrences of A, replace C with a new definer $Z \in \mathsf{N_C}$, and add $C \sqsubseteq Z$ to $\mathcal{O}$ if X contains a concept of the form $\exists R.C$ at surface level with $\mathsf{A} \in \mathsf{sig}(C)$;
NR3 For each instance of $X \sqsubseteq Y$ with multiple occurrences of A, replace C with a new definer $Z \in \mathsf{N_C}$, and add $Z \sqsubseteq C$ to $\mathcal{O}$ if Y contains a concept of the form $\exists R.C$ at surface level with $\mathsf{A} \in \mathsf{sig}(C)$;
NR4 For each instance of $X \sqsubseteq Y$ with a single occurrence of A, replace C with a new definer $Z \in \mathsf{N_C}$, and add $C \sqsubseteq Z$ to $\mathcal{O}$ if X contains a concept of the form $\exists R.C$ at surface level with $\mathsf{A} \in \mathsf{sig}(C)$ but $C \neq \mathsf{A} \sqcap D$ (per A-NF VI);

NR5 For each instance of $X \sqsubseteq Y$ with a single occurrence of A, replace C with a new definer $Z \in \mathsf{N_C}$, and add $Z \sqsubseteq C$ to $\mathcal{O}$ if Y contains a concept of the form $\exists R.C$ at surface level with $\mathsf{A} \in \mathsf{sig}(C)$ but $C \neq \mathsf{A} \sqcap D$ (per A-NF II).

Lemma 8. *Let $\mathcal{O}$ be an $\mathcal{ELIH}$-ontology and $\mathcal{O}'$ the normalized one obtained from $\mathcal{O}$ using the normalization rules NR6 – NR10. Then we have*

$$\mathcal{O} \models \alpha \text{ iff } \mathcal{O}' \models \alpha,$$

for any $\mathcal{ELIH}$-axiom α such that $\mathsf{sig}(\alpha) \subseteq \mathsf{sig}(O)$.

Lemma 9. *Let $\mathcal{O}$ be an $\mathcal{ELIH}$-ontology. The transformation of $\mathcal{O}$ into A-NF or r-NF $\mathcal{O}'$ exhibits the following complexity properties:*

1. *The transformation requires a linear number of normalization rule applications;*
2. *The size of the resulting ontology $\mathcal{O}'$ is linear in the size of $\mathcal{O}$;*
3. *The number of introduced definers is bounded by $\mathsf{O}(n)$, where n represents the number of $\exists$-restrictions in $\mathcal{O}$.*

Lemma 8 shows that the r-NF transformations are semantically conservative, preserving all entailments for axioms within the original signature. Lemma 9 shows that our normalization is computationally efficient, requiring only linear time and space complexity relative to the input ontology size.

Our forgetting method implements a linear definer-based normalization strategy that fundamentally differs from existing approaches such as LETHE, which introduces definers with exponential complexity bounded by $O(2^n)$, where n denotes the number of $\exists$- and $\forall$-restrictions in the input ontology [19]. This optimization achieves significant computational gains by maintaining linear space complexity during normalization, thereby enhancing the method's overall efficiency and scalability.

IR1. $C \sqsubseteq \mathsf{A}, \mathsf{A} \sqcap E \sqsubseteq G \Longrightarrow C \sqcap E \sqsubseteq G$

IR2. $C \sqsubseteq \mathsf{A}, \exists R.(\mathsf{A} \sqcap E) \sqcap F \sqsubseteq G \Longrightarrow \exists R.(C \sqcap E) \sqcap F \sqsubseteq G$

IR3. $C \sqsubseteq \exists R.(\mathsf{A} \sqcap D), \mathsf{A} \sqcap E_1 \sqsubseteq G_1, \ldots, \mathsf{A} \sqcap E_n \sqsubseteq G_n$
$\Longrightarrow C \sqsubseteq \exists R.(E_1 \sqcap \ldots \sqcap E_n \sqcap G_1 \sqcap \ldots \sqcap G_n \sqcap D)$
provided that: $\mathcal{O} \models \mathsf{A} \sqcap D \sqsubseteq E_1 \sqcap \cdots \sqcap E_n$
$C \sqsubseteq \exists R.(\mathsf{A} \sqcap D), \mathsf{A} \sqcap E \sqsubseteq G \Longrightarrow C \sqsubseteq \exists R.D$
provided that: $\mathcal{O} \not\models \mathsf{A} \sqcap D \sqsubseteq E$

IR4. $C \sqsubseteq \exists R.(\mathsf{A} \sqcap D), \exists S.(\mathsf{A} \sqcap E) \sqcap F \sqsubseteq G$
$\Longrightarrow C \sqsubseteq \exists R.D, C \sqcap F \sqsubseteq G$
provided that: $\mathcal{O} \models \mathsf{A} \sqcap D \sqsubseteq E$ and $\mathcal{O} \models R \sqsubseteq S$
$C \sqsubseteq \exists R.(\mathsf{A} \sqcap D), \exists S.(\mathsf{A} \sqcap E) \sqcap F \sqsubseteq G \Longrightarrow C \sqsubseteq \exists R.D$
provided that: $\mathcal{O} \not\models \mathsf{A} \sqcap D \sqsubseteq E$ or $\mathcal{O} \not\models R \sqsubseteq S$

Fig. 1. Inference rules for eliminating concept name A

4 Single Name Elimination

4.1 Calculus for Eliminating A

We now describe a two-step calculus for eliminating a single concept name A from an $\mathcal{ELIH}$-ontology $\mathcal{O}$:

Step 1: Transform $\mathcal{O}$ into A-NF using the normalization rules;
Step 2: Eliminate A through exhaustive application of inference rules (Fig. 1) to the normalized ontology.

In contrast to LETHE and UI-FAME, which operate on clausal representations, our method works directly with CIs and RIs, enabling more natural and efficient inference.

Given an $\mathcal{ELIH}$-ontology in A-NF, the elimination procedure operates on A-axioms using the inference rules shown in Fig. 1. These rules are schemata rather than concrete rules: meta-variables A, C, D, E, F, G represent concepts, while R, S represent roles. Each rule consists of *premises* (left of $\Longrightarrow$) and a *conclusion* (right).

The inference process systematically reveals logical entailments over $\mathsf{sig}(\mathcal{O}) \setminus \{\mathsf{A}\}$ by combining positive occurrences of A (forms A-NF I or II) with negative occurrences (forms A-NF III or IV). This results in four distinct combination cases (IR1–IR4), shown in Fig. 1. The process continues until reaching saturation, i.e., when no inference rule applications yield new entailments.

Our combination strategy extends the binary resolution principle [35], which traditionally combines clauses with complementary literals (e.g., deriving conclusion $A \vee C$ from premises $A \vee B$ and $\neg B \vee C$). However, $\mathcal{ELIH}$ resolution poses a unique challenge: A may appear under $\exists$-restrictions or within $\sqcap$-conjunctions, with complementarity only visible through first-order representation [48]. Our inference rules address this by directly resolving $\exists$ and $\sqcap$ literals on r. The final result of forgetting, which we denote by $\mathcal{O}^{-\mathsf{A}}$, is obtained by removing all A-CIs from the saturated ontology, yielding an ontology that preserves all relevant entailments over the remaining signature.

We provide a detailed explanation of the two 'provided that' conditions in inference rules IR3 and IR4 to clarify their semantic foundations. Taking IR3 as an example, the distinction between the two conditional clauses is essential for ensuring inference completeness. We must differentiate between the cases where $\mathcal{O} \models A \sqcap D \sqsubseteq E$ and $\mathcal{O} \not\models A \sqcap D \sqsubseteq E$, corresponding to the two distinct 'provided that' conditions in IR3. In the latter case, if the entailment $\mathcal{O} \models A \sqcap D \sqsubseteq E$ were to hold, the semantically correct inference would yield $C \sqsubseteq \exists R.(E \sqcap G \sqcap D)$, which is logically stronger than the current derivation $C \sqsubseteq \exists R.D$. However, this stronger conclusion is already captured by the first conditional clause when $\mathcal{O} \models A \sqcap D \sqsubseteq E$ holds. The side-condition mechanism thus ensures that the appropriate inference variant is selected based on the specific entailment relationships present in the ontology, preventing both inference gaps and redundant derivations.

Equivalence-preserving simplifications are applied eagerly throughout the elimination process to maintain the ontology in its simplest form. This process includes the systematic removal of subsumed axioms and all tautologies, including trivial axioms such as $A \sqsubseteq A$. By eliminating redundant and logically trivial content, this approach prevents the accumulation of superfluous axioms and ensures optimal ontological conciseness during the forgetting procedure.

Example 10. Consider the following $\mathcal{ELIH}$-ontology $\mathcal{O}$:

$$\{1.\ E \sqsubseteq \exists r^{-}.(F \sqcap \exists t.A), 2.\ \exists t.\ A \sqcap \exists t^{-}.E \sqsubseteq D\}$$

Let $\mathcal{F} = \{A\}$. The first step is to compute the A-NF of $\mathcal{O}$ by applying the normalization rules described earlier, where $Z_1 \in N_D$ is a fresh definer:

$$\{3.\ E \sqsubseteq \exists r^{-}.Z_1, 5.\ Z_1 \sqsubseteq F, 6.\ Z_1 \sqsubseteq \exists t.\ A, 2.\ \exists t.A \sqcap \exists t^{-}.E \sqsubseteq D\}$$

The above ontology is now in A-NF. The second step is to apply the inference rules in Fig. 1. Applying IR4 to CIs 2 and 6 gives:

$$\{3.\ E \sqsubseteq \exists r^{-}.Z_1, 5.\ Z_1 \sqsubseteq F, 7.\ Z_1 \sqcap \exists t^{-}.E \sqsubseteq D, 8.\ Z_1 \sqsubseteq \exists t.\top\}$$

Definers are treated as regular concept names, and are eliminated once all $\mathcal{F}$-names have been eliminated. Applying IR3 to CIs 3 and 7 gives:

$$\{9.\ E \sqsubseteq \exists r^{-}.\top\}$$

Applying IR3 to CIs 3, 5 and 8 gives:

$$\{10.\ E \sqsubseteq \exists r^{-}.(F \sqcap \exists t.\top)\}$$

CI 9 is redundant w.r.t. CI 10 and can thus be removed. In this case, $\{10\}$ is a uniform Σ-interpolant of $\mathcal{O}$, where $\Sigma = sig(\mathcal{O}) \setminus \mathcal{F}$.

Lemma 11. *For any $\mathcal{ELIH}$-ontology $\mathcal{O}$ in A-NF, the elimination procedure preserves all logical entailments over the signature $sig(\mathcal{O}) \setminus \{A\}$:*

$$\mathcal{O}^{-A} \models \alpha \text{ iff } \mathcal{O} \models \alpha,$$

for any $\mathcal{ELIH}$-axiom α with $sig(\alpha) \subseteq sig(O) \setminus \{A\}$.

Lemma 11 establishes the semantic preservation property of our calculus—$\mathcal{O}^{-A}$ satisfies the entailment preservation condition required for forgetting A from $\mathcal{O}$ (Condition 2 of Definition 4). However, the signature containment condition (Condition 1) may be violated due to the presence of auxiliary definers in $\mathcal{O}^{-A}$ that extend beyond $sig(\mathcal{O}) \setminus \{A\}$. We address this signature expansion challenge in a later subsection by a definer elimination procedure.

IR5.	$C \sqsubseteq \exists R.D, F \sqcap \exists R.E \sqsubseteq G \implies F \sqcap C \sqsubseteq G$ provided that: $\mathcal{O} \models \exists R.D \sqsubseteq \exists R.E$
IR6.	$C \sqsubseteq \exists R.D, F \sqcap \exists R^-.E \sqsubseteq G \implies F \sqcap C \sqsubseteq G$ provided that: $\mathcal{O} \models \exists R.D \sqsubseteq \exists R^-.E$
IR7.	$C \sqsubseteq \exists R.D, R \sqsubseteq T \implies C \sqsubseteq \exists T.D$
IR8.	$C \sqsubseteq \exists R.D, R^- \sqsubseteq T \implies C \sqsubseteq \exists T^-.D$
IR9.	$S \sqsubseteq R, F \sqcap \exists R.E \sqsubseteq G \implies F \sqcap \exists S.E \sqsubseteq G$
IR10.	$S \sqsubseteq R, F \sqcap \exists R^-.E \sqsubseteq G \implies F \sqcap \exists S^-.E \sqsubseteq G$

Fig. 2. Inference rules for forgetting role name r

4.2 Calculus for Eliminating r

Role name elimination follows a parallel structure to concept name elimination, employing a two-step calculus:

Step 1: Transform $\mathcal{O}$ into r-NF using the normalization rules;
Step 2: **Step 2**: Eliminate r through exhaustive application of inference rules (Fig. 2) to the normalized ontology.

The inference process combines positive occurrences of r (forms r-NF I, II, V, VI) with negative occurrences (forms r-NF III, VI, VII, VIII), resulting in a total of $4 \times 4 = 16$ combination cases. By introducing an involution mapping Inv where $\mathsf{Inv}(R) = r^-$ if $R = r$ and $\mathsf{Inv}(R) = r$ if $R = r^-$, we can express these 16 cases with 6 generalized cases (IR5—IR10). Upon achieving saturation and removing all r-axioms, we obtain an ontology $\mathcal{O}^{-\mathsf{r}}$ free of r.

Example 12. Consider the following $\mathcal{ELIH}$-ontology $\mathcal{O}$:

$$\{1.\ A \sqsubseteq \exists r.B \sqcap \exists s.C, 2.\ D \sqcap \exists r.E \sqsubseteq \exists r^-.F, 3.\ B \sqsubseteq E, 4.\ r \sqsubseteq t\}$$

Let $\mathcal{F} = \{r\}$. The first step is to compute the r-NF of $\mathcal{O}$ by applying the normalization rules described earlier. First, applying NR6 to CI 1:

$$\{5.\ A \sqsubseteq \exists r.B, 6.\ A \sqsubseteq \exists s.C, 2.\ D \sqcap \exists r.E \sqsubseteq \exists r^-.F, 3.\ B \sqsubseteq E, 4.\ r \sqsubseteq t\}$$

Since r appears multiple times, we apply NR7 to CI 2, where $Z_1 \in N_C$ is a fresh definer:

$$\{5.\ A \sqsubseteq \exists r.B, 6.\ A \sqsubseteq \exists s.C, 7.\ D \sqcap Z_1 \sqsubseteq \exists r^-.F, 8.\ \exists r.E \sqsubseteq Z_1, 3.\ B \sqsubseteq E, 4.\ r \sqsubseteq t\}$$

The above ontology is now in r-NF. The second step is to apply the inference rules in Fig. 2. Applying IR7 to CI 5 and RI 4, to CI 7 and RI 4 gives:

$$\{9.\ A \sqsubseteq \exists t.B, 10.\ D \sqcap Z_1 \sqsubseteq \exists t^-.F\}$$

Since $\mathcal{O} \not\models \exists r.F \sqsubseteq \exists r.E$, no inference rules are applicable to CIs 7 and 8. However, since $\mathcal{O} \models \exists r.B \sqsubseteq \exists r.E$, IR5 is applicable to CIs 5 and 8. This gives:

$$\{11.\ A \sqsubseteq Z_1\}$$

No further inference rules are applicable for the generation of r-irrelevant entailments, and the intermediate result contains CIs 3, 6, 9, 10, and 11. Applying IR1 to CIs 10 and 11 to eliminate the definer Z_1 gives:

$$\{12.\ D \sqcap A \sqsubseteq \exists t.F\}$$

In this case, $\{3, 6, 9, 12\}$ is a uniform Σ-interpolant of $\mathcal{O}$, where $\Sigma = \mathsf{sig}(\mathcal{O}) \setminus \mathcal{F}$.

Lemma 13. *For any $\mathcal{ELIH}$-ontology $\mathcal{O}$ in r-NF, the elimination procedure preserves all logical entailments over $\mathsf{sig}(\mathcal{O}) \setminus \{r\}$:*

$$\mathcal{O}^{-r} \models \alpha \text{ iff } \mathcal{O} \models \alpha$$

for any $\mathcal{ELIH}$-axiom α with $\mathsf{sig}(\alpha) \subseteq \mathsf{sig}(\mathcal{O}) \setminus \{r\}$.

The side conditions of the inference rules are verified using an external DL reasoner; we use HermiT [8]. Subsumption checking in $\mathcal{ELIH}$ is ExpTime-complete [2].

4.3 The Forgetting Process

Algorithm 1 illustrates the forgetting process. It takes as input an $\mathcal{ELIH}$-ontology $\mathcal{O}$ and a forgetting signature $\mathcal{F}$ comprising the names to be forgotten. A notable feature is the flexibility of the elimination sequence, which accommodates any order.

While each iteration may introduce definers requiring elimination from $\mathcal{O}^{-\mathcal{F}}$ using the concept elimination calculus, complete definer elimination is not always achievable. As already mentioned, UI cannot be guaranteed to be complete for $\mathcal{ELIH}$, as a finite uniform interpolant may not always exist within the logic. When the original ontology contains cyclic definitions, forgetting can yield an infinite set of axioms that cannot be finitely axiomatized within $\mathcal{ELIH}$. For instance, given $\mathcal{O} = \{B \sqsubseteq A, A \sqsubseteq \exists r.A\}$, forgetting A would yield $\{B \sqsubseteq \exists r.\top, B \sqsubseteq \exists r.\exists r.\top, \ldots\}$, an infinite sequence.

Our method addresses this challenge through a blocking-like technique that ensures termination by detecting when forgetting a definer produces a syntactic pattern identical to a previous intermediate result. This indicates entry into a forgetting cycle where eliminating one definer introduces another that takes its place. Importantly, cycles do not necessarily prevent finding finite uniform interpolants, as some names may be removed during the forgetting of other names, eliminating many cyclic definitions. However, when cycles persist, our approach halts computation and declares forgetting unsuccessful rather than entering infinite loops.

Algorithm 1. The Forgetting Process

Require: An $\mathcal{ELIH}$-ontology $\mathcal{O}$, a forgetting signature $\mathcal{F}$
Ensure: An $\mathcal{ELIH}$-ontology $\mathcal{V}$ with $\mathsf{sig}(\mathcal{V}) \cap \mathcal{F} = \emptyset$

function FORGET($\mathcal{O}, \mathcal{F}$)
  $\mathcal{V} \leftarrow$ SIMPLIFY($\mathcal{O}$) ▷ Apply simplifications
  $\mathcal{D} \leftarrow \emptyset$ ▷ Track introduced definers
  for each name $X \in \mathcal{F}$ **do** ▷ Eliminate $\mathcal{F}$-names
    $\mathcal{V}, \mathcal{D}_X \leftarrow$ NORMALIZE($\mathcal{V}, X$) ▷ Apply normalization rules NR1–NR10
    $\mathcal{V} \leftarrow$ FORGET($\mathcal{V}, X$) ▷ Apply inference rules IR1–IR10
    $\mathcal{D} \leftarrow \mathcal{D} \cup \mathcal{D}_X$ ▷ Collect introduced definers
    $\mathcal{V} \leftarrow$ SIMPLIFY($\mathcal{V}$)
  end for
  if $\mathcal{D} \neq \emptyset$ **then**
    for each definer $Z \in \mathcal{D}$ **do** ▷ Eliminate definers
      $\mathcal{V} \leftarrow$ FORGET($\mathcal{V}, Z$) ▷ Apply inference rules IR1–IR4
      $\mathcal{V} \leftarrow$ SIMPLIFY($\mathcal{V}$)
    end for
  end if
  return $\mathcal{V}$
end function

In the example above, our method would yield $\{B \sqsubseteq Z, Z \sqsubseteq \exists r.Z\}$ where $Z \in \mathsf{N_C}$ is a newly introduced definer. Recognizing the syntactic similarity between the original pattern $\{B \sqsubseteq A, A \sqsubseteq \exists r.A\}$ and the resulting pattern $\{B \sqsubseteq Z, Z \sqsubseteq \exists r.Z\}$, our method retains Z in the result and declares forgetting unsuccessful. This approach maintains semantic structure by introducing and preserving definers, whereas approaches like LETHE and FAME employ fixpoints to obtain finitely represented uniform interpolants. While fixpoint solutions exist [3], their implementation faces practical constraints due to limited support in mainstream reasoning tools and the OWL API.

Our termination strategy ensures that the method always produces a finite set of axioms, even when cycles exist over symbols to be forgotten. This guarantees that our forgetting procedure terminates with a finite result, albeit potentially incomplete in cases involving irreducible cyclic structures.

Theorem 14. *For $\mathcal{ELIH}$-ontology $\mathcal{O}$ and forgetting signature $\mathcal{F} \subseteq \mathsf{sig}(\mathcal{O})$, our method has the following properties:*

- *Always terminates and produces an $\mathcal{ELIH}$-ontology $\mathcal{V}$*
- *If $\mathcal{V}$ is definer-free, it constitutes:*
  - *A result of forgetting $\mathcal{F}$ from $\mathcal{O}$, and*
  - *A uniform Σ-interpolant of $\mathcal{O}$ where $\Sigma = \mathsf{sig}(\mathcal{O}) \setminus \mathcal{F}$.*

Table 1. Statistical information about Oxford-ISG and NCBO BioPortal

Oxford-ISG		Min	Max	Median	Mean	90th%ile	BioPortal		Min	Max	Median	Mean	90th%ile
I	$\|N_C\|$	0	1582	86	191	545	I	$\|N_C\|$	0	784	127	192	214
	$\|N_R\|$	0	332	10	29	80		$\|N_R\|$	0	122	5	15	17
	|Onto|	0	990	162	262	658		|Onto|	0	982	283	312	346
II	$\|N_C\|$	200	5877	1665	1769	2801	II	$\|N_C\|$	5	4530	1185	1459	1591
	$\|N_R\|$	0	887	11	34	61		$\|N_R\|$	0	131	12	30	33
	|Onto|	1008	4976	2282	2416	3937		|Onto|	1023	4977	2401	2619	2782
III	$\|N_C\|$	1162	9809	4042	5067	8758	III	$\|N_C\|$	432	8340	4363	4387	4806
	$\|N_R\|$	1	158	4	23	158		$\|N_R\|$	0	135	17	30	34
	|Onto|	5112	9783	7277	7195	9179		|Onto|	5084	8836	6934	6912	7109

5 Empirical Evaluation

We have implemented our method as a Java prototype using OWL API 3.5.7[3] and conducted comparative evaluations against LETHE, the current state-of-the-art system.[4] The evaluation utilized two industry benchmarks (Table 1): (i) Oxford ISG Library[5] featuring 797 ontologies from diverse sources and (ii) NCBO BioPortal (March 2017 snapshot) [29] featuring 438 biomedical ontologies. For systematic analysis, we selected ontologies with axiom count $|\text{Onto}| < 10000$ and categorized them by size:

Oxford ISG Corpus (488 ontologies after acyclic $\mathcal{ELIH}$-fragment refinement, leading to 8.9% axiom reduction):
- PART I: 355 ontologies ($10 \leq |\text{Onto}| < 1000$)
- PART II: 108 ontologies ($1000 \leq |\text{Onto}| < 5000$)
- PART III: 25 ontologies ($5000 \leq |\text{Onto}| \leq 10000$)

BioPortal Corpus (326 ontologies after refinement):
- PART I: 202 ontologies ($10 \leq |\text{Onto}| < 1000$)
- PART II: 104 ontologies ($1000 \leq |\text{Onto}| < 5000$)
- PART III: 20 ontologies ($5000 \leq |\text{Onto}| \leq 10000$)

To simulate real-world forgetting scenarios, we conducted three series of experiments varying the size of the signature $\mathcal{F}$: (i) forgetting 10% of concept and role names (small-size); (ii) forgetting 30% of concept and role names (medium-size); (iii) forgetting 50% of concept and role names (large-size).

The forgetting signatures were constructed using a shuffling algorithm to ensure unbiased testing. All experiments were conducted on an Intel Core i7-9750H processor (6 cores, 2.70 GHz) with 12 GB DDR4-1600 MHz RAM and 9 GB heap allocation. A forgetting attempt was considered successful if it: (i) eliminated all names in $\mathcal{F}$; (ii) produced a definer-free result; (iii) completed within 300 s (timeout threshold); and (iv) operated within allocated memory constraints (memory allowance).

[3] http://owlcs.github.io/owlapi/.

[4] https://lat.inf.tu-dresden.de/~koopmann/LETHE/ comparison with NUI was not possible due to its unavailability (as of February 20, 2025).

[5] http://krr-nas.cs.ox.ac.uk/ontologies/lib/.

Table 2. Experimental results (Time (sec.): Time Consumption, Mem (MB): Memory Consumption, SR: Success Rate, TR: Timeout Rate, MR: Memory Overflow Rate, RER: Runtime Error Rate)

Oxford	$\mathcal{F}$%	PART	Time	Memory	SR	TR	RER	BioPortal	$\mathcal{F}$%	PART	Time	Memory	SR	TR	RER
LETHE	10%	I	4.23	37.06	92.42	4.10	3.48	LETHE	10%	I	5.03	39.96	92.33	5.04	2.63
		II	9.72	58.76	86.68	11.07	2.25			II	11.16	59.04	85.58	10.58	3.57
		III	14.58	88.54	77.86	22.14	0.00			III	14.89	95.83	75.46	24.54	0.00
	30%	I	12.46	52.24	87.09	9.45	3.48		30%	I	14.07	53.26	83.29	14.08	2.63
		II	29.23	75.16	75.41	22.35	2.24			II	32.11	88.33	73.01	23.42	3.57
		III	41.36	123.11	67.82	32.18	0.00			III	46.06	133.20	65.50	34.50	0.00
	50%	I	14.63	71.36	79.91	16.61	3.48		50%	I	14.23	76.48	77.24	20.13	2.63
		II	43.16	134.65	71.31	26.45	2.24			II	45.73	140.11	69.00	27.43	3.57
		III	74.02	189.13	64.55	35.45	0.00			III	81.53	187.93	60.60	39.40	0.00
Proto	10%	I	0.17	24.33	100	0.00	0.00	Proto	10%	I	0.16	21.34	100	0.00	0.00
		II	0.46	38.54	100	0.00	0.00			II	0.43	34.01	100	0.00	0.00
		III	0.85	59.21	100	0.00	0.00			III	0.83	52.03	100	0.00	0.00
	30%	I	0.27	35.66	100	0.00	0.00		30%	I	0.31	31.23	100	0.00	0.00
		II	0.74	51.02	100	0.00	0.00			II	0.67	47.54	100	0.00	0.00
		III	1.05	86.77	100	0.00	0.00			III	1.04	78.27	100	0.00	0.00
	50%	I	0.80	48.13	100	0.00	0.00		50%	I	0.76	44.09	100	0.00	0.00
		II	1.33	91.21	100	0.00	0.00			II	1.34	88.55	100	0.00	0.00
		III	1.54	130.32	100	0.00	0.00			III	1.53	120.81	100	0.00	0.00

The experimental results (Table 2) demonstrate notable performance differentials between our prototype and LETHE. Specifically, our prototype maintained consistent success rates of 100% across all test configurations. In contrast, LETHE exhibited performance degradation patterns correlated with ontology size and forgetting percentage. On the Oxford-ISG corpus, LETHE's success rate dropped from 92% for small ontologies with 10% forgetting to 65% for large ontologies with 50% forgetting, with timeout rates reaching 35% for large-scale forgetting operations. Similarly, on the BioPortal corpus, performance declined from 92% success rate for small ontologies with 10% forgetting to 61% for large ontologies with 50% forgetting, with timeout rates peaking at 39% for large-scale operations. Additionally, LETHE encountered consistent runtime errors across both corpora, most likely because of compatibility issues coming up between the OWL API version LETHE employed and the test ontologies.

Regarding computational efficiency, our prototype demonstrated substantial advantages in both time and memory usage. Time-wise, our implementation proved significantly faster, operating 52 times faster on Oxford-ISG and 37 times faster on BioPortal datasets. This performance gap became more pronounced with larger forgetting signatures. For instance, with PART III ontologies and 50% forgetting, our prototype completed tasks in 1.54 s compared to LETHE's 74.02 s, while maintaining consistent scaling factors across different ontology sizes.

Memory utilization patterns also favored our prototype, showing consistently lower memory footprints across all test cases. Memory usage scaled more grace-

Table 3. Performance metrics for forgetting tasks on consecutive SNOMED CT releases

Tasks	$\|\mathcal{F}_\mathsf{C}\|$	$\|\mathcal{F}_\mathsf{R}\|$	$\|\sqsubseteq\|$	Time	Tasks	$\|\mathcal{F}_\mathsf{C}\|$	$\|\mathcal{F}_\mathsf{R}\|$	$\|\sqsubseteq\|$	Time	Tasks	$\|\mathcal{F}_\mathsf{C}\|$	$\|\mathcal{F}_\mathsf{R}\|$	$\|\sqsubseteq\|$	Time	Tasks	$\|\mathcal{F}_\mathsf{C}\|$	$\|\mathcal{F}_\mathsf{R}\|$	$\|\sqsubseteq\|$	Time
(2303,2304)	834	2	771K	75	(2308,2309)	1495	28	774K	115	(2401,2402)	876	1	771K	80	(2406,2407)	451	0	774K	50
(2304,2305)	1127	4	772K	95	(2309,2310)	1236	12	774K	98	(2402,2403)	523	1	772K	55	(2407,2408)	871	1	774K	78
(2305,2306)	1718	35	772K	125	(2310,2311)	1367	2	775K	105	(2403,2404)	128	0	773K	9	(2408,2409)	928	2	775K	83
(2306,2307)	962	3	773K	85	(2311,2312)	473	0	775K	48	(2404,2405)	287	2	773K	35	(2409,2410)	1382	0	776K	110
(2307,2308)	1743	19	773K	130	(2312,2401)	937	0	776K	85	(2405,2406)	916	3	774K	82	(2410,2411)	715	0	776K	65

fully with ontology size: for PART III ontologies with 50% forgetting, our method required 130.50 MB versus LETHE's 189.13 MB (31% reduction). This performance gap widened proportionally as ontology size and forgetting percentage increased.

A key distinction between the two systems lies in their definer introduction strategies. LETHE employs a clause-flattening algorithm with exponential complexity, introducing $O(2^n)$ definers in the worst case, where n is the number of input clauses [19]. In contrast, our method implements an optimized strategy that maintains linear growth w.r.t. input size by introducing definers only when structurally necessary.

6 Case Study Semantic Difference in SNOMED CT

We conducted an extensive evaluation of our UI method's practical efficiency through analyzing semantic evolutionary changes in SNOMED CT, examining 20 consecutive international releases. This analysis aimed to validate our method's potential as a back-end technology for SNOMED's knowledge base management system, with particular emphasis on QA in healthcare data. We developed a UI-Diff framework that integrates (i) our prototype for uniform interpolant computation (**Step 1**), and HermiT [8] for semantic difference detection (**Step 2**). This integration enables precise identification of evolutionary semantic changes.

The performance analysis (Table 3) across the evolving SNOMED CT releases (formatted as YYMM, e.g., 2309 for September 2023) reveals several key insights into our method's effectiveness and efficiency. Our method successfully handled a range of forgetting signature sizes, from minimal changes ($|\mathcal{F}_\mathsf{C}| = 128$, $|\mathcal{F}_\mathsf{R}| = 0$) to substantial modifications ($|\mathcal{F}_\mathsf{C}| = 1718$, $|\mathcal{F}_\mathsf{R}| = 35$). Processing time scaled efficiently with signature size: negligible time for minor changes (2403,2404), up to 150 s for major changes (2308,2309), with most tasks completing in 100 s despite the substantial terminology scales. This consistent performance shows robust handling of both incremental updates and major modeling changes throughout the evolution of SNOMED CT.

Figure 3 shows evolutionary changes across SNOMED CT releases, with version pairs on the x-axis and UI-witness counts on the y-axis. These witnesses include both explicit ones (verified through HermiT's entailment checking) and implicit ones (computed via both UI and entailment checking). This visualization captures the dynamic evolution of the SNOMED CT International edition over time. Notably, the number of UI witnesses, which were derived using our UI prototype, averages 69.1% of the total derived witnesses, indicating a substantial portion of implicit knowledge capture. This underscores the practical utility and robustness of the UI approach in identifying and preserving essential semantic elements through successive ontology versions.

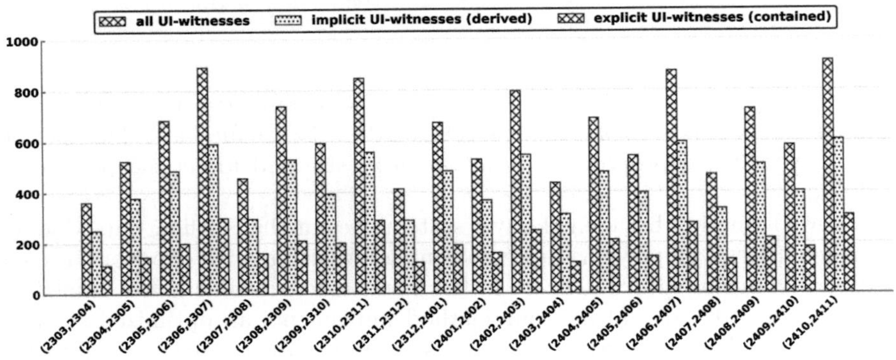

Fig. 3. Semantic difference across 20 consecutive releases of SNOMED CT (2023–2024)

Our UI method serves three purposes: to identify semantic changes between ontology versions, to ensure that changes are safe in the sense of being conservative extensions [7,27], and to identify unexpected semantic consequences in new releases. This implementation has strengthened SNOMED's QA framework by enabling systematic validation of ontological evolution and early detection of semantic inconsistencies.

7 Conclusion and Future Work

We have developed a highly optimized UI and forgetting method tailored for semantic change detection in large-scale ontologies. Our approach overcomes major limitations of existing methods, demonstrating superior performance on standard benchmarks through linear complexity normalization and efficient inference calculi specialized for $\mathcal{ELIH}$-ontologies. The method's practical effectiveness is evidenced by extensive testing on SNOMED CT's monthly releases, where it successfully handles large-scale semantic change detection tasks that are beyond the capabilities of existing tools.

Future work will focus on enhancing the system's analytical capabilities through fine-grained UI-witness classification and change justification generation [11]. We also plan to extend our approach to support more expressive DLs and investigate optimization strategies for larger ontological structures. These enhancements will advance automated ontology management and facilitate maintaining high-quality, semantically consistent knowledge bases across diverse domains.

Acknowledgments. We thank the reviewers for their useful comments and suggestions. This work was (partially) supported by NSFC under Grant (62476125), Jiangsu Province Innovation and Entrepreneurship Team Project under Grant (JSSCTD202202), the Xiaomi Foundation, and the Royal Society (IEC/NSFC/242439).

Disclosure of Interests. The authors declare that they have no competing interests relevant to the content of this article.

References

1. Antoniou, G., van Harmelen, F.: Web Ontology Language: OWL, pp. 67–92. Springer, Heidelberg (2004)
2. Baader, F., Horrocks, I., Lutz, C., Sattler, U.: An Introduction to Description Logic. Cambridge University Press (2017)
3. Calvanese, D., Giacomo, G.D., Lenzerini, M.: Reasoning in expressive description logics with fixpoints based on automata on infinite trees. In: Proceedings of the IJCAI'99, pp. 84–89. Morgan Kaufmann (1999)
4. Chen, J., Alghamdi, G., Schmidt, R.A., Walther, D., Gao, Y.: Ontology extraction for large ontologies via modularity and forgetting. In: K-CAP'19, pp. 45–52. ACM (2019)
5. D'Agostino, G., Lenzi, G.: Bisimulation quantifiers and uniform interpolation for guarded first order logic. Theor. Comput. Sci. **563**, 75–85 (2015)
6. Day-Richter, J., Harris, M.A., Haendel, M., Group, T.G.O.O.E.W., Lewis, S.: OBO-Edit: an ontology editor for biologists. Bioinformatics **23**(16), 2198–2200 (2007)
7. Ghilardi, S., Lutz, C., Wolter, F.: Did I damage my ontology? A case for conservative extensions in description logics. In: Proceedings of the KR'06, pp. 187–197. AAAI Press (2006)
8. Glimm, B., Horrocks, I., Motik, B., Stoilos, G., Wang, Z.: HermiT: an OWL 2 reasoner. J. Autom. Reason. **53**(3), 245–269 (2014). https://doi.org/10.1007/s10817-014-9305-1
9. Grau, B.C., Horrocks, I., Motik, B., Parsia, B., Patel-Schneider, P.F., Sattler, U.: OWL 2: the next step for OWL. J. Web Semant. **6**(4), 309–322 (2008)
10. Herzig, A., Mengin, J.: Uniform interpolation by resolution in modal logic. In: Hölldobler, S., Lutz, C., Wansing, H. (eds.) JELIA 2008. LNCS (LNAI), vol. 5293, pp. 219–231. Springer, Heidelberg (2008). https://doi.org/10.1007/978-3-540-87803-2_19
11. Horridge, M.: Justification based explanation in ontologies. Ph.D. thesis, The University of Manchester, UK (2011)
12. Horridge, M., Gonçalves, R.S., Nyulas, C.I., Tudorache, T., Musen, M.A.: WebProtégé: A cloud-based ontology editor. In: Proceedings of the WWW'19, pp. 686–689. ACM (2019)
13. Kalyanpur, A., Parsia, B., Sirin, E., Grau, B.C., Hendler, J.A.: Swoop: a web ontology editing browser. J. Web Semant. **4**(2), 144–153 (2006)
14. Klein, M., Fensel, D., Kiryakov, A., Ognyanov, D.: Ontoview: comparing and versioning ontologies (2002). http://iswc2002.semanticweb.org/posters/klein-etal.pdf
15. Konev, B., Ludwig, M., Walther, D., Wolter, F.: The logical difference for the lightweight description logic $\mathcal{EL}$. J. Artif. Intell. Res. **44**, 633–708 (2012)

16. Konev, B., Walther, D., Wolter, F.: The logical difference problem for description logic terminologies. In: Armando, A., Baumgartner, P., Dowek, G. (eds.) IJCAR 2008. LNCS (LNAI), vol. 5195, pp. 259–274. Springer, Heidelberg (2008). https://doi.org/10.1007/978-3-540-71070-7_21
17. Konev, B., Walther, D., Wolter, F.: Forgetting and uniform interpolation in large-scale description logic terminologies. In: Proceedings of the IJCAI'09, pp. 830–835. IJCAI/AAAI Press (2009)
18. Kontchakov, R., Wolter, F., Zakharyaschev, M.: Logic-based ontology comparison and module extraction, with an application to DL-Lite. Artif. Intell. **174**(15), 1093–1141 (2010)
19. Koopmann, P.: Practical Uniform Interpolation for Expressive Description Logics. Ph.D. thesis, The University of Manchester, UK (2015)
20. Koopmann, P.: LETHE: forgetting and uniform interpolation for expressive description logics. KI - Künstliche Intelligenz **34**(3), 381–387 (2020). https://doi.org/10.1007/s13218-020-00655-w
21. Koopmann, P., Schmidt, R.A.: Uniform interpolation of $\mathcal{ALC}$-ontologies using fixpoints. In: Proceedings of the FroCoS'13. LNCS, vol. 8152, pp. 87–102. Springer (2013)
22. Koopmann, P., Schmidt, R.A.: Saturated-based forgetting in the description logic $\mathcal{SIF}$. In: Proceedings of the DL'15, vol. 1350. CEUR Workshop Proc. (2015)
23. Liu, H., Lutz, C., Milicic, M., Wolter, F.: Updating description logic ABoxes. In: Proceedings of the KR'06, pp. 46–56. AAAI Press (2006)
24. Liu, Z., Lu, C., Alghamdi, G., Schmidt, R.A., Zhao, Y.: Tracking semantic evolutionary changes in large-scale ontological knowledge bases. In: Proceedings of the CIKM'21, pp. 1130–1139. ACM (2021)
25. Ludwig, M., Konev, B.: Practical uniform interpolation and forgetting for $\mathcal{ALC}$ TBoxes with applications to logical difference. In: Proceedings of the KR'14, pp. 318–327. AAAI Press (2014)
26. Lutz, C., Seylan, I., Wolter, F.: An automata-theoretic approach to uniform interpolation and approximation in the description logic $\mathcal{EL}$. In: Proceedings of the KR'12, pp. 286–296. AAAI Press (2012)
27. Lutz, C., Wolter, F.: Deciding inseparability and conservative extensions in the description logic $\mathcal{EL}$. J. Symb. Comput. **45**(2), 194–228 (2010)
28. Lutz, C., Wolter, F.: Foundations for uniform interpolation and forgetting in expressive description logics. In: Proceedings of the IJCAI'11, pp. 989–995. IJCAI/AAAI Press (2011)
29. Matentzoglu, N., Parsia, B.: BioPortal Snapshot 30.03.2017, March 2017. https://doi.org/10.5281/zenodo.439510
30. Musen, M.A.: The Protégé project: a look back and a look forward. AI Matters **1**(4), 4–12 (2015)
31. Nikitina, N., Rudolph, S.: (Non-)succinctness of uniform interpolants of general terminologies in the description logic $\mathcal{EL}$. Artif. Intell. **215**, 120–140 (2014)
32. Noy, N.F., Musen, M.A.: PROMPTDIFF: a fixed-point algorithm for comparing ontology versions. In: Proceedings of the AAAI/IAAI'02, pp. 744–750. AAAI/MIT Press (2002)
33. Pitts, A.M.: On an interpretation of second order quantification in first order intuitionistic propositional logic. J. Symb. Log. **57**(1), 33–52 (1992)
34. Rector, A.L., Rogers, J., Zanstra, P.E., van der Haring, E.J.: OpenGALEN: open source medical terminology and tools. In: Proceedings of the AMIA'03. AMIA (2003)

35. Robinson, J.A.: A machine-oriented logic based on the resolution principle. J. ACM **12**(1), 23–41 (1965)
36. Robinson, J.A., Voronkov, A. (eds.): Handbook of Automated Reasoning (in 2 volumes). Elsevier and MIT Press (2001)
37. Sioutos, N., de Coronado, S., Haber, M.W., Hartel, F.W., Shaiu, W., Wright, L.W.: NCI thesaurus: a semantic model integrating cancer-related clinical and molecular information. J. Biomed. Inform. **40**(1), 30–43 (2007)
38. Spackman, K.A.: SNOMED RT and SNOMED CT. Promise of an international clinical ontology. M.D. Comput. **17** (2000)
39. Staab, S., Studer, R. (eds.): Handbook on Ontologies. IHIS. Springer, Heidelberg (2009). https://doi.org/10.1007/978-3-540-92673-3_35
40. The Gene Ontology Consortium: The gene ontology resource: enriching a gold mine. Nucleic Acids Res. **49**(Database-Issue), D325–D334 (2021)
41. Visser, A.: Bisimulations, Model Descriptions and Propositional Quantifiers. Logic Group Preprint Series. Utrecht University (1996)
42. Wang, K., Wang, Z., Topor, R.W., Pan, J.Z., Antoniou, G.: Eliminating concepts and roles from ontologies in expressive descriptive logics. Comput. Intell. **30**(2), 205–232 (2014)
43. Wu, X., Deng, W., Lu, C., Feng, H., Zhao, Y.: UI-FAME: a high-performance forgetting system for creating views of ontologies. In: Proceedings of the CIKM'20, pp. 3473–3476. ACM (2020)
44. Yang, Z., Zhao, Y.: What a surprise! Computing rewritten modules can be as efficient as computing subset modules. In: Proceedings of the CIKM 2024, pp. 2940–2949. ACM (2024)
45. Zhao, Y.: Efficient computation of signature-restricted views for semantic web ontologies. In: Proceedings of the WWW'24, pp. 1945–1953. ACM (2024)
46. Zhao, Y., et al.: Tracking logical difference in large-scale ontologies: a forgetting-based approach. In: Proceedings of the AAAI'19, pp. 3116–3124. AAAI Press (2019)
47. Zhao, Y., Schmidt, R.A.: Forgetting concept and role symbols in $\mathcal{ALCOIH}\mu^+(\nabla, \sqcap)$-ontologies. In: Proceedings of the IJCAI'16, pp. 1345–1352. IJCAI/AAAI Press (2016)
48. Zhao, Y., Schmidt, R.A.: On concept forgetting in description logics with qualified number restrictions. In: Proceedings of the IJCAI'18, pp. 1984–1990. IJCAI/AAAI Press (2018)

Concrete Domains Meet Expressive Cardinality Restrictions in Description Logics

Franz Baader[1,2], Stefan Borgwardt[1], Filippo De Bortoli[1,2(✉)], and Patrick Koopmann[3]

[1] Institute of Theoretical Computer Science, TU Dresden, Dresden, Germany
franz.baader@tu-dresden.de, stefan.borgwardt@tu-dresden.de
[2] Center for Scalable Data Analytics and Artificial Intelligence (ScaDS.AI), Dresden/Leipzig, Germany
filippo.de_bortoli@tu-dresden.de
[3] Department of Computer Science, Vrije Universiteit Amsterdam, Amsterdam, The Netherlands
p.k.koopmann@vu.nl

Abstract. Standard Description Logics (DLs) can encode quantitative aspects of an application domain through either *number restrictions*, which constrain the number of individuals that are in a certain relationship with an individual, or *concrete domains*, which can be used to assign concrete values to individuals using so-called features. These two mechanisms have been extended towards very expressive DLs, for which reasoning nevertheless remains decidable. Number restrictions have been generalized to more powerful comparisons of sets of role successors in $\mathcal{ALCSCC}$, while the comparison of feature values of different individuals in $\mathcal{ALC}(\mathfrak{D})$ has been studied in the context of ω-admissible concrete domains $\mathfrak{D}$. In this paper, we combine both formalisms and investigate the complexity of reasoning in the thus obtained DL $\mathcal{ALCOSCC}(\mathfrak{D})$, which additionally includes the ability to refer to specific individuals by name. We show that, in spite of its high expressivity, the consistency problem for this DL is ExpTime-complete, assuming that the constraint satisfaction problem of $\mathfrak{D}$ is also decidable in exponential time. It is thus not higher than the complexity of the basic DL $\mathcal{ALC}$. At the same time, we show that many natural extensions to this DL, including a tighter integration of the concrete domain and number restrictions, lead to undecidability.

Keywords: Description Logics · Automated Deduction · Concrete Domains · Cardinality Constraints

1 Introduction

Description logics (DLs) [6,9] are a well-investigated family of logic-based knowledge representation languages, which can be used to formalize the terminological

C. Barrett and U. Waldmann (Eds.): CADE 2025, LNAI 15943, pp. 676–695, 2025.
https://doi.org/10.1007/978-3-031-99984-0_35

knowledge of an application domain in a machine-processable way. For instance, the popular Web Ontology Language OWL[1] is based on an expressive DL and large medical ontologies such as SNOMED CT[2] and Galen[3] have been developed using appropriate DLs. A key feature of DLs is the ability to construct descriptions of complex concepts (i.e., sets of individuals sharing certain properties) using concept names (unary predicates) and role names (binary predicates). For example, the concept of a parent can be described as $\mathsf{Human} \sqcap \exists \mathsf{child}.\mathsf{Human}$.Knowledge about the relationship between concepts can then be expressed using concept inclusions (CIs), such as $\mathsf{Human} \sqcap \exists \mathsf{child}.\mathsf{Human} \sqsubseteq \exists \mathsf{eligible}.\mathsf{TaxBreak}$, which says that parents are eligible for a tax break.

Such purely qualitative statements are not always sufficient to express quantitative information (e.g. the number of children required for a tax break) that is relevant for an application domain. *Qualified number restrictions* that constrain the number of role successors belonging to a certain concept by a fixed natural number can be employed in DLs to express such quantitative information; e.g., $\mathsf{Human} \sqcap (\geq 3\,\mathsf{child}.\mathsf{Human}) \sqsubseteq \exists \mathsf{eligible}.\mathsf{TaxBreak}$ says that a tax break isavailable if one has at least three children.*Concrete domain restrictions* can represent a different type of quantitative information, where concrete objects such as numbers or strings can be assigned to individuals using partial functions (*features*). For example, a tax break might only be available if the annual salary is not too high. The CI $\mathsf{Human} \sqcap (\geq 3\,\mathsf{child}.\mathsf{Human}) \sqcap \exists \mathsf{salary}.{<_{100{,}000}} \sqsubseteq \exists \mathsf{eligible}.\mathsf{TaxBreak}$ specifies at least three children and an annual salary of less than 100,000 € as eligibility criteria for a tax break.

Both (qualified) number restrictions [17,18] and concrete domain restrictions [8] have been introduced early on in DL research, but it turned out that they create considerable algorithmic challenges. For $\mathcal{ALCQ}$, the extension of the basic DL $\mathcal{ALC}$ with qualified number restrictions, it was open for a decade whether the increase in expressivity also increases the complexity of reasoning if numbers in number restrictions are assumed to be represented in binary, until Tobies [30,31] was able to show that it stays the same (PSPACE without and EXPTIME with CIs). It also turned out that the unrestricted use of transitive roles within number restrictions can cause undecidability [20].In [3], it was shown that reasoning in $\mathcal{ALCSCC}$, which extends $\mathcal{ALCQ}$ with very expressive counting constraints on role successors expressed in the logic QFBAPA [22], still has the same complexity as in $\mathcal{ALC}$ and $\mathcal{ALCQ}$. In this logic, one can, e.g., describe humans that have exactly as many cars as children as $\mathsf{Human} \sqcap \mathsf{succ}(|\mathsf{own} \cap \mathsf{Car}| = |\mathsf{child} \cap \mathsf{Human}|)$, without having to specify the exact numbers of cars and children. Such statements cannot even be expressed in full first-order logic [7].

The decidability result for $\mathcal{ALC}(\mathfrak{D})$, i.e., $\mathcal{ALC}$ extended with an admissible concrete domain $\mathfrak{D}$, in [8] did not take CIs into account. In the presence of CIs, integrating even rather simple concrete domains into the DL $\mathcal{ALC}$ may cause undecidability [10,26]. In [27], it was proved that integrating a so-called ω-

[1] https://www.w3.org/TR/owl2-overview/.
[2] https://www.snomed.org/.
[3] https://bioportal.bioontology.org/ontologies/GALEN.

admissible concrete domain into $\mathcal{ALC}$ leaves reasoning decidable also in the presence of CIs. That paper gives two examples of such concrete domains (Allen's interval algebra [1] and RCC8 [29]). Using well-known notions and results from model theory, additional ω-admissible concrete domains were exhibited in [10,11], for example the rational numbers with comparisons $\mathfrak{Q} := (\mathbb{Q}, <, =, >)$. Decidability results for $\mathcal{ALC}(\mathfrak{D})$ in the presence of CIs for concrete domains $\mathfrak{D}$ that are not ω-admissible can be found in [14,15,23].A simpler, but considerably more restrictive way of achieving decidability is to use unary concrete domains [19].

In this paper, we study $\mathcal{ALCOSCC}(\mathfrak{D})$, a combination of the DLs $\mathcal{ALCSCC}$ and $\mathcal{ALC}(\mathfrak{D})$ with ω-admissible concrete domains $\mathfrak{D}$ as well as nominals ($\mathcal{O}$). However, our logic goes beyond a pure combination of number restrictions and concrete domains by additionally allowing them to interact. For a numerical concrete domain, it seems natural to use the values of concrete features directly in the QFBAPA constraints, e.g. to describe people that own more books than their age. We show, however, that this unrestricted combination easily leads to undecidability. Instead, we use concrete domain constraints to define roles, which can then be employed within QFBAPA constraints. For example, the *concrete role* $(\mathsf{salary} < \mathtt{next}\,\mathsf{salary})$ connects an individual to all individuals that have a higher salary. One can use this to describe all persons that have a lower salary than at least half of their children with $\mathsf{succ}(|\mathsf{child} \cap (\mathsf{salary} < \mathtt{next}\,\mathsf{salary})| > |\mathsf{child} \cap (\mathsf{salary} \geq \mathtt{next}\,\mathsf{salary})|)$. However, we show that the unrestricted use of such concrete roles also leads to undecidability. Hence, we additionally restrict them to pairs of individuals that are already connected by a role name.

Our main result is that the complexity of reasoning in $\mathcal{ALCOSCC}(\mathfrak{D})$ stays in ExpTime if the complexity of reasoning in $\mathfrak{D}$ is in ExpTime. There are few results in the literature that determine the exact complexity of reasoning in DLs with concrete domains [13,15,23,25]. Only [25] and [13] consider ω-admissible concrete domains, and the ExpTime-completeness result in the former is restricted to a specific temporal concrete domain. Our paper extends the results of the latter from $\mathcal{ALC}(\mathfrak{D})$ to $\mathcal{ALCOSCC}(\mathfrak{D})$ and is generic since it holds for all ω-admissible concrete domains with a decision problem in ExpTime. Finally, apart from the aforementioned undecidability results, we show that adding transitive roles also makes reasoning undecidable, even under strong syntactic restrictions. All proof details can be found in [5].

2 Preliminaries

Concrete Domains. We adopt the term *concrete domain* to refer to a relational structure $\mathfrak{D} = (D, P_1^D, P_2^D, \dots)$ over a non-empty, countable relational signature $\{P_1, P_2, \dots\}$, where D is a non-empty set, and each predicate P_i has an associated arity $k_i \in \mathbb{N}$ and is interpreted by a relation $P_i^D \subseteq D^{k_i}$. An example is the structure $\mathfrak{Q} := (\mathbb{Q}, <, =, >)$ over the rational numbers $\mathbb{Q}$ with standard binary order and equality relations. Given a countably infinite set V of variables, a *constraint system* over V is a set $\mathfrak{C}$ of *constraints* $P(v_1, \dots, v_k)$, where

$v_1, \ldots, v_k \in V$ and P is a k-ary predicate of $\mathfrak{D}$. We denote by $V(\mathfrak{C})$ the set of variables that occur in $\mathfrak{C}$. The constraint system $\mathfrak{C}$ is *satisfiable* if there is a mapping $h\colon V(\mathfrak{C}) \to D$, called *solution* of $\mathfrak{C}$, such that $P(v_1, \ldots, v_k) \in \mathfrak{C}$ implies $(h(v_1), \ldots, h(v_k)) \in P^D$. The *constraint satisfaction problem* for $\mathfrak{D}$, denoted CSP($\mathfrak{D}$), asks if a given finite constraint system $\mathfrak{C}$ over $\mathfrak{D}$ is satisfiable. The CSP of $\mathfrak{Q}$ is decidable in polynomial time, by reduction to $<$-cycle detection: for example, the clique $x_1 < x_2,\ x_2 < x_3,\ x_3 < x_1$ is unsatisfiable over $\mathfrak{Q}$.

To ensure that reasoning in DLs with concrete domain restrictions remains decidable, we impose further properties on $\mathfrak{D}$ regarding its predicates and the compositionality of its CSP for finite and countable constraint systems. We say that $\mathfrak{D}$ is a *patchwork* if it satisfies the following conditions:[4]

JEPD if $k \geq 1$ and $\mathfrak{D}$ has k-ary predicates, then these predicates partition D^k;

JD there is a quantifier-free, equality-free first-order formula $\phi_=(x, y)$ over the signature of $\mathfrak{D}$ that defines equality between two elements of $\mathfrak{D}$;

AP if $\mathfrak{B}$, $\mathfrak{C}$ are constraint systems and
$P(v_1, \ldots, v_k) \in \mathfrak{B}$ iff $P(v_1, \ldots, v_k) \in \mathfrak{C}$

holds for all $v_1, \ldots, v_k \in V(\mathfrak{B}) \cap V(\mathfrak{C})$ and all k-ary predicates P over $\mathfrak{D}$, then $\mathfrak{B}$ and $\mathfrak{C}$ are satisfiable iff $\mathfrak{B} \cup \mathfrak{C}$ is satisfiable.

If $\mathfrak{D}$ is a patchwork, we call a constraint system $\mathfrak{C}$ *complete* if, for all $k \in \mathbb{N}$ for which $\mathfrak{D}$ has k-ary predicates and all $v_1, \ldots, v_k \in V(\mathfrak{C})$, there is exactly one k-ary predicate P over $\mathfrak{D}$ such that $P(v_1, \ldots, v_k) \in \mathfrak{C}$. The concrete domain $\mathfrak{D}$ is *homomorphism ω-compact* if every countable constraint system $\mathfrak{C}$ over $\mathfrak{D}$ is satisfiable whenever all its finite subsystems $\mathfrak{C}' \subseteq \mathfrak{C}$ are satisfiable. We introduce ExpTime-ω-admissible concrete domains, which differ from ω-admissible ones as defined in [11,27] by a stronger requirement on the decidability of CSP($\mathfrak{D}$).

Definition 1. *A concrete domain $\mathfrak{D}$ is* ExpTime-ω-admissible *if it has a finite signature, it is a patchwork, it is homomorphism ω-compact and its CSP is in* ExpTime.

The finiteness of the signature of $\mathfrak{D}$ is necessary to ensure decidability. Without this assumption, one can find instances of $\mathfrak{D}$ that satisfy all the other conditions of Definition 1 such that reasoning in $\mathcal{ALC}(\mathfrak{D})$ is undecidable. One such example is given by the concrete domain $(\mathbb{Z}, \{+_m \mid m \in \mathbb{Z}\})$ where $+_m$ relates those integers whose difference is equal to m [11]. The conditions of Definition 1 are satisfied by Allen's interval algebra, RCC8 and $\mathfrak{Q}$ [11,27].

The Logic QFBAPA. Set terms are built using the operations intersection $\cap$, union $\cup$ and complement ^{c} from *set variables* and the constants $\emptyset$ and $\mathcal{U}$. Set terms s, t are then used in *inclusion-* and *equality constraints* $s \subseteq t$, $s = t$. *Presburger Arithmetic (PA) expressions* ℓ, ℓ' of the form $n_0 + n_1 t_1 + \cdots + n_k t_k$,

[4] Originally [27] used JEPD (jointly exhaustive, pairwise disjoint) and AP (amalgamation property), while JD (jointly diagonal) was later added by [11].

where $n_i \in \mathbb{N}$ and each t_i is the cardinality $|s_i|$ of a set term s_i or an integer variable, are used to form *numerical constraints* $\ell = \ell'$, $\ell < \ell'$ and $n \operatorname{div} \ell$ (n divides ℓ), where $n \in \mathbb{N}$. A *QFBAPA formula* is a Boolean combination of set- and numerical constraints.

A *solution* σ of a QFBAPA formula ϕ assigns a *finite* set $\sigma(\mathcal{U})$ to $\mathcal{U}$, subsets of $\sigma(\mathcal{U})$ to set variables and integers to integer variables such that ϕ is *satisfied* by σ, which is defined in the standard way. ϕ is *satisfiable* if it has a solution.

The satisfiability problem for QFBAPA formulae is NP-complete. Membership in NP is proved in [22], using the notion of Venn regions. If ϕ is a QFBAPA formula containing the set variables $X_1, \ldots, X_k$, a *Venn region* for ϕ is a set term of the form $X_1^{c_1} \cap \cdots \cap X_k^{c_k}$ where each c_i is either empty or the set complement c. For a Venn region v for ϕ and a set variable X in ϕ, we write $X \in v$ to indicate that X occurs without complement in v, and $X \notin v$ if X^c occurs in v. The following characterization, proved in [22] and strengthened in [3], guarantees the existence of solutions with a polynomial number of non-empty Venn regions for satisfiable QFBAPA formulae, as follows.

Lemma 1. *([3]). For every QFBAPA formula ϕ, one can compute in polynomial time a number N_ϕ, whose value is polynomial in the size of ϕ, such that for every solution σ of ϕ there exists a solution σ' fulfilling the following conditions:*

- *there are at most N_ϕ Venn regions v for ϕ for which $\sigma'(v) \neq \emptyset$;*
- *if v is a Venn region for ϕ and $\sigma'(v) \neq \emptyset$, then $\sigma(v) \neq \emptyset$.*

3 Syntax and Semantics of $\mathcal{ALCOSCC}(\mathfrak{D})$

We now introduce the classical description logic $\mathcal{ALCO}$, its extension $\mathcal{ALCOSCC}$, and finally our new logic $\mathcal{ALCOSCC}(\mathfrak{D})$.

Given at most countable, disjoint sets $\mathsf{N_C}$, $\mathsf{N_R}$ and $\mathsf{N_I}$ of *concept-*, *role-* and *individual names*, $\mathcal{ALCO}$ *concepts* are built using negation $\neg$ and conjunction $\sqcap$ from concept names $A \in \mathsf{N_C}$, *nominals* $\{a\}$ with $a \in \mathsf{N_I}$ and *existential restrictions* $\exists r.C$ with $r \in \mathsf{N_R}$ and C an $\mathcal{ALCO}$ concept [9]. As usual, we use $C \sqcup D := \neg(\neg C \sqcap \neg D)$ (disjunction) and $\top := A \sqcup \neg A$. An *interpretation* $\mathcal{I}$ consists of a *domain* $\Delta^\mathcal{I} \neq \emptyset$ and a mapping $\cdot^\mathcal{I}$ assigning sets $A^\mathcal{I} \subseteq \Delta^\mathcal{I}$ to $A \in \mathsf{N_C}$, relations $r^\mathcal{I} \subseteq \Delta^\mathcal{I} \times \Delta^\mathcal{I}$ to $r \in \mathsf{N_R}$ and individuals $a^\mathcal{I} \in \Delta^\mathcal{I}$ to $a \in \mathsf{N_I}$. For $d \in \Delta^\mathcal{I}$, we define $r^\mathcal{I}(d) := \{e \in \Delta^\mathcal{I} \mid (d,e) \in r^\mathcal{I}\}$. We extend $\cdot^\mathcal{I}$ to concepts by $(\neg C)^\mathcal{I} := \Delta^\mathcal{I} \setminus C^\mathcal{I}$, $(C \sqcap D)^\mathcal{I} := C^\mathcal{I} \cap D^\mathcal{I}$, $\{a\}^\mathcal{I} := \{a^\mathcal{I}\}$ and $(\exists r.C)^\mathcal{I} := \{d \in \Delta^\mathcal{I} \mid \exists e \in r^\mathcal{I}(d) \cap C^\mathcal{I}\}$. In this DL, the concept of all individuals that are human and have a child who is not $\mathtt{Sam}$ can be written as $\mathsf{Human} \sqcap \exists \mathsf{child}.\neg\{\mathtt{Sam}\}$.

$\mathcal{ALCOSCC}$ extends $\mathcal{ALCO}$ concepts with *role successor restrictions* (or succ-*restrictions*) $\mathsf{succ}(\mathtt{con})$, where $\mathtt{con}$ is a set- or numerical constraint with role names and concepts as set variables and no integer variables, e.g. $r \subseteq C$ [3]. This DL requires interpretations $\mathcal{I}$ to be *finitely branching*, i.e. such that the set of all role successors $\mathsf{ars}^\mathcal{I}(d) := \bigcup_{r \in \mathsf{N_R}} r^\mathcal{I}(d)$ is finite, for all $d \in \Delta^\mathcal{I}$. Then, each $d \in \Delta^\mathcal{I}$

induces a QFBAPA assignment σ_d, where $\sigma_d(\mathcal{U}) := \mathsf{ars}^{\mathcal{I}}(d)$, $\sigma_d(r) := r^{\mathcal{I}}(d)$ for $r \in \mathsf{N_R}$ and $\sigma_d(C) := C^{\mathcal{I}} \cap \mathsf{ars}^{\mathcal{I}}(d)$ for concepts C. The mapping $\cdot^{\mathcal{I}}$ is extended to succ-restrictions by defining $d \in \mathsf{succ}(\mathfrak{con})^{\mathcal{I}}$ iff σ_d is a solution of $\mathfrak{con}$.

$\mathcal{ALCOSCC}$ does not need existential restrictions $\exists r.C$, as they can be expressed as $\mathsf{succ}(|r \cap C| \geq 1)$. Moreover, succ-restrictions can compare quantities of successors, e.g. $\mathsf{succ}(|\mathsf{own} \cap \mathsf{Car}| = |\mathsf{child} \cap \mathsf{Human}|)$ describes people who own as many cars as they have children, without specifying the exact amount.

To integrate the concrete domain $\mathfrak{D}$, we complement $\mathsf{N_C}$, $\mathsf{N_R}$ and $\mathsf{N_I}$ with an at most countable set $\mathsf{N_F}$ of *feature names* that connect individuals with values in D [8]. A *feature path* p is of the form f or rf with $r \in \mathsf{N_R}$ and $f \in \mathsf{N_F}$. For instance, salary is a feature name as well as a feature path, while child salary is a feature path including the role name child. *Concrete domain restrictions* (or *CD-restrictions*) are concepts $\exists p_1, \ldots, p_k.P$, where p_i are feature paths and P is a k-ary predicate of $\mathfrak{D}$. An interpretation $\mathcal{I}$ assigns to each $f \in \mathsf{N_F}$ a *partial* function $f^{\mathcal{I}} \colon \Delta^{\mathcal{I}} \rightharpoonup D$. A feature path p is mapped to $p^{\mathcal{I}} \subseteq \Delta^{\mathcal{I}} \times D$ by defining $p^{\mathcal{I}}(d) := \{f^{\mathcal{I}}(d)\}$ if $p = f$[5] and $p^{\mathcal{I}}(d) := \{f^{\mathcal{I}}(e) \mid e \in r^{\mathcal{I}}(d)\}$ if $p = rf$. Then we can define

$$(\exists p_1, \ldots, p_k.P)^{\mathcal{I}} := \{d \in \Delta^{\mathcal{I}} \mid \textit{some} \text{ tuple in } p_1^{\mathcal{I}}(d) \times \cdots \times p_k^{\mathcal{I}}(d) \text{ is in } P^D\}.$$

For example, one can describe individuals whose salaries are greater than that of some of their children using $\exists\mathsf{salary}, \mathsf{child\ salary}.>$. Furthermore, due to JEPD, we can encode *universal CD-restrictions* $\forall p_1, \ldots, p_k.P$ using the conjunction of all concepts $\neg\exists p_1, \ldots, p_k.P'$ where $P' \neq P$ is a k-ary predicate of $\mathfrak{D}$ [27].

A naive extension of $\mathcal{ALCOSCC}$ with concrete domain reasoning that simply combines succ- and CD-restrictions offers limited expressive power. To improve that, we introduce *feature pointers* α of the form f or $\mathtt{next}\, f$ with $f \in \mathsf{N_F}$ and define *feature roles* $\gamma := P(\alpha_1, \ldots, \alpha_k)$, where each α_i is a feature pointer and P is a k-ary predicate of $\mathfrak{D}$. For example, salary is a pointer to the salary of a given individual d, while next salary is a pointer to the salary of an individual e that we want to compare to d; the feature role $(\mathsf{salary} < \mathtt{next}\,\mathsf{salary})$ describes a binary relation that contains (d, e) iff the salary of d is smaller than that of e.

We define $\mathcal{ALCOSCC}(\mathfrak{D})$ as the extension of $\mathcal{ALCOSCC}$ with CD-restrictions and succ-restrictions $\mathsf{succ}(\mathfrak{con})$ where $\mathfrak{con}$ can also contain feature roles as set variables. We can now describe individuals that earn less than the majority of their children by

$$C_{\mathsf{ex}} := \mathsf{succ}(|\mathsf{child} \cap (\mathsf{salary} < \mathtt{next}\,\mathsf{salary})| > |\mathsf{child} \cap (\mathsf{salary} < \mathtt{next}\,\mathsf{salary})^c|).$$

Feature roles $\gamma := P(\alpha_1, \ldots, \alpha_k)$ are mapped by interpretations $\mathcal{I}$ to relations $\gamma^{\mathcal{I}} \subseteq \Delta^{\mathcal{I}} \times \Delta^{\mathcal{I}}$ such that $(d, e) \in \gamma^{\mathcal{I}}$ iff $(c_1, \ldots, c_k) \in P^D$, where $c_i := f_i^{\mathcal{I}}(d)$ if $\alpha_i = f_i$ and $c_i := f_i^{\mathcal{I}}(e)$ if $\alpha_i = \mathtt{next}\, f_i$. The QFBAPA assignment σ_d is extended to map feature roles γ to $\gamma^{\mathcal{I}} \cap \mathsf{ars}^{\mathcal{I}}(d)$, and $\mathsf{succ}(\mathfrak{con})^{\mathcal{I}}$ is defined as before.

An $\mathcal{ALCOSCC}(\mathfrak{D})$ *TBox* $\mathcal{T}$ is a finite set of *concept inclusions (CIs)* $C \sqsubseteq D$ between concepts C, D. For example, we can describe an individual Jane that

[5] In a slight abuse of notation, we view $f^{\mathcal{I}}(d)$ both as a value and as a singleton set.

earns more than $\mathtt{Sam}$, where the role $\mathsf{ref}_{\mathtt{Sam}}$ always points to $\mathtt{Sam}$:

$$\mathcal{T}_{\mathsf{ex}} := \{\, \top \sqsubseteq \mathsf{succ}(\mathsf{ref}_{\mathtt{Sam}} = \{\mathtt{Sam}\}),\ \{\mathtt{Jane}\} \sqsubseteq \exists \mathsf{salary}, \mathsf{ref}_{\mathtt{Sam}}\ \mathsf{salary}.{>}\,\}.$$

A finitely branching interpretation $\mathcal{I}$ is a *model* of $\mathcal{T}$ if $C^{\mathcal{I}} \subseteq D^{\mathcal{I}}$ holds for every CI $C \sqsubseteq D$ in $\mathcal{T}$. A TBox $\mathcal{T}$ is *consistent* if it has a model.

We mentioned above that feature roles make $\mathcal{ALCOSCC}(\mathfrak{D})$ more expressive. Precisely, we can show that some concepts with feature roles cannot be equivalently expressed by only using feature names in CD-restrictions; two concepts are *equivalent* if they are always interpreted by the same sets of individuals.

Theorem 1. *There is no $\mathcal{ALCOSCC}(\mathfrak{Q})$ concept without feature roles that is equivalent to C_{ex}.*

Proof. Assume that there is an $\mathcal{ALCOSCC}(\mathfrak{Q})$ concept D without feature roles that is equivalent to C_{ex}.Consider the interpretation $\mathcal{I}$, where d has salary 0 and five child-successors, two whose salary is 0 and three whose salary is 1. Then, $d \in C_{\mathsf{ex}}^{\mathcal{I}} = D^{\mathcal{I}}$.Construct $\mathcal{J}$ from $\mathcal{I}$ by changing the salary of one of the successors from 1 to 0.Since every individual in $\mathcal{J}$ satisfies the same CD-restrictions, concept names and succ-restrictions without feature roles as in $\mathcal{I}$, we deduce that $d \in D^{\mathcal{J}}$. However, d has more successors with equal salary in $\mathcal{J}$ than successors with greater salary, hence $d \notin C_{\mathsf{ex}}^{\mathcal{J}} = D^{\mathcal{J}}$ must hold, which is a contradiction. □

4 Deciding Consistency

Let $\mathfrak{D}$ be an ExpTime-ω-admissible concrete domain and $\mathcal{T}$ an $\mathcal{ALCOSCC}(\mathfrak{D})$ TBox. In this section, we assume w.l.o.g. that $\mathsf{N_C}$, $\mathsf{N_R}$, $\mathsf{N_I}$ and $\mathsf{N_F}$ are finite and contain exactly the names occurring in $\mathcal{T}$ and that there is at least one individual name; indeed, $\mathcal{T}$ is consistent iff $\mathcal{T} \cup \{\{a\} \sqsubseteq \{a\}\}$ is consistent, where a is a fresh individual name. We define the notion of *individual types*, describing sets of equivalent individual names in an interpretation.

Definition 2. *An* individual type $\mathfrak{a}$ *w.r.t.* $\mathsf{N_I}$ *is a non-empty subset of* $\mathsf{N_I}$, *and a set of individual types* $\mathbb{I}$ *is an* individual type system *for* $\mathsf{N_I}$ *if* $\mathbb{I}$ *partitions* $\mathsf{N_I}$.

Given an interpretation $\mathcal{I}$, *an individual* $d \in \Delta^{\mathcal{I}}$ has individual type $\mathfrak{a}_{\mathcal{I}}(d) := \{a \in \mathsf{N_I} \mid a^{\mathcal{I}} = d\}$ *if this set is non-empty, and* d *is* anonymous *otherwise.*

We now fix an individual type system $\mathbb{I}$. Let $\mathcal{M}$ be the set of all subconcepts appearing in $\mathcal{T}$, as well as their negations. We define the notion of *type* as usual.

Definition 3. *A* type *w.r.t.* $\mathcal{T}$ *is a set* $t \subseteq \mathcal{M}$ *such that:*

- *if* $C \sqsubseteq D \in \mathcal{T}$ *and* $C \in t$*, then* $D \in t$*;*
- *if* $\neg C \in \mathcal{M}$*, then* $C \in t$ *iff* $\neg C \notin t$*;*
- *if* $C \sqcap C' \in \mathcal{M}$*, then* $C \sqcap C' \in t$ *iff* $C \in t$ *and* $C' \in t$*.*

The type *of* $d \in \Delta^{\mathcal{I}}$ *w.r.t.* $\mathcal{T}$ *is the set* $t_{\mathcal{I}}(d) := \{C \in \mathcal{M} \mid d \in C^{\mathcal{I}}\}$.

If $\mathcal{I}$ is a model of $\mathcal{T}$, then $t_{\mathcal{I}}(d)$ is indeed a type w.r.t. $\mathcal{T}$. A type t is *named with* an individual type $\mathfrak{a}_t$ if for all $a \in \mathsf{N_I}$, $a \in \mathfrak{a}_t$ iff $\{a\} \in t$, and is *anonymous* if it is not named with any individual type.

Following the approach used in [3], we construct a QFBAPA formula ϕ_t that is induced by the succ-restrictions $\mathsf{succ}(\mathfrak{con})$ in a type t and enriched with constraints derived from the individual type system $\mathbb{I}$ and the set of role names $\mathsf{N_R}$. Formally, ϕ_t is defined as the conjunction of

- $\phi_{\mathfrak{con}}$ if $\mathsf{succ}(\mathfrak{con}) \in t$ and $\neg\phi_{\mathfrak{con}}$ otherwise, where $\phi_{\mathfrak{con}}$ is derived from $\mathfrak{con}$ by replacing role names r, feature roles γ and concepts C with set variables X_r, X_γ and X_C, respectively;
- $|\bigcap_{a \in \mathfrak{a}} X_{\{a\}}| \leq 1$ for every $\mathfrak{a} \in \mathbb{I}$; and
- $\mathcal{U} = \bigcup_{r \in \mathsf{N_R}} X_r$.

All formulae ϕ_t contain exactly the same set variables and thus have the same Venn regions (cf. Sect. 2), called the *Venn regions of* $\mathcal{T}$. A Venn region v of $\mathcal{T}$ *has individual type* $\mathfrak{a}_v = \{a \in \mathsf{N_I} \mid X_{\{a\}} \in v\}$ if this set is non-empty, and v is *anonymous* otherwise. The following example shows that ϕ_t does not yet account for the numerical constraints induced by the CD-restrictions in t.

Example 1. Let $\mathcal{T} = \{\top \sqsubseteq (\exists \mathsf{salary}, \mathsf{child\ salary}.<) \sqcap (\mathsf{succ}(|\mathsf{child}| \leq 0))\}$. For every model $\mathcal{I}$ of $\mathcal{T}$ and $d \in \Delta^{\mathcal{I}}$, the type $t := t_{\mathcal{I}}(d)$ contains both conjuncts appearing in this CI. The QFBAPA formula $\phi_t := |X_{\mathsf{child}}| \leq 0 \wedge \mathcal{U} = X_{\mathsf{child}}$ is satisfied by any solution assigning the empty set to $\mathcal{U}$. However, t cannot be realized: the first conjunct implies that d has a child-successor $e \neq d$ such that $\mathsf{salary}^{\mathcal{I}}(d) < \mathsf{salary}^{\mathcal{I}}(e)$, while the last conjunct forces d to have no child-successor.

To realize the CD-restrictions in t, we may need up to $M_{\mathcal{T}} := R_{\mathcal{T}} \cdot P_{\mathcal{T}}$ distinct role successors, where $R_{\mathcal{T}}$ is the number of CD-restrictions in $\mathcal{M}$ and $P_{\mathcal{T}}$ is the maximal arity of predicates of $\mathfrak{D}$ occurring in $\mathcal{M}$. We add this information to the QFBAPA formula ϕ_t with additional constraints over a set of pre-selected Venn regions, representing sets of role successors whose existence is implied by the CD-restrictions in t. Let S be a set of at most $M_{\mathcal{T}}$ Venn regions v, each associated to a natural number $0 \leq n_v \leq M_{\mathcal{T}}$. By Lemma 1, the QFBAPA formula $\phi_{t,S}$, which extends ϕ_t with a conjunct $|v| \geq n_v$ for each $v \in S$, is satisfiable iff there is a natural number $N_{\mathcal{T}}$ of polynomial size w.r.t. the size of ϕ_t and $M_{\mathcal{T}}$ s.t. $\phi_{t,S}$ has a solution in which at most $N_{\mathcal{T}}$ Venn regions are non-empty. Moreover, since all formulae ϕ_t are nearly of the same size (except for the difference between $\phi_{\mathfrak{con}}$ and $\neg\phi_{\mathfrak{con}}$) and $|S|$ and the numbers n_v are bounded by $M_{\mathcal{T}}$, we can assume that the bound $N_\mathcal{T}$ is independent of the choice of S and t, is polynomial w.r.t. the size of $\mathcal{T}$ and can be computed in polynomial time.

To formalize these additional restrictions, we consider *bags*, i.e. functions V assigning to every Venn region v of $\mathcal{T}$ a *multiplicity* $V(v) \in \mathbb{N}$, whose *support* $\mathsf{supp}(V)$ is the set of Venn regions of $\mathcal{T}$ with multiplicity $V(v) \geq 1$. The associated QFBAPA formula ϕ_V is the conjunction of the constraint $\mathcal{U} = \bigcup \mathsf{supp}(V)$ and all constraints $|v| \geq c$ where $v \in \mathsf{supp}(V)$ and $c = V(v)$.

Definition 4. *A* Venn bag *for a type t w.r.t. $\mathcal{T}$ is a bag V of Venn regions of $\mathcal{T}$ s.t. $|\mathsf{supp}(V)| \leq N_\mathcal{T}$, $V(v) \leq M_\mathcal{T}+1$ holds for all $v \in \mathsf{supp}(V)$ and the QFBAPA formula $\phi_{t,V} := \phi_t \wedge \phi_V$ is satisfiable.*

By Lemma 1, $\phi_{t,S}$ is satisfiable iff there is a Venn bag V for t such that $\phi_{t,V}$ includes all constraints from $\phi_{t,S}$.

Finally, we take care of actually satisfying the CD-restrictions occurring in a type by using complete constraint systems to describe all relevant feature values. Feature values that are not represented in these systems correspond to undefined values. To ensure that all types agree on the feature values of individual names, we fix an *individual constraint system* $\mathfrak{C}_\mathbb{I}$ w.r.t. $\mathbb{I}$, i.e. a complete constraint system over variables of the form $f^\mathfrak{a}$, where $f \in \mathsf{N_F}$ and $\mathfrak{a} \in \mathbb{I}$, that refer to the feature values of named individuals. Then, we define constraint systems $\mathfrak{C}_{t,V}$ representing the relations between the feature values associated with an individual of type t and those of its role successors as specified by a Venn bag V for t. The system $\mathfrak{C}_{t,V}$ extends $\mathfrak{C}_\mathbb{I}$ by adding variables of the form

- $f^\star$, representing the value of the feature $f \in \mathsf{N_F}$ at the current individual;
- $f^{(v,j)}$ with $v \in \mathsf{supp}(V)$ and $1 \leq j \leq V(v)$ for the f-values at the successors, in order to express the relevant CD-restrictions.

Again, not all these variables actually need to occur in the constraint system, only the ones whose associated feature values should be defined. To handle named types and named Venn regions, we define the indexing functions

$$\iota(t) := \begin{cases} \star & \text{if } t \text{ is anonymous} \\ \mathfrak{a}_t & \text{otherwise} \end{cases} \qquad \text{and } \iota((v,j)) := \begin{cases} (v,j) & \text{if } v \text{ is anonymous} \\ \mathfrak{a}_v & \text{otherwise} \end{cases}$$

for all $v \in \mathsf{supp}(V)$ and $1 \leq j \leq V(v)$. Additionally, we do not allow more variables of the form $f^\mathfrak{a}$ than those already contained in $\mathfrak{C}_\mathbb{I}$.

Definition 5. *Let t be a type w.r.t. $\mathcal{T}$ and V a Venn bag for t.*

A local system *for t, V is a complete constraint system $\mathfrak{C}_{t,V}$ that includes $\mathfrak{C}_\mathbb{I}$ and no additional variables of the form $f^\mathfrak{a}$, $\mathfrak{a} \in \mathbb{I}$, such that:*

1. *if $C := \exists p_1, \ldots, p_k.P \in \mathcal{M}$, then $C \in t$ iff $P(f_1^{x_1}, \ldots, f_k^{x_k}) \in \mathfrak{C}_{t,V}$ such that*

$$x_i = \begin{cases} \iota(t) & \text{if } p_i = f_i, \text{ or} \\ \iota((v,j)) & \text{if } p_i = rf_i, \text{ for some } 1 \leq j \leq V(v) \text{ and } X_r \in v; \end{cases}$$

Algorithm 1. Type elimination algorithm for $\mathcal{ALCOSCC}(\mathfrak{D})$

Input: An $\mathcal{ALCOSCC}(\mathfrak{D})$ TBox $\mathcal{T}$
Output: CONSISTENT if $\mathcal{T}$ is consistent, and INCONSISTENT otherwise

guess an individual type system $\mathbb{I}$ and an individual constraint system $\mathfrak{C}_{\mathbb{I}}$
guess augmented types $\mathsf{t}_{\mathfrak{a}} = (t_{\mathfrak{a}}, V_{\mathfrak{a}}, \mathfrak{C}_{\mathfrak{a}})$ for $\mathfrak{a} \in \mathbb{I}$ s.t. $t_{\mathfrak{a}}$ is named with $\mathfrak{a}$
$\mathbb{T} \leftarrow \{\mathsf{t} = (t, V, \mathfrak{C})$ augmented type $\mid t$ is anonymous$\} \cup \{\mathsf{t}_{\mathfrak{a}} \mid \mathfrak{a} \in \mathbb{I}\}$
while there is $\mathsf{t} \in \mathbb{T}$ that is not patched by $\mathbb{T}$ **do** $\mathbb{T} \leftarrow \mathbb{T} \setminus \{t\}$
if $\mathsf{t}_{\mathfrak{a}} \in \mathbb{T}$ for all $\mathfrak{a} \in \mathbb{I}$ **then return** CONSISTENT
else return INCONSISTENT

2. *for all set variables* $X_{P(\alpha_1,\ldots,\alpha_k)}$, *all* $v \in \mathsf{supp}(V)$, *and* $1 \leq j \leq V(v)$ *it holds that* $X_{P(\alpha_1,\ldots,\alpha_k)} \in v$ *iff* $P(f_1^{x_1}, \ldots, f_k^{x_k}) \in \mathfrak{C}_{t,V}$, *where*

$$x_i = \begin{cases} \iota(t) & \text{if } \alpha_i = f_i, \text{ and} \\ \iota((v,j)) & \text{if } \alpha_i = \texttt{next}\, f_i. \end{cases}$$

In the following definition, we denote with S_v the subset of $\mathcal{M}$ that contains $C \in \mathcal{M}$ if $X_C \in v$ and $\neg C \in \mathcal{M}$ if $X_C \notin v$ (cf. Sect. 2).

Definition 6. *An* augmented type *for* $\mathcal{T}$ *is a tuple* $\mathsf{t} := (t, V, \mathfrak{C}_{\mathsf{t}})$, *where* t *is a type w.r.t.* $\mathcal{T}$, V *is a Venn bag for* t, *and* $\mathfrak{C}_{\mathsf{t}}$ *is a satisfiable local system for* t, V. *The* root *of* t *is* $\mathsf{root}(\mathsf{t}) := t$.

An augmented type $\mathsf{t}' = (t', V', \mathfrak{C}_{\mathsf{t}'})$ patches t *at* (v, i), *where* $v \in \mathsf{supp}(V)$ *and* $1 \leq i \leq V(v)$, *if* $S_v \subseteq t'$ *and the* merged system $\mathfrak{C}_{\mathsf{t}} \lhd_{(v,i)} \mathfrak{C}_{\mathsf{t}'}$ *has a solution, where* $\mathfrak{C}_{\mathsf{t}} \lhd_{(v,i)} \mathfrak{C}_{\mathsf{t}'}$ *is obtained as the union of* $\mathfrak{C}_{\mathsf{t}}$ *and the result of replacing all variables in* $\mathfrak{C}_{\mathsf{t}'}$ *as follows:*

$$\begin{array}{lll} f^{\star} & \mapsto f^{(v,i)} & \text{if } t' \text{ is anonymous;} \\ f^{(w,j)} & \mapsto f^{(w,j)'} & \text{for all anonymous } w \in \mathsf{supp}(V') \text{ and } 1 \leq j \leq V'(w); \\ f^{\mathfrak{a}} & \mapsto f^{\mathfrak{a}} & \text{for all } \mathfrak{a} \in \mathbb{I}. \end{array}$$

A set of augmented types $\mathbb{T}$ patches t *if, for all* $v \in \mathsf{supp}(V)$ *and* $1 \leq i \leq V(v)$, *there is a* $\mathsf{t}' \in \mathbb{T}$ *that patches* t *at* (v, i).

The merging operation identifies all features associated to (v, i) in $\mathfrak{C}_{\mathsf{t}}$ with those associated to t' in $\mathfrak{C}_{\mathsf{t}'}$, while keeping the remaining variables associated to anonymous individuals separate. If t' is not anonymous (and thus $\mathfrak{C}_{\mathsf{t}'}$ contains no variable of the form $f^{\star}$) then the condition $S_v \subseteq t'$ ensures that $\mathfrak{a}_v = \mathfrak{a}_{t'}$, and thus the variable $f^{\iota((v,i))} = f^{\mathfrak{a}_v} = f^{\mathfrak{a}_{t'}}$ in $\mathfrak{C}_{\mathsf{t}}$ is already identical to $f^{\iota(t')} = f^{\mathfrak{a}_{t'}}$ in $\mathfrak{C}_{\mathsf{t}'}$.

The augmented types are now used by Algorithm 1 to decide consistency of an $\mathcal{ALCOSCC}(\mathfrak{D})$ TBox via a type elimination approach. We show that Algorithm 1 is indeed sound and complete.

Lemma 2. *If there is a run of Algorithm 1 that returns* CONSISTENT, *then* $\mathcal{T}$ *is consistent.*

Proof. We construct a model $\mathcal{I}$ of $\mathcal{T}$ using the individual type system $\mathbb{I}$ and the set $\mathbb{T}$ of augmented types constructed by Algorithm 1. The domain $\Delta^{\mathcal{I}}$ consists of tuples $(\mathfrak{a}, w)$, where $\mathfrak{a} \in \mathbb{I}$ and w is a word over the alphabet Σ of all tuples $(\mathfrak{t}, v, i)$ with $\mathfrak{t} \in \mathbb{T}$, v a Venn region of $\mathcal{T}$ and $i \geq 1$ a natural number. We associate to each tuple $(\mathfrak{a}, w)$ the augmented type $\mathsf{end}(\mathfrak{a}, w) \in \mathbb{T}$ defined as $\mathsf{end}(\mathfrak{a}, \varepsilon) := \mathfrak{t}_{\mathfrak{a}}$ and $\mathsf{end}(\mathfrak{a}, w' \cdot (\mathfrak{t}, v, i)) := \mathfrak{t}$ for $w' \in \Sigma^*$.

We define $\Delta^{\mathcal{I}}$ as the union of sets Δ^m with $m \in \mathbb{N}$, where Δ^0 contains $(\mathfrak{a}, \varepsilon)$ for every $\mathfrak{a} \in \mathbb{I}$ and Δ^{m+1} is defined inductively in the following. Given $(\mathfrak{a}, w) \in \Delta^m$ with $\mathsf{end}(\mathfrak{a}, w) = \mathfrak{t} = (t, V, \mathfrak{C}_{t,V}) \in \mathbb{T}$ we observe that

- the QFBAPA formula ϕ_t has a solution $\sigma_{\mathfrak{a},w}$ such that $\sigma_{\mathfrak{a},w}(|v|) \geq V(v)$ if $v \in \mathsf{supp}(V)$ and $\sigma_{\mathfrak{a},w}(|v|) = 0$ otherwise for all Venn regions v of $\mathcal{T}$,
- for $v \in \mathsf{supp}(V)$ and $i = 1, \ldots, V(v)$ there exists an augmented type $\mathfrak{t}_{(v,i)} \in \mathbb{T}$ patching $\mathfrak{t}$ at (v, i), as otherwise $\mathfrak{t}$ would have been eliminated from $\mathbb{T}$.

Using these augmented types, we define for $r \in \mathsf{N_R}$ the set $\Delta_r^{m+1}[\mathfrak{a}, w]$ containing $(\mathfrak{a}, w \cdot (\mathfrak{t}_{(v,i)}, v, j))$ iff $X_r \in v$, $\mathsf{root}(\mathfrak{t}_{(v,i)})$ is anonymous, $j = 1, \ldots, \sigma_{\mathfrak{a},w}(|v|)$ and $i = \max(j, V(v))$. We now define Δ^{m+1} as the extension of Δ^m by all sets $\Delta_r^{m+1}[\mathfrak{a}, w]$ for which $r \in \mathsf{N_R}$ and $(\mathfrak{a}, w) \in \Delta^m$.

The extensions of $a \in \mathsf{N_I}$, $A \in \mathsf{N_C}$ and $r \in \mathsf{N_R}$ are defined as:

$$a^{\mathcal{I}} := (\mathfrak{a}, \varepsilon), \text{ where } \mathfrak{a} \text{ is the unique individual type in } \mathbb{I} \text{ containing } a;$$

$$A^{\mathcal{I}} := \{(\mathfrak{a}, w) \in \Delta^{\mathcal{I}} \mid \mathsf{end}(\mathfrak{a}, w) = \mathfrak{t} \text{ and } A \in \mathsf{root}(\mathfrak{t})\};$$

$$r^{\mathcal{I}} := \{((\mathfrak{a}, w), (\mathfrak{b}, \varepsilon)) \mid \mathsf{end}(\mathfrak{a}, w) = \mathfrak{t} \text{ and } \mathfrak{t}_{\mathfrak{b}} \text{ patches } \mathfrak{t} \text{ at } (v, i) \text{ with } X_r \in v\} \cup$$
$$\{((\mathfrak{a}, w), (\mathfrak{a}, w')) \mid (\mathfrak{a}, w) \in \Delta^m \text{ and } (\mathfrak{a}, w') \in \Delta_r^{m+1}[\mathfrak{a}, w] \text{ with } m \in \mathbb{N}\}.$$

For $f \in \mathsf{N_F}$, $f^{\mathcal{I}}$ is defined as follows. If $(\mathfrak{a}, w) \in \Delta^{\mathcal{I}}$ and $\mathsf{end}(\mathfrak{a}, w) = (t, V, \mathfrak{C}_{t,V})$, we extend $\mathfrak{C}_{t,V}$ with all variables $f^{(v,i)}$ where $i > V(v)$ and $f \in \mathsf{N_F}$ such that $f^{(v,V(v))}$ occurs in $\mathfrak{C}_{t,V}$ and $(\mathfrak{a}, w \cdot (\mathfrak{t}', v, i))$ occurs in $\Delta^{\mathcal{I}}$. Then, we add all constraints $P((f_1^{x_1})', \ldots, (f_k^{x_k})')$ obtained by replacing every occurrence of $f^{(v,V(v))}$ in a constraint $P(f_1^{x_1}, \ldots, f_k^{x_k}) \in \mathfrak{C}_{t,V}$ with some variable $f^{(v,i)}$ among those occurring in the extended system with $i \geq V(v)$.In this way, the feature values of all role successors of $(\mathfrak{a}, w)$ are handled correctly w.r.t. one another and w.r.t. those of $(\mathfrak{a}, w)$.Next, we replace all variables $f^{\mathfrak{a}}$ with $f^{\mathfrak{a},\varepsilon}$, all variables $f^{\star}$ with $f^{\mathfrak{a},w}$ and all variables $f^{(v,i)}$ with $f^{\mathfrak{a},u}$ where u is the unique word of the form $w \cdot (\mathfrak{t}', v, i)$ for which $(\mathfrak{a}, u) \in \Delta^{\mathcal{I}}$.

Let $\mathfrak{C}_{\mathfrak{a},w}$ be the resulting complete constraint system and $\mathfrak{C}^m$ with $m \in \mathbb{N}$ be the union of all $\mathfrak{C}_{\mathfrak{a},w}$ with $(\mathfrak{a}, w) \in \Delta^m$. We show in [5] (Lemma 6) that for every $m \in \mathbb{N}$, the constraint system $\mathfrak{C}^m$ has a solution. Let $\mathfrak{C}^{\mathcal{I}}$ be the union of all systems $\mathfrak{C}^m$ with $m \in \mathbb{N}$. Every finite subsystem of $\mathfrak{C}^{\mathcal{I}}$ is a subsystem of $\mathfrak{C}^m$ for some $m \in \mathbb{N}$ and is thus satisfiable. Thus, by homomorphism ω-compactness of $\mathfrak{D}$, we can infer that $\mathfrak{C}^{\mathcal{I}}$ has a solution $h^{\mathcal{I}}$. For every $f \in \mathsf{N_F}$ and $(\mathfrak{a}, w) \in \Delta^{\mathcal{I}}$, we now define $f^{\mathcal{I}}((\mathfrak{a}, w)) := h^{\mathcal{I}}(f^{\mathfrak{a},w})$ if $f^{\mathfrak{a},w}$ occurs in $\mathfrak{C}^{\mathcal{I}}$ and leave it undefined otherwise.

We show in [5] (Lemma 7) that for all $d = (\mathfrak{a}, w) \in \Delta^{\mathcal{I}}$ and $C \in \mathcal{M}$, we have $C \in \mathsf{root}(\mathsf{end}(d))$ iff $d \in C^{\mathcal{I}}$. It is a direct consequence that $\mathcal{I}$ satisfies all CIs in $\mathcal{T}$ and is thus a model of $\mathcal{T}$. Hence, $\mathcal{T}$ is consistent. □

Lemma 3. *If $\mathcal{T}$ is consistent, then there is a run of Algorithm 1 that returns* CONSISTENT.

Proof. Let $\mathcal{I}$ be a model of $\mathcal{T}$ and $\mathbb{I}$ be the individual type system that contains an individual type $\mathfrak{a}$ iff $\mathfrak{a} = \mathfrak{a}_{\mathcal{I}}(d)$ for some $d \in \Delta^{\mathcal{I}}$ (cf. Definition 2).Then $\mathbb{I}$ is well-defined, as every $a \in \mathsf{N_I}$ is uniquely assigned to $a^{\mathcal{I}} \in \Delta^{\mathcal{I}}$. For $\mathfrak{a} \in \mathbb{I}$, we denote by $\mathfrak{a}^{\mathcal{I}}$ the unique $d \in \Delta^{\mathcal{I}}$ with $\mathfrak{a} = \mathfrak{a}_{\mathcal{I}}(d)$. Further, let $T_{\mathcal{I}} := \{t_{\mathcal{I}}(d) \mid d \in \Delta^{\mathcal{I}}\}$ be the set of all types that are realized in $\mathcal{I}$.

For each individual type $\mathfrak{a} \in \mathbb{I}$, we define $t_{\mathfrak{a}} := t_{\mathcal{I}}(\mathfrak{a}^{\mathcal{I}})$. Using $\mathbb{I}$ and $T_{\mathcal{I}}$, we build a constraint system $\mathfrak{C}_{\mathbb{I}}$ and a set $\mathbb{T}_{\mathcal{I}} := \{\mathfrak{t}_{\mathcal{I}}(d) \mid d \in \Delta^{\mathcal{I}}\}$ of augmented types, containing unique types $\mathfrak{t}_{\mathfrak{a}}$ whose roots are named with $\mathfrak{a} \in \mathbb{I}$. We define the individual constraint system $\mathfrak{C}_{\mathbb{I}}$ over all variables $f^{\mathfrak{a}}$ with $f \in \mathsf{N_F}$ and $\mathfrak{a} \in \mathbb{I}$ for which $f^{\mathcal{I}}(\mathfrak{a}^{\mathcal{I}})$ is defined, such that $P(f_1^{\mathfrak{a}_1}, \ldots, f_k^{\mathfrak{a}_k}) \in \mathfrak{C}_{\mathbb{I}}$ iff $(f_1^{\mathcal{I}}(\mathfrak{a}_1^{\mathcal{I}}), \ldots, f_k^{\mathcal{I}}(\mathfrak{a}_k^{\mathcal{I}})) \in P^D$. Clearly, $\mathfrak{C}_{\mathbb{I}}$ is complete.

Next, we associate to each $d \in \Delta^{\mathcal{I}}$ an augmented type $\mathfrak{t}_{\mathcal{I}}(d) := (t_{\mathcal{I}}(d), V_d, \mathfrak{C}_d)$. If e is a role successor of d, let v_e be the Venn region of $\mathcal{T}$ whose variables X_r, X_C, X_γ for role names r, concepts C and feature roles γ satisfy the following:

- $X_r \in v_e$ iff e is an r-successor of d;
- $X_C \in v_e$ iff $C \in t_{\mathcal{I}}(e)$;
- $X_\gamma \in v_e$ iff $e \in \gamma^{\mathcal{I}}(d)$.

For every non-negated CD-restriction $\exists p_1, \ldots, p_k.P \in t_{\mathcal{I}}(d)$, we can find values $c_i \in p_i^{\mathcal{I}}(d)$ for $i = 1, \ldots, k$ such that $(c_1, \ldots, c_k) \in P^D$. If $p_i = r_i f_i$, this implies that there is $e_i \in r_i^{\mathcal{I}}(d)$ such that $f_i^{\mathcal{I}}(e_i) = c_i$. We collect all these successors of d, which are at most $M_{\mathcal{T}}$ many distinct elements, in the set $\mathsf{S_{cd}}$. For $e \in \mathsf{S_{cd}}$, let n_e be the number of elements $e' \in \mathsf{S_{cd}}$ such that $v_e = v_{e'}$. We show in [5] (Lemma 8) that there is a Venn bag V_d for $t_{\mathcal{I}}(d)$ w.r.t. $\mathcal{T}$ such that $V_d(v_e) = n_e$ for all $e \in \mathsf{S_{cd}}$, and for all other $v \in \mathsf{supp}(V_d)$ we have $V_d(v) = 1$ and there is a role successor $e \in \Delta^{\mathcal{I}} \setminus \mathsf{S_{cd}}$ of d such that $v = v_e$.

It remains to define the local system $\mathfrak{C}_d$. Consider the set X_d that contains $\iota(t_{\mathcal{I}}(d))$ (either $\star$ or $\mathfrak{a}_{t_{\mathcal{I}}(d)}$), all $\mathfrak{a} \in \mathbb{I}$, and all pairs (v, j) with anonymous Venn bags $v \in \mathsf{supp}(V_d)$ and $1 \leq j \leq V_d(v)$ (cf. Definition 5). Let λ_d be a bijection mapping every such (v, j) to an anonymous successor e of d satisfying $v_e = v$, such that $\lambda_d((v_e, j)) \in \mathsf{S_{cd}}$ for all $e \in \mathsf{S_{cd}}$. Such a bijection exists due to Lemma 8 in [5]. We extend this bijection to $\mathbb{I}$ by setting $\lambda_d(\mathfrak{a}) := \mathfrak{a}^{\mathcal{I}}$. Furthermore, we extend λ_d to ξ_d with $\xi_d(\iota(t_{\mathcal{I}}(d))) := d$. Then, ξ_d is injective except for $\star$: if d is its own role successor, it can happen that $\xi_d(\star) = d = \xi_d((v, j))$. We define the complete constraint system $\mathfrak{C}_d$ over variables f^x with $f \in \mathsf{N_F}$, $x \in X_d$, such that $P(f_1^{x_1}, \ldots, f_k^{x_k}) \in \mathfrak{C}_d$ iff $\big(f_1^{\mathcal{I}}(\xi_d(x_1)), \ldots, f_k^{\mathcal{I}}(\xi_d(x_k))\big) \in P^D$ holds for all $x_1, \ldots, x_k \in X_d$. If $f^{\mathcal{I}}(\xi_d(x))$ is undefined, then f^x does not occur in $\mathfrak{C}_d$.

We show in [5] (Lemma 9) that $\mathfrak{C}_d$ is a satisfiable local system for $t_{\mathcal{I}}(d)$ and V_d. Thus, $\mathfrak{t}_{\mathcal{I}}(d) = \big(t_{\mathcal{I}}(d), V_d, \mathfrak{C}_d\big)$ is an augmented type. Furthermore, we can show (cf. Lemma 10 in [5]) that every augmented type in $\mathbb{T}_{\mathcal{I}}$ is patched in $\mathbb{T}_{\mathcal{I}}$. If Algorithm 1 guesses $\mathbb{I}$, $\mathfrak{C}_{\mathbb{I}}$, and $\mathfrak{t}_{\mathfrak{a}}$, where $\mathfrak{a} \in \mathbb{I}$, then the initial set $\mathbb{T}$ must contain $\mathbb{T}_{\mathcal{I}}$, and no augmented type from $\mathbb{T}_{\mathcal{I}}$ can ever be removed from $\mathbb{T}$. This shows that the augmented types $\{\mathfrak{t}_{\mathfrak{a}} \mid \mathfrak{a} \in \mathsf{N_I}\} \subseteq \mathbb{T}_{\mathcal{I}}$ remain in $\mathbb{T}$ throughout the execution of the algorithm. Since the algorithm terminates, it thus returns CONSISTENT. □

Because Algorithm 1 runs in exponential time, we obtain a matching upper bound to the ExpTime-hardness inherited from $\mathcal{ALC}$. Indeed, as there are at most exponentially many individual type systems and polynomially many individual types in such a type system, all guesses can be implemented by enumerating all choices in exponential time. The main elimination procedure also runs in exponential time as the number of augmented types is exponentially bounded, and all required tests can be performed in exponential time, provided that $\mathfrak{D}$ is ExpTime-ω-admissible. We thus obtain the following result.

Theorem 2. *Let $\mathfrak{D}$ be an* ExpTime-*ω-admissible concrete domain. Then, consistency checking in $\mathcal{ALCOSCC}(\mathfrak{D})$ is* ExpTime-*complete.*

5 Reasoning with ABoxes

In DLs, a TBox is often complemented by an *ABox* containing *concept assertions* $C(a)$ and *role assertions* $r(a, b)$, where $a, b \in \mathsf{N_I}$, $r \in \mathsf{N_R}$, and C is a concept, with the obvious semantics. In our DL, those assertions can be expressed in the TBox using nominals [9]. In the presence of a concrete domain, however, we may want to use additional kinds of assertions: *predicate assertions* $P(f_1(a_1), \ldots, f_k(a_k))$ with $f_i \in \mathsf{N_F}$, $a_i \in \mathsf{N_I}$, $i = 1, \ldots, k$, and a k-ary predicate P of $\mathfrak{D}$, and *feature assertions* $f(a, c)$ with $f \in \mathsf{N_F}$, $a \in \mathsf{N_I}$, and a constant $c \in D$. The former requires every model $\mathcal{I}$ to satisfy $(f_1^{\mathcal{I}}(a_1^{\mathcal{I}}), \ldots, f_k^{\mathcal{I}}(a_k^{\mathcal{I}})) \in P^D$, and the latter states that $f^{\mathcal{I}}(a^{\mathcal{I}}) = c$.

Using predicate assertions, we can rewrite the TBox $\mathcal{T}_{\mathsf{ex}}$ in Sect. 3 into a single, intuitive assertion $\mathsf{salary}(\mathtt{Sam}) < \mathsf{salary}(\mathtt{Jane})$. This also demonstrates how predicate assertions can be simulated by CIs: instead of $P(f_1(a_1), \ldots, f_k(a_k))$, we can use $\top \sqsubseteq \mathsf{succ}(\mathsf{ref}_{a_i} = \{a_i\})$ for $i = 1, \ldots, k$ and $\top \sqsubseteq \exists \mathsf{ref}_{a_1} f_1, \ldots, \mathsf{ref}_{a_k} f_k.P$.

On the other hand, with feature assertions, we can give specific values and state, for instance, that Sam's salary is 100,001 € with salary(Sam, 100,001). Feature assertions seemingly increase the expressivity, since we can use them to refer to constant values. However, we first have to specify how these constants are actually encoded. For the following results, we consider *concrete domains $\mathfrak{D}$ with constants*, which extend concrete domains with an encoding for arbitrary constants $c \in D$ and constraint systems that can use such constants in addition to variables. For ExpTime-ω-admissible concrete domains with constants, we also require the extended CSP($\mathfrak{D}$) to be decidable in exponential time. In particular, the main known examples of ExpTime-ω-admissible concrete domains ($\mathfrak{Q}$, Allen's relations, and RCC8) satisfy this requirement under the reasonable assumptions that all numbers are given as integer fractions in binary encoding and the constants in RCC8 refer to polygonal regions in the rational plane [21,24]. We can now use this encoding to represent the constants in feature assertions $f(a, c)$.

Unfortunately, we cannot directly use constants in constraints to extend Algorithm 1 to support feature assertions, since this would result in infinitely many possible local constraint systems. Another idea to deal with feature assertions is that, if $\mathfrak{D}$ has *singleton predicates* $=_c$ with $(=_c)^D = \{c\}$, then one can express $f(a, c)$ by $\{a\} \sqsubseteq \exists f.{=_c}$. Since an ω-admissible concrete domain $\mathfrak{D}$ has a finite signature, however, this only works for a fixed, finite set of values $c \in D$. Due to the JD and JEPD conditions, it turns out that feature assertions are actually equivalent to *additional singleton predicates* $=_c$ that are not part of $\mathfrak{D}$, but can be used in concepts with the same semantics as defined above.[6]

Lemma 4. *For $\mathcal{ALCOSCC}(\mathfrak{D})$ with an ω-admissible concrete domain $\mathfrak{D}$ with constants, the following problems are reducible to each other: (a) consistency with additional singleton predicates, and (b) consistency with feature assertions.*

The reductions take exponential time, but produce ontologies of polynomial size.

Additionally, feature assertions can be expressed by *predicate assertions* if $\mathfrak{D}$ is *homogeneous*, i.e. such that every isomorphism between finite substructures of $\mathfrak{D}$ can be extended to an isomorphism from $\mathfrak{D}$ to itself [11]. All known ω-admissible concrete domains are homogeneous [11].

Lemma 5. *For $\mathcal{ALCOSCC}(\mathfrak{D})$ with an ω-admissible and homogeneous concrete domain $\mathfrak{D}$ with constants, consistency with feature assertions can be reduced to consistency without feature assertions in exponential time. The resulting ontology is of polynomial size.*

Together, Lemma 4 to 5 show that, under these conditions, we can freely use constant values (either in feature assertions or additional singleton predicates) in $\mathcal{ALCOSCC}(\mathfrak{D})$, without increasing the complexity of reasoning. The following result then follows together with Theorem 2.

Theorem 3. *If $\mathfrak{D}$ is an* ExpTime*-ω-admissible and homogeneous concrete domain with constants, then consistency in $\mathcal{ALCOSCC}(\mathfrak{D})$ with feature assertions and additional singleton predicates is* ExpTime*-complete.*

6 Undecidable Extensions

To conclude our investigations, we show that several extensions of $\mathcal{ALCOSCC}(\mathfrak{D})$, inspired by existing DLs or obtained by seemingly harmless tweaks to the syntax and semantics, are undecidable. Hereafter, we assume that the domain set of $\mathfrak{D}$ is infinite and that $\mathfrak{D}$ is JD (cf. Sect. 2). In this case, we allow w.l.o.g. the usage of set terms ($f = \texttt{next}\, g$) expressing equality of the values assigned to f and $\texttt{next}\, g$ (we detail the construction of this term in [5]).

[6] The results in this section also hold for $\mathcal{ALC}(\mathfrak{D})$, since they can be shown without succ-restrictions, nominals, or restricting to finitely-branching interpretations [13].

Comparing Set Cardinalities and Feature Values. If $\mathfrak{D}$ is a numerical concrete domain where D is either $\mathbb{N}$, $\mathbb{Z}$ or $\mathbb{Q}$, it is natural to consider comparisons between feature values of an individual d and the cardinalities of sets of role successors of d. For example, we could describe individuals whose age is twice the number of their children using the concept $\mathsf{succ}(\mathsf{age} = 2 \cdot |\mathsf{child}|)$. This could be achieved by allowing succ-restrictions to contain *mixed numerical constraints* $f = \ell$, where ℓ is a PA expression (cf. Sect. 2) that is allowed in $\mathcal{ALCOSCC}(\mathfrak{D})$ and $f \in \mathsf{N_F}$; then, we extend $\cdot^{\mathcal{I}}$ by defining $d \in \mathsf{succ}(f = \ell)^{\mathcal{I}}$ iff $f^{\mathcal{I}}(d) = \sigma_d(\ell)$. Unfortunately, for the CDs considered here, this leads to undecidability, which can be shown by a reduction to $\mathcal{ALC}(\mathfrak{D})$ with the concrete domain $\mathfrak{D} = (\mathbb{N}, +_1)$ where $+_1$ is the successor relation, which is known to be undecidable [11].

Theorem 4. *If $\mathfrak{D}$ is a numerical concrete domain that is JD, then consistency of $\mathcal{ALCOSCC}(\mathfrak{D})$ TBoxes with mixed numerical constraints is undecidable.*

Proof. We force $r \in \mathsf{N_R}$ to be functional with the CI $\top \sqsubseteq \mathsf{succ}(|r| \leq 1)$.
We encode the CD-restriction $C := \exists p_0, p_1.+_1$ using $C_0 \sqcap C_1$, where

$$C_i := \begin{cases} \mathsf{succ}(f_i = |S| + i) & \text{if } p_i = f_i \\ \mathsf{succ}(f_i' = |S| + i) \sqcap \mathsf{succ}(|r_i \cap (f_i' = \mathtt{next}\ f_i)| \geq 1) & \text{if } p_i = r_i f_i. \end{cases}$$

for $i = 0, 1$, with fresh names $S \in \mathsf{N_C}$, $f_i' \in \mathsf{N_F}$.

□

Local and Global Cardinality Constraints. It is possible to extend $\mathcal{ALCSCC}$ by replacing succ-restrictions, ranging over sets of role successors, with sat-*restrictions* $\mathsf{sat}(\mathfrak{con})$ ranging over the whole domain of an interpretation. For the resulting DL, called $\mathcal{ALCSCC}^{++}$, the consistency problem is NExpTime-complete [4]. In this DL, we can state that an individual likes *all* existing cars using the concept $\mathsf{sat}(\mathsf{likes} \cap \mathsf{Car} = \mathsf{Car})$; in contrast, $\mathsf{succ}(\mathsf{likes} \cap \mathsf{Car} = \mathsf{Car})$ describes an individual that likes all cars to which it is related by some role.

If we consider the DL $\mathcal{ALCSCC}^{++}(\mathfrak{D})$ obtained by adding sat-restrictions in the presence of concrete domains, then these restrictions may additionally contain feature roles. For example, the concept $\mathsf{sat}(\top = (\mathsf{age} \geq \mathtt{next}\ \mathsf{age}))$ describes the *overall* oldest individuals, by saying that their age is greater or equal to those of all individuals, while $\mathsf{succ}(\top = (\mathsf{age} \geq \mathtt{next}\ \mathsf{age}))$ describes individuals that are not younger than any individuals related to them by some role name.

Formally, both $\mathcal{ALCSCC}^{++}$ and $\mathcal{ALCSCC}^{++}(\mathfrak{D})$ are evaluated over *finite* interpretations. In [4], this has been used to show that the consistency problem for the extension of $\mathcal{ALCSCC}^{++}$ with inverse roles is undecidable. Similarly, we can use sat-restrictions with feature roles to simulate multiplication of cardinalities of *finite* sets, and thus reduce Hilbert's tenth problem [28] to the consistency of a $\mathcal{ALCSCC}^{++}(\mathfrak{D})$ TBox, provided that $\mathfrak{D}$ is JD. Writing $C \equiv D$ as a shorthand for $C \sqsubseteq D$ and $D \sqsubseteq C$, we can encode the equation $\mathfrak{e} = (x = y \cdot z)$ over integers as a product of cardinalities $|A_x^{\mathcal{I}}| = |A_y^{\mathcal{I}}| \cdot |A_z^{\mathcal{I}}|$, in three steps. First, we enforce

$r_{\mathfrak{e}}^{\mathcal{I}} = A_y^{\mathcal{I}} \times A_z^{\mathcal{I}}$ to hold with $A_y \equiv \mathsf{sat}(|r_{\mathfrak{e}}| \geq 1)$ and $A_y \equiv \mathsf{sat}(r_{\mathfrak{e}} = A_z)$; then, we enforce $|s_{\mathfrak{e}}^{\mathcal{I}}| = |A_x^{\mathcal{I}}|$ by adding $\top \sqsubseteq \mathsf{sat}(s_{\mathfrak{e}} = (f_{\mathfrak{e}} = \mathtt{next}\, g_{\mathfrak{e}}))$ and the CIs

$$\top \sqsubseteq \mathsf{sat}(|(g_{\mathfrak{e}} = \mathtt{next}\, f_{\mathfrak{e}})| \leq 1) \text{ and } A_x \sqsubseteq \mathsf{sat}(|(g_{\mathfrak{e}} = \mathtt{next}\, f_{\mathfrak{e}})| \geq 1).$$

Finally, we add $\top \sqsubseteq \mathsf{sat}(|r_{\mathfrak{e}}| = |s_{\mathfrak{e}}|)$, so that, for every finite model $\mathcal{I}$ of all these CIs, $|A_x^{\mathcal{I}}| = |s_{\mathfrak{e}}^{\mathcal{I}}| = |r_{\mathfrak{e}}^{\mathcal{I}}| = |A_y^{\mathcal{I}} \times A_z^{\mathcal{I}}| = |A_y^{\mathcal{I}}| \cdot |A_z^{\mathcal{I}}|$ holds.

Theorem 5. *If the concrete domain $\mathfrak{D}$ is infinite and JD, then the consistency problem for $\mathcal{ALCSCC}^{++}(\mathfrak{D})$ TBoxes is undecidable.*

Transitive Roles. Often, we may want a role name to be interpreted as a transitive relation: for instance, trans(ancestor) in the TBox expresses the fact that the ancestor of an ancestor is also an ancestor. The interaction between number restrictions and transitivity axioms in the presence of role inclusions is known to lead to undecidability [20]. It is possible to regain decidability by disallowing transitive roles within number restrictions, even in the presence of inverse roles [20]. Another restriction that leads to decidability is to replace number restrictions with role functionality axioms; in this case, decidability holds even if one additionally allows nominals and inverse roles [16].

In the DL $\mathcal{SSCC}$ that extends $\mathcal{ALCSCC}$ with transitivity axioms, consistency is undecidable even under all syntactic constraints mentioned above. In particular, we require that numerical constraints contain no transitive roles and no constants other than 0 or 1. By adapting the reduction [20] from the tiling problem, which is known to be undecidable [12], we obtain the following.

Theorem 6. *Consistency in $\mathcal{SSCC}$ is undecidable, even if numerical constraints contain no transitive roles and no constants other than* 0 *or* 1.

7 Conclusion

We have presented the very expressive DL $\mathcal{ALCOSCC}(\mathfrak{D})$ that supports concrete domain restrictions and role successor restrictions involving feature values. We have shown that consistency in this logic is ExpTime-complete, the same as for the basic DL $\mathcal{ALC}$. Moreover, we have discussed the consequences of adding assertions, transitive roles, unrestricted semantics, or mixed constraints, most of which make the logic undecidable. While feature roles can already express a restricted form of inverse roles, in the future, we would like to investigate the decidability and complexity of $\mathcal{ALCOISCC}(\mathfrak{D})$ with full inverse roles, for which it is known that they increase the complexity of classical DLs with nominals and number restrictions to NExpTime [30]. Another avenue of research is to implement a reasoner for $\mathcal{ALCOSCC}(\mathfrak{D})$, based on a suitable tableaux algorithm [27] that needs to integrate a QFBAPA solver and a concrete domain reasoner. Currently, reasoners for DLs with non-trivial concrete domains only exist for $\mathcal{ALC}(\mathfrak{D})$ and $\mathcal{EL}(\mathfrak{D})$ with so-called p-admissible concrete domains and without feature paths [2].

Acknowledgments. This work was partially supported by DFG grant 389792660 as part of TRR 248 – CPEC, by the German Federal Ministry of Education and Research (BMBF, SCADS22B) and the Saxon State Ministry for Science, Culture and Tourism (SMWK) by funding the competence center for Big Data and AI "ScaDS.AI Dresden/Leipzig".

Disclosure of Interests. The authors have no competing interests to declare that are relevant to the content of this article.

References

1. Allen, J.F.: Maintaining knowledge about temporal intervals. Commun. ACM **26**(11), 832–843 (1983). https://doi.org/10.1145/182.358434
2. Alrabbaa, C., Baader, F., Borgwardt, S., Koopmann, P., Kovtunova, A.: Combining proofs for description logic and concrete domain reasoning. In: Fensel, A., Ozaki, A., Roman, D., Soylu, A. (eds.) Rules and Reasoning - 7th International Joint Conference, RuleML+RR 2023, Proceedings. LNCS, vol. 14244, pp. 54–69. Springer (2023). https://doi.org/10.1007/978-3-031-45072-3_4
3. Baader, F.: A new description logic with set constraints and cardinality constraints on role successors. In: Dixon, C., Finger, M. (eds.) Proceedings of the 11th International Symposium on Frontiers of Combining Systems (FroCoS'17). LNCS, vol. 10483, pp. 43–59. Springer-Verlag, Brasília, Brazil (2017). https://doi.org/10.1007/978-3-319-66167-4_3
4. Baader, F., Bednarczyk, B., Rudolph, S.: Satisfiability and query answering in description logics with global and local cardinality constraints. In: ECAI 2020, pp. 616–623. IOS Press (2020). https://doi.org/10.3233/FAIA200146
5. Baader, F., Borgwardt, S., De Bortoli, F., Koopmann, P.: Concrete domains meet expressive cardinality restrictions in description logics (extended version) (2025). https://doi.org/10.48550/arXiv.2505.21103
6. Baader, F., Calvanese, D., McGuinness, D.L., Nardi, D., Patel-Schneider, P.F. (eds.): The Description Logic Handbook: Theory, Implementation, and Applications. Cambridge University Press (2003). https://doi.org/10.1017/CBO9780511711787
7. Baader, F., De Bortoli, F.: On the expressive power of description logics with cardinality constraints on finite and infinite sets. In: Herzig, A., Popescu, A. (eds.) FroCoS 2019. LNCS (LNAI), vol. 11715, pp. 203–219. Springer, Cham (2019). https://doi.org/10.1007/978-3-030-29007-8_12

8. Baader, F., Hanschke, P.: A scheme for integrating concrete domains into concept languages. In: Mylopoulos, J., Reiter, R. (eds.) Proceedings of the 12th International Joint Conference on Artificial Intelligence, IJCAI 1991, pp. 452–457. Morgan Kaufmann (1991). http://ijcai.org/Proceedings/91-1/Papers/070.pdf
9. Baader, F., Horrocks, I., Lutz, C., Sattler, U.: An Introduction to Description Logic. Cambridge University Press (2017). https://doi.org/10.1017/9781139025355
10. Baader, F., Rydval, J.: Description logics with concrete domains and general concept inclusions revisited. In: Peltier, N., Sofronie-Stokkermans, V. (eds.) IJCAR 2020. LNCS (LNAI), vol. 12166, pp. 413–431. Springer, Cham (2020). https://doi.org/10.1007/978-3-030-51074-9_24
11. Baader, F., Rydval, J.: Using model theory to find decidable and tractable description logics with concrete domains. J. Autom. Reason. **66**(3), 357–407 (2022). https://doi.org/10.1007/s10817-022-09626-2
12. Berger, R.: The undecidability of the domino problem. Mem. Am. Math. Soc. **66**, 72 (1966). https://mathscinet.ams.org/mathscinet-getitem?mr=216954
13. Borgwardt, S., De Bortoli, F., Koopmann, P.: The precise complexity of reasoning in $\mathcal{ALC}$ with ω-admissible concrete domains. In: Giordano, L., Jung, J.C., Ozaki, A. (eds.) Proceedings of the 37th International Workshop on Description Logics (DL 2024). CEUR Workshop Proceedings, vol. 3739. CEUR-WS.org (2024). https://ceur-ws.org/Vol-3739/paper-1.pdf
14. Carapelle, C., Turhan, A.: Description logics reasoning w.r.t. general TBoxes is decidable for concrete domains with the EHD-property. In: Kaminka, G.A., et al. (eds.) ECAI 2016 – 22nd European Conference on Artificial Intelligence. Frontiers in Artificial Intelligence and Applications, vol. 285, pp. 1440–1448. IOS Press (2016). https://doi.org/10.3233/978-1-61499-672-9-1440
15. Demri, S., Quaas, K.: First steps towards taming description logics with strings. In: Gaggl, S.A., Martinez, M.V., Ortiz, M. (eds.) Logics in Artificial Intelligence – 18th European Conference, JELIA 2023, Proceedings. LNCS, vol. 14281, pp. 322–337. Springer (2023). https://doi.org/10.1007/978-3-031-43619-2_23
16. Gutiérrez-Basulto, V., Ibáñez-García, Y.A., Jung, J.C.: Number restrictions on transitive roles in description logics with nominals. In: Singh, S., Markovitch, S. (eds.) Proceedings of the Thirty-First AAAI Conference on Artificial Intelligence, pp. 1121–1127. AAAI Press (2017). https://doi.org/10.1609/AAAI.V31I1.10678
17. Hollunder, B., Baader, F.: Qualifying number restrictions in concept languages. In: Allen, J.F., Fikes, R., Sandewall, E. (eds.) Proceedings of the 2nd International Conference on Principles of Knowledge Representation and Reasoning (KR'91), pp. 335–346. Morgan Kaufmann (1991)
18. Hollunder, B., Nutt, W., Schmidt-Schauß, M.: Subsumption algorithms for concept description languages. In: 9th European Conference on Artificial Intelligence, ECAI 1990, pp. 348–353 (1990)
19. Horrocks, I., Sattler, U.: Ontology reasoning in the $\mathcal{SHOQ}$(D) description logic. In: Nebel, B. (ed.) Proceedings of the Seventeenth International Joint Conference on Artificial Intelligence, IJCAI 2001, pp. 199–204. Morgan Kaufmann (2001)

20. Horrocks, I., Sattler, U., Tobies, S.: Practical reasoning for very expressive description logics. Log. J. IGPL **8**(3), 239–263 (2000). https://doi.org/10.1093/JIGPAL/8.3.239
21. Jonsson, P.: Constants and finite unary relations in qualitative constraint reasoning. Artif. Intell. **257**, 1–23 (2018). https://doi.org/10.1016/j.artint.2017.12.003
22. Kuncak, V., Rinard, M.: Towards efficient satisfiability checking for boolean algebra with presburger arithmetic. In: Pfenning, F. (ed.) CADE 2007. LNCS (LNAI), vol. 4603, pp. 215–230. Springer, Heidelberg (2007). https://doi.org/10.1007/978-3-540-73595-3_15
23. Labai, N., Ortiz, M., Simkus, M.: An ExpTime upper bound for $\mathcal{ALC}$ with integers. In: Calvanese, D., Erdem, E., Thielscher, M. (eds.) Proceedings of the 17th International Conference on Principles of Knowledge Representation and Reasoning, KR 2020, pp. 614–623 (2020). https://doi.org/10.24963/KR.2020/61
24. Li, S., Liu, W., Wang, S.: Qualitative constraint satisfaction problems: an extended framework with landmarks. Artif. Intell. **201**, 32–58 (2013). https://doi.org/10.1016/j.artint.2013.05.006
25. Lutz, C.: The complexity of description logics with concrete domains. Ph.D. thesis, RWTH Aachen University, Germany (2002). http://sylvester.bth.rwth-aachen.de/dissertationen/2002/042/index.htm
26. Lutz, C.: NExpTime-complete description logics with concrete domains. ACM Trans. Comput. Logic (TOCL) **5**(4), 669–705 (2004). https://doi.org/10.1145/1024922.1024925
27. Lutz, C., Miličić, M.: A tableau algorithm for description logics with concrete domains and general TBoxes. J. Autom. Reason. **38**(1), 227–259 (2007). https://doi.org/10.1007/s10817-006-9049-7
28. Matiyasevich, Y.V.: Hilbert's tenth problem. With a foreword by Martin Davis. MIT Press, Cambridge, MA (1993)
29. Randell, D.A., Cui, Z., Cohn, A.G.: A spatial logic based on regions and connection. In: Nebel, B., Rich, C., Swartout, W.R. (eds.) Proceedings of the 3rd International Conference on Principles of Knowledge Representation and Reasoning (KR'92), pp. 165–176. Morgan Kaufmann (1992)
30. Tobies, S.: The complexity of reasoning with cardinality restrictions and nominals in expressive description logics. J. Artif. Intell. Res. **12**, 199–217 (2000). https://doi.org/10.1613/JAIR.705
31. Tobies, S.: PSPACE reasoning for graded modal logics. J. Log. Comput. **11**(1), 85–106 (2001). https://doi.org/10.1093/LOGCOM/11.1.85

A Real-Analytic Approach to Differential-Algebraic Dynamic Logic

Jonathan Hellwig(✉) and André Platzer

Karlsruhe Institute of Technology, Karlsruhe, Germany
{jonathan.hellwig, platzer}@kit.edu

Abstract. This paper introduces a novel axiomatic proof calculus for differential-algebraic dynamic logic (dAL). The calculus enables deductive verification and sound transformation of differential-algebraic programs (DAPs), which generalize differential-algebraic equations, while remaining compatible with differential dynamic logic (dL) for hybrid programs. One central contribution is the ghost switching axiom which establishes precise conditions to decompose multi-modal DAPs into equivalent hybrid systems with ordinary differential equations. The applicability of the calculus is demonstrated through a formal equivalence proof, showing the reduction of the Euclidean pendulum from a differential-algebraic formulation to an equivalent system of ordinary differential equations.

Keywords: Differential dynamic logic · Differential-algebraic equations · Proof calculus · Theorem proving

1 Introduction

Hybrid systems with explicit (vectorial) ordinary differential equations (ODEs) $x' = f(x)$ are important models for cyber-physical systems [13,3,8] and have been axiomatized in differential dynamic logic (dL) [21,25,23,26], which is the basis of the theorem prover KeYmaera X [10] that was used to prove correctness properties of aircraft, train and robotics systems [7,14,17]. This paper extends (modern differential-form) differential dynamic logic [25] with *differential-algebraic programs (DAPs)*. DAPs allow the relation of x and its time-derivative x' to be defined by a formula of first-order real arithmetic. In particular, DAPs include ordinary equations given by implicit equations such as $f(x', x) = 0$. Beyond that, DAPs also support composition using logical operators such as conjunctions $\wedge$ and disjunctions $\vee$, enabling modular and flexible specification of system behavior. This gives rise to easy combinations and extensions of systems.

Consider a model of an electric circuit consisting of a resistor r, a capacitor c and a source s. Each component of the circuit can be given by a local equation:

$$v_r = R\, i_r, \quad i_c = C\, v_c', \quad v_s = 0,$$

where $v_\bullet$ and $i_\bullet$ are the voltage and the current of each component, and R and C are constants. Assuming these three elements are connected in series, Kirchhoff's

C. Barrett and U. Waldmann (Eds.): CADE 2025, LNAI 15943, pp. 696–714, 2025.
https://doi.org/10.1007/978-3-031-99984-0_36

laws contribute two connection constraints $i_r = i_c$ and $v_r + v_c = v_s$. Putting everything together, the electric circuit is described by the single real-arithmetic formula

$$v_r = Ri_r \wedge i_c = Cv_c' \wedge v_s = 0 \wedge i_r = i_c \wedge v_r + v_c = v_s.$$

The complete model emerges by simply joining each component's constitutive equation with the corresponding connection constraints. This illustrates the key advantage of differential-algebraic programs: complex systems are built compositionally from independent components. For that reason, differential-algebraic equations are the mathematical foundation for the popular modeling tool *Modelica* [9]. However, the DAPs presented in this paper extend beyond differential algebraic equations by allowing inequality and quantified constraints such as $x' \leq f(x)$ and $\exists y(g(x, y) = 0 \wedge x' = f(x))$. This added expressiveness supports modelling of uncertainty and of dynamics with non-polynomial right-hand sides.

Yet, the expressive power and flexibility of DAPs comes with added complexities in numerical and symbolic analysis. DAPs may have hidden constraint that are only revealed when differentiating one of their algebraic constraints. Consider the *Euclidean pendulum*[1] [18, p. 13] — a classical example of a system of differential-algebraic equations. Its dynamics are given by the formula

$$x' = v \wedge v' = \lambda x \wedge y' = w \wedge w' = \lambda y - g \wedge x^2 + y^2 = 1,$$

where x, y are the pendulum's position coordinates, and v, w are the velocities. The scalar λ is a Lagrange multiplier implicitly constrained by the holonomic condition $x^2 + y^2 = 1$, and g denotes the gravitational constant. Suppose we wish to analyze the pendulum's behavior with respect to some safety property. Although x and y are confined to the unit circle, their time derivatives $x' = v$ and $y' = w$ are governed by the equations $v' = \lambda x$ and $w' = \lambda y - g$, so the evolution of x and y depends on the unknown multiplier λ. This multiplier is not a free parameter of the system: solutions exist only if λ satisfies the hidden constraint

$$\lambda = gy - (v^2 + w^2).$$

That relation is not explicit in the original model. It is only uncovered after repeatedly differentiating the algebraic constraint $x^2 + y^2 = 1$ and performing algebraic manipulations. Without this hidden constraint, we cannot directly analyze the behavior of x and y, because λ would remain undetermined. While such derivations are feasible for small examples, carrying them out by hand is tedious and error-prone, and doing so outside a formal logical framework forfeits any end-to-end guarantee of correctness. Because hidden constraints are a fundamental feature of DAPs, we need systematic and sound principles to uncover them, and a logic expressive enough to state and prove the resulting properties.

To meet this need, this paper introduces the *differential-form differential-algebraic dynamic logic* (dAL). This new logic gives native support to hybrid

[1] Its equations follow from the Lagrangian $\mathcal{L}(x, y, \lambda) = gx - \frac{1}{2}(v^2 + w^2) + \frac{\lambda}{2}(x^2 + y^2 - 1)$.

programs whose continuous behavior is specified by DAPs and provides an axiomatic proof calculus for reasoning about their dynamic properties. This calculus fulfills two roles. First, it guarantees correctness-preserving transformations of DAPs. Second, it enables rigorous proofs of system properties such as safety and reachability.

A first precursor, *differential-algebraic dynamic logic* (DAL) [22,23], already extended the original, non-differential-form variant of differential dynamic logic. The differential-form logic dAL presented in this paper builds on DAL and changes it in several essential ways. The main contributions of this paper are:

1. *Logical foundations for model transformations*: This calculus establishes a rigorous basis for differential and algebraic transformations of DAPs — an indispensable capability for practical work with DAPs that was not available in DAL. It also lays the groundwork for future integration with larger-scale modelling frameworks.
2. *Axioms for non-normalized differential constraints*: The prior DAL proof calculus required a syntactic normalization of DAPs. The new axioms remove that prerequisite: they apply directly and modularly to *non-normalized* formulas, streamlining proofs and simplifying implementation.
3. *Ghost switching axiom*: We introduce a new *ghost switching axiom* that gives exact criteria for when a multi-mode DAP can be split into a hybrid systems containing simpler, single-mode components. This axiom formally justifies a transformation that has previously been used without proof in the literature [28,15].
4. *Differential-form reasoning*: Our proof calculus employs differential forms, linking it to existing differential-invariant completeness results [27]. The same completeness guarantee now applies to every DAP that can be reduced to a polynomial ordinary differential equation.
5. *Local Hilbert-type proof calculus*: Compared to the prior DAL sequent calculus, our formulation represents a significant step toward a uniform substitution calculus for dAL. Uniform substitution externalizes side-condition checking, simplifying proof manipulation and theorem prover implementations [25].

2 Differential-algebraic Dynamic Logic

This section briefly introduces the syntax and semantics of (differential-form) differential-algebraic dynamic logic, with a focus on its continuous fragment. For a full treatment of the discrete fragment, the interested reader is referred to the foundational work on dL [25,26].

2.1 Syntax

The set $\mathcal{V}$ contains all variables and for each variable $x \in \mathcal{V}$, there is a differential variable $x' \in \mathcal{V}$. By $\mathcal{V}' \subseteq \mathcal{V}$ we denote the set of all differential variables. A differential variable x' represents the instantaneous rate of change of x, much like a derivative in calculus. However, rather than being a function of time explicitly it is treated as an independent variable within the system. This abstraction allows differentials to be represented algebraically, making it possible to manipulate them syntactically.

Definition 1 (Syntax of terms and formulas [25,26]). *The language of* dAL terms *is generated by the following grammar, where x is a variable, c is a rational constant, and f is a function symbol:*

$$e, g ::= x \mid c \mid f(e_1, \ldots, e_k) \mid e \cdot g \mid e + g \mid (e)'.$$

The language of dAL formulas *is generated by the following grammar, where x is a variable, P a predicate symbol, and α a differential-algebraic program (Def. 2):*

$$F, G ::= e \leq g \mid P(e_1, \ldots, e_k) \mid F \wedge G \mid \neg F \mid \forall x F \mid [\alpha] F.$$

Remark 1. The usual logical and modal operators such as $<, \geq, >, \neq, \vee, \rightarrow, \exists$ and $\langle \cdot \rangle$ are *definable* in terms of more primitive constructs. For instance, disjunction can be defined as $A \vee B \equiv \neg(\neg A \wedge \neg B)$, and the diamond modality as $\langle \alpha \rangle P \equiv \neg [\alpha] \neg P$. Throughout this work, we adopt vectorial notation: $\bar{x} = (x_1, \ldots, x_n)$ denotes a tuple of variables. For vector-valued function symbols $f(\bar{x}) = (f_1(\bar{x}), \ldots, f_n(\bar{x}))$, the expression $\bar{x} = f(\bar{x})$ abbreviates the conjunction $\bigwedge_{i=1}^{n} x_i = f_i(x_1, \ldots, x_n)$. The square of the Euclidean norm is defined as $\|\bar{x}\|^2 \equiv \sum_{i=1}^{n} x_i^2$.

Remark 2. For a variable x and formula F we write $x \in F$ to mean that x is a free variable of that formula [25, Def. 7].

Definition 2 (Syntax of programs [25,26]). *The language of* dAL *programs is generated by the following grammar, where x is a variable, $\bar{x}$ is a tuple of variables, e is a term, and F is a formula of first-order real arithmetic:*

$$\alpha, \beta ::= x := e \mid ?F \mid \{\bar{x} : F\} \mid \alpha; \beta \mid \alpha \cup \beta \mid \alpha^*.$$

Remark 3. In this syntax, an assignment is denoted by $x := e$, a test by $?F$, a nondeterministic choice by $\alpha \cup \beta$, and a nondeterministic loop by α^*. For any $n \in \mathbb{N}$, the notation α^n denotes the n-fold sequential composition of α.

Remark 4. Unlike ordinary differential equations, where the bound variables are syntactically evident form $x' = f(x)$, DAPs may involve arbitrary first-order real arithmetic formulas. For this reason, the notation used here explicitly indicates which variables evolve in the DAPs: in $\{\bar{x} : F\}$, the bound variables are given by the tuple $\bar{x}$.

2.2 Semantics

A dAL state is a function $\omega : \mathcal{V} \to \mathbb{R}$ that assigns a real value to each variable in the set of all variables $\mathcal{V}$. The set of states is denoted by $\mathcal{S}$. Given a subset

$X \subseteq \mathcal{V}$, we write $X^{\complement} = \mathcal{V} \setminus X$ for its complement. For a variable x and a real value $r \in \mathbb{R}$, we write ω_x^r to denote the state obtained from ω by replacing its value at x with r. For a state $\omega \in \mathcal{S}$ and a tuple $\bar{x}$, we write $\omega(\bar{x})$ as a shorthand for $(\omega(x_1), \ldots, \omega(x_n))$. Finally, the partial derivative of a differentiable function h with respect to x is written as $\frac{\partial h}{\partial x}$.

Definition 3 (Semantics of terms [25]). *The* semantics $\omega[\![e]\!] \in \mathbb{R}$ *of a* dAL *term e in state $\omega \in \mathcal{S}$ is inductively as follows:*

1. $\omega[\![x]\!] = \omega(x)$ *for a variable* $x \in \mathcal{V}$,
2. $\omega[\![f(e_1, \ldots, e_k)]\!] = f(\omega[\![e_1]\!], \ldots, \omega[\![e_k]\!])$ *for a function* $f : \mathbb{R}^k \to \mathbb{R}$,
3. $\omega[\![e + g]\!] = \omega[\![e]\!] + \omega[\![g]\!]$,
4. $\omega[\![e \cdot g]\!] = \omega[\![e]\!] \cdot \omega[\![g]\!]$,
5. $\omega[\![(e)']\!] = \sum_{x \in \mathcal{V}} \omega(x') \frac{\partial \omega[\![e]\!]}{\partial x}$.

The differential $(e)'$ characterizes how the value of e changes locally in response to variations in its free variables x. Specifically, it expresses this dependence as a function of the corresponding differential symbols x', which represent the rate of change of x. We note that each term e can only have finitely many free variables. Therefore, the sum in the definition of $(e)'$ is always finite.

Definition 4 (Semantics of formulas [25]). *The* semantics of a dAL formula *F is the subset $[\![F]\!] \subseteq \mathcal{S}$ of states in which F is true and defined as:*

1. $[\![e \leq g]\!] = \{\omega \in \mathcal{S} \mid \omega[\![e]\!] \leq \omega[\![g]\!]\}$,
2. $[\![P(e_1, \ldots, e_n)]\!] = \{\omega \in \mathcal{S} \mid (\omega[\![e_1]\!], \ldots, \omega[\![e_n]\!]) \in [\![P]\!]\}$,
3. $[\![\neg F]\!] = \mathcal{S} \setminus [\![F]\!]$,
4. $[\![F \wedge G]\!] = [\![F]\!] \cap [\![G]\!]$,
5. $[\![\forall x F]\!] = \{\omega \in \mathcal{S} \mid \forall r \in \mathbb{R} : \omega_x^r \in [\![F]\!]\}$,
6. $[\![[\alpha]F]\!] = \{\omega \in \mathcal{S} \mid \forall (\omega, \nu) \in [\![\alpha]\!] : \nu \in [\![F]\!]\}$.

The *box modality* $[\alpha]F$ is used to express *safety properties*, statements that hold after all possible executions of the system. If $[\alpha]F$ is true in a given state, it guarantees that no matter how the system evolves according to the program α, the condition F will always hold. The *diamond modality* $\langle\alpha\rangle F$, on the other hand, is used to express reachability properties, statements asserting that some execution of the system can lead to a desired state. If $\langle\alpha\rangle F$ holds, then there exists at least one execution of the program α that reaches a state where F is true.

Definition 5 (Real-analytic function). *On an open set $U \subset \mathbb{R}$ the function $f : U \to \mathbb{R}$ is said to be* real-analytic, *if for every $t_0 \in U$ there exist $\varepsilon > 0$ and coefficients $a_k \in \mathbb{R}$ such that for all $t \in (t_0 - \varepsilon, t_0 + \varepsilon)$*

$$f(t) = \sum_{k=0}^{\infty} a_k (t - t_0)^k.$$

Definition 6 (Flow). *A mapping $\varphi : (a, b) \to \mathcal{S}$ is called a* flow *in $\bar{x}$, if $\varphi(\cdot)(\bar{x})$ is real-analytic on (a, b) and satisfies the following two properties:*

1. $\varphi(t)(\bar{x}') = \frac{d\varphi(t)(\bar{x})}{dt}(t)$ *for all* $t \in (a, b)$,
2. $\varphi(t) = \varphi(0)$ *on* $(\bar{x} \cup \bar{x}')^{\complement}$ *for all* $t \in (a, b)$.

We write $\mathcal{A}_{\bar{x}}(a, b)$ *to denote the set of flows in* $\bar{x}$ *defined on the interval* (a, b). *For a formula* F *and an interval* I, *we also write* $\varphi(I) \subseteq [\![F]\!]$ *to denote* $\varphi(t) \in [\![F]\!]$ *for all* $t \in I$.

Remark 5. There always exists a flow $\varphi \in \mathcal{A}_{\bar{x}}(-\varepsilon, \varepsilon)$ that satisfies a given state $\omega \in \mathcal{S}$ at time 0. Define $\varphi : (-\varepsilon, \varepsilon) \to \mathcal{S}$, $\varphi(t)(\bar{x}) = \omega(\bar{x}')t + \omega(\bar{x})$. We can verify that $\varphi(0)(\bar{x}) = \omega(\bar{x})$ and $\varphi(0)(\bar{x}') = \frac{d\varphi(t)(\bar{x})}{dt}(0) = \omega(\bar{x}')$.

Definition 7 (Semantics of programs). *The* semantics of a dAL program α *is the transition relation* $[\![\alpha]\!] \subseteq \mathcal{S} \times \mathcal{S}$ *and is defined as follows:*

$$
\begin{aligned}
&[\![\alpha \cup \beta]\!] = [\![\alpha]\!] \cup [\![\beta]\!],\\
&[\![\alpha; \beta]\!] = [\![\alpha]\!] \circ [\![\beta]\!],\\
&[\![x := e]\!] = \{(\omega, \omega_x^r) \mid r = \omega[\![e]\!]\},\\
&[\![?F]\!] = \{(\omega, \omega) \mid \omega \in [\![F]\!]\},\\
&[\![\alpha^*]\!] = \textstyle\bigcup_{n \in \mathbb{N}} [\![\alpha^n]\!],\\
&[\![\{\bar{x} : F\}]\!] = \{(\omega, \nu) \mid \textit{There exist } T \geq 0, \varepsilon > 0 \textit{ and a flow } \varphi \in \mathcal{A}_{\bar{x}}(-\varepsilon, T + \varepsilon),\\
&\qquad \textit{with } \varphi([0, T]) \subseteq [\![F]\!] \textit{ and } \omega = \varphi(0) \textit{ and } \varphi(T) = \nu\}.
\end{aligned}
$$

Remark 6. The semantics of DAPs require flows to be real-analytic functions on an open neighborhood of $[0, T]$. In contrast, the differential constraint F only needs to hold on the smaller closed set $[0, T]$. This property is crucial for the soundness of the proof calculus in Section 3.

Example 1. To better understand the open-neighborhood assumption on flows, consider the following two DAPs:

$$\alpha \equiv \{x : x' = -1 \land x \geq 0\} \text{ and } \beta \equiv \{x, y : x' = -1 \land y^2 = x \land x \geq 0\}.$$

Fix the initial state $\omega(x) = 1$, $\omega(x') = -1$, $\omega(y) = 1$, and $\omega(y') = -1/2$. For some $\varepsilon > 0$, a flow $\varphi_\alpha \in \mathcal{A}_x(-\varepsilon, 1 + \varepsilon)$ of system α is given by $\varphi_\alpha(t)(x) = 1 - t$. Since $\varphi_\alpha(\cdot)(x)$ is a polynomial, it extends analytically beyond the interval [0,1], even though the differential constraint only holds on [0,1]. For system β, a flow $\varphi_\beta \in \mathcal{A}_{x,y}(-\varepsilon, 1 + \varepsilon)$ is given by $\varphi_\beta(t)(x) = 1 - t$ and $\varphi_\beta(t)(y) = \sqrt{1 - t}$ for any value $0 \leq T < 1$. However, $\varphi_\beta(\cdot)(y)$ does not extend to $[0, 1]$, because its first derivative exhibits finite-time blow-up (see Fig. 1):

$$\lim_{t \to 1} \frac{d\varphi_\beta(t)(x)}{dt} = \lim_{t \to 1} -\frac{1}{2\sqrt{1 - t}} = -\infty.$$

While for both system α and β there exists a flow that satisfies their respective constraint each closed subinterval $I \subset [0, 1]$, only system α has a flow that also satisfies it on $[0, 1]$. More generally, Def. 6 ensures that φ remains well-behaved in a small neighborhood of $[0, T]$ and ensures all derivatives are bounded on $[0, T]$.

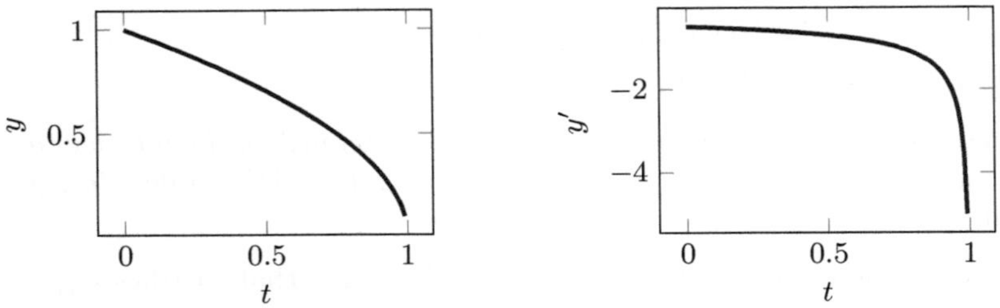

Fig. 1. The behavior $\varphi_\beta(\cdot)$ at y and y' as $t \to 1$.

Differential-algebraic programs are strictly more expressive than ODE systems in dL. Below, we show three key examples:

1. **Modeling Uncertainty**: Differential-algebraic programs can represent systems with continuous uncertainty by incorporating disturbances. For instance, the system

$$\{x, w : x' = f(x, w) \wedge w^- \leq w \leq w^+\}$$

describes a dynamical system where the evolution of x is governed by $f(x, w)$ with a disturbance w, constrained within the range $[w^-, w^+]$.
2. **Implicit System Characterization**: Differential-algebraic programs can define systems implicitly using existential quantification. Consider:

$$\{x : \exists y(x' = y \wedge y^2 = x \wedge x > 0)\}$$

Here, the derivative of x is characterized by the square root of x, as $x' = y$ must hold for some y satisfying $y^2 = x$. This implicitly defines the nonpolynomial differential equation with nonunique solutions:

$$x' = \pm\sqrt{x}, \quad \text{for } x > 0.$$

3. **Multimodal Systems**: These programs can naturally represent multimodal continuous programs. For example, the system

$$\{x : (x' = f(x) \wedge x \leq 0) \vee (x' = f(x) \wedge x \geq 0)\}$$

models an evolution in the two domains $x \leq 0$ and $x \geq 0$. In Section 3, we see that such programs can be decomposed into a loop with a nondeterministic choice between the two modes, provided that the handoff points are carefully managed. Note that there is no arbitrary switching between these two modes, because flows are real-analytic.

Remark 7. All ODE solutions in the dL sense are real-analytic (By the Cauchy-Kovalevskaya Theorem [16, Theorem 1.7.1], all ODE solution with real-analytic right-hand side are real-analytic). Thus, the dAL DAP semantics generalize the dL ODE semantics, allowing for a broader class of systems. In particular, the expressive term language of DAPs in dAL permits non-Lipschitz differential constraints (See 2 above). Non-Lipschitzian systems exhibit an implicit nondeterminism, such as spontaneous movement from rest [2]. To avoid unintended implicit behavior, we restrict flows to be real-analytic. When nondeterminism is needed, it can be explicitly introduced using discrete program constructs. For instance, a flow of the system $\{x : x' = f(x) \vee x' = g(x)\}$ never switches between two distinct right-hand sides. Because the flows of both modes are real-analtyic, the Identity Theorem for real-analytic functions [16, Cor. 1.2.6 p. 14] guarantees that any two flows agreeing on an open time interval must agree along their whole trajectories. If switching is desired, it must be made explicit with discrete assignments:

$$\left(x' := f(x); \{x : x' = f(x)\} \cup x' := g(x); \{x : x' = g(x)\}\right)^*.$$

Choosing flows to be real-analytic strikes the balance between flexible modeling and control over system behavior while still allowing for a powerful proof calculus.

3 Axiomatic Proof Calculus

In this section, we introduce a proof calculus for DAPs from Section 2. The complete proofs of the statements in this section are presented in [12].

3.1 Progress, Exit and Entry formulas

For reasoning about DAPs and the soundness of our proof calculus, it is crucial to understand how DAPs evolve locally and under what conditions they transition between modes. For discrete-time programs, the notion of *next step* is unambiguous: given a current state, there is a distinct next state at the subsequent time step. In the loop $(x := -x)^*$, a state with $x > 0$ is followed by a state with $x < 0$; each state has a distinct successor state. In contrast, continuous-time programs differ fundamentally, because the state evolves on real intervals of time. There is no smallest positive time instance, so there is no notion of next state — one can speak only of states that are arbitrarily close in the future.

Example 2. Let us consider the differential-algebraic program

$$\{x : x' = 1 \wedge -1 < x \wedge x \leq 1\},$$

started in the initial state $\omega \in \mathcal{S}$. The unique flow of this system is given by

$$\varphi(t)(x) = \omega(x) + t$$

as long as $-1 < \varphi(t)(x) \leq 1$ is satisfied. We consider three cases for the initial condition:

(i) Strictly inside the domain: If $-1 < \omega(x) < 1$, there always exists a positive time increment $\varepsilon > 0$ such that $\omega(x)+\varepsilon < 1$. Hence, the system can advance by every such ε, and the flow may continue until $\omega(x)$ reaches 1.

(ii) On the boundary: If $\omega(x) = 1$, the inequality $\varphi(t)(x) \leq 1$ is already tight. Any positive advance would violate it, so the only admissible evolution is the *blocked* flow $\varphi(t)(x) = \omega(x) + t$ for $t = 0$.

(iii) Outside the domain: If $\omega(x) > 1$, the initial state breaks the constraint $\varphi(t)(x) \leq 1$ — no execution is possible.

This example illustrates that there exist states in which the system can evolve and others where further progress is impossible. This distinction motivates the following definition:

Definition 8 (Local progress formula [27, p. 24]). *Let $\bar{y}$ and $\bar{y}'$ be two tuples of variables that do not occur in the formula F. The* local progress formula *of the system $\{\bar{x}:F\}$ is defined as*

$$\langle\{\bar{x}:F\}\rangle\bigcirc \equiv \exists\bar{y}\exists\bar{y}'\,(\bar{x} = \bar{y} \wedge \bar{x}' = \bar{y}' \wedge \langle\{\bar{x}:F \vee (\bar{x} = \bar{y} \wedge \bar{x}' = \bar{y}')\}\rangle(\bar{x} \neq \bar{y}))\,.$$

The formula expresses that, from the current state, the system can evolve to a different state—that is, make local progress. The right disjunct in the diamond modality includes all the points on the boundary of F that may not be strictly contained in F. In this way, the formula captures all states from which there exists a positive time step such that the state advances into F.

Example 3 (continued). Continuing Example 2, the progress formula $\langle\{x:x' = 1 \wedge x \leq 1\}\rangle\bigcirc$ precisely captures the concept we previously discussed: the characterization of states in which the system can locally evolve. In this particular instance, the progress formula is equivalent to $x' = 1 \wedge -1 < x \wedge x < 1$.

Equipped with the notion of progress formulas, we now define *local exit formulas*, which identify the state from which a flow may no longer continue within a mode, and *local entry formulas*, which mark the states from which a mode may start. Together, these formulas make it possible to describe the exact conditions under which a system leaves one mode and enters the next. The following definition is inspired by the approach in prior work [11].

Definition 9 (Local exit and entry formulas). *Let $F^- \equiv [\bar{x}' := -\bar{x}']F$ denote the reverse-flow formula of a formula F. The* local exit formula $\langle\{\bar{x}:F\}\rangle{\uparrow}\bigcirc$ *and the* local entry formula $\langle\{\bar{x}:F\}\rangle{\downarrow}\bigcirc$ *of the system $\{\bar{x}:F\}$ are defined as*

$$\langle\{\bar{x}:F\}\rangle{\uparrow}\bigcirc \equiv (\langle\{\bar{x}:\neg F\}\rangle\bigcirc \wedge F) \vee (\langle\{\bar{x}:F^-\}\rangle\bigcirc^- \wedge \neg F),$$
$$\langle\{\bar{x}:F\}\rangle{\downarrow}\bigcirc \equiv (\langle\{\bar{x}:F\}\rangle\bigcirc \wedge \neg F) \vee (\langle\{\bar{x}:\neg F^-\}\rangle\bigcirc^- \wedge F).$$

Remark 8. A state ω satisfies the *exit formula*, if and only if, one of two situations occurs:

(i) *Forward flow*: Starting from ω, there exists a flow of positive duration that satisfies the constraint F initially, but enter its negation $\neg F$ immediately.

(ii) *Reverse flow*: Alternatively, beginning in ω, there exists a time-reverse flow of positive duration that starts in the negation $\neg F$ and enters the constraint F .

Including the reverse-flow disjunct may seem surprising at first, but it is essential when the system's constraint is *open*. Open constraints do not contain their boundary, so no forward flow can reach the boundary while staying in the constraint. By considering a reverse flow starting form the negation, we can capture the exit points on the boundary.

Example 4 (continued). We now apply the notions of *entry formula* and *exit formula* to the differential-algebraic program

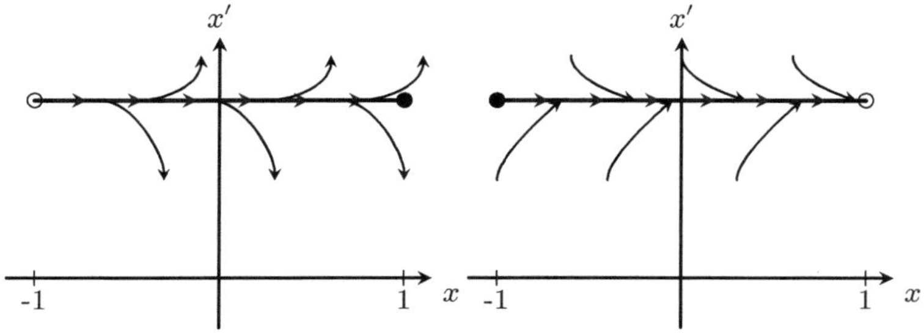

Fig. 2. Entry and exit formula for $\{x : x' = 1 \wedge -1 < x \wedge x \leq 1\}$. Left: The exit formula includes all points from which a trajectory can locally leave the constraint region (black arrows). The excluded left endpoint is shown as an open circle, the included right endpoint as a filled circle. Right: The entry formula includes all points where trajectories can locally enter the region.

$$\{x : x' = 1 \wedge -1 < x \wedge x \leq 1\}$$

from Example 2. *Exit formula:* A state satisfies the exit formula, if there exists a flow of positive duration that makes progress into the constraint's negation or a reverse flow can progress from the negation into the constraint. For the present system this reduces to

$$\langle\{x : x' = 1 \wedge -1 < x \wedge x \leq 1\}\rangle{\uparrow}\bigcirc \;\leftrightarrow\; x' = 1 \wedge -1 < x \wedge x \leq 1.$$

The left-hand inequality remains strict, because each flow starting in the domain immediately evolves away from the left boundary, i.e., it is no exit point (See Fig. 2 left). *Entry formula:* In contrast to the exit formula, a flow may enter into the constraint through its left open boundary, even though it is not part of the constraint (See Fig. 2 right). Consequently, both disjuncts from Def. 9 contribute to the entry formula. It reduces to

$$\langle\{x : x' = 1 \wedge -1 < x \wedge x \leq 1\}\rangle{\downarrow}\bigcirc \;\leftrightarrow\; x' = 1 \wedge -1 \leq x \wedge x < 1.$$

A central lemma, ensuring the correctness of the definition of exit and entry formulas, is the following generalization of the intermediate value theorem:

Lemma 1. *Let $T \geq 0, \varepsilon > 0$, $\varphi \in \mathcal{A}_{\bar{x}}(-\varepsilon, T+\varepsilon)$ be a flow and F be a semi-algebraic formula. Then, if we have $\varphi(0) \in [\![\neg F]\!]$ and $\varphi(T) \in [\![F]\!]$, there exists a $\xi \in [0,T]$ such that $\varphi(\xi) \in [\![\langle\{\bar{x}:F\}\rangle{\downarrow}\bigcirc]\!]$ and $\varphi(\xi) \in [\![\langle\{\bar{x}:\neg F\}\rangle{\uparrow}\bigcirc]\!]$.*

This lemma formalizes our intuition of entry and exit formulas: when a system's trajectory transitions from a state not satisfying F to one satisfying F, then there must be an intermediate point simultaneously satisfying the entry formula $\langle\{\bar{x}:F\}\rangle{\downarrow}\bigcirc$ and the exit formula $\langle\{\bar{x}:\neg F\}\rangle{\uparrow}\bigcirc$. Now, we finally have the necessary tools to formally define when two modes of a DAP are consistent:

Definition 10 (Mode consistency). *Let F and G be two formulas of first-order real arithmetic. The* mode consistency formula *$F \rightsquigarrow_{\bar{x}} G$ of F and G is defined as*

$$F \rightsquigarrow_{\bar{x}} G \equiv (\langle\{\bar{x}:F\}\rangle{\uparrow}\bigcirc \land \langle\{\bar{x}:G\}\rangle{\downarrow}\bigcirc) \rightarrow (F \leftrightarrow G).$$

Intuitively, the formula $F \rightsquigarrow_{\bar{x}} G$ states that if a state satisfies both the exit formula of F and the entry formula of G, then both constraints must agree at that point. If this condition is satisfied along every trajectory of a system, the disjunctive DAP $\{\bar{x}:F \lor G\}$ can be safely decomposed into a two distinct DAPs without losing any of its original behavior. The role of this definition for ensuring correct decompositions is illustrated in the following example:

Example 5. Consider the unrestricted system $\alpha \equiv \{x:x' = 1\}$. *Inconsistent decomposition:* One might try to decompose the system into the loop

$$\beta \equiv (\{x:x' = 1 \land x < 0\} \cup \{x:x' = 1 \land x \geq 0\})^*.$$

The two modes meet at the single boundary state $x' = 1 \land x = 0$. That state is precisely the conjunction of the exit formula of the first mode and the entry formula of the second mode. Because the first mode excludes $x = 0$, it creates an implicit infinitesimal barrier, preventing a continuous transition between the two modes. In the original system α, the value of x evolves continuously from negative to positive values without restriction. Hence, α has distinct behavior from β and the consistency condition fails. *Consistent decomposition:* Including the boundary in both modes resolves the issue:

$$\gamma \equiv (\{x:x' = 1 \land x \leq 0\} \cup \{x:x' = 1 \land x \geq 0\})^*.$$

With the notion of mode consistency formally defined, we now present an axiomatic proof calculus for dAL, which allows rigorous reasoning about mode transitions and model transformations:

Theorem 1 (Soundness). *The following formulas are sound axioms of* dAL, *i.e., they are valid in all states:*

DW $[\{\bar{x} : F\}]F$

C $[\{\bar{x} : F \wedge G\}]P \leftrightarrow [\{\bar{x} : G \wedge F\}]P$

DE $[\{\bar{x} : e = 0\}](e)' = 0 \quad (\bar{x}' \notin e)$

DX $[\{\bar{x} : F\}]P \rightarrow [?F]P$

DI $(F \rightarrow [\{\bar{x} : F\}](P)') \rightarrow ([?F]P \rightarrow [\{\bar{x} : F\}]P) \quad (\bar{x}' \notin P)$

DR $[\{\bar{x} : F\}]P \rightarrow \forall \bar{y} \forall \bar{y}' [\{\bar{x}, \bar{y} : F \wedge G\}]P \quad (\bar{y}, \bar{y}' \notin P, F)$

AG $[\{\bar{x} : F\}]G(h(\bar{x}, \bar{x}')) \rightarrow$
$(\forall \bar{y} \forall \bar{y}' [\{\bar{x}, \bar{y} : F \wedge G(\bar{y})\}]P \rightarrow [\{\bar{x} : F\}]P) \quad (\bar{y}, \bar{y}' \notin P, F, G(\cdot), h(\cdot, \cdot))$

BDG $[\{\bar{x}, \bar{y} : F \wedge \bar{y}' = g(\bar{x}, \bar{x}', \bar{y})\}] \; \|\bar{y}\|^2 \leq h(\bar{x}, \bar{x}') \rightarrow$
$([\{\bar{x} : F\}]P \leftrightarrow [\{\bar{x}, \bar{y} : F \wedge \bar{y}' = g(\bar{x}, \bar{x}', \bar{y})\}]P) \quad (\bar{y}, \bar{y}' \notin P, F, h(\cdot, \cdot))$

GS $[\{\bar{x} : F \vee G\}](F \rightsquigarrow_{\bar{x}} G \wedge G \rightsquigarrow_{\bar{x}} F) \rightarrow$
$((F \vee G \rightarrow [(\{\bar{x} : F\} \cup \{\bar{x} : G\})^*]P) \rightarrow [\{\bar{x} : F \vee G\}]P)$

The axioms for DAPs in Theorem 1 capture essential properties of their evolution. The *Differential Weakening (DW)* axiom ensures that the formulas representing differential-algebraic program remain valid throughout the system's execution. The *Commutativity (C)* axiom allows syntactic exchange of conjunctive formulas. The *Differential Effect (DE)* axiom justifies that the differential $(e)' = 0$ of any algebraic equation $e = 0$ also holds when following $e = 0$ since equations are closed under differentials. Thereby, the DE axiom also enforces consistency between a variable x and its derivative x', ensuring that x evolves in accordance with the specified dynamics. The *Differential Skip (DX)* axiom guarantees the existence of a trivial solution with zero duration whenever a formula F is initially satisfied, meaning the system may remain in place (see Remark 5). The *Differential Invariant (DI)* axiom provides a key condition for proving properties under the box modality. For instance, if $x \geq 0$ initially and $x' \geq 0$ throughout, then $x \geq 0$ at all future times, allowing reasoning about system invariants. The *Differential Refinement (DR)* axiom captures a simple principle: adding additional constraints only restricts the system's behavior. The *Algebraic Ghost (AG)* axiom generalizes differential cuts [25,22] from dL to encode observable system behavior. This is particularly useful when applying the DE axiom to derivatives. Since the side condition prevents DE from being directly applied to differential variables, we can introduce a new dummy variable $y = x'$ to track the behavior of x', allowing the reasoning to proceed. The *Bounded Differential Ghost (BDG)* axiom allows expressing new differential relationships between variables as long as the new variable y has bounds expressible in terms of prior variables. The *Ghost Switching (GS)* axiom allows modularly decomposing multi-mode differential-algebraic programs into a loop over a non-deterministic choice. This decomposition exploits analyticity and is *only* sound if the mode consistency formula is preserved along the evolution of the system. The key property, that the GS axiom needs for soundness is that a real-analytic function can only switch finitely many times in and out of a semi-algebraic set in bounded time. This is captured in the following lemma:

Lemma 2. *Let $T \geq 0$ and $\varepsilon > 0$. Further, let $\varphi \in \mathcal{A}_{\bar{x}}(-\varepsilon, T+\varepsilon)$ be a flow and F be a semi-algebraic formula. Let $(\tau_k)_{k\in\mathbb{N}} \subseteq [0,T]$ be a strictly monotone sequence with $\varphi(\tau_k) \in [\![F]\!]$ for all $k \in \mathbb{N}$. Then, there exists a $k_0 \in \mathbb{N}$ such that $\varphi(\tau) \in [\![F]\!]$ for all $\tau \geq \tau_{k_0}$ if the sequence is increasing and for all $\tau \leq \tau_{k_0}$ if the sequence is decreasing.*

The intuition behind this lemma is that if there exists a sequence of distinct time points where the flow satisfies F, then eventually, the system must satisfy F continuously from some point onward. Otherwise, the flow would have to switch infinitely many times in and out of F, which is incompatible with the regularity of real-analytic functions and semi-algebraic sets.

Remark 9. The formula $[\{\bar{x}:F\}][\{\bar{x}:F\}]P \leftarrow [\{\bar{x}:F\}]P$ is not a valid axiom of dAL, even though a corresponding axiom holds in dL. Consider, for instance:

$$\{x,t:(x' = t \wedge t \leq 0 \vee x' = -t \wedge t \geq 0) \wedge t' = 1\}.$$

This system exhibits a discontinuity in the second derivative of x at $t = 0$, which prevents the existence of a real-analytic flow from $t < 0$ to $t > 0$, because real-analytic functions are smooth. However, it is possible to construct two separate flows—one for $t \leq 0$ and one for $t \geq 0$—that agree in both x and x'. This shows a mode transition can occur via a composition of two flows, even though a single real-analtyic flow may not exist.

Some derived axioms are quite useful in practice:

Theorem 2. *The following are derived axioms of* dAL*:*

AR $\quad \forall\bar{x}\forall\bar{x}'(F \to G) \to ([\{\bar{x}:G\}]P \to [\{\bar{x}:F\}]P)$

DC $\quad [\{\bar{x}:F\}]G \to ([\{\bar{x}:F \wedge G\}]P \leftrightarrow [\{\bar{x}:F\}]P)$

∧DE $\quad [\{\bar{x}:F \wedge e = 0\}]P \leftrightarrow [\{\bar{x}:F \wedge e = 0 \wedge (e)' = 0\}]P \quad (\bar{x}' \notin e)$

The *Algebraic Refinement (AR)* axiom is for purely algebraic transformations. If F implies G, then all ways of following F also satisfy P if all ways of following the more general G do. For instance, AR allows rewriting $[\{x,y:x' = 1 \wedge y' = x'\}]P$ to $[\{x,y:x' = 1 \wedge y' = 1\}]P$. The *Differential Cut (DC)* axiom is one of the standard differential axioms of dL [25], allowing a DAP to be equivalently augmented with an invariant property G. It can be derived by AG and does not introduce a new variable each time. The *Conjunctive Differential Effect (∧DE)* axiom is useful to augment the system with its differential properties. For examples, we can transform the system $[\{x:y' = 2y \wedge x = y\}]P$ to $[\{x:y' = 2y \wedge x = 5y \wedge x' = 5y'\}]P$, deriving the differential properties of x from its algebraic relationship to y.

Example 6. Based on the derived $\wedge$DE axiom, one might be tempted to assume the following equivalence holds:

$$[\{\bar{x} : F \vee e = 0\}]P \leftrightarrow [\{\bar{x} : F \vee (e = 0 \wedge (e)' = 0)\}]P.$$

However, this equivalence in not valid in general. To see why, consider the following differential-algebraic systems:

$$\alpha \equiv \{x : x' = 1\} \equiv \{x : (x' = 1 \wedge x \neq 0) \vee (x' = 1 \wedge x = 0)\},$$
$$\beta \equiv \{x : (x' = 1 \wedge x \neq 0) \vee (x' = 1 \wedge x = 0 \wedge x' = 0)\}.$$

In system α, x evolves according to $x' = 1$, allowing continuous progression from $x < 0$ to $x > 0$ without obstruction. In contrast, system β imposes an additional constraint at $x = 0$, requiring $x' = 0$ at that point. This restriction causes the system to get stuck at the transition between modes, as x' cannot jump from $x' = 1$ to $x' = 0$. Consequently, the behavior of the DAPs α and β is not equivalent.

3.2 Completeness

Prior work has shown that the natural number are definable using differential equations [19]. As a consequence, Gödel's incompleteness theorem applies to dAL's proof calculus. Nevertheless, there are completeness results for differential invariants in dL [27]. Since our proof calculus builds on top of dL's proof calculus, it inherits these completeness results for systems which are reducible to polynomial ordinary differential equations.

4 Applications

In this section, we demonstrate the usefulness of our proof calculus through two examples. Both examples focus on the *index reduction* of DAPs. The *differentiation index* of a differential-algebraic equation is the minimum number of times it must be differentiated in order to uniquely determine the derivative of each state variable in terms of the others [4, p. 179, Def. 4]. In the first example, we apply the AR and DE axioms in a straightforward manner, successively differentiating the algebraic constraints to obtain a reduced system. In the second example, a state-dependent singularity in the differentiated constraint necessitates careful case distinction using the GS axiom.

Example 7. We now address the Euclidean pendulum from the introduction, showing how our dAL calculus can be used to eliminate the unknown multiplier λ. Let $\bar{x} = (x, y, v, w)$ denote the state variables, and define the differential-algebraic constraint

$$D(\lambda) \equiv x' = v \wedge v' = \lambda x \wedge y' = w \wedge w' = \lambda y - g \wedge x^2 + y^2 = 1.$$

Our goal is to simplify the dAL-formula $[\{\bar{x}, \lambda : D(\lambda)\}]P$, which states that a postcondition P holds after every evolution of the system. Since dAL only defines the box modality, we use an arbitrary predicate P as a placeholder to reason about system equivalence. For simplicity, we focus only on one part of the equivalence, as the reverse is analogous. The derivations are presented as inference chains, read bottom-up. In the following, we write $\mathbb{R}$ to denote proof steps justified by real-arithmetic, and $\mathbb{F}$ for steps justified by first-order logical reasoning.

The multiplier λ appears explicitly in the constraint, but its time-derivative is unspecified. To uncover its implicit dynamics, we differentiate the holonomic constraint $x^2 + y^2 = 1$ twice, thereby obtaining an explicit expression for λ.

$$\begin{array}{rl}
 & \vdash [\{\bar{x}, \lambda : D(\lambda) \land xv + yw = 0 \land \lambda = gy - (v^2 + w^2)\}]P \\ \hline
\mathbb{R},\mathrm{AR} & \vdash [\{\bar{x}, \lambda : D(\lambda) \land xv + yw = 0 \land x'v + xv' + y'w + yw' = 0\}]P \\ \hline
\land\mathrm{DE} & \vdash [\{\bar{x}, \lambda : D(\lambda) \land xv + yw = 0\}]P \\ \hline
\mathbb{R},\mathrm{AR} & \vdash [\{\bar{x}, \lambda : D(\lambda) \land 2xx' + 2yy' = 0\}]P \\ \hline
\land\mathrm{DE} & \vdash [\{\bar{x}, \lambda : D(\lambda)\}]P
\end{array}$$

Finally, we use algebraic refinement and differential refinement to remove λ from the formula with $h(x, y, v, w) = gy - (v^2 + w^2)$:

$$\begin{array}{rl}
 & \vdash [\{\bar{x} : D(gy - (v^2 + w^2)) \land xv + yw = 0\}]P \\ \hline
\mathrm{DR} & \vdash \forall\lambda\forall\lambda'[\{\bar{x}, \lambda : D(h(x, y, v, w)) \land xv + yw = 0 \land \lambda = h(x, y, v, w)\}]P \\ \hline
\mathbb{F},\ \mathrm{AR} & \vdash [\{\bar{x}, \lambda : D(\lambda) \land xv + yw = 0 \land \lambda = gy - (v^2 + w^2)\}]P
\end{array}$$

The open goal contains the transformed system, in which the multiplier λ has been eliminated. The result is a fully specified ODE, enabling the application of completeness results for differential invariants [27].

Note that we did not need to use the GS axiom in the previous example, because we were able to find a globally defined explicit expression for λ. We see that this is not always the case in our next example:

Example 8. Consider the system:

$$\{x, y : x' = y \land x^2 + y^2 = 1\}.$$

The variable x evolves depending on the value of y, and both variables are constrained to a circle of radius one. Our goal is to derive an explicit expression for y'. We start by differentiating the circle constraint using the $\land$DE axiom and do some equivalence transformations with the AR axiom:

$$\begin{array}{rl}
 & \vdash [\{x, y : x' = y \land x^2 + y^2 = 1 \land (x + y')y = 0\}]P \\ \hline
\mathbb{R},\ \mathrm{AR} & \vdash [\{x, y : x' = y \land x^2 + y^2 = 1 \land xx' + y'y = 0\}]P \\ \hline
\mathbb{R},\mathrm{AR},\land\mathrm{DE} & \vdash [\{x, y : x' = y \land x^2 + y^2 = 1\}]P
\end{array}$$

Now, we observe that there are two cases for the constraint: $x + y' = 0$ or $y = 0$. Next, we define

$$F(x, y) \equiv x' = 0 \land x^2 = 1 \land y = 0,$$
$$G(x, y) \equiv x' = y \land x^2 + y^2 = 1 \land y' = -x.$$

Here, $F(x, y)$ represents the special case where x is at its extrema (± 1) and remains constant, while $G(x, y)$ describes the general evolution of the system along the unit circle. We split the system into a disjunction of two modes using the AR axiom:

$$\dfrac{\mathbb{R},\ \text{AR}\ \dfrac{\vdash [\{x, y : F(x, y) \vee G(x, y)\}]P}{\vdash [\{x, y : x' = y \wedge x^2 + y^2 = 1 \wedge (y' = -x \vee y = 0)\}]P}}{\mathbb{R},\ \text{AR}\ \vdash [\{x, y : x' = y \wedge x^2 + y^2 = 1 \wedge (x + y')y = 0\}]P}$$

Finally, applying the GS axiom we have:

$$\text{GS}\ \dfrac{\vdash [\{\{x, y : F(x, y) \vee G(x, y)\}\}](F(x, y) \rightsquigarrow_{\bar{x}} G(x, y) \wedge G(x, y) \rightsquigarrow_{\bar{x}} F(x, y)) \quad \vdash [(\{x, y : F(x, y)\} \cup \{x, y : G(x, y)\})^*]P}{\vdash [\{x, y : (x' = 0 \wedge x^2 = 1 \wedge y = 0) \vee (x' = y \wedge x^2 + y^2 = 1 \wedge y' = -x)\}]P}$$

The top goal closes by simplification of progress formulas and real arithmetic (See [12]). The second goal contains a decomposed version of the original system, formulated as a loop over a nondeterministic choice of two simplified systems. This representation shows how singularities in the differentiated constraints give rise to distinct modes of evolution. To further illustrate these dynamics, Fig. 3 provides a visualization of the system in phase space, showcasing its trajectory and behavior over time.

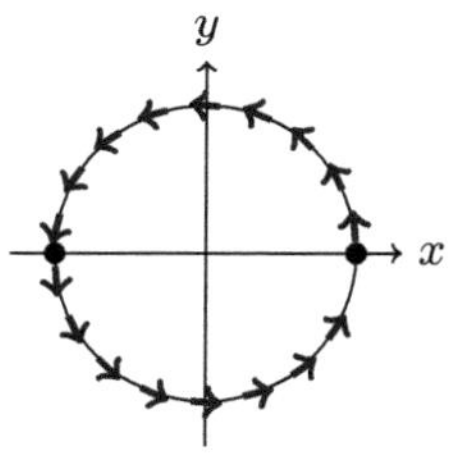

Fig. 3. Phase portrait on the unit circle with two stationary modes.

Remark 10. The pattern observed in the previous example can be formulated in a more general way: Given a semi-explicit system of the form

$$\{\bar{x}, \bar{y} : \bar{x}' = f(\bar{x}, \bar{y}) \wedge g(\bar{x}, \bar{y}) = 0\},$$

we can transform it using the $\wedge$DE axiom into the equivalent system:

$$\{\bar{x}, \bar{y} : \bar{x}' = f(\bar{x}, \bar{y}) \wedge g(\bar{x}, \bar{y}) = 0 \wedge \frac{\partial g}{\partial x}(\bar{x}, \bar{y}) f(\bar{x}) + \frac{\partial g}{\partial y}(\bar{x}, \bar{y}) y' = 0\}.$$

This transformation introduces an implicit constraint on $\bar{y}'$, but solving for $\bar{y}'$ is only possible if $\frac{\partial g}{\partial y}(\bar{x}, \bar{y})$ is non-singular. When this condition fails, the system encounters a singularity, highlighting the necessity of the GS axiom to distinguish between different cases.

5 Related Work

Differential dynamic logic dL has established the logical foundations for reasoning about hybrid systems [24,25]. However, dL does not support reasoning about differential-algebraic equations, which are natural for modeling many physical systems. To fill this gap, an extension of dL to differential-algebraic equation systems was proposed previously in a sequent calculus formulation [22]. However, each rule of this formulation requires a special normalization of differential-algebraic systems. In contrast, our calculus is given by a small set of axioms and does not require such special transformation. Additionally, a challenge in reasoning about differential-algebraic systems is understanding the conditions under which systems can be correctly decomposed. For our calculus, we exploit progress formulas, which have been used for reasoning about invariant properties of differential equations [27,11]. Contributions by Mattsson [18], Pantelides [20], and Benveniste [1] have addressed the challenge of consistently initializing differential-algebraic systems, primarily in the context of simulation. Other works, such as [5,6], focus on the minimization of polynomial ODE systems using bisimulation techniques, also with a focus on simulation. These approaches rely on model transformation techniques aimed at simulation and are not grounded in rigorous logical reasoning principles. In contrast, dAL enables transformations within an axiomatic proof calculus and goes beyond mere model simplifications as it enables the specification and verification of dynamic properties such as safety and liveness.

6 Conclusion

This paper introduced a sound axiomatic proof calculus for (differential-form) differential-algebraic dynamic logic dAL, providing a firm logical foundation for reasoning about differential-algebraic programs. This allows more flexible specification of continuous-time models, along with a framework for their rigorous transformations to obtain logically equivalent forms. The Euclidean pendulum example demonstrated how dAL supports the specification of systems with undetermined dynamics and their reduction to ordinary differential equations. Future work will explore how the sound logical reductions of dAL support automatic model transformation.

Acknowledgements

This work was funded by an Alexander von Humboldt Professorship.

Declaration of Interests

The authors are not aware of any conflicts of interest related to the content of this work.

References

1. Benveniste, A., Caillaud, B., Elmqvist, H., Ghorbal, K., Otter, M., Pouzet, M.: Structural Analysis of Multi-Mode DAE Systems. In: Proceedings of the 20th International Conference on Hybrid Systems: Computation and Control. pp. 253–263. ACM, Pittsburgh Pennsylvania USA (Apr 2017). doi: 10.1145/3049797.3049806
2. Bhat, S.P., Bernstein, D.S.: Example of indeterminacy in classical dynamics **36**(2), 545–550. doi: 10.1007/BF02435747
3. Branicky, M.S.: General hybrid dynamical systems: Modeling, analysis, and control. In: Alur, R., Henzinger, T.A., Sontag, E.D. (eds.) Hybrid Systems III. pp. 186–200. Springer, Berlin, Heidelberg (1996). doi: 10.1007/BFb0020945
4. Campbell, S.L., Gear, C.W.: The index of general nonlinear DAEs. Numerische Mathematik **72**(2), 173–196 (Dec 1995). doi: 10.1007/s002110050165
5. Cardelli, L., Tribastone, M., Tschaikowski, M., Vandin, A.: Symbolic computation of differential equivalences. In: Proceedings of the 43rd Annual ACM SIGPLAN-SIGACT Symposium on Principles of Programming Languages. pp. 137–150. ACM, St. Petersburg FL USA (Jan 2016). doi: 10.1145/2837614.2837649
6. Cardelli, L., Tribastone, M., Tschaikowski, M., Vandin, A.: ERODE: A Tool for the Evaluation and Reduction of Ordinary Differential Equations. In: Legay, A., Margaria, T. (eds.) Tools and Algorithms for the Construction and Analysis of Systems. pp. 310–328. Springer, Berlin, Heidelberg (2017). doi: 10.1007/978-3-662-54580-5_19
7. Cleaveland, R., Mitsch, S., Platzer, A.: Formally Verified Next-generation Airborne Collision Avoidance Games in ACAS X. ACM Trans. Embed. Comput. Syst. **22**(1), 10:1–10:30 (Oct 2022). doi: 10.1145/3544970
8. Davoren, J., Nerode, A.: Logics for hybrid systems. Proceedings of the IEEE **88**(7), 985–1010 (Jul 2000). doi: 10.1109/5.871305
9. Fritzson, P., Engelson, V.: Modelica — A unified object-oriented language for system modeling and simulation. In: Jul, E. (ed.) ECOOP'98 — Object-Oriented Programming. pp. 67–90. Springer, Berlin, Heidelberg (1998). doi: 10.1007/BFb0054087
10. Fulton, N., Mitsch, S., Quesel, J.D., Völp, M., Platzer, A.: KeYmaera X: An axiomatic tactical theorem prover for hybrid systems. In: Felty, A., Middeldorp, A. (eds.) CADE. LNCS, vol. 9195, pp. 527–538. Springer, Berlin (2015). doi: 10.1007/978-3-319-21401-6_36
11. Ghorbal, K., Sogokon, A.: Characterizing positively invariant sets: Inductive and topological methods. Journal of Symbolic Computation **113**, 1–28 (Nov 2022). doi: 10.1016/j.jsc.2022.01.004
12. Hellwig, J., Platzer, A.: A Real-Analytic Approach to Differential-Algebraic Dynamic Logic (May 2025). doi: 10.48550/arXiv.2505.19323
13. Henzinger, T.: The theory of hybrid automata. In: Proceedings 11th Annual IEEE Symposium on Logic in Computer Science. pp. 278–292 (Jul 1996). doi: 10.1109/LICS.1996.561342
14. Kabra, A., Mitsch, S., Platzer, A.: Verified Train Controllers for the Federal Railroad Administration Train Kinematics Model: Balancing Competing Brake and Track Forces. IEEE Transactions on Computer-Aided Design of Integrated Circuits and Systems **41**(11), 4409–4420 (Nov 2022). doi: 10.1109/TCAD.2022.3197690
15. Kabra, A., Mitsch, S., Platzer, A.: Verified train controllers for the Federal Railroad Administration train kinematics model: Balancing competing brake and track forces. IEEE Trans. Comput. Aided Des. Integr. Circuits Syst. **41**(11), 4409–4420 (2022). doi: 10.1109/TCAD.2022.3197690

16. Krantz, S.G., Parks, H.R.: A Primer of Real Analytic Functions. Birkhäuser, Boston, MA (2002). doi: 10.1007/978-0-8176-8134-0
17. Lin, Q., Mitsch, S., Platzer, A., Dolan, J.M.: Safe and Resilient Practical Waypoint-Following for Autonomous Vehicles. IEEE Control Systems Letters **6**, 1574–1579 (2022). doi: 10.1109/LCSYS.2021.3125717
18. Mattsson, S.E., Söderlind, G.: Index Reduction in Differential-Algebraic Equations Using Dummy Derivatives. SIAM Journal on Scientific Computing **14**(3), 677–692 (May 1993). doi: 10.1137/0914043
19. Olivetti, N. (ed.): Automated Reasoning with Analytic Tableaux and Related Methods, 16th International Conference, TABLEAUX 2007, Aix en Provence, France, July 3-6, 2007, Proceedings, LNCS, vol. 4548. Springer, Berlin (2007)
20. Pantelides, C.C.: The Consistent Initialization of Differential-Algebraic Systems. SIAM Journal on Scientific and Statistical Computing **9**(2), 213–231 (Mar 1988). doi: 10.1137/0909014
21. Platzer, A.: Differential dynamic logic for hybrid systems. J. Autom. Reas. **41**(2), 143–189 (2008). doi: 10.1007/s10817-008-9103-8
22. Platzer, A.: Differential-algebraic dynamic logic for differential-algebraic programs. J. Log. Comput. **20**(1), 309–352 (2010). doi: 10.1093/logcom/exn070
23. Platzer, A.: Logical Analysis of Hybrid Systems: Proving Theorems for Complex Dynamics. Springer, Heidelberg (2010). doi: 10.1007/978-3-642-14509-4
24. Platzer, A.: Logics of dynamical systems. In: LICS. pp. 13–24. IEEE, Los Alamitos (2012). doi: 10.1109/LICS.2012.13
25. Platzer, A.: A complete uniform substitution calculus for differential dynamic logic. J. Autom. Reas. **59**(2), 219–265 (2017). doi: 10.1007/s10817-016-9385-1
26. Platzer, A.: Logical Foundations of Cyber-Physical Systems. Springer (2018). doi: 10.1007/978-3-319-63588-0
27. Platzer, A., Tan, Y.K.: Differential equation invariance axiomatization. J. ACM **67**(1), 6:1–6:66 (2020). doi: 10.1145/3380825
28. Tan, Y.K., Mitsch, S., Platzer, A.: Verifying switched system stability with logic. In: Bartocci, E., Putot, S. (eds.) Hybrid Systems: Computation and Control (part of CPS Week 2022), HSCC'22. ACM (2022). doi: 10.1145/3501710.3519541

SAT

Entailment vs. Verification for Partial-Assignment Satisfiability and Enumeration

Roberto Sebastiani(✉)

DISI, University of Trento, Trento, Italy
roberto.sebastiani@unitn.it

Abstract. Many procedures for SAT-related problems, in particular for those requiring the complete enumeration of satisfying truth assignments, rely their efficiency and effectiveness on the detection of (possibly small) *partial* assignments satisfying an input formula. Surprisingly, there seems to be no unique universally-agreed definition of formula satisfaction by a partial assignment in the literature. In this paper, we analyze in depth the issue of satisfaction by partial assignments, raising a flag about some ambiguities and subtleties of this concept, and investigating their practical consequences. We identify two alternative notions that are implicitly used in the literature, namely *verification* and *entailment*, which coincide if applied to (tautology-free) CNF formulas, but differ and present complementary properties if applied to non-CNF or to existentially-quantified formulas. We show that, although the former is easier to check and as such is implicitly used by most current search procedures, the latter has better theoretical properties, and can improve the efficiency and effectiveness of enumeration procedures.

1 Introduction

Motivations. Many search procedures for SAT-related problems (e.g., Analytic Tableaux [38], DPLL [14], circuit AllSAT [17]) and many formula compilers (e.g., d-DNNFs [11,13], OBDDs [4] and SDDs [12]) rely their efficiency and effectiveness on the detection of *partial* truth assignments μ satisfying an input propositional formula φ, which allows to state that not only φ is satisfiable, but also all total assignments extending μ satisfy φ. In particular, when it comes to SAT-based problems requiring the *complete enumeration* of satisfying assignments (e.g. #SAT [20], Lazy SMT [3,34], OMT [37], AllSAT and AllSMT [6,17,24], #SMT [7,31], Projected #SAT [2], Projected AllSAT/AllSMT [18,24,40], knowledge compilation into d-DNNF [11,23], satisfiability in modal and description logics [36], Weighted Model Integration [29,39]), the ability of enumerating satisfying partial assignments which are as small as possible is essential, because each of them avoids the enumeration of the whole subtree of total assignments extending it, whose size is exponential in the number of unassigned atoms.

We start by raising a very-basic question: *What should we mean by "a partial assignment μ satisfies a formula φ"?* We notice that, quite surprisingly and despite its widespread implicit usage in algorithms, there is no unique and universally-agreed definition for formula satisfaction by partial assignments in the literature: most authors do

C. Barrett and U. Waldmann (Eds.): CADE 2025, LNAI 15943, pp. 717–735, 2025.
https://doi.org/10.1007/978-3-031-99984-0_37

not define it explicitly; a few others define it only when dealing with CNF formulas (e.g. [22]); the very few who define it, adopt one of the following distinct definitions:

"*applying μ to φ makes φ true*" (e.g., [10,17]). We say that μ *verifies* φ;[1]
"*all total assignments extending μ satisfy φ*" (e.g., [19,34]). We say that μ *entails* φ.

Notice that this is not simply an issue of the meaning of the word "satisfy": regardless which verb we may use for it (e.g. "satisfy", "entail", "verify", "imply",...), it should be desirable to have a unique and universally-agreed criterion to establish it.
Contributions. In this paper, we analyze in depth the notion of *partial-assignment satisfiability*, in particular when dealing with non-CNF and existentially-quantified formulas, raising a flag about the ambiguities and subtleties of this concept, and investigating their consequences. Our contributions are both theoretical and practical.
Theoretical Analysis. We show, analyze and discuss the following theoretical facts.

(a) Whereas for (tautology-free[2]) CNF formulas partial-assignment satisfiability can be indifferently be interpreted either as verification or as entailment because in this case the two concepts coincide, *for non-CNF formulas verification is strictly stronger than entailment*, and they have complementary properties.
(b) Whereas two equivalent formulas are always entailed by the same partial assignments, *they are not always verified by the same partial assignments*.
(c) Verification checks that the residual $\varphi|_\mu$ of a formula φ under a partial assignment μ—i.e., the formula obtained by applying the assigned truth values from μ to the atoms in φ—is *the true formula*, whereas entailment checks it is *a valid formula*. Thus verification can be computationally much cheaper to check than entailment.
(d) (a)–(c) apply also to existentially-quantified formulas, *even those in CNF*.
(e) (a)–(c) apply also to existentially-quantified formulas resulting from CNF-ization.

We stress the fact that (b) (and (d) and (e) consequently) would be an embarrassing fact if we adopted verification as the definition of partial-assignment satisfiability. As such, we champion the idea that the latter should be defined as entailment [19,34,36], and that verification should be considered an easy-to-check sufficient condition for it.
Practical Consequences. The above facts have the following practical consequences.

1. In satisfiability, we need to find only one total assignment η extending μ, so that entailment produces no benefits wrt. verification and is more expensive (c). Also, due to (a), when the input problem is natively in CNF, the distinction between verification and entailment is not relevant, because these two concepts coincide.

[1] The etymology of "to verify" derives from Latin "*verum facere*", meaning "to make true".
[2] A CNF formula is tautology-free if it contains no tautological clause in the form $(l \vee \neg l \vee \ldots)$. Since tautological clauses can be easily removed upfront by simple preprocessing, hereafter we often assume w.l.o.g. that CNF formulas are tautology-free.

Consequently, both the algorithms for satisfiability and those for enumeration with CNF formulas typically use verification as satisfiability criterion for the current partial assignments, because it is much cheaper and easier to implement than entailment.

This is the case, e.g., of classical procedures like Analytic Tableaux [38] and DPLL [1, 14], or enumeration, counting, or knowledge compilation procedures, e.g. [2, 11, 17, 18, 23, 24]. A few notable exceptions are the Dualiza procedure [27] and the procedures we described in [16, 28, 30]; also OBDDs [4] and SDDs [12] formula compilers implicitly use entailment to prune branches so that to guarantee canonicity (see below and §4).

The scenario changes when we deal with enumeration-based algorithms applied to non-CNF formulas, or to existentially-quantified formulas, or to CNF-ized formulas.

2. Due to (a), a partial assignment may entail a formula without verifying it. Thus, adopting entailment as partial-assignment satisfiability criterion during the search allows for detecting satisfiability earlier than with verification, and thus for producing smaller partial truth assignments.

Although this fact is not very interesting for satisfiability, it may become fundamental for enumeration, because the detection of a satisfying partial assignment avoids the enumeration of the whole subtree of total assignments extending it, whose size is exponential in the number of unassigned atoms: *the earlier satisfiability is detected, the (up to exponentially) fewer assignments are enumerated.*

3. Due to (d), a partial assignment may entail an existentially-quantified formula, even a CNF one, without verifying it. Thus, as with non-CNF formulas (b), adopting entailment as partial-assignment satisfiability criterion during the search allows for detecting satisfiability earlier than with verification.

This is important because in many application domains fundamental operations—like *pre-image computation* in symbolic model checking (see e.g. [5]) or *predicate abstraction* in SW verification (see e.g. [21, 24]) or *projected enumeration* (see e.g. [18, 24, 40]) or *projected model counting* (see e.g. [2])—require dealing with existentially-quantified formulas and with the enumeration of partial assignments satisfying them.

4. Due to (e), CNF-izing upfront the non-CNF formula with the standard techniques [32, 42] does not fix issues (a)–(c), since fresh atoms are introduced, and *a partial assignment over the original atoms may entail the existentially-quantified CNF-ized formula without verifying it.*

This is important because it shows that, although verification and entailment coincide for CNF formulas, Fact 2. Above cannot be fixed by simply CNF-izing a formula upfront and running a CNF enumeration procedure based on partial-assignment verification, projecting out the fresh variables introduced by the CNF-ization.

5. Due to (c), checking verification is polynomial, whereas checking entailment is co-NP-complete, since it consists of checking the validity of the residual formula.

This is the main argument in favour of verification vs. entailment. We notice, however, that if μ entails φ, then the residual of φ under μ is typically much smaller than φ with a much smaller search space, since its atoms are only (a subset of) those that are not assigned by μ. Notice also that, when this happens, entailment prevents from enumerating a number of assignments which is exponential in the number of the atoms in the residual. Therefore, unlike with satisfiability, for enumeration the tradeoff may be favourable to entailment checks.

Based on the considerations above, not only we suggest to adopt entailment rather than verification as unique definition of partial-assignment satisfiability, but also we champion its usage inside enumeration-based search procedures.

Related Work. This paper is a revised version of a 2020 unpublished paper [35], which at that time was not published due to lack of algorithmic support and empirical evidence. These came afterwards. Based on the theoretical analysis in [35] in combination with the idea of dualized search from [15,27], in [28,30] we proposed novel enumeration and counting procedures based on entailment. Unfortunately we were not able to produce any implementation efficient enough to compete with current enumeration procedures based on verification. Only very recently, in [16] we have enhanced the HALL enumeration tool for circuits from [17] by substituting verification checks with entailment checks for partial-assignment reductions ("generalizations" in [16]), boosting its performance in terms of both time efficiency and size of partial-assignment sets.

In [25] we addressed a problem which is different although related to (e), showing that adopting a form of CNF-ization different from [32,42] improves the efficiency and effectiveness of enumeration. Such encoding, however, does not fix fact (e) (see §3.3).

Content. The rest of the paper is organized as follows. §2 provides the necessary notation, terminology, and concepts used in the paper. §3 presents our theoretical analysis: §3.1 introduces verification and entailment for generic propositional formulas and discusses their relative properties; §3.2 lifts the discussion to existentially-quantified formulas; §3.3 discusses the role of CNF-ization in this context; §3.4 analyzes other candidate forms of partial-assignment satisfaction. §4 discusses the practical consequences of entailment vs. verification. §5 provides conclusions and suggestions for future research.

2 Background

In this section we introduce the notation and terminology adopted in this paper, and we recall the standard syntax, semantics and basic facts of propositional logics.

Notation. In what follows T, F, ? denote the truth values "true", "false" and "unknown" respectively; $\top$, $\bot$ denote the logic constants "true" and "false" respectively; A, B denote propositional atoms; φ, ψ denote propositional formulas; μ, η, γ denote truth value assignments. The symbols $\mathbf{A} \stackrel{\text{def}}{=} \{A_1, ..., A_N\}$ and $\mathbf{B} \stackrel{\text{def}}{=} \{B_1, ..., B_K\}$ denote disjoint sets of propositional atoms. More precisely, φ and ψ denote generic propositional formulas built on $\mathbf{A}$, $\mathbf{B}$ and $\mathbf{A} \cup \mathbf{B}$ respectively; η and μ denote total and a partial assignments on $\mathbf{A}$ respectively; δ denote total assignments on $\mathbf{B}$. (All above symbols may possibly have subscripts.)

Syntax. A *propositional formula* is defined inductively as follows: the constants $\top$ and $\bot$ (denoting the truth values true and false) are formulas; a propositional atom

$A_1, A_2, A_3, ...$ is a formula; if φ_1 and φ_2 are formulas, then $\neg\varphi_1$ and $\varphi_1 \wedge \varphi_2$ are formulas. We use the standard Boolean abbreviations: "$\varphi_1 \vee \varphi_2$" for "$\neg(\neg\varphi_1 \wedge \neg\varphi_2)$", "$\varphi_1 \rightarrow \varphi_2$" for "$\neg(\varphi_1 \wedge \neg\varphi_2)$", "$\varphi_1 \leftrightarrow \varphi_2$" for "$\neg(\varphi_1 \wedge \neg\varphi_2) \wedge \neg(\varphi_2 \wedge \neg\varphi_1)$". A *literal* is either an atom (a *positive literal*) or its negation (a *negative literal*). (If l is a negative literal $\neg A_i$, then by "$\neg l$" we conventionally mean A_i rather than $\neg\neg A_i$.) A *clause* is a disjunction of literals $\bigvee_j l_j$. A *cube* is a conjunction of literals $\bigwedge_j l_j$. φ is in *Conjunctive Normal Form (CNF)* iff it is a conjunction of clauses: $\bigwedge_{i=1}^{L} \bigvee_{j_i=1}^{K_i} l_{j_i}$.

Semantics. Given $\mathbf{A} \stackrel{\text{def}}{=} \{A_1, ..., A_N\}$, a map $\eta : \mathbf{A} \longmapsto \{\mathsf{T}, \mathsf{F}\}$ is a *total truth assignment* for $\mathbf{A}$. We assume $\eta(\top) \stackrel{\text{def}}{=} \mathsf{T}$ and $\eta(\bot) \stackrel{\text{def}}{=} \mathsf{F}$. We represent η as a *set of literals* $\eta \stackrel{\text{def}}{=} \{A_i \mid \eta(A_i) = \mathsf{T}\} \cup \{\neg A_i \mid \eta(A_i) = \mathsf{F}\}$. We sometimes represent η also as a *cube* $\bigwedge_{\eta(A_i)=\mathsf{T}} A_i \wedge \bigwedge_{\eta(A_i)=\mathsf{F}} \neg A_i$ which we denote as "$\bigwedge\eta$" so that to distinguish the set and the cube representations. We denote by $|\eta|$ the number of literals in η.

Given a *total* truth assignment η on $\mathbf{A}$ and some formulas $\varphi, \varphi_1, \varphi_2$ on $\mathbf{A}$, the sentence "η *satisfies* φ", written "$\eta \models \varphi$", is defined recursively on the structure of φ as follows: $\eta \models \top$, $\eta \not\models \bot$, $\eta \models A_i$ if and only if $\eta(A_i) = \mathsf{T}$, $\eta \models \neg\varphi_1$ if and only if $\eta \not\models \varphi_1$, $\eta \models \varphi_1 \wedge \varphi_2$ if and only if $\eta \models \varphi_1$ and $\eta \models \varphi_2$. (The definition of $\eta \models \varphi_1 \bowtie \varphi_2$ for the other connectives follows straightforwardly from their definition in terms of $\neg, \wedge$.)

φ is *satisfiable* iff $\eta \models \varphi$ for some total truth assignment η on $\mathbf{A}$. φ is *valid* (written "$\models \varphi$") iff $\eta \models \varphi$ for every total truth assignment η on $\mathbf{A}$. φ_1 *entails* φ_2 (written "$\varphi_1 \models \varphi_2$") iff, for every total assignment η on $\mathbf{A}$, if $\eta \models \varphi_1$ then $\eta \models \varphi_2$. φ_1 and φ_2 are *equivalent* (written "$\varphi_1 \equiv \varphi_2$") iff $\varphi_1 \models \varphi_2$ and $\varphi_2 \models \varphi_1$. Consequently: φ is unsatisfiable iff $\neg\varphi$ is valid; $\varphi_1 \models \varphi_2$ iff $\varphi_1 \rightarrow \varphi_2$ is valid; a clause $\bigvee_i l_i$ is valid (aka is a *tautology*) iff both A_i and $\neg A_i$ occur in it for some A_i; a CNF formula φ is valid iff either it is $\top$ or all its clauses are tautologies. We say that a CNF formula is *tautology-free* iff none of its clauses is a tautology.

$\neg\top$	$\Rightarrow \bot$	$\neg\bot$	$\Rightarrow \top$
$\top \wedge \varphi, \varphi \wedge \top$	$\Rightarrow \varphi$	$\bot \wedge \varphi, \varphi \wedge \bot$	$\Rightarrow \bot$
$\top \vee \varphi, \varphi \vee \top$	$\Rightarrow \top$	$\bot \vee \varphi, \varphi \vee \bot$	$\Rightarrow \varphi$
$\top \rightarrow \varphi$	$\Rightarrow \varphi$	$\bot \rightarrow \varphi$	$\Rightarrow \top$
$\varphi \rightarrow \top$	$\Rightarrow \top$	$\varphi \rightarrow \bot$	$\Rightarrow \neg\varphi$
$\top \leftrightarrow \varphi, \varphi \leftrightarrow \top$	$\Rightarrow \varphi$	$\bot \leftrightarrow \varphi, \varphi \leftrightarrow \bot$	$\Rightarrow \neg\varphi$

Fig. 1. Propagation of truth values through the Boolean connectives.

$\mu(\varphi_1)$	T	T	T	?	?	?	F	F	F
$\mu(\varphi_2)$	T	?	F	T	?	F	T	?	F
$\mu(\neg\varphi_1)$	F	F	F	?	?	?	T	T	T
$\mu(\varphi_1 \wedge \varphi_2)$	T	?	F	?	?	F	F	F	F
$\mu(\varphi_1 \vee \varphi_2)$	T	T	T	T	?	?	T	?	F
$\mu(\varphi_1 \rightarrow \varphi_2)$	T	?	F	T	?	?	T	T	T
$\mu(\varphi_1 \leftrightarrow \varphi_2)$	T	?	F	?	?	?	F	?	T

Fig. 2. Three-value-semantics of $\mu(\varphi)$ in terms of $\{\mathsf{T}, \mathsf{F}, ?\}$.

Partial Truth Assignments. A map $\mu : \mathbf{A}' \longmapsto \{\mathsf{T}, \mathsf{F}\}$ s.t. $\mathbf{A}' \subseteq \mathbf{A}$ and $N' \stackrel{\text{def}}{=} |\mathbf{A}'|$ is a *partial truth assignment* for $\mathbf{A}$. As with total assignments, we can represent μ as a set of literals or as a cube, denoted with "$\bigwedge\mu$".

By "*apply a partial assignment* μ *to* φ" we mean "substitute all instances of each assigned A_i in φ with the truth constants in $\{\top, \bot\}$ corresponding to the truth value assigned by μ, and then apply recursively the standard propagation of truth constants through the Boolean connectives described in Fig. 1. We denote by "$\varphi|_\mu$" ("*residual of φ under μ*") the formula resulting from applying μ to φ.

We introduce a three-value logic to extend μ to $\mathbf{A}$ as $\mu : \mathbf{A} \longmapsto \{\mathsf{T}, \mathsf{F}, ?\}$ by assigning to ? (unknown) the unassigned atoms in $\mathbf{A} \backslash \mathbf{A}'$. Then we extend the semantics of μ to any formula φ on $\mathbf{A}$ as described in Fig. 2.

The following facts follow straightforwardly and are of interest for our discussion.

Property 1. *Let η be a total truth assignment on $\mathbf{A}$ and $\varphi, \varphi_1, \varphi_2$ be formulas on $\mathbf{A}$.*

(i) $\eta \models \varphi$ *iff* $\bigwedge \eta \models \varphi$.
(ii) *If φ_1 and φ_2 are equivalent, then $\eta \models \varphi_1$ iff $\eta \models \varphi_2$.*
(iii) $\eta \models \varphi$ *iff* $\varphi|_\eta$ *is* $\top$.
(iv) *Checking $\eta \models \varphi$ requires at most a polynomial amount of steps.*

Notice that Property 1(i) justifies the usage of "$\models$" for both satisfiability and entailment.

Property 2. *Let μ be a partial assignment on $\mathbf{A}$ and φ be a formula on $\mathbf{A}$. Then $\varphi|_\mu$ is $\top$ iff $\mu(\varphi) = \mathsf{T}$ and $\varphi|_\mu$ is $\bot$ iff $\mu(\varphi) = \mathsf{F}$.*

Notice that total assignments are a subcase of partial ones, so that the definition of residual and Property 2 apply also to total assignments η.

Existentially-Quantified Formulas. A total truth assignment η satisfies $\exists \mathbf{B}.\psi$, written "$\eta \models \exists \mathbf{B}.\psi$", iff exists a total truth assignment δ on $\mathbf{B}$ s.t. $\eta \cup \delta \models \psi$. We call the *Shannon expansion* $\mathsf{SE}[\exists \mathbf{B}.\psi]$ of the existentially-quantified formula $\exists \mathbf{B}.\psi$ the propositional formula on $\mathbf{A}$ defined as

$$\mathsf{SE}[\exists \mathbf{B}.\psi] \stackrel{\text{def}}{=} \bigvee_{\delta_i \in \{\mathsf{T},\mathsf{F}\}^{|\mathbf{B}|}} \psi|_{\delta_i} \tag{1}$$

where $\{\mathsf{T}, \mathsf{F}\}^{|\mathbf{B}|}$ is the set of all total assignments on $\mathbf{B}$. Notice that some $\psi|_{\delta_i}$ may be inconsistent or $\bot$. The following property derives directly from the above definitions.

Property 3. *Let ψ be a formula on $\mathbf{A} \cup \mathbf{B}$ and η be a total truth assignment on $\mathbf{A}$. Then $\eta \models \exists \mathbf{B}.\psi$ iff $\eta \models \mathsf{SE}[\exists \mathbf{B}.\psi]$, that is, $\exists \mathbf{B}.\psi \equiv \mathsf{SE}[\exists \mathbf{B}.\psi]$.*

CNF-ization. Every generic formula φ on $\mathbf{A}$ can be encoded into a CNF formula ψ on $\mathbf{A} \cup \mathbf{B}$ for some $\mathbf{B}$ by applying (variants of) Tseitin CNF-ization $\mathsf{CNF}_{\mathsf{Ts}}(\varphi)$ [42], consisting in applying recursively bottom-up the rewriting rule:

$$\varphi \Rightarrow \varphi[(l_{j1} \bowtie l_{j2}) \mapsto B_j] \wedge \mathsf{CNF}_{\mathsf{DM}}(B_j \leftrightarrow (l_{j1} \bowtie l_{j2})) \tag{2}$$

until the resulting formula ψ is in CNF, where l_{j1}, l_{j2} are literals, $\bowtie \in \{\wedge, \vee, \rightarrow, \leftarrow, \leftrightarrow\}$ and $\mathsf{CNF}_{\mathsf{DM}}()$ is the validity-preserving CNF conversion based on DeMorgan rules (e.g., $\mathsf{CNF}_{\mathsf{DM}}(B \leftrightarrow (l_1 \wedge l_2)) \stackrel{\text{def}}{=} (\neg B \vee l_1) \wedge (\neg B \vee l_2) \wedge (B \vee \neg l_1 \vee \neg l_2)$). The size of ψ is linear wrt. that of φ. With Plaisted&Greenbaum CNF-ization $\mathsf{CNF}_{\mathsf{PG}}(\varphi)$ [32] the term $B_j \leftrightarrow (l_{j1} \bowtie l_{j2})$ in (2) is substituted with $B_j \rightarrow (l_{j1} \bowtie l_{j2})$ [resp. $B_j \leftarrow (l_{j1} \bowtie l_{j2})$] if $(l_{j1} \bowtie l_{j2})$ occurs only positively [resp. negatively] in φ.

Property 4. *If $\psi \stackrel{\text{def}}{=} \mathsf{CNF}_{\mathsf{Ts}}(\varphi)$ or $\psi \stackrel{\text{def}}{=} \mathsf{CNF}_{\mathsf{PG}}(\varphi)$, then $\eta \models \varphi$ iff exists a total assignment δ on $\mathbf{B}$ s.t. $\eta \cup \delta \models \psi$, that is, $\varphi \equiv \exists \mathbf{B}.\psi$.*

3 A Theoretical Analysis of verification and entailment

We address the following basic question: *What should we mean by "a partial assignment μ satisfies φ"?* We wish to provide a satisfactory definition of partial-assignment satisfiability for a generic propositional formula—i.e., not only for (tautology-free) CNF. Ideally, a suitable definition of partial-assignment satisfiability should verify all statements in Property 1, in particular (ii) and (iv). In practice, unfortunately, at least for generic (i.e., non-CNF) formulas, we show this is not the case.

3.1 Verification and Entailment of Formulas

Definitions. The first candidate definition of partial-assignment satisfaction, which extends to partial assignments Property 1(iii), is *verification*.

Definition 1. *We say that a* partial *truth assignment μ* **verifies** *φ iff $\mu(\varphi) = \mathsf{T}$—or, equivalently by Property 2, iff $\varphi|_\mu = \top$. We denote this fact with "$\mu \models\!\!\approx \varphi$".*

We stress the fact that verification is a *semantic* definition ($\mu(\varphi) = \mathsf{T}$) which, due to Property 2, captures exactly the *syntactic* and easy-to-check satisfaction criterion ($\varphi|_\mu = \top$) which is implicitly used in many procedures.

The second candidate definition of partial-assignment satisfaction, which extends to partial assignments Property 1(i), is *entailment*.

Definition 2. *We say that a* partial *truth assignment μ* **entails** *φ if and only if, for every total truth assignments η s.t.$\mu \subseteq \eta$, η satisfies φ—or, equivalently, iff $\varphi|_\mu$ is valid. We denote this fact with "$\mu \models \varphi$".*

Verification vs. Entailment. We show the following facts. When the formula φ is a tautology-free CNF then verification and entailment coincide: $\mu \models\!\!\approx \varphi$ iff $\mu \models \varphi$. Unfortunately, *with generic formulas verification and entailment do not coincide, the former being strictly stronger than the latter.*

Theorem 1. *Let φ be a formula and μ be a partial truth assignment over its atoms.*

(a) If φ a tautology-free CNF, then $\mu \models \varphi$ iff $\mu \models\!\!\approx \varphi$.
(b) If φ is a generic formula, then $\mu \models \varphi$ if $\mu \models\!\!\approx \varphi$, but the converse does not hold in general.

Proof. (a): Let φ be a tautology-free CNF. If $\mu \models \varphi$, then $\varphi|_\mu$ is a valid CNF formula which does not contain valid clauses, so that $\varphi|_\mu = \top$, hence $\mu \models\!\!\approx \varphi$ by Property 2.
(a) and (b): If $\mu \models\!\!\approx \varphi$ then, for every η s.t. $\eta \supseteq \mu$, $\eta \models\!\!\approx \varphi$ and thus $\eta \models \varphi$, hence $\mu \models \varphi$.
(b): The fact that the converse does not hold in general is shown in Example 1. □

Example 1. If $\varphi \stackrel{\text{def}}{=} (A_1 \wedge A_2) \vee (A_1 \wedge \neg A_2)$ and $\mu \stackrel{\text{def}}{=} \{A_1\}$, then $\mu \models \varphi$ but $\mu \not\models\!\!\approx \varphi$. ◇

Hereafter we implicitly assume w.l.o.g. that all CNF formulas are tautology free.

We try to build a counterpart of Property 1 for Definitions 1 and 2 respectively, but in both cases we fail to achieve all points (i)–(iv), resulting into complementary situations. The following properties follow straightforward from Definitions 1 and 2. (Here "✓" [resp. "✗"] denotes facts from Property 1 which are [resp. are not] preserved.)

Property 5. *Let μ be a partial truth assignment on* $\mathbf{A}$ *and* $\varphi, \varphi_1, \varphi_2$ *be formulas on* $\mathbf{A}$.

(i) × *If* $\mu \models\!\!\approx \varphi$ *then* $\bigwedge\mu \models \varphi$, *but not vice versa.*
(ii) × *If* φ_1 *and* φ_2 *are equivalent, this does not imply that* $\mu \models\!\!\approx \varphi_1$ *iff* $\mu \models\!\!\approx \varphi_2$.
(iii) ✓ $\mu \models\!\!\approx \varphi$ *iff* $\varphi|_\mu$ *is* $\top$ *(also, iff* $\mu(\varphi) = \mathsf{T}$ *by Property 2).*
(iv) ✓ *Checking* $\mu \models\!\!\approx \varphi$ *requires at most a polynomial amount of steps.*

Property 6. *Let μ be a partial truth assignment on* $\mathbf{A}$ *and* $\varphi, \varphi_1, \varphi_2$ *be formulas on* $\mathbf{A}$.

(i) ✓ $\mu \models \varphi$ *iff* $\bigwedge\mu \models \varphi$.
(ii) ✓ *If* φ_1 *and* φ_2 *are equivalent, then* $\mu \models \varphi_1$ *iff* $\mu \models \varphi_2$.
(iii) × $\mu \models \varphi$ *iff* $\varphi|_\mu$ *is a valid formula, not necessarily* $\top$ *(also, in general* $\mu(\varphi) \neq \mathsf{T}$*).*
(iv) × *Checking* $\mu \models \varphi$ *is* co-NP-complete.

Example 2. Let $\varphi_1 \stackrel{\text{def}}{=} (A_1 \wedge A_2) \vee (A_1 \wedge \neg A_2)$, $\varphi_2 \stackrel{\text{def}}{=} A_1$ and $\mu \stackrel{\text{def}}{=} \{A_1\}$. Then $\varphi_1 \equiv \varphi_2$, $\varphi_1|_\mu = A_2 \vee \neg A_2 \neq \top$ and $\varphi_2|_\mu = \top$. Thus $\bigwedge\mu \models \varphi_1$, $\mu \models \varphi_1$ and $\mu \models \varphi_2$, whereas $\mu \not\models\!\!\approx \varphi_1$ but $\mu \models\!\!\approx \varphi_2$. ◇

From a theoretical viewpoint, Example 2 spotlights the difference between Property 5(i) and Property 6(i) and, even more importantly, that between Property 5(ii) and Property 6(ii): *whereas entailment matches the intuition that equivalent formulas should be satisfied by the same (partial) assignments, verification does not.* The latter fact looks theoretically awkward. In particular, if we adopted verification as the definition of partial-assignment satisfiability, then we believe that it would be embarrassing to have that equivalent formulas were not "satisfied" by the same assignments.

3.2 Verification and Entailment of Existentially-Quantified Formulas

We extend the analysis of §3.1 to existentially-quantified propositional formulas, wishing to provide a satisfactory definition of partial-assignment satisfiability for this case as well. Property 3 paves our way, telling how to extend the definitions of verification and entailment to existentially-quantified formulas.

The first possibility is to see partial-assignment satisfiability as *verification*, leveraging Definition 1 to the existentially-quantified case by exploiting Shannon expansion.

Definition 3. *We say that a* partial *truth assignment* μ *on* $\mathbf{A}$ **verifies** $\exists\mathbf{B}.\psi$ *if and only if, there exists a total truth assignment* δ *on* $\mathbf{B}$ *s.t.* $\mu \cup \delta \models\!\!\approx \psi$, *that is,* $\psi|_{\mu\cup\delta} = \top$.

Theorem 2. *Let* ψ *be a formula on* $\mathbf{A} \cup \mathbf{B}$ *and* μ *be a partial assignment on* $\mathbf{A}$. *Then* $\mu \models\!\!\approx \exists\mathbf{B}.\psi$ *iff* $\mu \models\!\!\approx \mathsf{SE}[\exists\mathbf{B}.\psi]$.

Proof. By Definition 1, $\mu \models\!\!\approx \mathsf{SE}[\exists\mathbf{B}.\psi]$ iff $(\mathsf{SE}[\exists\mathbf{B}.\psi])|_\mu = \top$, that is, by (1), iff there exists some δ_i s.t. $\psi|_{\delta_i}|_\mu = \top$ (i.e., $\psi|_{\delta_i\cup\mu} = \top$), that is, by Definition 1, iff there exists some δ_i s.t. $\mu \cup \delta_i \models\!\!\approx \psi$, that is, by Definition 3, iff $\mu \models\!\!\approx \exists\mathbf{B}.\psi$. □

Notice that Theorem 2 is *not* a straighforward consequence of Property 3, because equivalent formulas are not necessarily verified by the same assignments (Property 5(ii)).

One second possibility is to see partial-assignment satisfiability as *entailment*, leveraging Definition 2 and Property 3 to the existentially-quantified case. This leads to the following definition and relative Property.

Definition 4. *We say that a* partial *truth assignment* μ *on* $\mathbf{A}$ **entails** $\exists \mathbf{B}.\psi$, *written* $\mu \models \exists \mathbf{B}.\psi$, *if and only if, for every total truth assignment* η *on* $\mathbf{A}$ *extending* μ, *there exists a total truth assignment* δ *on* $\mathbf{B}$ *s.t.* $\eta \cup \delta$ *satisfies* ψ.

Theorem 3. *Let* ψ *be a formula on* $\mathbf{A} \cup \mathbf{B}$ *and* μ *be a partial assignment on* $\mathbf{A}$. *Then* $\mu \models \exists \mathbf{B}.\psi$ *iff* $\mu \models \mathsf{SE}[\exists \mathbf{B}.\psi]$.

Proof. $\mu \models \mathsf{SE}[\exists \mathbf{B}.\psi]$ iff $\eta \models \mathsf{SE}[\exists \mathbf{B}.\psi]$ for every total assignment η s.t. $\eta \supseteq \mu$, that is, by Property 3, iff for every total assignments η s.t. $\eta \supseteq \mu$ exists a total assignment δ on $\mathbf{B}$ s.t. $\eta \cup \delta \models \psi$, that is, iff $\mu \models \exists \mathbf{B}.\psi$. □

Notice the nesting order of forall/exists in Definition 4: "for every η exists δ s.t. ...". In fact, distinct η's may satisfy distinct disjuncts $\psi|_{\delta_i}$ in $\mathsf{SE}[\exists \mathbf{B}.\psi]$, requiring distinct δ_i's.

Theorem 4. *Let* ψ *be a formula on* $\mathbf{A} \cup \mathbf{B}$ *and* μ *be a partial truth assignment over* $\mathbf{A}$. *Then* $\mu \models \exists \mathbf{B}.\psi$ *if* $\mu \models\!\approx \exists \mathbf{B}.\psi$, *but the converse does not hold in general.*

Proof. From Theorem 1(b) with $\varphi \stackrel{\text{def}}{=} \mathsf{SE}[\exists \mathbf{B}.\psi]$ we can deduce that $\mu \models \mathsf{SE}[\exists \mathbf{B}.\psi]$ if $\mu \models\!\approx \mathsf{SE}[\exists \mathbf{B}.\psi]$. By Theorem 2 and Theorem 3 we have that $\mu \models \exists \mathbf{B}.\psi$ if $\mu \models\!\approx \exists \mathbf{B}.\psi$. The fact that the converse does not hold in general is shown in Example 3. □

Example 3. Consider $\mu \stackrel{\text{def}}{=} \{A_1\}$ and the tautology-free CNF formula on $\mathbf{A} \cup \mathbf{B}$:

$$
\begin{aligned}
\psi \stackrel{\text{def}}{=} \quad & (B_1 \vee B_2) \wedge \\
& (\neg B_1 \vee A_1) \wedge (\neg B_1 \vee A_2) \wedge (B_1 \vee \neg A_1 \vee \neg A_2) \wedge \\
& (\neg B_2 \vee A_1) \wedge (\neg B_2 \vee \neg A_2) \wedge (B_2 \vee \neg A_1 \vee A_2).
\end{aligned}
$$

$\mathsf{SE}[\exists \mathbf{B}.\psi] = \xcancel{(A_1 \wedge A_2 \wedge \neg A_2)} \vee (A_1 \wedge A_2) \vee (A_1 \wedge \neg A_2) \vee \xcancel{\bot}$.

Thus $\mu \models \mathsf{SE}[\exists \mathbf{B}.\psi]$ but $\mu \not\models\!\approx \mathsf{SE}[\exists \mathbf{B}.\psi]$, so that $\mu \models \exists \mathbf{B}.\psi$ but $\mu \not\models\!\approx \exists \mathbf{B}.\psi$. ◇

Thus verification is strictly stronger than entailment also with existentially-quantified formulas. Remarkably, and unlike with the un-quantified case, this is the case *even if* ψ *is a tautology-free CNF formula*! (See Example 3.) Intuitively, this can be seen as a consequence of the fact that $\mathsf{SE}[\exists \mathbf{B}.\psi]$ is not in CNF even if ψ is in CNF.

3.3 Verification and Entailment of CNF-ized Non-CNF Formulas

One might argue that in SAT-related problems the distinction between verification and entailment in §3.1 is not relevant in practice, because we could CNF-ize upfront the input non-CNF formulas and then remove tautological clauses, exploiting Property 4 and the fact that the above distinction does not hold for (tautology-free) CNF formulas.

Unfortunately, the following result shows this is not the case.

Theorem 5. *Let φ be a non-CNF formula on $\mathbf{A}$ and $\psi \stackrel{\text{def}}{=} \mathsf{CNF}_{\mathsf{Ts}}(\varphi)$ or $\psi \stackrel{\text{def}}{=} \mathsf{CNF}_{\mathsf{PG}}(\varphi)$, and let μ be a partial truth assignment over $\mathbf{A}$. Then $\mu \models \exists \mathbf{B}.\psi$ if $\mu \models\!\!\approx \exists \mathbf{B}.\psi$, but the converse does not hold in general.*

Proof. As an instantiation of Theorem 4 we have $\mu \models \exists \mathbf{B}.\psi$ if $\mu \models\!\!\approx \exists \mathbf{B}.\psi$. The fact that the converse does not hold in general is shown in Example 4. □

Example 4. Consider $\varphi \stackrel{\text{def}}{=} (A_1 \wedge A_2) \vee (A_1 \wedge \neg A_2)$ and $\mu \stackrel{\text{def}}{=} \{A_1\}$. Then $\psi \stackrel{\text{def}}{=} \mathsf{CNF}_{\mathsf{Ts}}(\varphi)$ is the formula in Example 3. Then $\mu \models \exists \mathbf{B}.\mathsf{CNF}_{\mathsf{Ts}}(\varphi)$ but $\mu \not\models\!\!\approx \exists \mathbf{B}.\mathsf{CNF}_{\mathsf{Ts}}(\varphi)$.
Let $\psi \stackrel{\text{def}}{=} \mathsf{CNF}_{\mathsf{PG}}(\varphi)$ instead. Since ψ is $\mathsf{CNF}_{\mathsf{Ts}}(\varphi)$ minus its two ternary clauses, we also have that $\mathsf{SE}[\exists \mathbf{B}.\psi] = \cancel{(A_1 \wedge A_2 \wedge \neg A_2)} \vee (A_1 \wedge A_2) \vee (A_1 \wedge \neg A_2) \vee \cancel{\bot}$.
Thus $\mu \models \exists \mathbf{B}.\mathsf{CNF}_{\mathsf{PG}}(\varphi)$ but $\mu \not\models\!\!\approx \exists \mathbf{B}.\mathsf{CNF}_{\mathsf{PG}}(\varphi)$. ◇

Intuitively, the whole point is that both $\mathsf{CNF}_{\mathsf{Ts}}(\varphi)$ and $\mathsf{CNF}_{\mathsf{PG}}(\varphi)$ introduce fresh variables $\mathbf{B}$, which must be implicitly existentially quantified away in order to preserve equivalence and thus produce the set of original satisfying assignments (Property 4). Although these variables do not affect entailment, they may affect verification. In fact, since φ and $\exists \mathbf{B}.\mathsf{CNF}_{\mathsf{Ts}}(\varphi)$ [resp. $\exists \mathbf{B}.\mathsf{CNF}_{\mathsf{PG}}(\varphi)$] are equivalent, they are entailed by the same partial assignments, but they are not verified by the same partial assignments.

To this extent, in [25] we addressed a different though related problem: we proved that—unlike with $\psi \stackrel{\text{def}}{=} \mathsf{CNF}_{\mathsf{Ts}}(\varphi)$ or with $\psi \stackrel{\text{def}}{=} \mathsf{CNF}_{\mathsf{PG}}(\varphi)$—if $\psi \stackrel{\text{def}}{=} \mathsf{CNF}_{\mathsf{PG}}(\mathsf{NNF}(\varphi))$ and $\mu \models\!\!\approx \varphi$, then $\mu \models\!\!\approx \exists \mathbf{B}.\psi$. Notice, however, that this fact does not apply to our problem, because Theorem 5 holds also for $\psi \stackrel{\text{def}}{=} \mathsf{CNF}_{\mathsf{PG}}(\mathsf{NNF}(\varphi))$.

Example 5. Consider φ and μ as in Example 4. Since φ is already in NNF, then we have that $\psi \stackrel{\text{def}}{=} \mathsf{CNF}_{\mathsf{PG}}(\mathsf{NNF}(\varphi)) = \mathsf{CNF}_{\mathsf{PG}}(\varphi)$. Therefore $\mu \models \exists \mathbf{B}.\mathsf{CNF}_{\mathsf{PG}}(\mathsf{NNF}(\varphi))$ but $\mu \not\models\!\!\approx \exists \mathbf{B}.\mathsf{CNF}_{\mathsf{PG}}(\mathsf{NNF}(\varphi))$. ◇

3.4 Other Candidate Forms of Partial-Assignment Satisfaction

Given the above facts, we wonder if we could use other notions of partial-assignment satisfiability. (E.g., we could enrich $\models\!\!\approx$ with some form of formula simplification.) In particular, we wonder if there exists some suitable notion of partial-assignment satisfaction which is strictly stronger then entailment and fixes the "embarrassing fact" for verification of Property 5(ii). The following theorem states this is not the case.

Theorem 6. *Let $\models\!\!\simeq$ denote some relation such that*

(a) for every μ and φ, $\mu \models \varphi$ if $\mu \models\!\!\simeq \varphi$;
(b) for every η and φ, if η is total for the set of atoms in φ, then $\eta \models\!\!\simeq \varphi$ iff $\eta \models \varphi$;
(c) for every μ, φ_1 and φ_2, if $\mu \models\!\!\simeq \varphi_1 \wedge \varphi_2$, then $\mu \models\!\!\simeq \varphi_1$ and $\mu \models\!\!\simeq \varphi_2$;
(d) for every μ, φ_1 and φ_2, if $\varphi_1 \equiv \varphi_2$, then $\mu \models\!\!\simeq \varphi_1$ iff $\mu \models\!\!\simeq \varphi_2$

Then, for every μ, φ, we have that $\mu \models\!\!\simeq \varphi$ if and only if $\mu \models \varphi$.

Proof. The "only if" part is hypothesis *(a)*.
The "if" part: By absurd, suppose there exist μ and φ s.t. $\mu \models \varphi$ and $\mu \not\models\!\!\simeq \varphi$.
Let $\varphi_1 \stackrel{\text{def}}{=} \bigwedge\mu$ and $\varphi_2 \stackrel{\text{def}}{=} \bigwedge\mu \wedge \varphi$. Then we have that:
$\varphi_1 \equiv \varphi_2$, because $\mu \models \varphi$, and hence $\bigwedge\mu \models \varphi$ because of Property 6(i);
$\mu \models\!\!\simeq \varphi_1$, because of hypothesis *(b)*;
$\mu \not\models\!\!\simeq \varphi_2$, because of hypothesis *(c)*.
The latter three facts violate hypothesis *(d)*. □

Theorem 6 says that entailment is the only relation which (a) is stronger or equal than entailment, (b) extends to partial assignments the standard notion of total-assignment satisfaction, (c) maintains the standard semantics of $\wedge$, and (d) verifies Property 6(ii). Thus, any such relation $\models\!\!\simeq$ which is strictly stronger that $\models$ suffers for the same "embarrassing fact" of Property 5(ii).

Example 6. Let "$\models\!\!\simeq$" denote a variant of $\models\!\!\approx$ such that $\mu \models\!\!\simeq \varphi$ implements a syntactic check that adds "$l \vee \neg l \Rightarrow \top$", l being a literal, to the rules used in Fig. 1 for computing the residual $\varphi|_\mu$. Thus, considering the formula φ_1 of Example 2 we have $\mu \models\!\!\simeq \varphi_1$.

Nevertheless, let $\mu \stackrel{\text{def}}{=} \{A_1, .., A_M\}$ s.t. $\varphi \stackrel{\text{def}}{=} \bigvee_{i=1}^{M}(A_i \wedge cube_i)$ s.t. each $cube_i$ is a non-unary cube and $\bigvee_{i=1}^{M} cube_i$ is valid and does not contain occurrences of the atoms $A_1, .., A_M$. Then $\mu \models \varphi$ but $\mu \not\models\!\!\simeq \varphi$, because $\varphi|_\mu$ is the valid formula $\bigvee_i cube_i$ which is not simplified by the above reduction. If $\varphi_2 \stackrel{\text{def}}{=} \bigwedge \mu$, then $\varphi \equiv \varphi_2$, $\mu \not\models\!\!\simeq \varphi$ but $\mu \models\!\!\simeq \varphi_2$, whereas $\mu \models \varphi$ and $\mu \models \varphi_2$. Thus the "embarrassing fact" above applies also to $\models\!\!\simeq$. ◇

4 Practical Consequences of Using Verification or Entailment

In this section we analyze the practical consequences of adopting verification or entailment as a partial-assignment satisfiability tests in search procedures for satisfiability and enumeration and in formula compilation. In particular, when entailment and verification do not coincide, we analyze the tradeoff between the extra cost of entailment versus the benefits it may produce.

4.1 Verification vs. Entailment in Solving, Enumeration and Compilation

Verification vs. Entailment for Native CNF Formulas. When the input formula is natively in CNF, the distinction between verification and entailment is not relevant, because these two concepts coincide. (We conjecture that this is the main reason why the distinction between verification and entailment has been long overlooked in the literature.) For satisfiability of CNF formulas, CDCL SAT solvers directly produce *total* truth assignments, because it is not worth to perform intermediate satisfiability checks.
Verification vs. Entailment in Satisfiability. In satisfiability we need finding only one total assignment η extending μ which satisfy φ. Therefore entailment produces no benefits wrt. verification and is more expensive, so that the latter is always preferred.

The scenario changes when we deal with enumeration-based algorithms applied to non-CNF formulas, or to existentially-quantified formulas, or to CNF-ized formulas.

Verification vs. Entailment for Enumeration on Non-CNF Formulas. The analysis in §3.1 shows the following facts. On the one hand, the advantage of adopting verification rather than entailment for checking partial-assignment satisfiability is that it matches the intuition and practical need that satisfiability checking should be fast, since checking verification is polynomial (Property 5(iv)) and easier to implement, whereas checking entailment is co-NP-complete (Property 6(iv)), because it is equivalent to checking the validity of the residual $\varphi|_\mu$. We stress the fact, however, that if $\mu \models \varphi$, then the residual $\varphi|_\mu$ is typically much smaller than φ with a much smaller search space, since its variables are only (a subset of) the variables which are not assigned by μ, so that in many actual situations the above fact could not be a major issue.

On the other hand, a main advantage of adopting entailment on enumeration is that, due to Theorem 1, every partial assignments entailing the input formula is a *sub-assignment* of some other(s) verifying it. Consequently, as soon as one verification-based enumeration procedure produces (a branch corresponding to) an assignment μ s.t. $\mu \models \varphi$ but $\mu \not\approx \varphi$, it cannot realize this fact and thus proceeds the search to extend μ to some $\mu' \supset \mu$ s.t. $\mu' \approx \varphi$. This causes an extension of the search tree of up to $2^{|\mu'|-|\mu|}$ branches. Therefore, for an assignment-enumeration algorithm, being able to enumerate partial assignments entailing the input formula rather than simply verifying it may (even drastically) reduce the number of the satisfying assignments enumerated.

Also, the analysis in §3.4 shows that alternative forms of partial-assignment satisfiability extending verification—e.g., adding further simplifications for the residual $\varphi|_\mu$ like unit-propagation or the removal of basic valid subformulas—cannot fill the gap wrt. entailment, whose theoretical properties are specific.

Verification vs. Entailment for Projected Enumeration. The analysis in §3.2 shows that the above considerations for non-CNF formulas extend automatically to procedures for projected enumeration (e.g. projected AllSAT/AllSMT, projected #SAT/#SMT), even on CNF formulas, because projected enumeration consists in enumeration on an existentially-quantified formula $\exists \mathbf{B}.\psi$, $\mathbf{B}$ being the non-relevant atoms to be projected away. The same considerations apply also to other applications like preimage computation in symbolic model checking [5] or predicate abstraction in SW verification [21,24].

Verification vs. Entailment for CNF-ized Non-CNF Formulas. The analysis in §3.3 shows that, although verification and entailment coincide for CNF formulas, the problem with non-CNF formulas cannot be fixed by simply CNF-izing a formula upfront [32,42] and running a CNF enumeration procedure based on partial-assignment verification, projecting out the fresh variables introduced by the CNF-ization. In fact, a partial assignment over the original atoms may entail the existentially-quantified CNF-ized formula without verifying it. Also, even adopting the CNF-ization technique $\mathsf{CNF}_{\mathsf{PG}}(\mathsf{NNF}(\varphi))$ we proposed in [25], although improving the enumeration process, does not fill the gap between verification and entailment in this case.

Verification and Entailment in Formula Compilation. With formula compilers a formula φ is encoded into a format which makes assignment enumeration straightforward [13]. d-DNNF formulas are NNF DAGs which are *decomposable* (i.e., all conjunctive subformulas $\varphi_1 \wedge \varphi_2$ are such that φ_1 and φ_2 do not share atoms) and *deterministic* (i.e., all disjunctive subformulas $\varphi_1 \vee \varphi_2$ are such that φ_1 and φ_2 are mutually inconsistent)

[11]. The d-DNNF compilers typically implement a top-down search, implicitly adopting verification ($\varphi|_\mu = \top$) as partial-assignment satisfiability test [10].

OBDDs [4] and SDDs [12] are subcases of d-DNNFs [13] which are canonical under some order condition—i.e., two equivalent subformulas φ_1 and φ_2 are encoded into the same OBDD or SDD, and as such are shared inside the DAG representation. The OBDD and SDD compilers typically build the encoding bottom-up, and they are able to encode $\varphi|_\mu$ into $\top$ as soon as $\varphi|_\mu$ becomes valid. (That is, they implicitly use entailment as partial-assignment satisfiability test.)

Verification and Entailment for #SMT and WMI. With some enumeration-based techniques (e.g. #SMT [7,31] and WMI [29,39]) the total cost of *processing* each enumerated partial assignment dominates that of the enumeration itself. (E.g., with WMI each satisfying assignment μ corresponds to a polytope, and for each μ it is necessary to compute the integral of some multivariate function over such polytope.) Therefore, in this context the *effectiveness* of enumeration in reducing the number of assignments generated is even more important that the *efficiency* in terms of CPU time required to enumerate them.

Therefore, with entailment-based enumeration the reduced number of assignments produced, and hence of integrals computed, should definitely compensate the extra cost of entailment checking.

4.2 Verification vs. Entailment in Search Procedures and Formula Compilers.

When applied to satisfiable formulas, algorithms like *Analytic Tableaux*[3] [38] or "classic" *DPLL* [4] [14], or even recent sophisticated AllSAT procedures for circuits [17], produce branches representing partial assignments which *verify* the input formula. The same happens with enumeration algorithms for d-DNNF formulas, which resemble the tableaux enumeration algorithm, with the restriction that the formulas they are applied to are deterministic and decomposable NNFs, so that the enumerated assignment are pairwise disjoint and straighforward to compute, because the enumeration reduces to the traversal of the and-or DAG without encountering inconsistent branches [10].

Example 7. Consider $\varphi \stackrel{\text{def}}{=} ((A_1 \wedge A_2) \vee (A_1 \wedge \neg A_2)) \wedge ((\neg A_3 \wedge A_4) \vee (\neg A_3 \wedge \neg A_4))$. Notice that the single assignment $\mu \stackrel{\text{def}}{=} \{A_1, \neg A_3\}$ subsumes all total truth assignments satisfying φ and is such that $\mu \models \varphi$ but $\mu \not\approx \varphi$, since $\varphi|_\mu = (A_2 \vee \neg A_2) \wedge (A_4 \vee \neg A_4)$.

Figure 3 represents the search trees corresponding to AllSAT executions of Analytic Tableaux and (non-CNF) DPLL on φ[5,6]. Since (the DAG version of) φ is already in d-DNNF (Fig. 4), in this case the d-DNNF enumeration resembles the tableaux enumeration. In all cases, the enumeration produces:
$\{\{A_1, A_2, \neg A_3, A_4\}, \{A_1, A_2, \neg A_3, \neg A_4\}, \{A_1, \neg A_2, \neg A_3, A_4\}, \{A_1, \neg A_2, \neg A_3, \neg A_4\}\}$.

[3] Notice that Analytic Tableaux may generate duplicated or subsumed assignments (see [9,19]).

[4] Classic DPLL procedure [14] was designed to work for CNF formulas. Nevertheless it is easy to produce a non-CNF version of this procedure (see e.g. [1]).

[5] Here in DPLL the pure-literal rule [14] is not used because in All-SAT it may hinder the enumeration of relevant models (see, e.g., [33]).

[6] The search trees may vary with the ordering by which variables and subformulas are analyzed.

Notice that all the assignments produced are total. Notice also that neither Analytic Tableaux nor DPLL nor d-DNNF enumeration in this case can produce $\{\{A_1, \neg A_3\}\}$, regardless the adopted strategy. The same applies also to the verification-based AllSAT circuit enumeration of [17], see Example 9. ◇

OBDDs [4] contain branches representing partial assignments which *entail* the input formula, because if $\mu \models \varphi$ then $\varphi|_\mu$ is valid (Property 6(iii)), so that its corresponding sub-OBDD is reduced into the $\top$ node. (SDDs [12] behave similarly.)

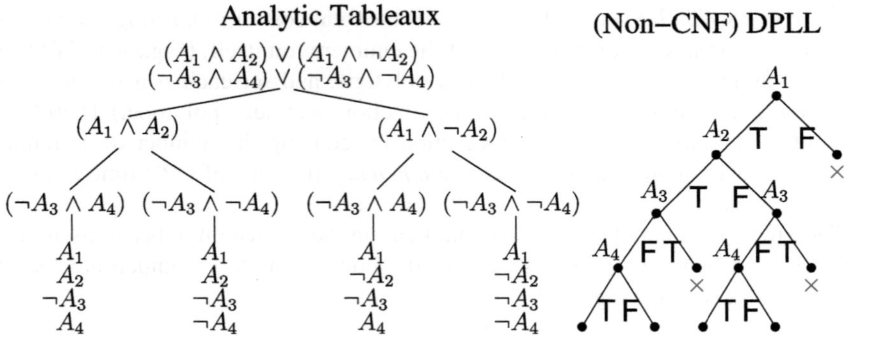

Fig. 3. $\varphi \stackrel{\text{def}}{=} ((A_1 \wedge A_2) \vee (A_1 \wedge \neg A_2)) \wedge ((\neg A_3 \wedge A_4) \vee (\neg A_3 \wedge \neg A_4))$.Enumeration by analytic tableaux (left) and (non-CNF) DPLL (right).

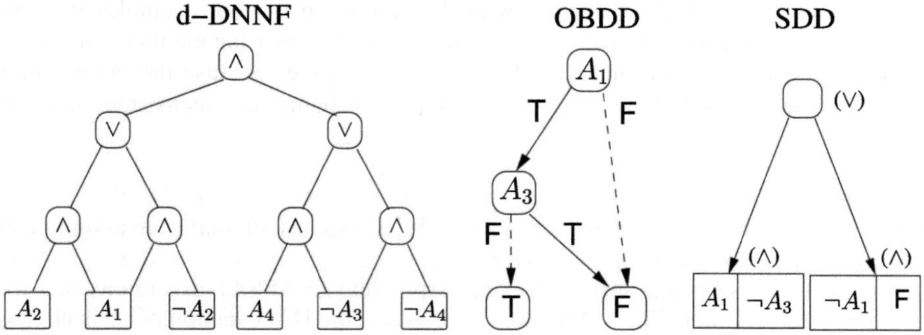

Fig. 4. $\varphi \stackrel{\text{def}}{=} ((A_1 \wedge A_2) \vee (A_1 \wedge \neg A_2)) \wedge ((\neg A_3 \wedge A_4) \vee (\neg A_3 \wedge \neg A_4))$.Compilation of φ into: d-DNNF (left), OBDD (center), SDD (right).

Example 8. Consider φ as in Example 7. Figure 4 represents possible compilations of φ into d-DNNF, OBDD and SDD respectively.[7] Notice that, unlike with OBDDs and

[7] The outcome may vary with the ordering by which variables and subformulas are analyzed.

SDDs which collapse equivalent subformulas into one, the two $\vee$-subformulas in the d-DNNF are not recognized to be equivalent to the nodes A_1 and $\neg A_3$ respectively.

Applying enumeration to the d-DNNF we obtain the total assignments of Example 7. By applying enumeration to the OBDD or to the SDD, we obtain the single-assignment $\{\{A_1, \neg A_3\}\}$, so that $\{A_1, \neg A_3\} \models \varphi$ but $\{A_1, \neg A_3\} \not\approx \varphi$. $\diamond$

4.3 Implementing Entailment Within Enumeration Procedures

Implementing efficiently entailment-based enumeration procedures can be tricky. One possible approach is to integrate AllSAT/AllSMT with OBDDs, exploiting the capability of OBDD to implicitly perform entailment-based reductions [6]. The main problem with this approach is the fact that OBDDs quickly blow up in memory as soon as the input formula increases in size.

[15,27] proposed a formal reasoning framework based on the idea of *dualized search*: while the main enumerator produces partial assignments μ for the input formula φ, another "dual" SAT solver is incrementally called on $\mathsf{CNF}_{\mathsf{Ts}}(\neg\varphi) \wedge \bigwedge\mu$: if it is unsatisfiable then the main enumerator produces μ and backtracks. Based on the analysis in [35] and noticing that the above dual check in [15,27] is an entailment ($\mu \models \varphi$) rather than a verification ($\mu \approx \varphi$), in [28,30] we proposed enumeration and model counting frameworks and algorithms based on dual search, enhanced with chronological backtracking. Unfortunately no implementation efficient enough to compete with state-of-the-art enumeration procedures was produced.

[17] presented HALL, a sophisticated AllSAT procedure for circuits which, among other techniques, exploited a form of (verification-based) *generalization* (aka minimization or reduction): as soon as a total truth assignment η satisfying φ is produced, the literals in η are removed one by one and the resulting partial assignment is tested to verify φ. In [16] we have enhanced HALL generalization procedure by substituting verification checks with entailment checks based on dualized search, boosting its performance in terms of both time efficiency and size of partial-assignment sets.

Example 9. Consider $\varphi \stackrel{\text{def}}{=} ((A_1 \wedge A_2) \vee (A_1 \wedge \neg A_2)) \wedge ((\neg A_3 \wedge A_4) \vee (\neg A_3 \wedge \neg A_4))$ as in Example 7 and assume some total assignment satisfying it is produced, e.g. $\eta \stackrel{\text{def}}{=} \{A_1, A_2, \neg A_3, A_4\}$. Since there is no literal $l \in \eta$ s.t. $\eta \backslash \{l\} \approx \varphi$, no assignment reduction based on verification can be successfully applied to η. Consequently, even the sophisticated verification-based circuit AllSAT procedure in [17] produces the set of four un-reduced total assignments of Example 7.

Instead, since $\eta \backslash \{A_2, A_4\} \models \varphi$ whereas $\eta \backslash \{A_1\} \not\models \varphi$ and $\eta \backslash \{\neg A_3\} \not\models \varphi$, the entailment-based assignment-reduction technique of [16] shrinks η into $\{A_1, \neg A_3\}$, so that the enumeration procedure returns $\{\{A_1, \neg A_3\}\}$. $\diamond$

5 Conclusions and Future Work

In this paper we have analyzed in depth the issue of formula satisfaction by partial assignments. We have identified two alternative notions that are implicitly used in the literature, namely verification and entailment, and we have showed that, although the former is easier to check and as such is implicitly used by most current search procedures, the latter has better theoretical properties, and can improve the efficiency and effectiveness of enumeration procedures.

From a theoretical viewpoint, we highlight the need for a unique universally-agreed definition of partial-assignment satisfaction[8], and we champion the idea that it should be defined as entailment, considering verification an easy-to-check sufficient condition for it. From a practical viewpoint, we suggest that entailment should be adopted as partial-assignment satisfaction check inside enumeration-based procedures in place of verification, so that to reduce the number of enumerated assignments.

The analysis presented in this paper opens several research avenues. First, we wish to investigate and evaluate empirically novel entailment-based techniques for both (projected) enumeration and (projected) model counting. In particular, we wish to enhance our (projected) AllSAT procedure in [40,41] with entailment tests. Second, we wish to implement entailment-based enumeration techniques to enhance our AllSMT procedures in MATHSAT [8] and evaluate them empirically. In particular, we wish to embed and evaluate such entailment-based AllSMT procedure inside our WMI tools [29,39]. Third, we wish to embed novel entailment-based AllSMT procedures inside our SMT compilers for $\mathcal{T}$-OBDDs and $\mathcal{T}$-SDDs [26], extending it also to generic $\mathcal{T}$-d-DNNFs.

Acknowledgements. The analysis described in this paper has strongly benefitted from interesting discussions, either in person or via email, with (in alphabetic order): Armin Biere, Alessandro Cimatti, Dror Fried, Allen van Gelder (R.I.P.), Alberto Griggio, Gabriele Masina, David Mitchell, Sibylle Möhle, Paolo Morettin, Andrea Passerini, Alexander Nadel, Yogev Shalmon, Laurent Simon, Giuseppe Spallitta, Armando Tacchella, Stefano Tonetta, and Moshe Vardi, whom are all warmly thanked.

The author was supported in part by the MUR PNRR project FAIR - Future AI Research (PE00000013) funded by the NextGenerationEU; he was partially funded under the NRRP, Mission 4 Component 2 Investment 1.4, by the European Union âĂŞ NextGenerationEU (proj. nr. CN 00000013); he was supported in part by the TANGO project funded by the EU Horizon Europe research and innovation program under GA No 101120763. Views and opinions expressed are however those of the author only and do not necessarily reflect those of the European Union, the European Health and Digital Executive Agency (HaDEA) or The European Research Council. Neither the European Union nor the granting authority can be held responsible for them.

Disclosure of Interests. The author has no competing interests to declare that are relevant to the content of this article.

References

1. Armando, A., Giunchiglia, E.: Embedding complex decision procedures inside an interactive theorem prover. Ann. Math. Artif. Intell. **8**(3–4), 475–502 (1993)
2. Aziz, R.A., Chu, G., Muise, C., Stuckey, P.: #∃SAT: projected model counting. In: Theory and Applications of Satisfiability Testing – SAT 2015, pp. 121–137. Springer (2015)

[8] In 2020 we ran an online poll among SAT and SMT PC members about the meaning of partial-assignment satisfiability: 35% said "entailment", 35% said "verification", 30% said both (!).

3. Barrett, C.W., Sebastiani, R., Seshia, S.A., Tinelli, C.: Satisfiability modulo theories. In: Biere, A., Heule, M., van Maaren, H., Walsh, T. (eds.) Handbook of Satisfiability - Second Edition, vol. 336, pp. 1267–1329. IOS Press (2021)
4. Bryant, R.E.: Graph-based algorithms for boolean function manipulation. IEEE Trans. Comput. **C-35**(8), 677–691 (1986)
5. Burch, J.R., Clarke, E.M., McMillan, K.L., Dill, D.L., Hwang, L.J.: Symbolic model checking: 10^{20} states and beyond. Inf. Comput. **98**(2), 142–170 (1992)
6. Cavada, R., Cimatti, A., Franzén, A., Kalyanasundaram, K., Roveri, M., Shyamasundar, R.K.: Computing predicate abstractions by integrating BDDs and SMT solvers. In: FMCAD, pp. 69–76. IEEE Computer Society (2007)
7. Chistikov, D., Dimitrova, R., Majumdar, R.: Approximate counting in SMT and value estimation for probabilistic programs. In: TACAS, pp. 320–334. Springer (2015)
8. Cimatti, A., Griggio, A., Schaafsma, B.J., Sebastiani, R.: The MathSAT 5 SMT solver. In: TACAS 2013. LNCS, vol. 7795, pp. 95–109. Springer (2013)
9. D'Agostino, M.: Are tableaux an improvement on truth-tables? J. Logic Lang. Inform. **1**, 235–252 (1992)
10. Darwiche, A.: Decomposable negation normal form. J. ACM **48**(4), 608–647 (2001)
11. Darwiche, A.: A compiler for deterministic, decomposable negation normal form. In: Proceedings of the AAAI Conference on Artificial Intelligence, pp. 627–634. American Association for Artificial Intelligence, July 2002
12. Darwiche, A.: SDD: a new canonical representation of propositional knowledge bases. In: 22nd International Joint Conference on Artificial Intelligence, IJCAI'11, Barcelona, Catalonia, Spain, July 2011, vol. 2, pp. 819–826. AAAI Press (2011)
13. Darwiche, A., Marquis, P.: A knowledge compilation map. J. Artif. Intell. Res. **17**(1), 229–264 (2002)
14. Davis, M., Longemann, G., Loveland, D.: A machine program for theorem proving. J. ACM **5**(7) (1962)
15. Fazekas, K., Seidl, M., Biere, A.: A duality-aware calculus for quantified Boolean formulas. In: SYNASC, pp. 181–186. IEEE Computer Society (2016)
16. Fried, D., Nadel, A., Sebastiani, A., Shalmon, Y.: Entailing generalization boosts enumeration. In: 27th International Conference on Theory and Applications of Satisfiability Testing. LIPIcs, vol. 305, pp. 13:1–13:14. Schloss Dagstuhl – LZI (2024)
17. Fried, D., Nadel, A., Shalmon, Y.: AllSAT for combinational circuits. In: 26th International Conference on Theory and Applications of Satisfiability Testing, LIPIcs, vol. 271, pp. 9:1–9:18. Schloss Dagstuhl – LZI (2023)
18. Gebser, M., Kaufmann, B., Schaub, T.: Solution enumeration for projected Boolean search problems. In: van Hoeve, W.-J., Hooker, J.N. (eds.) CPAIOR 2009. LNCS, vol. 5547, pp. 71–86. Springer, Heidelberg (2009). https://doi.org/10.1007/978-3-642-01929-6_7
19. Giunchiglia, F., Sebastiani, R.: Building decision procedures for modal logics from propositional decision procedures - the case study of modal K(m). Inf. Comput. **162**(1/2) (2000)
20. Gomes, C.P., Sabharwal, A., Selman, B.: Model counting, 2nd edn. In: Biere, A., Heule, M., van Maaren, H., Walsh, T. (eds.) Handbook of Satisfiability, vol. 336, pp. 993–1014. IOS Press (2021)
21. Graf, S., Saïdi, H.: Construction of abstract state graphs with PVS. In: CAV. Springer (1997)
22. Kleine Büning, H., Kullmann, O.: Minimal unsatisfiability and autarkies, 2nd edn. In: Biere, A., Heule, M., van Maaren, H., Walsh, T. (eds.) Handbook of Satisfiability, vol. 336, pp. 571–633. IOS Press (2021)
23. Lagniez, J.-M., Lonca, E.: Leveraging decision-DNNF compilation for enumerating disjoint partial models. In: 21st International Conference on Principles of Knowledge Representation and Reasoning, November 2024

24. Lahiri, S.K., Nieuwenhuis, R., Oliveras, A.: SMT techniques for fast predicate abstraction. In: Computer Aided Verification. LNCS, August 2006, pp. 424–437. Springer (2006)
25. Masina, G., Spallitta, G., Sebastiani, R.: On CNF conversion for disjoint SAT enumeration. In: 26th International Conference on Theory and Applications of Satisfiability Testing. LIPIcs, vol. 271, pp. 15:1–15:16. Schloss Dagstuhl – LZI (2023)
26. Michelutti, M., Masina, G., Spallitta, G., Sebastiani, R.: Canonical decision diagrams modulo theories. In: 27th European Conference on Artificial Intelligence, ECAI 2024, vol. 392, pp. 4319–4327. IOS Press (2024)
27. Möhle, S., Biere, A.: Dualizing projected model counting. In: 30th IEEE International Conference on Tools with Artificial Intelligence, November 2018, pp. 702–709 (2018)
28. Möhle, S., Sebastiani, R., Biere, A.: Four flavors of entailment. In: Pulina, L., Seidl, M. (eds.) SAT 2020. LNCS, vol. 12178, pp. 62–71. Springer, Cham (2020). https://doi.org/10.1007/978-3-030-51825-7_5
29. Morettin, P., Passerini, A., Sebastiani, R.: Advanced SMT techniques for weighted model integration. Artif. Intell. **275**, 1–27 (2019)
30. Möhle, S., Sebastiani, R., Biere, A.: On enumerating short projected models. Discret. Appl. Math. **361**, 412–439 (2025)
31. Phan, Q., Malacaria, P.: All-solution satisfiability modulo theories: applications, algorithms and benchmarks. In: ARES. IEEE Computer Society (2015)
32. Plaisted, D.A., Greenbaum, S.: A structure-preserving clause form translation. J. Symb. Comput. **2**(3), 293–304 (1986)
33. Sebastiani, R.: From KSAT to delayed theory combination: exploiting DPLL outside the SAT domain. In: 6th International Symposium on Frontiers of Combining Systems, FroCoS. LNCS, vol. 4720, pp. 28–46. Springer (2007)
34. Sebastiani, R.: Lazy Satisfiability Modulo Theories. J. Satisfiability Boolean Model. Comput. (JSAT) **3**(3–4), 141–224 (2007)
35. Sebastiani, R.: Are you satisfied by this partial assignment? arXiv preprint arXiv:2003.04225, February 2020
36. Sebastiani, R., Tacchella, A.: SAT techniques for modal and description logics, 2nd edn. In: Biere, A., Heule, M., van Maaren, H., Walsh, T. (eds.) Handbook of Satisfiability, vol. 336, pp. 1223–1266. IOS Press (2021)
37. Sebastiani, R., Tomasi, S.: Optimization modulo theories with linear rational costs. ACM Trans. Comput. Logics **16**(2) (2015)
38. Smullyan, R.M.: First-Order Logic. Springer (1968)
39. Spallitta, G., Masina, G., Morettin, P., Passerini, A., Sebastiani, R.: Enhancing SMT-based weighted model integration by structure awareness. Artif. Intell. **328**, 104067 (2024)
40. Spallitta, G., Sebastiani, R., Biere, A.: Disjoint partial enumeration without blocking clauses. Proc. AAAI Conf. Artif. Intell. **38**, 8126–8135 (2024)
41. Spallitta, G., Sebastiani, R., Biere, A.: Disjoint projected enumeration for SAT and SMT without blocking clauses. Artif. Intell. **345**, 104346 (2025)
42. Tseitin, G.: On the complexity of derivation in propositional calculus. In: Studies in Constructive Mathematics and Mathematical Logics, pp. 115–125 (1970)

Unfolding Boxes with Local Constraints

Long Qian ✉, Eric Wang ✉,
Bernardo Subercaseaux ✉, and Marijn J. H. Heule ✉

Carnegie Mellon University, Pittsburgh PA 15213, USA
{longq, ebwang, bsuberca, mheule}@andrew.cmu.edu

Abstract. We consider the problem of finding and enumerating polyominos that can be folded into multiple non-isomorphic boxes. While several computational approaches have been proposed, including SAT, randomized algorithms, and decision diagrams, none has been able to perform at scale. We argue that existing SAT encodings are hindered by the presence of global constraints (e.g., graph connectivity or acyclicity), which are generally hard to encode effectively and hard for solvers to reason about. In this work, we propose a new SAT-based approach that replaces these global constraints with simple local constraints that have substantially better propagation properties. Our approach dramatically improves the scalability of both computing and enumerating common box unfoldings: (i) while previous approaches could only find common unfoldings of two boxes up to area 88, ours easily scales beyond 150, and (ii) while previous approaches were only able to enumerate common unfoldings up to area 30, ours scales up to 60. This allows us to rule out 46, 54, and 58 as the smallest areas allowing a common unfolding of three boxes, thereby refuting a conjecture of Xu et al. (2017).

Keywords: Box folding · SAT encodings · Graph connectivity · Graph cyclicity · Local constraints.

1 Introduction

Folding two-dimensional surfaces into a three-dimensional structure is a fundamental problem in computational geometry, with many applications ranging from the arts (e.g., origami) to diverse fields of engineering (e.g., packaging, protein folding) [4]. Perhaps the simplest example, usually introduced to children, is that of folding a $1 \times 1 \times 1$ box (Figure 1b) from a *net* corresponding to a polyomino of area 6 (Figure 1a). Interestingly, as depicted in Figure 1c, multiple nets can fold into the same box, and the problem of enumerating all the nets that fold into a given $a \times b \times c$ box is already non-trivial (see Table 5).

An even more surprising fact, depicted in Figure 2, is that sometimes multiple non-isomorphic boxes can be obtained from the same net, simply by folding along different edges. These *common unfoldings* (also known as *common developments* [12]) allow for interesting engineering applications: a single two-dimensional piece of cardboard can be used for different types of boxes, depending on the dimensions of the object to be packed.

C. Barrett and U. Waldmann (Eds.): CADE 2025, LNAI 15943, pp. 736–754, 2025.
https://doi.org/10.1007/978-3-031-99984-0_38

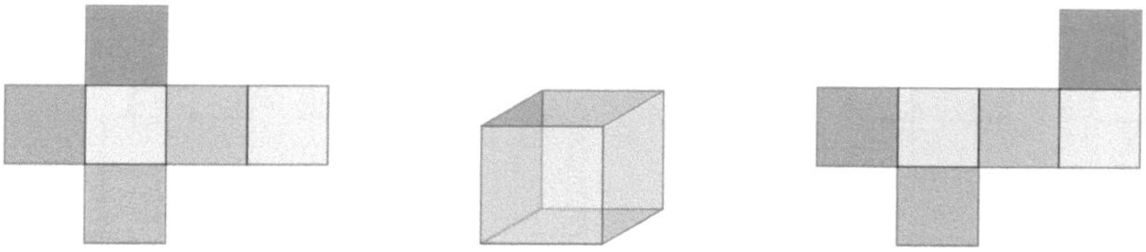

(a) Standard net. (b) 1×1×1 box. (c) Non-standard net.

Fig. 1: Illustration of the non-uniqueness of nets that fold into a box.

A body of work has focused in the particular case in which the nets are *polyominos*, and one can only fold along the edges of the unit squares forming the polyomino (cf. Figure 2) [6,8,10,11,12]. Nonetheless, several important questions remain open. To state them, let us define some notation.

For a positive integer s representing a surface area, let $P(s)$ be the set of all triples (a, b, c) with $a \leq b \leq c$ such that $s = 2(ab + ac + bc)$. In other words, $P(s)$ is the set of all possible integer dimensions of a box with surface area s. For example, $P(22) = \{(1, 1, 5), (1, 2, 3)\}$, and as shown in Figure 2, it turns out that both boxes in $P(22)$ can be folded from the same net of area 22. For a positive integer k, let $\Psi(k)$ be the smallest integer s such that there is a subset $P' \subseteq P(s)$ with $|P'| = k$ and all boxes in P' have a common unfolding. The example in Figure 2 shows that $\Psi(2) \leq 22$, and it can be easily checked that no smaller value of s works. An impressive result by Shirakawa and Uehara is that $\Psi(3) \leq 532$, as they showed a common unfolding for boxes 7×8×14, 2×4×43, and 2×13×16. Xu et al. [12] conjectured $\Psi(3) = 46$, which is the smallest value for which $|P(s)| \geq 3$. For $k \geq 4$, it is not even known whether $\Psi(k)$ is finite. We define as well the opposite quantity, $\Delta(k)$, as the smallest integer s such that there is a subset $P' \subseteq P(s)$ with $|P'| = k$ where **no** common unfolding for P' exists. The work of Mitani and Uehara [6] shows that $\Delta(2) > 38$, and suggests $\Delta(2) > 88$. On the other hand, no upper bounds for $\Delta(2)$ are known.

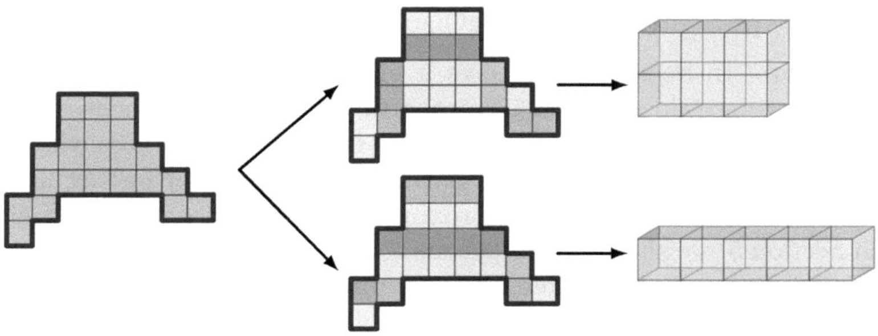

Fig. 2: Two non-isomorphic boxes that can be folded from the same net.

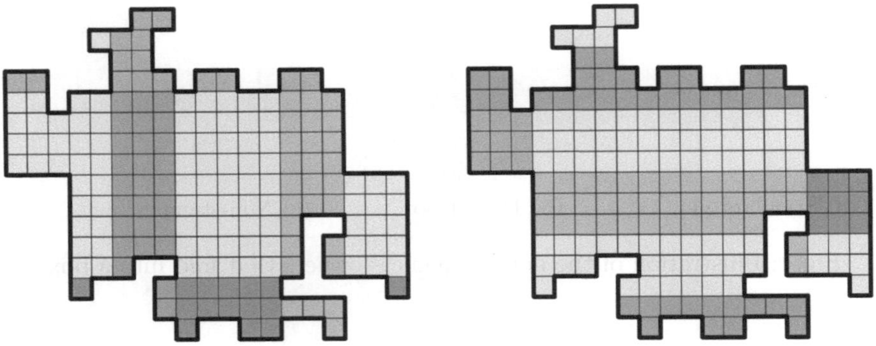

(a) 3×5×9 (b) 3×3×13

Fig. 3: A common unfolding of area 174.

In this work, we show that $\Psi(3) > 58$, that $\Delta(3) = 46$. We show as well that $\Delta(2) > 86$, and using heuristics we manage to compute solutions for certain very large areas (see Figure 3). More importantly, the SAT-based approach we developed to prove these results showcases a more general idea that might be applicable in a wide variety of contexts: global constraints, for which conflicts can be detected only after long propagation chains, can be approximated by local constraints for which conflicts are detected much earlier, leading to substantially better performance. To illustrate the power of our approach, let us present some brief elements in comparison with previous research. In 2011, Abel et al. [1] enumerated all common unfoldings for boxes 1×1×5 and 1×2×3 in about 10 hours [12], whereas our approach allows a complete enumeration in 2 minutes on a personal computer. Xu et al. [12] remarked that using the same approach for area 30 would have taken *"too huge memory even on a supercomputer"*, and their more efficient ZDD-based approach took only 10 days for area 30; ours takes 10 minutes. Moreover, Xu et al. conjectured that $\Psi(3) = 46$, saying *"However, the number of polygons of area 46 seems to be too huge to search"*. On a supercomputer [3], our approach took 3 hours to refute this conjecture.

Code. Our code and the instructions to reproduce our results are publicly available at https://github.com/LongQianQL/CADE30-BoxUnfoldings.

Organization. In Section 2, we give a high-level overview of our approach. Then, Section 3 introduces necessary properties that box unfoldings must satisfy, and that guide our encoding. In Section 4, we detail the differences with previous SAT encodings for a spanning tree (a natural subproblem for finding unfoldings) as we use local constraints that approximate both connectivity and acyclicty. Then, in Section 5, we show how to encode that a folding net, which our encoding keeps implicit, maps to two different boxes. In Section 6 we show how we break rotational symmetries of the problem. Section 8 discusses related work, and in particular, the limitations of previous SAT encodings. In Section 7 we present our experimental results.

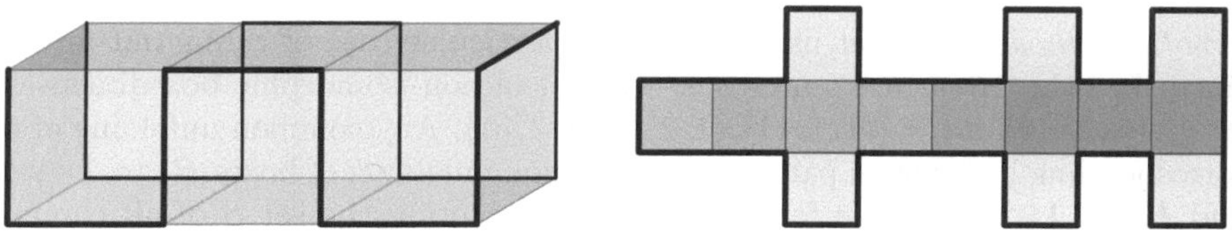

(a) A $1 \times 1 \times 3$ box with cut edges. (b) The corresponding folding net.

Fig. 4: The correspondence between cuts in a box and its folding nets.

2 Overview of our approach

The first step toward finding common unfoldings of multiple boxes is finding unfoldings of a single box. As in previous work (e.g., [4,10,12]), we frame the search for unfoldings of a given box B in terms of a search for *"cut edges"* in B (see Figure 4) which after being physically cut, would allow to unfold the box into a flat net without overlaps. For instance, if one were to cut the blue edges of the $1 \times 1 \times 3$ box depicted in Figure 4a, and then proceed to unfold[1] the box, the result would be the net depicted in Figure 4b. More precisely, any net N that folds into a box B through a sequence $\gamma_1, \ldots, \gamma_k$ of folding motions in space can be obtained by cutting a subset of the edges of the unit-squares that compose the different faces of B, and then reversing the folding motions as $\gamma_k^{-1}, \ldots, \gamma_1^{-1}$ to obtain the net N.

Note, however, that not all sets of cut edges are *"valid"*, in the sense of allowing for an unfolding of the box into a flat net. For example, one can easily see that cutting a single edge of a box never allows for an unfolding, and furthermore in Section 3 we will describe a simple argument showing one needs at least 4 cut edges to unfold a box. Similarly, another requirement for a set of cut edges to be valid is not contain cycles; cutting along a cycle would separate the box into disconnected pieces!

Nonetheless, provided an efficient method to find valid sets of cut edges for a box B, we can search for common unfoldings of multiple boxes. Indeed, to find a net N that folds into different boxes $B_1, \ldots, B_m$, we need to find a valid set C_i of cut edges in each box B_i such that the different sets C_i are *"compatible"*, which intuitively means that for each pair B_i, B_j, the unit squares of B_i can be mapped to those of B_j so that two adjacent squares in B_i without their common edge cut map to two adjacent squares in B_j without their common edge cut. The details of this mapping presented in Section 5.

Now, to illustrate our general methodology, let us present a concrete result and a high-level sketch of how we obtain it.

Theorem 1. *No set of three non-isomorphic boxes of area* 58 *or less has a common unfolding. In other words,* $\Psi(3) > 58$.

[1] A precise mathematical definition of folding/unfolding turns out to be pretty intricate, using the entirety of Chapter 11 in the book of Demaine and O'Rourke [4]. We will thus mostly stick to intuition.

Proof (Methodology). Let us consider the particular case of ruling out area 46, since the other areas are analogous. The set of non-isomorphic box-dimensions for area 46 is $P(46) = \{(1, 1, 11), (1, 2, 7), (1, 3, 5)\}$. Any common unfolding of the corresponding boxes is, in particular, a common unfolding of boxes $B_1 := 1{\times}1{\times}11$ and $B_2 := 1{\times}2{\times}7$, so we focus first on constructing the set S of all common unfoldings of these two boxes, where each common unfolding can be represented as a pair (C_1, C_2), where C_1 (resp. C_2) is the set of edges to cut in B_1 (resp. B_2). However, instead of computing S exactly, we compute a superset $S' \supseteq S$, that contains all common unfoldings of B_1 and B_2, but also potentially pairs (C_1, C_2) where the sets of cut edges do not necessarily allow to unfold the boxes into a common net. The set S' is obtained by enumerating all satisfying assignments of a CNF formula $\Phi(B_1, B_2)$, whose constraints will be detailed throughout the paper. Then, for each pair $(C_1, C_2) \in S'$, we do another SAT call to check whether it is possible to unfold box $B_3 := 1{\times}3{\times}5$ in a way that is compatible with (C_1, C_2). Since none of the $|S'|$ calls is satisfiable, we can conclude that no common unfolding of B_1, B_2, B_3 exists. □

While a SAT encoding for the problem of finding common unfoldings of two (or more) boxes was already presented by Tadaki and Amano [10], our approach represents a significant improvement in allowing to search and enumerate common unfoldings for significantly larger dimensions. At a high-level, the key improvements of our encoding are:

1. When encoding the unfolding of a single box, that is, whether a set of cut edges is *"valid"*, we do not explicitly encode the net as [10], but rather properties that the set of cut edges must satisfy, and moreover, our encoding of these properties is a very efficient under-approximation, that replaces global constraints (i.e., the connectivity constraint of [10]) with local constraints.
2. When encoding a 2-box common unfolding, we do not use a net as intermediary, and instead encode the existence of a direct mapping between the unit-squares of box B_1 and those of B_2, that *"preserves"* the cut edges.
3. We exploit the symmetry of the boxes to reduce the search space. For example, in a $1{\times}1{\times}11$ there are several rotational symmetries that we break.

Before we detail the improvements, let us describe what it means for a set of cut edges to be *"valid"*, or more precisely, some necessary conditions for it.

3 Valid sets of cut edges

Let us first briefly describe 4 well-known (cf. [4, Ch. 21], [6]) necessary properties for a set of cut edges to be valid for a box B:

P1. **Connectivity:** The graph induced by the cut edges (taking the set of their endpoints as vertices) must be connected.

P2. **Cut corners:** The graph induced by the cut edges must touch all the 8 corners of the box B.

P3. **Acyclicity:** The graph induced by the cut edges must be acyclic.

P4. **Necessity:** For every set of four unit-squares $\{s_1, s_2, s_3, s_4\}$ that forms a 2×2 square on B, it cannot be the case that *exactly one* edge between these unit-squares is cut, as such cuts are not necessary [6, Lemma 1].

We suggest the reader inspects Figure 4a to check that these constraints are satisfied, and to try to obtain some insight into their necessity. Intuitively, P1 is justified by the fact that the cut edges unfold into the boundary of the net, as exemplified in Figure 4, and that boundary is connected. P2, on the other hand, can be justified by noting that every non-cut edge connecting adjacent unit-squares s_1, s_2 in a box B will remain an edge connecting two adjacent squares in the net N that folds into B. Thus, if none of the three edges incident to a corner are cut, then the three squares incident to that corner will remain adjacent in the net N, which is a contradiction since in a polyomino there cannot be three pairwise adjacent squares, as illustrated in Figure 5. P3 is justified by the fact that if the graph induced by the cut edges contained a cycle C, then the unit squares inside C would be disconnected from the rest when unfolding the box B. Finally, P4 is intuitively justified by noticing that if exactly one such edge is cut, then this edge can always be "glued" back without affecting the underlying unfolding, a rigorous proof of P4 can also be found in earlier works [6, Lemma 1].

To represent whether an edge $\{s_1, s_2\}$ is cut or not, we can simply use a boolean variable e_{s_1,s_2} that is true if and only if $\{s_1, s_2\}$ is *not cut*. Then, P2 can be trivially encoded by 8 clauses of the form $(\overline{e}_{s_1,s_2} \vee \overline{e}_{s_1,s_3} \vee \overline{e}_{s_2,s_3})$, where s_1, s_2, s_3 are the three adjacent squares on a corner of the box. Similarly, for each 2×2 square $\{s_1, s_2, s_3, s_4\}$ on B (with $\{s_1, s_4\}$ non-adjacent), P_4 can be encoded by 4 clauses of the form $(e_{s_1,s_2} \wedge e_{s_1,s_3} \wedge e_{s_2,s_4} \rightarrow e_{s_3,s_4})$ The difficulty, however, arises when encoding properties P1 and P3, which are *"non-local"* properties, and despite a body of research, remain challenging to encode without resulting in either a large number of clauses or poor propagation properties [5,13].

Our approach replaces these constraints by a set of local constraints that intuitively pursue a similar goal as P1 and P3: ensuring that the graph of cut edges has sufficiently many edges (P1) without having too many (P3). Concretely:

1. To force cutting a significant number of edges, we leverage the work of Tadaki and Amano [10], and assign orientations to each square of the box, which then allows for enforcing consistency constraints between adjacent squares whose common edge is not cut. To satisfy those constraints, a significant number of edges must be cut.

Fig. 5: Illustration of the necessity of the cut-corners property.

2. In contrast to the encoding in [10], which forbid cutting too many edges by enforcing the connectivity of the resulting 2D net, explicit in their encoding, we use a fully novel idea: assigning orientations to the edges of the box, and then forbidding a small number of local directed patterns that every valid unfolding can avoid, but most disconnected nets contain. Intuitively, since disconnected nets correspond to cycles of cut edges, our encoding attempts to prevent such cycles.

4 Local constraints

As described in Section 3, our goal is to impose constraints that ensure that sufficiently many, but not too many, variables e_{s_1,s_2} (representing that the edge $\{s_1, s_2\}$ is not cut) are set to true. We achieve these goals independently: we enforce cutting edges using *"square-orientation constraints"* in a similar (albeit with important differences) way to Tadaki and Amano [10], and use a fully novel approach, based on *"edge directions"* to forbid too many edges from being cut.

4.1 Square orientations

Inspired by [10], we think of each square in a box B as having an *"orientation"*, that intuitively represents whether, on an unfolding of the net, the square would be rotated by 0°, 90°, 180°, or 270°. As Figure 6a indicates, each square is labeled with a dot, which then induces an orientation value on the square once it is unfolded onto the 2D plane. Naturally, this requires a labeling of squares on the box with such dots. Any consistent labeling will work. We adopt the convention that the dot is labeled at the corner that is diagonally the furthest away from the origin when the box is placed in the positive octant. Equivalently, one can directly extend the labeling shown in Figure 6b to general boxes. Once such a labeling has been fixed, it is clear that any unfolding of the box will induce an orientation assignment $o : B \to \{1, 2, 3, 4\}$.

Importantly, any orientation assignment $o\colon B \to \{1, 2, 3, 4\}$ induced by a valid unfolding will necessarily preserve *"relative orientations"* between connected

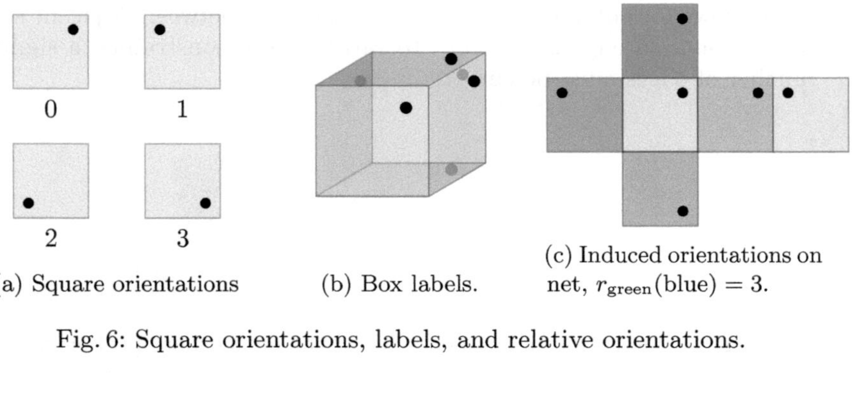

(a) Square orientations (b) Box labels. (c) Induced orientations on net, $r_{\text{green}}(\text{blue}) = 3$.

Fig. 6: Square orientations, labels, and relative orientations.

squares. For a pair of connected squares s_1, s_2, define the relative orientation of s_2 with respect to s_1, $r_{s_1}(s_2)$, to be the orientation of s_2 if s_1 was rotated to have orientation 0 (Figure 6c). Note that $r_{s_1}(s_2)$ *only* depends on the canonical labeling chosen for the box, and in particular does not depend on potential unfoldings. Since unfolding is an orientation-preserving geometric transformation, for any edge $e = \{s_1, s_2\}$ that is *not cut*, the relative orientations between s_1, s_2 must remain invariant. Thereby necessarily implying $o(s_2) = o(s_1) + r_{s_1}(s_2)$ (and vice versa), where addition is carried out in $\mathbb{Z}_4$. In fact, these are the only constraints that we enforce in our encoding for square orientations. The constraints are:

- Variables $o_{s,d}$ for $s \in B$, $d \in \{1, 2, 3, 4\}$ encoding a function $o : B \to \{1, 2, 3, 4\}$ representing the orientation values. For this to be a well-defined function, we have the following constraints for all $s \in B$.

$$\sum_{d=1}^{4} o_{s,d} = 1$$

- For each edge $e = \{s_1, s_2\}$ in B that is not cut (i.e. e_{s_1,s_2} is true), it must be the case that $o(s_2) = o(s_1) + r_{s_1}(s_2)$ (and vice versa). This is encoded as follows for every $d \in \{1, 2, 3, 4\}$.

$$\left(e_{s_1,s_2} \wedge o_{s_1,d} \to o_{s_2,r_{s_1}(s_2)+d}\right) \wedge \left(e_{s_1,s_2} \wedge o_{s_2,d} \to o_{s_1,r_{s_2}(s_1)+d}\right)$$

4.2 Edge directions

Let G_B be the graph with the squares of box B as vertices, and where neighboring squares have a graph edge if and only if their common geometrical edge is not cut. Recall now that forbidding cycles of cut edges is equivalent to making the graph G_B connected, which is our goal. The SAT encoding in [10] encodes graph connectivity by choosing one vertex $s^\star \in V(G_B)$ as the source of a *Breadth First Search* (BFS), and then encoding that every vertex is reached by that BFS.

Concretely, variables $t_{v,k}$ represent that vertex v is reached on step k or earlier of the BFS, with k ranging up to $|V(G_B)| - 1$ in the worst case. Then, the encoding consists of:

- The source vertex $s^\star$ is reached at step 0, enforced by unit clause $t_{s^\star,0}$.
- Each vertex is reached at some step, enforced by the formula

$$\bigwedge_{v \in V(G_B)} \bigvee_{k=0}^{|V(G_B)|-1} t_{v,k}.$$

- Let $N(v)$ denote the set of four neighbors of $v \in V(G_B)$. A vertex v is reached at step at most k if and only if one of its neighbors (or itself) was reached at step at most $k - 1$:

$$\bigwedge_{k=1}^{|V(G_B)|-1} \bigwedge_{v \in V(G_B)} \left(t_{v,k} \leftrightarrow \bigvee_{u \in N(v)} (t_{u,k-1} \wedge e_{u,v}) \right).$$

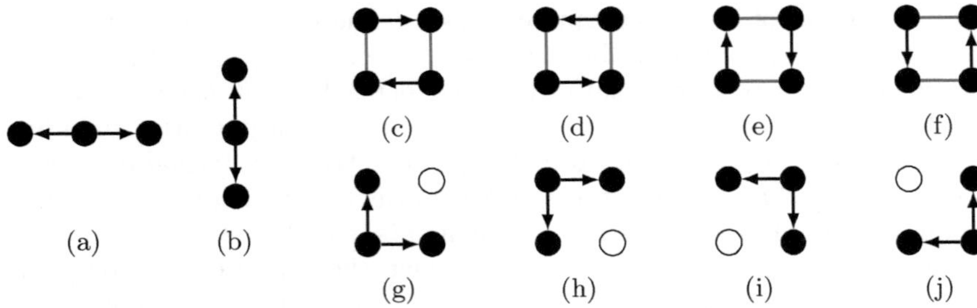

Fig. 7: The set $\mathcal{F}$ of forbidden subgraphs. The blue edges represent that the graph belongs to $\mathcal{F}$ regardless of the orientation of its blue edges. For the forbidden patterns 7g to 7j, the white node must not be present in the graph. Blocking the patterns 7a to 7b requires one binary clause per pattern. Blocking the patterns 7c to 7f requires two ternary clauses. Finally, blocking the patterns 7g to 7j requires two ternary clauses. The ternary clauses make use of the observation that it is impossible to preserve exactly 3 of the 4 edges.

As a result, the number of variables and clauses in their encoding is quadratic in $|V(G_B)|$, the number of squares of the box. It is possible to upper-bound $k \leq T$ for some $T \leq |V(G_B)| - 1$ to improve performance at the cost of potentially missing solutions, thus such bounds cannot be used if one wants to enumerate all solutions. Table 1 illustrates this for a typical sub-problem (Section 6) between boxes $1\times1\times7, 1\times3\times3$.

We approximate connectivity using a constant number of clauses per square. First, for each neighboring pair of squares (s_1, s_2), we create two variables, d_{s_1,s_2} and d_{s_2,s_1} representing that the preserved edge $\{s_1, s_2\}$ will be directed from s_1 toward s_2 (or from s_2 toward s_1, respectively). We have clauses $(\overline{d}_{s_1,s_2} \vee \overline{d}_{s_2,s_1})$ to prevent both directions per preserved edge. If an edge $\{s_1, s_2\}$ is preserved, it has at least one direction, this is enforced by $(e_{s_1,s_2} \rightarrow d_{s_1,s_2} \vee d_{s_2,s_1})$. Finally, if the edge $\{s_1, s_2\}$ has a direction, it is necessarily preserved. This is enforced by $d_{s_1,s_2} \rightarrow e_{s_1,s_2}$ and $d_{s_2,s_1} \rightarrow e_{s_1,s_2}$.

Now, we encode that a special vertex $s^\star$ is a *unique sink* by enforcing that (i) it has outdegree 0 according to the edge directions, so $\bigwedge_{u\in N(s^\star)} \overline{d}_{s^\star,u}$, and (ii) every other vertex has outdegree at least 1:

$$\bigwedge_{v\in V(G_B)\setminus\{s^\star\}} \bigvee_{u\in N(v)} d_{v,u}$$

Note that for us, $s^\star$ is a *"sink"*, instead of a *"source"*. To approximate further that our edge directions correspond to a *reverse BFS* from $s^\star$, we forbid all local patterns depicted in Figure 7 as subgraphs. Since this forbids a constant number of possibilities around each vertex, it totals $O(|V(G_B)|)$ clauses. While this is insufficient in theory to guarantee connectivity, it almost always results in connected nets in practice. We prove in the extended arXiv version of this paper [7] that these constraints are sound, meaning that every valid unfolding must satisfy them.

Table 1: Runtimes with BFS/forbidding local patterns at $|V(G_B)| = 30$.

$T = 15$	$T = 16$	$T = 17$	$T = 18$	$T = 19$	$T = 20$	**Local patterns**
79.66 s	240.53 s	385.56 s	504.43 s	947.83 s	1823.88 s	**36.51 s**

5 Common unfoldings of two boxes

An important feature of our approach is the *implicit* representation of nets via their corresponding cut edges, in contrast to *explicitly* representing them as subsets of the 2D plane. Utilizing such implicit representations, the search for a net N that folds into different boxes $B_1, \cdots, B_m$ naturally reduces down to the search for cut edges $C_1, \cdots, C_m$ that are "compatible". Importantly, such constraints are *intrinsic* to the boxes and cut edges (B_i, C_i) and do not concern the explicit 2D representation of nets. This allows for much more compact and efficient encodings compared to earlier work [10], which uses explicit representations.

Figure 8 shows how the search for a common net can be done explicitly by enforcing equivalence on the resulting 2D unfoldings, which is costly and introduces additional auxiliary variables. In contrast, we achieve this by encoding an equivalence mapping $M: B_2 \to B_1$ directly on the level of boxes, and thereby alleviating the need to consider the nets explicitly.

Figure 9 depicts the constraints imposed on $M: B_2 \to B_1$. If a square $s'_1 \in B_2$ is mapped to $s_1 \in B_1$ *and* the edge $e = \{s_1, s_2\}$ is not cut, then it must necessarily be the case that the corresponding neighbor of s'_1, in this case s'_2, maps to s_2

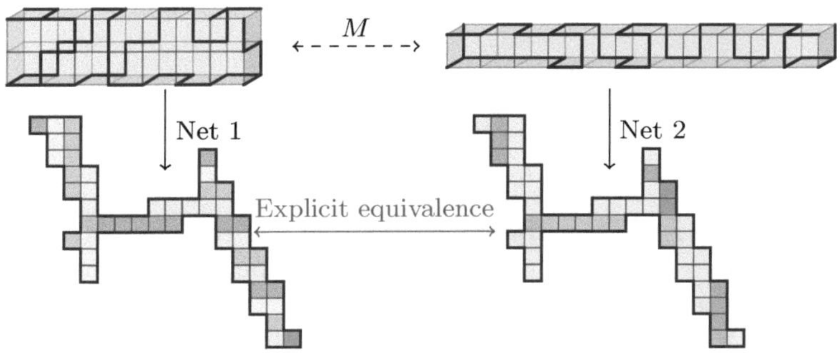

Fig. 8: Equivalence of nets of boxes 1×2×7 and 1×1×11, explicitly via nets (red) and implicitly via cut edges (M).

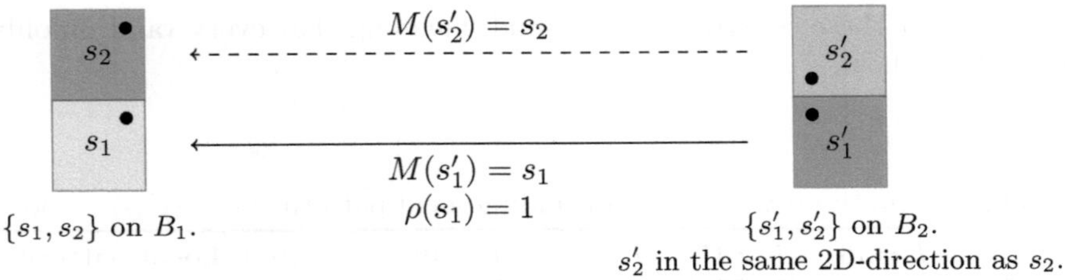

Fig. 9: Constraints on M with relative change in orientation ρ.

and the edge $e = \{s_1', s_2'\}$ is *not cut* in box 2. Furthermore, notice that s_2' is the unique neighbor of s_1' in the same direction as s_2, and can be computed from $o(s_1') - o(s_1)$, the relative change in orientations. These constraints are encoded as follows.

- Mapping variables $m_{s,s'}$ for $s' \in B_2, s \in B_1$ that encode a bijection $M\colon B_2 \to B_1$. For each $s' \in B_2$ we have the constraint
$$\sum_{s \in B_1} m_{s,s'} = 1$$
- Auxiliary variables $\rho_{s,d}$ for $s \in B_1, d \in \{1,2,3,4\}$ that encode a function $\rho\colon B_1 \to [4]$ indicating the change in orientation between s and the unique $s' \in B_2$ where $M(s') = s$. I.e. $o(s') = o(s) + \rho(s)$ holds. This is encoded via the following where $s' \in B_2, s \in B_1$ and $d, r \in \{1,2,3,4\}$.
$$m_{s,s'} \wedge o_{s',d+r} \wedge o_{s,d} \to \rho_{s,r}$$
- Constraints that enforce the preservation of relative positions as shown in Figure 9. Let $\{s_1, s_2\}$ be an edge in B_1, $s_1' \in B_2$ and $d, r \in \{1,2,3,4\}$ be such that $\rho(s_1) = r$ and d indicates the 2D-direction of s_2. Let s_2' be the unique neighbor of s_1' in the same direction as s_2. The constraints are:
$$m_{s_1,s_1'} \wedge \rho_{s_1,r} \wedge e_{s_1,s_2} \to m_{s_2,s_2'}$$
$$m_{s_1,s_1'} \wedge \rho_{s_1,r} \wedge e_{s_1,s_2} \to e_{s_1',s_2'}$$
$$m_{s_1,s_1'} \wedge \rho_{s_1,r} \wedge e_{s_1',s_2'} \to e_{s_1,s_2}$$
where the latter two constraints encode that the edge $e = \{s_1, s_2\}$ is cut if and only if $e' = \{s_1', s_2'\}$ is cut. Only the first type of constraint is necessary. The other two types help with performance.
- Finally, we write EQUIV_{B_1,B_2} to denote the overall encoding for equivalence obtained by taking the conjunction of all constraints above. Equivalence of more than 2 boxes can easily be encoded by enforcing EQUIV_{B_1,B_n} for all $n \geq 2$.

6 Symmetry breaking

Geometrically, if a box B unfolds into a net N, then the symmetries of B can certainly be unfolded into the same net N. To efficiently enumerate all unfoldings, it is important to avoid the computation of repeated solutions by breaking these symmetries. In this section, we describe how symmetry breaking is carried out and show experimentally that this greatly improves the performance.

As a first step, notice that a geometric (2D) rotation of a net only affects the orientations of squares and preserves the edges. Indeed, constraints on the orientation of squares introduced in Section 4 only enforce relative equality, and therefore if $o\colon B \to \{1,2,3,4\}$ gives a satisfying assignment of orientations, then a constant shift (e.g. $o'(s) = o(s) + 1$ for all s) will also be satisfying and corresponds to a 2D rotation of the underlying net. Thus, we may without loss of generality pick a distinguished square $\hat{s} \in B$ and enforce $o(\hat{s}) = 0$ with a unit clause.

To further break symmetries when searching for common unfoldings (of two boxes B_1, B_2), consider the image of pairs of squares under the equivalence mapping M (Section 5) of a common unfolding. First, fix a pair of squares (s_1, s_2) on B_1. Since M is a bijection, some pair of squares (s_1', s_2') on B_2 satisfies $(M(s_1'), M(s_2')) = (s_1, s_2)$, as illustrated in Figure 10. If $Q \in \mathrm{Sym}(B_2)$ is a symmetry of B_2, then certainly the same unfolding can be carried out on $Q(B_2)$ (as Q is a symmetry), inducing a common unfolding between $Q(B_2)$ and B_1 where the pair $(Q^{-1}(s_1'), Q^{-1}(s_2'))$ now maps to (s_1, s_2). Therefore, if P_2 denotes the set of all pairs of B_2 up to symmetry, then the search for common unfoldings can be reduced to the cases $(M(s_1'), M(s_2')) = (s_1, s_2)$ for every pair $(s_1', s_2') \in P_2$. Furthermore, if (s_1, s_2) are chosen on B_1 such that s_1 is in the orbit of s_2 under symmetries of B_1, then it suffices to consider the pairs in P_2 as unordered, thereby reducing the number of cases by a factor of 2. Table 2 depicts the number of such pairs relative to the total number of pairs $\binom{\text{Area}}{2}$. As shown, the number of pairs up to symmetry is relatively small compared to the number of all pairs.

Finally, when the dimensions of B_1 is of the form $1\times1\times n$, we always pick the pair (s_1, s_2) to be the 1×1 faces. In addition to them being symmetric, B_1 has full rotational symmetry about these faces and therefore the orientation of s_1

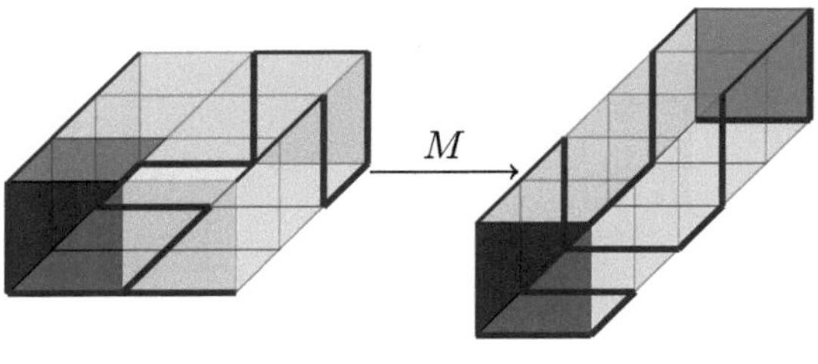

Fig. 10: Image of pairs of squares under M, mapping the (black, red) pair on B_2 to the (black, red) pair on B_1.

Table 2: Number of pairs

Area	Dimensions		#Pairs	Total%
22	1×1×5	1×2×3	45	9.74%
30	1×1×7	1×3×3	47	5.40%
34	1×1×8	1×2×5	97	8.64%
38	1×1×9	1×3×4	120	8.53%
42	1×1×10	2×3×3	77	4.47%
46	1×1×11	1×2×7	169	8.16%
54	1×1×13	1×3×6	231	8.07%
58	1×1×14	1×2×9	261	7.89%

can be altered by applying such rotations *without rotating the underlying net.* Consequently, this implies that we may always assume without loss of generality that $o(s_1) = 0$, in addition to fixing the orientation of a square $s'_1 \in B_2$. To summarize, when enumerating common unfoldings between two boxes B_1, B_2, the following symmetry-breaking procedure is carried out.

1. Fix a pair of squares (s_1, s_2) on B_1 that belong to the same equivalence class under symmetry.
2. If B_1 is of the form $1\times1\times n$, choose (s_1, s_2) to be the 1×1 faces and enforce $o(s_1) = 0$ using a unit clause.
3. Let P_2 be the set of (unordered) pairs of squares on B_2 unique up to symmetry. For each pair $(s'_1, s'_2) \in P_2$, encode $M(s'_1) = s_1, M(s'_2) = s_2, o(s'_1) = 0$ using 3 unit clauses.
4. Solve the corresponding sub-problem for each pair $(s'_1, s'_2) \in P_2$. Note that since each sub-problem is independent, they can be run in parallel.

7 Experimental results

Using the encodings given in Sections 4 and 5 without symmetry-breaking, we were able to compute unfoldings between all pairs of boxes with equal area up to 86 (Table 3), thereby establishing $\Delta(2) > 86$. As indicated in Table 3, most of such unfoldings with high area were previously unknown. The first missing

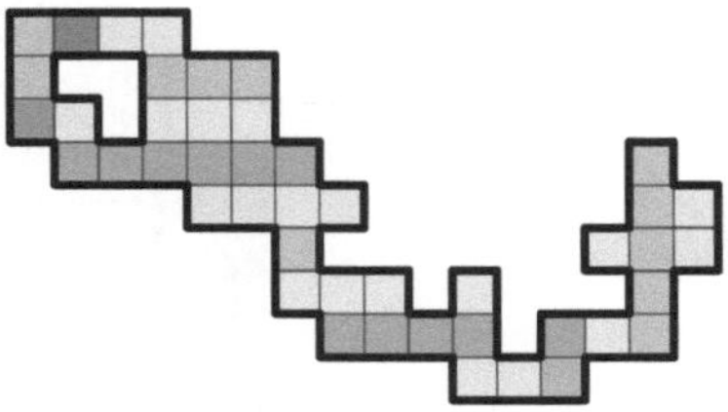

Fig. 11: Overlapping net (left) and touching net (right) of 1×1×11.

Table 3: Existence of common unfoldings.

Area	Dimensions		First	Area	Dimensions		First	Area	Dimensions		First
22	1×1×5	1×2×3	[6]	78	1×1×19	1×3×9	✓	108	1×4×10	3×4×6	✓
30	1×1×7	1×3×3	[6]	78	1×1×19	1×4×7	✓	110	1×3×13	1×6×7	✓
34	1×1×8	1×2×5	[6]	78	1×1×19	3×3×5	✓	110	1×3×13	3×5×5	✓
38	1×1×9	1×3×4	[6]	78	1×3×9	1×4×7	✓	112	2×2×13	2×4×8	✓
40	1×2×6	2×2×4	[10]	78	1×3×9	3×3×5	✓	112	2×3×10	4×4×5	✓
42	1×1×10	2×3×3	✓	78	1×4×7	3×3×5	✓	112	1×2×18	4×4×5	✓
46	1×1×11	1×3×5	[6]	80	2×2×9	3×4×4	✓	118	1×4×11	1×5×9	✓
46	1×1×11	1×2×7	✓	82	1×1×20	1×2×13	✓	118	1×3×14	1×5×9	✓
46	1×2×7	1×3×5	[6]	82	1×1×20	1×5×6	✓	118	1×4×11	2×5×7	✓
48	1×4×4	2×2×5	✓	82	1×1×20	2×3×7	✓	118	1×3×14	2×5×7	✓
54	1×1×13	3×3×3	[6]	82	1×2×13	1×5×6	✓	120	2×2×14	2×6×6	✓
54	1×1×13	1×3×6	[6]	82	1×2×13	2×3×7	✓	124	1×6×8	2×4×9	✓
54	1×3×6	3×3×3	[6]	82	1×5×6	2×3×7	✓	126	1×3×15	3×5×6	✓
58	1×1×14	1×2×9	✓	86	1×1×21	1×3×10	✓	126	1×7×7	3×5×6	✓
58	1×1×14	1×4×5	[6]	86	1×2×14	1×4×8	✓	126	1×7×7	3×3×9	✓
58	1×2×9	1×4×5	✓	86	1×2×14	2×4×6	✓	126	3×3×9	3×5×6	✓
62	1×1×15	1×3×7	✓	88	1×4×8	2×2×10	[6]	128	1×4×12	4×4×6	✓
62	1×1×15	2×3×5	✓	88	1×4×8	2×4×6	✓	128	2×2×15	4×4×6	✓
62	1×3×7	2×3×5	[6]	88	2×2×10	2×4×6	[6]	132	2×3×12	2×5×8	✓
64	1×2×10	2×2×7	[6]	90	2×5×5	3×3×6	✓	136	2×4×10	2×6×7	✓
64	1×2×10	2×4×4	✓	94	1×5×7	3×4×5	✓	136	2×6×7	3×4×8	✓
64	2×2×7	2×4×4	[6]	94	1×3×11	3×4×5	✓	138	1×4×13	1×6×9	✓
66	1×1×16	3×3×4	✓	94	1×3×11	1×5×7	✓	138	1×6×9	3×3×10	✓
70	1×1×17	1×2×11	✓	96	1×6×6	2×2×11	✓	142	1×5×11	1×7×8	✓
70	1×1×17	1×3×8	✓	96	1×6×6	4×4×4	✓	142	2×3×13	3×5×7	✓
70	1×1×17	1×5×5	[6]	100	1×2×16	2×4×7	✓	142	1×5×11	2×3×13	✓
70	1×2×11	1×3×8	[6]	102	2×3×9	3×3×7	✓	142	1×7×8	2×3×13	✓
70	1×2×11	1×5×5	✓	102	1×3×12	2×3×9	✓	142	1×5×11	3×5×7	✓
70	1×3×8	1×5×5	✓	104	2×2×12	2×5×6	✓	144	2×2×17	3×6×6	✓
72	2×2×8	2×3×6	✓	106	1×1×26	1×2×17	✓	148	1×4×14	4×5×6	✓
76	1×2×12	2×4×5	✓	106	1×2×17	1×5×8	✓	174	3×3×13	3×5×9	✓

entry is the pair 1×2×14, 2×2×10 at area 88. It is worth noting that common unfoldings can always be scaled up by subdividing squares, e.g. a common unfolding of 1×1×5, 1×2×3 directly implies the existence of a common unfolding for 2×2×10, 2×4×6 by dividing each square into 4 sub-squares [6].

With the symmetry-breaking procedure described in Section 6, we were able to completely enumerate all solutions for the pairs of boxes shown in Table 4. Local computations were conducted using a standard laptop, computations labeled with "cluster" were conducted on a supercomputer [3] running 64 SAT solvers in parallel. Solutions were obtained by enumerating all solutions for each fixed pair of squares on the second box (Section 6), using an allsat variant of CaDiCaL [2], available at https://github.com/jreeves3/allsat-cadical. Through these computations, we

Table 4: Exhaustive enumeration of solutions. The columns labeled $|S|$, $|T|$, and $|O|$ show the number of simple, touching, and overlapping solutions, respectively.

Area	Dimensions		#SAT	Unique	$\|S\|$	$\|T\|$	$\|O\|$	Time	First
22	1×1×5	1×2×3	3 942	2 303	2 263	27	13	2 mins (local)	[1]
30	1×1×7	1×3×3	1 790	1 080	1 070	10	0	10 mins (local)	[12]
34	1×1×8	1×2×5	131 054	35 700	35 675	22	3	1 hour (local)	✓
38	1×1×9	1×3×4	5 854	4 509	4 469	36	4	6 hrs (local)	✓
42	1×1×10	2×3×3	128 558	111 948	111 387	559	2	1 day (local)	✓
46	1×1×11	1×2×7	16 928	15 236	14 971	16	249	3 hrs (PSC)	✓
54	1×1×13	1×3×6	56 087	51 884	51 836	48	0	1 day (PSC)	✓
58	1×1×14	1×2×9	2 150 373	551 935	551 923	7	5	2 days (PSC)	✓

Table 5: Exhaustive enumeration of 1×1×n nets

Dimensions	#SAT	Unique	$\|S\|$	$\|T\|$	$\|O\|$	Time
1×1×1	384	11	11	0	0	0.05 s
1×1×2	12 124	723	723	0	0	1.79 s
1×1×3	240 304	15 061	14 978	79	4	77.78 s
1×1×4	3 708 380	231 310	228 547	2 603	160	9 hrs

found unfoldings with diameter close to the surface area (we include examples in the extended arXiv version [7]) making it difficult to compute using a BFS-style encoding for connectivity.

In addition to standard nets (simply connected, no overlaps), our encoding is also capable of finding non-standard unfoldings, which we classify into "touching" and "overlapping". Both are nets in the sense that one can obtain them by unfolding a box, however they are non-standard as the resulting shape is not simply-connected. The gray square in the overlapping net shown in Figure 11 is an overlapping green and yellow square. Touching nets can always fold into the original box if cuts were allowed, e.g. the touching net shown in Figure 11 can fold into 1×1×11 if a cut is made along the red edge.

Beyond common unfoldings, we also enumerated all nets for boxes of the form 1×1×n for $n \leq 4$ (Table 5). To the best of our knowledge, the number of such nets was previously unknown except for $n = 1$. Such computations were carried out locally on a standard laptop.

8 Related work

The algorithmic search for common unfoldings of non-isomorphic boxes has been investigated in many earlier works [1,6,8,10,11,12] using various techniques. One body of work is the complete enumeration of all unfoldings [1,12], computing all possible unfoldings between two boxes. The best previous result was due to

[12], providing a complete enumeration of all unfoldings at area 30. Our efficient approach allows us to completely enumerate all unfoldings up to surface area 58, providing complete enumerations for many pairs of boxes that were previously unknown (Table 4). Furthermore, solutions of area 22 were enumerated by [1] taking 10 hours, whereas our approach takes 2 minutes. Solutions of area 30 were enumerated by [12] taking 10 days using a computer with 128 GB memory, our approach only takes 10 minutes using a standard laptop.

We were also able to find many new common unfoldings between boxes that were previously unknown. The best lower-bound for $\Delta(2)$ from earlier works was 40 and already at area 42 it was not known if boxes of dimensions $1\times1\times10, 2\times3\times3$ admit a common unfolding. Using our approach, we compute all possible common unfoldings between all boxes up to surface area 86, more than doubling the previous best bound.

The use of SAT solvers to find common unfoldings has also been explored in earlier work [10], our approach has two fundamental improvements over the previous approach. The first being the use of implicit equivalences which alleviates the need to consider nets as subsets of the 2D plane (Section 5). This significantly improves the efficiency of the encodings by eliminating the auxiliary variables needed to represent the nets in 2D. Secondly, the use of local constraints (Section 4) allows us to efficiently detect connectedness in the cut edges of boxes, and furthermore this does not place an *a priori* restriction on the radius of the underlying net. Thereby allowing us to completely enumerate *all solutions* between boxes and establishing $\Psi(3) > 58$ rather than only finding solutions with a bounded radius. One can theoretically enumerate all solutions by using the surface area as the upper-bound, but this is too costly on performance [10].

9 Concluding remarks

We have presented a new SAT-based approach for finding and enumerating polyominos that can be folded into multiple non-isomorphic boxes, outperforming previous approaches. We have introduced a technique that could be applicable to searching for other combinatorial objects: approximating constraints that are hard to encode, or result in large numbers of clauses, with simpler local constraints, and then discard the solutions that do not satisfy the original constraints.

Further supporting the correctness of our encoding, we were able to reproduce the common unfolding of 3 boxes at area 532 [8] as shown in Figure 12. This was obtained by specifying the cut edges for one of the boxes ($2\times13\times16$) with unit clauses and using a SAT solver to solve for the remaining variables.

The quest for the smallest area allowing a common unfolding of three boxes remains open, and part of our future work. Another promising direction is to formally verify our work, in the line of [9], given how intricate the encoding is and the delicate arguments for its completeness. We suspect that a particularly challenging aspect of that verification will be to formally define *(un)foldings* (cf. Demaine and O'Rourke [4, Ch. 15]).

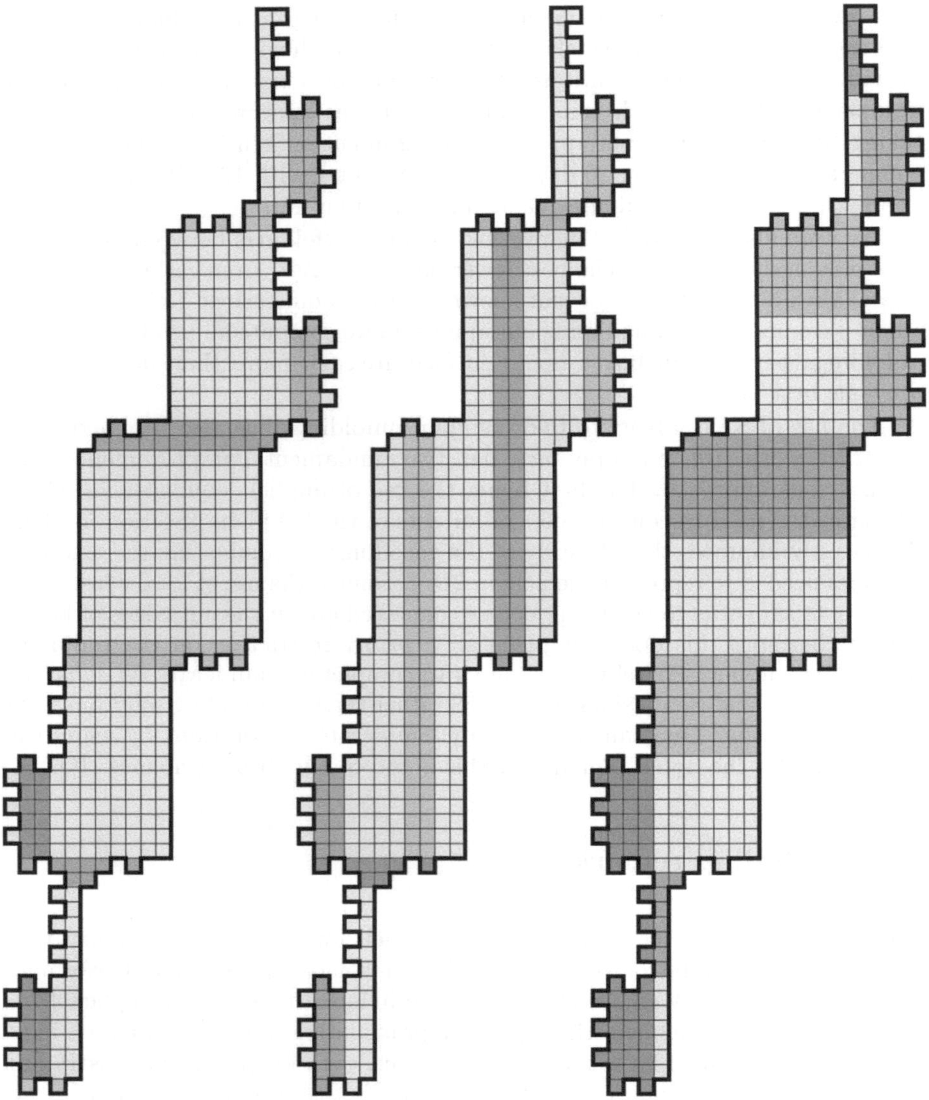

(a) 2×13×16 (b) 2×4×43 (c) 7×8×14

Fig. 12: Common unfolding of 3 boxes at area 532 [8].

Acknowledgements. We thank Joseph Reeves for implementing solution enumeration in CaDiCaL, which was crucial to performing the experiments. This work was supported by the U. S. National Science Foundation under grant DMS-2434625.

Disclosure of Interests. The authors have no competing interests to declare that are relevant to the content of this article.

References

1. Abel, Z., Demaine, E.D., Demaine, M.L., Matsui, H., Rote, G., Uehara, R.: Common developments of several different orthogonal boxes. In: Proceedings of the 23rd Annual Canadian Conference on Computational Geometry, Toronto, Ontario, Canada, August 10-12, 2011 (2011), http://www.cccg.ca/proceedings/2011/papers/paper49.pdf
2. Biere, A., Faller, T., Fazekas, K., Fleury, M., Froleyks, N., Pollitt, F.: CaDiCaL 2.0. In: Gurfinkel, A., Ganesh, V. (eds.) Computer Aided Verification - 36th International Conference, CAV 2024, Montreal, QC, Canada, July 24-27, 2024, Proceedings, Part I. Lecture Notes in Computer Science, vol. 14681, pp. 133–152. Springer (2024). https://doi.org/10.1007/978-3-031-65627-9_7
3. Brown, S.T., Buitrago, P., Hanna, E., Sanielevici, S., Scibek, R., Nystrom, N.A.: Bridges-2: A Platform for Rapidly-Evolving and Data Intensive Research. In: Practice and Experience in Advanced Research Computing. PEARC '21, Association for Computing Machinery, New York, NY, USA (2021). https://doi.org/10.1145/3437359.3465593
4. Demaine, E., O'Rourke, J.: Geometric Folding Algorithms: Linkages, Origami, Polyhedra. Cambridge University Press (2007)
5. Gebser, M., Janhunen, T., Rintanen, J.: SAT Modulo Graphs: Acyclicity. In: Fermé, E., Leite, J. (eds.) Logics in Artificial Intelligence. pp. 137–151. Springer International Publishing, Cham (2014)
6. Mitani, J., Uehara, R.: Polygons folding to plural incongruent orthogonal boxes. In: The 20th Canadian Conference on Computational Geometry (CCCG'08) (2008)
7. Qian, L., Wang, E., Subercaseaux, B., Heule, M.J.H.: Unfolding boxes with local constraints (2025), https://arxiv.org/abs/2506.01079
8. Shirakawa, T., Uehara, R.: Common developments of three different orthogonal boxes. In: The 24th Canadian Conference on Computational Geometry (CCCG'12) (2012)
9. Subercaseaux, B., Nawrocki, W., Gallicchio, J., Codel, C., Carneiro, M., Heule, M.J.H.: Formal Verification of the Empty Hexagon Number. In: 15th International Conference on Interactive Theorem Proving (ITP 2024). Leibniz International Proceedings in Informatics (LIPIcs), vol. 309, pp. 35:1–35:19. Dagstuhl, Germany (2024). https://doi.org/10.4230/LIPIcs.ITP.2024.35
10. Tadaki, R., Amano, K.: Search for developments of a box having multiple ways of folding by SAT solver (2020), https://arxiv.org/abs/2005.02645
11. Uehara, R.: A survey and recent results about common developments of two or more boxes. In: Origami ^{6}: proceedings of the sixth international meeting on origami science, mathematics, and education (2015)
12. Xu, D., Horiyama, T., Shirakawa, T., Uehara, R.: Common developments of three incongruent boxes of area 30. Computational Geometry **64**, 1–12 (2017). https://doi.org/10.1016/j.comgeo.2017.03.001
13. Zhou, N.F., Wang, R., Yap, R.H.C.: A Comparison of SAT Encodings for Acyclicity of Directed Graphs. In: 26th International Conference on Theory and Applications of Satisfiability Testing (SAT 2023). Leibniz International Proceedings in Informatics (LIPIcs), vol. 271, pp. 30:1–30:9. Dagstuhl, Germany (2023). https://doi.org/10.4230/LIPIcs.SAT.2023.30

Correction to: Automated Deduction – CADE 30

Clark Barrett and Uwe Waldmann

Correction to:
C. Barrett and U. Waldmann (Eds.): *Automated Deduction – CADE 30*, LNAI 15943, https://doi.org/10.1007/978-3-031-99984-0

The original published CADE 2025 proceedings volume, LNCS 15943, and conference papers included production editing mistakes. These have been corrected in a revised version. Springer Nature apologizes for any inconvenience.

The updated version of this book can be found at
https://doi.org/10.1007/978-3-031-99984-0

C. Barrett and U. Waldmann (Eds.): CADE 2025, LNAI 15943, p. C1, 2025.
https://doi.org/10.1007/978-3-031-99984-0_39

Author Index

C. Barrett and U. Waldmann (Eds.): CADE 2025, LNAI 15943, pp. 755–756, 2025.
https://doi.org/10.1007/978-3-031-99984-0

MIX
Papier aus verantwortungsvollen Quellen
Paper from responsible sources
FSC® C105338

If you have any concerns about our products,
you can contact us on
ProductSafety@springernature.com

In case Publisher is established outside the EU,
the EU authorized representative is:
Springer Nature Customer Service Center GmbH
Europaplatz 3, 69115 Heidelberg, Germany

Printed by Libri Plureos GmbH
in Hamburg, Germany